THE OXFORD HANDBOOK OF

APPLIED
LINGUISTICS

THE OXFORD HANDBOOK OF

APPLIED LINGUISTICS

SECOND EDITION

Edited by
ROBERT B. KAPLAN

Editorial Advisory Board
WILLIAM GRABE
MERRILL SWAIN
G. RICHARD TUCKER

OXFORD
UNIVERSITY PRESS
2010

OXFORD
UNIVERSITY PRESS

Oxford University Press, Inc., publishes works that further
Oxford University's objective of excellence
in research, scholarship, and education.

1006524l7X

Oxford   New York

Auckland   Cape Town   Dar es Salaam   Hong Kong   Karachi
Kuala Lumpur   Madrid   Melbourne   Mexico City   Nairobi
New Delhi   Shanghai   Taipei   Toronto

With offices in

Argentina   Austria   Brazil   Chile   Czech Republic   France   Greece
Guatemala   Hungary   Italy   Japan   Poland   Portugal   Singapore
South Korea   Switzerland   Thailand   Turkey   Ukraine   Vietnam

Published by Oxford University Press, Inc.
198 Madison Avenue, New York, New York 10016

www.oup.com

Oxford is a registered trademark of Oxford University Press

Library of Congress Cataloging-in-Publication Data
The Oxford handbook of applied linguistics / [edited by] Robert Kaplan.–2nd ed.
p. cm.
Includes bibliographical references and index.
ISBN 978-0-19-538425-3   1. Applied linguistics.   I. Kaplan, Robert B.
p129.095 2010
418–dc22   2009030287

1 3 5 7 9 8 6 4 2
Printed in the United States of America
on acid-free paper

Preface to the First Edition

THE work of organizing this volume began in the fall of 1998. Peter Ohlin of Oxford University Press (OUP) contacted me, indicating his interest in organizing *The Handbook of Applied Linguistics*. The suggestion was of interest to me—after all, I had been the editor of the *Annual Review of Applied Linguistics* from 1980 to 1991 and had continued on the editorial board through 2000 (Kaplan and Grabe, 2000); in addition, in 1980 I had edited *On the Scope of Applied Linguistics* (Kaplan, 1980), and in 1991 William Grabe and I coedited *Introduction to Applied Linguistics* (Grabe and Kaplan, 1991); finally, together with Henry Widdowson, I had served as coeditor for applied linguistics for the *International Encyclopedia of Linguistics* (IEL), edited by William Bright (Kaplan and Widdowson, 1992), and at present I'm engaged again in the same context for the second edition of the IEL (Kaplan and Grabe, in preparation), this time under the general editorship of William Frawley and with William Grabe serving as coeditor for applied linguistics in lieu of Henry Widdowson. In other words, I've been interested in the scope of applied linguistics for more than 20 years.

In October 1998, a preliminary proposal for the *Handbook* was developed, and, following appropriate review, in November a contract with OUP was signed. William Grabe, Merrill Swain, and G. Richard Tucker were invited to constitute an editorial advisory board for the project. In December 1998 and January 1999, the editorial advisory Board and I developed a revised outline for the volume and identified 43 contributors to write for the *Handbook* (out of a tentative list of more than 100 applied linguists who constituted a preliminary pool of potential contributors). Three contributors dropped out along the way. The first letters of invitation were mailed out in February 1999. Through March, April, and May 1999, negotiations were carried out; in June, the list of contributors was finalized. Contributors were asked to write scholarly articles on the topics for which they were responsible, placing their topics within the field of applied linguistics and, insofar as possible, suggesting the ways in which the several subdisciplines might develop in the future. Contributions began to arrive during late December 1999, though the deadline for contributions had been set for March 2000; contributions trickled in through March, April, and May 2000, and the last contribution was received in November 2000.

There are at least three holes in the design of this volume; work with the hearing impaired with teacher education, and with corpus development. Rachell Mayberry had agreed to provide an article on the first of these topics, JoAnn Crandall on the second, and Simon Murison-Bowie on the third; regrettably, these authors withdrew from the project in a time frame that made it impossible to replace them.

A book of this type will be judged not only on what it included, but on what it excluded. The editorial group spent quite a bit of time debating whether critical (applied) linguistics/critical pedagogy/critical discourse analysis should be included; on the grounds that critical applied linguistics rejects all theories of language, expresses "skepticism towards all metanarratives" (Lyotard, 1984), and rejects traditional applied linguistics as an enterprise because it has allegedly never been neutral and has, rather, been hegemonic (Rampton, 1997b), it was the decision of the editorial group not to include the cluster of *critical* activities.

In a way, the editorial group for this volume constitutes an entirely inappropriate set of editors for such a volume. Tucker had been president of the Center for Applied Linguistics (CAL) from 1978 and 1992; Swain, working at the Ontario Institute for Studies in Education (OISE) in Toronto, together with Michael Canale, had authored the seminal "Theoretical Bases of Communicative Approaches," which had appeared in volume 1, number 1 of the journal *Applied Linguistics;* Grabe was the second editor of the *Annual Review of Applied Linguistics*, serving from 1991 to 2000. Both Swain and Grabe (and I) had at various times been elected to the presidency of the American Association for Applied Linguistics (AAAL), and Tucker, in his CAL role, had served for a number of years as an ex officio member of its governing board. As a matter of fact, I happen to be the eldest of the editorial group by at least a dozen years; indeed, I am since 1995 formally retired from the University of Southern California (USC), holding the title professor emeritusus.

Thus, although the editorial group represents an enormous amount of experience, and although these four individuals have lived through much of the last 3 or 4 decades of the development of applied linguistics not only in the United States but in the world (through their participation in the International Association of Applied Linguistics [AILA] and their wide individual and collective familiarity with applied linguists around the world), they unquestionably know the history of applied linguistics; they know how and why applied linguistics has arrived at its present stage of development. Unfortunately, they are less well qualified to discuss the future of applied linguistics. That is a task for younger scholars. As a result, every effort has been made to allow a mix of younger and more established scholars to have their say through the 39 contributions to this volume. (Five of the chapters have two collaborating authors.) The distribution of scholars by country of residence and by gender is shown in table I.

Applied linguistics is a difficult notion to define; indeed, it should not be assumed that this volume will provide a definitive definition of the field. Rather, this volume offers a snapshot of some of the subfields of applied linguistics at the beginning of the third millennium—and thus, a kind of overview of the field. The term *applied linguistics* came into existence in the 1940s through the efforts of language teachers who wished to ally themselves with "scientific" linguists and to disassociate themselves from teachers of literature. By the mid-1950s, the term was given credence by the opening of the School of Applied Linguistics at the University of Edinburgh (1956) and by the creation of the Center for Applied Linguistics (CAL, 1959) in the United States. Soon thereafter, during the 1960s, the term was

Table I. Distribution of Contributors

By Country		By Gender	
Australia	05 (12.0%)	Male	24 (57%)
Belgium	01 (02.5%)	Female	18 (43%)
Canada	05 (12.0%)	TOTAL	42 (100%)
Hungary	02 (04.5%)		
Netherlands	02 (04.5%)		
United Kingdom	04 (09.5%)		
United States	23 (55.0%)		
TOTAL	42 (100.0%)		

institutionalized in the International Association of Applied Linguistics (*Association Internationale de Linguistique Appliquée* [AILA]; 1964) and in the evolution of a series of national associations of applied linguistics (e.g., the British Association of Applied Linguistics, 1967). Further, the field was given scope and substance by the publication of *Introducing Applied Linguistics* (Corder, 1973) and by the publication of *The Edinburgh Course in Applied Linguistics* (Allen and Corder, 1973–1975). The range and quality of research was soon being identified through the founding of a number of journals, including *Language Learning* (1948), *TESOL Quarterly* (1967), *Applied Linguistics* (1980), and the *Annual Review of Applied Linguistics* (1980).

Because the field came into being during the ascendancy of the structuralist linguistics movement, of Skinnerian psychology, and of the audiolingual method—a combination that gave rise to the notion that linguistic and psychological theory could easily be translated into practice—early applied linguistics was dominantly associated with language teaching. Indeed, although that relationship continues in the present (see, e.g., Davies, 1999; Spolsky, 1999), the field has diversified, with some segments splitting off to become essentially independent: Language testing has its own organization and its own journal; second language acquisition has its own journal though not yet an independent organization; and language policy and planning commands several journals (e.g., *Current Issues in Language Planning*) and a website (www.tandf.co.uk/journals/rclp) but no independent organization yet.

The current diversity of the field can be seen in the range of topics included in this volume, in the list of the "scientific commissions" of AILA, and in summary pieces written at various times over the past decade or so by Angelis (1987), Grabe and Kaplan (1991: 3–6), Kaplan (1999), Kaplan and Grabe (2000), and others (cf. Davies, 1999). It is clear that applied linguistics lacks a central organizing theory. In some ways, the field seems to be fragmenting into segments. At the Twelfth World Congress of AILA, held in Tokyo in August 1999, there were a number of fairly heated public discussions of the nature and scope of applied linguistics; there was little consensus among the participants in these discussions, but in part at least the lack of agreement may have been the result of the fact that six quite different questions were being addressed simultaneously:

1. What is the place of applied linguistics in the architecture of the "university"?
2. Where does applied linguistics fit in the sociology of knowledge?
3. What are the kinds of questions that applied linguistics ought to be addressing? That is, what are the dominant paradigms guiding research in the field?
4. What part(s) of linguistics can be applied to the real-world, language-based problems that applied linguistics presumes to mediate?
5. What kind(s) of problems can be solved through the mediation of applied linguistics?
6. What does an aspiring applied linguist need to know? That is, what should the content of graduate curricula in applied linguistics contain?

These questions are impacted by the assumption that applied linguistics ought to be unitary:

- That the training of incipient applied linguists ought to be based on the notion of a curriculum in which "one size fits all"
- That the work of applied linguists ought to be driven by a single unified theoretical paradigm
- That the place of applied linguistics in the academy ought to be conceived in terms of a model of the traditional academic department

This assumption is quite ironic, because applied linguists have repeatedly argued that their field is not merely "linguistics applied," but rather is, by definition, multidisciplinary and interdisciplinary. For example, the charge of some English departments includes at least the following:

American literature (divided into chronological components)
Comparative literature
Creative writing

English literature (divided into chronological components—sometimes with Anglo-Saxon language and literature and Middle English language and literature as separate components, sometimes with special components in Irish language and literature, sometimes with special components in EL2 literatures)

History of English language
Journalism
Rhetoric and composition
Teaching English as a first language
Teaching English as a second language
World literature

Such hydra-like monstrosities do exist (not always happily). If applied linguistics is to be conceived as having a traditional academic departmental structure, one could conceive of something as diverse and ecumenical as that suggested above. Although such a structure is not to be highly recommended, it does illustrate the point that diversity is possible in an administrative sense.

Because the real-world language-based problems that applied linguists try to mediate are enormously diverse, having in common only the probability that they are language based, it is unlikely that any single paradigm can speak to the diverse activity of the field. Depending on the setting of a given problem, the applied linguist practitioner may be expected to know something about at least the following:

Anthropology	Economics
Education theory	Gerontology
History	International relations
Language learning and teaching	Lexicography
Planning	Policy development
Political science	Psychology
Public administration	Sociology
Teacher training	Text production

Indeed, Christian (1999: 7) points out that the current staff of the Center for Applied Linguistics contains individuals holding graduate degrees in the following: particular languages, cognitive and social psychology, educational psychology, multicultural education, bilingual education, educational measurement, health administration, in addition to linguistics, applied linguistics, and sociolinguistics. In sum, the applied linguist has to have a broad exposure to all the social sciences. Of course, because the common element is language, the applied linguist ought to be well grounded in linguistics, psycho- and neurolinguistics, and sociolinguistics, including literacy, individual bilingualism, and societal multilingualism. And all applied linguists must be highly computer literate and able to deal with statistical data.

With respect to the training of incipient applied linguists, a curriculum grounded in linguistics and its various hyphenated subcomponents should be considered basic. Beyond that, perhaps a wide variety of academic minors ought to be available, or, alternatively, joint degrees in applied linguistics and any of the fields mentioned above ought to be possible, assuming that bureaucratic obstacles can be overcome. "While these demands on new students may seem daunting, they are probably no more demanding than new and increasing expectations in other disciplines. It is an exciting time to be an applied linguist, and also an exciting time to become one" (Kaplan and Grabe, 2000: 16).

The contributions to this volume will, I hope, explicate and demonstrate the breadth of applied linguistics and the depth of knowledge required of one who aspires to practice this discipline in the real world. Although the field is diverse and multidisciplinary, it need not be thought of as Balkanized. Although there is no unifying paradigm yet, it is likely that one may evolve in the future. What is unlikely, however, is that applied linguistics and autonomous linguistics will merge into a single enterprise. That is so because the two activities take quite distinct views of language: For the autonomous linguist, language is self-contained and independent of human use, whereas for the applied linguist language must be considered in the context of its uses and users.

Procedural Notes

Each of the contributions to this volume may be taken as a complete, freestanding discussion. Each is printed with its own end notes (if any are used), but the reference lists are compiled into one single alphabetical list at the end of the volume. This compilation of references is provided in part to eliminate duplication, but in part also to give a sense of the scope of the field, of the key players, and of the disciplinary history. There is also an index at the end of the volume, as well as a brief biographical listing of the contributors. The biographic entries were written by the contributors. Each entry provides an e-mail address at which the author can be contacted. Aside from these features, the approach is intentionally conservative, offering no special features and deliberately avoiding cross-reference among the contributions. Readers are invited to contact the editor or the members of the editorial with questions or comments.

Robert B. Kaplan
Port Angeles, Washington
November 2000

Preface to the Second Edition

EVERY academic discipline must, from time to time, reflect on its origins, its history, and its conflicts in order to understand its identity and its objectives. It appears, however, that the field of applied linguistics has entered a phase that might be called the "second coming of the Encyclopedists." The original Encyclopedists were the participants in the creation of *L'Encyclopédie*, produced between 1751 and 1776, directed by Denis Diderot (1713–1784) and Jean Le Rond D'Alembert (1717–1783), in 35 volumes, with essays that were said to be marked by love of truth and contempt for superstition, embodying the philosophical spirit of the eighteenth century and attempting to give a rational explanation of the universe—a notion that may have seemed perfectly plausible in the middle of the eighteenth century but that must appear, from the vantage point of the early twenty-first century, as somewhat arrogant—even the title (simply "The Encyclopedia," as if there were no other) is a bit over the top. (The relation between the two eras is more fully developed in Kaplan, 2009b.)

The task implied in the first sentence of this preface is actually quite impossible because applied linguistics is "a diverse discipline with many scholarly areas incorporated into the mainstream" (Gass and Makoni, 2004: 1). This second edition of *The Oxford Handbook of Applied Linguistic*, like its predecessor, aims to acquaint the reader with a range of perspectives that will allow the reader to understand how researchers across this wide-ranging field approach various issues that attempt to solve real-world problems in some way implicating language. This volume is *not* intended to represent all areas of applied linguistics, nor is it intended to cover the entire global geography, nor is it intended to review work relevant to all the world's languages.

The organizing principles that underlie the first edition were summarized in the preface to that volume. In terms of organization, little has changed. The distribution of scholars by country of residence and by gender for this edition is shown in table II.

The emphasis in this revision is (1) adding chapters intended to introduce some areas that have rapidly entered the field and were not represented in the prior volume and (2) deleting others in which there has been limited activity during the intervening years. For the existing chapters, authors were asked to update their reference lists and to add representative new citations; in addition, they were asked to update their texts to show important new developments over the years since the publication of the first edition and (briefly) to indicate where they think the area may now be moving.

Table II. Distribution of Contributors

By Country		By Gender	
Australia	05 (12%)	Male	22 (51%)
Belgium	01 (02.3%)	Female	21 (49%)
Canada	04 (09%)	TOTAL	43 (100%)
Hungary	02 (05%)		
Italy	01 (02.3%)		
Netherlands	01 (02.3%)		
United Kingdom	03 (07%)		
United States	26 (60%)		
TOTAL	43 (99.9%)		

In addition, the organization of the volume has been modified to show more clearly the implicit three-part structure—Where did applied linguistics come from? Where has applied linguistics arrived? Where does applied linguistics seem to be going? The chapter titled "Whence Applied Linguistics: The Twentieth Century" represents one major addition designed to support this structure. The remaining chapters of the volume (except the last, titled "Where to from Here?") indicate where applied linguistics has arrived. The last chapter tries to gather the several views of the future and to suggest what that future may involve. This is a most dangerous undertaking, because predictions often serve more to embarrass the futurist than to predict what will happen with any degree of accuracy.

Robert B. Kaplan
Port Angeles, Washington
June 2009

ACKNOWLEDGMENTS

I am deeply indebted to William Grabe, Merrill Swain, and G. Richard Tucler, who graciously agreed to serve a second time as members of the editorial advisory board and who helped enormously in the organization of this volume. I am also indebted to the authors, who contributed to this volume either for a second time or *de nouveau*, adding to the quality of this edition.

Contents
....

PART IX. LANGUAGE POLICY AND PLANNING

PART X. TRANSLATION AND INTERPRETATION

PART XI. LANGUAGE ASSESSMENT AND PROGRAM EVALUATION

PART XII. TECHNOLOGICAL APPLICATIONS IN APPLIED LINGUISTICS

PART XIII. CONCLUSION

CONTRIBUTORS

....

Colin Baker is pro vice chancellor at the University of Wales, Bangor. He is the author of 15 books and over 50 articles on bilingualism and bilingual education, with specific interests in language planning and bilingual education. His book *Foundations of Bilingual Education and Bilingualism* (Multilingual Matters, 1993, 1996, 2001, 2006) has sold over 50,000 copies and has been translated into Japanese, Spanish, Latvian, Greek, Vietnamese, and Mandarin. His *Encyclopedia of Bilingualism and Bilingual Education* (with S. P. Jones, Multilingual Matters) won the British Association for Applied Linguistics Book Prize Award in 1999. He edits three Multilingual Matters Book Series and is editor of the *International Journal of Bilingualism and Bilingual Education*. In addition to his academic activities, Colin Baker has held three U.K. government appointments. He can be reached at colin@rhodribaker.com.

Richard B. Baldauf, Jr., is professor of TESOL education in the School of Education at the University of Queensland. From 1999 to 2008 he was a member of the Executive of the International Association of Applied Linguistics (AILA). He has published several books and numerous articles in refereed journals. He is coeditor of *Language Planning and Education in Australasia and the South Pacific* (Multilingual Matters, 1990), coauthor with Robert B. Kaplan of *Language Planning from Practice to Theory* (Multilingual Matters, 1997) and *Language and Language-in-Education Planning in the Pacific Basin* (Kluwer, 2003), as well as coeditor of nine volumes in the Language Policy and Planning Series (Multilingual Matters, 2004–2008). He is coauthor with Zhao Shouhui of *Planning Chinese Characters: Evolution, Revolution or Reaction* (Springer, 2007). He can be reached at rbaldauf4@bigpond.com.

Kathleen Bardovi-Harlig is professor of second language studies and adjunct professor of linguistics, cognitive science, and Germanic studies at Indiana University, where she teaches and conducts research in second language acquisition. Her work on interlanguage pragmatics and on the acquisition of pragmatics has appeared in *Language Learning, Studies in Second Language Acquisition, Discourse Processes, ROLSI*, and *Pragmatics and Language Learning*. She is the coeditor of three volumes on the L2 acquisition of pragmatics and the means used to investigate it: *Pragmatics and Language Learning* (Vol. 11, 2006 University of Hawai'i: National Foreign Language Resource Center), *Interlanguage Pragmatics: Exploring Institutional Talk* (2005, Lawrence Erlbaum), and *Teaching Pragmatics* (2003, United States Department of State, http://exchanges.state.gov/englishteaching/resforteach/pragmatics.html). She can be reached at bardovi@indiana.edu.

Douglas Biber is Regents' Professor of English (applied linguistics) at Northern Arizona University. His research efforts have focused on corpus linguistics, English grammar, and register variation (in English and in synchronic and diachronic cross-linguistically). His publications include four books published with Cambridge University Press (1988, 1995, 1998, in press) and the coauthored *Longman Grammar of Spoken and Written English* (1999). He can be reached at douglas.biber@nau.edu.

Jill Burstein received a PhD in linguistics from the City University of New York, Graduate Center, in 1992. Dr. Burstein is currently a researcher at Educational Testing Service. Her research applies natural language processing methods to the development of text assessment applications. Dr. Burstein is a coinventor of *e-rater*, an automated essay scoring system, currently used to score essays on the Graduate Management Admissions Test, and of *Criterion*, a web-based writing instruction system. She may be reached at jburstein@ets.org.

Martin Bygate lectures in TESOL at the School of Education, University of Leeds. His main areas of interest are instructed second language acquisition, oral second language proficiency, and the role of tasks in language learning. He has directed research projects, coedited two volumes, and published a book and various research articles on the teaching and learning of oral skills. Prior to his appointment at Leeds, he taught in France, Morocco, and Brazil as well as at the Universities of Reading and London. He is currently coeditor of *Applied Linguistics* journal. He can be reached at m.bygate@education.leeds. ac.uk.

Micheline Chalhoub-Deville has a PhD from Ohio State University. She is university professor of educational research methodology at the University of North Carolina at Greensboro. She is recognized internationally for her work in the field of second language assessment. She has published in various journals, including *Annual Review of Applied Linguistics, Foreign Language Annals, Language Learning, Language Testing*, and *World Englishes*. She has edited a book on computer adaptive testing, titled *Issues in Computer-Adaptive Testing of Reading Proficiency* and coedited *Inference and Generalizability in Applied Linguistics: Multiple Research Perspectives*. Dr. Chalhoub-Deville has received the International Language Testing Association Award for Best Article on Language Testing. She has chaired the TOEFL Committee of Examiners and served on the TOEFL Policy Council. She can be reached at chalhoub-deville@uncg.edu.

Carol A. Chapelle, professor of TESL/applied linguistics, is coeditor of the Cambridge Applied Linguistics Series. Her research explores issues at the intersection of computer technology and applied linguistics. Recent books are *Computer Applications in Second Language Acquisition: Foundations for Teaching, Testing and Research* and *English Language Learning and Technology:*

Lectures on Applied Linguistics in the Age of Information and Communication Technology. Other books that focus on language assessment and research methods include the following: *Assessing Language through Technology* (Chapelle and Douglas) *Inference and Generalizability in Applied Linguistics* (Chalhoub-Deville, Chapelle, and Duff, eds.), and *ESOL Tests and Testing: A Resource for Teachers and Administrators* (Stoynoff and Chapelle). Her most recent books are *Building a Validity Argument for the Test of English as a Foreign Language* and *Tips for Teaching with CALL*. She can be reached at carolc@iastate.edu.

Martin Chodorow received a PhD in cognitive psychology from the Massachusetts Institute of Technology in 1976. After completing a postdoctoral research assignment at IBM's Thomas Watson Research Center, he joined the faculty of the psychology department at Hunter College of the City University of New York. Dr. Chodorow has worked on a number of natural language processing projects at IBM, at Princeton University's Cognitive Science Laboratory, and, most recently, at Educational Testing Service. He can be reached at martin.chodorow@hunter.cuny.edu.

Kees de Bot graduated from the University of Nijmegen in general linguistics and applied linguistics. His research concerns a number of topics including foreign language attrition, language and dementia in multilingual settings, maintenance and shift of minority languages and the psycholinguistics of bilingual language processing, early and late forms of bilingual education, and immersion and the application of dynamic systems theory in SLA and multilingualism. He is chair of applied linguistics and director of the Research School for Behavioral and Cognitive Neurosciences (BCN) at the University of Groningen. He is a trustee of the TESOL International Research Foundation and a member of the Program Committee of the Department of Modern Languages of Carnegie Mellon University. He is also coeditor of the series *Studies in Bilingualism*. He has published books and articles on various topics in the field of applied linguistics. He can be reached at c.l.j.de.bot@rug.nl.

Patricia Duff is professor of language and literacy education and Distinguished University Scholar at the University of British Columbia. She is also director of the newly established Centre for Research in Chinese Language and Literacy Education there. Her main areas of interest are language acquisition and language socialization, qualitative research methods, classroom discourse in a variety of educational contexts, including second/ foreign language courses, mainstream and L2-immersion content-based courses, and the teaching, learning, and use of English and Chinese as international languages. Her recent work includes three books and many book chapters and articles primarily dealing with language socialization across bilingual and multilingual settings; quantitative research methods (especially employing case study and ethnography) and generalizability in applied linguistics; issues in teaching and learning English, Mandarin and other international languages; the integration of second-language learners in high schools, universities and society; multilingualism at work; and sociocultural sociolinguistics and sociopolitical aspects of language(s) in education. She can be reached at patricia.duff@ubc.ca.

William G. Eggington is professor of English language and linguistics and associate chair of the English department, Brigham Young University. Originally from Australia, he received his MA and PhD in linguistics from the University of Southern California. He specializes in studying macrorelationships between language and society, specifically language policy and planning. He has published nationally and internationally in language planning; his most recent publication is a coedited book, *The Sociopolitics of English Language Teaching*. He is actively involved in professional organizations including TESOL International, having served as chair of the Sociopolitical Concerns Committee and chair of the Applied Linguistics Interest Section. He can be reached at wegg@byu.edu.

Eric Friginal is assistant professor in the Department of Applied Linguistics and English as a Second Language at Georgia State University. His main research interest lies in using corpus linguistics to explore linguistic variation in professional, cross-cultural discourse in the context of outsourced call centers in the Philippines serving American customers. He is the author of *The Language of Outsourced Call Centers: A Corpus-Based Study of Cross-Cultural Interaction*. He can be reached at efriginal@gsu.edu.

Ofelia Garcia is presently the dean of the School of Education at the Brooklyn campus of Long Island University. She has published extensively in the areas of bilingualism, bilingual education, sociology of language, and U.S. Spanish. She is the editor of the new journal *Educators for Urban Minorities*. She can be reached at ogarcia@gc.cuny.edu.

Robert C. Gardner is a professor emeritus in psychology at the University of Western Ontario. He has written two books, coauthored a third one, and coedited another. In addition, he has published approximately 150 journal articles and book chapters. The majority of his publications are concerned with the role of attitudes and motivation in second language learning, but in addition he has made contributions to the literature on ethnic relations, ethnic stereotypes, ethnic attitudes, psycholinguistics, and statistics. In 1999, he was honored by the Canadian Psychological Association with the Award for Distinguished Contributions to Education and Training. He can be reached at gardner@uwo.ca.

Susan Gass is University Distinguished Professor in the Department of Linguistics, Germanic, Slavic, Asian, and African Languages at Michigan State University. She is the director of the English Language Center, codirector of the Center for Language Education and Research, and director of the Second Language Studies PhD program. She has published widely in the field of SLA, focusing on a number of different areas, including language transfer, language universals, and input and interaction. She is the author of *Input, Interaction, and the Second Language Learner*, coauthor with Larry Selinker of *Second Language Acquisition: An Introductory Course*, and coauthor with Alison Mackey of *Second Language Research: Methodology and Design* and *Data Elicitation for Second and Foreign Language Research*. She can be reached at gass@msu.edu.

William Grabe is Regents' Professor of applied linguistics in the English Department at Northern Arizona University, where he teaches in the MA-TESL and PhD in applied linguistics programs. He is interested in reading, writing, literacy, written discourse analysis, and content-based L2 instruction. His most recent book is *Reading in a Second Language: Moving from Theory to Practice*. He has also coauthored *Theory and Practice of Writing* and *Teaching and Researching Reading* and coedited *Directions in Applied Linguistics*. He served as editor of the *Annual Review of Applied Linguistics*. He is a past president of the American Association for Applied Linguistics (2001–2002). He received the 2005 Distinguished Scholarship and Service Award from the American Association for Applied Linguistics. He can be reached at william.grabe@nau.edu.

Michael Harrington is a senior lecturer in second language acquisition at the University of Queensland, Brisbane, Australia. He has an MA in English as a second language (ESL) from the University of Hawaii, and a PhD in experimental psychology from the University of California, Santa Cruz. His research and teaching interests are in second language acquisition, research methods, second language vocabulary development, Japanese as a second language, and computer-mediated language processing and use. He has published articles and chapters in the areas of second language cognitive models, working memory, sentence processing, and computer-mediated second language acquisition. He may be reached at m.harrington@uq.edu.au.

Eli Hinkel has taught ESL and applied linguistics, as well as trained teachers, for almost 30 years. She has published numerous books and articles on learning second culture, and on second language grammar, writing, and pragmatics. Her recent books deal with research in second language learning, the effects of culture on second language learning, approaches to teaching L2 grammar, syntactic and lexical features of L2 written text, and practical techniques for teaching L2 academic writing. She is also the editor for the ESL and Applied Linguistics Professional Series of books and textbooks for teachers and graduate students. She can be reached at elihinkel@yahoo.com.

Nancy H. Hornberger is professor of education and director of educational linguistics at the University of Pennsylvania in Philadelphia. Her research interests include sociolinguistics in education, ethnography in education, language policy, bilingualism and biliteracy, indigenous language revitalization, and heritage language education. Recent publications include the 10-volume *Encyclopedia of Language and Education* and *Can Schools Save Indigenous Languages? Policy and Practice on Four Continents*. She can be reached at nancyh@upenn.edu.

Alan Juffs is currently associate professor and chair of the Department of Linguistics, University of Pittsburgh. He is the director of the English Language Institute at the University of Pittsburgh and coeditor of the Pitt Series in ESL textbooks published by the University of Michigan Press. He is currently vice-president of the University and College Intensive English Programs Consortium (UCIEP) and committee chair of the English as a Second Language Committee of the Pittsburgh Science of Learning Center. His research interests include the semantics-syntax interface and second language sentence processing. He has published in a variety of scholarly journals, including *Language Learning*, *Studies in Second Language Acquisition*, *Second Language Research*, *Language Teaching Research*, and *Transactions of the Philological Society*. In addition to more theoretical aspects of SLA, he maintains a keen interest in classroom research, vocabulary teaching, and materials development, as well as advocacy for intensive English programs. He may be reached at juffs+@pitt.edu.

Robert B. Kaplan is emeritus professor of applied linguistics in the Department of Linguistics at the University of Southern California. He was the founding editor of the *Annual Review of Applied Linguistics* and has served as an editor of the applied linguistics entries for both the first and second editions of the *International Encyclopedia of Linguistics*. In addition, he is founding coeditor (with Richard B. Baldauf, Jr.) of *Current Issues in Language Planning*. He has authored or edited some 50 books, more than 165 articles in scholarly journals and as chapters in books, and more than 90 book reviews and other more ephemeral pieces in various newsletters, as well as 10 special reports to government and to various institutions in the United States and elsewhere. Over a relatively long career, he has presented more than 200 talks, papers, and invited plenary addresses at national and international conferences. He has served as president of NAFSA (1983–1984), TESOL (1989–1990), and AAAL (1993–1994). He can be reached at rkaplan@olypen.com.

Judith Kroll is Distinguished Professor of psychology, linguistics, and women's studies and codirector of the Center for Language Science at Pennsylvania State University. Together with Annette de Groot, she edited *Tutorials in Bilingualism: Psycholinguistic Perspectives* and the *Handbook of Bilingualism: Psycholinguistic Approaches*. She served as a coeditor of *Bilingualism: Language and Cognition* from its founding in 1997 until 2001 and as its coordinating editor from 2001 to 2002. She serves on the editorial boards of *Journal of Memory and Language*; *Journal of Experimental Psychology, Learning, Memory and Cognition*; *International Journal of Bilingualism*; and *Psychological Science*. The research that she and her students conduct concerns the acquisition, comprehension, and production of two languages during second language learning and in proficient bilingual performance. Their work, using behavioral and neurocognitive methods, is supported by grants from the National Science Foundation and the National Institutes of Health. Together with Suparna Rajaram and Randi Martin, she was one of the founding organizers of *Women in Cognitive Science*, an organization supported by the National Science Foundation and developed to promote the advancement of women in the cognitive sciences. She may be reached at j.kroll@nici.kun.nl.

James P. Lantolf is the Greer Professor in language acquisition and applied linguistics in the Department of Applied Linguistics at Pennsylvania State University. He is also director of the Center for Language Acquisition and codirector of CALPER (Center for Advanced Language Proficiency Education and Research). He was president of the American Association for Applied Linguistics (2004–2005). He served as coeditor of *Applied Linguistics* (1995–2000). He has published numerous articles and book chapters, coauthored the book *Sociocultural Theory and the Genesis of Second Language Developmen*, and is editor or coeditor of three books: *Vygotskian Approaches to Second Language Research*, *Sociocultural Theory and Second Language Learning*, and *Sociocultural Theory and the Teaching of Second Languages*. He can be reached at jpl7@psu.edu.

Sara Laviosa is a lecturer in EFL and translation at the University of Bari (Aldo Moro) and a visiting lecturer at the University of Rome (Tor Vergata). From 1999 to 2002, she was lecturer in Italian at the University of Salford, Greater Manchester, United Kingdom. She has taught Italian as a foreign language, EFL, and translation in British and Italian universities. Her research interests lie in corpus translation studies and translation pedagogy. She is editor of the first volume of *Translation Studies Abstracts* and *L'Approche Basée sur le Corpus / Corpus-Based Approach* (Special Issue of *Meta*, 43 (4),1998). She is coeditor (with Anke Hübner and Toni Ibarz) of *Assessment and Accreditation for Languages: The Emerging Consensus?* She is also the author of *Corpus-Based Translation Studies: Theory, Findings, Applications* and *Linking Wor(l)ds: Lexis and Grammar for Translation*. She serves as consulting editor of *Translation Studies Abstracts and The Bibliography of Translation Studies* and as coeditor (with Dorothy Kelly) of the series Translation Practices Explained (St. Jerome Press). She can be reached at saralaviosa@gmail.com.

Ilona Leki is professor of English and director of ESL at the University of Tennessee. Her books include *Understanding ESL Writers: A Guide for Teachers*, *Academic English*, and *Reading in the Composition Classroom* (with

Joan Carson). She coedits (initially with Tony Silva, subsequently with Rosa Manchon) the *Journal of Second Language Writing*. Her research interests center around the development of academic literacy, and she is the winner of the 1996 TESOL/Newbury House Distinguished Research Award. She can be reached at leki@utk.edu.

Tony Lynch is senior lecturer at the Institute for Applied Language Studies, University of Edinburgh, Scotland, where he is involved primarily in teaching English to international students and in second language teacher education. His books include *Listening* (cowritten with Anne Anderson), *Communication in the Language Classroom*, and a new edition of *Study Listening*. He recently completed *Teaching Second Language Listening*. He is now researching second language listeners' informal practice strategies and is happy to respond to messages at A.J.Lynch@ed.ac.uk.

Mary McGroarty is professor in the applied linguistics program of the English department at Northern Arizona University, where she teaches courses in sociolinguistics, language pedagogy, and assessment. She has also been on the faculty at the University of California, Los Angeles. Her research addresses language policy, pedagogy, and assessment and has appeared in *Applied Linguistics, Language Learning, Language Policy, TESOL Quarterly*, and several anthologies. She is a past president (1997–1998) of the American Association for Applied Linguistics and has served on the editorial boards of *Applied Linguistics, Canadian Modern Language Review, Journal of Language, Identity and Education*, and *TESOL Quarterly*. From 2000 through 2006, she was editor-in-chief of the *Annual Review of Applied Linguistics*. She can be reached at mary.mcgroarty@nau.edu.

Péter Medgyes is ambassador of Hungary posted to Syria. Previously, he was a schoolteacher, teacher trainer, vice rector of his university, and deputy state secretary at the Hungarian Ministry of Education. Professor Medgyes has written numerous books and articles, including *The Non-Native Teacher* (winner of the Duke of Edinburgh Book Competition), *Changing Perspectives in Teacher Education* (coedited with Angi Malderez), *The Language Teacher*, and *Laughing Matters*. His main professional interests lie in curriculum studies, language policy, and teacher education. He can be reached at medgyes@citromail.hu.

Peter Mühlhäusler is the Foundation Professor of Linguistics at the University of Adelaide and Supernumerary Fellow of Linacre College, Oxford. He has taught at the Technical University of Berlin and in the University of Oxford. He is an active researcher in several areas of linguistics, including ecolinguistics, language planning, and language policy and language contact in the Australian-Pacific area. His current research focuses on the Pitkern-Norf'k language of Norfolk Island and Aboriginal languages of the West Coast of South Australia. His recent book publications are *Pidgin and Creole Linguistics, Language of*

Environment-Environment of Language, Early Forms of Aboriginal English in South Australia (with Foster and Monaghan), and *Herrmann Koeler's Adelaide-Observations on Language and Culture of South Australia* (with Amery and Gara). He continues to publish on theoretical and applied ecolinguistics. He can be reached at peter.muhlhausler@adelaide.edu.au.

Peter Hans Nelde died on August 31, 2007, after a long illness. Despite his passing, the contribution he wrote for the *Oxford Handbook of Applied Linguistics* was considered to be of such importance that it was decided to retain it in its original form. Dr. Nelde established *contact linguistics* as an integral part of the discipline, supported by annual international symposia dealing with contact and conflict between linguistic minorities and majorities. In addition, he established the series Plurilingua that he maintained as editor-in-chief during his life. Dr. Nelde was professor and chair of German and general linguistics at the Katholieke Universiteit Brussel (Belgium) and visiting professor in Nijmegen (the Netherlands) and Leipzig (Germany). He directed Languages in a Network of European Excellence (LINEE), the international research project on linguistic diversity sponsored by the European Union. In 1977 he founded the Research Centre on Multilingualism and had been its director ever since. He was responsible for the publication of the Euromosaic reports on the linguistic minorities of Europe. He was also one of the editors of *Sociolinguistica: International Yearbook of Sociolinguistics* (Niemeyer, Tübingen) and the editor in chief of *Contact Linguistics: An International Handbook of Contemporary Research*. His main research areas were multilingualism, contact linguistics, language policy, and language planning. He shall be sorely missed.

Marianne Nikolov is professor of English applied linguistics at the University of Pécs, Hungary, where she teaches undergraduate and graduate courses. Her research areas include early learning and teaching of modern languages, assessment of processes and outcomes in language education, individual differences, and language policy. Her papers have been published in *Language Learning, Language Teaching Research*, and *Annual Review of Applied Linguistics*. She is the author of several edited volumes. She can be reached at nikolov@nostromo.pte.hu.

Bonny Norton is professor and Distinguished University Scholar in the Department of Language and Literacy Education, University of British Columbia, Canada. She is also visiting senior research fellow in the Department of Education, King's College, University of London, and honorary professor in the School of Education, University of Witwatersrand, South Africa. Her award-winning research addresses identity and language learning, education and international development, and critical literacy. Recent publications include *Identity and Language Learning, Critical Pedagogies and Language Learning* (with K. Toohey), and *Gender and English*

Language Learners (with A. Pavlenko). She is currently coediting a Multilingual Matters book series, Critical Language and Literacy Studies (with several others). In 2003, she was awarded a UBC Killam Prize for Excellence in Teaching and in 2007 a UBC Killam Prize for Excellence in Research. Her website can be found at http://lerc.educ.ubc.ca/fac/norton/, and she can be contacted at bonny.norton@ubc.ca.

Terence Odlin is associate professor of English and adjunct associate professor of linguistics at Ohio State University. He has also taught in Washington DC, Texas, Algeria, Iran, France, Ireland, and Finland, where he was a Fulbright Scholar in 1997. Along with the psycholinguistic issues involved in language transfer and contrastive analysis, his research interests are focused on sociohistorical factors in language contact situations in the Celtic lands and elsewhere. He is the author of *Language Transfer*, the editor of *Perspectives on Pedagogical Grammar*, and coeditor of *Language Contact, Variation and Change*. He can be reached at odlin.1@osu.edu.

Deborah Poole is an associate professor of applied linguistics at San Diego State University. Her research focuses on classroom interaction as related to pedagogy, literacy, and language socialization. Her publications include articles in *Linguistics & Education, Reading Research Quarterly, Discourse Processes*, and *Language Learning*. She has also coauthored several ESL textbooks. She can be reached at dpoole@mail.sdsu.edu.

Randi Reppen is professor of applied linguistics in the Department of English at Northern Arizona University. Her research interests include exploring how corpus linguistics can inform language teaching and materials development. She can be reached at randi.reppen@nau.edu.

Betty Samraj is associate professor of linguistics at San Diego State University. Her research interests are in genre analysis and writing across the disciplines. Her publications include articles in journals such as *English for Specific Purposes, Journal of English for Academic Purposes*, and *TEXT*. She can be reached at bsamraj@mail.sdsu.edu.

John H. Schumann is professor of applied linguistics and former chair of the Department of Applied Linguistics and TESL at UCLA. His research focuses on the neurobiology of the language, the neurobiology of learning, language acquisition, and language evolution. He is coauthor of the book *The Interactional Instinct: The Evolution and Acquisition of Language*. He can be reached at schumann@humnet.ucla.edu.

Nancy L. Schweda Nicholson, PhD (Georgetown University), is professor of linguistics and cognitive science with a joint appointment in the Legal Studies Program at the University of Delaware. Dr. Nicholson is widely published in the areas of interpreting theory and practice, interpreter training, and language planning for court interpreter services. The late Honorable William

H. Rehnquist, Chief Justice of the United States, appointed her to the Federal Court Interpreters Advisory Board. She is a member of the Committee on Court Interpreters and Legal Translation of the *Fédération Internationale des Traducteurs* (International Federation of Translators, FIT). In September 2008, Professor Nicholson was invited to address the Supreme Court of Korea on court interpreting in the United States. In addition to her interpreter policy research at the International Criminal Tribunal for the Former Yugoslavia (ICTY) and the International Criminal Court (ICC), Dr. Nicholson is currently studying proposed European Union legislation that would require comparable language services in criminal matters throughout the 27 member states. She can be reached at nsn@UDel.Edu.

Jeff Siegel, currently associate professor of linguistics at the University of New England in Australia, has an MA in English as a second language from the University of Hawai'i and a PhD in linguistics from the Australian National University. He has done extensive research on pidgins, creoles, and other language contact varieties and their use in education and is author of *Language Contact in a Plantation Environment*, *Vernacular Education in the South Pacific*, and *The Emergence of Pidgin and Creole languages*. Since 1990, he has been editor of the *Pidgin and Creoles in Education (PACE) Newsletter*. He can be reached at jsiegel@une.edu.au.

James W. Tollefson is Emeritus professor of English at the University of Washington and Professor of Media, Communication, and Culture at International Christian University in Tokyo. He is the author or editor of eight books, including *Language Policy, Culture, and Identity in Asian Contexts* (co-edited with Amy B.M. Tsui); *Medium of Instruction Policies: Which Agenda? Whose Agenda?* (co-edited with Amy B.M. Tsui); *Language Policies in Education: Critical Issues*; *Power and Inequality in Language Education*; *The Strength Not to Fight: An Oral History of Conscientious Objectors of the Vietnam War*; *Planning Language, Planning Inequality*; *Alien Winds: TheReeducation of America's Indochinese Refugees*; and *The Language Situation and Language Policy in Slovenia*. His articles appear in *Journal of the Sociology of Language*, *TESOL Quarterly*, *Language Problems and Language Planning*, *Studies in Second Language Acquisition*, and many other journals. He may be reached at tollefso@u.washington.edu.

Kelleen Toohey is professor in the faculty of education at Simon Fraser University, Canada. Her current research examines literacy instruction and learning in child English language learners' classrooms. Recent publications include *Learning English at School: Identity, Social Relations and Classroom Practice*, *Critical Pedagogies and Language Learning* (with B. Norton). She is coauthor of *Collaborative Research in Multilingual Classrooms* (with C. Denos, K. Neilson, and B. Waterstone). She can be contacted at toohey@sfu.ca.

Marjorie Bingham Wesche was professor from 1978 to 2005 at the University of Ottawa (Second Language Institute and Graduate Studies in Education), and former director of the Institute, and serves as adjunct professor since her retirement. Her main research and teaching interests have involved second language acquisition, instruction, content-based second language instruction (immersion and postsecondary initiatives) language aptitude and assessment, and vocabulary acquisition. She has published widely on these topics, coauthored *Content-Based Second Language Instruction* and *Lexical Inferencing in a First and Second Language: Cross-Linguistic Dimensions* (2010), and co-edited *Second Language Performance Testing* and *Language Testing Reconsidered*. She also guest-edited two special issues of journals: *Incidental L2 Vocabulary Acquisition: Theory, Current Research and Instructional Implications, Studies in Second Language Acquisition,* 21 (1999), and *French Immersion and Content-Based Language Teaching in Canada, Canadian Modern Language Review,* 58 (2001). She can be reached at mwesche@xplornet.com.

PART I

INTRODUCTION

CHAPTER 1

WHENCE APPLIED LINGUISTICS: THE TWENTIETH CENTURY

ROBERT B. KAPLAN

EVERY academic discipline must, from time to time, reflect on its origins, its history, and its conflicts in order to understand its identity and its objectives. The *Oxford Handbook of Applied Linguistics* was an attempt to provide such a reflection, though it was by no means the only publication undertaking to record the history and spread of applied linguistics. (See, e.g., Allen and Corder, 1973, 1974, 1975; Allen and Davies, 1977; Bright, 1991; K. Brown, 2006; Brumfit, 1997a; G. Cook, 2003; Cook and Kasper, 2005; Davies, 1999; Davies and Elder, 2004b; K. de Bot, 2008; Doughty and Long, 2003; Finegan and Rickford, 2004; Frawley, 2003; Gass and Makoni, 2004; Grabe, 2004; Grabe and Kaplan, 1991; Halliday, McIntosh, and Strevens, 1964; Hinkel, 2005; Hornberger, 2008b; K. Johnson and Johnson, 1998; Joseph and Waugh, in press; Kaplan, 2002b, 1980; Kaplan and Grabe, 2000; Knapp and Antos, in press; Rosenthal, 2000; Schmitt, 2002; Spolsky, 1999; Spolsky and Hult, 2007; Tucker, 2000.)

Neither this review nor the second edition of the *Oxford Handbook* it introduces can possibly cover the world—it cannot represent all areas of applied linguistics or cover all countries of the world in which applied linguistics is being practiced. Both this synoptic history and the *Handbook* are intended to present a snapshot of the history of applied linguistics as well as of applied linguistics research from a variety of approaches, and, consequently, they celebrate the diversity that is applied linguistics. But, given such diversity, applied linguistics has emerged in different geographic spaces, having evolved through diverse histories.

This brief look at the history focuses on the evolution of applied linguistics in the English-speaking polities of Australia, Canada, New Zealand, the United Kingdom, and the United States. There is important work being done in Europe and in Africa, Asia, and Latin America that is not reflected in this historical overview, but there is only so much that one history can cover without becoming a bibliographic notation. (See, e.g., Gass and Makoni, 2004, for coverage of applied linguistics worldwide.) In time, the limiting of this history up to the year 2000 is also entirely arbitrary, but the *Handbook* chapters are a product of the twenty-first century, opening up the exciting applied linguistic work being done during the first decade of the twenty-first century.

It has been alleged that the term *applied linguistics* arose, in the 1940s, among a group of English composition teachers who wanted to be identified with scientific linguistic concepts rather than with less precise literary concepts. Conventional wisdom claims that the term first appeared in print in the title of the journal *Language Learning: A Journal of Applied Linguistics* that began publication in 1948 (Angelis, 2001), but Angelis found an earlier reference—in a speech by Hermann Collitz (1855–1935) of Johns Hopkins University presented at the foundational meeting of the Linguistics Society of America (LSA) on December 28, 1924, and Andresen (1990) traces the work, if not the title, back to the end of the eighteenth century. (See endnote 24 for more recent discussion.) Whatever the case, applied linguistics is a relatively new discipline, having sprung into existence slightly over 60 years ago. In its early life it was believed that the field was exclusively constrained to teaching English as a second language, though, as this chapter tries to demonstrate, the field has expanded and has professionalized enormously in the more recent past. However, interest in language teaching and learning still constitutes an important aspect of the field. (For encyclopedic views of this aspect of the field at the end of the 1960s, see, e.g., W. F. Mackey, 1965; Rivers, 1968a, 1968b. For an extensive list of periodicals available in the late 1960s, see, e.g., Mackey, 1967: 469–472.)

The 1950s and 1960s constituted a period of great ferment for applied linguists and for language teachers generally—only three key events in the field predate the beginning of the 1950s:

1. The Summer Institute of Linguistics, the sister organization of Wycliffe Bible Translators, "a worldwide U.S.-based nonprofit evangelical Christian organization whose main purpose is to study, develop and document lesser-known languages in order to expand linguistic knowledge, promote literacy and aid minority language development," was founded by William Cameron Townsend (1896–1982) in Arkansas in 1934.[1]
2. *Language Learning: A Journal of Applied Linguistics* began publication in 1948, having its base in
3. The English Language Institute (ELI) at the University of Michigan, which began its work under Charles C. Fries (1887–1967) in 1941. (See, e.g., Fries, 1945.)

A Historical Framework

A great flurry of events occurred from the 1950s through the 1960s (Kaplan, 2003, 1997):

- In 1951 the English Language Institute in Mexico City was established (Albert Marckwardt, director).
- In 1956 the School of Applied Linguistics at the University of Edinburgh was inaugurated (J. C. Catford, first director).
- In 1957 the Bourguiba Institute in Tunis was created (Rafik Said, director).
- In 1958 the Central Institute of English (CIEFL) in Hyderabad, India, was established (Ramesh Mohan, director[2]).
- In 1959 the Center for Applied Linguistics (CAL) opened its doors in Washington, DC (Charles Ferguson, director).

The momentum carried over well into the 1960s:

- In 1962 the Philippine Normal College Language Study Center was opened (Bonifacio Sibayan, director).
- In 1964 a linguistic development program at the National University of San Marcos, Peru, was initiated (Alberto Escobar presiding).
- In 1964 the International Association for Applied Linguistics/ *Association Internationale de Linguistique Applique* (AILA) was organized (see Valdman, 2004, for an excellent history of AILA in its formative years).
- In 1965 the English Language Institute of the American University in Cairo opened (Clifford Prator, director).
- In 1966 the Teachers of English to Speakers of Other Languages (TESOL) was organized (Harold Allen elected first president).
- In 1967 the British Association of Applied Linguistics (BAAL) was organized (S. Pit Corder presiding).
- In 1967 the International Association of Teachers of English as a Foreign Language (IATEFL) was organized (W. R. Lee presiding).
- In 1968 the Regional English Language Centre (RELC, later Regional Language Centre) of the Southeast Asia Ministers of Education Organization (SEAMEO)[3] was organized in Singapore (Tai Yu-Lin, director).
- In 1968, the Modern Language Centre at the Ontario Institute for Studies in Education, in Toronto, Canada, was founded (H. H. [David] Stern, director).[4]
- In 1969 the Caribbean Language Research Program at the University of the West Indies opened (Albert Marckward presiding).

In the United States

The Ford Foundation supported the development of the centers in Cairo, Hyderabad, Manila, Tunis, Washington DC, and the West Indies (M. J. Fox, 1975). Starting with the funding of the Central Institute of English in Hyderabad, the Ford Foundation began working closely with the British Council. However, because the Ford Foundation was a U.S.-based charitable foundation headquartered in New York, not surprisingly, the majority of the first directors of these various organizations were either North American or had been trained in North America. The Bureau of Educational and Cultural Affairs of the U.S. Department of State substantially supported the work of English language teachers and teacher-trainers in some areas abroad.[5]

In the years following the end of WWII, there was a significant migration of international students into academic institutions in the United States. It was recognized early on that these students had clear problems with immigration matters, with respect to the interpretation of foreign credentials, and with English language proficiency. NAFSA was founded in 1948 to address these various problems.[6] Its sections on foreign student advising, CAFSS, and on admissions issues, ADSEC, developed procedures for dealing with those matters, and its section on teaching English language, ATESL, was created somewhat later to address the particular problems of English language fluency. (See, e.g., H. M. Jenkins, 1982.) By 1953, thousands of students were enrolled in English-language programs at more than 150 institutions.[7] This development created a need for teachers specifically trained to teach and to prepare materials for that special population.

Driven by these developments, the Ford Foundation supported a conference on linguistics and the teaching of English as a foreign language at the University of Michigan in 1957. The direct outcome of that conference was a grant from the Ford Foundation to the Modern Language Association to support the development of center for applied linguistics. The center (known as CAL), soon operating independent of the MLA, served as the secretariat for the National Advisory Council on Teaching English as a Foreign Language (NACTEFL).

Amid all this ferment, the idea of TESOL was born. In May 1964, NACTEFL[8] recommended the development of a national register of specialists in teaching English to speakers of other languages (ESOL) from which individuals might be drawn to staff overseas programs (sponsored and funded by the U. S. government) in the teaching of English, teacher training, and administration; in October 1964, NACTEFL proposed the development of a professional association to facilitate its earlier recommendation. In response to the NACTEFL recommendations, an ad hoc committee meeting was called by Harold Allen (University of Minnesota), Robert Lado (dean of the School of Languages and Linguistics, Georgetown University, trained at the University of Michigan under C. C. Fries) and Serarpi Ohannesian (CAL). The committee, chaired by Robert Lado, met in Chicago in January 1965, with Virginia French Allen (Columbia University, Teachers College) and Betty Wallace Robinette (Ball State University) serving as recorders, and including, among others, James Alatis (U.S. Office of Education, later executive secretary, TESOL), Harold Allen (later first president, TESOL), Edward Anthony (later second president, TESOL), Charles Ferguson (CAL), Mary Finocchiaro (later fifth president, TESOL), David Harris (later fourth president, TESOL), Robert Hogan (executive secretary, NCTE), Albert Marckwardt (Princeton University), Sirarpi Ohannesian (CAL), Clifford Prator (UCLA), and Mamie Sizemore (Division of Indian Education, Arizona Department of Public Instruction).

The first anticipatory conference on the teaching of English to speakers of other languages, organized by Harold Allen and a number of distinguished colleagues, was held in Tucson, AZ, in May 1964; some 800 persons attended. The second such conference was held in San Diego, CA, the following year, and TESOL was officially organized as a professional association at a meeting in New York in 1966 (attended by 357 individuals, each paying annual dues of $6.00), where Harold Allen was elected as its president (Alatis, 1989). The organization of TESOL had been supported by a consortium of professional bodies including the Center for Applied Linguistics (CAL), the Modern Language Association (MLA), the National Association For Foreign Student Affairs (NAFSA),[9] the National Council of Teachers of English (NCTE), and the Speech Association of America (SAA). Their participation was, in part, altruistic and professional, but in part it was purely practical— intended to get those annoying ESL people from eating up valuable time in their respective conference agendas. By 1969, The Institute for International Education (IIE) was reporting that 23 academic institutions were offering graduate studies and certificate programs in the teaching of English as a second language (TESL), and an additional 40 institutions were at least offering methods courses. With the growing demand for English language proficiency world wide, many of the teachers produced by these academic programs sought and found teaching opportunities in various parts of the world, often funded by foundations or by the U.S. government.

Over the next 2 years, as TESOL's political structure gradually matured, its constitution was revised (1968–1969) to allow for the creation of geographic affiliates and of professional interest sections. The Applied Linguistics Interest Section (among the earliest sections formed) constituted the primary (and for a time, the sole) venue for applied linguistics activity and research in the United States. As a capstone to all this activity, Harold Allen disseminated the first issue of the *TESOL Newsletter* (later *TESOL Matters*) in June 1966. The *TESOL Quarterly*—a refereed academic journal—began publication in 1967 under the editorship of Betty Wallace Robinette; this journal was (and continues to be) a major carrier of applied linguistics research in North America.

The applied linguistics monopoly of TESOL was broken in 1978 with the creation of the American Association of Applied Linguistics (AAAL, http://www.aaal.org/). It wasn't merely a political monopoly that was disrupted:[10] an important theoretical distinction needed to be worked out (see, e.g., Kaplan, 1993b; Davies 1997; Davies and Elder, 2004b). In 1980, the applied linguistics functions of *TESOL Quarterly* were, to some extent, assumed by the journal *Applied Linguistics* (*AL;*

published by Oxford University Press and having both a British and a North American coeditor) and by the *Annual Review of Applied Linguistics* (*ARAL;* initially [1981–1984] published by Newbury House, but then continuously to date by Cambridge University Press).

The history of AAAL has been published elsewhere (see Kaplan and Grabe, 2000: 3–17). It seems redundant to repeat it here in its entirety. In brief, discussions began at the annual TESOL conference in Puerto Rico in May 1973 and continued from there:

- At the Summer Institute of the Linguistic Society of America (LSA) in Ann Arbor, MI, in August 1973
- At the annual business meeting of the LSA in December 1973
- At the then newly created Special Interest Section for Applied Linguistics at TESOL in March 1975 in Los Angeles
- At the annual business meeting of the LSA in San Francisco in December 1975
- At special program segments at the TESOL Conferences in New York in 1976, in Miami in 1977, and in Mexico City in 1978
- And especially at a roundtable discussion during the 1977 TESOL Miami Conference, where an informal vote of those attending was taken

During the summer months of 1977, an executive committee and several other committees were convened. A formal constitutional convention was organized in conjunction with the ACTFL convention in San Francisco in November 1977; the association came into existence, and Wilga Rivers was elected the association's first president.

In more recent years, a large number of attempts to define the field have been published (see, e.g., Candlin and Sarangi, 2004; Corder, 1973; Davies, 1999; Davies and Elder, 2004a; Grabe, 2002; Grabe, 2004; Grabe and Kaplan, 1991, 2006; Hinkel, 2005; Johnson and Johnson, 1998; Kaplan, 1980, 1993b, 2002a; Kaplan and Widdowson, 1992; Schmitt, 2002; Spolsky, 1999; Widdowson, 1979, 1984; Widdowson and Kaplan 2003), and two journals devoted to the field have appeared since 1980 (see, e.g., *Applied Linguistics, Annual Review of Applied Linguistics*).

As noted, however, the field has diversified into a range of specialties (this list merely suggests the increasing diversity of the field; for more detailed analysis, see, e.g., Grabe 2002, 2004):

1. Bilingualism (Cummins, 2000b)
2. Language for academic purposes (see, e.g., Benesch, 2001; Canagarajah, 2002)
3. Learning (see, e.g., Schumann et al., 2004)
4. Linguistic diversity (see, e.g., Finegan and Rickford, 2004; Valdez, 2001)
5. Pedagogy (see, e.g., Kumaravadivelu, 2001; McGroarty et al., 2004; VanPatten, 2003)
6. Policy and planning (see, e.g., Crawford, 2003; Cummins, 2000b; Fishman, 2001; Kaplan and Baldauf, 1997b; Tucker, 2003)

7. Professional uses (see, e.g., McGroarty, 2002)
8. Reading (see, e.g., Koda, 2005)
9. Second language acquisition (see, e.g., Cohen, 1998; Doughty and Long, 2003; Swain, 2000b; White, 2000)
10. Teaching SL/FL (see, e.g., Celce-Murcia, 2001; Hinkel, 2005; Kern, 2000; Klee, 2000; Widdowson, 2003)
11. Testing (see, e.g., Bachman and Palmer, 1996)
12. Variation (see, e.g., Conrad and Biber, 2001)
13. Writing (see, e.g., Ferris and Hedgcock, 2004; B. Kroll, 2003)

Not only have new areas of specialization come into the fold, but there has also been a certain amount of fragmentation. Areas such as language assessment, language policy and planning, second language acquisition, and writing, for example, have developed more rapidly than other areas, so that what were once splinters have grown into full-fledged separable trees. Indeed, these four areas have produced their own journals and their own internal structures. The Language Testing Research Colloquium has given birth to a new organization (International Language Testing Association) and a new journal (*Language Testing*), while language policy and planning, second language acquisition, and writing have spawned new journals to manage the rapidly growing body of specialized research. Language policy and planning is now represented by three dedicated journals—*Current Issues in Language Planning, Language Policy*, and *Language Problems & Language Planning*—but occasional pertinent articles also appear in the *International Journal of the Sociology of Language*, the *Journal of Multilingual and Multicultural Development*, and *World Englishes*. Second language acquisition has not yet produced a new organization, but it does have a dedicated journal, *Studies in Second Language Acquisition*. Writing has not developed an independent political structure, but it is represented in several journals—*Journal of Second Language Writing, English for Specific Purposes, Written Communication*, and *Text*. Such more general journals as *Language Learning, Modern Language Journal*, and *TESOL Quarterly* often contain pertinent articles.

The fragmentation described here can be seen either as a Balkanization of the field or rather as a healthy specialist branching; it seems likely, however, that the development is primarily a healthy one, because the extant applied linguistics journals were unable to deal with the rapidly increasing quantity and quality of scholarship.[11]

In the United Kingdom

Although the term *applied linguistics* may have originated in the United States, interest in what came to be called *applied linguistics* can be documented to the early nineteenth century in Britain and Europe. The "reform movement" (Howatt, 1999:

622–623) was, essentially, a pan-European reaction against the widely proliferated and marginally successful "grammar/translation" model of foreign and/or second language teaching during the nineteenth century. Henry Sweet (1845–1912) is sometimes credited as "the prime originator of an Applied Linguistics approach to the teaching of language" (Howatt, 1984: 180), although such other important figures as Otto Jesperson (1860–1943) in Denmark, Paul Edouard Passy (1859–1940) in France, and Wilhelm Vitor (1850–1918) in Germany must also be given appropriate credit.[12] The reformists focused on spoken language—a notion that helped to spread the direct method—and their rejection of the use of grammar rules independent of coherent texts provided an important intellectual foundation for early twentieth-century language teachers. In turn, the establishment of monolingual methodology as the norm for teaching English worked to set English language teaching (ELT) apart from foreign language teaching.

THE EMERGENCE OF ENGLISH LANGUAGE TEACHING (ELT)

Henry Palmer (1877–1949) did more than any other individual to turn ELT into an autonomous branch of education (Howatt, 1999), and was also a major influence on the applied linguistics that developed during and after World War II in the United States. Starting his teaching career in Belgium before World War I, Palmer's interest in transcribing speech led to an offer to give lectures on language-teaching methodology at London University—he had been forced by the 1914 start of WWI to escape to England. The London University offer brought him into contact with the university's new School of Oriental Studies, and that connection subsequently resulted in an invitation to go to Tokyo to advise the Japanese Department of Education. He remained in Japan until 1936.

The person responsible for bringing Palmer to London—and hence, indirectly, to Japan—was Daniel Jones (1881–1967), a fellow member (and later president) of the International Phonetic Association (IPA). Jones started lecturing at London University in 1907; 5 years later he became head of Britain's first department of phonetics. In addition to his analyses of English (notably the seminal *An Outline of English Phonetics*, 1918), Jones was also involved in the phonetic description of several African and Asian languages.

Through the Japanese Institute for Research in English Teaching (IRET), which he helped found in 1923, Palmer promoted the development of language-teaching methodology with a particular emphasis on graded listening exercises and on lexically restricted texts. Lexical restriction had been stimulated by his interest in the "British-American Scientific International Commercial English" (BASIC), developed by C. K. Ogden (1889–1957) and I. A. Richards (1893–1979). In the course of his first trip to the United States during the summer of 1926, Palmer met Edward Sapir (1884–1939), and, during a subsequent visit in 1934, Palmer played a key role in the Carnegie Conference on lexically restricted teaching materials.

Another important figure whose path crossed with Palmer's was reformist A. S. Hornby (1898–1978), who had been recruited from a provincial Japanese college in order to research lexical collocations at the IRET; Hornby became director of that institute in 1936. His *Idiomatic and Syntactic Dictionary*, published in Tokyo in 1942,[13] was an important model for monolingual learner dictionaries, including Hornby's own *Oxford Advanced Learners' Dictionary of Current English*. Forced to return to England by the outbreak of WWII, Hornby joined the British Council in 1942, and 4 years later founded the influential journal *English Language Teaching*, A Periodical Devoted to the Teaching of English as a Foreign Language.

Meanwhile Michael West (1888–1973), who had been involved in lexical research in the Indian Education Service in Bengal, urged the development of materials using controlled vocabulary; he published the first learner's dictionary, *New Method English Dictionary*, in 1935. Increasingly, he became critical of Ogden and Richards's BASIC, and joined Palmer and Hornby at the Carnegie Conference of 1936, adding his own views concerning lexical restriction.

The Organization of the British Council

Britain had had to deal with its empire during the last years of the nineteenth century as well as during the years between the wars, especially during the first quarter of the twentieth century.[14] In 1932 a joint committee representing the Boards of Trade and of Education was formed to consider the need for an organization to promote British culture and science across the Commonwealth and beyond. As a result, The British Council for Relations with Other Countries was created, leading to the establishment 2 years later of (and known from 1936 simply as) the British Council. Although funded partly from the Foreign Office, the council had its own chairman and considerable freedom over policy formulation.

In addition to government sources, private enterprises (e.g., initially, the oil giant Shell, and the Ford Foundation in the years immediately following WWII) were approached to support ELT projects overseas (with the intent to counter the influence of Fascist Italy and Germany), having a particular focus on the Middle East, the Balkans, Portugal (even though Portugal was a fascist state until 1971), and South America. Early activities included the support of teachers and teaching institutions through funding, supply of books and periodicals, and organization of lecture tours.

The outbreak of WWII in 1939 dramatically altered council activities. Although military and financial constraints curtailed many overseas operations, there was a new preoccupation in Britain with the linguistic needs of unprecedented numbers of refugees. The council announced a priority on producing texts for self-instruction, including, for example, adaptations of Ogden and Richard's *BASIC Step-by-Step* for Dutch and Czech speakers. The war also brought a huge expansion in the role of the central government.[15]

Postwar reconstruction and the need to repay war loans brought austerity to Britain that was in many ways more severe than it had been during the war years, resulting in the closure of many council offices, especially in the Middle East and Latin America, and raising questions about the future viability of the organization. Indeed, the renewal of council activity in Europe was short-lived in the many countries that happened to fall behind the iron curtain. But with its role more clearly defined as educational and cultural, rather than overtly propagandist, there was growing recognition of the council's potential not only for curbing anticolonialism, but also for helping to maintain British influence where decolonization was inevitable.[16]

After initial doubts about what to do with the empire, the postwar Labor government began to pursue a vigorous colonial and foreign policy—a policy that was continued by its Conservative successors. Although some signs of government interest in centralizing imperial educational policies can be traced to the period before the war—notably the 1927 first Colonial Conference Committee on Education, and the creation of a unified Colonial Education Service 10 years later—in general it was the clear decline of empire itself that provided the impetus to continue British cultural influence in postcolonial contexts. As a consequence, there was a significant expansion of council activity in India and Pakistan after 1948, following their independence. Breaking from a tradition of restricting the spread of English in the colonies, governments in the 1950s began to see reasons for promoting English as a medium of instruction. As Fox observed in retrospect in 1975,

> Ford Foundation experience over the past two decades [i.e., 1952–1974] has shown that language projects that are designed to further national development cannot be limited to establishing resources to teach English...as a second language, or to creating linguistics and language scholars only at the university level, or to encouraging basic research about language use, or to training language specialists for work as educators or administrators, or to innovation in language curricula based on an appropriate experimentation. (1975: 147)

In this single sentence, Fox succeeds in summarizing the errors underlying the bulk of the work supported by the council, the foundations and the U.S. agencies during the 1950s and 1960s.

In 1954, a committee of inquiry into overseas information services identified a key role for the council's ELT activities in managing public opinion, both in the colonies themselves and in other countries where British influence was being questioned. Two years later, the Official Committee on the Teaching of English Overseas reported on opportunities for expanding ESL throughout the non-Anglophone world. It recommended closer collaboration with the United States in order to draw on the latter's wealth of experience derived from domestic ELT. In the same year, a conference at Nutford House formulated plans to expand British academic interests overseas, with ELT as an important element of that activity.

In 1961, the council established the English Teaching Information Centre (ETIC), which both published its own, and archived other, language teaching materials. However, ETIC was to be overshadowed by the Centre for Information on Language Teaching (CILT), established under George Perren in 1966. (The center endured until 1986.) Many of its materials, including those donated by IRET, were subsequently transferred to the University of Edinburgh.

It is important to bear in mind that, until the start of World War II, imperial policy tended to work toward restricting the spread of English to strategic elites, with a heavy focus on literature and on cultural assimilation, quite different from the methods espoused by disciples of the reform movement. By the end of the WWII, Britain had ceded the task of serious research into language pedagogy to the United States, offering nothing to challenge the likes of C. C. Fries's work at the English Language Institute at the University of Michigan. The reversal of colonial expansion brought about by the war seems to have been paralleled by restricted professional and intellectual activity in ELT, the main protagonists tending to inhabit a small circle connected with the British Council, London University's Institute of Education, the Colonial Office, and the BBC, and the main aim of these professionals was to refine existing models rather than to innovate.

Nevertheless, the expansion of applied linguistics in the United States and the potential rewards from collaborating with the United States did not go unnoticed. In July 1955, the British Council sponsored a conference at Ditchley House, near Oxford, to which representatives of the United States Information Agency and the State Department's Bureau of Educational and Cultural Affairs were invited, as was a representative of the Ford Foundation. Unfortunately, written records from this collaboration no longer exist (Phillipson, 1992: 164). However, in the following year, the *Report of the Official Committee on the Teaching of English Overseas* (Ministry of Education, 1956) noted the extent to which linguistics had become established in universities in the United States and how this phenomenon had helped to improve the production of teaching materials. At the same time, the report commented that the U.S. interest in promoting ELT overseas might benefit from British experience, and the report anticipated possibilities for increasing ESL throughout the non-Anglophone world if the two nations were to combine their respective strengths. Hornby pushed for closer ties between the British Council and the universities in the United Kingdom (notably Edinburgh, Leeds, and London University's Institute of Education).[17]

Ways of expanding British academic interests overseas were discussed at the Nutford House Conference of 1956, during which the central importance of ELT was acknowledged. A year later, the Hill Report recommended greater emphasis on training and supporting local teachers rather than on sending out teachers from Britain. (At that time, the only British institution offering TEFL training was London University's Institute of Education.)

Britain's first School of Applied Linguistics was founded in 1957 at the University of Edinburgh under the directorship of J. C. (Ian) Catford (a pupil of Daniel Jones) with the aid of David Abercrombie (1909–1992) at the Department of Phonetics. In addition to their interest in phonetics, both shared a background of teaching English overseas with the British Council.

Leeds University was another important center of applied linguistics at that time, producing Julian Dakin (1939–1971), who was to take over at Edinburgh in 1964.[18] His colleague, Stephen Pit Corder (1918–1990) also moved into the renamed Department of Applied Linguistics. Dakin was a pioneer in the field of language laboratory-based learning. Corder's "The Significance of Learners' Errors" (1967), seminal to research on interlanguage, was published the same year that he became the first chair of the British Association of Applied Linguistics (BAAL). From the late 1960s, Edinburgh started running summer schools at which ELT publishers exhibited, and in 1968 it hosted the Second Annual General Meeting of BAAL. In 1970, the Applied Linguistics Department (which had recently merged with the Linguistics Department) turned its ELT materials collection into a resource center, later expanded into the Institute of Applied Language Studies (IALS) archive. In the 1970s, the Edinburgh Course in Applied Linguistics (ECAL) was established (Corder, 1974, 1978a; see also Allen and Corder 1973, 1975; Allen and Davies, 1977).

Other universities active in establishing applied linguistics in the United Kingdom include Essex (which created a chair in the discipline in 1965), Cambridge (where the Department of Linguistics was organized by John Trim, 1922–, in 1965 having a distinctly sociolinguistic outlook), and Reading (which had been active in the field of sociolinguistics under Peter Trudgill and started an MA program in applied linguistics in 1974).

Although Oxford University does not figure prominently in the teaching of applied linguistics, its publishing house, Oxford University Press (OUP), played a crucial role in producing academic and pedagogical materials and in supporting language teaching. OUP's representatives—for example, Peter Collier and Christina Whitecross—traveled the world and worked not merely to market OUP's publications but also to serve an important role in bringing people together, in stimulating research, and in linking strands of research across the continents. Several works produced by IRET, for example, were reprinted by OUP, including Hornby, and Gatenby and Wakefield's (1948) *Idiomatic and Syntactic English Diction* (A. S. Hornby, 1898–1978; E. V. Gatenby, 1892–1955; A. H. Wakefield, 1892–1962). The founding of the Edinburgh School of Applied Linguistics prompted all the main U.K. ELT publishers (Cambridge University Press [CUP], Longman, Macmillan, and OUP) along with several presses in the United States (including the American Council of Learned Societies) to donate materials.

By the 1970s, U.K. universities were producing over 100 applied linguistics professionals every year, and the number of applied linguistics doctoral candidates was increasing rapidly at a time when applicants for linguistics were being turned away because of the lack of jobs in the field (Strevens, 1978) and at a time when those trained in the field of linguistics were turning to applied linguistics for the better employment opportunities available (Corder, 1978b).

In the 1970s and 1980s, the council and the major publishers regularly funded attendance at U.S. academic meetings for distinguished British scholars and council officers (e.g., several controllers of the English Language Division including Roger Bowers, Matthew Macmillan, Alan Maley, and John Munby), so that such names as Richard Allright, Christopher Brumfit, Christopher Candlin, J. C. Catford, S. Pit Corder, Peter Strevens, and H. G. Widdowson are as well known in the United States as they are in the United Kingdom.

In 1977, the Bureau of Educational and Cultural Affairs, in cooperation with the council, dispatched two U.S. linguists to visit British universities in a program intended to reciprocate for the frequent presence of British scholars visiting U.S. institutions; Louis Trimble and Robert B. Kaplan visited the Universities of Edinburgh, Lancaster, London, and Manchester. Unfortunately, the program was not renewed in subsequent years.

THE FOUNDING OF THE BRITISH ASSOCIATION OF APPLIED LINGUISTICS (BAAL)

Before the founding of BAAL in September 1967, applied linguistics research in the United Kingdom had been spread across such organizations as the Philological Society (PS), the Audiovisual Language Association (ALA), the Modern Language Association (MLA), the International Association of Teachers of English as a Foreign Language (IATEFL), and the Language Association of Great Britain (LAGB). In a paper written to commemorate BAAL's tenth anniversary, Strevens (1978) argued that there were two main reasons for its establishment: (1) the perceived need for a single body devoted to applied linguistics and the need for an organization to take on those activities not covered by LAGB (e.g., communication research and language planning), and (2) the need for an organization that would reflect the multidisciplinary nature of the field. Trim (2004) points out that the decision to hold the Third Annual General Meeting (AGM) of the Association Internationale de Linguistique Appliqué (AILA) in Britain provided organizational urgency. Strevens (1922–1989, formerly lecturer at Edinburgh's Department of Phonetics and subsequently appointed chair of applied linguistics at Essex) had organized preliminary discussions at London University's Birkbeck College, among an elite group of participants including James Britton (then active in the field of research into writing at London), Frank Palmer (Professor of Linguistic Science at Reading), John Trim (head of Cambridge University's Department of Linguistics), and Michael Halliday (a former pupil of John Firth brought from Edinburgh by Randolph Quirk to a professorship in linguistics at London). In 1961, the newly created school council had appointed Halliday director of the Nuffield Project in Linguistics and English Teaching. The project's report—*Language in Use*—and a collaboration among Halliday, Macintosh and Strevens, *Linguistic Sciences and Language Teaching* (1964), illustrate Halliday's intent to promote sociolinguistic awareness in all aspects of education.

Trim opposed the initial proposal that the new body be devoted to foreign language teaching and translation, reflecting growing concern that the dominance of Chomskyan linguistics in the United States was leading to neglect of the social dimensions of langauge learning (see, e.g., Chomsky, 1988, 1986, 1981, 1966). At the founding meeting at Reading in 1967, a wider aim of applying linguistic knowledge to language problems in society was agreed upon (Trim, 2004). Corder was appointed chair and Trim treasurer, the rest of the executive committee consisted of Strevens, George Perren (CILT director), Eric Hawkins (York—researcher in language awareness), David Wilkins (Reading—notional-functionalism pioneer), Norman Denison (sociolinguist), and Brian Gomes da Costa.

Under the constitution adopted at the 1968 annual general meeting (AGM) in Edinburgh,[19] the association's objective was defined: "to promote the study of problems of language acquisition, teaching and use, and to foster interdisciplinary collaboration in this study." Seminars and the annual conference were defined as the principal means for achieving the objective. Chairs were to serve 3-year terms, with Strevens taking over from Corder in 1970, followed by Walter Grauberg (Nottingham) in 1973, Alan Davies (Edinburgh) in 1976, Sam Spicer (Essex) in 1979, Christopher Brumfit (London) in 1982, and John Trim in 1985.

There appears to have been an early commitment to prevent BAAL from becoming another language teachers' association. Membership was thus restricted to those with knowledge of applied linguistics, however acquired—that is, formal credentials were not required. There were 255 members by 1974, 411 in 1980, and over 500 after membership restrictions were eased in the late 1980s. A large proportion of members had EFL backgrounds. Associate membership was granted to CILT, the British Council, the Institute of Linguistics, and to various publishers including Collins, Heffers, Multilingual Matters, OUP, and Pergamon.

There were close early ties between BAAL and AILA: Strevens was the first AILA secretary and Corder its second president, while Trim served on its executive committee. The third BAAL AGM was held at Cambridge, to coincide with the 1969 AILA congress there, and the latter's unexpected success not only provided intellectual stimulus but seems to have assured BAAL's financial standing.[20] Subsequent BAAL AGMs were held at Essex, the West Midlands College of Education, Nottingham, Edinburgh, York, Exeter, and again at Essex (for the 10th anniversary). There seems to have been some dissatisfaction with the quality of conference papers, and it was decided to devote each conference after the Essex conference to a particular theme. The conference themes were: "Bilingualism" at Cardiff (1978), "Applied Linguistics vs. Linguistics Applied" at Manchester (1979), "Grammar in Applied Linguistics" at Leeds (1980) and "Linguistic Variation and the Death of Language Teaching" at Sussex (1981). From 1969 BAAL started to organize seminars, the proceedings of several of which were published by CILT. Early seminar themes included language laboratory cost effectiveness, preparation of foreign language teaching materials, science and technology in language teaching, and German applied linguistics.

Although BAAL considered itself too small to embark upon a journal, its mailings to members developed into a regular newsletter. In 1978, BAAL and the newly founded American Association of Applied Linguistics (AAAL) agreed jointly to sponsor a journal to be published by OUP, leading to the launching of *Applied Linguistics* in 1980 under the editorship of Patrick Allen in Canada, Bernard Spolsky in the United States, and Henry Widdowson in the United Kingdom.

Applied Linguistics and British Education at the End of the Twentieth Century

Although EFL remained a driving concern for applied linguistics in the United Kingdom, the 1970s saw an increasing focus on more immediate language problems. A conference on professional standards at Lancaster in 1976, motivated by perceived commercialization of British Council operations and fears for declining teaching conditions and standards, did not move BAAL to take on professional accreditation, but the association was active in protesting against post-oil-shock cuts to the council's budget and also against fee increases for students from overseas. The increase in the number of foreign students in British universities coincided with the multiculturalisation of schools in the wake of mass immigration, accelerating convergence with applied linguistics in the United States and its ESL concerns.

In 1966 Leeds University's Institute of Education set up a program for immigrant primary school children. Seven years later, in 1973, BAAL wrote to the Bullock Committee on the teaching of English in U.K. schools. A 1975 BAAL seminar in Birmingham addressed the problems of overseas students in higher education and included a paper by Christopher Candlin and Helen Moore titled "Problems and Issues in Developing Study Skills in English." The 1970s had seen a rapid growth in ESL in the United Kingdom and corresponding concerns within applied linguistics for communicative teaching and genre analysis of texts—two areas of particular concern to Candlin, whose emphasis on methods and materials based on authentic language was somewhat different from Widdowson's approach of creating manipulated material in such a way that learners could engage with it authentically. (In 1988, the eighth volume of *ARAL*, guest edited by Christopher Brumfit, was concerned with communicative language teaching.)

A BAAL seminar in 1978 looked at linguistics and the teaching of language in schools, and a 1980 seminar "Linguistics as a School Subject" debated whether a standard form of English should be taught and what effect this might have on social identities. This debate included the role of dialects such as West Indian Creole and the special needs of bilingual children. Another seminar, in 1982, addressed the topic of language and ethnicty. In 1985, BAAL published comments on the Report of the Swann Committee on the Education of Ethnic Minorities, and 2 years later BAAL addressed the Kingman Committee report on teaching English language. In this activity, an effort to put language awareness at the heart of educational policy can be identified, but BAAL's influence on mainstream government policies seems to have been quite limited.

Although BAAL's activities have remained extensive over the turn of the millenium, it is clear that the influence on government policy of BAAL, like that of AAAL, seems to have decreased.

In Canada

An important Canadian player during the last half of the twentieth century was H. H. (David) Stern (1913–1987),[21] whose career began in Dorset as a teacher of French and German in the 1930s. He completed his MA in 1948 at the University of London Institute of Education, and subsequently lectured at the University of Hull until 1965. He completed a PhD at the University of London in 1956, and he worked in the early 1960s as a research officer on the IEA studies of educational achievement in 22 countries at the UNESCO Institute for Education in Hamburg (see, e.g., Purves, 1989); that research led to the publication of two major books on language education in primary schools (1967, 1969). After a period as reader in applied linguistics at the University of Essex, Stern moved in 1968 to Toronto, Canada, where he founded the Modern Language Centre of the Ontario Institute for Studies in Education (OISE; Stern, 1970: v), which he directed as professor until his retirement in 1981 (Cumming, 2000; McCuaig and Stern, 1981; Mollica, 1981). Stern serves to tie together applied linguistics activity in the United Kingdom and that in North America, specifically in Canada. (See also Canadian Association of Applied Linguistics.) OISE faculty have produced a steady stream of important work in applied linguistics over the years (e.g., Allen, 1989; Canale and Swain, 1980; Cumming, 1994, 1998, 2000; Cummins, 1984, 1986, 1996, 1999, 2000a, 2000b; Moore, 2001; Naiman et al.,1978; Spada, 1997; Spada and Fröhlich, 1995; Stern, 1983, 1989, 1992; Swain, 1985, 1993, 1995, 1998, 2000a, 2000b, 2005, 2006; Johnson and Swain, 1997; Swain and Lapkin, 1982, 1995, 1998, 2000, 2001, 2002).

Still another important Canadian researcher in the last half of the twentieth century was William F. Mackey, who taught for many years at Laval University—Canada's oldest university, located in Québec. He had earlier taught at the University of London. His *Language Teaching Analysis* (1965) was widely used in courses for preparing applied linguists because it offered a taxonomy of a typology of language-teaching drill types classified according to the four skills and recognizing the added capabilities of the language laboratory. His elaborate typology of bilingual education (1972)—which distinguishes 90 different potential varieties depending on the intersection of languages of the home, neighborhood, and country—had special significance in Canada as that polity implemented its bilingualism. Like Stern, he served to tie together applied linguistics activity in the United Kingdom with that in North America, specifically with Canada.

The Canadian Association of Applied Linguistics (http://www.aclacaal.org/) held its first meeting in 1969 and was officially incorporated in 1978. More commonly known as ACLA, it is an officially bilingual scholarly association whose members derive from across Canada and elsewhere. It was created to promote research and teaching in all areas of applied linguistics across Canada. At present, it has approximately 200 members. Its official journal, published continuously since 1978, is the *Canadian Journal of Applied Linguistics*. This scientific and professional French/English bilingual journal is published twice each year and deals with a wide range of applied linguistics research (e.g., mother tongue and second language teaching, first and second language acquisition, bilingual education, sociolinguistics, language planning, sociology of language, psycholinguistics, literacy, applied phonetics, translation/terminology, and multimedia and language teaching).

A group of secondary resources lies in the regional affiliates of TESL Canada. TESL Canada (Teaching English as a Second Language in Canada) is a national organization dedicated to promoting communication and coordinating awareness of issues for those concerned with English as a second language and English skills development. The national umbrella organization promotes advocacy for ESL learners, unifies teachers and learners by providing a forum and network capabilities, supports the sharing of knowledge and experiences across Canada, and represents diverse needs and interests in TESL nationally and internationally.

The provincial members represent Alberta, Manitoba, New Foundland/ Labrador, Ontario, Saskatchewan, British Columbia, New Brunswick, Nova Scotia, Prince Edward Isle, and the Yukon. In the interests of brevity, only the British Columbia affiliate will be discussed in any detail. The affiliate carries the name B.C. TEAL (Teaching English as an Additional Language). Among the honorary members of this organization are Mary Ashworth, British Columbia; Catherine Eddy, Nova Scotia; and Patricia Wakefield, British Columbia. This organization is more clearly education centered. According to its mission statement, B.C. TEAL advances the profession of teaching English as an additional language in British Columbia through professional development and research, organizational development, promotion of standards, advocacy, and representation:

1. It encourages a high standard of professional teacher training in public and private institutes throughout the province of British Columbia.
2. It supports research and encourages professional development of educators of English as an additional language throughout British Columbia.
3. It advocates on behalf of teachers and learners of English as an additional language in British Columbia.
4. It represents the profession of teaching English as an additional language in the development of policy at all levels of government.

In Australia

The origins of applied linguistics in Australia are distinctively different from those in the United Kingdom and the United States. As has been shown, in the United Kingdom and the United States, applied linguistics arose out of a concern for the teaching of English as a second/foreign language. That tradition was enhanced through the need to teach English in the British colonies during the nineteenth century and subsequently to teach English in the United States and the United Kingdom to international students and to immigrants during the twentieth century (McNamara, 2001a, 2001b). In Australia, however, applied linguistics originated not from English but rather from the modern foreign languages and the languages of immigrants (Kleinsasser, 2004; McNamara and Lo Bianco, 2001). The academic leadership in the establishment of applied linguistics as a viable academic endeavor arose significantly from among teachers involved in the teaching of English as a second or foreign language, whereas in Australia, although there was a significant effort to teach English to speakers of other languages, the academic leadership arose significantly from the community of teachers of foreign languages; indeed, many of the leading figures in Australian applied linguistics were teachers of French. The Australian tradition shows a surprisingly strong influence from continental Europe and the United States rather than from Britain, a somewhat surprising development given the powerful general influence of British educational traditions in Australia. A concern with teaching English appeared in Australia rather late, having arrived in Australia only in the 1980s, and then largely in the context of first-language teaching and of the teaching of English to immigrants (ESL; Horvath, 1985).

Australia, a country of about 20 million people living in an area a little smaller than the United States, has a 40,000-year-old indigenous cultural history surviving from cultures that were violently displaced as a result of European colonization developing after 1788. The English-speaking Australian colonies federated and achieved technical independence from Britain in 1901, but racist immigration policies restricted immigration largely to English-speaking Europeans. After 1945, however, the population's small size and the experience of invasion during World War II led to widespread support for an increase in immigration, initially from European countries but expanded on a nondiscriminatory basis after the early 1970s so that the majority of immigrants coming into Australia are presently from Asia. A well-funded government program of teaching English to adult immigrants and their children accompanied the introduction of the expanded immigration policy, and that program has increasingly been the site of significant applied linguistics research.

Since the 1970s, Australia's official policy has been favorable to multiculturalism and to the increasing ethnic diversity of the country. To a much greater extent than in the past, Australia has tried to redefine itself and to perceive itself as part of the Asian-Pacific region; its main trading partners have changed from those characteristic of Britain and North America to those located in Continental Europe and in Asia, especially Japan, South Korea, and China. Australia no longer looks exclusively to Britain for its models.

Some Significant Events

1947   Massive expansion of the immigration program.

1948   Establishment of the Adult Migrant English Program.

1960s   Applied linguistics begins among modern language teachers. Research initiated on language shift in immigrant communities.

1972   Policy of multiculturalism enacted; immigrant languages taught.

1976   Applied Linguistics Association of Australia founded; the association organizes an annual conference, produces the journal *Australian Review of Applied Linguistics*, edits occasional papers in applied linguistics, provides scholarships for high-quality student research in areas of applied linguistics, and jointly with the Australian Linguistics Society sponsors the Australian Linguistics Institute; as of the time of writing, the association recognized the following life members: Michael Clyne (see, e.g., 2001, 1997b, 1994, 1987a, 1987b, 1982; Clyne and Kipp, 1997), M. A. K. Halliday, Ian Malcolm, Brian McCarthy, Terry Quinn (who established the foundations for the graduate program in applied linguistics at Monash University; see, e.g., Quinn, 1985), Gay Reeves, and Ross Steele, all of whom played significant roles in the founding of the association.

1978   Galbally Report recommends language teaching research. M. A. K. Halliday (and his wife, Ruquaiya Hasan; see, e.g., Halliday, 1993; Halliday and Hasan, 1976, 1989) begin work in Australia—University of Sydney MA program initiated.

1987   *National Policy on Languages* is published (Lo Bianco, 1987); research centers are established; new emphases placed on Asian languages and on adult literacy; growth develops in the international student market, resulting in the birth of the private EFL industry.

         Australian Advisory Council on Languages and Multicultural Education (AACLAME; Lo Bianco, chair) was authorized and funded for 3 budget years (1987–1988, 1988–1989, 1989–1990) to support and administer five new programs (Australian Second Language Learning Program [ASLLP], Adult Literacy Action Program [ALAC], Multicultural and Cross-Cultural Supplementation Program [MACSP], National Aboriginal Languages Program [NALP], and Asian Studies) and to supplement one existing program. Funding ended in 1992, and AACLAME ceased to exist.

         VOX (issue 1 of the journal of AACLAME) published. Journal had a run of six issues; funding expired in 1992.

1988   National Center for English Language Teaching and Research at
        Macquarie University founded (Candlin, director).
1992   National Language and Literacy Institute of Australia (replacing
        discontinued AACLAME) is founded (Lo Bianco, director)
        coordinating a number of national projects:

Language Acquisition Research Centre (Universities of Sydney and Western
    Australia)
Language and Society Centre (Monash University)
Language and Technology Centre (University of Queensland)
The Centre for Deafness and Communication (Griffith University)
The Language Testing Centre (University of Melbourne) and Language
    Testing and Curriculum Centre (Griffith University)
Workplace Communication and Culture (University of Technology, Sydney,
    and University of Wollongong)
Unit for Professional Training (Australian TESOL Training Centre)
Unit for Language Training (Multi-Function Polis, Adelaide)
Child Literacy and ESL Research Network and Adult Literacy Research
    Network (in formation). The Commonwealth budget of May 1998
    terminated Commonwealth funding for NLLIA, leaving it entirely
    dependent on contracts.

As previously noted, the origins of Australian applied linguistics lie largely, though
not exclusively, in the teaching of modern languages in the universities. Major figures in that development were Terry Quinn and Keith Horwood at the University of
Melbourne, Wilga Rivers (among others) at Monash University, and David Ingram
at Mt. Gravatt College of Advanced Education. From the early 1960s, university language teachers attended the annual meetings of the Australasian Universities
Languages and Literatures Association (AULLA), the individual state Modern
Language Associations, and the Australian Federation of Modern Language Teachers'
Associations (AFMLTA), where they discussed language teaching, particularly in
the light of the new technology offered by the language laboratory. This concern
created a submeeting that became known as the Language Laboratory Workshop.
At the time, language laboratories were being sold to university language departments, but the expertise to exploit them was often lacking. The topics discussed in
the workshop soon extended beyond the specifics of the language laboratory. The
Applied Linguistics Association of Australia (ALAA) grew directly out of that
workshop.

    Terry Quinn, arguably the most distinctive figure in the history of Australian
applied linguistics, was originally (like the better known Wilga Rivers[22]) a high
school French teacher. In 1969, he went on to earn a PhD in Foreign Language
Education in the United States and subsequently he returned to Australia, in 1972,
to take up a position in French at Monash University in Melbourne. Unlike Rivers,
Quinn stayed in Australia, becoming director of the Horwood Language Centre at
the University of Melbourne[23] from 1975 to 1989 and the founder of that institutions

graduate applied linguistics program. With extraordinary timing, Rivers's thesis delivered the critique of audiolingualism the field had been waiting for. Ironically, the "new approach" to language teaching that Rivers espoused was precisely the audiolingualism that her doctoral thesis had critiqued (1968a, 1968b; Rivers and Temperley, 1978).

As noted, the Applied Linguistics Association of Australia (ALAA) was formed in 1976 at a conference at the University of Newcastle organized by Gay Reeves, a lecturer in French there. She was its first secretary; Ross Steele, a lecturer in French at the University of Sydney, was its first president. Quinn became editor of the association's journal, the *Australian Review of Applied Linguistics;* he was also editor of *Babel*, the journal of the Australian Federation of Modern Language Teachers Associations. Ingram served in various capacities, was heavily involved in language testing, and gradually became more concerned with planning (e.g., Ingram, 1989, 2003).

Two major issues disturbed applied linguistics in Australia over the more recent years of its work:

1. The serious matter of the death of many of the Australian Aboriginal languages that had existed when European arrived in the late eighteenth century
2. The questions surrounding the articulation of a national policy on languages following the publication of the initial incentive work by Lo Bianco (1987, 1990, 1997).

The first has been argued powerfully by advocates of steps to protect those languages from extinction (though, unfortunately, there have been few Aboriginal voices among them; see, e.g., Devlin et al., 1995; Eggington and Baldauf, 1990; Fesl, 1987; Lo Bianco and Freebody, 2001; Lo Bianco and Rhydwen, 2001; Russo and Baldauf, 1986; Schmidt, 1990). The second marked the gradual drift of Australia's official policy from a broadly liberal understanding of multilingualism and multiculturalism to a policy (and accompanying debate) about English literacy for all Australians (see, e.g., Clyne, 1991, 1997a; Department of Education and Training (DEET), 1991; Department of Employment, Education, Training and Youth Affairs (DEETYA), 1998; Eggington, 1994; Freebody, 1997; B. J. Green, Hodgens, and Luke, 1994; Hammond, 2001; Ingram, 1994; Liddicoat, 1991; Lo Bianco and Wickert, 2001; Ozolins, 1993).

In New Zealand

The total population of New Zealand is around four million people. Of that number, something on the order of 90% are *Pakeha;* in other words, they are themselves, or are descendents of, English-speaking Europeans whose primary affiliation is to cultural and educational values deriving from Europe. The remaining 10% consists of the Mäori people, Pacific Islanders, and a scattering of non-English-speaking

Europeans, Asians, Latin Americans, and so forth. If one were to remove the Mäori people from the computation, the remainder would constitute only about 2% of the total population—fewer than 70,000 people. Pacific Islanders (Cook Island Mori, Niuean, Samoan, Tokelauan, Tongan) make up about 40% of that group.

Despite New Zealand's apparent linguistic heterogeneity (Hirsh, 1987), interest in languages and in applied linguistics was a more recently emerging concern in New Zealand. The Applied Linguistics Association of New Zealand (ALANZ) was formed in 1993, holding its first AGM on May 13, 1994. The association publishes an occasional newsletter (*ALANZ Newsletter*) and offers the Christopher Brumfit PhD Thesis Award. Membership in the association provides access to a network of individuals interested and active in applied linguistics research. Applied linguistics research had been undertaken before 1993 (see, e.g., Benton, 1981; Hawley, 1987; Kaplan, 1979; Kennedy, 1982; Peddie, 1991a, 1991b; Spolsky, 1987), and academic programs in the field are available at five universities (Kleinsasser, 2004). Scholars have been engaged in world-class research for many years—for example, Nation (1990) has been pursuing pioneering work in morphology and vocabulary acquisition at Victoria University of Wellington, and his colleague, Kennedy (receiving his doctorate from UCLA), has been involved in critical research since 1982. ALANZ publishes a newsletter, and, since 1995, the refereed journal *New Zealand Studies in Applied Linguistics* (NZSAL) has appeared twice a year.

The Applied Linguistics Association attempts to cover areas of research of interest to its members including foreign and second language education, Mäori language, cross-cultural pragmatics, speech and language disorders, language planning, and community languages (Hoffmann, 1998). This list demonstrates that the field has been fractured in New Zealand probably since the late 1960s.

- First, New Zealand, like Australia, liberalized its immigration policy after World War II, resulting in significant inflows from both Western and Eastern Europe (i.e., Holland, France, Yugoslavia) and, more recently, from Asia (i.e., Cambodia, China, India, Laos, Vietnam). The government organized English language instruction for new arrivals, but there has been a long-standing concern about the loss of these languages among immigrant communities (Chrisp, 1997b).
- Second, great amounts of work have been invested in the preservation of Mäori language and culture (D. L. Bates, 1991; Fishman, 1991a; Harlow, 1991; Hohepa 2000; Karetu, 1991; McCafferty, 1999; Reedy, 2000; Research New Zealand, 2007). Richard Benton (1981, 1991a, 1991b) and his wife Nena (1998; see also R. A. Benton and Benton, 2001) have been especially active in this area.
- Third, for nearly half a century, relatively large numbers of individuals have migrated to New Zealand from the Pacific Islands with which New Zealand has had a political relationship. This migration has created a number of serious problems. The languages of these migrants are under threat not only in New Zealand but in their home territories as well. Small communities like

Niue and Tokelau, constantly in contact with English as well as with local pidgins and creoles (see, e.g., Baldauf and Luke, 1990), are in danger of losing their languages entirely and, even in fairly robust areas like Western Samoa, language change appears to be occurring rapidly. In New Zealand, until relatively recently, the Pacific Island languages have received little formal attention. The Samoan community has supported "language nests" for the preschool teaching of the language and culture, but other Pacific Island languages do not yet enjoy even this hostage against language loss.

- Fourth, there has been a complementary (but sometimes conflicting) interest in the English language as the *de facto* national language of New Zealand and in Mäori as the primary indigenous language. The Mäori people, *inter alia*, have mounted a substantial grassroots effort to preserve their language, and the government has been embarrassed into taking official note of such developments as *kohanga reo* (preschools teaching Mori language and culture to youngsters, emulated subsequently by the Samoan community) and other significant activities extending through the grades and into higher education (Grin and Vaillancourt, 1998). English research has focused on the differences between New Zealand dialect and other varieties of English (Bell and Holmes, 1990; Holmes, 1997; Hundt, 1998). Additionally, there has been work in translation and in relation to language of the disadvantaged (e.g., Lane et al., 1999). As a consequence of these four directions of research, a discussion of the need for a language policy erupted in the early 1990s and continues, though much attenuated, in the present (Hawley, 1987; Kaplan, 1993b, 1994; Peddie, 1991a, 1991b; Waite, 1992).

DÉNOUEMENT

The subdiscipline of applied linguistics [AL] is an inquiry into the relevance of linguistic expertise to actual language experience. Whenever such expertise is drawn on to resolve a basic language-related problem, one may say that AL is being practiced. In this sense, AL is a technology that makes abstract ideas and research findings accessible and relevant to the real world; it mediates between theory and practice. (Strevens, 2003: 112)

If we accept a definition of applied linguistics along the lines proposed at the start of this article, two questions follow from it. First, what kind of real-world problems does AL typically address? Second, which areas of theoretical inquiry have provided relevant insights? (Widdowson and Kaplan, 2003: 114)

These quotations from a pertinent encyclopedia section serve in the broadest terms to frame what applied linguistics is.[24] Given such a definition, the discipline whose roots are sought through this essay serves to support the definition. Although the history of applied linguistics is dynamic—is in a constant state of development—that history demonstrates that applied linguistics has sprung up in response to the recognition of real-world language-related problems. Real-world language-related problems surface first in language teaching and learning—the point at which language encounters the constraints of the real world.

It appears that applied linguistics emerged out of the contention between a widely proliferated and marginally successful "grammar/translation" model of foreign and/or second language teaching popular during the nineteenth century and the needs of teachers and students caught in the immediacy of practical learning and reflective of the European "reform movement" together with the coincident rise of modern linguistics. In the years following the end of WWII, there was a significant migration of persons displaced by the war as well as large numbers of international students looking for educational systems not disrupted by the war or by the political compromises immediately following from it. These forces coalesced in various attempts to meet the immediate and urgent needs of linguistic populations seeking to exist in new linguistic environments. From what more logical site could applied linguistics appear?

Modern linguistics was thought to provide solutions that were actually beyond the reach of other academic disciplines. Linguistics was not perceived as useful when applied directly in the language classroom with its solutions arrived at in the abstract study of language. In short order, a breed of scholars emerged who were able to mediate between theory and practice. A number of the tangents pursued in the formative years of applied linguistics were precisely the results of attempts to apply theoretical findings directly in the solution of real-world needs. Skinner brought psychology into union with structural linguistics theory to create the audiolingual approach; Chomsky showed that the audiolingual approach ignored some key matters in language theory (Chomsky, 1959). A long series of attempts to find a functional compromise have served to confuse students and teachers. Inevitably, more successful approaches have emerged.

At the same time, new problems have developed. The movement of significant population segments from one linguistic-cultural environment to another created legal, political, social, educational, and cultural problems; consequently, applied linguistics has enjoyed a rich set of opportunities to try to develop and apply different approaches to the point of intersection between language and society. This volume presents a map of those various undertakings, sometimes frankly reflecting the absence of practical solutions, alternatively showing patterns that suggest parts of the solution, still not yet always capable of developing complex models leading to genuine solutions. The next century may provide time and scope to make possible more viable responses—but because problems slide out of sight just as they approach solution, it would appear that applied linguistics may yet enjoy a golden age because new problems emerge at a rate far more rapid than applied linguists can fashion and adjust solutions. The race between ignorance and survival assures growth in attempts to find solutions—unless ignorance wins. I cannot conceive what the third edition of the *Oxford Handbook of Applied Linguistics* might look like, but I am reasonably confident that a third edition—even perhaps an nth edition—will be needed.

Acknowledgments

I wish to acknowledge the most helpful reading of an earlier draft of this chapter and the corrections and emendations offered by Richard B. Baldauf, Jr., William Grabe, and G. Richard Tucker. I remain responsible for all remaining errors.

NOTES

1. The Summer Institute of Linguistics (now SIL International) started as a small summer session program to train missionaries; it was associated with the University of Oklahoma from the early 1950 to 1987. One of the students at the first summer institute in its second year (1935) was Kenneth L. Pike (1912–2000), who was to become a major figure in early applied linguistics, founder of Tagmemics (and coined the words *emic* and *etic*), and SIL president from 1942 to 1979 and then president emeritus until his death. He worked at the University of Michigan for many years, and in that position trained many of the first generation of applied linguists in the United States. A major contribution that SIL has made to linguistics has been SIL's data, gathered in and analyzed from over 1,000 minority and endangered languages. SIL has compiled an enormous bibliography under the title *Ethnologue* (Gordon, 2005), listing some 20,000 items, updated monthly and revised at four-year intervals. *Ethnologue* includes work by such well-known figures as Ruth Brend, H. L. Gleason, Archibald Hill, Martin Joos, Sydney Lamb, Robert Longacre, Adam Makkai, Eugene Nida, and George Trager. See, for example, http://en.wikipedia.org/wiki/SIL_International. SIL field workers have been helpful to various projects undertaken by other linguistics groups (personal communication, G. R. Tucker, February 18, 2008).

2. Actually, Mohan was not the initial director; however, he was the first to try to accomplish the stipulated objectives of the institute.

3. Opened in July 1968 at Watten Estate, Singapore, moved to new facility July 1972, adjacent to the Shangri-la Hotel in Orange Grove Road, Singapore, built with substantial funding from United States, as one of six SEAMEO regional centers, intended to improve "the standards of teaching and learning English as a second or foreign language in the member countries [Indonesia, Khmer Republic, Laos, Malaysia, Philippines, Singapore, Thailand] of SEAMEO" (Pusponegroro, 1972: 8).

4. H. H. (David) Stern (1913–1987) was an influential theorist of foreign and second language teaching. His thinking helped to shape policies for, and research on, language curriculum, instruction, and teacher education, particularly in North America and Europe from the 1960s to the 1990s. (See, e.g., Mollica, 1981; McCuaig and Stern, 1981.) The founding of the International Centre for Research on Bilingualism at Laval was quite another matter. The Canadian Government approached the Ford Foundation saying that they wished to "make a gesture," to establish such a center, and that it must be located in Quebec (G. R. Tucker, personal communication).

5. Similar developments occurred in the United Kingdom; the British Council (established in 1934 as the British Committee for Relations with Other Countries) is believed to have contributed to the development of the schools of applied linguistics (at the Universities of Edinburgh, London [Institute of Education], Leeds, and York) and, of course, to have supported the work of English language teachers and teacher trainers

through its posts in various countries around the world (62 countries in 1955—the point of widest distribution). (See the following section, "In the United Kingdom"; for the British Council, see http://www.britishcouncil.org/history.htm. For more recent information, see Elaina Loveland's "An Interview with British Council Chair Lord Kinnock" in *International Educator* (November/December 2006), pp. 20–23. *International Educator* is a journal published by NAFSA (q.v.).

6. Originally (1948) entitled the *National Association of Foreign Student Advisors*, later (1964) renamed the *National Association for Foreign Student Affairs*, and currently (since 1990) known as *NAFSA: Association of International Educators*. At the present time, there are five "sections" in the Association: ADSEC (Admissions Section), ATESL (Administrators and Teachers in English as a Second Language; originally, Association of Teachers of English as a Second Language), CAFSS (Council of Advisors to Foreign Students and Scholars), COMSEC (Community Section), and SECUSSA (Section concerned with the needs of U.S. students abroad). The association is also geographically divided into 12 regions across the United States (the "lower 48" states, and including Alaska, Hawaii, Puerto Rico, and the Virgin Islands). The association's central office is in Washington, DC (http://www.nafsa.org). For many years, the liaison between NAFSA and the Bureau of Educational and Cultural Affairs was Maurita Houlihan.

7. The Institute for International Education (IIE, 809 United Nations Plaza, 7th Floor, New York, NY 10017; http://www.iie.org/), an independent, nonprofit organization founded in 1919, has become a world leader in the exchange of people and ideas. IIE administers over 200 programs (including the prestigious Fulbright Program), serving more than 20,000 individuals each year. It publishes an annual report (*Open Doors*) on the enrollment of international students in U.S. colleges and universities, analyzed by nationality, gender, type of institution, major field of study, and other demographic factors.

8. Membership in the council included, among others, Harold Allen (University of Minnesota), J. Milton Cowan (Cornell University), Robert Lado (Georgetown University), Albert Marckwardt (Princeton University), Melvin Fox (Ford Foundation), David Harris (Georgetown University), Serarpi Ohannesian (CAL), Harry Freeman and Myron Vent (U.S. Agency for International Development), Richard Beym (U.S. Defense Language Institute), James Alatis and William Shamblin (U.S. Office of Education), and Jane Alden (Bureau of Educational and Cultural Affairs, U.S. Department of State). The educational functions of the Bureau of Educational and Cultural Affairs have, over the past 40 years, had several reincarnations, first within the United States Information Agency (USIA), with officers in U.S. embassies in many countries (USIS), and currently again within the Bureau of Educational and Cultural Affairs in the U.S. Department of State.

9. NAFSA consisted of five "sections"; the one involved in these developments was the Association of Teachers of English as a Second Language (ATESL), whose first president had been David P. Harris (Georgetown University). At the time of these developments (1966–1967), William R. Slager (University of Utah) represented ATESL/NAFSA. ATESL was in part the father of TESOL.

10. Up to the founding of AAAL, there had been no professional applied linguistics association in the United States that could affiliate with AILA; TESOL was not an association of applied linguists. Although there was no associational representative from the United States to AILA, CAL was the "official" institutional rep from the inception of AILA until the creation of AAAL (G. R. Tucker, 2008, pers. comm.).

> Soon after its founding, AAAL joined AILA. As Sridhar (1990: 171–172) has
> observed, formal linguistics... identifies language with grammar and linguistic

theory with grammatical theory, leading to an exclusive preoccupation with form and disregard of, or skepticism toward, language use and function. If linguistics is defined as the scientific study of language, why should it be limited to the study of ... syntax, semantics, morphology, and phonology? ... Chomsky (1966) has steadfastly asserted the autonomy of grammar and its independence from considerations of language use and function.

11. This review is not intended to represent all areas of applied linguistics, nor is it intended to overview the entire global geography, nor is it intended to review work pertaining to all the world's languages. Gass and Makoni (2004) provide brief analyses of applied linguistics activity in Africa, Asia, Brazil, Europe, New Zealand, and North America (in addition to some reflections on the history of AILA). The journal *Current Issues in Language Planning* publishes studies of the language situation in various polities; to date it has published studies of the following: (1) Algeria, (2) the Baltics, (3) Botswana, (4) Cameroon, (5) Côte d'Ivoire, (6) Czech Republic, (7) Ecuador, (8) European Union, (9) Fiji, (10) Finland, (11) Hungary, (12) Ireland, (13) Italy, (14) Malawi, (15) Mexico, (16) Mozambique, (17) Nepal, (18) Nigeria, (19) North Ireland, (20) Paraguay, (21) the Philippines, (22) South Africa, (23) Sweden, (24) Taiwan, (25) Tunisia, (26) Vanuatu, and (27) Zimbabwe. A 28th monograph on Chinese character modernization is also available.

12. See, for example, Sweet's *The Practical Study of Languages* (1899) (which proposed progressive and rational language teaching); Jesperson's *Language: Its Nature, Development and Origin* (1921), Passy's *La phonétique et ses applications* (1929) and Viëtor's *Elemente der Phônetik der Deutschen, Englischen und Französischen* (1884). In 1886, Passy was, with a number of others, involved in the founding of the Phonetic Association of Teachers of English—a body with the stated purpose of reforming existing methods of teaching languages. The association rapidly acquired an international character. In 1897, with the encouragement of Jesperson, it became the *Association Phonetique Internationale* (i.e., the International Phonetic Association [IPA]), with Sweet serving as president.

13. This date of publication follows the entry of the United States into the war in 1941. One may speculate about the effect of events on the early distribution and availability as well as the reputation of this work.

14. Over much of this period, British language policy tended to follow the advice provided in Thomas Babington Macaulay's 1835 "Minute." Macaulay had been sent to Calcutta in an official capacity (as "advisor" to the government). He knew nothing about any of the South Asian languages; indeed, he appears to have actually despised them. His "minute" or "message" concerned the intent of education and colonial language policy in India, dealing particularly with the use of English in the education of Indian people. The wide adoption of his advice introduced the future leaders of India to English literature and history, providing a common language in multilingual India and laying the groundwork in the traditions of English law. More specifically, Macaulay's advice was

> ... to form a class Indian in blood and colour, but English in tastes, in opinions, in morals, and in intellect; a class who could serve as interpreters between the government and the masses, and who, by refining the vernaculars, would supply the means of widespread dissemination of western knowledge. (quoted in Phillipson, 1992: 110)

Subsequently, Macaulay's policy was also applied widely in British colonial Africa.

15. Although the council was able to escape amalgamation into the new Ministry of Information, it was required to relinquish information-gathering activities to that ministry.

16. The recognition of a more clearly defined distinction between activities that were educational and cultural as opposed to those that were overtly propagandist, and a growing recognition of the council's potential not only for curbing anticolonialism, but also for helping to maintain British influence where decolonization was inevitable were quickly modifying council activities abroad. The absence of a similar distinction, however, continued to confuse the situation in the United States as the Bureau of Educational and Cultural Affairs was moved about within the government, and the functions dealing with language education have been, on a number of occasions, redistributed. For example, as recently as November 2, 2002, CNN posted this item on its website:

> Richard Brecht, Director of the National Foreign Language Center, a Washington think tank, observed that the government commits money to language education only in a time of international crisis, and then as the crisis wanes interest lags. "We've never made that investment [in language education]."

17. Beginning in 1948, Bruce Pattison occupied England's first chair with responsibilities for EFL. In 1945 the Inter-University Council for Higher Education Overseas was created (representing all U.K. universities), with the aim of coordinating higher education standards throughout the Commonwealth. The council drew heavily on these arrangements.

18. Catford moved to the University of Michigan in 1964, replacing Lado, who had moved to Georgetown University.

19. The Association of Teachers of English as a Foreign Language (ATEFL, later IATEFL) was established in the same year.

20. It must be noted, however, that, with the exception of an executive committee meeting in 1974, no other AILA conference has taken place in the United Kingdom; it appears that there had been some disagreement between the two bodies.

21. H. H. (David) Stern was an influential theorist of foreign and second language teaching, His thinking helped to shape policies for and research on language curriculum, instruction, and teacher education, particularly in North America and Europe from the 1960s to the 1990s. His major book, *Fundamental Concepts of Language Teaching* (1983), elaborated an analytic framework of fundamental concepts of which language teachers and policies should necessarily be cognizant, both to be aware of foundational theories and research and to guide their ongoing educational practices. These foundational concepts include knowledge of one's own learning and teaching experiences, the history of language teaching, concepts of language, the role of language in societies, the psychology of learning languages, and educational policies and theories. A later companion volume—*Issues and Opinions in Language Teaching* (1992, edited posthumously by his colleagues Patrick Allen and Birgit Harley)—presented a multidimensional curriculum that aimed to broaden the range of objectives and content options conventional to language education while highlighting core issues in teaching, such as whether to present second languages in an intralingual mode (in reference to the second language and culture) or a cross-lingual mode (in reference to the first language) and whether to approach language learning analytically or experimentally (or both). These books, like Stern's numerous journal articles and contributed chapters (e.g., Stern, 1969, 1967), stressed the logical importance and humanistic value of closely interrelating language teaching practices, policies, theories, and research.

22. Rivers was another high school teacher of French in Melbourne who, after the early years of a successful career in language teaching in Australia, had moved to Europe for further study and enhanced professional experience, and then to the United States to

do a PhD. Subsequently, she earned a professorship at Harvard University and completed her career there.

23. Keith Horwood had a background in German, and in the 1960s had been appointed lecturer in Science German at the university to help Faculty of Science students meet the requirement to complete the compulsory reading course in a foreign language (one or more of German, French, and Russian). Harwood eventually became head of the science language section in the faculty.

24. The *Handbook of Multilingualism and Multicultural Communication*, (Eds. Peter Aver and Li Wei, 2007; of the nine parts of the *Handbooks of Applied Linguistics*, vol. 5) has an obvious European perspective in a long introductory discussion, by Karlfried Knapp and Gerd Antos, of theoretical/pure science and applied science and linguistics, alleging that the term *applied linguistics* emerged in 1948 in the first issue of *Language Learning*, though actually the term/concept can be traced back to nineteenth-century Europe.

LIST OF PUBLICATIONS EXPLORING THE NATURE AND STATUS OF APPLIED LINGUISTICS

Brown, K. (Ed.). (2006). *Encyclopedia of Language and Linguistics* (2nd ed., 14 vols.). Amsterdam: Elsevier.

Candlin, C., and S. Sarangi (2004). Making applied linguistics matter. *Journal of Applied Linguistics* 1, 1–8.

Cook, G. (2003). *Applied Linguistics*. Oxford: Oxford University Press.

Cook, G., and G. Kasper (2005). Applied linguistics and real world issues [Special issue]. *Applied Linguistics* 26(4).

Davies, A. (1999). *An Introduction to Applied Linguistics: From Practice to Theory*. Edinburgh: Edinburgh University Press.

Davies, A., and C. Elder (Eds.). (2004). *The Handbook of Applied Linguistics*. Malden, MA: Blackwell.

Doughty, C., and M. Long (Eds.). (2003). *The Handbook of Second Language Acquisition*. Malden, MA: Blackwell.

Frawley, W. (Ed.). (2003). *Oxford International Encyclopedia of Linguistics* (2nd ed., 4 vols.). New York: Oxford University Press.

Gass S. M., and S. Makoni (Eds.)(2004). *Applied Linguistics: A Celebration of AILA at 40* Philadelphia/Amsterdam: John Benjamins[SPECIAL ISSUE, AILA Review 17]

Grabe, W. (2004). Perspectives in applied linguistics: A North American view. *AILA Review* 17, 105–132.

Hinkel, E. (Ed.). (200). *Handbook of Research in Second Language Teaching and Learning*. Mahwah, NJ: Lawrence Erlbaum.

Hornberger, N. (Gen. Ed.). (2008). *Encyclopedia of Language and Education* (2nd ed., 10 vols.). New York: Springer.

Johnson, K., and H. Johnson (Eds.). (1998). *Encyclopedic Dictionary of Applied Linguistics*. Oxford: Blackwell.

Joseph, J., and L. R. Waugh (in press). *Cambridge History of Linguistics*. Cambridge: Cambridge University Press.

Kaplan, R. B. (Ed.). (2002). *The Oxford Handbook of Applied Linguistics*. Oxford: Oxford University Press.

Kaplan, R. B., and W. Grabe (2000). Applied linguistics and the *Annual Review of Applied Linguistics*. In W. Grabe et al. (Eds.), *Annual Review of Applied Linguistics: Vol. 20. Applied Linguistics as an Emerging Discipline* (pp. 3–17). New York: Cambridge University Press.

Schmitt, N. (Ed.). (2002). *An Introduction to Applied Linguistics*. London: Arnold.

Spolsky, B. (Ed.). (1999). *Concise Encyclopedia of Educational Linguistics*. Amsterdam: Elsevier.

Spolsky, B., and F. M. Hult (Eds.). (2008). *The Handbook of Educational Linguistics*. Malden, MA: Blackwell.

Waugh L. R., and Joseph, J. (Eds.).(2009) *Cambridge History of Linguistics*. Cambridge: Cambridge University Press.

Widdowson, H. G. (2006). Applied linguistics and interdisciplinarity. *International Journal of Applied Linguistics* 16, 93–96.

APPENDIX A: PAST PRESIDENTS OF U.S. TESOL

Harold Allen (1966–1967)*
Edward Anthony (1967–1968)
Paul Bell (1968–1969)*
David Harris (1969–1970)
Mary Finocchiaro (1970–1971)*
Russell N. Campbell (1971–1972)*
Alfonso Ramirez (1972–1973)*
Betty Wallace Robinette (1973–1974)
Muriel Saville-Troike (1974–1975)
Mary Galvan (1975–1976)*
Christina Bratt Paulston (1976–1977)
Donald Knapp (1977–1978)
Bernard Spolsky (1978–1979)
Ruth Crymes (1979)*
H. Douglas Brown (1979–1981)
John Fanselow (1981–1982)
Darlene Larson (1982–1983)*
John Haskell (1983–1984)

Charles Blatchford (1984–1985)
Jean Handscombe (1985–1986)
Joan Morley (1986–1987)
JoAnn Crandall (1987–1988)
Richard Allwright (1988–1989)
Jean McConochie (1989–1990)
Robert B. Kaplan (1990–1991)
Lydia Stack (1991–1992)
Mary Hines (1992–1993)
Fred Genesee (1993–1994)
Joy Reid (1994–1995)
Denise E. Murray (1995–1996)
Mary Ann Christison (1996–1997)
Kathleen M. Bailey (1997–1998)
David Nunan (1998–1999)
Barbara Schwarte (1999–2000)

* = Deceased

APPENDIX B: PAST PRESIDENTS OF AAAL

Wilga Rivers (1978–1979)*
Roger Shuy (1979–1980)
Eugene Brière (1980–1981)*
Muriel Saville-Troike (1981–1982)
Betty Wallace Robinette (1982–1983)
Thomas Scovel (1983–1984)
Braj. B. Kachru (1984–1985)

Leslie Beebe (1990–1991)
Elaine Tarone (1991–1992)
Sandra Savignon (1992–1993)
Robert B. Kaplan (1993–1994)
Claire Kramsch (1994–1995)
Jodi Crandall (1995–1996)
Elinor Ochs (1996–1997)
* = Deceased

CHAPTER 2

APPLIED LINGUISTICS: A TWENTY-FIRST-CENTURY DISCIPLINE

WILLIAM GRABE

A realistic history of the field of applied linguistics would place its origins at around the year 1948 with the publication of the first issue of the journal *Language Learning: A Journal of Applied Linguistics* (cf. Davies, 1999; Kaplan, elsewhere in this volume). Although there are certainly other possible starting points, particularly from a British perspective, this dating still accords roughly with most discussions of the beginning of applied linguistics.

Over the years, the term *applied linguistics* has been defined and interpreted in a number of different ways, and I continue that exploration in this overview. In the 1950s, the term was commonly meant to reflect the insights of structural and functional linguists that could be applied directly to second language teaching and also in some cases to first language (L1) literacy and language arts issues as well. In the 1960s, the term continued to be associated with the application of linguistics to language teaching and related practical language issues (Corder, 1973; Halliday, McIntosh, and Strevens, 1964; Rivers, 1968a; 1968b). At the same time, applied linguists became involved in matters of language assessment, language policies, and the new field of second language acquisition (SLA), focusing on learning, rather than on teaching (Ortega, 2009). So, by the late 1960s, one saw both a reinforcement of the centrality of second language teaching as applied linguistics, as well as an expansion into other realms of language use. In this respect, applied linguistics began to emerge as a genuine language-centered problem-solving enterprise (see Davies, 1999a).

In the 1970s, the broadening of the field of applied linguistics continued, accompanied by more overt specification of its role as a discipline that addresses real-world language-based problems. Although the focus on language teaching remained central to the discipline, it additionally took into its domain the growing subfields of language assessment, SLA, L2 literacy, multilingualism, language-minority rights, language policy and planning, and language teacher training (Kaplan, 1980; Widdowson, 1979/1984). The notion that applied linguistics is driven first by real-world language problems rather than by theoretical explorations of internalized language knowledge and (L1) language development is largely what set the field apart from both formal linguistics and later from sociolinguistics, with its own emphasis on language description of social variation in language use (typically minus the application to language problems). This separation has had four major consequences:

- The recognition of social situated contexts for inquiry and exploration and thus an increase in the importance of needs analysis and variable solutions in differing local contexts
- The need to see language as functional and discourse based, thus the reemergence of systemic and descriptive linguistics as resources for problem solving, particularly in North American contexts
- The recognition that no single discipline can provide all the tools and resources to address language-based real-world problems
- The need to recognize and apply a wide range of research tools and methodologies to address locally situated language problems

These trends took hold and evolved during the 1980s as major points of departure from an earlier, no longer appropriate, "linguistics applied" perspective (cf. Davies and Elder, 2004b). The central issue remained the need to address language issues and problems as they occur in the real world. Of course, because language is central to all communication, and because many language issues in the real world are particularly complex and long-standing, the emerging field has not simply been reactive, but rather, has been and still is, fluid and dynamic in its evolution (cf. Brumfit, 2004; Bygate, 2005; Grabe, 2004; Seidlhofer, 2003; Widdowson, 2005, 2006). Thus, definitions of applied linguistics in the 1980s emphasized both the range of issues addressed and the types of disciplinary resources used in order to work on language problems (Grabe and Kaplan, 1991; Kaplan, 1980). In the 1980s, applied linguistics truly extended in a systematic way beyond language teaching and language learning issues to encompass language assessment, language policy and planning, language use issues in professional settings, translation, lexicography, bilingualism and multilingualism, language and technology, and corpus linguistics (which continues to hold more interest for applied linguists than for formal linguists). These extensions are well documented in the first 10 years of the journals *AILA Review, Annual Review of Applied Linguistics, Applied Linguistics*, and *International Journal of Applied Linguistics*, among others. (See Kaplan, elsewhere in this volume, for a detailed discussion.)

By the beginning of the 1990s, a common trend was emerging to view applied linguistics as incorporating many subfields and drawing on many supporting disciplines in addition to linguistics (e.g., anthropology; education; English studies—including composition, rhetoric, and literary studies; modern languages; policy studies; political sciences; psychology; public administration; and sociology). Combined with these two foundations (subfields and supporting disciplines) was the view of applied linguistics as problem driven and real-world based rather than theory driven and disconnected from real language use data (Davies, 1999; Kaplan and Widdowson, 1992; Strevens, 1992). Applied linguistics has evolved still further during the 1990s and 2000s, breaking away from the common framing mechanisms of the 1980s. A parallel coevolution of linguistics itself needs to be commented upon to understand how and why linguistics, broadly defined, remains a core resource for applied linguistics.

From the 1960s to the early 1990s, generative linguistics dominated the linguistics landscape. Although other competing formal theories (tagmemics, systemic-functional linguistics, descriptive grammar, and others) were always available, and sociolinguistics claimed language variation, spoken discourse analysis, and social uses of language as descriptive areas of inquiry, Chomskean linguistics, and its offshoots, almost defined linguistics, at least in North America. This situation was especially true for many practicing applied linguists during that time. However, the growing abstractness of generative linguistics, the assumption of a language acquisition device (LAD, an innate language learning mechanism), and the assumption that a theory should be universally applicable to all languages has, for the most part, taken generative linguistics out of the running as a foundation for language knowledge that is relevant and applicable to real-world language uses and real-world language problems. In its place, applied linguists have been turning back to more cognitive and descriptive approaches to language knowledge (K. de Bot, 2008; Huddleston and Pullum, 2002; Robinson and Ellis, 2008), language explanations that are explicitly driven by attested language uses rather than intuitions (corpus linguistics, descriptive grammars, sociolinguistics; Biber et al., 1999; Carter and McCarthy, 2006), and theories of language representation that have more realistic applicability to the sorts of language issues explored by applied linguists (Doughty and Long, 2003; Kroll and de Groot, 2005; Robinson and Ellis, 2008).

Linguistics, viewed from this larger perspective, is still central to the overwhelming majority of applied linguistic areas of inquiry that are generally recognized as falling under the umbrella discipline of applied linguistics. After all, applied linguists, and training programs for applied linguists, universally recognize that language knowledge of various types is crucial for careful description and analysis of language, language learning, language uses and abuses, language assessment, and so forth. Applied linguists must draw on knowledge bases of phonetics, phonology, morphology, syntax, semantics, pragmatics, and written discourse because they are relevant to an applied linguistics issue, even if a given area of applied linguistics may not draw specifically on this knowledge at all times (e.g., L2 teacher training, language policy and planning). What has changed is the recognition that linguistic foundations do not need to be narrowly prescribed by theoretical fashion; instead, they must be relevant to language description in specific contexts and provide resources that help address language-based problems and issues in real-world contexts.

For applied linguistics research, the shift to discourse analysis, descriptive data analysis, and interpretation of language data in their social/cultural settings all indicate a shift in valuing observable language data over theoretical assumptions about what should count as data (van Lier, 1997). One of the most useful perspectives that has arisen out of this evolution of a more relevant linguistics has been the development of register analysis, genre analysis, and the resource of corpus linguistics as they apply to a wide range of language learning and language use situations (A. M. Johns, 2002; McCarthy, 2008). All of these approaches to linguistic analysis, along with more refined techniques for discourse analysis, are now hallmarks of much applied linguistics research. In fact, many applied linguists have come to see the real-world, problem-based, socially responsive research carried out in applied linguistics as the genuine role for linguistics, with formal linguistics taking a supporting role. As van Lier (1997) notes,

> I think that it is the applied linguist who works with language in the real world, who is most likely to have a realistic picture of what language is, and not the theoretical linguist who sifts through several layers of idealization. Furthermore, it may well be the applied linguist who will most advance humankind's understanding of language, provided that he or she is aware that no one has a monopoly on the definitions and conduct of science, theory, language research, and truth. (1997: 103)

TRENDS AND PERSPECTIVES IN THE 1990S AND THE 2000S

In this section, I only note various developments that have emerged over the last 20 years and that will probably continue to define applied linguistics in the coming decade. The present volume provides the details to expand much of the brief sign posting that this section provides. For much the same reason, I refrain from a long catalog of appropriate references on the assumptions that these ideas will be well-referenced elsewhere (Davies and Elder, 2004b; Grabe, 2004; Hinkel, 2005).

First, under the umbrella of applied linguistics, research in language teaching, language learning, and teacher education is now placing considerable emphasis on notions of language awareness, attention and learning, "focus on forms" for language learning, learning from dialogic interactions, patterns of teacher-student interaction, task-based learning, content-based learning, and teacher as researcher through action research. Research in language learning has shifted in recent years toward a focus on information processing, the importance of more general cognitive learning principles, the emergence of language ability from extended meaningful exposures and relevant practice, and the awareness of how language is used and the functions that it serves (Doughty and Long, 2003; N. Ellis, 2007; Robinson and Ellis, 2008; Tomasello, 2003; VanPatten and Williams, 2007). Instructional research and curricular issues have centered on task-based learning, content-based learning, strategies-based instruction, and a return to learning centered on specific language skills (Cohen and Macaro, 2007; elsewhere in this volume; Long and Doughty, 2009; McGroarty et al., 2004; Samuda and Bygate, 2008).

Language teacher development has also moved in new directions. Widdowson (1998) has argued forcefully that certain communicative orientations, with a pervasive emphasis on natural language input and authenticity, may be misinterpreting the real purpose of the language classroom context and ignoring effective frameworks for language teaching. He has also persuasively argued that applied linguists must support teachers throughout their mediation with all aspects of Hymes's notion of communicative competence, balancing language understanding so that it combines grammaticality, appropriateness, feasibility, and examples from the attested (Widdowson, 2000). A further emphasis for language teacher education has been the move to engaging teachers in the practice of action research. The trend to train teachers as reflective practitioners inquiring into the effectiveness of teaching and learning in local classroom settings will increase in the coming decade.

A second emphasis that has taken hold in discussions among applied linguists themselves is the role for critical studies; this term covers critical awareness, critical discourse analysis, critical pedagogy, student rights, critical assessment practices, and ethics in language assessment (and language teaching; Davies, 1999; Fairclough, 1995a; McNamara, 1998; McNamara and Roever, 2006; Pennycook, 2001; van Lier, 1997). At the same time, there are a number of criticisms of this general approach and its impact on more mainstream applied linguistics that highlights weaknesses in much of the critical studies theorizing (Seidlhofer, 2003; Widdowson, 2004). At present, the notion of critical studies also constitutes an emphasis that has not demonstrated strong applications in support of those who are experiencing "language problems" of various types. The coming decade will undoubtedly continue this debate.

A third emphasis is on language uses in academic, disciplinary, and professional settings (Biber, 2006b; elsewhere in this volume; Connor and Upton, 2004a; Swales, 2004). This research examines ways in which language is used by participants and in texts in various academic, professional, and occupational settings. It also emphasizes how language can act as a gatekeeping mechanism or can create unfair obstacles for those who are not aware of appropriate discourse rules and expectations. In academic settings, the key issue lies in understanding how genre and register expectations form the basis for successfully negotiating academic work (Hyland, 2004a, 2008; A. M. Johns, 2002; Swales, 2004). Analyses of language use in various professional settings are described in Gibbons (2004), Grabe (2004), Master (2005), and McGroarty et al. (2003). More specific to English for specific purposes (ESP), Swales (2000) and Widdowson (2004) provide relevant overviews.

A fourth emphasis centers on descriptive (usually discourse) analyses of language in real settings and the possible application of analyses in corpus linguistics, register variation, and genre variation. A breakthrough application of corpus linguistics remains the *Longman Grammar of Spoken and Written English* (Biber et al., 1999). It is based entirely on attested occurrences of language use in a very large corpus of English. The key, though, lies not in the corpus data themselves but in the innovative analyses and displays that define the uniqueness of the grammar (see also Carter and McCarthy, 2006). Other important applications of corpus linguistics include more teacher- and learner-directed resources (see McCarthy, 2008).

A fifth emphasis in applied linguistics research addresses multilingualism and bilingual interaction in school, community, and work and in professional settings or policy issues at regional and national levels. Because the majority of people in the world are to some extent bilingual, and because this bilingualism is associated with the need to negotiate life situations with other cultural and language groups, this area of research is fundamental to applied linguistics concerns. Multilingualism covers issues in bilingual education, migrations of groups of people to new language settings, equity and fairness in social services, and language policies related to multiple language use (or the restriction thereof). Key issues are addressed in Baker (2006), Brisk (2005), McGroarty et al. (2003, 2006), and van Els (2005).

A sixth emphasis focuses on the changing discussion in language testing and assessment. During the past decade, the field of language assessment has taken on a number of important issues and topics that have ramifications for applied linguists more generally. Validity remains a major theme for language testers, and it has been powerfully reinterpreted over the last 10 years (Chapelle, Enright, and Jamieson, 2008; Kane, 2006). In its newer interpretation, validity has strong implications for all areas of applied linguistic research and data collection and is not merely an issue for assessment practices (Chapelle, 1999). An additional major shift in language assessment with significant implications for applied linguistics more generally is the greater emphasis being given to *assessment for learning* (sometimes discussed as *formative assessment*).

The goals for assessment have shifted from assessing what students can do at a given moment to using assessment as a way to improve learning effectiveness on an ongoing basis. The goal is to see continuous learner assessment for learning purposes. This trend is likely to grow considerably in the coming decade (Black et al., 2004; Davison, 2007; Grabe, 2009; Rea-Dickins, 2006; Wiliam and Thompson, 2007). More generally, emphases on technology applications, ethics in assessment, innovative research methodologies, the roles of standardized assessment, standards for professionalism, and critical language testing are all reshaping language assessment and, by extension, applied linguistics.

A seventh emphasis focuses on the resources and perspectives provided by neurolinguistics and brain studies associated with language learning and language use (Schumann et al., 2004; see also Schumann elsewhere in this volume). The potential and the benefits of research in neurolinguistics and the impact of language learning on brain processing is perhaps not an immediate concern of applied linguistics. However, significant advances in the relations between brain functioning and language learning (including literacy development) suggest that research insights from neurolinguistics may soon become too important to ignore. The impact of literacy training, literacy learning in different languages, and training with language disability learners on brain processing has accelerated in recent years (J. R. Anderson, 2007; Berninger and Richards, 2002; Schumann et al., 2004; elsewhere in this volume; Ward, 2006; Wolf, 2007). A sure sign of this change is the extraordinarily accessible explanations relating neuroscience to reading ability in Wolf (2007) and the recent inclusion of four chapters on neuroscience and reading comprehension in a recent volume on comprehension instruction (Block and Parris, 2008). This emphasis will probably become an important sub-area of applied linguistics within the decade.

THE PROBLEM-BASED NATURE OF APPLIED LINGUISTICS: IT'S THE PROBLEMS, NOT THE DISCIPLINES

In the many discussions of trends and disciplines, and subfields, and theorizing, the idea is sometimes lost that the focus of applied linguistics is on trying to resolve language-based problems that people encounter in the real world, whether they be academics, dictionary makers, employers, lawyers, learners, policy developers, service providers, supervisors, teachers, test takers, those who need social services, translators, or a whole range of business clients. A list of major language-based problems that applied linguists typically address (across a wide range of settings) follow. The list is necessarily partial, but it should indicate *what* it is that applied linguists try to do, if not *how* they go about their work.

Applied linguists address subsets of the following problems:

- Language assessment problems (validity, reliability, usability, responsibility, fairness)
- Language contact problems (bilingualism, shift, spread, loss, maintenance, social and cultural interactions)
- Language inequality problems (ethnicity, class, region, gender, and age)
- Language learning problems (emergence of skills, awareness, rules, use, context, automaticity, attitudes, expertise)
- Language pathology problems (aphasias, dyslexias, physical disabilities)
- Language policy and planning problems (status planning, corpus planning, acquisition planning, ecology of language, multilingualism, political factors)
- Language teaching problems (resources, training, practice, interaction, understanding, use, contexts, inequalities, motivations, outcomes)
- Language and technology problems (learning, assessment, access, use)
- Language translation problems (access, effectiveness, technologies)

- Language use problems (dialects, registers, discourse communities, gatekeeping situations, limited access to services and resources)
- Literacy problems (orthography development, new scripts, resource development, learning issues)

These categories could be expanded further, and themes in each category could be elaborated into full articles and books in and of themselves. The key point, however, is to recognize that it is the language-based problems in the world that drive applied linguistics. These problems also lead applied linguists to use knowledge from other fields apart from linguistics, and thereby impose the interdisciplinarity that is a defining aspect of the discipline.

Defining Applied Linguistics

Over the past decade, Widdowson (1998, 2000, 2004, 2005) has argued consistently that applied linguistics is not an *interdisciplinary* discipline as much as a *mediating* field or domain between the theoretical plane of linguistics and language knowledge on the one hand and its applications to problems that arise in a number of real-world settings. As such, applied linguistics is problematic as a discipline or as an interdisciplinary field. Rather than create unique knowledge or work within unique disciplinary principles and resources, it is identified by its role mediating between theoretical knowledge from disciplines and practitioners who encounter real-world language problems. However, other applied linguists do not see applied linguistics through such a problematized lens. Brumfit (2004), Bygate (2005), Davies (1999a), and Kaplan (2002a) all see the complexity, fuzziness, and dynamism of applied linguistics as not so distinct from other disciplines. This debate on the definition of applied linguistics will surely continue for at least another decade.

A further debate has centered around the connection between applied linguistics as an academic discipline and the domain of real-world language problems (e.g., Widdowson, 2005). It is certainly true that much research under the umbrella of applied linguistics retains a somewhat detached, descriptive quality to it, contributing to knowledge about a language problem in a real-world context, but not suggesting ways to ameliorate that problem or demonstrating success in addressing the problem. This criticism is a legitimate one, but not one that undermines the definition of applied linguistics itself. There are certainly cases in which applied linguists have drawn on combined disciplinary resources, including language and language learning knowledge, and taken the key steps from basic resource knowledge, to specific research applications, to learning outcome comparisons, to curriculum development, and to instructional use and evaluation of outcomes (and then leading to a new cycle in this problem-solving process). Consequently, it remains reasonable to see applied linguistics as a discipline that engages interdisciplinary resources (including linguistic resources) to address real-world language problems.

As a result (and much like Brumfit, Bygate, Davies, and Kaplan), I have defined applied linguistics as a practice-driven discipline that addresses language-based problems in real-world contexts. This general definition certainly does not come to terms with all of the claims that applied linguistics is not a discipline. Aside from the major issues noted above, critics have also noted that applied linguistics is too broad and too fragmented, that it demands expert knowledge in too many fields, that it does not have a set of unifying research paradigms. However, it is possible to interpret applied linguistic as a discipline much in the way that many other disciplines are defined. Applied linguistics, like many disciplines, has a core and a periphery, and the periphery blurs into other disciplines that may—or may not—want to be allied. This picture may not be very different from that of several other disciplines, particularly those that are relatively new, give or take a hundred years.

A quick look at a number of well-recognized disciplines will reveal that they too are open to charges that their fields are too fragmented and too broad, that they demand expertise in too many related subfields, and that they do not have a set of unifying research paradigms. Obvious, recognizable disciplines that can be included under these criticisms include chemistry, biology, education, English, history, and psychology, just to note some of the larger fields. We tend to note the messiness that is close at hand and see distant disciplines as tidier and better-defined entities. Disciplinary histories, current controversies, blurred borders, and new technologies and taxonomies of subfields within each discipline would suggest some of the same issues that confront applied linguists as they seek to describe disciplinary status. In the case of other disciplines, time and recognition have provided a much greater sense of inevitability, a sense that is likely to accrue to applied linguistics over the next 50 years.

Accepting the messiness of a newer discipline and the controversies that are inevitable in describing an intellectual territory, applied linguistics, nonetheless, exhibits many defining disciplinary characteristics. These points reflect commonalities that most applied linguists would agree on:

1. Applied linguistics has many of the markings of an academic discipline: many professional journals, many professional associations, international recognition for the field, funding resources for research projects. The field contains a large number of individuals who see themselves as applied linguists, as trained professionals who are hired in academic institutions as applied linguists, as students who want to become applied linguists, there is a need for a recognized means for training these students to become applied linguists.
2. Applied linguistics has conferences with well-articulated subareas for conference-abstract submissions. These subareas generally define applied linguistics in ways quite similar to the problem-based list previously provided; categories for submission for the American Association for Applied Linguistics (AAAL) have, for example, remained remarkably stable over the past 10 years.

3. Applied linguistics recognizes that linguistics must be included as a core knowledge base in the training and work of applied linguistics, although the purpose of most applied linguists' work is not simply to *apply* linguistics to achieve a solution. Moreover, direct applications of language knowledge is not necessarily a criterion that defines applied linguistics work. How one trains effective language teachers may involve research that does not refer directly to aspects of language knowledge, but rather to aspects of learning psychology (cognitive processes), educational practice (task development and sequencing), and social interactions (autonomy, status, turn taking).

4. Applied linguistics is grounded in real-world language-driven problems and issues (primarily linked by practical matters involving language use, language evaluation, language contact and multilingualism, language policies, and language learning and teaching). There is also, however, the recognition that these practically driven problems have extraordinary range, and this range tends to dilute any sense of common purpose or common professional identification among practitioners.

5. Applied linguistics typically incorporates other disciplinary knowledge beyond linguistics in its efforts to address language-based problems. Applied linguists commonly draw upon and are often well trained in areas of anthropology, computer programming, education, economics, English, literature, measurement, political science, psychology, sociology, or rhetoric.

6. Applied linguistics is, of necessity, an interdisciplinary field, because few practical language issues can be addressed through the knowledge resources of any single discipline, including linguistics. For example, genuinely to influence language learning, one must be able to call upon, at the very least, resources from educational theory, ethnomethodology (sociology), and learning theory as well as linguistics.

7. Applied linguistics commonly includes a core set of issues and practices that are readily identifiable as work carried out by many applied linguists (e.g., second language assessment, second language curriculum development, second language learning, second language teaching, and second language teacher preparation).

8. Applied linguistics generally incorporates or includes several identifiable subfields: for example, corpus linguistics, forensic linguistics, language testing, language policy and planning, lexicography, second language acquisition, second language writing, and translation and interpretation.

9. Applied linguistics often defines itself broadly in order to include issues in other language-related fields (e.g., first language composition studies, first language literacy research, language pathology, and natural language processing). The great majority of members in these other fields do not see themselves as applied linguists; however, the broad definition for applied

linguistics licenses applied linguists to draw upon and borrow from these disciplines to meet their own objectives.

These nine points indicate the developing disciplinary nature of applied linguistics. There are certainly difficulties for the field, and there are problems in attempting to define and differentiate the core versus the periphery. There are also problems in deciding how one becomes an applied linguist and what training (and what duration of training) might be most appropriate. But these problems are no more intractable than those faced by many disciplines, even relatively established ones.

Conclusion

The coming decade of research and inquiry in applied linguistics will continue the lines of investigation noted in the second and third sections of this chapter. Applied linguists will need to know more about computer technologies, statistical applications, sociocultural influences on research, and new ways to analyze language data. Testing and assessment issues will not be limited to testing applications but will also have a much greater influence on other areas of applied linguistics research. Issues such as validity, fairness, and ethics will extend into other area of applied linguistics. These issues will also lead to continued discussions on the most appropriate research methods in different settings. Additionally, applied linguistics will direct more attention to issues of motivation, attitudes, and affect because those factors potentially influence many language-based problems. Similarly, learning theories (as discussed and debated in educational and cognitive psychology) will become a more central concern in language learning and teaching. Finally, neurolinguistic research will undoubtedly open up new ways to think about language learning, language teaching, and the ways in which language is used.

All of these issues also ensure that applied linguistics will remain essentially interdisciplinary. The resolution of language-based problems in the real world is complex, dynamic, and difficult. It seems only appropriate that applied linguists seek partnerships and collaborative research if these problems are to be addressed in effective ways.

CHAPTER 3

RESEARCH APPROACHES IN APPLIED LINGUISTICS

PATRICIA A. DUFF

INTRODUCTION

In a field as vast as applied linguistics (AL), representing the range of topics featured in this volume and across the many fascinating subdisciplines in the field, an overview of research approaches must be highly selective. Duff (2002a) described many of the developments in research approaches in AL in the 1990s and early 2000s. In this revised and updated chapter, I discuss recent quantitative, qualitative, and mixed-method approaches to AL research, especially in the areas of second language learning and education. I also highlight important new ways of conceptualizing, analyzing, and/or representing knowledge about language issues and at the same time embracing new contexts of language learning and use and a wider range of research populations in the twenty-first century.

More comprehensive and in-depth recent discussions of research methods in AL can be found in recent volumes by Dörnyei (2007), King and Hornberger (2008), A. Mackey and Gass (2005), and Wei and Moyer (2007), with respect to second-language acquisition (SLA), bilingualism, and language education in particular. Many other publications have highlighted specific analytical approaches or methods for conducting research, typically within a particular realm of AL, such as the following:

- L2 classroom research and classroom-based discourse analysis (McKay, 2006; Zuengler and Mori, 2002)
- Ethnomethodology and conversation analysis (Markee, 2000, 2004; Seedhouse, 2004)

- Case study research (Duff, 2008)
- Corpus linguistics (Barlow, 2005; Biber, Conrad, and Reppen, 1998; Myles, 2005; Gries, 2008)
- Ethnography (Duff, 2002b; Hammersley and Atkinson, 2007; Toohey, 2008)
- Language analysis (R. Ellis and Barkhuizen, 2005)
- Stimulated recall (Gass and Mackey, 2000)
- Data elicitation methods (Gass and Mackey, 2007a)
- Discourse analysis and critical discourse analysis (Fairclough, 1989, 2003; Wooffitt, 2005)
- Critical applied linguistics more generally (Pennycook, 2001)
- Multimodal semiotic analysis (Kress and Van Leeuwen, 2002)
- Complex systems approaches (Larsen-Freeman and Cameron, 2008a, 2008b)
- Survey methods (C. Baker, 2008)

Scholars have also given careful consideration to the processes of drawing inferences or making generalizations in applied linguistics research:

- Across a variety of types of research (Chalhoub-Deville, Chapelle, and Duff, 2006)
- To meta-analysis and other important approaches to research synthesis regardless of paradigm (Norris and Ortega, 2006a, 2006b, 2007)
- To the benefits of longitudinal research (Ortega and Byrnes, 2008; Ortega and Iberri-Shea, 2005)

J. D. Brown (2004) produced a recent overview chapter on the theme of research approaches in AL in another handbook in applied linguistics, and Hinkel's (2005) *Handbook* also reflects the current range of approaches to second-language/AL research. Finally, a number of journals and handbooks are also dedicated to such particular research methods or approaches as critical discourse analysis or narrative research. In addition, the recently revised 10-volume Springer *Encyclopedia of Language and Education* contains many chapters on current or emerging approaches to research in language and education.

Research Approaches: Contrasting, Combining, and Expanding Paradigms

Most research methodology textbooks in education and the social sciences (e.g., Cresswell, 2005; J. P. Gall, M. D. Gall, and Borg, 2005; M. D. Gall, J. P. Gall, & Borg, 2003), as well as in some of the AL overview textbooks referred to above, continue to distinguish between quantitative (nomothetic) and qualitative (hermeneutic) research, as two distinct but by no means mutually exclusive approaches to systematic and rigorous inquiry in the social sciences. They also emphasize that the approach or method is crucially linked to the kind of research question or problem under investigation, to the purpose of the study (e.g., exploratory, interpretive, descriptive, explanatory, confirmatory, predictive), and to the type of data and population one is working with. Quantitative research is often associated with experiments, surveys, and other research with large samples of people or observations, whereas qualitative research is associated with ethnography, case study, and narrative inquiry, often with a smaller number of participants but fuller and more holistic accounts from (or of) each one. However, each paradigm actually represents a collection of approaches to research that share some common principles but at the same time reflect major differences.

Any research paradigm or approach reflects a number of components:

- A philosophical basis or belief system regarding epistemology, or the nature of truth and of knowing (e.g., that research is ideally objective, unbiased, and value free versus more subjective)
- An ideology concerning ontology, or the nature of reality (e.g., that an objective reality exists, or that reality is constructed socially and multiple perspectives on reality exist)
- A corresponding methodology (e.g., one that is experimental/manipulative and hypothesis testing, or is not) with various designs, methods, techniques, and devices for eliciting and analyzing phenomena (Denzin and Lincoln, 2005a, 2005b; Duff, 2008)

Therefore, there are many levels at which research can be analyzed and categorized. Comparison and categorization in AL has traditionally been based primarily on methods or techniques, with less reflection on epistemological and ontological issues. Quantitative approaches tend to be associated with a positivist or post-positivist orientation, a realist ontology, an objectivist epistemology, and an experimental, manipulative methodology. Qualitative approaches, on the other hand, are more often associated with an interpretive, humanistic orientation, an ontology of multiple realities, a nonobjectivist epistemology and a naturalistic, nonmanipulative methodology (Guba and Lincoln, 1994). However, what is ostensibly quantitative research may involve qualitative analysis (e.g., discourse analysis) and vice versa. Case study, for example, normally considered qualitative research, may actually reflect a more positivist approach than an interpretive one, or it may be part of a quantitative one-shot (experimental) case study or a single- or multiple-case time series design (Duff, 2008). Similarly, statistical techniques can be used in both quantitative and qualitative research, but inferential statistics are mostly associated with quantitative research (Gall et al., 2003, 2005).

Quantitative research includes a variety of approaches and designs, as well as such tools as correlations, surveys, and multifactorial studies, in addition to experimental or quasi-experimental studies. Qualitative research, on the other hand, encompasses a broad, expanding assortment of approaches, including narrative research, life history, autobiographical or biographical accounts, content analysis, historical and archival studies, conversation analysis, microethnography, and discourse analysis. These types of research draw on a variety of theoretical traditions as well, such as ethnomethodology, symbolic interactionism, structuralism, interpretivism and social constructivism, poststructuralism, phenomenology, hermeneutics, feminism, social/educational anthropology, and cultural studies (Denzin and Lincoln, 2005b).

In recent years, government-funded quantitative research in the United States has enjoyed a privileged status within education and the social sciences because it is considered by some authorities to be more robust, rigorous, "scientific," theoretical, and generalizable and, therefore, it is argued to have more to contribute to knowledge, theory, and policy than qualitative research (Freeman et al., 2007). Of course, claims of rigor or generalizability should not be taken for granted in quantitative research—they must, rather, be demonstrated by the researcher. Neither should it be assumed that qualitative research is atheoretical, unscientific, lacking in rigor or generalizability (transferability), or intellectually insignificant. However, again, the onus is on the researcher to demonstrate the credibility and importance of the methods and findings (Duff, 2006). Fortunately, qualitative research of different types has gained a major foothold in AL in the past 10 years, creating a better balance between quantitative and qualitative publications in the major AL journals than had been reported earlier (Lazaraton, 2000).

Critical (or "ideological") research is sometimes accorded a category of its own, separate from quantitative and qualitative paradigms. According to Pennycook (2008), critical applied linguistics is

> an emergent approach to language use and education that seeks to connect the
> local conditions of language to broader social formations, drawing connections
> between classrooms, conversations, textbooks, tests or translations and issues of
> gender, class, sexuality, race, ethnicity, culture, identity, politics, ideology or
> discourse. (p. 169)

Perhaps critical research is considered an independent category because certain approaches to research constitute explicitly ideological lenses or frames (e.g., critical or feminist) through which any data or situation can be analyzed using a variety of methods, quantitative or qualitative. Thus, critical perspectives can be applied to ethnography or to census data, and feminist perspectives can be applied to test score data or case studies. Alternatively, it could be claimed that these overtly ideological perspectives constitute different approaches, purposes, underlying assumptions, methods, subject matter, and reporting styles and that they are therefore not simply new lenses, frames, or values to be applied to otherwise orthodox academic pursuits with reified categories and objectification.

Such other types of research as program evaluation research and action research can take the form of either—or both—quantitative and qualitative research.

DEVELOPMENTS IN QUANTITATIVE RESEARCH

The last 3 decades have been very productive for the development, explanation, and application of quantitative research design and statistics and other analytical techniques in AL research using a variety of types of research: experimental, quasi-experimental, correlational, survey, and other carefully controlled, sometimes multivariate designs. As a result, careful attention has been paid to the reliability and validity of research constructs, instruments, scales, rating protocols, and analytical procedures; sampling procedures; measurement; variables and parametric and nonparametric statistics and power effects (Hatch and Lazaraton, 1991; Lazaraton, 2000). Some additional developments are reported in this section.

N. C. Ellis (1999) discusses three quantitative approaches to cognitive and psycholinguistic research: observational research (e.g., using language corpora), experimentation (e.g., in studies on form-focused instruction and SLA; Doughty and Williams, 1998), and simulations (e.g., connectionist models of SLA; Kempe and MacWhinney, 1998). Although there is a greater understanding among applied linguists of the criteria of good quantitative research currently, it is also evident that true experimental research is often difficult to conduct for logistical and ethical reasons, particularly in research with children or adults in educational contexts. In many institutions, for example, pretesting, random assignment to treatment types (e.g., instructional interventions or experimental stimuli), and control or normative/baseline groups may be difficult to arrange. Norgate (1997) provides an interesting example of this dilemma in research on the L1 development of blind children. Rather, quasi-experimental research examining cause-effect relationships among independent and dependent variables and research looking for other kinds of relationships among variables predominate. Experimental SLA laboratory studies are an exception; that research often involves artificial or semi-artificial L2 structures, control groups, random assignment, and pre- and posttesting (e.g., Hulstijn and DeKeyser, 1997). The downside of this carefully controlled research is that it lacks ecological validity because the language(s), contexts, and activities do not represent those ordinarily encountered by language learners and users.

In another area of AL, language testing, which has made great strides in tackling issues of validation, ethics, and psychometric precision in recent years, Kunnan (1999) describes new quantitative methods, such as structured equation modeling, that permit sophisticated analyses of relationships among groups of learner (test taker) variables such as L2 proficiency, language aptitude, and intelligence. Chalhoub-Deville and Deville (2008) also note developments in testing based on generalizability theory, multidimensional scaling, multifaceted Rasch analysis, rule-space methodology, and computer-based and computer-adaptive testing, typically found in articles in the journal *Language Testing*.

In L1/L2 survey research, C. Baker (2008) describes large-scale and small-scale initiatives in Europe, South America, and elsewhere, dealing with such issues as language vitality among minority language groups and social-psychological variables (e.g., attitudes and motivation) connected with successful L2 learning. He also illustrates how more readily available census data with specific items about language has facilitated certain kinds of analysis for language policy and planning purposes. Finally, Baker notes that a growing trend in European research lies in examining practices related to community (heritage) language schooling and surveying attitudes toward trilingualism and multilingualism (which others might refer to as language ideologies).

Developments in Qualitative Research

Whereas qualitative AL research in the past may have leaned toward (post)positivism and structuralism, relying on researchers' structured elicitations, analyses, and interpretations of a relatively narrow band of observed linguistic (or other) behavior sometimes designed to test specific hypotheses, current strands of research lean toward more unapologetically subjective, dialectical accounts, incorporating different, sometimes contradictory perspectives of the same phenomenon and grappling more intentionally with issues of positioning, voice, and representation (Duff, 2008; Edge and Richards, 1998). The omission of qualitative research methodologies from many textbooks, key journals, graduate courses, and programs in applied linguistics even a decade ago has been corrected to a significant degree in the interim (K. Richards, 2003, 2009), particularly with the *social* and *narrative turns* that applied linguistics has witnessed during this decade in second language learning research as well as in language testing. Baker (2008), the researcher in bilingualism referred to above, dryly observes, "within language and education, the methodological pendulum has partly swung towards a preference for qualitative, ethnographic and phenomenological types of approach. Although quantitative approaches have been much criticized within the study of language and education, it is unlikely that they will disappear" (p. 65).

A growing enthusiasm for qualitative poststructural, postcolonial, and critical L2 research (e.g., Pennycook, 1999, 2008) is indeed evident in many areas of AL. Critical and poststructural perspectives have been applied to ethnographies (e.g., T. Goldstein, 1997, 2001; Madison, 2005; Talmy, 2008), to in-depth studies of language and social identity (e.g., Norton, 2000), and to research on language and gender (e.g., Cameron, 1992; Ehrlich, 1997; R. D. Freeman, 1997; Mills, 1995), some of which is explicitly feminist, emancipatory, reflexive, and postmodern. Yet a comprehensive overview textbook of qualitative research approaches in AL still seems to be lacking, though a plethora of generic qualitative textbooks exist in education and the social sciences.

The "Research Issues" section of the *TESOL Quarterly*, which I edited for 12 years, featured many qualitative developments: in narrative research, interview and focus group research, corpus research, classroom observation, testing, research guidelines, and software tools for qualitative data analysis. Special issues of the *Modern Language Journal* in 1997 and 2007, centering on the so-called Firth and Wagner debates, also marked salient turning points in both theory and methodology in AL. The current expansion of qualitative approaches in AL reflects trends across the health sciences, social sciences, humanities, and education in recent years (Denzin and Lincoln, 2005a, 2005b) and a growing interest in ecological validity and the social, cultural, situational, embodied, and performative nature of language, knowledge, representation, and learning. Journals that have been established in AL this decade, such as the *Journal of Language, Identity and Education*, as well as many other journals with *qualitative* or *narrative* in their titles, are further evidence of the emphasis on more subjective, discursive aspects of learning that are often approached through interpretive, inductive, and sometimes critical methods. I have observed, however, that in many parts of the world (e.g., in East Asia and Central Europe) the status of qualitative research is still considerably lower (and often poorly understood) in comparison with quantitative research, a situation that has fortunately changed in North American AL. Sociocultural research in those same geographical domains also seems to have had less visibility or traction than it has, for example, in the United Kingdom, Canada, United States, and Australia.

However, in such traditionally very quantitative subfields as language testing, more nonpsychometric and qualitative studies have been published in recent years in the English-speaking world, particularly in such journals as *Language Assessment Quarterly* (Chalhoub-Deville and Deville, 2008). Lazaraton (2008) describes the kinds of (qualitative) discourse or conversation analysis that have been done of transcribed oral-proficiency interview talk (including her research) and especially of interviewers' accommodations of interviewees (test takers), based on such factors as the test takers' proficiency level or the familiarity of test takers and testers. Other studies she reviews deal with test takers' discourse and their negotiation for meaning, the dynamics of interaction and discourse in tests that pair up test-takers, or use group formats (e.g., on Cambridge ESOL proficiency tests). The qualitative analyses prove very useful for test validation and especially to ascertain whether the interaction during testing has an inadvertent effect on test takers' scores. Other research that Lazaraton reviews describes the use of think-aloud protocols (verbal reports) by test raters and of research that looks at the impact or consequences of testing through ethnographic observation or case study.

Ethnography, Case Study, and Interview Research

Ethnographies of language learning and teaching, literacy practices, and workplace encounters, as well as methodological discussions about cultural aspects of knowledge and behavior, have become more prominent and commonplace since Watson-Gegeo's influential (1988) article first appeared in the *TESOL Quarterly*. Harklau (2005), Heath and Street (2008), and Toohey (2008) provide recent reviews of ethnographic research in AL. Ethnographic research typically describes the cultural patterns of groups as they evolve and settle over time, such as language learners in a class or workers at job sites. It aims to elicit insiders' (*emic*) perspectives as well as those of the researcher, undertaking participant observation (*etic*) perspectives. Increasingly, too, this research looks at the positioning of research participants not only by the others they interact with in their natural settings but also by how the researcher herself positions the participants and their behaviors—and herself. Harklau noted that relatively little ethnographic research has been conducted outside of the United Kingdom or North America by non-White, non-Anglophone researchers on languages other than English and their cultures. However, L. C. Moore (2008) subsequently described numerous ethnographic accounts of multilingual socialization in a variety of non-Western, non-English-dominant settings, including her own work in French postcolonial Africa. Indeed, many of the other invited chapters in the Springer 2008 *Encyclopedia of Language and Education* series likewise involved researchers reviewing describing practices in communities where various languages are spoken.

Case studies remain one of the most common forms of qualitative research in AL, on their own or in combination with quantitative research (Duff, 2008; Gomm, Hammersley, and Foster, 2000; Merriam 1998; Yin, 2009). Like ethnographic research, case studies typically place great importance on contextualization and holistic accounts of individuals, groups, or events. In some instances researchers are also able to track participants longitudinally, as Kanno (2003) did with several Japanese students who had previously studied English and other curriculum content abroad and then returned to Japan. Morita (2004), in her multiple-case study of Japanese women studying at a Canadian university, documented their academic and linguistic socialization as well as the meanings and factors behind, and social construction of, their apparent silence in some of their classes. The study revealed that far from representing a monolithic group based on ethnicity, gender, first-language, and academic status, each woman's experience in her new English-speaking academic environment was highly situated, contingent, and unique and also changed over time.

Another common approach to research at present concerns involved interviews as an important mediating tool and site for linguistic processes and for social semiotic action. Although interviews are used in many kinds of research for different purposes, the actual interactional structures, positioning, footings, framing, and so on are commanding renewed attention by AL researchers and others in the social sciences, in medicine, and in other fields (Campbell and Roberts, 2007; Kvale, 2006; Talmy and Richards, forthcoming; Gubrium and Holstein, 2002; Silverman, 2001). Some of the work compares a content analysis of interview discourse with other kinds of analyses of the interview itself as a speech event.

Narrative Inquiry and Art-Based Research

Personal accounts and narratives of the experiences of language teachers, learners, and others—often across a broad span of time, space, experience, and languages—have increasingly become a major focus in some qualitative research. Evidence includes first-person narratives, diary studies, autobiographies, and life histories of learning, teaching, or losing aspects of one's language and identity (e.g., Belcher and Connor, 2001; Kouritzen, 1999; Pavlenko and Lantolf, 2000; Schumann, 1997). At present, studies also examine individuals using language in and across social contexts that had been investigated to a lesser degree in the past (e.g., in professional or academic settings, in the home/family, in the community, in the workplace, and in other social institutions). New meta-methodological discussions about the range of directions, data collection approaches, forms of analysis, and criteria for good narrative research are presently abundant both in AL (Coffey and Street, 2008; Pavlenko, 2007a, 2007b) and in the social sciences and education (Atkinson and Delamont, 2006; Clandinin, 2007; Clandinin and Connelly, 2000; Polkinghorne, 2007; Riessman, 2008). In addition to these narrative approaches to exploring linguistic experience, other important but less emic accounts of language and behavior have attracted renewed attention from scholars across disciplines, particularly in studies of the discursive structure and social-interactional accomplishment of narrative texts (e.g., Bamberg, 1998). Arts-based research involving dramatic enactments, representations through nonprint visual modes of representation, multimodal analysis, poetics, and fictionalized accounts are gradually gaining visibility in AL as well (e.g., T. Goldstein, 2001; M. C. Taylor, 2008).

Although often compelling and highly engaging as both a process and as research output, these emerging approaches do not supplant existing ones (whether quantitative or qualitative) but rather complement them and provide new topics, genres, analyses, and conclusions, as well as different notions of authenticity and legitimacy (Edge and Richards, 1998). There is a growing emphasis on social, cultural, political, and historical aspects of language and language research, in addition to narrative aspects (Creese, Martin, and Hornberger, 2008; Hinkel, 1999; McKay and Hornberger, 1996; Norton and Toohey, 2004; Duff and Hornberger, 2008). Categorical labels and unacknowledged bias have therefore been the subject of analysis and critique (in connection with race, class, culture, language, gender, heterosexism, native versus nonnative speakers, inner and outer circle in World Englishes [or Chineses], and indigenous versus nonindigenous voices and knowledge[s]). Drawing on different (psychological) traditions but also concerned with social aspects of language and literacy are neo-Vygotskyan, sociocultural, and constructivist accounts, which have been adopted by growing numbers of applied linguists over the past decade (Lantolf, 2000; Lantolf and Thorne, 2006, 2007), particularly in research in classrooms, in therapeutic, counseling, or dynamic assessment encounters, and in community settings. Like other primarily qualitative approaches, sociocultural research often involves conversation analysis, discourse analysis, narrative analysis, and microethnography, and examines language and content in an integrated manner.

Reflecting another change in AL research approaches and objects of study, at the present time text and discourse analyses investigate not only the structure of, say, scientific research articles, but also the linguistic messages, symbols, and genres associated with ostensibly nonscientific media and interactions—for example, in popular culture, mass media, and everyday social encounters (e.g., dinnertime discussions). Some of this research is framed in terms of critical or poststructural theory and the constructs of literacy and discourse like that of identity have been theorized and analyzed as plural—not singular—entities, and as social, multifaceted, and fluid (Gee, 1996; Norton, 2000). Finally, the concern for understanding contextual features of linguistic phenomena—the hallmark of much qualitative (or at least nonquantitative) AL research—has also been applied to analyses of the historical, political, social, cultural, rhetorical, and intellectual contexts and consequences of AL theories, research, and practice/praxis (Rampton, 1995; Thomas, 1998).

DEVELOPMENTS IN MIXED-METHOD RESEARCH

Quantitative and qualitative approaches are currently viewed as complementary rather than fundamentally incompatible, and more mixed-paradigm research is recommended (Bergman, 2008; Dörnyei, 2007; Tashakkori and Teddlie, 1998, 2003; Teddlie and Tashakkori, 2009). However, a balanced combination of the two is not yet commonplace in AL research. According to Denzin (2008) and Lincoln and Guba (2000), the paradigm "wars" of the last two decades have transformed into paradigm "dialogs."

An example of mixed-method research in foreign language learning is the full-length research monograph by Kinginger (2008), a multiple-case study of American students in French-language study abroad programs in France. Another example is an evaluation of a Japanese foreign-language elementary school program by Antonek, Donato, and Tucker (2000) in the United States. Both studies provided measurement (test) data for students at different points in their programs but also included case studies of focal participants as well as the students' experiences and perspectives together with an analysis of their narrative or interview data to help shed light on the quantitative findings.

THE IMPACT OF TECHNOLOGICAL ADVANCES ON RESEARCH APPROACHES IN AL

At the present time, technological and computational advances play a crucial role in most AL research, whether for collecting, inputting, managing, coding, storing, and retrieving data or for analyzing it. The availability of high-quality, affordable tape recorders, digital video cameras, personal and handheld computers, scanners, smart pens/boards, wikis, and means of incorporating data of different types from multiple sources in computer files and in publications (e.g., with accompanying compact disks or linked websites) has major practical and theoretical implications for education, testing, and research. Developments in digital technologies have been particularly useful in applied psycholinguistics, corpus linguistics, discourse analysis, and testing (N. C. Ellis, 1999; Markee, 2007). Videotaped data or other audiovisual representations of data can presently be posted online, can be linked to more traditional print-based reports, or can appear in stand-alone online publications. In research involving graphic imaging or analyses of the intersection of sound and image or multimodal analysis, this development is very important and enriches what would otherwise be limited to static, black-and-white, print- and transcript-based written accounts of linguistic phenomena that are often primarily oral but are represented through writing. New technologies have also enhanced research with minority populations in AL, such as the blind and deaf (Hornberger and Corson, 1997) and have enabled diaspora communities to remain connected and able to communicate freely using the languages and sometimes hybrid symbol systems at their disposal (Lam, 2008). Technology has also facilitated the documentation of endangered languages. Increasingly AL research involving computer-mediated communication conceives of language and literacy as social practice in which linguistic, social, and other identities can be constructed, displayed, and transformed (or resisted) and in which rich intertextuality, multimodality, and creativity are the norm and are the object of analysis (Snyder, 2008).

In addition, the use of data management and analysis software designed specifically for qualitative research has become more accessible and more widely used in AL than it had been earlier (e.g., Dörnyei, 2007; Séror, 2005). Furthermore, the development and accessibility of such L1 and L2 databases as TalkBank by MacWhinney (2001) at Carnegie Mellon University (http://www.talkbank.org), represent a significant language database of vocal interactions of humans and animals that is continually being updated and currently incorporates child language data (CHILDES) and data related to aphasia, conversation analysis, bilingualism, and second language acquisition, with linked digital audio and video data. This electronic database provides a tremendous resource for researchers as well as tools for analyzing their own and others' data. In addition, corpora and concordances for collecting and analyzing oral and written texts (Biber, Conrad and Reppen, 1998; Thomas and Short, 1996) and new databases resulting from the use of computers in language testing, as well as online language interactions in CALL or other electronic networks, have also engendered new possibilities for AL research. Thus, such diverse subfields as language acquisition, text analysis, syntax and semantics, assessment, sociolinguistics, and language policy are affected. Research involving functional neuroimaging tools (e.g., functional magnetic resonance imaging, fMRI) and positron emission tomography (PET) provide valuable real-time information about the inner workings of the brain, especially in relation to different languages and tasks among monolinguals, bilinguals, and multilinguals (Wattendorf and Festman, 2008). The relationships between age of additional-language acquisition, proficiency level, and differential cortical functioning and localization of functions have long been of interest to neurolinguists and neurobiologists, and these new technologies literally provide a window into the brain's inner workings.

In addition to the *Journal of Language Learning and Technology*, which has become one of the most respected journals for digital technologies in applied linguistics, the recent survey of research across applied linguistics mediated by technology in Markee's (2007) special issue of the *Annual Review of Applied Linguistics* is particularly helpful. Possibilities are changing almost daily with what is presently known as Web 2.0 and the many other applications and tools for linguistic research in laboratories and in natural everyday settings and texts. Digital tools are ubiquitous for conversation analysis, teleconferencing, self-access podcasting, detecting plagiarism, modeling pronunciation and other aspects of speech or writing, tracking one's own or others' activities and progress online, text messaging, and test taking, and scoring tests.

Future AL research will no doubt continue to be greatly influenced by ongoing technical developments in natural language processing, machine and other translation systems, artificial intelligence, brain imaging techniques, CALL, gaming, aural/visual recognition, (eye gaze and other) tracking, and transcription devices. AL-tailored statistical packages and procedures will also become more sophisticated. Also, as more research focuses on languages other than English—including signed languages and those with different orthographies or with no orthographies at all—and seeks to accommodate a greater range of information about messages (e.g., phonetic, temporal, visual, contextual, material, embodied), new electronic tools and theoretical insights are bound to result.

PARTICIPANTS AND POPULATIONS IN APPLIED LINGUISTIC RESEARCH

Although the *populations* that are the focus of applied linguistics are distinct from research *approaches*, the characteristics of groups under investigation certainly have implications for both methodology and theory. For example, work about/with indigenous language learners, their communities and cultures, and their languages, literacies, and other symbol systems, long underrepresented in applied linguistics, is currently beginning to flourish. Important developments have also occurred in the past decade in indigenous and postcolonial/decolonizing epistemologies and knowledges (e.g., Denzin, Lincoln, and Smith, 2008; L. T. Smith, 1999). Expanding the research participant pool and the languages they represent has implications for the way the research is theorized, conducted, interpreted, and disseminated with these populations as well as the form it ultimately takes. Given the endangered status of many such indigenous languages and related cultures and ideologies, this work is urgently needed.

However, just as great care is being taken to expand the collective research agenda to include a wider range of language users and geolinguistic contexts and to reflect on their experiences, poststructural and critical scholars remind us not to essentialize or reify these same populations. Applied linguistic and sociolinguistic research on gender and language, for example, has been carried out for more than a generation. But many scholars are at present very cautious about making grand claims based on gender (or sexuality, race, ability/disability, nativeness, etc.) as a set of predetermined, stable, always relevant, mutually exclusive categories (e.g., male/ female) to which certain behaviors and perspectives can be uniquely ascribed (e.g., Bucholtz, 2003; Kyratzis and Cook-Gumperz, 2008). Rather, scholars are at present increasingly seeking evidence of how membership in such categories is socially coconstructed and *performed* through discourse not as a "preformed" category (Pennycook, 2008) but as a situated identity and by the various ways in which inter- locutors position one another and themselves through their interactions and other behaviors and discourse and how they may also negotiate and transgress the expec- tations placed on them in relation to these social categories (Cameron and Kulick, 2003; Pavlenko, 2008b; Pavlenko and Piller, 2007).

Elderly learners and users of language are also being included in more AL research as are people with degenerative cognitive or physical conditions affecting their language and communication capacities. Groups that in the past were not given special attention, such as generation 1.5 learners, heritage-language learners, transnationals, asylum seekers or refugees, very young or very old language learners/ users, multilingual/multiliterate people, and the so-called generation of digital natives (youth and young adults immersed in new digital information and commu- nication technologies) have, when included as research participants in AL (e.g., in SLA, language testing, language policy, sociolinguistics, and language/literacy edu- cation), yielded important new theoretical understandings that have often required new methodological approaches not previously used because these populations were excluded from earlier research.

Conclusion

In this chapter, I have provided a brief overview of both dominant and emerging approaches to AL research, particularly those typically described as quantitative, qualitative, or mixed-method, and as how these have been discussed and utilized in the field. The research topics and approaches discussed, much like the field of AL, involve various philosophical and theoretical commitments as well as meth- odological preferences and practices. AL research this past decade has demon- strated greater pluralism and rigor, an increased sensitivity to the contexts of research, the characteristics and diversity of research participants, the need to draw meaningful theoretical insights from findings and to consider carefully constraints on generalizability (or transferability) of results. Explicit discussion and reflection on researchers' own histories, investments, and roles in the research process are also expected to a greater degree than before not only in AL but across the humanities and social sciences more generally (Duff, 2008). Explicit discussion of criteriology in the assessment of research has underscored the responsibility that scholars have to know not only how to conduct and assess work in their own immediate areas of scholarship but also the different criteria, norms, genres, and expectations in other areas in AL (Edge and Richards, 1998; Lazaraton, 2003; cf. M. Freeman et al., 2007). There is a growing recognition of and respect for fundamental issues of ethics, fairness, and validity in AL research and practice (e.g., Cameron et al., 1992; Davies, 1997; Davis, 1995; Ortega, 2005), attention to the consequences of research for educational policy and practice, and an awareness that some issues, populations, languages, and geographic areas have received considerable research attention (and funding) whereas others have remained invisible or on the margins. This last point not only suggests imbalances in the global research enterprise, but also has implications regarding the limitations of the theoretical conclusions drawn from work confined to particular areas, languages, and participants at the expense of others.

The development of criteria for exemplary quantitative, qualitative, and mixed-method research and reporting has resulted in many carefully conceived studies and programs of research. In addition, a greater collective awareness and understanding of different research methods and areas of study is occurring. Collaboration among researchers looking at similar phenomena in different (socio)linguistic, cultural, and geographical contexts (as in earlier work by Blum-Kulka, House, and Kasper, 1989, with respect to interlanguage pragmatics) would certainly benefit theory development and practical applications. Combining the expertise of applied linguists espousing different research paradigms in complementary types of analysis of the same phenomenon would also yield richer analyses of complex issues (Koshmann, 1999). One recent project reflecting multiperspectival research was undertaken by Barnard and Torres-Guzman (2009), who had chapter authors present their own analyses of classroom discourse and language socialization in schools in various parts of the world and then asked other researchers to do a "second take" (an independent analysis) of the same data to see how their analyses and interpretations differed. More multiperspectival research and theoretical triangulation involving researchers either from the same or from different traditions and disciplines (e.g., anthropology, psychology, education, and linguistics) examining the same data from their own frames of reference would enrich applied linguistics.

Although much AL research is chiefly concerned with abilities, behaviors, or sociolinguistic conditions and phenomena at one point in time (typically the present and/or immediate past), research sustained over larger periods of time, space, and activities is also needed, especially in developmental studies, studies trying to establish the long-term effectiveness of particular interventions, or those related to (academic) language socialization or language loss (Heath, 2000). Ortega and Byrnes's (2008) study represents a real contribution to AL precisely because it deals with both *longitudinal* research and research on *advanced* language learners. Replication studies, meta-analyses, cross-linguistic, cross-generational, and cross-medium (e.g., oral/written) studies have been used in limited ways in AL, with particular combinations of languages, media, and age groups. Recent work by Tarone, Bigelow, and Hansen (2009) highlights the theoretical benefits for SLA of examining alphabetic literacy levels of learners in studies of oral language development and processing. Thus, looking beyond one modality of language ability and use to see connections across modalities is very important.

More multimethod AL research would provide a greater triangulation of findings and help identify and interpret "rich points" in research (Hornberger, 2006a). Research has started to take into account in more significant ways not only individual (e.g., cognitive, linguistic, affective) and (social) group aspects of language behavior and knowledge, but also sociocultural, historical, political, and ideological aspects. Consequently, more emphasis is being placed on the multiple, sometimes shifting identities, perspectives, and competencies of research participants and researchers, as well as the multiple contexts in which language is learned, produced, interpreted, translated, forgotten, and even eliminated (Norton, 2000; Duff, 2008).

Finally, all basic or pure research is meant to contribute to the knowledge base and theoretical growth of a field; thus, with more conceptually sound research, new discoveries, insights, and applications are certainly in store for the field of AL. In applied research that aims to yield a greater understanding of phenomena in the mind/world and also help to improve some aspect of the human condition, increased social and political intervention and advocacy is required. These, then, are just some of the issues and challenges that applied linguists must address in the future from different perspectives and using a variety of approaches. Indeed, as new perspectives, genres, and media for reporting and disseminating research are transformed, new areas for AL research and new challenges, too, will surface for the evaluation of innovative, nontraditional forms of research.

PART II

THE FOUR SKILLS: SPEAKING, LISTENING, READING, AND WRITING

CHAPTER 4

....

SPEAKING

....

MARTIN BYGATE

I. INTRODUCTION

....

The study of speaking—like the study of other uses of language—is properly an interdisciplinary enterprise. It involves understanding the psycholinguistic and interpersonal factors of speech production, the forms, meanings, and processes involved, and how these can be developed. This chapter views speaking as a multilevel, hierarchical skill, in which high-level plans, in the form of speaker intentions, are realized through the processes of formulation and articulation under a range of conditions. For the purposes of this chapter, spoken language is taken to be *colloquial* in the two senses of representing dialogue and of representing the features typically associated with the everyday use of language.

This chapter first outlines the need for an integrated account of oral language processing. It then presents such an account, considers the range of formal features that characterize spoken language, and reviews oral language pedagogy in the light of this account. The conclusion outlines issues for further exploration.

II. ASPECTS OF SPOKEN LANGUAGE

....

We start from the distinction between language as system and language in contexts of use. A speaker's language proficiency can be seen as a pool of systemic resources and the ability to use them in real contexts. Systemic knowledge can be described in relatively decontextualized terms, as in a grammar or dictionary. To communicate, speakers have to exploit those resources for real purposes and under real constraints.

An applied linguistic model of speaking needs to explain how and why speakers adapt systemic knowledge of language to real world use, involving judgments of appropriacy at all levels, whether discourse, lexico-grammatical, or articulatory.

Consider the following example, from a recording of a family evening meal:

Example 1
Mother: Oh:: you know what? you wanna tell Daddy what happened to you
            today?=

(Ochs and Taylor, 1992: 324)

We can assume that behind the mother's utterance lie a number of intentions:

- To attract attention
- To announce a potentially interesting topic
- To indicate familiarity with it
- To invite her child to recount it
- To invite others present to listen

In other words, the content of the communication reflects judgments of appropriacy based on speaker intention.

In addition, formulation of the message is also subject to judgments of appropriacy based on the speaker's intentions. For example, the speaker chose to formulate her intentions through uninverted questions (requiring the realization of appropriate intonations). Other choices include the use of the first question to announce a new topic; use of the word *Daddy* rather than, say, *your father*; and *you wanna* as an invitation implying strong encouragement. Issues of appropriacy, then, are not limited to the level of discourse structure or message content, but permeate the processes of message formulation and phonological articulation.

This example suggests the desirability of an account that presents the speaker's judgments of feasibility, appropriacy, and frequency as affecting the whole speech process. Although underlying this process there must be a robust systemic knowledge of the language, this chapter focuses on how our systemic resources are used across the full hierarchy of language levels.

III. AN INTEGRATED MODEL OF
ORAL LANGUAGE PRODUCTION

An account of oral language production needs to represent the main types of decision that speakers typically make. Building on the work of Levelt (1989) Levelt et al. (1999; see also Poulisse, 1997, and Scovel, 1998, for an accessible introduction), these can be accommodated to a considerable extent in terms of four different *levels* of decision making: discourse modeling, message conceptualization, message formulation, and message articulation. We consider each of these in turn.

Discourse Modeling

In speaking, we have to construct a discourse plan that represents a number of general intentions: our overall topic and intended outcome, the way we would like the interaction to proceed, our relationships with our interlocutor(s), our personality, and our relationship with the world. One aspect of this concerns the kinds of relationships, identity, and formality we wish to establish and maintain. This dimension has been researched in relation to cross-cultural talk and its capacity to lead to misleading perceptions of the speakers in various contexts (e.g., in relation to communication at the workplace, in the law courts, in the context of academic tutorials, in doctor-patient interviews). Studies have shown how language is used to negotiate particular interactional roles and relationships in the family, and studies in cross-cultural pragmatics have explored the ways in which speakers negotiate the dimension of face (see Scollon and Scollon, 1983; Spolsky, 1998).

A second dimension concerns the expected patterns of oral discourse (Hoey, 1991). Studies have demonstrated the structuring of classroom talk (e.g., Sinclair and Coulthard, 1975; Coulthard, 1991) and of service encounters, and have shown the differences in the organization of talk across cultures and from a cross-cultural perspective (e.g., Gumperz, 1983). This suggests differences in cultural expectations toward particular types of interpersonal interactions or discourse types (such as narrative structure) that can give rise to significant misinterpretations.

A third dimension, content knowledge, is clearly also relevant to managing communication on different topics (e.g., Selinker and Douglas, 1985). The speakers' knowledge of their topic has been shown to have an impact on their ability to speak. To participate in any form of interaction, then, speakers need knowledge of types of identity and relationship, knowledge of discourse patterns and patterns of interaction, and topic structures.

Further, in practice, these aspects of discourse have to be negotiated by speakers through joint interaction, rather than resulting from the unilateral decisions of individual speakers or the application of fixed patterns. Speakers might therefore commonly develop strategic routines for purposes such as the offering of invitations, or the giving of directions, including preparatory as well as summarizing moves (Widdowson, 1983). Speakers improvise around familiar structures in order to achieve satisfactory outcomes. In addition, in interacting with others we commonly identify discourse features preferred by our interlocutors. We can borrow or adopt these ourselves, if we feel that by so doing interaction will be facilitated. This is referred to as the process of *converging* or *diverging* from the dialect feature of one's interlocutor (Preston, 1989; Spolsky, 1998).

So the discourse level provides speakers with frames of reference for planning their utterances, anticipating interlocutors' knowledge and expectations, evaluating utterances produced, and deciding whether any repair work might be needed. It provides, then, a key reference point for the production process.

Message Conceptualization

The production of specific utterances begins by conceptualization of the particular pragmatic purpose, content, speaker orientation, and appropriate speech acts in terms of contextual appropriacy and relevance (Yule, 1996). This is undertaken against a mapping of the preceding discourse, and with anticipation of the interlocutors' knowledge and expectations, and of the likely ensuing talk. The output from this phase is the mental activation of a set of lexical concepts (Levelt et al., 1999: 9).

This level is important for two main reasons. First, whether we are concerned with first or second language production, it is important to be able to work with the notion that thought underlies talk. Work with first language users in secondary school, or more generally with second language users, might for instance aim to raise awareness among students of the strategic implications of the choice of different kinds of content that they could select in particular contexts (such as contexts of group work, formal presentation, or in different kinds of interview situations). See Bardovi-Harlig and Hartford (1990) for a discussion of these issues in the context of student/tutor advising sessions, and L. Cameron et al. (1996) on the language of study among British ESL students in secondary classrooms.

Second, it provides a basis for understanding how speakers solve communication problems through the use of communication strategies. Communication strategies are part of the formulation phase and involve improvising the communication of meanings in which conventional language is lacking. This can only occur if speakers already have a meaning to convey. This is the framework proposed by Færch and Kasper (1983) for the study of communication strategies. (See also Færch and Kasper, 1983b; Bialystok, 1990; Kasper and Kellerman, 1997.) Dörnyei and Kormos (1998) use this as a basis for bringing together all problem-solving processes, whether these are prearticulatory or postarticulatory, and whether they resolve problems in the speaker's own output or in that of their interlocutor. Conceptualization then provides a basis for formulation, pre- and postarticulatory monitoring and, if necessary, reformulation or reconceptualization.

Message Formulation

Formulation is the phase in which the speaker selects language to convey the conceptual content of their intended message. This involves accessing speakers' systemic language store and making a number of distinct but interrelated decisions. Levelt et al. (1999) consider that this involves the following processes:

Selection of lemmas—identifying a relevant lexical family

Formation of a rough syntactic frame on the basis of initial awareness of the word classes needed

Selection of relevant lexemes, including multiword items

Selection of grammatical lexemes

Accessing of relevant grammatical morphemes, such as inflections

Preparation of a phonological plan for the utterance

The process has a strong pragmatically developed dimension. Several aspects of native-speaker production appear to be based on speakers' prototypical memories of the characteristics of different lexical items (such as the likelihood of their occurring as singular or plural nouns, and their typical meanings). Further, many decisions depend on the use of rapidly fading traces—on the part of speaker and listener—in short-term memory (for instance, in the production of anaphoric and cataphoric markers, relative clauses, or verb-adverbial particle combinations). In addition, accessing involves drawing on a range of different types of collocational information (Lennon, 1996, 1998; Pawley and Syder, 1983; Wray, 2002; see also below for further discussion). We should note that it is not known how far the precise characteristics of native speaker processing can, or need be, replicated by nonnative learners, but clearly the process is complex and demanding.

The complexity and time pressures may help explain why unscripted spoken language is typically found to be less dense than written language (Biber et al., 1994; G. Brown and Yule, 1983; Chafe, 1985). It also explains why patterns of pausing typically change as speakers become more proficient: On the one hand, too much intraclause pausing will interfere with various aspects of processing, providing an in-built motivation to increase fluency; on the other hand, more intraclause pausing can be predicted when speakers need more accessing time, whereas, as accessing becomes quicker and other processing loads get lighter, pausing will retreat to clauses boundaries, resulting in longer runs. This occurs whether the talk is produced by native speakers (Beattie 1980) or by less proficient, nonnative speakers (Lennon, 1990; Towell, Hawkins, and Bazergui, 1996).

It is evident from this account that relevant practice should engage speakers as active decision makers in the task of formulation. Rote repetition clearly cannot provide sufficient appropriate practice (although thought-provoking types of *drill* will be useful if they involve learners in active decisions of linguistic appropriacy).

Message Articulation

Articulation involves the execution of the prearticulatory plans prepared in the formulation phase. Just two points need noting here about this phase of operation. First, articulation is generally a relatively automated phase. This means that plans can be executed with minimal conscious attention. An indication of this is that speakers often fail to correct their speech errors and, when they do, it is with a delay, suggesting that errors are picked up after, rather than during, articulation.

The fact of automation is important, particularly within a limited capacity model of attention, according to which channeling attention to articulation would divert it from the phases of conceptualization and formulation in which it is particularly needed (Levelt, 1989). However, although articulation in proficient speakers is usually automated, it is nonetheless open to some degree of active monitoring. This can be seen in speakers' articulation when addressing children, speaking against background noise, or to those thought to have comprehension difficulties. A limited capacity model suggests that attention to pronunciation will be difficult when learners are simultaneously encountering other problems in oral communication, that articulatory skills need integrating into the full hierarchy of oral production, rather than relying on pronunciation practice in isolation.

Monitoring

From the foregoing account it is clear that all aspects of speech production are subject to active monitoring (see particularly Dörnyei and Kormos, 1998). In this view, maintaining formal accuracy is only one facet of the more general process of ensuring that conceptualization, formulation, and articulation of the message conforms to the speaker's underlying intentions. That is, accuracy (Hymes's category of "possibility") joins feasibility, appropriacy, and frequency in being subject to online monitoring.

IV. Processing Demands and Quality of Performance

Drawing on current views of cognition and memory, Skehan (1998) proposes an account of language processing that describes quality of performance in terms of fluency, accuracy, and complexity. Skehan suggests that in producing language, speakers have two kinds of memory to draw on (Peters, 1983). One is an extensive memory store of lexical items, including formulaic *chunks* (Bolinger, 1975; Nattinger and DeCarrico, 1992; Pawley and Syder, 1983; Wray, 2000). The second is a lexico-grammatical repertoire for generating novel utterances. According to this view, speakers can access their item store for rapid production, avoiding the trouble of having to assemble novel lexico-grammatical combinations. The item store then enables speakers to maintain fluency of output.

However, this resource is not without limitations. First, formulaic phrases may not be appropriate to any particular communicative intentions, and second, they may contain inaccuracies, constituting a source of communication problems or impeding the learner's development. In contrast, although generating new utterances is more time-consuming, it is more likely to: (a) enable learners to monitor the accuracy of their output, and (b) enable learners to develop new ways of express-ing themselves. Working within a limited capacity model, Skehan suggests that effort in each of the dimensions of fluency, accuracy, and complexity can affect our capacity to process the others, suggesting the possibility of a trade-off in performance between them.

There is growing evidence supporting this account of language processing. However, P. Robinson (2000) argues for a multiple capacity model, suggesting that by manipulating task factors, speakers can be induced to increase fluency and com-plexity without loss of accuracy. Clearly this issue remains to be resolved. However, three points need making. First, the existence of a trade-off effect should not dis-tract from the fact that fluency, accuracy, and complexity have to be managed simul-taneously in any circumstances, and it is far from clear how they can be effectively integrated in language learning. Second, it is worth noting that language use is typ-ically a constant blend of the formulaic and the generative, speakers being unable to rely exclusively on either one or the other in the vast majority of situations. And third, the construct of *complexity* requires investigation given that it sometimes involves complex language, but sometimes involves the complex matching of simple language to new concepts. Nonetheless, the framework discussed here is one with clear interest for teachers and testers, and with considerable potential for development.

V. Forms of Oral Language

Finally, the lexico-grammatical features of speech need consideration. Most speech conditions affect the patterning of grammar and vocabulary in four major ways. First, as G. Brown and Yule (1983) point out, the lack of planning time for the speaker, combined with the fact that in most speech the listener has to cope with a fleeting and often imperfect signal, leads speech to be less lexically dense, notably with less noun premodification (Chafe, 1985). These conditions also account for the fact that speakers will often repeat and rephrase aspects of their message, and help to explain part of the function of pausing (Pawley and Syder, 1983). A second impor-tant condition is the fact that speech is usually situated in the same time and space for both speaker and listener. This means that speakers can typically refer directly to the environment ("this here") and can orient to the same temporal context ("now") without having to make these points of reference explicit (Chafe, 1985). A further effect of this condition is that speakers assume the shared knowledge and coopera-tion of the listener, which enables various forms of ellipsis (Chafe, 1985; Eggins and Slade, 1997). The third important condition of speech is that the interlocutors are both normally involved and have speaking rights during the event. This has the effect that the speaker can typically refer directly to the listener (using second-person pronouns) and that the speaker can expect the listener to take turns at talk.

Finally, the fact that the speaker knows the listener and the context of the interaction enables a wide range of informality in speech style (Preston, 1989).

These four conditions can clearly affect writing as well as speech. However, the range of speech functions is wider than that in writing, and the informal end of the range is more common in speech. (See the findings of corpus linguistics; e.g., Biber 1988.) However, although education needs to consider the informal aspects of speech, other features will also be important for learners, such as more formal speech styles and contexts, and the ability to handle cross-cultural or cross-dialectal differences. Hence these should not be neglected. Features of spoken language are explored in Carter and McCarthy (1997) and in Eggins and Slade (1997) and are reviewed in Riggenbach (1999).

VI. PEDAGOGY

Against this background it is instructive to consider developments in the teaching of spoken language. It can be argued that in most approaches to language pedagogy, the teaching of speaking began to emerge as a concern in its own right only in the 1940s. For one thing, many approaches to language teaching had largely ignored speech, as in the grammar-translation method, and most were based on the use of texts (apart from the use of phrase books and written dialogues—according to Howatt, 1984: 8, a tradition going back to the Middle Ages). It is true that the European reform movement had as two of its three main principles the primacy of speech and the centrality of an oral methodology in the classroom (Howatt, 1984: 171). However, even within this context, speech was used first (particularly because of its "here-and-now" dimension) as an effective conduit for presenting and demonstrating grammatical structures without using the first language, as in the direct method, and in Palmer's use of question-answer sequences in his "oral method" (e.g., Palmer, 1930) and, second, as a way of facilitating memorization. Spoken discourse, then, was mainly represented through question-answer interactions or the use of written dialogues.

These assumptions continued through the audiolingual approach of the 1940s. Building on the insights of the reform movement, this approach began from the insistence that new language should be taught initially through listening and speaking. The reasons for this, however, had little to do with the aim of fostering spoken interaction. Rather, it was based on the assumptions that accurate speaking depended on habit formation, which was taken to imply a need for substantial practice at responding to oral stimuli, that the orthography of a language was likely to interfere with the development of accurate pronunciation, and that oral drills were an effective way of promoting memorization (Fries, 1945). This approach could be described, then, as one that used oral activities as a way of teaching pronunciation skills and grammatical accuracy and of promoting memorization. The language content of materials was substantially (e.g., Broughton, 1968–1970) or even exclusively (e.g., Lado and Fries, 1957; or *English 900* (English Language Services, 1964)), defined in terms of the formal grammatical structures of the language, although often the structures were to some extent related to typical conversation patterns (e.g., Alexander, 1967).

Clearly, this neglected significant aspects of speaking as a skill. During the 1960s there was a growing awareness that drills were inadequate for real-world needs and that it would be necessary to try to prepare learners to handle a range of commonly occurring real-life situations in terms of dialogues (e.g., Ockenden, 1972; O'Neill, 1970, 1981). In the 1970s critics began to suggest that audiolingual drills were also limited in that they failed to teach the typical forms and functions of oral language and that a "functional" approach might be more effective (e.g., Munby, 1978; Wilkins, 1976). This led to the introduction of drills and exercises that taught learners to express a range of speech functions (such as invitations, requests, apologies, offers, refusals) and to vary the degrees of formality (particularly in terms of politeness; e.g., Abbs and Freebairn, 1977; O'Neill, 1981), though some began to include role-play activities (e.g., Morrow and Johnson, 1979). The nature of spoken language was, then, one of the central concerns of this period, but the issue was addressed mainly in terms of identifying typical speech acts. The kinds of *activity* provided for learners to practice on still mainly took the form of drills.

To summarize developments so far, speaking was attended to in terms of system rather than contextual appropriacy. Audiolingual approaches aimed to develop speaking only in terms of pronunciation and fluent, accurate manipulation of grammar. Situational approaches introduced dialogue patterns into the range of features to be taught, and functional approaches added speech acts into the syllabus. However, these approaches, on the whole, omitted to develop the interactive grammar and discourse patterns of typical speech; that is, they neglected typical "modes" of speech. Further, the types of exercise used to practice them omitted to situate practice within the contexts of genuine communication. In terms of the integrated model outlined in this chapter, audiolingual, situational, and functional approaches concentrated on providing practice at the levels of formulation and articulation; the level of conceptualization was broadly ignored, so that practice was largely isolated from the conceptual planning and decision making typical of the communicative use of language. To resolve this problem required the development of different kinds of activities and not merely broaden the scope of drills. Awareness of this need led to the development of a communicative approach to language teaching.

The communicative approach stressed the importance of enabling learners to develop fluency and not just accuracy (e.g., Brumfit, 1984) and advocated exercises containing problems to resolve and requiring learners to communicate with each other in order to resolve them (Allwright, 1984). Littlewood (1981) outlined the possibility of a range of different types of oral exercise: precommunicative, communicative, and socio-interactional. G. Brown and Yule (1983) sketched the elements of an oral syllabus, including the desirability of teaching short turns, long turns, interactional language, and transactional language. A key area of concern for them was that of "reference"—the ability to identify effectively referents (such as participants in a narrative), time, and place. (See also Yule, 1997.)

These general developments resulted in the publication of supplementary materials (e.g., Dörnyei and Thurrell, 1992; Geddes and Sturtridge, 1979, 1981; Hadfield, 1987; Klippel, 1984; Matthews and Read, 1981; Porter-Ladousse, 1987; Ur, 1981) that were largely based on the use of various kinds of jigsaw or opinion-gap tasks in the context of pair and group work. (See Pica, Kanagy, and Faludon, 1993, for an attempt to map an extensive inventory of task types.) Course books similarly incorporated many of these insights (e.g., Abbs and Sexton, 1978; Geddes, 1986; J. C. Richards, Hull, and Proctor, 1991), the output of one task often serving as input to the next (e.g., Nunan, 1995b; Swan and Walter, 1992; Willis and Willis, 1988).

The communicative movement was also sensitive to the fact that speaking in a second language can be stressful, particularly if it is not supported by adequate exposure to the vernacular forms of the language. This insight gave rise to a movement which favored delaying oral production at the beginning of language programs, instead introducing students to the oral language through a more or less extensive period of listening activities (e.g., Asher, 1977). Concern for the personal affective aspects of language learning gave rise to the development of materials with subject matter likely to engage learners' personal interest and curiosity (e.g., Maley, Duff, and Grellet, 1980; Geddes, 1986; Legutke and Thomas, 1991; Riggenbach and Samuda, 2000).

VII. Conclusion

Most of the conditions of speech have been broadly attended to in these pedagogical developments, although perhaps issues of identity, register, topic familiarity, and discourse type have been less well addressed than the contextualized practice of formulation skills. In addition, broader scale methodological controversies also remain.

A central concern lies in the ways in which the different parts of the skill hierarchy can best be practiced. Although it is agreed that the main teaching and learning objective is for learners to be able to exploit all levels of the hierarchy in order to be able to communicate, five alternative approaches have been proposed. One is that oral skills should first be learned in a controlled form, essentially at the level of lexico-grammatical system, before extending into the broader areas of spoken discourse. This is suggested by Widdowson (1998a), drawing on Rivers and Temperley's (1978) distinction between "skill-getting" and "skill-using" phases of learning. This view seems to see it as preferable to practice speaking initially in a decontextualized manner, bringing communication tasks into operation only once the "skill" has been learned.

A second view is that provided the conceptual load is constrained so as to enable learners to focus on particular aspects of the lexico-grammar and to avoid over-loading them with complex communication problems, it would be perfectly possible to follow a communication task with a decontextualized grammar practice activity. This has been described as a "whole-skill: part-skill" approach (Littlewood, 1981), the decontextualized activities being used to provide "part-skill" practice, whereas the communication tasks provide "whole-skill" practice.

A third approach argues that it is possible to use tasks to provide a context in which the focus can alternate between different aspects of language performance, such as fluency, accuracy, and complexity. Skehan (1998), Bygate (1996, 1999), and Lynch and MacLean (2001) suggest that adjusting task variables (such as the provision of planning time, structuring, relevant background knowledge, and task repetition) can be deployed to vary the focus on language in similar ways; some suggest ways teachers can switch students' attention from discourse pattern and function to formal features within (Samuda, 2001) or around (J. Willis, 1996) a given task. Similarly K. Johnson (1996) argues that it is possible for a speaker either to proceduralize declarative knowledge or to start with proceduralized knowledge and work at analyzing it.

The fourth approach, stressing the importance of integrating attention to form and attention to meaning, argues that attention to language form should be handled only within the context of a focus on meaningful communication (e.g., papers in Doughty and Williams, 1998b). Finally, outlining a fifth approach, Brumfit's (1984) account argues for seeing the contrast from a number of perspectives. For one thing, the same task may be accuracy focused for some students, and fluency focused for others, depending on their language and content knowledge; further, the overall language program might best be characterized by a proportionate shift from a concern with accuracy in the early stages toward a predominant focus on fluency as students become more advanced.

It is worth noting that these controversies are far from adequately researched and to recall the well-documented failure to find clear-cut results in favor of one pedagogical approach or another (Ellis, 1994: 571). Further, they do not address the broader issues of the potential interactive content of the oral language syllabus. Although, as we have seen earlier, this issue has not been totally ignored, much remains to be done in this area if the potential content of the oral syllabus is to be as thoroughly mapped as those in the areas of reading and writing. It is the range of areas that deserve attention, rather than the particular route to be adopted in addressing them, that this chapter has aimed to highlight.

CHAPTER 5

··

LISTENING: SOURCES, SKILLS, AND STRATEGIES

··

TONY LYNCH

THE chapter on listening in the first edition of this handbook closed with the comment "Listening is hard work, and deserves more analysis and support" (Vandergrift, 1999: 168), which seems a suitable starting point for this updated version. The sheer complexity of listening is beyond doubt. Even in one's first language (L1) one may encounter difficulties in understanding speech, including internal factors such as emotional distraction, or toothache, or lack of interest in the topic, or negative reaction to the speaker, or having to prepare a response to what is being said. When listening to a second language (L2), one faces additional problems due to external factors related to speaker or to text: novel expressions, speed of speaking, accent, unfamiliar content and cultural references, and so on. Unsurprisingly, the terms used to characterize the process of coping with L2 speech tend to emphasize physical pressure (*load, burden, barrier,* and *obstacle*), transience (*transitory, ephemeral,* and *temporary*), lack of clarity (*buzz, fog, fuzzy,* and *blur*) and the sense of being overwhelmed (by the *stream, flood, torrent,* and *cascade*).

A second type of complexity arises from increasingly advanced digital technology, which is something of a double-edged sword: on the one hand, it allows L2 learners to do more listening to more languages at less cost than ever before; on the other, effective use of the technology makes ever-growing demands on teachers' professional and technical skills. There is no denying that the new digital media have put listening experiences within the reach of many learners, but the key question is this: Has the technology changed the *ways* in which learners listen to L2 speech? The consensus among researchers seems to be that the *internal* processes of listening to and viewing material on computer are not radically different from watching the same event live, or on television, or via a video recorder or DVD player, although the *social* processes may be different.

Third, conducting effective research into listening is also a complex under-taking, given the number of factors that stand in the researchers' way, not least the inaccessibility of what goes on in the listener's head and the variety of influences on the success or failure of his or her attempts to understand spoken language. Listening rarely has an observable product, and even when a listener does provide such responses suggesting successful comprehension as "Uhuh" or "Really?" there is no guarantee that the listener has in fact understood what the speaker intended to convey. Under some circumstances, listeners might even want to give the impres-sion they have understood, particularly if the interaction is in L2 and they want to avoid imposing socially on the speaker by continually asking for clarification of points they have not heard or grasped. For these reasons, "We cannot base our anal-ysis completely on what we judge, from the discourse, to be comprehended by the non-native speaker. The determination of comprehension is, in fact, rather elusive" (B. Hawkins, 1985: 176). Given this elusiveness, listening researchers have adopted such various strategies to access mental activity during listening tasks as the use of stimulated recall (Farrell and Mallard, 2006; S. Ross, 1997), listening journals (Y. Chen, 2005; Rost, 1994), and think-aloud protocols (Goh, 2000).

Despite the potentially daunting complexity of comprehension processes, most of us rarely encounter serious problems in everyday listening—at least in our L1 and under reasonable acoustic conditions. However, L2 listening is a qualitatively different experience, requiring more conscious attention to information at different levels, especially when potential cues to meaning in what is being said are rendered inacces-sible by our lack of L2 knowledge. "How well L2 listeners cope with these limitations will depend on their ability to make use of all the available resources to interpret what they hear" (Vandergrift, 2007: 193). In this chapter, I focus first on the sources of listening experience, sources of comprehension difficulty, and the sources of help the listener can draw on in the form of background knowledge, visual context, and linguistic knowledge. I then turn to the role played by listening skills and listening strategies, touching on the debate over the relationship between them. Finally, I con-sider the implications of comprehension research for listening instruction and point to likely areas of future investigation. In the course of the chapter, I concentrate mainly on L2 listening, though much of the discussion necessarily applies to L1 listening, too (cf. A. Anderson, and Lynch, 1988; G. Brown, 1995; G. Brown and Yule, 1983).

SOURCES OF LISTENING EXPERIENCE

The technological advances in the digital media over the last decade have given learners and teachers access to a wider range of sources than have been available to previous generations: DVDs, web-based listening libraries, MP3 players, and so on. Strong claims have been made for the benefits of the novel facilities offered in computer-enhanced language learning materials—for example, that "the computer and interactive technologies will allow teachers to select materials of all kinds, support them as learners' needs dictate and use the visual options of screen presentation or the interactive capabilities of computer control to help students develop good listening techniques" (Garrett, 1991: 95).

Although successive generations of technology—from the reel-to-reel recorder to the handheld computer—have led to similar predictions of a revolution in language teaching, the hardware has tended to run ahead of the pedagogic purposes for which it might be exploited. In an article on the value of multimedia software in the teaching of listening skills, Hulstijn (2003) expressed the view that the major milestone in the history of L2 listening instruction was *not* in fact the arrival of modern digital multimedia technology, "but rather the invention, more than 100 years ago, of the phonograph and similar devices with which sound could be recorded, stored, played and replayed" (p. 420). Hoven (1999) had made a similar point about the ways in which teachers use computer-enhanced language learning (CELL) materials for listening and viewing comprehension: "Although the presence of new technology and new means of using it entail the development of new models [of second language instruction], there is no reason to start completely afresh" (p. 88). What the more "advanced" technologies do is *complement*, rather than replace, existing ones, and offer a *more convenient* way of delivering spoken language to learners than was available in the past.

SOURCES OF DIFFICULTY

In the effort to make sense of what they hear, listeners have to work simultaneously at various levels of the message: phonetic, phonological, prosodic, lexical, syntactic, semantic, and pragmatic. The dominant paradigm in listening comprehension is that of information processing, derived from Anderson's three-stage comprehension model: perception, parsing, and utilization (J. R. Anderson, 1985). Although this implies that understanding is achieved through a linear series of steps, it is clear that the only way that listeners can cope with the multilevel task of understanding is by some form of parallel distributed processing (PDP). PDP models of language processes, based on neural networks (e.g., Sharkey, 1996), are biologically plausible because they resemble the way brain cells work—in particular, their capacity for the simultaneous integration of information from multiple sources. A full picture of how listening works—or rather how listeners work—will need to incorporate the various levels at which simultaneous processing takes place. For reasons of space, I will comment here only on the level of prosody (stress, rhythm, and intonation) and how it impacts listeners' comprehension.

There is now a substantial body of evidence that, as we try to identify words in the stream of L2 speech, our early experiences of L1 listening exert a very powerful influence on the recognition of what is being said in the other language. In the first 3 or 4 years of life, our immersion in L1 prosody creates a mental "metrical template," enabling us to recognize what we hear. English and Dutch, for example, are predominantly *trochaic* (strong syllable followed by weak), whereas French is *iambic* (weak syllable followed by strong), and L1 listeners exploit these characteristics to identify words in fluent spontaneous speech, which typically offers few cues to signal word boundaries. As a result, English and Dutch speakers tend to segment speech at the onset of strong syllables, whereas French speakers do so after what they perceive to be the final syllable of a rhythmic group (Cutler, Dahan, and van Donselaar, 1997). Spanish listeners, whose first language uses variation of syllable stress placement to differentiate between meanings, have been found to be more skilled at discriminating stress placement in nonsense strings than French listeners, whose language does not exploit stress phonologically in that way (Dupoux, Paillier Pallier, Sebastien, and Mehler, 1997). It is only at relatively advanced levels of L2 proficiency that we are able to inhibit our misapplication in L2 of our native language strategies (Cutler, 2000; Delabatie and Bradley, 1995).

A recent study has highlighted the extent to which English native listeners may use main syllable stress as the *primary* means of lexical recognition in speech, not only in interaction with fellow native speakers but also when listening to L2 speakers (Zielinski, 2008). Zielinski asked Australian native English speakers to transcribe extracts from the unscripted conversational English produced by three native speakers of Korean, Mandarin, and Vietnamese with postintermediate levels of English (TOEFL score 580 or higher). She focused on *sites of reduced intelligibility*—parts of the speakers' utterances in which one or more of the transcribers failed, or found it difficult, to identify what the speaker intended to say. Analysis showed that the listeners relied heavily and consistently on two features: the placement of syllable stress and the speaker's production of the consonants and vowels in strongly stressed syllables. The listeners appeared to find it especially difficult to recognize words in which both the syllable-initial consonant and the main-stressed vowel were pronounced in a nonstandard way. For example, in pronouncing the word *before*, the Korean speaker changed both consonants [b] and [f] to [p], and also placed the main stress on the first syllable, resulting in ['piːpoː], which all three Australian listeners understood and transcribed as "people." Interestingly, their transcriptions of the three L2 speakers suggested that they made no apparent adjustment to their routine L1 speech processing strategies when listening to speakers who they knew to be foreign users of English.

SOURCES OF HELP

Background Knowledge

The key role of relevant background knowledge in comprehension is long established and is often traced back to the work on memory of the psychologist Charles Bartlett (1932), whose concept of *schema* has been influential in a number of cognitive fields, including both human comprehension and artificial intelligence. However, as Bartlett showed in his early experiments, schemata have the power to *distort*, as well as to support, listening comprehension and memory.

In one of the most widely cited studies of schematic influences on listening comprehension, D. Long (1990) compared the effects of background knowledge and L2 proficiency level of American undergraduate learners of Spanish. They were played recordings of two passages: one concerned a recent gold rush in Ecuador and served as the less familiar topic; the other was about the rock band U2 and served as the more familiar topic. Prior to the listening experiment, Long used a questionnaire to establish the individual students' knowledge of previous gold rushes and rock bands, their previous course grades in Spanish, and a self-rating of their ability to understand spoken Spanish. As expected, their questionnaire responses showed that the learners possessed significantly less background knowledge about gold rushes than rock music. They were played each of the two passages twice, were not allowed to take notes, and were then asked to summarize in English what they had understood of the text. They were also given a checklist of statements on the passage topic and asked to indicate which ones they had heard mentioned.

On the English summary recall test, the listeners produced a significantly higher proportion of main ideas from the U2 text than from the Ecuadorian gold rush passage. However, on the checklist recognition test, there were no significant differences in scores. Long argued that this difference in achievement on the two types of listening test arose because the recognition (checklist) test was less challenging and because its format may have encouraged the students to guess correctly. She concluded that L2 proficiency plays an important role when listeners do *not* possess the relevant background knowledge, but a lesser role when they have that knowledge available. Interestingly, in a set of additional results, Long discussed recall summaries written by a small number (roughly 7%) of the listeners that showed the distorting effect of schemata on comprehension. For example, these listeners *overextended* their schema of the California gold rush of 1848 and produced summaries that conflated Ecuador with California, placed modern artifacts like plastic and Coca-Cola in the mid-nineteenth century, or merged the exploits of the Spanish conquistadores of the sixteenth century with modern-day Ecuador. Yet the students who produced these odd summaries had rated their Spanish listening ability between "average" and "very good." There was similar overextension of content schemata in some students' summaries of the U2 text, leading her to comment, "It is clear that schemata can hurt, as well as help" (D. Long 1990: 73)—a useful reminder of the validity of Bartlett's original warning that schemata can work negatively as well as positively.

A number of studies have compared the relative impact of background knowledge and L2 proficiency on listening comprehension (e.g., Chiang and Dunkel, 1992; Jensen and Hansen, 1995; for a comprehensive review, see Macaro, Vanderplank, and Graham, 2005). In an unusually large scale study, Tsui and Fullilove (1998) investigated two possible reasons for poor L2 comprehension ability that could be rooted at the "bottom" level: if poor listeners are unable to recognize words rapidly and construct an accurate representation, they have, therefore, to rely more on contextual information and guessing. Alternatively, poor listeners might fail because they are overreliant on either the top-down or bottom-up route. Using a data set of some 150,000 listening test item performances, Tsui and Fullilove compared how listeners performed on questions in which the correct answer matched the likely schema with their degree of success on questions in which the correct answer conflicted with the schema. Analysis showed that the candidates who gave the correct answer for nonmatching schema items tended to be more skilled listeners; presumably, the less skilled could rely on guessing for matching items, but not for nonmatching ones. They also found that bottom-up processing seemed more important than top-down processing in discriminating listening performance on test items.

From the information processing perspective, it seems plausible that background knowledge assists the comprehension process by freeing up the listener's mental resources and allowing more attention to be directed at processing the specific L2 forms in the input. Direct evidence for this comes from a study by Tyler (2001), which compared the responses of L1 and L2 listeners to the same spoken texts. When they were given advance warning of the topic of the passage they were about to hear, the two groups displayed no significant difference in working memory consumption. When that prior information about the topic was not provided, the working memory consumption for the L2 listeners was significantly higher than for the native listeners.

Visual Context

Although conventionally (including in this chapter) we may talk of *listening*, it is important not to lose sight of the key role played by nonverbal expression in support of the spoken word, especially in the case of L2 comprehension. In most cases, the listener has access to visual information, in the form of gestures and facial expressions of the interlocutor in face-to-face interaction and of supplementary on-screen information in the case of digital listening/viewing. The potential wealth of these nonverbal resources was captured in an early paper (Riley, 1981) that remains, even after nearly 3 decades, one of the best discussions of the role of the visual in listening comprehension. Writing at a time when video materials were beginning to make their mark in language teaching, Riley argued that the visual aspects of communication "are not to be despised; true, they lack the semantic referential precision of the verbal component, but in pragmatic and relational terms they are generally far more important" (Riley, 1981: 145). Among the key functions in Riley's analysis of the visual element of communication are the following:

- *Deictic*, pointing to nearby objects
- *Interactional*, signals of turn taking, such as adjustments of body position
- *Modal*, expressing the speaker's commitment to what they are saying (e.g., mouth turned down at the corners and eyebrows raised, to indicate they may be relaying someone else's opinion)

- *Indexical*, indicators of 'self' (e.g., posture and clothes)
- *Linguistic*, replacing certain verbal expressions, such as beckoning to indicate "come here"

A fully competent language user has to be able to integrate these signals with the spoken message—a point made again recently in a paper whose title, "Listening with Your Eyes" (T. Harris, 2003) echoes that of Riley's "*L'oeuil coute*" from 2 decades earlier.

The power of the visual component of communication should not be underestimated; even very limited visual support has been found to enhance listening comprehension. Long before the advent of today's multimedia, including moving image, G. Mueller (1980) and Wolff (1987) had established the beneficial effect of simple static illustrations on the understanding of L2 speech, in the form of narratives. Wolff (1987) investigated German secondary school learners' understanding of English stories—one relatively easy, the other relatively difficult—told by two native speakers, recorded and played on videotape. Each story came in two versions: for some listeners, a simple drawing of an element of the story was inserted into the video recording; the others watched the video without the illustration. Analysis of listeners' answers indicated clear benefits of access to the illustration: in the case of the more difficult narrative, the listeners who had seen the drawing remembered significantly more details and also made more text-based inferences. Wolff concluded that the more linguistically demanding a text is, the greater the listener's need to exploit any available contextual cues.

One of the obvious benefits of the spread of CELL materials in L2 instruction is the additional support they provide for successful comprehension. There is empirical evidence from a range of recent work (e.g., Guichon and McLornan, 2008; Jones and Plass, 2002; H. Williams and Thorne, 2000) that access to the moving image, combined with static graphic and textual information in the form of diagrams and subtitles, brings measurable benefits for L2 listeners, both in the short term—as enhanced comprehension, and in the longer term—as increased motivation and acquisition.

L2 Knowledge

It would seem reasonable to assume that a listener's knowledge of L2 vocabulary and grammar will play a significant role in his or her ability to understand spoken language, and the evidence is that lexical knowledge plays the larger role. P. Kelly (1991) compared the transcription errors made by an advanced user of English (a French teacher of English) with those made by a group of French undergraduates at intermediate level. Finding that around two-thirds of errors in which there was evidence of severely impaired comprehension were connected with unfamiliar vocabulary, Kelly concluded "lexical ignorance is by far the most frequent cause of lack of comprehension" (1991: 147). Mecartty (2000) investigated the possible relationship between knowledge of L2 grammar, L2 vocabulary, and listening performance in a study of English-speaking students of Spanish. She found that although grammatical knowledge was not a significant factor in listening comprehension, knowledge of

Spanish vocabulary accounted for some 15% of listening success. Comparing her findings with those of previous studies of L2 reading, Mecartty concluded "lexical knowledge appears to be more crucial to reading than it is to listening" (Mecartty, 2000: 340). It seems likely that lexical knowledge is accessed differently in reading, in which the text is visible, than in listening, in which the learner has, in a sense, to recreate the text.

Vandergrift (2006) extended research into the impact of L2 proficiency on listening by examining the possible relationship between L2 knowledge, L2 listening ability, and L1 listening ability. The learners in his study were English-speaking Canadian secondary learners of French, who were given similar tests of their English and French listening comprehension, based on short dialogues. Analysis of their scores showed that both L2 proficiency and L1 listening ability contributed to the L2 listening scores, but to different degrees, with L2 proficiency having the greater influence. However, when the listeners' scores were broken down by type of comprehension (literal and inferential), it emerged that L2 proficiency was a more important factor in success in *literal* comprehension. It seems that lexical knowledge is essential for literal questions, because "students cannot draw on world knowledge as much when it comes to answering questions concerning details that require knowledge of specific L2 words" (Vandergrift, 2006: 14). Both Mecartty and Vandergrift argue that given the evidence of an effect of L2 vocabulary knowledge in success in listening, instruction in L2 vocabulary development should include and highlight practice in aural lexical recognition of the natural form(s) of words in connected speech—the word in the ear, rather than the word on the page.

SKILLS

The Strategy/Skill Relationship

The debate over the status of, and interrelationship between, listening skills and listening strategies in L2 instruction was encapsulated in an exchange of views in *ELT Journal* (Ridgway, 2000; Field, 2000), which was partly related to the wider issue of whether strategies are conscious or unconscious. Ridgway (2000) argued that there could be no clear distinction between what is conscious and what is not, and, moreover, what is a conscious action for one person may be unconscious and automatic for another. He concluded that teaching cognitive strategies such as guessing is a waste of lesson time, because in authentic (one-way) listening situations L2 learners do not have enough spare processing capacity to adopt strategies in real time. He did, however, agree that it made sense to teach the use of negotiating strategies for clarifying in (two-way) conversational listening. In his response to Ridgway, Field (2000) called for a distinction to be made between the terms *skill* and *strategy*. He defined a *skill* as an ability that the L1 listener possesses and uses automatically, but which an L2 listener has yet to acquire; and a *strategy* as a technique that the L2 listener resorts to, consciously, to compensate for incomplete L2 knowledge or ability that has caused a problem of comprehension. In Field's view, strategies are useful as temporary compensatory devices, whereas the L2 learners are practicing, improving, and automatizing their L2 listening skills.

Skills in Action

Rubin (1994) pinpointed five elements of a listening event that influence the perceived ease or difficulty of listening: text, speaker, task, listener, and process These influences hold in both L1 and L2 listening; work done by Gillian Brown and colleagues on the cognitive difficulty of listening texts involved interactive tasks carried out by competent native speakers (Brown, 1986, 1995; Brown and Yule, 1983), providing baseline data against which to evaluate the performances of L1 speakers undergoing communication skills training, as well as those of L2 learners (Lynch, 1991).

As previously noted, among the listener characteristics contributing to effective comprehension are relevant topic knowledge and L2 lexical knowledge. In addition, the individual's phonological decoding ability plays a key role in the deployment of skills. Rost (1990) set out the components of listening ability in a hierarchy from *perception* (e.g., lexical segmentation and literal recognition of an utterance), through *interpretation* (such as inferencing and establishing speaker intention), to *enacting* (for instance, requesting clarification or responding to the content of what the speaker has said).

Investigation of these skills is problematic, but a particularly enlightening study is that of Ross (1997) exploring the hypothesis that listeners at different levels of L2 proficiency apply different skills. Ross asked Japanese learners of English to match an array of icons (e.g., a train) with a recorded message in English (e.g., about a rail journey) and then to introspect in Japanese about how they decided which icon to choose. Their self-reports suggested eight *processing stages* ranging from the more primitive and unsuccessful to more complex and successful:

1. *Noise*—no response
2. *Distraction*—process overload
3. *Syllable restructuring*—mishearing
4. *Syllable identification*
5. *Key word association*
6. *Linking* with more than one key word
7. *Phrase recognition;*
8. *Whole utterance recognition*

Ross found that Stage 5, key word association, was the commonest level of processing for the weaker listeners, who produced an initial mental model and kept to it without searching for confirming cues; the more proficient listeners also frequently operated at Stage 5 but had sufficient capacity to hold the key word in short-term memory while they searched for support in the message.

Wu (1998) applied a similar retrospective commentary method to examine skill performance on a listening test by relatively advanced Chinese learners of English in order to explore their use of linguistic and nonlinguistic processing. Wu's analysis of his subjects' test performance and retrospective commentaries showed that partial success in linguistic processing often forced the listeners to activate general knowledge, as compensation for linguistic failings, and partial success in linguistic processing could also lead them to override what they had correctly abstracted from that processing, in favor of schema-based interpretation. He concluded that, for L2 listeners, linguistic processing is basic, in two senses: failure or partial success in it may result in learners allowing activated schematic knowledge to dominate their decision-making inappropriately, and competence in linguistic processing constrains but does not rule out nonlinguistic activation.

Buck and Tatsuoka (1998) applied the "rule-space" statistical technique to language testing for the first time; previously it had been used to assess mastery of skill components in other academic subjects. The technique breaks test items down into cognitive attributes representing the underlying knowledge and skills that the items assess, and then analyzes each candidate's pattern of responses to calculate an individual's chances of having mastered each attribute. Buck and Tatsuoka established 15 attributes accounting for virtually all the variance in the performance of the test population. These attributes involved the following abilities:

- Recognize the task by deciding what constitutes task-relevant information
- Scan fast spoken text automatically and in real time
- Process a substantial information load
- Process dense information
- Use previous items to locate information
- Identify relevant information without explicit markers
- Understand and utilize heavy stress
- Make text-based inferences
- Incorporate background knowledge into text processing
- Process L2 concepts with no literal equivalent in L1
- Recognize and use redundancy
- Process information scattered throughout a text
- Construct response quickly and efficiently (Buck and Tatsuoka, 1998: 141–142)

They concluded, "Second-language listening ability is not a point on one linear continuum, but a point in a multi-dimensional space, and the number of dimensions is large" (1998: 146).

STRATEGIES

Research has focused on learners' use of listening strategies, categorized into three main groups drawn from the wider framework of language learning strategy research:

- *Metacognitive*—those to do with planning, regulating, and managing
- *Cognitive*—those that facilitate comprehension, such as inferencing based on context or background knowledge
- *Social and affective*—for example, requests for clarification and positive self-talk

The consensus from a range of studies—for example, Thompson and Rubin (1996), Goh (1997), and Vandergrift (1999)—is that metacognitive strategy use increases with learner proficiency level. Such leading researchers in this area as Vandergrift and Goh (Goh, 1997, 2000, 2002; Goh and Taib, 2006; Vandergrift, 1999, 2003; Vandergrift, Goh, Mareschal, and Tafaghodtari, 2006) have employed a variety of methods including learner diaries, learner interviews and questionnaires, and retrospective recall. Again, though, one should note that investigations based on self-reported behavior are inevitably one step removed from the behavior itself.

From the instruction perspective, perhaps the most tangible outcome to date of some 2 decades of work on L2 listening strategy use is the study by Vandergrift, Goh, Mareschal, and Tafaghodtari (2006). Drawing on the findings of a wide range of previous work, Vandergrift and colleagues developed and validated a *Metacognitive Awareness Listening Questionnaire* (MALQ) that has undergone extensive trials in Canada, Singapore, and the Netherlands. When listeners' self-reports were compared with their performances on listening tests, it was found that five factors derived from the MALQ responses correlated statistically with listening ability:

- *Problem solving* (guessing and monitoring of guesses)
- *Planning and elaboration* (preparing for listening and assessing success)
- *Mental translation*—or, rather, avoiding it
- *Person knowledge* (confidence or anxiety)
- *Directed attention* (ways of concentrating on aspects of the task)

Taken together, these five factors accounted for some 13% of the variability in the listeners' performance, which the researchers described as a moderate relationship. (Alternatively, one can say that almost 90% of success in listening appeared to be attributable to *other* factors).

Vandergrift et al. (2006) argued that the statistical relationship between those five principal factors is evidence for the complex and interrelated nature of meta-cognitive processes in listening; they used the term *orchestration* to refer to the way in which L2 learners have to coordinate different aspects of strategy use. In choosing that word, they were echoing Flavell's early work on learning strategies, in which *metacognition* was described as "active monitoring and consequent regulation and orchestration of these processes in relation to the cognitive objects or data on which they bear" (Flavell, 1976: 232). Despite some evidence that strategy instruction can be successful, there remains an element of doubt, with opinions divided between enthusiastic—and mainly North American—advocates of strategy instruction and more skeptical voices that point to the lack of clear evidence that such instruction actually produces *more effective* listeners, as opposed to *more self-aware* listeners or *more knowledgeable* listeners.

Account also has to be taken of the potential influence of home culture on the L2 learner's use of strategies. There is wide agreement that culture exerts a key influence on individuals' learning processes in general and on their language learning style and learning strategies in particular (Oxford, 1993; Oxford and Anderson, 1995). One element of cultural disposition is *tolerance of ambiguity* (TOA)—the willingness to accept uncertainty, vagueness, and fuzziness. According to Oxford (2002), cultures with low TOA resort to rules and regulation to avoid uncertainty, whereas high-TOA cultures are open to change and taking risks. Because guessing is a form of communicative risk tasking, it would be interesting to research the possible implications of TOA for L2 listeners' willingness to guess at meaning when they encounter unfamiliar or ambiguous input.

Writers of all shades of opinion agree on the pressing need for long-term research to assess whether and how L2 listening strategies develop over time, with or without explicit training. Among the likely reasons for the lack of longitudinal research are the methodological difficulty of isolating the possible effects of such instruction from other real-life influences and the fact that learners naturally improve their second language proficiency over time, a phenomenon that may help make them better listeners, irrespective of any strategic training. Graham, Santos, and Vanderplank (2008) monitored the progress over 6 months in L2 listening strategy use by two English secondary school learners of French, chosen because of their high and low scores on a listening test. The learners' strategy use was investigated by asking them to give a "running commentary" of their thoughts in the process of doing a multiple-choice listening test. Analysis of their commentaries revealed very little change in their strategy use over the 6 months, leading the researchers to conclude that listening strategy use is relatively stable and closely tied to proficiency level.

FUTURE DIRECTIONS

The comment with which I opened this chapter—that listening is hard work and deserves more analysis and support—encapsulates the themes I have touched on:

- The intensity and scale of the resourceful listener's efforts after meaning
- The complex interrelationship between the microskills of listening
- The importance of empirical assessment of programs intended to help L2 learners to listen strategically to compensate for linguistic difficulties

The wider range of multimedia resources now available through advances in digital technology brings learners the prospect of ever-increasing availability of the experience of listening to their target languages. In addition, digital listening formats allow the provision of accompanying visual and textual support, which has been shown to enhance comprehension. Given the primary role claimed for listening in L2 learning (e.g., Ellis, Tanaka, & Yamazaki, 1994; Faerch and Kasper, 1986; Vandergrift, 2007), it would seem that this easier access to oral sources should open up beneficial learning opportunities. Yet, although there is some evidence that the visual component of multimedia listening can assist L2 acquisition in the longer term, the number of studies is as yet limited. Thus, one area of likely expansion in research lies in investigation of the different replay and support modes in CELL applications, such as L2 subtitles, L1 translation and other graphic representations of speech, and the degree to which their short-term comprehension benefits might be matched by the increased likelihood of longer term L2 learning.

This chapter has provided a flavor of the professional debate over "skills or strategies" in listening. Many of us would agree that the (mainly) strategic approach has been taken too far and that a better balance should be struck between skill teaching and strategy teaching, especially in the light of the evidence (e.g., Tsui and Fullilove, 1998; Wu, 1998) that what differentiates skilled and unskilled listeners is the ability to cope with linguistic processing, rather than the ability to use appropriate strategies. The current arguments for a problem-orientated, skill-focused approach to listening instruction can be traced back to Gillian Brown's comment that "comprehension teaching...is very much a hit-or-miss affair....Until the teacher is provided with some sort of method of investigating the student's problems, the teacher is really not in the position of being able to help the student 'do better'" (Brown 1986: 286). Arguably, as Hulstijn (2003) has reminded us, teachers could do more by using *repetition* of recorded material. Repetition is something that many language teachers avoid, by intuition or training, but there is increasing evidence from a wide variety of research that repetition helps develop listeners' ability to segment the speech flow, understand the speaker's message, and notice new L2 features. In particular, there is scope for teachers to do more to exploit the pedagogic potential of misunderstandings as starting points—not only at the level of perception (such as the lexical segmentation activities proposed by Tauroza, 1997, and Field, 1998), but also at the level of interpretation—by encouraging learners to share and contrast their individual understandings of what they have heard (Lynch 2009).

The capacity of listening strategy instruction (rather than plentiful practice and postlistening study) to help learners become more effective listeners has been called into question, as we have seen. In response to some of these objections, it had been suggested that the relatively disappointing findings of listening strategy research could have been due to the absence of any or all of five essential features of successful strategy training (Mendelsohn 1998):

> First, in-depth teacher education in the efficacy of strategy use
> Second, a strong individual teacher commitment to a strategic approach

Third, the gradual implementation of strategic instruction, maintained over time rather than in short, enthusiastic bursts

Fourth, a consistent focus on the listening process (i.e., on how to listen)

And last, the use of video rather than audio materials

Future investigations of listening strategy instruction, carried out in circumstances that provide the optimal conditions Mendelsohn outlined, should help us to decide whether some of the educational time and effort invested in strategic training would be better diverted to listening skill development.

CHAPTER 6

READING IN A
SECOND LANGUAGE

WILLIAM GRABE

I. INTRODUCTION

The ability to read in a second language (L2) is one of the most important skills required of people in multilingual and international settings. It is also a skill that is one of the most difficult to develop to a high level of proficiency. Any current understanding of reading requires attention to a number of basic issues:

1. Different purposes for reading
2. Definitional criteria for fluent reading (varying by context)
3. Processes underlying reading as an individual skill
4. Institutional and social context influences on L2 reading
5. Determining unique features of L2 reading (as opposed to L1 reading) and recognizing difficulties central for L2 reading instruction
6. Using L2 research implications to improve instruction and student learning

These topics will form the framework for the ensuing discussion.

II. DIFFERENT PURPOSES FOR READING

People read for a variety of purposes, and many of these purposes require distinct combinations of skills in order to achieve the reader's purpose. Because of this variation, it is not easy to define L2 reading as a single notion or a unitary ability. It is true that differing purposes draw on many of the same cognitive processes, but they do so to differing extents and sometimes in different ways. Having said this, I will nonetheless state that the most fundamental ability for L2 reading is the basic comprehension of main ideas from a text. Few purposes for reading disregard this ability, and most purposes build upon this foundation (cf. Alderson, 2000; Grabe, 2009, for other discussions of reading purposes).

Purposes for reading can include the following:

- To find information (scanning, searching)
- To learn, critique, and evaluate
- For basic comprehension (there are other purposes).

In the case of reading to find information, the crucial skill constitutes scanning for a specific word, phrase, form, or number. Meaning in the text is not critical initially, though a reader may slow down to skim (a different purpose) to see if he or she is perhaps in the right neighborhood. This skill is typically carried out at a very rapid rate of words per minute (WPM) processing of the text.

Reading to learn, in contrast, requires reading for the main ideas, but it also requires awareness of many of the details of the text and a strong organizing frame by which to connect information from various parts of the text. Such textual coherence making on the part of the reader increases the text's memorability and aids recall when the relevant information is needed. The cognitive processing is carried out at a relatively slow rate of WPM processing (perhaps around 175–200 WPM for fluent L1 readers, much slower for most L2 readers). Reading to critique and evaluate will require, in addition, reflection on and evaluations of the text information and a strong integration with prior knowledge, including the reader's attitudes, emotions, motivations for reading, and level of topic-specific background knowledge. Reading rate will likely be even slower for this purpose.

The most common, and most basic, reading purpose is reading for general understanding. It is saved for last in this discussion because it is the primary goal of most L2 reading instruction, even though it may not be the easiest type of reading to teach. Reading for general understanding typically occurs at a rate of about 250–300 WPM by fluent readers (but this rate applies to relatively few L2 readers). This purpose satisfies most reading expectations for understanding main ideas and a subset of supporting ideas and information. Although it is often noted as "basic," and "general," it is by no means easy to carry out fluently. Reading for general understanding, under normal processing rates, requires a very large recognition vocabulary, automaticity of word recognition for most of the words in the text, a reasonably rapid overall reading speed for text-information integration, and the ability to build overall text comprehension under some time pressure.

This set of processing abilities is the common goal of most advanced L2 reading instruction, though many reading teachers and curriculum developers have only a limited concept of the processing demands of reading for general comprehension under relatively rapid time constraints. Instead, instructors and text materials often end up teaching slow translation of texts; with fairly short texts, they treat reading as problem solving. Reading in this way may, in fact, be a purpose for reading in settings with much more limited L2 educational goals, though such a limitation is not often explicitly recognized. This mismatch among goals is explored in more detail in the next two sections.

III. A Definition of Reading

Reading can easily be defined simply as the ability to derive understanding from written text. However, this brief definition belies the complexity inherent in the ability to read (now assuming reading for general understanding as the primary purpose). L2 reading can best be understood as a combination of skills and abilities that individuals bring to bear as they begin to read. The following five abilities should be seen as definitional, though others may be added under a finer specification of reading:

1. A rapid and automatic process
2. An interacting process
3. A flexible and strategic process
4. A purposeful process
5. A linguistic process (cf. Grabe, 2009)

First, fluent **reading is by definition a rapid process:** The various bits of information being activated at any moment in working memory (Baddeley, 2006) need to be active simultaneously if the information (from both the text and the reader's background knowledge) is to be integrated for understanding. Slow reading rates make the assembling of text comprehension a more inefficient and laborious process. Assisting in a rapid and efficient process is the ability to recognize words automatically; reading, in any normal sense, is not possible without this ability.

Second, reading is an interactive process in two ways. Reading requires many skills and abilities—some of which are automatic and some of which are attentional (where one's attention is focused)—to be carried out nearly simultaneously. At the same time, such higher level comprehension processes as identifying the main ideas of the text require an interaction between textual information and background knowledge. This latter interaction is also needed to determine whether immediate goals are being met, whether information is being understood, and whether strategies for reading are being used effectively to achieve the reading purpose.

Third, reading is strategic and flexible in that readers assess whether or not they are achieving their purposes for reading. If not, readers must then flexibly adapt various processing and monitoring activities. This ability to adapt strategically is the hallmark of a good reader (Hudson, 2007; Koda, 2005).

Fourth, reading is purposeful in the ways noted earlier; it is also purposeful in a more immediate way. As readers, we monitor not only our efficiency of processing, but also whether the immediate activity fits with our larger expectations, whether the task is sufficiently interesting to continue, and whether our purposes might be better served by changing the current activity or task. Reading in academic contexts also often has the reading purpose set by the teacher; in such a context, individual students then analyze purposes in terms of prior successes (or failures) with similar tasks. It is also worth remembering that the most central purpose for reading is to comprehend the text.

Fifth and finally, reading is a linguistic process (as opposed to a reasoning process). Fundamentally, we derive understanding and new meaning as we interact with the text information by means of linguistic processing. It is sometimes said that for meaning to be developed from text, reading is primarily a reasoning activity. However, this view is the result of researchers who are fluent readers and who cannot recognize the obvious language struggles that a beginning reader or an L2 reader has with texts. One has only to try to read a text in Chinese when one knows no Chinese characters to realize that reading is first and foremost a linguistic processing activity.

IV. How Reading Works: Individual Processes in Reading

Fluent reading requires efficient cognitive processing. Two basic types of processing are required: lower level processing, and higher level processing (without assuming that either type is more difficult than the other type; rather, understanding that they are simply different). Within lower level processing, readers must be rapid and automatic word recognizers; they must be able to pull out and use basic structural information; and they must begin to assemble clause-level meaning units (Perfetti, Landi, and Oakhill, 2005). Within higher level processing, readers must be able to assemble clause-level information into a text model of their understanding—strengthening repeated and salient ideas and pruning ideas that do not get reactivated. Readers also need to build an interpretation of the text that conforms to their goals, attitudes, and background knowledge (a situation model of interpretation). They also have to make appropriate inferences and determine whether they are staying on task and achieving their reading purpose (Grabe, 2009; Kintsch, 1998).

Lower level processes most importantly involve activating word meanings for use in working memory. In this respect reading centrally involves word recognition even though researchers recognize that word recognition itself is not equivalent to the *reading comprehension* process. However, many researchers argue that reading comprehension cannot be carried out without strong word recognition and lexical access skills (potentially two separable abilities for L2 readers; e.g., Stanovich, 2000). The average fluent L1 reader can recognize 4–5 words per second and can actually take time to look at these words each and every second of reading time. This fact may well be the central miracle of a human's fluent reading abilities. Moreover, the words and meanings are accessed automatically in the vast majority of cases because readers do not take the time to think consciously about what each new word means (Samuels, 2006). Research has shown that fluent readers cannot suppress the activation of known word meanings when they are visually exposed to a word for as little as a twentieth of a second. (Automaticity entails an inability to suppress information.)

The syntax and semantics of clauses in a text also play a role in lower level processing. In fluent reading, as a clause is read, information about word order (and which word or phrase constitutes the grammatical subject), about main versus adjunct phrase, and about relations among phrases in the clause unit are all extracted. Usually this process is attempted quickly in line with certain default expectations, so syntactic information is pulled automatically from a clause, assuming there is no complication that confuses the reader's processing. At the same time, basic information about the word meanings, in combination with the syntactic information, lead to initial meaning units being assembled (propositional units). Unless there is some complication or unexpected outcomes of these processes, they take place relatively automatically; that is, we don't have to think about them (and actually aren't able to think about them very easily; Grabe, 2009).

The higher level processing that a reader carries out includes the combining of clause-level meaning information into a basic text representation (a text model of reading). This text model represents the basic *summary* of the text, as the reader understands it to be intended by the author. At the same time, a more elaborate copy is created that combines the text model with stronger reader views about the purposes of the author in writing the text, the attitude of the reader to the material in the text, past experiences with reading similar texts, reader motivations for reading, and reader evaluation of the text itself (i.e., the reader's likes, agreements, interests, surprises, supports for opinions, disagreements with the text). This second model is often described as a situation model of text interpretation (Kintsch, 1998; Kintsch and Rawson, 2005). Thus, a good reader creates two levels of comprehension for a text. Both levels of text understanding require processing interactions with reader knowledge; both levels require extensive inferencing and reasoning about the text (and reasoning becomes important at this point). Finally, a fluent reader is able to monitor his or her reading (an executive control process) to decide if it is achieving the intended purpose and, if needed, to take some actions to make adjustments for better understanding.

V. Social Factors Influencing Reading

One outcome of this explanation of fluent reading processing is the impression that learning to read is an individual activity. It is true that at any given moment when a reader engages with a text, reading is primarily a cognitive activity, but the longer developmental process cannot be understood without recognizing social influences on reading development. Social contexts influencing reading include those deriving from the home, the school and other institutions, from peers, and resulting from student-teacher interactions. Much research has shown that home factors in early reading development have a significant and lasting impact, though they do so in many complex ways, depending on the settings and interactants (C. E. Snow et al., 2007). Peer interactions over time and student-teacher interactions also have a major role to play in a developing reader's motivations, attitudes, task successes, and reading experiences. The educational institutional setting more generally also plays a powerful role. Students develop differing proficiencies in reading depending on school administrations, library resources, classroom resources, amount of curricular time set aside specifically for reading development, teacher training, teacher practices and preferences, and teacher interest in books and in student learning. The picture is very complex and difficult to sort through, but that does not give anyone the license to ignore such major influences on a person's learning to read (Grabe, 2009).

In L2 reading contexts, the picture becomes even more complex because readers deal with the following:

- Two languages
- Two general educational experiences (including patterns of success and failure on a wide range of learning tasks)
- Varying motivations and attitudes towards tasks in both L1 and L2 contexts
- Different impositions by an L2 culture
- Differing levels of expected success in L2 instruction

Moreover, in many L2 academic settings, the assumption may be made that L2 reading abilities (often poorly defined) can be acquired in a much briefer time span than typically occurs in L1 contexts, creating unrealistic expectations and often destroying motivation for reading in the L2. Complicating the fact that there are unending variations in L2 social contexts for reading, there are also relatively few empirical studies of social context influences on L2 reading. Nonetheless, most L2 reading researchers recognize the powerful impact that social contexts will have on L2 reading development (Koda, 2008a; 2008b).

VI. Specific L2 Reading Issues

To this point, the discussion of reading has been general, combining L1 and L2 reading issues. However, the purposes, processes and practices of L2 reading invoke a number of specific issues that deserve attention, including the following:

- More limited language knowledge of the L2 reader (as compared with the L1 reader)

- Relative importance of L2 language proficiency versus L1 reading abilities as the strongest factor in L2 reading development
- Issues surrounding transfer of skills more generally
- Role of strategy uses unique to L2 learners (e.g., bilingual dictionaries, cognates, mental translation, glosses)
- Recognition that texts and educational institutions themselves may work differently for L2 learners
- More limited total exposure of learners to the L2 and to L2 reading experiences

In comparison with L1 readers, L2 readers begin to learn to read without the initial language base that can be assumed to be present among L1 readers. Most L1 readers begin their formal reading instruction with a vocabulary of at least 6,000 words already known in their language and with a firm tacit knowledge of most basic grammatical structures of the language. The L2 reader, in contrast, may have relatively little L2 spoken language knowledge at the time reading instruction begins. A major debate has arisen as to the primary way that a learner gains L2 reading abilities and whether L2 reading development is supported

> *via L2 language knowledge* (i.e., knowledge of L2 vocabulary, L2 structure, L2 task successes, exposure to L2 reading) or
> *via prior L1 reading skills* (i.e., L1 reading strategies, metalinguistic knowledge, L1 task successes, L1 word learning skills)

This debate is otherwise known as the *language threshold hypothesis*. Over the past 10 years, the evidence has grown steadily that L2 language knowledge plays a much greater role until some general (and very variable) threshold of language knowledge is passed, confirming a general version of the language threshold hypothesis. For most L2 students, the key lies in developing a large recognition vocabulary, a reasonable command of language structure and discourse marking devices, and many positive experiences with manageable L2 reading tasks. At some point, most words are recognized rapidly and automatically, and most structural parsing automatically provides the needed processing information. At that point, the reader will be more successful in using the full range of reading skills and strategies that already support successful fluent L1 reading—in other words, reading with greater metalinguistic awareness, monitoring comprehension efficiently, engaging in a range of reading strategies with more difficult texts, and using background knowledge to support appropriate inferences.

More generally, the issue of L1 transfer has also been explored extensively and a useful set of findings may be provided (Dressler and Kamil, 2006; Koda, 2008a; 2008b). L2 readers almost certainly transfer underlying cognitive reading skills such as working memory processing, phonological processing, and orthographic processing for word recognition (Genesee et al., 2006). It appears that L2 readers do transfer L1 syntactic knowledge of various types to their L2 reading, even at relatively advanced stages. Sometimes the transferred knowledge is supportive, and sometimes it causes interference (Koda, 2005). On this issue, L2 reading strongly overlaps with SLA research on transfer. More specifically for reading, research on orthographic transfer seems to show an L1 impact at early stages of L2 reading, though the impact diminishes at advanced L2 levels. Much of this research can be linked to the *orthographic depth hypothesis*, which states that readers of differing orthographies will develop somewhat different word recognition processing skills, depending on the L1 orthography. There is growing evidence that this hypothesis does reflect the learning behavior of certain groups of beginning L2 readers (e.g., Japanese readers of English, English readers of Japanese, Spanish readers of English, English readers of Hebrew; see Koda, 2008b).

Another area that focuses specifically on L2 reading issues involves the use of certain reading strategies and the role of bilingual resources for reading. In strategy research, for example, it is found that mental translation (a uniquely L2 strategy) is not necessarily a "poor habit" but can be a useful early L2 reading strategy for students who are dealing with difficult texts. Strategies for the use of cognates have also proven to be important for L2 readers, but often only after learners receive explicit instruction in recognizing and using potential cognates. Bilingual dictionaries and the use of word glosses for comprehension purposes are two further useful resources for L2 reading not common to L1 reading instruction. Even though the use of bilingual dictionaries has been an ongoing issue for many teachers, recent research over the past decade suggests that dictionaries can be useful supports for L2 reading. However, students should be trained in the effective use of dictionaries. Recent research on the use of glosses with L2 reading texts has also demonstrated that glosses can provide benefits for comprehension and do not seem to interfere with reading comprehension tasks.

Another issue that involves L2 readers uniquely concerns the patterns of text organization that may be uncommonly read by learners in their L1 contexts. Students moving to L2 reading may encounter text organization patterns that are unfamiliar to them or to which they have not had extensive exposure and practice. In some cases, the cultural and literacy practices of a culture privilege certain types of text patterns and organization structures, particularly with informational expository prose texts. The point is not that such texts cannot be understood by L2 readers, but that learners will need more explicit instruction in how texts are structured and how information is organized. In some cases, the issue is not a matter of no exposure to rhetorical preferences in the L2, but a need for more practice with such texts. This problem is part of a more general problem of L2 exposure.

L2 readers are almost always at some disadvantage (in comparison with L1 readers) because they seldom have exposure to similar amounts of text for L2 reading purposes. Given that reading efficiency is dependent on rapid and automatic word recognition and a large recognition vocabulary, extensive exposure to L2 texts through reading is the only learning option available to L2 students seeking to develop advanced L2 reading abilities. Yet most L2 students do not receive nearly the amount of exposure to L2 texts that would be necessary for the development of fluent L2 reading skills. A large factor in this L2 issue is that most teachers, curricula, and instructional materials do not recognize the severely limiting impact of relatively small amounts of exposure to L2 reading texts. The solution, theoretically, is obvious and simple; in practice, however, the solution (reading extensively) is quite difficult to implement for a variety of reasons (Grabe, 2009).

Overall, the research on L2 reading shows that the factors that influence reading development are quite complex. One example of this complexity involves transfer: Research shows that the transfer of L1 reading skills and strategies is itself complex. One cannot assume that the transfer of all reading skills and strategies from the L1 is easy, automatic, or uniformly positive. Only three useful generalizations can be made at present:

- Many instances of transfer lead to interference for L2 reading comprehension.
- Researchers do not know the full range of situations in which positive transfer does or does not occur, or when transfer occurs.
- L2 reading ability is the product of the L2 reader's dual-language processing system. (Koda, 2008b)

A second example of complexity involves extensive exposure to L2 reading material. A reading specialist would be hard-pressed to miss the linkage in research between amount of exposure texts and reading development. However, the goal of increasing the amount of learners' exposure to L2 reading material is commonly resisted in instructional practice and curriculum planning, or it is given a low priority (Grabe, 2009). Reliable research on the direct effects of extensive reading is limited, but the great majority of this research points to the benefits of more extensive exposure to print.

A third example involves vocabulary development. Vocabulary knowledge is at the heart of fluent reading abilities—a large recognition vocabulary is essential. Vocabulary consistently ranks as one of the strongest predictors of growth in reading ability. Yet vocabulary growth and vocabulary instruction is not emphasized in many L2 instructional contexts. Admittedly, vocabulary instruction is not an easy instructional focus, but ignoring the need will not solve the learner's difficulties in this area (Han and Anderson, 2009).

VII. Reading Instruction

Based on research in both L1 and L2 reading contexts, a number of general implications for L2 reading instruction can be established. These implications, many of which have been supported in the above discussion, provide guidance for the development of reading curricula and instructional practices (even if each teaching context is unique and requires its own combination of instructional emphases). These 10 implications offer a useful starting point for instructional practice:

1. The need for a large recognition vocabulary
2. The need to provide explicit language instruction to help students move through the L2 language threshold
3. The need for knowledge of discourse organizing principles
4. The usefulness of graphic representations for comprehension instruction
5. The importance of metacognitive awareness and strategy learning—the need for students to become strategic readers
6. The need for practice in reading fluency to develop automaticity
7. The importance of extensive reading and broad exposure to L2 texts
8. The benefits of integrating reading and writing instruction in academic settings
9. The need to develop effective content-based instruction for reading development
10. The need to motivate students to read

Describing in detail how such implications can be transformed into applications would require another full chapter (see N. Anderson, 2009). However, some comments on these implications are in order. Points 1 and 2 follow directly from research on the reading processes of the individual; a large recognition vocabulary and reasonable structural knowledge are central resources for reading improvement. Points 3 and 4 follow from the need to work with academic texts or text types to which learners may not have received sufficient exposure, particularly in reading-to-learn situations (see also Point 8; Pressley, 2006). Point 5 highlights the need to develop the strategic reader (rather than reading strategies), a key aspect of skilled reading comprehension, especially in academic settings (Grabe, 2009). Points 6 and 7 highlight the importance of reading efficiency, appropriate reading rates, automaticity, and broad exposure to L2 texts (Krashen, 2004; Samuels, 2006). Point 8 stresses the link between reading and writing, the academic and occupational demands that assume this linkage, and the need to develop skills for linking reading and writing (Hudson, 2007). Points 7, 9, and 10 also combine under the need to motivate student to read in the L2. Extensive reading provides learners with opportunities to become engaged with interesting ideas and topics as does the framework provided by effective content-based curricula. Both reinforce motivation for L2 reading, a crucial component of any successful L2 reading instruction. More generally, content-based instruction, if done well, provides an effective curricular framework for carrying out all of the 10 implications for L2 reading instruction as previously noted (Grabe, 2009).

VIII. Further Issues for Consideration

There are a number of additional issues that should be addressed in a longer review of L2 reading. A number of these deserve mention and some brief commentary. These issues include new directions in reading assessment, reading and writing interactions, neurolinguistics and reading, child L2 reading development, reading in new modes and new media (e.g., e-mails, Internet hypertext, blogging, text messaging, Facebook, twittering), teacher training, the role of authentic materials, and motivational factors. Volumes by Alderson (2000), Grabe (2009), and Khalifa and Weir (2009) offer important insights into L2 assessment research and practice. The exploration of reading and writing relationships primarily examines the various type of reading and writing tasks assigned in university settings and the variable abilities that L2 students demonstrate when carrying out such tasks. Grabe (2001) and Hudson (2007) address reading-writing relations in some detail.

Neurolinguistics and reading is a rapidly growing field of exploration (see Schumann elsewhere in this volume). Even a recent volume on L1 comprehension instruction devoted four chapters to this issue (C. Block and Parris, 2008; see also Shaywitz and Shaywitz 2004; Wolf, 2007). Little neurolinguistic research has been carried out involving L2 readers. Child L2 reading development has grown tremendously over the past 10 years. A number of findings involving L1 transfer to L2 reading development have emerged from this research (Dressler and Kamil, 2006; Genesee et al., 2006). The issue of reading from a computer screen, reading new media, and reading new text types is no longer a marginal theme, and research in this area is beginning to appear. As younger readers move through to adulthood, distinct reading processes and reading strategies are likely to become a major locus of research. As present, relatively little in the way of empirical research with L2 students in this context has been carried out.

Another unexplored area for L2 research is the issue of effective teacher training for L2 reading instruction. This theme has become an important one for L1 research in the past 5 years; comparable attention has not yet been given to teacher training for reading instruction in L2 contexts (C. E. Snow, Griffin, and Burns, 2005). Issues of authenticity and appropriateness of instructional texts are addressed very thoughtfully by Day and Bamford (1998) and Widdowson (2004). Both make powerful arguments for rethinking simplistic notions about authenticity for reading instruction and reading materials. Finally, research concerning reading motivation has grown considerably in the past 10 years. The role of motivation in L2 reading development has been relatively untouched but needs serious exploration (Grabe, 2009).

IX. Conclusion

One outcome of a careful review of L2 reading is that it is almost impossible to get a firm grasp on all the issues and complexities that influence learner success or failure, particularly in the endlessly varying L2 settings. But complexity, in and of itself, should not be a cause for despair. The situation of L2 reading instruction may actually be seen to be generally positive. Despite all the complexities and difficulties that can go into reading success or failure, it is extraordinary that so many L1 and L2 learners become good readers. We should celebrate this miracle at the same time that we look for ways to improve this pattern of success for more learners.

CHAPTER 7

SECOND LANGUAGE WRITING IN ENGLISH

ILONA LEKI

In his discussion of theoretical issues in L2 writing, Cumming comments, "Writing is text, is composing, and is social construction" (1998: 61). His analysis is appropriate not only synchronically, as he uses it in his discussion of current theoretical issues, but also diachronically. Modern L2 writing instruction and research have gradually broadened their perspective by shifting focus from texts, to processes (i.e., composing), to disciplinary and sociopolitical contexts (i.e., social construction).

The fortunes of L2 writing have certainly expanded in modern times. At one time L2 writing was viewed as no more than a handmaid (Rivers, 1968a) to all other language skills, a means of reinforcing the acquisition of grammatical and vocabulary knowledge. Now construed primarily as composing rather than as language practice, writing is considered by some as a privileged or particularly potent means for effecting democratic change toward a more just and equitable sociopolitical order (Clark and Ivanic, 1997) through the potential participation in public written debate of traditionally dominated voices. Less grandly, L2 writing (in particular in English) is also constructed as a primary means for participation in international disciplinary conversations through publications in international journals. At the level of pedagogy, researchers, especially in foreign language (FL) contexts (see Manchn, in press) are now beginning to shift back toward consideration of writing as a language skill, but in a more judicious way; that is, writing not as the handmaid of other language skills, but rather as the affordance of a potential opportunity to enhance those other skills as writing skill develops.

On the other hand, and more ominously because of writing's usefulness as a gatekeeping mechanism, writing is also at the center of the contested terrain of access to knowledge, power, and resources (see Leki, 2003; see also Crowley, 1998; D. Russell,

1991, for discussion of this issue for English L1 writing). In secondary and especially tertiary academic settings in English dominant countries, for example, L2 writing in English is a primary vehicle for establishing proficiency in disciplinary courses. In professional settings, as English has increasingly become the international language of science and technology publications, and as academics and other professionals are required to publish in international journals (Braine, 2005; Casanave, 1998; Curry and Lillis, 2004; Flowerdew, 2000; Gosden, 1996), the ability to write in L2 English has become, for some, a sometimes irritating and costly necessity (Phillipson and Skutnabb-Kangas, 2000). In short, the heightened status of L2 writing as an English language skill, and the prevalence of English L2 and FL writing instruction world-wide, have brought with them serious implications for writers' material lives.

L2 writing has historically been studied across a variety of languages for centuries (Kaplan and Grabe 2002). But because of the current dominance of English as an international language, the many millions of learners of English and the economic wherewithal of English dominant countries to invest in researching English writing and in exporting their language teaching technologies, research into L2 writing in the last 60 years has often meant research into L2 writing in English. Although for many users—perhaps most, outside academic and professional circles—L2 English writing may be limited to functions such as writing short notes or even simply filling out forms (Cumming and Gill, 1991), the vast majority of published research on L2 writing has dealt with extended writing in academic (particularly tertiary) and professional settings. The goal of research into extended L2 writing has often centered on how best to teach it.

Yet such a research question is, in a sense, premature, because before determining how L2 writing might best be taught, it would seem necessary to understand and to characterize good writing. Although examples of admired texts abound, it has become clear that the characteristics of good writing are slippery, perhaps unspecifiable, because decontextualized good writing cannot exist. In fact, given current understandings of meaning as constructed (rather than as residing in text), the quality of writing comes into being only in the reading of the text. In a postmodern intellectual climate, the insight that judgments about the quality of writing depend on the context in which the writing is done and read seems unobjectionable, even trivial. However, the following questions have profound implications and have long been at the center of intellectual and disciplinary debates about L2 writing research and instruction:

• What is good writing?
• What is good writing good *for*?
• What does it mean to be a good writer?
• How can we teach good writing?
• Can good writing even be taught, particularly by an L2 writing teacher (rather than by someone familiar with the thematic content of the writing)?

In the effort to develop an understanding of the responses to these questions, modern L2 writing research has set itself the goal of accounting for the following:

1. L2 texts through examination of contrastive or intercultural rhetorics, genre analysis, and written discourse analysis, including the study of linguistic and rhetorical text features
2. Writers' processes through the study of individual writers at varying levels of expertise at a particular point in their L2 writing development and across time as expertise develops, including the role of the L1 in L2 writing
3. Contexts of L2 writing, such as the personal histories of writers, their linguistic and cultural backgrounds, their disciplinary formation, the institutional constraints under which they operate, and the influence of a variety of sociopolitical factors
4. Pedagogical practices in L2 writing, including assessment at all levels

Although the themes that thread through historical and current L2 writing research and instruction overlap and cross-fertilize, making division into separate strands difficult, I have attempted to group the core research interests noted above into three orientations that represent the primary concerns of L2 writing practitioners and researchers in modern times (i.e., in the last 60 years):

1. Text- and classroom-based orientations
2. Process-based orientations
3. Orientation to contexts for writing

I. Text- and Classroom-Based Orientations

In the early years of L2 writing research, the core of text- and classroom-based issues was concern about error in writing, text structure, and rhetorical differences across languages/cultures (contrastive rhetoric), teacher and peer response to writing, and assessment of L2 writing. Although each of these threads has persisted over time, the degree of research attention each commands has shifted considerably and moved in parallel with pedagogical focuses in L2 writing.

Interest in errors in writing and in their correction, reduction or prevention—arguably the overriding issues of concern in early modern L2 writing instruction—has fluctuated considerably. These fluctuations have followed trends in part from language teaching (i.e., from an emphasis on avoiding error in, for example, audiolingual methodology, to a de-emphasis in communicative approaches) and in part from L1 English writing instruction (also moving from emphasis to de-emphasis). The professional conversation about L2 writing errors moved from how best to eliminate them from L2 student writing to whether to bother dealing with them at all and more recently, with the focus-on-form movement (Doughty and Williams, 1998), back to how to deal with them as a means of building language accuracy and grammatical understanding. The more recent perspective, however, gives errors far less importance and exhibits far less faith that error correction can have much of an effect on reducing the numbers of written errors. Although students express a desire for error correction, among researchers the debate about the effectiveness of attention to errors has continued (Ferris, 1999; Guénette, 2007; Truscott, 1996). Supported by research in second language acquisition (SLA) concerning the importance of attention in language acquisition, rather than concentrating on grammar instruction on predetermined grammatical forms or their correction, the more generalized focus on form emphasizes heightened awareness of linguistic form and strategic corrective interventions.

As L2 writing instruction was pondering its initial move away from a focus on sentence-level error, a new interest had begun to captivate L2 writing teachers and researchers, contrastive rhetoric, or the idea that different cultures produce culturally influenced and rhetorically distinguishable types of text (Kaplan, 1966). Because providing students with model texts to imitate was a familiar feature of L2 writing classrooms of the 1960s and 1970s, contrastive rhetoric's focus on organizational patterns smoothed its ready incorporation into L2 writing classrooms at that time. As with error correction, however, after a period of fairly intense interest, arguments began to emerge in the professional literature challenging the validity of early contrastive rhetoric research and ultimately granting it a much-diminished pertinence in L2 writing instruction. However, the kernel insight of contrastive rhetoric, that cultures affect texts, has recently dovetailed with and been partially subsumed by interest in the idea that knowledge (and judgments about the quality and appropriateness of texts) is socially constructed (Connor, 1996), a notion introduced into L2 writing though genre studies (Johns, 1997). Genre studies have strongly influenced textual analyses generally (Swales, 1990), examining generic requirements across disciplines and within different sections of texts, management of author-reader relations and author positioning and self-presentation, and textual and linguistic manipulations of claim strengths (see Hyland, 2004). These more recent and complex approaches to textual variation depart from cross-national and essentializing cultural explanations that characterized early contrastive rhetoric and analyze cross-cultural variation in text as arising, not cross-nationally, but rather in the "small cultures" (Matsuda and Atkinson, 2008) of, for example, organizational settings and histories (see, e.g., Thatcher, 2000). Other descendents of the original contrastive rhetoric studies include "intercultural" rhetoric research with a greater emphasis on context (Connor, 2004) and critical contrastive rhetoric with attention to issues of race, class, and gender (Kubota and Lehner, 2004). In addition, study of the traces of L1 rhetorical preferences in L2 writing expanded to recognize a reciprocal effect—that is, bidirectional transfer, with evidence that instruction and experience in L2 writing leave traces on a writer's L1 writing as well as the other way around (Kobayashi and Rinnert, 2004). Writers are viewed less as struggling with L2 text than as "multicompetent" L1 and L2 language users (Ortega and Carson, in press).

How readers respond to a writer's text probably has more influence on a writer's motivation and progress than any other single feature of writing instruction.

With the arrival in the mid 1980s of process approaches[1] to teaching writing and their emphasis on multiple drafting, it became clear that merely giving L2 writers model texts to imitate and marking their errors did not produce better writers. Thus, the attention of researchers and teachers turned to investigations of other kinds of responses to L2 writing, by teachers (Conrad and Goldstein, 1999) and by peers (Nelson and Carson, 1998), in writing (Ferris, 1997) and in oral conferences (L. Goldstein and Conrad, 1990) that could lead to appropriate revision beyond sentence-level corrections.

Results of these investigations reveal the complexity of the impact of response to L2 writing. L2 writers who are more advanced in their disciplines may resist teacher suggestions beyond the level of grammar/mechanical errors (Radecki and Swales, 1988); writers may also resist suggestions for revision that target macro text features and that would require revisions deemed too extensive (Leki, 1990). Writing teachers are warned not to substitute their own "ideal" text for the emerging texts their L2 students are creating, but also are urged to realize that intervention in learner writing is not the same as appropriating text (Reid, 1994). Peer response is sometimes too gentle (Nelson and Carson, 1998), sometimes too forceful (Nelson and Murphy, 1992), sometimes ignored in preference to teacher response (Zhang, 1995). Conferencing appears to work best when the students actively invest themselves in the conference rather than simply accepting teacher commentary (L. Goldstein and Conrad, 1990). Some evidence suggests that self-directed revision, without response from any reader at all, also results in improvement in subsequent drafts (Polio, Fleck, and Leder, 1998). Finally, even response that corresponds to a student's expressed desire for a particular response type may lead to unanticipated and adverse affective reactions in the writer (Hyland, 1998b).

Although L2 writing professionals now have some idea about effective response strategies, given the central importance of responding to writing and the complexity of its effects, it is clear that just as there is no prototypical good text, there is no simple relationship between response and writing improvement (Ferris, 2002; L. Goldstein, 2005). Furthermore, L2 writing professionals have recognized that writing response is crucially embedded in complex and inescapable disciplinary, social, and political contexts that may be beyond the control of both the writer and the teacher.

In most academic contexts (and less directly in professional settings), writing is evaluated. Like many other forms of assessment, L2 writing assessment often serves a sorting and gatekeeping function. However repugnant such a function may be, if this type of assessment is unavoidable (an arguable supposition), assessment specialists insist that it is the responsibility of L2 practitioners to do it well (Hamp-Lyons, 2001). One of several tortured issues in writing assessment is, what is a fair sample of writing to assess?

- Single-shot exams written within a restricted period of time on an arbitrarily chosen topic that the writer sees for the first time at the exam session, such as in the former Test of Written English and many placement tests?

- Tests based on a reading passage from the test taker's disciplinary area (Hamp-Lyons, 1991a)?
- Essays that writers have the opportunity to revise before evaluation?
- Portfolios of a variety of writing produced over time?

Each of these types of evaluative measures has been used at one time or another to decide the educational fate of L2 writers. Despite continued pressure to move away from single-shot writing exams, their relative ease of administration keeps them alive.

In addition to the problem of which texts to evaluate comes the question of who should evaluate them. Research studies have shown the negative results of allowing inappropriate raters to evaluate texts, for example, language teachers evaluating texts in disciplinary areas in which they have no expertise, as has happened with the IELTS examination (Hamp-Lyons, 1991b), or L1 writing teachers (and teachers from other disciplinary areas) evaluating L2 writing with no understanding of L2 writing issues, as may happen in exit or proficiency exams (Sweedler-Brown, 1993). When the same writing proficiency examination is used with L1 and L2 writers, problems arise with selecting culturally appropriate writing topics that do not disadvantage the L2 writers (Johns, 1991). Furthermore, in situations in which L1 and L2 writers are tested together, a question of standards seems unavoidable: Should different standards be used to evaluate the writing of these two groups? That question in turn evokes the issue of how to determine where to draw the line between L1 and L2 writers, and even beyond that, of how to treat second dialect writers. Balancing between a perceived need, or institutionally enforced requirement, to test writing and a desire to be fair to L2 writers, L2 writing professionals have worked to develop consistent, satisfactory answers to these vexed questions:

1. What is an appropriate text to rate?
2. Who should read it?
3. What writing topic is fair?
4. What accommodations should be made in rating L2 writers' texts? (Weigle, 2002)

Finally, an important element in some classroom-oriented research has been a focus on possible classroom uses of corpus linguistics, Internet resources, and computer-mediated communication systems, especially for interacting with writing teachers and peers. (See, e.g., Warschauer, 1996, 1999, 2000.)

II. Process-Based Orientations

Questions about texts, tests, and teaching methodologies continue. However, these issues were displaced from center stage by explorations oriented toward individual writers, first synchronically toward their cognitive processes while composing, and then diachronically toward their development as writers and as initiates into academic and professional disciplines. Emulating Emig's seminal (1971) study of English L1 high school students' cognitive processes while writing, early L2 writing researchers developed a significant body of research reviewed in, for example, Krapels (1990), focusing on such topics as writing processes of strong L2 writers (Zamel, 1983), those of less proficient L2 writers (Raimes, 1985), use of L1 in L2 writing (Roca de Larios, Murphy, and Manchn, 1999), and threshold levels of L2 proficiency (Cumming, 1989). The most significant results of these studies include the following findings:

- Proficient L2 writers focus on content, and not only on form, as they write.
- L2 writers may need to reach a threshold level of proficiency in L2 before they can engage the efficient writing processes they use in L1.
- Writers' processes vary fairly widely across individuals, though they may remain more or less consistent from L1 to L2 (Arndt, 1987).
- Shifting to L1 can be a very useful strategy for generating ideas and stimulating more complex thinking in L2.

Pursuit of the question of how mental processes are engaged in L2 writing has tapered off somewhat in English-dominant countries, but it remains an active part of the research agenda in EFL settings, particularly in Europe. (See, e.g., the *Journal of Second Language Writing*, special issue, "Writing in Foreign Language Contexts: Research Insights," 2008; see also Manchón, in press; Wang and Wen, 2002; Zimmerman, 2000). These studies have focused on time allocated to various tasks while writing (e.g., planning versus transforming ideas into language versus editing), focus of attention during writing, and impact of task type and previous experience and instruction.

In addition to investigating L2 writing processes, researchers have also examined the intersection of L2 writing and SLA, particularly in the EFL studies. On the whole, however, this cross-fertilization has been fairly limited, with little examination, for example, of language acquisition through L2 writing. (See, however, Weissberg, 2000, who argues that new L2 forms first emerge in writing, not in speech).[2] No doubt part of the astonishing lack of interdisciplinary interface with SLA heretofore is the result of L2 writing's historical, and sometimes misguided, dependence on L1 writing research; another part is perhaps SLA's historical focus primarily on speech rather than on writing. The implications for writing of theoretical models of SLA, such as connectionism, also remain unexplored. Yet the focused attention required by writing and the repetition of forms occasioned by writing cannot but have an effect on SLA. Insights from SLA research might help to clarify, for example, the apparent disconnect students experience between the writing done for L2 writing classes and that done in other disciplinary areas, for which the L2 writing classes purportedly prepare them (Leki and Carson, 1997). Similarly, socio-culturally influenced theories of SLA that consider the relationship between L1 and L2 communities and learner purposes should find natural coincidence with issues of differential L2 writing success and learning transfer (from one writing context to another), but again these links have been little explicitly explored. (See, however, M. James, 2006.)

Perhaps the most significant link between SLA and writing processes comes in the extensive work on output, primarily by Swain and her colleagues (see, e.g., Swain and Lapkin, 1995, 1998). The underlying assumption in this work is that the attention required to produce output, such as writing, causes semantic understandings of the target language to become syntacticized. Furthermore, when that written output potential is combined with oral output in the form of collaborative writing with a peer, learners' linguistic resources are extended and scaffolded, and on-the-spot advances in language proficiency are better remembered.

III. Orientation to Contexts for Writing

As a clearer picture of L2 writers' mental processes during single moments of writing began to develop, disciplinary interest shifted toward the question of how individuals' writing processes and skills developed over time. Consistent with a growing trend in L2 writing research away from decontextualized examinations of texts or of the writing processes of disembodied writers, the focus on L2 writers' development has demonstrated how personal, social, cultural, linguistic, institutional, educational, and political contexts are necessarily entwined. At the more micro level, context has been construed as the writing task, the reading associated with writing, the teacher's goals in assigning a task, and the writer's goals in carrying out the task (Cumming, 2006). Important theoretical influences in these studies have been activity theory (Engeström, 1987), sociocultural theories of language learning (Lantolf, 2000), and theories of situated learning (Lave and Wenger, 1991), each of which places the individual within a network of other individuals, tasks, tools, goals, and settings in an effort to explain both experiences and progress, or lack of it. In broadening its scope to include more than just learners' L2 writing, much of this research has been qualitative or naturalistic, going into classrooms, offices, and workplaces. These studies of L2 writers' development have provided the field with a better sense of how specific individuals, with names, histories, personalities, and voices, negotiate their way in the L2, over time, through educational institutions, toward academic literacy. (See McCarthey, Garcia, Lopez-Velasquez, Lin, and Guo, 2004, for child writers; Harklau, 1999, 2000, for high school students, including *generation 1.5* students; and Leki, 2007, and Spack, 1997, for college students in the United States.)

Other studies have looked at how individuals come to be initiated into disciplinary domains. Here, personal intellectual, academic and literacy growth is shown to be actively and firmly shaped by academic disciplines. These studies focus on graduate students and professionals working in L2 English, tracing such formative experiences as writing for graduate seminars (Prior, 1998; Riazi, 1997), experiencing conflicting assumptions about the chosen discipline (Casanave, 1992), writing dissertations in L2 (Belcher, 1997), writing in L2 on the job (Parks, 2000), and publishing in L2 (Flowerdew, 1999). Less traditionally noted groups have also been studied for their interactions with L2 writing, revealing the amazing complexity of the uses of literacy as distributed in whole communities rather than located only autonomously within a single individual (Street, 1984; Weinstein-Shr, 1993).

A significant aspect of all the contexts for writers is related to sociopolitical environments, with many L2 writing professionals emphasizing that none of the issues discussed above can be viewed apolitically (Matsuda, Ortmeier-Hooper and You, 2006). Rather, political dimensions subsume and permeate all the focuses, concerns, and themes discussed above, whether or not we choose to recognize this, as aptly argued by Benesch (1993).

Reflecting a growing awareness of the interested or nonneutral nature of education, increasing numbers of L2 writing researchers have begun to address sociopolitical questions, in some cases primarily in relation to general cross-cultural issues and stereotyping (for example, Kubota, 1999). Others, however, have dealt more directly with L2 writing—for example, how identity issues influenced one South African L2 writer's decisions about where and how to ally himself politically through his writing choices (Angelil-Carter, 1997) or how local knowledge can function as a means of resisting the spread of the hegemonic and normative influences of Western academic writing (Canagarajah, 1993).

Another significant L2 writing domain explored through a sociopolitical lens has been the issue of plagiarism. Resisting the hysteria sometimes surrounding plagiarism, researchers have examined historical, cultural, and economic roots of Western notions of plagiarism (Pennycook, 1997) and the legitimate and transgressive uses of L2 intertextuality (Abasi, Akbari, and Graves, 2006; Currie, 1998; Pecorari, 2008).

L2 writing researchers have also been active in arguing for a critical pedagogy that would encourage and instruct L2 students on how to use writing to counter economic and political forces that have a negative impact on their lives (see e.g., Benesch, 2001). Australian genre researchers (for example, Christie, 1987; Cope and Kalantzis, 1993) have all argued for the empowerment of the disempowered, particularly children from nonprivileged classes and ethnic backgrounds, through teaching them the "power genres" favored in school settings. References in L2 writing research to theorists and researchers of critical language awareness and the new literacies movements—such as Street, Rampton, Gee, and Fairclough—are commonplace. Many of these writers reflect postmodern perspectives, which help to deepen our understanding of certain writing issues. Postmodernism challenges the belief in individual agency, in the unitary self, and in freely chosen, self-motivated actions, feelings, and opinions. The speaker/writer is viewed instead as a juncture of shifting experiences, beliefs, and ideological discourses. Such a perspective works against the ever-present temptation to exoticize L2 learners and essentialize their home cultures.

CONCLUSION

Although L2 writing studies have a long history, they did not coalesce in modern times until the late 1980s. The early 1990s saw an explosion of published research into L2 writing in addition to the development of a journal devoted specifically to the field (the *Journal of Second Language Writing*), a TESOL interest section, and an annual conference (Symposium on Second Language Writing). If disciplinarity is marked by, among other things, a theoretical foundation and a disciplinary history, L2 writing is hitting its stride as fragments of theoretical models surface along with disciplinary histories (Matsuda, 1998, 1999; Silva, 1993). Thus, the historical trajectory of L2 writing has moved from narrow focuses and tight control over L2 writing toward a growing interest in the context in which that writing takes place, both the individual context and the broad sociopolitical and historical context. We have partial answers to such central questions as what constitutes good writing and what good writing is good for, how L2 writing is done, and how we should teach L2 writing. But explorations continue from perspectives that shift over time, as they should. Perhaps disciplines evolve in ways similar to the ways natural language acquisition appears to take place, with each important new perspective unsettling and causing a salutary restructuring of previous, presumed-settled understandings.

NOTES

1. In brief, process approaches emphasize the recursive nature of writing by encouraging prewriting activities to generate ideas for writing, attention to audience and purpose for writing, consultation with peers and other potential responders on drafts of texts, and decreased focus on sentence-level correctness, among other features. Process approaches are often juxtaposed against previous "product" approaches that tended to feature single-draft, error-free texts that were read only by instructors with a view to evaluation, not consultation.

2. One notable exception to this generalization is the impact of Krashen's SLA work (1984, 1993), which certainly did its part to move L2 writing teachers away from a narrow focus on language errors toward a more comprehensive understanding of L2 writing. Krashen's interest in literacy and the power of reading has also influenced L2 writing.

CHAPTER 8

INTEGRATING THE FOUR SKILLS: CURRENT AND HISTORICAL PERSPECTIVES

ELI HINKEL

In the contemporary world of second and foreign language teaching, most professionals largely take it for granted that language instruction is naturally divided into discrete skill sets, typically reflecting speaking, listening, reading, and writing, and usually arranged in this order. That is, the primacy of speaking skills has remained unquestioned, at least in North America, for almost the entire past century, since the rise and preeminence of structural linguistics in second and foreign language teaching (*Language Teaching*, 2007).

Based on the principles of Bloomfieldian linguistic analyses and their applications to language pedagogy, the structural division of language teaching in the four skill areas has the learning objective of imitating the native speaker. The continual separation of the four skills lies at the core of research and testing in speaking, listening, reading, and writing.

Some current approaches to teaching language, however, strive to integrate the four skills in pedagogy whenever possible. Integrated language teaching and various integrated pedagogical paradigms are usually associated with outgrowths of communicative teaching. Relative to its predecessor, the audiolingual method, integrated teaching of the four skills represents a central innovation. On the other hand, in the United Kingdom, the path toward integrated teaching of the language skills did not derive from a strong audiolingual focus but rather from an evolution of older situational and functional teaching methods that were developed prior to and concurrent with the structural method in the United States. Current models of integrated language teaching are not without their shortfalls. Nor is integrated instruction appropriate in all contexts of language teaching and for all purposes of language learning. The advantages and disadvantages of integrated teaching may crucially determine its usefulness in second or foreign language contexts.

This chapter begins with a brief look at the historic and methodological reasons for the continual separation of the four skills in teaching. Modern-day perspectives on skill integration and integrated curriculum designs will also be discussed, together with problems and issues typically associated with integrated teaching. The chapter will then address the highly idiosyncratic and limited designs of major English language tests in the United Kingdom and the United States, as well as the indelible effect of tests on the separation of the four skills. The chapter concludes with an overview of the pedagogical and methodological currents in integrated language instruction.

How the Four Skills Became Separated

Contemporary methods for teaching second and foreign languages in the United States and the United Kingdom have followed two distinctly different routes, primarily due to the divergent histories of the two countries during the second half of the twentieth century. The reasons for separating or integrating the teaching of the four skills in the United States and the United Kingdom are reviewed in turn and in their historical contexts.

In the early 1940s and during World War II, a group of specialists under the auspices of the Linguistic Society of America were called on to develop effective, efficient, and intensive language teaching to members of the U.S. Armed Forces. Based on methods for linguistic field studies, and in keeping with the outline developed by Bloomfield (1942), the program worked with a wide range of languages, such as Chinese and Hungarian, and was designed for target language instruction in small classes of specially selected learners who were highly motivated. The students were tutored by native-speaking informants together with linguists whose task was to interpret the structural, lexical, and phonetic patterns of the language for teaching purposes. The learners then drilled the elicited systematic patterns of spoken language to replace their first-language "habits" with second language behaviors (Mitchell and Vidal, 2001).

In this way, following the principles of structural linguistics in conjunction with the prevailing behaviorist learning theories, the primacy of speaking skills was established in a famously successful language-teaching program. The instruction in, and the learning of, spoken patterns was accompanied by similar structure-based teaching and learning of listening skills, needed for conversing in a target language. Learning to read—or write—in another language was not a focus of the linguistic analyses or of teaching simply because these skills were not expected of the learners in their practical and required language uses in the field.

In a parallel development and in conjunction with teaching English as a second language in the United States, Charles Fries and his successor, Robert Lado, undertook to design a similar program—one solidly rooted in structural linguistics—intended to teach English as a second or foreign language. The implementation of the English language courses at the University of Michigan led to the creation of the first North American set of teaching materials incorporating the English sound system, common grammatical structures, and lexical patterns, excerpted from the available linguistic analyses (Fries, 1945, 1952). In accordance with the principles of structural linguistics, linguistic knowledge was methodically arranged for instruction in the first North American course of its kind. The structural separation of second language skills and the primacy of speaking served as a model for course and materials development. In later years, Robert Lado (1957, 1964) formalized methods for contrastive and structural analyses of languages and their application to the teaching and testing of discrete language skills. Lado's (1957) study was the first systematic application of contrastive analysis to curriculum development, preparing teaching materials and the discrete testing of such incremental language skills as phonemic discrimination, vocabulary, and grammar.

The structural and behaviorist approach to language teaching and learning, with an almost exclusive focus on speaking and grammar drills and listening comprehension, became known as the *oral method*, the *aural-oral method*, the *structural method*, and in the 1950s as the *audiolingual method*. Ellis (1990: 21) comments, however, that "audiolingualism was very much an American method. In its purist form it was never very popular in Britain and Europe, where less attention was paid to teaching the formal patterns of the second language and more to their situational uses." Nonetheless, Ellis continues, "Many of the audiolingual assumptions regarding the way language is learnt can be found in pedagogical prescriptions of British and European methodologists writing at this time."

In the United Kingdom, the separation of the four skills had to do with the utilitarian purposes of language teaching, rather than with matters of a particular methodology. According to Howatt and Widdowson (2004), in the United Kingdom, the period immediately after World War II was characterized by "continuation and consolidation rather than change" in English language teaching (ELT). Generally speaking, prior to the late 1950s, much of the British work in second or foreign language pedagogy was devoted to teaching English to school-age children in the colonies. Thus, teaching efforts were largely directed toward learners outside the United Kingdom without much prominence attached to listening and speaking skills, but with a primary instructional focus on learning grammar needed for translating written texts. The teaching of English as a second—rather than a foreign—language was conducted primarily in London, and second language teaching and learning there required listening and speaking skills, essential in basic communication and routine interactions.

In the 1960s, however, with the influx of foreign workers and students, as well as former colonials, British perspectives on ELT began to change. One of the top priorities in teaching English as both a second and foreign language lay in the need for specialized instruction for technical and highly trained personnel, for academic linguistic skills for college students, as well as for grade school teachers of the children of immigrants. The emerging learning needs of these new populations of learners brought about curricular and methodological work in two novel directions: English for specific purposes for technical and professional learners and English for academic purposes for university students. Thus, the language learning needs of specific groups of learners led to pivotal shifts in the types of language that were taught, but not necessarily in the specific skills that were taught. Howatt and Widdowson (2004: 247) comment that in the 1960s "history intervened in a somewhat dramatic way in the United Kingdom, creating a wholly new professional alignment." New and urgent demands arose for teaching the language needed in technical and academic fields, as well as for integrated teaching of the discrete skills.

To this end, in the United Kingdom, the emphasis on situational, rather than structural, language skills became predominant in the curricula, similar to the syllabi developed by A. S. Hornby in the 1950s. The *situational approach* (also called the *situational-structural method*, the *structural-situational approach*, or *situational language leaching*) resembled the pragmatic—and situationalized—version of the audiolingual method, with a primary emphasis on speaking and listening skills. These were, however, socially, rather than structurally, driven. According to Howatt and Widdowson (2004: 299–300), the principles underlying language instruction between the 1950s and 1970s postulated that "all four language skills (listening, speaking, reading, and writing) should be taught, but the spoken skills should be given priority."

Real-world situational contexts of instruction, with lessons built around specific topics, such as "at the post office," "at the doctor's," or "a visit to the theater," served as a backdrop for teaching language *chunks* and contextually relevant grammar and vocabulary. The emergence of the *situational approach* also gave rise to the classroom teaching technique currently known as *PPP* (presentation, practice, and production). The PPP model of instruction implies that learners can be guided from controlled practice of language features to free and automatic production of language in any or all of the four skills. By the end of the 1960s, however, many linguists and ELT methodologists arrived at the conclusion that the situational method was somewhat limited in scope and its interactional foci—in other words, speaking and listening—and did not provide clear principles that could guide curricula and instruction (Strevens, 1977).

Although Stern (1983: 167) called the 1960s "disorienting" in language teaching and new theories about language, the 1970s and 1980s ushered in humanistic approaches to language pedagogy in North America and in Europe. It should be noted, however, that in the United Kingdom the strongly pragmatic goal orientation in teaching the four skills and the impact of social factors on language usage continued to occupy a prominent place in ELT. (See, e.g., the work of Stevick and Widdowson published in the 1970s for thorough discussions.)

The introduction of the concept of *communicative competence* (Hymes, 1971, 1972) brought about a change in the perspectives on how language skills were to be taught and used for communication inside and outside of the classroom. Although not directly associated with language teaching per se, Hymes's work emphasized the key role of the social context in communication and the centrality of the sociolinguistic norms of appropriateness in speech communities and their cultures. Hymes was particularly interested in language as social behavior. New perspectives began to emerge that authentic representations and uses of language in the classroom were nearly impossible—particularly so within the established models associated with the audiolingual method. The structural separation of the four skills, pattern practice, error avoidance, and native-speaker imitation in second and foreign language production contrasted markedly with teaching language as a means of communication.

Communicative language teaching (CLT) places a great deal of value on teaching language skills with the goal of enabling learners to communicate meaningfully both inside and outside of the classroom, as in, for example, asking for information, seeking clarification, relying on circumlocution when necessary, and in general, negotiating meaning by all linguistic and nonlinguistic means at one's disposal. In their seminal publication on learners' coping strategies, Canale and Swain (1980) developed a three-component framework of language competence that learners needed to achieve: communicative competence, grammatical competence, and sociolinguistic competence. Canale and Swain's empirical findings demonstrated convincingly that practicing a range of language skills simultaneously and in the context of communication allowed learners to attain levels of grammatical competence similar to those achieved by students who concentrated on audiolingual structural patterns. In addition, however, the communicative competence of the learners who practiced their skills in interaction, measured in terms of language fluency, comprehensibility, and effort, substantively exceeded that of learners without comparable practice. As an outcome of this and other studies published at the time (e.g., Paulston, 1974; Savignon 1972, 1983), CLT and its subsequent methodological offshoots have presently come to dominate integrated approaches to teaching of the central four skills. (See also chapter 19 content-based language teaching chapter 23.)

Linguistic and Methodological Bases for Integrating the Four Skills

As early as the 1970s, many researchers and methodologists noted that the teaching of language skills cannot be conducted through isolable and discrete structural elements (Corder, 1971, 1978b; Kaplan, 1970; Stern, 1992). In reality, it is rare for language skills to be used in isolation; for example, both speaking and listening comprehension are needed in a conversation, and, in some contexts, reading or listening and making notes is likely to be almost as common as having a conversation. The central innovative characteristic of the communicative approach in second or foreign language teaching was the integration of the four macroskills and their components.

Widdowson (1978) was one of the first linguists to call for integrating the four language skills in instruction to raise learners' proficiency levels and enable advanced language learning. In his proposal for integrated and communicative language teaching in general and in particular in English for specific purposes, Widdowson emphasized that virtually all language uses take place in the form of discourse and in specific social contexts. Although he notes that the separated teaching of language skills is probably more administratively convenient, as in "divide and rule" (1978: 144), language comprehension and production does not in fact take place in discrete "units." Thus, to attain proficiency, learners need to develop receptive and productive skills in both spoken and written discourse. Widdowson's (1978) strong emphasis on the integration of the four skills, as well as discourse-based teaching, have had a considerable impact on the emergence of discourse-oriented curricula and teaching methods in English for specific purposes and English for academic purposes. Widdowson's (1978) and Halliday's (1978) early work and their insights into the importance of discourse in language usage provided highly influential theoretical foundations in linguistic analyses and language teaching. These works have led to the subsequent rise and prominence of content-based and integrated language instruction, especially in English as a second language in Australia, in the United Kingdom, and, to some extent in North America.

In the 1980s and 1990s, a great deal of elaboration and refinement took place in communicative and integrated teaching of the four skills. In light of the fact that opportunities for meaningful communication in the language classroom are limited—particularly so in the regions where English is taught as a foreign language—a great need arose for integrated communicative activities. These had to be interaction-centered and as authentic as possible to enable students to use the language for purposeful communication (Savignon, 1983, 1990). The need for integrated activities led to the evolution of task-based instruction that gained currency in the early to mid-1980s. (See chapters 22 and 23 for additional discussion.) At present, the ubiquitous language practice exercises for groups or pairs of learners typically combine listening and speaking, reading and speaking, or reading, writing, and speaking. Such integrated classroom activities (also called tasks) include, for example, listening to language tapes, playing games, or working on information gap and problem-solving exercises. These types of practice require learners to engage in interaction and integrated language usage because group or pair work can be carried out only if the participants share and discuss, or read and pool their information. Task-based teaching is probably the most widely adopted model of integrated language teaching today, and it is often considered to be the closest classroom simulation of real-life interaction.

In his highly acclaimed book, Nunan (1989) outlines the principles that should guide the design of teaching materials and modules for integrating a variety of language skills. (See also Willis, 1996, for another set of such principles.) According to Nunan, effective integrated modules are characterized by uses of authentic language models and exemplars, continuity of language work from comprehension to production, explicit connections of classroom language practice to real-world uses (e.g., a business presentation or a job interview), and a systematic language focus that enables learners to identify and analyze language regularities. In his later work on designing integrated syllabi, Nunan (2001) explains that the first step is to identify the contexts and situations in which learners will need to communicate. After the communicative events are identified in general terms, the next phase should work toward learners' functional goals along with the linguistic elements required to achieve them. According to Nunan, in integrated instruction, language skills are taught and practiced depending on the students' learning objectives, rather than in the context of the four separate instructional areas.

Key Considerations in Integrated Language Teaching and Curricula

Richards, Platt, and Weber (1985: 144) define the teaching of integrated skills in the *Longman Dictionary of Applied Linguistics*: "the teaching of the language skills of reading, writing, listening, and speaking in conjunction with each other as when a lesson involves activities that relate listening and speaking to reading and writing." There are several principled models for integrating the teaching of two or more language skills. Such models can vary substantially in their complexity and in the types of skills that can be integrated to benefit learning, and virtually all have their advantages and disadvantages in particular contexts.

The simplest and most basic type of integrated teaching incorporates the skills in the same language medium, either spoken to include listening and speaking or written to include reading and writing. A typical instructional paradigm found in many locations around the world deals with employing learners' receptive skills to provide input and modeling for productive skills. For instance, in the spoken medium, listening selections are used as models for speaking, interaction, or pronunciation skills, and in the written medium, reading input supplies models for writing.

More complex integrated curricula combine a range of language skills. For instance, instructional activities can bring together listening and reading input to promote speaking or writing, or to facilitate both speaking and writing. In complex integrated teaching methods, such as *text-based* (also called *genre-based*) language input materials are usually organized thematically. In this way, theme, register, and language content can be made consistent and cohesive to expose learners' to contextually linked vocabulary, relevant grammar constructions, and discourse organization features. For example, if the theme of the instructional materials has a focus on, say, weather, climate, or geography, then in speech or writing, the register is likely to be somewhat more formal than it would be in a module on friends and family. The vocabulary on weather and geography is bound to include common climate-related terms, and the grammar constructions are likely to deal with the present (but not the past) tenses, several kinds of adverb clauses, and locational prepositions.

In practically all methods and techniques geared toward integrated teaching, curricula typically include at least two essential teaching and learning objectives:

- Language features needed for communication and used in the context of communication
- Thematic and cohesive stretches of discourse for language input, rather than a focus on discrete vocabulary items, patterns, or grammar points

Discourse-based approaches to instruction afford learners an opportunity to focus on the linguistic and sociocultural features of organizing and presenting information in particular contexts. (See Kaplan 1997, 2001, 2005, for a more thorough analysis.) Teaching the language with a discourse focus also greatly facilitates an integration of a broad range of skills when incremental skills can be transferred from one aspect of language to another. For example, learning to organize and explain one's ideas in writing can prove to be highly useful in structuring oral presentations. Similarly, the language features—for example, vocabulary and grammar, associated with the formal register in speech—can also be applicable to constructing semiformal written text, such as an e-mail to a colleague. McCarthy (2001: 54) comments that transferability of skills from one type of discourse to another provides for "a greater integration of the traditional four skills in language teaching, where writing tasks might be 'spoken' in their mode, and vice versa."

It should be noted, however, that the teaching of integrated language skills can also have a number of disadvantages (e.g., McDonough and Shaw 2003; Widdowson, 1978, 1993, 2003). To begin with, a curriculum that concentrates on a single language skill at a time can permit more focused teaching and more intensive learning. Furthermore, in various regions and cultures in which the instruction in discrete language skills is highly valued, both teachers and learners have been known to resist skill integration (Richards and Rodgers, 2001). In such settings, integrated instruction may not be well suited to the local traditions of how teaching and learning are to be conducted.

Additionally, complex integrated instruction with more than two language skills addressed in tandem places greater demands on both the teacher and the learner. Curricula and syllabi that integrate a range of language skills require the teacher to be reasonably versatile and well trained. In most cases, the teachers need to be at least somewhat familiar with discourse-based instructional models, such as those noted earlier. At the same time, teachers can be expected to devote more time and effort to preparing materials appropriate for integrated instruction. In many regions around the world, where teachers are required to teach very large classes, the teaching of integrated skills may not be a very practical option.

Another notable disadvantage of integrated instruction is that many (if not most) learners have unevenly developed proficiencies across the four macroskills (Hinkel, 2002, 2003; Stern, 1983). For example, second language learners who live in English-speaking countries may have stronger skills in listening and speaking than in reading and writing. Conversely, English as a foreign language learners are likely to be better readers and writers than listeners and speakers. For this reason, the teaching of integrated skills can become complicated, when instructional materials and practice have to account for a considerable variance in learners' abilities. In complex integrated teaching, a frequent tendency is for a particular language skill or set of skills to receive less attention than learners' proficiencies might require. In light of the fact that the integrated curricula concentrate primarily on purposeful communication and meaning making, typically, the teaching of grammar and vocabulary, as well as accuracy in learner language production, may receive less emphasis than they should (J. C. Richards, 2005). Some experts and methodological authorities also contend that integrated language teaching with its main focus on the learning process tends to overlook the quality of the learning product (e.g., Swan, 2005; Widdowson, 1990, 2003).

LANGUAGE TESTS AND TESTING OF THE FOUR SKILLS

It seems reasonable to expect that the methodological currents in language testing would follow those prevalent in language teaching. However, the evolution of major standardized tests has not coincided with the shifts and developments in teaching. In the 1960s, the newly emerging standardized tests of English as a foreign language were constructed in keeping with the prevailing influence of structural linguistics and the audiolingual method. At that time, standardized English language tests were designed to assess learners' proficiencies in the skills considered to be important for the overall mastery of the language. These incremental skills included sound discrimination and listening comprehension, conversational and idiomatic expressions, grammatical and structural knowledge, and vocabulary needed for reading comprehension. In line with the standards in psychometric measurements of the time, to ensure their reliability and validity, language tests consisted of large numbers of discrete-point multiple-choice items.

Generally speaking, the design of discrete-point tests (also called discrete-item tests) assumes that language proficiency and its measurements encompass an array of components, such as speaking, listening, reading, and writing and their smaller increments—for example, the sound system, vocabulary, clause- and phrase-level grammar, or morphology (word forms and word grammar; see, e.g., Bachman, 1990; Bachman and Palmer, 1996; Brindley, 2001; for earlier discussions, see D. P. Harris, 1969; Jones and Spolsky, 1975; Lado, 1961; Northeast Conference on the Teaching of Foreign Language, 1962; Oller and Perkins, 1978; Valette, 1977). These incremental units of language—in other words, the discrete points—have been the backbone of language testing for the more than a century in practically all regions of the world.

In the United Kingdom, the shift in the prevailing methodology was prominently reflected in the design of language tests. The British English language examinations, such as the University of Cambridge Local Examinations Syndicate (UCLES), were revised to make them communicative and integrated. However, these tests were famously unreliable and error-prone. According to Spolsky (1995b), for example, written compositions were marked subjectively, listening comprehension was scored by clerical personnel according to a key, and the speaking segments of the examinations were rated locally wherever they were administered across several dozens of examination sites around the world.In fact, Spolsky refers to three sources of measurement error:

1. A lack of consistency in the discrete-point listening and reading comprehension sections with consistency coefficients so low as to make them statistically invalid
2. Subjective marking of compositions without a means of establishing rater consistency
3. A high degree of variation in different forms of the test and of examiners' scoring methods

To some degree, the complex integrative and communicative nature of the examinations, the complexities of their interconnected design, and the administration and scoring procedures also caused a substantial amount of variation in test scores. As a result, UCLES examinations scores were frequently seen as markedly unreliable and inconsistent (Bachman and Palmer, 1996). After several studies and attempts to make Cambridge examinations more consistent and equivalent across the forms and ratings, the integrative connections between the reading and the speaking segments were removed in 1989, and between the reading and the writing modules in 1995. The examination flyer announced that both changes were widely welcomed by teachers and students.

Spolsky (1995a: 341) notes sardonically, "UCLES managed for a long time to resist the claims of objective testing," just as the Educational Testing Service that constructs, administers, and scores language tests in North America "managed to hold off the claims of integrative communicative testing for some decades." Test design in North America did not adapt to the shift from discrete-point testing of vocabulary, grammar, and listening comprehension until 2005, and even then, the integration of vocabulary testing went only as far as being incorporated in the reading comprehension section. As an outcome, since the 1970s, important philosophical and practical disparities have remained between the objectives of integrated language teaching and the methods of language testing; that is, if the goal of communicative language teaching is to enable learners to communicate meaningfully and appropriately in various contexts then, clearly, discrete-point tests are inadequate and unsuitable for measuring learners' communication abilities. For example, Paulston and Bruder (1975) argued that in real-life interaction, there is always more than one way of effectively accomplishing a speaker's communicative goals. On the other hand, even in carefully designed test items, there is only one correct answer, and such an approach to testing that seems to resemble "the cue-response pattern" (1975: 15) conflicts with the very purpose of teaching language for communication.

When communicative language teaching became the gold standard, the disconnect between the foci of integrated instruction and the means of testing language proficiency, as well as the mastery of communicative skills, gave rise to strong demands for similarly integrative tests and testing. It was at that time that innovative types of language tests were created for the purposes of institutional or local assessment; for example, dictation tests that integrate listening and writing abilities, or cloze tests that integrate vocabulary, grammar, and discourse skills (see, for example, Oller, 1979; Oller and Perkins, 1978, 1980). In the 1970s and 1980s, a number of integrative testing models were proposed for indirect measurements of learners' overall general proficiency and communicative competence. However, after a series of experimental studies, such test designs did not prove to be valid in different contexts for a variety of reasons.

For instance, research on proficiency measurements in various regions of the world—for example, Brazil and the Philippines—demonstrated convincingly that language proficiency was not a unitary trait, but that proficiency consists of complex and multifaceted linguistic and communicative components (e.g., Cohen, 1994; Farhady, 1982). Research in students' language performance found that the mastery of one language skill does not necessarily translate to competencies in any other skills. Furthermore, a great deal of evidence was obtained to show that overall language proficiency cannot be adequately assessed by means of indirect tests; for example, a successful performance on an integrative vocabulary and grammar test has little to say about a learner's writing abilities. Consequently, the separation of the four skills and the reliance on testing discrete skills has been considered essential for accurate measurements of learners' language proficiency—or subsets of proficiencies. For example, an individual can have excellent listening comprehension skills but a comparatively low speaking ability, and, as most teachers know from experience, having had a great deal of grammar practice does not necessarily lead learners to writing well.

Language tests and assessment instruments have remained largely unaltered in their separation of the four skills since at least the 1960s. In the 1990s and early 2000s, a few modifications have been made to provide at least some degree of integration in writing, grammar, and vocabulary in North American standardized tests. For instance, overt and direct testing of discrete grammar points has been eliminated, and assessments of grammar mastery are now embedded in the essay tests, similar to the incorporation of vocabulary testing in reading comprehension tests. By and large, however, language testing methods and test designs have continued to rely on the separation of the four skills and skill subsets probably because a better model for measuring language abilities has not yet been discovered. A fundamental issue in language testing is that the skills needed for communication and communicative competence seem to be enormous in their range and scope. There is little doubt, however, that the dichotomy between communicative—and integrated—language teaching and discrete-point language testing has had an indelible effect on the continued separation of the four skills in pedagogy, research, curricular models, and teacher training (e.g., Hinkel, 2004; A. Hughes, 2003; Stern, 1992). One of the greatest ironies associated with integrated teaching is that language proficiency testing—and hence much of the administrative gatekeeping— has remained discrete-point-based. Not surprisingly, though, not all learners set out to learn another language in order to do well on tests.

CURRENT PERSPECTIVES ON INTEGRATED TEACHING

With the spread of English as a lingua franca and as the medium for worldwide dissemination of information and knowledge, in many cases, the pragmatic objectives of language learning underscore the importance of integrated and flexible instruction. In many regions around the world, learning English has the objective of enabling learners to gain access to social, vocational, educational, or professional opportunities (Celce-Murcia, 2001; Kaplan, 1986, 1988, 1991). In common perspectives on contemporary language curricula, teaching reading is typically connected to instruction on writing and vocabulary, teaching writing can be easily tied to reading and grammar, and speaking skills readily lend themselves to teaching listening, pronunciation, and cross-cultural pragmatics (Hinkel, 1999, 2001).

According to Richards and Rodgers (2001: 165), integrated language instruction that engages learners in meaningful communication and enables them to attain their learning objectives can be found in an "unlimited" array of models, teaching materials, and techniques. Such integrated models with a communicative and contextualized focus include the following: content-based (sometimes also called theme-based), task-based, text-based (also called genre-based), discourse-based, project-based, network-based, technology-based, corpus-based, interaction-based, literature-based, literacy-based, community-based, competency-based, or standards-based.

With the current emphasis on both fluency and accuracy in language production, it seems clear, however, that integrated language teaching and learning, as well as integrative instructional models, will need to continue to be refined and developed (e.g., Breen, 2001; Swain, 1991). For instance, exposure to and experience with L2 speaking and meaningful interaction, but without the benefit of explicit and focused instruction, leads to learners' developing high degrees of fluency but not necessarily accuracy and advanced L2 proficiency (e.g., Lightbown and Spada, 1990; Swain, 1991).

In regard to communication-oriented principles that guide much of integrated language teaching, critics have contended that with its focus on communication in interaction, second or foreign language instruction frequently lacks depth and substance. As Howatt and Widdowson (2004) note, naturalistic and integrated language learning tends to meet the communicative needs that people would have as tourists in, for example, simple service transactions and casual conversational exchanges. Widdowson (2003: 24) explains, for instance, that "coping with written language is also a communicative objective," but the contemporary focus on face-to-face encounters lacks a teaching focus on "an understanding of writing, literary and otherwise, of the past." He also points out that outside English-speaking areas where English is taught as a school subject, current methodologists would do well to consider "what kind of language is to be specified for the subject to fulfill its educational objective" (2003: 27).

On the other hand, in recent years, standards- and outcomes-based language teaching curricula have become one of the foremost educational priorities in a number of English-speaking nations. To this end, innovative integrated methodological models have been proposed to concentrate on advancing learner proficiencies in a range of language skills. Specifically, the objectives of these models are geared toward clearly defined language competencies that students need to achieve within the educational system. Stern (1992) is to be credited with the first set of guidelines for an integrated curriculum that address the major goal of advancing students' language proficiency. His model effectively combines the learning of the central language skills with the achievement-oriented syllabus in culture learning, communicative skills, and general education. Stern also notes (1992: 76) that "as useful expressions of proficiency, however, the 'four skills' continue to be important categories in language pedagogy."

In Canada, for example, the instructional model is based on Stern's "proficiency as competence" (1992: 73) and on communicative competence together with "the mastery of such skills as listening, speaking, reading and writing." Canadian Language Benchmarks and common sets of proficiency standards have been a recognized success in nationwide second language teaching. Canadian language assessments and national achievement standards also account for the fact that many learners' language proficiencies vary from skill to skill. In part, the effectiveness of the Canadian achievement-oriented curriculum can be attributed to its design supporting learners with different levels of mastery in the four skills (Breen, 2001). Other types of integrated syllabi are currently adopted in national educational movements and in the United States, Australia, and New Zealand. These standards-based curricula reflect an ongoing work in the refinement and elaboration of integrated instruction that can raise learners' language proficiency and the quality of production in the contexts of real-life communication. (See, e.g., McDonough and Shaw, 2003 for detailed discussion.)

CONCLUSION

In the past several decades, much evidence has emerged that, in order for learners to attain language competence, teaching needs to integrate linguistic and communicative skills. The overarching goal of integrated instruction is to advance learners' language proficiency required for communication in various contexts. In general, the learning of language for communication in both speaking and writing entails achieving mastery in discourse, language strategies, sociocultural and interactional norms, and the communicative culture of the people who use the language (Stern, 1992). Today, after decades of research in language teaching and learning, it seems clear that in many cases and for many purposes, the separation of the four macroskills is likely to be less effective than integrated instruction simply because, in reality, communication does not take place in terms of discrete linguistic skills.

The early models of integrated and communicative teaching largely eschewed explicit instruction in any of the four skills, and in particular in grammar. Typically, the teaching of reading was integrated with writing, and listening with speaking. Classroom instruction concentrated predominantly on activities and interactions—for example, on games, role-plays, skits, and problem solving in groups or pairs of learners. These exercises sought to promote authentic language usage with the goal of developing learners' fluency. The overarching objective of integrated and thematic language input was to facilitate language acquisition naturalistically. At the time, the purpose of engaging with language in classroom interactions was to enable learners to attain communicative competence. By and large, learners' engagement in integrated communicative activities without deliberate teaching led to incidental learning of such various linguistic features as conversational expressions, vocabulary associated with daily and routine interactions, and informal reading and writing skills (Hinkel, 2006).

In the mid-1990s, a number of studies found that many years of exposure to and immersion in integrated classroom instruction does in fact lead to the development of language fluency. It also became clear, however, that learners' productive language lacked accuracy and sociocultural appropriateness, in other words, advanced communicative competence that the integration of language skills in teaching sought to achieve (e.g., Lightbown and Spada, 1990; Swain, 1991).

The current models of integrated teaching of the four language skills have the objective of developing learners' fluency and accuracy, as well as their sociocultural communicative competence requiring adapting the language from context to context and from genre to genre. In light of the fact that at the present time English is widely employed as the medium of international communication, it seems easy to predict that integrated language teaching will continue to dominate among the various types of pedagogical models. There is little doubt, however, that the evolution and change of integrated teaching models and methods will remain one of the main—if not the main—defining characteristics of language teaching around the world.

PART III

DISCOURSE ANALYSIS

CHAPTER 9

DISCOURSE ANALYSIS AND APPLIED LINGUISTICS

DEBORAH POOLE AND
BETTY SAMRAJ

Since their initial convergence in the 1970s, the relationship of discourse analysis and applied linguistics has been a fluid and multifaceted one, driven by a variety of theoretical perspectives across an increasingly diverse range of contexts. From its initial—and still largely central—focus on second language learning, applied linguistics is now more widely seen as relevant to any real-world, language-related problem that an interdisciplinary, as opposed to purely linguistic, approach can address (e.g., Brumfit, 1997a; Gunnarsson, 1997; Widdowson, 1980). With an explosion of work over the past 2 decades, this wider perspective has been realized with more frequency throughout the discipline (Kramsch, 2000). The expanded focus has resulted in closer ties with discourse analysis, as applied linguists have recognized its potential to specify how language is integral to the constitution and maintenance of complex social phenomena. Accordingly, discourse analysis has increasingly become a methodology of choice for investigating such broader concerns in applied linguistics as the language of education, politics, professions, and community settings.

The following discussion focuses on some of the varied contexts and strands of discourse analysis methodology as they have developed in applied linguistics. To begin, we focus on ways that discourse analysis has been employed in the traditional second language focused areas of applied linguistics. Though narrower than the whole, this work remains one of the most fully developed areas of interface between the two areas (cf. Kaplan and Widdowson, 1992) and is itself characterized by considerable variation in terms of what counts as discourse analysis and the purposes for which it is used.

LANGUAGE LEARNING AND DISCOURSE ANALYSIS

Discourse analysis initially converged with L2 concerns in relation to a variety of subfields in applied linguistics, especially, communicative language teaching, English for specific purposes, contrastive rhetoric, classroom-based research, and interlanguage pragmatics. Across these areas of inquiry or application, applied linguists drew from multiple perspectives associated with the analysis of language use: speech act theory, functional linguistics, conversation analysis, the ethnography of speaking, and text linguistics (see, e.g., Coulthard, 1977; Hatch, 1992; Hatch and Long, 1980; Widdowson, 1978). Hence, the types of analyses have varied widely and included a range of foci such as the following:

- Form-function relations of grammatical features
- Lexical and grammatical characteristics of texts
- Written text structure
- Sequential organization of talk in speech activities
- Frequency, scope, and distribution of specific interactional sequences or speech acts

Throughout these domains and types of L2 discourse inquiry, one unifying feature has been the goal of drawing pedagogical implications from a research base in actual language use. Through a focus on learner goals—or the target discourses that learners *aim for*—communicative language teaching (CLT) and its related movements led to the most significant initial influences of discourse analysis on second language teaching. Early CLT, especially in the oral/aural domain, strove for a pedagogical "authenticity" that paralleled speech events and activities beyond the classroom setting, thus necessitating understanding and analysis of such authentic, nonclassroom contexts. In developing prescriptions for syllabi and pedagogy to reflect this concern, language teaching theory turned to perspectives focused on language use in interactional settings beyond the classroom, especially to the work of Austin (1962), Searle (1969), Halliday (1978), and Hymes (1971). As widely documented, speech act theory in particular motivated the development of functional-notional syllabi, which in turn were appropriated by a more broadly focused communicative approach drawing from Hymes's notion of communicative competence and the Hallidayan perspective of language as a system of meaning potential through which individuals and communities fulfill their communicative purposes.[1]

The tenets and methodologies of the communicative approach arguably still constitute the dominant paradigm in English language teaching and in much L2 teaching in general. However, although pedagogical theory in CLT was initially based on existing theories and analyses of discourse, it was not tied to a well-articulated research agenda. The consequence was that, over time, the original link between discourse analysis and the communicative teaching of spoken language receded in importance, and comparative analyses of recommended classroom practices, as well as the authentic communication on which they are purportedly based, have been less common than the original CLT theorists might have hoped.

Discourse Analysis and English for Specific Purposes

A contrast to the relationship of spoken discourse analysis and L2 classroom teaching can be found in developments in the literatures of language for specific purposes (LSP). Swales (2000), in an overview chapter on LSP, traces the "descriptive base for pedagogical materials" in this subfield of applied linguistics to an early call to provide linguistic studies of specialized registers for language teaching by three British linguists (Halliday, McIntosh, and Strevens, 1964, referred to in Swales, 2000). The field of English for specific purposes (ESP), a prominent part of LSP, has been characterized by a steady stream of systematic analyses of the sorts of discourses produced in the target communities to which EAP/ESP students are seeking membership. The nature and foci of such discourse analyses have varied over the past 40 years, with early studies focusing on grammatical and lexical elements (Dudley-Evans and St. John 1998), followed by a shift to research on the organization of genres in terms of rhetorical moves, leading to a renewed interest in lexical and grammatical features of texts produced for specific purposes through use of corpus analytic tools (see the chapter by Leki elsewhere in this volume).

As Belcher (2004: 166–167) notes in her recent overview of trends in teaching ESP, "The means and ends of ESP and genre studies are so similar that it is difficult to disentangle the two, [and, in fact, m]any in ESP would argue that genre analysis is a tool of ESP." It is therefore not surprising that most studies of the discourses of target communities employ some form of genre analysis.[2] Swales's (1990) classic monograph, *Genre Analysis*, and earlier work on the structure of research articles can be argued to have inspired a substantial number of studies of the genre structure of academic and nonacademic written and spoken genres, although the bulk of the studies have focused on written academic genres. Overall, greater attention has also been placed on written rather than spoken genres. These genre studies have tended to identify the rhetorical moves that characterize the ways texts fulfill their communicative purposes and the constituent steps or moves, which spell out "more specifically the rhetorical means of realizing the function" of a move (Yang and Allison, 2003: 370). Another essential component of these genre analyses is the lexical and grammatical realization of these rhetorical moves (see, e.g., Lim, 2006: 370).

As noted earlier, corpus analytic techniques have also facilitated the sorts of discourse analyses not common in early ESP research. Instead of a focus on rhetorical moves and the overall organization of genres, focus has shifted to a consideration of lexico-grammatical features such as reporting clauses and metadiscoursal elements in an endeavor to explore discourse issues such as hedging and writer stance (Charles, 2006; Hyland, 2005). Another recent development within genre analysis has been a consideration of related genres that members of a discourse community might engage in both "receptively and productively" (Swales, 2004: 20). The relationship across genres that belong to genre sets and more complex genre networks, described as "the totality of genres available for a particular sector" (Swales, 2004: 22), has also been explored in terms of discourse structure. Such analyses have revealed, for instance, the relationship between published research articles and graduate student dissertations (e.g., Dong, 1998; Thompson, 1999), and research article introductions and abstracts (Samraj, 2005).

Due mostly to the influence of studies from an area within composition referred to as new rhetoric (Hyon, 1996), more recent genre analyses conducted within ESP have given social context a more significant role in the discourse analyses performed. Studies of academic discourse in particular have been richly informed by the views of disciplinary experts and an acknowledgment of the heteroglossia inherent in the discourses produced in the academy (e.g., Hyland, 2000; Prior, 1998; Samraj, 2005).

The underlying pedagogical motivation for the large number of careful discourse analyses of genres produced in target discourse communities for which students are being prepared has led to the creation of materials strongly influenced by the results of such analyses especially in the last 15 years. This direct relation is perhaps best seen in the volumes by Swales and Feak (2000, 2004 [second edition of 1994]), where, for example, the results of extensive analyses on the structure of research article introductions have been transformed into a set of useful pedagogical materials, intended to raise the rhetorical consciousness of students. These materials reflect findings not only on the rhetorical move level but also those from the lexico-grammatical level. Studies indicating the discourse variations across genres have prompted such key ESP scholars as Flowerdew (1993) and Johns (1997, 2002) to advocate that EAP students be trained to discover the discursive practices of their own disciplinary communities. The effects of genre-based instruction on reading and writing development (e.g., A. Henry and Roseberry, 1998; Hyon, 2001, 2002; Swales and Lindemann, 2002) have received serious attention only in recent years. These studies have provided growing support for the efficacy of such instructional methods as well as a more nuanced understanding of the sorts of literacy developments that students exposed to such instruction undergo (Cheng, 2007, 2008a, 2008b).

Discourse Analysis and Contrastive Rhetoric

Research in contrastive rhetoric (Connor, 1996; Kaplan, 1966, 2005), which includes some of the earliest connections between discourse analysis and applied linguistics, represents a complementary body of work that has, over time, become more closely linked to ESP/LSP. Because of its aim to contribute to the teaching of ESL and EFL writing, many studies in contrastive rhetoric over the last 30 years have been discourse analyses of ESL and EFL student writing, contrastive studies of academic and professional genres, and studies of the acculturation of L2 writers into academic and professional communities. The overlap in the pedagogical aims of ESP and contrastive rhetoric can be seen as reason for the growing convergence of research methodologies in ESP and contrastive rhetoric. In particular, recent research in contrastive rhetoric has also included the analysis of various academic and professional genres and considerations of the social contexts that give rise to these genres (Connor, 2004). Although the field of study was characterized by "more or less decontextualized text analytic models" (Connor, 2002: 496) in the 1980s, the last 20 years have seen a greater use of genre analysis, corpus linguistics, and ethnographic approaches (Connor, 2004: 294). As Connor (2002: 506) points out, the "increasingly context-sensitive research approach often involves studying the talk that surrounds text production and interpretations as well as writing processes and written products themselves." The change in discourse analytic methodologies employed has been paralleled by a change in the kinds of discourses analyzed, with a growing interest in contrastive analysis of particular genres, such as the book review or letter of recommendation, instead of analyses of student texts, which characterized earlier studies.

DISCOURSE ANALYSIS AND INSTRUCTION IN L2 SPOKEN INTERACTION

Consideration of ESP/LSP and contrastive rhetoric approaches highlights the fact that for purposes of L2 pedagogy, discourse analysis research has traditionally focused more on written language, though a renewed focus on spoken language has taken hold in recent years. The comparatively greater focus of discourse analysis and the teaching of writing can be viewed in light of the classroom as a social context. Written genres, including those typical of nonschool settings, can be taught *through* the practice of routine classroom interaction, so that the norms of classroom speaking are largely unaffected. In spoken language instruction, however, inherent differences characterize the authentic language representing the goals of instruction and the authentic interactional environment of the classroom (cf. Ellis, 1990; Sinclair, 1987; Widdowson, 1978). The analysis of classroom discourse has the potential to address this contradiction by revealing how communicative tasks affect interaction and, in turn, how that interaction compares with traditional activities or more authentic contexts beyond the classroom. However, until recently, the fundamental characteristics of classroom discourse and its realizations in foreign and second language settings were largely marginal to mainstream L2 pedagogical concerns.

A sizable body of classroom discourse work (e.g., Cazden, 1987; 2001; Mehan, 1979; Nassaji and Wells, 2000; Sinclair and Coulthard, 1975) has existed for some time, however, some of which is directly focused on the L2 context (Coulthard, 1977; Duff, 1995, 2002a; Hall and Walsh, 2002; Lin, 1999; Riggenbach, 1999; Rymes, 2003a; Sinclair, 1987; Van Lier, 1988). These and numerous other studies acknowledge the basic IRF sequence of classroom interaction[3]—what Cazden has termed the "default" script, in that it is "what happens unless deliberate action is taken to achieve some alternative" (1987: 53). In the default script, the teacher constructs the overwhelming proportion of initiating and responding turns, as well as framing utterances that function to bring the activity into being, move it forward, and draw it to a close. The teacher also has the right to determine when and how to relinquish the floor to a student, as well as to select which student can respond. In such a sequence, the student's verbal role can be a limited one (i.e., a response to the teacher's initiation), so that the full repertoire of communicative acts needed for L2 competence becomes, for all practical purposes, difficult to practice and thus unlikely to be achieved.

For CLT, the relevance of the default pattern similarly lies in its differences from interaction beyond the classroom—exactly the sort CLT tries to teach in the name of authenticity. In face-to-face conversation, initiations and responses are shared between and among interlocutors, a speaker can select him- or herself as next speaker, and a single turn often includes both a response and subsequent initiation (Sacks, Schegloff and Jefferson, 1974). Hence, in classrooms, the dispreference for student self-selection as next speaker, the low proportion of student initiation turns, and the unlikelihood of a student responding and initiating in the same utterance mark the interaction as fundamentally distinct from most nonclassroom (or "authentic") talk (Cazden, 2001; Goldenberg and Patthey-Chavez, 1995; Nassaji and Wells, 2000).

Hints of this mismatch emerged in at least one early study (Long and Sato 1983), which found that interaction in communicative classrooms bore little resemblance to conversations but was characterized by more typical teacher-talk features such as display questions.[4] As a result, Long and Sato suggested that "contrary to the recommendations of many writers on SL teaching methodology, communicative use of the target language makes up only a minor part of typical classroom activities. 'Is the clock on the wall?' and 'Are you a student?' are still the staple diet, at least for beginners" (1983: 280). Seen in light of the differences between the default pattern of classroom interaction and the characteristic features of face-to-face interaction, however, the findings of Long and Sato are not surprising, given that the teachers in their study acted appropriately according to the norms of classroom speech activities (cf. Byon, 2006; Duff, 1995; Poole, 1992).

The attempt in CLT to facilitate language learning useful for nonclassroom contexts has most often been represented through the use of role plays, jigsaw activities, and various types of pair and small-group work, because these allow students to assume interactional roles outside those afforded by the default script. The problem, however—reminiscent of the caution offered by A. M. Johns and Dudley-Evans (1991)—is that much of CLT practice draws from materials developers' intuitive notions of interaction beyond the classroom but is not tied to a research base in the analysis of spoken discourse. Attempts to address this situation are found in the work of a few pedagogical theorists, such as Burns (1998; see also Burns and Moore, 2008), who proposes clusters of pedagogical activities (both spoken and written) based on sets of activities linked in contexts beyond the classroom (such as making a doctor's appointment and taking a prescription to the pharmacist).

Others—such as Nunan (1991), Duff (1993), and Kinginger and Savignon (1991)— have investigated the interactional and pedagogical effects of task design. However, this body of work has not yet achieved the critical mass necessary to provide clear implications for practice. The substantial work that *does* exist in the area of L2 class-room-based research has, until recently, been less concerned with pedagogy than with what classroom practices will motivate second language acquisition (SLA). The result is that the findings have largely been addressed in the SLA rather than in the pedagogical literature, without a significant impact on L2 classroom practice, despite the impressive efforts of some (e.g., Chaudron, 1988; R. Ellis, 1990; Van Lier, 1988) to link the two.

Discourse Analysis in Classroom-Based Research

For a number of years, L2 classroom-based discourse analysis was not only focused on SLA, but was motivated primarily by the question of whether the interactional modifications of L2 learners or their interlocutors would promote acquisition of the target language (Doughty and Pica, 1986; Pica, 1987; see chapter by Gass else-where in this volume). This work has focused on phenomena such as clarification requests, confirmation checks, repair sequences, and, more recently, recasts. Perhaps due to its greater focus on acquisition than on pedagogy, this substantial body of L2 classroom-based research has had surprisingly little effect on classroom practice. For example, one of the most widely cited findings (Doughty and Pica, 1986) is that *two-way* tasks (such as information gap or jigsaw activities) promote more interac-tional modifications than *one-way* tasks (such as decision making and problem solving) and are therefore preferable.[5] However, pedagogical recommendations for L2 speaking or interactional activities (e.g., P. Gibbons, 2002; Nunan, 1991; Ur, 1996) have seldom recommended one task type over the other, stressing instead the importance of task variation. In addition, even a cursory survey of current text-books reveals little preference for so-called two-way tasks.

The goal of locating interactional modifications in the types of SLA-driven discourse studies referred to here has necessitated a form of discourse analysis based on quantification of predetermined categories such as recasts or response turns. As a whole, it is also grounded in the common input-output metaphor of SLA research. In both senses, it differs from a second, growing strand of spoken discourse analysis that has now taken a more prominent role, largely eclipsing the SLA-focused interactional research as the center of discourse analysis research in applied linguistics. This second strand takes a qualitative approach to spoken data, viewing interaction as the joint, embedded activity of all coparticipants. It aims to avoid imposing predetermined analytical categories, identifying them instead through a process involving repeated readings of transcript data, often triangulated with such other qualitative data as ethnographic observations, interviews, or situational artifacts.

NEW DIRECTIONS IN INTERACTIONAL AND CLASSROOM-BASED RESEARCH

In recent years, as the balance of L2 classroom discourse studies has shifted away from the SLA-oriented quantitative approach, the scope and depth of qualitative interactional analyses have increased. This newer work investigates L2 classrooms, and the second language experience more generally, without the motive of locating interactional modifications or even of relating its findings to SLA theory and research. Hence, it represents a major departure from the SLA-motivated study of talk in second language classrooms and offers a new orientation to the link between analysis of spoken discourse and second language classroom-related issues as well as to a range of complex phenomena linked to the L2 experience (e.g., cultural expectations and practices, and issues related to bilingualism and the immigrant experience). Moreover, within applied linguistics, classroom-based research is becoming less focused on the clearly identified L2 classroom, reflecting the increasingly diverse contexts within which much contemporary second language learning occurs.

Like the earlier connections of applied linguistics and discourse analysis, this more recent qualitative work in classroom discourse research is grounded in a variety of theoretical and methodological perspectives and hence does not represent a fully unified orientation. However, regardless of theoretical motivation, the majority of such work builds on and incorporates the findings of the early seminal studies in classroom discourse (Cazden, 1987; Sinclair and Coulthard, 1975) and constitutive ethnography (Mehan, 1979) previously mentioned. For example, work by scholars such as Boyd and Maloof (2000), Goldenberg and Patthey-Chavez (1995), Hall (1998), Hall and Walsh (2002), Nassaji and Wells (2000), Nystrand (1997), and Wells (1993) has focused on the issue of tripartite or IRF interaction and the ways in which, given its near universal occurrence, it can be employed effectively in ways that support student learning. Rymes (in press) takes knowledge of classroom discourse research, in fact, to be a resource for teachers' pedagogical development. This body of research, though it draws from a range of theoretical perspectives, seems to take effective pedagogy as a primary goal and focus of inquiry. Moreover, these studies represent a range of settings that cannot be neatly divided into L1 and L2 research contexts. Many, for example, are situated in contexts with high percentages of diverse immigrant and bilingual students (e.g., Duff, 2002b; Zappa-Hollman, 2007; Zuengler, 2003) in which it might be difficult to find a class with all interaction conducted in the L1 of any particular group of students. Hence, the increasingly prominent work in classroom discourse analysis can also be seen as a reflection of the growing scope of applied linguistics beyond the second language teaching/learning experience.

In addition, although multiple perspectives and methodologies underlie this work, it is unified in its assumption that language use is inextricably linked with features of context. In essence, this view considers language and context to be mutually constitutive phenomena (Goodwin and Duranti, 1992), although perspectives on relevant contextual features vary widely. On the one hand, a range of approaches assume that broader (i.e., institutional, historical, ideological, or cultural) dimensions of context are reflected and sustained through features of language use. At the other end of the spectrum, conversation analysis considers the most relevant contextual features to include gesture, gaze, bodily orientation, and the turn-by-turn unfolding of a sequence of talk. Both perspectives, however, represent a departure from earlier discourse research within applied linguistics. More expansive approaches such as language socialization, for example, consider multiple layers of context in much broader ways than the traditional approach to discourse in applied linguistics. Moreover, they take the notions of discourse community and the social embeddedness of language as relevant to both spoken *and* written language, as well as to ways they interact. In these ways, current spoken discourse analysis also echoes the trends in genre analysis and contrastive rhetoric previously noted.

CONVERSATION ANALYSIS IN APPLIED LINGUISTICS

Conversation analysis (CA), since the mid-1990s, has become one of the increasingly influential paradigms in applied linguistics research, often in L2 classroom contexts but recently as applied to SLA as well. Because CA did not evolve within linguistics and often rejects traditional linguistic categories, it has typically been distinguished from discourse analysis (e.g., Levinson, 1983). Moreover, CA research typically does not incorporate or blend with other recent influential perspectives in applied linguistics such as language socialization or sociohistorical theory (cf. Hall, 2007). Given its complexities, even a cursory overview of CA is beyond the scope of this chapter, but a comprehensive discussion of the methodology in relation to applied linguistics is available in Schegloff et al. (2002).

A major strand of CA in applied linguistics focuses on interaction in such common L2 activities as small group work (Frazier, 2007; Mori, 2004; Olsher, 2004) and teacher-student writing conferences (Koshik, 2002). This work seeks to understand at an in-depth, local, fine-grained level what constitutes student experiences in common L2 pedagogical practices. In some instances, these studies have important implications for common conceptions or practices related to L2 instruction. Y. A. Lee (2006) and Koshik (1999), for example, consider how display questions can assist student performance in teacher-student writing conferences, thus calling into question their traditional negative treatment in applied linguistics. Recently, CA has also been considered as a methodology for investigation of SLA. Although this is somewhat controversial (Larsen-Freeman, 2004; Mori, 2007), a growing number of researchers are either exploring the possibility of "CA-for-SLA" (e.g., Kasper, 2006) or incorporating CA methodology for the purpose of longitudinal studies of particular learners (Markee, 2008).

CULTURAL DIMENSIONS AND PERSPECTIVES

Another major development of the past decade has been an increase in the focus on classroom interaction from a cross-cultural perspective. Early on, Chick (1988) argued for the importance of understanding classroom interactional differences across cultures but lamented that the research perspectives and methodologies employed in applied linguistics "tend to be narrow" (Chick, 1988: 3). His analysis focused on student choral responses in a KwaZulu classroom and grew from his participation in a CLT program dedicated to the improvement of English language teaching in South Africa. From his perspective, this program tended to view existing teaching practices as incompatible with (and inferior to) those advocated in CLT. Chick considered the chorusing practices from the perspective of politeness theory (P. Brown and Levinson, 1988) and pointed to their role in satisfying wider sociocultural norms for preserving face. He called upon applied linguists to view such phenomena with deeper understanding of their underlying dimensions rather than with a "deficit" perspective toward practices seemingly at odds with communicative ideology (cf. Chick, 1996; Poole, 1992).

The sort of cross-cultural perspective recommended by Chick, though slow to develop, is being realized with increasing frequency in recent applied linguistics research. In one of the most significant studies to encourage more cross-cultural focus, Duff (1995) analyzed language in a dual-language program in Hungary, documenting the changing interactional characteristics of a recitation event and linking them to the rapid sociopolitical changes characteristic of the school's wider context. L. C. Chen's (1999) study of Chinese TEFL classrooms recalled Chick's in considering the predominance of student choral responses and the corresponding low frequency of individual student responses (cf. Poole, 2005). More recently, work by a growing number of scholars (e.g., Abd-Kaidir and Hardman, 2007; Forman, 2008; Lin, 1999; Luk and Lin, 2006; Vaish, 2008) has brought cultural dimensions of language learning to the fore, focusing on a range of contexts including both second and foreign language settings as well as a variety of age groups, from preschool to university level. Drawing from a variety of theoretical approaches to discourse, including language socialization, sociohistorical theory, and constitutive ethnography, this work is undertaken in part to dispel cultural stereotypes through in-depth contextualized analyses that can support grounded, but not deterministic, understanding of cross-cultural differences. In some instances, these studies document interaction characterized by heavy reliance on a teacher-centered default script that provides little opportunity for student initiation or individual participation. However, they also assume the possibility of change and human agency, documenting ways that both teachers and students can affect the nature of interaction in ways that promote a different type of interactional script, one with more possibilities for student influence and participation (e.g., Lin, 1999; Vaish, 2008).

A LANGUAGE SOCIALIZATION PERSPECTIVE

A major thread in the focus on discourse and culture in applied linguistics is the work conducted within or informed by a language socialization perspective, a theoretical framework that seeks to understand the role of language in the socialization of novices to group membership (Ochs, 1988; Schieffelin and Ochs, 1986). For example, in an analysis of Japanese teacher-student interaction, H. M. Cook (1999) considered an interactional sequence in which one student is called upon to comment on a previous student's utterance. She interpreted this sequence as a linguistic means through which students are socialized to the importance of listening and the ability to interpret nuances of another speaker's intended meaning (cf. F. Anderson, 1995).

Where the language socialization perspective might have been marginal in applied linguistics a decade ago (cf. Poole, 1992), it now occupies a far more influential role—one which also accompanies a growing interest in issues of agency, hybridity and learner identity. Hence, classroom discourse research by scholars such as Duff (2002a), He (2000), Ohta (1999), Rymes (2003b), Talmy (2008), and Zappa-Holman (2007) does not necessarily undertake language socialization as a single motivating theoretical perspective. Rather, language socialization is one thread interwoven with other orientations such as a Vygotskyan or sociohistorical perspective and/or the ethnography of communication.[6]

In a way that parallels proposals to approach SLA research through a conversation analytic approach, some language socialization proponents have argued for its appropriateness as an investigative framework for SLA (e.g., Watson-Gegeo, 2004; cf. Zuengler and Miller, 2006). Despite the differences of the two approaches, each is motivated by a similar goal of broadening or changing what they see as the relatively narrow goals and assumptions of much SLA research to data. In each case, the aim is to bring a more prominent focus to the naturally occurring discourse within which L2 learning occurs so as to avoid the common focus on specific linguistic features in the absence of the interactional context within which they occur. The language socialization advocates, however, are of course especially focused on the cultural and more macro-contextual dimensions of the acquisition process.[7]

SPOKEN DISCOURSE AND ITS LINK TO LITERACY

The discussion to this point has illustrated a widespread phenomenon in discourse analysis as well as applied linguistics more generally—namely, the tendency to focus on speech and writing separately with minimal acknowledgment of their interconnectedness. As noted earlier, research in ESP/LSP has tended to focus more on written language, though more analyses of spoken interaction are emerging. Similarly, the interactional analyses, previously described, in large part have an exclusive speaking focus. There are, however, indications of increased interest in understanding the interplay of interdependence of the two modes (Poole, 2003).

Theoretical motivation for acknowledging the relationship of speech and writing more fully is originally found in the literatures of CLT, in that one of its original premises was the notion that everyday language use involves the complex interplay of both speech and writing (Savignon, 1991). Similarly, seminal ethnographic studies of literacy document the interconnectedness of spoken and written language (Heath, 1982; Scribner and Cole, 1981), whereas large-scale multidimensional corpus analyses have failed to find distinct linguistic differences between spoken and written genres (Besnier, 1988; Biber, 1986).

Research that acknowledges this more complex view of the speech-writing relationship is emerging on a variety of fronts. Patthey-Chavez and Clare (1996), for example, analyze the spoken interaction of reading lessons and its impact on student writing. As mentioned earlier, Connor (2002) notes that research in contrastive rhetoric, as it attends more to the intricacies of context, is beginning to focus not only on written texts but also on the talk that surrounds them. Similarly, from a literacy socialization perspective, researchers (e.g., Poole, 2008; Sterponi, 2007) have applied the language socialization model to literacy contexts (Schieffelin and Ochs, 1986), an approach that necessitates investigation of the talk-text connection.[8]

CURRENT TRENDS AND FUTURE DIRECTIONS

In addition to the multiple developments discussed above, the focus of discourse-oriented applied linguistics has also broadened to include issues related to "communication in institutions, media discourse, political discourse, discourse and gender [and] racist discourse" (Wodak, 1993: 1), as well as to topics more readily linked to traditional applied linguistic concerns such as bilingualism, language minority issues, and NS classroom interaction. As the disciplinary boundaries of applied linguistics expand, however, they also become increasingly blurred, a tendency amplified through its closer association with discourse analysis. Large bodies of research in areas such as the ethnography of education or doctor-patient communication, for example, employ some form of discourse analysis on which to base interpretations of and implications for real-world situations. Much of this work has a tradition outside of applied linguistics, however, and has not typically acknowledged applied linguistics as a home discipline. Hence, the potential exists for nonreciprocal relationships with a number of fields even if their purposes of inquiry match those of applied linguistics. Conversely, in some areas, particularly those linked to education, the insights provided through the discourse analytical investigations of applied linguistics have resulted in a ready willingness to acknowledge and foster cross-disciplinary bridges (e.g., Tharp and Gallimore, 1991).

At this stage, discourse analysis research of the sort described in this chapter has become a central focus within applied linguistics. Across an expanding range of contexts and settings, as well as from a variety of theoretical perspectives, research proceeds in ways that take ever more complexities into account. Much of this work remains focused on issues related to language learners and classrooms; however, it does so in ways that increasingly reveal the multifaceted dimensions of the many diverse contexts of contemporary language learning and use.

NOTES

1. Although Hymes's term *communicative competence* has been widely adopted within applied linguistics for well over 30 years, the meaning differs from Hymes's original meaning—namely, the ability to use language appropriately in one's speech community. Applied linguists have used the term in a more transparent way to simply mean competence in communicating. An early case in point is Bruder's (1973) widely used textbook, *Developing Communicative Competence (in English as a Second Language)*, largely a drill-based audiolingual textbook. Applied linguistic models of communicative competence (e.g., Canale and Swain, 1980) acknowledge the appropriateness dimension, but only as one among others such as discourse, grammatical, or strategic competence.

2. A substantial number of studies using genre analysis have also been conducted within the framework of systemic-functional linguistics, but discussion of this work is beyond the scope of this chapter. See Martin (2002) and Christie (1999) for overviews.

3. IRF represents the common three-turn sequence of classroom interaction: initiation, reply, and follow-up (or feedback). In U.S. contexts it is often referred to as IRE (initiation, reply, evaluation; e.g., Cazden, 2001; Mehan, 1979).

4. The term *display question* is used in the literature to refer to the familiar classroom question type to which a teacher already has an answer in mind.

5. Two-way tasks, it is argued, necessitate an exchange of information that is optional, though encouraged, in one-way tasks. Doughty and Pica (1986) argued that it is the *requirement* to exchange information that promotes more interactional modifications.

6. Recent work in interlanguage pragmatics (Kasper and Blum-Kulka, 1993) has also begun to highlight the role of cross-cultural research for SLA. Like contrastive rhetoric, interlanguage pragmatics takes the perspective that discourse norms in the first language—in this case, interactional rather than written—can influence a learner's acquisition of related norms in the second. This work has been less influential and prominent, however, than the language socialization, ethnographic, or sociohistorical perspectives and tends not to focus on naturally occurring discourse. See also the chapter by Bardovi-Harlig elsewhere in this volume.

7. A third discourse perspective to gain recent prominence in SLA research is sociohistorical (Vygotskyan) theory. See Lantolf (elsewhere in this volume) for discussion. In applied linguistics more broadly, critical discourse analysis (CDA), which addresses issues of power and language, has also become a significant research strand. Full discussion of this body of work is beyond the scope of this chapter; however, a number of studies mentioned here incorporate (or focus on) issues of power in the contexts they investigate (e.g., Duff, 2002a; Lin, 1999; Talmy, 2008) and could thus be considered CDA studies, though they may not necessarily define themselves as such.

8. These studies build on a large body of work that, although it has assumed the socially contextualized nature of literacy, has employed more ethnographic than linguistic methodologies (cf. Poole, 2003).

PART IV

....

THE STUDY OF SECOND LANGUAGE LEARNING

....

CHAPTER 10

PERSPECTIVES FROM
FORMAL LINGUISTICS ON
SECOND LANGUAGE
ACQUISITION

ALAN JUFFS

1. INTRODUCTION

Before considering the contributions of formal linguistics to the study of second language acquisition (SLA), a definition of *formal linguistics* is necessary. Linguists disagree on the scope of formal linguistics (even within a theory of syntax; R. Van Valin and La Polla, 1997: 12–15), so any definition of the field will be controversial. For clarity, this chapter understands formal linguistics to be a theory of natural language that meets the requirements of *explanatory adequacy* (Chomsky, 1981, 1986; Van Valin and La Polla, 1997). A formal grammar is an explicit description of a speaker's knowledge of his or her language(s); it means that all the properties are specified fully and precisely as a system of operations on linguistic categories (C. Hall, 1995: 171). The grammar will achieve explanatory adequacy if it can account both for how the semantics, morphosyntax and phonology of language derive from the grammar *and* how the grammar might have arisen in the mind of the speaker (Van Valin and La Polla, 1997: 8). Formal linguistics, then, seeks the answers to two main questions: "What is the content of linguistics knowledge?" and "How does that knowledge arise in the mind of the speaker—in other words, how is it acquired?"

Many researchers have written on the relationship between formal linguistics and second language acquisition; this review owes much to previous work, which readers should also consult (Cook and Newsom, 1996; Epstein, Flynn, and Martohardjono, 1996; Gregg, 1989; Lightbown and White, 1987; L. White, 2003). Lightbown and White (1987: 483) wrote that (formal) linguistic theories have an "essential but not exclusive" role to play in studies of language acquisition. Their position is adopted in this overview—formal theories have a major role to play in one subdomain of a general theory of SLA: the development and ultimate attainment of linguistic competence. Linguistic competence is the tacit knowledge of the abstract properties of the language(s) we speak. Formal linguistics does not address issues of language *use* directly; that is, it does not claim to be a comprehensive theory of communicative competence (Canale and Swain, 1980; Hymes, 1972a) but of only one subcomponent of communicative competence. Performance on language-related tasks is of great interest for what it reveals about underlying competence. It is worth emphasizing, as others have, that formal approaches neither deny the importance of pragmatics and sociological constraints in language use and learning, nor do they underestimate their importance in a unified theory of SLA; they simply do not claim to address them (Schwartz, 1999).[1]

Formal linguistics has contributed to SLA in the following ways:

First, it has provided a detailed description of principles underlying human languages, particularly in the area of sentence-level morphosyntax and phonology. With these descriptions, researchers can make *falsifiable* claims about the nature of second language (L2) competence. Formal theory also provides a framework for investigating how that knowledge is related to native language (L1) competence and to linguistic universals.

Second, through various detailed linguistic descriptions, researchers have been able to discover facts about second language grammars that had not previously been described, much less explained.

Third, research that is grounded in formal linguistics has created an evolving methodology for evaluating L2 grammar and enabled the field to adopt methods from such other disciplines as psychology.

Finally, in some cases, questions in formal linguistics have led to the development of materials and interventions in instructed second language acquisition (Toth, 2000, 2008; Trahey and White, 1993; L. White, 1991a, 1991b).

2. MORPHOSYNTAX

Most formal linguistic research in second language acquisition has been conducted within the principles and parameters paradigm (Chomsky, 1981, 1986) and its successor theory, minimalism (Chomsky, 1995; Marantz, 1995).[2] I focus on three main areas. The first area concentrates on the development of a class of grammatical categories called *functional categories* and the relationship between the development of these categories, the acquisition of morphology, and word order. The second area focuses on second language learners' knowledge of constraints on wh- questions. These two areas are only examples, and interested readers should consult L. White (2003) for recent summary research concerning formal theories of syntax and morphology.

2.1 Functional Categories and the Development of Morphosyntax

In principles-and-parameters (P&P) syntax, the morphosyntactic system consists of principles that determine the order and combination of syntactic categories into sentences and constrain reordering operations and possible interpretations. In addition to these principles, the theory includes a lexicon in which words are divided into two basic types: open-class, lexical categories (noun, verb, adjective, adverb) and closed-class, functional categories (FCs). One can think of the lexical categories as the "bricks" of a sentence and the functional categories as the "mortar" that holds the bricks together and affects how they are interpreted. More specifically, functional categories have been proposed as the hosts for such free and bound grammatical morphemes as determiners (*the, a*), complementizers (*whether, that, if*), negation, tense, aspect, agreement and so on. Early formulations of P&P syntax contained two important functional categories. The first one is the complementizer phrase (CP), which is the outer "shell" of the clause; in English it is a position to which auxiliaries and question words can move in interrogative sentences. The second is the inflectional phrase (IP), which was the host of tense, number, and agreement. Pollock (1989) and Chomsky (1991) proposed that IP be split into separate categories of tense, agreement, and even aspect. Hence, the formal description of a clause for English will appear as in figure 10.1 (Marantz, 1995: 364), where AgrS = subject agreement, and Agr O = object agreement:

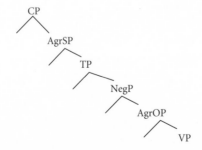

Figure 10.1 Split Inflectional Phrases (IP or INFL)

Functional categories, and the "split" INFL categories in figure 10.1, are important because, by the mid-1990s, they had become the part of universal grammar where constrained variation among languages was accounted for. For some researchers, these functional categories are assumed to exist in all languages, even when those languages do not have overt morphemes to show that they exist.[3] The claim is that they form the common core of the syntactic computational component of the language module.

In order to understand the role of functional categories in word order variation, consider first the sentences from French and German in (1) and (2). The descriptive generalization to be made is that the verb "eat" is not next to the object NP, "beef," in sentences with questions, negation, and with an adverb.

(1) a. *Mange- t-il le   boeuf?*
        eats   he   the   beef
        "Does he eat beef?"

     b. *Il   (ne) mange pas le   boeuf.*
        He   (ne) eats   not   the beef
        "He doesn't eat beef."

     c. *Il   mange souvent le   boeuf.*
        he   eats   often   the beef
        "He often eats beef."

     d. *Il   a   mangé le   boeuf*
        he   has eaten   the beef
        "He has eaten the beef."

(2) a. *Ißt   er   Rindfleisch?*
        eats he   beef?
        "Does he eat beef?"

     b. *Er   ißt   nicht (kein) Rindfleisch*
        he   eats not   (no)   beef
        "He doesn't eat beef."

     c. *Er   ißt   oft   Rindfleisch*
        he   eats often beef
        "He often eats beef."

     d. *Er   hat   das   Rindfleisch gegessen*
        he   has the   beef   eaten
        "He has eaten the beef."

Although both French and German permit the verb to be separated from the object, note that in German the verb phrase is head-final; this means that in the abstract representation of all clauses, the verb comes after the direct object NP in German. This is clear in the "surface" structure of some clauses: note that "eaten" appears after the object NP "the beef" in (2d). I will say more about this directly.

In contrast, languages like English require the finite verb to be next to the object. The English glosses and translations of the examples in (1) and (2) show that English employs "do" support for questions and negation. The examples in (3) through (6) show that Chinese behaves much like English with respect to the placement of the main verb and the object. However, Chinese uses no auxiliary for negation or "yes/no" questions.

(3) a. *Bao   Yu   xihuan   Dai   Yu   ma?*
       Bao   Yu   like   Dai   Yu   Question Part?
       "Does Bao Yu like Dai Yu?"

   b. **Xihuan*   *Bao   Yu   Dai   Yu*
       like   Bao   Yu   Dai   Yu
       Intended: "Does Bao Yu like Dai Yu?"

(4)   *Zhang   San   bu   xihuan   niurou.*
       Zhang   San   not   like   cow-meat
       "Zhang San does not like beef."

(5) a. *Li   Si   changchang   chi   jüzi.*
       Li   Si   often   eat   orange
       "Li Si often eats oranges."

   b. **Li   Si   chi   changchang   jüzi.*
       Li   Si   eat   often   oranges.
       Intended: "Li Si often eats oranges."

(6)   *Huangdi   zuotian   qu   le   Nanyue*
       emperor   yesterday   go   ASP   South Mountain
       "The Emperor yesterday went to the South Mountain."

The theory of functional categories explains these differences in word order as follows. Functional categories are the host of syntactic features such as [±wh] for questions in CP and [±PAST] in TP. Functional category features may be "strong" or "weak" in different languages (Chomsky, 1995: 348–354). In French and German the functional category TENSE is [+ STRONG]; in English and Chinese it is [– STRONG]. The specific tense value—for example, [±PAST]—on the verb must agree with the [±PAST] tense value of the functional category TP; otherwise the representation will be ungrammatical. This agreement occurs through a process of "checking" in which the verb "moves" up to the functional category. Features in [+ STRONG] functional categories must be checked *before* the representation is encoded in the phonology. The result is that the finite main verb appears in a position that is not next to its NP arguments in questions and in negative sentences. Weak features are checked *after* phonological processing, so the verb usually cannot appear in a position that is not directly next to the object in a sentence. Hence, the difference between French and German on the one hand and English and Chinese on the other can be represented schematically in (7) and (8). In French, V raises to C for yes/no questions, as shown in (1a). In German, the finite verb always moves to C, even in declarative, finite main clauses. This property of German explains the requirement that the verb is always the second constituent in a finite main clause.

(7) Strong: [CP [C [TP [T· [$_T$V$_i$]   [ADV/NEG]   [VP [V' [t$_i$] NP]]]]]]
                          |_____|
                          Verb raises from VP to TP for checking

(8) Weak:
     [CP [TP [T· [$_T$ Ø] ADV/NEG] [VP [V' [**V**] NP]]]]

This theory has several strengths for SLA researchers: It *describes* structure with details that can handle a range of unrelated languages. The theory provides precisely defined categories and a single operation carried out on those categories to explain cross-linguistic variation in word order. It reduces several superficially unrelated structures (word order in question formation, negation and declarative clauses) to one simple property of the grammar, [±STRONG] functional category. The grammar is *learnable* based on existing knowledge of the categories provided by UG and the binary values of the categories. In addition, the data available to the learner—for example, exposure to sentences such as those in (1) through (6) in the appropriate language—will *trigger* the correct strength value.

  Not surprisingly, these proposals have formed the basis of intense debate in SLA about the status of such categories in second language development and the relationship of such knowledge to the acquisition of inflectional morphology and the position of the verb in the clause. The theory permits questions such as the following:

  • Do second language learners show evidence of acquiring the correct strength value(s) of features in language they are learning across a range of structures?
  • Do strength values of FCs transfer from the L1 to the L2 (L. White, 1991a, 1991b; Schwartz and Sprouse, 1996)?
  • Does the acquisition of tense and agreement morphology coincide with the correct placement of verbs (Lardiere, 2000, 2006; Prévost and White, 2000; Sprouse, 1998)?
  • Is there an advantage for native speakers of a language with a strong or a weak functional category system?

Note that such questions are more precise than a range of similar, but theoretically simpler, questions—"Are second language learners able to acquire tense and agreement?" or "Can second language learners acquire new word orders?"

  A significant finding of research on the knowledge of functional categories in SLA since the work of L. White (1991a, 1991b, 1992) is that second language grammars seem to exhibit an optionality that first language grammars do not always show, at least in the end state (Sorace, 2000). For instance, it appears that learners of English as a second language permit the verb both to appear adjacent and nonadjacent to the verb. This behavior violates the expected pattern if learners know that weak features must be checked after phonological processing. Violations even occur with learners whose L1—for example, Chinese,—is also a weak feature language (Eubank et al., 1997).

The acquisition of German has been the focus of intense scrutiny because of its variable word order, richer (than English) inflectional morphology, and the availability of a large corpus of data from a variety of learners (Eubank, 1993; Schwartz and Sprouse, 1994). As pointed out already, in German the verb raises to the head of the CP (complementizer) in German main clauses but not in subordinate clauses. The finite verb must be the second constituent, but infinitives remain in the verb phrase, which is head-final. At the beginning stages, second language learners of German often fail to "raise" finite verbs; moreover, these verbs appear to lack inflectional morphology. To account for these facts, Vainikka and Young-Scholten (1994, 1996, 1998b) have proposed that the *gradual* emergence of functional categories is the best account for the developmental facts both for morpheme order development and knowledge of L2 word order. They claim that L2 learners begin by building a grammar of the L2 that has only the lexical VP in figure 10.1. The initial acquisition of agreement would trigger the development of a functional projection and permits optional raising of the verb; this initial FP is not specified in terms of type but provides a position to which a verb may move and is the source of initial agreement marking. The acquisition of full inflectional paradigms would result in fully specified functional projections and obligatory raising if that is required by the language. Zobl (1998) adopts a similar proposal in his account of the acquisition order of morphemes in English by two Russian speakers.

In contrast, Schwartz and Sprouse (1994, 1996) argue that all functional projections, which are present in the L1, are transferred and available in the L2; in other words, the final state of the L1 serves as the basis for the beginning of the L2 grammar. Development is based on restructuring of the values of the functional categories or adding new ones from UG to cope with the new demands of the L2 input data.

Eubank (1993/1994), Eubank et al. (1997), and Beck (1998) adopt a third position: Knowledge of the functional categories exists, but the values [±STRONG] and [±TENSE] are somehow impaired. Eubank's claim seeks to account for the variability in the interlanguage data—in other words, sometimes morphemes are supplied correctly, sometimes the verb is in the correct position with regard to its complements; at other times learners make errors. Eubank does not attribute these errors to performance but instead claims that variability is inherent in the grammar and therefore must be accounted for in terms of the system of categories and features.

More recently, Hawkins and Chan (1997) and Hawkins and Liszka (2003) argue that abstract features [±wh] in CP and as tense in the L1 can be transferred and learned appropriately, but features that are new in the L2 cannot be acquired. This position is known as the *failed functional features hypothesis*. An example would be English-speaking learners of L2 French; tense is acquirable for them in French because their English L1 has tense, but noun class (gender) and adjective agreement marking in determiner phrases is not acquirable because English does not have masculine and feminine classes of nouns as French does, nor does it have noun-adjective agreement.

Hence, the issue of current interest is the knowledge learners have of the overt morphology associated with features such as tense and agreement. In other words, formal linguists see a difference between a representation of the syntactic functional category and the morphemes that represent the category. This is so because the morphophonological forms of tense and agreement vary and thus must be learned for each language (e.g., *-ed* in English, *-te* in German), and even within one language—for example, the regular past "walk-walk*ed*" and irregular past "dive-dove." Therefore, if learners do not produce them correctly, it does not necessarily mean that the knowledge of the abstract categories *themselves* is deficient. L. White (2003) points out that research in this area of the grammar is critical to the debate on whether adult L2 grammars (1) are fundamentally different in nature from L1 grammars (e.g., Bley-Vroman, 1989; Clahsen and Muysken, 1986), (2) show local impairment (e.g., Beck, 1998), or (3) are essentially the same in terms of the computational mechanism, but show either L1 influence or surface failure at the morphophonological level (e.g., Haznedar and Schwartz, 1997; Lardiere, 2000, 2006). This latter position is called *missing surface inflection* (MSIH).

One example of research in MSIH is Prévost and White (2000). Based on data from two Arabic-speaking learners of French, they argue that if the [±strong] values in functional categories are missing or "impaired" in some way, the position of finite and nonfinite verbs should be random and not predictable on the basis of the type of morphophonological inflection they carry. Their data show that "finite verb forms are associated with finite features and appear in raised positions. Nonfinite forms appear correctly in non-finite contexts and also as a default in finite positions" (Prévost and White, 2000: 119). The lack of random placement suggests a syntactic system that is unimpaired.

Recall that Hawkins (Hawkins and Chan, 1997; Hawkins and Liszka, 2003) has suggested that if these abstract features are available in the first language of the learner, then acquisition should be easier than if they are absent. However, in a recent paper, Spinner and Juffs (2008) compare a Turkish learner of German (no gender in the L1) to an Italian learner (gender in the L1). They show that the acquisition of grammatical gender in German as a second language is not helped by have gender marking on nouns in the first language. Spinner and Juffs suggest the need to consider a range of other issues where functional category acquisition is involved. These factors include inadequate lexical learning, mapping difficulty, processing pressure, and parsing errors that cause inflectional paradigms to be inadequately learned.

Although no consensus on the exact status of the development of functional categories yet exists, the framework nevertheless permits research on what learners know and when they know it. It is worth reemphasizing that such theories permit researchers to ask questions about second language development *in general* and not just questions concerning the acquisition of a specific language or a specific structure. Global questions are made possible because functional category theory constitutes a theory about all human languages, not just about English or Indo-European languages. As such, the use of the theory had been a significant step toward a general theory of SLA for this domain.

Hawkins (in press) concludes his overview of research in this area by drawing attention to the results that these formal approaches have produced: (1) It is clear that the forms learners use when they speak is not a *direct* reflection of their underlying morphosyntactic system, and (2) it is not the second language input alone that contributes to the development of their systematic knowledge. He suggests that future research will continue to tackle the question of whether L2 grammars suffer from an underlying deficit (failed functional features), or whether there are more superficial problems of lexical learning of the correct forms (missing surface inflection). Future questions will be driven by an exploration of what relationship exists in L2 grammars between the different levels of abstract syntactic categories and more overt morphophonological representation.

2.2 Wh- Movement: An Enduring Source of Theory Development and Empirical Research

The study of the syntax of human languages has focused to a large degree on clause structure and the constraints governing the interpretation and the ordering of constituents within and across clause boundaries. It has been argued that some of the constraints must be part of a specific linguistic endowment—namely, universal grammar (UG; Chomsky, 1981, 1986, 1995; papers in Hornstein and Lightfoot, 1981). This claim is based on the finding that adult speakers know more about the clause structure and meanings of their native language than they could possibly have induced from the input they receive. This argument is now well known as the "poverty of the stimulus" or the "logical problem of language acquisition."[4]

Hence, the second question that formal theories of morphosyntax have sought to answer is whether learners of a second language have knowledge of constraints on representation that native speakers of that language have (L. White, 2003, 2007). One example is represented by knowledge of possible and impossible forms of wh-questions. A wh- question is a question that involves "who," "what," "why," "how," and so forth. This program of research on questions has endured for over 40 years, since the publication of Ross's (1967/1974) work on constraints on wh- questions that evolved into a principle that has become known as subjacency (Chomsky, 1977). Ross showed that speakers know that sentences such as "Who does Mary know the doctor examined __ in the hospital?" are grammatical, whereas sentences such as "Who did the nurse meet the patient who the doctor examined __ in the hospital?" are not. The assumption is that the wh- word moves from the position indicated by a dash in each example to the front of the clause. Ross (1967/1974) pointed out that there must be something about the structure of the second ungrammatical sentence that prevents this movement. Children are never taught the difference between sentences such as this, and in fact even the grammatical sentences of this type are very rare. Given the absence in the input for this kind of knowledge, Chomsky and other researchers have assumed that knowledge of constraints derives from built-in limits on the computational system. In other words, constraints on wh- movement are neither learned nor acquired but rather are part of universal grammar (de Villiers and Roeper, 1995).

The question in second language acquisition has focused on whether L2 learners know the same restrictions on wh- questions as native speakers do. A particularly interesting question has been whether speakers of languages such as Chinese, Indonesian, and Japanese, which do not "move" a wh- word to the front of the clause to create a wh-question, also know constraints on wh- questions in English. In general, a consensus has emerged that they do know such restrictions and therefore UG is available to L2 learners, at least in this domain of grammar (Hawkins and Chan, 1997; Schachter, 1989). However, a question has remained concerning the acceptance of *correct* long-distance movement. In particular, learners were observed to be better at correctly accepting sentences such as (9), containing an object moved from an embedded clause, than (10), containing a subject moved from an embedded clause:

(9)   Who does the nurse think the doctor saw __ in the hospital?
(10) Who does the nurse think __ saw the patient in the hospital?

If the learners have *no* knowledge of long-distance wh- movement, they should reject both. This finding led some researchers to consider whether the problem with sentences such as (10) was related to processing. Schachter and Yip (1990) first pointed out that there was a tendency for learners to reject subject extraction in (10) and that this might be a processing problem. This view was supported by White and Juffs' (1998) data. However, given that learners were reading whole sentences, it was unclear *where* the problem in processing might be. Juffs and Harrington (1995)—in a study that was published before, but actually carried out after the White and Juffs (1998) study—used a technique from mainstream psycholinguistics to look at this issue. Specifically, they asked learners to read sentences word by word. They found a similar pattern of accuracy in acceptance of grammatical wh- movement, with subject extraction being more difficult. More important, they found that the Chinese speakers in their experiment had greatly increased reading times on the embedded verb (e.g., "saw" in [10]).

Juffs and Harrington (1995) attributed this difference between native speakers of English and Chinese speakers to a lack of familiarity with "wh- movement" in surface syntax. In addition, given the assumptions concerning reading, in which each word is integrated into a sentence word by word, with revisions in structure being made only when necessary, subject extraction involves manipulating both case and semantic role features. In other words, a subject extraction required the reader to switch from an analysis of "who" as the object of the verb "think" to "who" as the subject of the verb "saw" in (10). However, Juffs and Harrington did not have learners whose first language was one that did in fact have wh- movement with which to compare. Consequently, Juffs (2005) recruited participants whose language did have wh-movement. These learners read and judged sentences such as these:

(11) a. * Who did Tom believe the claim that Ann saw __ at school? (noun complement)
      b. * Who did Tom hear the woman who saw __ on television? (relative clause)
      c. * Who did Ann meet the teacher after she saw __ last week? (adjunct)
      d.   Who does the nurse know __ saw the patient at the hospital? (finite, subject)
      e.   Who does the nurse know the doctor saw __ in his office? (finite, object)
      f.   Who does the boss expect __ to meet the customers next Monday? (nonfinite, embedded subject)
      g.   Who does the boss expect to meet __ next Monday? (nonfinite, object)

Juffs found that the learners all knew that sentences in (a)–(b) were not possible. This confirms previous findings. However, once again, the sentences containing a subject wh- word from an embedded clause proved to be more challenging. This fact is clear from the reading times for each word. Figure 10.2 provides an illustration of subject extraction that can be compared to the object extraction sentences in figure 10.3.

The spike in reading time on the embedded verb that can be observed in figure 10.2 is similar to that found in Juffs and Harrington (1995); however, the Japanese subjects also show an increase in reading time on the head noun of the object in figure 10.2, whereas all other learner groups show a decrease in reading time. Results such as these suggest that all learners, regardless of L1, have problems with subject extraction. In other words, it is not the presence or absence of wh- movement in the L1 that is the principal problem.

Juffs (2004, 2005, 2006) and Rodríguez (2008) propose that similarities between L1 and L2 processing indicate that L1 and L2 processing share some similar features such as structure dependency. However, Clahsen and his colleagues (e.g., Marinis et al., 2005; Silva and Clahsen, 2008) have argued strenuously against this view. They have suggested that second language learners have only "shallow" processing both in syntax and morphology. In other words, L2 learners do *not* use structural principles that are used by L1 speakers to process language. Clahsen and Felser (2006a) summarize a range of experiments with different structures in which second language learners fail to process in a way that is predicted by linguistic theory. Regardless of the outcome of these debates, it is formal linguistics, together with methods from mainstream psycholinguistics, that permits researchers to ask detailed questions about representation and processing in a second language.

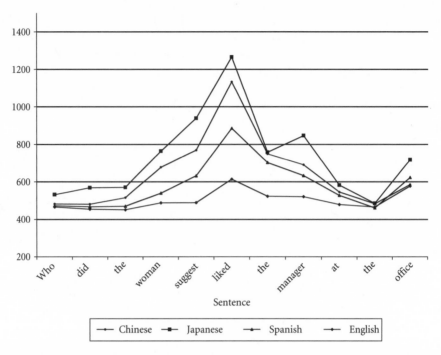

Figure 10.2 Word-by-word reading times of extraction of a subject from a finite clause.

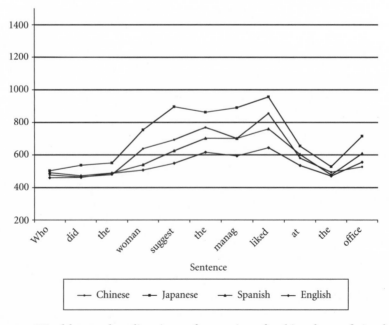

Figure 10.3 Word-by-word reading times of extraction of a object from a finite clause.

One potential drawback to all of these findings is that linguistic theory evolves as formal linguists develop and abandon models of competence. L. White (2000: 4) does not believe that such changes are always detrimental; however, Schwartz and Sprouse (2000) point out that analyses of interlanguage data that rely only on theory internal analysis cannot show conclusively that learners' grammars are, or are not, constrained by principles that constrain first language acquisition. Instead, they advocate concentrating on the logical problem of acquisition in SLA: that is, showing that the learners' knowledge of the L1 either does, or does not, go beyond the input data they receive from data concerning wh- movement and interpretation. For example, recent work by Dekydtspotter and colleagues (e.g., Dekydtspotter, 2001; Dekydtspotter and Sprouse, 2001) has sought to show that very subtle semantic interpretations of quantifier phrases, described as formal operations in logic and constrained by syntax, are available to second language learners. In this case, a formalism is also needed to describe the grammar that is the target of acquisition and that permits researchers to ask sophisticated questions about L2 knowledge.

3. Semantics and the Lexicon

It is uncontroversial that the links between sounds and concepts is completely arbitrary, and that new words have to be learned from the linguistic environment. However, recently some researchers have argued that not *all* aspects of lexical knowledge are entirely arbitrary (Gleitman, 1990; Pinker, 1989; see Juffs, in press, for a complete review of lexical issues in SLA). Hale and Keyser (1993), Pinker (1989), and Jackendoff (1990) have proposed that the number of noun phrases and prepositional phrases that are permitted in a clause, as well as their position within the clause, are in part predictable from the underlying semantic representation of the main verb. They propose that a verb's meaning can be broken down into semantic concepts. They developed formal representations for "decomposing" the meaning of verbs, as well as operations on those representations that express the relationship between different sentence types. For example, English has a well-known alternation between some, but not all, locative verbs. Locative verbs describe the movement of an object to a destination or location. The issue with locative verbs is that some allow one syntactic pattern, in which only theme (the moving object) can be the direct object in the syntax (12), whereas others allow only the goal (the destination of movement) to be the direct object (13).

(12)   a. John poured the soup into the bowl.
           [X ACT + effect [Y GO [PATH]]]
        b. * John poured the bowl with soup.

(13)   a. John covered the bed with the blanket.
          [X ACT + effect [Y GO [STATE]]]
       b. * John covered the blanket onto the bed.

(14)   a. John sprayed insecticide onto the tree.
          [X ACT + effect [Y GO [PATH]]]
       b. John sprayed the tree with insecticide.

(15)   a. John loaded the hay onto the truck.
       b. John loaded the truck with hay.
          [X ACT + effect [Y GO [STATE]]]

Underneath each sentence, a proposed semantic decomposition is provided. Verbs that have the decomposition structure [GO [PATH]] in (12) allow only theme direct objects; those with meaning components in (13) [GO [STATE]] allow only goal direct objects. Verbs of both classes may allow alternations that are expressed as a rule that changes semantic structure from the type in (12) to the type in (13) or vice versa. This is possible only if verbs belong to *narrow* classes within the main semantic classes of (12) and (13), in which the movement of a specific type of theme is specified. For example, *spray* in (14) belongs to a class that specifies ballistic motion in a specified trajectory; *load* in (15) belongs to a class that involves a mass that is put onto/into an object intended for that use. Pinker maintains that verb learning involves acquiring these narrow range classes and that once these classes are established errors will cease.

Recently, knowledge of semantic constraints of this type has been investigated by researchers in SLA (Juffs, 1996; Montrul, 1998, 1999). An overview of this research and the results that have been achieved so far is available in Juffs (2000) and, more recently, in L. White (2003). A full account of the details is not possible in this chapter, but it appears that language learners are able to acquire new semantic structures in the L2 lexicon, even if they are not instantiated in the first language grammar. The important point in the context of this chapter is that these developments show the clear role theory plays in SLA research—until a theory of a certain type of linguistic knowledge develops, researchers have no way of asking interesting or important questions in the relevant domain. Formal theories are not merely useful; they are a *requirement* for investigation of the nature of SLA.

4. PHONOLOGY

Studies of L2 phonology have not been as numerous as studies of morphosyntax. However, with new developments in theories of the internal structure of the segment and new theories of prosody, together with developments in acoustic recording and analysis, the field of second language phonology is rapidly developing (Archibald, 1998; Eckman, 2004; Hansen-Edwards, Zampini and Zampini, 2008). The Hansen-Edwards and Zampini volume is an important recent collection of articles on theory, and includes chapters on the increasingly important role of technology in L2 perception and production research. Several proposals concerning L2 phonology have been made in the past 20 years based on both perception and production data from learners. These proposals include Best's (1995) perceptual assimilation model, Flege's (1995) speech learning model (see Flege et al., 2005, for a recent paper), Major's (2001) ontogeny model, and Hancin-Bhatt and Bhatt's (1997; Hancin-Bhatt, 2008) model based on optimality theory. Finally, as in syntax studies, processing and frequency in phonology is becoming a focus of attention (e.g., Trofimovich, Gatbonton, and Segalowitz, 2007). This section highlights three areas in which recent advances have been made.

4.1 Segments

It is well known that some languages employ certain (sounds) segments as part of the system of contrasts (i.e., the segments are *phonemes*), whereas these same sounds in other languages are merely phonetic variants of an underlying phoneme (*allophones*). For example, the sound [t] and aspirated [tʰ] are allophones of the phoneme /t/ in English, but they are separate phonemes in Thai and Chinese. French only has the plain phoneme /t/ and phone [t]. This formal distinction has been important in explaining L2 phonological development, and versions of it remain of interest in SLA to this day (e.g., Eckman, 2004, 2008). Standard generative theory, for example, the sound pattern of English (SPE; Chomsky and Halle, 1968), proposed that segments consisted of bundles of unorganized features, for example, [± voice], [±coronal]. This view of the segment was challenged because some features influence other segments beyond the specific segment with which they are associated and those immediately adjacent to it; for example, [+ nasal] and [+ round] can spread in predictable but constrained ways across multiple segments in nasal and vowel harmony, yet SPE theory provided no principled way of accounting for these phenomena (Goldsmith, 1976).

In the 1980 and 1990s, a segment's features were said to have an internal organization, know as feature geometry (e.g., Clements, 1985; Piggott, 1992). For example, one proposal is that features are organized into groups, as indicated in Figure 10.4. Like the schematic of functional categories in figure 10.1, such geometry is assumed to be a part of universal grammar (UG) that limits the range of possible phonologies in human languages. It is meant as a constraint on the hypothesis space and a guide to interpreting the data from the language that the learner hears. However, not all languages will make use of all nodes in their representation of segments. For instance, C. Brown (1998, 2000) suggests that Japanese does not make use of the coronal node anywhere in its feature geometry. The absence of this node has implications for the acquisition of a second language that *does* make use of this node.

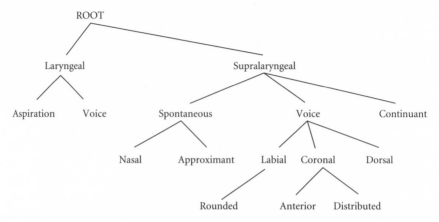

Figure 10.4 A Model of Feature Geometry (Brown, 2000: 12)

This theory of the internal structure of the segment has been particularly useful in giving precision to such problematic concepts as Flege's (1990, 1995) "old" versus "new" sounds (cf. Leather and James, 1996: 276, n. 1). For example, C. Brown (2000) uses feature geometry to discuss how the theory defines new sounds. She describes three experiments in which she claims to show that it is not the *segmental* level, but rather at the level of the *node* in features in which some more satisfying explanations can be reached concerning L1 phonological effects. For example, Brown shows that the well-known difficulty that Japanese speakers have with the [l] versus [r] contrast in English is due to the absence of the coronal node in the phonological representation of their L1. Although Chinese speakers do not have segments that are exactly similar to English [l] and [r], they are nevertheless more successful than Japanese speakers because the coronal *node* is present in the phonology of Chinese.

4.2 Suprasegmentals

Suprasegmental phenomena have also seen some considerable advances recently. In addition to Archibald's (1993) work on metrical parameters, there have been other developments in approaches to suprasegmental phonology (see papers in Hannahs and Young-Scholten, 1997; Hansen-Edwards, Zampini and Zampini, 2008). In their wide-ranging and thorough review of L2 phonology, Young-Scholten and Archibald (2000) investigate knowledge of syllable structure in second language acquisition. They demonstrate that a theory of the syllable that includes internal structure (illustrated in figure 10.5) allows for interesting cross-linguistic comparisons and predictions to be made. The independence of syllable onsets from syllable rhymes has been especially relevant to SLA research.

Young-Scholten and Archibald (2000) explain that segments are associated with positions in syllable structure by two principles: (1) segments must attach to

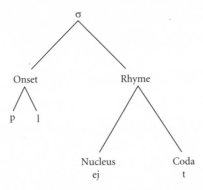

Figure 10.5 Syllabification of the word *plate* [plejt]

onset first; (2) other segments must attach to the onset until the vocalic peak is reached. This attachment must be in compliance with a segment sonority hierarchy (highest: stops-fricatives-nasals-liquids-glides VOWEL -glides liquids-nasals-fricatives-stops). Languages vary with respect to principle 2 in the number of consonants they allow in the onset. For example, Mandarin Chinese does not allow complex onsets (other than some restricted to glides), nor does it allow consonants in coda position other than alveolar and velar nasals.

Interestingly, Young-Scholten and Archibald (2000) link syllable structure with a theory of feature geometry of the type discussed in section 4.1. It is impossible to do justice to the sophistication of their analysis in this chapter, but a sketch of their ideas follows. They suggest that the acquisition of a contrast between liquids ([l] and [r]) at the level of feature geometry, and the presence of such a contrast cross-linguistically, is related both to the acquisition of complex onset clusters and to the presence of such onset clusters in a particular language. In other words, the nodes used in the feature geometry of a language for phonemic contrasts have implications for syllable structure.

This fact about languages has implication for second language acquisition. Korean, like Japanese, does not make the [l]/[r] distinction and also does not allow complex onsets such as that for [pl] in figure 10.5. Finnish, however, does make the [l]/[r] contrast and like Korean does not allow complex onsets. Now, Korean-speaking learners of English make syllabification errors in speaking L2 English with complex onsets containing liquids; for example, in producing the words *floor* and *plate*, they insert a schwa [´] between the [f] and the [l] (and the [p] and the [l]), creating two syllables (e.g., *floor* is pronounced [f´lçr], and *plate* is pronounced [p´lejt]). However, the Finnish learner that Young-Scholten and Archibald (2000) report on does not do this even though complex onsets are disallowed in Finnish as they are in Korean. According to this analysis, then, the errors of Korean learners are attributable more to the structure of the segment inventory than to the phonotactics of syllable onsets. The analysis that Young-Scholten and Archibald (2000) make here is not possible with simple accounts of cross-linguistic *phonetic* contrasts; rather, they claim that an explanation is possible only with a formal phonological representation.

The third area involved in the explanation of Ls data formal phonology is described by Hancin Bhatt and Bhatt (1997) and Hancin Bhatt (2008). They make the case for the role of the current dominant theory in phonology, optimality theory, in second language phonology studies. Optimality theory, like most current generative approaches, sees universal grammar as a set of constraints on possible human languages. The theory of constraints is grounded in acoustic and articulatory phonetics as well as in frequency and typological data from a variety of languages. As Hancin-Bhatt (2008) points out, optimality theory consists of two basic forms of constraints. The first type concerns markedness constraints that describe universal tendencies. For example, two markedness constraints are (a) the onset constraint, which stipulates that syllables must have onsets, and (b) the no coda constraint, which stipulates that syllables may not have codas. The second family of constraints is the so-called faithfulness constraints, which are constraints on how input is processed and represented. Two faithfulness constraints are (a) MAX-10, which states that the output must preserve all segments in the input (i.e., no deletion), and (b) DEP-10, which states that all output segments must have counterparts in the input (i.e., no insertion—for example, epenthesis is not permitted). In this theory, all constraints can be violated, and in general the markedness constraints have more force than the faithfulness constraints. Language variation is captured by the degree to which each language can violate these constraints and in the ranking of the importance of the constraints within a particular language. For example, Chinese and English obviously vary with respect to the coda constraint, with English being more marked than Chinese because it allows highly complex codas that can contain voiced stops.

This approach makes interesting predictions for second language acquisition that appear to be supported by the data. For example, Chinese-speaking learners of English as a second language have difficulty with complex syllable codas. Syllable codas in English violate a markedness constraint; one way for the Chinese learner to handle this is to violate a lower ranked faithfulness constraint, DEP-10, "no epenthesis." This conflict in constraint ranking leads to the well-known errors of Chinese learners who will say [bQg´] instead of [bQg] for *bag*: the voiced coda [g] violates markedness in the L1 and is resolved by violating DEP-10, which prohibits epenthesis.

Overall, Hancin-Bhatt (2008) suggests that a progressive reordering of constraint rankings can explain the developmental patterns in L2 phonology. Initially, the L2 is represented by the L1 constraint rankings, with beginning stages being dominated by markedness constraints and reranking (= reordering of constraints) from the L1 to the L2 input. As L2 phonological development progresses, the L2 input is represented more precisely, and faithfulness constraints assume greater importance than markedness constraints.

5. METHODOLOGICAL CONTRIBUTIONS

In addition to production data, the standard tool for investigating competence has been the grammaticality judgment task. However, it is well known that there are several problems with using such tasks out of context (e.g., Birdsong, 1989). In response to these difficulties, researchers have developed the use of pictures to give context to the sentences that they are investigating. In this way, they can be more certain that learners' intuitions are the relevant ones. Researchers have also developed narrative contexts that force certain interpretations on the sentences that learners are supposed to judge (L. White et al., 1997). Bley-Vroman and Loschky (1993) suggest that this type of task may be used in developing pedagogical materials because they force learners to pay attention to both form and meaning.

The past 10 years have seen the increasing use of methods from psycholinguistics in L2 acquisition (Juffs, 2001; Marinis, 2003). The methods include eye tracking and self-paced reading, event-related potentials (ERP) that monitor brain activity during grammaticality judgments or processing of linguistic stimuli (e.g., Tokowicz and MacWhinney, 2005), and increasingly sophisticated truth-value judgment tasks in semantics. In phonology, acoustic phonetics technology that measures formant structure and ultrasound technology that measures tongue position and laryngeal activity (e.g., Gick, Bernhardt, Bacsfalvi, and Wilson, 2008) are being used to evaluate second language phonetic and phonological systems.

6. CONCLUSION

Formal linguistic theory has a crucial role in the explanation of second language linguistic competence and performance. Without it, researchers cannot hope to ask sophisticated questions about what it means to know and use a second language. Formal theory captures generalizations about the structural properties of languages and makes it possible to ask whether these generalizations hold in the development of second language grammars as well (Schwartz, 1999). As linguistic theory develops and incorporates more views from alternative perspectives (e.g., Jackendoff, 2002), it is becoming possible to map more and more aspects of a learner's interlanguage grammar(s) and to ask more precise and more nuanced questions. The field has reached the stage at which dialogue between frameworks such as generative linguistics and more functional perspectives is possible as Juffs (2004) and Ellis (2005) have suggested. Moreover, linguistic theory provides the constructs that can be exploited by new technologies and experimental techniques. Although the results of this research often do not have immediate pedagogical applications, the results can inform an understanding of the process of second language acquisition and provide a background for teachers to understand the progress or lack of progress learners make in the classroom.

Acknowledgments

The research for this article was supported in part by a grant to the Pittsburgh Science of Learning Center from the National Science Foundation, award number SBE-035442, for which I am grateful.

NOTES

1. It is possible that pragmatics and semantics cannot be completely excluded from a theory of grammar, even in the narrowest sense of constraints on formal operations on linguistic categories (e.g., Van Valin and La Polla, 1997).

2. Other candidate theories are lexical-functional grammar (Bresnan, 2001) and head-driven phrase structure grammar(Pollard and Sag, 1994). See Borsley (1998) for a comparative treatment of generative theories.

3. However, it is not the case that all languages have all FCs. For example, L. White (1996: 341) assumes that French has functional projections that host clitic pronouns, but that English does not.

4. See articles in P. Robinson and Ellis (2008) for alternative views of the issue of innateness.

CHAPTER 11

···

SOCIOCULTURAL THEORY AND THE PEDAGOGICAL IMPERATIVE

···

JAMES P. LANTOLF

Since the papers authored by Frawley and Lantolf (1985) and John-Steiner (1985), which were among the first to explore the implications of sociocultural theory (henceforth, SCT) for second language learning, there have been, by my count, over 300 publications (including doctoral dissertations) informed by the theory.[1] Virtually all of these up to 2003 have used SCT as a theoretical lens to observe and explain the processes involved in second language learning and instruction. The reader might well wonder why one should make such a patently obvious assertion, given that the assumed purpose of any theory is to provide the framework for interpreting (i.e., explaining) some observed phenomenon in the world. The argument that I want to make in this chapter, however, is that Vygotsky made a different proposal with regard to how theories come to explain the object of study—a proposal that in my view at least has, until very recently, been overlooked by the vast majority of SCT-informed SLA researchers, the present author included. In making this argument, my aim is to encourage researchers to broaden their orientation to include Vygotsky's approach to theory and research methodology. This is not to say that previous research has failed to produce important findings—it has (see Lantolf and Thorne, 2006, 2007; Lantolf, 2006). However, because it has adopted the theory-as-analytical-lens perspective, it has not taken full advantage of the power of Vygotsky's theory.

The chapter will first discuss the relevant features of SCT that I believe have been overlooked in previous SLA research. It will then present selected data and findings from a recent study by Ferreira (2005) on ESL writing instruction that adopts Vygotsky's original perspective on theory and research. Ferreira's study is by no means the only one to have taken up Vygotsky's original orientation. Two studies, by Negueruela (2003) and Poehner (2008), have focused heavily on grammar learning and are already well known in the literature. These studies have approached grammar not as sets of rules to be learned but as conceptual knowledge that may help learners more effectively to create meanings that express their particular communicative intentions. A third study by Yáñez-Prieto (2008) broadens this focus to include not only grammar but also figurative language and the connection between everyday communication and literary texts. Unfortunately, space does not allow me adequately to address the complexities of this important study here, where my goal is not to survey the literature but rather to argue for a different way of working within Vygotsky's theory than has been the case for most of the past 25 years (see especially Lantolf and Poehner, 2008).

THE PURPOSE OF THEORY

The purpose of any theory is to explain some observed phenomenon: in the case of SLA, the acquisition of languages beyond the first. Theory not only informs but also guides research, often, though not always, carried out under controlled laboratory conditions, which includes the classroom setting when it is treated as a quasi-experimental venue.[2] One of the concerns of many, though not all, SLA researchers is how to connect the findings of basic, theoretically informed, research with pedagogical practice. A typical expression of this worry is found in Gass and Mackey (2007b: 190), in which the authors state that "like most SLA researchers, however, [Rod] Ellis is cautious about making direct connections between theory, research, and teaching practice." With regard to their own theory of SLA, the authors state that their direct concern is "how languages are learned" and that "direct application [of the theory] may be premature" (Gass and Mackey, 2007b: 190). Vygotsky, as I argue below, makes a decidedly different claim with regard to theory/research interface.

Although there would be little disagreement that Vygotsky's most important single work is *Thinking and Speech* (Vygotsky, 1934/1986), I think a strong case can be made that his foundational work is "The Historical Meaning of the Crisis in Psychology," originally written in 1927 (Vygotsky, 1927/2004). The former opus is significant because it presents Vygotsky's most mature and coherent theoretical thinking; but it is in the latter manuscript that he lays down the foundational principles on which the theory was to be developed. These principles are firmly anchored in Marx's dialectical materialist philosophy, a fact that has been largely overlooked in much SCT-informed SLA research (and I would say the same thing for a fair amount of general SCT research as well). This oversight comes at a price— continuance of the *theory (research) versus practice divide* that Vygotsky sought to overcome in his effort to develop a unified psychology (Cole, 1996). The following excerpt from "The Crisis" illustrates Vygotsky's commitment to overcoming the theory-practice divide:

> Previously theory was not dependent on practice; instead practice was the conclusion, the application, an excursion beyond the boundaries of science, an operation, which lay outside science and came after science, which began after the scientific concept operation was considered completed. Success or failure had practically no effect on the fate of the theory.... Now the situation is the opposite. Practice pervades the deepest foundations of the scientific operation and reforms it from beginning to end. Practice sets the tasks and serves as the supreme judge of theory, as its truth criterion. It dictates how to construct the concepts and how to formulate the laws. (Vygotsky, 2004: 304)

Vygotsky argued that the distinction between general and applied psychology, including educational psychology, was inappropriate and that in fact applied psychology *is* psychology. This was, for Vygotsky, the full implication of *Marx's Eleventh Thesis on Feuerbach* (Marx, 1972), which he paraphrased in his first book-length publication, *Educational Psychology* (Vygotsky, 1926/1997: 9), as follows: "Marx has said that it was enough for philosophers to have interpreted the world, now it's time to change it."

The unification of theory and practice is known *praxis* (see Bernstein, 1971; Sanchez Vasquez, 1977). In order for practice to evoke change in a systematic and intentional way, it must be informed and guided by theory. In turn, the outcome of practical activity informs and (potentially) changes theory. Through this dialectical interaction, humans change the world in which they live and as a consequence change themselves as well. At the same time, we improve our knowledge of the world.[3]

Educational Praxis and Artificial Development

A long-standing debate in education research has revolved around the nature of the relationship between the everyday and the schooled setting. The focus of the debate is whether mental processing, including its formation, is universal, or whether it differs with variation in the material circumstances in which it occurs. Educational approaches such as the *apprenticeship model* proposed by Rogoff (1995), as well as by Lave and Wenger (1991), support the universalist assumption and thereby undertake to import the everyday into the schooled. As Daniels (2007: 324) cautions, however, the apprenticeship model may very well undermine the unique contribution that schooling can make toward transcending "the constraints of the everyday."

Accepted wisdom in SLA also supports a universalist stance on the acquisition process. Long (1998: 93), for instance, makes the following assertion:

> Remove the learner from the social setting, and the L2 grammar does not change
> or disappear. Change the social setting altogether, e.g., from street to classroom,
> or from a foreign to a second language environment, and, as far as we know, the
> way the learner acquires does not change much either, as suggested, e.g., by a
> comparison of error type, developmental sequences, processing constraints, and
> other aspects of the acquisition process in and out of the classroom.[4]

The universal acquisition hypothesis underpins pedagogical approaches that advocate "natural language learning experiences for classroom learning" (Larsen-Freeman and Long, 1991: 221). Included among these are communicative language teaching, which often privileges small-group interactions, input-processing pedagogy, task-based language instruction, and Krashen's natural approach (Krashen, 1981; Krashen and Terrell, 2000).

Vygotsky considered educational praxis to be a special form of cultural activity that had important and unique developmental consequences for the individual. Education is far more than the acquisition of knowledge. Unlike the spontaneous and unintentional development that occurs during upbringing in the everyday world, education is "the artificial mastery of natural processes of development. Education not only influences certain processes of development, but restructures all functions of behavior in a most essential manner" (Vygotsky, 1926/1997: 88). By *artificial*, Vygotsky meant intentional and conscious control of mental activity directed at a specific object or goal. In the everyday world, development is largely unintentional. It happens as we participate in the various forms of interpersonal relationships (e.g., play, work, religion) made available by our cultural communities (Rogoff, 1995). In everyday contexts, development is "not a goal but a means or a by-product" of participatory activity (Kinard and Kozulin, 2008: 25), whereas in educational praxis, development is the "ultimate goal and objective" of "specially designed" educational activity (Kinard and Kozulin, 2008: 25). The key difference between schooled and everyday development is located in the different ways in which mediation is organized and implemented in the two settings.

MEDIATION: EDUCATIONAL VERSUS EVERYDAY KNOWLEDGE AND DEVELOPMENT

As is by now well known, SCT proposes that uniquely human forms of development arise from three principle types of mediation: "through another human being, via symbolic tools, and through specially designed sociocultural activity" (Kinard and Kozulin, 2008: 51). Although each form of mediation can be considered as a separate process for analytical purposes, in reality they always co-occur. Thus, for example, when parents interact with their children, they do so most often through linguistic means and during such activities as family meals, play time, joint reading of books, and so forth. Space does not permit a full elaboration of each of the three media-tional means (see Vygotsky, 1934/1986, 1978). The important point for the present discussion, however, is that mediation—which occurs in everyday ontogenetic development of the person—is by and large nonconscious, unsystematic, and built on knowledge derived from direct empirical observation of the world, whereas mediation that takes place during schooling should be conscious, systematic, and grounded in scientific understanding of the object of study—in other words, it should be based on the concept of praxis.[5]

A particularly important difference between everyday and educational media-tion relates to the type of symbolic tools that are featured in the respective activities. Although both rely primarily on language as the symbolic tool *sine qua non*, the meanings imparted through everyday linguistic interaction are distinctly different from those meanings imparted through educational interaction. Vygotsky (1934/1986) captures the distinction with the concepts of *spontaneous* and *scientific* (also referred to as *theoretical*) knowledge.

Spontaneous knowledge is comprised of concepts that are internalized in the activity of becoming a participant in one's community. It is empirical in nature because it is formed on the basis of "an immediate observable property of an object" (Kozulin, 1995: 123) and usually requires lengthy periods of practical experience to develop. Children's understanding of a kinship concept such as *uncle* normally arises spontaneously and unconsciously, is usually learned through empirical exem-plars of concrete individuals (e.g., uncle Harry), and is something they have a hard time systematically explaining (i.e., the male sibling of either parent). Another example, which persists into adult life (unless changed through formal education), is the concept of circle. Most of us derive our concept through direct empirical comparison of objects that have a particular geometric shape (e.g., coins, cakes, wheels, bracelets).

Scientific concepts "represent the generalizations of the experience of humankind that is fixed in science, understood in the broadest sense of the term to include both natural and social science as well as the humanities" (Karpov, 2003: 66). These concepts are domain specific and are "aimed at selecting the essential characteristics of objects or events of a certain class and presenting these characteristics in the form of symbolic and graphic models" (Karpov, 2003: 71). The essential features of phenomena are most often hidden from direct empirical observation by untrained individuals and require the special proce-dures of rigorous scientific research to become explicit. The scientific concept of *circle*, for instance is "a figure that appears as the result of a movement of a line with one free and one fixed end" (Kozulin, 1995: 124). This definition encom-passes all possible circles and "requires no previous knowledge of round objects to understand" (Kozulin, 1995: 124).

To give an example from language, I will briefly consider how temporal aspect is traditionally explained to students of Romance languages. Pedagogical explana-tions of verbal aspect, especially those found in texts situated within the CLT tradi-tion, present learners with rules reminiscent of empirical everyday knowledge. For example, students are told that perfect aspect expresses actions that are completed in the past, whereas imperfect aspect expresses actions that are incomplete or ongoing in the past and to describe emotions or mental states (see Whitley, 1986). Students may be provided with terse rules of thumb such as the following: Use perfect aspect when a sentence contains an adverb that expresses past time (e.g., yesterday, last year, 2 weeks ago). Sample sentences are then constructed to illustrate specifically the correctness of the assertions expressed in the rules. The problem is not that the rules are wrong; it is that at best they illustrate use of aspect in a restricted subset of concrete contexts. The result is that learners end up "being able to 'apply formulas' only in a situation that is precisely as described in the textbook" (Ilyenkov, 1974).

Full knowledge of, and ability to use, aspect are more effectively built upon the concept of lexical aspect in which events and states in the world have inherent temporal perspective. That is, some events are inherently perfective, or bounded, and therefore of limited duration (e.g., jump, throw, fall, build a house, run a race), whereas others are inherently imperfective, or unbounded, and of extended duration (e.g., run, walk, talk, study).[6] Grammar allows a language user to bring events into discourse, and consequently the understanding of an interlocutor, as other than their inherent aspect. Thus, one can talk about a limited duration event "as if it were" an extended-duration event. It does not matter whether the event (or state) is in reality terminated. What does matter is how a user wishes to talk/think about the event.[7]

The type of complex knowledge briefly discussed above is rarely if ever made explicitly available to learners, especially in the early stages of instruction. Krashen (1981), in fact, argued strongly against direct instruction in knowledge that is as complex as aspect with the claim that such knowledge would not serve as input for acquisition and therefore would be inaccessible for spontaneous communication. In Vygotskyan developmental theory, it is precisely complex knowledge that calls for explicit instruction, and from early on in the process, because this type of knowledge is difficult for learners to figure out on their own through trial-and-error intuitive learning. Students must be "provided with the tools for a meaningful orientation in the implicit rules that govern each language" and if they are not they are likely to perceive the system as "a meaningless collection of isolated cases rather than a coherent system of relationships based on general regularities" (Stetsenko and Arievitch, 2002: 90).

One of the primary, if not the primary, site for the transmission of theoretical knowledge is school. The developmental value of theoretical knowledge is that it liberates learners from the constraints of their everyday experiences of the world and enables them to function appropriately in a broad array of concrete circumstances. Theoretical knowledge enables us to "reproduce the essence of an object [physical or symbolic] in the mental plane" (Kozulin, 1995: 124), and, in so doing, we can carry out an activity ideally before doing so concretely. The advantages of this procedure are clear.

Avoiding Verbalism

The proposal that education must be organized around scientific knowledge does not reduce educational activity to mere presentation and memorization of scientific definitions. Vygotsky recognized that, because such definitions are abstract and "detached from reality" (Vygotsky, 1934/1986: 148–149), memorizing them per se will not result in mental development. Such an approach to education he characterized as *verbalism*—activities that must be avoided as definitions alone cannot result in true development (Vygotsky, 1986: 159). Although Vygotsky failed to offer concrete proposals for overcoming verbalism, two of Vygotsky's followers, Gal'perin (see Haenen, 1996; Talyzina, 1981) and Davydov (2004), did formulate pedagogical programs designed to proceduralize scientific concepts—that is, to foment educational praxis whereby theoretical knowledge is integrated with concrete practical activity. As Rowlands (2000: 564) points out, verbalism disappears as scientific knowledge becomes embedded in concrete practical activity.

Previous research has exemplified and discussed Gal'perin's educational theory as it relates to L2 instruction (see Kabanova, 1985; Lantolf, 2007; Negueruela, 2003; and Yáñez-Prieto, 2008, among others). In the present chapter, I wish to focus instead on the educational model proposed by Davydov.

To counter the fact that schools by and large rely on, and reinforce, empirical everyday-based concepts, Davydov, following Vygotsky, "advocated theoretical knowledge and principles of theoretical learning" (Kinard and Kozulin, 2008: 62), which he built into an approach referred to as *developmental education* (Davydov, 2004). Developmental education seeks to realize Vygotsky's argument, contrary to Piaget, that formally organized education must promote development rather than wait for students to be developmentally ready to learn.[8]

Davydov's approach presents students with systematic conceptual knowledge in a given academic domain (e.g., physics, biology, mathematics, language). This knowledge is then visualized in what he calls a *germ-cell model* of the concept (see figure 11.1 in the next section). Davydov, as well as Gal'perin, argue that visual depictions of concepts are material, holistic, and, if properly designed (a skill instructors need to develop over time), more concise and coherent than linguistic representations alone. As a consequence, germ-cell models are more readily employed by students to guide their learning actions (explained presently) and are therefore more easily internalized (the SCT equivalent of proceduralized) than are purely linguistic explanations. This is so because linguistic representations of conceptual knowledge are sequential, encourage rote memorization, and they are less viable guides for carrying out concrete activities (see Davydov 1988; Talyzina, 1981).

To achieve internalization of conceptual knowledge, developmental education engages learners in what Davydov calls *quasi-investigation*, whereby they rely on the germ-cell model to guide rigorous and systematic exploration of specific instantiations of the concept, including their own, in practical activity (Davydov and Markova, 1983: 67). The quasi-investigation is segmented into a series of six learning actions:

1. Identifying the problem situation
2. Modeling
3. Modifying the model
4. Applying the model to solve tasks
5. Monitoring the actions
6. Evaluating the actions (Davydov and Markova, 1983: 61)

Some of these are elucidated in the ensuing section, where I consider, though in nowhere near the thoroughness it deserves, an extensive study on ESL writing instruction that implemented Davydov's educational model.

Educational Development in the L2 Writing Classroom

The course, a 16-week university ESL writing course, was developed and carried out by the researcher/instructor M. Ferreira and is reported in her dissertation (Ferreira, 2005). Fourteen students from five different L1 backgrounds participated in the course. With one exception (an international student from Korea), all students had immigrated to the United States with their families when they were in their early or mid-teen years and had begun the study of English upon arrival.

The aim of the course was to develop student theoretical thinking around the concept of genre and to help them systematically deploy this knowledge to improve their writing ability in English. The long-term goal of developing students' theoretical knowledge of genre as a general category of language was to enable them to eventually deal with any type of text, including those to which they had not been previously exposed, and figure out its structure in order to be able to use the genre effectively if need be. To help the students reach this point, however, required that they have guided experience in analyzing and producing specific genres. To this end, three genres served as the focus of the course: (1i) public announcement, (2) cover letter for job applications, and (3) argumentative text. These genres were selected for their relevance in the life of students in the North American academic setting. Public announcements, for instance, are commonplace as a means of advertising events such as lectures, social events, blood drives, and so forth. Moreover, it was assumed that the reduced language typical of this type of text would facilitate introduction of the core concept, language-based communication realized in the notion of genre as defined in systemic functional linguistics. The cover letter was important because students are often concerned about applying for jobs upon graduation, and it was felt this need would motivate their interest in exploring the features of this genre. In addition, its enhanced complexity would enable the instructor to expand the concept of mode via cohesion and thematic progression. The argumentative genre was chosen because it is one of the major text types that students are expected to master in tertiary education. The three focal genres were supplemented at different points in the course with additional genres (e.g., letters of invitation, obituaries, wedding invitations, letters to the editor, and research abstracts) selected because of their relevance to specific features of genre that the instructor wished to highlight. The relevant core concept as presented to the students is given in the germ-cell model depicted in figure 11.1.

The germ-cell model was inspired by the aspect of SFL theory that focuses on the mutual influence of language and context (see Eggins, 1994; Martin, 1993) in which context takes account of the subconcepts of *field, tenor,* and *mode.* Following Eggins (1994), the additional concept of culture was incorporated into the model, given that culture exerts a strong influence on the various combinations of field, tenor, and mode and on "how the culturally determined purpose of the genre will be realized in stages known as schematic structure or generic moves" (Ferreira, 2005: 28).[9] The bidirectional arrows are intended to capture inherent relationship in language use between creativity and contextual constraints, which are often strongly normative, especially in the case of formal written genres. This tension was explored in the specific genres analyzed in the course. For example, in the cover letter there is a tension, according to Ferreira (2005), between the applicant's need for self-promotion while complying with the norms of the genre that, among other things, proscribe excessive use of "I."

The course implemented the six learning actions proposed by Davydov previously listed. These were embedded in a general instructional framework whereby the students were expected to carry out a series of tasks designed to guide their analysis of texts and to stimulate their thinking about genre-based communication. Space does not permit a full examination of each learning action; I have, instead,

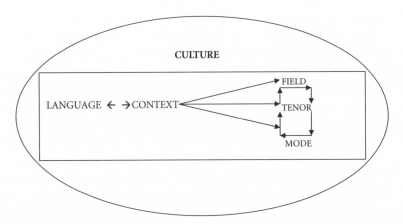

Figure 11.1 Germ-cell Model Depicting Theoretical Concept of Communication
(Ferreira 2005: 79)

selected a subset in order to illustrate how a language education program grounded in Davydov's theory might unfold.

One of the ways of implementing learning action 4, *applying the model*, was to modify an activity from Bhatia (1993) in which students conducted a cross-cultural comparison of cover letters (South Asia versus United States) guided by the germ-cell model supplemented by a set of leading questions:

- *Field:* What is the text about and what is its goal? What is the specific content of each subpart of the text?
- *Tenor:* Who is the author? Who is the text addressed to? How does the author approach the audience?
- *Mode:* How is the text constructed? Are there fully developed sentences (with subject + verb + complement), or are key words and fragments used? What is the effect of this usage?

Ferreira analyzed the students' comparative work for evidence of empirical and theoretical thinking. The criteria she applied were as follows: whether they used the model; whether they referred to field, tenor, and mode; and whether they showed an understanding of the interrelationship among the three features of genre. According to Ferreira, the following excerpt from student *Chg* evidences empirical thinking, because it fails to integrate any of her criteria:

> In the South Asia cover letter, they show too much emotion such as using different adjective to describe their thoughts. But in American, the rules show the lay out clearly, only a few paragraphs can describe all the information which they need. We should never use the adversary glorification and self-degradation moves in the cover letter, all you have to do which is to show the employers your best abilities and skills. Let them know you are the best of those employees. (2005: 170)

In the following excerpt, the student identified as *Ma* exhibits signs of theoretical thinking. Although he fails to meet all of the criteria, he does frame his discussion in terms of tenor and mode differences between the two cultures:

> Cover letters in America have to be very professional. If you make at least a minor error, you may be discarded right away. In America, people do not beg for a job position while in South Asia it is permitted. In South Asia, this letters can be seen as professional, but they are greatly different from the ones in America. The tenor in the two letters is somewhat similar but at the same very different. In both countries you say good things about the company but in South Asia people also beg too much for the job. The mode in America is different to the one in South Asia because in American Cover letters people try to diversify the beginning of every sentence. They try not to be too I centered. In South America [sic], it seems to be permitted because to what I see, the sender of the letter talks too much about himself. (Ferreira, 2005: 173–174)

Learning action 6, evaluating ones own actions and abilities as they relate to what took place in the course, was effected through regularly produced student logs. In the logs the students were asked to comment on their own performances as well on their impressions of any aspects of the course they considered positively or negatively noteworthy. In compliance with the university's Office of Research Protection, students knew that these would not be made available to the instructor until after grades had been assigned. It is therefore likely that the contents of the logs would be more balanced than otherwise might have been the case.

The most interesting, though in many ways not all that surprising, aspect of the logs was that they reflected a strong sense of empirically based expectancy for what should transpire in an ESL writing course. Even though some of the students began to develop an appreciation for, and an understanding of, the value of theoretical knowledge, throughout the course they continued to wonder about the connection between such knowledge and their ability to write in English. As Ferreira points out (2005: 255), the students questioned the relevance of some of the genres they were asked to work with in the course, in particular, announcements, invitations, and obituaries. They considered the cover letters to be particularly important because of their need to apply for jobs. Only some of the students were able to make the connection between the conceptual model and practical writing activity. The excerpts that follow illustrate this important point.

In the early part of the course, student N wrote the following in his log: "I do not think I learned anything yet in this English class because we are focusing and in to different kinds of announcements and I do not see how I could prove my writing skill and English grammar" (2005: 256). Another student, Xn, produced a similar evaluation: "I don't understand why we spend a lot of time on those topics. I don't think that is really helpful for everybody....Not everybody need to know how to make an announcement...I still think they are not helpful for me" (p. 257).

Such comments, as Ferreira notes (2005: 258), most likely emanate from a long history of immersion in empirically based education, in which students are given procedures for solving problems or for carrying out specific kinds of tasks (e.g., writing a cover letter) and subsequently they do what they have been instructed to do. Even though the instructor made it clear that the reason for analyzing the public announcement genre was to illustrate how field, tenor, and mode function in texts within and across cultures, most students continued to perceive the course as a *how-to* activity. For this reason they saw value and relevance in learning about cover letters, as illustrated in this quotation from student X: "We started the second unit finally. This time we are doing something more meaningful, because we are here to […] apply for jobs. What we learn will be really useful, I hope! But why don't we learn to do resume first?" (p. 258).

A fair number of students, however, did overtly comment in their logs on the significance of the link between the germ-cell model and writing. The following extensive excerpt from K not only incorporates field, tenor, and mode, but it also reflects the importance of the relationship among these:

> To evaluate myself that what I know or our performance, I think the best way is to ask our self questions about how much do I know before writing a kinds of genre. I will ask some questions such as what is this genre's field which is the content and goal, what is it tenor which is the audience and writer and the ways to approach audiences. What is the genre's mode, which is the layout, sentence

> structure, and how are they related to each other. Beside all these, I still have to look if this genre have discourse community or not. Discourse community were the people who discover the rules of different genre. For example, the cover letter has discourse community because it had rules and the writers must following those rules, otherwise he or she will not get the reader attention. Therefore, I evaluate myself by keep asking what is this genre and what should I do to convince the audience. (2005: 264–265)

Student *X* remarked that had he known earlier in his academic career about the concept of genre, he might have been more successful in his application for a scholarship: "I did write a biography for a scholarship before. But I didn't considered much about these problems [where/how are the mode, tenor, field would be? Who is the audience? What is the goal?]. Maybe that was why I was not selected it" (p. 265).

Writing Ability

Development of theoretical thinking is not in itself the goal of developmental education; rather, it is the link between thinking and relevant practical activity. As one of the students in the course wrote in his log from an early point in the course, "Although I'm learning from ESL class, I wonder how it can be good at my writing skill" (Ferreira, 2005: 260).

To assess writing development, Ferreira submitted the written performance of six of the students who exhibited evidence of development in their theoretical thinking to an objective assessment conducted by a team of three independent raters who were experienced writing instructors.[10] The students were given two preinstruction and two postinstruction activities in which they were asked to produce a job application cover letter (based on openings posted in the local newspaper) and an argumentative text (selected from one of three topics provided by the instructor). They were given 60 minutes to complete the cover letter task, and on the following day were given 75 minutes to write the argumentative text. The same activity was carried out at the conclusion of the course. The texts were evaluated using a 4-point scale (1 = low, 4 = high) tailored to the genres in question. The level descriptors were based on Macken and Slade (1993), whose criteria are grounded in the concepts of genre (generic moves or schematic structures) and register variables (field, tenor, and mode).

Table 11.1 presents the ratings for each of the six students on all four of the pre and postinstructional tasks. The results of the Wilcoxon Signed Ranks Test performed by Ferreira showed statistically significant improvement for the cover letter but not for the argumentative text.[11] A possible reason for this was, as Ferreira notes (2005: 211), that only 2 weeks of instruction toward the end of course were dedicated to argumentative texts, a shortcoming that the instructor acknowledges as resulting from the overly ambitious nature of the syllabus. The students who exhibited the most noticeable improvement in their writing in both genres were *X* and *Cho*. On the other hand, *K* and *H* showed very little change in their writing ability. *M* improved in his ability to produce cover letters but not in his argumentative writing.

Table 11.1 Mean scores for the pretests and posttests

Students	Precourse Activity		End-of-Course-Activity	
	CL	A	CL	A
K	1	1	1.5	1.5
Cho	1.5	1.5	2.5	2.5
M	1	1	2.5	1.5
H	1.5	2	2	2
Chl	1.5	3	3	3
X	1.5	1.5	3.5	3

CL = Job application cover letter; A = Argumentative.
Source: Ferreira, 2005: 210.

X and *Cho* showed noticeable improvement in both genres from the pre- to the end-of-course writing activity, whereas *K* and *H* exhibited very little improvement in either genre. *Chl* improved in his writing of cover letters but did not show much change in his ability to produce argumentative texts. However, for whatever reason, not explained by Ferreira, he already had a high level of ability with regard to this genre from the outset of the course.

Conclusion

The full impact of Vygotsky's theory can be appreciated only when it is understood not as a theoretical lens but as a commitment to praxis—that is, the dialectical unity of theory and practical activity that results in development of the person. Thus, research within this framework is not about observing change; it is instead about causing change through active, intentional, and systematic intervention in the very process one wishes to understand. The intervention must take account of the various forms of mediation that affect development: symbolic (i.e., conceptual), activity based, and social relationships. Different types of cultural activities (education, play, work, politics, etc.) entail different types of cultural concepts (academic, everyday, work-related, religious, etc.) and call for different forms of social relationships between those participating in the activities (teacher-student, parent-child, supervisor-worker, etc.). Ideally, the three forms of mediation should be taken into account in any research project. This is a complex matter that is not so easily achieved. In her study, for example, Ferreira focused on the function of academic/scientific concepts in educational activity but paid much less attention to the social relationships between the instructor and her students as well as to relationships among the students.

Although she did consider to some extent what transpired between the instructor and the students during one-on-one office consultations, that was not the focus of her project.

Yet, any account of development without serious consideration of social mediation leaves out an important component of the process. This observation is not intended as a criticism of Ferreira's study; rather, it is meant to point out the complexities involved in researching higher forms of mental activity. Instruction, the fundamental form of social relationship in educational activity, cannot be a one-size-fits-all proposition. For instruction to be maximally effective, it must be sensitive to the zone of proximal development (Vygotsky, 1978) in which instructor and student negotiate the appropriate form of mediation needed to help the learner develop (see Poehner, 2008). Thus, even though theoretical concepts are essential components of educational development, without mediation tailored to the ZPD of individual learners, development will at best be uneven and at worst completely absent. The fact that not all of the learners showed improvement in writing performance could very well be traced to the instructor's not having dealt adequately with the learners' ZPD. Effective developmental education relies on the interaction of all three forms of mediation.

NOTES

1. This estimate is based on the bibliography on sociocultural theory and second language learning compiled by the Center for Language Acquisition at Penn State University. The bibliography will be available as a searchable database shortly at http://language.la.psu.edu.

2. Of course, not all SLA research is experimental. Many researchers rely on ethnographic observational research to collect the data of interest and prefer to analyze it through a qualitative rather than inferential statistic orientation.

3. At least one interpreter of Vygotsky's theory, Rowlands (2000), argues that the relationship between theory and practice need not be construed as praxis. Rowlands proposes that practice may also include the changes made during the conduct of experiments in laboratory settings, as Vygotsky and his colleagues often did when assessing the effects of external mediation in the conduct of a task (see the account of forbidden colors experiment reported in Vygotsky, 1934/1986).

4. Tarone (2007) discusses evidence from different learning contexts, which presents a substantial challenge to the universal acquisition hypothesis particularly with regard to the claim that developmental sequences are the same everywhere.

5. I use the modal verb *should* because, as many SCT researchers have noted (e.g., Davydov, 2004; Karpov, 2003), schooling frequently fails to implement an instructional program that promotes qualitatively different forms of development from the everyday world. That is, it does not provide the "'educational break' from the community in which it is situated" that it should provide (Rowlands 2000: 561).

6. In cognitive linguistics *boundedness* is a concept that generalizes beyond verbal aspect and functions to distinguish different categories of nouns as well. Thus, nouns that

refer to unitary concrete entities, such as chair, pen, and book, are bounded, whereas those that refer to entities traditionally categorized as mass nouns, such as snow, coffee, paper, are unbounded. In my view, the distinction also distinguishes the two copula verbs of Spanish, each equivalent of English "to be." *Ser*, derived from Latin *essere*, "to be or exist," is unbounded, and *estar*, derived from Latin *stare*, "to stand," is bounded. Boundedness is an excellent example of the principle of generalization that is central to scientific knowledge.

7. For a full treatment of verbal aspect see Salaberry (2008).

8. Stetsenko and Arievitch (2002), for example, discuss an early elementary school program in which children identified as Piagetian nonconservers developed the ability to conserve liquid volume as a result of instruction organized around Gal'perin's educational principles. For a full discussion of such programs at different educational levels and in different subject domains, see Karpov (2005).

9. For the reader not familiar with SFL, *field* refers to the content or the social action involved in the text; *tenor* is the relationship between the language users in terms of familiarity, power differential, and so forth; and *mode* refers to how language is employed in a particular text (e.gs., cohesion and thematic progression; see Martin 1993).

10. The comments have not been edited for style.

11. Ferreira (2005) also carried out a qualitative analysis of samples of the students' writing, but I am unable to discuss this component of her project here.

CHAPTER 12

LANGUAGE LEARNER IDENTITIES AND SOCIOCULTURAL WORLDS

KELLEEN TOOHEY AND BONNY NORTON

I. Introduction

In this chapter, we briefly review an increasingly large body of research that seeks to understand the relationship between language-learner identities and their sociocultural worlds. Rather than seeing learner identities as developed individually and as expressive of the essence of individuals, current identity theorists have argued that identities are complex, multilayered, often hybrid, sometimes imagined, and developed through activity by and for individuals in many social fields. This complex notion of selves has been accompanied by a great deal of recent research on language and learning, drawing primarily on postmodern and poststructuralist theories. We begin with a consideration of current understandings of these fundamental concepts, and then review some of the foundational studies, before focusing on more recent research on identity and language learning.

II. A Focus on Language Use, Not System

In recent years, *usage* theories of language have become increasingly attractive to identity and to language learning researchers. Previous structuralist theories of language, associated initially with the work of Swiss linguist F. de Saussure ([1916]

1966), posited that languages had patterns and structures, and that the proper foci of a scientific study of language were those stable and idealized patterns and structures and how idealized native speaker/hearers utilized them ("competence"). Actual instances of language usage ("performance") were of lesser interest because they were subject to exigencies (memory lapses, fatigue, slips, errors, and so on), and were not reflective of language competence. By contrast, poststructuralist theories of language, associated particularly with the work of Russian literary theorist M. M. Bakhtin (1981, 1984), who argued that language should be investigated not as a set of idealized forms independent of their speakers or their speaking but rather as situated utterances in which speakers, in dialogue with others, struggle to create meanings. For Bakhtin, language learning was not best seen as a gradual individual process of internalizing a set of rules, structures, and vocabulary of a standard language but rather as a process of struggling to use language to engage in participation in a specific speech community. Using words that have been used by many others previously, speakers are constrained—as well as enabled—to make their own meanings. His view was that language was characterized simultaneously by convention (customary discourse), as well as by innovation, as individuals struggled to use language to express their own voices. Bakhtin recognized that the customary discourse practices of any particular community may privilege or debase certain speakers. Finding answering words for the words of others, joining the chain of speech communication, was, for him, as much a social as a linguistic struggle. Thus, the notion of the *individual* voice was a fiction, as he saw all speakers constructing their utterances jointly, on the basis of their interaction with others, both in historical and contemporary—actual and imagined—communities.

Another social theorist, P. Bourdieu, a French sociologist, has also been influential in shaping poststructuralist understandings of language and learning (see Albright and Luke, 2008). Bourdieu (1977; Bourdieu and Passeron, 1984) focused on the often unequal relationships between interlocutors and on the importance of power in structuring speech. He suggested that the value ascribed to speech cannot be understood apart from the person who speaks, and that the person who speaks cannot be understood apart from larger networks of social relationships. To redress the inequities between what he called "legitimate" and "illegitimate" speakers, he argued that an expanded definition of competence should include the "right to speech" or "the power to impose reception" (Bourdieu, 1977: 648). The fact that there is no guarantee to the right to speech follows from Bourdieu's theorizing of discourse as "a symbolic asset which can receive different values depending on the market on which it is offered" (1977: 651). Simply put, "language is worth what those who speak it are worth" and dominant usage is associated with the dominant class (Bourdieu, 1977: 659). Bourdieu's foregrounding of power relations in language use has important implications for how language learners are positioned by others, for the opportunities they get to speak, and for the varieties of language that are taught and used.

Hall, Chen, and Carlson (2006) have also recently argued for a usage-based view of language knowledge. They see language knowledge as a dynamic constellation of linguistic resources in which meanings emerge in specific contexts, thus "an inherently dynamic set of patterns of use which, in turn, is subject to a variety of stabilizing influences that are tied to the constancy of individuals' everyday lived experiences" (2006: 229). Hall et al. show that Bakhtin's metaphor, which suggests that we take words from one another's mouths, is empirically demonstrated in research in both child language development (e.g., Tomasello, 2003) as well as in sociolinguistic research that shows the variability of language knowledge across speakers and contexts (Coupland and Jaworski, 2006). Hall et al. claim that such understandings should transform our concepts of language knowledge from a mentalist "system" perspective to one that recognizes the social contingency and dynamism of all language knowledge. As we shall attempt to show, this usage-based notion of language is congruent with current theory and research regarding identity, language learning, and sociocultural worlds.

III. Learning to Use Language

Usage theories of language competence direct attention not only to the social dynamics obtaining in any language situation but also to the activities that learners engage in as they are learning languages. Drawing on Vygotskyan notions of the sociality of learning (Vygotsky, 1978), postmodern learning theorists see learning as "an integral and inseparable part of social practice" (Lave and Wenger, 1991: 31) as people engage with the practices of their communities in particular ways and from particular positions. Rogoff (2003) supported this perspective, pointing out that development (or learning) involves "changing participation in the sociocultural activities of a community, which also change" (Rogoff, 2003: 368). Vygotsky (1978) emphasized the central role of mediation in these human activities, with language being the primary tool mediating such activity.

A shift from seeing learners as individually internalizing stable systems of language "knowledge," to seeing them as differentially positioned members of social and historical collectivities using (and thus learning) language as a dynamic tool, moves observers toward examining the conditions for learning and the issues of access of learners for appropriation of practices, in any particular community. Lave and Wenger's (1991) construct, legitimate peripheral participation, represented their view that communities are composed of participants who differentially (peripherally) engage with the practices of their communities and that such engagement or participation in practice is "learning." Stressing the importance of local analysis of communities, they pointed out that conditions vary with regard to ease of access to expertise, to opportunities for practice, to consequences for error in practice, and so on. Lave and Wenger discussed the importance of not sequestering newcomers away from participation in community activities, if they are to learn. They noted that learners must "see," or be in the presence of, mature practice.

A usage-based theory of language competence and a sociocultural perspective on learning are often foundational assumptions of recent work in identity and language learning. Below, we first review some early studies and then examine work undertaken primarily from the year 2000 on. Our chapter in the first edition of this book reviewed earlier studies in more detail (Norton and Toohey, 2002).

IV. Early Identity and Language Learning Studies

Although much research on language learning in the 1970s and 1980s was directed toward uncovering the personalities, learning styles, motivations, and other unique characteristics of individual learners (conceived of as relatively fixed and long-term traits or characteristics), more recent work on language learners and their learning is informed by poststructural understandings of learners' identities. As Luke (2009) put it, "The concept of multiple subjectivity suggests that people are simultaneously and differentially positioned by discourse and practice—and that identity is an amalgam of different characteristics" (Norton, 2000). This perspective stresses that, as much as people are positioned, they also struggle to position themselves, and such struggles should be of interest to researchers. Luke (2009), and many other scholars (e.g., Block, 2007; Menard-Warwick, 2006; Ricento, 2005; Swain and Deters, 2007; Zuengler and Miller, 2006), cited Norton's mid- and late 1990s theorizing on identity and language learning (Norton, 1997a; Norton, 2000; Norton Peirce, 1995) as pivotal in reframing debates on language and identity in the field of language learning. Drawing on poststructuralist theories of language and subjectivity, particularly those associated with the work of Weedon (1987/1997), Norton argued that people use language to negotiate a sense of self within and across a range of sites at different points in time, and that social relations in those historically specific sites enable or constrain opportunities for social interaction and human agency. In her work with immigrant language learners in Canada, she theorized the individual—the subject—as diverse, contradictory, dynamic, and changing over historical time and social space. Drawing on an extensive body of data, she demonstrated that her learners assumed and were assigned various identity positions in the various communities in which they participated and, as such, had greater or lesser possibility for participation in community activities and for using language in particular ways. Investigating how power operates in social interaction, and with reference to larger sets of social relationships, was central in her analysis.

Norton further developed the notion of *investment* as a way to understand the learners' variable desires to engage in social interaction and community practices. Norton's notion of *investment* is best understood with reference to the economic metaphors that Bourdieu (1977) used in his work—in particular the notion of "cultural capital." Bourdieu and Passeron (1977) used the term *cultural capital* to reference the knowledge, credentials, and modes of thought that characterize different classes and groups in relation to specific sets of social forms. They argued that cultural capital is situated, in that it has differential exchange value in different social fields. Norton observed that if learners "invest" in a second language, they do so with the understanding that they will acquire a wider range of symbolic and material resources, which will in turn increase the value of their cultural capital. As the value of their cultural capital increases, so learners' sense of themselves and their desires for the future are reassessed. Hence, she argued, there is an integral relationship between investment and identity. (For an economist's view of *cultural capital*, see, e.g., Grin and Vaillancourt, 2000.) We review more recent explorations of this relationship in part V.

V. Recent Identity and Language Education Research

In the first decade of the twenty-first century, there has been an explosion of interest in identity in the language education literature. In 2002, the first volume of the quarterly *Journal of Language, Identity and Education* was published, an event that has generated a high degree of interest in these matters. Some of the topics that authors in the journal have considered, with respect to identity and language learning and teaching, include the following:

- Deafness and disability
- Gender sexual orientation
- Multilingual, monolingual, multicompetent identities
- National, religious, imagined affiliations
- Situated roles (teacher, researcher, writer)
- Race and class, and other bases of identity

These categories are, of course, not mutually exclusive, and their variety points out the complexity of how language learning and identity interact. A number of edited and single-authored books have taken identity as a major focus. Recent examples include Block (2007), Clarke (2008), Day (2002), T. Goldstein (2003), Heller (2007), Kanno (2008), Kubota and Lin (2009), Lin (2008), May (2008), Miller (2003), Nelson (2008), Norton (2000), Norton and Toohey (2004), Pavlenko and Blackledge (2003), Potowski (2007), Stein (2008), and Toohey (2000). Space precludes comprehensive review of these (and a good deal of other) recent works, so we have decided to organize our review in terms of some of the conceptual categories and themes that have generated a good deal of interest, are present in a variety of studies, and may well continue to be important in future research. We begin with the notion of investment.

Investment

The construct of *investment* in language learning (from Norton Peirce, 1995; Norton, 2000) has been of considerable interest in the field of applied linguistics and language education (see, e.g., Cummins, 2006; Haneda, 2005; Pittaway, 2004; Potowski, 2007; Skilton-Sylvester, 2002; and a special issue on the topic in the *Journal of Asian Pacific Communication* [Arkoudis and Davison, 2008]). As discussed earlier, Norton recruited this construct to complement existing theories of *motivation* in the field of second language acquisition and to capture the sometimes contradictory desires of learners to appropriate a second language. Unlike notions of motivation, which often conceive of the language learner as having a unitary, fixed, and ahistorical "personality," the construct of *investment* conceives of the language learner as having a complex identity, changing across time and space, and reproduced in social interaction. Thus although motivation can be seen as a primarily psychological construct (Dörnyei, 2001; Gardner, 2007), investment must be seen within a sociological framework, and it seeks to make a meaningful connection between learners' desire and commitment to learn a language, and their changing identity.

The construct of *investment* provides for a different set of questions associated with a learner's commitment to learning the target language. In addition to asking, for example, "To what extent is the learner motivated to learn the target language?" the researcher asks, "What is the learner's *investment* in the target language practices of this classroom?" A learner may be a highly motivated language learner, but may nevertheless have little investment in the language practices of a given community, practices that may, for example, be racist, sexist, elitist, or homophobic. Thus, despite being highly motivated, a learner could be excluded from the language practices of a classroom, and in time positioned as a "poor" or unmotivated language learner (see Norton and Toohey, 2001).

Skilton-Sylvester (2002) argued that traditional views of adult motivation and participation inadequately represented the complex experiences of the four Cambodian women in her study, and she made the point that understanding of women's domestic and professional identities is necessary to explain their investment in adult ESL programs. Haneda's (2005) work with two university students in an advanced Japanese literacy course also drew on *investment* to show that these adults' multimembership in differing communities may have shaped the way they invested in writing in Japanese, whereas Potowski (2007) argued that learners' investment in the target language should be consistent with the goals of their educational programs if language learning is to be successful. Indeed, Cummins (2006), who used the construct of *investment* to develop the notion of the "identity text," argued that the construct has emerged as a "significant explanatory construct" (2006: 59) in the second language learning literature.

Imagined Communities

Language learners desire to become members of other communities. Because those communities are not yet sociocultural worlds for the learners, they might be termed "imagined communities" (Kanno and Norton, 2003; Norton, 2001). These imagined communities may be, to some extent, a reconstruction of past communities and historically constituted relationships, and may offer possibilities for an enhanced range of identity options in the future. Norton (2001) showed that teachers' lack of awareness of learners' imagined communities hindered the teachers' ability to construct learning activities that engaged learners and that contributed to their desired trajectories toward participation in their imagined communities. She drew on the work of Lave and Wenger (1991), Wenger (1998), and later B. Anderson (1991) to argue that in many second language classrooms, all of the members of the classroom community, apart from the teacher, are newcomers to the language practices of that community. The question that arises, then, is this: What community practices do these learners seek to learn? What, indeed, constitutes "the community" for them? Learners have different investments in particular members of the target language community, and the people in whom learners have the greatest investment may be the very people who provide access to the imagined community of a given learner. Of particular interest to the language educator is the extent to which such investments are productive for learner engagement in both the classroom and the wider target language community. In essence, an imagined community assumes an imagined identity, and a learner's investment in the target language must be understood within this context.

Such issues have been taken up more extensively in publications such as those by Pavlenko and Norton (2007) and in a coedited special issue of the *Journal of Language, Identity, and Education*, "Imagined Communities and Educational Possibilities" (Kanno and Norton, 2003), in which a number of scholars have explored the imagined communities of learners in diverse regions of the world, following up this initial research in more recent publications. In the Japanese context, for example, Kanno (2008) examined the relationship between school education and inequality of access to bilingualism in five different Japanese schools promoting bilingual education. She found that although additive bilingualism was promoted for upper-middle-class students, subtractive bilingualism was far more common in schools serving immigrant and refugee children. Kanno argued that in the schools she researched, different visions of children's imagined communities called for different forms of bilingual education, exacerbating existing inequities among students with unequal access to resources.

In Canada, Dagenais, Moore, Lamarre, Sabatier, and Armand (2008) investigated the linguistic landscape in the vicinity of two elementary schools in Vancouver and Montreal, illustrating the ways in which the children imagined the language of their neighborhoods and constructed their identities in relation to them. Dagenais et al. described the innovative ways in which researchers and students drew on such multimodal resources as digital photography to document the linguistic landscape of these neighborhoods and the way children in both cities were encouraged to exchange letters, posters, photographs, and videos. Dagenais et al. argued that documenting the imagined communities of neighborhoods as seen by children can provide much information on the children's understanding of their community, an understanding that has important implications for identity and language learning.

In another region of the world, Kendrick and Jones (2008) drew on the notion of imagined communities to analyze the drawings and photographs produced by primary and secondary schoolgirls in Uganda. Their research, drawing on multimodal methodologies, sought to investigate the girls' perceptions of participation in local literacy practices and to promote dialogue on literacy, women, and development. What they found was that the girls' visual images provided insight into the imagined communities, which were associated with command of English and access to education.

Positioning

Bakhtin's work offers us ways to think about the learning of language within particular contexts and with particular interlocutors, and many identity and language learning researchers and theorists stress the importance of considering *positioning* in contexts and among interlocutors. As a theoretical construct, positioning is most often associated with the work of Davies and Harré (1990), who sought to challenge the adequacy of the concept of *role* in developing a social psychology of selfhood. They and other postmodern theorists have reminded us of the contingent, shifting, and context-dependent nature of identities, and emphasized that identities are not merely given by social structures or ascribed by others, but are also negotiated by agents who wish to position themselves. As Bourdieu (1977) pointed out, language usage is a complex social practice in which the value and meaning ascribed to an utterance is shaped in part by the value and meaning ascribed to the person who speaks. Heller, building on the work of Bourdieu (1977), drew attention to how linguistic and other resources of both individuals and groups are "produced, attributed value and circulated in a regulated way, which allows for competition over access and typically, unequal distribution" (Heller, 2008: 50). Thus, not only individuals' but also groups' ascribed identities are important in structuring access to and opportunities for language use and learning.

The recognition of *positioning* in social structures, but also individual agency, has been important in many studies of language learning. Menard-Warwick (2007), for example, described a vocational ESL class in which she was able to identify particular episodes of positioning on the part of both the teacher and her Latina students that had effects on how learners were able to claim "voice" in the classroom. She commented that although vocational teachers often aim at "empowering" their students, nevertheless classroom materials and activities, as well as powerful societal discourses, often constrain students' possibilities for claiming identities they previously held or identities to which their efforts are directed. She concluded that teachers need to "listen for and support [students'] reflexive positionings" (2007: 286) of themselves and to integrate language practice and social criticism so that learners are able to name some of the disempowering tendencies of the linguistic practices of their new cultures.

In an earlier study, Toohey (2001) wrote about how two girls in primary classrooms were positioned, and how they claimed positions, and consequently how that affected their language learning. One child was able to claim a powerful identity in classroom play and, as such, was able to negotiate new meanings or to negotiate or display her powerful position in relation to classmates, and to participate in many classroom activities with peers. Her "powerful" identity derived from a particular arrangement of classroom practices that displayed her as powerful. Her enhanced access to many conversations resulted in her observable progress in language learning. Another child, positioned more subordinately, was frequently denied access to classroom playgroups and, as such, did not seem to progress as quickly in her language learning. Toohey argued that teachers might better assist students to speak from powerful and desirable positions by addressing issues of dominance and subordination directly and by analyzing how classroom practices are arranged to display some children as dominant and others as subordinate.

Race

Positioning and identity are, of course, linked to *race* (see, e.g., Amin, 1997; Curtis and Romney, 2006; Lin et al., 2004; Ng, 1993), and we would like to review some of the studies that have examined the relationship between racial identities and language learning. The 2006 special issue of *TESOL Quarterly*, edited by Kubota and Lin, offered several articles that investigate this relationship; all authors made the case that TESOL practitioners need to examine critically how ideas about race and racial identities influence what we teach, how we teach, and how we see our students. As Kubota and Lin observed, "[Although] the field of teaching English to speakers of other languages (TESOL) brings people from various *racialized* backgrounds together,...the field of TESOL has not sufficiently addressed the issue of race and related concepts" (2006: 471). Motha supported Kubota and Lin's assertion that race is central in language teaching, noting that "school and classroom practices provide the terrain in which meanings of *racialized* identities are dynamically and continuously constructed and negotiated" (Motha, 2006: 497). Motha examined how four American teachers attempted to create antiracist pedagogies, showing what complexities such a commitment involved. For example, the Korean American teacher (the only teacher of color of the research subjects) described her belief that her legitimacy as a professional was judged inadequate by colleagues, and that this contributed to her feelings of inequality within her professional context. Motha's analysis of the conversations around race of the four research subjects underlined for her the importance of critical examination, with students, of how language ideologies can oppress or liberate and how the equation of Whiteness with "standard English" should be challenged.

Shuck (2006) explicitly examined how public discourse in the United States links language with race as a way of positioning groups. In interviews with White undergraduates who speak English as a first language at a southwestern U.S. university, Shuck found that nonnative speakers having non-European origins were seen by the students as incomprehensible, intellectually weaker, and responsible for their "nonintegration" in American society. In particular, she found the onus was always on the nonnative speaker, not the White student, to create comprehensibility, and drew on the analysis of R. Schmidt (2002: 142) to support her analysis:

> [A] conjunction of the hegemonic position of the dominant English language and the socially constructed normalization of *Whiteness* creates an ideological context within which Americans speaking languages other than English, and whose origins lie in continents other than Europe, are *racialized* as alien outsiders, as *Others*. (Shuck, 2006: 261)

Blackledge (2003) linked the notion of imagined communities with racialization to investigate racial discourses embodied in educational documents. He found that a monocultural and monolingual community, imagined by educational decision makers as normative and natural, stigmatized the cultural practices of Asian minorities who made regular visits to their heritage countries. He argued that this normative imagined community valued homogeneity over diversity, and "positioned particular cultural practices as aberrant, 'Other,' and damaging to the educational prospects of minority children (2003: 332)." In essence, he made the case that the normalizing discourses of the dominant group *racialized* the cultural practices of Asian groups by proposing a set of apparently commonsense arguments to undermine them.

Digital Representations and Identity

The affordances of digital technology have been investigated by a number of scholars interested in identity and language learning (e.g., Kramsch and Thorne, 2002; Lam, 2006; Lewis and Fabos, 2005; Mutonyi and Norton, 2007; Snyder and Prinsloo, 2007; Warschauer, 2003; C. White, 2007). Lam (2006), for example, found that immigrant youth in the United States were fashioning identities for themselves in computer-mediated transnational networks as multilingual, multicompetent actors. In so doing, they were able to provide for themselves new language learning opportunities that seemed denied to them in their schools in which they were stigmatized as immigrants and incompetent language users. In another part of the world, L. White (2007) examined two at-distance language-teaching programs in Australia, both of which were responding to the need for a wider range of foreign languages in schools. She concluded that as innovations in distance learning and teaching expand, it will be imperative that the field find ways of addressing the philosophical, pedagogical, and professional issues that arise, and that issues of identity, for both teachers and learners, are significant factors in each of these domains. C. Lewis and Fabos (2005) examined the functions of instant messaging (IM) among seven youths to see how their social identities shaped, and were shaped by, this form of digital literacy. They found that the youths engaged in IM to enhance their social relationships and sta-tuses across contexts, sometimes assuming alternative identities online. They noted that IM permitted these youths to engage in literacy practices in ways they were not able to do in school and that schools must take into account these new forms of literacy. The research of Kramsch and Thorne (2002) indicated, however, that not all Internet communication leads to positive identity outcomes. In their study of the synchronous and asynchronous communication among American learners of French in the United States and French learners of English in France, they found that students had little understanding of the larger cultural framework within which each party was operating, leading to problematic digital exchanges.

In general, most of the studies that investigate how digital technologies affect identity and language learning have been commendatory, with the following com-ment by Lam representing current thinking: "Networked electronic communica-tions have given rise to new social spaces, linguistic and semiotic practices and ways of fashioning the self beyond the national context for immigrant youths in the United States" (2006: 171). However, she also cautioned that these technologies may not "necessarily provide the analytical tools that may empower youths to critique and change existing social structures in positive directions" (2006: 186). It may be that mentoring is a crucial element in supporting learner use of multimodality for critical purposes (Hull, 2007). The interest of many emerging scholars in what digital technologies may mean for language learning and learner identities will no doubt add to an increased understanding of this relationship in the future.

VI. Toward the Future

As can be seen from this brief review of foundational and more recent studies in identity and language learning, this is an exciting field that is stimulating many researchers and much debate. Increasingly, the field is being informed in diverse ways by work in anthropology, sociology, postcolonial and cultural studies, and education. The researcher who investigates identity and language education in the future will need to be comfortable with this interdisciplinarity and, as scholars such as Luke (2004) and Morgan and Ramanathan (2005) have remarked, will need to understand that learners live in globalized and cosmopolitan sociocultural worlds. We have made the case that current language education scholars have seen a static view of language as system and learning as internalization of system as an inade-quate representation of dynamic and complex processes. What has remained of interest is the notion of complex and embodied language learners living in socially stratified worlds that constrain as well as enable the exercise of human agency. The goal we see for future research on identity and language learning lies in contributing to efforts to promote language teaching and learning in ways that can enhance human agency in more equitable worlds.

CHAPTER 13

COMPUTATIONAL MODELS OF SECOND LANGUAGE SENTENCE PROCESSING

MICHAEL HARRINGTON

SENTENCE comprehension draws on multiple levels of linguistic knowledge, including the phonological, orthographic, lexical, syntactic, and discoursal. Understanding the computational mechanisms responsible for using this knowledge in real time provides basic insights into how language and the mind work. For a cognitive theory of second language acquisition, a better understanding of how the second language (L2) learner develops the capacity to process sentences fluently also has important implications for theories of acquisition and instruction (Segalowitz and Hulstijn, 2003).

This chapter examines two perspectives on written sentence comprehension in the L2. The two approaches considered are:

Syntax-based (Clahsen and Felser, 2006b; Felser and Roberts, 2007; Juffs, 1998a, 1998b; Juffs and Harrington, 1995; Marinis et al., 2005; J. N. Williams, 2006; Williams, Möbius, and Kim, 2001)
Constraint-based (Ellis, 2006; MacWhinney, 2005; Sasaki, 1994; Ying, 1996)

The approaches make fundamentally different assumptions concerning the nature of linguistic representation and how the human speech processing mechanism uses this knowledge in online comprehension. The two perspectives also represent a basic division in cognitive theory in SLA between formalist and functionalist/usage-based approaches to L2 learning and use (Gregg, 2003).

Syntax-Based Approaches to Sentence Processing

The syntax-based approach ascribes a central role to syntactic processes in driving comprehension. Syntactic knowledge is characterized as a set of atomic syntactic units and rules that relate these units in a hierarchical structure. This structural knowledge incorporates an abstract level of representation whose features may not be explicitly represented in surface forms (R. Hawkins, 2001). Sentence processing, or *parsing*, is characterized as a process of structure building driven by the application of these syntactic rules. Parsing is an incremental process in which each incoming word is incorporated into the structure as it is built and possibly revised online (Pickering and Van Gompel, 2006). Syntactic knowledge is modular in that it is represented as discrete, language-specific entities, or *symbols*, that are applied automatically in the course of comprehension. Lexico-semantic, frequency, and contextual information can affect the parse in various ways, but all approaches assume that parsing is primarily a syntax-driven process. The perspective is strongly influenced by the generative grammar tradition (Chomsky, 1986) and related assumptions concerning the (un)learnability of key principles of language structure from exposure alone (Marcus, 1998). The symbolic rule-based view of language has traditionally been the dominant approach in cognitive science in general and in L1 sentence processing in particular (MacDonald and MacDonald, 1995). The syntax-based approach has also been the main approach in L2 sentence processing research over the past decade, with virtually all the major online comprehension studies carried out in this framework. In this section the basic assumptions of the syntax-based approach are described and studies applying the framework to L2 processing are presented.

Grammar Knowledge as a Rule-Based Symbol System

There is a long tradition in cognitive science that characterizes sentence comprehension as a symbol manipulation process. This symbolic approach assumes that linguistic knowledge is represented in the mind in the form of localist representations, which in natural language include phonemes, morphemes, syntactic rules, and so forth. Computations, specified in rules, are carried out directly on these representations to yield an interpretation. Syntactic rules are assumed to be independent of the semantics of the specific items in a manner similar to an algebraic equation (e.g., $a + b = c$). The computation is carried out in the same way regardless of the specific values of a and b. Syntactic knowledge is compositional in the sense that constituents can be plugged into hierarchical structures, which in turn determine how the constituents are interpreted. These knowledge structures are also recursive in that they allow embedding within larger structures (Stilling et al., 1995).

As an account of processing the perspective has been less concerned with how these rules and representations are learned, although many of the syntax-based models below have been closely associated with generative views of language acquisition (e.g., Frazier and Fodor, 1978).

Syntax-Based Processing

Sentence comprehension in the syntax-based perspective is a process of structure building in which syntactic rules play a primary role. Fundamental insights into how this structure building proceeds have come from examining how individuals process structures that make significant demands on comprehension. These include sentences that are temporarily ambiguous, as in *garden path* sentences like *The horse raced past the barn fell*... or nonlocal dependencies encountered in relative clause and *wh-* structures, for example, *Which girl do you believe John loves _____ a lot?* (Frazier, 1987). The latter are assumed to involve movement of elements out of structural trace or gap positions that do not appear in the surface form and thus presumably require an abstract level of representation (Stowe, 1986).

One of the earliest syntax-based models was the two-stage "sausage" model proposed by Frazier and Fodor (1978). Strictly modular, the model made a sharp distinction between the principles, or *heuristics*, responsible for the initial parse of the input string into constituent syntactic structure in the first stage, and a thematic processor that drew on lexical and contextual information to interpret the initial output in the second stage. If the output of the first parse was not appropriate for the context, the structure was reanalyzed. One type of ambiguity studied was attachment preferences in relative clauses, as in (1):

(1a)   The spy saw the cop with the binoculars.
(1b)   The spy saw the cop with a revolver.

In (1a) the phrase *with the binoculars* can modify either the NP *The spy* or the VP *saw the cop*. The minimal attachment heuristic was proposed to account for observed attachment preferences in processing. Minimal attachment stipulated that the parser attaches a new phrase to the preceding tree structure in the structurally simplest manner—that is, the one involving the fewest additional nodes. In (1a) this would yield the interpretation in which the spy used the binoculars, and this indeed appeared to be the preferred attachment preference for English readers (Frazier, 1987). Rayner, Carlson, and Frazier (1983) tested the psychological reality of the minimal attachment proposal by comparing reading times for sentences like (1a) with the unambiguous (1b), in which the VP attachment reading is not possible. Eye-tracking results showed that readers found (1b) more difficult than (1a), the slowdown being attributed to the need to reanalyze the initial, and ultimately erroneous, parse in light of second stage thematic information—in other words, that revolvers cannot be used to see.

The two-stage approach accorded a primary role to syntactic principles, but it was also evident that the application of these principles was strongly influenced by nonsyntactic factors. These include lexico-semantic information, exposure (frequency), and prior context. All these factors have been shown to influence the course and outcome of the parsing operation in given settings, effects extensively demonstrated in the processing of temporarily ambiguous main verb/reduced relative structures as in (2) (MacDonald & Seidenberg, 2006: 592):

(2a)   Temporary main verb/reduced relative ambiguity: The three men arrested...

(2b)   Main verb interpretation: The three men arrested the burglary suspects...

(2c)   Reduced relative ambiguity: The three men arrested by the local police...

When the parser first encounters the verb *arrested* in (2a) there are two possible interpretations. It could either be the main verb (2b) or part of a reduced relative clause (2c), with relatively longer reading times having been observed for (2c) in a number of studies. Early syntax-based accounts attributed the longer reader times to the need for the parser to reanalyze the original parse, which favored the simpler structural interpretation stipulated by the minimal attachment heuristic (Rayner, Carlson and Frazier, 1983). However, alternative constraint-based accounts have shown that the predicted structural effects can be neutralized or even reversed by nonsyntactic factors that act together to account for the observed behavioral outcomes.

Factors affecting interpretation include the following:

- The animacy of the preverbal noun (Trueswell, Tanenhaus, and Garnsey, 1994)
- Verb frequency in the respective structures (MacDonald, Perlmutter, and Seidenberg, 1994)
- The agenthood plausibility of the preverbal noun (Tanenhaus and Trueswell, 1995)
- The thematic role of preverbal noun (Tabor, Juliano, and Tanenhaus, 1997)
- Broader discourse constraints (Altmann and Steedman, 1988)

These constraints and their interaction explain why the main verb/reduced relative clause ambiguities can be extremely difficult for some readers and easy for others. This variation cannot be easily explained by the application of strict grammatical principles alone (Pickering and Van Gompel, 2006). At issue, however, is not whether this nonsyntactic information can influence processing outcomes, but whether such knowledge can completely eliminate difficulties encountered in, for example, garden path structures and by doing so remove the need to posit a syntax-based processing mechanism (Gibson, 1998; McKoon and Ratcliff, 2003; Pickering, Traxler and Crocker, 2000).

Syntax-Based Accounts of L2 Processing

L1 sentence processing research has been primarily concerned with developing normative models of adult processing. Research on L2 processing shares this goal but also has a primary interest in the relationship between acquisition and processing

(Harrington, 2001). As in L1 research, L2 researchers attempt to understand the mechanisms and knowledge bases responsible for successful L2 processing by examining performance on target linguistic structures that place significant demands on learners. This performance is typically compared with L1 baseline performance (Juffs and Harrington, 1995; Williams, Möbius, and Kim, 2001) and assessed as a reflection of the learner's L1 (Marinis et al., 2005) or as a function of L2 proficiency (Hopp, 2006). A central question implicit in the research discussed here concerns the degree to which observed L2 processing difficulties can be attributed to fundamental differences between the learner's L2 grammar knowledge and the L1 grammar—that is, a *knowledge deficit*, or whether the observed difficulties arise from online *processing limitations* that vary according to such learner-based factors as proficiency, working memory capacity, or automaticity.

An early syntax-based study of L2 sentence processing was Juffs and Harrington (1995, 1996). The study examined online reading of *wh-* question structures by advanced Chinese ESL learners, focusing on the observed asymmetry evident in L2 learner performance on grammatical judgments for *wh-* question structures (Schachter and Yip, 1990). The sentences in (3) are from a class of structures that are assumed to be governed by constraints on how constituents can be moved across structural element (Chomsky, 1986). In (3a) it is assumed that the *wh-* element is moved, or *extracted*, from the underlying subject position, as indicated by the empty gap in (3a), or from the object position in (3b):

(3a)   Who did Ann believe _____ likes her friend? (subject extraction)
(3b)   Who did Ann believe her friend likes _____? (object extraction)

ESL learners experience more difficulty accepting grammatical subject extraction sentences (3a) than the object counterparts on these structures. Poorer performance on the subject structures (3a) by, for example, Chinese ESL learners has been used as evidence for lack of access to UG principles by these learners, given the assumed absence of *wh-* movement constraints in Chinese (Schachter and Yip, 1990). However, although L2 learners had difficulties with the subject structures (3a), they were sensitive to movement constraints in other types of *wh-* structures, including (3b). This raised the possibility that knowledge of the movement constraints per se was not the source of difficulty. Juffs and Harrington (1995, 1996) compared reading times on the two structures by advanced Chinese ESL learners using a self-paced reading task. They found the participants produced significantly longer reading times in the target region in the subject structures, in line with the parsing predictions made by Pritchett's (1992) thematic role assignment model.[1] This led the authors to conclude that the parser, rather than the underlying L2 grammar knowledge, was responsible for the observed subject-object asymmetry (Juffs and Harrington, 1995, 1996). The findings were replicated in Juffs (2005).

Structures involving these nonlocal dependencies are a testing ground for syntax-based accounts, as the accounts assume that abstract linguistic structures represented in the underlying grammar are used in syntactic processing. A question of interest is to what extent L1 processing preferences can influence L2 processing outcomes on these structures. L1 influence has been demonstrated in processing L2 phonological, lexical, and morphosyntactic properties (Juffs, 1998a; Marian and Spivey, 2003; Weber and Cutler, 2003), but there is little evidence for the transfer of L1 syntactic processing preferences in the online processing of the nonlocal dependencies in structures like (4). There is substantial evidence that native English readers reactivate the fronted *wh*-structures at the structural gaps, even when the gap is not the target for the structure—that is, when the structure does not occur immediately after the subcategorizing verb (Gibson and Warren, 2004). Here is an example:

(4)   The nurse who the doctor argued (i) that the rude patient had angered (ii) is refusing to work late.

L2 learners do not appear to process the gaps in the same manner as L1 readers, especially those who have learned the L2 as adults (Clahsen and Felser, 2006b; Dallas and Kaan, 2008; Marinis et al., 2005). Marinis et al. (2005) used a self-paced reading task to compare reading times by native English speakers and L2 learners on sentences like example (4). The structures contained intermediate (i) and target (ii) gaps, allowing the processing of the empty gap and any lexical effect of the adjoining verb to be examined separately. The L2 participants were from typologically distinct Chinese, German, Japanese, and Greek L1s.

Relative faster reading times were evident for the native speakers at the target *angered* (ii) in structures containing an intermediate gap (i) compared to control sentences with no intermediate gap. In contrast, the L2 readers did not seem to be affected by the availability of the intermediate syntactic gap, regardless of L1 background. The authors attributed the results to differences in use of abstract syntactic features in the course of processing, with the L2 readers relying more on lexical information from the verb and other semantic information in the sentence for comprehension. Felser and Roberts (2007) reported similar results using a cross-modal priming technique to study sentences containing a single indirect object gap.

Papadopoulou and Clahsen (2003) also examined language-specific attachment preferences for relative clauses as a potential source of L1 transfer. Prior exposure has been shown to affect the initial parsing preference in complex noun phrases like (5) (Mitchell et al., 1995):

(5)   The journalist interviewed the daughter of the colonel who had the accident.

The preference for attaching the relative clause *who had the accident* "low" to *the colonel* (the colonel had the accident), or "high" to *the daughter* (the daughter had the accident) appears to differ cross-linguistically according to frequency of occurrence. English readers tend to prefer a low reading, whereas French, German, and Dutch readers prefer the high reading (Mitchell et al., 1995), though other research (Mitchell and Brysbaert, 1998) did not support these preferences. Reading time performance of advanced learners of Greek from Spanish, German, and Russian L1s was compared (Papadopoulou and Clahsen, 2003). The participants showed native-like knowledge of the structures in an offline task, but also showed online processing preferences that were different from the native Greek controls and that did not show any influence from L1 processing strategies. Other studies have also failed to demonstrate L1 effects on L2 parsing (Marinis et al., 2005; Williams, Möbius, and Kim, 2001).

However, the nonequivalence of L1 and L2 syntactic processing has been challenged. Hopp (2006) showed that highly proficient L2 learners can exhibit native-like processing outcomes on complex structures. The study compared performance on German subject and object relative clause structures by L1 Dutch and L1 English learners of low and near-native proficiency. Contrary to Clahsen and Felser (2006b) the results indicated that the near-native group for both L1s showed reliable use of syntactic features in phrase-structural reanalysis, especially in a condition in which lexical, semantic, pragmatic, and frequency-based cues to sentence interpretation were not available. Moreover, the near-natives showed an interaction of syntactic feature type and phrase-structural parsing principles in parsing the ambiguous grammatical sentences as well as the ungrammatical ones. The study suggests that the difference between L1 and L2 syntactic knowledge may be one of degree and not of kind. See Sabourin and Stowe (2008) for a similar discussion.

It remains to be established whether L2 readers are able to reach native-like processing fluency on complex syntactic structures in the L2. The weight of the evidence to date has led Clahsen and others to propose that the abstract syntactic representations available to native speakers are not used in the same way by adult L2 learners. Adult L2 processing in this view is characterized as being *shallower* in that it makes less use of syntactic or phrase-structural information in the course of parsing (Townsend and Bever, 2001). L2 parsing decisions seem to be guided to a greater extent by lexical-semantic cues and associative knowledge than those in the L1 (Clahsen and Felser, 2006a, 2006b; Dallas and Kaan, 2008).

Evidence that L2 learners do not access abstract linguistic features when processing the target L2 grammar indicates that knowledge shortcomings may be a factor in L2 processing difficulties. It also raises the question as to how abstract linguistic features are represented in the L2 grammar and how those features might interact with other types of knowledge. Although Clahsen and others maintain that L2 learners do not use this abstract knowledge in the same way as native speakers, presumably L2 grammar knowledge remains essentially a rule-based entity, though one that differs from the L1 in important respects (Hawkins, 2008; Williams and Kuribara, 2008).

Whatever differences and similarities may be evident between the L1 and L2 grammars, more studies are needed to assess how knowledge representations interact with processing limitations. Two key processing limitations are individual differences in working memory capacity and the degree of automaticity attained in L2 processing. Although individual differences in L2 working memory capacity have been related to L2 language performance in a number of domains (Harrington and Sawyer, 1992; Kormos and Safar, 2008; Leeser, 2007), the effect of capacity differences on L2 syntactic processing outcomes has yet to be shown. The few studies that have been done show little or no effect for differences in working memory on processing the type of structures examined here (Felser and Roberts, 2007; Juffs,

2005). Automaticity in accessing and using linguistic knowledge in real-time discourse is an essential aspect of fluent processing. Reduced automaticity in even advanced L2 learners in phonological and lexical processing has been widely observed, and the assumption is that automaticity in syntactic processing will be similar (Segalowitz and Hulstijn, 2003). Recent research using evoked-response potentials (ERP) to track the time course of processing provides some evidence that L2 learners also display less automaticity in the processing of complex syntactic structures (Clahsen and Felser, 2006b). More research in both areas is needed.

Syntax-Based Models of L2 Processing and SLA Theory

Syntax-based approaches assume that syntactic knowledge is a primary driver of online comprehension. L1 accounts provide evidence for the need to posit an abstract level of syntactic representation to account for the processing of the complex structures discussed here (Traxler and Van Gompel, 2006; though see Van Valin, 1995, for a counter view). The L2 syntax-based accounts examined make the same assumptions about syntactic knowledge and processing as their L1 counterparts. However, a number of studies show that L2 processors do not use this knowledge in the same way. Whether this abstract knowledge is available at all to the L2 learner remains an open question, as does the extent to which the adult L2 reader can achieve native-like processing skill overall, or just in certain parts of the grammar (Dallas and Kaan, 2008; Dussias and Sagarra, 2007; Osterhout et al., 2006; Sabourin and Stowe, 2008).

Clahsen and colleagues propose a model of L2 processing that is shallower and is driven by lexicalist and associative knowledge to a greater extent than in the L1 (see Clahsen and Felser, 2006a). This proposal suggests that L2 grammatical knowledge is not a unitary construct in which one set of mechanisms can account for all the effects observed. It is also consistent with the long-standing view that adult SLA is fundamentally different from L1 acquisition—a difference evident here at the computational level (Bley-Vroman, 1989). The less important abstract linguistic features become in determining L2 processing outcomes, the more overlap the L2 accounts discussed in this section share with the constraint-based approaches considered in the next.

Constraint-Based Approaches to L2 Sentence Processing

The constraint-based approach characterizes sentence processing as an interactive process in which different sources of information compete and converge in the course of comprehension (MacDonald and Seidenberg, 2006). The approach is nonmodular, with grammatical knowledge being but one source of information influencing (or *constraining*) processing outcomes. Word order regularities, morpho-syntax, number agreement, and so forth are not represented as abstract rule-based knowledge but rather as statistical form-function regularities that arise as the result of use. These knowledge representations emerge as the result of the interaction of linguistic, pragmatic, contextual, and physical features (or *cues*) available in the input that are stored in memory at the time of processing (Ellis, 1998). The relative weight of a cue depends on its distribution and frequency in the input and will determine its availability during processing. The associative mechanisms responsible for the learning of the cues are also directly implicated in the processing of a specific instance (MacWhinney, 1999).

The multiplicity of potential cues in the input and the interactive nature of their use make the approach less amenable to testing specific effects. As a result, online accounts of the processing of the complex syntax discussed above have yet to appear in the L2 literature. Constraint-based studies of L2 processing have focused on the cross-linguistic development of cue knowledge—particularly as a source of L1 transfer (Harrington, 1987; Rounds and Kanagy, 1998)—and on the development of these cues in connectionist-learning studies (Ellis and Schmidt, 1998, 1997). Recent work in usage-based construction grammar (P. Robinson and Ellis, 2008) shares basic assumptions with these approaches. In this section, these assumptions are described and L2 studies in the framework are discussed.

Grammar Knowledge as a Graded Probabilistic System

Grammar knowledge in the constraint-based approach is represented as interconnected units in memory and not as a set of abstract rules. In connectionist approaches, these units take the form of distributed features connected in complex associative networks. Structure-like patterns corresponding to traditional rule-based representations (phonemes, morphemes, syntactic rules) emerge from these networks (Ellis, 2006), producing rule-like behavior in production and comprehension. Crucially this behavior does not assume the abstract level of syntactic representation central to principle-based approaches (MacWhinney, 1999). In more recent grammar accounts these units take the form of individual grammatical constructions (Tomasello, 2003).

Grammar knowledge develops as the result of experience with the language; hence, the approach is termed *usage-based* (Bybee, 2006). The effect of this experience is graded, with representations undergoing constant modification and strengthening with use. The graded nature of the patterns contrasts with traditional symbolic approaches, in which these linguistic representations are assumed to be learned in a discrete, all-or-none manner. The graded nature of language knowledge also means proficiency can be characterized in probabilistic statistical terms (Seidenberg and McDonald, 1999). The application of grammar knowledge in this view is not an either/or computation of a rule but rather an estimation of which alternative is the most probable. Probabilistic models have an advantage over rule-based models in being able to capture the variable nature of behavior, both across individuals and across time. The approach is particularly advantageous in SLA theory and research, in which variation itself is of primary theoretical and methodological interest. Although probabilistic approaches are not incompatible with discrete rule approaches, they are more consistent with constraint-based view of cognition (Chater and Christiansen, 2008).

The constraint-based approach assumes a direct and immediate relationship between processing and learning. Novel input is processed via previously stored experience, with the act of comprehension or production itself changing the strength of the existing knowledge representations. As a result, the mechanisms involved in processing existing forms are also responsible for learning new ones. Furthermore, unlike the modularity of the syntax-based approaches, these mechanisms draw on the same cognitive mechanisms as those used by other cognitive processes; that is, they are not specific to language. Language learning is thus characterized as an *emergent* property of the interaction between the learning environment and general learning capacities of the individual, and not as the result of some prespecified principles or capacities (Ellis, 1998).

Sentence Processing as Cue Competition and Convergence

The constraint-based perspective characterizes sentence processing as an interactive process in which multiple sources of information—semantic, syntactic, discourse, and referential—compete and converge to yield a particular interpretation. This process is exemplified in the competition model (MacWhinney and Bates, 1989), a paradigmatic constraint-based model. The model was developed to account for how readers or listeners assign agenthood in simple active sentences like *Tom saw the sunset*. The main English cues to agenthood in these sentences are *word order* (the first noun is usually the agent), *preverbal position* (the agent usually precedes the action), and *animacy* (animate entities can do things like "see"), and in certain contexts these cues all bias the assignment of agenthood to *Tom* in the canonical sentence above. But cue assignment is probabilistic, and the second noun could be the agent, as when the object is left-dislocated for effect (*The sunset Tom saw*). In this case, word order biases agent assignment to *the sunset*, whereas animacy and preverbal cues converge to bias the selection of *Tom* as the agent. Native English speakers will typically assign agenthood to *the sunset* in nonsensical but grammatically acceptable strings like *The sunset saw Tom*. This reflects the importance of word order as a cue in English—a condition not universally shared across languages; for example, Italians accord less weight to word order cues than English speakers (MacWhinney and Bates, 1989). Cross-linguistic differences in cue types and cue weights provide a means to quantify differences among languages and across levels of learner proficiency within a language.

The available cues are simultaneously activated in the course of processing, with the ultimate interpretation the result of the cooperation and competition among the varying cues strengths (MacWhinney, 2005). The competition model embodies the crucial characteristics of the constraint-based approach, and has, as a research program, had a significant influence on research on cross-linguistic differences and on how cues are learned by children. However, application of the model has been limited to the domain of agent assignment, not addressing how these multiple cues are integrated online.

Constraint-Based Accounts of Sentence Processing

The constraint-based view of processing is best exemplified by connectionist models of cognition and language. A variety of constraint-based accounts of learning and processing have been modeled within the connectionist framework, with early ones focusing on phonological, lexical, and morphosyntactic phenomena (O'Reilly and Munakata, 2000). Connectionist models have been trained to learn the following:

- How to form English past tense verbs (Rumelhart and McClelland, 1986)
- How to assign verb tense (Plunkett and Marchman, 1993)
- How to resolve lexical ambiguity (Kawamoto, 1993)

These early studies were highly influential because they demonstrated the ability of the approach to learn and process language by a general associative learning mechanism that provided a uniform account of processing across linguistic levels, perceptual, lexical, and syntactic (MacDonald and Seidenberg, 2006). However, the adequacy of associative learning alone as the means to develop the capacity to process complex structural relations has been challenged (Marcus, 1998; Pinker and Prince, 1988). Such relations include the nonlocal dependencies discussed earlier as well as other relations like embedding and agreement. These domains have been assumed to require an abstract level of syntactic representation that entails a rule-based system of grammatical knowledge (Pinker and Prince, 1988).

A major advancement thus was that of Elman (1993), who showed how a certain class of connectionist models could in principle capture nonlocal dependencies. Elman used a simple recurrent network (SRN) model to predict word sequences in sentences generated by a small, context-free grammar. The grammar contained key syntactic structures (including subject-verb agreement and subject-object relative clauses), and the model was able to extract these grammatical regularities from the input. Most notable was the ability to identify agreement relations across intervening words (Elman, 1993).

Elman's findings were extended to show that connectionist models were able to capture the difficulties encountered by human readers processing complex syntax. Christiansen and Chater (1999) examined the processing of center-embedded structures by comparing results of an SRN simulation with reading data from human subjects. They found that the connectionist simulation did a good job of predicting the structural complexity effects evident in the reading data. The resolution of garden path ambiguities was also examined in a two-component model consisting of an SRN and a weighting mechanism (Tabor, Juliano, and Tanenhaus, 1997). The lexical and syntactic interactions obtained from the simulation were fitted to human reading times from previous studies. The foregoing indicated that these structures can be handled in the connectionist framework. However, although interactive connectionist accounts have shown the potential to capture the complex syntactic relations needed in online comprehension, these structures remain a challenge for models of language processing that depend on statistical learning alone (MacDonald and Seidenberg, 2006).

Constraint-Based Accounts of L2 Processing

Constraint-based accounts of L2 processing include those done in the competition model framework (Bates and MacWhinney, 1989) and connectionist studies (Ellis and Schmidt, 1998). Unlike the syntax-based accounts, the focus in these studies has not been on online comprehension processes, but rather on identifying the linguistic factors that contribute to learning and processing outcomes.

The earliest constraint-based studies of L2 processing were applications of the competition model. These studies modeled L2 learning in terms of the development of cue strengths in the target L2. The focus was on relative differences in cue strengths across the learner's L1 and L2. These cue strengths were of interest as a source of cross-linguistic processing transfer, and as a measure of proficiency within the specific languages. Results from off-line agent-assignment tasks showed that cue weights provided a reliable and quantifiable way to describe L2 development in both areas (Harrington, 1987; Kilborn, 1989; Rounds and Kanagy, 1998; Sasaki, 1994). The competition model was limited in that it was applied to a single domain—agent assignment—and the off-line nature of the experimental task provided little insight into how these cues might be used in real-time processing. Recent studies have attempted to extend the model to argument structure (Dong and Cai, 2007).

Connectionist accounts of L2 development have focused on learning specific grammatical features. Early research examined the mapping of lexical items onto the following:

- Thematic roles (Gasser, 1990)
- The learning of gender in French (Sokolik, 1990; Sokolik and Smith, 1992)
- The development of verb morphology (Broeder and Plunkett, 1994)
- Tense in English (Ellis and Schmidt, 1998)

Ellis and Schmidt (1998) investigated the frequency by regularity-interaction observed in the production of English past tense verbs (Prasada and Pinker, 1993). English native speakers differ in the time taken to produce regular (*play-played*) and irregular (*run-ran*) past tense forms, the production of the latter being closely related to stem frequency. Past tense forms of high-frequency stems are produced more quickly than those from low-frequency stems, whereas regular past tense verb take approximately the same time to produce, regardless of stem frequency. To account for this result, two separate mechanisms have been proposed:

1. Frequency-sensitive irregular verbs are stored as individual items in associative memory, with production based on retrieval from memory.

2. In contrast, regular forms are generated by a rule binding stem and affix at the time of production. (Pinker and Prince, 1994)

Ellis and Schmidt (1998) tested this proposal in a study comparing human and connectionist simulation data on learning plural morphology.[2] They found a frequency-by-regularity interaction similar to the earlier study and consistent with earlier connectionist models (Rumelhart and McClelland, 1986). The results demonstrated that, in principle, a separate symbolic rule-based mechanism was not required to account for learning in this domain. The researchers also attempted to show that a connectionist model could account for the learning of number agreement by L2 learners (Ellis and Schmidt, 1997). The study tested Ellis's (1996) bootstrapping account of SLA in which the interaction of short-term and long-term memory processes allows the learner to extract nonlocal grammatical dependencies on the basis of exposure alone. The results were consistent with the account, as better memory performance correlated with more accurate performance on the structures (Ellis and Schmidt, 1997). However, the indirect nature of evidence from memory tasks, the fragmentary nature of the language used, and the off-line nature of task leaves open how generalizable these findings are to actual acquisition and online processing.

The accounts considered so far have not directly examined online comprehension processes in the same way as the syntax-based models discussed in the first part of this chapter. The formal linguistic theories that inform the latter provide the means to make specific processing predictions that can be tested in a controlled manner. To date, constraint-based accounts have been successful in identifying what knowledge is important for explaining L2 outcomes, but they have been less successful in explaining how that knowledge is integrated in real-time processing.

Complex syntax thus remains an issue for constraint-based approaches to processing. These domains are receiving increasing attention from researchers in construction grammar (Goldberg, 2006; Tomasello, 2003). The construction grammar approach shares basic assumptions of the constraint-based approach as it has been outlined here. Principal among these is the usage-based nature of grammar knowledge, its graded representation, and the emphasis on memory retrieval in processing in lieu of the application and evaluation of syntactic principles in processing. The processing of nonlocal *wh-* dependencies has been addressed in recent work in the area (Ambridge and Goldberg, 2008; Dąbrowska, 2008). Although the current empirical data (consisting of questionnaire and production data) is off-line, the insights may be applicable to testing in online studies of L2 processing in the future (Goldberg and Casenhiser, 2008).

Constraint-Based Models of L2 Processing and SLA Theory

Constraint-based models of L2 sentence processing remain underspecified in terms of the online effect studied by the syntax-based approaches. However, although empirical findings are limited, the constraint-based perspective remains appealing, as it embodies key properties of L2 learning and performance. The graded, probabilistic nature of grammar knowledge that is characteristic of the approach is well suited to capturing the variation evident across learners, languages, and settings—an integral part of adult SLA. The unified approach to learning and processing also provides an explicit characterization of the transition mechanisms that must be specified as part of a complete theory of SLA (Gregg, 2003).

As more explicit processing predictions are developed, more on-line processing studies in the constraint-based framework can be expected. Although the discussion so far has contrasted syntax-based and constraint-based accounts, there may also be a middle ground between the two. The less that abstract linguistic knowledge is seen to play a role in L2 processing outcomes (Clahsen and Felser, 2006a), the more tenable constraint-based approaches become as an account of the computational basis of SLA. Adult L2 grammar learning and processing may turn out to be a hybrid process in which constraint learning processes combine in some manner with structural representations that are primarily rule-based (Mellow, 2004).

Conclusion

The two perspectives examined here differ significantly in how they approach L2 sentence processing and in the domains of L2 performance studied. Three questions emerge from the comparison of the two perspectives and from the research produced to date:

1. *Are L1 and L2 sentence processing fundamentally different?* The evidence from syntax-based research is mixed, though an increasing number of studies suggest that abstract syntactic relations are handled differently by the L2 processor. The constraint-based approach assumes the two are the same on theoretical grounds. The ability to answer this question will depend in part on being able to identify and isolate the effect of nonstructural factors (frequency, plausibility, etc.) on syntactic processing outcomes.

2. *Is L2 sentence processing a unitary behavior?* The evidence from the syntax-based studies suggests it is not. Some domains (e.g., nonlocal dependencies) appear to be governed by some mechanisms, whereas other aspects (e.g., verb subcategorization) may be governed by others; individuals may be strategic in how they process a particular sentence at a particular time (Townsend and Bever, 2001). Constraint-based accounts assume that the same memory-based mechanisms are responsible for all processing outcomes in a uniform way.

3. *Can adult L2 learners attain native-like processing proficiency?* Again, the findings from the syntax-based accounts are mixed, but they suggest that overall native-like processing proficiency may not be attainable, at least in some

domains. The usage-based nature of the constraint-based approach implies that native-like fluency in the L2 is possible, given the appropriate experience.

L2 sentence processing as a research area is still developing, and the answers given above are highly tentative. It has been only in the last decade that online studies have appeared, and the number of such studies will undoubtedly grow. The studies discussed in this chapter have used primarily behavioral data, examining online reading behavior through self-paced reading tasks (Papadopoulou, 2005) or eye movement monitoring (Frenck-Mestre, 2005). Recent neurolinguistic research is applying increasingly sophisticated tools to study online sentence processing in the L2. Techniques such as event-related brain potentials (ERPs; Mueller, 2005; Osterhout et al. (2006); Sabourin and Stowe, 2008), and brain imaging (Indefrey, 2006) will allow researchers to study online comprehension processes at a level of sensitivity not possible with the current behavioral methods.

NOTES

1. The generalized theta attachment (GTA) model is a serial processing model that assigns thematic roles (that is, agent, theme, goal, etc.) to elements in the input string. Processing difficulties arise as the result of unfulfilled thematic role assignments. The key comparison was for reading times in the region following the word *believe* in the example sentences. In the subject extraction sentences this region follows the extraction gap, and in the object structures it occurs before. It was predicted that the parser will initially interpret the main verb *believe* in the subject structures as an NP complement and will posit a complete grammatical sentence with an object gap—that is, *Who does Ann believe* ____? (Pritchett, 1992). This is a version of the active filler strategy in which the processor is assumed to favor any analysis that allows gap filling over one that does not (Stowe, 1986). The subsequent appearance of the word *like* then forces the object gap to be reanalyzed as a subject gap structure, resulting in longer reading times.

2. Input units were singular word stems, and output units were plural prefixes, either regular or irregular. The network was trained by presenting the input units, each presentation activating either of the output units. At the outset, the mappings were random. Each time a given input unit activated a particular output unit, the model would compare the activation weight of that mapping with that of the correct output unit for that input unit. A backpropagation learning mechanism was used to calculate the difference between the observed and the desired mappings and then to make an incremental adjustment in the weight of the observed mapping. As a result, the next time the input unit was presented, it was closer to the weight of the correct output unit. All the input-output mappings were thus trained separately over thousands of trials. Subsequently, an untrained singular stem was used to test the model's ability to handle novel input; the result showed a small but statistically significant tendency for the novel unit to activate the appropriate output unit (regular plural; Ellis and Schmidt, 1998).

CHAPTER 14

SECOND LANGUAGE ACQUISITION: A SOCIAL PSYCHOLOGICAL PERSPECTIVE

ROBERT C. GARDNER

I. INTRODUCTION

The basic premise underlying a social psychological perspective of second language acquisition is that language is a defining characteristic of the individual.[1] It is involved in one's thoughts, self-communication, social interaction, and perception of the world. Moreover, language is a defining attribute of cultural groups. It serves to distinguish one group from another, and thus to reflect one's cultural identity. Thus, to learn a second language involves, to some extent, making part of another cultural group part of one's self, even if this is only the vocabulary, sounds, verbal forms, and so forth of that group. That is, the language is more than a symbolic system that facilitates communication among individuals; it is a defining feature of self-identity linked directly to the very social existence of the individual.

A related issue that must be considered from this perspective is what constitutes learning a language. As initially formulated, the social psychological perspective viewed second language learning in terms of bilingual skill. Taking a few courses or being able to make oneself understood in the language in a halting fashion was not the criterion. The criterion was the development of a free-flowing and automatic use of the language comparable to native speakers. Thus, the social psychological perspective is concerned with the development of bilingualism, not the achievement of an A grade in the course or a high mark on a test. These achievements might represent stages along the way to the development of bilingual skill, but they are not the ultimate goals in the social psychological perspective. Having said this, however, it must be confessed that in those studies that assess the relationship between affective variables and achievement, most, if not all, assess proficiency in terms of grades in courses, scores on tests, ratings of oral proficiency, and so forth, and it is a testament to the validity of the social psychological perspective that it is able to explain proficiency even when it is defined in terms of these types of criteria.

Prior to the 1950s, the main determinants of success in learning a second language were thought to be intelligence and language aptitude. In his review of research on bilingualism, however, Arsenian (1945) devoted a section on social psychology of language and bilingualism in which he raised questions about the relation between language and acculturation, the role of affective factors in second language acquisition, intergroup relations and language learning, and so forth. Then, in the lead article of the inaugural issue of *Language Learning*, Marckwardt (1948) identified five motives that were influential in promoting the acquisition of another language. He described three of them as practical (assimilation of an ethnic minority, promotion of trade, and scientific utility), and two as nonutilitarian (self-cultural development and the maintenance of ethnic identity of a minority group). Later, Nida (1956) reported a case study of a missionary who was unable to learn the language of the group with which he was to work. He noted that the individual, who was the son of immigrant parents, had identified strongly with English-speaking America. Nida claimed that this extreme identification and an emotional block against anything "foreign" interfered with his being able to learn another language. The social psychological perspective of second language acquisition grew out of this background.

II. THE EARLY PERSPECTIVE

The initial empirical studies with a social psychological perspective were conducted by Lambert (1955, 1956a, 1956b, 1956c). His research was concerned with the assessment of bilingual dominance and the development of bilingualism. He investigated developmental changes in French and English among students differing in terms of language training—undergraduate students majoring in French, graduate students majoring in French, and native French speakers who had lived in an English-speaking country for an average of 7 years. Two of his observations are noteworthy here. One was that two of the graduate students measured dominant in French. In both cases, these students could be described as particularly motivated—one because of her career as a French teacher, and the other because of his extreme identification with France (Lambert, 1955). We can note the foundation of the integrative and instrumental dichotomy that still pervades much of the research in this field today.

The second observation was that the developmental changes in second language acquisition appeared to involve at least two plateaus. Lambert (1956c) described the first plateau as reflecting a "vocabulary" cluster because those measures that involved vocabulary strength distinguished the undergraduate students from the other two groups. He defined the second plateau as reflecting a "cultural" cluster because these measures differentiated between the native speakers on the one hand and the undergraduate and graduate groups on the other, and involved such features as habitual word order, stereotypy of response, and so forth. He proposed, therefore, that second language acquisition entails a series of barriers to overcome, with the vocabulary barrier being the easiest and the cultural barrier the most difficult. Although Lambert did not discuss other barriers, Gardner (2007) contrasted first and second language learning, identifying four phases common to both: the elemental, consolidation, conscious expression, and automaticity and thought stages. In this sense, the true acquisition of a second language can be seen to involve the development of expert performance in that language.

Conceptualizing second language acquisition in terms of the development of expert performance has important implications. Ericsson, Krampe, and Tesch-Römer (1993) reviewed the literature on expert performance in many facets of human behavior and concluded that it is not dependent primarily on innate talent or ability, as is commonly believed. They reviewed many studies on such diverse topics as typing speed, artistic prowess, chess mastery, and so forth, and found that expert performance results from repeated practice (i.e., from consistent and persistent motivated behavior). They concluded that it requires approximately 10 years of sustained practice to develop expertise and noted that it takes about this long to acquire the vocabulary of a normal adult. If, therefore, we view second language acquisition as equivalent to the development of expert behavior, it follows that the motivation to learn the second language must be long-standing. From the social psychological perspective, learning a second language means the acquisition of near-native facility with the content and structure of the language, and near automaticity in its use both conceptually and behaviorally. Such acquisition takes time and dedicated effort for an adult to achieve! Thus, when we speak of motivation to learn a second language, we are speaking not about some transient motivation but instead about a long-term commitment to the task (with the associated effort, desire and satisfaction).

The term *motivation* has been variously defined in the literature (see, for example, Kleinginna and Kleinginna, 1981), largely because it has many characteristics. The individual who is motivated has a goal, wants to achieve it, exerts effort to achieve it, enjoys activities associated with it, is persistent and attentive, has expectations, makes attributions, is self-confident, and so forth (cf. Gardner, 2006). It is general in nature in that it pervades much of the individual's behavior, and it is specific to activities or goals in which it is aroused. The important point is that motivation is multifaceted, not unidimensional, and is a characteristic of the individual, not the environment. That is, regardless of whether motivation is defined as intrinsic or extrinsic, integrative or instrumental, and so forth, it is an attribute of the individual that displays itself in all of the characteristics listed above, and it is the degree of motivation, not the source, that influences one's degree of success in learning the language. For example, if intrinsic motivation is superior to extrinsic motivation in promoting achievement, or if integratively orientated learners are more successful than instrumentally oriented ones, it is because one is more strongly associated with all the characteristics of motivation, not that the source is different.

The first investigation of individual differences in second language acquisition from the social psychological perspective was conducted by Gardner and Lambert (1959). They studied high school students learning French as a second language in Montreal and found that two factors were associated with achievement in French. One was aptitude; the other was motivation. They concluded that the motivation was *"characterized by a willingness to be like valued members of the language community"* (p. 271 [italics in the original]). Since then there have been numerous studies of the relation between attitudes and motivation and achievement (e.g., Gardner, 1985; Gardner and Lambert, 1972). Clément and Gardner (2001) present a graph, based on an unpublished survey of three databases (*PsycLIT, ERIC,* and *Linguistics and Language Behavior Abstracts*) of the number of investigations published between 1985 and 1994 that dealt with individual difference variables in second language acquisition. In this 10-year period, 496 studies dealt with attitudes and 218 with motivation. Obviously, some articles referred to both attributes, and not all of them referred just to attitudes directly related to the social psychological perspective, but it is clear that there was an active interest in the field.

III. Social Psychological Models of Second Language Acquisition

The initial social psychological model was outlined by Lambert (1967, 1974), who proposed that aptitude, attitudes, orientation, and motivation promote the development of bilingual proficiency and that this can have an effect on one's self-identity. Lambert (1974) distinguished between two types of bilingualism— additive and subtractive—that reflect the effect of second language acquisition on self-identity, and linked them to different language contexts. Additive bilingualism was seen to apply to members of the majority learning the language of a minority, in which they did not lose any of their own ethnic identity but developed proficiency in the other language. Subtractive bilingualism, on the other hand, was more characteristic of minority group members who, in learning the language of the majority, ran the risk of losing some of their own cultural identity.

Since then there have been a number of models presented, each changing the focus slightly and adding and subtracting elements. Gardner and Smythe (1975) proposed a model that retained the elements of Lambert's social psychological model but expanded it to take into account the language learning situation, distinguishing between formal and informal language learning contexts. This model, now referred to as the socio-educational model, has evolved since then (Gardner, 1985, 2000, 2007), and has become much more formal, operationalizing the concepts in terms of measures of specific attributes. Currently, it focuses on six latent constructs: *language aptitude, attitudes toward the learning situation, integrativeness, motivation, language anxiety*, and *language achievement* (characterized in terms of linguistic and nonlinguistic outcomes). Gardner and Smythe also developed and standardized the Attitude/Motivation Test Battery (AMTB) that assessed 11 relevant affective variables.[2] The concept of the integrative motive is hypothesized to comprise the three constructs: *attitudes toward the learning situation, integrativeness*, and *motivation;* it can be assessed by aggregating scores on eight of the variables assessed by the AMTB. A measure of *instrumental* orientation is included in the measures, but it is not a construct emphasized in the model. With the exception of *attitudes toward the learning situation* and *language anxi*ety, this model shares constructs with Lambert's model and, though self-identity is not explicitly identified in it, the concept of integrativeness involves the willingness to identify with the other language community.

A third model in this tradition is the social context model (Clément, 1980). It has many constructs that are similar to those in Gardner's model, with the exception of *attitudes toward the learning situation*, but it sometimes conceptualizes and measures them differently. A major feature of this model is that it focuses on the linguistic nature of the community, distinguishing between unicultural and multicultural communities. Moreover, it contains additional constructs such as *fear of assimilation, contact with the language* (which is influenced in part by the linguistic nature of the community), and *self-confidence with the language.* Later developments (Clément, Dörnyei, and Noels, 1994) added *appraisal of the classroom environment* (similar conceptually to Attitudes toward the Learning Situation in the Socio-educational model).

A fourth model was proposed by Dörnyei (1994) as the extended motivational framework. It referred to three levels of motivation—: *language level, learner level*, and *learning situation level,*—and involved 17 constructs, some of which involve more than one measure. Many of the constructs associated with the third level are different from those proposed in the preceding models, but those in the first two levels are comparable to those in at least one of the Lambert, Gardner, or Clément models.

A fifth formal model was proposed by MacIntyre, Clément, Dörnyei, and Noels (1998) referred to as a situated model of confidence and affiliation. This model, unlike those referred to above that focus on second language achievement, has a pyramidal structure comprised of six levels, with *communication behavior* at the top and *social and individual context* at the bottom. Twelve major constructs form the elements of these levels, but the ultimate criterion is the willingness to communicate in the second language, not second language achievement.

There are other models that could be discussed (see, e.g., Dörnyei, 2001, 2003), but the above five are most representative of the social psychological perspective because each involves the concept of motivation and some form of involvement with the other cultural community. One thing that is obvious from these models is that they involve a series of overlapping constructs, and each time a new model is proposed it tends to be more complex than its predecessor, often encompassing more variables. This tendency is valuable in that it focuses attention on more variables that might be important, but it has drawbacks too in that with greater complexity comes less parsimony, making empirical verification more difficult.

This particular approach was criticized in the 1990s as not being education friendly. For example, Crookes and Schmidt (1991) called for a new approach to the investigation of motivation, and this was augmented by a lively exchange in the 1994/1995 issues of the *Modern Language Journal*. There have been a number of models and approaches proposed since then (see, e.g., Dörnyei and Otto's [1998] process model of second Language Motivation and Williams and Burden's [1997] social constructivist model), but these are more focused on classroom learning and performance than on the development of bilingual skill. This is not intended as a criticism of these models. This type of approach is important to the area of second language education, to be sure, but the motivation involves performance in the classroom environment. One cannot argue against the importance of motivation in the classroom, but it is an open empirical question whether the motivation that might be promoted by teachers in this context eventuates in the development of bilingual skills as discussed above, or even if it is that unrelated to motivation as defined, for example, in the socio-educational model of second language acquisition.

IV. Research Issues

This has been a very active research field over the years with many different issues under consideration. Some of them are long-standing and were discussed in an earlier edition of this chapter (Gardner, 2002) but are still very much a part of the research literature. Among the long-standing issues, the first concerns some disagreement about which is the more important for second language acquisition: integrative or instrumental motivation. Despite the disagreement, there has been relatively little research devoted to resolving the issue. Instead, most studies concerned with this distinction focus primarily on integrative and instrumental orientations and do not assess any other aspect of motivation. In this context, there have been a number of studies focused on identifying other orientations (see, e.g., Clément and Kruidenier, 1983), generally by factor analyzing a number of different reasons for studying a language. Many of the studies do not relate the orientations to either motivation or achievement.

This distinction between integrative and instrumental motivation is often made in the context of a second issue—the distinction between foreign and second language learning—where it is often hypothesized that the social environment governs which type of motivation is the more dominant. For example, Oxford (1996) proposed that a foreign language is typically learned in an environment in which the language is seldom used or experienced, whereas a second language is learned in a setting in which that language is typically used by the majority of individuals for everyday communication. This distinction has been made by many others, and it has even been suggested that the motivations of individuals in the two different environments would be quite different. Thus, Dörnyei (1990) proposed that instrumental motivation may be more important for foreign language learners than for second language learners, for whom integrative motivation may be the more influential. This is a compelling hypothesis, and it is certainly reasonable to assume that the language context will influence the dynamics of language acquisition (cf. Clément, 1980); however, it is unwise to tie this distinction to the labels *foreign* and *second language acquisition*. Instead, it should be associated with an analysis of the ethnolinguistic vitality of the language in the community in terms of the relevant demographics (Giles, Bourhis, and Taylor, 1977). Simply using the labels *foreign* and *second language* as indicators of this vitality can be very misleading. For example, French and English are both considered second languages in Canada, but this is simply because they are the official languages. Some parts of Canada are relatively French/English bilingual, but many are not. For example, according to the 1996 Canada census, only 12% of the population in the province of Ontario knows French. Interestingly, this is where much of the research by Gardner has been conducted, and his research is often referred to by others as demonstrating why integrative motivation is important for the learning of a second language. Sometimes the added meaning associated with foreign and second language simply does not apply. Thus, based on these types of numbers, much of Gardner's research would be characterized as taking place in a foreign language environment.

A third issue concerns the notion of causation in the motivation–achievement sequence. That is, does motivation facilitate achievement in the second language or does achievement in the second language promote motivation? This issue has been raised by a number of researchers (see, e.g., Ellis, 1994), and it seems likely that both causative directions are applicable. Wherever individual differences are concerned, however, the question of directionality can never be answered unequivocally, regardless of the context. The only way to establish causation in a scientific sense is to randomly assign individuals to conditions, and this is not possible when the focus is on individual differences (see, e.g., Gardner, 2000). One can use structural equation modeling to test the validity of a particular "causal" model, but it is not proof of the direction of causation—rather, it is a test that the data are consistent with that model. One can test any number of models and find that they are relatively consistent with the data, but to compare one with another requires that one model be nested in the other, and this is not feasible in contrasting different directions of causation. This does not mean that the study of the correlation between these two classes of variables is meaningless. From the perspective of Bayesian statistics, a positive correlation between two variables indicates that given a particular score on one of the variables (say, *motivation*), there is a given probability that one's score on the other variable (language achievement) will be greater than some given score and vice versa. That is, there is enhanced value in knowing the nature of the correlation. To the extent that a correlation has been demonstrated in a sample of individuals, it is reasonable to expect that it exists in the population for which the sample can be considered representative. This correlation has implications in that it links the two underlying constructs. The question of which "causes" which, or if anything does at all, is indeterminate and immaterial.

A fourth issue concerns the role of the classroom in motivation. This was initiated in part by Crookes and Schmidt (1991), who proposed that more attention should be directed to the motivation in the classroom, a stated motivation that was viewed as less stable and more susceptible to environmental characteristics (cf. Boekaerts, 1986). Those models that focus attention on motivation in the classroom (see, e.g., Dörnyei and Csizér, 1998; Dörnyei and Otto, 1998; Williams and Burden, 1997) are concerned with the more situationally relevant elements of motivation. It is true that they might endure for the length of the course, and perhaps beyond, but the focus in the models and associated research is the effect of the classroom environment. In this respect, they do not differ that much from the research in educational psychology that applies to any school subject, and generally the findings that have been reported are comparable to those obtained with other school subjects. It is meaningful to ask, however, whether this classroom-based motivation is that different from and unrelated to the more general form of motivation characterized in a social psychological perspective. One possible hypothesis is that there is a functional relationship between the two and that there is in fact a correlation between levels of motivation in the classroom and motivation socially defined. This hypothesis was investigated recently by Bernaus, Moore, and Azevedo (2007), who adapted measures from the socio-educational model (Gardner, 1985, 2007) and the process model (Dörnyei and Otto, 1998). They found that executive motivational influences from the process model loaded on an integrative motive factor, that motivational influences on intention formation and motivational influences on intention enactment shared variance in common with Gardner's measure of interest in foreign languages, and that postactional evaluation contributed to an attitude toward the learning situation factor defined by two measures from the socio-educational model.

A fifth issue concerns the concept of integrative motivation. Is the integrative motive to be conceived in the same way as various social motives, or is it different? Some researchers appear to consider it as a trait-like characteristic of the individual that is relatively stable and long lasting (like many social motives), whereas Gardner (2005) has argued that integrative motivation is an inference made on the basis of a number of characteristics of the individual. That is, individuals can be said to be integratively motivated if they have an open willingness to take on (often linguistic) features of another community, are motivated to learn their language, and view the language learning situation positively (see also Gardner, 1985). As a consequence, it is reasonable to believe that features of integrative motivation can change over time. This was even demonstrated by Gardner (1985) in which significant decreases in attitudes toward the learning situation, motivation, and integrativeness (the three defining characteristics of integrative motivation in the socio-educational model of second language acquisition) were shown to take place within individuals in many settings from one year to the next. Furthermore, there was little evidence in those results that the decreases were moderated by the level of achievement (high versus low defined by a median split in grades obtained in the first year).

More recent research has considered this further. Gardner, Masgoret, Tennant, and Mihic (2004) investigated a sample of university students studying French as a second language. The students were tested with the AMTB at the beginning and end of the academic year, and the results compared for students obtaining A, B, and less than B grades at the end of the year. The results demonstrated that students who obtained A grades at the end of the year had relatively high scores on the measures of attitudes and motivation at the beginning of the year and showed very little change over time, whereas those obtaining B grades started the year with lower levels of attitudes and motivation and evidenced slight decreases, and those obtaining less than B grades began with lower levels of attitudes and motivation and showed much greater decreases. Gardner (2005) reports similar results obtained in a study conducted in Spain with secondary students learning English as a foreign language.

This leads to a sixth and final issue, namely, the role of the teacher in influencing the level of motivation in the classroom. This topic has been considered from a number of different perspectives in recent years revealing some inconsistencies in the perceptions of teachers and students and in the generalizations that might be drawn. Three studies demonstrate this.

Madrid (2002) considered the relationships between the perceptions of 18 teachers and their students regarding the power of 18 strategies to motivate students as well as the students' self-perceptions of their motivation. He found that some strategies, such as the use of audiovisual aids, were seen as motivational by many of the students whereas others, such as individual work, were not. Furthermore, there were few significant correlations between the students' and teachers' perceptions of the power of the different strategies. The highest positive correlation was for the use of audiovisual aids, whereas the highest negative correlation was for satisfying students' needs and interests. A 2 4 (Gender Grade Level) analysis of variance for each strategy revealed only 1 effect due to gender but 13 for grade level differences, indicating primarily grade level differences in the perceived power of some strategies. In addition, it was found that global motivation level varied across grade levels.

In another study, Guilloteaux and Dörnyei (2008) investigated 25 strategies in a sample of 40 classrooms in English as a foreign language. However, rather than having teachers and students rate the use of specific strategies, the behavior of both the teachers and the students with respect to these strategies were observed in a time sampling scheme in terms of a set of categories. In addition, a teacher evaluation scale was administered immediately after each class, and students completed three

Likert scales: attitudes toward the course, linguistic self-confidence, and classroom anxiety. The classroom observations produced two aggregate variables, teacher's motivational practice and learners' motivated behavior, whereas the aggregate of the Likert scales was used as a measure of motivation. The results demonstrated significant correlations among the three measures, with the highest correlation between the two classroom observation measures, and lower and comparable correlations with the Likert measure of *motivation*.

Bernaus and Gardner (2008) investigated the effects of teachers' and students' perceptions of the use of 12 innovative and 14 traditional teaching strategies on students' attitudes, motivation, and English achievement in 31 classes of English as a foreign language. The results demonstrated significant correlations between teachers' and students' perceptions for 10 of the traditional strategies and 6 of the innovative ones. Separate aggregate scores for traditional and innovative strategies were computed based on teachers' perceptions, class perceptions, and individual student perceptions, and these were correlated with English achievement and the six composite scores on the mini-AMTB. None of the correlations based on teacher perceptions were significant, but when class perceptions were investigated, significant correlations were obtained between traditional strategy use and integrativeness, attitudes toward the learning situation, motivation, instrumental orientation, and parental encouragement, and between innovative strategy use and attitudes toward the learning situation and motivation. When the student was the unit of analysis, significant positive correlations were obtained with all of the composite measures except language anxiety with both the traditional and innovative strategies. The only significant correlation with the measure of English achievement was with traditional strategy use and this correlation was negative. That is, students who rated the use of traditional strategies as being used frequently obtained lower English scores.

VI. Future Directions

In the previous edition of this chapter (Gardner, 2002) we focused on five issues that seemed to be important in future considerations:

- Employing meta analysis to investigate the consistency of findings
- The use of laboratory studies as analogues to test hypotheses about process
- The investigation of immigrant populations learning a second language
- The study of both societal and educational environmental factors in second language learning
- The validity of the various models

To some extent, some of these issues have been dealt with in the interim, and I have been able to integrate them into the preceding paragraphs, and some have not been considered to any great extent.

In this edition, I will discuss four issues that appear necessary to strengthen the scientific foundation for the investigation of factors that influence second language acquisition. Although I will elaborate on them using research from the socio-educational model of second language acquisition, all of the points apply equally to the other models.

As proposed in the previous edition (Gardner, 2002), there is considerable need for further research to assess the validity of the various models that have been, and are continuing to be, developed and especially to clearly articulate the differences between them. It is often the case that the various models use somewhat different concepts and measures but do not make predictions that are in disagreement, so to some extent the results of many studies can be seen to apply to all the models. It is necessary, however, to obtain more information making use of measures that are specific to the various models. It is unlikely that discrepant results will be obtained, but clarifying the role of these other variables would be an important advance. To elaborate, a study by Tremblay and Gardner (1995) included measures of attributions and goal salience along with many of the measures generally used in the context of the socio-educational model. The results demonstrated how these variables could be incorporated into the model, but there was no indication that they appreciably improved prediction of measures of achievement.

This gives rise to the second issue, namely, the need to clarify concepts in this research area and eliminate the use of multiple definitions for a given construct. For example, Gardner (1985) operationally defined *integrativeness* as the sum of scores on three scales from the AMTB—in other words, attitudes toward French Canadians, ratings of an integrative orientation—and interest in foreign languages and concluded that it "thus reflects attitudinal reactions toward the cultural aspects of language learning" (p. 93). The operational definition has been employed in the bulk of his research since, though it is the case that recently he has chosen to define *integrativeness* more generally. For example, Gardner (2006) states "individuals who are high in integrativenss do not focus on their own identity but instead are willing and able to take on features of another language group (if only just the language) as part of their own behavioral repertoire" (p. 247). More recently, Gardner has referred to *integrativeness* as cultural openness, pointing out that concepts such as Kraemer's (1993) *social/political attitudes* and Yashima's (2002) *inercultural posture* are comparable to *integrativeness* because they also focus on the intercultural basis of language acquisition. Cultural openness incorporates all three conceptions. Other researchers, however, have defined the concept of *integrativeness* differently, varying all the way from attitudes toward the language group to perceptions of the ideal self as a language learner. Of course, researchers can define concepts in ways that are most meaningful to themselves and their research, but using the same labels for clearly different operational definitions can cause confusion in communication. It would seem that, at a minimum, various operational definitions of the same construct should yield measures that are correlated with one another.

The third issue that I believe is important to the advancement of research in the area of second language acquisition is the proper use of data analytic procedures to answer specific questions. Thus, the correlation coefficient is an indicator of the relationship between two variables, but a regression coefficient in multiple correlation is not. It is an indicator of the extent to which a variable adds to prediction given the other variables in the equation (i.e., increases the correlation of the composite with the criterion variable). Structural equation modeling is a powerful analytic procedure that permits one to determine how well a predefined model fits the data, but it does not "prove" the model. There are an infinite number of models that might fit the data as well or better for the particular data set. Finally, there is a relatively new data analytic procedure, hierarchical linear modeling (Raudenbush and Bryk, 2002), which could be very instructive in studies of individual differences when the data are derived from students in different classes. It is comparable to multiple regression except that in addition to determining the coefficients in the model, it also permits an assessment of the variability of these coefficients in the different classes as well as the relationship between these coefficients and characteristics of the classes themselves (see, e.g., Bernaus and Gardner, 2008). Thus, it is a procedure that allows for a data analytic linking of individual difference variables and classroom characteristics, and represents an exciting new frontier.

The fourth, and I believe the most important, issue is the need for improved measurement in our research. As noted previously, there are a large number of constructs that have been hypothesized as important for learning a second language. Moreover, the majority of these variables are measured through the use of verbal report, often in the form of questionnaires. Too often these questionnaires are made up of items written for a particular study, and a common procedure in this area is to factor analyze the correlations among the items to identify common clusters of items. These are then aggregated to produce scales, and often these are correlated with other variables to assess their validity. This is useful in the initial stages of research, but if new scales are continually developed in this way without cross-validation, one must be cautious of interpretation. Scales formed in this way will evidence artificially high estimates of internal consistency reliability because of sampling error that contributes to the factor structure, and these sampling errors can artificially inflate validity coefficients. At a minimum, such results should be cross-validated with an independent sample to determine whether the scales maintain their internal consistency reliability as well as their discriminant and convergent validity with other constructs in the area of research. Only when measurement improves will advances be made in this research area.

The value of employing reliable and valid measurement can be illustrated with an example involving measures associated with the socio-educational model of second language acquisition. Earlier it was noted that some researchers have claimed that the research associated with the socio-educational model of second language acquisition was applicable to Canada because it was a bilingual country and that different results would be obtained in different settings, particularly if the language being learned was a foreign as opposed to a second language. Studies purporting to support this conjecture generally made use of measures that were not the same as those in the AMTB. When such research is conducted using the AMTB, the results do not support this conjecture. Gardner (2006) presents results obtained with eight samples involving students in two different grade levels studying English as a foreign language in four European countries (Croatia, Poland, Romania, and Spain). The results demonstrated that the internal consistency reliability coefficients of the 12 scales from the AMTB were consistent across all eight samples and similar to those obtained in Canadian samples. Furthermore, factor analyses of the 12 scales in each country revealed structures that were very similar to each other and comparable to those obtained in Canada. A table of 54 correlations assessing factor congruence in the eight samples revealed that all but 4 of the correlations were .90 or higher. Furthermore, when the predictive validity of final grades in English by the six constructs was investigated, it was found that significant correlations were obtained in all eight samples for the measures of integrativeness, motivation, and language anxiety, and that these results were shown to be comparable to those obtained in Canada. Thus, when uniform measures are employed, there is considerable stability in the results obtained.

Attention to these four issues will, I believe, be beneficial. As can be seen, this is an active area of research with great potential. The future looks bright, but continued research focusing on empirical findings to support or clarify theoretical models and hypotheses represents its greatest strength.

NOTES

1. The terms *acquisition* and *learning* are used interchangeably in this chapter, as are the terms *foreign* and *second language* (except where stated otherwise).

2. When used with young students, there was an additional measure, parental encouragement (to learn the language).

CHAPTER 15

INTERACTIONIST PERSPECTIVES ON SECOND LANGUAGE ACQUISITION

SUSAN GASS

I. Introduction

The field of *second language acquisition* (SLA) has been studied from many angles. This broad scope is due in part to the myriad disciplinary backgrounds of scholars in the field. This chapter deals with the interactionist perspective and, as such, is primarily concerned with the environment in which second language learning takes place. It is important to note from the outset that this perspective is by and large neutral as to the role of innateness. In other words, it is compatible with a view of SLA that posits an innate learning mechanism (e.g., universal grammar [UG]); it is also compatible with a model of learning that posits no such mechanism. A word of caution is in order, however, as the situation is far more complex than these few terse statements suggest. It is not the case that interaction does not relate to issues of UG. Rather, what is intended is that the relationship of interaction to acquisition per se does not depend on whether there is or is not an innate mechanism that guides the learning of a second language. To provide an example of what the relationship between interaction and a UG account of learning might be, one notes that there are two kinds of evidence that are available to learners:[1] positive evidence and negative evidence. Positive evidence refers to the language that a learner hears or reads and is clearly available through the linguistic environment; negative evidence is more complex. Negative evidence refers to information about what is incorrect in the language produced by a learner but not necessarily about what is needed to make an appropriate correction. Thus, overt correction is a form of negative evidence that not only indicates an error but also provides information about what is wrong. It may be that for complex syntax, negative evidence is necessary; it may also be that negative evidence is difficult to provide in other than an explicit (pedagogical) format. In other words, issues that form part of learnability theory (e.g., UG) may find answers in the conversational interactions in which learners engage in that these interactions provide the forum for both positive and negative evidence.

I have argued elsewhere (Gass, 1997) that the dichotomy between innatist and environmental approaches is ill-conceived in the sense that a presumed dichotomy leads only to a discussion of "which is correct" rather than of "how they complement one another." But the goal of second language research must be the determination of how these approaches are intertwined, assuming that both are indeed relevant, even though they provide different sorts of explanations (see also Pinker, 1994). This chapter deals with interactionist approaches focusing on how learners use their linguistic environment (in particular, conversational interactions) to build their knowledge of the second language. To summarize briefly, the interaction approach considers exposure to language (input), production of language (output), and feedback on production (through interaction) as constructs that are important for understanding how second language learning takes place. Gass (2003) argues that interaction research "takes as its starting point the assumption that language learning is stimulated by communicative pressure and examines the relationship between communication and acquisition and the mechanisms (e.g., noticing, attention) that mediate between them" (p. 224). Long (1996) makes a similar claim, proposing that "environmental contributions to acquisition are mediated by selective attention and the learner's developing L2 processing capacity," and that these resources "are brought together most usefully...during *negotiation for meaning*. Negative feedback obtained...may be facilitative of L2 development" (p. 414). A related construct, output was emphasized in Swain's (1993) research: "Learners need to be pushed to make use of their resources; they need to have their linguistic abilities stretched to their fullest; they need to reflect on their output and consider ways of modifying it to enhance comprehensibility, appropriateness, and accuracy" (pp. 160–161).

In what follows, I discuss the basic tenets of the interaction approach (see Gass and Mackey, 2007a) and then discuss learner-internal variables that impact how learners do and do not utilize language information stemming from interaction.

II. Input

Input has had an uneven history in the development of (second) language research. In behaviorist views of language learning, input was central to an understanding of how learners acquired a language, first or second. Imitation and habit formation were primary concepts in the acquisition process. If habits were formed through imitation, then it was necessary to examine the input to learners to determine what they were imitating. It was also necessary to examine the relationship between the input (what was to be imitated) and production (the product of imitation).

From the mid-1950s on, behaviorism was on the wane, and as a consequence so too was the importance ascribed to input. A new era of language research emerged, and acquisition research followed, deemphasizing the significance of input and focusing on the nature of the internal linguistic resources that a learner brings to the learning task.

By the early 1970s, scholars began to take a more balanced view of what was relevant and not relevant to the study of second language learning. With specific regard to input, Ferguson (1971, 1975) began to investigate the nature of input to nonproficient speakers of a language. In particular, he considered special registers such as "baby talk" (i.e., language addressed to young children) and "foreigner talk" (i.e., language addressed to nonnative speakers of a language). His focus was on the similarities between these two language systems, and his ultimate goal was understanding the nature of human language. With regard to foreigner talk, the system of particular interest to researchers in second language acquisition, certain common features became apparent. Speech directed towards nonproficient nonnative speakers was found to include speech modification ranging from phonological to syntactic. For example, speech tends to be slower, more clearly enunciated, and even louder. In terms of the lexicon, vocabulary tends to have a preponderance of common words. Syntax is simple, often including two sentences when one might normally expect to find one complex sentence. These characteristics are commonly found in speech to learners, although clearly there is variation among individuals.[2]

What function does modified speech serve? A lengthier discussion and exposé on this topic may be found in Gass (1997). For present purposes, it is important to point out that there are two perspectives from which one can answer this question. First is the perspective of the fluent speaker of the target language. It is likely that the purpose is to aid comprehension. One does what one can to ensure that one's conversational partner is able minimally to understand the general meaning and to be in a position to respond appropriately. The example below shows how a native speaker (NS), upon realizing that an original question may have been too difficult for a learner (NNS), modifies her speech to give the learner a greater opportunity to comprehend.

1. NNS: How have increasing food costs changed your eating habits?
→ NS: Uh well that would I don't think they've changed 'em much right now, but the pressure's on.
   NNS: Pardon me?
→ NS: I don't think they've changed our eating habits much as of now....
   (From Gass and Varonis, 1985)

In this example the reduced pronoun ('em ← them) is modified to include full information (our eating habits).

A second way of considering the function of modified speech is to examine the question from the perspective of the learner. Modified speech contributes to the likelihood that the learner can understand and can therefore get through what is essentially a social interaction. In other words, modified speech helps the learner participate in a conversation as fully as possible. Assuming that a learner is able to participate in a conversation, she is assured of receiving a greater quantity of input, can produce output, and can receive much-needed feedback on his/her production.

III. Interaction

The interactionist hypothesis—which was given initial prominence by Wagner-Gough and Hatch (1975) and refined by Long (1980, 1981, 1983) and others (Gass and Varonis, 1985, 1989; Mackey, 1999; Pica, 1987, 1988; Pica and Doughty, 1985; Pica, Doughty, and Young, 1986; Pica, Young, and Doughty, 1987; Schmidt and Frota, 1986; Varonis and Gass, 1985a)—has as its main claim that one route to second language learning is through conversational interaction (Gass, 1997; Long, 1996; Pica, 1994).

In Wagner-Gough and Hatch's original work, the role of conversation was valued, not just as a means for providing opportunities to practice previously learned language, but also as a locus of learning itself. Long, in his early work, showed how conversations involving nonfluent nonnative speakers of a language were quantitatively different from conversations in which both parties (assuming dyadic conversation) were equal and fluent participants. Wagner-Gough and Hatch (1975) and Long (1980, 1981, 1983) went beyond modified speech (e.g., simpler syntactic structures, easier vocabulary) to consider the structure of conversation itself. Following are examples of typical patterns found in conversations involving nonfluent, nonnative speakers of a language. This is not to say that these patterns do not exist in conversations involving fluent speakers—only that they are more frequent in nonnative learner speech.

2. **Confirmation Check**
     NNS: *c'è una verdi, uh…*
          there is a green, uh.
     NS: *una verdi?*
          a green?
          (From Mackey, Gass, and McDonough, 2000)

In this example from an English-speaking learner of Italian, the NS's questioning the word *verdi*, which in fact is inappropriate in Italian, resulted in a subsequent negotiation until the correct word *pianta* (plant) was recognized later in the exchange.

Examples 3–7 are crucial to an understanding of the interaction hypothesis and to an understanding of how modified interactions contribute to learning. In these examples, one can see various means of modifying a conversational structure, resulting in a greater likelihood of comprehension.

3.   Comprehension Check
      NNS1: And your family have some ingress.
      NNS2: yes ah, OK, OK?
➜   NNS1: more or less OK?
             (From Varonis and Gass, 1985a)

4.   Clarification request
      NS: there's there's just a couple more things
      NNS: a sorry? Couple?
      NS: couple more things in the room only just a couple
➜   NNS: couple? What does it mean couple?
             (From Mackey and Philp, 1998)

5.   Or-choice
      NS: Where did you go yesterday?
      NNS: What?
➜   NS: Did you go to the zoo or to the garden?
             (Original data)

6.   Topic-focused
      NS: Did your friend travel with you to Italy and Switzerland?
      NNS: What?
➜   NS: Your friend, did she travel with you?
             (Original data)

7.   Elaboration
      NNS: How have increasing food costs changed your eating habits?
      NS: Well, we don't eat as much beef as we used to. We eat more chicken and uh, pork, and uh, fish, things like that.
      NNS: Pardon me?
➜   NS: We don't eat as much beef as we used to. We eat more chicken and uh, uh pork and fish.... We don't eat beef very often. We don't have steak like we used to.
             (From Gass and Varonis, 1985)

Long (1996) defined the interaction hypothesis as

> *negotiation for meaning*, and especially negotiation work that triggers *interactional* adjustments by the NS or more competent interlocutor, facilitates acquisition

> because it connects input, internal learner capacities, particularly selective
> attention, and output in productive ways. (pp. 451–452)

In addition,

> it is proposed that environmental contributions to acquisition are mediated by
> selective attention and the learner's developing L2 processing capacity, and that
> these resources are brought together most usefully, although not exclusively,
> during *negotiation for meaning*. Negative feedback obtained during negotiation
> work or elsewhere may be facilitative of L2 development, at least for vocabulary,
> morphology, and language-specific syntax, and essential for learning certain
> specifiable L1-L2 contrasts. (p. 414)

It is through negotiation that the learner may direct attention to an area of the
target language (1) about which she may be entertaining an hypothesis (or about
which she is trying to formulate a hypothesis) or (2) about which she has no
information. This is not to say that learning necessarily takes place during a
conversation; the interaction itself may only be the first step in recognizing that
there is something to learn. Interaction may be a priming device representing the
setting of the stage for learning. The following examples represent two ways in
which conversation can lead to learning: (1) on the spot learning and (2) delayed
learning.

Example 8 comes from a study that used stimulated recall (see Gass and Mackey,
2000) to determine what a learner was thinking during a prior interaction. The relevant part of the interaction is provided, followed immediately by the learner's
comments on the interaction.

8. On the Spot Learning
    NNS: so the people make a line in front of the place
    NS: they are standing in line?
➜   NNS: ahh, they are standing in line
          (Twelve turns later)
➜   NNS: Beside the people standing in line
          (From Mackey, Gass, and McDonough, 2000)

    Learner's retrospective comment:
    Make a line is the same meaning as stand in line, actually I thought of this
    situation as make a line but after she said standing in line, her expression is better
    than mine so I changed mine.

The learner in this instance used the conversation as a way of obtaining new
linguistic information, as is evidenced by her retrospective comments. She then
tried out her newly learned information later in the conversation.

But sometimes learning does not take place immediately; time to "digest" the
new linguistic input is often needed. This is illustrated in 9, which took place over
the time period of a class.

9.   Delayed Learning
→   NNS1: Kutsu o shiroi no kutsu o <u>hamete imasu</u> ka?
             Shoes ACC white (GEN [*sic*] shoes ACC wearing [*sic*] INT?
             Is the person wearing white shoes" ((wrong verb for "wear,"
             underlined))
     NNS2: Iie <u>haite imasen</u>. Ano:::
             No, he's not. Uh:: (correct verb for "wear," underlined))
→   NNS1: Ano: ano: kuroi no kutsu o <u>hai- hamete imasu</u> ka?
             U:h u:h black (GEN [*sic*] shoes ACC wea-wearing [*sic*] INT?
             U'h u"h is the person wearing black shoes ((wrong word for "wear,"
             underlined))
     NNS2: *Hai haite imasu*
             Yes, he is ((correct verb for "wear," underlined))
     NNS1: Anoo uh jiinzu o::: jeans? Jinzu o ha uh::::: <u>haite imasu</u> ka?
             U:h uh: you're um jeans? Are you u:::h wearing Jeans?
     NNS1: Sorekara shiroi no kutsu ga kutsu o how do you say it? Kutso o:::
             And white shoes shoes how do you say it for shoes?
     NNS3: haitemasu. haki-
             Wearing. Wear-
→   NNS1: what? <u>Haite imasu</u> ka?
             What? Is it "haite imasu?"
→   NNS4: Hanjiinzu o:: um oh what is it? Hare- <u>haite imasu ka</u>?
             Shorts ((*sic*)) ACC um oh what is it? Do you we-wear shorts?
     NNS4: (inaudible)
→   NNS1: Sorekara::: kiroi to shiroi no kutsu g- o::: yeah. <u>Haite imasu ka</u>?
             And::: are you wearing yellow and white shoes?(From Ohta, 2001)

In this example the learner initially uses the incorrect form for the verb *wear, haimete*,
rather than the correct form, *haite*. She begins to receive input with the correct form and
eventually asks about the correct form, but it isn't until quite a bit later in the class that
she finally, presumably as a result of the interaction, begins to use the correct form.

   Learners do not always use a conversation to obtain new information; there are
times when she or he uses it to test certain hypotheses about the second language
and to receive feedback on production. Example 10 below shows how a learner uses
a conversation to test a hypothesis:

10.   NNS: *poi un bicchiere*
              then a glass
       INT: *un che, come*
              a what, what?
       NNS: *bicchiere*
              Glass
              (From research reported on in Mackey, Gass, and McDonough, 2000)

Learner's retrospective comment:
I was drawing a blank. Then I thought of a vase but then I thought that since
there was no flowers, maybe it was just a big glass. So, then I thought I'll say it and
see. Then, when she said "*come*" [what] I knew that it was completely wrong.

In this instance, the learner is throwing out a word to see where it gets her.

3.1 Recasts

Feedback to learners can be explicit (e.g., an overt correction) or implicit, as often
illustrated through negotiation work. Perhaps the most subtle type of feedback
comes in the form of a recast, a reformulation of an incorrect utterance while maintaining the original meaning of the utterance. An example is given in 11 in which the
native speaker recasts the nonnative speaker's incorrect question:

11. NNS: I think some this girl have birthday and and its big celebrate
➔   NS: big celebration
      NNS: oh (From Mackey and Philip, 1998)

A question arises as to the effectiveness of recasts. Are they noticed, and, if so, are
they taken as a form of correction? Lyster and Ranta (1997) collected data from
grades 4–6 children in French immersion programs. They were primarily concerned
with the reaction by the student immediately following a recast inasmuch as this
reveals what the student does with the feedback. Despite the preponderance of
recasts in their database, recasts were not found to have an impact on subsequent
production. Using the same database, Lyster (1998) found that there was some confusion between the corrective and approval functions of recasts, thereby questioning their usefulness in terms of corrective feedback.

Other studies, however, do show a positive effect for recasts (for reviews, see
Long, 2007, and Nicholas, Lightbown, and Spada, 2001). Mackey and Philp (1998)
argue that using the production immediately following a recast may not be the most
appropriate way to determine effectiveness. They make the point that if one is to
consider effectiveness (i.e., development/acquisition), then one should more appropriately measure delayed effects (see, e.g., Gass, 1997; Gass and Varonis, 1994;
Lightbown, 1998). The study on the acquisition of English questions (Mackey and
Philp, 1998) showed that for more advanced learners, recasts plus negotiation were
more beneficial than negotiation alone. This was the case even though there was not
always evidence for a reaction by the learner in the subsequent turn (see Oliver,
1995). Thus, the effectiveness of recasts may be in part dependent on developmental
stages (see, e.g., Iwashita, 2003; Philp, 2003). Further, as Egi (2007) has shown, the
value of recasts may be dependent on their interpretation—in other words, are they
thought to be a comment on content (a practice that is not effective), or are they
taken to be a form of positive and/or negative evidence (in which case they appear
to be of some benefit)?

Recent meta-analyses (Mackey and Goo, 2007; Russell and Spada, 2006) have addressed the effects of recasts. Both studies reported large effect sizes for implicit feedback (including recasts), but both also report that their data are based on very few studies given their inclusion criteria for their meta-analyses. Mackey and Goo also note that although there are strong effects on learning from recasts, there is little data on longer term effects.

3.2 Does Interaction Contribute to Learning?

In recent years, the question has moved from the arena of speculation to serious investigation of the effects of interaction. Three early studies led the way in this regard:

1. Loschky (1994), in an investigation of English learners of Japanese, found that interaction had a positive effect on comprehension but did not find an effect on the acquisition of vocabulary or on the acquisition of morpho-syntax (locative expressions; see also Ellis, Tanaka, and Yamazaki (1994).
2. Gass and Varonis (1994) did show that the effects of interaction went beyond a subsequent turn. As in previous studies, vocabulary did not appear to be affected, although general discourse organizational strategies were affected.
3. Mackey (1999) provides the most detailed support in favor of the effects of interaction. In her investigation of a single grammatical structure, question formation, she found a relationship between conversational interaction and development in that those who were involved in structure-focused interaction moved along a developmental continuum more rapidly than those who did not. Mackey's study supports the notion of interaction not necessarily (or not always) being the locus of immediate learning but often being the catalyst for later learning. She found that for the developmentally advanced structures, the effects of interaction were noted in delayed posttests rather than immediately.

In the past 30 years or so, numerous studies have been conducted on the relationship between interaction and learning, most showing a positive relationship (e.g., Adams, 2007; Trofimovich, Ammar and Gatbonton, 2007; Carpenter, Jeon, MacGregor, and Mackey, 2006; Ellis, 2007; Ellis, Loewen, and Erlam, 2006; Gass and Alvarez-Torres, 2005; Gass and Lewis, 2007; Jeon, 2007; Kim and Han, 2007; Loewen, 2005; Loewen and Nabei, 2007; Loewen and Philp, 2006; Lyster and Mori, 2006; Mackey, 2006; Mackey and Silver, 2005; McDonough, 2005, 2006, 2007; McDonough and Mackey, 2006; Pica, Kang, and Sauro, 2006; Sachs and Suh, 2007; Sagarra, 2007; Sato and Lyster, 2007; Sheen, 2007; Tarone and Bigelow, 2007; Tocalli-Beller and Swain, 2007). Only studies published since 2005 have been included due to limitations of space; for a more complete listing, see Mackey (2007).

In their meta-analysis, Mackey and Goo (2007) found that interaction is facilitative of the acquisition of both vocabulary and grammar. There is a stronger immediate effect for vocabulary, but a delayed and lasting effect on grammar. Both feedback and modified output were significant factors in promoting learning, but Mackey and Goo recommend a more nuanced investigation of these interactional components.

There is little doubt as to the facilitative effects of interaction on learning, but many questions remain unanswered. Some of the questions are descriptive, as was previously alluded to; that is, what types of feedback contribute to learning and under what circumstances? The second type of question is explanatory; that is, why does interaction contribute to learning? There are four areas that will be examined next:

a. Attention
b. Working memory (including inhibitory control)
c. Output
d. Contrast

IV. ATTENTION

Central to the interaction hypothesis is the concept of attention or noticing. If interaction is to have an effect (either through negotiation or recasts), the learner must notice that his/her conversational partner is explicitly or implicitly making a correction.[3] If there is no attention to a particular part of language during an interaction, then it is difficult to attribute the source of change to the interaction itself. Example 12 illustrates how the direct questioning of an utterance makes the learner notice the discrepancy between her pronunciation of *yellow* and the native speaker interviewer's pronunciation:

12.   NNS: The color is /**wellow**/
      NS: Is what?
      NNS: /wellow/ /wellow/ color
      NS: Yellow?
      NNS: Yellow.
             (From Mackey, Gass and McDonough, 2000)

Learner's retrospective comment:
My pronounce is different. I say /wellow/ but yellow is the exact pronounce.
Yellow, yellow.

The question remains as to what learners do notice. J. Williams (1999) considered learner-generated attention to form. She points out that most of the focus on form research within a classroom context focuses on teacher-generated attention. (See also Sharwood Smith's [1991, 1993] discussion of enhanced input and internally and externally induced salience). Williams found that learners are indeed capable of focusing attention to language form, but that there is variation according to proficiency level and even to activity types.

Mackey, Gass, and McDonough (2000) also investigated what learners notice in an interaction. Their investigation differed from that of Williams in that they were concerned with interactional feedback and how learners actually interpreted that feedback. Through a postinteraction stimulated recall of learners of English and learners of Italian, they found that learners do notice interactional feedback, but they do not do so in a uniform manner. Lexis and phonology are more likely to be noticed than aspects of morphosyntax. The results also suggest that the manner of feedback (e.g., recasts or negotiation) have different effects when occurring alone or in combination. A related study of heritage and nonheritage learners (Gass and Lewis, 2007) found that both nonheritage language learners and heritage language learners perceive phonological and lexical feedback much more accurately than morphosyntactic feedback, as had been observed in Mackey, Gass, and McDonough (2000). However, differences were noted in the area of semantic feedback, with nonheritage language learners generally not accurate in their perceptions about semantic feedback, whereas heritage language learners were. Neither of these studies investigated the next step; that is, the determination of what happens after learners notice a gap between their knowledge of the second language and the second language itself.

V. Working Memory

Within an interactive context, learners produce language, receive feedback, and, in an ideal situation, use the information contained in the feedback in a productive way. In so doing, a learner must notice the feedback given, determine what is relevant, and retain that information long enough to identify the precise part of language that is being corrected. The question remains as to why some individuals are more successful at this than others. One possible explanation relates to working memory capacity. Why some learners are able to focus attention on certain parts of an interaction better than others may be related to their ability to regulate their focus of attention, either through selectively attending to some part of language or by inhibiting others. Working memory is generally considered to incorporate both processing and storage functions of memory. Miyake and Shah (1999) define working memory as "those mechanisms or processes that are involved in the control, regulation, and active maintenance of task-relevant information in the service of complex cognition, including novel as well as familiar, skilled tasks" (p. 450). In other words, following work by Baddeley and Hitch (1974), working memory keeps representations in temporary storage, allowing operations on those representations to take place (Caplan, Waters, and Dede, 2007).

There have not been many studies that relate interactional success and working memory capacity. One of the early ones was by Philp (2003), who studied noticing.

She did not measure working memory capacity, but did point the way to research involving working memory when she suggested that attentional resources may be at the base of understanding when learners do notice differences between their own utterances and those of the target language. Two studies by Sagarra (2007, 2008) indirectly looked at working memory capacity and interaction. In one—a computer-based study of feedback—Sagarra (2007) found that working memory capacity predicted learners' ability to benefit from recasts. In the second, Sagarra (2008) found that redundant grammatical information is not processed by low proficiency L2 learners (English as an L1; Spanish as an L2) with low working memory capacity.

In the most directly relevant study, Mackey, Philp, Egi, Fujii, and Tatsumi (2002) investigated the relationship among individual differences in verbal working memory, noticing of interactional feedback, and the L2 development of English question formation. Their study compared the interactional benefits of two groups of L2 learners (L1 Japanese; L2 English): those with low working memory capacity and those with high working memory capacity. The former group benefitted immediately from interaction, but the results did not persist on a delayed posttest (2 weeks after the treatment). Those with higher working memory capacity demonstrated more lasting benefits from communicative interaction as demonstrated in the delayed posttest. A possible explanation is that learners with higher working memory capacities engage in cognitive comparisons between target language forms and their own versions of the forms, impacting processing loads and immediate performance. Learners with lower working memory capacities, in contrast, may be better equipped to engage in immediate modifications to output, at a potential longer term cost to comparison, storage, and subsequent retrieval mechanisms. Thus, the emphasis for high-working memory capacity individuals may be on processing, whereas the emphasis for low-working memory capacity individuals may be on storage (for differing results, cf. Trofimovich, Ammar, and Gatbonton, 2007).

Initial analysis in a study of English-speaking learners of Italian (Gass, Behney, and Uzum, in preparation) suggests that more significant than working memory differences are differences in inhibitory control (a construct related to working memory)—that is, the ability to suppress information that is not relevant.

In sum, second language learners are exposed to more input than they can process; consequently, they must have a mechanism that enables them to sort through that input (see, e.g., Gass, 1997) to determine what is (momentarily) relevant and what is not. Working memory capacity may be one such mechanism and inhibitory control may be another.

VI. OUTPUT

In preceding sections, the nature of language that is directed toward learners and the function of modified language and/or modified conversational structure have been considered. However, in any discussion of the interaction hypothesis, there is a third prong to examine, and that is the role of output. In earlier conceptualizations of second language acquisition, output served little learning purpose, other than, perhaps, to reinforce previously learned linguistic knowledge. Swain's (1985) pioneering work (see also Swain, 1995, 2005) in this area came from observations of immersion programs in Canada (see also Kowal and Swain, 1997; Swain and Lapkin, 1995, 1998). She noted that children who had spent many years in immersion programs were still lagging in target-language-like abilities. In looking more carefully at the classroom context in which the target language was used and in which it was the prime source of information about the target language for these children, she noted that what was lacking was consistent and frequent use of the second language. She proposed that one needed more than input; learning a second language required a significant amount of output. Output, or language production, forces learners to focus on the syntax of an utterance and, consequently, on formulating hypotheses about how the target language works. This is different from receiving input because input involves primarily comprehension and comprehension often requires little syntactic organization. As a result, Swain introduced the notion of comprehensible output or "pushed" output.

Comprehensible output refers to the need for a learner to be "pushed toward the delivery of a message that is not only conveyed, but that is conveyed precisely, coherently, and appropriately" (Swain, 1985: 249). In a more recent explication of the concept, Swain claimed output may stimulate learners to move from the semantic, open-ended, nondeterministic, strategic processing prevalent in comprehension to the complete grammatical processing needed for accurate production. Output, thus, would seem to have a potentially significant role in the development of syntax and morphology (1995: 128).

Mackey (2002) conducted a study in which learners reflected on a previous interaction through a stimulated recall procedure. Example 13 provides insight into what the learner was thinking as she was engaged in a conversation.

13. Example of Pushed Output
    NNS: And in hand in hand [sic] have a bigger glass to see.
    NS: It's err. You mean, something in his hand?
    NNS: Like spectacle. For older person.
    NS: Mmmm, sorry I don't follow, it's what?
    NNS: In hand have he have has a glass for looking through for make the
          print bigger to see, to see the print, for magnify.
    NS: He has some glasses?
    NNS: Magnify glasses he has magnifying glass.
    NS: Oh aha I see a magnifying glass, right that's a good one, ok.
          (Mackey 2002)

Retrospective comment:
In this example I see I have to manage my err err [sic] expression because he does not understand me and I cannot think of exact word right then. I am thinking thinking [sic] it is nearly in my mind, thinking bigger and magnificate and

> eventually magnify. I know I see this word before but so I am sort of talking
> around around [sic] this word but he is *forcing* me to think harder, think harder
> for the correct word to give him so he can understand and so I was trying. I carry
> on talking until finally I get it, and when I say it, then he understand it, me
> [emphasis mine].

As can be seen, the learner was pushed (note the word *forcing*) through the negotiation sequences to make her language clearer.[4]

McDonough (2005) tested the output hypothesis directly in her study of Thai learners of English. In a study investigating the acquisition of English questions, four groups carried out communicative tasks. The groups focused on salience (enhancement) and opportunity to modify following feedback. She found that the best predictor of acquisition lies in the opportunity to modify one's speech. A later study (McDonough and Mackey, 2006), however, noted that mere repetition of an interlocutor's form (in their case, recasts) did not impact learning, whereas primed production (use of a form in the recast in later production) did.

Output, in sum, is important for a number of reasons, including forcing a learner to produce language about which feedback may often be given. However, precisely how it benefits learning is still open for investigation. Further, as noted by Sato and Lyster (2007), the interlocutor partner (native speaker or another learner) may impact the amount of modified output; learners tend to produce more when interacting with other learners than with a native speaker (see also Varonis and Gass, 1985a).

VII. Theory of Contrast

What sort of mechanism allows for learning to take place as a result of negative evidence derived from conversational interaction? One possibility to account for learning through conversation is the direct contrast hypothesis (Saxton, 1997), defined within the context of child language acquisition as follows:

> When the child produces an utterance containing an erroneous form, which is
> responded to immediately with an utterance containing the correct adult
> alternative to the erroneous form (i.e., when negative evidence is supplied), the
> child may perceive the adult form as being in CONTRAST [emphasis in original]
> with the equivalent child form. Cognizance of a relevant contrast can then form
> the basis for perceiving the adult form as a correct alternative to the child form.
> (1997: 155)

Attention alone is not sufficient. A contrast must be attended to, or in SLA parlance, a gap must be noticed. And conversation provides a forum for the contrast to be detected, especially when the erroneous form and a correct one are in immediate juxtaposition.

VIII. Conclusion

It is likely that there are limitations to what can and cannot be learned through negative evidence provided through conversation. One possibility is that surface-level phenomena can be learned but abstractions cannot. This is consistent with Truscott's (1998) claim that competence is not affected by noticing. Negative evidence can probably not apply to long stretches of speech, given memory limitations (see Philp, 2003). But it may be effective with low-level phenomena such as pronunciation or the basic meanings of lexical items. In fact, these are precisely the areas that Mackey, Gass, and McDonough (2000) have isolated as those that are sensitive to feedback. Future research will need to determine the long-term effects of interaction on different parts of language (see also Gass, Svetics, and Lemelin, 2003; Trofimovic, Ammar, and Gatbonton, 2007).

Research on interaction began descriptively. In the past decade, as it became clear through empirical research that there was a positive relationship between interaction and learning, research moved toward an explanation of how this relationship works: What individual factors can help to explain differential benefits? In looking toward future research, individual cognitive differences will undoubtedly lead the way in attempting to answer this question, but other factors such as motivation, learning strategies, language aptitude, cognitive styles, learning context (e.g., second versus foreign language learning), language background (heritage versus nonheritage language learners), and social context will also likely have a role.

NOTES

1. There is a third type of evidence, indirect negative evidence (see Plough, 1994, 1995). To simplify matters, we do not deal with this complex type of evidence.

2. It is beyond the scope of this paper to comment on whether these systems are learned or not. It is important to note, however, that the extent to which an individual adopts foreigner talk characteristics in her speech may depend to an individual's experience with nonnative speakers. Varonis and Gass (1985b) describe an interaction in which a salesperson adopts very few foreigner talk features (she speaks rapidly, uses idioms, and uses anaphoric pronouns with no obvious referent). It was speculated that this is so precisely because of her lack of experience with noncomprehending individuals.

3. This is not to say that attention cannot come from a learner noticing a new form on her own (i.e., without an interlocutor's correction).

4. It is not clear from the description in the original article whether the learner had actually seen the phrase *magnifying glass* as part of the input (although she does say that she had seen the word [sic] before) and was trying to recall it or if she was generating it from what she had heard in the exchange. Regardless, it is through the interaction that this learner was able to come up with the correct word.

CHAPTER 16

PRAGMATICS AND SECOND LANGUAGE ACQUISITION

KATHLEEN BARDOVI-HARLIG

THE study of pragmatics is traditionally held to encompass at least five main areas:

- Deixis
- Conversational implicature
- Presupposition
- Speech acts
- Conversational structure (Levinson, 1983)

Within second language studies, work in pragmatics is narrower than it is in the field of pragmatics at large, including the investigation of speech acts and to a lesser extent conversational structure and conversational implicature. It is also broader, investigating areas traditionally considered to be sociolinguistics (Stalnaker, 1972). For example, Kasper and Dahl (1991: 216) included speech acts, conversational management, discourse organization, and sociolinguistic aspects of language use such as choice of address forms as part of pragmatics. In the intersection of second language studies and pragmatics, research is best characterized by Stalnaker's definition of pragmatics (1972: 383): "the study of linguistic acts and the contexts in which they are performed."

The most dominant area of pragmatics in second language studies is the study of speech acts. Speech act theory views utterances as not just stating propositions, but as a way of doing things with words; hence the concept of act (Searle, 1969, 1976). Speech acts include five categories: Representatives (asserting, explaining), Directives (requesting, advising), Commissives (promising, threatening), Expressives (apologizing, complimenting), and Declarations (declaring war, hiring/firing someone from a job).

Every speech act has two forces: the intended force of an utterance (the illocutionary force) and the actual effect on the hearer (the perlocutionary force). As an illustration, by arguing (the intended illocutionary force) I may convince or persuade someone (the perlocutionary force). Second language studies have typically investigated illocutionary force, although perlocutionary force, the effect of learners' utterances, would be relevant in second language research and consequently represents an area for future investigation. A recent review of articles on second language pragmatics that were published in major applied linguistics journals found that 99 studies of the 152 studies surveyed (65%) employed a speech act framework (Bardovi-Harlig, in press).

The second area of pragmatics addressed in second language studies is conversational structure. The study of conversational structure includes the investigation of turn taking, how turns are constructed, back channeling (signaling comprehension or lack thereof without claiming the floor), adjacency pairs (e.g., question and answers), and conversational boundaries (such as opening and closing conversations; Schegloff and Sacks, 1973). Studies in the area include the acquisition of openings and closings in Kiswahili (Omar, 1992, 1993), closings in English (Hartford and Bardovi-Harlig, 1992), and the acquisition of disagreement turn structure (Bardovi-Harlig and Salsbury, 2004). This is a rapidly growing area of research in second language pragmatics (see, for example, *Pragmatics and Language Learning*, 2006, and in press) due to interest and skill in microanalysis promoted by the adoption of and subsequent training in conversation analysis by researchers of second language acquisition.

The third and least investigated area in second language pragmatics is conversational implicature. Often referred to simply as *implicature*, conversational implicature is one of the most important concepts in pragmatics (Levinson, 1983). The identification of an implicature allows speakers to comprehend the message behind an illocutionary act. Implicature plays a significant role in the interpretation of indirect speech acts. To account for conversational implicature, Grice (1975) introduced the cooperative principle and the following four related maxims: quantity, quality, relation, and manner (Grice 1975: 45–46).

- *The cooperative principle:* Make your contribution such as is required, at the stage at which it occurs, by the accepted purpose or direction of the talk exchange in which you are engaged.
- *Quantity:* (1) Make your contribution as informative as is required for the current purposes of the exchange; (2) do not make your contribution more informative than is required.
- *Quality:* Try to make your contribution one that is true: (1) Do not say that which you believe to be false; (2) do not say that for which you lack adequate evidence.
- *Relation:* Make your contributions relevant.
- *Manner:* (1) Avoid obscurity; (2) avoid ambiguity; (3) be brief; (4) be orderly.

Best known is Bouton's work on the comprehension of conversational implicature in second language (Bouton, 1994a, 1994b); additionally, others have recently begun to investigate implicature as well (Taguchi, 2005). Studies of comprehension of implied meaning and indirection (Carrell, 1979; Koike, 1996) also contribute to this area of investigation.

In addition to the classic views of pragmatics, there are more socially oriented views that accord well with the broader, sociolinguistic orientation that research in second language pragmatics has adopted. In their monograph on second language pragmatic development, Kasper and Rose (2002) adopt two such definitions by Mey and Crystal:

> Mey (1993: 315) defines *pragmatics* as "the societally necessary and consciously interactive dimension of the study of language."
>
> Crystal (1997: 301) defines *pragmatics* as "the study of language from the point of view of users, especially of the choices they make, the constraints they encounter in using language in social interaction and the effects their use of language has on other participants in the act of communication." (Cited in Kasper and Rose, 2002: 2)

With their focus on interaction, both definitions will help to shape research in second language pragmatics in the future.

Transition to SLA Studies: Interlanguage Pragmatics

The study of L2 pragmatics has come to be known as *interlanguage pragmatics* and, more recently, simply as *ILP* (Kasper and Schmidt, 1996). Interlanguage pragmatics has developed two strands of research: comparative-sociolinguistic and acquisitional. In interlanguage pragmatics research, the comparative and sociolinguistic studies dominate the field. As Kasper observed,

> The bulk of interlanguage pragmatics research derived its research questions and methods from empirical, and particularly cross-cultural, pragmatics. Typical issues addressed in data-based studies are whether NNS differ from NS in the 1) range and 2) contextual distribution of 3) strategies and 4) linguistic forms used to convey 5) illocutionary meaning and 6) politeness—precisely the kinds of issues raised in comparative studies of different communities.... Interlanguage pragmatics has predominantly been the sociolinguistic, and to a much lesser extent a psycholinguistic study of NNS' linguistic action. (1992: 205)

Comparative studies have resulted in a significant body of research in four main areas:

1. Development and refinement of elicitation tasks
2. Description of L1 speech acts

3. Description of L2 speech acts (especially by advanced NNS)
4. The comparison of L1 and L2 production by native and nonnative speakers

In applied linguistics, the face of pragmatics was forever changed by the introduction of the discourse completion task (DCT) to study speech acts (Blum-Kulka, 1982) and by the subsequent publication of the results of the Cross-Cultural Speech Act Realization Project (Blum-Kulka and Olshtain, 1984; Blum-Kulka, House, and Kasper, 1989). The DCT introduced a means by which the performance of speech acts could be compared cross-linguistically and cross-culturally, thus offering a methodology that was understandably absent from a tradition derived from philosophy. The use of the DCT surpassed even the collection of natural conversation in the decade that followed. Traditionally, discourse completion tests take at least three formats, all of which provide a description of the speech context called a scenario:

- Example (1) shows the open questionnaire format in which only the scenario is provided but no turns of talk.
- Example (2) shows the dialogue completion task format with an initiating turn to which participants respond.
- Example (3) shows a dialogue completion task with a rejoinder (Larry's reply, which follows the turn to be supplied by the respondent).

(1)   Open Q
      You were in a hurry to leave on a trip, and you asked your roommate to mail an express letter for you. When you get back a few days later, the letter is still lying on the table.
      You: _____
      (Johnston, Kasper, and Ross, 1998: 163)

(2)   Dialogue Completion with Initial Turn
      It is winter and you are in Moscow. You have a meeting with your advisor at the university at noon and you are a half-hour late because of the traffic delays caused by the snowstorm. Your bus that was taking you to the metro station was cancelled. Since you couldn't get a taxi, you had to walk and it took you thirty minutes longer to get to the metro station. When you arrived to the office your professor greeted you with the phrase: "Вы опоздали на 30 минут." ["You are 30 minutes late."]
      You: _____
      (Shardakova, 2005: 450–451)

(3)   Dialogue Completion with Rejoinder
      At a student's apartment
      Larry, John's roommate, had a party the night before and left the kitchen in a mess.
      John: Larry, Ellen, and Tom are coming over for dinner tonight and I'll have to start cooking soon; _____

Larry: OK, I'll have a go at it right away.
(Blum-Kulka and Olshtain, 1984: 198)

Although many researchers recognize written DCTs to be "an indirect means for assessing spoken language in the form of a written production measure" (Cohen and Shively, 2007: 196), many continue to employ them. Written production tasks have played a significant role in the development of ILP, but nevertheless they do not match the oral mode or the interactivity of conversation. For investigations that require the control of the DCT, but not interactivity, researchers have developed DCTs supplemented by pictures (Nickels, 2006; Pearson, 2006) and various oral DCTs including the cartoon oral production task (COPT; Rose, 2000), multimedia DCTs (Schauer, 2007), and computer-delivered DCTs that supply an oral turn to which the participant responds (Bardovi-Harlig et al., in press). (See also Bardovi-Harlig, 1999b, in press; Kasper and Rose, 2002, for a review of tasks employed in ILP research.)

Role-plays allow researchers to control speakers and situational variables while eliciting oral, interactive data. Role-plays, which have been used since the beginning of ILP investigations (Cohen and Olshtain, 1981; Edmondson, House, Kasper, and Stemmer, 1984; Trosborg, 1987), are increasingly found in papers published in major journals in applied linguistics (Bardovi-Harlig, in press). The studies that employ role-plays investigate a range of speech acts and languages including refusals and requests in L2 Spanish (Félix-Brasdefer, 2004, 2007, respectively), compliment responses in English (Huth, 2006), and postweekend greetings in French (Liddicoat and Crozet, 2001); Gass and Houck's (1999) monograph on the acquisition of English refusals by Japanese learners is also based on role-plays and includes a chapter of nonverbal communication that shows how rich role-play data can be.

Through its comparative studies, ILP has contributed significantly by describing the realization of a range of speech acts by native speakers in a number of languages. ILP has also yielded a description of speech acts in a variety of second languages. More important, it has resulted in a number of comparisons of native speaker and nonnative speaker production.

Nonnative speakers can differ from native speakers in the production of speech acts in at least four ways (Bardovi-Harlig, 1996):

1. Native and nonnative speakers may perform *different speech acts* in the same contexts, or one group may not perform any speech act.
2. Speakers may use *different semantic formulas*. Semantic formulas represent the primary content of the parts of an utterance. An apology may contain the head act "I'm sorry" as well as an explanation or an offer to restore the damage.
3. The *content of semantic formulas may also differ*, even when speakers use the same semantic formulas. "My printer is jammed" and "I didn't feel like doing the assignment" are both explanations for why an assignment is late, but the content is significantly different.
4. The *form of a speech act may also differ*. In a study of requests, S. Takahashi (1996) found that learners of English favored monoclausal request formulas ("Would you verb?" or "Could you verb?"), whereas NS preferred biclausal

request formulas ("Would it be possible for you to verb?" or "I was wondering if you could verb.")

The comparisons serve a number of functions: as primary research into L2 pragmatics; as a type of pragmatic error analysis; as a needs assessment for the development of pedagogical methods and materials for teaching pragmatics; and as models for pedagogical materials. They may also serve to define research areas for acquisitional ILP studies.

The Study of Pragmatics within SLA

The second, smaller, area of investigation within ILP concerns the acquisition of second language pragmatics. Kasper and Dahl (1991: 216) defined interlanguage pragmatics as referring to nonnative speakers' comprehension and production of pragmatics, and how that L2-related knowledge is acquired—not a new area, just an underdeveloped one. The definition of interlanguage pragmatics as referring to NNS comprehension and production of pragmatics was made first by Kasper (1992) and has been addressed more recently by others (Bardovi-Harlig, 1999a; Kasper and Rose, 1999; Kasper and Schmidt, 1996; Rose, 2000). The crucial distinction between comparative and acquisitional studies is the concern for the development of pragmatic knowledge. The central question driving SLA pragmatics research must be "How does L2 pragmatic competence develop?"

As with other areas of SLA research, the investigation of development is carried out through cross-sectional or longitudinal studies, ideally ranging from beginners through advanced learners. In contrast, the comparative studies are often single-moment studies (Rose, 2000). Early longitudinal studies include Schmidt's (1983) well-known report on Wes, a learner of English, Schmidt and Frota's (1986) study of a beginning learner of Brazilian Portuguese, and Billmyer's (1990) study of instructed learners of English. Later studies included Ellis's (1992) longitudinal study of two children's untutored acquisition of English requests, and Sawyer's (1992) study of the acquisition of the sentence-final particle *ne* by American learners of Japanese. Bouton (1992) investigated the development of comprehension as related to implicature, and Bardovi-Harlig and Hartford (1993) studied the changes in the speech acts of advanced nonnative speakers during their first year of postgraduate study. Siegel's (1996) ethnographic longitudinal study followed the acquisition of sociolinguistic aspects of Japanese by four Western women in Japan, and Cohen (1997) reported on his own acquisition of Japanese in a foreign environment by means of a diary study. Kanagy and Igarashi (1997) studied the acquisition of pragmatic routines in a Japanese immersion kindergarten by L1 speakers of English. Churchill (1999) investigated the acquisition of requests by Japanese enrolled in a partial immersion content-based English program in Japan.

The number of longitudinal studies compares favorably to the number of cross-sectional studies done in the same period. The emphasis on speech acts reflects the importance of the framework in ILP. A number of cross-sectional studies of requests were carried out in a range of target languages and included Blum-Kulka and Olshtain (1986, Hebrew), Takahashi and DuFon (1989, English), Svanes (1992, Norwegian), Takahashi (1996, English), Hassall (2003, Bahasa Indonesian), and Hill (1997, English). Studies of refusals in English were carried out by Takahashi and Beebe (1987), M. A. Robinson (1992), and Houck and Gass (1996). Apologies in English were studied by Trosborg (1987) and Maeshiba, Yoshinaga, Kasper, and Ross (1996). Omar (1992) studied greetings and leave takings in Kiswahili. Takenoya (1995, 2003) studied the acquisition of Japanese address terms by Americans. Multiple speech acts were investigated by Scarcella (1979, English), Olshtain and Blum-Kulka (1985, Hebrew), Trosborg (1995, English), Koike (1996, Spanish), and Rose (2000, English). Assessment of assertiveness was studied by Kerekes (1992, English), and pragmatic and grammatical awareness was studied by Bardovi-Harlig and Dörnyei (1998). For a review of the longitudinal and cross-sectional studies, see Kasper and Rose (1999, 2002).

Framing the Questions of Acquisition

Long (1990) distinguished description and explanation as dual goals for a theory of second language acquisition, stating that a theory of SLA needs to account for the accepted findings. As a starting point, investigations of the acquisition of interlanguage pragmatics would provide a description of the development of L2 pragmatics, which would constitute the body of "accepted findings." Because the overarching question of acquisitional ILP research—"How does L2 pragmatic competence develop?"—has such a broad scope, specific questions of smaller scope are also necessary. Kasper and Schmidt (1996) posed fourteen guiding questions that I have arranged by topic.

Measurement

1. How can approximation to target language norms be measured?

Kasper and Schmidt (1996) identify the lack of a common means to measure pragmatic development as one factor that has contributed to the underrepresentation of acquisitional studies.

Development

What are the stages of L2 pragmatic development?

2. Is there a natural route of development as evidenced by difficulty, accuracy, or acquisition orders or discrete stages of development?
3. Does (must) perception or comprehension precede production in acquisition?

    4. Does chunk learning (formulaic speech) play a role in acquisition?
    5. Does L1 influence L2 pragmatics?

Comparisons

Comparisons between L1 and L2 pragmatics lead to distinguishing the universals of acquisition of pragmatics from the particulars of (adult) second language acquisition. Kasper and Schmidt pose these questions:

    6. Is the development of L2 pragmatics similar to that in learning a first language?
    7. Are there universals of pragmatics, and do they play a role in interlanguage pragmatics?

Variables

Research in comparative ILP, acquisitional ILP, and SLA more generally suggest the following variables and corresponding research questions:

    8. Do children enjoy an advantage over adults in learning a second language?
    9. Does type of input make a difference?
   10. Does instruction make a difference?
   11. Do motivation and attitudes influence level of acquisition?
   12. Does personality play a role?
   13. Does a learner's gender play a role?

Among these questions, the most broadly investigated is the influence of the first language, but, as Rose (2000) has pointed out, the results from comparative studies on transfer may have to be reassessed when more acquisitional studies have been completed. Acquisitional studies on the influence of instruction represent a growing area of investigation (Billmyer, 1990; Bouton, 1994b; House, 1996, and the many empirical studies included in Rose and Kasper, 2001). As Long said, the seed of explanation often lies in the description itself, and any of the above variables may potentially play a part in an explanation of how or why L2 pragmatics is or is not acquired.

Mechanisms of Change

As part of an explanation, a theory of (pragmatics in) SLA must also be able to account for the mechanisms of change: How do learners move from one pragmatic stage to another?

   14. What mechanisms drive development from stage to stage?

This is the least researched area in ILP, although Schmidt (1993) and Bialystok (1993) address this issue. Kasper and Schmidt (1996) point out that there should be overlap in the mechanisms that drive change in other areas of SLA.

INVESTIGATING THE PRAGMATICS OF
GRAMMATICALLY LOWER PROFICIENCY LEARNERS

This final section explores some of the issues that arise in studies of beginning language learners. Although descriptions of L2 pragmatic competence necessarily include a linguistic component, it seems that they are not formulated to account for the acquisitional process but rather promote comparison between learner and native speaker production, as reported at the beginning of this chapter. Note, for example, that definitions often refer to deviations from the target, as a sampling of three classic descriptions shows. Blum-Kulka posits a three-way division between social acceptability (this determines when to perform a speech act, sequencing and appropriacy, and degree of directness), linguistic acceptability (deviations from which result in utterances that are "perfectly grammatical, but fail to conform to the target language in terms of what is considered an 'idiomatic' speech act realization," 1982: 52), and pragmatic acceptability (that an utterance has the intended illocutionary force). Blum-Kulka identifies unintended shifts in illocutionary force as the most serious consequence of nonnative speech act realization. Such shifts can occur with both linguistically acceptable and unacceptable utterances. Thomas (1983) identified *sociopragmatic failure* (inappropriate utterances due to a misunderstanding of social standards) and *pragmalinguistic failure* (utterances that convey unintended illocutionary force). Cohen suggests a third division, between sociocultural and sociolinguistic ability. *Sociocultural ability* refers to a speaker's ability "to determine whether it is acceptable to perform the speech act at all in the given situation and, if so, to select one or more semantic formulas that would be appropriate in the realization of the given speech act" (1996: 254). In contrast, *sociolinguistic ability* consists of speakers' control over their selection of language forms used to realize a speech act (e.g., *sorry* versus *excuse me*).

None of these distinctions is explicitly designed to deal with emergent interlanguage grammar. In fact, the practice of separating grammatical development (stated below in terms of errors) from pragmatic development is well established:

> Very often, of course, it is not pragmatic failure which leads non-native speakers to misinterpret or cause to be misinterpreted the pragmatic force of an utterance, but an imperfect command of the lower-level grammar.... I do not in any way underestimate the importance of these factors [grammatical error and covert grammatical error], but they have already been dealt with extensively. (Thomas 1983: 94)

Although such a separation between grammar and pragmatics has been productive in the analysis of language samples of relatively proficient learners—whose grammaticality was no doubt enhanced by the use of written elicitation tasks—with low-level learners linguistic and pragmatic development are intertwined (Bardovi-Harlig, 1999a). It may not be possible to make a clear distinction as studies of low-level learners show.

Rose's (2000) cross-sectional study of oral elicited requests by second- to sixth-grade children learning English in Hong Kong reveals an early development of a conventionally indirect request formula, *can you/I*, and subsequent development of grammar:

(4)   Can you McDonald, please? (second grade)
(5)   Can I eat lunch in McDonald? (fourth grade)
(6)   Can you take me to McDonald's for lunch? (sixth grade)

Data from spontaneous requests show a closer relationship between the linguistic and the pragmatic (Churchill, 1999; Ellis, 1992). Ellis (1992) investigated the classroom requests of two boys, aged 10 and 11, who were enrolled in an ESL language unit designed to help primary schoolchildren learn enough communicative English to join appropriate content classes. As example (7) shows, the use of nominal utterances, an early stage of language development, corresponds to the pragmatic request strategy of naming the desired item. The *give me* strategy in (8) and the *want* strategy (softened with *Miss*) in (9) emerge before the learner produces a direct object:

(7)   Sir / Big Circle (R wanted to staple his card/a cutout of a
       big circle)—Term 1
(8)   Give me (R wanted a ruler from another student)—Term 2
(9)   Miss I want [the stapler]—Term 3
(10) Tasleem, have you got glue?—Term 4
(11) Can I take my book with me? / Can you pass me my pencil?—Term 5

Churchill's (1999) yearlong study of 37 teenage learners of English (intermediate to high beginners on the ACT OPI) enrolled in a partial immersion content-based high school EFL language program shows similar interdependence of pragmatics and linguistic development:

(12) Tomomi: File...Return...
       NS: Huh? What do you want?
       Tomomi: Return to me.

(13) Reiko: Please...Colored pencils....
       NS: no response
       Tomoko: Lend us.

The requests in (12) and (13), constructed cooperatively by two learners, are quite direct, at least in part due to the low level of language development. In spite of the form of the early requests, the learners in the two observational studies demonstrate competence at the social level. As students they are expected to ask for what they need so they can go about the business of being students, whether they are in primary school or high school. These learners' production of requests shows social acceptability

(Blum-Kulka, 1982) or sociocultural ability (Cohen, 1996) in the appropriacy of performing the act. The second part of the social component—degree of directness and/or selection of semantic formulas—depends on grammatical development.

As a final exploration of the relation of pragmatic and grammatical development, consider a pair of spontaneous disagreements by adult learners during conversational interviews collected over a period of a year (Salsbury and Bardovi-Harlig, 2000). Compare the linguistic mitigation in (14) used by Mousa, an adult learner in an intensive English program in his ninth month of study, with the lack of mitigation in (15), recorded in his tenth month. In (14), Mousa disagrees with the interviewer over the use of the term *test anxiety* to characterize his feelings. Mousa mitigates his disagreement with the hedge *quite* and a partial agreement *I have a little:*

(14)   Mousa (21, male); Interviewer (32, male, PhD candidate)
       M: I don't know, maybe when ah, I'm taking like TOEFL, I have, a kind of
            feeling, sometimes I don't see, I don't—
       I: —It's called *test anxiety.*
       M: I don't have *quite* like this, but *I have a little,* but not quite like this...

In (15), Mousa disagrees with a classmate's opinion on polygamy, a topic that Mousa introduced. In the final line, Mousa goes bald on record with his disagreement, saying *no, no, no, you care!*

(15)   Mousa (21, male); Takako (19, female, classmate)
       M: you said like, if your, you don't care if your, your, your husband has
            other wife?
       T: I don't know.
       M: you don't care about that?
       T: like, now, I'm a little bit thinking, before I didn't like it, but now
       M: if you say that, I will say no, no
       T: I don't care
       M: no, no, no, you care!

On the one hand, Mousa's disagreement in (14) might be seen as more pragmatically successful than his disagreement in (15)—especially if we take a target-like perspective. His disagreement in (14) is mitigated and shows a higher degree of grammaticalization than that in (15). The difference between (14) and (15) could be due to a topic effect that prevents monitoring. On the other hand, the difference between (14) and (15) could be viewed as an indication of Mousa's developing L2 pragmatic competence.

Consider also the structure of the disagreement (Pomerantz, 1984). In the first two adjacency pairs, Mousa asks for clarification, a turn that is associated with dispreferred turns such as disagreement. Mousa then warns his classmate (using an emergent conditional) that he will disagree. At this point, it is still possible for the disagreement to be withheld, but his classmate again repeats that she does not care, and Mousa disagrees (Bardovi-Harlig and Salsbury, 2004). Mousa has a well-established pragmatic sense of the turns that constitute oppositional talk and their sequencing (part of Blum-Kulka's *social acceptability*). Mousa also uses greater mitigation with the male interviewer, 11 years his senior, than with his female classmate, 2 years his junior. Mousa shows what Cohen called *sociolinguistic ability*, the ability to control the selection of forms for pragmatic purposes; in Mousa's case he selects among the forms in his interlanguage inventory. Note that Takako, too, uses her emergent skills to mitigate her contribution, "I'm a little bit thinking." Although her turn is not grammatical, she clearly uses linguistic forms for pragmatic purposes. Cohen's definition of *sociolinguistic ability* seems to be the definition of linguistic ability that is most compatible with developmental aspects of L2 pragmatics.

As in other areas of SLA, it is important to develop frameworks that encourage and support the investigation of acquisitional stages—the process of second language acquisition—rather than the final outcome alone. As illustrated in the previous examples, one promising area for continued research is the exploration of the competencies that combine in the acquisition of L2 pragmatics. Learners develop grammatical and lexical knowledge that may form the basis of *pragmalinguistic knowledge* and social sensitivity that forms the basis of *sociopragmatic knowledge*. The question of primacy of one over the other seems to be a less promising research question than the question of how each contributes to the other.

Another necessary area of investigation, largely absent from early work on pragmatics (with the exception of work that used conversational data), is the effect of a learner's contribution on others. Success or failure is measured not in target-like performance but in success or lack of success in communication or conveying illocutionary force as seen, for example, in the requests of the preceding section. The analysis of conversation provides a contextualized reaction to a learner's contribution and removes the researcher from the position of judge. Studies that elicit noninteractive data have begun to use judges or raters as an alternative to comparison of learner to native speaker production by the researcher. Taken together, research in these areas will lead to a better understanding of form, function, and effect of production, and the nature of L2 pragmatic success. The research in pragmatics and SLA of the future promises not only to describe and explain development of L2 pragmatics, but also to contribute to our fundamental knowledge of what constitutes pragmatic competence.

CHAPTER 17

··

APPLIED LINGUISTICS AND THE NEUROBIOLOGY OF LANGUAGE

··

JOHN H. SCHUMANN

NEUROSCIENCE has made enormous strides in the last 2 decades. The brain is no longer a black box, and the exploration of language from a neurobiological perspective has become a major research focus in the language sciences.[1] These developments have been fostered by the availability of such neuroimaging technologies as *event-related potentials* and *functional magnetic resonance imaging*. This chapter will not directly review these technologies and the language research that they have generated because several excellent discussions already exist in the applied linguistics literature (C. L. J. de Bot, 2008; Dörnyei, in press; Ellis, 2008; Indefrey, 2006; Paradis, 2004; Ullman, 2006). This chapter will focus on some issues related to the development of a neurobiology of language in applied linguistics. The first section will discuss research on the neural underpinnings of language from a conceptual/theoretical perspective, laying out hypotheses about what systems may support language acquisition and use. These proposals about the biological substrate for language are made even though the technology to investigate them may not yet exist. The second section will address some reservations linguistics researchers have had about the relevance of neuroimaging research, and it will also explore the profound attraction such research has for scientists, the general public, and applied linguists in particular. Next, the problem of finding of cognitive ontology that is appropriate for research on the brain will be discussed. Essentially, this issue has to do with finding matches between psychological terms and neurobiological regions and processes. Finally, the problem of deciding what aspects of language are relevant for neurobiological investigation will be the focus.

Possible Neural Systems Underlying Language Acquisition and Use

Primary Language Acquisition

Lee et al. (in press) present an evolutionary theory of language as a complex adaptive system that exists as a cultural artifact without any requirement for innate abstract grammatical representations. From this perspective, language acquisition is seen as an emotionally driven process relying upon an innately specified "interactional instinct." This genetically based tendency provides neural structures that entrain children acquiring their native language to the faces, voices, and body movements of conspecific caregivers. It is essentially an innate attentional and motivational system driving children to pay attention to the language interaction in their environment and to acquire the ambient language by general learning mechanisms that subserve declarative and procedural knowledge. This brain mechanism guarantees the ubiquity of language acquisition for all biologically normal children. Second language acquisition by older adolescents and adults no longer has recourse to this mechanism, and therefore success in second language learning is extremely variable. Sometimes, however, a learner with sufficient second language learning aptitude may develop affiliative bonds with language speakers that are sufficiently strong to recapitulate the attentional and motivational power of first language acquisition.

Based on research by Depue and Morrone-Strupinsky (2005) and Luciana (2001), Lee et al. (in press) have proposed a model of social affiliation that may subserve the interactional instinct. It is divided into two parts: an appetitive component and a consummatory phase. The biology underlying consummation develops first and involves the expression of endogenous opiates during child–caregiver interaction. These opiates provide the child and the adult feelings of calmness, attachment, and affiliation with each other. This process, we argue, entrains the child's attentional mechanisms to the caregivers and serves as a hardwired motivational mechanism that ensures socialization in general and language acquisition in particular.

The intensely rewarding aspects of the attachment bond become part of the child's memory and serve as a template for subsequent affiliative relationships. The child in encountering conspecifics more distal than immediate caregivers responds to such affiliative stimuli as friendly vocalizations, gestures, smiles, and touch with positive appraisals and a desire to approach. The appraisals are communicated via the medial orbital cortex with contextual information relating to the affiliative stimuli coming from the hippocampus and the basolateral and extended amygdala. Dopaminergic innervation of the nucleus accumbens facilitates the integration of these various inputs, forming affiliative memories that may be retrieved and acted upon.

Second Language Acquisition

Since 1997, my students and I have been attempting to explore the neurobiology underlying motivation in second language acquisition. We began with the notion of stimulus appraisal and demonstrated how motivations could be reduced to appraisal dimensions, and how appraisal dimensions could then be related to neural structures.

Following on the work of Scherer (1984) and others, we argued that learners make evaluations of stimulus situations occurring along several parameters: novelty, pleasantness, goal or need significance, coping potential, and self- and social image. A novelty appraisal determines whether the stimulus is new or whether it has been experienced previously. Novelty can be appraised positively or negatively. A stimulus might be seen as novel and therefore interesting or as so unusual that it is threatening. An evaluation along the goal/need dimension determines whether the stimulus situation is conducive to achieving one's goal or satisfying one's needs. Coping potential refers to the individual's determination of whether or not he or she is capable of dealing with the physical or psychological consequences of this in a situation. Appraisals on the self- and social image dimension determine how engaging the stimulus situation would affect the individual's notion of his or her ideal self or how it would affect the evaluation of the individual by significant others (Schumann, 1997).

Using these five categories of stimulus appraisal, Schumann (1997) examined the major questionnaires used to assess motivation in SLA and demonstrated that each question on these instruments could be categorized on one or more of the appraisal dimensions. The analysis also revealed that different motivational frameworks focus on different appraisal dimensions. For example, in the early research done by Gardner (1985) and associates, approximately 70% of the appraisals were elicited on the appealingness (pleasantness) dimension. In motivation research by Clement, Dörnyei, and Noels (1994), appraisals of appealingness and goals were dominant. Schmidt and Savage's (1992) work focused strongly on appraisals of coping potential, and to a lesser extent on goal significance and self- and social compatibility, with appealingness playing a lesser role. In Schmidt et al. (1996) goal relevance received major focus, with a substantial number of items eliciting appraisals of coping potential and appealingness (Schumann, 1997).

We then were able to relate the appraisal functions to neural structures such as the amygdala, the orbital frontal cortex, and the body proper (the endocrine, autonomic, and musculoskeletal systems; Damasio, 1994). At present, continued research is extending this model to areas such as the insular cortex and specific components of the autonomic nervous system such as the vagus nerve, to additional areas of the prefrontal cortex (medial and lateral) and to the temporal poles.

Motivation, of course, is of no use unless it leads to action. Therefore, in order to understand the neurobiology that would subserve learners' efforts to acquire a language he or she is motivated to learn, we studied the neurobiology underlying the transformation of motivation and behavior. The literature on this topic demonstrated that animals—when foraging for food or to mate—engaged the neural mechanisms described above. The resulting appraisals generate signals that are passed from such structures as the amygdala and orbital frontal cortex to the ventral striatum in the basal ganglia and then to cortical and subcortical motor systems and finally to the spinal cord. We then reasoned that humans could use the same system to achieve not just biological goals (feeding and mating) but also such symbolic goals as acquiring a second language (Schumann, 1997; Schumann et al., 2004).

Relating this model of SLA to the one we developed for first language acquisition, it appears that the process is reversed in SLA, with the affiliative phase coming first. The learner appraises one or more speakers of the target language positively and makes efforts in the appetitive phase to affiliate with them. This affiliative goal is based upon a positive appraisal of the target language speaker in terms of novelty, pleasantness, coping potential, and self- and social image. The individual makes efforts to come into physical proximity with the valued other, and as it pursues that goal, when it contacts stimuli that are predictive of success, dopamine is released into the ventral and dorsal striatum. This neurotransmitter provides a reward similar to those generated by the ingestion of alcohol, amphetamines, cocaine, nicotine, or caffeine. The reward serves as a "go" signal, indicating to the organism that it is on the right path to achieve its goal to affiliate. The dopamine is modulated by neuropeptides (oxytocin and vasopressin) that have evolved to mediate social affiliation. If affiliation with the target conspecific is successful, the hypothalamus releases opiates that provide a reward similar to that generated by exogenous substances such as heroin and morphine. Successful affiliation leads to calmness, engagement, attachment, and gratifying pleasure (Lee et al., 2009; Schumann et al., 2004).

As the child passes into adolescence and adulthood, changes take place in the hormone—peptide—and neurotransmitter systems that support affiliation in primary language acquisition. Dopamine levels increase until the onset of puberty and then gradually reduce throughout life. The opiate system is modulated by oxytocin and vasopressin. These neuromodulators are also found at high levels in the child and become lower as the individual ages. The abundance of dopamine, opiates, oxytocin, and vasopressin in the child's brain supports interaction with conspecifics and guarantees primary language acquisition. The reduction of these substances in the mature brain may contribute to the difficulties in SLA experienced by older learners (Lee et al., in press).

Willingness to Communicate

MacIntyre (2007), working within the psychological construct "willingness to communicate," shows how a complex trait function can collapse in a moment into a state function and affect an individual's willingness to interact in a second language.

As MacIntyre indicates, there comes a point in any affiliative contact when a second language learner has to make a decision about whether or not to talk. At this point, we leave the realm of traits and must consider the learner's state. What becomes important is the learner's willingness to communicate at a particular moment with a specific person. As MacIntyre points out, in that precise moment, "WTC integrates motivational processes and communication competencies and perceived self-confidence" (2007: 4). McIntyre also implies that although a person may genuinely desire to learn the L2, and may even have an integrative motivation, he or she may, in certain situations (and these could be frequent), decide *not* to engage in verbal interaction in the L2.

The neurobiology of what might be going on in that moment is suggested by the social engagement system within Stephen W. Porges's *polyvagal theory* (2003). Porges argues that in order to become socially engaged, the organism must reach an appraisal that such engagement would be safe. This is accomplished when the face recognition areas of the brain judge the facial expression of the conspecific as friendly, welcoming, and sympathetic, when the learner's auditory perception appraises the conspecific's vocalizations as welcoming and comforting, and when the conspecifics body movements indicate friendliness and receptiveness. Under these conditions, the learner's ventral vagal complex operates to release oxytocin in the bloodstream and to induce the nucleus ambiguous to signal various cranial nerves to prepare the facial and head muscles, the larynx and pharynx, the muscles of the middle ear, and the heart and lungs for social engagement.

Safety is the crucial issue; if the organism feels threatened either physically or socially, then the amygdala signals the sympathetic nervous system for flight or fight, or it signals the dorsal vagal complex to induce immobilization. The trait variables with respect to capacity for social affiliation ultimately have to interact with a state variable (willingness to talk). That willingness will be manifest only if the organism's appraisal system determines that the target language speaker and the context in which he/she is embedded will not be a threat to the learner's physical being, self-image, or social image. The perception of threat may be accurate or inaccurate, but in either case it will control the willingness to talk.

From Declarative to Procedural Skill

One of the most important questions in SLA research is whether declarative knowledge can become procedural skill. Schumann et al. (2004) address this question by asking whether there is a neural route whereby the hippocampus, which mediates declarative knowledge, can get information to the basal ganglia, which mediates procedural skill. Extensive examination of the neural circuits that subserve the transformation of motivation to action offered a clue. The appraisal areas of the brain (the amygdala and the orbital frontal cortex) project to the hippocampus that has access to declarative knowledge about the target language. The hippocampus projects to the shell of the nucleus accumbens, which is a part of the ventral striatum of the basal ganglia. From there information can be transmitted to the ventral pallidum, which has efferents to the thalamus. From the thalamus, there are projections to the motor cortex, which then projects to the dorsal basal ganglia (caudate, putamen, and globus pallidus). This circuit potentially allows declarative information to become procedural, but we must note that this transformation may require substantial motivation generated by appraisals from the amygdala and the orbital frontal cortex as well as by dopamine reward signals from the ventral tegmental area. Schumann et al. (2004) also hypothesize that the engagement of this circuit would be required to correct fossilized interlanguage forms.

This conceptual/theoretical perspective on neurobiology in language acquisition has allowed us to hypothesize a set of systems at the biological level that generate appraisal functions, motivation, and willingness to communicate at the psychological level. It also allows us to move in the other direction, from willingness to communicate, to motivation, to appraisal, to neural mechanisms. Explanation at either the psychological level or the neurobiological level alone is inadequate. Both must be considered. There are advantages to such a conceptual/theoretical approach. Knowledge about the brain is developing exponentially. The neural story we have suggested will be expanded with new information and corrected on the basis of new discoveries. Current technology (e.g., neuroimaging) could test the model in minor ways, but the technology is expensive and access is limited. Of course, if the opportunity arose to do some imaging, it would be worth attempting experiments. But continued conceptual integration of the neurobiological and language acquisition literature is necessary and, indeed, primary if we are to be able eventually to seriously test a serious model.

LANGUAGE USE

Pragmatics

Research by Damasio (1994) demonstrated that patients with ventromedial prefrontal damage have severe difficulties in personal and social reasoning. Classic cases such as those of Phineas Gage and Elliot showed that insults to the prefrontal cortex left individuals with knowledge of social rules but an inability to implement them. The patients were said to have normal language. However, we reasoned that if one's social and personal reasoning were disrupted, one would also have deficits making appropriate decisions in language pragmatics. In other words, such patients would likely have problems in appropriately choosing what to say, when to say it, how to say it, and to whom to say it. Schumann (1997) made this hypothesis, and 10 years later the opportunity arose to test it. Alan Fiske, a cognitive anthropologists, and Mario Mendez, a neurologist at UCLA were interested in the social consequences of frontotemporal dementia (FTD), a disease that leads to progressive degeneration of the frontal lobe and the temporal lobes. Five of our students, Sam Torrisi, Lisa Mikesell, Andrea Mates, Netta Avineri, and Michael Smith, who were trained in neurobiology, conversational analysis, and ethnographic methods, began doing research in the patients' homes and during daily activities such as shopping and visits to the doctor. As we expected, pragmatic deficits were evidenced—some of them quite obvious and others more subtle.

Torrisi (in press) laid out the neurobiology of the brain's social cognition and social regulation systems. He identified the temporal poles, the orbital frontal cortex (including the ventromedial prefrontal cortex), the medial prefrontal cortex (including the dorsal medial, rostromedial regions), and the anterior cingulate. He also points out the pervasive connections between the temporal pole and the prefrontal regions via the uncinate fasciculus. Interconnections between brain regions have to be reckoned with in any understanding of neural function. In neurobiology, it's not simply "location, location, location"; it is also "connection, connection, connection." Mates (in press) noticed that the patient with whom she worked had difficulty in person reference. For example, when showing family pictures to Mates, the patient repeatedly overidentified his wife. Apparently he was unable to intuit the knowledge his interlocutor had about persons previously identified. This suggests difficulties with aspects of theory of mind. Mikesell (in press) examined all caregivers' efforts to manage FTD patients' behavior. She noticed that they used three strategies: reasoning, distracting, and physically directing. Avineri (in press) studied a patient's deficits in insight about her problems. Avineri's analysis indicates that her patient is unaware of her difficulties, but she knows that her caregivers believe she has problems. Therefore, when asked by a doctor, for example, about whether she had any difficulties, she suggested that he ask her caregiver. So, although the patient is unaware of her deficit, she can call on another person to fill that gap. Smith (in press) has demonstrated that FTD patients perform better in conversation when the discourse is about them. This self-bias seriously skews normal conversational interaction.

What seems to emerge from these studies is that FTD patients' difficulties with appropriate behavior, theory of mind, self-awareness, and egocentricity all contribute to pragmatic distortions in their verbal interaction with others. These results indicate that prefrontal cortex and the anterior temporal lobes are part of the neural substrate for language. This finding is consonant with the speculation previously articulated that the orbitofrontal cortex is integral in stimulus appraisal and, therefore, in motivation for learning.

Ethnographic researchers have examined the socialization of children in the home, in preschool, and in elementary school (see, e.g., H. J. Ahn, 2005; Bhimji, 2002; Han, 2004; He, 2000; Howard, 2004; Kremer-Sadlick and Kim, 2004; Lowi, 2007). The socialization efforts that emerge in this research seem to be building the neural structures that are later destroyed in FTD—patients were in many ways behaving like children/adolescents. As previously mentioned, Damasio (1994) had proposed that the ventromedial prefrontal cortex was a region of the brain that subserved socialization, enculturation, and education. Anna Joaquin (in press), a member of our Neurobiology Language Research Group (NLRG), analyzed the socialization literature and related it to the loss of socialization in FTD. She provided both arguments and evidence for Damasio's proposal. She is now casting this perspective within Vygotskyan sociocultural/activity theory (Lantolf and Thorne, 2006), showing how human neurobiology has evolved to receive and to incorporate the socialization from the society in which it develops.

READING

A particularly good example of an effort to understand that neural underpinnings of a language process is Maryanne Wolf's (2007) account of the biology of reading. Wolf integrates the literature on linguistics, psychology, and neuroscience and provides an analysis of the reading process and the acquisition of reading skill. In particular, she lays out a neurobiological account of the first 500 ms of the reading process. Then she analyzes the neurobiological research on dyslexia, using that neurological deficit to amplify her model of neurobiology of reading. She is careful to point out that reading is not a skill for which the brain evolved. It is an enterprise in which each individual reader has to co-opt brain regions and systems that have evolved other purposes. In her effort, she is able to offer an example for how language acquisition researchers might conceive of the neurobiology underlying language learning. If language is a cultural artifact, as Lee et al. (2009) and others suggest, then language acquisition itself (first and second) operate in the same way. Language acquisition colonizes neural systems that have evolved for other sensory and motor processes. Under these conditions, we can expect to see in the neurobiology of language the brain's ability to reuse neural tissue for any of our higher cognitive processes. But Wolf's exposition also serves as a caution against assuming that neurobiological research examining the reading process constitutes research that is automatically relevant to language acquisition. The mechanisms that language acquisition and reading co-opt in the brain may have substantial overlap, but they will also have substantial differences. Therefore, research involving reading tasks may not provide direct information about the neural substrates for oral language acquisition and use. Wolf points out that the many ways in which reading skills change the brains of children who have already had their brains changed by learning to speak. This perspective on the neurobiology of language in which brain mechanisms designed for other purposes are exapted for language is, of course, a radical departure from the traditional view of language as governed by innate domain-specific linguistic representations of a universal grammar.

WHY IS NEUROIMAGING SO ATTRACTIVE?

In recent years, the availability of neuroimaging technology (ERP, fMRI, etc.) has allowed some neurobiological investigation of SLA, multilingual processing, and bilingualism in general.[2] Scholars in the field have been extremely interested in this research, but at the same time many have been disappointed with the results. Now there exists the possibility that applied linguists may dismiss the neurobiology of language by implicitly equating neuroimaging with neurobiology; in other words, because of the limitations of neuroimaging, some researchers may think applied linguists should stick to the examination of the SLA at the psychological and behavioral levels only. I think the problem arises, in part, from the attempt to appreciate neuroimaging results without knowing neurobiology. For example, an fMRI study of SLA may indicate activity in a brain area during certain aspects of second language processing. This result provides locational information about such processing. If this research were complemented with an ERP study, one would also have information about the temporal duration of that activation. But then what does an applied linguist who doesn't know neuroanatomy or neurophysiology do with such information? In fact, he or she can do relatively little. More knowledge is needed. For example, one would want to know what other parts of the brain project to the activated area and what neural regions receive innervation from that region. Additionally, it would be important to know what other types of processing have been identified within the activated area. Most neuroimaging information is not likely to be informative to someone who is nave about neurobiology. However, there is a danger in this observation. As mentioned earlier, it might lead to the conclusion that applied linguists should stay with psychological and behavioral research. But the field has already recognized the enormous difficulties that are presented by trying to infer mechanism from behavior. It is this observation that has led linguists to place some hope in neuroscience.

Another impediment to developing a neurobiology of SLA is a rather compulsive empiricism that seems to characterize social science. The field is not patient with efforts to work out theoretical models of mental processing in SLA. This is particularly true when the neurobiological technology to test these hypotheses does not yet exist. I would argue that such models are absolutely necessary because, without them, all we will have are inferences about mental mechanisms based on behavior and neuroimaging. Applied linguistics researchers interested in processing might have to take the processors seriously; a brainless approach will sooner or later hit a wall.

The most successful sciences appear to be those in which the phenomena of interest are easily indexicalized. If a phenomenon can be observed with the naked eye or with some visual prosthesis (e.g., telescope, microscope), and if words can unambiguously refer to the phenomenon, then facts can be accrued and some degree of certainty can be attained. Therefore, in science one is always looking for indexicalization; we are trying to move from symbolic conceptualizations to indexical reference in which the words used can, as directly as possible, refer to physical phenomena and processes in the world. The kind of indexicalization we seem to prefer is through vision; if we can see it, we are more likely to consider that we have truth than if we hear it, feel it, taste it, or know it merely via definitions built on other definitions (i.e., symbolic conceptualizations).

An example of indexicalization through vision leading to a verifiable fact and therefore truth can be found in the history of neurobiology. At one time there was a theoretical debate as to whether the cortex was composed of a reticulum, in which all units were connected without breaks between them, and an opposing view, in which it was hypothesized that individual units were separated from others by small gaps. The neuroscientist Golgi represented the former theory, and Cajal the latter. Both received the 1906 Nobel Prize in Physiology or Medicine and presented their Nobel lectures proclaiming opposite points of view. Some years later the light microscope was invented and then the electron microscope that allowed us to visualize (i.e., see) actual neurons, and it was discovered that Cajal was correct. The brain was not a reticulum; it consisted of billions of individual units (neurons) that were connected across spaces called synapses. However, subsequent research has shown that there are some connections between neurons that are characterized by synaptic space but with tissue intermittently extending across the space connecting the two neurons. These connections are called lap junctions.

In physics a major task has been to "see" subatomic particles. This was first made possible in the 1950s and 1960s by bubble chambers. These chambers were large tanks filled with hydrogen in which atoms collided and the particles that comprise them created trails of bubbles that could then be photographed (Amato, 2003). This allowed an indexicalization of subatomic particles in which the tracks of the bubbles served as reliable indexes of the particles that produce them.

Moving in the other direction, telescopes have allowed us to indexicalize (i.e., see) large bodies at great distances. Speculations about the structure of the solar system have been settled by telescopic observations. The amazing images provided to astronomers via the Hubble Space Telescope are well known. Amato (2003) describes a less well-known telescope called The Chandra X-ray Observatory that can capture x-rays that penetrate the clouds and Milky Way. This telescope can detect x-rays from galaxies beyond the dust of the Milky Way. Thus the x-rays indexicalize for scientists the existence of astronomical bodies at enormous distances and through galactic regions obscured by clouds and dust.

When we move from science to engineering, indexicalization becomes virtually automatic. Any technology that we produce is visible one way or another. Thus we can generate words to refer unambiguously to the various components of any piece of technology. Therefore, with the right expertise, it is possible to understand completely how some technological instrument operates. We make it from visible parts, and we observe its visible processes, and therefore, the technology is thoroughly indexicalized, and we can say we know it; we understand it. If we confuse the production of technology and the certainty we have about its components and processes with what should be expected of all scientific endeavors, we become greatly disappointed. In the social sciences it is very difficult to get clear indexicalization; frustration with this fact, and implicit comparisons of social scientific endeavors with those of engineering frequently leave us feeling that the enterprises of sociology, anthropology, and psychology are either less deserving of the label *science* or that they must be done more rigorously so that they can behave like the sciences and technologies that are lucky enough to be easily indexicalized. I believe that neuroimaging is so attractive because it appears to allow us to see cognition, to see mental processing, to verify with our eyes the neural basis of the phenomenon we are interested in. However, fMRI images are not unproblematic representations of brain functioning (Dörnyei, in press). These images must undergo several transformations in order to provide even limited locational information. First of all, baseline neural activity must be determined, and then later it must be subtracted from task-generated activity. Then averaging across subjects is necessary in order to make general statements about the location of the activity. Nevertheless, when one looks at the images of individuals, there is often a great deal of variation in the location of activity. "Seeing" is such a valued source of information for humans that, among nonneuroscientists, the idea of getting brain images of the phenomena you're interested in becomes irresistible. When these images appear in newspapers, magazines, and on television, and especially in social science journals, reader or viewer tends to believe he or she is seeing a scientific reality.

Problem of Words: Cognitive Ontology

A major problem in the study of the brain is matching psychological categories to neural regions and neural circuits. The problem revolves around the fact that a single neural area can subserve many psychological functions, and many neural regions can be part of the substrate for a single psychological function. This situation is exacerbated by the fact that psychological categories/functions have developed over the past 400 years by inferring function from behavior. The typical procedure has been to design an experiment requiring some behavior or action, then to observe the behavior over many subjects, and finally to assign a mental label to that function. Because the label did not have to refer to a physical entity, it inevitably referred to a concept; consequently, the term was inherently symbolic, not indexical. The resulting psychological terms reference symbolic constructs that are understood only in relation to other psychological terms. Neuroanatomy, on the other hand, is largely indexical. Words are used to point out specific structural entities in the brain, and anatomists can index biological structures with relatively unambiguous terms. Therefore, when cognitive neuroscience came along, there was the problem of how to match the symbolic terms to indexical anatomical entities. For example, a task that was designed to test the concept *attention* might be linked to the anterior cingulate cortex because imaging has indicated activity in that area was generated in experiments designed to examine attention. Essentially, the attempt was to map the psychological notion of attention onto some physical entity in the brain. But one might also notice that certain areas of the dorsal lateral prefrontal cortex become active when an animal attempts to hold information about a stimulus that is no longer present. The brain's neurons active under these conditions are called *working memory* neurons (Fuster and Alexander, 1971). But a moment's thought allows us to realize that if information is in current use (i.e., in working memory), then that information can be considered as *attended to* (either implicitly or explicitly). Thus, the question could be, "What is the difference between working memory and attention?"

This issue has been identified in the biological literature as the problem of cognitive ontology, and the question posed is, "How does the cognitive ontology of psychology map on to neurobiology?" Price and Friston (2005) argue that we should be able to predict a neural structure from psychological function, and we should also be able to predict psychological function from neural structure. They lay out a research program to determine what psychological function is at play when a particular brain region is active. They noted that if a neural region became active during a psychological task, then the function of that region could be labeled according to a characterization of the task demands. Therefore, "different investigators assigned different labels to the same area" (Price and Friston, 2005: 265). They noted that the left posterior lateral fusiform (PLF) area might be labeled as the "visual word form area" (p. 265) based on experiments that showed it became active during reading tasks. However, the research also showed that part of the fusiform cortex is active in the naming of objects and nonobjects, that, during visual priming, the fusiform cortex is active in tactile identification of words and objects, and in the auditory perception of spoken words. So the problem is how to label this area in the light of the disparate (and seemingly unrelated) functions it subserves. The authors note that the PLF responds most strongly in each sensory modality "when a motor response (name or action) is retrieved from sensory clues" (p. 267). They suggest that an appropriate function for this region might be *sensory motor integration*, because different cognitive tasks elicit input to the PLF from various other neural regions. They concluded that a particular psychological function may emerge depending on what other neural areas are coactivated with, and/or have input to, the region of interest.

This problem was illustrated in a course I taught for my students who were involved in the study of frontotemporal dementia (FTD). We were to examine the literature on the prefrontal cortex with the idea that if we knew where an FTD patient had prefrontal degeneration, we should be able to predict his/her behavioral problems, and given an account of the patient's behavioral deficits, we should be able to predict the location of his/her prefrontal damage. However, the literature did not provide unambiguous characterizations of the functions of the various prefrontal subregions (lateral, orbital, ventromedial, medial). Typically, researchers labeled them according to the nature of the tasks eliciting activation. The result was that several subregions would elicit the same or similar functions, and individual subregions would have function that also characterized other regions. In the light of the research by Price and Friston (2005), we would assume that this smearing of psychological function could be the result of various inputs to these areas from outside the prefrontal cortex and from the interconnection among the various parts of the prefrontal cortex. Price and Friston say that "mapping [psychological] function to anatomy depends on a clear understanding of the cognitive processes that are being tapped by the experimental paradigm" (2005: 264). However, this "clear understanding" may be difficult to achieve and, in many cases, the turn to neurobiology occurs because attempts to achieve a "clear understanding" at the psychological level have not been successful.

Nielson, Hansen, and Balslev (2004) also tackled the cognitive ontology problem by associating psychological terms in the abstracts of 121 neuroimaging articles with terms in those abstracts referring to locations in the brain (i.e., sets of Talairach coordinates). They found that a set of psychological terms was associated with sets of locations. Essentially, the results pointed to a many-to-many relationship with multiple psychological functions associated with multiple regions.

Poldrack (2006) also confronts the cognitive ontology problem when investigating the process of *reverse inference*, in which cognitive processes are inferred from the activation particular brain regions. He observes that the cognitive ontology of the neuroimaging databases is rather coarse (indicating such very broad categories as attention, language, memory, music, reasoning, soma, space, and time), and therefore, the database ontology provides poor fits with the processes as described in cognitive psychology.

Therefore, a serious problem that applied linguists face when they try to match terms for processes in language acquisition and use to regions and circuits in the brain is that these terms—coming from psychology, psycholinguistics, and cognitive science—may not fit the structure of the brain. There are a couple of possible outcomes to this dilemma. First, it may be the case that as we learn more about the brain and develop technology that allows us to image neurocircuitry (not simply brain regions), we may find a more satisfying fit between psychological constructs and neural structure. On the other hand, we may find that neural processes, in very many instances, do not correspond to the labels we have given to psychological processes derived from observations of behavior. A possible solution could be to remain with a psychological label. But it was precisely the dissatisfaction with psychological characterizations that led many researchers to try to understand processes at a neurobiological level. It is not clear that we can go back.

To What Aspects of Language Should Neurobiology Be Responsible?

An important issue in establishing a neurobiology of language asks, "To what aspects of language should neurobiology be responsible?" Here the biology of language links to the evolution of language. If we want to understand the basic human capacity for language, we have to consider language as it may have existed during the environment of evolutionary adaptation. Written language has been around for about 5,000 years. Spoken language might conservatively be estimated at about 50,000 years, but there are arguments that it may have been a characteristic of our species for as long as 200,000 years.

It is generally accepted that language is acquired without overt instruction. On the other hand, literacy skills are usually learned through explicit instruction in school. Therefore, reading and writing may be things that the brain can do, but not what it would do spontaneously, naturally, and without pedagogical intervention. In addition, there is evidence that the language of writing differs substantially from oral language (Chafe, 1985; Hopper, 1998; Tao and Meyer, 2008, Thompson and Hopper, 2001).

It would seem that language most directly representing what evolved would be spontaneous conversational interaction among illiterates, particularly those who have had little or no exposure to the oral language of literates. A comparable situation might exist if a neuroscientist wanted to learn how the nervous system generates basic bipedal locomotion. In that case, the scientist would not want to begin by trying to study the motor activity of a professional basketball player or a professional tap dancer. With training, human motor systems can develop elite skills in basketball or tap dancing, but those are not the skills the nervous system evolved to execute. Therefore, we have argued (Lee et al., in press; Schumann, 2007) that a neurobiology of language might be best seen as responsible to ordinary conversational interaction. Of course, speakers who have not had schooling would be the best source of relevant data, but where such speech is not available, any informal, natural conversational interaction among speakers would be preferable to written language (or sentences invented by highly literate persons). Therefore, conversational analytic transcription of spontaneous interaction probably provides the data the brain has to deal with in comprehension and production. Such data, however, indicate that language may be very different from what linguists have supposed. Lee et al. (in press) and Mikesell (2004) have shown that in ordinary English conversation, subjects, verbs, and objects do not have to be expressed if they are recoverable from the linguistic or situational contexts. This forces us to question the very nature of grammar that the brain processes.

For a very long time, the sentence has been considered a major unit of language analysis, and in the past 50 years it has been the central object of linguistic inquiry. But several lines of investigation raise questions about whether the sentence merits this singular attention. The questioning may be particularly important with respect to the neurobiology of language. If we want to understand the biological basis of language, we must conceive of it in evolutionary terms—in other words, as it existed prior to the development of writing. Analyses of early English language manuscripts by Robinson (1998) indicate that the notion of sentence did not emerge in writing until the 1700s. Prior to that time, manuscripts lacked spaces between words, and when punctuation did appear, it was used to indicate pauses for reading. The ancient and medieval grammarians were concerned with meaning units and logical units (i.e., truth and falsity), not with syntactic units. Indeed, Robinson (1998) suggests that during the Middle Ages, Latin was taught without reference to the notion of *sentence*, not because *sentence* was being ignored, but rather because the concept of *sentence* did not yet exist.

Conversational annalists have noted that sentences are difficult to identify in normal interaction; consequently, they use conversational turn as the basic unit of analysis. Comparisons of the language processing abilities of literates versus illiterates (Tarone and Bigelow, 2007) and of people with less education versus those with more education (Dąbrowska, 1997, 2004) show that those subjects with less schooling rely on lexical and contextual information to interpret sentences, whereas, educated subjects are able to use syntactic and grammatical information. (See Schumann, 2007, for a short review.) Thus, education seems to have profound effects on how humans process language, and sentences are what students are exposed to in school.

This evidence seems to indicate that sentences are, in fact, units of written language, and therefore neurobiological studies of their processing may tell us very little about the human language faculty as it emerged during the environment of evolutionary adaptation. As mentioned earlier, analyzing how the brain comprehends and produces sentences may be like studying tap dancing when you want to understand the basic human ability for bipedal locomotion. Therefore, it might be reasonably argued that sentences are units of written language, and studies of sentence processing may tell us about what the brain can be trained to do, but not necessarily what it evolved to do.

Conclusion

When one field attempts to enhance its knowledge of a phenomenon by incorporating information from another field, it may amplify its understanding, but it must also face the problems arising from the adopted field. Therefore, applied linguists who study the neurobiology of language have to become interested in the brain qua brain. They have to know what is not understood about the brain, and they have to enjoy working in that vacuum. For example, current investigation of the neural substrate shows little evidence of anything that might be the basis for universal grammar (UG). This fact has led some researchers (such as those in our group at UCLA) to pursue a research program with the assumption that UG does not exist. But there is always the possibility that new technology that allows exploration of the brain with finer resolution may find the biological basis for innate representations of grammatical knowledge.

The brain is like no other machine. It is often analogized to a computer, but that analogy is basically misleading. The massive interconnectivity of neural regions, and the chemical as well as electrical nature of neural processing, make the brain a machine that could never have been built—the brain is not a machine; it had to evolve (Edelman, 1987). It is the product of slow biological change, not the product of intelligent engineering. Its innovations have come out of older systems that have not disappeared. They still exist and still influence processing. Such issues make the neurobiology of language an important complement to the traditional psychology of language. Applied linguists have a role not only in discovering the neural basis for language and use, but also in discovering the nature of the brain itself. In order to advance our field, we have to borrow, but at the same time we have the opportunity to contribute.

NOTES

1. A glossary and illustrations of brain areas have not been provided in this chapter for two reasons: (1) in any single publication, only a very limited number of glosses or figures can be provided, and (2) readers are generally quite varied in terms of their knowledge of neuroanatomy. Therefore, these aids are often out of sync with readers' needs. The best way to handle this problem is to refer the reader to the Internet. A single Google search for a term (e.g., "ventral striatum") will provide a definition and a discussion of this neural area. In addition, if one adds the term "image" to the search, several illustrations of the brain will appear, and the readers can use the ones that make the most sense, given the reader's current knowledge of neuroscience.

2. Much of the material in the section "Why Is Neuroimaging So Attractive" was previously published in Schumann et al. (2006). It is reproduced with permission of the online journal *Marges Linguistique*.

PART V

THE STUDY OF SECOND LANGUAGE TEACHING

CHAPTER 18

....

CURRICULUM DEVELOPMENT IN FOREIGN LANGUAGE EDUCATION: THE INTERFACE BETWEEN POLITICAL AND PROFESSIONAL DECISIONS

....

PÉTER MEDGYES AND MARIANNE NIKOLOV

THIS chapter falls into two main sections. The first section is concerned with general aspects of curriculum development and innovation. It sets out to define the curriculum in relation to its sister concept, the syllabus, and further it examines the connection between theoretical and practical aspects of curriculum development. The chapter goes on to address the issue of curriculum innovation, an undertaking aimed at resolving the conflict between what is desirable and what is acceptable and feasible. In view of pressing needs, this contradiction has become more acute in recent years, giving rise to various kinds of friction between curriculum designers and teachers on the one hand and specialists and policymakers on the other. Among the conditions supposed to ensure the success of curriculum reforms, the primary one requires concerted efforts among all participants in education. Turning to language education in particular, the first section of the chapter concludes by taking stock of the major curriculum models adopted in the past 40 years. The second section is devoted to illustrating the main aspects of curriculum design postulated in the first section. The country chosen to exemplify these assumptions is Hungary, a country in which curriculum reforms were necessitated by pervasive political, economic, and social changes during the last decade of the twentieth century. Through an analysis of interim versions of the National Core Curriculum, the way political decisions are brought to bear on curriculum reform in general and on the development of the foreign language syllabus in particular is demonstrated.

What Is the Curriculum?

Issues relating to the curriculum have been of interest to philosophers and educators since the time of Plato, but its formal study really began only in the twentieth century. However, as in the case of many other new disciplines, there was no consensus over the meaning and scope of curriculum, and definitions varied according to academic allegiance and geographical location.

It was not until the last quarter of the century that debates over definition had subsided, and the term *curriculum* had come to refer to the whole educational process, including the design, implementation, and evaluation of language programs (Richards 2001). In this broad sense, curriculum also comprises methods and approaches, measures of evaluation, teaching materials and equipment, and even teacher education (Stern 1983). In contrast to curriculum, *syllabus* refers to a more circumscribed document generally taken to refer to the content of an individual subject, such as history, physics, or English as a second or foreign language (Dubin and Olshtain, 1986; Yalden, 1987).

Curriculum studies is an umbrella term covering both theoretical and practical issues; in fact, researchers differ mainly in their choice either to move toward deeper immersion in academic scholarship, with only an indirect or tangential interest in practical issues, or to become more closely involved with school affairs and the mechanics of curriculum innovation (Jackson, 1992). In this regard, Pratt and Short complained that although "a considerable body of knowledge concerning curriculum [studies] has emerged in the course of the twentieth century, so far its impact on actual school practice has been minimal" (1994: 1325). This outcome is not only a result of the lack of a widely accepted and explicitly formulated theoretical paradigm (Johnson, 1989) but also of the adoption of a top-down model of curriculum development. According to this model, the theorists' job is to articulate well-defined general educational aims and behavioral objectives, design detailed content specifications, and set valid and reliable assessment criteria, whereas practitioners are relegated to the task of implementation.

Challenging this distribution of work, Stenhouse (1975) argued that it forces teachers to adopt a *hidden curriculum*, that is, an alternative teaching program in the face of official dictates. This contradiction can be resolved only by offering teachers the chance to subject their professional skills and attitudes to critical scrutiny through continuous and active involvement in curriculum research and development. The underlying images in Stenhouse's line of argument are those of the *reflective teacher* (Schön, 1983) and the *teacher researcher* (Freeman, 1998), which have become catchphrases in educational literature. To drive home the same message, Graves substitutes *enactment* for *implementation* in order to reflect the central role that teachers and learners play in the educational process, asserting that "curriculum must be enacted to exist" (2008: 152).

What Is Curriculum Innovation?

Attempts at innovation are spurred and justified by human needs, which, for the purpose of this discussion, may be defined as "a discrepancy between an actual and a preferred state" (Pratt and Short, 1994: 1321). The key attributes of innovation are that (a) it is a change that involves human intervention, and (b) it is aimed at bringing about improvement (White, 1993.) This is more a regular sentence than a list. Obviously, certain needs specifically call for innovation in education, even though sociologists seem to agree that education basically serves a socially and culturally reproductive function and is therefore conservative and resistant to change.

Until the 1970s, educational and curriculum reforms followed one another at a steady pace, and most of them were limited to the introduction of minor modifications. In the final decades of the century, however, the pace of curriculum reforms accelerated, and their scope widened in response to the demands of a rapidly changing world. Fundamental measures were taken to reform and centralize the curriculum even in such countries as the United Kingdom, the United States, and Australia, which earlier had taken little interest in curriculum issues (Skilbeck, 1994).

Curriculum reform, like any other innovation, involves several kinds of participants, each assigned distinct roles. Five main types of role may be distinguished:

1. *Policymakers*, who take the major decisions (politicians, ministry officials, deans, heads of departments)
2. *Specialists*, who provide the necessary resources (curriculum and syllabus designers, materials writers, methodologists, teacher trainers)
3. *Teachers*, who deliver the services
4. *Students*, who receive the services

5. *Mediators*, who liaise among all the participants (government agencies, such as the British Council, the United States Information Agency, and the Goethe Institut, or nongovernmental organizations, such as the Soros Foundation)

POLICY CONSTRAINTS

In theory, any participant may initiate action, but in practice teachers (not to speak of students) can seldom make their voices heard beyond their classrooms or schools. Specialists, but especially curriculum and syllabus designers, are usually in a better position to influence policymakers (Kaplan, 1992). However, the right of policymakers to act at their own discretion is rarely challenged, in recognition of the responsibility they assume for their decisions. Judicious specialists are willing to admit that a policy decision may be beneficial even when it runs contrary to current educational or research wisdom (Judd, 1992). After a decision has been made, it is the professional and moral duty of specialists to state their views on feasibility, costing, and other aspects of implementation; again, it is up to policymakers whether or not to seek expert advice.

Nevertheless, it appears that curriculum innovation suffers from what the American sociologist Ogburn (cited in Skilbeck, 1994) once defined as *social lag*. Driven by economic, financial, and social constraints, policymakers often find that the rate at which educational reform is being introduced is too slow. In Pratt and Short's view, "curriculum is not successfully developed and installed until political pressure is strong enough to overcome the forces of tradition, inertia, and vested interest that work against change in educational institutions" (1994: 1320). To make matters worse, there is growing dissatisfaction with the quality of education delivered, from which policymakers conclude that

> the curriculum should no longer be considered the "secret garden" for the professionals to tend and enjoy....The content of schooling and methods of teaching are held to be too important to be left in the hands of teachers and other educational professionals. They must be brought into line with the overall objectives of society. (Skilbeck, 1994: 1339, 1341)

CONDITIONS FOR SUCCESS

Curriculum development is a complex activity, and its products usually have a slim chance of long-term survival; in Adams and Chen's estimate (1981, cited in Markee, 1997), 75% of all innovations fail to take root. However, if certain preliminary measures are not taken before designing the curriculum, the chance of success may be greatly enhanced. The first question to be asked is whether the reform is necessary, timely, and feasible. The continuation of a program that has lost steam usually causes less damage than the introduction of a reform that is unjustifiable, premature, or short of financial support and human resources. The second issue is that campaign-like reforms urged by agents with vested personal interests in their realization are dangerous. In general, evolution is a far more desirable goal than revolution in curriculum development (Johnson, 1989; Stenhouse, 1975). The third consideration is that curriculum design should be conducted with methodological rigor (Markee, 1997). Fullan is right in saying that "large plans and vague ideas make a lethal combination" (1982: 102). Finally, any innovative idea is bound to hurt those whose psychological and occupational security rests on the survival of the old system. Therefore, efforts should be made to convince opponents about the benefit that the new curriculum will bring them (Kaplan, 1992; Kaplan and Baldauf, 2007).

Once the decision to get the curriculum reform off the ground has been made, a team of specialists is invited to set to work. Experienced specialists are aware that curriculum development, like most human endeavor, is a hopelessly untidy business, rife with mismatches, uncertainties, and redundancies. It cannot be expected to work merely by legislative, decree, white papers, and centrally issued directives (Skilbeck, 1994). This being the case, every participant involved in the undertaking should be prepared to engage in continuous communication with every other agent. Only by dint of close collaboration and mutual responsiveness can problems be identified, precluded, and remedied.

CURRICULUM MODELS IN LANGUAGE EDUCATION

Let us now turn to issues that specifically relate to second and foreign language education. In analyzing the relationship between general curriculum theory and curriculum theory in language teaching, Stern noted that, in fact, "very little movement of thought across these two trends has taken place" (1983: 442). The two exceptions he referred to are Halliday, McIntosh, and Strevens (1964) and W. F. Mackey (1965), who had made elaborate attempts at designing a language curriculum based on theoretical underpinnings. With reference to language projects, Kennedy (1988) also complained that, whereas the literature in other fields of education was rich, there was a scarcity of research relating to language education. In a similar vein, Fettes wrote, "the exclusion of education research from the field of language planning…appears decidedly unhelpful" (1997: 17).

Investigating innovative language syllabuses in the last third of the twentieth century, one is dazzled by the variety of directions and models (Howatt, 2004). After the eclipse of the audiolingual method in the late 1960s, Stern (1983) advocated the need to break away from the method concept; indeed, *method* became a taboo word, as testified by the names of the most quoted language teaching models of the 1970s, including silent way, community language learning, suggestopedia, and total physical response (Richards and Rodgers, 2001; Stevick, 1980). Incidentally, despite the originality underlying their philosophies and practices, these models had limited currency in language classrooms.

However, the real breakthrough in language education came with the advent of communicative language teaching (CLT), a paradigm that has permeated the language teaching scene since the 1970s. Originally called the communicative approach, it had gone a long way before it shed the capital letters and metamorphosed from a method through a syllabus (i.e., the functional-notional syllabus; Munby, 1978; van Ek, 1977; Wilkins, 1976) to an all-encompassing humanistic philosophy of language education (Moskowitz, 1978; Rogers, 1969; Stevick, 1990; Tudor, 1997), begetting a plethora of syllabuses and methodologies, as well as classroom procedures and techniques (Breen and Candlin, 1980; Brumfit and Johnson, 1979; Krashen and Terrell, 1983; Littlewood, 1981; Widdowson, 1978). Among the best-known syllabuses are the process syllabus (Breen and Littlejohn, 2000; Clarke, 1991; Prabhu, 1987), the content-based syllabus (Snow, 1998; Snow, Met and Genessee, 1989), the task-based syllabus (Crookes and Gass, 1993; Ellis, 2003; Skehan, 1996), and the lexical syllabus (Willis, 1990). Nevertheless, two caveats may well be in place. One concerns critiques that have found fault with CLT on both theoretical and pragmatic grounds (Medgyes, 1986; Swan, 1985). The other has to do with the imposition of CLT under all circumstances, even in countries whose educational ideologies and cultural traditions are not in harmony with learner-centeredness and humanistic education as defined by the leading theoreticians and ambassadors of CLT (Holliday, 1994; Phillipson, 1992). Although CLT has become a buzzword, there is reason to believe that teachers have continued to follow more structural lines in their classroom practices (Karavas-Doukas, 1996).[1]

On a more general plane, Breen finds no fault with the mismatch between innovative ideas as they feature in the syllabus and the process of language teaching and learning, because the "syllabus is mediated by teaching and the encircling classroom context within which instruction is only one element" (1987: 159). Widdowson goes even further when he suggests that the classroom is largely unaffected by "shifts of thinking" (2004: 369).

The gap between advances in language syllabus design and slow progress in modification of classroom practice has to do, among other things, with inadequacies of teacher education. Most training institutions still fail to perceive teachers as facilitators of change and to prepare them for this role (Allwright, 2005).

HUNGARY: A CASE STUDY

To illustrate the process of curriculum development and the nature of curriculum innovation, the rest of the chapter will present a case study. The country chosen to exemplify the assumptions made in the previous sections is Hungary, the authors' country of origin. After a discussion of how political changes have influenced educational policy in the past decade, the investigation will focus on the processes that have interacted in the development of a new national core curriculum (NCC) in general and the foreign language syllabus in particular, as well as the degree of impact these processes have had on classroom practice.

The Political and Educational Context of Curriculum Innovation

By the mid-1980s, it had become obvious in Hungary, as in all the other countries of Central and Eastern Europe, that the communist system was not going to improve unless the entire political and economic structure underwent change. As a herald of an imminent cataclysm, the Education Act of 1985 undermined the communist educational system, while the 1990 Amendment, passed by the last communist government, gave it the *coup de grace*. By reducing heavy administrative and political control over education, these two acts gave more autonomy to individual schools, canceled the prescriptive control of the curriculum, and restored teachers' pedagogical sovereignty, offering them a free choice of methodology and teaching materials (Medgyes and Miklósy, 2000, 2005).

Communism imploded in 1989. The first free election, held in 1990, brought a conservative government to power, which, oddly enough, condoned a model of education more centralized than the one adopted by its reform-minded communist predecessors. Whereas the socialist-liberal government formed in 1994 was committed to liberalizing the education system, 4 years later the pendulum swung back at the push of another conservative government. The coalition government of socialists and liberals came back to power in 2002 and was reelected in 2006. As a result, a number of laws that had been abolished by the conservatives were reinstated, while several others were passed. A new law concerned the school-leaving examination, which gave priority to instruction providing practical skills rather than the rote learning of lexical knowledge. Incidentally, this shift of balance harmonized with general educational trends within the European Union.

There are at least two lessons to learn from this political tug-of-war. One has to do with the limited impact policy decisions taken by consecutive governments with differing ideologies seem to have had on classroom life; apart from a growing feeling of insecurity among teachers, no significant changes can be observed in their teaching practices. The second lesson relates to the academic performance of Hungarian students in the light of international comparative studies. Whereas Hungarian students did extremely well in the 1970s and 1980s, their results have gradually declined since the late 1980s, as evidenced by both national and international surveys (Csapó, 1998, 2002; OECD, 2006), and no government or political will has thus far proven capable of reversing this downward trend. In addition, these two lessons are indications of the *social lag*, referred to earlier, with which education responds to political, social, and economic changes.

Educational Policy and the National Core Curriculum

These fluctuations in Hungarian politics are reflected in curricular innovation and can be traced through the development of the National Core Curriculum (NCC). The need to design a new curriculum had already been recognized by the last communist government. Then, from the early 1990s on, several versions followed one another in quick succession until the final version came into effect in 2007.

The curriculum designers involved in developing the NCC had been randomly selected, and it was at the whim of policymakers that their services were retained throughout the process or dispensed with at some certain stage. In accordance with the consensus-seeking ethos of postcommunist democracies, specialists, including designers of local curricula, materials writers, and examination experts, were also invited to comment on the different versions of the NCC. Their suggestions, however, were often considered not so much on the basis of their intrinsic professional value as on the strength of the political message they were judged to carry. Furthermore, many schools, pedagogical institutes, and university departments were also invited to provide feedback, but it is unclear what actually happened to this feedback. As for teacher feedback, because teachers had not been asked to express views on curriculum matters, the scope of their responses was rather limited, and their voices could hardly be heard in the NCC.

From among the different versions of the NCC (1990, 1993; Hungarian Ministry of Education, 1995, 2003, 2007), the one published in 1995 may be considered innovative on several counts. To give an example, traditional subject areas were arranged in integrated cultural domains, in an attempt to loosen up subject boundaries across the curriculum. This approach came under heavy criticism on the grounds, on the one hand, that it was alien to Hungarian educational traditions and, on the other hand, that there were no teachers available to teach such integrated content areas. Despite the controversy, these cultural domains have been maintained in subsequent versions of the NCC as well.

To make matters worse, the idea of introducing cultural domains was not carried beyond the confines of the NCC, and the subsequent examination reform still structured its requirements around traditional school subjects, rather than around cultural domains. In other areas, too, although the NCC broke new ground, it was fraught with contradictions, which, combined with protests from specialists professing conservative views, rendered its implementation a daunting task. Confronted with both pragmatic and ideological constraints, the second conservative government decided to slow down the process of introducing the NCC and, simultaneously, to subject it to thorough revision. Revisions, however, were stalled until the second socialist-liberal coalition takeover in 2002.

Another controversy concerned the two-tier versus the three-tier curriculum hierarchy. According to the original two-tier idea, local educational bodies, particularly schools, were urged to develop (on the basis of the NCC) their own local curricula, which were intended to give schools the opportunity to meet local needs and to involve teachers in a worthwhile professional activity besides classroom teaching.

As a result, hundreds of local curricula were devised and implemented all over the country. However, when the second conservative government came to power, it decided to insert centrally prepared *frame curricula* between the NCC and the local curricula. Partly according to one's political allegiance, a frame curriculum could be regarded either as a helpful device to exempt schools and teachers from the burden of extra work or, conversely, as a pretext to curb their administrative and professional autonomy. Not long after the socialist-liberal coalition returned in 2002, the idea of the frame curricula simply fizzled out.

Foreign Languages in the National Core Curriculum

Modern languages, which represent one of the 10 cultural domains, may be perceived as a primary conveyor of innovation in the NCC. First, the most spectacular curricular change in 1989 ended the monopoly of Russian with the result that the study of other foreign languages became accessible on a large scale (Enyedi and Medgyes, 1998; Nikolov, 1999a). Second, the accession of Hungary to the European Union in 2004 increased the need to speak foreign languages and to adopt European norms. All the documents relating to foreign-language education since 1989 have been designed to be "euroconform"; more specifically, they have adopted the functional-notional syllabus and have advocated humanistic and communicative principles of education. A milestone in this process was the integration of levels of proficiency as defined in the *Common European Framework of Reference* (Council of Europe, 2001) into the Hungarian reform of school-leaving exams and the later versions of the NCC.

In the following, five versions of the NCC will be analyzed within the framework of foreign language education. Although all of them address the same political, linguistic, and pedagogical concerns, the points of departure are different, and they exhibit divergences in language policy and specialist opinion. Most important, whereas the earlier versions tended to satisfy needs rooted in the national past, the recent versions emphasize what Hungary has in common with contemporary European trends. To illustrate these differences, four issues will be examined:

1. *Native language versus foreign languages.* Versions 1 and 2 emphasized the isolation of Hungarian among Indo-European languages and elaborated on the role of foreign-language study in the learners' native language development. Whereas version 1 explicitly stated that teaching should shed light on similarities and differences between the first and the foreign language, this contrastive principle was softened into "awareness raising" in version 2, only to be pushed into the appendix in version 3 and ultimately to fade into oblivion in versions 4 and 5. These alterations testify to shifts of focus both in linguistic attitudes and in the political agenda.
2. *Choice of languages.* It is revealing how the role of Latin and English in relation to other foreign languages has changed over time. Whereas in version 1 only English and German were listed as examples of modern

languages, and Latin was referred to only indirectly, version 2 avoided specifying any languages. Perhaps with the purpose of making concessions to conservative policymakers, version 3 mentioned Latin as a second foreign language in the introduction but then supplied examples only for English, French, German, and Russian. In version 4 new categories were set up: frequently taught modern foreign languages (English and German), less frequently taught languages, languages of ethnic minorities, and dead languages. However, achievement targets were identified merely for the first two categories. Unlike in earlier versions, freedom in language choice in version 4 was declared, with no priority given to English or any other foreign language. Version 5 witnessed a major change in that it obliged all secondary schools to offer English for those students who requested it. Strangely enough, apart from a sheer mention of this new regulation in the introduction, the rest of the syllabus fails to discuss it at any length. This suggests that politicians had not bothered to consult professionals before the decision was made—or since then, for that matter.

3. *Starting age.* Before 1989, students started learning Russian in grade 4 (age 9), but as the regime became more liberal, so the opportunity for learning other foreign languages improved. Despite pressing social and individual demands for competence in foreign languages after 1989, neither version 1 nor version 2 specified the time when foreign language instruction should commence. To aggravate the situation, version 3 pushed the compulsory starting age back to grade 5 (age 10), that is, a year later than stipulated in the 1980s. Versions 4 and 5, however, not only set grade 4 as the initial year of compulsory foreign language study, but allowed—what has since become common practice—schools to launch language programs even earlier.

4. *Proficiency levels.* Whereas earlier versions alternately articulated two or three levels of language proficiency, versions 4 and 5 specified achievement targets at four levels out of the six defined in the *Common European Framework of Reference* (Council of Europe, 2001). A dual system was adopted, according to which students may take their school-leaving exams either at level B1 or B2. Version 5 includes a further specification: Students who participated in a year of intensive language learning program in grade 9 (Medgyes and Miklósy, 2005) are expected to sit the exam at level B2 by the end of grade 10.

Foreign Language Classrooms

While the NCC has undergone several alterations during the past 2 decades, teachers have kept teaching according to their own hidden curriculum, hardly affected by official dictates. A classroom observation study involving 118 English classes from disadvantaged backgrounds (Nikolov, 1999b) looked into what teachers and students were actually doing in the classroom. In a large-scale fol-low-up study, questionnaire data on frequencies of classroom activities in English and German classes, collected from representative samples of Hungarian learners, were analyzed (Nikolov, 2003). Both studies reveal that language teachers generally adopt an eclectic approach: Techniques of the grammar-translation method and those of the audio-lingual method mingle with ones more characteristic of the communicative classroom. The most frequent tasks invariably include translation, reading aloud, question-and-answer exercises, and the explanation of grammar rules in Hungarian—none of which have been favored by recent versions of the foreign language syllabus.

To aggravate the situation, at the end of the twentieth century 65% of teachers of modern languages in Hungarian primary schools were registered as retrained graduates, who had previously been employed as Russian teachers (Halász and Lannert, 1998). Worse still, 10% of English and German teachers have no teaching qualifications whatsoever (Halász and Lannert, 2003).

Returning to the issue of curricular reforms, it is no exaggeration to assert that the majority of foreign language teachers in Hungary have paid little heed to the unreasonable demands presented by the different versions of the NCC: They teach at the present time as they always did. In some sense, their immobility may well be regarded as a positive trait because teachers have thus managed to avoid falling victim to the effects of ill-considered and rash political decisions.

In light of the findings referred to earlier, it is no surprise that in terms of language proficiency, Hungary lags behind all the other member states of the European Union (*Europeans and Languages: A Eurobarometer Special Survey*, 2001). It is a sorry fact that a mere 19% of the Hungarian population claimed to know at least one foreign language in the last national census (2002). Nevertheless, compared to 12% in the early 1990s (Terestyéni, 1996), steady progress may be observed, and the 29% documented in 2005 (*Europeans and Languages*, 2005) gives sufficient reason for cautious optimism.

However, the growth of foreign language competence in Hungary appears to be attributable to positive changes in learners' attitudes and learning motivation rather than to progress in curriculum design, instruction methods, or teacher competence (Nikolov, 2003; Nikolov and Józsa, 2006). According to large-scale longitudinal studies investigating eighth-graders' motivation, learning efforts, and language choice (Dörnyei, Csizér and Németh, 2006), contemporary Hungarian learners were highly motivated and diligent to study modern languages, and their attitudes were favorable toward native speakers of the language of their choice. As for their choices, the majority studied English and German, but a pronounced shift toward English has been observed over the years.

Conclusion

This chapter has attempted to show curriculum development as a process furthered by agents who subscribe to different philosophies of education. Decisions made at policy and specialist levels are seldom based on consensus, and changes are often instituted over the heads of teachers and learners. The Hungarian National Core Curriculum (NCC) may be considered a typical example of a reform curriculum: While extolling the merits of communicative language teaching and setting "euro-conform" requirements, it disregards the genuine needs of classroom participants and connives at the use of outdated classroom methods. In some sense, perplexed by the ever-changing and often contradictory expectations of curriculum require-ments, teachers in Hungary and elsewhere may well be right in pursuing their own hidden agenda, instead of jumping on the bandwagon. Even though teachers obvi-ously belong to various age cohorts with different political and pedagogical experi-ences over their teaching career, the majority appear to find a gentle breeze in the form of a new technique more refreshing than a gale of disparate ideas formulated in a reform curriculum.

On a more general level, it has been argued in this chapter that if there is a gap between policymakers and specialists, the gap between both groups and teachers is far wider. Hence, it usually takes a long time before curriculum innovation, even at its best, permeates the thinking of those at the chalk-face and in turn rejuvenates their daily practice.

ACKNOWLEDGMENT

The second author gratefully acknowledges the support of the Research Group on the Development of Competencies, Hungarian Academy of Sciences (MTA-SZTE Kpessgkutat Csoport).

NOTES

1. Markee (1997) warns that case studies may prompt some readers to ask, "What does this project have to do with me?" This is a legitimate criticism, but only if the case study fails to demonstrate the issues raised or exhibit their relevance to the readers' own concerns and environments. The authors hope to have avoided both pitfalls.

CHAPTER 19

CONTENT-BASED SECOND LANGUAGE INSTRUCTION

MARJORIE BINGHAM WESCHE

CONTENT-BASED instruction (CBI) is a form of communicative language teaching (CLT) in which language instruction is integrated with school or academic content instruction. Content-based approaches to second and foreign language (L2) teaching have in recent decades become increasingly prominent at all levels of schooling and in postsecondary education (Brinton, Snow, and Wesche, 2003; Richards and Rodgers, 2001; M. A. Snow, 1998). In CBI, as in other experiential CLT approaches, the traditional L2 instructional focus on raising learners' awareness of linguistic form is secondary to a focus on their learning and sharing of information through the medium of the L2, in a curriculum based on the language needed for learning the particular content. As CBI evolves, there is, as well, increasing recognition of the need to draw learners' attention to formal properties of the language within communicative situations.

CBI AND CLT

"Weaker" forms of CLT (Howatt, 1984) tend to view spontaneous communication as an end rather than a means and to incorporate practice based on description of communicative language features (e.g., of appropriate forms for expressing given language functions). Such descriptions stem from early research in systemic or functional linguistics (see Halliday, 1978), dealing with patterns in language use well beyond the sentence level, and in sociolinguistics (see Hymes, 1972a, 1972b), on the nature of *communicative competence*, in other words, not only characteristics of the language code but also appropriate language behavior for given communicative goals. (For a review of the history of CLT, see Wesche and Skehan, 2002.)

In "stronger" forms of CLT, such as CBI, communicative language ability is considered to be largely acquired through purposeful language use, according to the *acquisition hypothesis* that emerged from early research on second language acquisition, perhaps best articulated by Krashen (1985; also see Hatch, 1978; Larsen-Freeman and Long, 1991, among others). The premise is that L2 development proceeds through intensive language use for comprehension and expression in communicative situations. As in L1 development, a "natural" syllabus for core grammatical and certain other language features will emerge through multiple, richly contextualized interactions in the language. Furthermore, lexical items relevant to the context at hand will be learned. Experiential CLT is for these reasons organized around situations, oral and written texts, skill or knowledge domains, or tasks requiring communicative language use of various kinds. Although quite diverse content may assure acquisition of underlying phonological and syntactic systems, content that is highly relevant to learners' interests and postlanguage needs will be most effective. This is so not only because it will be more motivating to learners, but also because much of what is learned is context specific (e.g., content vocabulary including lexical phrases; usage that respects given discourse communities) and of evident utility to them. Educational contexts provide a ready-made setting for such instruction, as is shown through CBI approaches.

The history of CBI, like that of CLT in general, has been closely tied to insights from SLA studies, themselves inspired by empirical research on first language acquisition in children, cross-Atlantic developments in linguistics in the 1960s and 1970s and demographic shifts that gave social and political importance to L2 learning. The emerging field of SLA was served with living laboratories by the bilingual education movement for non-English speaking children in the United States, the massive influx of immigrants and guest workers to North America and to western Europe—particularly Germany and France, and by Canada's national effort to find more effective ways of teaching French to English-speaking children through *immersion;* in other words, using the L2 as the medium of school instruction for majority language children. SLA researchers in the 1970s and 1980s increasingly directed their attention to the nature of the linguistic environment available to learners and its possible role in acquisition. They focused particularly on features of language directed to learners by different types of interlocutors, as modified from native speaker norms to accommodate their limited language proficiency. Systematic modifications to such linguistic *input*, as well as to accompanying interactional moves, were observed at all levels of language, with differences depending on the type of interlocutor, social relations among speakers, and the purpose of communication (see Hatch, 1983; Krashen, 1981; Long, 1983; Wesche, 1994; Wesche and Ready 1985). Research on input and acquisition has since highlighted the importance of purposeful interaction for learners' interlanguage restructuring, especially that involving negotiation, recasts, and other feedback, and related this to CLT and CBI practice (see reviews in Lightbown and Spada, 2006; Pica, 1994, 2002). When learners are involved in communication, their motivation to understand and express meanings is high; furthermore, such interaction may provide appropriate models, specific feedback, and other pertinent information at the very moment when the learner is attentive to language form or meaning and aware of a knowledge gap. The large body of research on input and interaction has provided empirical support for teaching language through communication as well as information on optimal conditions regarding the kinds of language exposure needed to support L2 acquisition. Later research has supplemented and refined this information in terms of pedagogical interventions that can help ensure the development of accurate and contextually appropriate language use.

CBI, or concurrent teaching of school or academic subject matter and a second language, is similar to other CLT approaches in that it generally

- requires frequent interaction among learners or with others to exchange information and solve problems.
- uses authentic (nonpedagogic) texts and communication activities linked to *real-world* contexts, and frequently emphasizes links across written and spoken modes and channels.
- is learner-centered, taking into account learners' backgrounds, language needs and goals, often allowing them some creativity and role in instructional decisions.
- may involve cooperative learning activities such as group or pair work and opportunities for learners to focus on the language learning process itself.
- provides opportunities for form-focused language activities, feedback, and practice within meaning oriented communication.

A major advantage of CBI over other CLT approaches is that the use of school or postsecondary subject matter as the content for language learning maximizes learners' exposure to the second language because they study both language and content at the same time. Furthermore, this exposure is to a highly contextualized and particularly relevant subset of the language, that builds on their previous knowledge in educational settings and in the subject area, and for those preparing for further study through the L2 incorporates the eventual uses they will make of it in terms of academic language and, as well, management and interpersonal discourse of the classroom community.

When the necessary conditions for successful CBI are met, learners are able to master both language and content through a reciprocal process as they understand and convey varied concepts through their second language. Language development progresses through repeated communicative encounters with language forms and patterns whose meanings and functions are related to a given topic, as learners comprehend the content being communicated and use the L2 productively in discussions and reformulations of it, generally through both oral and written modes. Repeated understanding and production of recently learned linguistic forms or of known ones in new contexts ensures their ongoing mental elaboration and practice, increasing their availability for new encounters and longer term retention. For these reasons, CBI can be very effective for both language development and content learning. However, this outcome depends on learners having adequate previous language knowledge and their receiving any needed instructional support to allow them to understand the content being conveyed through their L2. Although these conditions might be relatively easy to fulfill in a tailored one-on-one tutorial situation, there is considerable challenge in ensuring them for groups of students within institutional settings.

SHARED FEATURES OF CBI APPROACHES

Successful content-based L2 instruction allows students to master new concepts and learning skills through a language in which they have limited proficiency. All its forms share certain features, including:

- Dual learning objectives, for both content and language
- Enhanced motives for L2 learning
- Adaptation of language *input* for L2 learners
- Orientation into a new "*discourse community* (Kramsch, 1993)
- Expository discourse as the basis for a *content-driven* language curriculum
- Focus on developing academic L2 proficiency

Dual learning objectives: CBI links two different kinds of learner objectives: gains in both content knowledge and language proficiency. It implies that both kinds of learning will benefit from the link; in other words, learners will to some extent receive "two for one." This can happen under conditions that enable learners successfully to access and learn subject matter concepts through their L2.

Motivation for L2 learning: Learners' desire to understand and learn new subject matter—as promoted through the social environment of the school or academic institution—will generally enhance their motivation to master the L2 in which it is being taught—particularly if they are given the support they need to achieve this. Content-based instruction also solves the perennial L2 instructional problem of how to involve L2 users in meaningful communication with interlocutors and engage them with significant texts.

Adaptation of language input: As noted above, fluent speakers, when addressing less proficient speakers such as L2 learners and children, normally adapt their language and accompanying interactional moves to facilitate comprehension and use gestures and the immediate context to demonstrate or emphasize their intended meanings. In written language, principles such as simplification, redundancy, graphics, and illustrations are similarly used to accommodate readers' limited language proficiency. The conceptual and linguistic complexity of texts and learning activities in a given CBI context and their novelty for learners will largely determine the difficulty they experience in understanding the information conveyed and therefore the amount and kinds of support they will need for successful content comprehension and learning.

Aside from greater use of contextual illustration and adaptation of the oral and written language addressed directly to L2 speakers through lectures, interactions, and instructions, modification of the language load implied in assignments and evaluation of content learning is critical. It is essential that course designers and instructors keep in mind that L2 users are faced with learning new content through a language they have not fully mastered. Thus, for example, adaptations such as greater redundancy in instructions for assignments will facilitate learners' understanding of what is expected; in evaluation, adaptations such as the use of short-answer test formats instead of essay questions to evaluate content knowledge will allow learners to better demonstrate their subject matter mastery—rather than their poor mastery of L2 writing. Increased time for lessons, assignments, and evaluation will generally be needed for optimum results for students learning through their L2. As well, it may be necessary to lessen the amount, form, or complexity of a given unit of content presentation in comparison with L1 norms so that, for example, more time may be spent on explaining basic concepts and less on optional information in the curriculum. Ongoing support for L2 learners through explicit language instruction related to the content being learned is generally also needed, and is an excellent way to increase the redundancy of content presentation (see ensuing discussion).

A new discourse community: A new instructional situation may require considerable socialization even for first language (L1) students who have no experience in that discourse community, whether it be the appropriation of new understandings, roles, routines, and language use conventions in kindergarten or in postsecondary academic life. This gap will be strongly compounded for L2 speakers faced with a learning context and discourse that—in addition to the linguistic demands—may represent very different assumptions, roles, and customs from those they know. It is important that course designers and instructors take this factor into account, as well.

Centrality of expository discourse: In CBI language curricula, expository discourse and texts, mostly about nonlanguage phenomena, are the basis of the language curriculum. For younger learners, school discourse is largely oral; for older learners, *authentic* texts written for native speakers tend to drive the curriculum. Increasingly also, in both cases the ever-increasing instructional role of multimedia and Internet uses of language must be noted. In CBI, instructor explanations, texts, presentations through other media, and related activities and assignments are the main source not only of content knowledge but also of new language forms, patterns, functions, and meanings to be understood and internalized, thus providing opportunities for language-focused activities and feedback. These determine the sequencing and emphases in language study and practice; it is in this way that the language curriculum is *content-driven*.

Academic language proficiency: The second language abilities emphasized in CBI—again in contrast to most other CLT—are primarily those needed for dealing with instructional discourse. Much of this discourse conforms to

Cummins' (1984) characterization of *context reduced* and *cognitively demanding* dimensions of language use, such as listening to a lecture or reading an academic article. These contrast with *context-embedded, cognitively undemanding* dimensions of language use, in which familiar contexts and previous knowledge (such as conversations or e-mail exchanges with intimates about familiar events) support meaning comprehension. Because academic language proficiency is crucial to school success, CBI may be seen as particularly relevant to learners who are preparing for full-time study through their second (or weaker) language—at any level of education. Reading, writing, listening, speaking, and various kinds of interpersonal interaction all have an important place in school language.

Mohan and his colleagues (Mohan, 1986; Mohan, Leung, and Davison, 2001; Tang, 1992) have further characterized academic discourse in terms of the forms and patterns found in expository prose that correspond to basic human *knowledge structures* common in school curricula. These tend to evoke certain discourse markers to show relationships among phenomena; for example, the sequence of propositions may be flagged ("first...second...last") or their relative specificity ("in general...for example). These relationships can furthermore be represented through *key graphics* reflecting the different ways in which information is organized in discourse that can aid learners in their mastery of both new content and the language through which it is presented (Early, Mohan, and Hooper, 1989; Tang, 1992). Certain language forms are typically used to describe hierarchical classification systems—for example, categories of biological phenomena or historical events can be represented through classification trees. Likewise, sequencing patterns of such events as seasonal phenomena or natural processes can be represented in cyclical or linear diagrams or flow charts. In her broader characterization of *academic literacy*, a primary goal of CBI, M. A. Snow (2005) builds on these ideas. She distinguishes knowledge components:

- Linguistic characteristics (lexis, syntax and discourse, and academic language functions)
- Background knowledge (subject content, cultural understandings and scripts)
- Cognitive knowledge (knowledge structures, critical thinking patterns)
- Knowledge of the discourse community

PROTOTYPE CBI MODELS

Three prototype CBI models used at the postsecondary level: *theme-based, sheltered* and *adjunct* were described in a feature analysis and exemplified by Brinton, Snow, and Wesche (1989, 2003). All three models remain prominent in current CBI analysis and practice in college and university programs, and the first two have counterparts in school language programs. Theme-based CBI is frequently used with English as a second language (ESL) populations at all proficiency levels and may include academic content as preparation for mainstreaming students into regular school programs. Foreign language programs often include thematic CBI to present geographical and cultural information, as well as language instruction, in preparation for literature-based instruction. A now familiar form of sheltered L2 instruction at the school level is immersion, in which part or all of the regular school program is offered through a second or foreign language over a number of years. Such instruction has also been important in school-based efforts to revive or support declining indigenous languages; modern examples including Hawai'ian (Slaughter, 1997), Welsh (Dodson and Thomas, 1988), Cataln (Artigal, 1997), and Inuktitut (Fettes, 1998).

A number of CBI models that diverge from the three prototypes have been described that incorporate different sets of features to better serve particular contexts. The three models are presented here in greater detail, because they illustrate both the shared features of CBI approaches and important features that distinguish them. The most important differences among them are in their administrative arrangements, the relative L2 proficiency required of learners, the course format, instructor expertise and responsibility, and their relative focus of instruction and evaluation on language or content learning objectives.

In theme-based CBI, often found in host-country language programs for immigrants (such as English, Dutch, or German as a second language) or in foreign language school or postsecondary programs (such as Spanish, Arabic, or Chinese in English-speaking countries or English as a foreign language [EFL] in non-English speaking countries), the language curriculum is organized around specific topics of interest to the students, each of which may typically extend over several weeks. Although content learning is of both apparent and real importance, the primary objective is to promote learners' communicative L2 proficiency; thus the instructor— although familiar with the content—is generally a specialist in the language rather than in content instruction. Language learning is also the main focus of evaluation. Theme-based instruction is the most flexible type of CBI. It is administratively more flexible than other types, because it can be used in any type of language program and with any age or proficiency level; also, thematic units can be of different lengths and can form part or all of a course. It is generally the most feasible type of CBI, because administrative decisions are under the control of language departments.

Sheltered CBI, including school immersion programs and secondary or post-secondary courses in nonlanguage disciplines, groups second language speakers in a content program or course taught in the learners' L2; thus they are in a "sheltered" environment separate from L1 speakers in which instructional language can be tailored to their needs. The L2 is often a *foreign* or second language, but the format is also useful for immigrant students learning the language of their host country. The curriculum, schedule, and academic credit given are the same as for the corresponding regular (L1) course. Sheltered courses can provide excellent preparation for student mainstreaming into school or postsecondary courses for L1 speakers. Their primary objective is to promote learners' mastery of the subject matter, while at the same time improving learners' proficiency in the instructional language. The extra time and instructional attention devoted to course related language objectives varies, so that sheltered CBI may range from *language-sensitive content instruction* to systematic participation of language instructors and supplementary language learning activities. A major impediment to sheltered instruction (in the absence of a full-scale immersion program) administratively to justify a separate L2 section is assembling a sufficient number of L2 students at the appropriate proficiency level who wish to take a particular subject matter course.

In school immersion, language majority children spend half to most of the school day over a period of years studying the regular school curriculum through a foreign language—in courses generally taught by native speakers of that language. Very young learners generally begin kindergarten or primary school with little or no L2 knowledge but are expected to reach a high level of language mastery within a few years. Research has shown that an initial lag in L1 reading and spelling scores on standardized tests disappears within a year or two once L1 language arts instruction is introduced. In addition to taking some or most of their school subjects through their L2, immersion learners also receive regular L2 language arts instruction focusing on features of the L2 and on correct usage. Older learners entering immersion or sheltered courses at more advanced levels must already have the relatively high level of proficiency needed to cope with complex discourse and subject matter. (See immersion research reviews by, among others, Calvé, 1991; Cummins, 1998; Genesee, 1987; Met and Lorenz, 1997; Swain and Lapkin, 1982; Wesche, 1993a, 2002.)

At the postsecondary level, sheltered courses may provide an option for relatively advanced L2 users as preparation for regular study through their L2, or for advanced foreign-language speakers wishing to improve their L2 proficiency and subject matter knowledge in areas that are nontraditional for language programs. In the first context, the L2 is readily available in educational institutions, where L2 programs generally serve international students trying to perfect their language skills and immediate cultural knowledge for university study and social interaction. The surrounding community provides varied opportunities for them to use the language and further reinforces their motivation. In contrast, sheltered courses in foreign language contexts may have more diverse objectives, including language development, but often emphasizing humanistic and cultural knowledge. The goal—particularly at lower L2 proficiency levels—may be more one of *foreign language-enriched content instruction* (Anderson, Allen, and Narváez, 1993; Jurasek, 1993, 1996) than content-based language instruction. In situations in which perceived future needs for the language may include functional and culturally sensitive language skills for study abroad or future work in the foreign language, developing intercultural understanding may be an important objective. At advanced levels, the study of literature and culture generally retains its traditional importance.

In both kinds of context, sheltered courses in nonlanguage disciplines require interdisciplinary cooperation between language and relevant nonlanguage departments. In North America, ESL courses may be in any field when the goal is integration of international students into regular programs. The main issue that arises is finding subject matter experts who are excellent teachers or tutors willing to accommodate the needs of L2 speakers. In the case of foreign language programs,

interdisciplinary partnerships are likely to include both foreign language departments and departments in humanities or social science disciplines whose subject
matter deals with international issues or who are preparing students for international careers. (For North American examples of such programs see Anderson,
Allen, and Narváez, 1993; Brinton, Snow, and Wesche, 2003; Grandin, 1993; Jurasek,
1993, 1996; Klee, 2000; Klee and Tedick, 1997; Krueger and Ryan, 1993; Shaw, 1996;
Straight, 1994; Stryker and Leaver, 1997; Wesche 1985, 1993b, 2001.) In addition to
interdepartmental sponsorship of courses, sheltered CBI in foreign language settings requires instructors who are fluent users of the language, specialists in subject areas with wide appeal and relevance to the needs of potential students, and
who are able to assemble and use appropriate academic course materials in the L2.
For these reasons, such initiatives are more difficult to undertake and maintain.

Adjunct CBI instruction—mainly found in postsecondary situations—involves
a separate language course for advanced L2 speakers linked with a regular school or
university course offered for L1 speakers in a nonlanguage discipline, in which the
L2 students also enroll. Both courses generally offer equivalent academic credit in
their respective subject areas. Adjunct content instruction requires a higher level of
L2 proficiency than a sheltered course covering the same material, because L2 students must be able to follow the regular lectures and readings alongside native
speakers and also understand the sometimes colloquial language and in-group
cultural references of classroom discussions (Duff, 2001). The language course syllabus may be tightly coordinated with the content of a single course in a nonlanguage discipline, providing language support for the L2 enrollees (Burger, Wesche,
and Migneron, 1997). As an alternative, it may serve L2 speakers enrolled in several
different disciplinary courses, providing more general academic language instruction
and some individualized, course-related support (M. A. Snow and Brinton, 1997).
The primary goal of both the nonlanguage course and the language course in an
adjunct arrangement is students' successful learning of the subject matter, but the
adjunct model also offers a context in which higher proficiency students can
concentrate on improving their academic L2 skills—particularly in writing and
vocabulary building. Furthermore, they offer opportunities for interaction with L1
peers. Adjunct courses are not common because of the complex cross-departmental
collaboration and high L2 learner proficiency levels they require. For these reasons
they are mainly found in postsecondary programs in which international students
are preparing for regular study through the host language or in interdisciplinary
programs promoting students' foreign language abilities and international
knowledge base.

The University of Ottawa, Canada's oldest and largest bilingual university, with
a mandate to promote French/English bilingualism among its students and larger
community, offers a historical as well as a current example of sheltered and adjunct
CBI in both English and French. In 1982, it offered its first experimental sheltered
psychology courses in both English and French with ESL coinstructors (Edwards,
Wesche, Krashen, Clment, and Kruidenier, 1984). Given their efficacy, these courses
became regular offerings, and other courses in social sciences and humanities

disciplines were established. The first adjunct models were undertaken soon after-
ward for higher proficiency students (Burger, Wesche and Migneron, 1997; Hauptman,
Wesche, and Ready, 1988; Wesche, 2000). Some of these courses were offered for over
a decade; with one exception they were, however, gradually abandoned in the early
1990s due to financial constraints. (Sheltered and adjunct L2 courses are generally
more expensive than advanced ESL courses due to the difficulty of enrolling large
numbers of students at the right L2 proficiency level in a given content area at a given
point in time). A two-semester sequence of adjunct L2 courses linked to the introductory courses in second language teaching was maintained for non-native enrollees in the university's ESL Certificate Program for Foreign Trained Teachers for
several more years. In 2005, with a new source of financing to promote advanced
French L2 mastery among English-speaking students, the university was able to rees-
tablish CBI in the context of a new *Rgime d'immersion*, or French Immersion Studies
(FIS program, which offers multifaceted content-based opportunities for advanced
French learning; Burger and Weinberg, 2009; Ryan, Gobeil, Hope, and Toews-Janzen,
2008; Weinberg, Burger, and Hope, 2008). (Several new English adjunct courses were
also established at that time.) The FIS is aimed at graduates of secondary French
immersion programs and students who have otherwise reached advanced levels
through other school programs, exchanges, or work in bilingual environments, as
verified by an online admission test of receptive French skills. Its goal is to equip such
students to pursue their postsecondary education partially or entirely in French.
Participants take a minimum of 12 credit courses in French from among the advanced
French language courses, the adjunct language courses supporting some 50 selected
French courses in different disciplines, or the regular courses for francophone students. Further incentives include the option of pass/fail grades for up to eight adjunct
courses in the first 2 years of study, access to language monitors and conversation
groups, a student resource center, opportunities for one- or two-semester international exchanges, official French Immersion designation on their graduation diploma,
and if participants reach high enough levels on the French Language Certification
Test by the end of their studies, a French Second Language Certificate.

OTHER MODELS

Examples of some other models incorporating different sets of CBI features that have
been described for particular contexts in recent literature are subsequently provided.

   Sustained-content language teaching/instruction (SCLT/I) is a variant of
theme-based instruction that focuses on a single topic or theme content over the
length of a course rather than multiple topics. In this way, L2 speakers who are preparing for postsecondary study through their L2 are ensured greater depth of
treatment of the subject matter (M. A. Snow, Andrade, and Harper Makaafi, 2001;
Murphy and Stoller, 2001; Pally, 1997, 2000). Although SCLT may not have the

integrity of a sheltered credit regular-content course taught to L2 students by a subject expert as a bridge to the new discourse community, it allows a primary focus on language instruction and may offer particularly relevant content to learners entering a given discipline. It also has greater potential for adaptation of instruction and evaluation techniques for students at somewhat lower proficiency levels. Finally, SCLT is likely to be more feasible administratively than a sheltered course, because interdisciplinary arrangements are not required.

A *simulated adjunct* model that combines features of both theme-based and adjunct-content instruction with L1 speakers has been successfully implemented at UCLA, in a context in which true adjunct instruction is not feasible (Brinton and Jensen, 2002; Goodwin, 2001; Weigle and Jensen, 1977). Content-based units, taught by a language instructor, are organized around topics and materials drawn from existing university courses in different disciplines. Each unit consists of authentic video lecture excerpts and readings, supplemented with language activities that aim to develop students' academic language and study skills. With its multiple topics, this model can serve students preparing for different disciplines. A major advantage lies in the use of the oral and written materials from actual courses. Otherwise, the simulated adjunct model shares the curricular flexibility and administrative feasibility of SCLT, as well as the drawback of not being a credit regular-content course.

The practice of *mainstreaming* advanced second language speakers into classes for native speakers when accompanied by tutoring or other individual or small-group instructional support to help them succeed academically and continue their language development may be viewed as a form of CBI. This practice takes many forms; it is often found in ESL CBI at all school levels. One approach is to begin with partial mainstreaming into subject areas that rely relatively less on language and for which students may have more transferable background knowledge from L1 schooling (for example, music, physical education, or mathematics versus social studies or history) while providing ongoing CBI support.

A related variant of the adjunct model, known as *Project LEAP: Learning English for Academic Purposes*, was a multiyear project implemented at California State University Los Angeles (CSULA), an institution with a significant language minority student population. Given the impossibility of providing language support for enough students through sheltered or adjunct courses, the project focused on faculty development (M. A. Snow, 1997; M. A. Snow and Kamhi-Stein, 1997, Snow, Kamhi-Stein, and Brinton, 2006). A major activity in LEAP was a semester-long seminar for selected faculty instructors of core general education courses (e.g., history) on how to make their instruction more accessible to L2 speakers. They then applied these principles to the design of *language-enhanced* sections of their discipline courses for all students, including language minority students who also enrolled in special *study group* sections linked to these sections that were team taught by a regular study group leader and an ESL teacher. In these they received guidance and practice in academic language use and study skills directly related to the discipline courses.

A conceptually related approach to LEAP is the now common provision of training for preservice K–12 secondary teachers to understand and deal effectively with the needs of language minority students in their classes at different levels and in different subject areas (Crandall, 1994; see Walker, Ranney, and Fortune, 2005, for a recent discussion of considerations in the design of such a course.) Similar initiatives in many teacher education programs are responding to the fact that American schools face an average of almost 10% of children overall for whom English is a second language, with far higher enrollment averages in many urban contexts (Kindler, 2002).

Brinton (2007) has recently proposed *language enhanced instruction* (LEI), a variant of sheltered instruction for advanced students following postsecondary professional preparation programs around the world through their L2, typically English or some other language that functions as a lingua franca. Even though all students in such programs are studying through their L2, the content courses are often not organized to support language analysis, practice, and feedback. Such students frequently have significant gaps in their English academic language proficiency, exhibiting high levels of comprehension and fluency but lacking accuracy in their writing and speaking. Brinton sees LEI as having particular relevance to methodology courses in English teacher preparation programs embedded in institutions that function in a national language, she cites both an Outer Circle example in Uzbekistan and the European example of English studies programs in Spanish universities (also see Dueñas, 2004). At the Uzbek State University of World Languages, a Russian-medium institution in Tashkent, the Institute for English Language Teacher Education offers a 4-year English-medium teacher preparation program in which 2 years of intensive English language study are followed by 2 years of methodology courses. Brinton (2007) and Snow, Kahmi-Stein, and Brinton (2006) describe a recent multiyear project to revise the entire curriculum in which one of the main innovations was the introduction of LEI as the underlying approach to methodology course syllabi during years 3 and 4. The goal was to ensure ongoing attention to students' language development in these content courses, emphasizing such elements as integrated language and content goals, more interactive (as opposed to teacher fronted) activities, and systematic feedback on language accuracy. The Uzbek case may be seen as a model for language teacher preparation in a variety of settings—a model that can respond to locally perceived needs and possibilities.

Finally, the increased use of the Internet and other technologies in second/foreign language instruction have led to new kinds of CBI delivery to language learners. To date such initiatives generally supplement more traditional teaching modes; for example, Internet discussion forums and e-mail exchanges linking L1 and L2 speakers (Furstenberg, Levet, English, and Maillet, 2001; Warschauer and Meskill, 2000). These technologies are often focused on participants' perspectives regarding current social and cultural issues as well as on linguistic interaction. A Canadian example of synchronous computer-mediated communication (CMC), linking L1 and L2 Korean students for chat homework assignments from a weekly "heritage language and culture" course, demonstrates how such an approach can enhance the development of both language and cultural knowledge (Chung, 2005; Chung, Graves, Wesche, and Barfurth, 2005). A recent Malaysian example of CMC use in CBI involves an SCLT approach tailored for L2 computer students in a technological university (Shamsudin and Nesi, 2006). Practicum tasks that students worked on to design computerized software for given "clients" led to improved communicative language skills as well as to better performance in subsequent computer science projects. An innovation in concordancing software that can be used in CBI to help students develop specialized vocabulary in different fields is reported by Cobb (2005). His program allows students to access and compare excerpts from a given text exemplifying uses of a given word or phrase of interest and to create specialized dictionaries for literary or other specialized texts.

Language Instruction Issues in CBI

Language and Content Interface

The most important pedagogical issue for CBI at all program levels is the interface between language and content considerations. Learners tend to be highly motivated in CBI contexts, particularly if they are there by choice. However, a serious mismatch between course demands and learners' existing capabilities and knowledge in either the language or subject matter (or both) easily leads to frustration, loss of motivation, and lack of progress (see discussion in Cisar and Suderman, 1992, as well as examples in Johnson, 1997, and Shaw, 1996). Mohan (1986) referred to "the language factor in content" by which learners are handicapped in accessing content through lectures and texts in their L2. Likewise, assessment methods involving high language demands—such as lengthy oral presentations, essay tests, or unstructured research assignments—may furthermore mean that L2 learners are unable to demonstrate the content knowledge they do have (Brinton, Snow, and Wesche, 2003; Klee and Tedick, 1997; Weigle and Jensen, 1997). The "content factor in language" is also at work, so that learners for whom the subject matter is unfamiliar and difficult may be overwhelmed with content learning demands. In such cases they cannot adequately attend to the new language to which they are exposed or are required to produce (Johnson, 1997; Ready and Wesche, 1992). Interface problems are present in all forms of CBI; however, managing them is particularly critical at the postsecondary level due to the sheer quantity of disciplinary content to be learned, the sophisticated language expectations, and the high stakes for students. Even when lectures are modified for L2 users, as in sheltered instruction, heavy reading loads and complex written texts raise difficulties with both content learning and language development. The alternative, noted in the concern of content instructors that adaptations for L2 speakers may "water down" content, is not new. Neither is the solution. In the words of the Moravian bishop, Jan Amos Comenius (1638), if students do not understand the subject matter, how can they master the various devices for expressing it forcibly? The time is more usefully spent on less ambitious efforts, so devised that knowledge of the language and the general intelligence may advance together step by step (*The Great Didactic of Jan Amos Cometius* [1638], tr. M. W. Keatinge, 1920/1967: 204–205.).

In other words, adaptation of some kind may be required for successful progress of L2 users in their studies of other subjects, be it courses in somewhat familiar content areas, modifications in presentation, smaller doses of content, more time devoted to fewer courses, and/or content-related language instruction. Confirmation of this wisdom for CBI is found in reports of well-researched programs representing strong forms of CBI. All point to the crucial need for attention to the pedagogical and other conditions that can ensure that learners arrive at an in-depth understanding of the content and are able to reformulate it appropriately for relevant purposes. Through these efforts and those of the students themselves the learning of both will advance together step by step.

Emphasis on Accuracy

One way in which CBI approaches differ is with regard to their pedagogical focus on aspects of the code, or *language analysis* (Stern, 1989). Research findings indicate the importance of drawing learners' attention to formal characteristics of the L2 as part of communicative activity for the development of accurate language use (Harley, 1984, 1993; Lightbown and Spada, 2006; Lyster, 2007; Lyster and Ranta, 1997; Spada, 1997). This is particularly important with respect to learner errors that do not impede communication and thus attract little natural feedback. Although CBI in its stronger forms has often proceeded without instructional emphasis on language analysis, its contexts provide rich opportunities for an emphasis on accurate and culturally appropriate language. Accuracy in language use is an important educational goal and, in recent years, realization of the need for more attention to formal properties of language and discourse has brought change to many CBI contexts.

Methods for insuring such a focus within purposeful communicative activities include:

- Careful curricular formulation of specific language objectives for content units (M. A. Snow, Met, and Genesee, 1989)
- The systematic incorporation of tasks into the curriculum of tasks that promote interaction (Long and Crookes, 1992; Swain, 2001b; Tulung, 2008) or focus on formal aspects of language (Skehan 2003)
- An emphasis on accuracy as well as fluency in language production (Swain 1985, 1995) and incorporation of planning, structure, and feedback into the preparation of complex oral and written texts (Brinton, Snow, and Wesche, 2003; Burger and Chrétien, 2001; Skehan, 2003)
- Explicit content-related language instruction (Burger, Wesche, and Migneron, 1997; Harley, 1993)

Recent research on the topic of form focused activity in a sheltered Italian geography course (given as part of an Italian language program in an American university) found that intentional focusing on form in communicative frames when incidental or preplanned opportunities were present was effective in developing more accurate language use (Rodgers, 2006). It seems likely that in the future, L2 CBI approaches will increasingly incorporate form-focused activities.

Contact with Native Speaker Peers and Out-of-Class L2 Use

With the exception of adjunct courses, most forms of CBI for L2 speakers cannot provide either regular contact with peers who are native speakers of the target language or, in the case of foreign language contexts, broad exposure to out-of-class language use. In classes limited to L2 speakers, even when all instruction is in the instructional language, learners may exhibit L2 use patterns that diverge from accepted target language norms, particularly in grammatical aspects of the language (e.g., Harley, 1984, 1993). In classes where native speaker peers are present, such as the regular courses for L1 speakers in adjunct CBI arrangements and CBI supported mainstreaming, L2 learners observe and interact with L1 speakers in class and may also develop social relations with them. As a result, they are likely to become more aware of their own errors and of appropriate academic language norms and consequently gain greater ease in social situations, higher listening and speaking fluency, and more of what some have called "cultural literacy" regarding the target language community. The following are some other notable examples of CBI situations that involve significant contact with native speaker peers:

- The innovative Korean/English program, previously noted, designed to bring together Korean-speaking high school age immigrants to Canada and English-speaking second generation Korean peers in an international school Saturday class with a theme-based curriculum (Chung, 2005; Chung, Graves, Wesche, and Barfurth, 2005). Previously, separate instruction was given for the two groups due to differences in Korean proficiency, and cross-group social interaction was rare. In bilingual small-group Internet chat-room homework assignments, they became each other's tutors for themes comparing different phenomena across Korean and Canadian cultures, for example, a selected holiday or sport, with students using their respective L1s. In her ethnographic study Chung (2005) found that over time participants became effective peer tutors across groups for both language and cultural understandings.
- *Two-way immersion*, in which peers from two different L1s each separately study the their own language as an L1 and the other as an L2 in language arts classes, and attend together other subject area classes taught in either of the languages (Rhodes, Christian, and Barfield, 1997). Ongoing school programs of this kind are feasible only in areas where there are relatively large numbers of L2 or bilingual households, and where bilingual schooling attracts adequate enrollments from both groups.

- European schools, established primarily for children whose parents work for European institutions, aim to develop each learner's home language and culture and a "European" identity in at least three languages by graduation. This is accomplished through L2 study of the host country language and several other European languages as well as taking courses (including native-speaker peers) given in other disciplines and taught in those languages in different subject areas by native-speaker teachers (Baetens-Beardsmore, 1993). Fourteen such schools now exist through intergovernmental agreements.
- A postsecondary, multilingual "Languages across the Curriculum" (LAC) graduate program at the Monterey Institute of International Studies (MIIS, Monterey, CA), in which mixed classes of American and international students take courses in various disciplines together through different languages including English, so that all students experience study through one or several L2s as well as their L1 (Shaw, 1996)
- Organized out-of-class language activities, exchanges, and study abroad programs as a complement to classroom CBI. Freed's (1995) edited volume provides varied cases studies of mainly postsecondary exchange experiences and their outcomes, particularly in terms of language learning. MacFarlane and Wesche (1995), in a study of Ontario French immersion and Quebec Intensive English grade 6 students in a school group exchange, demonstrated the kinds of classroom-complementary language development that can be promoted in different contexts during extended contact experiences

RESEARCH FINDINGS

As is clear from the documents previously mentioned, an abundant and continually evolving literature on content-based instruction now exists, including 4 decades of documentation on school immersion. For reviews or edited collections on Canadian immersion, see Calvé (1991), Cummins (1998), Genesee (1987), M. A. Snow (1998), Swain and Lapkin (1982), and Wesche (2001), and in recent years, annual reports on French-language education in Canada, published by the national organization known as Canadian Parents for French (CPF; 2008), that provide a cumulative record of current issues in French immersion and other French programs. For immersion in other countries, see Johnson and Swain (1997) and Wesche (2002), and for CBI elements in a similarly vast literature on bilingual education, see Baker (2006). Excellent reviews and collections also cover school-level CBI for mainstreamed English as a second language (ESL) learners (e.g., Faltis and Hudelson, 1998; Genesee, 1994), and for postsecondary CBI and LAC (Crandall and Kaufman, 2002; Grabe and Stoller, 1997; Krueger and Ryan, 1993; Rosenthal,

2000; M. A. Snow and Brinton, 1997; Stryker and Leaver, 1997; Turlington and Schoenberg, 1996). Discussion of common implementation issues for CBI programs at different levels may be found in program handbooks, manuals, research reports, and university and college websites. The Center for Advanced Research on Language Acquisition (CARLA) at the University of Minnesota is an important source of such information.

Because studies have most often been undertaken to evaluate existing program initiatives, theory development has drawn heavily from research in related fields in the interpretation of patterns of program success and failure (Grabe and Stoller, 1997). Over time, program descriptions and data on learner outcomes have yielded to more detailed analysis of classroom processes (see, e.g., Duff, 2001; Early, 2001; Mohan and Beckett, 2001; Pica, 2002; Swain, 2001a). The development of shared concepts and models has led to comparisons within and across programs. The resulting literature provides guidance for diverse CBI initiatives. Two general points may be noted: (1) To be successful, a CBI program must respect the particularities of its context; each situation is unique; and (2) at the same time, shared issues arise over quite diverse contexts in implementing and maintaining CBI programs, so there is much to be learned from the experience of others. Overall, the research findings on the outcomes of a broad range of CBI programs are highly consistent, showing that successful subject matter learning, second/foreign language development superior to that achieved otherwise in school or academia and positive attitude changes (by both learners and instructional staff) can all be achieved—with willing learners—through CBI approaches. Several recent studies have also shown transfer of learning through greater success of L2 students with CBI preparation than those without it in subsequent L2 and regular subject matter courses for L1 speakers (James, 2006; Song, 2005), while a recent study of French language sheltered course outcomes at the University of Ottawa showed that participants were likely to move to nonsheltered, regular courses for L1 speakers following sheltered instruction (Ryan, Gobeil, Hope, and Toews-Janzen, 2008; Weinberg, Burger, and Hope, 2008). Studies have also shown that content-based second language instruction tends to be greatly appreciated by students for its relevance to their L2 needs and by participating staff for the satisfaction of truly helping students to prepare for "life after language instruction" (Burger and Weinberg, 2009; Grabe and Stoller, 1997; M. A. Snow, 1997, 1998; Wesche, 1993a, 1993b).

Stronger forms of CBI involving credit instruction in sheltered or L1 contexts nonetheless face significant obstacles, and their existence can usually be traced to highly committed individuals and to institutions that place a priority on multilingualism and intercultural education for a global citizenry. CBI initiatives often suffer from inconsistent administrative support and may face daunting obstacles to cross-disciplinary collaboration, in itself an extremely complex issue at secondary and postsecondary levels. The long-term survival of CBI activities depends crucially on continuing administrative commitment and adequate resourcing. Significant issues confronting most CBI programs include (among others) the following:

- Lack of specific teacher preparation, either of content instructors for L2 learners or language instructors for content-driven instruction (but see Peterson, 1997; Snow and Kamhi-Stein, 2002; Walker, Ranney, and Fortune, 2005)
- Inadequate or nonexistent curricular definition designed to integrate language and content objectives
- Related problems such as unrealistic expectations and inappropriate assessment practices

Again, it must be noted that, although CBI is founded upon sound principles, the outcomes depend upon the details of implementation.

CONCLUSIONS

CBI involves relatively intensive exposure of L2 speakers in school or academic settings to highly contextualized new language of particular relevance to them. It can provide enhanced motivation for L2 learning, a naturalistic learning context that provides the needed conditions for such learning, including social and other pragmatic dimensions, and offers the possibility of form-focused activity that can enhance accuracy in L2 use. Together these perhaps offer as close to a comprehensive environment for second language development as is possible in the classroom.

CBI may be a particularly evident choice for two clienteles. The first is young school learners (e.g., in kindergarten immersion) who readily accept a foreign instructional language and a native-speaker teacher as a language model to be imitated—thus minimizing the accuracy problem for oral language. Because the learners are preliterate, reading readiness and academic talent are not as decisive to their early language success as they would be for older learners. Thus the basis may be laid for L2 proficiency across a broader spectrum of learners than is likely when language study comes later and is less intensive. CBI also works well with able and motivated older learners who have had adequate L2 abilities and knowledge, often including systematic study of language structures—enabling them to cope, when supported, with high-level academic content when learners are motivated by an interest in the particular content as related to their eventual uses of the language. In such cases, learners can draw upon their preexisting grammatical knowledge and language use ability while focusing on understanding content. CBI for them can play an activating role for language known together with the conditions for ongoing acquisition of an L2.

Content-based instruction is distinguished by its application in school, academic, and similar training contexts that, although they may offer good conditions for language development, also constrain the language syllabus, and generally require tailor-made programs. It is nonetheless attractive because it offers simultaneous development of content knowledge that might have to be addressed anyway, as well as L2 ability, because it emphasizes academic language skills, and, perhaps most crucially, because it is a means of significantly increasing exposure to the L2. CBI is likely to continue to flourish, particularly in contexts in which learners' main opportunity for developing advanced L2 proficiency is a school or postsecondary context and in which they need to develop academic L2 ability.

CHAPTER 20

....

BILINGUAL EDUCATION

....

COLIN BAKER

INTRODUCTION

....

Bilingual education is not just about education and bilingualism. There are dimensions to bilingual education that require a multidisciplinary understanding. It is not just about the use of two languages in the classroom. There are dimensions to bilingual education that involve economics, philosophy, history, sociolinguistics, and, not least, politics as well as language planning. For example, bilingual education is a means of language planning that sometimes seeks to assimilate indigenous and immigrant minorities, or to integrate newcomers or minority groups. At other times, bilingual education is a major plank in language revitalization and preservation.

This means that politics is rarely absent from debates about bilingual education. Indeed, there is no understanding of international bilingual education without contextualizing it within the history and politics of a country (e.g., United States) or a region (e.g., Wales in the United Kingdom) or a state (e.g., New York, Arizona, California). Bilingual education can be fully understood only in relation to political ideology and political opportunism. Also, the increasing politicization of bilingual education has led to such key economic questions as whether the bilingual education option is expensive, cost efficient or cost effective.

Pedagogic, language planning, political, and economic perspectives are not the only perspectives on bilingual education. There are public (opinion), sociolinguistic, psychological, historical, and individual national perspectives (Baker, 2006; McCarty, 2004; Cummins and Hornberger, 2008). Also, any individual perspective is capable of extension into components (e.g., pedagogy into teaching methodology, learning strategies, curriculum resourcing, teacher training, and school organization) and overlap and interact (e.g., language planning and economics interact with politics).

Four major perspectives on bilingual education are presented.

1. Bilingual Education as Language Planning

First, there is the viewpoint of language planners (e.g., in Wales, Ireland, Catalonia, and the Basque country) who believe that bilingual education is one essential means of language maintenance, language revitalization, and reversing language shift. In this perspective, bilingual education is part of a framework for language revitalization.

For a language to survive and revive, it has to be lived and loved. Daily language use and a consistently favorable attitude to a language are all important. Imagine a minority language with rights to use enshrined in law, with radio and television, web pages, and computer programs in that minority language and bilingual signage, and yet everyone using the majority language at home, when experiencing the mass media, in leisure and in religious activities, in employment, and in all daily social interaction. It is theoretically possible to have many support systems for a language but for the language to be dying because it is not used in families and communities. Therefore, at the heart of language planning is planning for reproduction and usage. This suggests that language rights, mass media, signposts, and many other strategies and actions are not of first-order importance in themselves. Although each contributes to the status and institutionalization of a language, they are ultimately important to the extent to which they contribute to four priorities:

1. Language acquisition in the family
2. Language learning from preschool education through formal schooling to adult education
3. Using the minority language for economic purposes
4. Social, cultural, and leisure participation through the minority language

Minority languages decline when families fail to reproduce the language in their children. Where and when much higher proportions of older people speak a minority language than younger age groups, the language is imperiled. Where and when younger age groups are in larger proportions than older speakers of the language, a positive sign for the future of the language is present. Thus, family language planning is a top priority, quintessential but insufficient by itself. The family plants the seed and ensures early growth. The blossoming requires cultivation in bilingual education, the employment market, and social/cultural life.

For language planning to be successful, language learning in school is important to make up for a shortfall in language transmission at the family level and to increase the stock of minority language speakers. Language acquisition in preschool education, in elementary and high schools, at higher education levels, and in adult language learning classes becomes the lifeline to increase the supply of minority-language speakers. Language planning through bilingual education has succeeded in the Basque Country, Canada, Catalonia, and Wales, for example, and becomes a necessary but insufficient foundation, by itself, for language revitalization.

The case of Ireland signals a warning. The creation of the Irish Free State in 1922 made Irish the first official language of the country, and Irish was made compulsory in schools, compulsory to pass as a subject in order to matriculate from school, and compulsory for entrance to much public sector employment and to university. Despite constant state intervention and economic schemes to support the Irish language, the Irish language has declined in daily usage.

One reason for the decline in the Irish Language, despite language rights and central language planning, has been the lack of a strong economic dimension to Irish. Children leaving school found that the Irish was of little real value in most of the employment market. For many jobs, Irish was practically irrelevant. Instead, schoolchildren, their parents, and students in Ireland have become increasingly aware of the economic advantages of the European Union languages, particularly French, German, Spanish, and English. The economic value of a language is not the only determinant of its value and usefulness, but it is a crucial factor.

The more a minority language is tied in with employment, promotion in employment, and increasing affluence, the greater the perceived value and status of that language. The greater the number of jobs that require bilingualism (and often biliteracy), the more importance a minority language will have in the curriculum. Thus, an economic value to a minority language provides needed instrumental motivation for children to become proficient in that language in school.

The more a minority language is aligned with employment and the economy, the more parents may become motivated and encouraged to reproduce that language among their children. A strong economic value to a language gives added momentum for language reproduction in the family. It also gives momentum to preschool efforts for language acquisition—that is, learning the language when very young in an informal, subconscious, and enjoyable fashion.

The danger of promoting only the economic value of a minority language is that it may have short-term monetary associations. There is a possibility of doing the right thing for a temporary reason. Once economic motives are fulfilled, a minority language may not be used. For a language to be of increased value and to be used daily, it has to capture particular contexts (domains) in which people's noneconomic activity occurs. For a language to survive and multiply, it has to be used regularly in everyday interaction and relationships, in many positive aspects of cultural, leisure, and community life. The widest form of cultural participation needs to be encouraged, from festivities to discos, the rites and rituals of religion to the rhythms of rock music, from sports events to quiet group hobbies and pastimes.

When there is valued cultural and leisure use of a minority language, then language reproduction in the family becomes more encouraged and motivated. In the same way, language production through education becomes more meaningful when it is seen that a minority language has an enjoyable use in cultural and leisure activity.

Literacy in a minority language is also important for that language to live into the future. Any language lacking a literacy component in this century may be in grave danger of not surviving. Literacy in a minority language gives many more uses and functions to that language (e.g., in employment, leisure reading). A language lacking a literacy component is like a colonized language. When the British colonized areas of Africa and India, they frequently allowed literacy solely in the English language. The indigenous languages were relegated to lower status, noneconomic uses; English was the key to educational wisdom, employment, and wealth. Thus, a language lacking a literacy component has many fewer functions and much less status. Bilingual education has a crucial function in promoting biliteracy (except when there is a strong religious promotion of a literacy—e.g., in a mosque or synagogue).

The language planner's view of bilingual education necessarily focuses on the importance of producing more speakers of a minority language than are generated through the parents and the home. A language planner's view of bilingual education necessarily focuses on strengthening the minority language among first language speakers and on majority language children learning a minority language as a second language as early as possible and becoming fluent in that minority language so as to operate in the curriculum of the primary and secondary school. Also, a language planner's view of bilingual education is for a minority language culture to permeate throughout the formal and hidden curriculum. Thus a "minority language" cultural dimension added to every curriculum area becomes important to a language planner in giving a language rootedness, identity, and connectedness at a cognitive and affective level with the kaleidoscopic colors of a minority-language culture.

However, there are three particular overlapping limitations of the language planning perspective of bilingual education that need mentioning.

- There is a danger in the language planner's perspective in regarding bilingual education as for the sake of the language and not necessarily for the sake of the child. Bilingual education can be seen as a salvation for the language, whereas an alternative (but not a contradictory) viewpoint is that a minority language education is for the sake of the child. A humanistic educationalist may argue that bilingual education needs to be defended for its value and contribution to the development of the child rather than the language.
- The language planning perspective on bilingual education tends to have a limited view of the functions and purposes of education. Among both supporters and critics of bilingual education there are arguments that separate and artificially dissociate debates about language from debates about effective education. We shall be returning to this theme later in this chapter when the politics of bilingual education are considered.
- There is sometimes overoptimism among language planners about what can be expected from, and delivered by, bilingual education in revitalizing a language. When a language fails to be reproduced in the family, and when there are insufficient support mechanisms (e.g., language rights, mass

media) outside of schools, too high expectations of language reversal via bilingual education are not uncommon. Although bilingual education has an important role in language reproduction—and probably without it a minority language cannot survive except through intergenerational family language or intense religious usage—bilingual education cannot deliver language maintenance by itself.

2. BILINGUAL EDUCATION AS PEDAGOGY

Although bilingual education consists of many different types (see Baker, 2006), it has recently been greeted as typically superior to monolingual education (e.g., in achievement across the curriculum, in raising the self-esteem of language minority children, in producing bilingualism, biliteracy, and interculturalism). Although the critics of bilingual education (e.g., the anti-Latino lobby in the United States and the assimilationists in the United Kingdom) must not be underestimated, the philosophy, principles, policies, and practices of bilingual education have grown remarkably vibrant in recent decades. Educationalists have increasingly considered the value of two or three majority languages in schools, not just taught as languages but used to transmit curriculum content. For example, China, Scandinavia, and many Far East countries are increasingly seeing the importance of languages in the global market, and in intercontinental communication and information exchange, while educators interested in minority languages argue for the benefits of bilingual education as standard raising, child-centered, and responsive to parents and pupils as clients.

Among educationalists, arguments for bilingual education vary according to local politics and the status and power of majority and minority languages, but tend to revolve around eight particular advantages of bilingual education (Baker, 2007):

1. Bilingual education allows both languages (sometimes three languages) to develop fully. Rather than engaging in token second language learning, two or more languages are well developed. This allows children to engage in wider communication, having more options in patterns of communication across generations, regions, and cultural groups, and provides linguistic capital.

2. Bilingual education develops a broader enculturation and a wider and more sympathetic view of different creeds and cultures. Rather than token multicultural lessons, bilingual education gives deep insights into the cultures associated with the languages, fosters a broader understanding of differences, bequeaths cultural capital, and, at its best, avoids the tight compartmentalization of racism—the stereotyping of different social groups—and fosters a more multiperspective and sensitive-to-difference viewpoint.

3. Bilingual education often generates biliteracy. Being able to read and write in two or more languages allows more possibilities in uses of literacy (e.g., in employment), widening the choice of literature for pleasure, giving more opportunities for different perspectives and viewpoints, and leading to a deeper understanding of history and heritage, of traditions and territory.

4. Research suggests that when children have two well-developed languages, they enjoy certain cognitive benefits (Bialystok, 2001). Schools are often important in developing a child's two languages to the point where they may be more creative in thinking owing to their bilingualism and be more sensitive in communication because they may be interpersonally aware, for example, when needing to codeswitch and be able to inspect their languages more (that is, they enjoy metalinguistic advantages).

5. In heritage language education (developmental maintenance bilingual education) children's self-esteem may be raised. When a child's home language is replaced by the majority language, the child, the parents, and the child's community may seem to be rejected. When the home language is used in school, then children may feel themselves, their home, and community to be accepted, thus maintaining or raising their self-esteem. Positive self-esteem—a confidence in one's own ability and potential—interacts in an important way with achievement and curriculum success (Baker, 2006).

6. Not only Canadian immersion studies and dual language schools in the United States but also studies of developmental maintenance bilingual education suggest that curriculum achievement is increased through such education (Baker, 2006). The precise causes of raising standards via bilingual education are neither simple nor straightforward. There is likely to be a complex equation among the support of the home, the enthusiasm and commitment of teachers in school, the quality of the school, children feeling accepted and secure, and the relationship between language and cognitive development. All of these, and many other variables, act and interact in the complex equation of success in bilingual education.

7. The role of bilingual education in establishing security of identity at a local, regional, and national level may be important. As a basic psychological need, security and status in self-identity may be important. For example, bilingual education has aided the establishment of a Welsh identity in Welsh children.

8. The economic advantages of bilingual education are increasingly being claimed, particularly in jobs that require a customer interface and communications with bilinguals or multilinguals. Being bilingual can be important to secure employment in many public services and sometimes in niche private companies as well. To secure a job as a teacher, to work in the mass media, to work in local government, and increasingly in the civil service in areas such as Canada, Wales, the Basque Country, bilingualism has become important. Thus, bilingual education is increasingly seen as delivering relatively more marketable employees than monolingual education.

Although bilingual education worldwide has an increasing number of supporters (albeit not without some virulent critics, especially in the United States; see Cummins, 2000b), there are limitations in the pedagogical view of bilingual education. For example, bilingual education is no guarantee of effective schooling. Occasionally, there is a naiveté among those who support bilingual education in assuming that employing two or more languages in the school curriculum automatically leads to a raising of standards, to more effective outcomes, and to a more child-centered education. In reality, the languages of the school are but part of a wider matrix of variables that interact in complex ways to make schooling more or less effective. Among bilingual schools in every country, there appears to be a mixture of the outstanding and the ordinary, those in an upward spiral of enhancing their quality and those that depend on past glories rather than current successes. Bilingual education is only one ingredient among many.

Another limitation of the pedagogical perspective on bilingual education is the type and use of language learned at school. Canadian research suggests that the language register of formal education does not necessarily prepare children for language use outside the school (Cummins, 2000a). The language of the curriculum is often complex and specialized. The vernacular of the street may be different. Canadian children from English-speaking homes who have been to immersion schools and learned through the medium of French and English sometimes report difficulty in communicating appropriately with French speakers in local communities. Local French speakers may find their French too formal, inappropriate, or even off-putting.

A further concern about bilingual education is that language learning may stop at the school gates. The minority language may be effectively transmitted and competently learned in the classroom. However, once outside the school gates, children may switch into the majority language. Thus, the danger of bilingual education in a minority language is that the language becomes a language of school but not of play, a language of the content delivery of the curriculum but not of peer culture. Even when children are taught through the medium of a minority language at school, the common denominator language of the peer group in the street is often a majority language. When one child turns to English, often so does everyone else. The language of the screen, shop, or street may be different from the language of the school. Extending a minority language learned at school to use in the community is something that is difficult to engineer and difficult to plan but nevertheless vital if the language is to live outside the school gates.

3. BILINGUAL EDUCATION AS POLITICS

Wherever bilingual education exists, politics is close by. To assume that bilingual education is educationally justified and therefore, *ipso facto*, must be strongly supported is naive. Bilingual education is not simply an educational issue. Behind bilingual education there are always expressions of political ideology, tides of political change, and political initiative. To argue for bilingual education solely as a strong plank of language planning and language revitalization is simplistic. Language planning itself is predicated on language politics. Behind what might be posed as conservation of the threatened languages of the world lie other, more basic political assumptions and ideologies. Surrounding bilingual education are usually political debates about national identity, dominance and control by elites in power, power relationships among politicians and civil servants, questions about social order and social cohesion, and the perceived potential subversiveness of language minorities.

Cummins (1999) argued that research on bilingual education has become so unfocused, has sent out so many mixed messages, and in particular is so ignorant of underlying theory that politicians can selectively use research to fit and support their ideology. He contends that research reviews and meta-analyses (see Baker, 2006) all assume that research reviews can directly inform policy making. Cummins sees this as naive, owing to the "myriad human, administrative, and political influences that impact the implementation of programs over time" (Cummins, 1999: 26). There are hundreds of variables that affect program outcomes so that research cannot, by itself, directly inform policy, provision, and practice. Rather, Cummins (1999) argues that it is tested theory that should drive policy making. That is, research should commence from theoretical propositions, testing, refining, and sometimes refuting those propositions.

In complex educational and other human organizational contexts, data or "facts" become relevant for policy purposes only in the context of a coherent theory. It is the theory rather than the individual research findings that permits the generation of predictions about program outcomes under different conditions (Cummins, 1999: 26).

However comprehensive and elaborate are the theoretical foundations of bilingual education, however strong are the educational arguments for bilingual education, and however strong are the arguments for the preservation of dying languages in the world, it is the politics of power, status, assimilation, and social order that can deny bilingual education so readily.

4. The Economic Perspective on Bilingual Education

A highly original and essential economic perspective comes from Dutcher (2004), who analyzes developmental maintenance bilingual education through cost-effectiveness and cost-efficiency. In a World Bank paper on the use of first and second languages in elementary education, Dutcher (2004) examines international evidence from Haiti, Nigeria, the Philippines, Guatemala, Canada, New Zealand, the United States (Navajo), Fiji, the Solomon Islands, Vanuatu, and Western Samoa. She concludes that development of the mother tongue is critical for cognitive development and as a foundation for learning the second language. That is, sub-mersion and transitional models of bilingual education are internationally less effective in developing a child's thinking abilities. When such development is slowed considerably by learning in a second language (e.g., submersion), then the second language will itself be learned more slowly.

Dutcher (2004) concludes that the recurrent costs for bilingual education are approximately the same as for traditional programs. Bilingual education is not an expensive option, having similar costs to mainstream programs. However, the most important conclusion is that developmental maintenance bilingual education cre-ates cost savings for the education system and for society. For example, such bilingual education provides higher levels of achievement in fewer years of study. Student progress is faster, and higher achievement benefits society through less unemployment and a more skilled workforce.

In submersion and transitional models of bilingual education, there may be costs to a national economy due to slower rates of progress at school, lower levels of final achievement, and sometimes the need for special or compensatory education. Higher dropout rates mean lower potential for the employment market, and the economy suffers with a lower level of skills among the workforce and higher unemployment rates. In economic terms, students need to gain productive charac-teristics through education, and Dutcher (2004) indicates that this is achieved through early use of the native language.

Such cost-efficiency of developmental maintenance bilingual education is exem-plified in a World Bank cost-effectiveness study on Guatemala, where Dutcher (2004) found that bilingual education was a prudent policy. Repetition and dropout rates were decreased through a bilingual education intervention program, and standards of achievement rose (including in Spanish). It was estimated that education cost savings due to bilingual education were US$5.6 million per year, whereas cost benefits were in the order of US$33.8 million per year. Also, individual earnings rose by approximately 50%. In Guatemala, developmental maintenance bilingual education made economic sense because it produced a more skilled, highly trained, and employable workforce. Submersion and transitional forms of bilingual education in comparison tend to have higher dropout rates and lower levels of achievement and thus have less chance of serving and stimulating the economy through a skilled workforce.

5. CONCLUSION

This chapter has suggested that bilingual education derives its raison d'tre not only from a concern for language maintenance and revitalization but also from a variety of educational, economic, social, cultural, and political factors. An idealistic conclusion would be to suggest the possibility of integrating the five perspectives. When there can be a wholeness in the four perspectives between language planners, bilingual educationalists, and the politicians who influence the growth of bilingual education, then a mature, logical, rational, and smooth evolution in bilingual education is possible. However, it is apparent in this chapter that, more often than not, there is a separation between the perspectives. Each is a partial view, a view that could be enlightened and expanded by understanding the perspective of another. All four perspectives are present in international bilingual education.

In particular, educationalists who support bilingual education need to understand the politics behind, and sometimes against, bilingual education for there to be movement forward. The defense and expansion of bilingual education cannot come suddenly from language planning perspectives (language planning acquisition) or through purely stating the many and real advantages of bilingual education. Bilingual education may flourish or otherwise through the locus of political power, through the movement of political ideology, and through political influence. This is where language planners and educationalists in support of bilingual education can join forces. The future fortunes of bilingual education are open to political influence. The benefits of bilingual education are not self-apparent or intrinsically obvious. Therefore, the notion of bilingual education has to be marketed so that both the public and politicians are persuaded and convinced.

PART VI

VARIATION IN LANGUAGE USE AND LANGUAGE PERFORMANCE

....

CHAPTER 21

LANGUAGE TRANSFER AND CROSS-LINGUISTIC STUDIES: RELATIVISM, UNIVERSALISM, AND THE NATIVE LANGUAGE

....

TERENCE ODLIN

LANGUAGE transfer, or cross-linguistic influence, has long been a topic that many in applied linguistics have pondered, even though some have doubted its importance (e.g., Dulay, Burt, and Krashen 1982). In recent work on transfer, two different orientations have been prominent—one universalist and the other relativist. Although these orientations are opposed to each other in certain ways, research on both relativism and universalism intersects with the study of cross-linguistic influence. This chapter emphasizes the significance of the relativist orientation, but it also contends that any thorough understanding of transfer and universals necessitates a broad view of what characterizes all human languages.

Transfer as a Relativist Concern

Nonlinguists occasionally ask the question "What is the hardest language in the world?" The usual response of professionals is, of course, that children do not have any advantage in learning English, for example, as opposed to Swedish, Finnish, or Estonian. On the other hand linguists will normally acknowledge that adult language learning does not allow for such a categorical response. "It all depends" is one possible answer, even though this may not satisfy the person asking the question. However much or little linguists have thought about the issue of cross-linguistic influence, most would probably acknowledge that Swedish, a Germanic language like English, will take less time than Finnish for English-speaking adults to learn, even bearing in mind all the meanings that "learn" can have (cf. Ringbom 1987). On the other hand Finnish will prove relatively easy for Estonians (whose language is, like Finnish, Uralic), whereas these same learners will encounter much of the difficulty that Finns do when it comes to learning English. This point is perhaps so obvious to linguists as to seem uninteresting. However, ignoring it has resulted in surprisingly little discussion of the fact that language transfer entails a relativist approach to second language acquisition.

The link between relativism and transfer has recently received increased attention (e.g., Kellerman 1995; Jarvis 1998; Odlin 1998), but earlier research also considered that possibility. For example, Kaplan argued that "Logic (in the popular rather than the logician's sense of the word), which is the basis of rhetoric, is evolved out of a culture; it is not universal" (1966/1984: 44). From that position, Kaplan asserted that the difficulty encountered by speakers of other languages with English writing stems from rhetorical differences. The consequences of discourse differences have gotten considerable attention in subsequent work on contrastive rhetoric (e.g., Connor 1996) and also in the related field of contrastive pragmatics (e.g., Kasper 1992). Nevertheless, the issue of relativism remains controversial largely because of the complexities of the relation between linguistic relativity and linguistic universals. Much of the difficulty is evident in the hedge that Kaplan used to characterize "logic": "in the popular rather than the logician's sense…." The popular sense of the term can in fact mean *all* the ways of structuring arguments, not only emotional and ethical arguments but also rational ones (whether or not Aristotle offers the most reliable guide to understanding rhetoric). Accordingly, there exists an important overlap between the logic of rational arguments and the logic of logicians.

How much of an overlap there is remains controversial. Few if any philosophers nowadays would equate the logical systems they have developed with a general cognitive code, but there are widely varying opinions on the fit between invented logical systems and mental capacities. Some thinkers even deny the usefulness of positing a universal semantic code. Quine (1960), for example, has contended that logic is much less independent of the language spoken by the logician—even when the logician employs a modern calculus that supposedly eliminates the problems that ensue when syllogisms are formulated in English, Greek, or any other natural language.

Moreover, he argues against the notion of semantic equivalence as a neutral baseline to compare languages or to verify the accuracy of translations. Interestingly, he speculates on the difficulties encountered by an English-speaking linguist attempting to learn a very different kind of language and appeals to the notion of native language "habits" (1960: 70). The behaviorist stance on transfer here is, of course, widely challenged now (e.g., Sharwood Smith 1979). More telling, however, is the fact that Quine has little to say about the interlingual identifications made by bilinguals who have known two languages from early childhood, and so he cannot really account for the intuitions of ordinary child or adult bilinguals (cf. Fishman 1977a; Lyons 1977: 236).

However bilinguals establish their interlingual identifications, the process must rely on a calculus more or less independent of the two languages, a calculus providing something akin to "logic in the logician's sense." The cognitive basis for such a calculus is perhaps best understood as "the language of thought," a system flexible enough to allow children to acquire any language and also to accommodate other mental phenomena such as imagery. While Fodor (1975) allows for the possibility that a language of thought can coexist with language-specific schemata that might affect processing, Pinker has been more skeptical about linguistic relativism: "People do not think in English, Chinese, or Apache; they think in a language of thought. This language of thought probably looks a bit like all of those languages" (1994: 81).

Among linguists engaged in cognitivist or generativist research, Pinker's position probably has more adherents than Fodor's. However, recent work on linguistic relativity suggests that the latter position is more tenable. Lucy (1992) reports a highly detailed study of cognitive consequences of contrasting noun phrase patterns in English and Yucatec Maya, and the results were consonant with his general expectation that "language influences...do not affect a speaker's potential ability to see a referent at all or in a certain way, but rather affect a speaker's habitual dispositions towards, or ways of responding to, a referent" (1992: 91). Another recent study (Pederson et al. 1998) focused on the relation between linguistic structure and spatial memory. Like Lucy, the investigators obtained results that support the notion that linguistic structure can affect habitual thought. The investigations just described suggest that relativist approaches to language need to be taken seriously even by linguists who have questioned the significance of "Whorfian" ideas (a somewhat misleading term in view of the long history of linguistic relativism described by Janney and Arndt 1993). If the structural peculiarities of any language affect memory and other cognitive capacities, certain questions about bilingualism call for greater attention including these:

- Does acquiring a second language offer the possibility of new modes of habitual thinking?
- Can habitual thought patterns from L1 interfere with the acquisition of the new modes?

Wilhelm von Humboldt (1836/1988: 60) took an affirmative position on both questions, and he was probably right. Some research does support him on the first question, such as work by Bloom (1981) suggesting that bilinguals sometimes show a wider range of habitual thought patterns, though it must be noted that the Bloom study has proven very controversial (cf. Odlin 1989; Pinker 1994). The second question invites speculation about the conceptual roots of language transfer. The implications of Lucy's research, for example, may or may not be straightforward for second language research. Yucatec is a language where the count/noncount distinction matters little because of the absence of obligatory marking of plurality. Many other languages (e.g., Chinese) likewise show significant differences from English in their nominal systems, and even a language as similar to English as Spanish shows important contrasts with regard to noncount nouns. Such differences may well have consequences for the acquisition of grammatical targets such as the English article system. Master (1987) compared speakers of languages with no articles (e.g., Chinese) with speakers of languages with articles (e.g., Spanish). As with several other studies, Master's investigation showed that the presence of articles in the native language facilitates the acquisition of articles in English (cf. Odlin 1989). Even so, he noted that Spanish speakers did encounter difficulties that seemed to arise from an unclear sense of how noncount nouns function in English. Although problems with areas such as pluralization no doubt have other sources as well (e.g., word-final consonant clusters), differences in habitual thought may contribute to difficulties.

The study by Pederson et al. likewise invites speculation about how speakers of different languages might compare in the ways they tackle spatial relations in a second language. Tasks similar to those in the Pederson study have been used in second language research, as in work by Bongaerts, Kellerman, and Bentlage (1987) comparing how speakers of Dutch perform in their L1 and in L2 English, and the results indicate some influence from Dutch, although much of it may stem simply from inadequate lexical knowledge. In other types of spatial reference, however, there is strong evidence for conceptual transfer. Ijaz (1986) reports differences in the use of English prepositions by speakers of German and Urdu on items on a cloze test such as *The keys are hanging____the hooks*. The German speakers who did not supply the target language form *on* typically used *at* (corresponding to German *an*, 'at'), while Urdu speakers often chose *with* (corresponding to Urdu / say/, 'with').

Prepositional choices often depend not only on conceptions of static space but also on conceptions of motion. Jarvis (1998) discusses a frequent difference in the way that speakers of Finnish and speakers of Swedish described the part of the film *Modern Times* in which Charlie Chaplin and Paulette Goddard accidentally collide in the street. The Swedes often chose *ran on*, which corresponds to Swedish *springa på* ('run on'), while the Finns often chose *crash to*, which corresponds to Finnish *törmätä* ('crash') plus an illative case ending equivalent to English *to*. It is also significant that a Finnish control group describing the same film almost always used a verb denoting a crash (i.e., *törmätä*), whereas a Swedish group chose either a verb normally used to denote running (i.e., *springa*) or one to denote a crash (*krocka*). Accordingly, the differences in the Finnish and Swedish interlanguages may reflect not only structural differences but also the way that the two groups cognized the event seen in the film. Further evidence for differences in spatial cognition is evident in a recent study by Jarvis and Odlin (2000).

Other studies have also considered native language influence on choices of prepositions and/or verbs of motion (e.g., Harley 1989), and it seems quite clear that L1 patterns of spatial reference frequently find their way into interlanguage. Kellerman (1995) and Slobin (1993) note still other cases of such influence which involve temporal reference. As with space, time often shows language-specific mappings in tense, modality, and aspect (TMA) systems, and several studies indicate that the native language can affect TMA choices in the interlanguage (e.g., Ho and Platt 1993; Klee and Ocampo 1995; Sabban 1982; Wenzell 1989). If native language conceptions of space and time play an important role in structuring learners' adaptations of target language patterns, there is good reason to believe that semantic transfer should be considered an extension of linguistic relativity into second language acquisition.

On the Varied Bases for Language Universals

The growing importance of relativist approaches does not vitiate universalist insights, and if research in applied linguistics shifts toward a relativist framework, there will still be a need to look for the common thread (or threads) running through human languages. Even while there exist language-specific forms best interpreted within a relativist framework (as discussed earlier), panlinguistic patterns still inform human languages. Hockett (1961/1966) contends that all languages have deictic elements, and Anderson and Keenan (1985) consider spatial deixis to be a universal. With regard to temporal deixis, not all languages grammaticalize the notion of tense (Comrie 1985). On the other hand, aspect is probably a grammatical category applicable to all human languages, and Comrie (1976) argues that the perfective/imperfective semantic contrast is relevant to any language that codes aspect. Along with certain conceptions involving space and time, some other notions seem likely universals aiding all learners in their attempts to make interlingual identifications. Ijaz (1986), Jarvis (1998), and others have relied on conceptions of categories in terms of core and periphery, that is, prototype theory as developed by Rosch (1974) and others. Thus, for example, the prepositions and postpositions of many languages often show a core meaning that will match core meanings in other languages, even though there can be great cross-linguistic variation in the peripheral meanings, as well as in the patterns of morphological realization.

If semantic universals aid in making both first and second languages learnable, the problem of ascertaining the specific principles that assure learnability remains. The conceptions of Chomsky (1995) and others of such principles, often termed Universal Grammar (UG), have prompted numerous studies in second as well as first language acquisition, though there do exist other approaches to universals and acquisition (e.g., Greenberg 1991; Wolfe-Quintero 1996). Within the Chomskyan framework, transfer has attracted considerable attention, much of it in the context of arguments made by Bley-Vroman (1989). As he observes, adult learners may have no access to UG (and, of course, it is also possible that UG itself is simply nonexistent). On the other hand, there are two possible affirmative answers to the access question. Bley-Vroman notes that adults may have direct access, sharing with children some sense of what a language must look like (as this might be identified in the principles and parameters of UG); alternatively, whatever access adults have might be channeled through their native language. The logic of the second approach runs as follows: Like every other human language, the learner's native language instantiates UG principles and thus serves as a reference point for deciding what can or cannot be characteristic of any other language. Bley-Vroman acknowledges, of course, that not all learner intuitions are accurate and that they may often reflect only some language-specific characteristic (in which case negative transfer can occur). The access question has led to numerous studies, many of them reviewed by White (2000a), but no consensus has yet developed. Whatever the verdict on the access issue, both of the following points remain valid:

- The importance of transfer to second language acquisition does not stand or fall on the answer to the access question.
- UG research focuses on a subset of possible language universals, and accordingly there remains a need for universalist research that looks beyond the issues raised by UG theorists.

With regard to the first point, it will help to list just a few of the questions that have proved important to transfer researchers, even though they have gotten little attention in UG debates:

- What kind of cognate vocabulary can trigger interlingual identifications (e. g., Schweers 1993)?
- What ways do listening and reading comprehension interact with transfer to promote acquisition (Ringbom 1992)?
- How much do learners rely on genre conventions in their native language when writing, for example, a business letter or a résumé (e.g., Connor 1996)?

With regard to the second point, concerning universals, some linguists have opted for approaches outside the UG framework, as the following questions indicate:

- How may universals of language change and second language acquisition be related (Greenberg 1991)?
- Is the Topic/Comment category the basis for interlingual identifications made by speakers of English learning Chinese (Jin 1994)?
- Does the semantic similarity between existential and possessive constructions have any effects on acquisition (Duff 1993)?

While UG research has focused on a small number of principles that may or may not characterize human language generally, the examples just given indicate that the sources for language universals are highly varied. Gass and Ard (1984) identify six different sources: a physical, a perceptual/cognitive, a neurological, a diachronic, and an interactional, plus one possibly available only to children, a language acquisition device (LAD). The LAD (which has also gone by other names) is often hypothesized to work according to a genetic timetable that children apparently follow despite the fact that they acquire language in highly diverse circumstances. As Gass and Ard suggest, the six bases for universals may overlap considerably, though the possible uniqueness of the LAD to child language makes its status problematic for many issues, including transfer (cf. Selinker and Lakshmanan 1992; Singleton 1989). In any case, the clear diversity of the sources certainly argues against any reductionist approach to universals.

Chomsky and many others have foregrounded what they consider to be uniquely human cognitive capacities, and UG theorists in second language research have naturally maintained the same focus. Even so, it would be mistaken to conclude that the human race is the only species possessing any of the capacities involved in language, even if researchers finally agree that chimpanzees and other primates lack the capacity for syntax (cf. Bickerton 1990). However unique human syntactic capacities may be, it is no doubt true that human language can communicate notions that are, as best we can tell, unknown to other species, such as arguments about the constitutionality of laws. Nevertheless, humans, along with other mammals, communicate emotions, and, as Darwin (1872/1979), Lazarus (1991), and others have contended, affect is an area likely to show evolutionary continuity between other mammals and the human species. If emotional displays and language never interacted, the role of affect would hold little interest for linguists. However, one likely universal is that all languages can express affective states, and it is natural to wonder if there are any other universals involving emotion and language. On the other hand, considerable evidence indicates that language-specific patterns can have affective consequences, in which case transfer seems inevitable.

One instance noted by Schweers (1993) offers an intriguing example of how a semantic difference in cognate words has affective consequences. The English form *pregnant* and the Spanish *preñada* are transparently similar, but the latter has a restriction not found in English: *preñada* normally does not indicate the state of a *human* female. From this restriction, *preñada* may often seem to Spanish speakers to be the wrong word to guide them in their search for an appropriate English form. In fact, Schweers describes in detail the reluctance of one Spanish speaker to use *pregnant* to describe (in English) a picture of an expecting mother in a clinic. Although this evidence is anecdotal, it nevertheless has crucial implications for contrastive analysis. The actual similarity or dissimilarity of forms and meanings is only one factor at work in transfer; the *judgment* of each individual learner matters just as much. Kellerman (1977) emphasized the importance of judgments in the area of idioms a quarter of a century ago, and even though there are problems with his original claim, subsequent work has shown the value of considering learner perceptions of language distance (e.g., Odlin 1991; Sjöholm 1983).

Learners' subjective positions can lead to interlingual identifications in other areas of language besides lexis. Odlin (1998) discusses euphemistic and dysphemistic (i.e., strong) forms of negation in relation to learners' social perceptions. Along with the neutral *no one*, a dysphemistic choice, *devil a one*, was available to speakers of Irish and Scottish Gaelic learning English in the nineteenth century, as well as a euphemistic choice, *sorrow a one*. Both the dysphemistic and the euphemistic forms have parallels in Gaelic, and it appears that learners in the nineteenth century (and earlier times) made interlingual identifications with the affective loadings in mind. The transfer here involves syntax as well as lexis, since the negation patterns in Gaelic are realized in focusing constructions. Even when they do not involve negation, moreover, focusing structures interact with affective factors not only in the Celtic languages but in others as well (Irvine 1982; Odlin 1998). It is worth noting that the contrastive pragmatics of negation has also been investigated with actual learners, including a study of refusals in Japanese and English that indicates the influence of Japanese on learners' formulas in English (Beebe, Takahashi, and Uliss-Weltz 1990).

CONCLUSION

As noted, there is reason to believe, with Darwin, in the existence of pancultural emotions. On the other hand, relativists (e.g., Lutz and White 1986) have noted problems with a universalist position, and many empirical questions remain to be resolved. Beebe, Takahashi, and Uliss-Weltz (1990) argue that speech acts, such as refusals, reflect language-specific cultural values not readily given up when learners attempt a new language. The affective burdens that learners may thus experience are, as these researchers suggest, a crucial area for investigation. The growing interest of second language researchers in emotion (e.g., Rintell 1989; Schumann 1994) may lead to a wider discussion of language universals and relativism in the years to come. If so, studies of cross-linguistic influence may attract the interest of anyone concerned with how human beings share a common heritage yet differ in crucial ways.

LANGUAGE TRANSFER AND CROSS-LINGUISTIC STUDIES: AN UPDATE

Since the publication of the original *Handbook of Applied Linguistics* in 2002, trends observable then in the study of language transfer have continued, leading to new insights as well as new research issues (see Odlin, 2002: 253–261). Three trends in particular will be the focus of this update:

1. Growth in the literature on transfer
2. Growth in the interrelated study of transfer and relativity
3. Growth of work on transfer seen in universalist approaches

EXPANDING LITERATURE ON TRANSFER

Although transfer was hardly a neglected area in the 1990s, the study of cross-linguistic influence has expanded considerably since 2000. At least three recent monographs have appeared (DeAngelis, 2007; Jarvis and Pavlenko, 2008; Ringbom, 2007), and several edited collections focusing on transfer (e.g., Arabski, 2006; Cenoz, Hufeisen, and Jessner, 2001), as well as many other collections having at least a couple of chapters on the subject, have also appeared. There have likewise been numerous journal articles, and several of these, as well as chapters in edited collections, have been surveyed in recent review articles (Odlin, 2001, 2003, 2005, 2008a). Transfer has likewise continued to generate discussion in work as diverse as that focused on universal grammar (e.g., White, 2003), contrastive rhetoric (Casanave, 2004), and L2 speech production (Kormos, 2006). Certainly in the foreseeable future, one major challenge confronting transfer researchers will be simply finding enough time to read all the new (much less the earlier) research.

TRANSFER AND RELATIVITY

The study of linguistic relativity has also grown in recent years, as seen most prominently in the work of Levinson and colleagues (e.g., Levinson, 2003). Even while Benjamin Lee Whorf (1897–1941) remains controversial in linguistics, Levinson goes so far as to call himself a "neo-Whorfian," a position more strongly relativistic than what Slobin has termed the "thinking-for-speaking" approach (1993, 1996). Interestingly, Slobin (1997) has also considered what he calls the "rhetorical" consequences of language-specific structures evident in cross-linguistic differences between translations and original texts; so far, however, discussions of contrastive rhetoric (e.g., Casanave, 2004) have not yet pursued many of the interesting possibilities of this approach. On the other hand, Slobin's thinking-for-speaking approach has generated considerable interest in second language acquisition (SLA; e.g., Cadierno, 2008; Yu, 1996). Yu, for instance, has identified differences in the English motion constructions preferred by Chinese speakers, on the one hand, and Japanese speakers on the other. Other work with relativistic implications has likewise identified some differences that seem due to transfer, as in the type of motion structures preferred by English speakers using L2 German when compared with native speakers of German (von Stutterheim, 2003). Spatial reference in L2 German also shows the influence of English semantics (Carroll et al., 2000). Further evidence of the effects of L1 semantics and syntax is extensive in areas such as article use (e.g., Jarvis, 2002), grammatical gender (Sabourin, 2001), serial verbs (Helms-Park, 2003), verb tenses (e.g., Collins, 2002; Rocca, 2007), and focus constructions (Odlin, 2008b). Yet although there is abundant evidence for the transfer of certain meanings—and the morphosyntax implicated in such meanings—it is less clear how much such influence should be considered evidence of actual linguistic relativity. Such influence is now frequently called *conceptual transfer*. Odlin (2005, 2008a) has maintained that although all conceptual transfer is *meaning transfer*, not all meaning transfer is conceptual transfer (in which *meaning transfer* refers both to semantic and pragmatic transfer). If, as Levinson (1997) has argued, concepts and meanings are not the same, even though they obviously must be related, then the view of conceptual transfer as a subset of meaning transfer seems the most viable working hypothesis to adopt.

TRANSFER SEEN IN UNIVERSALIST APPROACHES

Although the thinking-for-speaking and other relativistic approaches have led to advances in the study of conceptual transfer, a wide range of universalist approaches can be found in both the literature of SLA and of applied linguistics. These approaches often attempt to integrate notions of transfer with other long-standing concerns, as in (1) the relation between putative universal grammar and parameters that lead to some kinds of syntactic transfer (e.g., White, 2003), (2) linguistic processing and supposed constraints on language transfer (e.g., Pienemann et al., 2005), and (3) connectionist models that seek to identify the common threads in first and second language acquisition even while acknowledging some kinds of transfer (e.g., MacWhinney, 2005, 2008).It is beyond the scope of this chapter to attempt a comprehensive review of such positions, but certain problems ought to be noted. Some oft-cited UG work (e.g., Vainikka and Young-Scholten, 1998) has made claims about a structural constraint on transfer that have long been untenable, the supposed constraint being the suggestion that the L1 plays no role in the acquisition of articles. In reality, earlier studies (some cited by Odlin, 2003: 461), as well as more recent ones (e.g., Jarvis, 2002), show that when there is considerable cross-linguistic similarity, L1 influence can contribute greatly to success with L2 articles. A developmental constraint on the transfer of some particular word order patterns proposed by Pienemann et al. (2005) likewise seems untenable in light of more credible research on just such word order patterns (Bohnacker, 2005). Connectionist models have accounted better for some types of transfer, although claims by MacWhinney (2005) about the nontransferability of morphosyntax do not hold up well when cross-linguistic similarity is taken into account (e.g., Orr, 1987). Despite such problems, a particular strength of connectionism that makes it promising is the interdisciplinary links being established with fields such as cognitive grammar and neurolinguistics (e.g., Ellis, 2003, 2008; MacWhinney, 2008). Indeed, one intriguing possibility recently pursued by Dodge and Lakoff (2005) is that there are verifiable neurolinguistic differences in the way that some linguistic structures are processed; the structures they investigated happen to be some that have figured prominently in research on thinking-for-speaking.

A Compromise Position?

Dodge and Lakoff thus attempt to account for cross-linguistic diversity while also stressing that every human has essentially the same kind of brain. If that view is taken into account, it may help to strike a continuing balance between relativist and universalist research and consequently may minimize the dangers of wild pendulum swings in theories of acquisition.

CHAPTER 22

LANGUAGE USES IN PROFESSIONAL CONTEXTS

MARY MCGROARTY

I. INTRODUCTION

Scholars in several disciplines have studied the language used in professional contexts for many different reasons, so this topic represents an unusually interdisciplinary panorama. Here I review some current work comprising the study of language in professional contexts with the dual goals of illustrating representative approaches taken to date and suggesting where additional efforts by applied linguists could be most productive. The discussion concentrates on areas not discussed elsewhere in this handbook. Hence, I will not comment in depth on language use in schools, on the implications of research on workplace language for societal multilingualism, on language policy and planning, on translation and interpretation (all specifically addressed elsewhere in this volume), or on language use in religion. These disclaimers reveal the extreme multidisciplinarity of academic attention to language employed in professional settings; it implicates many possible avenues of scholarship related to applied linguistics (see, e.g., Gunnarsson, Linell, and Nordberg, 1997) and thus typifies the richness of the field.

The study of language in professional contexts overlaps an area more widely recognized within applied linguistics, namely, language for specific purposes (LSP—or English for specific purposes, ESP), a subfield recognized since at least 1964 (see Halliday, McIntosh, and Strevens, 1964, cited in Swales, 2000). As Swales notes, early LSP work relied on two straightforward assumptions:

1. Descriptive structural analysis of language used in work settings would provide an adequate basis for the development of teaching materials.
2. Those engaged in teaching languages (most often, but not always, English) for defined groups of adult learners would be capable of conducting at least basic required descriptive research on which design of teaching materials would be based.

From the start, LSP has had a strongly pedagogical impetus.

The pedagogical motivation remains strong, and more recent LSP work has drawn on the growing awareness of the multiple text types and changing definitions of genre relevant to any disciplinary field (Belcher, 2006; Bhatia, 2000) and the wider range of research methodologies in applied linguistics that have come into greater prominence in the last 20 years. As illustrated in one field, chemistry, these include, among others, corpus linguistics (see, for example, Robinson and Stoller's 2008 textbook for novice writers in chemistry, developed on the basis of extensive analysis of four typical genres in chemistry, research articles, conference abstracts, scientific poster presentations, and research proposals) and the more widespread use of qualitative methods such as longitudinal case studies (Li, 2007).

Concurrent with LSP's establishment as a recognized focus within applied linguistics over the last 5 decades, investigators in other disciplines looked to the study of language used in specific professional or occupational settings as data germane to a gamut of theoretical and empirical questions ranging from issues of occupational socialization to the expression and constitution of social relationships. The social relationships highlighted in such research were usually those illustrating particular identities crucial to the occupational settings at hand: experts versus nonexperts, doctors versus patients, judges versus attorneys versus clients, teachers versus students, and supervisors versus workers. Various projects have, at times, included consideration of other demographic categories such as men versus women, native speakers versus nonnative speakers, and native residents versus immigrants to a country, all of which coexist with standard occupational hierarchies. Individuals can be part of many of these categories, with the relevance of each aspect of identity determined according to past history and present communicative situation (see Toohey and Norton elsewhere in this volume). The methodology used in these investigations has generally been that of discourse or conversation analysis (see Johnstone, 2000). In the last 20 years, propelled by more explicit theorizing of concerns related to gender (Kendall and Tannen, 1997; Leidner, 1993; Wodak, 1997) and political power (Benhabib, 1997, 1999) that have marked all social sciences, academic discussion of workplace language has produced more differentiated and often more subtle renderings and interpretations of the language used in various occupational settings. Thus, a survey of language uses in professional contexts must include more and less than LSP: more in that one of its goals is to illuminate not only language but also aspects of social structure; less in that it does not aim, necessarily, to serve as the basis for pedagogical methods and materials.

Because research in this area has generally been motivated by an interest in social relations, much of the foundational research on language uses in professional contexts has been done by social scientists in sociology, anthropology, or political science. Given these distinct disciplinary foci and research methods, there is considerable variation in the type and amount of language data gathered and the nature, systematicity, and level of detail and sophistication of the linguistic analysis applied. Schegloff has remarked on the need to balance the focus on social structure with a focus on conversational interaction in conversation analytic approaches, noting that "each makes its own claims in organizing observation and analysis of the data, and one can preempt the other" (1991: 57). Moreover, research done since the 1980s has emphasized the interconnectedness of oral and written language in any workplace setting (see, e.g., Spilka, 1993), presaging the interests in intertextuality and historicity now prevalent in critical theoretical discussions in many fields. Additionally, Bhatia (2008), a major scholar in analysis of professional communication, notes the importance of "interdiscursivity"—that is, of grounding investigation of disciplinary discourses in a more fully explicated vision of professional practices—so that investigators can produce findings that integrate analysis of discourse into the lived world of professional activity. Hence, there is considerable opportunity for applied linguists to supplement the research previously summarized either for the specific aim of developing pedagogical tasks and materials, the usual mandate of LSP, or for the more general goal of expanding knowledge of the relation between language use and social setting—the lodestar of contemporary sociolinguistics.

II. LANGUAGE USES IN TRADITIONAL STATUS-DIFFERENTIATED PROFESSIONS

Social scientists have examined the language used in traditional high-status professions of law and medicine and similarly status-sensitive fields of education and social work for decades; consequently, applied linguists find a substantial foundation for related work. More recent trends in these fields incorporate theory and scholarship related to expression and realization of gender and ethnicity and aspects of technological change as all these interact with occupational and institutional authority.

Law

Law is the professional arena in which the study of language has been preeminent, both because the practice of law is driven by verbal and textual exchange (scholars have asserted that "language *is* legal power"; Conley and O'Barr, 1998: 14) and because, for centuries, legal proceedings have been described and recorded, sometimes verbatim, yielding an enormous amount of publicly accessible material for analysis. Researchers based in applied linguistics (e.g., Schane, 2006; Shuy, 1996, 1998, 2008) have complemented the study of legal records with many of the tools of contemporary social scientific and applied linguistic analysis such as ethnographic interviews and detailed discourse analysis of court transcripts.

Contemporary research on actual language use in legal settings reflects concern for both the expressive and constitutive role of language in pertinent relationships.[1] Recent work also demonstrates awareness that legal language, a register complex enough to challenge the abilities of native speakers, must often be used as a regular part of job duties by nonlawyers (as when police officers inform suspects of their Miranda rights) and that such uses of language can pose additional problems for second language speakers, even those deemed highly skilled in everyday conversational interaction, as Pavlenko's (2008a) comprehensive case study of a university student, a native speaker of Russian indicted in the United States on a murder charge, demonstrates. Applied linguists have also turned their analytical lenses onto the issue of distinguishing truth from deception in testimony (Shuy, 1998; Singleton, 2000). Furthermore, many contemporary studies of legal language address not simply a two party (i.e., attorney-client) interaction, but language used in the courtroom, a highly ritualized setting in which at least three different status positions—judge, attorney, and members of the public (sometimes considered separately as members of a jury versus lay litigants, plaintiffs, or defendants versus onlookers)—affect the nature of communication. Often when the profiles of relevant interlocutors include differences in gender or cultural or ethnic group membership as well as role in legal interactions, such dual identities are foregrounded in the study of legal discourse (e.g., Eades, 1994, 2003; Walsh, 1994).

Whereas early studies of language uses in legal settings sought generally to characterize the role-related discourse used by various parties, more contemporary work (e.g., Conley and O'Barr, 1990, 1998; O'Barr and Conley, 1996) seeks to determine the development of, and differences among, the evolution of legal meanings for laypeople involved in legal proceedings compared to legal meanings for legal professionals. An extension of such work is the explication of legal language as the expression of a particular ideology, with judges, in their roles of substantive legal authorities and arbiters of courtroom procedure, as its principal exponents (Harris, 1994; Solan, 1993). Philips (1998) examines the interplay among three different ideological frameworks—due process, state policy, and courtroom control—manifested in the discourse of judges, and shows that the connections perceived by the judges across the three areas are usually invisible to outsiders, rendering judicial conduct at worst unpredictable and at least mysterious. Her work, that of O'Barr and Conley (1996) on the contrasting understandings of individuals in small claims courts, and that of Matoesian (1999) on the development of expert witness identity through court testimony exemplify the trend toward documenting the multivalent nature of discourse in multiparty legal settings. Many studies of courtroom language demonstrate the existence of conventionalized discourse roles during parts of a trial; some also show that certain participants can affect typical question-answer sequences by challenging the linguistic constraints implicit in attorneys' queries (e.g., Erlich and Sidnell, 2006).

Another important development in the study of language use in legal settings is the attention to effects of new technologies for communication and analysis within the legal system, in, for example, the use of videotaped depositions (Pearson and Berch, 1994), voice recognition technology (Jones, 1994; Nolan, 1994), and use of computerized linguistic analysis to establish or disprove authorship of a text (Eagleson, 1994; Grieve, 2007; W. Smith, 1994). These uses, and the situational and topical issues to which they would apply, are particularly germane to the subfield known as *forensic linguistics* (Coulthard and Johnson, 2007; Olsson, 2008; Shuy, 1996, 2002, 2008). The development of increasingly sophisticated technologies for language recording and analysis and concomitant application of the ever more powerful (in the statistical sense) analytical approaches stimulated, in part, by advances in corpus linguistics (see Burstein and Chodorow, chapter 36 in this volume) have enabled many parties to the legal system, notably attorneys and sometimes other law enforcement agencies, to employ various methods of text mining in analyzing large bodies of linguistic evidence such as transcripts of electronic communication exchanges that last for months or years or transcripts of telephone conversations. It should be noted that not all of these genres are open to public inspection, as are courtroom proceedings; hence, some of these bodies of data qualify as what Swales (1996) calls "occluded genres," or communicative exchanges hidden from some or all individuals for reasons of law, custom, convenience, or efficiency (see Schweda Nicholson, chapter 34 in this volume). Hence, although research on many linguistic aspects of language in legal settings can be productively conducted by applied linguists with appropriate expertise, results of such research might not appear in traditional academic venues immediately or at all. Nonetheless, there is tremendous potential for applied linguistic research in all these areas.

Medicine

Interest in more- and less-authoritative social roles enacted through the discourse between health professionals and lay patients parallels work on legal discourse in many ways. However, the context of most medical interactions, unlike much interaction in legal settings, does not regularly include public discourse. Many crucial interactions take place between doctors and patients or across several different parties (doctors, nurses, pharmacists, nurses' aides, housekeepers, patients, relatives of patients, and, in some multilingual settings, interpreters; see Angelelli, 2004a; Schweda Nicholson, chapter 34 in this volume) and, unlike court proceedings, are not routinely recorded verbatim, although conventions of clinical practice often include generation of and reliance on practitioners' dictated or written notes about patient care. Compared to law, then, the nature and amount of data from medical settings available for analysis has been somewhat more limited. Also, scholars from several disciplines have engaged in the study of medical discourse, but with diverse motivations, goals, methods, and access to data; there is as yet no universally accepted mode of analyzing clinical discourse (Candlin and Candlin, 2003; Frankel, 2000, 2001b). Early work (see, e.g., Fisher and Todd, 1983; Mishler, 1984) documented the ways physicians managed communication with patients to provide technical information in what they believed to be understandable language, direct the interactions efficiently, and minimize emotional responses. Related research (Engeström, 1993) used the discourse of medical consultations to explore whether reorganization of government-funded medical care had any impact on physicians' communication styles or typical modes of activity. Contemporaneous discussion of these topics (Todd and Fisher, 1993) adds documentation of various realizations of power and resistance through specific discoursal strategies used by providers and patients. The research on medical encounters between oncology and nononcology patients analyzed by Ainsworth-Vaughn (1998) offers detailed examples of types of questions, storytelling forms, and humor used to frame and propel interactions. Tensions related to the material conditions of medical practice, particularly the limited time physicians may have with patients, are foregrounded in Stivers's (2007) account of the language surrounding physicians' prescribing practices. Drawing on the fine-grained approach of conversation analysis, Heritage and Maynard (2006) and their contributors illustrate some of the typical exchange patterns prevalent in primary care settings. They, and Frankel (2001a), raise intriguing questions regarding the discursive tensions between provider- and patient-centered talk, the latter sometimes recommended as part of the movement toward patient-centered care. In an intriguing parallel development within applied linguistics, researchers (e.g., Sarangi, 2001) have called for research that documents and explores patients' linguistic behavior and interpretive frameworks in greater detail rather than concentrating principally (and sometimes inadvertently) on the providers' perspective; Martinez's (2008) study of health-care interactions on the U.S.-Mexican border reflects this mandate.

The role of language in the occupational socialization of doctors has attracted analytic attention from several social scientists and medical educators.[2] Current work has examined the functions of language used by experts to induct novices into the profession. During formal medical education, senior physicians' knowledge of the content of the lectures and lab sessions that medical students would have completed up to a certain point would determine whether they referred to patients' problems in more or less technical terms (Cicourel, 1992), documenting developmental constraints on discourse. Becoming a member of any profession, not only medicine, requires novices not only to know technical terms but also to be able to reproduce the decision processes that lead to designation as a competent member of the profession. Discourse analytic methods have been used to track the socialization of medical students and to explore the effectiveness of less teacher-dominated, more discussion-oriented, modes of medical training, the topic of a special issue of *Discourse Processes* in which several scholars analyze a segment of videotaped discussion of a clinical case by medical students and their faculty tutor (Koschmann, 1999). Frankel (2000), a veteran researcher of the interactional aspects of medical language, shows that medical students have not been consistently trained in presenting bad news or using empathic techniques during patient interaction, although their use increases patient satisfaction and compliance with therapeutic recommendations.

Feminist theory and scholarship have increased attention to the relationships between gender and communication in medical practice. Because women use medical care more than men do, both for themselves and as caregivers for other family members, communication between women patients or parents and male healthcare providers has frequently been investigated (e.g., Maynard, 1992; Tannen and Wallat, 1993; Todd, 1993). In the United States, most physicians have been male and many other health providers, such as nurses, female, although proportions are changing; thus the dynamics of workplace communication between providers in different occupational categories has inspired research highlighting some gender-related comparisons. Fisher's (1995) exploration of the differences in social psychological dimensions of health care received from doctors versus nurse practitioners is one such example. The relevance of gender distinctions to medical research, as well as direct medical care, is a topic of some complexity; Epstein's (2007) thorough consideration of such concerns suggests that the existence and extent of gender-linked differences should be neither assumed nor ignored, but require empirical and experiential verification. The same is certainly true of sociolinguistic dimensions of medical communication.

The study of language in *language-intensive* branches of medicine and such allied fields as psychiatry, psychology, and psychotherapy has been a favorite site of investigations that have used mainly discourse analytic methods, and there is growing interest in efforts to determine whether any aspect of language use can be meaningfully linked with health status (Wilce, 2003). Pennebaker (2003) has developed a computer program to examine connections between degree and type of self-disclosure in college students' written reflections and health outcomes; using a similar technique, other investigators have found that such effects varied by ethnic group (Booth and Davison, 2003). Although it would be misleading to pose a dichotomy between these specialties and other branches of medicine, the latter areas often rely relatively more heavily on procedures such as physical examinations, lab tests, and visual representations (x-rays, sonograms, other forms of physical imaging) as routine components of professional research and clinical practice.[3] Labov and Fanshel's (1977) work showed that conversational analysis methods could be productively applied to psychotherapy, a line of inquiry reaching back to the 1950s that continues to be active (Ferrara, 1994; Frankel, 2000; Morris and Chenail, 1995).

The impact of new technologies on the nature and frequency of medical communication between patients and caregivers and among various groups of healthcare providers represents another central area for theorizing and research. Multiple types of computerized equipment are now commonplace in many hospitals and medical offices, requiring that physicians, nurses, and other providers learn to manage communication with and through such devices in addition to the older channels of handwritten notes or telephone conversations. These technological changes interact with considerations of typical gender roles in emerging occupational identities within health care (Cook-Gumperz and Hanna, 1997). More widespread use of electronic medical records raises several crucial language-related issues such as the possible intrusiveness of computers during physician-patient interactions (Frankel, 2000) and the need for accurate ways to search for information (Currie, Cohan, and Zlatic, 2000), which is of central import because some of the potential value of such records depends on efficient searchability (Lohr, 2008). Although electronic medical records are, like some types of records of legal interactions, to some degree "occluded" genres, they nonetheless raise several issues readily suscep-tible to applied linguistic research.

Education

Whether education and social work qualify as high-status professions has long been debated (Etzioni, 1969; Freidson, 1973), but both the strong institutional structures and the status differential between teachers and students or social service providers and clients suggest that they merit inclusion in a general overview of language uses in professional settings. I mention education only briefly here because other chap-ters in this volume provide more detail, on, for example, the study of classroom discourse (see contributions by Poole and Samraj, chapter 9 in this volume; Lantolf, chapter 11 in this volume; and Gass, chapter 15 in this volume). Investigators have used the conversation analytic approaches employed in the legal and medical arenas to examine processes of student classification and advising in special education placement conferences (Mehan, 1986) and in language proficiency interviews (Young and He, 1998). Such work illuminates the gatekeeping function of language use in educational institutions.

Social Services

The nature and types of social services available in different national contexts and the types of bureaucracies established to deliver them are highly context-specific. However, wherever services exist, determinations of eligibility and benefits must be made, often through the mechanism of individual interviews; hence, the relevance of language as gatekeeper in this sphere as well (McGroarty, 1996). As in all professional uses of language addressed here, the problematics of status-differentiated interviews increase when populations to be served differ in native language and communicative orientation from service providers. Britain's Industrial Language Training Project, established to address conflicts around the nature of communication in workplaces and in provision of social services, represented a wide-ranging and influential research program in this area; it was one of the first efforts drawing on large-observations and discourse samples to suggest that related language training be developed not only for minority language background workers but also for those who interacted with them (Jupp, Roberts, and Cook-Gumperz, 1982; Roberts, Davies, and Jupp, 1992). Some similar methods have been used to document the second language acquisition of "guest workers" in their interactions with social service providers or employers in several European countries (Bremer et al., 1996).

III. Language Uses in Other Professional Arenas

The discourse analytic methods applied to interactions in high-status professions have also been employed in other occupational settings in which hierarchical role differentiation, though still present, is less marked. From a research perspective, it is particularly provocative to examine language use in organizations aspiring to the "transformative," or "best-practices" ethos touted by many commentators; in such settings, language becomes one of the principal modes of instrumental activity between presumably coequal participants (Deetz, 1995). Related studies have documented how workers engaged in verbal interaction mediated through speech, print, or both seek to influence each other during transactions such as fixing a machine, arranging schedules, negotiating future business arrangements, or making purchases. Given trends toward flattening hierarchies in many workplaces and developing less adversarial attitudes toward customers, understanding the complexities of workplace language use in such settings is even more crucial than it might be in status-differentiated settings, for participants' effectiveness may depend less on hierarchical authority and more on communicative abilities (Deetz, 1995). Indeed, much postmodernist scholarship on language use in the workplace forges explicit connections between language use and the kind of individual identity promoted by employers, especially large corporations. In an ironic extension of Goffman's (1959, 1961) theories of self-presentation in the context of total institutions, the total institutions of note in contemporary scholarship on workplace language use are not those to which individuals are consigned because of deviance or disease, but rather those with which interlocutors freely seek affiliation because of economic and emotional rewards. However, dramatic changes in economic conditions and their impact on employment in many sectors have also influenced workplace language use of and by individuals and organizations (Kunda and Van Maanen, 1999).

Manufacturing/Engineering

Studies of the nature of work in manufacturing settings offer insights into language as one form of activity that represents and contributes to accomplishment of corporate goals and, at the same time, contradicts some commonsense notions about the skills and language abilities needed to be a competent worker. Ethnographic work at a successful U.S. wire manufacturing plant has shown that rhetoric about the need for a highly skilled workforce (Hull, 1997) misrepresents the idiosyncratic but efficacious approaches to production job performance, including various combinations of using talk and referring to written job procedures and specifications and the possibility of decontextualizing supposedly prerequisite skills from contexts of use (Darrah, 1990, 1997). In another U.S. manufacturing plant, growing emphasis on an incentive system based on pay for knowledge and teamwork led to some new literacy demands, but workers did not always see these as useful, nor did they value the company's concomitant requirement to learn about additional jobs or offers of related training (Hart-Landsberg and Reder, 1997). Both studies suggest that effective language use is embedded in additional understandings of the physical requirements and social relationships governing production work and cannot be defined in the abstract.

In many English-speaking countries, changes in the manufacturing process have coincided with demographic changes in the workforce such that many work sites include employees from extremely varied linguistic and cultural backgrounds. In the United States, social scientists have shown that in areas characterized by high proportions of immigrants, entire industries may be dominated by workers sharing a linguistic and cultural affiliation other than English (Waldinger, 2001; Waldinger and Lichter, 2003). Applied linguists have documented some of the ways workers and supervisors succeed or fail at managing both the production processes and social relationships in multilingual, multicultural work sites. Their work has enhanced the understanding of the multiple functions of language at work as well as the connections across different language communities outside work. Clyne's (1994) study of multicultural workplaces in Melbourne showed that various cultural groups favored relatively different patterns of speech act sets in talk, and that these patterns interacted with turn-taking behavior to shape communication; further, members of different linguistic and cultural groups tended to employ characteristic discourse styles based on their native languages even when communicating entirely in English. Goldstein's (1997) data on the language choices made by Portuguese-speaking women workers at a Toronto factory indicated that because of participation in dense and active social networks, mastery of English was often unnecessary for workplace responsibilities, although many desired it for other personally significant purposes such as communicating with children's teachers. Both projects provide ample evidence that good communicators in the workplaces are those who can grasp and convey comprehension of the material, historical, social, and cultural presuppositions that shape their work duties, and that such understandings need not be achieved or communicated mainly or exclusively in English even when that is the language of the surrounding society.[4]

Studies of workplace language in many industries attest that language, like other aspects of workplace activity, can reveal tensions. Kunda's (1992) ethnography of a United States high-tech company foregrounded (1) the company's language practices as exemplified in written documents, (2) the constant stream of e-mail, and (3) often ritualized presentations of work groups to each other as powerful normative influences on members of the organization. In exploring relationships between workers' experiences and attitudes and corporate success in an industry known for dramatic shifts in products and organization, the study documented an atmosphere of "high pressure ambiguity" (Kunda, 1992: 234) that coupled high expectations with lack of clear directives on how to achieve them. While documenting the experience of nonnative speakers of English working at professional jobs in Australia, Willing and collaborators (1992) found that meetings generally posed more much complex linguistic and interactional demands than moment-to-moment performance of other job duties. In a study of a British manufacturing plant adjusting to a change in management after a takeover, T. J. Watson (1997) showed that the talk among the production managers revealed ongoing tensions between the bottom-line-oriented new ownership and the original owners' empowerment philosophy even as the managers sought to reconcile the two views.

Technology-oriented companies have been on the forefront of computer use for internal employee communication as well as regulation of production, and they have thus been settings for much work exploring the multiple and reciprocal influences of technology, language, and social groups on each other. Murray's (1995) study of computer usage for management and internal communication at a U.S. high-tech company showed that, like earlier communications technologies, computer "technology both transforms and is itself transformed by society" (1995: 5); this study documented the now widely recognized attributes of a simplified register found in computer-mediated communications and illustrated some of the context- and topic-sensitive reasons for choosing among a variety of communication modes (fax, e-mail, phone call, personal conversation). The interface between people and technology is attracting considerable innovative theorizing (Devlin and Rosenberg, 1996) and ever more sophisticated design expertise (P. Taylor, 2009). Empirical research using the many techniques available in applied linguistics has a central role in further specification of the reciprocal influences of technology and human communication on each other.

Another arena in which communication has been studied regularly by several different groups is that of transportation—particularly air transport, a setting in which achievement of clear communication, sometimes under extreme time pressure, is essential and consequences of misunderstanding potentially dire. As with some other fields previously discussed, investigations of linguistic aspects of occupational activity are often conducted by nonlinguists and some accounts of difficulties may not always be made public (another partially occluded genre). Cushing's (1994) seminal study documented how, among other linguistic problems, ambiguity of reference and polysemy in commonly used expressions can contribute to accidents. Using conversation analytic methods, later investigators (Grommes and Dietrich, 2000; Nevile, 2007, 2008) demonstrate how particular grammatical patterns contribute to the coherence of pilot-copilot communication and point out that excessive overlapping talk in a cockpit may often accompany unanticipated technical problems during flight.

Language in Business and Sales-Related Positions

The last 20 years have witnessed an explosion of interest in the language used to conduct business negotiations within and across various linguistic and cultural borders, among them the economic shifts due to the demise of command economies and the increasing internationalization of business (Harris and Bargiela-Chiappini, 1997, 2003). Although there are literally hundreds of manuals and how-to guides aimed at sharing techniques for successful negotiation and sales, relatively few are based on real language data derived from relevant settings. Within the last 15 years, scholars in applied linguistics and related areas have begun to fill this gap through empirical analyses of intercultural and interlingual negotiations; chapters in Bargiela-Chiappini and Harris (1997) provide several relevant comparisons of the discourse of negotiations and service encounters within and across diverse linguistic and cultural groups. Such work continues, and has grown even more interesting from the perspective of applied linguistics because of the expansion of English as a lingua franca (ELF; Seidlhofer, 2004), one of the factors explored as a possible explanation for differences in participation levels in international meetings explored by Rogerson-Revell (2008). Growing use of English has co-occurred with increased use of electronic communication for routine business transactions, a development nicely exemplified by Jensen's (2008) study of e-mails exchanged by the director of a small Danish company and the sales manager of a larger Taiwanese company. Over the 3-month period of initial contact during which the smaller company sought to negotiate exclusive distribution rights for products of the Taiwanese company, there was evidence of growing personalization in the language used by the correspondents even as they negotiated the eventual possibilities and limits on what a contract would permit.

The role of the job interview in attaining initial employment is another area in which prescriptive recommendation abounds but actual data are comparatively scant. Applicants are often urged to "sell themselves" in interviews, and current applied linguistic scholarship shows this is by no means a simple injunction; M. White's (1994) study of the language used in 80 genuine job interviews indicated the successful interviews (defined as those in which the applicant got the job) could be described based on set of linguistic dimensions identified using corpus analysis, and, further, that the relevant dimensions differed somewhat according to type of job (professional versus no degree requirements) and gender of applicant. In an investigation of 47 initial interviews at a temporary staffing agency, Kerekes (2006) used conversation analytic methods to identify the interactional achievement of supervisors' judgments of trustworthiness that determined candidates' eventual success.

The growth of the service sector characteristic of most developed economies has led to greater interest in related language issues, particularly the role of sales in shaping and meeting consumer demands. Contemporary social science scholarship offers many important insights into the contradictory impulses that, in the spirit of "best-practice" companies and total quality management, promote personal, individual engagement in job-related interactions while, at the same time, aiming for greater efficiency and standardization of outcome. These tensions are tellingly explored in Leidner's (1993) ethnography of the recruitment, training, and occupational experiences used by a McDonald's restaurant and by a life insurance company dependent on door-to-door sales calls. In both enterprises, trainees were exposed to the language forms and uses deemed appropriate by the companies with videos and actual scripts, which they had to rehearse, and successful performance of scripted language on the job was reinforced by supervisor comments and, eventually, by some employees' own self-monitoring. Leidner argues that the ubiquitous and routinized service encounters characteristic of much contemporary life are actually changing norms of language use and interpretation: "Scripted service work accustoms both workers and service-recipients to participation in interaction that violates basic norms" (Leidner, 1993: 215) of genuineness, authenticity, and individuality to which most North Americans adhere, and employees become habituated to these new interactional norms and carry them into areas outside the job. Empirical research in applied linguistics could assess the changes in language behaviors and attitudes suggested by such studies. Indeed, organizational theorists (Kunda and Van Maanen, 1999) have already suggested that the postindustrial economy alters individual and organizational perceptions and expectations regarding stability and mobility at work; related research could help to show whether this affects workplace language use and norms. The trend toward outsourcing many types of customer service has created new research opportunities for applied linguists; Friginal's (2007, 2009b) analysis of telephone communication between North American customers and Filipino customer service agents provides many insights into the language forms and interactional norms typical of success in such interactions. Such research exemplifies the detailed study of actual language called for by organizational theorists (Barley and Kunda, 2001) concerned with postindustrial conditions of workplace life. Anthropologists have already documented innovations in local styles of social interaction and communication brought about by the establishment of fast food outlets in parts of Asia (J. L. Watson, 1997); applied linguistic research can be used to gauge the impact of new forms of commercial transaction on language norms and attitudes, discourse conventions, and the politeness formulas and vocabulary items pertaining to interactions between employees and consumers in a globalized service economy.

Symbolic Language: Media and Advertising

Many of the developments related to recognition of the links between language use and creation and manipulation of power relationships that mark the study of language use in various professional contexts also apply to the study of language used in mass media (see, e.g., Bell, 1991; Fairclough, 1995b), though these have not been explored in detail. As with other aspects of language use in professional contexts, studies of media language also demonstrate trends toward a critical perspective on the contents of messages, as well as the language used, particularly as implicated in cross-cultural references (Piller, 2003; Riggins, 1997) and the reciprocal influences of various technological forms on media content and language (see Myers, 1999, 2000).

CONCLUSION

Scholarship on the language used in professional and occupational settings has been sponsored by a variety of institutions or agencies whose agendas affect the research purpose and phenomena chosen for study, the accessibility of data, and the ultimate use and dissemination of the results. Research has been conducted from a descriptive, a confirmatory, or a critical stance. Whatever the occupational focus or analytic stance, current scholarship on language and work is now more sensitized to issues of the way people construct and maintain their work worlds through talk and, frequently, through the generation, consultation, and interpretation of related print materials and electronic technologies. Social changes affecting the economic opportunities available to men and women have made gender an important variable in the study of workplace language. Demographic changes leading to more multiethnic and multicultural workplaces mean that applied linguistic research can be used to identify relevant communication issues whether work-site communication takes place in several languages or only in one. Finally, technological changes related to the integration of computer technologies into many workplaces coincide with other social and demographic developments, affecting many aspects of communication. Language used in the workplace is never only about work; it expresses and shapes the social realities experienced by workers and spills over into the understandings about work, life, and people—understandings that carry over into other realms of individual and social experience. Hence, ongoing research on language uses in professional and occupational activities belongs in the mainstream of contemporary applied linguistics. Without it, theorists, researchers, and policymakers are likely to oversimplify the complexities and contradictions connecting the study of language and society.

NOTES

1. The historical provenance of legal language, a line of research related to philology, has interested attorneys and legal scholars for decades; see, for example, Melinkoff's classic *The Language of the Law* (1963), which characterizes legal language as "wordy, unclear, pompous, and dull," 24 ff.) and a more recent exemplar, Tiersma's *Legal Language* (1999). I shall not discuss these works further here because they deal mainly with written language and word-level phenomena rather than the actual language used by participants in legal proceedings. Still, they represent a genre worth noting by applied linguists. Both books

provide the historical pedigree (going back, in some cases, more than 2 millennia to Celtic Britain) of technical legal terminology used most often in writing, and both admonish attorneys to eschew obfuscation and communicate clearly in "plain language." Melinkoff observes that even before the seventeenth century, lawyers and even judges made money based in part on lengths of documents prepared and filed, thus furnishing a strong incentive for wordiness (1963: 186ff). Tiersma's (1999) treatment begins to address the conflicting motivations for uses of language in legal settings (establishing and maintaining authority versus communicating with outsiders, be they clients or jury members) and the economic practices that promote relative wordiness (charging by the page or the hour) versus concision (charging based on contingencies or recovery). Though the latter observation is based on the writer's experience rather than a particular research study, it is one of many areas of language use in the law in which applied linguistic research using contemporary empirical methods would be well warranted.

2. A classic in this genre is *Boys in White* (Becker et al., 1961), an account of medical school life at the University of Kansas in 1956–1957. Although it is enlightening to read the book as a portrait of the social divisions affecting student experience at the time—one of the most important of which was whether or not the students were members of fraternities or "independents," and, secondarily, whether students were married or single—it contains little explicit attention to language, defined either as number and type of technical vocabulary items to learn or as communication skills students needed to acquire. Instead, investigators represent students as overwhelmingly engaged in figuring out what the faculty members would select for the frequent quizzes, tests, and practical laboratory exams, a preoccupation certainly not limited to medical students though it was, apparently, characteristic of them.

3. Because of the necessarily embodied nature of medicine and medical practice, studies of medical communication routinely include much greater attention to nonverbal behavior than studies of language use in legal settings or in most other professional or occupational arenas; see, for example, I. Robinson (1998) for a careful explication of the simultaneous functions of verbal and nonverbal elements in the initial moments of medical office visits. In this chapter, for reasons of length, I restrict discussion to studies that emphasize the linguistic aspect of medical communication but note that any overall consideration of communication in the provision of health care must reckon with the physicality of interactions between providers and patients.

4. These studies also suggest that the performance of successful bilinguals deserves reconceptualization on a theoretical level, a principal contention of Woolard (1999). See Kaplan (1979) for a discussion of immigrant Polynesian workers in New Zealand workplaces. Additional applied linguistic research on dimensions of language contact in the workplace could advance theoretical developments as well as provide data valuable for a wide range of practical decisions.

PART VII

BILINGUALISM AND THE INDIVIDUAL LEARNER

CHAPTER 23

COGNITIVE PROCESSING IN BILINGUALS: FROM STATIC TO DYNAMIC MODELS

KEES DE BOT

THIS chapter proposes a move from the current largely static models of multilingual processing to more dynamic models. As in the first edition of the *Oxford Handbook of Applied Linguistics*, the focus will be on language production because the models that have been developed for this are detailed, well supported, and have been accepted as the standard at this moment. The first section is largely similar to that previously presented (de Bot, 2002). Then, for the transition to a more dynamic model, Hartsuiker and Pickering's (2007) comparative study to evaluate different variants will be discussed and contrasted with a view that is based on a dynamic perspective on representation and processing in which change over time is seen as the most important aspect of processing.

1.1 Traditional Psycholinguistic Models and Their Multilingual Variants

For the discussion of language production and code-switching, Levelt's "speaking" model (1989) is taken as a starting point. This is arguably the most established psycholinguistic model available, and various researchers have shown its relevance for bilingual processing (Green, 1993; Myers-Scotton, 1995; Poulisse, 1997). The Levelt model will be discussed briefly here in order to give the reader an idea of the main line of argumentation. More elaborate versions of the model are described in Levelt (1989, 1993; Levelt, Roelofs, and Meyer, 1999; for bilingual processing, see Kormos, 2006).

In the speaking model, different modules are distinguished:

- The conceptualizer
- The formulator
- The articulator

Lexical items are stored in the lexicon in separate files for lemmas and lexemes. The different parts can be described briefly as follows:

The conceptualizer translates communicative intentions into messages that can function as input to the speech production system. Levelt distinguishes *macroplanning*—which involves the planning of a speech act, the selection of information to be expressed and the linearization of that information—from *microplanning*—which involves the propositionalization of the event to be expressed, the perspective taken, and certain language-specific decisions that have an effect on the form of the message to be conveyed. The output of the conceptualizer is a preverbal message, consisting of all the information needed by the next component, the formulator, to convert the communicative intention into speech. Crucial aspects of the model are the following:

- There is no external unit controlling the various components.
- There is no feedback from the formulator to the conceptualizer.
- There is no feedforward from the conceptualizer to the other components of the model.

This means that all the information that is relevant to the "lower" components has to be included in the preverbal message.

The formulator converts the preverbal message into a speech plan (phonetic plan) by selecting lexical items and applying grammatical and phonological rules. Lexical items consist of two parts, the lemma and the morphophonological form, or lexeme. The lemma represents the meaning and syntax of the lexical entry, whereas the lexeme represents the morphological and phonological properties. In production, lexical items are activated by matching the meaning part of the lemma with the semantic information in the preverbal message. Accordingly, the information from the lexicon is made available in two phases: Semantic activation precedes form activation (Schriefers, Meyer, and Levelt, 1990). The lemma information of a lexical item concerns both conceptual specifications of its use—such as pragmatic and stylistic conditions—and (morpho)syntactic information, including the lemma's syntactic category and its grammatical functions, as well as information that is needed for its syntactic encoding (in particular, number, tense, aspect, mood, case, and pitch accent). Activation of the lemma immediately provides the relevant syntactic information, which in turn activates syntactic procedures. The selection of the lemmas and the relevant syntactic information leads to the formation of a surface structure. While the surface structure is being formed, the morphophonological information in the lexeme is activated and encoded. The phonological encoding provides the input for the articulator in the form of a phonetic plan. This phonetic plan can be scanned internally by the speaker via the speech-comprehension system, which provides the first possibility for feedback.

The articulator converts the speech plan into actual speech. The output from the formulator is processed and temporarily stored in such a way that the phonetic plan can be fed back to the speech-comprehension system and the speech can be produced at normal speed.

> A *speech-comprehension system connected with an auditory system* plays a role in the two ways in which feedback takes place within the model: The phonetic plan as well as the overt speech are passed on to the speech-comprehension system, where mistakes that may have crept in can be traced. Speech understanding is modeled as the mirror image of language production, and the lexicon is assumed to be shared by the two systems.

1.2 Speech Production in Bilingual Speakers

The Levelt model has been developed as a monolingual model and, if one wants to apply it to code-switching and other bilingual phenomena, one needs to clarify to what extent the present model is capable of handling bilingual speech.

In her discussion of learners of a foreign language as bilingual speakers, Poulisse (1997) mentions the following factors that have to be taken into account in a bilingual model:

1. *L2 knowledge is typically incomplete.* L2 speakers generally have fewer words and rules at their disposal than L1 speakers. This deficiency may keep them from expressing messages they had originally intended to convey, may lead them to use compensatory strategies, or may lead them to avoid words or structures about which they feel uncertain.

2. *L2 speech is more hesitant, and contains more errors and slips, depending on the level of proficiency of the learners.* Cognitive skill theories such as Schneider and Shiffrin's (1977) or J. Anderson's ACT* (1982) stress the importance of the development of automatic processes that are difficult to acquire and hard to unlearn. Less automaticity means that more attention has to be paid to the execution of specific lower level tasks, which leads to a slowing down of the production process and to a greater number of slips because limited attention resources have to be expended on lower level processing.

3. *L2 speech often carries traces of the L1.* L2 speakers have a fully developed L1 system at their disposal, and may switch to their L1 either deliberately (*motivated* switches) or unintentionally (*performance* switches). Switches to the L1 may, for example, be motivated by a desire to express group membership in conversations in which other bilinguals with the same L1 background participate, or they may occur unintentionally, for example, when an L1 word is accidentally accessed instead of an intended L2 word. Poulisse and Bongaerts (1994) argue that such accidental switches to the L1 are very similar to substitutions and slips in monolingual speech.

Poulisse (1997) argues that the incomplete L2 knowledge base and the lack of automaticity of L2 speakers can be adequately handled by existing monolingual production models, but that the occurrence of L1 traces in L2 speech pose problems for such models. Paradis (1998), on the other hand, claims that neither switches to the L1 nor cross-linguistic influence (CLI) phenomena call for adaptations in existing models. In terms of processing, Paradis argues, CLI phenomena cannot be distinguished clearly from code-switching phenomena; both result from the working of the production system in an individual speaker, and the fact that CLI may sometimes be undesirable in terms of an external model of the target language is not relevant here.

1.3 Language Separation and Language Choice

In dealing with bilingual speakers, there are two aspects that have to be accounted for:

1. How do those speakers keep their languages apart?
2. How do they implement language choice?

Psycholinguistically, code-switching and keeping languages apart are different aspects of the same phenomenon. In the literature, a number of proposals have been made on how bilingual speakers keep their languages apart. Earlier proposals involving input and output switches for languages have been abandoned for models based on activation spreading.

On the basis of research on bilingual aphasia, Paradis (2004) has proposed the subset hypothesis, which he claims can account for most of the data found. According to Paradis, words (but also syntactic rules or phonemes) from a given language form a subset of the total inventory. Each subset can be activated independently. Some subsets (e.g., from typologically related languages) may show considerable overlap in the form of cognate words. The subsets are formed and maintained by the use of words in specific settings; words from a given language will be used together in most settings, but in settings in which code-switching is the norm, speakers may develop a subset in which words from more than one language can be used together. The idea of a subset in the lexicon is highly compatible with current ideas on connectionistic relations in the mental lexicon (cf. Roelofs, 1992).

A major advantage of the subset hypothesis is that the set of lexical and syntactic rules or phonological elements from which a selection has to be made is reduced dramatically as a result of the fact that a particular language/subset has been chosen. The claim in this chapter is that the subset hypothesis can explain how languages in bilinguals may be kept apart but not how the choice for a given language is made. The activation of a language specific subset will enhance the likelihood of elements of that subset being selected, but it is no guarantee for the selection of elements only from that language.

According to the subset hypothesis, bilingual speakers have files for lemmas, lexemes, syntactic rules, morphophonological rules and elements, and articulatory elements that are not fundamentally different from those of monolingual speakers. Within each of these files there will be subsets for different languages, but also for different varieties, styles, and registers. There are probably relations between subsets in different files; in other words, lemmas forming a subset in a given language will be related to both lexemes and syntactic rules from that same language, and phonological rules from that language will be connected with articulatory elements from that language. The way these types of vertical connections are made is, in principle, similar to the way in which connections between elements on the lemma level develop.

Activating a subset in the lexicon on the basis of the conversational setting can result in the activation of a particular language, but it can also result in the activation of a dialect, a register, or a style. These subsets can be activated both top down (when a speaker selects a language for an utterance) and bottom up (when language used in the environment triggers and activates a specific subset; de Bot, 2004). Triggers on different levels—in other words, sounds, words, constructions, but probably also gestures—can activate a subset. An interesting question remains: To what extent in normal conversation is it a conscious decision to use a specific subset? Research on speech accommodation (Street and Giles, 1982) has shown that conversational partners adjust their style of speaking to each other, but largely unconsciously, and the same may happen in bilingual settings in which many factors may define what is the most appropriate style of speaking in that setting.

2. A Comparison of Three Production Models

Hartsuiker and Pickering (2007) compare three models of language production in bilinguals:

1. The bilingual version of Levelt's speaking model (de Bot, 1992)
2. Ullman's (2001) declarative/procedural model
3. Their own model (Hartsuiker, Pickering, and Veltkamp, 2004)

Their main goal is to assess which model is best able to predict cross-linguistic influence (CLI) at the lexical and syntactic levels. The main characteristics of the Levelt model have been presented in the previous sections. The Ullman model (2001) is based on a fairly strict distinction between declarative and procedural knowledge. Ullman (2001) provides evidence from neuroimaging research to show that the two types of knowledge make use of different parts of the brain. Lexical processing is typically based on declarative knowledge, whereas syntactic processing, in particular in highly proficient speakers of a language, is procedural. Another assumption of this model is that age of exposure has more impact on procedural knowledge than on declarative knowledge. Late learners cannot develop procedural knowledge of the second language and therefore have to rely entirely on the declarative knowledge system. Consequently, the model predicts different ways of processing of syntactic aspects for late learners as compared to early learners or native speakers. The Hartsuiker, Pickering, and Veltkamp (2004) model is concerned primarily with the interface between the mental lexicon and syntactic processing. Figure 23.1 represents their model in condensed form. It represents the lexical entries in the lexicon of a Spanish-English bilingual.

The link between the lexical concept and the L2 lemma nodes is relatively weak, as indicated by the dotted lines. There is no direct link between the L2 lemma HIT and the L1 lemma GOLPEAR, but there are links with category nodes (VERB) and combinatorial nodes like ACTIVE. How the lemmas are connected to the lexemes and the phonetic realization of the word is not represented in this reduced representation of the model. A significant aspect of the model is that lemmas are labeled for language. So the activation of the conceptual node HIT (X, Y) and the language node L2 leads to the activation of the lemma HIT. There is no separate lexicon for L1 and L2; language selection takes place through the language nodes. Activation of a lemma leads to the activation of syntactic procedures. In this model there are no language specific sets of syntactic patterns: "Importantly, such combinatorial nodes are connected to all words with the relevant properties, irrespective of language" (Hartsuiker and Pickering, 2007: 481). This implies that grammatical rules may be shared by different languages.

In their comparison, Hartsuiker and Pickering (2007) look at what the three models predict for four specific aspects:

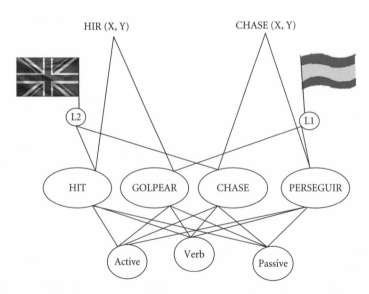

Figure 23.1 Hartsuiker and Pickering's integrated bilingual model (2007: 481)
Reprinted from *Acta Psychologica*, vol. 128, issue 3, by Robert J. Hartsuiker and Martin J. Pickering, entitled "Language integration in bilingual sentence production," July 2008, with permission from Elsevier.

1. Cross-linguistic influence, here restricted to the impact of L1 on L2
2. Syntactic influences within and between languages as measured by various forms of syntactic priming
3. The impact of linguistic distance on cross-linguistic influence
4. The impact of proficiency on cross-linguistic influence

Table 23.1 presents the predictions for the three models. For the first prediction, the authors show that all three models are able to handle cross-linguistic influence, though it would require a weak version of the Levelt/de Bot model in which there is interaction between the proposed separate formulators.

For the second prediction, an extensive analysis of the literature on syntactic transfer in production and syntactic priming is presented. Syntactic priming refers to the finding that speakers tend to have a preference for syntactic patterns that have been used shortly before. In a typical experiment (e.g., Bock, 1986) speakers are presented with a sentence with a particular pattern (e.g., a passive) and are then asked to choose between two versions of a target sentence, one with a similar pattern and one with a different one. Speaker will typically opt for the similar one. This syntactic priming effect has been shown not only in controlled experiments but also in natural conversation (Schoonbaert, Hartsuiker, and Pickering, 2007). All three models can deal with these findings, but the crucial aspect is whether there is a difference in priming between and within languages. In the Levelt/de Bot model, separate but connected formulators have been postulated, which would argue for more within than between syntactic priming. In a later version of the model (de Bot, 2004), this position is slightly modified by assuming that there are language specific subsets in the larger set of syntactic patterns, but this view has no consequences for this discussion. What the Ullman (2001) model predicts for within/between language priming is not so simple. Hartsuiker and Pickering explain:

> Less proficient speakers rely *more* on declarative knowledge than proficient and native speakers, who rely *more* on procedural knowledge. Thus, this model is

Table 23.1. Predictions for three models in Hartsuiker and Pickering (2007)

	Prediction Model		
	Levelt/De Bot	Ullman	Hartsuiker et al. (2004)
Cross-linguistic influence	Yes	Yes	Yes
Within CLI/between CLI	Within > between	Within > between	Within = between
Linguistic distance	More distance/more CLI	Unclear	No effect
Proficiency	More proficient/less CLI	More proficient/more CLI	No effect

> compatible with grammatical influences from one language on the other, but
> these cross-linguistic influences should be weaker than within language
> influences. (2007: 482)

However, it is not clear why this should be the case. Ullman (2001) makes a rather strict distinction between declarative and procedural knowledge and sees few connections between these two types of knowledge, so it is not clear how the L1 procedural knowledge can influence L2 declarative knowledge. If the two types of knowledge remain within their own domains, equal within-language priming would be expected within L1 and L2, whereas no predictions can be made with respect to between-language priming.

For the Hartsuiker et al. model (2004), the predictions are straightforward—because grammatical rules are shared by different languages, similar priming effects should be found for within- and between-language conditions. The findings on these effects in a series of experiments are mixed. Schoonbaert et al. (2007) compared all possible combinations (L1-L1/L1-L2/L2-L1/L2-L2) of priming with the same data set. They found similar within- and between-language priming effects when the prime and target verbs differed, and they found no differences when the same verb or translation equivalents were used. Hartsuiker and Pickering (2007) refer to several unpublished studies that show no differences between within- and between-language conditions. Therefore, the findings on priming seem to support the Hartsuiker and Pickering model more than the other two models.

The discussion on the impact of linguistic distance on CLI is somewhat muddy and oversimplified. "Hartsuiker et al. (2004) predict no difference between cross-linguistic priming in closely related languages (e.g., Dutch and English) or very distant languages (e.g., Korean and English), *as long as the languages have a similar syntactic rule*" (Hartsuiker and Pickering, 2007: 485, italics added). It is difficult to falsify such a statement; linguistic distance is defined by the degree of overlap between language systems, and more similar languages will have more overlap than less similar ones. But in all models, it is to be expected that rules that are highly similar between languages are likely to be transferred. The large literature on transfer (see Odlin, 1989, for an overview) convincingly shows that there is more CLI between similar languages than between dissimilar ones, but that does not mean that for equivalent patterns there will be no CLI. Accordingly, finding between-language syntactic priming for datives in English and Korean (Shin and Christianson, 2007, reported in Hartsuiker and Pickering, 2007) does not seem to constitute evidence against the general assumption that more linguistic similarity will lead to more CLI.

Finally, Hartsuiker and Pickering (2007) looked at the relation between level of proficiency and CLI. As they indicate, there are no data on syntactic priming to speak of this matter. The three models seem to have different predictions for this; in the Levelt/de Bot model, the assumption is that more proficiency will lead to a stronger network with more within- than between-language links and accordingly less CLI with higher proficiency. Hartsuiker and Pickering claim that in Ullman's (2001) model, higher proficiency should lead to more CLI, but it is not clear why they make such a claim. In their own model they predict no effect of proficiency on CLI.

Not surprisingly, Hartsuiker and Pickering conclude that their model best describes the process of CLI in bilingual speakers. The strong point of their contribution is that they have translated rather general theoretical notions into testable hypotheses, but, as the discussion presented may have elucidated, the translation is not without its pitfalls.

3. TOWARD DYNAMIC MODELS OF BILINGUAL PROCESSING

It can be argued that the Hartsuiker and Pickering article represents the state of the art at this moment in the sense that this type of model is the most prominent one. The whole literature on bilingual processes centers on this type of model. It will be argued in the remainder of this chapter, however, that there may be reasons to move beyond such models because they have a number of rather serious problems.

The main problem is that they are based on underlying assumptions that may no longer be tenable:

- Language processing is modular; it is carried out by a number of cognitive modules having their own specific input and output and functioning more or less autonomously.
- Language processing is incremental, and there is no internal feedback or feedforward.
- Language processing involves operations on invariant and abstract representations.

Because of these underlying assumptions, isolated elements (phonemes, words, sentences) are studied without taking into account the larger linguistic and social context of which they are a part. Also, the models are static and steady state models in which change over time has no role to play. Moreover, studies are based on individual monologue rather than on interaction as the default-speaking situation.

Within the tradition of which such models are a part, these characteristics may be unproblematic, but in recent years new perspectives on cognition have developed that lead to a different view. The most important development is the emergence of a dynamic perspective on cognition in general and on language processing in particular. The most important tenet is that any open, complex system (such as the bilingual mind) interacts continuously with its environment and will change continuously over time. Although a full treatment of dynamic systems theory (DST) as it has been applied to cognition and language is beyond the scope of the present chapter, a brief summary of some aspects is provided. Relevant publications on various aspects of DST and language include those by Port and van Gelder (1995), van Geert (1994), van Gelder (1998), and Spivey (2007). Specific for bilingualism and second language development are works by de Bot, Verspoor, and

Lowie (2007) and Larsen-Freeman and Cameron (2008b). The main characteristics of DST are:

- DST is the science of the development of complex systems over time—complex systems are sets of interacting variables.
- In many complex systems, the outcome of development over time cannot be predicted, not because the right tools to measure it are not available, but because the interacting variables keep changing over time.
- Dynamic systems are always part of another system, going from submolecular particles to the universe.
- Systems develop through iterations of simple procedures that are applied over and over again with the output of the preceding iteration serving as the input of the next.
- Complexity emerges out of the iterative application of simple procedures; therefore, it is not necessary to postulate innate knowledge.
- The development of a dynamic system appears to be highly dependent on its beginning state—minor differences at the beginning can have dramatic consequences in the long run.
- In dynamic systems, changes in one variable have an impact on all other variables that are part of the system—systems are fully interconnected.
- Development is dependent on resources—all natural systems will tend to entropy when no additional energy is added to the system.
- Systems develop through interaction with their environment and through internal self-reorganization.
- Because systems are constantly in flux, they will show variation, making them sensitive to specific input at a given point in time and some other input at another point in time.
- The cognitive systems as a dynamic system is typically
  - *situated*, in other words, closely connected to a specific here and now situation;
  - *embodied*, in other words, cognition is not just the computations that take place in the brain, but also the interactions with the rest of the human body, and
  - *distributed*, "knowledge is socially constructed through collaborative efforts to achieve shared objectives in cultural surroundings" (Salomon, 1993: 1)

van Gelder describes how a DST perspective on cognition differs from a more traditional one:

> The cognitive system is not a discrete sequential manipulator of static representational structures; rather, it is a structure of mutually and simultaneously influencing change. Its processes do not take place in the arbitrary, discrete time of computer steps; rather, they unfold in the real time of ongoing change in the environment, the body, and the nervous system. The cognitive system does not interact with other aspects of the world by passing messages and commands; rather, it continuously coevolves with them. (1998: 3)

With these notions in mind, let us look at the main characteristics of the models discussed that are part of the information processing tradition.

> Language processing is modular: It is carried out by a number of cognitive modules that have their own specific input and output and that function more or less autonomously.

The most outspoken opponent of a modular approach to cognitive processing at the moment is probably Michael Spivey in his book *The Continuity of Mind* (2007). His main argument is that there is substantial evidence against the existence of separate modules for specific cognitive activities such as face recognition and object recognition. For linguistic theories, this is crucial because in universal grammar (UG)–based theories, a separate and innate language module plays a central role. Distributed processing of language undermines the idea that language is uniquely human and innate because the cooperating parts of the brain are not unique for language, have no specific linguistic knowledge, and work in feedback and feedforward types of structures.

> Isolated elements (phonemes, words, sentences) are studied without taking into account the larger linguistics and social context of which they are a part.

If cognition is situated, embodied and distributed, studying isolated elements is fairly pointless: one needs to investigate them as they relate to other aspects of the larger context, both linguistic and extra-linguistic. For example, work by Eisner and McQueen (2006) has shown that the perception of ambiguous phonemes is strongly influenced by the semantics of the context in which that phoneme is used.

> Based on individual monologue rather than on interaction as the default speaking-situation.

As Pickering and Garrod (2004) have argued, it is necessary to move away from monologue as the default type of language production and look instead at interaction. The task for a speaker is fundamentally different in interaction as compared with monologue. The literature on syntactic priming mentioned earlier supports this way of looking at production; how language is used depends only partly on the intentions and activities of individual speakers and is to a large extent defined by the characteristics of the interaction.

> Language processing is seen primarily as operations on invariant and abstract representations.

In the models presented earlier, and in the information processing approach in general, the assumption is that language processing is the manipulation of invariant entities (words, phonemes, syntactic patterns). In a dynamic approach this invariance is highly problematic because every use of a word, expression or construction will have an impact on the way it is represented in the brain. As Spivey indicates:

> I contend that cognitive psychology's traditional information processing approach...places too much emphasis on easily labeled static representations that are claimed to be computed at intermittently stable periods over time (2007: 4).

He admits that static representations are the corner stone of the information processing approach and that it will be difficult to replace them with a concept that is more dynamic because what is presently available is too vague and underspecified.

> Language processing is incremental, and there is no internal feedback or feedforward.

One of the problems of this assumption is that many second-language speakers regularly experience a "feeling of knowing." They want to say something in the foreign language but are aware of the fact that they do not know or do not have quick access to a word they are going to need to finish a sentence (de Bot, 2004). This suggests at least some form of (L1) feedforward in speaking. Additional evidence against a strict incremental view is provided in an interesting experiment by Hald, Bastiaanse, and Hagoort (2006). In this experiment, speaker characteristics (social dialect) and speech characteristics (high/low cultural content) were varied in such a way that speaker and speech characteristics were orthogonally varied. Listeners heard speakers whose dialect clearly showed their high or low socioeconomic status talk about Chopin's piano music or about tattoos. The combinations of high cultural content and low social status in a neuroimaging experiment led to N 400 reactions that showed that these utterances were experienced as deviant. A comparison with similar sentences with grammatical deviations showed that the semantic errors were detected earlier than the syntactic ones—a problem for a purely incremental process from semantics to syntax and phonology. The semantics and pragmatics seem to override the syntax in this experiment.

> Isolated elements (phonemes, words, sentences) are studied without taking into account the larger linguistics and social context of which they are a part.

If cognition is situated, embodied, and distributed, studying isolated elements is fairly pointless: One needs to investigate them as they relate to other aspects of the larger context, both linguistic and extralinguistic. For example, work by Eisner and McQueen (2006) has shown that the perception of ambiguous phonemes is strongly influenced by the semantics of the context in which that phoneme is used.

> Language processing is based on individual monologue rather than on interaction as the default speaking-situation.

As Pickering and Garrod (2004) have argued, it is necessary to move away from monologue as the default type of language production and look instead at interaction.

The task for a speaker is fundamentally different in interaction as compared with monologue. The literature on syntactic priming mentioned earlier supports this way of looking at production; how language is used depends only partly on the intentions and activities of individual speakers and is to a large extent defined by the characteristics of the interaction.

> Language processing is seen primarily as operations on invariant and abstract representations.

In the models presented earlier, and in the information processing approach in general, the assumption is that language processing is the manipulation of invariant entities (words, phonemes, syntactic patterns). In a dynamic approach, this invariance is highly problematic because every use of a word, expression, or construction will have an impact on the way it is represented in the brain. As Spivey indicates, "I contend that cognitive psychology's traditional information processing approach…places too much emphasis on easily labeled static representations that are claimed to be computed at intermittently stable periods over time" (2007: 4). He admits that static representations are the cornerstone of the information processing approach and that it will be difficult to replace them with a concept that is more dynamic because what is presently available is too vague and underspecified.

So far, there has been hardly any research on the stability of representations. De Bot and Lowie (2009) report on an experiment in which a simple word-naming task of high frequency words was used. The outcome shows that correlations between different sessions with the same subject and between subjects were very low. In other words, a word that was reacted to rapidly in one session could have a slow reaction in another session or with another individual. This outcome points to variation inherent in the lexicon and resulting from contact interaction and reorganization of elements in networks. Elman puts it this way: "We might choose to think of the internal state that the network is in when it processes a word as representing that word (in context), but it is more accurate to think of that state as the *result* of processing the word rather than as a representation of the word itself" (1995: 207; emphasis added). Additional evidence for the changeability of words and their meanings comes from an ERP study by Nieuwland and van Berkum (2006), who compared ERP data for sentences like "The peanut was in love" versus "The peanut was salted." This type of anomaly typically leads to $N = 400$ reactions. Then they presented the subjects with a story about a peanut that falls in love. After listening to these stories, the $N = 400$ effects disappeared, which shows that through discourse information the basic semantic aspects of words can be changed.

To summarize, in research on the mental lexicon so far, the metaphor of a library in which books are opened and closed is often implicitly used to explain how access and storage work, reflecting the thinking in terms of static representations. From a dynamic perspective, the library metaphor no longer holds, because the book changes every time someone has read it!

2.2. Characteristics of DST-Based Models of Bilingual Processing

As may be clear from the argumentation so far, it is necessary to review some of the basic assumptions of the information processing approach in which current models of multilingual processing are based. In the previous section, the main characteristics and the problems related to them were listed. It follows from this that it is necessary to develop models that take into account the dynamic perspective in which time and change are the core issues. As Spivey argues,

> The fundamental weakness of some of the major experimental techniques in cognitive psychology and neuroscience is that they ignore much of the time course of processing and the gradual accumulation of partial information, focusing instead on the outcome of a cognitive process rather than the dynamic properties of that process. (2007: 53)

As a conclusion, some of the characteristics of dynamically based models are listed:

- Models should take into consideration that *languages* do not exist as entities in the brain and focus on situation-associated networks instead.
- Models should include time as a core characteristic—language use takes place on different but interacting time scales.
- Models should allow for representations that are not invariant but variant and episodic.
- Models should allow for feedback and feedforward information rather than a strict incremental process.
- Models should recognize that language use is distributed, situated, and embodied; therefore, linguistic elements should not be studied in isolation but in interaction with the larger units of which they are a part.
- Models should recognize that interaction, rather than monologue, is the focus of research.

Accepting that time and change are the core issues in human cognition implies that new models are needed, but, as Spivey (2007) readily admits, it is difficult to leave established notions and assumptions behind while there is as yet no real alternative. It is our conviction that we will move on to more dynamic models in the years to come, but how that will happen is unclear. Model development in itself is a dynamic process.

ACKNOWLEDGMENT

The author is indebted to Robert B. Kaplan, Ludmila Isurin, and Marjolijn Verspoor for their comments on an earlier version of this contribution.

CHAPTER 24

THE BILINGUAL LEXICON

JUDITH F. KROLL AND

TON DIJKSTRA

How do bilinguals recognize and speak words in each of their two languages? Past research on the bilingual lexicon focused on the questions of whether bilinguals represent words in each language in a single lexicon or in separate lexicons and whether access to the lexicon is selective or not.

These questions endured because they constitute a set of correlated assumptions that have only recently been teased apart. One concerns the relation between representation and process. As Van Heuven, Dijkstra, and Grainger (1998) note, it is not logically necessary to identify selective access with segregated lexical representations and nonselective access with an integrated lexicon; the form of representation and the manner of access can be treated as independent dimensions. Another issue concerns the way in which the lexicon itself has been operationalized. Different assumptions about the information required to recognize and speak a word in the first (L1) or second (L2) language have led to models of the bilingual lexicon that differ in the types and levels of codes that are represented. (See Francis 1999 and Pavlenko 1999 for a discussion with respect to semantic and conceptual representation.)

In this chapter we review the way in which models of the bilingual lexicon reflect different assumptions about the architecture and processing of words in two languages and then consider three central questions about lexical access:

1. What codes are activated?
2. When are these codes activated?
3. What are the critical factors that affect lexical selection?

We examine the answers to these questions first for comprehension and then for production. Because we assume that comprehension and production rely on a common representational system but differ in the problems that they pose for the system, we finally consider the implications of the comparison for reaching general conclusions about the nature of the bilingual lexicon.

MODELS OF THE BILINGUAL LEXICON

The Revised Hierarchical Model

Initial attempts to model the bilingual lexicon proposed a hierarchical arrangement to represent word forms and word meaning (e.g., Potter, So, Von Eckhardt, and Feldman 1984). These models solved the problem of whether there were integrated or separate lexicons by assuming that both alternatives were accurate but that they described different levels of representation; at the level of word form, they proposed independent lexical representations for each language, but at the level of meaning they assumed a single conceptual system. The empirical basis for these assumptions has been reviewed extensively in the recent literature, so we will not describe it here. (See Chen 1992; De Groot 1993, 1995; Kroll 1993; Kroll and De Groot 1997; Kroll, Michael, and Sankaranarayanan 1998; Smith 1997.) With these assumptions in place, the focus shifted to consider whether words in the bilingual's two languages are connected via the lexical representations or by direct access to the conceptual representations. Initial evidence suggested that the connections between lexical forms in L1 and L2 might be active early in L2 acquisition but that, by the time the bilingual achieved proficiency in L2, words in each language could access concepts directly (e.g., Chen and Leung 1989; Kroll and Curley 1988).

Kroll and Stewart (1994) proposed the revised hierarchical model (RHM) (Figure 24.1) to capture the developmental consequences of a shift from lexical to conceptual processing with increasing L2 proficiency. They argued that, early in acquisition, the reliance on lexical-level connections between words in the two languages provided a means for transfer; L1 could provide the meaning for an L2 word if L2 activated its respective translation equivalent. However, unlike other models, the RHM assumed that the lexical level links remained even after conceptual processing was established for L2. The implication of the sequential acquisition of these links was a set of hypothesized asymmetries. Lexical links were assumed to be stronger from L2 to L1 than the reverse, as this was the initial direction of transfer during acquisition, and L1 was assumed to have stronger connections to concepts than L2.

To test the predicted asymmetries between lexical and conceptual representations, Kroll and Stewart (1994) examined translation performance in a group of highly fluent Dutch-English bilinguals. In one condition, the words to be translated were presented in a semantically categorized list. In another, the words

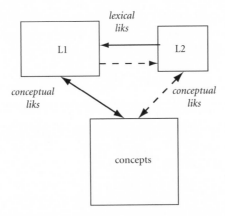

Figure 24.1 Revised hierarchical model (adapted from Kroll and Stewart 1994)

were randomly mixed. Under these conditions forward translation, from L1 to L2, was slower than backward translation, from L2 to L1, and only forward translation was affected by the semantic list manipulation, suggesting that only in that direction of translation was performance conceptually mediated. The absence of semantic processing for backward translation suggested that the task could be performed on the basis of lexical-level connections between words in the two languages.

Subsequent research provided mixed support for the RHM. On one hand, a set of studies showed that forward translation is more sensitive to semantic factors than backward translation (e.g., De Groot, Dannenburg, and Van Hell 1994; Sholl, Sankaranarayanan, and Kroll 1995) and that more semantic processing is observed in priming tasks from L1 to L2 than the reverse (e.g., Fox 1996; Keatley, Spinks, and De Gelder 1994), even when primes are masked and participants are unaware of the bilingual nature of the experiment (Gollan, Forster, and Frost 1997; Jiang 1999). However, other studies reported semantic effects in both directions of translation (e.g., De Groot and Poot 1997; La Heij, Kerling, and Van der Velden 1996) and also questioned the reliance on lexical links during early stages of acquisition (e.g., Altarriba and Mathis 1997; Frenck-Mestre and Prince 1997). (See Kroll and De Groot [1997] and Kroll and Tokowicz [2001] for a discussion of how these apparent discrepancies may be resolved.)

The RHM assumed independent lexical representations for words in each language. As we will see in the sections that follow, more recent studies on comprehension and production of words in two languages suggest that the assumption of independence at the lexical level was incorrect. (See also Brysbaert 1998; Van Heuven et al. 1998.) However, even models of the bilingual lexicon that assume an integrated lexicon and parallel access must address asymmetries in the way in which words in the two languages are processed by virtue of the relative dominance of one language over the other and the context in which they occur. In comprehension, these asym-

metries may be revealed in greater or faster activation of orthography and/or phonology associated with L1. In production, there may be a bias to activate and select
lexical candidates in L1 even when the task requires that words are spoken in L2.

The Bilingual Interactive Activation Model (BIA)

Which mechanisms should be incorporated in a processing model to implement
the assumptions of an integrated lexicon and parallel access and at the same time
allow simulation of asymmetric L1/L2 processing and context effects? In the domain
of language comprehension, Van Heuven, Dijkstra, and Grainger (1998; Dijkstra
and Van Heuven 1998; Dijkstra, Van Heuven, and Grainger 1998) have developed a
computer model for bilingual visual word recognition that incorporates one possible proposal. The bilingual interactive activation (BIA) model (Figure 24.2) is a
bilingual extension of the well-known interactive activation (IA) model for monolingual visual word recognition (McClelland and Rumelhart 1981).

It consists of a network of hierarchically organized representational units of
different kinds: features, letters, words, and language nodes. The model differs from
the original IA model in two main respects: First, it incorporates an integrated lexicon with words from two different languages rather than one, and, second, it
includes an extra layer of two language nodes that can be considered as language
labels (tags) that indicate the language membership of each word.

According to the model, presentation of an input letter string leads to parallel
activation of several possible words (the "neighborhood") irrespective of language.
Next, activated lexical candidates compete and suppress each other's activation until
one item surpasses its activation threshold and is recognized. Competition takes
place between items from the same and different languages through the mechanism
of lateral inhibition. By means of this mechanism, the model simulates the results
of several studies that showed both within- and between-language effects of the
number of lexical competitors (Dijkstra, Van Heuven et al. 1998; Van Heuven, and
Grainger 1998).

The BIA model accounts for asymmetries observed in unbalanced bilinguals
(stronger effects from L1 on L2 than vice versa) by assuming that, relative to L1
words, the subjective frequency of L2 words is lower for participants with lower
L2 proficiency. This is implemented in terms of the model's resting level activations,
which are generally lower for words in L2 than L1. As a consequence, L2 words on
the whole become activated more slowly and to a lesser extent than L1 words.

The language nodes in the BIA model account for context effects that are
dependent on specific characteristics of experiment and task. (Such context effects
are discussed in detail in the next section.) These nodes modulate the relative
activity in the L1 and L2 lexicons during lexical processing by exerting top-down
inhibitory effects on all words of the other language (e.g., the English language
node suppresses all active Dutch words). This mechanism induces stronger or
weaker interactions between words from L1 and L2, thus allowing the simulation

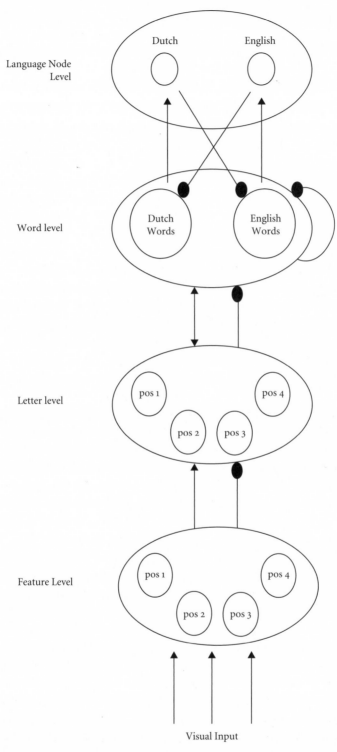

Figure 24.2 Bilingual interaction activation model (adapted from Dijkstra, Van Heuven, and Grainger 1998)

of the relative degree of language selectivity observed under various experimental circumstances.

We now review empirical studies in comprehension that support the language nonselective access hypothesis. Next, we specify under which experimental circumstances more or less selective results have been observed.

COMPREHENSION

What Codes Are Activated?

One of the most frequently used tasks in monolingual and bilingual word recognition research is lexical decision. In this task, participants decide as quickly and accurately as possible whether presented letter strings are words in a prespecified target language. In monolingual lexical decision, response times are usually in the order of 500–550 ms. The same experiments performed in L2 with relatively proficient Dutch-English bilinguals led to response times of about 600?ms in L2, but for less proficient participants considerably longer latencies may be obtained (e.g., Dijkstra, Grainger, and Van Heuven 1999).

It has been shown that presentation of a word to monolinguals induces activation not only of orthographic codes but of phonological and semantic codes, as well (e.g., Frost 1998; James 1975). Furthermore, monolingual studies involving ambiguous words (e.g., 'bug,' referring to an insect, a spy, or a programming error) suggest that different meanings of these words are initially activated during recognition (e.g., Kawamoto and Zemblidge 1992; Simpson 1984). In a study on word naming, Gottlob, Goldinger, Stone, and Van Orden (1999) found that English homographs (words with separate pronunciations and meanings, such as 'lead') were read slower than homonyms (with a single pronunciation but separate meanings, such as 'spring') and control words (e.g., 'clock'). Thus, during monolingual word recognition there is *intra*lingual coactivation of lexical candidates with overlap in meaning or form.

According to a nonselective access view, it should not matter very much whether the coactivated lexical candidates belong to the same language or to another. In other words, this view predicts that there will be *inter*lingual activation of similar words during bilingual word recognition as well. In contrast, according to a language-selective access view, a presented word will activate the form and meaning representations only from the language that is currently selected.

A study by Dijkstra et al. (1999) indicates that cross-linguistic competition between form-similar and meaning-similar words does indeed occur. In a series of experiments, Dutch-English bilinguals were tested with English words varying in their degree of orthographic (O), phonological (P), and semantic (S) overlap with

Dutch words. Thus, an English word target could be spelled the same as a Dutch word and/or could be a near-homophone of a Dutch word. Whether such form similarity was accompanied with semantic identity (translation equivalence) was also varied. This led to six different test conditions, exemplified by the following words: 'hotel' (overlap in S, O, and P codes), 'type' (S, O), 'news' (S, P), 'step' (O, P), 'stage' (O), and 'note' (P). The first three conditions are what are usually called "cognates," while the last three conditions contain "interlingual homographs" or "interlingual homophones." Lexical decisions were facilitated by cross-linguistic orthographic and semantic similarity relative to control words that belonged only to English. However, phonological overlap produced inhibitory effects. This study indicates that (at least for L2) a presented word form leads to the activation of all representations that it is associated with, irrespective of the target language.

When Are These Codes Activated?

The empirical evidence just discussed indicates that, under particular experimental circumstances, form and meaning representations of lexical candidates that belong to different languages become activated and may affect the pattern of results. A further question concerns the time course of such effects. At which moment in time is the necessary lexical candidate selected? Given that all three types of representations (S, O, and P) may affect the response, earlier views that assume that lexical selection always occurs at the orthographical level clearly cannot be correct.

A recent study by Dijkstra, Timmermans and Schriefers (2000) suggests that coactivation of lexical candidates from different languages occurs until relatively late in the word recognition process. In three experiments, bilingual participants processed the same set of interlingual homographs embedded in identical mixed-language lists, but each experiment had different instructions. Homographs of three types were used: High-frequent in English and low-frequent in Dutch (HFE-LFD); low-frequent in English and high-frequent in Dutch (LFE-HFD); and low-frequent in both languages (LFE-LFD). In the first experiment (involving language decision), one button was pressed when an English word was presented and another button for a Dutch word. In the second and third experiments, participants reacted only when they identified either an English word (English go/no-go) or a Dutch word (Dutch go/no-go). It turned out that participants were able to exclude effects from the nontarget language on homograph identification only to a limited degree. Target-language homographs were often "overlooked," especially if the frequency of their other-language competitor was high. The results suggest that the two readings of a presented homograph are involved in a "race to recognition" that is won by the fastest candidate. Even more interesting, it appeared that a slowing down of the response occurred if two candidates were relatively close to the "finish," that is, their recognition activation threshold. For instance, in the Dutch go/no-go task, responses to homographs were much slower in the HFE-LFD condition than in the LFE-LFD condition, although the proportion of responses did not differ between the two conditions. This suggests that selection takes place relatively late, implying coactivation of lexical candidates from different languages over a considerable period of time.

The observed effects were dependent on the relative word frequency of the two readings of the interlingual homograph. This factor, of course, is an approximation of the participants' subjective frequency, that is, the number of times they have encountered or used the word in question. For bilinguals, this subjective frequency is lower for items that belong to their L2 than to their L1, it being correlated to their L2-proficiency. If the subjective frequency of the L2-reading is negligible relative to its L1 frequency, the L2 reading will not be able to affect the lexical processing to any considerable extent. In other words, low proficiency bilinguals might show relatively weak effects from their L2 on their L1 lexicon (but strong effects from their L1 on their L2 lexicon). This point brings us to a consideration of critical factors that may affect the selection of lexical candidates during the bilingual word recognition process.

Critical Factors That Affect Lexical Selection

We have seen that different codes are activated and competition may occur even during response selection. However, we have already suggested, as well, that observed result patterns may not be a direct reflection of an underlying architecture. They may have been "changed" by processing or decision strategies from the participant that relate to task demands and stimulus presentation conditions. In other words, even though the bilingual word recognition system may be basically nonselective in nature, seemingly selective results may be obtained under particular experimental circumstances. A number of influential factors have been identified in earlier studies (e.g., Grosjean 1998), including L2-proficiency, language intermixing, task demands, and instruction. Apart from proficiency, which we referred to earlier, we now discuss these factors and their relative effect on the (non)selectivity of bilingual word recognition in more detail by summarizing a few recent studies that examined them.

Language Intermixing and Task Demands

Language intermixing refers to whether an experiment contains exclusively items that belong to one language (blocked presentation) or items from two languages (mixed presentation). The term thus refers to one aspect of "stimulus list composition." In a series of three lexical decision experiments, Dijkstra, Van Jaarsveld, and Ten Brinke (1998) showed that interlingual homographs may be recognized faster than, slower than, or as fast as single language control words, depending on language intermixing and task demands. In Experiment 1, Dutch bilingual participants performed an English lexical decision task on a list that included English/Dutch homographs, cognates, and purely English control words. Response times to interlingual homographs were unaffected by the frequency of the Dutch reading and did not differ from monolingual controls. In contrast, cognates were recognized faster than controls. The first result seems to be in support of selective access models, while the second result favors nonselective access. In Experiment 2, Dutch participants again performed an English lexical decision task on homographs, but, apart from nonwords, Dutch words were included that required a "no" response. Strong inhibition effects were obtained that depended on the relative frequency difference of the two readings of the homograph (as in the study by Dijkstra, Timmermans, and Schriefers 2000, discussed earlier).

In retrospect, the different pattern of results in Experiments 1 and 2 may be due to differences in language intermixing in the two experiments. The selective access view of bilingual word recognition is evidently rejected by the results of Experiment 2; therefore it must be that Experiment 1 created experimental circumstances in which null results for interlingual homographs arose in a language nonselective access system. Other studies have confirmed the importance of language intermixing for performance and have proposed accounts to explain the null effects (De Groot, Delmaar, and Lupker 2000; Dijkstra et al. 1999).

In Experiment 3, Dijkstra, Van Jaarsveld, and Ten Brinke (1998) used the same stimulus materials but changed the task demands. Participants now performed a general lexical decision task, responding "yes" if a word of either language was presented (rather than saying "no" to Dutch words). In this experiment, frequency-dependent facilitation effects were found for the interlingual homographs. Dijkstra et al. explain these results by pointing out that the task in Experiment 2 required the participants to make a distinction between the two readings of interlingual homographs, while they were able to use either reading in Experiment 3. Thus, the same underlying architecture (involving representations for homographs in different languages) could lead to both inhibition and facilitation effects.

Effect of Instruction

We have seen that several factors (proficiency, language intermixing, task demands) may affect the (non)selectivity of the result patterns in bilingual word recognition experiments. In this context, the question arises to which extent top-down factors, such as participant expectancies based on the instructions of the experimenter, may affect the observed result patterns.

While adequate evaluation of this issue will require additional empirical evidence, it appears that bottom-up factors, such as language intermixing and stimulus characteristics (e.g., frequency, code similarity), are the more important ones. Dijkstra, De Bruijn, Schriefers, and Ten Brinke (2000) contrasted the effect of instruction-induced expectancies and language intermixing in an English lexical decision task performed by Dutch-English bilinguals. At the start of the experiment, participants were explicitly instructed to respond "yes" to interlingual homographs and exclusively English words and "no" to English nonwords and to exclusively Dutch words. In the first part of the experiment the stimulus list did not contain any Dutch words. In the second part of the experiment, Dutch items were introduced. No significant differences were found between interlingual homographs and controls in the first part of the experiment, while strong inhibition was obtained for interlingual homographs in the second part. This effect is demonstrated for words with a low-frequency reading in Dutch and a high-frequency reading in English, as shown in Figure 24.3.

The reader will note that these results converge with those of Experiments 1 and 2 by Dijkstra, Van Jaarsveld, and Ten Brinke (1998), discussed earlier. They suggest that language intermixing, rather than instruction-based expectancies, drives the bilingual participants' performance. However, the issue is still not decided, because a study by Von Studnitz and Green (submitted) suggests that the result patterns may yet be modulated by participant strategies.

To summarize this section on bilingual comprehension studies, it appears that:

1. Lexical codes from different languages are activated in parallel on the basis of an input string.
2. Selection of the lexical candidate that is identified appears to take place rather late in the recognition process.
3. Several factors affect the ultimately arising result patterns, the most important of which are a participant's L2-proficiency level, the requirements of the task, and the blocked or mixed presentation of items from different languages.

We now examine the same issues on code activation and factors that affect lexical selection for the bilingual's language production process.

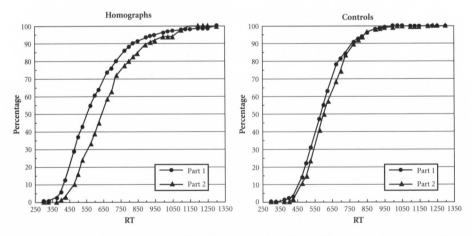

Figure 24.3 Cumulative response distributions to interlingual homographs and matched exclusively English controls. Data are from the first and second parts of the English visual lexical decision by Dijkstra, De Bruijn, Schriefers, and Ten Brinke (2000).

Note: Homographs had low-frequency Dutch and high frequency English readings. Exclusively Dutch words, which required a "no" response, occurred only in the second part.

PRODUCTION

What Codes Are Activated?

To speak a word in order to express a thought or to name a picture, the speaker must engage a sequence of processes to map the meaning of the intended utterance onto the phonology of the appropriate word. Even within a single language, the hypothesized process is quite complex (Bock and Levelt 1994; Dell 1988; Levelt 1989; Levelt, Roelofs, and Meyer 1999). An initial debate concerned the seriality of this process. Some researchers argued that phonology becomes specified only after a single meaning is identified (e.g., Levelt et al. 1991), and others claimed that as soon as meanings are activated, but before a single meaning is selected, there is corresponding activation of phonology (e.g., Dell and O'Seaghdha 1991; Starreveld and La Heij 1995). Recent evidence favors the view that language production is a cascaded process whereby some, but not all, close competitors may engage their associated phonology in overlapping stages (e.g., Cutting and Ferreira 1999; Damian and Martin 1999; Jescheniak and Schriefers 1998; Peterson and Savoy 1998).

For a bilingual, there is the additional matter of selecting the language in which a word should be spoken. It might seem that simply intending to speak in one language rather than the other would be sufficient. Unlike perception, which is to a large degree driven by the properties of the stimulus input, production, even of a single word, is a top-down process, initiated by conceptual activity. The language to be spoken could plausibly be selected from among other conceptual constraints prior to lexical access. (See de Bot and Schreuder 1993; Poulisse 1997). It is, therefore, surprising to discover that words in both of a bilingual's languages appear to be active well into the process of lexicalizing a concept into a single spoken word. The evidence that we will review suggests that, like perception, lexical access in production is nonselective. However, because production is conceptually driven and typically unfolds over a longer time than perception, the answer to the question of what is activated is not necessarily the same.

In past research, the primary task that has been used to investigate the form of the codes active during lexical access is picture-word interference, a variant of the Stroop (1935) task. In this paradigm, a picture is presented, and its name must be spoken aloud as quickly as possible. At some point before, during, or after the onset of the picture, a word distractor is presented visually or auditorily. By observing the consequences of the relation of the word to the name of the picture and the timing of its presentation, it is theoretically possible to infer the nature of the activated information at any given point during the process. The general pattern of results is clear: Semantically related words produce interference, form-related words (by orthography, phonology, or both) produce facilitation, and identical words (i.e., the picture's name) produce facilitation relative to unrelated controls (e.g., La Heij 1988; Schriefers, Meyer, and Levelt 1990). However, the goal of assigning a given code to a specific component stage of production has been only partly successful (e.g., Damian and Martin 1999; Starreveld 2000).

Two recent studies used the picture-word interference paradigm to investigate the activity of the nontarget language when words in only one of the bilingual's two languages are to be spoken. Hermans, Bongaerts, de Bot, and Schreuder (1998) had fluent Dutch-English bilinguals name pictures in English, their L2, with distractor words presented auditorily following a variable stimulus onset asynchrony (SOA). The main question was whether the name of the picture in L1 would be activated when the task required naming in L2. For example, if a picture of a mountain was to be named 'mountain' in English, would the Dutch word '*berg*' be active? Distractors that were semantically and phonologically related or unrelated to the picture's name were presented in L1 or in L2. In the critical condition, the distractor was a word that sounded like the L1 name of the picture (e.g., 'berm' or 'bench' instead of '*berg*'). The results for these "phono-Dutch" words were more like those for the semantic distractors than for the phonological distractors (i.e., they followed a similar time course), suggesting that the translation equivalent is active through the stage of selecting an initial lexical candidate but one not yet phonologically specified. Furthermore, semantically related distractors produced similar interferences regardless of the language in which they were presented, a result that also converges on the conclusion that lexical access is nonselective with respect to language, at least during the initial stages of production.

Similar studies by Costa, Miozzo, and Caramazza (1999) and Costa and Caramazza (1999), but using visual distractors, also revealed cross-language effects and demonstrated that even L2 distractors can influence L1 naming performance. However, Costa et al. also found some limits on the degree to which the phonology of translation equivalents was activated and argued that ultimately production proceeds on the basis of a selective process that favors lexical candidates in the language in which the bilingual intends to speak.

These studies provide evidence that lexical alternatives are available in both languages, at least during the early stages of production, when abstract lexical representations corresponding to the intended meaning of the utterance (sometimes called "lemmas") are activated. However, unlike evidence on monolingual production, which shows that close lexical competitors may be phonologically specified (e.g., Jescheniak and Schriefers 1998; Peterson and Savoy 1998), there is no indication from bilingual picture-word experiments that non target competitors are phonologically encoded.

When Are These Codes Activated?

Examining the time course of picture-word interference effects is one way to investigate the availability of meaning and phonology during production. However, because the distractor word itself is recognized, a process that cannot be viewed independently of the primary picture-naming task, the paradigm does not provide a pure window into the time course of production.

Kroll and Peck (1998) developed a new task, cued picture naming, to obtain a more direct measure of L1 activity during L2 production. Participants are presented with a pictured object and told to produce the object's name when they hear a tone cue. The cue is presented following a variable SOA. In pure conditions, the subjects are instructed to name the picture in their L1 or L2 when they hear the cue. In mixed conditions, they are instructed to name the picture in one language if the cue is a high tone and in the other if the cue is a low tone (Figure 24.4). Thus, in pure conditions, the language of naming is certain; only the onset of production depends on the presentation of the cue. In mixed conditions, the language of naming is uncertain until the cue has been processed.

Kroll and Peck (1998) investigated the time course of picture naming in the cued task for English-Spanish bilinguals. As expected, naming latencies decreased with increasing SOA, reflecting a general effect of preparation, and the time to name pictures was faster for L1 than L2, also expected because L1 is the first and dominant language. However, the results also suggested an asymmetry in the time course of activation of cross-language competitors, with greater cost to L1 than L2 under the mixed conditions. When the language of naming is uncertain, both languages must be simultaneously active. If L2 picture naming normally involves the activation and subsequent inhibition of L1, then mixing L1 and L2 should have little effect on L2 performance. However, if the more dominant L1 does not normally involve the activation and inhibition of L2, then mixing languages should have particularly deleterious effects for L1 picture naming, as these results suggest.

Furthermore, there was an indication that in the blocked condition there was a steeper decline in L2 than L1 naming latencies at the long SOAs. If L2 cannot be prepared until the activation of L1 has decayed or been inhibited, then L2 naming will be slow relative to L1 and relative to conditions in which L1 is not active. The pattern of results is consistent with the claim that additional time is needed to resolve com-

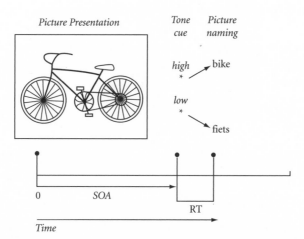

Figure 24.4 Illustration of the mixed cued picture naming task
Note: In the example shown, a Dutch-English bilingual is shown a picture of a bicycle. When a high tone is presented, the picture is to be named "bike" in English. When a low tone is presented, the picture is to be named "fiets" in Dutch.

petition from activated lexical candidates in L1 before L2 naming can proceed. The picture-word interference results also suggest that this is the case.

Kroll, Dijkstra, Janssen, and Schriefers (1999) examined performance in the cued picture naming task using conditions aimed at identifying the locus and form of these effects more precisely. Two sets of experiments were designed, one with Dutch-English bilinguals and the other with English-French bilinguals. In each experiment, the mixed task was performed with the tone cue presented at an SOA of 0, 500, or 1000 ms. The critical materials were pictures whose names were cognates, translation equivalents that share identical or similar word form (e.g., 'bed'-'bed' or 'tomaat'-'tomato' in Dutch and English).

If both language alternatives are active to the level of the phonology, then we might predict an effect of cognate status because of the high degree of phonological overlap between the L1 and L2 names. Results for both bilingual groups were similar. In each case there was facilitation for pictures with cognate names relative to controls for both L1 and L2 (Figure 24.5). A monolingual control group naming pictures in English only produced no effect of cognate status. For bilinguals, the time course data for L1 revealed a benefit for cognate pictures across all SOAs. For L2, the effects were present only at short SOAs; by 1000 ms the cognate facilitation was absent. The inhibitory process for L1 may have been complete by the time of the longest SOA, and thus no effect of cognate status was observed for L2. For both

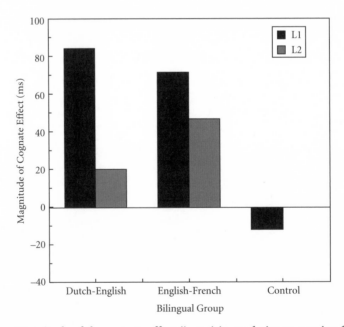

Figure 24.5 Magnitude of the cognate effect (in ms) in cued picture naming for Dutch-English and English-French bilinguals naming pictures in their L1 and L2
Note: Control data for native English speakers naming English-French cognate pictures in L1. Bars above the line indicate facilitation.

bilingual groups there was also a reversal of L1 and L2, with faster picture naming latencies for L2 than for L1. The finding of slower RTs for L1 than L2 (a result also reported by Meuter and Allport [1999] following a language switch) suggests that L1 was inhibited when L2 responses were required to be prepared.

To summarize, the data from the cued picture naming experiments show that when picture naming is performed in L1, there is not normally an influence of L2 unless the task requires that L2 be active, as in the mixed conditions. For L2, however, there is a persistent effect of L1 that appears well into the lexicalization process and regardless of whether or not the task requires L1 to be active. Whether lexical alternatives are specified to the level of the phonology appears to depend in these experiments on the nature of the task. It remains for future research to specify the conditions that determine the locus of language selection.

Critical Factors That Affect Lexical Selection

If lexical access is nonselective during production and the language to be spoken is not determined until a relatively late point in the process, then the factors that influence selection will play an important role in constraining the nature of the resulting utterances. For example, one might expect that the later in time that language is selected, the more likely we are to observe errors of language, with substitutions of words from the unintended language. These errors occur (Poulisse 1999), but they are relatively rare unless the bilingual is in a context in which code switching is likely—see de Bot, chapter 23, this volume, for a related discussion—or unless the speaker is less proficient in L2. Particularly for L2, for which the evidence reviewed suggests that L1 competitors are active well into the lexicalization process, we need to consider what mechanisms may be in place to control the consequences of unintended activation of L1.

Inhibitory Control

The issue of how bilinguals resolve competition across their two languages has been addressed at a theoretical level in terms of language mode (e.g., Grosjean 1997a, 1998, 2001) and by models that propose inhibitory control mechanisms (e.g., Green 1986, 1993, 1998). In the section on perception, we considered factors (e.g., list composition, instruction) that are thought to influence the relative activation of words in the two languages. Here we consider another factor, the recruitment of externally driven attentional resources, that may selectively bias the way in which the activation within the lexical system is utilized.

Green (1998) proposed the inhibitory control model to provide a mechanism that would allow the bilingual effectively to suppress activity in the nontarget language and thereby to avoid speaking words in the unintended language. For example, when translating from L1 to L2, the bilingual must avoid inadvertently naming the L1 target word itself. According to the model, before any task can be performed, a task schema must be engaged (e.g., for naming a picture in L1 or L2, for translating a word, or for making a lexical decision). The more resources that need to be allocated to inhibiting nontarget responses, the greater the predicted processing costs.

The effects of an inhibitory control mechanism have been examined in experiments on language switching in which bilinguals change the language of production over a predictable sequence of trials (e.g., Loasby 1998; Meuter and Allport 1999). The typical result is that larger switch costs are observed when bilinguals switch into their more dominant language (L1) than when they switch into the weaker language (L2). The interpretation of the asymmetric switch costs for the two languages is that L1 is more likely to be active, and therefore more likely to be suppressed during the processing of L2, than L2 is during the processing of L1.

A curious aspect of the language switching results is that the asymmetric pattern of switch costs occurs even when successive items are not related to one another, suggesting that this inhibitory mechanism is global rather than local. A related question is whether, in the presence of cues to the language of production, the relative activation of nontarget competitors can be reduced, thereby reducing the inhibitory control requirements. We consider this issue next.

Cues to Language Selection

If the goal of language production is to accomplish the task of lexical selection as quickly as possible, then the longer the language of speaking remains open, the longer selection will be delayed. One way to achieve early language selection is to rely on cues that signal one language. In picture naming, the drawings used as stimuli typically contain little information that biases them toward one language. In contrast, tasks such as translation provide clear cues to the language to be spoken. When a word is presented for translation it is, in a sense, the very competitor that the speaker must avoid producing. Having a specific cue (don't name that word, and, more generally, don't name a word in that language) may enable selection to occur earlier.

Two recent studies provide some evidence for the hypothesis that language cues available in the translation task permit language selection to occur earlier than in picture naming. Kroll, Dietz, and Green (in preparation) tested the hypothesis that switch costs would be greater in the picture-naming task than in translation, even though the actual spoken production in the two languages was identical. The results supported the predictions. Performance in the picture-naming task replicated the pattern of switch costs reported by Meuter and Allport (1999) for numeral naming. There were large costs to switch into the more dominant L1, but smaller costs to switch into L2. However, the same pattern was not observed in the translation task where the switch costs were not significant for either language.

A second source of evidence for the claim that the translation task provides cues that enable earlier language selection than picture naming comes from a recent Stroop translation study (Miller 1997). This version of the Stroop task is similar to picture-word interference, but with translation rather than picture naming as the primary task. When distractor words appeared in the language of production, Miller replicated the pattern of semantic interference and form facilitation that has been reported previously for the translation Stroop task (La Heij et al. 1990) and in bilingual picture-word interference (Costa, Miozzo, and Caramazza 1999; Hermans et al. 1998). However, Miller's study also included a condition in which distractor words were related to the language of the word to be translated, rather than to the language of production. In this condition, semantic interference and form facilitation were significantly reduced. Of interest is that both Costa, Miozzo, and Caramazza (1999) and Hermans et al. (1998) reported semantic interference in picture naming, regardless of the match between the language of the distractor and the language of production. The difference between picture naming and translation in these Stroop-type tasks mirrors the difference observed in the language switching tasks. In both cases, it appears that language selection may occur earlier in translation than in picture naming by virtue of the presence of the language cue contained within the input itself.

DISCUSSION: SIMILARITIES AND DIFFERENCES BETWEEN COMPREHENSION AND PRODUCTION

In this chapter, we have contrasted comprehension and production to reveal those aspects of bilingual lexical representation and processing that are common to both modes of language use. We now evaluate the outcome of this comparison. It is important to note that some of our conclusions will necessarily be influenced by the fact that most of the research on bilingual word recognition and comprehension has been in the visual domain. The small number of studies on the recognition of spoken words in bilinguals (e.g., Grosjean 1988; Li 1996; Spivey and Marian 1999) makes it difficult to compare the comprehension and production of spoken language alone.

Perhaps the most striking similarity between comprehension and production in bilinguals is the overwhelming evidence for nonselective access to words in both languages, regardless of whether the task logically permits the language of processing to be selected in advance. Comprehension and production also share the consequences of the lower L2 than L1 proficiency in unbalanced bilinguals. In both modes of language use, there appears to be more evidence for effects of L1 on L2 than the reverse, and a suggestion that the relative asymmetry in the magnitude of these cross-language influences may be larger for less fluent bilinguals.

Though the two domains share the aspect of language nonselective access, this does not imply that orthographic, phonological, and semantic codes are used in the same way or at the same moment in processing. For example, the bottom-up nature of comprehension requires that orthographic codes play a larger and earlier role in word recognition than they do in word production, although little is known about the activation of orthography during production. Likewise, the role of phonology is likely to be more critical in production than in comprehension, although, as we have seen, there is overwhelming evidence to suggest that phonology is involved in bilingual word recognition and that it determines, at least in part, the magnitude of cross-language influences. In both domains, there is evidence for semantic processing, but again the contribution of meaning is generally more reliable in production than in comprehension. In comprehension, semantics appear to play a role when there is a consistent correspondence between lexical form and meaning, as in the case of cognates, suggesting that semantic codes are activated even when they are not required by the task.

The time course over which these lexical codes are activated must also be different for comprehension and production. Because the longer time course associated with production provides additional opportunities for feedback and interaction between codes, there is the possibility that the cohort of activated lexical competitors will differ from those available in comprehension. The different nature of orthographic and conceptual representations makes such a difference all the more likely. For instance, it may be that more lexical alternatives are initially activated in comprehension than in production because there are simply more orthographic neighbors of the input word than semantic alternatives for the output concept.

The inherent different nature of comprehension and production also has its effects for factors that may potentially affect lexical selection. There are a large number of variables (e.g., stimulus list composition, language mixing, instructions, language cues, and aspects of attentional control) that may influence lexical selection in each domain. Because comprehension and production differ in the cognitive resources that they require, and because we know that the ability to understand precedes the ability to speak, it seems likely that the role that external factors play in moderating the relative activation of alternatives in each language and in potentially inhibiting the unintended language, will be different.

Furthermore, in production, the language of speaking can and must be determined by the language user; in comprehension the requirement to determine the language in which the task is performed depends in a more complex way on the nature of the task itself. For example, to perform a generalized lexical decision task, it is logically not necessary to specify the language of the activated lexical form. But, to speak a word in order to name a pictured object, it is mandatory that language be specified. Even in the case of highly similar cognate translations, words in two languages rarely have an identical pronunciation, so language must be known if performance is to be error-free.

CONCLUSION

The answers to the questions that we have posed about the bilingual lexicon are, of course, preliminary. As noted earlier, we have said nothing about the comprehension of spoken language in the bilingual, nor have we considered how these questions might be answered for bilinguals for whom the two languages do not share the same alphabet. Rather, our discussion reflects the fact that we are just beginning to develop a theoretical framework for how words in the bilingual's two languages are represented and processed. The current issue driving experimental research is no longer simply whether or not there are two lexical representations, or whether or not processing is language selective. Research has gone beyond that point and now focuses on investigating how the output of activity from the representational system interacts with the processing goals and context in which the languages are used.

The Bilingual Lexicon: An Update

The original chapter had been coauthored by Judith Kroll and Ton Dijkstra; this contribution to the second edition has been authored exclusively by Judith Kroll. Ton Dijkstra has chosen not to participate in this contribution. The conclusion in the original 2002 chapter was that lexical access is fundamentally nonselective with parallel activation of both languages when bilinguals read and speak in one language alone. The research that has been reported during the time since the original chapter first appeared (2002) supports, extends, and refines that conclusion. In the update that follows, progress on each of these topics is reviewed briefly.[1]

The Scope of Nonselectivity

In the domain of comprehension, the earlier review focused on evidence from visual word recognition, suggesting that bottom-up activation of information about orthography and phonology persisted during early stages of processing so that only at a relatively late point in the process was it possible to select the word in the target language. The new data extend these initial claims (see T. Dijkstra, 2005, for a review) showing that there are subtle modulations of cross-language activation sensitive to word frequency (e.g., Smits, Sandra, Martensen, and Dijkstra, 2009) and to the composition of the context in which words are recognized (e.g., Haigh and Jared, 2007). The more recent studies also show that under some circumstances, the L2 has more of an effect on the L1 than might be expected (e.g., Jared and Kroll, 2001; Van Hell and Dijkstra, 2002).

In the 2002 chapter, little evidence was available on bilingual spoken word recognition. There is now a substantial literature that has exploited a range of methods, including eye tracking, to examine the presence of cross-language activation in recognizing spoken words (e.g., Kroll, Gerfen, and Dussias, 2008; Marian, Blumenfeld, and Boukrina, 2008).

Constraining the Parallel Activity of the Two Languages

Although the demonstration of cross-language activation and competition in bilingual word recognition is compelling, it is based almost entirely on studies of isolated word recognition. A critical focus of the recent studies is to ask about the fate of cross-language activation when words appear in sentence context. Quite surprisingly, this newer work shows that the parallel activation of words in the unintended language cannot be overcome easily (e.g., Duyck, Van Assche, Drieghe and Hartsuiker, 2007; Schwartz and Kroll, 2006; Van Hell and De Groot, 2008). These studies show that only when sentence contexts are highly constrained semantically does reading become relatively language selective. However, the ability to maintain a selective focus when reading in the L2 appears quite fragile, with interference from the L1 easily disrupting the ability to "zoom in" to the L2 alone (e.g., Elston-Güttler and Gunter, 2009). The presence of cross-language activation in sentence context is counterintuitive. Knowing the language in which one is reading is not sufficient to overcome the parallel activation of the other language. However, other recent investigations of bilingual sentence processing suggest that not only words but also grammatical structures in each of the bilingual's two languages are active when bilinguals read in one language alone (e.g., Dussias, 2003). It remains for future research to demonstrate the way in which the engagement of the two grammars supports the observed lexical activity.

The Effects of L2 Proficiency

The research on language nonselectivity in bilingual word recognition is also surprising in that the presence of cross-language activity is not simply a matter of relative proficiency in the L2. Proficiency modulates the form of the observed cross-language interactions, but even highly proficient bilinguals show these effects, and, as previously noted, the L2 comes to influence the L1. In the earlier review, there was a suggestion that during early stages of L2 learning, there is evidence for activation of the translation equivalent in the L1 when processing words in the L2, but that once individuals are proficient in both languages, the observed effects tend to be restricted to the activation of lexical form neighbors. A recent study of native English speakers at different levels of proficiency in Spanish as the L2 provides some support for the earlier claims. Sunderman and Kroll (2006) found that only less skilled L2 users appeared to activate the L1 translation equivalent, whereas all learners, regardless of their proficiency, appeared to activate lexical form neighbors. However, Thierry and Wu (2007), using event-related potentials (ERPs), reported that highly proficient native Chinese speakers of English as the L2 were sensitive to the form of the Chinese translation of English words when recognizing words in English alone. Although it is possible that the timing required by the ERP paradigm may have induced the observed translation effects for relatively proficient L2 users, it remains to be seen under what circumstances the L1 translation is activated in comprehension.

CROSS-LANGUAGE ACTIVATION AND SELECTION IN SPOKEN PRODUCTION

There has been an increasing presence of research that examines bilingual spoken production. As noted in the 2002 chapter, finding limited evidence for cross-language activation and competition in comprehension is not surprising given that the task itself is not under the control of the reader or listener. In contrast, speaking is initiated by a thought that the speaker wishes to express. In theory, it should be possible for speakers to specify in advance the language in which they plan to speak in addition to the conceptual content of the message they hope to communicate. There is agreement among most production researchers that lexical alternatives in both languages are active, at least to some point in the process of planning spoken utterances (see, e.g., Costa, 2005, for a review). Like the evidence on bilingual comprehension, there is compelling data to suggest that not only are both languages active during speech planning, but that cross-language activity can be observed to the level of the phonology, even for bilinguals whose languages are quite distinct—in other words, Japanese and English (Hoshino and Kroll, 2008), or spoken English and American Sign Language (Emmorey, Borinstein, Thompson and Gollan, 2008).

There is less agreement on the issue of whether candidates in the unintended language compete for selection and, if so, what mechanism might characterize selection. One class of models assumes that alternatives may be active in both languages but that candidates are selected only from the language the bilingual intends to speak (e.g., Costa et al., 1999; Roelofs and Verhoef, 2006). Consequently, the bilingual is able to function in a language-specific mode by creating a mental firewall between the two languages, even though there may still be evidence of activity of the nontarget language itself. The alternative—that candidates in both languages compete for selection—assumes that parallel activation creates cross-language competition that must be resolved at a relatively late stage of speech planning. Given the latter assumption, it may be necessary to inhibit the unintended language prior to articulation (see Kroll, Bobb, Misra, and Guo, 2008, for arguments about the need for inhibition).

THE COGNITIVE CONSEQUENCES OF CROSS-LANGUAGE COMPETITION

An exciting development has been the report of cognitive advantages for bilinguals who spend a lifetime negotiating the competition across their two languages in selecting the intended words to speak. Although cognitive benefits for bilingual children have been investigated extensively in the past (see Bialystok, 2005, for a review), it is only in the last few years that similar benefits have been reported for the elderly. It is well known that executive control functions decline with aging; bilingualism appears to offer a measure of protection against these cognitive declines with elderly bilinguals outperforming their monolingual counterparts on tasks the require ignoring irrelevant information (e.g., Bialystok, Craik, Klein, and Viswanathan, 2004). The claim that these cognitive advantages are related to the dynamics of bilingual lexical activity is only speculation at this stage. It is tempting to argue that a lifetime of resolving cross-language competition might create the observed benefits, but at present these studies provide only correlational data. In the next stage of research, a priority will be to examine the causal basis of the observed cognitive advantage in executive function. The search for the neural basis of bilingual performance will also surely inform the investigation of these issues.

ACKNOWLEDGMENTS

The writing of this chapter was supported by NSF Grant BCS-9905850 to Judith F. Kroll at The Pennsylvania State University and by NWO Grant B 56–432 to the Nijmegen Institute for Cognition and Information to support collaborative research between Ton Dijkstra and Judith F. Kroll. We thank Albert Costa, Tamar Gollan, David Green, Kristin Lemhöfer, Nanda Poulisse, and Gabriella Vigliocco for helpful comments on the initial manuscript. The writing of the 2008 update was supported by NIH Grant R01-HD053146 to Judith F. Kroll. Correspondence should be addressed to Judith F. Kroll, 641 Moore Building, Department of Psychology, Pennsylvania State University, University Park, PA 16802 (e-mail:jfk7@psu.edu).

NOTE

1. It is beyond the scope of present update to discuss recent studies that have begun to consider the neural underpinnings of the observed activity across the bilingual's two languages. See recent papers by Van Heuven, Schriefers, Dijkstra, and Hagoort (2008) for neural evidence on cross-language competition in comprehension and Abutalebi and Green (2007) on the evidence for activation of brain areas associated with inhibitory control during spoken production. See also Schumann, chapter 17 in this volume.

PART VIII

MULTILINGUALISM IN SOCIETY

CHAPTER 25

LANGUAGE CONTACT

PETER HANS NELDE

I. Language Contact, Multilingualism, and Applied Linguistics

In the last 40 years, scientific research on multilingualism has experienced numerous stimuli, the majority of which can be attributed to language contact research in the Weinreich tradition, going back to his famous *Languages in Contact* (1953). Weinreich's work is based on the fact that speakers or language communities, rather than languages on an abstract level, are in contact with one another, and that any analysis of multilingual behavior is useless without consideration of the linguistic and cultural roots of the given situation. Today, research into language contact is manifest in two volumes of an international handbook (*Contact Linguistics*) which appeared for the first time in Dirven and Pütz (1996 and 1997). The interest of applied linguistics in language contact research or contact linguistics—a term used since the Brussels "Contact and Conflict" congress in 1979—begins with the recognition that the majority of the world's population is multilingual, so that multilingualism is to be regarded as the norm rather than the exception. Although multilingualism and language contact between individuals and groups are as old as the Babylonian confusion of tongues, language contact research first obtained a secure position in applied linguistics in the 1970s through the development of the social sciences. The great significance of multilingualism in the future of Europe and North America and its greater importance in many other parts of the world led to an interdisciplinary interest in contact linguistics, whose relation to multilingualism can be portrayed graphically: see figure 25.1.

Reprinted in Memory of Dr. Nelde.

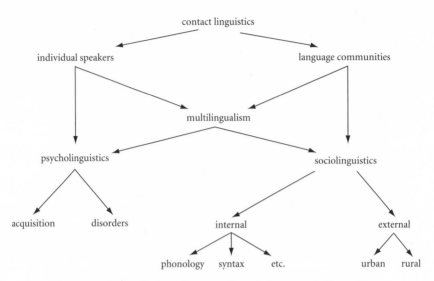

Figure 25.1 The relation of contact linguistics to multilingualism

II. What Is Contact Linguistics?

As an interdisciplinary branch of multilingual research, contact linguistics incorporates three areas of inquiry: language use, language user, and language sphere.

The significant parameters of contact linguistics are linguistic levels (phonology, syntax, lexicon) and also discourse analysis, stylistics, and pragmatics. In addition there are the external linguistic factors: for example, nation, language community, language boundaries, migration, and many others.

The type of multilingualism is also relevant; in other words, whether it manifests itself as individual, institutional, or state bilingualism, as social multilingualism, as diglossia or dialect, or as natural or artificial multilingualism, for which the immediate levels—such as so-called semilingualism or interlinguistics—also must be considered. In the process it is helpful to make a basic, simplifying distinction between autochthonous (native) and allochthonous (migrant, refugee) groups, because instances of language contact can rarely be isolated as single phenomena but, rather, usually as a cluster of characteristics.

The structuring of social groups is of crucial importance to the language user. Besides the conventional differences of age, sex, and social relationship, minority status receives special attention from researchers of multilingualism.

Above and beyond these factors, all of the sectors responsible for the social interplay of a language community play an essential role. Added to traditional sectors like religion, politics, culture, and science in the last few decades are others like technology, industry, city and administration and, most recently, also media, advertising, and data processing. In the educational/cultural sector, the schools occupy a special place, as they are constantly exposed to new forms and models of multilingual instruction from North America and—above all—from Canada. The question of whether bilingual and multilingual education will interfere with a child's right to use his/her mother (home, first, colloquial) tongue depends mainly on the intentions of the respective language planners, so that conformity and integration, instead of language maintenance, constitute the motivating forces of multilingual instruction. To oversimplify the issue, the underprivileged must submit to *bilingual* education and thus to assimilation, while *foreign language* instruction is available to the sociological elite. Contact processes that have concerned researchers in multilingualism since the beginning are partly diachronic and partly synchronic in nature. Besides language change, borrowing processes, interference, and language mixing, there are *linguae francae*, language alternation, language maintenance and loss, code-switching, pidginization, and creolization.

The effects of such language contact processes can be registered by measuring language consciousness and attitude. Language loyalty and prestige play a decisive role in the linguistic identity of a multilingual person, and extreme care must be taken in interpreting so-called language statistics (censuses and public opinion surveys).

The language spheres in which considerations of multilingualism have become indispensable extend over numerous areas of study and are, furthermore, dependent on the respective level of development and interest. These include, to name a few, language policy, language planning, language ecology, language contact in multinational industries and organizations, language care and revitalization among minorities, as well as single development, planned languages, and the role of English as a world language with all the concomitant effects on the respective individual languages. (For a complete list of topics see Nelde et al., 1996.)

Such a bird's-eye view shows well enough how extensive, interdisciplinary, and yet specialized the field of multilingualism is as related to contact linguistics.

III. Contact and Conflict

Ethnic Contact and Conflict and Sociology

Most contact between ethnic groups does not occur in peaceful, harmoniously coexisting communities. Instead, it exhibits varying degrees of tension, resentment, and differences of opinion that are characteristic of every competitive social structure. Under certain conditions, such generally accepted competitive tensions can degenerate into intense conflicts, in the worst case ending in violence. The possibility of conflict erupting is always present, because differences between groups create feelings of uncertainty of status, which could give rise to conflicts. Sociologists who have dealt with contact problems between ethnic groups define conflicts as contentions involving real or apparent fears, interests, and values, in which the goals of the opposing group must be opposed, or at least neutralized, to protect one's own interests (prestige, employment, political power, etc.; Williams, 1947). This type of contention often appears as a conflict of values, in which differing behavioral norms collide, because usually only one norm is considered to be valid. Conflicts between ethnic groups, however, occur only very rarely as openly waged violent conflicts and usually consist of a complex system of threats and sanctions in which the interests and values of one group are endangered. Conflicts can arise relatively easily if—as is usually the case—interests and values have an emotional basis.

The magnitude and the development of a conflict depend on a number of factors determined by level of friction between two or more ethnic groups, the presence of equalizing or mitigating elements, and the degree of uncertainty of all the participants. Thus, a one-sided explanation of the conflict, or one based on irrational prejudices, will fail. Very different factors that influence each other can reinforce and escalate to cause group conflict. This group conflict is part of normal social behavior in which different groups compete with each other, and should therefore not be connoted only negatively, because in this way new—and possibly more peaceful—forms of coexistence can arise. On the other hand, tensions between ethnic groups brought about by feelings of intimidation can give rise to new conflicts at any time—conflicts that can be caused by a minority as well as by a majority group. As long as society continues to create new fears, because of its competitive orientation, the creation of new conflicts appears unavoidable.

Political Language Contact and Conflict

Along with sociologists, political scientists also assume that language contact can cause political conflict. Language conflicts can be brought about by changes in an expanding social system when there is contact between different language groups (Inglehart and Woodward, 1972). Belgium and French Canada are examples of this. The reasons for such a situation are the following: A dominant language group (French in Belgium, English in Canada) controls the crucial authority in the areas of administration, politics, and the economy, and gives employment preference to those applicants who have command of the dominant language. The disadvantaged language group is then left with the choice of renouncing its social ambitions, assimilating, or resisting. Although numerically weak or psychologically weakened language groups tend toward assimilation, in modern societies numerically stronger, more homogeneous language groups possessing traditional values, such as their own history and culture, prefer political resistance, the usual form of organized language conflict in this century. This type of conflict becomes especially salient when it occurs between population groups of differing socioeconomic structures (urban/rural, poor/wealthy, indigenous/immigrant) and when the dominant group requires its own language as a condition for the integration of the rest of the population. Although in the case of French-speaking Canada, English appeared to be the necessary means of communication in trade and business, nearly 80% of the francophone population spoke only French, thus being excluded from social elevation in the political/economic sector. A small French-speaking elite, whose original goal was political opposition to dominant English, ultimately precipitated the outbreak of the latent, socioeconomically motivated language conflict.

Most current language conflicts are the result of differing social status and preferential treatment of the dominant language on the part of the government. In these cases, there are the religious, social, economic, or psychological fears and frustrations of the weaker group that may be responsible for the language conflict. However, a critical factor in the expansion and intensification of such conflict remains the impediment to social mobility, particularly of a disadvantaged or suppressed ethnic group (e.g., the numerous language conflicts in multiethnic Austria-Hungary).

Language problems in very different areas (politics, economics, administration, education) appear under the heading of language conflict. In such cases, politicians and economic leaders seize upon the notion of language conflict, disregarding the actual underlying causes, and thus continue to inflame "from above" the conflict arisen "from below," with the result that language assumes much more importance than it may have had at the outset of the conflict. This language-oriented "surface structure" is used to obscure the more deeply rooted, suppressed "deep structure" (social and economic problems). Furthermore, multilingual conflicts in Europe, especially in urban societies, show quite clearly that language conflicts are caused primarily by attempts on the part of the dominant group to block social mobility.

Language Conflict and Contact Linguistics

Even in contact linguistics the term *conflict* remains ambiguous, at least when it refers generally to social conflict that can arise in a multilingual situation. The notion appears to us essential here that neither contact nor conflict can occur between languages; they are conceivable only between speakers of languages. Oksaar (1980) correctly points out the ambiguity of the term *language conflict* as either conflict between languages within an individual or as conflict by means of language(s), including processes external to the individual. Similarly, Haarmann (1980, 191) distinguishes between interlingual and interethnic language conflicts.

Among the founders of modern research in language contact—running parallel to the rapidly developing sociolinguistics and sociology of language (e.g., Weinreich and Fishman), the term *conflict* rarely appears. Although Weinreich views multilingualism (bilingualism) and the accompanying interference phenomena as the most important form of language contact, without regard to conflict between language communities on the basis of ethnic, religious, or cultural incompatibilities, Fishman (1972: 14) grants language conflict greater importance in connection with language planning. Haugen (1966) was the first to make conflict presentable in language contact research with his detailed analysis of Norwegian language developments. Indeed, even linguists in multilingual countries (e.g., Yugoslavia, Switzerland, Belgium) resisted, up until the end of the 1970s, treating conflict methodically as part of language contact research, since such an "ideologicalization" of language contact appeared to them as "too touchy" (Fishman, 1980: xi). One reason for the late discovery of a term indispensable in today's contact research is to be found in the history of contact linguistics itself: In traditional language contact research (as well as in dialectology and research on linguistic change) the emphasis tended toward closed, geographically homogeneous and easily describable socioeconomic groups, rather than on urban industrial societies, ripe for social and linguistic strife, whose demand for rapid integration laid the groundwork for conflict. However, it is precisely in modern urban society that conflicts result essentially from the normative sanctions of the more powerful, usually majority, group, which demands linguistic adaptation to the detriment of language contact, and thus preprograms conflict with those speakers who are unwilling to adapt.

Despite a less than ideal research situation essentially limited to empirical case studies of language contact, the following statements can be made. Language conflict can occur anywhere there is language contact, chiefly in multilingual communities, although Mattheier (1984: 200) has also demonstrated language conflicts in so-called monolingual local communities. Language conflict arises from the confrontation of differing standards, values, and attitude structures, and strongly influences self-image, upbringing, education, and group consciousness. Thus, conflict can be viewed as a form of contact or, in terms of a model, as a complementary model to the language contact model.

Contact linguists have either described conflict research as an integral part of language contact research (Nelde et al., 1996) or have dealt with special topics from the perspective of conflict. The methods used are heterogeneous and come from numerous neighboring disciplines (psycholinguistics and sociolinguistics, communication research, sociology, etc.). For lack of its own methods, research still employs predominantly empirical procedures. Along with interview and polling techniques, privileged informants and representative sampling, prejudice research and stereotype and attitude observation, the past few years have seen combined investigation models such as socioprofiles and ethnoprofiles, community and polarity profiles (Nelde, 1995).

IV. Essential Principles of Contact Linguistics

These observations on language contact and conflict situations lead to some basic premises of contact linguistic, which, despite their occasional seeming triviality, merit consideration at this juncture:

1. Language contact exists only between speakers and language communities, not between languages. Comparison of one and the same language in different contexts is therefore possible only in a quite limited way.

2. The statement that there can be no language contact without language conflict ("Nelde's Law"; K. de Bot, 1997: 51) may appear exaggerated, but

there is in the realm of the European languages at present no imaginable contact situation that cannot also be described as language conflict.

3. Contact linguistics usually sees language as a significant secondary symbol of fundamental causes of conflict of a socioeconomic, political, religious, psychological, or historical sort. Thus, in a way, language conflict appears to be the lesser evil, because it apparently can be more easily corrected and neutralized than primary sociopolitical conflicts.

4. Contact linguistics, at the same time, makes it clear that conflicts should not be condemned as only negative, but, rather, it proves that new structures that are more advantageous than the foregoing ones can often result from conflicts.

V. Typology of Conflict

The current language conflicts in Europe, North and Central America, Southeast Asia, and parts of Africa can be viewed as situations of either *natural* or *artificial* language conflict.

Natural Language Conflict

Natural language conflicts are those situations that have traditionally existed between indigenous majorities and minorities. The extensive literature of language conflict abounds with examples of this type, particularly those of minorities pitted against official national or regional languages. Conflict has frequently arisen in these situations of language contact because the linguistic minority was not in a position to assimilate. This type of conflict can be found, for example, in Europe along the Germanic-Romance and the Slavic-Germanic linguistic boundaries, and in Canada involving the French-speaking minority and among a few indigenous peoples. Natural language conflicts can become problematic when ideology on either side—not only the majority but the minority as well—is used to intensify the differences that exist, and peaceful coexistence between language communities can easily be threatened when the banner of language is hoisted as the defining symbol of a people.

The conflict between Belfast (Northern Ireland) and Connemara (North of Galway in the Irish republic), for example, involves considerably more than just language: An urban, Protestant, working environment (Belfast) in fact has little if anything in common with a rural, Catholic region of high unemployment (Connemara). The issue of language only exacerbates these differences.

A similar situation is reflected in the ideologically motivated opposition between Afrikaans and English in Namibia (and also in South Africa). The vast majority of the Namibian populace, regardless of race or social status, speaks or at least understands Afrikaans. The country's official language, however, is English, cast as the "language of freedom," though less than 3% of the population speak it as their first language. Afrikaans, the former language of instruction and administration, remains the "language of oppression."

More recently, the study of Russian has witnessed a rapid decline in the former Eastern Bloc countries, and one can only speculate on the relationship between the sudden lack of interest in Russian and the "de-ideologicalization" of that language in the new republics. After 1992, in the Croatian part of Bosnia-Herzegovina (*Herzeg*), all mentions of the term *Serbo-Croatian* have been expunged from schoolbooks and replaced, not on linguistic but on ideological grounds, by the term *Croatian*.

Artificial Language Conflict

Artificial, or self-imposed, conflict arises out of situations of compromise in which one or more language communities are disfavored. These situations have existed in every society from Babel to Brussels. Symmetric multilingualism, in which equal numbers of speakers are invested with equal rights and in which both language prestige and linguistic identities are congruent, is impossible, because one of the language groups will always be subject to stigmatization and/or discrimination, with conflict the inevitable result.

Artificial language conflict occurs especially when, motivated by the need for rapid international communication, politically influential economic powers export their languages (and their resulting socioeconomic influence) to their trading partners. Thus, Russian (before 1990) and English have become languages of great economic expansion, despite a noteworthy lack of formal educational planning. Secondary schools in Strasbourg, for example, have abandoned study of the native German dialect for English (as the first foreign language), with the result that German is being lost as a local working language. It is offered as a second "foreign" language only to students over 12 years old, with the result that a passive knowledge of the mother tongue (a German dialect) is now all that remains.

The European Union has provided interesting examples of artificial language conflict. In the "Which language(s) for Europe?" debate, the Danes years ago, in a spirit of genuine cooperation, seemed to have opted to forgo the use of Danish. In retrospect, Denmark may appear to have resolved the issue, in the early years of the European Union, of reducing the number of official languages to at most two, with English and French destined to be the languages of international communication. The initial delight of London and Paris at this helpful suggestion was quickly dampened, however, because the Danes also suggested that the English should use French and the French should use English. After that suggestion, enthusiasm for the Danish solution quickly withered.

The presence of almost 4,000 translators and interpreters in Brussels suggests a return to the Tower of Babel. At the present time (the year 2000), the 11 working languages of the 15 member states generate a total of ($10 \times 11 =$) 110 language combinations. The enlargement of the European Union by six or more additional member states in the coming years, with several new languages, leads to so many mathematical combinations that no assembly hall in the world would be able to accommodate meetings for all the interpreters.

These examples amply demonstrate that the language contacts and conflicts that threaten the peaceful coexistence of peoples are not always the consequence of long-standing historical contacts and conflicts among language communities. The new orders and restructurings of recent years have also led to sources of conflict that were not fully grasped just a few years ago. In any event, neither *natural* nor *artificial* conflict should be judged only negatively; rather, we should hope that out of conflict there may ensue new alliances and new solutions that will function better than any of the efforts of the past.

VI. Future Prospects

There are hardly any areas of human life that do not have to do with language contact and multilingualism in some way. Since its renaissance in the 1950s and 1960s, research on multilingualism has been carried out on contact linguistic initiatives due to the inclusion of neighboring disciplines like sociology, psychology, and many others. In the new century, younger subdisciplines will probably play a leading role because of their pronounced orientation to practical applications. The difference between the so-called internal and external linguistic criteria that was stressed in the past will be abandoned, because the interdependence and inseparability of these factors has become apparent in the most recent research results. In addition to the traditional ("hyphenated") linguistic disciplines, these areas of research will surely include ecolinguistics, which has already provided research on language contact with many new stimuli. In the area of the conflict issues mentioned before, ecolinguistic initiatives have proved to be particularly successful, so much so that the constantly changing forms of language contact and multilingualism can be described more satisfactorily. More and more new migrant groups (evacuees, asylum seekers, refugees, expatriates) are being included in the traditional autochthonous and allochthonous forms of multilingualism, in addition to the native minorities. Here, we see, at the beginning of the new century, new language contact research fields arising. One example is connected to the development of the new media and their dominant role in changing societal structures by destroying traditional fields in the society. This also has an enormous influence on the central concept of contact linguistics that remains multilingualism. In future research, we have to develop new forms of multilingualism that are emerging from virtual contacts and from new economic-based minorities. It is one of the chief tasks of contact linguistics to meet this challenge and concern itself more intensively than in the past with a field that can serve as an outstanding example of applied science, the significance of which for life and survival on an overpopulated planet with hundreds of different languages cannot be overvalued.

CHAPTER 26

PIDGINS AND CREOLES

JEFF SIEGEL

I. INTRODUCTION

PIDGINS and creoles are new languages that develop in language contact situations because of a need for communication among people who do not share a common language. A pidgin continues to be used primarily as a second language for intergroup communication, whereas a creole has become the mother tongue of a particular group of speakers. The lexicon of a pidgin or creole is derived from the various languages originally in contact, with the majority usually coming from one particular language, called the *lexifier*. However, the grammar of a pidgin or creole is different from that of the lexifier or any of the other contributing languages.

Most scholars in the field of pidgin and creole studies (or "creolistics") would agree on these characterizations of the languages they study, but on little else. A great deal of controversy has existed in the field since it became a separate (and ultimately respectable) area of linguistics in the 1960s. There are disagreements about the precise definitions of *pidgin* and *creole*, about which language varieties are actually pidgins or creoles, and about the origins of the linguistic features of these languages. Because these theoretical controversies are given excellent coverage in other overviews, textbooks, and compilations (e.g., Singler and Kouwenberg, 2008; Rickford and McWhorter, 1997; Sebba 1997), I outline them only briefly here. Then I present some sociolinguistic background information on speakers, status, and attitudes. Finally, I go on to discuss some areas of applied linguistics that concern pidgins and creoles.

II. THE ORIGINS AND DEFINITIONS OF PIDGIN AND CREOLES

Pidgins most often arise in situations involving trading or large-scale population movement. An earlier *prepidgin* or *jargon*, which is quite variable in structure, may later become a *stable* pidgin, which has developed its own lexical and grammatical norms. However, compared to the contributing languages in contact, the stable pidgin is formally less complex, having a much smaller total lexicon and little if any morphological marking of grammatical categories. Two examples are Russonorsk and Pidgin Fijian.[1] A stable pidgin is normally quite restricted in function, but in some cases it may later extend into wider areas. As a result, the language becomes lexically and grammatically more complex. It is then called an *expanded* pidgin. An example is Melanesian Pidgin, now spoken as three main dialects: Tok Pisin in Papua New Guinea, Pijin in the Solomon Islands, and Bislama in Vanuatu.

When a pidgin (or prepidgin) is learned by children as their first language and becomes the mother tongue of a new community, it is called a creole. Unlike pidgins, creoles are not restricted in use and are like any other vernacular language in having a full range of informal functions. Creoles are also more complex than pidgins in terms of lexicon, morphology, and grammatical rules. Some creoles seem to have arisen very quickly, perhaps even before a stable pidgin had developed—for example, among children of slaves born in the Caribbean (e.g., Jamaican Creole). Other creoles clearly developed from a preexisting stable pidgin—for example, among Australian Aboriginal children in the Northern Territory who were brought up at a mission station where their parents took refuge from murderous White invaders (Northern Australian Kriol).

Terminological controversies in the field result from researchers focusing on different aspects of these languages. The perfect example is Melanesian "Pidgin." For those who consider sociolinguistic criteria, some call it a *pidgin* because it is a second language rather than the mother tongue for the large majority of its speakers. Others call it a *creole* because it has some native speakers and it is used in a wide range of functions. Those who consider only linguistic criteria call it a *creole* because the grammatical features that it has developed are just as complex as those of clearly recognized creoles. Closely related to this controversy is the recent debate over whether creoles can be defined as a coherent group of languages according to purely linguistic criteria and whether they actually have pidgin predecessors (DeGraff, 2001a, 2001b; McWhorter, 1998, 2001).

An issue that has dominated the field of pidgin and creole studies for a hundred years is explaining the origins of the grammatical features of creoles and the apparent grammatical similarities among creole languages the world over. There are basically three main camps: the substratists, the superstratists, and the universalists. The substratists (e.g., Alleyne, 1980; Lefebvre, 1998) believe that the features can be traced back to the substrate languages—for example, that the features of Caribbean creoles are derived from the West African languages of the slaves. The superstratists (especially Chaudenson, 1992, 2001) believe that the features can be traced back to both standard and nonstandard varieties of the lexifier language. The universalists (especially Bickerton, 1981, 1984) believe that creoles reflect characteristics of innate human linguistic endowment and that only this can explain the similarities between far-removed creoles.

Over the past decades, a lot of time and energy has been spent supporting one of these positions (and attacking others). However, most creolists these days believe in some kind of compromise (see Michaelis, 2008). In recent times, many scholars have moved on to concentrate on the cognitive processes and constraints that may be relevant to pidgin and creole genesis—for example, by looking more closely at research in first and second language acquisition (e.g., DeGraff, 1999; Lefebvre, White, and Jourdan, 2006; Siegel, 2008).

In some pidgin and creole situations, especially where English is the lexifier language as well as the language of government and education (as in Guyana, Hawai'i and Australia, for example), a continuum of varieties exists. These range from what is called the *basilect* (furthest from the lexifier) to the *acrolect* (closest to the lexifier), with intermediate varieties, the *mesolects*, in between. This kind of continuum was thought to have arisen from a process of *decreolization* that occurs when creole speakers come into greater contact with the lexifier language (for example, through more widespread education). In this process, the grammatical rules of the creole supposedly change to become more like those of the standard form of the lexifier. Linguists such as Bickerton (1975) believed that synchronic variation along the continuum reflected diachronic language change.

However, several issues have been debated with regard to the notions of decreolization and the creole continuum. First, there is the view that the continua of internal variation are not necessarily the result of decreolization but were present in many creoles from the beginning (e.g., Alleyne, 1971; Valdman, 1991). Second, many scholars have thought that linguistic change in creoles does not necessarily take place in the direction of the lexifier (e.g., Bailey and Maynor, 1998; LePage, 1977). In fact, some creolists (e.g., Mufwene, 2001) believe that creoles develop via a process of gradual basilectalization, in which a creole becomes more unlike its lexifier, rather than decreolization, in which it becomes more like its lexifier. Third, the whole concept of the creole continuum has been attacked on two fronts. Scholars such as LePage and Tabouret-Keller (1985) argue against the notion of variation in the continuum occurring along a single dimension. Other researchers reject the whole notion of a continuum in some situations, favoring a model with two discrete systems, the creole and the lexifier (W. Edwards, 1983; Lawton, 1980; Siegel, 1997a), or a model with an intermediate system as well (Winford 1997a), and code-switching between the systems. (For more recent work on creole continuum situations see, Patrick, 1999, and Inoue, 2007.)

Finally, there are debates about whether particular languages are (or were) creoles. The most well known example is African American Vernacular English (AAVE; see Rickford, 1999; Winford 1997b, 1998). Other languages with disputed "creoleness" are Afrikaans, Brazilian Portuguese, Kituba, Shaba Swahili, and various "mixed" languages, such as Michif. In order to avoid these controversies, I will be dealing only with undisputed creoles in this chapter, but many of the applied issues are also relevant to varieties such as AAVE.

III. Sociolinguistic Background

The applied issues discussed below are mainly relevant to expanded pidgins and creoles, which I will group together for convenience using the abbreviation P/C (pidgin/creole). There are at least 124 million speakers of P/Cs—101 million of expanded pidgins and 23 million of creoles (based on figures in Gordon, 2005).[2] They are spoken by indigenous populations in at least 50 countries or territories and by immigrants in many other places—for example, up to one million speakers of Haitian Creole in the United States (Joseph, 1997: 281). Note that *pidgin* and *creole* are technical terms used by linguists and not necessarily by speakers of the languages. For example, speakers of Jamaican Creole call their language *Patwa* (from *patois*).

In most places where a P/C is spoken, its speakers form a majority of the population—for example, in Cape Verde, Mauritius, Papua New Guinea, and most Caribbean nations. In other places, however, P/C speakers are a minority—for example, Kriol and Torres Strait Creole speakers in Australia, and Gullah and Louisiana Creole speakers in the United States. Creole-speaking immigrants are also substantial minorities in Britain, Canada, the Netherlands, the United States, and other countries. In some places, P/C speakers are the majority in a particular state or territory, but a minority in the country as a whole—for example, in Hawai'i in the United States.

In nearly all cases, P/Cs are spoken mainly in informal contexts, whereas a different language—most often the standard form of a European language—is the official language of government, the law, and education. An important factor is whether or not this official language is the same as the lexifier language of the P/C. When the lexifier and the official language are different, as with English-lexified Sranan and Dutch in Surinam, the P/C is recognized as a separate, autonomous language (Winford, 1994). When they are the same, the P/C is often perceived as nonautonomous.

Like other languages, P/Cs are valued by their speakers in the private domains of family and friendship. Speakers often have positive attitudes toward their language as a marker of solidarity and local social identity, as reported for Hawai'i Creole (Sato, 1991; Watson-Gegeo, 1994), Australian Kriol (Siegel, 1998), and Dominica Creole French (Fontaine and Leather, 1992). But unlike other languages, P/Cs are rarely valued in public formal domains and, as a result, they generally suffer from overall negative attitudes and low prestige (see, for example, Rickford and Traugott, 1985; Winford, 1994).

The stigmatization of P/Cs can in some ways be attributed to the nature of these languages and their origins as described above. First of all, as languages of former indentured laborers or slaves, P/Cs are associated with repression and powerlessness, and indeed to this day they are often spoken by disadvantaged sections of society. In contrast, it is the official language that has high prestige and is seen as the key to success. Second, as the new languages of relatively recently formed speech communities, P/Cs suffer from comparison to the official languages with their long historical traditions and bodies of literature (Alleyne, 1994). Third, P/Cs are often not considered to be legitimate languages but rather are seen as a deviant and corrupt form of their lexifiers. This is especially true in situations in which a P/C coexists with the standard form of its lexifier. This view is reinforced by the fact that, at least superficially, the P/C and the standard share the same lexicon. The P/C is not seen to have its own grammatical rules, and so the way it is spoken is considered to be the result of performance errors rather than of language differences. This lack of autonomy is exacerbated in countries like Jamaica and Guyana, where there is a creole continuum, as there seems to be no clear dividing line between the lexifier and the creole. In addition, in such situations the more creole-like varieties at the basilectal end of the continuum have lower social status than the more standard-like varieties at the acrolectal end.

Hawai'i Creole, locally known as *Pidgin*, is a good example of a P/C that has been denigrated over the years by teachers, administrators, and community leaders. A history of attitudes toward the language is presented in a recent position paper, "Pidgin and Education," by a group of interested staff and students at the University of Hawai'i (Da Pidgin Coup, 1999: 6–8). It notes that in publications starting from the 1920s, Pidgin was consistently labeled with negative terms such as "lazy," "ungrammatical," "faulty," "sloppy," "slothful" and "ugly." In the 1930s and 1940s, it was even considered a speech defect. In 1962, a major local newspaper compared Pidgin to the language of animals in an editorial entitled "Why Not Just Grunt?" (*Honolulu Star-Bulletin*, February 13, 1962). Such extreme statements are now getting harder to find, but the language is still commonly referred to as "bad English" or "broken English."

When the field of pidgin and creole studies emerged in the 1960s, linguists produced many studies showing that P/Cs are legitimate, rule-governed varieties of language that differ in systematic ways from recognized standard languages. These studies have had a limited effect, but they have led to more positive attitudes in some sections of P/C-speaking populations (see Mühleisen, 2002) and to efforts to raise the status and extend the functions of some P/Cs. This brings us to the issues of applied linguistics.

IV. Applied Issues

Following current trends in linguistics over the last quarter century, pidgins and creoles have often been abstracted away from the populations who speak them. As Alleyne (1994), Rickford (1997), and others have pointed out, most creolists have been more interested in working on the hot theoretical issues than on the applied issues that directly affect the speakers of the languages they study. Nevertheless, some applied work has been done in the areas of language planning, language and education, and language and the law.

Language Planning

Over the years, there have been many calls to expand the use of particular P/Cs into public and official areas such as government, broadcast media, and education. Most of the arguments for this expansion are sociopolitical, pointing out that a large proportion of the population is disenfranchised by not knowing the established official language. The use of the P/C in government and other official domains would give people greater access and allow them to participate in decision-making processes, thus counteracting neocolonialism and elitism. (See, for example, Bebel-Gisler, 1981; Devonish, 2007.) Therefore, the ideology behind language planning involving P/Cs has largely involved vernacularization (Cobarrubias, 1983), but in most cases the planning has been initiated by religious groups or popular movements, rather than by government organizations.

With regard to status planning efforts (Haugen, 1983), the aim in all cases has been to increase both the status and functions of the P/C so that it is used in official contexts alongside the existing official language (instrumentalization). With regard to corpus planning, the major activity has been codification: choosing a variety of the P/C to be used for these wider functions and developing a writing system for it (graphization).

The codification of a P/C does not involve developing a "standard" in the usual sense of the term. This is so because of two additional goals of codification in P/C contexts:

1. Developing a variety of the P/C that would be accessible to the majority of its speakers
2. Making the P/C autonomous from its lexifier so that it is perceived as a separate, legitimate language

For other languages, a standard is developed on the basis of a prestige variety used by the social elite and found in an established literary tradition. In addition, it is often modeled on an already established standard used in the community (such as Latin in the European context). In contrast, a P/C normally has no established literary tradition. The prestige variety is the form closest to the lexifier, and the established standard is often the lexifier itself—both spoken by only a small elite class (see Sebba, 1997). Obviously the goals of accessibility and autonomy would not be accomplished by developing a standard form of the P/C on the basis of the lexifier.

Instead, codification of P/Cs has involved selecting the varieties distinct from the lexifier that would be the most efficient to use for communication within the P/C-speaking community. Where there is a creole continuum, this could mean selecting the most common intermediate or mesolectal varieties considered to be acceptable forms of the creole. Although such a method has been advocated for the

English-lexified creoles of the Caribbean (Devonish, 2007: 122), it has not been accomplished to any degree. An alternative is to select the most widespread variety of the P/C that is furthest from the lexifier, usually the rural or basilectal variety as opposed to the urban variety more influenced by the lexifier. This is what has occurred with Tok Pisin in Papua New Guinea (Wurm, 1980). The argument there was that urban speakers would be more familiar with the more conservative rural varieties than rural speakers would be with the more innovative and anglicized urban varieties. Although Tok Pisin is usually seen as a success story in P/C language planning, with the language widely used in some official functions, Romaine (1992, 1994a) sees increasing "linguistic fragmentation" in the language with the gap between urban and rural varieties growing.

The extension of a P/C into formal domains necessarily involves its becoming a written language. The choice of an orthography is again influenced by the nature of P/Cs and people's attitudes toward them. There are basically two types of orthographies used for P/Cs: etymological and phonemic.[3] An etymological orthography is generally based on the conventional spelling of the lexifier language—for example, in Hawai'i Creole:

They wen' buy 'em las' night.
["They bought it last night."]

This type of orthography is easy to read for those literate in the lexifier, but it reinforces the view that the P/C is a deviant variety of that language. On the other hand, a phonemic orthography is based on the sounds that actually occur in the P/C without any reference to the lexifier, ideally with one symbol for each sound. Here is the same Hawai'i Creole sentence in a phonemic orthography:

Dei wen bai om ls nait.

This type of orthography reinforces the autonomy of the P/C, but it is not easy to read for those literate in the lexifier. Other advantages and disadvantages of each type are described by Winer (1990).

There are also two types of compromise orthographic systems. A modified etymological orthography distinguishes the salient linguistic features of the P/C and uses phonemic representation for words not from the lexifier (Winer, 1990). An intermediate phonemic orthography basically has one symbol (or digraph) for one phoneme, but in some cases it uses the spelling conventions of the lexifier—for example, <ou>for /u/ in French-lexified creoles (Schieffelin and Doucet, 1994).

Supporters of a phonemic orthography believe that it is easier for illiterate people to learn to read and that therefore, along with the autonomy factors, it is better suited to fulfill the libertarian goals of access and equity. Supporters of an etymological orthography believe that there will always be bilingualism and a need to become literate in the lexifier, and that similar orthographies will promote this biliteracy. Sociopolitical ideologies also affect orthographic preferences. For example,

Schieffelin and Doucet (1994) describe how some groups in Haiti oppose an etymo-logical orthography because of its association with French (the language of the former colonial power), whereas others oppose the phonemic orthography because it looks too much like English (the language of the English-speaking Americans, who occupied Haiti from 1915 to 1934).

The first Haitian Creole orthography was developed in the 1920s, and there have been several others proposed since then, all surrounded by vigorous ideological debates. The current official system, *òtograf IPN* (Institute Pédagogique National) is an intermediate phonemic orthography developed in the mid-1970s and made offi-cial in 1980. This system is now widely used by the writers of Haitian Creole, although it still has its pro-etymological detractors, such as Métellus (1998). Also in the Carib-bean, orthographies based on the Haitian IPN model were developed for the French-lexified creoles of Guadeloupe and Martinique in the mid-1970s and for those of St. Lucia and Dominica in the early 1980s. These are in general use, although alterna-tives have been proposed (Bernabé, 2001; Hazäel-Massieux, 1993). In the Indian Ocean, a phonemic orthography was developed for Seselwa in 1976 (Bollée, 1993), but this was later amended to be more similar to that of Haitian Creole (P. Baker, 1991). At least four different phonemically based orthographies have been devised for Mauritian Creole, but none of these have achieved official recognition. However, the Mauritius Ministry of Education has recently released a proposal for a standard orthography that appears to have wide acceptance (Hookoomsingh, 2004).

With regard to English-lexifier P/Cs, Tok Pisin had several different orthogra-phies being used from 1935 through the 1950s, when standardization efforts began. A standard finally emerged from that used in the Tok Pisin translation of the New Testament, published in 1968 (Wurm, 1985). Agreement on an orthography for Bislama did not occur until 1995 (Crowley, 2000). An orthography for Jamaican Creole (which could be adapted for other English-lexified creoles in the Caribbean) was developed by Cassidy (1961, 1993), and one for Hawai'i Creole was developed by Odo (see Bickerton and Odo, 1976). These orthographies are widely used by lin-guists but rarely by others. For example, nearly all literature in Hawai'i Creole and the recent translation of the New Testament use different modified etymological orthographies rather than the phonemic Odo orthography. Sranan (Surinam) also has an official (largely) phonemic orthography that is not widely accepted (Sebba, 2000). An intermediate "rule-based" orthography developed specifically for Belize Kriol in the mid-1990s seems to have more acceptance (Decker, 1995).

Regarding other creoles, Papiamentu has two official orthographies, both widely used: an etymological one used on the island of Aruba and a more phonemic one used on Curaao and Bonaire (Kouwenberg and Muysken, 1994). In 1998, the government of Cape Verde decided to support officially a unified orthography for Capeverdian (Gonsalvez, 1999).

In other aspects of corpus planning, there are at least 20 P/Cs that have a dictio-nary or a detailed grammar or both. Of course, some have more than one—for example, Haitian Creole with at least half a dozen dictionaries. However, govern-ment-sponsored language planning organizations for P/Cs are not very common.

I am aware of only three: *Instituto Lingwistiko Antiano* for Papiamento in the Netherlands Antilles (Dijkhoff, 1993), *Lenstiti Kreol* in the Seychelles (Bollée, 1993), and the Jamaican Language Unit (Brown-Blake, 2008: 33–34n). Nongovernment organizations that conduct some language planning activities exist in other countries—for example, the Folk Research Centre in St. Lucia (Frank, 1993) and *Komité pou Etid Kwéyòl* in Dominica (Stuart, 1993).

With regard to instrumentalization, one of the first extensions of the use of P/Cs has been their adaptation by various Christian churches for use in religion. There are translations of the New Testament in many P/Cs—for example, all three dialects of Melanesian Pidgin, Cameroon Pidgin, Sranan, Haitian Creole, St. Lucia Creole, Papiamento, and Sango. These P/Cs are also commonly used in religious services by most denominations.

Extension into secular written literature has also occurred for nearly all P/Cs, but with different degrees of popularity. For example, in the Seychelles, short stories in Seselwa began to appear in 1979, and by the late 1980s six novels and several collections of short stories and children's stories were in print (Bollée, 1993: 91). However, Mahoune (2000) reports that today very few people actually write in the standardized creole. On the other hand, literature in Haitian Creole has been more varied and more popular. The highly acclaimed novel *Dezafi* by Franketienne appeared in 1975 and a detailed historical work by Michel-Rolph Trouillot in 1977 (Schieffelin and Doucet, 1994: 183). Since then, a substantial body of Haitian Creole literature has developed in novels, short stories, plays, and poetry (St Fort, 2000).

Literature is one of the few areas into which most English-lexified P/Cs have extended. For example, poetry, short stories, and plays have been written in Nigerian Pidgin and Cameroon Pidgin (Todd, 1990: 75–77). Throughout the Caribbean, English-lexified creoles are used in stories, especially in dialogue, and also in songs, poems, and plays (Winer, 1990). Jamaican Creole is also widely used in cartoons and comics, and since the 1990s it has been used in stories as the voice of first- and third-person narration. In recent years, Hawai'i Creole has also become a literary language, with the appearance of many popular short stories and poems and several novels using dialogue in the language. Romaine observes that the emergence of Hawai'i Creole as a literary medium is "a sign of the vitality of a language coming of age and gaining status" (1994b: 551).

In contrast, Mühlhäusler (1995, 1996a) and Charpentier (1997) claim that literacy in Melanesian and Australian P/Cs is something that has been imposed by Europeans on speakers of these languages and that it is basically irrelevant to their societies. However, in a rebuttal of these claims (Siegel, 1998), I present evidence showing that although the idea of literacy has been introduced from the outside, it has been adopted by speakers of Melanesian and Australian P/Cs for their own purposes and now plays an important part in their communities.

The broadcast and print media is another area of expansion for most P/Cs, except for English-lexified creoles in which English is the official language. Most common is radio broadcasting, especially for news and announcements. Haitian Creole and Seselwa are also used on television. Use in the print media is somewhat limited in comparison, but Papiamento is widely used in daily newspapers and magazines. News reports in Seselwa and Tok Pisin can also be found on the Internet.

Some P/Cs are now used in politics—for example, in political speeches during election campaigns. This occurs in St. Lucia, but the creole is not used in Parliament. However, in other countries, such as Papua New Guinea, Vanuatu, and the Seychelle Islands, the P/C is the frequently the language of parliamentary debate. At least three countries have declared a P/C as a national and official language: the Seychelles (1979), Vanuatu (1980), and Haiti (1987). So certainly some P/Cs have gained a fair amount of status. But as Sebba (1997: 258) points out, no P/C has ever been the sole official language of a country. These official P/Cs share their official status with English or French (or both), which generally still have more prestige.

In summary, since the 1970s, linguists have been involved in language planning for P/Cs, particularly in instrumentalization and orthography development. In some places, especially where there is a creole continuum, their efforts have had little effect on actual language use and attitudes. But in others, the functions of P/Cs have expanded in to new areas and, as Dejean (1993: 80) notes for Haiti, at least creole voices are now being heard more often.

Language and Education

One official area into which P/Cs have been slow in expanding is education. (For an overview, see Simmons-McDonald, 2004.) Although P/Cs are sometimes used informally in the classroom, the official language of education in almost all contexts is still a standard variety that most P/C-speaking students do not know. As a result, these students face inequities in formal education, as reported for creole speakers in the Caribbean (Devonish, 2007; LePage, 1968; Winer, 1989) and for creole-speaking immigrants in Britain (Dalphinis, 1991; V. Edwards, 1979) and North America (Coelho, 1988; Winer, 1993). These inequities include

1. Negative attitudes and ignorance of teachers (Breinberg, 1986; Pratt-Johnson, 1993)
2. Negative attitudes and poor self-image of the students themselves because of denigration of their speech and culture (Fischer, 1992)
3. Repression of self-expression because of the need to use an unfamiliar form of language (Feldman, Stone, and Renderer, 1990)
4. Difficulty in acquiring literacy in a second language (UNESCO, 1968)

An obvious way to deal with these inequities would be to use the language of the students as a language of instruction or a subject of study. But this is rarely done. More common, in fact, are calls to ban the P/C from the schools, as has occurred in Hawai'i (Eades et al., 2006; Sato, 1991).

The reasons for not using P/Cs in education are closely related to the nature of these languages and the prevailing attitudes toward them. First of all, many people, including educators, still believe that P/Cs are deviant forms of the standard and thus not suitable for education. Such attitudes have been reported for many P/Cs, such as Carriacou Creole English (Kephart, 1992), other varieties of creole in the Caribbean (Alleyne, 1994; Winford, 1994), Krio in Sierra Leone (Fyle, 1994), Nigerian Pidgin (Elugbe, 1994), Hawai'i Creole English (Sato, 1985), Torres Strait Creole (Shnukal, 1992), and Tok Pisin (Nidue, 1988).

But even when P/Cs are recognized as legitimate languages, some educators, administrators, and linguists still argue that using them in education would be both impractical and detrimental to students. One argument concerns the lack of standardization. Especially in situations in which there is a creole continuum, it is difficult to select a norm to be used in education. Another "impractical" argument is that even if P/Cs could be standardized, the cost of developing written materials would be a disadvantage. Thus, linguists such as Todd (1990) advocate only the oral use of P/Cs in the classroom to facilitate communication in the early years, but not the written use.

The "detrimental" arguments are premised on the belief that a goal of the education system should be the acquisition of the standard language of education. Thus, learning in or about a P/C is seen as a waste of time—time that would be better spent learning the standard. Closely related is the "ghettoization" argument (C. E. Snow, 1990), which asserts that using a nonstandard variety of speech in the classroom deprives children of the instruction they need to get the economic benefits that speakers of standard varieties have and condemns them to permanent underclass status. This argument has been used, for example, to oppose Torres Strait Creole as an educational language (Shnukal, 1992: 4). Third is the "interference" argument, which claims that using a P/C in education will make it difficult for students to learn the standard because of negative transfer or confusion between the two closely related varieties. Thus, according to Charpentier (1997: 236), using Bislama along with English in education in Vanuatu would "lead to a social, psychological and pedagogical blockage, seriously compromising any passage to literacy."

The "impractical" arguments are countered by the existence of viable educational programs that use creoles as the languages of instruction and initial literacy in primary schools. One example occurs in the Seychelles, where Seselwa has been the primary medium of instruction in all schools since 1981 (Bollée, 1993). Another was in Australia, where a bilingual program using Kriol ran for more than 20 years at the Barunga Community Education Centre (Siegel, 1993). Both programs reported successful outcomes despite some initial problems in standardization, and the Barunga program illustrated how materials can be produced locally at very low cost using modern desktop publishing technology (Northern Territory Department of Education, 1995).

The major premise of the "detrimental" arguments is not accepted by many linguists. Devonish (2007), for example, argues that if creoles were used in more official capacities in creole-speaking countries, speakers would not need to learn the European standard. But even if the learning of this standard is accepted as the goal of education, there is no evidence that using a P/C in school is detrimental. On the contrary, research in Australia (Murtagh, 1982), in the Seychelles (Ravel and Thomas, 1985), in Carriacou (Kephart, 1992), and in Papua New Guinea (Siegel, 1997b) demonstrates that using a P/C in formal education has no negative effect on the subsequent acquisition of the standard language and may even be advantageous.[4]

Three types of educational programs using P/Cs are in existence: instrumental, accommodation, and awareness. Instrumental programs use a P/C as a medium of instruction to teach initial literacy and content subjects such as mathematics, science, and health. In addition to those in the Seychelles and Australia mentioned above, there are nationwide instrumental programs in primary schools using Haitian Creole (Bentolila, 1987; Dejean, 1993; Valdman, 1989) and Papiamentu (Appel and Verhoeven, 1994; Ferrier, n.d.). There are also some individual or experimental instrumental programs using Tok Pisin (Ray, 1996; Wiruk, 2000), Torres Strait Creole (Turner, 1997), Guadeloupean Creole (Faure, 2000), San Andres Creole (Morren, 2001), and Jamaican Creole (Devonish and Carpenter, 2007). In the United States, bilingual programs have existed for immigrants speaking Haitian Creole (Joseph, 1997; Zéphir, 1997) and Capeverdean (Gonsalvez, 1996). P/Cs are also used in nonformal adult educational programs in Britain, Dominica, Mauritius, Solomon Islands, St. Lucia, and Vanuatu (for references, see Siegel, 1999a).[5]

In accommodation programs, a P/C is accepted in the classroom, but it is not a medium of instruction or subject of study. In the early years of school, students are allowed to use their home varieties of language for speaking and sometimes writing, and teachers may utilize their students' own interactional patterns and stories for teaching the standard. Individual accommodation programs of this type have existed in Hawai'i (e.g., Boggs, 1985; Rynkofs, 1993). At the higher levels, literature and creative writing in local P/Cs may be accommodated into the curriculum, as has been done in Trinidad and Tobago (Winer, 1990).

Awareness programs make P/Cs a topic of study. The students' own varieties are put into context by teaching some basic sociolinguistics about different language varieties, standardization, and language attitudes. In some cases, the P/C's grammatical rules and pragmatics are explicitly contrasted with those of the standard variety. An objective here is helping students to acquire the standard by focusing on how its structure and use are different from their own varieties.[6] In Hawai'i, two of the government-funded programs for creole speakers referred to by Watson-Gegeo (1994) have had awareness components. But the most significant awareness programs have been developed in countries where creole speakers are a minority, namely, among Kriol speakers in Western Australia (Berry and Hudson, 1997) and Caribbean English Creole speaking immigrants in Britain (ILEA Afro-Caribbean Program in Further and Adult Education, 1990), Canada (Coelho, 1988, 1991), and the United States (Fischer, 1992).

These references for awareness programs in minority contexts are also important resources for teachers who are not creole speakers and know little about the language of their students. In Australia, a professional development course for teachers of Kriol-speaking students also exists (Catholic Education Office, 1994), and many other resources for teachers have been produced by the national and state governments (e.g., Siegel, 1999b, 2007). Other important resources for teachers, giving background information about creoles as well as suggestions for classroom activities, have been written by Pollard (1993) for Jamaican Creole; V. Edwards (1979) for Caribbean English creoles in Britain; Dalphinis (1985) and Nwenmely (1996) for French-lexified creoles in Britain; and Nichols (1996), Winer (1993), and Winer and Jack (1997) for English-lexified creoles in the United States. Craig (1999) has written a detailed guide to teaching speakers of English-lexifier creoles and other vernaculars.

Studies and reports evaluating programs of all three types describe various positive results from using P/Cs in education: greater participation rates, higher scores in achievement on tests measuring reading and writing skills in the standard language, and increases in overall academic achievement (see Siegel, 1999a, 2007). There seem to be several obvious reasons for these results. First, for the instrumental programs, students find it easier to acquire literacy skills in a familiar variety of language and then to transfer these skills to the standard. Second, in all types of programs, students can express themselves better in a familiar language (without fear of correction), leading to better cognitive development. Third, teachers have more positive attitudes because of the nature of the programs that make them aware of the legitimacy and complex rule-governed nature of their students' languages; therefore, they have higher expectations. Fourth, students have more positive attitudes toward their language and themselves, leading to greater interest and increased motivation.

Another reason, however, may be related to aspects of psycholinguistics and second language acquisition. As Craig (e.g., 1966, 1976, 1983) has pointed out, in educational situations involving a creole and the standard form of its lexifier, students often have trouble separating the two varieties because of the many similarities between them. Craig notes that in such cases "the learner fails to perceive the new target element in the teaching situation" (1966: 58). But when students look at features of their own varieties in the classroom, they have a greater chance of noticing features of the standard that are different. This helps them to build the separate mental representation of the standard that is necessary for language acquisition (Siegel, 1999a).

Although problems of autonomy and negative attitudes continue to exist, it is unlikely that many communities would allow their pidgin or creole to be used as the primary language of education in an instrumental program. However, most of the educational benefits of such programs can still be obtained from accommodation or awareness programs, which would be much more acceptable to P/C-speaking communities (Siegel, 2006). The establishment and evaluation of such programs will most likely be a future trend in the applied linguistics of pidgin and creole languages.

Language and the Law

Speakers of P/Cs also face inequities in the legal systems of most countries where a standard European language is the language of the law. Like others who do not know the official language, speakers of P/Cs suffer from not understanding police cautions, police interviews, and courtroom interactions (e.g., see Eades, 1997, in press). But these problems are exacerbated by the belief that P/Cs are not separate languages and therefore that interpreters are not necessary. For example, Devonish

(2007: 92–95) points out that English is the unquestioned language of the law in all Caribbean countries where English-lexifier creoles are spoken. Yet, monolingual creole-speaking witnesses often do not understand questions addressed to them in English, and lawyers, prosecutors, and magistrates have to translate them into the creole. Devonish contrasts this ad hoc court interpreting with that provided to speakers of other languages. He points out that a monolingual creole-speaking defendant is disadvantaged because "there is no official court-appointed interpreter, or anyone else for that matter, who ensures that he is able to follow the proceedings" (2007: 94). The erroneous assumption is that speakers of an English-lexifier creole should be able to follow the English used in court proceedings. Speakers of P/Cs are also disadvantaged by nonspeakers' mistaken impressions that they can understand evidence or testimony given in these languages (e.g., Koch, 1991).

An article by Brown-Blake and Chambers (2007) backs up this view. It examines intelligibility between Jamaican Creole and English in legal contexts by applying discourse analysis techniques to pretrial interviews in Britain. The article describes many instances of miscommunication and lack of comprehension by speakers of both languages in the course of the interviews and also by the transcribers. These findings demonstrate the problems faced in the criminal justice system by Jamaican immigrants and speakers of other creoles not only in Britain but also in their home countries.

Linguists have attempted to serve as expert witnesses in order to deal with some of these problems, but with varying success. Shuy (1993), for example, describes the case of a speaker of Hawai'i Creole on trial for perjury, and demonstrates the accused's misunderstanding, lack of comprehension, and confusion about the prosecutor's questions. Shuy notes, "The judge would not permit the expert witness testimony that could have clarified these issues" (1993: 148). The defendant was convicted on six counts of perjury.

In contrast, in the Supreme Court in Cairns, Australia, in 1995, Helen Harper was allowed to give evidence in the defense of a Torres Strait Creole speaker charged with attempted murder. Her evidence, based on an analysis of the recorded police interview, was that the accused did not have sufficient knowledge of standard English to deal with the complexities of the questions in the interview. Furthermore, she pointed out that in Torres Strait Creole, the word *kill* may mean "hurt or maim" rather than "kill," so that the accused's statement *I wanted to kill him with that thing* did not necessarily indicate an intention to murder. As a result of this testimony, the charge was reduced to unlawful wounding (Trezise, 1996).

Linguists in Australia have also been involved in the training of Kriol speakers as interpreters in courses held since 1994 in Western Australia and the Northern Territory. The emphasis of the courses has been Kriol-English interpreting in legal and medical contexts. Teaching materials in Kriol have been developed and several students have received paraprofessional accreditation from the National Association for Accreditation of Translators and Interpreters (NAATI).

Linguists in the United States, Canada, and Britain have also served as expert consultants and witnesses in cases involving creole speakers—in some for the defense and in some for the prosecution. In the most well known case, a bilingual speaker of Hawai'i Creole and standard English unsuccessfully sued his employer for accent discrimination (Lippi-Green, 1997: 44–45; Sato, 1991). Matsuda (1991: 1345–1346) notes, "The judge discounted the testimony of the linguist who stated that Hawaiian Creole pronunciation is not incorrect, rather it is one of the many varieties of pronunciation of standard English. The linguist, the judge stated, was not an expert in speech."

In another case in the United States, described by Patrick and Buell (2000), both wiretapped and consensual recordings of defendants speaking in Jamaican Creole were transcribed for the trial by a speaker of the language. The defense hired an unnamed linguist to contest the transcripts, and the prosecution hired Patrick (a near-native speaker of Jamaican Creole and an expert on the language) to review the defense version. He identified many examples of omissions, misunderstandings, mistranslation, misrepresentations, and other errors made by the defense linguist, and appeared as a witness during the proceedings. With regard to linguists acting as expert witnesses in cases involving creoles, Patrick and Buell (2000: 104) note

> Creole languages are typically widely-disrespected, unwritten vernaculars which have not undergone standardization or been formally admitted to public use in institutional discourse, even in their home settings.... Presenting expertise on creoles to an audience of nonlinguists (e.g., judges, juries and attorneys) who may be disinclined to credit them with the status or complexity afforded to recognized standard varieties, and even to their regional or social dialects, thus raises interesting problems.

Other forensic linguistic work by creolists has included the following: accent identification, determining the reliability of a confession supposedly given in standard English by a creole speaker, translating and interpreting documents and recordings in creoles, and rating intelligibility between a creole and standard English.

Applied research on creoles in legal contexts has recently been extended into the area of constitutional law. It has been proposed that the new Charter of Rights in the Constitution of Jamaica should prohibit discrimination on the basis of language in addition to the prohibition of discrimination on basis of race, place of origin, political opinions, color, and creed in the current constitution. Brown-Blake (2008) explores the complex legal implications of such a proposal in Creole language jurisdictions like Jamaica. These mainly concern what the legal responsibilities of the state would be in official areas that currently use English, such as the courts and the education system. As Creole-dominant or monolingual speakers could be perceived to be disadvantaged in these areas, would the state be obliged to provide, for example, translations and interpreting of all public communication (p. 33), or bilingual education? Brown-Blake (p. 71) also connects the establishment of language rights for Creole speakers to language planning efforts. A standardized variety with specialized terminology is needed to perform state communication functions alongside English: "This will close the legal window for denying the right on the basis of capacity of the Creole to perform adequately in relevant domains."

V. Conclusion

The nature of pidgin and creole languages, their role in society, and the continuing misconceptions about them provide a unique context for work in applied linguistics, especially in the areas of educational and forensic linguistics. But it remains to be seen whether or not more creolists shift their attention from theoretical to applied issues in the years to come.

Acknowledgments

I would like to thank the following people for providing information about various creoles for the original version of this chapter: Jacques Arends (who sadly died in 2005; Sranan), Ken Decker (Belize Creole), Michel DeGraff and Hugues St Fort (Haitian Creole), Emmanuel Faure (Guadeloupean Creole), Ron Morren (San Andres Creole), and Peter Patrick (Jamaican Creole).

NOTES

1. More information on any of the pidgins or creoles referred to here can be found in Holm (1989) or Arends, Muysken, and Smith (1994). See also the Language Varieties website: http://www.une.edu.au/langnet.

2. Nearly all expanded pidgins are English-lexified, and the largest, Nigerian Pidgin, has over 80 million speakers. Creoles lexified by French have the most speakers (10 million) followed by English (6.5 million), African languages (4.6 million), and Portuguese (1.5 million). The largest creoles are Haitian Creole (7.4 million speakers) and Jamaican Creole (3.2 million).

3. P. Baker (1991) calls the two types "nonautonomous" and "autonomous."

4. These results correspond with those of general research (such as Thomas and Collier, 2002) which clearly show that using a familiar language in early education is advantageous both in overall academic performance and in acquisition of the mainstream educational language.

5. P/Cs have also been used instrumentally at the tertiary level. A degree-level course on the grammar of Bislama has been offered at the University of the South Pacific in the medium of Bislama (Crowley, 1987). Furthermore, a successful master of arts thesis on the grammar of Tok Pisin was written in Tok Pisin by Dicks Raeparanga Thomas in 1996. (The two external examiners, Terry Crowley and Jeff Siegel, also wrote their evaluations and comments in Tok Pisin.)

6. This type of program is similar to some in the "language awareness" movement in Britain (see Hawkins, 1987), but the emphasis is on pidgins and creoles or on nonstandard minority dialects.

CHAPTER 27

···

LANGUAGE SPREAD AND ITS STUDY IN THE TWENTY-FIRST CENTURY

···

OFELIA GARCÍA

LANGUAGE spread is, according to Cooper, "an increase, over time, in the proportion of a communication network that adopts a given language or language variety for a given communicative function" (1982a: 6). It is generally taken for granted that language, as a concomitant of culture, can spread.

Schoolchildren learn of the spread of Greek culture and language throughout the Mediterranean world, of the spread of Roman influence and Latin throughout the Roman Empire, and of the spread of Islam as a new world religion that accompanied the spread of the language of the Koran, Arabic. As the children's world expands in historical and geographical dimensions, they begin to perceive how most historical change has been accompanied by the spread of a culture, and consequently of a language, usually that of the more powerful or high-status group. In some cases, the language of the more powerful has been forcefully imposed; in others, participation in the new sociocultural context has simply demanded the adoption of the new language or of new language features. Sometimes there is a social need for the new language or language variety in order to enjoy socioeconomic benefits or to achieve political integration; at other times, the need is communicative because the new messages that the new cultural context creates cannot simply be transmitted in the old way, and a new way of communicating is needed (García and Otheguy, 1989; Otheguy, 1993, 1995).

As children in the Americas grow up, they begin to understand that English, Spanish, Portuguese, and French were powerful languages that spread quickly and forcibly, as the Indigenous groups of the Americas were silenced and sometimes killed. They learn from history books that other languages were brought to the New World, but yet there was no spread of either the many languages of African slaves or of the languages of less powerful immigrant groups. When students later compare the fate of Spanish in Latin America, brought by powerful conquerors, with that of Spanish in the United States, spoken originally by the less powerful conquerors in remote areas such as Florida or eventually by darker-skinned Mexicans in the Southwest who had by then adopted the Spanish language of their conquerors, they start to realize that language spread has much to do with dominance, power, prestige, and privilege.

Three different, but not mutually exclusive, phases in the study of language spread (or language diffusion or language expansion as the phenomenon is also known) can be distinguished:

1. *The beginnings (1970s to 1980s)*: Language spread is described as a natural phenomenon to solve the language problems of the world, usually referring to those created by language diversity and multilingualism. Studies during this time were motivated by a modernist agenda following the independence of Asians and African countries. The imposition of language planning agencies and other forms of imperial and political control in spurring the spread is foregrounded. (See, e.g., Quirk, 1988, for English.)

2. *The critical period (1990s)*: Language spread is studied within the complex sociocultural processes that affect it in diverse ways. The role of class, ethnicity, race, and gender that causes asymmetrical power relations between speakers and that impacts adoption is given attention (McConnell, 1990). There is much criticism of language spread as a linguistic imperialist agenda within the context of language rights and of protecting endangered languages (Phillipson, 1992; Skutnabb-Kangas and Phillipson, 1994).

3. *The postmodern period (twenty-first century):* Language spread is studied from a postmodern perspective, within a language ecology framework in which languages do not compete, but readjust themselves to fit into an environment (Mühlhäusler, 2000). Globalization and technological advances spur this position. In language adoption, the agency of speakers—causing language spread while appropriating and penetrating it with their own intentions and social styles—is foregrounded.

Basing their formulations on Tsuda's work on communication (1994, 1997), Phillipson and Skutnabb-Kangas (1997) make a distinction between what they call the diffusion paradigm and the ecology of languages paradigm in the study of language spread. The *diffusion paradigm* refers to factors of imposition that are closely associated with the first period (modernization, monolingualism, capitalism) but also, as Tsuda (1997) has made clear in the case of English, to factors that are often associated with the second period (linguistic, cultural, and media imperialism) and the third period (globalization). The *ecology of languages* paradigm, on the other hand, includes factors that emphasize the sustainability of language diversity and multilingualism, and the equality of languages—factors associated with the third period. At the same time, Phillipson and Skutnabb-Kangas's (1997) ecology of languages paradigm includes the protection of local production and national sovereignties. Thus, although supporting linguistic diversity in the face of language spread, Phillipson and Skutnabb-Kangas's ecology of languages paradigm does not promote the flexibility in language use that Mühlhäusler's (2000) and other postmodernist scholars (e.g., Canagarajah, 1999; Pennycook, 1994) support. Many have proposed that the old imperialism-resistance analytical model is not relevant in postcolonial globalized contexts in which hybrid identities and flexible language practices are being constructed (Canagarajah, 1999). Pennycook (2000) has proposed that language spread is a result of "postcolonial performativity," the ability of local people to appropriate language practices for their own diverse intentions. In fact, one could say that the study of contemporary language spread is more about *languaging* spread—that is, about the spread of the ways in which people use language and about their discursive practices. (For additional explication of the concept *languaging*, see especially the discussion of Yngve, 1996, in Makoni and Pennycook, 2007.)

Brutt-Griffler (2002) has indicated that language spread is not always imposed by external factors, but rather that local situations may encourage the spread. In encouraging language spread, the speech community is involved in a process of language change in which the local interacts with the global. In this process of second language acquisition by speech communities that she terms *macroacquisition*, there is no language spread without local language change; in other words, language spread occurs because speakers adopt external language practices, while infusing them with their own. In the face of language spread, language change occurs. Thus, language spread does not promote additive bilingualism in the classical sense of two separate languages. Language spread encourages a dynamic bilingualism that supports flexible language use and translanguaging practices. (For additional explication of the concepts *bilingualism* and *translanguaging*, see García, 2009.) Dynamic bilingualism involves multiple language practices and translanguaging, in other words, using hybrid and multiple language practices simultaneously—practices that are associated with one or another autonomous language to perform different languaging acts (García, 2009).

This chapter synthesizes the theoretical literature on language spread, focusing on the defining characteristics of this field of study. The study of language spread has sometimes mimicked the phenomenon itself, thinly stretching to encompass many situations of different kinds of language change. This chapter also draws theoretical boundaries around the construct of language spread, making it easier to study it in the future.

The Study of Language Spread

What It Is, and What It Is Not

Fishman, Cooper, and Conrad (1977) formally introduced the complex conceptualization of the field of study in relationship to English-as-an-additional-language and as another perspective for the study of language maintenance and shift. Language spread studies were the object of attention at the Aberystwyth Conference in Wales in 1978. Cooper (1982b) compiled the first significant publication of studies devoted to language spread.

The modern study of language spread, made possible by advances in the sociology of language and in psycholinguistics, as well as in ways of gathering and analyzing macro- and microsociolinguistic data, was preeminently shaped by Cooper, who has offered the classic definition: "the increase over time in the proportion of a communicative network that adopts a given language or language variety for a given communicative function" (1982a: 6).

Both Fishman, Conrad, and Rubal-Lopez (1996) and Cooper (1982a) insist that the study of language spread is really not about language itself but is rather about *changes in the language behavior of speakers*. Sometimes these changes in behavior result in new speakers, but often they result simply in the adoption of the language, language variety, or language features for new societal or communicative functions by existing speakers (Fishman, Cooper, and Rosenbaum, 1977).

According to Cooper (1982a), the study of language spread is really about human variability in four aspects of behavior toward language: (1) awareness, (2) evaluation, (3), proficiency, and (4) use. These four behaviors have defining characteristics and are connected to different disciplines. The first two aspects—awareness and evaluation—involve being aware of being positively inclined toward a language or language variety and are of psychological import. Proficiency may be subdivided into (a) the underlying knowledge or competence and (b) the execution or speech performance in that language. Underlying competence is of psycholinguistic import, whereas performance is of sociolinguistic import and involves external behavior that may be directly observed and measured. Finally, the frequency of actual use, or adoption of the language or language variety or language practices, implicates both the narrower definition of sociolinguistics and the broader definition, sometimes explicitly referred to as sociology of language or macrosociolinguistics.

While studying the variance in human behavior toward language, language spread studies also focus on the contextual specificity and their dynamics in change in language behavior. Three aspects of contextual specificity and their dynamics are taken into account:

1. *Variance in overtness:* whether the behavioral change toward language is in speaking, hearing, reading or writing, and whether it includes receptive or productive language behavior;

2. *Variance in domain specificity:* whether the behavioral change toward language occurs in relation to an institutional domain—in other words, home and family, school, work, religion, government—and in a specific communicative situation;

3. *Variance in role-relationship specificity:* whether the behavioral change toward language depends on the social relationship of the interlocutors.

Language spread studies look not only at the degree and location of language behavior change but also at the dynamics and the interrelationship of the aspects of contextual specificity identified earlier (Fishman, Cooper, and Conrad, 1977). But language spread studies go beyond the degree and location of language behavior to include the *sociocultural processes* that accompany the change. For example, Brosnahan (1963) identified four sociocultural processes that explain the spread of Arabic, Greek, and Latin as mother tongues:

1. Military conquest or imposition
2. The length and duration of authority
3. The multilingualism and linguistic heterogeneity of the area in which the spread occurred
4. The material incentives for learning the language

The study of language spread focuses, then, on the pervasiveness and variance of change in human behavior toward language (even when those are affective or cognitive, instead of only interactional behavior per se), while identifying the contextual specificity and institutional domain of the behavior as well as the sociocultural processes that shape the language behavior (Fishman, Cooper, and Rosenbaum, 1977).

Working within a modernist development framework, Fishman, Cooper, and Rosenbaum (1977) and Lewis (1982) identify the following sociocultural processes as important for language spread:

1. Factors related to modernization, especially:
   • Economic development, particularly external exploitation of indigenous resources
   • Educational development
   • Political affiliation and global position vis-à-vis superpowers
   • Urbanization, with greater linguistic heterogeneity, presence of governmental agencies, and increased educational opportunity
   • Demographics and population mobility
2. Factors related to between-group interactions besides conquest, such as
   • Colonization
   • Nature of the colonial center and the periphery
   • Geographical contiguity
   • Ease of communication
3. Factors related to the religious and cultural characteristics of a group

Although early modernist work on language spread merely described the phenomenon and related it to these sociocultural processes, critical work on language spread has foregrounded the linguistic imperialism that accompanied development projects, including education. Phillipson (1992) describes the spread of English as an imperialist project conducted not through impositional force, as had been done in the past, but through persuasion and ideas. This critical language spread work questioned the role of modernization and the state, focusing not on the spread, but rather on the decline and loss of many of the world's languages (Krauss, 1992; Nettle and Romaine, 2000).

In the twenty-first century, globalization has become the most important sociocultural process in the study of language spread. The development of globalization and the end of the Cold War, coupled with technological advances, have accelerated the movement of peoples. Language spread is now more dynamic than ever, involving not simply replacement of languages as a result of language shift, but also the acquisition of additional languages and dynamic bilingualism (García, 2009).

De Swaan (1998) has proposed that there is a dynamic world system of languages that accounts for language spread. This system is held together by multilinguals. Languages that spread are *central* because there is a large percentage of multilinguals in that system whose repertoire contains that language. Thus, these central languages have more *Q-value*, in other words, their utility increases with an increasing number of users. De Swaan (1998: 71) explains that languages spread when speakers realize that they can increase the Q-value of their repertoire by a greater amount by adding a given language than any other. Q-value, the worth of a language, takes into account the language's prevalence (i.e., the number of people within a language constellation who speak it) and its centrality (i.e., the number of people knowing another language who choose to use this language to communicate). The difference at present in the study of language spread is that it is multilingualism and dynamism that stands at the center of the spread.

Language spread studies, as a subfield of sociology of language studies, attempt to answer the summarizing question posed by Cooper: "Who adopts what, when, why, and how?" (1982a: 31). The framework proposed by Cooper asks that language spread studies determine

Who: the sociolinguistic characteristics of individual and communicative
    network adopters
Adopts: the interaction of the different levels of language behavior previously
    identified
What: the structural/functional characteristics of the linguistic innovation
When: the time of adoption
Where: the kinds of social interaction within the type of societal domain that
    lead to the adoption
Why: the incentives for adoption
How: the language planning activities that accompany adoption

There are a number of well-known cases of language spread:

- The spread of Latin as a lingua franca in the western half of the Roman Empire until the Middle Ages
- The spread of Arabic during the Islamic expansion
- The spread of Spanish throughout Latin America during the conquest and colonization
- The spread of French, Portuguese, and English as colonial languages throughout Asia and Africa

But all these cases of language spread, which resulted from direct military conquest, often causing a language shift in the population, have little to do with the study of language spread as it is currently conceived. Studies of language spread beginning after Cooper (1982b) mark a change in scholarship brought about not only by advances in the sociology of language (Fishman, 1968) but also by the globalization of a new world order. Presently, the study of language spread looks at how global and discourse forces, less explicitly present than military conquest and interacting simultaneously at many social levels, impact language behaviors.

Language spread differs from language change, from language shift, from language maintenance, from reversing language shift, and from language policy. The term *language change* describes the change in the linguistic forms themselves, without considering the behavior of human beings as mediators (or sources) of change (Cooper 1982a) or the reason for the occurrence of language change within a given sociocultural context.

Language shift, the process by which a speech community abandons a language or language variety and takes up another one, most often starts with the displacement of a language or a variety for low (L) functions—in other words, with the erosion of diglossia. Language spread, however, most often responds to newly created communicative functions and language uses, usually for high (H) functions. Thus, in some ways, language spread disturbs what was previously a diglossic relationship between two particular languages. As two or more languages coexist within the same social spaces, a transglossia results with many languages in functional interrelationships. (For additional explication of the concept *transglossia*, see García, 2009.) The French sociolinguistic Louis-Jean Calvet (1999) has proposed that the contemporary spread of globally powerful languages can coexist with many other languages. For the individual, this means being able to engage in different language practices encompassing those of the expanding speech community.

Language shift situations constitute the other side of the coin of language spread. The study of language shift and language maintenance focuses on the more external human behavior toward language (i.e., proficiency and use), often using the more implicit behavior (i.e., awareness and evaluation) only as predictors of the change in external adoption, unlike language spread studies. Whereas studies of language shift and language maintenance concern themselves with measurement of habitual language use, language spread concerns itself with processes of sociocultural change and their impact on language behavior, including awareness, evaluation, proficiency, and use (Fishman, Cooper and Conrad, 1977).

Efforts to reverse language shift (RLS) often mimic in reverse the process of language spread, attempting to spread the use of a heritage language in communicative functions for which another language is being used. As in language spread, RLS results in macroacquisition that also produces differences in the local language practices.

Language spread is always spurred by the three components of language policy (Spolsky, 2004):

1. Language management—also known as language intervention, language engineering, or language planning in the context of direct efforts to manipulate language situations
2. Language practices or the habitual pattern of selecting among varieties that make up a linguistic repertoire
3. Language beliefs or ideology referring to the beliefs about language and language practices

THE CHARACTERISTICS OF LANGUAGE SPREAD: WHO, WHAT, WHERE, AND WHEN?

Language spread has been characterized as taking an upbeat perspective (Fishman, 1988), as the language adds speakers, functions, and ways of languaging. Additive, Dynamic, Dominant, Sustained over time, and Broad refers to contextualized language spread within an additive context. Each of these defining characteristics of language spread will be explicated individually.

Additive. Language spread results in additive language practices. According to Fishman (1977), language spread often begins with the acquisition of a language—or of a variety—for such H functions as technology, economics, government, high culture, religion, and literacy-related functions in education. The increased globalization occurring over the past 2 decades of the twentieth century has spurred the spread of languages, in particular of English, with bilingualism and multilingualism being desired outcomes. As globalization takes hold, new communicative functions are created that respond to the movement of capital and people around the globe and to a proliferation of new products and services. Speakers who wish to participate in this new world order are then increasingly aware and favorably inclined to learn and adopt the language or language variety that will enable them to participate in this new economic order. The increased use of English on the Internet is an obvious example. Phillipson (1994a, 1994b) claims that English has been globally marketed as the language of economic and technological progress, national unity, and international understanding. Thus, it has spread through ideological persuasion of access to socioeconomic incentives and favors.

Dynamic. Language spread is dynamic because the increase in pervasiveness of behavior toward language is a result of sociocultural change and results in socio-linguistic and sociocultural change. As a result, the bilingualism is not linearly additive, but dynamic. As Brutt-Griffler (2002) has suggested, language spread always results in language change for a speech community, and it is precisely this complex language use that results in dynamic language practices and translan-guaging. Although language spread is always upbeat, its dynamism can hide the painful social dislocation of the adopters, sometimes resulting in conflict and loss (Fishman, 1988).

Kachru (1986) refers to the "alchemy of English," suggesting that the spread of English has resulted in nonnative varieties of English, used extensively in non-English society for H functions, in other words, even in literature (Thumboo, 1987). It is precisely because of the bilingual nature of language spread that adoption of such language behavior usually begins and is enthusiastically embraced by indige-nous populations—populations that are the victims of extensive power inequalities and for whom use of a second language, whether an international language like English or a colonial language like French, constitutes an advantage.

Dominance. Combined with economic power, language spread occurs primarily among groups that have a secure group language identity and for whom an addi-tional language does not appear to be threatening. In countries of the Global South, where the division between the poor and rich is great, only the elite become bilingual. For example, Phillipson (1994a) points out that in such "English speaking coun-tries" as Kenya, Nigeria, and Pakistan, only a very few indigenous people are actually English speakers. There is a difference between language spread in the Netherlands and language spread among the indigenous people of the Americas. In the former case, English has spread throughout the Netherlands, both in the Dutch-speaking and in the Frisian-speaking areas, without posing any threat to the language iden-tity of the Dutch and the Frisians, because English does not compete with their languages. Yet the spread of Dutch threatens the existence of Frisian, whose speakers have adopted protective policies against the spread of Dutch. Although Spanish has spread extensively throughout Latin America and has been vigorously imposed through conquest and colonization, there continues to be resistance against total adoption of Spanish by members of impoverished and isolated indigenous groups who fear that the pull of economic advantages will lead to sure language death (Cobarrubias, 1990; García, 1999; Heath, 1972).

Language spread responds to dominance of some kind, whether economic, political, ideological, or demographic, or to dominance arising from communica-tive factors. The language that is contextually more powerful spreads as an addi-tional language because of the benefits that accrue to the adopters (Fishman, 1977, 1988). Scotton (1982: 85) recalls that in order for individuals to want to adopt another language or language variety, they must be dissatisfied with their socioeconomic status and confident that their lives will improve as a result of the new language behavior. Language spreads because there is dominance and because there are pros-pects for increased dominance.

To a lesser extent than economic, political, or demographic factors, religion can also account for the dominance that causes language spread. Religion, by insisting that prayer and ritual must be conducted in a certain language, may indeed be a very important factor in language spread, as in the case of Arabic (C. A. Ferguson, 1982).

Because language spreads through dominance, spread usually occurs from the top down; in other words, it is the government or the cultural elite who first adopt and promote the change. Dominance is also advanced through schools—especially through higher education—as well as through such other special mechanisms controlled by the elite as the mass media, business, and employment (Fishman, 1977), and testing and language in public space (Shohamy, 2006).

Language spread may be most effective in cities, where interaction is intensive and prevalent and where there is greater linguistic heterogeneity, creating a communicative need for the acquisition of different language practices and for their spread. Language spread may also be most effective where there are governmental agencies and schools that can promote the use of different languages.

Sustained over time. Language spread takes place over extended time. It is persistent, consistent, and repetitive, having lasting impact on language behavior. Mackey (1990) recalls that the study of language spread is usually diachronic; he uses demographic, geographic, and especially historic factors to explain spread.

Broad. Finally, language spread affects not only groups, as do both language shift and language maintenance, but also its impact is felt between groups. Thus, language spreads in a broad and extensive context is responsive to geopolitical interests. Language spreads among individuals and groups, as well as in sociopolitical contexts. Phillipson (2003) has, for example, examined the spread of English throughout the European Union (EU) and the laissez-faire EU policies that are moving the EU dangerously close to being an English-only union. (For additional details, see Council of Europe, 2000.) Scotton recalls that "it is misleading to study the spread of any language out of the context of change in the entire social system" (1982: 89).

Traditional diglossia allows for bilingual speakers who clearly differentiate between the "L" and "H" functions for which the two languages serve. Language spread makes possible multiple language acquisition for H functions and translanguaging practices, a transglossia (García, 2009) that is a consequence of living in the twenty-first century.

How and Why Language Spreads

The macro level of geopolitical interest may manifest itself consciously (as in language policy and language planning—management—efforts), or it may be unplanned, with the pull toward the spreading language being a result of what Fishman refers to as the *zeitgeist*, in which "social mobility aspirations, hungers for material and leisure time gratifications and stylishness of the pursuit of modernity itself" (1988: 2) constitute part of the picture. Yet Fishman himself believes that if left unattended, the spreading language will eventually erode the other language(s) in the environment. Phillipson (1994a, 1994b) also believes that because language spread is tied to linguistic hierarchies in the new world order, it is never really left to chance. This is a different position from that of Calvet (1999), who, in proposing a gravitational model of bilingualism, believes that the spread of global languages can coexist with official and national languages, with regional lingua francas, and with local vernaculars without threatening them in any way.

Language spread also occurs because of the communicative needs in language contact situations. The spread of a trade pidgin along contact borders, its subsequent acquisition as a creole, and its eventual decreolization constitute examples of language spread (Holm, 1988; Kaplan and Baldauf, 1997b; Stewart, 1989).

Language spread is not subconscious, as language maintenance is because of its static characteristics. Language spreads only when people believe that they will gain well-being, power, and control (Scotton, 1982); in other words, the educated and the middle-class are more likely to adopt new language behaviors than are those for whom the acquisition of a new language will offer little change in the socioeconomic and political structure. Scotton (1988) provides evidence from Africa that the spread of a lingua franca depends upon the degree of socioeconomic integration. Fishman notes that the spread of languages is facilitated by "the promise they hold to change the lives of their new speakers" (1988: 2).

Language spread policy, defined by Ammon, "attempts to entrench a language more deeply in its speakers, to increase their skills and improve their attitudes or to enhance its status or extend its functions in any domain" (1997: 51). Ammon (1997) identifies the following five goals of language-spread policy:

1. To increase communication
2. To spread one's ideology
3. To develop economic ties
4. To gain revenue from language study and products
5. To preserve national identity and pride

Language spread policy, according to Ammon (1992: 47), can be explicit and declared, but it can also be undeclared (as in the case of Japan), covert (as in the case of Nazi Germany), or implicit (as in the case of Brazil). Language spread policy is not always directed by government or by independent organizations; it also involves the media, business, the scientific community, and education, particularly institutions of higher education (Phillipson, 1994a: 20). There are many agencies that promote or limit the spread of language by acting as motivators, propagandists, and pressure groups (Lewis, 1982: 248). Among the most important agencies of language spread are the national language academies. Language planning deals with both corpus planning (especially standardization) and status planning. Ammon (1992, 1994) has described at length the Federal Republic of Germany's overt policy of spreading German. Although language spread policy is commonly top down, there have been various attempts to contain it and promote it through bottom-up efforts, such as those described in Hornberger (1997a), Rivera (1999), and Lin and Martin (2005).

LANGUAGE SPREAD AND ENGLISH

Since Cooper's seminal volume (1982b), there have been only a few serious comprehensive general studies of general language spread (Ammon, 1994; Ammon and Kleinedam, 1992; Laforgue and McConnell, 1990; Lowenberg, 1988). The term is absent from encyclopedic works on language such as those by Crystal (1987), Baker and Jones (1998), and Davies and Elder (2004b). Yet, *language spread* has been increasingly used to describe the growth of English as the language of science, technology, finance, and higher education (Crystal, 1997, 2003; Fishman, 1977; Fishman, Cooper, and Conrad, 1977; Fishman, Conrad, and Rubal-Lopez 1996; Graddol, 1997; 2006; Kachru, 1986, 1992; Lin and Martin, 2005; Phillipson, 1992; Tsui and Tollefson, 2007; Uysal, Plakans, and Dembovskaya, 2007). This emphasis on English responds to the more current definition of language spread as a consequence of modern globalization and local desire and agency, and not simply of military conquest or imposition.

How English has spread has been the object of intense disagreement. Some have argued that English happened to be in the right place at the right time (Crystal, 2003); others have proposed that English spread just came along with globalization (Block and Cameron, 2002; Fishman, Conrad, and Rubal-Lopez, 1996; Kumaravadivelu, 2006) and colonialism (Pennycook, 1994, 1998). Others have focused on the role that the English language teaching profession has had in spreading English (Canagarajah, 1999; Phillipson, 1992). Yet, other scholars have pointed to voluntary language choice as the explanation for the spread of English (de Swaan, 2001; Brutt-Griffler, 2002; Ferguson, 2006), while Kaplan (2001) has looked at the accidental confluence of forces following World War II.

> In 1988, Kachru observed that one reason for the spread of English was…its propensity for acquiring new identities, its power of assimilation, its adaptability to decolonization as a language, its manifestation in a range of lects and its provision of a flexible medium for literary and other types of creativity across languages and cultures. (Kachru, 1988: 222)

English spreads because it has increasingly become synonymous with globalization and with the economic and technological progress that accompanies it. English has also been widely disseminated, however, because as English has spread across cultures, cultures and languages have spread across English, enabling people to appropriate it differently to express global and local messages. Many different forms of English are spreading. For example, in Singapore, "Singlish" language practices are spreading, requiring government intervention to promote Standard English.

English has succeeded in shedding its Anglo-American identity. As it has spread, it has gained new speakers and spawned new nativized English varieties (Kachru, 1982, 1992) that include hybrid translanguaging practices (Chew, 2007). Because of its global identity, English has even spread in Cuba, isolated by the United States for almost a half century (Corona and García, 1996).

CONCLUSION

The questions raised in Cooper's (1982a) language spread framework ("Who adopts what, when, where, why and how?") can be summatively answered. Missing from such answers, however, are the complex interaction of all those factors that defines language spread:

1. Who adopts?
   - Those individuals who stand to gain, who need to achieve, and who are secure in their language identity, thus being open to change.
   - Those communicative networks that stand to gain from the spread of one language because it provides them with a lingua franca enabling both intergroup and intragroup communication, thus increasing trade, improving economic and educational opportunity, or promoting religious/ideological fervor.
2. How does adoption work?
   - Generally adopters first become aware of the language innovation and become favorably disposed to it. Behaviors of psychological import (awareness and evaluation) precede behaviors of psycholinguistic and sociolinguistic import (knowledge and use).
3. What structural and functional characteristics of language are associated with adoption?
   - Especially high-literacy/econo-technology spurs the adoption. Whether the adoption includes receptive or productive language behaviors depends on the communicative need.
4. When does adoption take place? Why does it take place at different speeds?
   - The higher the benefit of adoption, and the higher the density and repetitiveness of the language behavior, the faster the adoption.
5. Where does adoption take place?
   - Usually first in societal domains that have high value.
6. Why does adoption take place?
   - Because there are enough personal and societal incentives.
7. How does adoption take place?
   - It is most often spurred by language planning activities but many times without them, as long as the incentive is high enough.

To be adopted as an additional language, the spreading language must either be curbed by language planning efforts or even through explicit language management or it must be allowed to coexist flexibly in a stable multilingual ecology.

Language spread is not a new phenomenon, but it is a highly complex one. As the study of language spread has expanded and demanded a multidisciplinary and multidimensional level of analysis, the numbers of languages that are spreading have contracted. In this first decade of the twenty-first century, English is not the sole language that is spreading. Arabic, Spanish, and Swahili are spreading. And

Modern Standard Chinese—also known as *Putonghua* or Mandarin—is also spreading (Zhou, 2006). But, increasingly, the focus is on English, as it spreads not only around the Global South (which had been gaining English speakers since the days of colonization) but also significantly throughout the Global North. English has not only spread through cultures, but cultures have spread across English (García and Otheguy, 1989). Thus, although the number of autonomous languages that are spreading has shrunk, languaging practices that include features of different languages are spreading more rapidly than ever. This phenomenon has to do with the spread of new technology and of media throughout the world. The shrinking of geographical space, coupled with the dynamism of the concept of time, will certainly accentuate languaging spread in the twenty-first century, as it shifts the traditional understandings of language spread.

CHAPTER 28

LANGUAGE SHIFT AND LANGUAGE REVITALIZATION

NANCY H. HORNBERGER

I. LANGUAGE SHIFT, MAINTENANCE, AND REVITALIZATION DEFINED

Language shift refers to "the gradual displacement of one language by another in the lives of the community members" (Dorian, 1982: 44) manifested as loss in number of speakers, level of proficiency, or range of functional use of the language. The contrasting term has traditionally been language maintenance, which "denotes the continuing use of a language in the face of competition from a regionally and socially more powerful or numerically stronger language" (Mesthrie, 1999: 42). Implicitly, these terms connote a contact situation and power differential between two or more speech communities (Hyltenstam and Stroud, 1996: 568; Brenzinger, 1997: 274); it is usually speakers of the minority language (in numerical or power terms) who shift away from or maintain use of their own language vis vis the majority language.

Language shift and language maintenance as a field of inquiry dates back to the earliest days of sociolinguistics, in particular the work of Joshua Fishman (1964, 1965)—above all, his monumental and groundbreaking *Language Loyalty in the United States* (1966; see also a revisiting of Fishman's work on language loyalty in García et al., 2006; Hornberger and Pütz, 2006). Other early and influential studies in this field include Heinz Kloss's *American Bilingual Tradition* (1977) on immigrant language maintenance and shift in the United States, Susan Gal's *Language Shift*

(1979) on the social determinants of the shift from Hungarian to German in the Austrian village of Oberwart, and Nancy Dorian's *Language Death* (1981) on morphological manifestations of language loss in older and younger speakers of East Sutherland Gaelic in northern Scotland. More recent studies, outside the United States and Europe, include Jane and Kenneth Hill's *Speaking Mexicano* (1986) on central Mexican Nahuatl speakers' resistance to and incorporation of Spanish into their way of speaking and Don Kulick's *Language Shift and Cultural Reproduction* (1992) on the "cosmological" reasons behind one Papua New Guinea village's shift away from their local language, Taiap, and toward Tok Pisin.

Factors contributing to language maintenance and shift are diverse and complex, making the science of prediction elusive if not impossible, though scholars have proposed models and typologies of relevant factors. Conklin and Lourie (1983: 174–175) provide a comprehensive list of political, social, economic factors, cultural factors, and linguistic factors that influence language maintenance and shift. Giles, Bourhis, and Taylor (1977) construct a model of the vitality of an ethnolinguistic group (and their language) in terms of status, demographic, and institutional support factors, specifically: economic, social, sociohistorical, and language status; geographic distribution and numbers; and institutional support through mass media, religion, education, and government. (For recent studies using this model, see Evans, 1996, on Spanish language maintenance among Mexican Americans in the U.S. Southwest and Yagmur et al., 1999, on Turkish in Australia.) J. Edwards (1992) proposes a typology of minority-language-situation variables affecting language maintenance and loss, organized as a grid attending to demographic, sociological, linguistic, psychological, historical, political, geographic, educational, religious, economic, and media perspectives on the speakers, their language, and the setting, respectively. (This work follows Haugen, 1972, in taking an ecology of language approach; see Mühlhäusler, "Ecology of Languages," chapter 29, this volume.)

Language revitalization arose as a scholarly and activist focus of concern[1] primarily in the 1990s and has intensified in the two decades since then, in conjunction with the increasing recognition that an alarming portion of the world's languages are endangered (Krauss, 1992). Defined as "the attempt to add new linguistic forms or social functions to a threatened language with the aim of increasing its uses or users" (King, 2000), language revitalization is closely related to earlier sociolinguistic concerns with vitality (Stewart, 1968) and revival (J. Edwards, 1993; Fellman, 1974), and with more recent notions of renewal (Brandt and Ayoungman, 1989: 43) and reversing language shift (Fishman, 1991b).

Language revitalization, renewal, or reversing language shift goes one step further than language maintenance, in that it implies recuperating and reconstructing something that is at least partially lost, rather than maintaining and strengthening what already exists. The change in emphasis is at least in part a reflection of the changing and increasingly threatened circumstances of the world's languages, in particular indigenous languages, in the latter years of the twentieth century. Consider the case of Quechua, the largest indigenous language of South America with some 8 to 12 million speakers, but nevertheless a threatened language (Hornberger and

King, 2000). Although Hornberger's dissertation research on Quechua in Peru in the early 1980s was formulated around the question of language maintenance (Hornberger, 1988, 1989), a decade later her student King formulated her research on Quichua in Ecuador around the question of revitalization and reversing language shift (Hornberger and King, 1996; King, 2000), a change in research focus at least partially attributable to the growing threat to even such a large indigenous language as Quechua (Hornberger and Coronel-Molina, 2004; Note that Peru uses the spelling *Quechua* and Ecuador the spelling *Quichua*.).

Whereas work on language maintenance (and shift) has focused as much on immigrant as on indigenous languages (or perhaps more so), language revitalization work carries a particular emphasis on indigenous languages; for example, Fishman's *Reversing Language Shift* (1991b) includes, among its 13 cases, Irish, Frisian, Basque, Catalan, Navajo, Maori, and Australian aboriginal languages, and his *Can Threatened Languages Be Saved?* (2000) includes these plus Ainu, Andamanese, Quechua, and indigenous languages of Mexico and Nigeria as well. Likewise, although research on language maintenance and shift has been biased toward documenting cases of shift rather than maintenance (Hyltenstam and Stroud, 1996: 568), documentation on language revitalization emphasizes the positive side of the equation, despite seemingly insurmountable odds against survival of the languages in question.

Another difference between maintenance and revitalization work is the relative emphasis placed on conscious and deliberate efforts by speakers of the language to affect language behavior; in other words, on language planning. Although language maintenance has long been recognized as a language planning goal (e.g., Nahir, 1977, 1984) and language revitalization only more recently so, nevertheless it is also true that maintenance can describe a "natural" language phenomenon that does not require any deliberate planning on the part of its speakers, whereas revitalization cannot. Finally, whereas language maintenance efforts have often tended to emanate from the top down (in which someone takes benevolent initiative in "maintaining" someone else's language), language revitalization efforts tend to originate within the speech community itself. For that reason, and because there is another section in this volume devoted to the topic of language policy and planning, the present chapter emphasizes community-based rather than government-led language planning efforts (see the chapters in part IX, "Language Policy and Planning," this volume).

The following discussion focuses on work beginning in the latter half of the 1990s and, given the recent trend toward greater attention to language revitalization and to endangered languages in particular, those will also be emphasized here. I will provide, first, a brief overview of selected work on endangered language shift and revitalization by geographic region of the world, followed by a highlighting of themes and trends in the field; the chapter concludes with some unresolved conceptual and methodological issues. Much of the work cited here is published in two journals that readers may want to consult for further detail and additional cases: the *International Journal of the Sociology of Language* (IJSL), edited since its founding in 1974 by Joshua Fishman, and the *Journal of Multilingual and Multicultural Development* (JMMD), edited since its founding in 1980 by John

Edwards.[2] New journals which regularly take up language revitalization topics include *Current Issues in Language Planning* (CILP) beginning 2000, *Journal of Language, Identity, and Education* since 2002, and *Language Policy* also since 2002. In addition, a burgeoning number of full-length volumes (Grenoble and Whaley, 2006; Harrison, 2007), special journal issues (Liddicoat and Bryant, 2001), edited volumes (Huss et al., 2003; King et al., 2008), and how-to guides (Hinton, 2002; Hinton and Hale, 2001) on endangered language revitalization have begun to appear since 2000.

II. Endangered Language Shift and Revitalization around the World

Krauss announced (1992) and reaffirmed (1998: 103) that only an estimated 5–10% of the world's 6,000 extant languages are safe and 20–50% are moribund, thus leaving 40–75% endangered. His and others' calls to both scholarship and action on behalf of endangered languages have been resoundingly taken up, especially in the past half decade. (See Craig, 1997: 268–269, for a brief history of the Linguistic Society of America's response to the situation of endangered languages.) International nonprofit organizations such as Terralingua and the Endangered Language Fund promote and advocate language revitalization efforts through their websites, newsletters, and project funding. Long-standing scholarly organizations such as the Society for the Study of the Indigenous Languages of the Americas (SSILA; founded in December 1981) also currently report regularly on colloquia, news items, and strategies of support for endangered languages.

Research attention to the maintenance and revitalization of endangered languages has burgeoned since the 1990s as well. By way of sketching the recent richness of cases and coverage, I cite here only selected work appearing since 1996. Edited collections on endangered indigenous languages in the Americas include volumes on North, South, and Meso-America (Hornberger, 1996; McCarty and Zepeda, 1998, 2006); Latin America (Freeland, 1999); North American Indian and Alaska Native languages (Cantoni, 1996; McCarty, Watahomigie, and Yamamoto, 1999; Reyhner, 1997, Reyhner et al., 1999); and Alaska, California, Hawaii, and the Solomon Islands (Henze and Davis, 1999).

In addition to the American cases above, other cases of endangered language shift and revitalization discussed in recent literature include, by region of the world:

- *Australia*—immigrant languages (Clyne and Kipp, 1997) and aboriginal languages (Amery, 2000; Lowell and Devlin, 1999; Wurm, 1999)
- *New Zealand*—community languages (Holmes, 1997) and Mori language (Chrisp, 1997b; Durie, 1999; May, 1999; Spolsky, 1996, 2003)
- *Papua New Guinea*—revitalization of indigenous languages in education (Klaus, 2003; Nagai and Lister, 2003; Skutnabb-Kangas, 2003)

- *Africa*—language revitalization among Western Bantu speakers in Uganda (Bernsten, 1998), the rise of Lingala in eastern Zaire (Goyvaerts, 1997), the death of Berber in Tunisia (Battenburg, 1999), and the status of K'emant, one of the most threatened languages of Ethiopia (Leyew, 1998)
- *Asia*—Chinese speakers in Singapore (Wei et al., 1997), Sindhis in Malaysia (Khemlani-David, 1998), indigenous languages in Japan and the Solomon Islands (Wurm, 1999), and minority languages in Dehong, China (Xiao, 1998)
- *Siberia and Russia*—Estonians shifting to Russian (Viikberg, 1999), Evenki and Yukagir speakers shifting to Yakut or Russian (Wurm, 1999), and Karelians shifting to Russian (Pyöli, 1998)
- *Europe*—the Sámi of Scandinavia (Huss, 1999; Todal, 1999), Iranian immigrants in Sweden (Sohrabi, 1997), and Dutch language loss in French Flanders (Willemyns, 1997)
- *Middle East*—minority languages in Israel (Spolsky and Shohamy, 1999a, 1999b) and Judeo-Spanish speakers in Istanbul, Turkey (Altabev, 1998)

This is by no means a comprehensive listing of cases reported on, but it will serve as a sample and as the basis for the following highlighting of trends and unresolved questions in the field.

III. Themes and Trends in the Study of Language Shift and Revitalization

I highlight here only four themes that permeate recent work in language shift and revitalization:

- Linguistic human rights
- Literacy and education as vehicles for shift and revitalization
- Community-based revitalization efforts
- The controversial link between language and identity in revitalization initiatives

There is a natural affinity between language revitalization efforts and the advocacy of linguistic human rights (Freeland and Patrick, 2004; Skutnabb-Kangas, 2000a; Skutnabb-Kangas and Phillipson, 1994); after all, the impetus behind language revitalization is speakers' desire—and their right—to speak their own language. Two articles in Hamel's special *IJSL* issue on *Linguistic Human Rights from a Sociolinguistic Perspective* (1997) deal directly with language maintenance and shift (and others do so implicitly): Hamel (1997), based on his research in Hñähñú (Otomí) and other indigenous areas of Mexico, proposes a sociolinguistic framework for defining and implementing linguistic human rights in contexts of language conflict and shift; and Hornberger (1997) draws on ethnographic research with Quechua speakers in Peru and with Puerto Ricans and Cambodian refugees in Philadelphia to explore the degree to which the development of literacy in a minority language does, or does not, contribute to minority linguistic human rights and minority language maintenance.

The ambiguous role of literacy and education in language maintenance and shift is a concern presaged by Gaarder (1977) and taken up in subsequent book-length ethnographic studies by Hornberger (1988) on Quechua in southern Peru, and McLaughlin (1992) on Navajo in southwestern United States. Grenoble and Whaley, (1998: 32) consider the role of literacy so important (though controversial) in language endangerment that they argue for its inclusion as a variable in their modified version of J. Edwards's (1992) typology. Despite the demonstrably complex and ambivalent relationships among literacy, education, and language shift/maintenance/revitalization, literacy and education continue to be a productive focus of language revitalization efforts everywhere. McCarty and Zepeda (1995, 2006) bring together papers concerned with the aims and effects of American Indian/Alaska Native bilingual and bicultural programs in relation to the survival of indigenous languages. Hornberger (1996) provides evidence from Shawandawa in the Brazilian Amazon, Quechua in the Andes, East Indian communities of South Africa, Khmer in Philadelphia, Welsh in the United Kingdom, Mori in New Zealand, Turkish in the United Kingdom, and Native Californian languages that language education (and language policy) can serve as vehicle(s) for promoting the vitality, versatility, and stability of indigenous and immigrant languages, an argument further taken up in Hornberger (2008a).

Very often the confluence of linguistic human rights with literacy or educational initiatives directed toward language revitalization lies in community-based education efforts, such as those reported in May's (1999) edited volume. Indeed, May argues that indigenous community-based education is predicated on the principle of self-determination, which in turn encompasses the retention and promotion of indigenous languages and cultures (May, 1999a: 1). Community-based education initiatives are also reported in the *IJSL* issue edited by McCarty and Zepeda (1998), including efforts by Native California Indians to revive and maintain community languages via such measures as the Master-Apprentice Language Learning Program, which pairs older native speakers with younger members of the tribe who want to learn the ancestral language, as well as immersion preschool initiatives, the development of writing systems, and the formation of the committee Advocates for Indigenous California Language Survival (Hinton, 1998, 2002; Hinton and Hale, 2001), as well as approaches being attempted in the Tohono O'odham community of Arizona to maintain their language via oral tradition and computer technology, not to mention the potential role of the lucrative gaming industry in turning the tide of their language loss (Zepeda, 1998). In addition to accounts such as these by academic linguists, anthropologists, and educators, McCarty and Zepeda (1998, 2006) have interwoven narratives by speakers of indigenous languages—"language autobiographies," which attest powerfully to the compelling reasons why indigenous community members invest so much time, energy, and effort in revitalization efforts.

These narratives also point to the importance of identity in language revitalization efforts, a topic explored by Henze and Davis's (1999) contributors. Warner, for example, argues forcefully against "an ideology whereby language is viewed as an autonomous entity distinct from the people from whom it evolved" (1999: 78); such an ideology, he suggests, is promoted by non-Hawaiians for political reasons of their own but is ultimately damaging to the cause of Hawaiian revitalization. Similarly, McCarty's (2002) *A Place to Be Navajo*, published in honor of the thirtieth anniversary of the Rough Rock Community School, documents in rich detail how the community-based bilingual and bicultural program at the Rough Rock School provides a space not only for Navajo language to be maintained and revitalized but also for Navajo identity to flourish. Wurm asserts, with respect to Australian Aboriginal languages, that "it was the very strong reawakened feeling of ethnic identity and a strong resurgence of Aboriginal pride … that led to efforts at maintaining and revitalizing languages" (1999: 169). Bernsten regards the language revitalization effort by Western Bantu speakers as an example of "an ethnic group working to maintain its identity by maintaining its language and expanding its domain" (1998: 104). Others, such as Jones (1998) on Breton, Wong (1999) on Hawaiian, and King (2000) on Ecuadorian Quichua, document the tensions around authenticity and identity that can arise between traditional speakers of a threatened language and younger speakers who learn the revitalized language through schooling and become advocates for a newly articulated authenticity and identity that may be somewhat at odds with the traditional ones. (See also Dorian, 1994, on purism versus compromise in these matters.) Still others—such as Bankston and Henry (1998) on Cajun French in Louisiana, Khemlani-David (1998) on Sindhis in Malaysia, and Wei et al. (1997) on the Teochew community in Singapore—raise questions about the indissolubility of the language-identity bond, suggesting that speakers may place "the instrumental value of a language above [its] sentimental or symbolic value" (Wei et al., 1997: 380). Further, it has been suggested that the language-and-identity ideology is in direct conflict with another powerful ideology supporting minority language survival; namely, the ideology of language-and-territory (Myhill, 1999).

IV. Unresolved Conceptual and Methodological Issues in the Study of Language Shift and Revitalization

Myhill believes it is important to address the above-mentioned conflict in ideologies, because the language-and-identity ideology "undermine[s] the efforts of those working to preserve Indigenous minority languages threatened by demographic swamping, as speakers of mainstream languages move into areas historically dominated by Indigenous languages but do not learn or use these Indigenous languages"

(1999: 34), whereas the language-and-territory ideology "undermines the immigrant language supporter who is trying to fight for public acceptance of the immigrant language" (1999: 36); furthermore, he suggests not the choice of one ideology over the other, but rather a synthesis providing "general principles regarding when one ideology should take priority over the other" (1999: 47).

Grenoble, Whaley, and Lindsay (1998) argue for modifications to J. Edwards's (1992) typology, including the addition of literacy as a variable (mentioned above), the ranking of variables in terms of their predictive ability (e.g., the potential of economics to outweigh the other variables; Grenoble, Whaley, and Lindsay, 1998: 31), and the expansion of the *setting* category into local, regional, national, and extranational settings. While providing three case studies to justify these proposals (the general pattern of language endangerment in sub-Saharan Africa, the decline of Evenki in Siberia and the revitalization of Maori in New Zealand), they also acknowledge that many details remain to be filled in before the typology can be applied consistently (Grenoble, Whaley, and Lindsay, 1998: 52). Similarly, Fishman's eight-stage Graded Intergenerational Disruption Scale (GIDS) for reversing language shift is undergoing continuing criticism and refinement based on both theoretical concerns and the experience of applying it in different language revitalization contexts (e.g., J. Edwards, 1993; Fishman, 2000; Myhill, 1999; Romaine, 2006).

Scholars have recently begun to call for approaches to language shift and language revitalization that go beyond attention to surface linguistic structure on the one hand and macrolevel societal domains on the other. Wei and colleagues suggest that the "only coherent model which has been widely used in the study of language maintenance and language shift has been Fishman's domain analysis which focuses on the habitual language use of individual speakers" and that what is needed (and what they hope their work contributes to) is a model for analyzing underlying sociocultural processes, including both macrolevel social, political, and economic changes, as well as linguistic and psychological processes of individual speakers in interaction, as they relate to changes in habitual language use (Wei et al., 1997: 365). Similarly, Holmes (1997: 33) warns that survey methods in and of themselves may unwittingly hasten the demise of community languages because they focus on general trends and conceal detail; she recommends the use of census/survey methods to document change in sociolinguistic norms over time, complemented by more detailed ethnographic research to provide information on how those changes came about (Holmes, 1997: 26). In a recent issue of the *Journal of Language, Identity, and Education*, Hornberger (2006b) offers, and Hohepa (2006), May (2006), and McCarty (2006) comment and expand on, a heuristic approach drawing on Bakhtinian notions of voice in conjunction with the continua of biliteracy as a means of understanding why and how it is that the activation of indigenous voices can be a powerful force for both enhancing indigenous children's learning in school and promoting the revitalization of their languages. Hamel, too, recommends finding ways to get at an understanding of underlying processes of language shift as "constituted and reproduced in verbal interaction" (Hamel, 1997: 109); he argues for a sociolinguistic framework that takes into account not only linguistic structure (i.e., phonology, morphology, syntax, semantics) but also discourse structure (i.e., discourse strategies, organization of interaction) and cultural models (i.e., discourse styles, habitus).

Grappling with these unresolved conceptual and methodological issues can only strengthen work in language shift and language revitalization. The overriding unresolved issue is, of course, the defining question of the field, How do we predict which languages will shift, which will be maintained, and which successfully revitalized? Although this question is perhaps ultimately unanswerable given the complexity and unpredictability of human existence, the rewards of pursuing an answer are immeasurable.

NOTES

1. Language revitalization thus becomes the third in the trinity of logical alternatives for minority language use and change in situations of language contact—language shift and maintenance being the other two.

2. In preparation for this chapter in the first edition of the handbook, the 1996–1999 issues of the following journals were searched and consulted, in addition to the *IJSL* and *JMMD* mentioned above: *Anthropological Linguistics, Anthropology and Education Quarterly, Applied Linguistics, Bilingual Research Journal, Discourse and Society, International Journal of Bilingual Education and Bilingualism, Language and Education, Language in Society*, and *Language Problems & Language Planning*. I am especially grateful to Doris S. Warriner for her timely and strategic assistance in identifying and summarizing relevant literature and for her invaluable feedback on the first draft of that earlier version of the chapter. Thus, although the number of autonomous languages that are spreading has shrunk, languaging practices that include features of different languages are spreading more rapidly than ever. This phenomenon has to do with the spread of new technology and of media throughout the world. The shrinking of geographical space, coupled with the dynamism of the concept of time, will certainly accentuate languaging spread in the twenty-first century, as it shifts the traditional understandings of language spread.

CHAPTER 29

ECOLOGY OF LANGUAGES

PETER MÜHLHÄUSLER

I. Introduction

Ernst Haeckel, who coined the term *ecology* in 1866, characterized it in this way:

> By ecology we mean the body of knowledge concerning the economy of nature—
> the investigation of the total relations of the animal both to its inorganic and its
> organic environment; including, above all, its friendly and inimical relations with
> those animals and plants with which it comes directly or indirectly into contact—
> in a word, ecology is the study of all those complex interrelations referred to by
> Darwin as the conditions of the struggle for existence. (Translation by R. Brewer,
> 1988: 1)

Since this passage was written, a number of things have changed. One such change
is the extension of the ecology metaphor to new domains such as the "ecology of
mind" or the "ecology of language." A second change is the reevaluation of the
notion of "the conditions of the struggle for existence." Functioning ecologies are
characterized by predominantly mutually beneficial links and only to a small degree
by competitive relationships.

Ecological thinking has a number of distinguishing characteristics, including:

- Considerations not just of system internal factors but of wider environ-
  mental considerations
- Awareness of the dangers of monoculturalism
- Awareness of the limitations of both natural and human resources
- Long-term vision
- Awareness of those factors that sustain the health of ecologies

The first use of the ecology metaphor in linguistics is found in a paper by Voegelin,
Voegelin, and Schutz (1967) on the language varieties in Arizona, where a distinction

between intralanguage and interlanguage ecology is drawn. The metaphor was introduced independently in Haugen's seminal paper, titled "The Ecology of Language" (1972, based on a lecture given in 1970), in which he defines it as "the study of interactions between any given language and its environment" (1972: 325). The notion of environment includes the question "What concurrent languages are employed by speakers of a given language?" (1972: 336). Since then, there has been a great deal of descriptive work on a number of multilingual ecologies (e.g., Denison, 1982, for the European languages) as well as considerable conceptual refinement (e.g., Enninger and Haynes, 1984). By the early 1980s, the importance of this notion to applied linguistics had become established, particularly for the problem of language shift and loss (W. F. Mackey, 1980).

II. Ecology as a Struggle for Existence

Characteristic of much earlier work on language ecology is the dominance of the "struggle for existence" metaphor. Mackey highlights this competition:

> Languages too must exist in environments and these can be friendly, hostile or indifferent to the life of each of the languages. A language may expand, as more and more people use it, or it may die for lack of speakers. Just as competition for limited bio-resources creates conflict in nature, so also with languages. (1980: 34)

The same emphasis is encountered in Denison:

> There is a sense in which all the languages and varieties in an area such as Europe constantly act in supplementation of each other and in competition with each other for geographical, social and functional *Lebensraum;* hence the metaphorical appropriateness of the term "ecology." (1982: 6)

Again, Nelde argues,

> I would like to put forward the argument here that an ecological viewpoint is not of paramount importance for the description of stable diglossic or multilingual linguistic areas or for open bilingual conflict ones, but rather for linguistics/ ethnic contact areas in which one or more languages or variants are in danger of dying without any apparent political decisions—whether linguistic, administrative or repressive—being made. (1987: 189)

It seems extraordinary that Nelde reserves the ecological perspective to "pathological" situations and denies its use for gaining understanding of the many situations in the world in which language contact did not result in conflict and in which a large number of languages could coexist in a single communal community.

Denison's and Nelde's views can of course be explained by their concentration on the effects of nation-states and national languages, two constructs that indeed have led to a great deal of linguistic conflict and to the endangerment of many smaller forms of speaking. To regard European conditions as the measure of all things has not been helpful and remains problematic when it is applied to the strengthening of endangered languages around the globe. Empowering languages and making them more competitive by giving them grammars, lexicons, writing systems, and school syllabi is a recipe that ignores a basic ecological fact: What supports one language may not support another language. Each language requires its own ecological system.

The theme of a metaphorical struggle for existence has attracted the attention of creolists, as pidgin and creole languages are the result of imposing their patterns of communication and competition onto colonized language communities. Mufwene (2001) presents a detailed account of the emergence of creole languages in colonial contexts. He refines earlier notions of creoles being languages with European lexicon and non-European grammar by examining the selective advantages that individual grammatical features have in the competition between substratum and superstratum languages. The portrayal of language evolution as an essentially biological process, triggered off by external ecological conditions, offers only partial explanations. It ignores the importance of deliberate human choices and interventions resulting from the ability of the human inhabitants of linguistic ecologies to reflect on their languages. Calvet (2006: 53–56) has emphasized the importance of understanding the ecology of creole genesis and criticized Bickerton's proposed artificial creation of a creole.

III. On the Inhabitants of Language Ecologies

Denison (1982: 8) drew attention to a weakness of Haugen's ecological metaphor, the notion of language itself, which Haugen equates with a code: "However, the picture is greatly complicated by the fact that each language (variety), far from being a separate, independent organism or species, is rather to be seen as a symbiotic conglomerate" (1972: 325).

The characterization of languages as fixed grammatical codes is at best unnecessarily reductionist and at worst a contributing factor in the loss of linguistic diversity. Before the advent of European nation-states, there were a number of dialect continua such as the Germanic, stretching from the north of Scandinavia to the north of Italy and consisting of an indefinite number of varieties, of which the proximate ones were mutually intelligible and the more distant ones were not. At present, this continuum has been overlaid by a number of superimposed official (standard) languages such as Swedish, Norwegian, German, Dutch, and Letzebuergisch, each associated with a nation-state. Such national languages, as Haugen points out, are cultural artifacts. The ecological support system needed to

sustain them consists of political and educational institutions, information technology, and the like. It would be unwise to regard the species "European national
language" as the canonical case of an inhabitant of an ecology.

The label *language* is not applicable to the ways of speaking in pre–nation-state
Europe and indeed to the ways humans communicate in more traditional settings.
For the Pacific area, Grace (1993) has reexamined the notion of *languages* as employed
by mainstream linguistics and demonstrated its insufficiency in other than the cases
of few mainstream standard national languages.

As in the previously mentioned case of Europe, in many parts of the Pacific
we find long chains of interrelated dialects and languages with no clear internal
boundaries. In Micronesia, a group of very closely related languages are spoken all
the way from Truk in the east to Tobi in the west. As observed by Bender (1970),
"there are some indications that it is possible to establish a chain of dialectal connections from one end to the other with all contiguous dialects being mutually
intelligible." The question as to how many distinct languages can be counted in
the group remains difficult to answer, even for those who regard it as a sensible
question. Bender concludes that there are between 10 and 20 languages indigenous to the cultural-geographic area of Micronesia, the indeterminacy in numbers reflecting the indeterminacy as to the language limits among certain of the
nuclear languages.

Professional linguists, nevertheless, have identified such languages as Sonso-
rolese, Ulithian, Satawalese, Puluwat, Namonuito, and Trukese, the last having
become the language *par excellence* in this chain, as it is the best described variety
and spoken at the center of economic and communicational activities. In many
other areas, the places where missionaries, administrators, or linguists have settled
have become the focus for the development of linguistic systems of *language* status.
Arbitrary points on a linguistic continuum are made into discrete abstract entities
called *languages*, whereas all other reference points on the same continuum, unless
of course some important outsider has settled there, become marginalized, dialectal
deviations from the standard.

A particular problem arises when it comes to labeling the *languages* brought
into being by acts of power and other historical contingencies. The act of name
giving by European linguists and missionaries can be compared to Europeans
inscribing colonial landscapes with their place-names. An unintended but nevertheless real outcome is that only those ways of speaking that have been named are
regarded as languages and can potentially feature in catalogues such as the UNESCO
Redbook of Endangered Languages. Being a named language brings with it other
rights and privileges—for example, financial support for recognized minority languages within the European Union—and has led to considerable competition for
status and recognition. The emergence of named regional languages in post-Franco
Spain is another case in point: Galician, Asturian, and Valencian are examples of
ways of speaking that are becoming bounded and recognized, in the last case in an
atmosphere of considerable political conflict. Mühlhäusler (2006) has presented a
detailed criticism of language naming practices in Papua New Guinea.

Naming languages and imposing fixed boundaries has left numerous other ways of speaking behind, including some that have had tenuous labels attached to them. So-called controversial languages of Europe include Aromanian, Lallans, Piedmontese, Sater, Tsakonian, Zayrian, and about 50 others. One concludes (see Mühlhäusler, 1996b) that the notion of a language is not a description of the actual nature of most inhabitants of language ecologies but a metaphor, based on linguists' experience of European national languages whose applicability to other societies stands in need of explanation and justification.

The Western linguists' concept of language derives much of its importance from its use in reconstructing the past. Conventionally, such reconstruction has employed the metaphor of a family tree characterized by divergence and partheno-genesis. That the assumption of language splits and subsequent isolation is highly problematic has been a theme in the study of linguistic prehistory for some time—for instance, in the writings of Hill (1978). Newer ecologically oriented approaches to linguistic prehistory have been summarized by Nichols (1997). To understand the linguistic prehistory of the Pacific, for instance, one needs to work with linguistic units larger than single languages. Such units have been named language areas or language ecologies and describe the endemic interconnections between mutually dependent language groups.

IV. Contact without Conflict

Competition and conflict are the consequence of certain cultural practices among colonial powers that privilege particular ways of speaking, such as that of the Île de France located in the center of Paris, or in the case of Kâte of Papua New Guinea, the variety spoken around the main mission station. This is not to deny that a certain amount of linguistic conflict undoubtedly also occurred in pre–nation-state language ecologies, but it would seem unwarranted to characterize language ecol-ogies as a battlefield. Current understanding of natural ecologies suggests that, of the interrelationship between the inhabitants of any given ecology, the vast majority is mutually beneficial.

Ecological linguistics in recent years has begun to examine the question of how, in many parts of the world, a large diversity of ways of speaking manages to coexist side by side, several varieties often being used by the same communication community (e.g., Fill, 1993; Puetz, 1997).

When applied to the language ecologies of Melanesia and Australia, the useful-ness of Nelde's conflict hypothesis as a working hypothesis for sociolinguistic and applied sociolinguistic research seems much reduced. In a brilliant article about the functions of linguistic diversity in Melanesia, Laycock (1981), for instance, drew attention to the seemingly paradoxical situation in Papua New Guinea, where, in the most isolated areas, with the most difficult terrain (i.e., the New Guinea

Highlands), one finds not only the largest languages and the least linguistic diversity (languages with up to 150,000 speakers), but also the largest amount of violent intergroup conflict, whereas in the coastal areas, with a much easier terrain, we encounter the greatest linguistic variety, few languages with more than 500 speakers, extensive trade and cultural contacts, and, apparently, a much lower degree of inter-group conflict.

How is it, we might ask with Laycock (1979), that languages with as few as 50 speakers appear to have survived in an environment consisting of many larger surrounding languages? Or one may ask, with Sutton (1991: 63), about the language diversity of the Wik languages, in Northern Australia, where a dozen or more language groups manage to coexist in a very small geographical area over thousands of years in conditions of constant contact. A tentative conclusion would seem to be that social conflict and language contact are independent parameters, not part of the same package, and that unity and co-operation are compatible with both a high degree of linguistic diversity and contact as well as quasi-monolingualism and isolation. In many Australian languages, one encounters a special sublanguage, called *mother-in-law language*, which can differ lexically and structurally from the everyday languages spoken in a community. This additional language serves the principal function of conflict reduction when communicating with disharmonic relatives.

When one studies the complex language situation in Papua New Guinea, one will note that in addition to the very large number of languages spoken in the area, there were numerous structurally reduced intervillage pidgins used in trade relations between different language groups. The function of these intervillage pidgins appears to have been one of conflict reduction, as they were restricted to use in a small domain of discourse of the type that made it unlikely that controversial topics would arise. Dutton (1983), in his study of the ancient Hiri trade language of Papua, points out that the language was not used by women or for talking about women, a domain that might have caused violent conflict from time to time. One is reminded of a comment made somewhere by Hymes to the effect that a viable future for language study will require some complex comparisons between practices that bring people together and those that permit people to be apart, to consider what is shared and what is unique in verbal repertoires that include both *lingue franche* and personal choices.

The cases outlined here are suggestive of a class of languages whose principal function is that of conflict reduction. The mechanisms involved are of several types:

1. "Mother-in-law" language and a number of trade languages are referentially impoverished to such a degree as to reduce dramatically their ability to refer to conflict-generating topics. Modern sublanguages of English such as maritime English or aviation English are of a similar nature. They enable North and South Korean aircraft captains and pilots to communicate in one of the few domains in which neither party wishes to be confrontational. Pidgin languages, of course, are the reduced languages par excellence, and again and again one finds them used as neutral forms of speech between

politically hostile communities, one of the earliest pidgin Englishes, Chinese Pidgin English (CPE), being an example. It was used initially as a medium of communicating about a small range of trade commodities (see Baker and Mühlhäusler, 1990). Impoverishment of the type found in pidginization affords a balance between the desiderata of access (for trade) and privacy (for keeping interpersonal and cultural distance).

2. The flip side of the coin in creating social distance and conflict reduction is esotericity, making the language formally and lexically so complex as to make it virtually unlearnable to outsiders. Examples again abound in the traditional language ecology of areas such as Melanesia. Very small societies with only 100 or so speakers appear to have spent a great deal of energy on complicating the language. The Anm language, whose esotericity—described by Thurston in a number publications (e.g., 1987)—is one example. The members of such communities spend an enormous amount of energy on linguistic socialization. Such are the complexities of these languages that no one under about age 25 is regarded as a proficient speaker. Contact with outsiders is made by means of easier neighboring languages. In Western societies, legal English, Church languages, and such professional jargons as medical talk are the equivalent of such esoteric languages. Their very complexity makes it difficult for outsiders to come into conflict with their users.

3. A third solution to conflict reduction is that found in Kupwar village in India (Gumperz and Wilson, 1971), where a combination of phonetic and grammatical convergence and lexical divergence enables members of a highly multilingual community to function as a single communication network. More complex versions of this type of intercommunication and contact with little conflict used to be found in New Caledonia or in the Western Desert of Australia. Each small community actively used its own endolexicon but passively understood several synonyms (the exolexicon). This enabled them to communicate while overtly signaling one's own identity (Hansen, 1984).

The examples just elaborated would seem to afford some interesting generalizations:

a. All three conflict-reducing strategies involve people using two or more languages. This bi- or multilingualism is of a stable type and not transitional to monolingualism in a dominant language. There is no agenda—as found, for instance, among many Esperantists and other Western designers of world languages—to have a single language shared by all.

b. The solutions are very clearly intercultural, not monocultural. They exhibit a linguistic repertoire combining private language for intergroup identity with access languages for intergroup communication. In the cases surveyed, these access languages were relatively powerless.

c. The typical locus of the linguistic ecologies studied is not a nation-state.

d. None of the solutions is predicated on the idea that a shared code reduces conflict.

It is further noted that the reduction of linguistic conflict appears to require two functional types of languages: identity-preserving languages and linking languages (*lingue franche*). Conflict appears to arise most readily when these two functions are "fudged"—in other words, when a language, which is the language of identity of a community, is employed as a linking language. English or French as international languages, or indeed as languages of a nation such as Great Britain or France, are cases in point. Their dual function almost automatically enhances their power and thereby reduces the power of the other languages that come into contact with them. Additional conflict can arise if the speakers of a powerless language switch to English, or French, or whatever, as their language of identity.

V. THE INDEPENDENCY HYPOTHESIS
OF LANGUAGE

Mackey (1980) identifies another problem with Haugen's equation of language with a code—in other words, the impossibility of separating linguistic from other communicative behavior: "One may question the very existence of non-linguistic social behavior, since both language (*langue*) and language (language) are inseparably connected with all social activity" (Mackey, 1980: 36). This contrasts with the view of modern linguists that (a) languages are given and (b) language is independent of other external considerations.

N. V. Smith and Wilson, for instance, argue, "It seems to us that there is no way of describing or defining a given language without invoking the notion of a linguistics rule" (1979: 1); and "A human language...is a rule governed system, definable in terms of a grammar which separates grammatical from ungrammatical sentences, assigning a pronunciation and meaning to each grammatical sentence" (1979: 31).

The independency view of language is largely foreign to members of non-Westernized societies: In discussing the Javanese concept of *Basa*, B. R. Anderson argues,

> Basa, just like bahasa in Classical Malay, meant "language"; but it always included in its broad semantic field the notions of civility, rationality, and truth. This conception of "true" language meant that in the profoundest sense Javanese (or in their local habitats, Sundanese, Balinese and Buginese) was isomorphic with the world, as it were glued to it. It was this isomorphism, this inherence, which made for the efficacy of mantra. Because words, or particular combinations of them, contained Power, like *kings, grasses, banyan-trees* and *sacred images*, their utterance could unleash that Power directly on, and in, the word. (1990: 28)

Basa, thus, is an entirely different concept of language from modern *Bahasa* that emerged as a translation equivalent of Dutch *taal* in the sense of modern nation-state language defined by its grammar and lexicon. The absence of a clear boundary between linguistics and other cultural practices is also documented for numerous other groups as well. Australian indigenous ways of speaking, for instance, recognize the holistic package of speaking, knowledge, land, dreaming, people, and cultural practices, and this view has prevailed among many speakers of pre–nation-state languages of Europe despite a pretense among linguists and politicians to reduce them to closed systems of rules.

The metaphor of ecology, like all metaphors, has limitations. It does not lend itself readily to accommodating a holistic view of language and culture. Its etymology is *oikos* house/home—in other words, a cultural artifact that has boundaries and recognizes distinct inhabitants, furniture, fittings, and so forth. Although *oikos* denotes a static object, a holistic perspective sees speaking as an activity or mode of being.

VI. ECOLOGIES AS ADAPTIVE SYSTEMS

Language change in mainstream linguistics has been variably characterized as being governed by natural laws or by fashions. By contrast, an ecological perspective highlights adaptation to external circumstances as a major force. In support of this view, one can point to the coincidence of tribal and language boundaries and local natural ecologies in Australia (Tindale, 1974: 133) and a study by Nettle (1999) suggests a close correlation between language size, number of endemic species, and rainfall. Geographically spread out languages are encountered typically in dry areas, whereas small languages predominantly occur in high-rainfall areas. The unstoppable spread of English (a high-rainfall language) over the entire globe under this view suggests problems for discourses about the management of resources in desert areas.

Mühlhäusler (1998) argues that the hypothesis of adaptation can be tested most conveniently with evidence from recently occupied "desert islands": A particularly revealing case is that of the Pitkern/Norfolk language, which developed on Pitcairn after 1792 and which was transported to Norfolk Island in 1856. Although the constant scarcity of food and water on the overpopulated Pitcairn Island led to the development of a rich vocabulary for natural life forms, the subsistence affluence on the much larger Norfolk Island did not require the naming of every plant or animal and the lexicon for life forms in the Norfolk variety is far less developed as a consequence. A detailed study of language and of biological life forms on Pitcairn Island (Mühlhäusler, 2003b) shows a direct correlation between plants having no name and their endangerment or extinction. What is not named typically is not managed or is mismanaged.

Natural resources are not equally manageable everywhere, even if our ways of speaking suggest this. The predominance of grammar for effective causality in environments in which human actions can control nature (e.g., Central Europe) contrasts with predominant inherent causality in areas in which control over nature is difficult (e.g., in large desert areas). This hypothesis requires much additional research.

As languages get transported around the globe, the fit between them and the environment in which they are spoken of necessity weakens. As linguistic adaptation to a new environment takes several hundred years (e.g., the development of complex plant classification in Mäori after the arrival of Eastern Polynesian with a much less complex system in New Zealand), this misfit is likely to be a prolonged one and may turn out to be an important task for language planners.

VII. Types of Linguistic Ecologies

Ecolinguistics emphasizes the uniqueness of forms of human speaking rather than abstract universal principles, and the abstractions presented here have to be regarded as exploratory pretheoretical categories. This section draws on insights from a number of sources, most of them not written from a specifically ecolinguistic perspective.

An overview of writings on the psychology and sociology of language ecologies is given by Fill (1993: 14–17). The parameters determining ecological processes in language and society listed by Fill include

1. Status and intimacy
2. Similarity and difference of language in contact
3. Number of competing languages
4. Cultural, religious, and economic factors
5. Frequency of intermarriage
6. Functional distribution
7. Degree of codification
8. External intervention (1993: 15ff.)

Haarman (1980: 199) has argued that these variables have to be ecologically interconnected but does not provide a theoretical framework for achieving this. In my view, there are a number of additional parameters that need to be considered:

i. Whether languages are endemic or exotic to an ecology
ii. The degree of esotericity (closed in-group language) or exotericity (for intercommunication)
iii. The degree of vitality of the languages in an ecology
iv. Whether languages are 'packaged" with, or disconnected from, the ecology
v. Continuity (e.g., dialect or chains) or discontinuity (abrupt boundaries)
vi. Named or unnamed (i.e., degree of recognition by speakers and outsiders)

vii. Types of solutions for intergroup communication with outside groups
(bilingualism, *lingue franches*, pidgins)

I cannot offer a theoretical framework for connecting all these parameters, but I
believe that a number of typical ecologies that combine at least some of them. The
following are suggested:

Type 1: balanced equitable ecologies—Balanced ecologies are encountered in
highly multilingual regions such as Papua New Guinea (Laycock, 1979), the Cape York
Peninsula of Queensland (Sutton, 1991), or Brazil (Aikhenvald, 1999). Communication
among the speakers of multiple small languages is achieved by (a) multilingualism,
silent barter, or a layered language ecology in which local languages are employed
mainly to express local identity and discuss local knowledge, (b) intergroup pidgins
(often with a 50/50 mixed lexicon and a common core grammar) that are employed
mainly for transactions between villagers, and (c) regional *lingue franches* that are
employed mainly for signaling regional identity and exchanging regionally important
information. Examples of such layered ecologies have been documented for Native
(Indian) Americans in the southern United States by Drechsel (1997).

Type 2: mixed endemic/exotic ecologies—These are the consequence of large-scale
population movement such as have taken place many times in human history. The
coexistence, after initial disruptions, of earlier Papuan and later Melanesian languages in New Guinea or Timor prior to European colonization are examples, as are
such *Sprachbunds* as that of the Balkans or Arnhemland. Prolonged contacts tend to
result in the leveling of grammatical differences (familiarity leads to similarity),
with lexical differences sufficient to signal separate identities. The social structures
in such communities discourage social mobility, and both original endemic and
later introduced languages coexist side by side for prolonged periods of time. The
coexistence of Spanish and Guarani in postcolonial Paraguay is another instance.

Type 3: competitive ecologies—The stability of types 1 and 2 is the result of the
relative lack of power of the communities that inhabit these ecologies, whereas type
3 is characterized both by power differential and constant restructuring of the
ecology. The link between political and linguistic power is not a necessary one.
Before the advent of European nation-states, for instance, centralized political
power and tolerance of linguistic diversity were both present: Austria Hungary
before 1918 and Yugoslavia before its disintegration after Tito's demise are examples.
There is a continuing trend toward streamlining the linguistic ecologies of
nation-states, with the consequent marginalization and extinction of numerous
smaller ways of speaking. The spread of Bahasa Indonesia or Mandarin today
parallel the spread of French in France in the nineteenth century. With new transnational units becoming more important, smaller national languages are pushed
out by a small number of super languages such as English.

Type 4: language continuance and networks—These presuppose a lack of competition and an absence of national boundaries. Modern communication technology tends to require language standards and is ill suited to continua or structured
diversity.

Type 5: artificial ecologies—One can argue that diversity is natural whereas streamlining is artificial and further that most contemporary language ecologies are located at the artificial end of a continuum, with examples of instances in which exotic world languages were elevated to national languages being particularly artificial. Thus, the processes that have made English the national language of the Philippines and of Namibia are for the main part deliberate (artificial) interference in a language ecology. Attempts to create artificial languages as additions to, or replacements of, existing languages have been made from time to time. The promotion of Esperanto as the preferred language of the European Union is a recent example.

Type 6: isolated monolingual communities—Although isolated desert islands with a single language are an important discursive category, there are very few examples of prolonged isolation of monolingual communities. Easter Island Rapanui (Fischer, 1992) has been mentioned, though even in that instance there are doubts. Linguistic isolates (languages with no structural or historical affinity to surrounding languages, such as Basque) tend to be accounted in complex ecologies, and it can be argued that structured contacts rather than isolation promotes unique ways of speaking.

VIII. Discourse Analysis

Mühlhäusler and Peace (2006) have argued that over the years, the structural properties and metaphors of discourses about the ecology of languages and the relationship of language to ecological matters have developed into a distinct discourse category. Typically, the endangerment of the world's linguistic diversity is equated to the loss of biological diversity, and languages are increasingly being portrayed as inseparable parts of the biocultural environment.

Calvet's (2006) analysis of linguistic ecologies and discourses about them is one of the most comprehensive attempts to demonstrate how problems in prehistoric and historical linguistics can be solved by applying new ways of speaking to them.

IX. Applications of Ecological Linguistics

Applied linguistics involves the address of linguistic theories to a range of practical tasks such as language teaching, increasing document readability, decreasing obsolete racist and sexist aspects of language, and many other tasks. As a general principle, the applicability of a linguistic theory is determined by the number and type of parameters it contains; the fewer parameters, the smaller the range of its applications.

Time-free theory has little to contribute to problems of language development; monostylistic (monolectal) theory has little to contribute to problems of variable language use. A clear advantage of ecological linguistics over other theories is that it accounts for a large number of parameters and hence is particularly applicable to a range of practical tasks including at least the following:

1. Language planning
2. Language revival
3. Second language learning
4. Literacy teaching
5. Ecotourism language
6. Environmentally appropriate language

The importance of understanding language planning as ecological task was first raised by C. H. Williams (1991), and ecological language planning has since begun to replace technical structural planning worldwide (Liddicoat and Bryant, 2001).

It has become widely accepted that second language teaching involves more than structure and lexicon and that, for teaching/learning to be lasting, the learners, the classrooms, the attitudes of both teachers and students, and many other factors need to be included. Similarly, literacy is much more than skill in writing and reading. When the ecological conditions for a literate community are not given (e.g., Desert Schools, Department of Employment, Education, Training and Youth Affairs, 1996), literacy programs cannot take off.

Applied ecological linguistics begins with the question, What are the minimum ecological requirements to sustain a given linguistic practice over long periods of time? The ultimate aim of all ecological planning is to promote structured diversity—and such structural diversity implicates the different subdomains listed above:

a. The preservation of a number of smaller languages in a single communication ecology rather than the preservation of the most widely spoken/best documented language
b. The offering of a range of sociologically and structurally different languages for second language learners rather than the focusing on a single world language
c. The inclusion of native speakers and nonspeakers as well as semispeakers in language revival programs

Applied ecological linguistics also aims at greater harmony between languages and their physical environment rather than at mere "greenspeaking" (Harré, Brockmeier, and Mühlhäusler, 1999), which conceals and distorts this relationship. A study on the language of ecotourism (Mühlhäusler and Peace, 2006) suggests that nonecological focusing on a few charismatic species and heavy emphasis on "survival of the fittest" were common in this domain. Some observers have argued for environmentally more suitable language, paralleling arguments for gender, race, and age sensitivity.

Generally speaking, ecological linguists are weary of control and prescriptivism and particularly of single solutions. Because ecologies are complex and are generated by many parameters, understanding this complexity rather than focusing on single and simple formulae or universalist explanations is favored. As yet, streamlining and simple formulae remain the norm in applied linguistics, and genuinely ecological approaches are rare.

X. Outlook

The linguistics ecology of the earth, like its natural ecology, has become highly disturbed in the last 200 years, mainly as a result of European expansion with the consequent restriction and destruction of the habitats of the majority of the world's linguistic ecologies. The metaphor of ecology makes available both explanations for this process and solutions for reversing the current trends, which, if left unchecked, may result in the disappearance of up to 90% of the world's languages within two generations.

Since Haugen first created the term *language ecology* as an aid to description, there has been a gradual shift toward seeing it as a focus for action. Language ecologies provide a home in which different communities can coexist, and their diversity is seen as a valuable resource for restoring the disturbed relationship between human beings and their natural environment.

The notion of language ecology and ecological linguistics can't be reconciled with the system-focused and universalist trend in modern linguistics. Ecologically aware linguists (e.g., the contributors to Fill, 1996) regard modern linguistics as empirically unsustainable, as irrelevant, and as an obstacle to applied linguistics. This is also argued in the first English language textbook on ecolinguistics (Mühlhäusler, 2003a).

The themes of language and ecology and ecology of languages continue to be well represented at symposia and conferences in general and applied linguistics, and the number of younger (particularly European) scholars such as Döring (2002) who have made a name in this area is growing, as can be seen from the proceedings of the Thirty Years of Language and Ecology Conference (Fill, Penz, and Trampe, 2002). The effects of the ecological turn in linguistics require careful documentation, and it remains to be seen whether those effects will result in a paradigm shift in linguistics and whether the ecological turn lives up to its promise to contribute significantly toward improving the health of endangered languages and the natural environment.

PART IX

LANGUAGE POLICY AND PLANNING

CHAPTER 30

··

METHODOLOGIES FOR POLICY AND PLANNING

··

RICHARD B. BALDAUF, JR.

I. INTRODUCTION

···

Although a number of books have been written about research methodology appropriate for applied linguistics (e.g., Hatch and Lazaraton, 1991) and for the subfields of (second) language learning (e.g., Brown and Rogers, 2002; Makey and Gass, 2005; Mckay, 2006; Nunan, 1992) and language testing (e.g., Dörnyei, 2003; McNamara, 1996, 2000; McNamara and Roever, 2006; Weir, 2005), little attention has been paid to the methodology appropriate for one of the other major areas within applied linguistics—language policy and planning (cf. Eastman, 1983a: chapter 6; Kaplan and Baldauf, 1997a: chapter 4; Ricento, 2006a: chapters 8–12). Although journals like the *TESOL Quarterly* frequently discuss issues related to research methodology for language teaching (e.g., Brown 1991, 1992; *TESOL Quarterly* [28.4.] 1994), there is very little in the way of substantive discussion of language policy and planning (hereafter LPP) methodology in the journals or in related literature.

Given the lack of easily recognizable material explicitly relating to LPP methodology, this chapter has been developed as a survey based on a corpus review of published LPP literature as found in *Linguistic and Language Behavior Abstracts* (LLBA) from 1973 to 2008 and as available on WebSPIRS (up to 1988) and CSA Illumina (1989–2008). Using such a corpus of studies has advantages (e.g., there are abstracts, the material is published and usually readily available, the abstract is computer searchable, and it is widely used as an authoritative source) and disadvantages (e.g., it doesn't include government reports and other ephemeral material that may be the initial products of language planning; it probably has the limitations of other databases—selectivity, long lead time for item entry, different selection criteria at different times, bias in favor of articles in English or other "modernized languages"—for a discussion of these issues, see Baldauf and Jernudd, 1983). Nevertheless, the large number of studies in the corpus provides an initial starting point for doing a broadly based review of LPP methodology.

II. An Overview of Language Policy and Planning Publication

It has been asserted that LLP is a relatively new but growing field, dating back to the late 1960s as language planning and to the late 1940s as language engineering. Its initial focus on polity-level solutions for language problems in emerging states has been replaced with a broader emphasis both in geography and scope (micro, meso, and macro studies). The increased emphasis on the micro or local (Canagarajah, 2006; Liddicoat and Baldauf, 2008) has led to a recent greater focus on discourse and critical studies. The LPP literature has always been scattered and diverse, with only a few specialist journals, reflecting at least partly the variety of disciplines that contribute to the field. To better understand the nature and scope of the field, the LPP literature, as defined by the LLBA database, was examined to construct a LPP corpus. The LLBA used for this study was an online version that covers publications over the last 50 years but with most entries dating since 1973. The corpus for this study (see table 30.1) are the 10,999 articles related either to *language policy* or to *language planning* out of a total of 285,540 items related to *language* (26%) in the LLBA database. The references per 1,000 articles column shows how, in the 1970s, the LPP literature grew as a field relative to the language literature from only 6 articles per 1,000 in 1973 to 41.1 articles per 1,000 in 1979. The 10-year period from 1979 to 1988 saw 1,840, or 49 articles per 1,000 published, whereas the period from 1989 to 1998 saw 4,192, or 39.4 articles per 1,000 published, and 1999 to 2008 saw 4,114, or 39.4 articles per 1,000 published, indicating the emerging strength of the field in the 1980s with a leveling off of interest in relative terms since. However, from the total of 10,999 LPP articles, 1,917 book reviews must be deducted, leaving a corpus of 9,082 potentially research-related items. The decline in the number of articles published in 2008 (and 2007) is an artifact of the corpus data, as it takes several years for most articles from a particular year to be added to a database.

The diversity of sources in the total LPP corpus can be seen in part by the amount of non-English language material it contains; in other words, 6,896, or 62.7%, were in English—this is an increase from 57% in 1998; 1,150, or 10.4% (13.3% in 1998), were in German; 1,123, or 10.2% (12.4%, in 1998), were in French; 333, or 3% (2.9% in 1998), were in Spanish; 187, or 1.7% (2.6% in 1998), were in Russian; 185, or 1.7% (2.0% in 1998), were in Italian, whereas 1,125, or 10.2%, were in other languages (or the language was uncoded).

Table 30.1. Language planning and language policy items in the *Linguistics and Language Behavior Abstracts* database for 1973–1988 (WebSPIRS—shaded) and 1989–2008 (CSA Illumina)

Year of Publication	Language	Language Planning	Language Policy	Planning or Policy	References Per 1,000
2008	4,623	170	100	204	44.1
2007	9,990	339	246	426	42.6
2006	11,213	342	250	433	38.6
2005	10,912	327	228	424	38.9
2004	11,624	347	285	452	38.9
2003	11,377	307	231	390	34.3
2002[a]	10,705	350	280	455	42.5
2001	11,771	371	268	469	39.8
2000[b]	11,369	328	222	402	35.4
1999	10,718	377	280	459	42.8
1999–2008	104,302	3,258	2,390	4,114	39.4
1998	11,694	369	236	453	38.7
1997	13,019	409	306	549	42.2
1996	13,085	455	244	556	42.5
1995	12,689	376	186	446	35.1
1994	11,003	298	153	364	33.1
1993	10,103	333	173	407	40.3

(*continued*)

Table 30.1. Continued

Year of Publication	Language	Language Planning	Language Policy	Planning or Policy	References Per 1,000
1992	9,436	296	161	367	38.9
1991	9,244	324	176	390	42.2
1990	9,013	286	202	385	42.7
1989	7,232	205	148	275	38.0
1989–1998	106,518	3,350	1,985	4,192	39.4
1988	5,472	157	139	221	40.4
1987	5,077	224	172	310	61.1
1986	4,720	176	128	229	48.5
1985	3,349	108	93	154	46.0
1984	3,005	153	130	201	66.9
1983	2,981	126	98	163	54.7
1982	2,864	102	91	149	52.0
1981	3,250	94	92	146	44.9
1980[c]	3,349	64	81	124	37.0
1979	3,475	90	93	143	41.1
1979–1988	37,542	1,294	1117	1840	49.0
1978	4,451	113	83	166	37.3
1977[d]	4,550	69	48	104	22.8

1976	4,560	75	37	93	20.4
1975[e]	4,568	53	19	62	13.6
1974[f]	4,606	36	15	44	9.6
1973	4,337	16	15	26	6.0
1969–1972	3,003	9	9	16	5.3
1969–1978	30,075	371	226	511	17.0
Database[g]	285,540	8,547	5,853	10,999	38.5

[a]*Language Policy* begins publishing.
[b]*Current Issues in Language Planning* begins publishing.
[c]*Journal of Multilingual and Multicultural Development* begins publishing.
[d]*Language Problems & Language Planning* begins publishing.
[e]*Language Planning Newsletter* begins publishing.
[f]*International Journal of the Sociology of Language* begins publishing.
[g]Total in LLBA CSA Illumina online data base.

441

This compares to the remaining *language* related items[1] in LLBA in which 192,021 items, or 66.3% (70.6% in 1998), were in English; 21,938, or 8% (8.9% in 1998), were in German; 20,803, or 7.6% (8.3% in 1998), were in French; 6,265, or 2.3% (3.0% in 1998), were in Russian; 7,086, or 2.6% (1.8%, in 1998), were in Spanish; 4,934, or 1.8% (1.6% in 1998), were in Italian, whereas 21,494, or 7.8% (5.8% in 1998), were in other languages (or the language was uncoded). (See Ammon, 1998, for a discussion of the decline of languages other than English—especially German—in databases in general.) The LPP corpus had proportionally fewer items in English (62.7% versus 66.3%) and more items in German, French, and other languages than the non-LPP language items in the database. This percentage had declined markedly since 1998, suggesting that LPP items come from a slightly more diverse set of language backgrounds than language items in general, but that this distinction is narrowing.

III. Methodology as Represented in the LPP Corpus

A variety of methodologies have been identified as appropriate to LPP research (e.g., Eastman, 1983b; Kaplan and Baldauf, 1997; Ricento, 2006b). Methodologies are related to the kinds of questions that the researcher wants to answer and are often discipline based. The variety of techniques used in LPP research reflects in part the multidisciplinary nature of the field. The LPP corpus was searched for instances of various methodological terms or their equivalents, and the number of studies found were noted. Such searching is imprecise, as it depends on what terms were used in the abstracting process, their spelling (e.g., color, colour) or form (e.g., methodology, methodologies), and so on. The subsets of studies were then weeded for "false friends" (e.g., *methodology* was frequently found to be related to *language teaching* rather than *research; anthropology* was a term used in conjunction with the author's department rather than in *anthropological linguistics*) and then examined for examples that clearly demonstrated the methodology's use in LPP situations. Given a large number of potential examples, exemplary articles for this study were selected not only for their illustrative value, but to show the variety of work being done in LPP around the world, the wide range of publications for LPP material, and the range of authors working in the field.

The studies were also selected to illustrate different types of LPP studies in the literature. They were classified under four categories: (a) as a comment on methodology, on the basis of what LPP methodology actually had been used in (b) prelanguage policy and planning studies, or (c) what is reported in "evaluative studies of LPP and (d) in *ex post facto* or descriptive studies. Originally it was intended also to classify studies under "unplanned sociolinguistic change" (see Baldauf, 1994), but this proved too difficult to do, working primarily with the abstracts in this corpus. This analysis is summarized in table 30.2, in which articles are listed by methodology and by type of study. In the following sections, for each methodology, a number of illustrative studies are briefly summarized. With the exception of methodology, the topics are ordered from the most frequently to the least frequently occurring in the LPP corpus.[2]

Methodology(ical)

Although methodology is not the focus of articles being written for the field, this does not mean that methodology is not discussed. For example, Haarmann (1990) reviews the functional ranges of language planning and methodology and presents an ideal typology that argues for the need to consider prestige planning and the roles of individuals and groups in that planning. Hamel (1986) attempts for language policy purposes to formulate theoretical-methodological criteria for research into the relationships between national and indigenous languages in Mexico. Schiffman (1994) provides an alternative approach to language policy that puts greater emphasis on the role of linguistic culture in LPP development. Labrie, Nelde, and Weber (1994) summarize the methodology to be used to study the situation of minority languages in the European Community. Blommaert (1996) evaluates the past performance of the tradition of language planning from the perspectives of theory, concepts, and methodology to improve future LPP studies. Holmes (1997) examines methods used by New Zealand researchers to collect community language data and the relationship between methodology and theory and concludes that the expressive functions may provide a basis for reversing language shift. Baldauf (1994) argues that "unplanned" LPP occurs regularly and is an important aspect of much LPP implementation (see Eggington, chapter 31 in this volume). Poth (1996) provides a methodological outline of LPP for the introduction of national languages into schools in Africa. Although these articles deal with methodological issues, they do not deal with methodology as a topic in its own right, as was the case in the references in the first section of this chapter.

History(ical)

A large number of items in the LPP corpus have a major historical focus. A few examples of items with this focus include Daud's (1996) historical overview of the five stages of the development of the Indonesian language; a description of the functions and activities of the Academy of the Hebrew Language (Bar Acher and Kaufmann, 1998); an overview of the effect of the Soviet dictatorship on the Lithuanian language (Palionis, 1997); a review of the developments in Quebec French during the last 20 years (Poirier, 1998); a discussion of the implications of the historical context of African multilingualism for Ugandan language policy (Pawlikova-Vihanova, 1996), and the historical context for language policy in

Table 30.2. A summary of study methodologies used in language policy and planning

Methodology: Language Planning and Policy	Pre-LPP Studies	Evaluation of LPP Studies	Descriptive LPP Studies
Methodology/(ical) issues: Eastman (1983a: chapter 6); Baldauf (1994); Haarmann (1990); Hamel (1986); Kaplan and Baldauf (1997b: chapter 4); Ricento (2006a); Schiffman (1994)	Labrie, Nelde, and Weber (1994)	Blommaert (1996); Holmes (1997)	Poth (1996)
Historical analysis: Kaplan and Baldauf (1997b: 88); Wiley (2006)		Clyne (1997a); Henry (1997); Pawlikova-Vilhanova (1996)	Awoniyi (1975); Bar-Acher and Kaufmann (1998); Daud (1996); Poirier (1998); Palionis (1997)
Measurements of language attitudes: Eastman (1983a: 190); Gorter (1987); Winter (1992)	Verhoef (1998)	Guilford (1997); Kennedy (1996)	Bourhis (1997); Varro (1997)
Implementation and evaluation surveys: Eastman (1983: 196); Kaplan and Baldauf (1997b: 90); Rubin (1971)	Colomer (1996)	Dogançay-Aktuna (1995); Daoust (1992); Strubell (1996); Varga (1995)	Grin (1996)
Comparative method: Eastman (1983b: 185)		Michelman (1995); Pakir (1993)	Hornberger (1996); Robinson (1994); Sommer (1991); Sonntag (1996)
Proficiency measures: Contextualized proficiency test; Eastman (1983b: 199)	Van Weeren (1995)	Extra (1995); Strubell (1996)	Liddicoat (1996); Tucker (1997); Verhoeven (1997)
Corpus analysis: Kaplan and Baldauf (1997b: 99); Bailey and Dyer (1992)	Gouadec (1994)	Kennedy (1996); Piehl (1996); Planelles-Ivanez (1996)	Glinert (1998); Kenrick (1996), Otto (1991)

Anthropological linguistics: Kaplan and Baldauf (1997b: 100); Fishman (1993); Grillo (1989)		Hendry (1997); Henry (1997); Morphet (1996)	Jernudd (1971); Thornell (1997)
Sociolinguistic survey(s): Eastman (1983b: 192, 198); Gorter (1987); Kaplan and Baldauf (1997b: 102); Tse (1982)	Apronti (1974); Dieu (1991)	LePage (1986); O'Riagain (1988)	Crowley (1994); Kayambazinthu (1998); Mehrotra (1985); Shevyakov (1987)
Interlanguage: Eastman (1983b: 189)	Cavalli (1997)		Calvet (1997); Glenn (1997); Smalley (1988)
Ethnography of communication: Kaplan and Baldauf (1997b: 101); sociolinguistic interview: Eastman (1983b: 198); Fishman (1994)			Chick (1992); Cooper and Danet (1980)
Cost-benefit analysis: Eastman (1983b: 178); Kaplan and Baldauf (1997b: 94)	Colomer (1996); Markee (1991); Mühlhäusler (1996b)		

Australia (Clyne, 1997a). The historical context is nearly always important in understanding LPP in a particular polity and has been incorporated into a number of recent polity-wide LPP studies (e.g., those in Baldauf and Kaplan, 2000; Kaplan and Baldauf, 1999; and Spolsky and Shohamy, 1999b).

Language Attitudes

Attitudes (and values) are an important aspect of language planning (see Haarmann, 1990) because the attitudes of individuals can have a major impact on the success or failure of LPP or in the adoption of language change (e.g., Guilford, 1997, for the acceptance of English loanwords in French). There are a number of studies in the corpus that discuss the general issue of attitudes and language planning (e.g., Bourhis, 1997, in France and Canada, or Verhoef, 1998, about the new process to promote new language attitudes in South Africa). Winter (1992) discusses how discourse analysis can be used to collect information about language attitudes. Attitudes may also be an important indicator of the success (or failure) of certain language planning features (e.g., Kennedy, 1996, for the use of nonsexist language in job advertisements). Attitudes are also important in our understanding of particular language problems (e.g., in Varro, 1997, for the source of pejorative social attitudes toward immigrants in France).

Evaluation

As Rubin (1971) indicated nearly 30 years ago, there is a dearth of data on the processes that actually characterize LPP. Little has changed. Although the corpus contains a substantial number of items relating LPP and evaluation, most are not specifically about the evaluation of LPP but relate more narrowly to testing and proficiency issues. There are also a number of studies in the corpus using other methodologies that make evaluative statements about LPP (see the category "Evaluation of LPP Studies" in table 30.2). Examples of evaluation studies include those by Daoust (1992), who examined the effectiveness of Quebec's language planning program in bringing French use to private business by examining the language choice of workplace terminology; Grin (1996), who reviews the language economics literature, commenting on a range of matters including their use in the evaluation of language policies; Colomer (1996), who examines the economic efficiency of translation versus language learning in Europe; Dogançay-Aktuna (1995), who evaluates Turkish language reform after 60 years; Varga (1995), who evaluates the effects of the recent literary version of Rhaeto-Romance for the five dialect populations who speak and write the language in the Grisons canton of Switzerland; and Strubell (1996), who evaluated the Catalan government's language policy for normalizing Catalan. Most of these items represent quasi-evaluations, rather than detailed examinations of policy and practice. Perhaps such documents exist in the more ephemeral government literature, but they aren't abstracted in LLBA.

Comparative Studies

It is often possible to get a better understanding of language planning and policy situations by using comparative data. For example, Hornberger (1996) uses a comparative approach to indigenous languages and literacies to highlight the common challenges that such languages face, especially because individual language work is often undertaken in isolation; Michelman (1995) highlights the differing impact that British and French colonial language policies have had on the production of African literatures; Pakir (1993) provides a descriptive and evaluative look at bilingual education in Singapore, Malaysia, and Brunei Darussalam; Robinson (1994) compares policies to support minority languages in Canada and Cameroon; Sonntag (1996) compares the relationship between language and politics in India in Bihar State (relatively politically stable) and Uttar Pradesh State (marked by high political conflict); and Sommer (1991) compares factors affecting language maintenance and shift for the Nubian in Egypt and the Yai in Botswana. Comparisons such as these allow for the development of LPP commonalties or allow hypotheses about differences in LPP approaches to be examined.

Proficiency

Much of the LPP-related literature on proficiency talks about proficiency needs in the LPP context (see, for example, Liddicoat, 1996, for Australia; Tucker, 1997, for the United States; or Verhoeven, 1997, for bilingual proficiency) rather than actually evaluating proficiency. The literature also contains work about developing proficiency standards (e.g., Van Weeren, 1995), but as noted under evaluation, there is relatively little evaluation of proficiency (cf. Strubell, 1996, briefly evaluates policy outcomes for Catalan using language proficiency information from the census, whereas Extra, 1995, presents data on the language proficiency of ethnic minority children in Holland). Language proficiency is clearly an important LPP goal, but its assessment is difficult and not much of this sort of work is available in the literature.

Corpus Studies

The literature also contains a substantial number of corpus-related studies, although many of these relate to corpus planning rather than corpus as a methodology. Several other studies relate to lexicography (e.g., Glinert, 1998, for an overview of the revernacularization of Hebrew) or to terminological development (e.g., Gouadec, 1994, looks at official French computer terminological development). Although such work is an important component of corpus planning, its connection with some specific LPP may be more difficult to discern. Another use of corpus analysis is to examine particular bodies of LPP literature (e.g., Piehl, 1996, for Finnish language standardization; Kenrick, 1996, for the written corpus of Romani; or this chapter) for LPP-related directions or trends. In other uses, Bailey and Dyer

(1992) show how random samples from a corpus of speech data can be used to provide inferences about the language use of populations, whereas Planelles-Ivanez (1996), Kennedy (1996), and Otto (1991) use samples of written news media to look at linguistic policy related to the changing use of feminized job titles in French, sex discrimination in recruitment advertisements, or the promotion of German in France as assessed by language-related job advertisements.

Anthropology(ical)

Anthropological approaches normally involve the field study of a language in its social context. The corpus provided a substantial number of items that linked LPP and anthropology, but many were not clearly linked with fieldwork. Examples of this method include Hendry (1997), who, based on interviews in 1987 and 1995, examined the effects of the Spanish government's policy of official bilingualism in Rioja Alavesa (on the periphery of the Basque region) and found that the policy marginalized the identity of the population as neither Basque nor Spanish. Henry (1997) reviewed the impact of efforts since 1968 by the state government to develop French in Louisiana and noted modest success on the educational side. Thornell (1997) examined the social interaction and general characteristics of the lexicon of Songo—a newly developing lingua franca of the Central African Republic. Morphet (1996) provides an overview of an ethnographic study of the literacy practices of unschooled people in South Africa, showing that it was not illiteracy itself but issues of power and control that were problematic. Fishman (1993) argues for the necessity of ethnolinguistic consciousness; in other words, the involvement of the community in language maintenance and preservation is necessary for language revival. Jernudd (1971) used an anthropological linguistic approach to examine social change and Aboriginal speech variation in Australia. As an introduction to a volume on the topic of social anthropology and the politics of language, Grillo (1989) provides a review that explores how anthropologists are concerned with issues of language and power. These studies indicate the usefulness of an anthropological approach to LPP problems.

Sociolinguistic Survey(s)

The corpus contains a fairly small number of examples of this method. Two (Tse, 1982, for Taiwan, and Gorter, 1987, for Frisian in the Netherlands) had, as their primary focus, discussion of the method, whereas Mehrotra (1985) for South Asia and Apronti (1974) and Shevyakov (1987) for Ghana provide brief reviews of these respective situations using survey data. O'Riagain (1988) compared the results of the 1973 and 1983 national language surveys to describe and explain the evolving pattern of bilingualism in Ireland. This could be classified as an evaluation of the state's language policy aimed at the maintenance and revival of Irish. Dieu (1991) reports on the use of a sociolinguistic survey to determine the most practical language for use for literacy development in the northern Cameroon, whereas LePage

(1986) used a sociolinguistic survey to collect data on Creole language development in Belize. Census data can also be used to provide sociolinguistic and LPP-related data (see Clyne, 1997a; Crowley, 1994). Although sociolinguistic surveys can arguably be a foundation methodology for polity LPP (see Kaplan and Baldauf, 1997a), as well as for more micro situations, their reported used is not great, and it is noteworthy that 16 of the 18 studies in the corpus were published in the 1970s or 1980s. Although not part of the LLBA corpus, Kayambazinthu (1999) provides a more recent example of how survey data (for Malawi) can contribute to LPP.

Interlanguage

The traditional micro use of this term for learners at a stage of second language acquisition between L1 and L2 has been broadened to reflect the social extent to which languages, or certain deviations from mainstream language, are suggestive of a stable ethnic usage or dialect (Eastman, 1983b: 190). Whereas Cavalli (1997) uses interlanguage in the individual sense, Calvet (1997—for the use of lingua francas of African cities), Glenn (1997—for the preservation of minority languages in Europe and North America), and Smalley (1988—for the hierarchy of languages in Thailand) use interlanguage in a macro context, examining the sociolinguistic and LPP relationship between languages. When searching the LPP corpus for the terms *interlanguage* (or *ethnography of communication*) and *LPP*, there was often a false relationship between co-occurrence of the two because they were found in volumes of collected papers, but in separate chapters.

Ethnography of Communication

Marxist and poststructuralist critiques of language planning have suggested that ethnographic LPP research would help to avoid the elitism, inequality, and modernist approaches as well as the lack of support for multiculturalism found in classical LPP. Fishman (1994), although acknowledging the validity of such critiques, takes a minority language perspective, arguing that such critiques focus more on theory than on actual practice, and that one needs to be careful not to replace one set of exploitations with another. Despite the call for the use of the technique, very few items were found in the corpus in which LPP was examined from the viewpoint of the ethnography of speaking/communication. Cooper and Danet (1980) discuss it in relation to language planning in Israel, whereas Chick (1992) uses it in a comparative micro LPP study of compliment and response in a South African university as an indicator of changes in postapartheid power relations.

Cost-Benefit Analysis

Cost-benefit analysis was an early method suggested in the LPP literature for evaluating language decision making. However, the difficulties of assigning monetary values to benefits in the language area, and the fact that many language decisions are often made for political rather than for economic reasons, has limited the use of this technique. Colomer (1996) examines the economic efficiency of translation versus language learning in Europe using cost-benefit analysis; Mühlhäusler (1996a) discusses the benefits of learning lesser taught/learned languages in terms of their costs and benefits; whereas Markee (1991) uses cost-benefit analysis to look at language planning of communicative innovations. Reagan (1983) examines cost-benefit analysis as part of the potential of economics for LPP. As Fasold (1984) and J. Edwards (1985) indicate, very few cost-benefit analyses have been done or are available for scrutiny.

Other Methods

A number of methods originally suggested by Eastman (1983b) as possible tools for LPP that seem not to have been taken up in the corpus of LPP literature include *mutual intelligibility studies* (1983a: 195; cf. Rahman, 1995; Gonzalez, 1989), *language distance* (Eastman, 1983a: 186; cf. Khubchandani, 1989), *transaction theory* (Eastman, 1983b: 200; cf. Laitin and Eastman, 1989), *degrees of bilingualism* (Eastman, 1983b: 184; cf. Garmendia, 1994), *glotoeconomics* (Eastman, 1983a: 180), *ethnic decision making* (Eastman, 1983b: 182), and *dominance configuration* (Eastman, 1983b: 185). Her analysis of emerging methodology was based on work in the 1970s (when LPP was in its formative stages as a field) and indicates that a wide range of methodologies have been considered for LPP work.

Misuses of Method

This is a difficult area to document, especially based on a corpus study such as the one employed here. However, from LPP theses/dissertations I have been asked to read in which the methodological component was weak, and from verbal reports of problematic survey questions in large national studies I have heard about, methodology seems to be a problem. Although these do not constitute a large or random sample, they further strengthen the suggestion that issues of methodology may be undervalued in the LPP field.

IV. Summary and Conclusions

This corpus study demonstrates that LPP has grown into a substantial field of study since it first formally appeared in the database literature (as represented by LLBA). Around 4% of studies abstracted in LLBA related to language are related to language policy and planning. This literature is scattered across a wide range of publications related to many different disciplines and is published more frequently in a language other than English than is the LLBA literature in general. Unlike some other areas of applied linguistics, methodology and theory are, by and large, not issues for metadiscussion in the literature. It appears scholars bring to their LPP studies the more general traditions of the humanities and social sciences, with a lot of the work having an historical or comparative component or being merely descriptive. Statistical surveys or quantitative-data-based studies and evaluations seem to be relatively infrequent.

Based on this initial analysis of the LPP literature, the question needs to be asked whether this is a satisfactory state of affairs or whether, on the other hand, there are unique methodological demands studies of LPP make on scholars that should be better represented in the literature. What this brief survey of the literature points up, however, is the widely dispersed theoretical base of LPP—the nature of the underlying views of language, of language change, and of the politics of language change.

NOTES

1. The 285, 540 *language* items, less the 10,999 *language planning or policy* items, leaves 274,541 non-LPP language items.

2. As previously indicated, the imprecision of the search techniques makes the actual number of studies found relatively meaningless without detailed analysis of the focus of each of the studies located. Such an exercise was beyond the scope of this corpus review that sought primarily to illustrate the methodologies in use.

CHAPTER 31

UNPLANNED LANGUAGE PLANNING

WILLIAM G. EGGINGTON

INTRODUCTION

The concept of "unplanned language planning" might appear to be an oxymoron but, as this chapter will indicate, unplanned language planning plays an important role in any language planning process. Because the term includes the semantic notion of an "unplanned" planned activity, precise definitions of something that is unplanned are difficult to construct. Kaplan and Baldauf (1997b: 297–299), with reference to Baldauf (1994) and Luke and Baldauf (1990), suggest that unplanned language planning may involve language modification affected by accident, by a shared set of *laissez-faire* attitudes toward a language situation, and/or by an ad hoc solution to an immediate problem.

Recognizing the potential impact of unplanned language planning with respect to formal language planning, Kaplan and Baldauf (1997b: 298–299) and Baldauf (1994) offer four reasons that a formal language planning activity needs to consider unplanned language planning activities in its planning stages:

1. Planned and unplanned language planning attempts can coexist in a symbiotic relationship, and thus a formal language plan is incomplete unless it considers existing unplanned language plans within the social ecosystem.
2. The existence or nonexistence of unplanned language planning can offer vital information, allowing the language planner to consider the social- and language-related factors as to why an unplanned language planning exists or does not exist.

3. The relationship between planned and unplanned language planning and social power and control are such that any formal language plan needs to consider the power relationships revealed in all the unplanned language planning activities in the society.

4. The almost universal language competency that human beings share seems to give most people all the authority they need to become involved in language planning activities especially at the local and microplanning level. This situation can create a myriad of mostly unplanned language planning activities and attitudes. Language planners need to address these attitudes and activities in any formal plan.

Obviously, when language planners attempt to develop and implement a formal language plan, unplanned language planning activities in the society need to be thoroughly considered. Ironically, neglecting the importance of unplanned language planning could easily lead to the formal language plan being "sucked into" an unplanned morass. Ridge (2004: 210) suggests such a process may be occurring with South African language planning efforts.

As the above brief review indicates, to date, the discussion of unplanned language planning tends to allocate rather benign descriptive attributes to this phenomenon. However, it could be argued that, when something happens in the social ecosystem by accident, or because of *laissez-faire* attitudes, or because of an ad hoc solution, underlying ideologies are being revealed. In a sense, unplanned language planning does not just "happen." There are reasons that "unplanning" occurs. Consequently, rather than blandly reviewing instances of unplanned language planning, the following discussion attempts to get to the heart of unplanned language planning in terms of the ideologies and motivations that cause the accident, create the *laissez-faire* attitudes, and develop the ad hoc solutions. In so doing, the definition of unplanned language planning may be extended to include an ideological component that suggests that matters involving language issues in society do not unaccountably spring forth from the language ecosystem.

An Overview of Ideologies in Unplanned Language Planning

A review of some of the types of contemporary unplanned language planning activities suggests that there are at least two somewhat overlapping categories that reveal the ideological nature of unplanning in language planning: (1) unplanned language planning in social engineering planning and (2) unplanned language planning conducted by nonspecialists.

Space does not permit an extensive elaboration of these two types of unplanned language planning in all settings and contexts, but it is evident that they occur at the national level, the state and regional level, the local level, and the site-specific level. What follows is an elaboration of a number of unplanned language planning activities across a selection of these levels.

UNPLANNED LANGUAGE PLANNING IN SOCIAL ENGINEERING PLANNING

The closest that formal language planning gets to *social engineering* is probably through *social purpose language planning* as described by Kaplan and Baldauf (1997 B[1997b]: 122–152). However, it does appear that unplanned language planning is frequently utilized by those wishing to undertake various forms of social engineering. With respect to national social engineering, Sir Karl Popper, renowned philosopher of science, offers a typical "Popperian" critique. Popper divides social engineers into two groups—those who engage in *piecemeal* engineering and those with a more utopian, ideologically driven outlook who engage in *holistic* engineering. At the risk of relying excessively on his work, he states,

> The piecemeal engineer [as opposed to the *holistic* or *Utopian* engineer] knows, like Socrates, how little he knows. He knows that we can learn only from our mistakes. Accordingly, he will make his way, step by step, carefully comparing the results expected with the results achieved, and always on the look-out for the unavoidable unwanted consequences of any reform; and he will avoid undertaking reforms of a complexity and scope which make it impossible for him to disentangle causes and effects, and to know what he is really doing....
>
> The holists reject the piecemeal approach as being too modest. Their rejection of it, however, does not quite square with their practice; for in practice they always fall back on a somewhat haphazard and clumsy although ambitious and ruthless application of what is essentially a piecemeal method without its cautious and self-critical character. The reason is that, in practice, the holistic method turns out to be impossible; the greater the holistic changes attempted, the greater are their unintended and largely unexpected repercussions, forcing upon the holistic engineer the expedient of piecemeal improvisation. In fact, this expedient is more characteristic of centralized or collectivistic planning than of the more modest and careful piecemeal intervention; *and it continually leads the Utopian engineer to do things which he did not intend to do; that is to say, it leads to the notorious phenomenon of unplanned planning.* (Popper, 1961: 68–69, emphasis added).

The relevance of Popper's lengthy definition of unplanned planning to language planning is obvious. Language planning is an extremely complex undertaking with a host of controllable and uncontrollable variables. As Kaplan and Baldauf (1997b) explicate in detail, language planners, working within a human resource management mind-set, follow theories and practices that Popper would have no difficulty labeling as "piecemeal." This mind-set has no doubt arisen because experienced language

planners recognize the complexities involved in any language planning activity—
and the potential for unintended consequences deriving from any overlooked variable. Consequently, piecemeal, language-as-human-resource language planners
tend to construct elaborate empirical procedures for information gathering usually
through surveys. They then use the information analyzed in a survey report to
inform their policy development and to develop their implementation plan. This
plan is then implemented. At all stages in the language planning procedure, there
are a series of "feedback" loops to ensure that there are no unintended consequences
of any action. Most of these feedback loops involve seriously valuing the wishes and
desires of the people immediately affected by the implementation of the policy
within a bottom-up, top-down meeting of minds. As much as possible, the inculca-
tion of scientific objectivity into this process reduces the potential for language
planners to imprint their personal ideologies into language planning outcomes. In
this way, language planners hope to avoid being enmeshed in the repercussions that
follow when resistance to a plan develops from segments in society that had been
overlooked in the planning process.

On the other hand, language plans motivated by a desire to engineer a holistic
solution to a perceived problem often fall into Popper's unplanned planning trap.
An ideological framework that either longs for some form of Utopian society or
attributes failure to achieve a Utopian ideal to a single causality usually motivates
these "social engineers." As such, any behavior exhibited by people in the society
that does not fit "desired" behavior is seen as a "problem" that needs to be fixed—
and because it is a problem, it needs to be fixed as quickly, efficiently, and directly as
possible.

Instances of this mentality to language-related issues in social contexts are plentiful. This is probably because of the binding relationship between language and
identity—and between identity and ideology. In short, just about everyone in a
speech community has an opinion of what should happen when that community is
confronted with a perceived language problem, even though the problem may not
really exist. Indeed, because there is some form of language behavior that does not
meet the preferred or ideologically driven set of desired behaviors, the "problem"
may be a figment of an ideologically driven imagination. Ironically, the solution to
this virtual problem is also found in the ideologies that established the presence of
the problem. To people outside of the ideological loop, this process can be described
as "a solution in search of a problem" (see, for example, former Utah State House
minority leader Dave Jones, as quoted in the *Deseret News*, January 22, 1999).

Nevertheless, for many people, a solution for the "problem" must be found—
and it is found in some form of language planning process that usually leads to the
enactment of a language policy. Not surprisingly, those most affected by the policy
(those with the "problem") are seldom consulted or, if they are consulted, they are
presented with a set of simplistic solutions to the virtual problem. Some form of
straw man argumentation often supports these solutions. Eventually, the ideologically driven language plan is implemented through a top-down, bottom-up compliance process, and it is here that the plan encounters its unplanned consequences.

The people who were supposed to change their language behavior do not change. In fact, sometimes they behave in ways that suggest that the top-down language plan has contributed to the problem rather than provided a solution to the problem. Benrabah (2007: 226) describes such a process in his overview of language-in-education planning in Algeria: "The imposition of an exclusively Arabic monolingual schooling system implemented during the nationalist phase is considered to be a major source of its current 'failure,' of the rise of religious fanaticism, and of the civil war that has ravaged Algeria since the early 1990s." (See also Benrabah, 2005.)

Popper provides an additional insight into this phase of an unplanned language planning project:

> It seems to escape the well-meaning Utopianist that this programme implies an admission of failure, even before he launches it. For it substitutes for his demand that we build a new society, fit for men and women to live in, the demand that we "mould" these men and women to fit into his new society. This, clearly, removes any possibility of testing the success or failure of the new society. For those who do not like living in it only admit thereby that they are not yet fit to live in it; that their "human impulses" need further "organizing." (Popper, 1961: 70)

Considering the ideological foundations of this type of unplanned planning, it is not surprising that specific examples of unplanned language planning in social engineering can be provided from across the political spectrum; two are reviewed here. They are the *Official English movement* in the United States and the *language rights movement* also found in the United States, as well as in many international contexts.

OFFICIAL ENGLISH

As implied above, it appears that most people have a full and varied set of opinions about language behavior (grammar, pronunciation, usage, use) and behavior toward language (attitudes, motivations, opinions regarding existing formal or informal language policies and practices). Often, such a body of ideologies, if correctly implemented, would drive these opinions to create a Utopia. Eggington (1997) describes these ideologies in terms of socially shared metaphors. For example, dominant metaphors in English-as-first-language nations include "English as national language," whereby "English" is defined at a level of proficiency closely approximating educated standard, and "English as *our* language"—the language of "us." These dominant metaphors create a set of corollary socially shared ideologies that can be scripted as "If you don't speak (standard) English, you are not one of *us* or are not a part of *our* nation."

Throughout the history of the United States, resistance to large, non-English speaking immigration movements usually is revealed through concerns that the preeminence of English (and "us") is under threat and that the essential national character will disappear. Even Benjamin Franklin weighed in on this subject by asking the following:

> Why should the Palatine Boors be suffered to swarm into our Settlements, and by herding together establish their Language and Manners to the exclusion of ours? Why should Pennsylvania, founded by the English, become a Colony of Aliens, who will shortly be so numerous as to Germanize us instead of our Anglifying them, and will never adopt our Language or Customs, any more than they can acquire our Complexion? (as quoted in Labaree, 1959: 234)

In recent times, responses to the current wave of non-English speaking immigration have included various attempts to legislate English as the official language of the United States or of an individual state. Perhaps motivated by Utopian ideologies that might include the "English as 'us'"[1] set previously discussed, and by a nostalgic longing for the mythological melting pot of the past (Dicker, 2003: 38–81), most native English speakers, as well as a large number of nonnative English speakers, seem to agree with sundry forms of legislation that would provide government services—except for a narrow range of circumstances involving health and legal issues—only in the English language. Obviously, the legislators proposing official English laws are engaging in a form of language planning. However, a careful analysis of the underlying assumptions motivating such pieces of legislation reveals that the reality of the problem is questionable. Non-English speaking immigrants living in the United States are highly motivated to acquire English, and they are doing so at a remarkable rate (Dicker, 2000: 54–55; Mejias et al., 2002; Mora et al., 2006; Porcel, 2006; Portes and Schauffler, 1994; Potowski, 2004; Romero-Little et al., 2007; Schreffler, 2007; D. J. Smith, 2006; Tamosiunaite, 2008). The English language has become the most powerful language in the macrohistory of humankind, and thus is not under any form of threat (Graddol, 1997, 2006). Indeed, far from being a language under threat, the English language is threatening numerous world languages through linguistic imperialism to a degree that some have labeled it a "killer language" (Skutnabb-Kangas, 2000b: 22).

The proposed language planning solutions to such virtual problems are equally problematic and have the potential to usher in a host of unintended consequences. There is no evidence that offering government services only in English will motivate people to acquire English any more efficiently or effectively than they are currently doing. Indeed, by withdrawing government services in languages other than English, class conditions are established that encourage immigrants to maintain closer ties to their ethnic and linguistic groupings (Picone, 1997) that, in turn, retard *assimilation*—the primary objective of U.S. English. In addition, there is valid evidence that in those states with official English laws, limited English speakers are paid less by nongovernment employers than in those states without official English laws primarily because of the second-class status the state extends to non-English speakers by declaring English as the "official" language (Zavodny, 1998). Once again, the Official English "language plan" promotes conditions that increase the likelihood of creating in reality the perceived problem that the plan is designed to solve (see, e.g., Kaplan and Baldauf, 2001).

Space and the objectives of this chapter will not allow for a full rebuttal of the Official English position. Suffice it to say that the proponents of official English are engaged in an ideologically motivated enterprise trying to solve a perceived problem with recommendations that will instead lead to a host of unintended consequences—consequences that could easily devolve into further tribalization of the nation and ultimately create repercussions that will require solutions that in effect are the reverse of the intent of Official English. The Official English movement in the United States is an example of Popper's unplanned language planning.

A second instance of ideologically driven unplanned language planning comes from those who appear to have knowledge of piecemeal objectives (and scientific) language planning procedures designed to reduce the subjectivity and ideology of the planners. However, such planners seem to have accepted the postmodern notion that ideologies of power inform and control every action regardless of any attempts to create objective, or scientific, procedures in the language planning process. (See, for example, Moore, 1996.) Having accepted the notion that "all is power," these language planners have demonstrated a tendency to disregard and even to denigrate Popperian piecemeal language planning procedures substituting for them holistic "ideologies of power," implying singular causality and singular outcome templates. Moore (1996: 474), for example, in her description and discussion of Australian language policy, introduces the topic by stating, "In this article, I use insights from Dorothy Smith and Anna Yeatman, both feminist scholars, to explore the nature of policy formation. They start with the premise that all description is partial and interested." Discounting the disturbing notion that Moore is either admitting that her subsequent discussion of Australian language policy is partial and interested or claiming that she alone holds the key permitting her to rise above partiality and self-interest, one must ask what one will find when one examines anything from the perspective of a predetermined ideology other than what one's ideology predetermines. A cookie cutter, when applied to pastry, will always produce the desired outcome. Similarly, an ideologically driven template, regardless of whether it is from the political left or the political right, will always create the desired outcome, especially if that ideology rejects scientific objectivity. Thus, any language plan derived from an ideological template is predetermined to create unplanned consequences requiring improvised unplanned solutions.

One such ideological cookie cutter is the notion of "linguistic human rights"— as defined by Skutnabb-Kangas—for example, as the right of all children to "have the opportunity to learn their parents' idiom fully and properly so that they become (at least) as proficient as the parents" (Skutnabb-Kangas, 2000b: 25). In theory, such a right is a worthy objective, supported by the majority of applied linguists, and I include myself in this company. However, in most social contexts (except Utopia), significant problems may lie in the development and implementation of any plan that is exclusively built on total, or at least widespread, acceptance of the outcomes of a language-rights template (see Bruthiaux, 2008; Wright, 2007). Regardless of the worthiness of the end objective, a language plan established solely upon this ideo-logically driven foundation is likely to obstruct perception of variables that could invalidate the success of the plan.

For example, in both Australia and the United States, numerous maintenance and transition bilingual education plans for linguistic minorities—including immi-grants and indigenous peoples—were implemented during the 1970s (the decade during which the language rights ideology initially flowered). These programs either have ceased to exist or have floundered, consequently facing severe opposition partially because generations of holistic language-in-education planners who played a role in the construction of such programs were so eager to implement an ideolog-ical Utopia that they ignored a host of significant processes and variables, including:

- The fervent desires of language minority parents to ensure that their children receive a quality education in the dominant language (English)—a notion shared among many minority parents, assuming that it is their responsibility to ensure that their children speak the family language and the educational system's to teach in English (Eggington, 1985)
- A realistic cost-benefit analyses
- The difficulties faced in training high-quality bilingual teachers
- The complexities and expenses of creating quality materials
- The articulation of realistic bilingual education outcomes
- The development of quality testing and feedback mechanisms
- Most important, the creation of an ongoing procedure ensuring that the bilingual education plan reflect a meeting of the minds of those school administrators wishing to implement and continue the plan with those parents and students directly affected by the plan (Eggington and Baldauf, 1990; Hansen, 1999)

It is impossible to determine whether, had these more piecemeal approaches been followed, bilingual education programs would be flourishing. However, it is likely that, had piecemeal approaches been established—especially early in the development of bilingual education implementation models—procedures might have been put in place that would have identified growing resistance to bilingual education not only from the dominant English-speaking society, but also from parents eager for their children to acquire English as quickly as possible. Through community educa-tion programs and the involvement of parents in local language-in-education planning, many legitimate parental concerns could have been addressed. It should be noted that in both the Australian Aboriginal context and the California bilingual education program context, early and meaningful resistance to bilingual education came from parents of bilingual children (Hansen, 1999). At present, in both Aboriginal Australia and California's bilingual education program, bilingual educa-tion has come to be seen by many as a huge and costly mistake—yet another example of the wrongheadedness and ideologically driven "political correctness" of professional educators. And language-minority children are daily facing the personal consequences of what was clearly an exercise in unplanned language planning.

As the Official English and bilingual education movements demonstrate, ideologically driven unplanned language planning is not confined to a particular wing of the political spectrum. Rather, the commonality lies in the attempt to impose top-down, holistic, ideologically based solutions to a perceived language problem without considering the probability of a host of unintended consequences.

Unplanned Language Planning
Conducted by Nonspecialists

Although the term *global village* appears trite, it accurately reflects what is happening globally with regard to communication, immigration patterns, trade and business interactions, global information storage and retrieval systems, international media, and tourism. Only 60 years ago, most speech and discourse communities (using Swales's [1990] definitions of these terms) had very limited intra- and/or intermultilingual contact. However, in contemporary society, individuals are regularly engaged in some activity that requires interaction with people who do not speak a common language. In addition, the unanticipated arrival and rapid growth of the Internet has vastly increased cross-linguistic interactions. This situation often involves nonspecialists in a form of language planning.

Recently, I witnessed the creation, design, construction, and implementation of a complex computer animation project in which the clients, initial design team, and production center were in Japan, the coordination group was in Los Angeles, the programmers were in Iceland, and the animators were in Utah. All communication among the various teams was conducted via the Internet in a specialized variety of English. Aside from the requirement for all project teams to be available during Tokyo business hours, one could easily come to the conclusion that the project was being undertaken by teams housed in a single building in an English-speaking city. It is doubtful that there had been a conscious decision to implement an English-as-language-of-project language plan. The decision probably just happened, and in that respect it is an example of unplanned language planning conducted by nonspecialists.[2]

This rather one-dimensional example does not imply that unplanned language planning by nonspecialists will always result in the desired outcomes. When complexities increase, so-called commonsense language-related solutions can easily lead to a host of unintended consequences, making any plan vulnerable to Popper's unplanned planning trap. Burningham (1998), in her study of language policy and planning in an urban U.S. school district, found an absence of any formal planning designed to address the needs of language-minority students. One administrator stated that the district language policy was "fairly clear," but when asked to produce the policy, the administrator explained that he couldn't because the district has distributed the plan via "just kind of memos." When asked about how they deal with language planning issues, other administrators responded:

- "Kind of operate from my own beliefs."
- "Basically it's whatever you feel like as a humanitarian."
- "...professional and personal tendency."
- "Anything in effect is kind of what [administrator #4] and I have decided to do." (Burningham, 1998: 42–43)

After conducting extensive interviews with administrators and faculty, and after surveying language-minority parents, students, and teachers, Burningham concluded that the absence of a formal language plan in the district and the presence of a series of uncoordinated unplanned language plans were linked to what Wiley and Lukes (1996) label as *individualism*—an attitude or ideology in which the responsibility for any student failure is placed on the individual, thus freeing the institution and the society from any liability and, in turn, forming the foundation for significant, widespread student failure in the near future with all the unintended consequences that accompany minority-group low academic achievement.

CONCLUSION

As is probably painfully obvious, this chapter has only skimmed the surface of the available instances of ideologically driven unplanned language planning. There are, however, a number of lessons that can be gleaned from this discussion. Applied linguists and, more specifically, those applied linguists engaged in language planning activities need to examine carefully the ideologies informing and constructing unplanned language planning efforts. At the same time, they need to ensure that their own Utopian-driven ideological proclivities do not contribute to the creation of unplanned consequences arising from any language planning recommendations they may make. The necessary assurances can be achieved only by relying on established objective procedures and "piecemeal" approaches to language planning enterprises rather than on attempts at holistic, sweeping social reconstruction.

A final lesson comes from Forrest Cuch, Head of Utah's Office of Indian Affairs. When asked for his suggestions of what needs to be done to overcome a host of unplanned and uncoordinated language plans in Utah (see Sayers, 1996), he suggested that

> What you have to do is sit down and take a look at the needs and develop a policy systematically.... There's one thing that our state has going for it. Although we appear to be very narrow in our perceptions, at least I've found that the people at the top, once they hear the truth about the history of the state, once they obtain the information, they do change. They're not static; they don't resist the information.... It's just that they lack some information—some of the people at

the top. But they do have a willingness to try to improve things. (McCrea, 1998: 102–103)

By and large, public officials are amenable to the application of language planning procedures and they generally will enact those recommendations that are supported by strong evidence. Consequently, it is the responsibility of language planners to be proactive in sharing their expertise with those outside of academia (Kaplan and Baldauf, 2007).

NOTES

1. It is no coincidence that the national organization sponsoring official English legislation has named itself "U.S. English," playing on the ideologies of English as "U.S." and English as "us."

2. Those scholars invested in power ideologies might assume that the language plan was a result of the continuing hegemony of the English language. However, it is equally valid to assume that the decision was motivated by a practicality often overlooked by power-is-everywhere ideologues. That ideological factor might be labeled as "communicative need," and it fits along the social solidarity axis—an axis not encompassed by the plus/minus power construct.

PERSPECTIVES ON LANGUAGE POLICY AND PLANNING

JAMES W. TOLLEFSON

I. INTRODUCTION

When language policy and planning (LPP) first became widely practiced in the 1960s and 1970s, LPP specialists believed that their newly emerging understanding of language in society could be implemented in practical programs of "modernization" and "development" that would have important benefits for "developing" societies. Noting that "there is still no institution in the United States in which students can be adequately trained for either theoretical or applied involvement in the language problems of developing nations," Fishman, Ferguson, and Das Gupta, in their groundbreaking collection, argued that "few areas are more fruitful or urgent with respect to interdisciplinary attention" (1968: x–xi). The early period of LPP was characterized by an explosive growth in research (e.g., Fishman, 1968, 1971, 1972, 1974; Rubin and Jernudd, 1971; Rubin and Shuy, 1973), as the new field of LPP was widely seen as having practical significance for the many newly independent states of the postcolonial period, as well as theoretical value in providing "new opportunities to tackle a host of ... novel theoretical concerns" (Fishman, 1968: x) in sociology and political science.

Despite this early optimism, in less than 20 years, by the mid-1980s, disillusionment with LPP was widespread (Blommaert, 1996; G. Williams, 1992). The rapid disillusionment with LPP was due to several factors, which I will outline. More recently, a modest revival in academic interest in LPP has begun, though research is characterized by important differences from the early period. Following analysis of the limitations of early LPP, I will summarize these recent trends in research and suggest future directions for the field.

II. Early Development in LPP

Major Concerns of Research

The linkage of LPP with development and modernization was crucial for the early history of the field. Influenced by modernization theory (e.g., Rostow, 1960), early research focused primarily on the role of LPP in developing societies. For instance, of the 19 case studies in Fishman, Ferguson, and Das Gupta (1968), 11 focused on Africa, the others examining developing countries such as India, Haiti, Papua New Guinea, and Paraguay. (One article focused on Scandinavia.) Indeed, much of this early research seemed to restrict LPP to developing nations, as indicated by the subtitle of Rubin and Jernudd's (1971) influential book: *Can Language Be Planned? Sociolinguistic Theory and Practice for Developing Nations*. It was widely believed that LPP could play a major role in achieving the goals of political/administrative integration and socio-cultural unity (Das Gupta, 1970). Thus, a major focus of this early research was analysis of the language planning needs specific to newly independent states, particularly language choice and literacy in processes of *nationism*, and language maintenance, codification, and elaboration in processes of *nationalism* (Fishman, 1968).

Although LPP was borne out of a concern with development, researchers soon extended their work to include developed societies. By the end of its early "formative half decade" (Fishman, 1971: 7), LPP research was being applied to language problems in the Soviet Union (Lewis, 1972), Israel (Rabin, 1971), Belgium, Luxembourg, and France (Verdoodt, 1971), the United States (Entwisle, 1971), and Ireland (Macnamara, 1971), as well as to an expanding number of developing countries, including China, Indonesia, Malaysia, Pakistan, and the Philippines.

The major achievement of this early period of LPP was a deeper understanding of the relationship between language structure and language functions on the one hand and various forms of social organization (communities, ethnic groups, nations) on the other. On the theoretical level, this early work linked LPP with important research in microsociolinguistics on such issues as sequencing in interactions, code-switching, and systematicity in style and register variation.

Three Assumptions in Early LPP

In early LPP research, practitioners were seen as having the expertise to specify ways in which changes in the linguistic situation would lead to desired social and political transformations (e.g., enhancing sociocultural unity, reducing economic inequalities, opening access to education). The historical link between LPP modernization/ development ensured that the implicit assumptions in LPP reflected widely held assumptions in the social sciences that have been subject to a great deal of critical reflection. Especially striking in hindsight is the optimism of early LPP, which conveyed an underlying ideological faith in development and modernization. This belief in economic and social progress was perhaps best expressed in Eastman's introduction to language planning (1983a), in which language planners are depicted at the forefront of fundamental shifts in the organization of global society: "Modernization and preservation efforts are seemingly happening everywhere, to provide all people with access to the modern world through technologically sophisticated languages and also to lend a sense of identity through encouraged use of their first languages" (Eastman, 1983a: 31). The belief that LPP would benefit ethnic and linguistic minorities was widespread in early LPP research, and cases could be found to confirm this optimism. For instance, the remarkable spread of Malay-Indonesian from the 1960s until the early 1980s indicated that LPP could have important consequences for newly independent multilingual and multiethnic states (Alisjahbana, 1971). Subsequently, however, the failure of LPP to achieve its goals in many contexts and the intimate connection between early LPP and modernization theory meant that LPP was subject to the same criticisms as modernization theory generally, including the following (Foster-Carter, 1985; Worsley, 1987):

- Economic models appropriate for one place may be ineffective elsewhere.
- National economic development will not necessarily benefit all sectors of society, especially the poor.
- Development fails to consider local contexts and the conflicting needs and desires of diverse communities.
- Development has a homogenizing effect on social and cultural diversity

A second key assumption of the early period of LPP was the emphasis on *efficiency*, *rationality*, and *cost-benefit analysis* as criteria for evaluating plans and policies in all contexts. For instance, Tauli (1968) proposed *clarity* and *economy* whereas Haugen (1966) proposed *efficiency* as key criteria for evaluating the effectiveness of LPP decisions. The emphasis on the technical aspect of LPP led Jernudd and Das Gupta (1971) to argue that planners may be more able than political authorities to apply rational decision making in the solution to language problems. Such attempts to separate LPP from politics reflected not only a belief in the skills of technical specialists but also a broader failure to link LPP with a political analysis. The wide failure of early LPP to acknowledge that LPP is fundamentally political, involving a powerful mechanism for disciplining societies, is central to subsequent critiques of LPP.

A third assumption central to early LPP was that the nation-state is the appropriate focus for LPP research and practice. Indeed, this assumption is implicit in the perspective of LPP as a tool for political/administrative and sociocultural integration of the nation-state. Focusing on the nation-state had two important consequences. First, the main actors in LPP were assumed to be government agencies, and thus most research examined the work of such agencies. Second, many researchers adopted a top-down perspective, in which they were interested in national plans and policies rather than local language practices. This emphasis on the nation-state continued in later LPP research as well, including research critical of other early assumptions in the field, such as research on linguistic imperialism (Phillipson, 1992).

III. DISILLUSIONMENT AND CRITIQUE

The critique of early LPP was, in part, a manifestation of the general collapse of social planning that took place during the 1980s, as centrally planned economies gave way to market economies in which planning plays a relatively limited role. Yet criticisms specifically directed at the field of LPP can also be identified. I will examine three of these criticisms here.

Perhaps the most important criticism of early LPP was the failure to analyze adequately the impact of local context on national policies and plans. In part, this failure was due to the emphasis on technical rather than political evaluation of plans and policies, as well as the general separation of LPP from political analysis. As Blommaert (1996) argues, LPP "can no longer stand exclusively for practical issues of standardization, graphization, terminological elaboration, and so on. The link between language planning and sociopolitical developments is obviously of paramount importance" (p. 217). One consequence of the failure to link LPP to politics was that planners could not predict the impact of their plans and policies. Although early LPP specialists believed that unexpected outcomes could be avoided as long as adequate information was available, recent work in LPP assumes that unexpected outcomes are a normal feature of highly complex social systems, in which linear cause-effect relationships between language and society do not apply and social groups may have covert goals for LPP (Ammon, 1997).

With the failure of many plans and policies to achieve the goals of political/administrative and sociocultural integration, the optimism of early LPP was soon replaced by skepticism about the work of language planners (e.g., Cluver, 1992). Yet the failure of LPP to achieve its lofty goals is not surprising, given the complex forces affecting various forms of national integration. As a result, researchers have proposed a "systems approach" or "ecological" perspective for LPP (Clayton, 1999; Cluver, 1991; Ohly, 1989; Skutnabb-Kangas, 2000a). Although such work varies in the factors considered central to LPP, proponents agree that specialists must understand the wide range of social, economic, and political forces that affect, and are affected by, LPP processes. Within this framework, a widespread belief is that not enough is known about the complex relationships between language and society for

LPP to be used for "social engineering" (Cluver, 1991: 44; also see Kashoki, 1982). Thus, recent work examines the capacity of LPP to achieve limited aims, such as reducing social distance and stereotyping or increasing language learning and communicative interaction among groups speaking different primary languages (e.g., Musau, 1999).

A second criticism of early LPP was that it paid too little attention to the language practices and attitudes of communities affected by LPP, particularly the ways in which linguistic minorities accommodate, subvert, or transform national plans within their local communities. In addition, early LPP research did not adequately examine the involvement of business enterprises, nongovernmental organizations, professional associations (e.g., teachers' groups), and other institutions and organizations involved in LPP practice. In contrast, more recent work emphasizes the capacity of local communities (even those having relatively little political power) to adopt multiple identities only partly determined by LPP and to alter significantly the outcomes of plans and policies (Pennycook, 1995, 1998).

A third criticism of early LPP is that despite the hope that LPP would bring a broad array of benefits to minority populations in developing nations, in practice LPP was often used by dominant groups to maintain their political and economic advantage. The clearest example is apartheid South Africa, where LPP isolated Black populations, increased conflict, and aided the White minority in its efforts to hold on to power (Cluver, 1992; de Klerk and Barkhuizen, 1998; Kamwangamalu, 1997; Ohly, 1989). Indeed, the Afrikaner nationalist government promoted mother tongue instruction and used codification and standardization as tools for segregating different ethnic groups among the Black population, whereas other policies promoted Afrikaans rather than English (de Klerk, 2000). As Cluver (1992) shows, LPP was used in apartheid South Africa to confirm the ideology of racial separation that was at the heart of apartheid, and thus resistance to language policies was an important factor behind the important Soweto uprising in June 1976 and the eventual end of apartheid. In other states in Africa, LPP was used to overcome the immediate postindependence crisis of national integration, but often this goal was achieved only within the educated elite, leaving masses of the population largely cut off from economic and political power (Mazrui and Tidy, 1984).

The use of LPP by dominant groups is not limited to developing nations. In the Soviet Union, for instance, the spread of Russian was selectively encouraged in regions where central planners sought to extend their authority (Kirkwood, 1990). In the United Kingdom, the renewed prominence of standard English in the schools in the 1990s was linked to a wider effort to limit the role of immigrants' languages in education; in the United States, federal policies suppressed indigenous languages (Shonerd, 1990) and, more recently, Official English legislation in some states is an effective tool for restricting the political power of Latinos (Donahue, 2001).

IV. RECENT DEVELOPMENTS IN LPP

New Concerns of Research

One of the most important changes since the 1980s is the recognition that LPP is not necessarily an aspect of development. Indeed, the recent revival in academic interest in LPP is due in part to the growing recognition that LPP is involved in a broad range of social processes. Among the most important of these processes are migration and the rise of nationalism in Europe and Central Asia.

Migration is one of the major reasons for the increase in the number of people worldwide who are learning languages and for the resulting revival in LPP. With 10 million refugees worldwide, more than 20 million people displaced within their own countries, and countless millions of economic migrants such as Bosnians and Turks in Germany, Filipinos in Hong Kong, South Asians in the United Kingdom, and Latinos in the United States, language teaching programs have been dramatically affected throughout the world. In many countries, LPP in education has been central to efforts to deal with this massive movement of people (Tollefson, 1989). As a result of the global process of migration, new questions have gained importance in LPP:

- What should be the role of migrants' languages in education and other official domains of use?
- How are local languages affected by migrants?
- What should be the status of new varieties of English and other lingua francas?
- How can acquisition planning be most effectively carried out?
- What factors constrain acquisition planning?

A second area for LPP has emerged from the collapse of the Soviet Union and the realignments in political boundaries in Eastern Europe and Central Asia. In these new states, language issues are intimately linked with ideological and political conflicts. Minority issues, including LPP, are at the center of conflicts between Russia and Ukraine, Georgia and South Ossetia, Armenia and Azerbaijan, Russia and Chechnya, Hungary and Slovakia, Slovenia and Austria, Turkey and its Kurdish minority, and elsewhere in the region, and they are central also to the efforts of new states to establish effective local institutions (e.g., Estonia, Latvia, and Lithuania; see Hogan-Brun et al., 2007). In the states of former Yugoslavia, for example, language policy has been a key issue for government leaders (Tollefson, 1997, 2004). Indeed, the violent destruction of Yugoslavia has focused attention on the fundamental political problem of Europe and Central Asia: the relationship between minorities and nation states. The LPP choices made by state planners, legislative bodies, and citizens will play a key role in the management of political conflict in these new states for decades to come.

A third area of research is the movement to deconstruct the ideology of monolingualism that has pervaded much LPP research (G. Williams, 1992). This work involves a reexamination of traditional assumptions about the costs of multilingualism and the benefits of monolingualism. Particularly influential has been innovative language policies in postapartheid South Africa, which developed an ideology of multilingualism as a symbol of national revival and adopted a Constitution declaring 11 official languages to enhance the process of democratization (Blommaert, 1996). Moreover, the linkage of multilingual policies and democratization is also an important part of political debates elsewhere (e.g., in Guatemala, where official recognition of the country's indigenous languages was an important part of the peace accords ending the country's civil war).

Closely related to the critique of monolingual ideology is the movement for linguistic human rights. Whereas some LPP scholars have advocated mother tongue–promotion policies (e.g., Skutnabb-Kangas, 2000a), others have linked language rights to political theory and to efforts to develop a theory of LPP (e.g., Cooper, 1989; Dua, 1996; May, 2001). Calls for expansion and implementation of language rights can be expected to continue, with LPP research heavily involved in developing better understanding of the role of language rights in state formation, international organizations, political conflict, and other important social processes. Similarly, recent research on the links between LPP and social theory, long advocated by G. Williams (1992) and Fishman (1992), can contribute to more complex understandings of language rights and to new applications of research methods in LPP (Ricento, 2006b).

Although early LPP research seldom considered the local legal framework of plans and policies, more recent research has examined how LPP processes are constrained by constitutional and statutory law. For example, in the United States, the body of law surrounding the concept of *free speech* directly affects LPP debates about the English-only movement, state efforts to restrict languages other than English, and the use of nonstandard varieties in schools. Indeed, language policy decisions have been overturned by courts as violations of free speech (Donahue, 2001; Grove, 1999; Stephan, 1999). Similarly, language policies in the Philippines can be understood only within the framework of a long history of constitutional debates about the appropriate official role for English, Filipino, and other languages; in Bangladesh, medium of instruction debates involving Bengali and English must be understood within the constitutional provisions for Bengali as a core symbol of Bangladeshi nationalism (Hossain and Tollefson, 2007). Such *local* legal concerns are increasingly incorporated into LPP research (Sonntag, 2003).

New Approaches and Methods

Along with a focus on new areas for research, LPP specialists have greatly expanded their research models and methods, drawing from work in anthropology, political sociology, and other disciplines. Particularly important are the ecology of language, application of discourse analysis to LPP, and use of ethnographic research methods:

1. *Ecology of language:* Ecological approaches to LPP have evolved from their application in a wide range of language studies, including literacy, language learning, language change, and language spread (e.g., Mühlhäusler, 1996a; van Lier, 2004). Drawing on biological models of diversity, ecological models place linguistic diversity as a fundamental "natural" condition that is essential for the well-being of human social systems. Applied to LPP, an ecological perspective provides a framework for evaluating the impact of language plans and policies, including a concern for language maintenance and revival, acceptance of multiple forms of linguistic diversity, and concern for language rights. In sum, ecological models present a powerful framework for LPP that includes a goal for planning and policymaking (i.e., promoting linguistic diversity) and a general approach for its implementation (community participation in policymaking). Future research within ecological models will have to confront recent criticisms: that they are metaphors rather than serious theories of language in society, that they include unjustified assumptions (e.g., that languages will survive if left free from the pressures of human intervention), and that they implicitly reflect a neoliberal fascination with small, isolated communities whose members want access to dominant languages and institutions in order to overcome serious economic deprivation (Edwards, 2001; Pennycook, 2004). Nevertheless, the widespread influence of ecological models suggests that they will continue to be influential in future LPP work.

2. *Discourse analysis in LPP:* An important recent direction in LPP is work within a discourse analytic framework, in which LPP research and policy documents are examined as a discourse on language in society (Blommaert, 1996). One of the most important applications has been the discourse-historical approach to LPP developed by Lemke (1995), Wodak (2003, 2006), and Titscher et al. (1998). By examining LPP topics and texts, including their historical development and their "representation" within elite discourse (Chilton, 2004), this approach seeks to integrate LPP with social theory. In practice, this approach focuses on policy documents, public policy debates (particularly within mass media), and LPP programs. All are viewed as implicit ideological struggles that shape and are shaped by social relations. Particularly important are the visions of language and social identities, and the representation of languages and social groups that are implicit in LPP. Future research is likely to continue to examine the role of public political discourse and the mass media in LPP processes, particularly the role of political leaders in shaping public discussion of language issues.

3. *Ethnography:* In response to the criticism that early LPP failed to examine the impact of LPP on communities, some LPP researchers have adopted an

ethnographic approach to LPP, because it is concerned with the microlevel language of everyday life of communities. By examining the "unconscious 'lived culture'" of a community (Canagarajah, 2006: 153), researchers seek to understand community support and resistance to plans and policies, the impact of policy alternatives on communities, and the value of community involvement in LPP processes. One key to ethnographic research in LPP is participant observation over relatively long periods of time, with the goal of rich, multilayered analysis of language use, including code-switching, code-mixing, and language maintenance and shift. Application of ethnography to LPP has been carried out in a variety of contexts, including Quechua language maintenance in Peru (Hornberger, 2003) and Ecuador (King, 2001), education in Solomon Islands (Gegeo and Watson-Gegeo, 2004), and bilingual classrooms in Wales (Jones and Martin-Jones, 2004). Use of ethnographic methods offers great promise for LPP. It permits macrolevel policy analysis along with analysis of microlevel local practices. Integrating policy and discourse analysis is crucial if researchers are to understand how local practices are situated within the broader social and political order.

IV. Future Directions in LPP

Since the 1990s, researchers in LPP have proposed new models, such as the systems approach or ecological model, incorporating new metaphors, such as networks (Cluver, 1991; Kaplan and Baldauf, 1997a). This attention to the complex array of social forces involved in LPP presents a major challenge for LPP theory: Which social processes and factors are most relevant to LPP? Although LPP theory is not yet sufficiently developed to answer this question, it is likely that attention to both the local and global context and an interdisciplinary approach that considers issues of power and identity will be essential. With these general guidelines in mind, I believe the following issues will receive attention by LPP researchers in the years ahead:

1. Although early LPP specialists assumed that LPP would lead to a general improvement in the economic conditions of both countries and minority groups, recent research has examined how LPP exacerbates rather than reduces economic, social, and political inequalities (Phillipson, 1992; Skutnabb-Kangas, 2000a; Tollefson, 1995, 2001). In many instances, state policymakers have used LPP to further marginalize already dominated populations (e.g., Albanians in Kosovo). Rather than being a result of failed plans and policies, such exploitation is typical of LPP in many contexts, and thus should be a major focus for research.

2. Research on how the recipients of LPP control the process of social change has led to a more complex understanding of social identity, the various community affiliations that characterize individuals and groups, and the importance of institutions other than the state for language use and acquisition (Norton, 1997a). Innovative work on language and social identity should explore how communities undergo social change, quite apart from actions of the state. Analysis of "real-life language planning" (Dasgupta, 1990: 87) should particularly examine the role of contact languages in promoting grassroots dialogue. In this way, LPP research can move away from a restricted focus on lingua francas as mechanisms for state control and toward a deeper understanding of how they are involved in the multiple ways that power may be exercised in social life. Especially important is the role of LPP in identity politics (Kymlicka, 1995).

3. The diminishing role of the state and the growing importance of multinational corporations as institutions of global decision making require new approaches to LPP research (Schubert, 1990). How will global corporations manage the communication needs of business? What will be the different functions within a united Europe for official languages and for regional languages such as Catalan and Welsh? How will educational systems respond to the language needs of foreign workers? How will languages serve local community identity and communication needs, while also meeting the demands of globalization? How will the global economy change language acquisition and the structure of international languages? These and many other important questions of language and globalization will require new forms of LPP research, no longer focused exclusively on the actions of state agencies but instead linking LPP to related work in the ethnography of communication, in mass media, and in microsociolinguistics, as well as in sociology and political theory.

4. The link between LPP and national security concerns is only beginning to be examined. How is LPP related to globalization, conflict over the control of natural resources (e.g., oil), political violence, and the "war on terror"? For example, how are English-promotion policies integrated with national security goals of the United States? In a provocative call for research on such questions, Karmani (2005: 101) argues that the U.S. policy of "more English and less Islam" in the Arabian Gulf region is implemented by American and other foreign educational institutions using English as medium of instruction in order to promote U.S. interests, undermine local educational institutions, and block the adoption of Arabic-English bilingual policies. Such research responds to important contemporary issues in which LPP plays a role. With increased recognition of the need for LPP specialists to play a more visible role in public policy debates, we can expect such research to expand in the years ahead.

PART X

TRANSLATION AND INTERPRETATION

CHAPTER 33

TRANSLATION

SARA LAVIOSA

I. INTRODUCTION

Within the broad interdisciplinary field of translation studies, a title that has been used in the English-speaking world since 1972, translation is investigated from a wide array of theoretical perspectives drawn from disciplines as varied as linguistics, literary studies, cultural studies, language engineering, and philosophy (Hatim and Munday, 2004: 8). There are almost as many formal definitions of translation as there are theories that endeavor to account for the multifarious nature and functions of this complex, language-based, sociocultural phenomenon that is rapidly spreading in multiple directions within and across nations in the increasingly globalized, multilingual world, characterized by the constant movement of peoples, goods, and cultures.

The definition provided by the *Dictionary of Translation Studies* (Shuttleworth and Cowie, 1997: 181) makes a distinction between translation as a process (translating) and translation as a product. Some of the major types of written translation are labeled: for example, literary translation, technical translation, subtitling, and machine translation. It also points out that although the term generally refers to the transfer of written texts, it sometimes subsumes *interpreting*, which refers more specifically to "the oral translation of a spoken message or text" (Shuttleworth and Cowie, 1997: 83).

In this chapter, *translation* is used in the more restricted sense of written transfer. Moreover, in line with Hatim and Munday (2004: 6), the ambit of translation is intended:

- The process of transferring a written text from the source language to the target language, conducted by a translator, or translators, in a specific sociocultural context
- The written product, or target text, that results from that process and that functions in the sociocultural context of the target language

- The cognitive, linguistic, visual, cultural, and ideological phenomena that are an integral part of ambit 1 and ambit 2.

This chapter provides an overview of the theoretical, descriptive, and applied aspects of the study of translation as they have been investigated since the late 1960s and early 1970s, when translation studies became established as a new field of scholarly inquiry in the West. The conclusion suggests the ways in which this rapidly expanding field might develop in the future.

II. Overview of Translation Studies

In his famous paper "The Name and Nature of Translation Studies," presented at the 3rd World Congress of Applied Linguistics (Copenhagen, August 21–26, 1972),[1] the Amsterdam-based American literary translator and theorist James S. Holmes outlined the scope and structure of the emerging field of research concerned with the description, theory, and praxis of translation. Holmes's programmatic presentation of translation studies was based on his observations of the state of the art of translation study and his vision for the future (Toury, 1995: 7–8). Holmes's proposal for the development of a new "disciplinary utopia" (as intended by Hagstrom, 1965, cited in Holmes, 1987: 10) was put forward after more than 2 decades of sustained interest for the problems of translating and translation by scholars coming from linguistics, linguistic philosophy, literary studies, information theory, logic, and mathematics (Holmes, 1987: 10), as well as psychology, anthropology, sociology, and sociolinguistics (Steiner, 1992, as cited in Tymoczko, 2007: 24). The expansion of translation study in the postwar period, observes Tymoczko (2007: 24–26), had sprung from the important role fulfilled by translation in all those wartime activities involving intercultural communication and propaganda. Since then, the study of translation has been influenced by postpositivist thinking, which recognizes "that knowledge in any field is affected by time and space, viewpoint, immediate context, and long-term history, as well as by factors such as social context, subject position, and place of enunciation" (Tymoczko, 2007: 25).

Holmes shared his vision of a new discipline at a time when linguistic-oriented approaches to translation study had been elaborated (see, e.g., Catford, 1965; Jacobson, 1959; Mounin, 1963; Nida, 1964; Vinay and Darbelnet, 1958/1995) and when the practice-oriented North American workshop approach to literary translation had been developing in American universities since 1963. That is when translated modern literature was growing in popularity, a trend that continued throughout the 1960s and 1970s (Gentzler, 2001: 5–7; Venuti, 1995: 12–13, 1998: 311). Meanwhile, in the United Kingdom, the first specialized university postgraduate courses in translation and interpreting were being established (Munday, 2001: 6).

Over the years, Holmes's framework of translation studies has been presented, interpreted or rewritten in various ways (Toury, 1987, 1995; Hermans, 1999; Munday, 2001; Quah, 2006). The following summary is based on Holmes's paper, initially published in the posthumous collection edited by Raymond van den Broeck in 1988 (second ed., 1994) and reprinted in the second edition of *The Translation Studies Reader* (Venuti, 2004).

Holmes states two main objectives for the empirical discipline of translation studies. The first objective was to describe the phenomena of translating and translation(s); this activity is the concern of *descriptive translation studies* (or *translation description*). The second objective was to establish general principles that explain and predict these phenomena; this activity is the concern of *theoretical translation studies* (or *translation theory*). More specifically, translation description focuses on three research areas:

- Synchronic and diachronic text-focused analyses of translations (*product-oriented studies*)
- The influence of translations in the recipient sociocultural context (*function-oriented studies*)
- The mental processes involved in the translation act (*process-oriented descriptive studies*)

Translation description and translation theory constitute the two branches of pure research. The third branch, *applied translation studies*, concerns itself with:

1. *Translator training* (teaching methods, testing techniques, and curriculum planning)
2. *Translation aids* (translation-specific lexicographical or terminological resources and grammars)
3. *Translation policy* (giving sound advice on the place and role of translators and translations in society)
4. *Translation criticism* (translation interpretation and evaluation)

The three main branches of translation studies are interdependent, because each provides data and insights for the other two: translation theories and models, for example, are elaborated by combining the observational and experimental findings of descriptive and/or applied studies with the theoretical insights of neighboring fields. "In view of this dialectical relationship," affirms Holmes (2004: 190), "[...] attention to all three branches is required if the discipline is to grow and flourish." Holmes also briefly outlines the historical and methodological dimensions of the discipline. The former deals with the history of translation theory, translation description and applied translation studies; the latter discusses issues concerning the object of study of the discipline together with the methodologies that are most appropriate for research carried out in the different subdivisions of the field.

While the dawn of translation studies was breaking, a new approach to translation study saw the light of day after a decade of preparation by Holmes with

- Czech and Slovak scholars Jiří Levý, Anton Popovič, and František Miko
- Two researchers at Tel Aviv University, Itamar Ivan-Zohar and Gideon Toury
- A group of scholars in the Low Countries including Jos Lambert, Raymond van den Broeck, and Andr Lefevere.

The approach is variously called *descriptive translation studies*, *polysystems approach*, *manipulation school*, *Tel Aviv-Leuven axis*, *Low Countries group*, and even *translation studies*. Elaborated at a series of conferences (Leuven in 1976, Tel Aviv in 1978, and Antwerp in 1980), the new descriptive paradigm gained ground in the 1980s with the publication of Susan Bassnett's *Translation Studies* (1980) and Hermans's edited volume *The Manipulation of Literature* (1985), and was consolidated, extended, and reexamined in the 1990s (Hermans, 1999).

The new school of thought advocated a descriptive, functional, target-oriented, and systemic approach to translation study. In this paradigm, translators' behaviour, translations and translating are intimately interrelated within a complex, dynamic network of relations of a linguistic, textual, literary, and sociocultural nature. Translations are studied as target language texts in their own right rather than being viewed merely as derivative, imitative texts that are to reproduce and represent the originals by establishing a relationship of equivalence based on *a priori* criteria, such as fidelity, accuracy, or fluency. Descriptive translation studies view the actual relationships linking each individual target text with its source text as similarity relationships involving samenesses and differences, hence "equivalence is not a postulated requirement, but an empirical fact" (Toury, 1980: 39) that is conceived in terms of balance between invariance and transformation, a balance that is determined by historical and cultural factors reflected in norms.[2]

From a target-oriented perspective, a whole range of comparative analyses may be carried out to gain an insight into the nature of translation *qua* translation; for example, a translation may be investigated vis--vis other translations of the same source text. Translated and nontranslated texts of the same or similar genre are also regarded as legitimate objects of study, and so is the discourse about translation in synchronic or diachronic studies, as well as the relation between translation and other forms of intercultural or mediated communication.

The target orientation of descriptive translation studies is congruent with the principles informing *Skopos* theory.[3] Proposed in the late 1970s and early 1980s by Katharina Reiss and Hans J. Vermeer, as cited in Nord (1997), it played a major role in the development of modern functionalism in translation studies. The generic notion of *Skopos* subsumes the related concepts of *aim*, *purpose*, *intention*, and *function* of a translational action and is the prime principle determining the translation process (Reiss and Vermeer, 1984: 101, cited in Nord, 1997: 29). *Skopos* theory is a pragmatic, culture-oriented translational model whose principles are formulated in two *Skopos* rules. The first is this: "Translate/interpret/speak/write in a way that enables your text/translation to function in the situation in which it is used and with the people who want to use it and precisely in the way they want it to function" (Vermeer, 1989: 20, cited in Nord, 1997: 29).

The second rule states that the *Skopos* can be described as "a variable of the receiver" (Reiss and Vermeer 1984: 101, in Nord, 1997: 29). It follows that translators' decisions are governed by the target-text *Skopos* and are not bound to any preconceived idea about the relationships linking the target text with its source text. "What the Skopos states," in fact, "is that one must translate, consciously and consistently, in accordance with some principle respecting the target text. The theory does not state what the principle is: this must be decided separately in each specific case" (Vermeer, 1989: 182). Hence, the *Skopos*, which is or should be defined in the commission, widens the range of possible translation strategies and enlarges the accountability of the translator (Vermeer, 1989: 186). Moreover, the addressee is the main factor determining the target-text *Skopos;* the source text, like any other text, is seen as merely an "offer of information" from which receivers select the items they find interesting and important (Vermeer, 1982, cited in Nord, 1997: 31).

In the late 1980s and early 1990s, the meeting of Translation Studies and Cultural Studies gave rise to "the cultural turn" of the descriptive paradigm (Bassnett and Lefevere, 1990), entailing the analysis of translation in its cultural, political, and ideological context. From this perspective, translation is viewed as a form of rewriting alongside adaptations, summaries, reviews, editing, anthologies, critical commentaries, or literary histories (Lefevere, 1992). Unlike other meta-texts, however, translation is potentially the most influential form of text processing "because it is able to project the image of an author and/or those works beyond the boundaries of their culture" (Lefevere, 1992: 9). The literary system, which comprises translated literature, is claimed to be constrained by professionals (i.e., critics, reviewers, teachers, and translators), patronage (i.e., persons or institutions that further or hinder the production of cultural goods), and poetics. More specifically, the latter comprises literary devices and the relationship of literature to the social system, which, through its institutions, tries to enforce the dominant poetics of a period "by using it as the yardstick against which current production is measured" (Lefevere, 1992: 19). The cultural turn in translation studies was part of a trend also occurring in other disciplines: in other words, linguistics, literary studies, history, classsical studies, and geography. It arose from the need to understand the rapidly changing patterns of cultural interaction in the world (Bassnett, 2007).

Cultural studies continued to influence the field of translation throughout the 1990s, bringing about a shift of emphasis toward translation and power. The "power turn" of descriptive translation studies, as it was named by Tymoczko and Gentzler (2002), is evident in two main research areas: (i) translation and gender, and (ii) postcolonial translation studies, whose concerns include "the ways translation can affect cultural change, and the relation of translation to dominance, cultural assertion, cultural resistance, and activism" (Tymoczko, 2007: 44).

Starting from the observation that "translators are handmaidens to authors, women inferior to men" (Simon, 1996: 1), feminist translation theory endeavors to examine critically how cultural differences—be they social, sexual, or historical— are construed in language, and how these differences are transferred across languages by communicating, rewriting, and manipulating the source text (Simon, 1996: 1–2). Translation is, therefore, about difference and often accentuates difference (Von Flotow, 1997: 98) by using language as cultural intervention to resist or subvert expressions of domination and marginalization in society and in literature.

Studies inspired by postcolonial theory consider translation within contexts characterized by the power imbalance between languages and their profound linguistic and cultural differences (Tymoczko, 2007: 45).[4] Moreover, being viewed as an agent of social change, the literary translator is called upon to unveil and oppose the means by which the colonizer represses and marginalizes the identity of the colonized not only in literature but also in education, theology, historiography, and philosophy (Munday, 2001: 133–138).

At the start of the new millennium, descriptive translation studies entered a new phase, "the international turn," which shares many of the concerns of postcolonial translation studies (Tymoczko, 2007: 45). From this perspective, scholars have begun to question the suitability of Eurocentric models for the study of translation across the world (see, e.g., Fenton, 2004; Gaddis Rose, 2000; Hung and Wakabayashi, 2005; Hermans, 2006, as cited in Tymoczko, 2007: 4). These scholars argue that the increasing multiculturalism of contemporary society, driven by migration and globalization, challenges the traditional view of translation as a phenomenon occurring among distinct languages and cultures belonging to separate nations and ethnic groups. The case of the Americas is exemplary in this regard, where translation "is less something that happens between separate and distinct cultures, and more something that happens between and/or among different but often interconnected hybrid cultures" (Gentzler, 2002: 9). The voice of the international turn of translation studies is the International Association of Translation and Intercultural Studies (IATIS), which has already held three conferences: one in Seoul, Korea (August 12–14, 2004), another in Cape Town, South Africa (July 12–14, 2006), and a third in Melbourne, Australia (July 8–10, 2009). A fourth is scheduled to be held in Belfast, Northern Ireland (July 24–27, 2012). See: http://www.iatis.org/content/conferences.php.

III. Translation Models and Research Methods

From the turn of the millennium onward, translation studies has reflected on the variety of methodologies elaborated by the different approaches and theories of translation, their relationship with existing paradigms, and the extent to which they can be applied across the wide range of phenomena considered to be legitimate data for the discipline (Hermans, 2002; Olohan, 2000). Starting from a general definition of *models of translation* as "preliminary, pretheoretical ways of representing the object of research," Chesterman (2000: 16) identifies three types of models: comparative, process, and causal. Each of these models influences the way of testing and developing a theory as well as of producing and exploring new data.[5]

The comparative model posits a relation of similarity between two entities—for example, source text(s) and target text(s), or corpora of translated texts and comparable nontranslated texts in the same language. Research based on this model aims to gain an insight into the nature of the assumed similarity relation with respect to a particular linguistic feature. The dynamic, process model represents translation as a process involving a change of state over a time interval. It underlies research aimed at unveiling the relations between different phases of the translation process. Comparative and process models are essentially descriptive; they do not seek to account for the phenomena they investigate.

More specifically, the comparative model makes use of probabilistic descriptive and interpretive hypotheses. Descriptive hypotheses make claims about the generality of a given phenomenon (e.g., English-Italian translations of economics articles tend to use fewer lexical Anglicisms than comparable Italian nontranslated articles). Instead, interpretive hypotheses are based on the concept *as* (e.g., the lower frequency of lexical Anglicisms in translated versus nontranslated Italian economics articles can be seen as a way of resisting the influence of English in intercultural professional communication). Moreover, the process model puts forward predictive hypotheses claiming that under given conditions a particular phenomenon will (tend to) occur; for example, in professional translating, a literal translation will be the first step during the writing phase, immediately followed by a nonliteral translation (Englund Dimitrova, 2005).

On the other hand, the causal model posits a chain of cause-effect relations between the different elements that come into play before, during, and after the production of a translation: sociocultural conditions, translation event, translation act, translation profile, cognitive effects, behavioral effects, and sociocultural effects. The causal model, argues Chesterman (2000: 21), "is the richest and most powerful of the three models [...] because it also contains the other two," and it posits explanatory predictions, which suggest the cause of a given phenomenon as well as predict that the phenomenon will (or probably will) occur as a result of the presence of given causal factors. For example, a causal model allows one to put forward:

a. The explanatory hypothesis that writing down a literal translation at the beginning of the translation process is (probably) caused by the limitations of working memory capacity
b. The predictive hypothesis that owing to the limitations of working memory capacity, the professional translator will (tend to) write down a literal translation before a nonliteral one

A causal model of translation, contends Chesterman (2000, 2005), can make a significant contribution to the development of translation theories. It can also be applied in translator training and quality assurance because it accommodates prescriptive statements. Stating what translators and translator trainees should or should not do in a given context is in fact the same as formulating implicit predictive hypotheses of effect. These prescriptive hypotheses (e.g., if a given norm is accepted/broken under given conditions, certain desirable/undesirable effects will be produced) can be explicitly formulated and tested in the translation classroom. The results will provide a translator, a translator trainee, or a teacher of translation with information on how to produce high-quality translations as well as information about the likely effects of a specific translation choice; for example, lexical variety is one of the stylistic effects produced by avoiding the use of lexical Anglicisms when translating English economics articles into Italian (Laviosa, 2007; Musacchio, 2005).

More recently (drawing on Croft, 1990/2003, as cited in Chesterman, 2008: 368), Chesterman affirms that the line between description and explanation is not clearly a dividing line because a generalizing description is already a kind of preliminary explanation (Chesterman, 2008: 377). For example, if a set of shifts concerning explicitation is found not only in a particular translation but also in other translations involving more than one language pair, this fact would offer some explanation of the existence of these shifts.[6] It would, therefore, be reasonable to affirm that the shifts occurred because all translations contain these kinds of shifts regardless of the language combination (Chesterman, 2008: 368). Moreover, the linear causal model of translation, he admits, is an oversimplification; "[i]t would be more realistic to model multiple causality as a cluster of factors that may all influence each other, at the same time or at different times" (Chesterman, 2008: 375–376).

Each of the above translation models underlies different scholarly endeavors that are carried out with a variety of research methods. The comparative model, for example, informs corpus-based descriptive studies of the textual features of translation,[7] whereas studies of the cognitive aspects of the translation act, which make use of experimental methods, such as the think-aloud (or thinking-aloud) method of data collection, are based upon process and causal models.[8] The discovery and justification procedures proposed by Toury (1995: 36–39) offer an illustrative example of a research method elaborated for descriptive translation studies and derived from a comparative translation model.

Toury's methodological point of departure is target-oriented: translations are regarded as "facts of the culture that hosts them" (Toury, 1995: 24). Their position and function in the target culture, the form they have, and hence the relationships that tie them to their source texts and the strategies used during their production are interconnected. Toury's research methodology is articulated in three phases:

> The first phase involves the selection of a corpus[9] of translated texts and the examination of their acceptability[10] in the target language—a process that can be carried out by comparing different translations of the same source text either synchronically or diachronically.
>
> The second phase starts with the identification of the source text(s) and proceeds by mapping the segments of each target text onto the source text's counterparts to determine target-source relationships, translation problems, translation solutions, and shifts.
>
> In the third phase, these relationships become the basis of first-level generalizations about the norm underlying the concrete way in which equivalence is realized, this being expressed in terms of the balance between invariance and transformation.

At each stage of this gradual discovery, facts about the nature of translation and translating hypotheses are formulated on the basis of empirical descriptions and are verified through further procedures that are applied to an expanding corpus, aiming to achieve higher and higher levels of generalization.

The shared ground between Toury's descriptive approach to translation and the neo-Firthian[11] empirical approach to language studies adopted by corpus linguistics, particularly since the 1980s, gave rise in the mid-1990s[12] to a new research methodology: the corpus-based approach.[13] Corpora are becoming increasingly used in descriptive studies of translation, in translator training, and in translation technology.[14]

IV. Applied Translation Studies

Since the mid-1990s, translator training has been a much investigated applied field of Translation Studies, as testified by the growing number of publications, ranging from handbooks for translator trainers and practical courses in translation to scholarly individual monographs, collective volumes, and academic articles. As Kelly and Way (2007: 5–6) observe, the increasing scholarly interest in translator training is linked to the internationalization of tertiary level education in the twenty-first century. This is a phenomenon that in Europe is reflected in the reforms implemented to achieve the aim of the "Bologna Process," namely, the creation of a European higher education area.[15]

Essentially interdisciplinary, this substantial body of research brings together reflections derived from the theoretical and descriptive branches of translation studies and a host of neighboring disciplines and areas of scientific inquiry, most notably constructivism, corpus linguistics, education, information and communication technologies, language teaching methodology, linguistics, second and foreign language learning, as well as second language acquisition.

These studies have focused on subjects as varied as:

- The design of translator training programs
- The development of trainer training
- The impact of international mobility
- Collaborative and task-based learning
- The professional status of translator trainer
- Student expectations and motivation
- Translator training and translator education
- The link between language teaching and translation

- Curriculum and syllabus design
- Teaching and learning materials
- Translation quality assessment
- The development of creativity
- Graduate employability

- Directionality in training
- Aptitude profiles

- Methods and tools
- The acquisition of general and/or specific
  translator competences
- The balance between theory and practice
  in designing a translation course
- The implications of translation theory for
  translator training (Kelley and Way, 2007;
  Vermeer, 1998)

Three influential single-authored monographs illustrate the variety of theories and approaches underpinning recent research in the field: Nord (1991/2005), Robinson (1997/2003), and Kiraly (2000).[16] Inspired by the functionalist approach to translation and an action-oriented concept of textuality (whereby a text is an element of a communicative interaction that takes place in a given situation), Nord develops a model of translation-oriented source-text analysis intended for students and teachers of translation as well as for professional translators. According to this model, the process of translation involves the production of a functional target text whose relationship with the source text is determined by the translation Skopos (see note 3). The target text's communicative function in a new situation with new participants deriving from a different culture, contends Nord, can be fulfilled only by means of a thorough source-text analysis informed by the principles of pragmatic text linguistics. These principles state that the communicative function of a text:

- is fulfilled by the verbal and non-verbal elements of a text (the intratextual
  factors of analysis), and
- is determined by the factors of the communicative situation in which a text
  is embedded (the extratextual factors of analysis)

The text's function is inferred from the analysis of the following interdependent extratextual factors:

- author (or sender if the author is not named)
- author's intention,
- audience
- medium (or channel)
- place
- time
- the motive for communication

Then, by reading the text, the interdependent intratextual factors are identified:

- subject matter
- knowledge presuppositions made by the author
- content
- text composition

- non-verbal elements (i.e., the non-linguistic or paralinguistic elements accompanying the text)
- lexis
- sentence structure, and
- the suprasegmental features: i.e., intonation, prosody, and stress.

Finally, the effect of the text is detected through the interplay between the extratextual and intratextual factors.

In the translation classroom the above text-analytic model is first applied to the source text. The model is then combined with the translation brief: a set of instructions that resemble, insofar as possible, the real world of professional translation, giving detailed information about the extratextual and intratextual factors of the target-text profile. The analysis of the source text together with the translation brief enables students to single out the source text's intratextual features that are relevant for the production of the target text. It is at this stage that translation problems are considered and functionally adequate solutions are put forward. Nord's model also provides criteria for grading the text material to be used in class; it adopts a systematic approach to problems and procedures and elaborates principles for assessing learning progress and evaluating translation quality. The perspective adopted lies midway between the learner-centered approach and the teacher-centered approach, because "[w]ith their greater knowledge and experience teachers should guide the learning process, but take account of the needs and potential of the students" (Nord, 2005: 161).

Robinson's departure point is the belief that shifting from traditional pedagogy—which presents a subject in a conscious, analytical, systematic way—toward a pedagogy that encourages holistic, subliminal learning, enabling students to acquire relevant competences at a much faster pace and in a more effective, enjoyable way. Drawing on suggestopedia, psychology, terminology, linguistics, and sociocultural theory, Robinson aims to harmonize translation theory and professional practice, as well as traditional and subliminal teaching methods, in order to provide translation teachers with a variegated learner-centered methodology through which students can develop the linguistic and cultural skills they need to meet contemporary market demands for effective, rapid, and accurate translations. By adapting to the translation classroom the pedagogical techniques of suggestopedia developed for foreign language learning, students are encouraged to process information through a vast array of channels: visual, auditory, and kinesthetic; drawing, storytelling, acting, and miming; imaging, discussing, and moving (Robinson, 2003: 241).

For this method to work, stresses Robinson (2003: 242–243), the teacher has to create a learner-centered environment with the students:

- The teacher is not the source of all knowledge but a facilitator of students' learning experience and a learner together with the students.

- The students are not passive recipients of knowledge or know-how but rather are active generators; hence, they are teachers along with the teacher.
- There are no right or wrong answers or solutions to the discussion activities because these are intended to help learners draw on what they already know in order to discover things they do not yet know.
- Because people are different, some discussion activities may prove fruitless, so the teacher must be creative and always be prepared to assign new tasks.

Finally, a social-constructivist educational epistemology and a vision of translation as a multifaceted, highly skilled professional activity form the basis of Kiraly's (2000, 2003) collaborative, learner-centered, and praxis-relevant approach to translator education. Central to social constructivism is the idea that learning is a constructive, active, and dynamic process in which meaning is developed through cumulative experience that is constantly open to change. If meaning derives from a personal interpretation of experience, then there can be no right or wrong answers during the learning process, but only solutions that learners believe to be plausible on the basis of norms and conventions inferred from the experience acquired by performing in class the actual work of the professional community of which they aim to become members. As expertise studies show, "knowing is *in* the action" (Schön, 1987: 25, cited in Kiraly, 2003: 10). Consequently, social-constructivist teaching methods advocate carrying out authentic professional tasks in a collaborative learning environment in which students engage in a real, rather than a simulated, translation project together with peers, in pairs, and then in teams. In these "translation praxis classes" (Kiraly, 2003: 20), the teacher-facilitator assumes the role of project coordinator and acts as project manager, native-speaking informant, mediator to facilitate negotiations between the students and the client, and supportive guide providing feedback and suggestions on how to resolve complex problems (Kiraly, 2003: 21). The project-based classroom, as envisioned by Kiraly and actually realized in his home institution, constantly reminds translator educators that their primary goal is to help students become competent, reflective, self-confident, and professional colleagues—a goal, contends Kiraly (2003: 24), that can best be accomplished through participation in praxis rather than through practice.

V. TRANSLATION AND TECHNOLOGY

The computer revolution has deeply transformed the translation industry, particularly since the advent of the Internet. The information technology boom has increased the volume and diversity of multilingual document production and widened the range and complexity of electronic tools and resources available to translators. Moreover, it has broadened the skills expected of a translator, skills that presently include teamwork, flexibility, and highly developed intercultural communication skills. Also, such new professional functions have been created as bilingual editor, multimedia designer, research and information specialist, cultural assessor, multicultural software designer, software localizer, terminologist, and project manager (Shreve, 2000: 228, cited in Koby and Baer, 2003: 213)—new functions that require translators to gain both declarative knowledge (i.e., specific technical skills) and procedural knowledge (i.e., the ability to recognize and contextualize technical issues) of translation technology (Koby and Baer, 2003: 216).

Alcina (2008: 96–99) classifies translation technologies in five blocs:

1. The translator's computer equipment—the elements related to the general functioning of the computer.
2. Communication and documentation tools—the concepts, tools, and resources used by translators to retrieve information and data from other computers or servers and interact with clients, other translators, or specialists.
3. Text editing and desktop publishing—the tools for writing, correcting, and revising texts. Word processors, for example, incorporate spelling, grammar, and style checkers as well as revision functions that allow the translator(s) to modify a document while keeping the different revisions separate, so they can later be accepted or rejected.
4. Language tools enabling translators to carry out a series of functions or tasks with their linguistic data and language resources—such sets of previously gathered data available online or on CD-ROM as dictionaries, glossaries, corpora, or terminological databases.
5. Translation tools further subdivided into machine translation systems (commercial or online) and computer-assisted translation (CAT) tools (e.g., translation memory systems and terminology management systems).

CAT tools, in particular, are increasingly combined with tools and resources belonging to the other four categories. A workbench (or workstation) is an example of a single integrated system made up of a translation memory, an alignment tool, a tag filter, electronic dictionaries, terminology databases, a terminology management system, and spelling checkers, and grammar checkers (Quah, 2006: 93–94). Moreover, translation memory systems and terminology management systems are used together with localization tools for the translation of software applications, product documentation, and websites, which require changes to make them appropriate and acceptable to the target locale—that is to a group of people sharing a particular language and culture (Quah, 2006: 19–20, 113).

VI. Conclusion

The conception that translation involves a linguistic transposition of texts, observes Tymoczko (2007: 56–57), is enshrined in the etymology of the word itself, deriving from the Latin *trans* (across/beyond) and the past participle of the verb *ferre* (carry). The meaning of *carrying across* is, in turn, associated with Christian religious practices in the later Middle Ages in Europe—in other words, the movement of religious relics, and the translation of the Bible into vernacular languages. Arguably, the current English word *translation* "is *not* a neutral word; it is saturated with Western history, Western ideology, and Western religious meanings and practices" (Tymoczko, 2007: 57). In order to move toward a truly cross-cultural understanding of the practices and products of translation throughout the world, the task of defining translation, suggests Tymoczko (2007: 53), "will continue to be a central element of translation research in the foreseeable future." Continuing to define translation so that it is viewed cross-linguistically, cross-culturally, and cross-temporally as an open concept will encourage further reflection on methodological issues; it will lead to a greater internationalization of the field, and ultimately it will result in a greater empowerment of translators. Having gained a better understanding of translation products and processes worldwide, translators will in fact be able to appreciate the full range of possibilities offered by their profession, and to meet the ethical, ideological, and intellectual challenges of the contemporary world (Tymoczko, 2007: 189).

Professional empowerment is also the ultimate goal of scholars engaged in developing and applying new pedagogic methods that will equip students with the self-reliance, authentic experience, and expertise they need to become full members of the expanding, highly skilled professional community of translators (Kiraly, 2003). Moreover, fully recognizing that technology is of central importance to the translation activity in the twenty-first century (Koby and Baer, 2003), translation pedagogy will certainly rise to the challenge of incorporating, within a task-based, collaborative, and learner-centered framework, the general and specialized software tools that are transforming the professional landscape of the modern language industry.

NOTES

1. As recalled by Toury (1995: 8), in 1972 the full English text of Holmes's lecture was available only as a brochure at the Translation Studies Section, University of Amsterdam, Department of General Literary Studies. Holmes's paper was then reprinted by Toury (1987: 9–24) in his collected volume. A year later, it was included in the posthumous collection of Holmes's (1988) papers. More recently, this latter version of Holmes's paper has been reprinted (Holmes, 2000, 2004).

2. Here, *norm* refers to "[a] regularity in behaviour, together with the common knowledge about and the mutual expectations concerning the way in which members of a group or community ought to behave in certain types of situation" (Hermans, 1999: 163).

3. In German *Skopostheorie*, the theory that applies the notion of *Skopos*, a Greek word for "purpose," to translation (Nord, 1997: 27).

4. Here, as in Tymoczko (2007: 192), the term *postcolonial* refers to cultural conditions after the beginning of colonialism.

5. Here, *theory* refers to "a set of concepts and statements (claims, hypotheses) that provides a systematic perspective on something, a perspective that allows us to understand it in some way, and hence perhaps to explain it" (Chesterman, 2000: 15).

6. *Explicitation* is broadly defined by Klaudy (1998: 80) as "the technique of making explicit in the target text information that is implicit in the source text."

7. Corpus-based studies investigate translation through computer corpora—in other words, through collections of machine-readable, authentic texts (including transcripts of spoken data), which are sampled to be representative of particular languages or language varieties (McEnery, Xiao, and Tono, 2006: 5).

8. Borrowed from psychology, the think-aloud method involves asking a translator to translate a text and, at the same time, to verbalize as much of his/her thoughts as possible. Subjects' performances are recorded on audio- or videotape. The term *think-aloud protocols* (TAPs) refers to the written transcripts of such recordings (Jääskeläinen, 1998: 266).

9. Here, the term *corpus* does not have the same meaning as *computer corpus* (see note 7); rather, it refers to a small collection of texts assembled according to specified criteria and analyzed manually. These collections include, for example, the texts produced by a particular translator or school of translators. Of course, the automated analysis of a computer corpus is not incompatible with the methodological approach proposed by Toury.

10. *Acceptability* is the extent to which a translation or a corpus of translated texts adheres to the linguistic and cultural norms prevailing in the target language for a particular text genre.

11. The neo-Firthian approach to language studies was developed by the British scholars Michael A. K. Halliday and the late John McH. Sinclair from the 1960s onward. Their perspective on language was inspired by the work of Jonathan R. Firth. A pioneer of the new discipline of linguistics in the United Kingdom, Firth established the so-called British tradition from the mid-1930s to the 1950s (Stubbs, 1996).

12. Baker (1993) first proposed the idea of using corpora for the study of the product and process of translation from a descriptive rather than a prescriptive stance.

13. See Laviosa (1998) for an overview of corpus translation studies in their early stages.

14. See Olohan (2004) for an excellent introduction to the use of corpora in research across the board in translation studies. See Anderman and Rogers (2008) for a balanced overview of recent corpus translation studies in a number of European areas.

15. The Bologna Process aims to create a European area where all higher education degrees are harmonized, mutually intelligible, and accepted for professional purposes. To achieve this end, such different mechanisms as diploma supplements, a common grading system and a two-cycle program structure are to be implemented by the year 2010. The process also intends to encourage student-centered teaching and learning (Kelly, 2005: 158).

16. The ideas presented in this volume are summarized in Kiraly, 2003.

CHAPTER 34

INTERPRETING

NANCY L. SCHWEDA NICHOLSON

I. INTRODUCTION

Almost 15 years ago, in an article that presented an overview of the fields of translation and interpreting, I wrote, "Research trends (especially in interpretation) clearly
reveal a heightened awareness among many scholars of the value of interdisciplinary
studies which provide enlightening psychological and physiological data on . . . simultaneous interpretation" (Schweda Nicholson, 1995: 44). This statement remains true
at present as the body of literature in interpreting continues to focus on the *cognitive*
approach. Whereas in the past, publications tended to include personal accounts of
interpreting experiences, lists of linguistic challenges presented by various language
combinations, and pedagogical frameworks offering training advice, the current
emphasis is placed on interdisciplinary studies that incorporate various components of processing activities (such as perception, comprehension, memory, monitoring, communication strategies, and so on). Journals such as *Interpreting* highlight
research studies that look at interpreting from a wide range of perspectives. Currently
there is a growing trend in articles and books that focus on quantitative as well as
qualitative data.

Moreover, although writings in the period from 1952 to 1988 are primarily by
French authors (many associated with the *Ecole Supérieure d'Interprètes et de
Traducteurs* [ESIT]), recent work provides evidence of an increasing internationalization in the field. Authors from other European countries (i.e., Austria, Italy, and
Switzerland), the United States, Canada, and Japan figure prominently (Pöchhacker,
1995). Perhaps one of the reasons for this is that the Internet and e-mail now provide an almost effortless medium of communication, making access to colleagues
across the world as easy (and inexpensive) as getting in touch with someone across
town. There has also been a growing tendency toward collaboration among

interpreting researchers and scholars working in related fields. Such cooperation is typified by the interdisciplinary efforts of Kurz (interpreting) and Petsche (neuro-physiology; Kurz, 1995). In this connection, simultaneous interpreting (SI) is a more frequent subject of study than is consecutive interpreting (CI), probably because its real-time overlap of two codes permits the examination of interference, input-output, monitoring, ear-voice span (EVS) and other language interface issues as the process takes place.

Pöchhacker (1995) also identified another trend: During the 6-year period he investigates (1989–1994), the majority of the publications are written in English. Finally, pedagogy still plays an important role in research and writing, because fully 25% of the material published during this interval concentrates on the teaching of interpreting, stressing the value of specific techniques and strategies. Additionally, many quantitative studies are conducted using interpreting students as subjects. (See, e.g., Russo, 1995; Tonelli and Riccardi, 1995.)

II. Conference Interpreting

As in the past, conference interpreting continues to be a popular research subject. Riccardi, Marinuzzi, and Zecchin (1998) describe interpreter stress, specifically in the context of remote interpreting (typified by videoconferencing). Braun (2007) also analyzes remote interpreting, most specifically when the primary participants as well as the interpreters are all in different locations.

Seeber and Zelger (2007) focus on interpreter renditions in simultaneous inter-pretation, highlighting the ethical side of the decisions interpreters make. They comment on output that, at first sight, appears to be a "betrayal" of the source lan-guage (SL) version. Under closer scrutiny, however, the material is often deemed to be a "truthful rendition." Gubertini (1998) discusses the validity of interpreter addi-tions, making a case for the importance of producing a comprehensible rendition rather than a mere *transcodage*. Sergio (1998) examines the interpreter's role(s) in terms of mediating cultural differences. Ondelli (1998) deals with the interpreter's oral text production and also focuses on the text type of the SL material. Kohn and Kalina (1996) stress that interpreting differs sharply from monolingual communi-cation. They provide a detailed description of the strategies employed by inter-preters in order initially to understand and subsequently to produce coherent output.

A. Simultaneous Interpreting (SI)

Kurz (1995) reports on her continuing research into SI processing activities using electroencephalograms (EEGs). Although the experiments were performed in a rather artificial situation—subjects were asked to interpret silently so as to avoid any motor activity interference in the EEG readings—Kurz states that a control experiment (in which interpreters did utter their renditions aloud) provided essentially the same outcome. She stresses that the aim of her study was to investigate cognitive processing activity, not articulatory or motor elements in SI. Kurz's results confirm right hemisphere involvement during language tasks in bilinguals (A. Green et al., 1994, 1990). She also suggests that interpretation into a nonnative language creates "greater coherence increases in the temporal region of the non-dominant hemisphere" (Kurz, 1995: 13).

Messina (1998) revisits the ongoing problem of speakers who read prepared texts at conferences (Déjean le Féal, 1978; Schweda Nicholson, 1989). He offers some good suggestions regarding the preparation of speeches to be read aloud (which, unfortunately, are largely ignored by conference participants). Setton (1998) also touches on text type and delivery format in his discussion of how meaning develops incrementally as a speech unfolds during SI.

Van Besien (1999) analyzes German to French data taken from Lederer (1980, 1981) regarding simultaneous interpreters' use of anticipation techniques. He concludes that anticipation does play a role in SI, proposing that the approaches employed may also be language-specific. His data show that verbs were anticipated most frequently. He attributes this to the different syntactic patterns of the two languages (German = SOV and French = SVO). Von Besien also highlights the role of such extralinguistic information as context in the application of anticipation strategies. Chang and Schallert (2007) examine Mandarin Chinese/English SI in terms of the methods employed based on directionality and conclude that interpreters utilize specific techniques associated with working from an A to a B language and vice versa. Riccardi (2005) discusses how interpreters' SI strategies evolve throughout their training and professional careers. Rennert (2008) reports on an SI study that analyzes the effects of the presence or lack of visual input. Focusing on Arabic and English, Al-Salman and Al-Khanji (2002) discuss SI in terms of the efficiency of decoding from a nonnative language into the mother tongue. Using a computer-assisted analytical technique, T.-H. Lee (2002) looks at EVS in a set of approximately 800 sentences gathered during English-into-Korean SI.

Darò (1997) provides an overview of memory studies in conference interpreting. She stresses that memory is a multipartite and multifaceted phenomenon, not a single entity. In this connection, Darò indicates that different types of memory may be more or less involved in CI and SI. For example, she suggests that episodic memory may play a greater role in CI than in SI. Mizuno (2005) discusses the role of working memory in SI. Gran and Bellini (1996) report on a study of short-term memory in SI, focusing on verbatim recall. The recency effect played an important role in recall, as other studies have also demonstrated. Chincotta and Underwood (1998), as well as Gernsbacher and Shlesinger (1997), discuss the consequences of concurrent articulation and suppression during SI. More specifically, the latter study examines a wide variety of material that may be suppressed during processing. This includes literal expressions as well as syntactic, anaphoric, and lexical interference. Frauenfelder and Schriefers (1997) propose a psycholinguistic approach to SI.

Drawing on advances in the field of cognitive science, Balliu (2007) comments on the "deverbalization" process in terms of memory and attention among both interpreters and translators. From a historical perspective, Kaufmann (1998) traces the history of SI in Israel. Mizuno (1995) reviews recent theoretical research in Japan.

1. *Errors and Monitoring*

Error analysis in interpreting has frequently been the subject of research (Barik, 1994, 1969; Falbo, 1998). Braun and Clarici (1997) describe the challenges posed to interpreters to represent numerals correctly in SI. Their study examines data collected from students working in a German-Italian combination, and includes shadowing, translation, and SI tasks.

Carlet (1998) tests Chernov's (1994) concept of probability prediction by including semantically unrelated, meaningless information in a SI passage. Subjects are jarred by these sentences, which do not fit into the logical progression of information input to that point in the speech. This material causes them to reevaluate what they have already heard in terms of the new and implausible information. The effect results in frequent omissions. Carlet concludes that Chernov's approach is a valid tool for examining psycholinguistic processes in SI.

Over the years, a frequent topic of discussion has been the deleterious effects of simultaneous interpreters working longer than the average 30-minute stint. Moser-Mercer, Künzli, and Korac (1998) report on a small-scale study that reveals that not only is there an increase in meaning errors during extended interpreting but interpreters become less effective at (a) monitoring their output and (b) recognizing the resulting reduction in the quality of their renditions. Zeier (1997) presents a broad overview of research on psychophysiological stress. He suggests that in cases of mental overload in SI, interpreters may exhibit a careless attitude and take their work less seriously. Zeier stresses that this change in attitude occurs quite automatically and interpreters are generally not conscious of decremental performance. Such results as these on extended turns and stress are currently being used to further the argument that court interpreters should also work in teams in order to combat the negative consequences of physiological and psychological fatigue (Festinger, 1999).

B. Consecutive Interpreting (CI)

Hamidi and Pöchhacker (2007) describe a small experiment with new technology designed to enhance consecutive interpreters' performance. A digital voice recording device allows for "simultaneous consecutive" interpreting. The interpreters who tested this hybrid technique consider it a viable option. Albl-Mikasa (2008) offers a cognitive approach to "note taking" (as opposed to the more common "memory trigger" perspective) and stresses the importance of propositional analysis. Laurenzo (2008) provides general information on "note taking," including the use of symbols, the language chosen and the organization of notes on the page. Szabo (2006) and

Dam (2004) examine the language of choice in consecutive "note taking," and each advances different perspectives on this activity. Falbo (1995) presents a general discussion of CI and focuses on the relevance of two preinterpreting exercises—namely, sight translation and memorization. Nguyen and Tochon (1998) discuss the role of concept maps and summaries during consecutive training of Vietnamese interpreters; they conclude that the concept map is a useful learning tool. Kellet (1995) focuses not only on the importance of public speaking skills in consecutive texts but also videotapes trainees in order to gather extralinguistic data regarding demeanor and presentation techniques. Giambagli (1998) questions whether or not attentional resource allocation to consecutive "note taking" detracts from efficient listening activity. Gillies's text offers a complete course in "note taking" (2005).

In a study that looks at Portuguese to German interpreting of a political speech, Meyer (1998) applies the functional pragmatic framework with the goal of demonstrating that a reconstruction of mental processing activity during interpreting can be accomplished by examining transcriptions of output.

Dam (1998) reports on a Spanish-to-Danish study that examines lexical similarity and dissimilarity between SL and target language (TL) consecutive texts in an attempt to identify meaning-based versus form-based interpreting. Her results suggest that more interpretations are form-based rather than meaning-based. This outcome is antithetic to the widespread belief that the identification of SL meaning and its transfer to the TL are at the heart of all interpreting.

Although not consecutive "conference interpreting" per se, Wadensj (2008) writes about an interview of Mikhail Gorbachev through his interpreter, Pavel Palazchenko, on a BBC talk show, *All Talk*. She discusses the "invisibility" of interpreters (or lack of it) based on the interlocutors' interactional style and behavior.

III. TRAINING

"Teaching Translation throughout the World" is the title of a special issue of *Meta* that examines both translator and interpreter education on a global scale (2005). Also most welcome is a complete issue of *Meta* dedicated to interpreting and translation in Korea ("Theories and Practices," 2006). Many of the interpreting articles focus on training and include discussions of interpreter schools in Korea, how to interpret neologisms, SI with text in English, SL interference, teaching CI, and pronunciation pedagogy (Korean/English). Ahn (2005) examines coherence challenges related to the linguistic structures of Korean and German.

Viaggio (1995) believes that exercises in sight translation are perhaps the most effective presimultaneous tool available to the interpreter trainer. Kremer (2005) offers a rationale for the introduction of three basic exercises early in interpreter training: "contextualization, prioritization of ideas and mental images" (2005: 795). Fusco (1995) presents a long list of problems and strategies in the context of training students to work between cognate languages. Nolan (2005) provides much peda-gogical information for the interpreter trainer and trainee alike.

Based on the results of research that examines speech proportion and accuracy during English-to-Korean SI, T.-H. Lee (1999) suggests that training programs emphasize techniques that develop automatic (as opposed to controlled) processing capabilities and strengthen both prediction and anticipation skills.

In a study that examined speech errors during shadowing tasks, Tonelli and Riccardi (1995) found that phonological errors are identified less frequently than are lexical and morphological ones. They conclude that subjects tend to be more con-scious of mistakes at "deeper linguistic levels" rather than at the surface phonolog-ical level (1995: 72). Inasmuch as shadowing has always generated considerable controversy regarding its usefulness as a presimultaneous training technique, the authors propose some possible applications based on their findings. Tonelli and Riccardi suggest that in order to strengthen phonological focus, students shadow number lists in no apparent order. They also propose shadowing of prose passages that are characterized by frequent insertions of numbers and nonsense words that fit the phonotactic constraints of the specific language. The authors believe that the requirement of attention to surface form is most particularly evidenced in scientific and technical meetings.

Russo (1995) reports on a survey of 135 conference-interpreting students at the University of Trieste regarding their impressions after simultaneously para-phrasing a 5-minute political talk in Italian. In this activity, no interpreting was involved, but the difficulty of the dual-task exercise of speaking and listening at the same time was compounded by the requirement to paraphrase (an assign-ment that is quite challenging even when the subject has a written text and simply paraphrases as s/he proceeds, reading the source text silently before uttering the paraphrased material aloud). After the exercise, an overwhelming majority (111 of the 135; 82%) indicated that it was hard for them to continue listening and focus on the source content while at the same time trying to generate a paraphrase and utter it without reiterating the lexical items in the original. Trainees responded that even though the task was an intralingual one, they still encountered diffi-culties with comprehension.

Déjean le Féal (1997) makes her case for preceding simultaneous training with consecutive skills acquisition. This approach is not new, for it has been the accepted norm for many years, especially in the European schools. She suggests a number of exercises to facilitate the transition from consecutive to simultaneous activities, and offers critical comments on their usefulness.

Looking at SI from Arabic into English, Shakir and Farghal (1997) take a text-linguistic perspective on student error analysis when trainees fail to recognize the pragmatic effects of specific conjunctives and lexical items in Arabic. The trainees frequently misinterpret these components, resulting in a distortion of the source text's message when rendered in the TL. Taylor Torsello (1996) also employs a text-linguistic approach, stressing the important role of theme as a speech develops. She offers suggestions for training, including stopping a video- or audiotape just after important thematic components are introduced, and having students predict what will follow based on context and information up to that point.

Kurz et al. (1996) gathered data using a questionnaire developed by Casse (1981) to create a personality profile of translation and interpretation students at the University of Vienna. Based on their results, translation students are primarily "*process* and *people oriented*," whereas interpretation trainees are "*people* and *action oriented*" (Kurz et al., 1996: 17). They also include comments about differences between beginning and advanced students. A related study examines aptitude for the study of interpreting, focusing on potential trainees' ability to paraphrase (Russo and Salvador, 2004). Schweda Nicholson (2005e) employed the Myers-Briggs Type Indicator (MBTI) to investigate personality characteristics in student interpreters and discovered that there is a great variety of behavioral traits and qualities represented.

The role of technology in interpreter training is growing. Hansen and Shlesinger (2007) discuss positive results obtained from the use of software for practice and self-study in CI. They also highlight an increase in motivation and a reduction in stress among interpreter trainees who take advantage of the out-of-class opportunities for practice. Merlini (1996) suggests that students utilize computer software to assist them with the development of CI note-taking skills. She proposes her "Interprit" computer module, which presents a combination of aural and written tasks.

Viaggio (2006) provides a detailed examination of the theory and practice of both interpreting and translation. Replete with examples and anecdotal illustrations of the challenges of "interlingual mediation," this book always informs and often entertains. Viaggio (1996a) offers a very practical and novel look at training strategies related to building context and inferences. He selected a speech text in which the speaker neither (a) identifies himself, (b) nor states his country of origin, nor (c) names his employer. Viaggio played the speech for students, stopping at various intervals to gather input regarding their comprehension level and how they were going about constructing a mental framework of the unfolding text.

IV. Research Questions, Frameworks, and Techniques

Gambier et al., (1997) provide an overview of research trends in SI. In the same vein, Danks et al., (1997) offer interdisciplinary viewpoints on a wide variety of cognitive processing aspects of SI. Roberts and Schweda Nicholson (2003) discuss theory and research in both interpreting and translation, including historical perspectives as well.

Déjean le Féal (1998b) selects three of the most widely debated issues in the interpretation field:

1. Does deverbalization exist?
2. How does one choose interpreter trainees?
3. Should SI into a B language be encouraged or frowned upon?

She then proceeds to discuss various sides of each issue "in as dispassionate and impartial a fashion as possible" (1998b: 41). Déjean le Féal concludes her analysis with suggestions for research that might provide some definitive answers to these contentious debates. She calls for cooperation among practitioners and researchers in the field, focusing on solidarity from within as a unifying force against those outside the interpreting world (whose effects are increasingly felt).

Garcia-Landa (1998) proposes a theoretical structure for research in both oral and written translation. Marzocchi (1998) examines the variety of settings in which interpreting takes place at the European Parliament. He suggests future research studies to investigate the goals of any given organization with respect to interpreting services, examining such factors as the treatment of culture within a particular context and the constraints imposed on interpreting by institution-specific parameters.

Focusing on SI, Massaro and Shlesinger (1997) discuss language processing and describe a computational approach to its study, including an examination of the fuzzy logical model of perception, top-down and bottom-up processing, the role of introspection, and some methodological challenges for SI researchers. Lonsdale (1997) presents a variety of methodological questions and concerns regarding the development of a cognitive model of SI. Among many other issues, he examines the potential relevance of research techniques available through technological advances, suggests which properties could be modeled, and questions how such a framework would function. Pöchhacker (2005) reviews several processing models of interpreting, stressing a cognitive approach and the importance of context. Viaggio (1996b) offers an "outsider's" point of view on current research in interpreting.

Yagi (1999) applies a new technique—digital discourse analysis—to the study of SI. It is interesting to note that Yagi compared the time management data gathered via digital discourse analysis with traditional subjective measures and found a strong correlation between the two evaluation types. Shlesinger (1998) discusses the relevance of corpus-based studies (as used in translation) to interpreting. Armstrong (1997) also writes about corpus-based methodology in natural language processing.

Alexieva (1997) proposes a typology to be applied to all events that involve interpreters (i.e., those that are "interpreter-mediated"). She discusses the topic in terms of general human communication theory as well as intercultural communication. Alexieva focuses on two basic categories: (i) the delivery mode and (ii) the components of the communicative situation.

Grosjean (1997b) suggests some new parameters for the study of bilingualism that stress a holistic approach. He encourages "researchers to move away from the monolingual yardstick and develop a true linguistics and cognition of bilingualism" (1997: 184).

Hoffman (1997) presents an overview of psychological research on expertise and proposes several "knowledge elicitation" techniques that may provide some insight into reasoning and memory activities during SI.

The age-old issue of the identification of quality in interpreting is still a subject of interest (Chen, 2007; Grbi, 2008; Kalina, 2005; Kurz, 2001; Moser-Mercer, 1996; Pöchhacker, 2001; Setton and Motta, 2007). These authors propose a number of methodological questions and a variety of perspectives regarding quality assessment and measurement.

In a paper that examines 10 network websites for interpreters and translators, Gambier (2007) discusses the various orientations of the online resources, including the promotion of humanitarian and political goals.

V. COURT INTERPRETING

A. General Overview of History, Theory, and Practice

Although conference interpreting is still the focus of numerous articles, the last 20 years have witnessed a proliferation of court interpreting conferences, training courses, and research (Crooker, 1996; de Jongh, 1992; A. B. Edwards, 1995; González et al., 1991; Hale, 2004; Mikkelson, 2000; Moore, 1999). Schweda Nicholson (2005b, 2005c) offers a 25-year retrospective on court interpreting in the United States, and Lowney (2005) discusses progress in the federal judiciary over a 10-year period as well as the challenges that remain.

Although no new certification tests have been developed for additional languages at the federal level since the 1980s, the National Center for State Courts (NCSC) has contributed much at the state level in terms of testing and certification of court interpreters. In 1995, it established the Consortium for State Court Interpreter Certification, a group that states may join for a fee (Gill and Hewitt, 1996). Membership in the consortium entitles the current 40 member states to use certification tests developed by the NCSC. There are now 18 languages represented, and multiple versions of the most popular language examinations (i.e., Spanish, Russian, and Vietnamese) exist. This program has obviated the need for each state to invest significant funds and human resources in test development, pilot testing, administration, and grading. The National Association of Judiciary Interpreters and Translators (NAJIT) has also developed a certification examination in the Spanish/English combination (Orrantia, 2002). Even with the federal program, the NCSC Consortium, and the NAJIT test, certification still remains an issue in the United States (Kelly, 2007).

The literature continues to examine weighty issues, especially ethics. Camayd-Freixas (2008) describes his participation in a case involving an Immigration and Customs Enforcement (ICE) raid on a meatpacking plant in Iowa, highlighting the ethical issues he faced. Rudvin (2007) suggests that the development of a universal code of ethics for community interpreters is not a workable solution, because the interpreter's role is often dictated by the setting and organization. Moreover, specific cross-cultural differences preclude a one-size-fits-all guideline. Mikkelson (1998) questions whether or not the role of the interpreter should be expanded to allow for elucidation on often very disparate source and target cultural practices. Fenton (1997), writing about New Zealand, examines the interpreter's role in the adversarial courtroom setting. Schweda Nicholson (1994b) presents an overview of critical ethical concerns, offering information taken from a variety of professional codes of ethics. Grabau (1996) writes about the role of the court interpreter from the perspective of a judge.

Court interpreting publications also deal with linguistic challenges as well as analytical tools. Paulsen Christensen (2008) discusses judges' use of direct and indirect speech in Danish courtroom proceedings in which interpreters facilitate communication. Angermeyer (2006) examines code-switching and interpreter use in New York small claims courts from a sociolinguistic perspective. He also describes problems with ambiguity in language, especially with respect to the use of *you* when interpreters participate (Angermeyer, 2005). Hale (2004) applies discourse analysis techniques to the study of court interpreting. She also writes about the importance of maintaining the same register when interpreting from the SL to the TL (Hale, 1997). Hewitt and Lee (1996) examine a number of linguistic issues in terms of accuracy and completeness, commenting especially on false cognates, slang, and idioms. They furnish test data illustrating a wide variety of TL answers provided by examinees for specific scoring units. Richardson (1996) discusses the linguistic and cultural difficulties inherent in court interpreting for the deaf.

Comparative work continues to inform an international body of researchers and practitioners. A variety of articles on court interpreting has appeared in Australia (Spring, 1999), Canada (Bergeron, 2002), Denmark (Jacobsen, 2008; Schweda Nicholson, 1997), Ecuador (Berk-Seligson, 2008), England (Fowler, 1997), England and Wales (Banton, 1998), Israel (Hefer, 2007; Morris, 1998), Japan (M. Tsuda, 1997), Mexico (Walker, 2008; Weller, 2008), South Africa (Moeketsi, 1999; Moeketsi and Mollema, 2006; Moeketsi and Wallmach, 2005), Spain (Miguelez, 1999), and Spain and Colombia (Sherr, 1999a). Morris (2008) offers a comparison between judicial attitudes to interpreting in Canada and Israel. Sherr (2008) and Clementi (2008) write about Iraqi interpreters who have assisted the U.S. military in that war-torn land and are now in the United States. Schweda Nicholson (2007a, 2007b, 2005d) describes the journey of a European Union (EU) proposal for a council framework decision on the use of interpreters in criminal proceedings through various legislative bodies and committees.

The need for client education has grown as the number of cases involving non-English speakers and limited English proficient (LEP) speakers continues to increase.

Interpreters recognize the importance of informing attorneys, judges, and other courtroom personnel, as well as the defendants and witnesses themselves, as to the role of the court interpreter. Patrick (2008), an Ohio attorney who provides legal services to low-income individuals, offers her insights into the process and stresses the value of using competent interpreters. In this connection, NAJIT has published a glossary for the users of interpreter services ("Terms of the Profession," 2008) and has also created nine position papers, on such topics as "Direct Speech in Legal Settings," "Information for Court Administrators," "Modes of Interpreting," "Language Assistance for Law Enforcement" and "Team Interpreting in the Courtroom" (http://www.najit.org). All are designed not only to educate legal personnel but also to assist the users of interpreter services as they make critical language services decisions.

Currently, two of the most hotly debated issues in the court-interpreting field are telephone interpreting and team interpreting. Regarding telephone interpreting, J. Lee (2007) provides information collected from telephone interviews with Korean interpreters who work in Australia. Lee gathered information on interpreters' personal perspectives on this specialized interpreting activity. Mintz (1998) offers firsthand observations of the procedure. Heh and Hu (1997; representing the AT&T Language Line Services) discuss the history of the program and present data from surveys that measured both customer satisfaction and job satisfaction among the language line interpreters. They call for standards development and the professionalization of over-the-phone interpreting (OPI). (See, e.g., Australian Telephone Interpreting Service, from 150 languages into English, http://www.appliedlanguage. com/interpreting_services.shtml.) Vidal (1998) is skeptical about OPI, stating, "The question is one of the inherent unreliability of the telephone for meaningful communication of important legal matters" (1998: 1). One of the major concerns of the opponents of telephone interpreting is the fact that all of the extralinguistic and nonverbal cues present in face-to-face interaction are missing in an OPI situation. Vidal asks whether OPI is a "technological advance or due process impediment" (1998: 1). Samborn (1996) offers an overview of the changing world of court interpreting, highlighting the development of testing for additional languages and the role of technology in evolving services, such as OPI. (See also, section II.A.1(earlier in this chapter), regarding stress in remote interpreting; additionally, see V. Kim, 2009).

In 1997, the NCSC launched an OPI initiative for the courts in the hopes of "assess[ing] the feasibility of providing high quality interpreting services to courts on short notice and at an affordable cost" (Hewitt, 1997). This pilot project continued for 6 months and encompassed about 1,100 OPI calls. The conclusion of the study is that interpreters' preferences are not strongly against OPI. Furthermore, interpreter participants do not view OPI as a severe threat to quality interpreting. The most common response in favor of in-person interpreting is that the quality of the sound transmission is sometimes compromised, resulting in hearing difficulties (Hewitt, 2000).

A more important concern is that court interpreters be competent to work in the judicial system. "[T]he use of unqualified individuals as interpreters in court *in person* is a far more commonplace and serious problem than those that arise when *qualified* interpreters work over the phone" (Hewitt, 2000: 12, italics in original). The key lies in reducing the number of incompetent interpreters, regardless of whether services are provided via telephone or in person.

At the federal court level, a pilot project was launched in 1989 using special equipment developed by Chandler Thompson, a federally certified Spanish/English interpreter from Las Cruces, New Mexico. The apparatus permits *simultaneous* OPI (as opposed to consecutive only, which is the normal practice when one phone line is involved). In the late 1990s, the Administrative Office of the United States Courts (AO) devoted additional financial resources to the production of advanced proto-types. The new equipment was installed in the Houston, Los Angeles, Miami, New Mexico, Puerto Rico, and Washington DC courts. It has proven to be dependable, efficient, and user-friendly. Rauch Companies, LLC, manufactures this kind of OPI equipment (Hewitt, 2000).

Team interpreting (Festinger, 1999; Resolution, 1997) has been the norm in simultaneous conference interpreting. Inasmuch as working in court is extremely physically taxing, there has been a move in recent years to establish teams in the legal arena. Progress has been made, although some courts are resistant to it on financial grounds. Practitioners have reported on the success of effective teamwork at national and international conferences, and this approach has gained further acceptance as the new millennium unfolds.

A final comment on court interpreting is warranted. Judicial interpreters have been working for many years toward greater professionalization within the field. A constant bone of contention has been the generally low rates paid to contract, freelance interpreters as well as the lack of benefits and job security in the work-place. Choate (1999) examines these issues in the California context. Aranguen and Moore (1999) respond to the issues raised by Choate. Roder (2000) writes about the decision of the 200-member Bay Area Court Interpreters (BACI) to join the Newspaper Guild-Communications Workers of America (CWA), Northern California Media Workers Guild Local 39521 in October 1999. This unionization agreement was approved by more than 90% of BACI's voting members. M. Paz Perry, chair of the BACI stated, "Interpreters have realized that if we are to have any control over our profession, we must ally ourselves with the labor movement" (Roder, 2000: 18). Herrara (2001) discusses a variety of issues related to the collective bargaining efforts of interpreters. Barbassa (2003) reports on State of California court interpreters who are now considered to be court employees. This status permits them to negotiate for improved working conditions and to join a large union like the CWA, for example. In New Jersey, an extensive interview with Karla Katz, president of Local 1034 of the CWA, describes the numerous options available to contract court interpreters in the realm of unionization ("New Jersey Per Diems Seek a Fair Deal," 2001). Court interpreters in North Carolina call for fairness in payment practices. When uncertified interpreters are used, they are paid at the same or a very similar rate as those who are certified (Thuerk, 2006). It will be interesting to see if the aforementioned efforts to deal with widespread problems such as pay equity and overall working conditions will result in additional future collective bargaining agreements for court interpreters in other parts of the United States.

B. International Tribunals and Military Courts

Inasmuch as there are three major international tribunals currently in operation, the interpreting literature over the past decade has included a variety of articles on the challenges presented in this specialized legal domain. From a historical perspective, Takeda (2008) provides information on interpreting at the Tokyo War Crimes Tribunal after World War II, and Sonnenfeldt's 2006 autobiography recounts his experiences as the chief interpreter for the prosecution during the investigative stage prior to the Nuremberg Trials. The International Criminal Tribunal for the Former Yugoslavia (ICTY) was created in 1993 in response to an international outcry for justice related to the commission of atrocities in Serbia, Croatia, Bosnia, and Kosovo (Der-Kévorkian, 2008; Nikolic, 2005; Schweda Nicholson; 2005a, forthcoming). The International Criminal Tribunal for Rwanda was established in November 1994 to investigate alleged genocide and other horrific acts in Rwanda and surrounding countries (http://www.ictr.org). Finally, the International Criminal Court (ICC) was formed in 1998 by the Rome Statute to look into crimes against humanity and war crimes throughout the world. Cases are currently in progress against governmental and military leaders in such countries as the Sudan, the Democratic Republic of the Congo, and Uganda (http://www.icc-cpi.int). Language services play an important role in the day-to-day functioning of these three courts. Of greatest interest in the context of this chapter is legal interpreting, especially inside the courtrooms. Inasmuch as interpreting is provided in several languages, all courtroom interpreting in these three international bodies is in the simultaneous mode. For example, although the official languages at the ICTY are English and French, most witnesses testify in Bosnian/Croatian/Serbian (BCS). Moreover, when cases are heard that involve Albanian-speaking regions of Kosovo (as in the prosecution of Slobodan Milosevic), interpreting to and from Albanian is also furnished. The six official languages of the ICC are English, French, Spanish, Russian, Arabic, and Chinese (identical to those at the United Nations). The working languages are English and French, but numerous additional indigenous languages will be needed as prosecutions proceed against people from all over the world (Keating, 2005; "Interpretation and Translation," 2005). The use of SI in the courts is quite different from the norm, in that most jurisdictions in the United States and abroad use CI for witness testimony. On a smaller scale, Lipkin (2008) offers an overview of interpreting in the Yehuda Military Court near the city of Jerusalem during a 1-year period. The author includes a discussion of ethics, procedures, and training. Lipkin laments the fact that there are no clear rules governing the work of interpreters and that training is strictly on-the-job, providing no guidance prior to employment.

VI. Medical/Healthcare Interpreting

Community interpreting as a whole is a growing field, especially in formerly English-dominant countries that are now faced with burgeoning ethnic and linguistic minority populations (Benmaman, 1997; Brunette et al., 2003; Carr et al., 1997; Hale, 2007; Mikkelson, 1996; Penning, 1996; Schweda Nicholson, 1994a; 1994c).[1] Medical/healthcare interpreting now figures prominently in the literature. Of particular interest are training, client education, and ethical considerations. Angelelli (2004a) provides a detailed look at medical interpreting and stresses the relevance of cross-cultural communication to the process. On the ethical side, Angelelli (2006, 2004b) reviews the standards and codes for medical interpreters and reports on the role of the interpreter in medical, court, and conference settings in North America. Bot (2005) looks specifically at CI in the mental health arena. Several organizations are working on the development of certification examinations for medical interpreters. These groups include the National Coalition on Health Care Interpreter Certification and the International Medical Interpreters Association (http://www.imiaweb.org).

VII. A Look to the Future

Déjean le Féal (1998a) describes the changing world of the conference interpreter from the perspective of differing employer requirements in the private and institutional (primarily government) markets. It used to be possible for a freelance interpreter to move easily between both types of markets. Now, however, a shift in focus regarding working languages has made this virtually impossible. To be more specific, in the private market, companies look for a bilingual combination: the national language and English. On the other hand, the institutional framework (most notably, the EU and other international organizations) looks for an "A" language (one of the 23 official languages of the EU) and as many "C" languages as possible.[2] Technological advances are also reshaping the interpreter's world. Videoconferences and telephone interpreting are becoming more and more prevalent in both the private and public sectors (Mouzourakis, 1996).

Déjean le Féal (1998a) boldly predicts that the profession of conference interpreter will not exist 50 years from now. She believes that the growing dominance of English throughout the world will result in the great majority of conferences being conducted exclusively in that language. A brief analysis of selected international conferences I have attended over the past several years provides evidence regarding interpreter use. A November 2004 EU meeting brought together representatives from most member states (MSs) to discuss a proposal for a council framework decision to regulate and standardize language services in criminal proceedings throughout the EU. I was honored to be invited to present the American perspective on legal interpreting. Held in The Hague at the International Court of Justice in the main court chamber that was equipped with SI booths, the conference took place entirely in English. In May 2004, the EU had expanded to 25 MSs, and many of the newcomers were former Soviet bloc countries. As a participant at this conference, it was impossible not to notice the limited English skills of many of the delegates. Their lack of English fluency prevented them from participating fully in the numerous discussions and question-and-answer sessions. It was a surprise that an important EU meeting such as this one would not include interpreter services. At the 50th Anniversary *Meta* Conference in Montreal in 2005, the working languages were French and English (because Canada is an officially bilingual country). As might be expected, some speakers delivered their presentations in English, and others spoke in French. Although there were many in attendance who were fully bilingual and moved easily from one session to the next (no matter what the language), there were quite a number of participants who spoke only English. No interpreting services were provided at this meeting, which resulted in many attendees missing out on the content of the papers that were delivered in French. At the 9th International *Fédération Internationale des Traducteurs* (FIT) Forum on Legal Interpreting and Translating at Court and for Public Authorities at the University of Tampere in Finland in May 2008, SI was provided from English to Finnish and Finnish to English. Moreover, at the conference entitled "Court Interpretation Cases in Selected Countries and South Korea's Position" at Hankuk University of Foreign Studies in Seoul, in September 2008, SI was furnished from Korean to English and English to Korean. It is also worthy of mention that the American Translators Association (ATA), the largest professional organization of translators and interpreters in the United States, has never (to the best of the author's knowledge) provided interpreting services at its annual conferences, which bring together over a thousand participants each year. The ATA meetings do include sessions in a variety of languages, but those who attend must speak those languages in order to take advantage of the information presented.

The preceding overview of international conferences demonstrates that, on the one hand, conference interpreting is alive and well. On the other hand, though, some meetings at which one would have expected interpreting were held without it. Informal inquiries about the lack of interpreter services at meetings such as those cited have consistently been met with the response that interpreting is too costly.

Launer, Launer, and Pedro (1998) ask the question, "Do U.S.-based interpreters have a future?" The authors conducted a survey as well as personal interviews of primarily male, Russian native speakers who work in English and Russian. The sample consisted of interpreters with extensive experience. Overall, they found that with increasing frequency, interpreters for various U.S.-based companies and some federal agencies are now being hired abroad. Past policy involved taking U.S. interpreters along with a visiting delegation. The primary reason offered for this shift to foreign nationals is cost. Although this study looks at a small segment of the

U.S. interpreting population, one can hypothesize that the same thing may be happening with other language groups as well. On the other hand, some private U.S. companies continue their policy of taking U.S. interpreters with them. They indicate that they feel more comfortable working with people they know, get along with, and trust—those who most definitely have their interests at heart in all types of business negotiations. The trust factor is critically important. Related to this consideration is that confidentiality must be strictly maintained when sensitive material or trade secrets are involved. The authors conclude by mentioning that many of the overseas interpreters are actually contracted out by U.S.-based agencies, and that this practice appears to violate the popular "Buy American" approach to securing goods and services.

In spite of these recent developments and potentially disturbing trends in conference interpreting, it appears clear that court interpreting will not disappear. This is especially true in the United States, where due process rights outlined in the Constitution provide the basis for the appointment of an interpreter when a non-English speaker is charged with a crime and/or comes into contact with the judicial system.

Based on Déjean le Féal's outlook, will more and more conference interpreters become involved in court interpreting? It is not always an easy task for a conference interpreter to make the transition to court interpreting. There are a number of important skill-related, linguistic, and subject matter considerations. First, many conference interpreters work primarily in SI; some have never done CI and do not possess the requisite note-taking skills. Strong consecutive skills are required for witness testimony.[3] From the linguistic perspective, one trend previously outlined is for conference interpreters to have an "A" language and a number of "C" languages. The rule in SI has traditionally been that interpreters never work into a "C" language. A solid "B" language is required for court interpreting. If the interpreter is a non-native English speaker (and this is often the case), active English skills must be very strong because the language of the record is English.[4] In addition to substantial CI skills and a sound "B" language, court interpreters must be knowledgeable about the law in general (both in the United States and in the countries from which defendants and witnesses come), as well as legal procedure and terminology. The court interpreter must be comfortable being "in the thick of things," because the isolation of the interpreting booth is not an option.

Moreover, conference interpreters working in SI are permitted to paraphrase and omit redundancies. The courts, however, require a verbatim translation of SL input and TL output (no additions, deletions, register changes, or editing of any kind). Conference interpreters may have difficulty adjusting their "mental set" to the stringent standards of the courts regarding completeness and pinpoint accuracy (Perez-Chambers, 2000).

From a financial perspective, many conference interpreters are not interested in courtroom work because the pay is generally much less than they are accustomed to earning. For example, on January 2, 2008, federally certified interpreters (Spanish, Haitian Creole, and Navajo) received a pay raise to $376 per day (http://www.

uscourts.gov). Many conference interpreters (depending on language combination and geographic location) make significantly more.

Some conference interpreters object to court interpreting on purely aesthetic grounds. Those who are used to jetting all over the world and interacting with individuals who are at the top of their professions may not be interested in the prospect of sitting next to a defendant who is accused of serial murders or multiple rapes.

VIII. Conclusion

Moser-Mercer (1997) writes about the Ascona workshops in which researchers from a wide variety of disciplines got together to share their areas of expertise. These individuals brought different methodological perspectives to the study of processing components, all of which are relevant to interpreting. The goal of the workshops was to foster and advance an interdisciplinary approach to interpreting research.

It is clear that the growing emphasis on empirical, quantitative inquiry will continue. As technological advances become more accessible to interpreting researchers, the field will expand to include even more precise studies of neurolinguistic and cognitive processing activity. The search for more effective teaching tools will endure. Interpreter trainers will be able to take advantage of the information gleaned from detailed investigations and develop instructional strategies that are empirically based. Additional quantitative and linguistic studies of court interpretation are definitely on the horizon as well. Medical interpreting in the United States is a growing field, and certification is in the early stages of development at this writing. The twenty-first century holds much promise for those who strive to better understand SI and CI. Slowly but surely, researchers and practitioners alike are chipping away at the shell that protects the secrets of the brain's processing activities during these complex cognitive tasks.

NOTES

1. There is some disagreement within the profession regarding the use of the term *community interpreting*. For some, it is an umbrella term that includes interpreting in the courts, in medical settings, and in social service and other government venues. Others prefer to distinguish between court interpreting and community interpreting, recognizing the former as a separate category. (See Benmaman, 1997, for a discussion of this issue.)

2. An "A" language is considered to be one's dominant language. It is usually one's first language. Simultaneous interpreters work *into* an "A" (output); it is characterized as an *active* language. On the other hand, a "C" language is considered *passive*. In other words, an interpreter would work *from* a "C" language (input) into an "A," but not *into* a "C." A "B" language has traditionally been considered one that one can also work *into*, but only in CI.

3. Many courts (especially at the federal level) own SI equipment that has traditionally been used to provide a running interpretation of the English proceedings to non-English-speaking defendants. In recent years, some courts have begun to use SI for witness testimony as well, thereby speeding up the proceedings.

4. The language of the court record in the United States is English. In the great majority of federal and state courts, court reporters are employed to keep a written verbatim account of what transpires. The presiding judicial officer can, at his/her discretion, require audio recording of the proceedings (Judicial Improvements and Access to Justice Act, 1988). However, in the courts of the Executive Office for Immigration Review (which hear political asylum and deportation cases, for example), an audio recording is made of all proceedings (Schweda Nicholson, 1999).

PART XI

LANGUAGE ASSESSMENT AND PROGRAM EVALUATION

CHAPTER 35

TECHNOLOGY IN STANDARDIZED LANGUAGE ASSESSMENTS

MICHELINE CHALHOUB-DEVILLE

INTRODUCTION

Within the past generation, computer technological advances have transformed the work environment, leisure activities, and educational practices. People have even argued that the emergence of computers represents a major turning point in civilization, not unlike that experienced with the invention of the printing press in the late fifteenth century (Provenzo, Brett, and McCloskey, 1999). It is to be expected, therefore, that computers have had and will have a large and even a defining impact on second language (L2) assessment as well. Indeed, computer-based tests (CBT) are not at all uncommon in the L2 field today. The computerized delivery of tests has become an appealing and a viable medium for the administration of standardized L2 tests in academic and nonacademic institutions. Given the growing use of CBT, an important issue to reflect on is the nature of the change that CBTs have brought and may bring to L2 assessment.

Researchers in various fields have characterized changes introduced by technology, including computers, in terms of two differentiated outcomes. Maddux (1986), in education, and Christensen (1997), in business, differentiate between two categories of computer technology applications. Maddux refers to these as "Type I" versus "Type II," and Christensen (1997) identifies them as "sustaining" versus "disruptive" applications. Type I application—or sustaining technology—refers to innovations intended to simplify and facilitate current practices and products.

Examples of this category in education include the use of the computer to administer learning drills. Type II—or disruptive technologies on the other hand—lead to the accomplishment of something that previously had not been considered plausible, such as utilizing the computer as part of new models for instruction—for example, distance learning.

An examination of the changes introduced by L2 CBT shows that technology has been intended primarily to enhance current assessment practices—that is, as Type I or sustaining innovations. CBT allows, among other things, more flexible and individualized test administration, tracking of student performance, immediate test feedback, new item/task types, and enhanced test security.Perhaps one of the most exciting capabilities of L2 CBT, which may be viewed as a disruptive technology, is the adaptive approach. Computer adaptive testing (CAT) enables tailoring item difficulty to test takers' performance, allowing a more accurate assessment of test takers' L2 ability. In short, apart from the adaptive innovation, CBT has been utilized mainly to facilitate test delivery and administration. What is now needed, however, is an exploration of how computer technology can lead to innovations in fundamental aspects of L2 testing.

This chapter discusses issues in various areas of the CBT operation that will help promote this assessment more as the disruptive type of technology. Areas covered in this discussion include the representation of the L2 construct, overall test design and measurement issues, item/task construction, and test purpose. Although the discussion mainly highlights the advantages—not the shortcomings—of certain models, measures, and procedures, this discussion is not intended to promote any of these advantages specifically but rather to explicate the type of changes needed. As background information to the central discussion, the chapter first provides an overview of several L2 CBTs that have been described in the literature. The review outlines the main features of these instruments, including test purpose, content, and scoring.

Second Language CBT Instruments

Because of space limitations, appendix A provides a tabular description of several CBT and CAT projects that are either currently operational or under development. The ensuing discussion presents a brief description of a representative sample of these operational projects that have been developed in academic and nonacademic institutions. For more complete information on these projects see Chalhoub-Deville and Deville (1999) and Chalhoub-Deville (1999).

The Brigham Young University (BYU) assessments are among the first CBTs developed in the L2 field (Larson, 1987, 1989; Madsen, 1991). The instruments include placement tests in French, German, Spanish, Russian, and English as a second language (ESL). They assess test takers' language ability in grammar, reading, and vocabulary. The ESL instrument includes a listening comprehension component.

Items are of the restricted response type with an emphasis on multiple-choice. The BYU instruments use an adaptive algorithm based on the Rasch item response theory (IRT) model.

Another French placement test is the Computer Adaptive Proficiency Test (CAPT), developed by Laurier (1991, 1999) at the University of Montreal. CAPT uses multiple-choice items to assess test takers' reading and listening comprehension, sociolinguistic judgment, lexical and grammatical knowledge, and self-assessment of oral skills. A three-parameter IRT and graded-response models are used for the adaptive algorithm.

Dunkel at Georgia State University has developed an ESL and a Hausa CAT (1997, 1998, 1999). These instruments are used to assess test takers' listening comprehension for placement into and exit from Hausa language programs. Both instruments use Rasch estimation procedures for the adaptive algorithm. Included are a variety of such selected-response item types as multiple-choice, matching, and identifying appropriate elements in a graphic.

Southern Illinois University also has an ESL placement CAT (Shermis, 1996; Young et al., 1996). The instrument assesses test takers' reading comprehension as they move from one course level to another within the ESL program. The instrument uses multiple-choice items and employs the Rasch model for the adaptive algorithm.

In the previous edition of this volume (Chalhoub-Deville, 2002), I addressed the CBT version of the Test of English as Foreign Language (TOEFL), which was introduced in 1988 (Educational Testing Service [ETS], 1998). The purpose of CBT TOEFL, just like the paper-and-pencil (P&P) version, is to measure the English language proficiency of nonnative speakers of English who seek admission into postsecondary institutions in North America. Also like the P&P version, CBT TOEFL includes a listening, structure, and reading component. CBT TOEFL includes traditional multiple-choice items, as well as other selected-response items, including selection of a visual or part of a visual, matching, and ordering of objects or text. Unique to CBT TOEFL is a writing component—a replication of the P&P Test of Written English. The listening and structure segments of the CBT TOEFL are adaptive and use a three-parameter IRT model.

A major development since the publication of the previous edition of this book is the introduction of iBT TOEFL, including numerous features that distinguish it from the CBT TOEFL. Texts and tasks represent extended language use (e.g., a reading passage could be 750 words long) and incorporate integrated skills.

The iBT TOEFL has made a serious effort to respond to developments in the field. In line with the L2 literature (see, e.g., Widdowson, 1978; Grabe, 1999) calling for integrated tasks that require the use of more than one skill at a time, iBT TOEFL measures separate as well as integrated modalities. For example, iBT TOEFL includes test tasks that require students to read, then listen, and then speak or write on a given topic. Such integrated tasks have the potential to provide a clearer representation of how well the test taker can communicate in English. A case could be made that the integration of skills is a good step toward a disruptive application of technology from a construct representation perspective. However, the orientation of language used in iBT TOEFL—and in all other tests discussed in this section—continue to operate with a cognitive representation of the L2 construct. The L2 field (see, e.g., Chalhoub-Deville, 2003; Chalhoub-Deville and Deville, 2005; McNamara, 1997; Swain, 2001a; Young, 2000) is increasingly calling for the exploration of a sociocognitive depiction of language use. This issue is discussed subsequently.

The iBT TOEFL has also moved away from continuous to fixed-date testing; based on volume and test center capacity, ETS offers approximately 40 administrations per year. Finally, unlike the CBT TOEFL, the iBT TOEFL does not utilize the adaptive approach. The adaptive feature of item delivery, which is perceived to be a disruptive technology, has proven to be quite challenging to implement in large-scale international tests such as TOEFL. From an academic perspective, it is possible to discuss CAT benefits/shortcomings and to make positive judgments as to their merits on balance. From an operational program perspective, judgment rendered may differ given the serious challenges presented:

- Resources for continuous item development to accommodate the larger demands for the item bank
- Costs and challenges of ongoing individual administration
- Immediate score reporting constraints with more constructed responses
- The serious threat to the integrity of the item bank in which larger chunks of items could be more easily compromised with repeated exposure

One example can be found in the lawsuit filed by ETS in early 2000 against the New Oriental School in China alleging widespread use and dissemination of confidential GRE and TOEFL test questions. (See "ETS Statement Concerning Copyright Violations by New Oriental School and Various Websites," published in *People's Daily*, Thursday, April 5, 2001, downloaded from http://english.peopledaily.com.cn/200104/05/eng20010405_66873.html.)

In conclusion, the above description of the various L2 CBTs illustrates that, except for the adaptive feature of item delivery, the tests employ largely P&P thinking in their approach to assessment. These instruments focus on the same aspects of the L2 construct as P&P tests; they

- use unidimensional IRT models,
- employ predominantly selected-response items types (mainly multiple-choice), and
- generate an overall score(s) used for selection and placement purposes.

In short, the various advantages of L2 CBTs function mainly to help make assessment more efficient and serviceable. As such, they can be characterized as Type I, or as representing sustaining technologies. Advances that can help make this assessment become Type II or disruptive technologies are still needed. The ensuing discussion enumerates some of the changes needed in several key areas in the CBT operation.

REPRESENTATION OF THE CONSTRUCT

Researchers (e.g., Bernhardt, 1991, 1999; Buck, 1994; Grabe, 1999) present strong arguments that standardized tests, including CBT, are not based on well-articulated theories of the L2 construct. These researchers question a representation of the L2 construct that depicts separate language skills or components and utilizes an additive unidimensional measurement framework. A number of researchers (e.g., Bernhardt, 1991, 1999; Buck, 1994; Grabe, 1999; Schoonen et al., 2000) have argued persuasively that the L2 construct is multidimensional and involves a variety of interacting components and processes. The construct comprises a complex constellation of components, including knowledge of the language system, knowledge of the world, knowledge of the particular situation of language use, and knowledge of a variety of strategies and processing skills needed to access, plan, and execute the communicative intents.

These researchers also contend that the makeup of the construct changes with different ability levels. The language ability of more proficient test takers is different from that of less proficient ones—not simply in quantity but also in the nature of the construct. Test takers at different ability levels differ in their command of linguistic and nonlinguistic concepts and knowledge, of the richness of the connections among knowledge structures, of the kinds of processes they employ, and of the degree of automaticity governing those processes. Although some abilities and processes are critical for beginning language learners, these become less salient and others emerge among more proficient learners. For example, Bernhardt (1991) shows that phono-graphemic features and word recognition are more critical in the early stages of reading language development. As the processing of these word-based features becomes more automatic, learners can attend to more complex syntactic attributes of the text. Syntactic processing of text features becomes more critical as learners advance in their reading language proficiency.

Test developers can use computer technology to measure such critical aspects of the construct more effectively and to trace learners' development. For instance, in reading, "a variety of measures of reading rate, word recognition and vocabulary and reading fluency could be developed for computer delivery" (Grabe, 1999: 36). Additionally, the computer can collect reading protocols (Bernhardt, 1991) or summary completion tests (Taylor, 1993) that allow test developers to investigate how test takers organize and reconstruct texts. Although they are not readily available, computerized scoring templates can be feasibly incorporate (see, e.g., Bernhardt, 1991; Heinz, 1993) for such assessments. Similarly, in assessing writing, the computer can be used to capture test takers' outlines, drafts, uses of spell checkers, dictionary look-ups, references to grammatical help, time spent on each of these aspects, and so on.

Such a process would permit a more detailed examination of the linguistic and nonlinguistic components and the metacognitive processes that test takers use while writing. The real challenge with such assessments lies in organizing, analyzing, and interpreting those rich data. This challenge is pertinent not only to language testing researchers but also to applied linguists in general. As Alderson (1999) argues, applied linguists need to make explicit the nature of the interactive components and processes involved in L2 performances in order to utilize the information to help explicate test performances.

Another issue to reconsider is the operationalization of the L2 construct in terms of separate skills. Current CBTs continue to emphasize the separation of the language skills, something incompatible with typical language use. As Widdowson (1978) and Grabe (1999) point out, language use typically involves more than one skill. For example, Widdowson (1978) states that *conversations* involve listening and speaking, and *correspondence* involves reading and writing. In short, the integration of skills provides for a more meaningful and appropriate depiction of language use.

Another issue worth exploration is a current L2 CBTs practice that emphasizes a cognitive representation of the L2 construct. In cognitive-based L2 tests, knowledge and skills are treated as stable entities that reside within a language user and are transferable across contexts. This practice is probably a reflection of the dominant models in language testing—for example, communicative language ability (CLA; Bachman, 1990; Bachman and Palmer, 1996)—which tend to be cognitive/psycholinguistic in their representation of L2 use and interaction. Interaction in CLA is said to be person-focused, and the L2 construct is viewed as residing within language users. Such researchers as McNamara (1997), Young (2000), and Swain (2001b) reject this notion of individual performance, which is the manifestation of an L2 user's fixed cognitive abilities. L2 use from a sociocognitive perspective is contextually mediated, jointly constructed by the interactants, and local.

L2 use within a sociocognitive approach can be represented using the notation *ability-in language user-in context*. Briefly, this notation underscores that the ability components language users bring to a communicative context interact with situational features to change those features as well as to be changed by them. The perspective summarized in the notation "maintains that ability and context features are intricately connected, and it is difficult or impossible to disentangle them" (Chalhoub-Deville, 2003: 372). Additionally, this sociocognitive approach requires that researchers address two fundamental challenges in language testing: reconsidering the construct of individual ability and exploring how to accommodate the coconstructed language use, and paying more serious attention to the types of contexts to which scores can generalize given the view the L2 use is local. It is important to note that the issues raised by a sociocognitive approach to language testing have not been accorded the attention needed, and much theoretical exploration is required before CBT language testing, among other testing applications, could be realized. This area merits focused research effort. For more discussion on the issues raised, see, for example, Chalhoub-Deville (2003) and Chalhoub-Deville and Deville (2006).

In conclusion, CBT should allow test developers to move beyond P&P tests. Computer technology can be employed to advance assessment practices in terms of the representation of the L2 construct. Language testers need to utilize technology to design measures that increasingly explore and measure components and processes identified as salient to language abilities in specific contexts.

Overall Test Design

The other area in which technological innovation can be explored to improve assessment lies in overall test design, with a related issue being the measurement model. Standardized P&P and CBT test developers have invested in procedures that seek to provide overall scores intended to rank students rather than to provide rich documentation of the salient linguistic and nonlinguistic structures that underlie test takers' performances. One important factor that has influenced current test design is related to the unidimensional measurement models used for ability estimation and item/test analysis. Unidimensional measurement models are at odds with the multidimensional representation of the L2 construct. The multidimensional conceptualization of the L2 construct previously discussed necessitates an extension of current measurement models and, perhaps, the use of a different measurement model. Extensions of and alternatives to current models (e.g., multidimensional IRT models, Bayesian inference networks, and latent class models) have been advanced in the measurement literature. These models differ in the way they represent the construct; for example, whereas multidimensional IRT assumes a continuous latent trait, the latent class model assumes an underlying categorical variable. (See publications by such researchers as Haertel, 1984; Embretson, 1985; Tatsuoka, 1993; Mislevy, 1995; Samejima, 1995, for a thorough discussion of these measurement models.)

In addition to an alternative measurement model, an overall test design that yields meaningful representation of test takers' abilities requires a coherent approach that closely links performance on test items to intended inferences about the underlying components and processes. An example of such an integrated overall test design is based on Tatsuoka's (1993) work using rule-space methodology. This approach has been employed in the L2 field with reading and listening assessments (Buck and Tatsuoka, 1998; Buck, Tatsuoka, and Kostin, 1997). The approach entails a close examination of such stimulus attributes as text features, item/task characteristics, and the types of knowledge and processes these are likely to tap in test takers. The researchers "begin with item characteristics, examine how these affect person performance, and then make assumptions about how these item characteristics map on to important aspects of linguistic knowledge or cognitive processes" (Buck and Tatsuoka, 1998: 125). Rule-space methodology generates attributes related to text length, density of information, type of information, location of relevant information, processing speed, type of inferences, response requirements, and so on. The research conducted so far with rule-space methodology has focused on exploring the feasibility of the methodology to uncover attributes of existing, operational, standardized L2 tests. The ultimate contribution of the approach occurs when performed at the test-design stage with items under development. In summary, although exploratory at this time, research using rule-space methodology points to the future of test design that emphasizes an explicit link among the intended knowledge and processes, targeted performances, and score interpretation.

Portal is an example of an approach that utilizes computer technology and alternative measurement models to advance a principled and construct-based approach to CBT design from the early stages of test construction. This test design system, under development by Mislevy and his colleagues (see Frederiksen, Mislevy, and Bejar, 1993; Mislevy, 1996; Mislevy, Steinberg, Breyer, Almond, and Johnson, 1999), is intended to develop assessments that systematically link task characteristics to test takers' abilities on the basis of test performance. The system is grounded in evidence-centered design (ECD); and it combines three models: the studentmodel, the task model, and the evidence model.

1. The student model includes variables that describe the knowledge and processes to which the test developer makes inferences.
2. The task model includes items/tasks that are, on the basis of task analysis, supposed to elicit performances that target identified aspects of the learner's knowledge and processes.
3. The evidence model makes use of probabilistic modeling to relate salient features of test takers' performance to the student model variables.

Such a test design approach works to create interrelations among task characteristics, test takers' performances, and inferences about intended underlying abilities.

The thinking behind Portal has continued to evolve. Mislevy and Riconscente (2005) argue that recent developments in terms of cognitive and psychometric research, as well as technological tools that undergird educational assessment, compel researchers to "bring the exciting array of possibilities to bear in designing coherent assessments" (2005: 61). For example, in recent years Mislevy and his colleagues have been working on the development of Principled Assessment Design for Inquiry (PADI), which emphasizes and makes explicit a systematic, comprehensive approach to test design and delivery (e.g., Mislevy, Hamel, Fried, Gaffney, Haertel, and Hafter, 2003; see also http://padi.sri.com/publications.html for links to 18 technical reports and a variety of presentations related to PADI). PADI is a coherent, interdisciplinary online assessment design system, utilizing ECD (Mislevy, Almond, and Lukas, 2003). PADI also integrates task templates that are reverse-engineered (i.e., intended tasks are analyzed to identify their underlying features and generate templates) from popular complex-problem assessment tasks with a multidimensional IRT-based scoring engine, data management component, and diagnostic scoring.

Other researchers have been making similar arguments. Under the label of assessment engineering (AE), Luecht and his colleagues (Luecht, 2006, 2008; Gierl,

Zhou, and Alves, 2008) emphasize the importance of a principled test design and development framework, integrating construct maps that delineate:

- Performance features at different proficiency levels
- Task templates aligned with different levels of the construct maps intended to direct the item writing process
- Evidence models and cognitive task models that replace traditional test specifications
- Psychometric procedures serving as statistical quality assurance, together with automated test assembly and diagnostic score interpretation

The approaches just described capitalize on recent developments in technology to advance overall test design models and to represent a clear departure from traditional practices. The individual components of the systems may not be new, but their integration and principled interconnections are innovative. These integrated, principled approaches have been favorably received in the measurement field—see, for example, presentations given at the National Council on Measurement in Education's (NCME's) invited symposium "Assessment Engineering: An Emerging Discipline," (including presentations by Gierl (2007), Luecht (2007), Pellegrino (2007); Wilson (2007), as well as Mislevy and Haertel (2007). Language testers have also shown interest in these systems—see, for example, presentations at the East Coast Language Testing annual meetings by Kenyon (2007), Luecht (2008), and Mislevy (2006).

In conclusion, technological innovations and measurement advances can help CBT move beyond conventional test design practices. Information generated by the use of alternative measurement models and by the use of an integrated test design can greatly enhance the information and quality of inferences made about test takers' L2 abilities.

ITEM/TASK CONSTRUCTION

The third area in which technological innovation can facilitate needed change lies in item/task (hereafter task) construction. Whereas the previous section focuses on overall test design, the present one addresses issues specifically related to test tasks. This section emphasizes a rational approach to task construction that can help facilitate the systematic links discussed earlier.

Typically, task development in standardized tests is an intuitive process rather than a principled procedure deliberately representing the complex L2 construct and providing explicit links between task characteristics and the abilities needed to perform these tasks. (See Pierce, 1994, for an example.) A meaningful approach to task development provides a clear understanding of the ability features that are likely to be engaged in the test task. Bachman and Palmer (1996) provide a frame-work of "distinctive task characteristics" (1996: 107) intended as a tool to guide a principled approach for L2 task development. The framework requires considering characteristics related to:

- The setting (e.g., participants, time of task)
- The characteristics of the input and the expected response (e.g., organizational, pragmatic features, topical properties, and format—channel, form, language, length, speededness, type)
- The relationship between input and expected response (e.g., scope of relationship, directness of relationship, and reactivity—reciprocal, nonreciprocal, adaptive)

Such a principled mechanism to constructing tasks helps test developers better to understand and to manipulate task features so as to target intended ability aspects. Hence, it affords more meaningful and appropriate test score inferences.

The measurement literature has been discussing use of computer technology to promote a principled approach to task construction. One example involves response generative modeling (RGM; Bejar, 1993; Bennett, 1999). RGM is intended to develop task prototypes entailing task analysis similar to that described using Bachman and Palmer's (1996) framework. These prototypes and their characteristics are then fed into a database used to generate new tasks with the desired linguistic, situational, cognitive, and measurement characteristics. Such prototypes enable test developers to draw more defensible inferences by establishing a close link between task creation and underlying abilities.

RGM can be used to generate a variety of task types, such as selected response multiple-choice or more elaborate types such as simulations. Simulations have long been used in instructional settings (e.g., BaFá BaFá; Shirts, 1977)—and to some extent in assessments (e.g., role plays, interviews, and other authentic tasks). (See projects in Bachman and Palmer, 1996.) Computer advances now permit the use of such complex tasks in standardized tests as well. As Mislev et al. (1999) state, "Tasks in standardized tests are encap-sulated and observations are spare mainly because, historically, we could not handle more. Computers and simulation capabilities shatter this barrier" (1999: 372). Simulation tasks would allow language test developers to elicit contextual-ized, integrated language performances that closely resemble those in real-life interactions. Remembering that such real-world task features as face validity are not the end goal when designing simulations, test developers must ensure that simulations tap intended ability features. Controlled simulations allow relevant features to be manipulated in a structured manner in order to target intended knowledge and processes. Finally, CBT simulations are increasingly being used in professional licensure and certification, and it is only a matter of time before L2 CBT simulations will be developed as well. (For an example of a CBT simu-lation, see Mislevy et al., 1999.)

TEST PURPOSE

The main purpose of most standardized assessments, including CBT, is to help test users make, accept/reject, or classification decisions. Contemporary L2 CBT purposes reflect the "gatekeeping" practices (Spolsky, 1997) that emerged in the early part of the twentieth century as a response to the educational situation. The demands and constraints educators faced at the beginning of the twentieth century—the introduction of education on a broader scale, coupled with limited instructional resources—led to the creation of large-scale standardized assessments for selection purposes (Messick, 1999). A similar situation developed in the L2 field, in which, because of limited learning opportunities, "efforts were made in the USA and elsewhere to develop prognostic tests that would justify decisions to exclude unqualified students from high school foreign language classes. In the USA, after the second world war, USA government language programs supported research to improve selection techniques" (Spolsky, 1995a: 321).

The Modern Language Aptitude Test (Carroll and Sapon, 1959), Pimsleur's Language Aptitude Battery (Pimsleur, 1966), the Defense Language Aptitude Battery (DLAB; MacWhinney, 1995a), and TOEFL (see discussion in Spolsky, 1995b) are examples of such prognosis/selection tests.

Although historical circumstances have led to the creation of these selection tests, today's technological advances are changing learning environments (Bennett, 1999; Layne and Lepeintre, 1996; Messick, 1999). In the L2 field,

> [i]ncreased demands for language instruction, together with advances in communication technology, have resulted in a proliferation of distance instruction programs.... With each advance in communication technology, the potential for meeting pedagogical requirements through distance instruction has increased, and it is now technically possible to provide effective distance instruction to widely diverse language learners scattered around the world.
> (Layne and Lepeintre, 1996: 235)

Such changes in language learning opportunities will likely alter the traditionally dominant purpose of standardized assessment. Selection tests to limit students' access to universities will be needed less, as more students will be involved in distance instruction. Computer-delivered tests to assess students' progress in this environment will be more in demand.

Some of the circumstances that have led institutions to demand assessments for selection are changing and making way for an increased emphasis on achievement and diagnostic tests. Bunderson, Inouye, and Olson (1989) point out that this shift will result in a new generation of CBT assessment, to which they refer as "continuous measurement" (CM) CBT. The CM CBT generation has distinct features:

- It emphasizes a close relationship between assessment and the curriculum in terms of learning objectives, tasks, and procedures.

- It is integrated into instructional plans in the form of exercises and activities related to instructional units.
- It is intended to produce a rich profile of learners' strengths and weaknesses to inform teaching and learning.

CM CBTs are learner centered with an emphasis on meeting individual needs. Although the CM generation of CBT corresponds in principle to current classroom assessments, its significance lies in its ability to transform large-scale standardized L2 assessment purposes and practices to accommodate changing learning and instructional environments.

The CM model of CBT may sound futuristic to some. Visualizing such changes is difficult because of entrenched educational thinking. Nevertheless, continuing technological advances that produce new learning contexts and opportunities mean new CBTs in the future—CBTs that will address changing purposes and needs.

CONCLUSION

CBT has made many of our L2 testing practices more efficient and introduced notable innovations such as CAT. But L2 CBTs, as currently conceived, fall short in providing any radical transformation of assessment practices. Rapidly changing computer technology should expand test developers' thinking beyond the realm of P&P testing. For CBT to be described as Type II, or disruptive, it needs to be reconceptualized in terms of the opportunities computer technology can engender to make fundamental changes in the representation of the L2 construct, overall test design, task development, and even the context and purpose of tests. Changes along these lines can genuinely transform not only L2 CBTs but also the way language testers think about their field.

APPENDIX: COMPUTER WEB-BASED PROJECTS

Instrument/institution	Purpose	Components and item types	Scores/algorithm
Test of English as a Foreign Language–CBT—ETS. References: Educational Testing Service, 1998; TOEFL CAT Scorer Guide (online).	Proficiency test to measure the English proficiency of nonnative speakers who intend to study in institutions of higher learning in the United States and Canada.	Listening: MC, selection of visual, selection of 2–4 choices, matching/ordering. Structure: Complete sentence, ID 1 of 4 acceptable words/phrase/sentences. Reading: MC, word/phrase selection, insert appropriate sentence. Writing: an essay.	Each section scored 0–30; Structure and Writing are combined and converted to scaled score of roughly 50% each. Listening and Structure parts are adaptive. 3-parameter IRT is used.
ESL Listening Comprehension—Georgia State University. References: Dunkel, 1997, 1998.	Listening comprehension test for placement into/exit from adult ESL programs.	Topics and authentic excerpts varying in extensiveness and cultural references; items require comprehension from discrete words and phrases to variable-length mono/dialogs, radio segments, scripted texts. Item types include MC, matching, and identifying appropriate elements in a graphic.	Rasch IRT is used; scores reported according to a 9-level scale representing the ACTFL scale continuum.
Hausa Listening CAT (HAST)—Georgia State University. References: Dunkel, 1997, 1998.	Listening comprehension test for placement into/exit from adult Hausa programs in the United States.	Comparable to ESL Listening Comprehension CAT.	Rasch IRT is used; scoring is comparable to ESL Listening Comprehension CAT.
French Computer Adaptive Proficiency Test (CAPT)—University of Montreal. References: Laurier, 1991, 1999.	Placement test for English speakers enrolled in French courses at the postsecondary level.	MC for reading comprehension; sociolinguistic knowledge; lexical and grammatical knowledge; listening comprehension; and self-assessment of oral skills.	3-parameter IRT is used; score from each subtest provides entry point to subsequent subtest; final score determined by obtaining average of the five subtest scores.

(continued)

Instrument/institution	Purpose	Components and item types	Scores/algorithm
Dutch Reading Proficiency CAT—Brigham Young University, CIA Language. Training Division. References: Larson, 1999.	Reading proficiency; the test simulates four phases of the OPI: warm-up, level check, probe, and wind-down.	Texts are balanced in terms of content, context, abstract/concrete passages, and cultural understanding. MC items are used; they focus on best meaning, best misfit, best restatement, best summary, and best logical completion.	Rasch IRT is used; scores span ILR reading proficiency scale, levels 1–5.
Spanish-CAPE, French-CAPE, German-CAPE, and ESL-CAPE—Brigham Young University References: Larson and Madsen, 1985; Larson, 1987, 1989; Madsen, 1991; CAPE informational website (online).	Placement tests for incoming students in language curricula at the postsecondary level.	Each CAPE includes a grammar, reading, and vocabulary section; ESL also includes a listening section. Content sampling is random within each segment. MC items are used.	Rasch IRT is used; placement according to overall score obtained from the various sections.
ESL Reading Comprehension—SSouthern Illinois University. References: Shermis, 1996; Young, Shermis, Brutten, and Perkins 1996.	Assess reading comprehension when progressing levels in a four-course ESL program.	Includes variable-length reading passages on diverse topics. Items used are MC.	Rasch IRT is used. Scores classify test takers into one of the four courses.
Multimedia Placement CAT (MultiCAT) in French, German, Spanish—Ohio State University. References: MultiCAT website.	Placement tests; also suggested as entrance/exit types of proficiency tests.	MultiCAT includes 3 subtests: Reading: Authentic texts, MC questions in English or target language, one question per text; Language in Context: Cloze passages with MC options; Listening: (still under development) MC based on audio or video clip.	Rasch IRT is used; scores rank students from beginning to superior.

Instrument/institution	Purpose	Components and item types	Scores/algorithm
Contextualized Reading Assessment (CoRA)—University of Minnesota. References: Chalhoub-Deville, Alcaya, Lozier, 1997; Chalhoub-Deville, 1997; CARLA website.	Entrance/Exit Reading Proficiency Tests for French, German, and Spanish language programs.	Authentic reading texts from a variety of sources are used. MC items are used.	Algorithm information is not provided. Scores are based on total number of correct items within given time.
COMPASS—ACT References: ACT COMPASS Planform (online).	English Placement Test into ESL or mainstream classes.	The test includes 3 segments: math, reading, and writing. MC items are used. The reading segment measures vocabulary and comprehension of a variety of text types. The writing segment focuses on mechanics, grammar, organization, and style.	3-parameter IRT is used. The 3 segments produce 7 possible scores (1 each in writing and reading skills and up to 5 in math).
International English Language Testing System (IELTS)—UCLES. References: Charge and Taylor, 1997.	English placement test with 2 foci: Academic and General Training.	Listening: MC, short answer/ sentence completion, chart completion, label diagrams, classification, and matching. Reading: Same as listening plus identifying page/section, identification of writer's views.	Algorithm information is not provided. IELTS P&P band scores are used.

(continued)

Instrument/institution	Purpose	Components and item types	Scores/algorithm
CommuniCAT—University of Cambridge. References: UCLES CommuniCAT (online).	Assess proficiency in English, French, German, and Spanish for placement purposes and for monitoring learner progress to determine appropriate certificate exam to take.	The tests include several question types, including MC listening and reading exercises, Cloze tests, and sentence transformations.	Algorithm information is not provided. Levels of Ability categorized as with P&P KET, PET, FCE, CAE, and CPE exams.
DIALANG—European Commission. References: DIALANG website (online).	Diagnostic assessment in 14 languages.	The tests combine self-assessment information with other measures related to reading, writing, listening, speaking, vocabulary, and structure. Item type information is not provided.	Algorithm information is not provided. Scores are based on the Council of Europe Proficiency Scale.

PART XII

TECHNOLOGICAL APPLICATIONS IN APPLIED LINGUISTICS

CHAPTER 36

PROGRESS AND NEW DIRECTIONS IN TECHNOLOGY FOR AUTOMATED ESSAY EVALUATION

JILL BURSTEIN AND MARTIN CHODOROW

I. INTRODUCTION

Computers have been used to analyze essays since the early 1960s (Burstein, Kukich, Wolff, Lu, Chodorow, Braden-Harder, and Harris, 1998; Foltz, Kintsch, and Landauer, 1998; Larkey, 1998; Page, 1966; Page and Petersen, 1995). Rapid technological advances in natural language processing (NLP) over the past 10 years have made it possible for computer systems to evaluate student essays in high-stakes testing, as well as low-stakes writing practice environments. This chapter describes some of the linguistic and computational bases for automated essay evaluation. Computer systems have been developed for *holistic scoring* and for the generation of *diagnostic feedback*. For *holistic scoring*, a reader (human or computer) assigns a single numerical score to the quality of writing in an essay. For *diagnostic feedback*, a reader (again, human or computer) identifies features in a writing sample, such as errors in grammar, usage and mechanics, style issues, organization and development, and text coherence.

An important issue for all forms of evaluation is test validity. Messick (1988) defines *validity* as the degree to which the empirical evidence and theoretical rationales support the appropriateness of interpretations and actions based on test scores. In the context of automated essay evaluation, the validity question might be phrased as "How adequately do computer-based scoring and other feedback appropriately represent the underlying aspects of an assessment?" Such an assessment might be standardized or classroom-based.

When people rate essays, they are instructed to follow a set of scoring criteria that characterize different aspects underlying the writing construct. Specifically, these are the aspects that can be measured (evaluated) in a writing task. For expository writing tasks, for instance, readers are typically instructed to focus on a number of features in writing that contribute to a high-quality essay. These include the writer's organization and development of ideas, the variety of syntactic constructions, the use of appropriate vocabulary, and the technical correctness of the writing in terms of its grammar, usage, and mechanics. All of these features are aspects of the writing construct that need to be evaluated to assign an appropriate rating for an essay. The challenge for computational linguistics is to develop methods automatically to identify these features in student writing. In the case of *holistic scoring*, the task is to combine the features into a single score that represents the overall quality of an essay; for purposes of *diagnostic feedback*, the goal is to accurately highlight the different features of an essay that contribute to overall essay quality and to the final score.

In the next three sections, we describe research on computational analyses of features that commonly contribute to essay evaluation for providing either a *holistic score* or *diagnostic feedback*. These analyses include lexical (vocabulary-based) measures, syntactic analyses, and evaluations of an essay's discourse structure. We discuss how these analyses are handled in the context of three systems—an influential, early project known as the *Writer's Workbench* (WWB), and two contemporary automated essay evaluation systems, Educational Testing Service's e-rater and Pearson Education's *Intelligent Essay Assessor* (IEA). In the final section, we discuss progress and future research directions in automated essay evaluation technology.

II. Three Essay Evaluation Systems

The Writer's Workbench (WWB; MacDonald, Frase, Gingrich, and Keenan, 1982) was an early application designed to be a general aid for text analysis. WWB was constructed by implementing *rules* for good writing (e.g., avoid passive voice) in such style guides as *Elements of Style* (Strunk and White, 1955). This computer-based tool looked for violations of these rules and analyzed text in three main categories:

1. Proofreading (primarily spelling and punctuation)
2. Stylistic analysis (e.g., readability measures, percentage of passives, and nominalizations)

3. English usage (online reference information about confusable words like *affect/effect*).

The *rule-based methodology* in WWB contrasts sharply with the *data-driven, statistical approaches* of the IEA and e-rater automated scoring engines. Both e-rater (Attali and Burstein, 2006; Burstein et al., 1998) and IEA (Landauer, Foltz, and Laham, 1998) base their assessment of an essay on a comparison between the essay and other essays that have been evaluated by human readers.

For *holistic scoring*, e-rater is trained on a few hundred essays representing the full range of scores assigned by readers. (On standardized tests, a 6-point scale is often used, with 1 indicating the lowest quality of writing and 6 the highest.) From this training set, e-rater measures up to 12 writing features reflecting grammar, usage, mechanics, style, vocabulary, and organization and development. E-rater then uses a regression model to assign weights to these features, for topic-specific and grade-level-specific models (Attali and Burstein, 2006). Topic-specific models are trained on essays written about the same topic, or prompt. Grade-level-specific models are trained on essays written for many different prompts by students in the same grade at school. In this way, the system can easily adapt to new topics or grade levels. IEA's essay scoring capability uses a method called *Latent Semantic Analysis* (LSA) and rates essays primarily based on content (vocabulary). The LSA methodology is described in detail in the following section about *content analysis*. IEA's capability also uses human-scored essay data for training scoring models.

Both e-rater and IEA are used in commercial applications. One of e-rater's uses is within Educational Testing Service's *Criterion* application—a web-based essay evaluation service. In terms of its essay evaluation capabilities, *Criterion* offers an e-rater score *and* diagnostic feedback that highlights and details the following writing features: errors in grammar, usage and mechanics, style issues, and an essay's organizational structure (*introductory material, thesis statement, main points, supporting details*, and *conclusion*). Pearson Education's IEA scoring engine is integrated into their WriteToLearn product, a web-based reading and writing tool. The automated essay scoring capability in IEA provides an overall essay score *and* a trait-based essay scores, including audience and purpose, organization, elaboration, and use of language. The system also produces feedback about grammar and spelling errors.

III. Content Analysis

Traditional readability measures (e.g., Coleman and Liau, 1975; Kincaid, Fishburne, Rogers, and Chissom, 1975; Chall and Dale, 1995) reflect aspects of lexical content, such as overall word frequency and number of syllables in words. WWB calculates standard readability indices and also provides information about the relative abstractness of writing by computing the percentage of words in the text that appear in a list of words rated as abstract in psychological research. Good documents were found to have less than 2.3% abstract terms, so that, when this value is exceeded, the user is given an indication that the text should contain more concrete examples to increase its clarity.

For topic-specific scoring models, e-rater evaluates the vocabulary of an essay by comparing its vocabulary to the vocabulary found in manually graded training essays for a particular topic. Higher quality essays better reflect the assigned topic. They also tend to use a more specialized and precise topic-specific vocabulary than do lower quality essays. Therefore, we expect a higher quality essay to resemble other higher quality essays in its choice of words and, conversely, a lower quality essay to resemble other lower quality ones. Resemblance is computed with *content vector analysis* (CVA), an adapted technique originally developed for information retrieval (Salton, 1989).

The first step in CVA is to convert each training essay into a word frequency vector—a one-dimensional array in which each element represents the number of times a particular word type occurs in the essay. (Because this procedure discards syntactic information and position, it is referred to as the "bag of words" approach.) Usually, high-frequency function words (e.g., *the*, *of*) are excluded, and each remaining word is converted to its base form using a morphological analyzer. The vectors can be viewed as representing points in a multidimensional space, and similarity between two essays can be measured as the cosine of the angle between their vectors. To illustrate this with highly simplified examples, suppose that each of the three sentences below is an entire essay. Their word frequency vectors are shown in table 36.1.

> Essay 1 = *Training essays are converted into word frequency vectors, and new essays are compared to the training.*
> Essay 2 = *The words in a new essay are counted and transformed into a vector of frequencies.*
> Essay 3 = *Essays are represented by word counts.*

The cosine is a measure of correlation; the more similar two vectors are, the closer their cosine will be to 1.0; the less similar two vectors are, the closer their cosine will be to 0. Cosines calculated for the frequency data in table 36.1 would show essays 2 and 3 to be most similar.

For use in essay scoring, a variant of the procedure described above is implemented in the following manner. Word weights are used instead of frequencies (Salton, 1989). The weights are computed so as to give greater importance to a word that is extremely frequent in an essay. In Essay 1, the base form *train* is more frequent than *convert*, for example and therefore has a higher weight. Additionally, the weighting scheme gives less importance to a word that is commonly found in many essays. If we consider our small collection to be the entire essay corpus, then the weights for *essay* and *word* are set to 0 because they appear in every essay and therefore do not discriminate among them. Cosines between the weight vectors show essays 1 and 2 to be most similar, a result that better captures our intuitions about the three essays than the frequency vector analysis did.

In its topic-specific scoring, e-rater uses two different lexical measures based on content vector analysis. The training essays at each of the score points are combined

Table 36.1. Word frequency (weight) vectors for three
example essays

Word	Essay 1	Essay 2	Essay 3
train	2 (1.1)	0 (0.0)	0 (0.0)
essay	2 (0.0)	1 (0.0)	1 (0.0)
convert	1 (0.5)	0 (0.0)	0 (0.0)
word	1 (0.0)	1 (0.0)	1 (0.0)
frequency	1 (0.2)	1 (0.4)	0 (0.0)
vector	1 (0.2)	1 (0.4)	0 (0.0)
new	1 (0.2)	1 (0.4)	0 (0.0)
compare	1 (0.5)	0 (0.0)	0 (0.0)
count	0 (0.0)	1 (0.4)	1 (0.4)
transform	0 (0.0)	1 (1.1)	0 (0.0)
represent	0 (0.0)	0 (0.0)	1 (1.1)

to produce one content vector representing each score point. The value of the first lexical measure is the score point whose content vector is most similar to the essay's score point, based on the cosine correlation. The second lexical measure is the cosine between the essay's content vector and the vector for the best training essays, that is, those at the highest score point. This feature indicates how similar the essay vocabulary is to the vocabulary in the best writing examples. Together these two features provide a measure of the level of topic-specific vocabulary used in the essay (Attali and Burstein, 2006.)

The actual *word × essay* matrices constructed from training sets tend to be extremely sparse (have numerous 0-frequency cells). These gaps can occur because of a failure to recognize synonymous word forms. For example, in our example, *convert* and *transform* appear in Essays 1 and 2, respectively, but the vectors miss the similarity of meaning of these two words as each is represented on an independent row of the matrix. This issue can be addressed by using the LSA approach, in the ensuing description. LSA is used in IEA's scoring engine to evaluate text meaning.

LSA begins with the same rectangular *word × document* matrix used in content vector analysis but applies to it a mathematical procedure known as singular value decomposition (SVD)—a generalized form of factor analysis. SVD decomposes the overall matrix into a set of independent dimensions, a word matrix locating each word in the space of these dimensions and a document matrix locating each document in the same space. Together, the set of dimensions, the word matrix and the document matrix can be used to reconstruct the original *word × document* matrix. However, the real value of the decomposition is that it allows "noise" to be eliminated by leaving out dimensions that account for only small amounts of variability in the original data. When only the most important dimensions are retained, the vectors for words with similar meaning (similar distributions across documents) are close together, and vectors for documents that are composed of similar word meanings are also proximate to one another. If LSA is used to process large corpora of general text (e.g., encyclopedia articles), it can create a kind of statistical thesaurus of the language. Thus, LSA can generalize across synonyms in ways that standard content vector analysis cannot.

It should be noted that although LSA can help with the issue of synonyms, and alone can score essays accurately, CVA, in combination with other writing-relevant features used in e-rater, also scores essays with *at least* comparable accuracy. *Accuracy of automated essay scoring systems is typically measured by examining agreement between human and system score assignments.*

IV. Computational Modeling of Writing Components

The WWB was an early example of a system that provided feedback using a pedagogical approach and defining good features of writing based on style guides. The approach is most similar to the kinds of corrections that can be expected from grammar checkers in current word processing software. The effectiveness of the WWB's feedback is documented in studies of those who have used it. MacDonald, Frase, Gingrich, and Keenan (1982) reported that writers' final draft documents had fewer passives, abstract words, and awkward phrases than did their first drafts. Proofreading was also shown to be more accurate using the system.

Significant progress has been made beyond generating *only* a score for writing. *Criterion*, IEA, and a number of other commercial writing evaluation systems offer diagnostic feedback related to a number of aspects of writing, including grammatical error detection, spelling error detection, and evaluation of discourse structure (Burstein, Chodorow, and Leacock, 2004). Diagnostic feedback will be illustrated primarily by using the *Criterion* essay evaluation application as an example.

Grammatical Analysis

Computational linguistics has developed many tools for syntactic analysis that range from tagging words for part of speech to chunking words into phrases to full-scale parsing of a sentence. The selection of syntactic analysis tools for use in essay scoring depends in part on the application. The WWB uses a part-of-speech tagger and heuristics to locate and count passive constructions. It then compares the proportion of passives to that found in a corpus of good documents of the same type, such as technical papers. In e-rater, syntactic analysis is used both for diagnostic feedback and essay scoring, as well as for detection of errors in grammar, usage, and mechanics.

Grammar, Usage, and Mechanics

Criterion identifies five main types of errors:

- Agreementerrors
- Verb formation errors
- Wrong word use
- Missingpunctuation
- Typographical errors

For some error types, e-rater uses a *rule-based approach* that relies on syntactic analyses and looks for specific predetermined syntactic patterns to identify errors. For example, to detect a subject-verb agreement error, the system would look for a singular subject and an adjacent plural verb (e.g., *The boy walk*). For other types of errors, an approach is used for detecting violations of general English grammar that is *corpus-based and statistical*. The system is trained on a large corpus of edited text, from which it extracts and counts sequences of adjacent word and part-of-speech pairs called *bigrams*. The system then searches student essays for bigrams that occur *much less often* than would be expected based on the corpus frequencies. The expected frequencies come from a model of English that is based on 30-million words of newspaper text. Every word in the corpus is tagged with its part of speech using aversion of the MXPOST (Ratnaparkhi, 1996) part-of-speech tagger that has been trained on student essays. For example, *a* is labeled as a singular indefinite article (abbreviated AT), *good* is tagged as an adjective (JJ), and *job* gets the label for a singular common noun (NN). After thecorpus is tagged, frequencies are collected for each tag and for each function word (determiners, prepositions, etc.), and also for each adjacent pair of tags and function words. The individual tags and words are called *unigrams*, and the adjacent pairs are *bigrams*. To illustrate, the word sequence,"*a good job*" contributes to the counts of three bigrams: *a*-JJ, AT-JJ, and JJ-NN. To detect violations of general rules of English, the system compares observed and expected frequencies in the general corpus. The statistical methods that the system uses are also commonly used by researchers to detect combinations of words that occur *more frequently* than would be expected based on the assumption that the words are independent. These methods are usually used to find technical terms or collocations. To identify errors in grammar, usage, and mechanics, *Criterion* uses the measures for the opposite purpose—to find combinations that occur *less often* than expected and that therefore might be evidence of a grammatical error (Chodorow and Leacock, 2000). For example, the bigram for *this desks*, and similar sequences that show number disagreement, occur much less often than expected in the newspaper corpus based on the frequencies of singular determiners and plural nouns.

Confused Words

Some of the most common errorsin writing are due to the confusion of homo-phones—words that sound alike. *Criterion* detects errors among *their/there/they're*, *its/it's*, *affect/effect*, andmany other word-confusion sets. For the most common cases, the system uses 10,000 training examples of correctusage from newspaper text and builds a representation ofthe local context in which each word occurs. The context consists of a set of features based on the two words and part-of-speech tags that appearto the left, and the two that appear to the right, of thetarget word. For example, a context for *effect* mightbe "*a typical effect is found*," with the features of an article-and adjective to the left, and a form of the verb "BE" and apast participle to the right. For *affect*, a local context mightbe "*it can affect the outcome*," with the features of a pronoun and modal verb on the left, and a determiner and noun on the right. Some easily confused words, such as *populace/populous*, are so rare that a large training set cannot easily be assembled from published text. In this case, generic representation-sare used. The generic local context features for nouns consist of all the part-of-speech tags found in the two positions to the left and in the two positions to the right of nouns in a large corpus of text. In a similar manner, generic local contexts are cre-ated for verbs, adjectives, adverbs, and so forth. These serve the same role as the word specific representations built for more common homophones.Thus, *populace* would be represented as a genericnoun and *populous* as a generic adjective.

Once the contextual representations have been extracted from the training examples, weights are assigned to the features by the machine learning technique known as maximum entropy (ME) or multinomial logistic regression (Ratnaparkhi, 1998). When a new essay is evaluated, it is searched for words that are members of easily confused sets. For each word that is found, the context is extracted, and the ME model is used to compute the probability of each member of the word's confu-sion set. A word will be highlighted as a possible error if it is not the highest proba-bility member of its set, in which case the system will suggest the highest probability member as a correction.

Discourse Analysis

Although the WWB does not analyze discourse structure per se, it does give the user an abstract of the essay by extracting the first and the last sentence of each para-graph. For writers who use the standard methods of beginning and ending para-graphs with topic and conclusion sentences, respectively, the claim is that viewing these sentences provides the writer with a sense of the organization of the essay and its flow of ideas.

When grading students' essays, teachers often comment on an essay's discourse structure. A well-written essay typically contains well-developed discourse ele-ments, which include *introductory material*, a *thesis statement, main ideas, support-ing ideas*, and a *conclusion*. When teachers are grading student essays, for example, they may make explicit that there is no thesis statement or that there is only a single main idea with insufficient support. This kind of feedback is designed to assist students in the organization and development of discourse structure and elements in their writing.

E-rater contains a discourse analysis system that was designed to model how teachers perform this task. The system identifies the presence and absence of expected discourse elements in an essay. For the discourse analysis system to learn how to identify discourse elements, humans annotated a large sample of student essays with essay-based discourse elements. The annotation schema reflected the discourse structure of essay writing genres, such as *persuasive* writing, in which a highly structured discourse strategy is employed to convince the reader that the thesis or position that is stated in the essay is valid. Using machine-learning techniques, the discourse analysis system maps each sentence in an essay to a corresponding discourse element: in other words, *introductory material, thesis statement, main points, supporting ideas*, and *conclusion* (Burstein, Marcu, and Knight, 2003).

V. Assessing Validity

From a purely data-driven, statistical point of view, the validity of scores obtained from a holistic scoring model is measured by R^2—the proportion of variation in writing scores accounted for by the model. For example, e-rater builds a statistical model using a sample of training essays that have been scored by at least two human readers. Depending on the model type (prompt-specific *or* grade-level-specific), up to 12 features related to vocabulary, technical correctness, sentence length, and discourse structure are identified for each essay in the training sample, and a multiple linear regression assigns weights to each feature. The regression weights are used to assign scores to new essays. The degree of match between predicted and reader-assigned scores form the basis for R^2.

There is, however, another sense of validity (more closely related to Messick's [1988] definition) that asks how adequately scores from the model represent the underlying aspects of assessment. The distinction between these two senses can be seen when considering a feature such as *essay length* (number of words)—a feature that is reliably correlated with score but is not one of the scoring criteria given to human readers. Including length in the model increases statistical measures of validity used for scoring, but it does so at the expense of construct validity, or evaluation of the writing construct. In e-rater, an attempt has been made to base scores *only* on the kinds of features that human readers use.

How well, then, do automatically generated essay scores correlate with other indicators of writing ability, such as grades in courses that require considerable writing, self-evaluations, and writing-related accomplishments (e.g., authoring a published paper)? An early study by Powers, Burstein, Chodorow, Fowles, and Kukich (2000) addressed this question by comparing e-rater scores on Graduate

Record Examination (GRE) essays to these nontest indicators. In this study, the original version of e-rater was used (Burstein et al., 1998). This version has since been upgraded (Attali and Burstein, 2006). The results showed that automated scores correlated significantly with the external criteria, though not quite as highly as the human reader scores. Similarly, Landauer, Laham, Rehder, and Schreiner (1997) used the IEA scoring engine to evaluate student essays in content areas such as the structure and function of the human heart. IEA scores and human reader scores were significantly correlated with student performance on a 40-item, short-answer test on the same topic, but scores from IEA were correlated more strongly with this external measure than were scores from the human readers.

More recently, in a study using 9,000 essays from sixth- to twelfth-graders, Attali (2004) reported that students' first submission and revised final submission showed improved writing outcomes when *Criterion* was used. Specifically, Attali's results showed that errors were reduced, on average, in students' final submissions, and that, furthermore, the reduction in errors reflected the feedback error types in *Criterion*. In addition, Attali noted that students' revised essays typically showed an increase in production of those essay-based discourse elements for which *Criterion* offers feedback (i.e., *introductory material, thesis statement, main points, supporting ideas,* and *conclusion*). The outcomes of this study suggest *Criterion* feedback supports meaningful aspects of the writing construct (e.g., technical quality and organization) and facilitates students' progress in developing writing skill.

VI. FUTURE DIRECTIONS

A goal of current research in automated essay analysis and scoring is to develop applications ensuring that systems maintain a relevant link to what writing experts believe are factors critical to the teaching and learning of writing. The WWB began with this approach by consulting classic style guides, and e-rater and IEA use data-driven techniques that relate scoring models and diagnostic feedback to scoring criteria. It is also critical that as new capabilities are developed, we continue to consider the needs of English language learners (ELLs), a rapidly growing student population. Some capabilities already include grammatical error detection that is designed with ELLs in mind (Han, Chodorow, and Leacock, 2006; Tetreault and Chodorow, 2008).

Future research should continue to enhance the validity of scores based on automated evaluation of writing, so that computer-based methods of essay analysis will be in line with educational goals in writing instruction and so that systems can adequately represent the underlying aspects of writing tasks in the classroom and on assessments.

CHAPTER 37

COMPUTER-ASSISTED LANGUAGE LEARNING

CAROL A. CHAPELLE

I. INTRODUCTION

Computer-assisted language learning (CALL), defined as "the search for and study of applications of the computer in language teaching and learning" (Levy, 1997: 1), covers a broad spectrum of concerns, but the central issues are the pedagogies implemented through technology and their evaluation. The variety of technologies available to teachers and learners include:

- Interactive tutorial programs designed specifically for language teaching
- Websites in which target language resources and interlocutors are found
- Electronic communication tools
- Linguistic aids for helping learners with spelling and grammar

In view of the range of complex materials included under the umbrella of CALL, research and practice in this area draws from other areas within and beyond applied linguistics for conceptual and technical tools to develop practices and evaluate success. However, because other areas only begin to address the relevant pedagogical and evaluative needs for the many technologies that are used by second language (L2) learners, the perennial issue in CALL has been how best to apply research and practice in L2 pedagogy to CALL as well as to develop new pedagogies effective in helping students learn in ways that were impossible in the past.

Almost 20 years ago, Underwood took up these challenges by drawing on the then-current comprehensible input theory of Krashen (1982) to develop pedagogical principles for designing CALL activities. In summary, he wrote, "Input theory tells us that classroom activities should be directed more toward the unconscious acquisition of language than the conscious learning of rules. Acquisition will take place if we provide our students with sufficient quantities of comprehensible input" (Underwood, 1984: 18). Based on the dominant view of second language acquisition at the time, Underwood developed principles for "communicative" CALL such as "Communicative CALL will aim at acquisition practice rather than learning practice" and "grammar will always be implicit rather than explicit (Underwood, 1984: 52).

Underwood illustrated the implications of the principles by describing CALL activities that, for example, allowed learners to "communicate" with CALL programs through interactive written language concerning topics such as family. At that time, the idea that students might communicate with machines using natural language was very forward looking, but today it is not unusual for language users to interact with computers (e.g., checking a flight status with an airline), to interact with other people through the use of computers (e.g., sending an e-mail to, and receiving one from, a colleague), and even to receive linguistic help from the technology (e.g., receiving error mark-up on spelling) while communicating with other people through technology. These changes in everyday language practices are in large part prompted by advances in technology, which have offered new opportunities for second language learning (Heift and Schulze, 2007; Kern, 2006). Attempts to understand the new opportunities are made regularly by teachers and researchers who draw upon theory in instructed second language acquisition to return to the basic issue that Underwood tackled: How can our understanding of second language acquisition (SLA) inform the design, use, and evaluation of second language learning activities that make use of technology?

II. Theory in Instructed SLA and CALL

Like technologies for language learning, theories of instructed SLA have evolved dramatically over the past 20 years. One change is the evolution in the input theory that Underwood drew upon. Whereas that theory asserts that the L2 is acquired unconsciously, Schmidt claims the opposite: "that subliminal language learning is impossible, and that [what might be learned] is what learners consciously notice. This requirement of noticing is meant to apply equally to all aspects of language (lexicon, phonology, grammatical form, pragmatics…)" (1990: 149). Schmidt's claim is consistent with findings indicating benefits of interaction with the target language rather than exposure to input alone (Gass, 1997; Long, 1996); interaction draws attention to language. Recognition of the importance of interaction in addition to an expanded view of factors related to selection of pedagogical materials (Doughty and Long, 2003; Doughty and Williams, 1998; Skehan, 1998) has resulted in the need to reconsider the relationship between theory-based L2 pedagogy and CALL.

A second change in instructed SLA theory is the development of useful socially oriented theoretical perspectives toward language acquisition. Sociocultural theory views language development as part of what can occur through learners' "participation in culturally organized practices, life-long involvement in a variety of institutions, and humans' ubiquitous use of tools" (Lantolf and Thorne, 2006: 1). Tools can refer to both language and technology, and therefore this theoretical perspective provides a window for a broad view of how and why technology is chosen by particular learners as well as the effects of their choices. Such a broad view has been particularly useful in studying such communication technologies as e-mail, instant messaging, blogs, wikis, and iPods in L2 learning activities (e.g., Thorne and Payne, 2005).

A third change in instructed SLA is the expanded number of theoretical perspectives—both cognitive and social—on SLA that may be brought to bear on the design and evaluation of learning activities. Whereas, in 1984, Underwood drew upon the pioneering work of the day, teachers and researchers wishing to draw upon theory in SLA at present can choose from many theoretical perspectives. The volume edited by VanPatten and Williams (2007) summarizes 10 theoretical perspectives used to investigate SLA, and one could add such others as complex systems theory (Larsen-Freeman and Cameron, 2008a). As Ortega (2007) points out, each of these theories can be analyzed in terms of whether or not it is relevant to instruction, and if it is, what kind of contribution it makes. In view of the wealth of ideas embodied in these theories, it seems worth exploring the theory-technology relationship more fully in design and research on learning tasks.

III. Empirical Research on CALL

Empirical research on CALL is conducted for a variety of audiences and purposes (Chapelle, 2007). Program directors and curriculum designers wish to assess the effectiveness of instruction provided by computer to make decisions about how and how much technology should be used in the curriculum. Publishers wish to demonstrate the quality of their materials. Teachers want to assess the success of the technological innovations they try in their classes. Teacher educators ask for the bases for technology-related pedagogies they advocate to their students. Researchers in computer-assisted language learning and applied linguistics attempt to learn how well particular technological techniques work for students in order to develop a foundation of knowledge in this area. The variety of needs and audiences for research on CALL, as well as the many theoretical perspectives from which CALL can be studied, has created a vibrant area of inquiry within applied linguistics. Dividing the territory into *product-oriented research* and *process-oriented research* can provide a broad overview.

Product-Oriented Research

Many applied linguists agree with Pederson's statement about product-oriented comparative research for assessing the effects of technology of second language learning: "Comparative research on computer-assisted versus non-computer-assisted language instruction is incapable of providing generalizable results" (Pederson, 1987: 106). Product-oriented research aims to identify increases in language ability that can be attributed to learners' participation in technology-based tasks. Such research can be conducted using between-subjects experimental and quasi-experimental designs and within subjects pretest/posttest designs. In studies conducting comparisons, a point of comparison must be identified—a point that depends on the purpose of the research. The lack of generalizability that Pederson was concerned about pertains to experimental and quasi-experimental studies comparing outcomes from CALL with those from classroom instruction. Such research has not been satisfying to applied linguists who hope better to understand how, when, and why technology can be used for second language learning because it focuses on the technology alone rather than on the pedagogy implemented through technology (Dunkel, 1991).

Many administrators, in contrast, are very interested in such research because they need to make decisions about expenditures of funds and curriculum design, and for them the point of comparison *is* the teacher-led classroom. Recent research has sought to compare classes that are teacher-led for the complete language course with hybrid courses consisting of some parts that are teacher-lead and others that are provided online (Chenoweth and Murday, 2003; Scida and Saury, 2006). Although such research can offer context-specific information about curriculum, and in some cases can identify areas of language study in which the technology or the teacher were superior, the generalizability of research results as indicative of the superiority of teachers or computers is not warranted from such research, and therefore if such comparisons are really needed in a particular setting, research needs to be conducted in that setting.

Developers of CALL tasks and teacher educators would like to work from research-based knowledge about how, when, and why technology is effective for language learning. Some such knowledge is gained by comparisons of outcomes obtained from different types of learning tasks. Such research has found evidence for the positive effects of such particular task features as

- subtitles in an interactive listening task (Borrás and Lafayette, 1994)
- highlighting linguistic form in texts (Doughty, 1991)
- interactive glosses for learners reading and listening online (Yoshii and Flaitz, 2002); and
- specific error identification and corrective feedback (Nagata, 1993)

Positive effects on vocabulary retention (De la Fuente, 2003) and speaking ability (Payne and Whitney, 2002) have been found in research comparing tasks that require student-student interaction through computer-mediated communication with other types of tasks. Other research has found that some types of online communication tasks (focusing on both meaning and form) are related to better outcomes than other online communication tasks focusing either on meaning or on form alone (Fiori, 2005).

Teachers are also interested in such work, but teachers and many researchers would simply like to demonstrate that something taught using technology has actually been learned by the students. This interest can be pursued in research using a within-subjects design, particularly when it is possible to give students both a pretest and a posttest. The question in such cases is whether the students have been able to learn through technology rather than whether or not they learned better through one mode rather than through another.

Product-oriented research is important for providing evidence about the learning potential of particular types of CALL activities. However, such research can be criticized for its narrow scope, because assessment of outcomes typically requires the researcher to define a specific body of knowledge (or of a set of abilities) to be tested. Moreover, SLA is a gradual process affected my many factors, one of which may be learners' work on CALL. Therefore, researchers have explored a range of process-oriented approaches to investigating CALL use to examine the extent to which learners

- engage in interactions expected to prompts noticing,
- produce language providing evidence for development, and
- expand their access to and engagement with the target language and culture

Process-Oriented Research

Process-oriented research investigates *interactions*, *discourse*, and other aspects of learner performance as well as the dynamic *contexts* of CALL use. Such research typically does not address the question of whether or not CALL is better than something else. Such research is of greater interest to researchers attempting better to understand the use of CALL than to practitioners attempting to link pedagogy with learning outcomes, but practitioners can also gain insights about technology for language learning by examining what learners do.

When researchers investigate learners' interactions in CALL, these can refer to interactions between the learners and the computer as well as the interactions among the learners and their interlocutors using computer-mediated communication (Chapelle, 2003; Chen, Belkada, and Okamoto, 2004). These interactions can be theorized within a conceptual framework on the role of interaction in L2 development (Gass, 1997; Pica, 1994). Learners can interact with the computer by typing at the keyboard or by clicking their mouse; advances in natural language processing have made possible some interactions with the computer through language as well (Chapelle, 1998). The questions researchers ask about such interactions are how frequently they occur and how successful they may be for language learning.

From an interactionist perspective, such interactions may reveal that learners have noticed linguistic form, engaged in interactional modifications, and corrected errors in their linguistic output (Chapelle, 2005). Noticing linguistic form, of course, is not directly observable; however, some researchers infer that noticing is taking place when they observe learners engaging in *reflective conversation* (i.e., conversation about language) during CALL tasks (Lamy and Goodfellow, 1999) or when learners simply produce the types of modifications (e.g., self-correction) that are the object of investigation in classroom research.

During computer-learner interactions, interactional modifications are evident whenever the learners interrupt their language processing to request help. For example, when learners read or listen to a text that provides opportunities for them to request modified input, "normal" interaction for reading a text on a screen is considered to consist of the learner's receiving input and requesting more input (e.g., scrolling down the page); this normal sequence is interrupted, or modified, when the learner clicks on a word to receive a definition (Chun and Plass, 1996). Similar interactions can be seen as students work on listening comprehension materials (Jones and Plass, 2002).

Modified interaction may also be apparent when a learner requests and receives a clarification during a chat room conversation (Jepson, 2005) or when learners interrupt their writing to request help. The latter behavior was documented in research by Bland, Noblitt, Armington, and Gay (1990), who examined the process learners used to construct a text using *System-D*, a technology that supports queries about the vocabulary and grammar of French while the learners are writing their French texts. The error correction tools available in contemporary commercial communication tools, which provide error mark-up, spelling help, and an online dictionary, have superseded such innovative systems from many years ago. Moreover, texts on the Web can be used by skillful learners as a repository of examples of idiomatic phrasal units that are essential for proficient writing. Process-oriented research is needed to see the moment-by-moment utility of sequences of interaction that may lead gradually to improved performance.

One such sequence is error correction, which can be observed in data consisting of the learners' unsuccessful attempts at expression followed by their linguistic modification. Such modifications can occur as the result of feedback from the computer or as a result of the learners' own reflection on their language. In the latter case, the data would include the learner's original form, the process of correction, and the learner's final form; this sequence might be used to infer self-monitoring (Jamieson and Chapelle, 1987). In computer-mediated communication tasks, both types of corrections have been noted as well. When communication tasks conducted through synchronous communication are framed by a teacher as a language learning activity, students can be observed correcting their own linguistic production and acting on the feedback from other learners (Pellettieri, 2000).

Process-oriented research also examines the discourse in which learners engage while they work on CALL. Computer-learner interaction can be interpreted as consisting of a set of discourse moves (Chapelle, 1990), but the large majority or discourse-oriented research on CALL has focused on the discourse taking place among learners sitting at a computer doing collaborative work and on the discourse of computer-mediated communication. Research investigating learners' oral discourse as they worked on CALL has shown how various activities stimulate different types of language-for-doing (Abraham and Liou, 1991; Mohan, 1992; Piper, 1986). The dynamic aspects of the computer program play a role in keeping the conversation moving as learners use language to make decisions, to initiate moves, and to react to the action that the computer program takes.

When researchers and teachers began looking at the potential of synchronous interactive written communication, Chun (1994) conducted a study to identify the nature of the discourse moves that learners of German made in such conversations. This fundamental question about the discourse of computer-mediated communication has been investigated in many different ways in the past in order better to understand the role such activities can play in language learning (Levy and Stockwell, 2006). For example, Kern (1995) examined the linguistic characteristics of his students' language in a computer-assisted classroom discussion, finding that learners engage in meaning-focused language at an appropriate level of complexity for their development (see also Blake, 2000; Kelm, 1992). Warschauer (1995/1996) examined the levels of participation of learners in computer-mediated communication, finding that learners participate more evenly than one is typically accustomed to in a classroom.

Research on the larger context of technology use expands beyond the learner-technology interface to include the contextual affordances and constraints that affect learning in which technology can be chosen by teachers and learners (Russell, 2001; Thorne, 2003) in and out of the classroom (Lam, 2000). Much of this research draws upon sociocultural theory (e.g., Lantolf and Thorne, 2006) because, as Belz and Thorne (2006) point out, many of the tele-collaborative pedagogies associated with Internet use encompass a broad set of issues. Research needs to take into account the dynamic interactions among the learner, the teacher, the language, the technology, and the institution in addition to the cultural and power relations that intersect with those interactions. The aim is to seek an understanding of the factors affecting learners' development of language and their intercultural competence as learners work with people from other cultures.

Such research can draw upon multiple methods to examine the context, the learners' language, and their perspectives on the use of technology. For example, Belz (2001) gathered multiple forms of data that together revealed the institutional and cultural factors affecting the communication learners had with their international *keypals* as they engaged in communication tasks. Thorne's (2003) case studies examined the influence of students' histories of using technologies before coming to their language classes and how these past experiences shaped their technology choices and use in connection with the class. The study of learners' histories and choices demonstrate the importance of learners' agency in their technology use and learning.

Such research can examine pedagogical interventions in these contexts as well. Belz and Vyatkina (2008) investigated the connection between instructional interventions in a German class and performance. They did a microgenetic analysis that entails tracing the development of learners' language in order to understand how it is connected with the activities in which the learner engages. In all of these studies, the object of inquiry extends beyond the learner, the teacher, and the technology alone to encompass the larger context in which activity and learning as well as their antecedents take place. Technology provides learners the opportunity for cultural contact and, consequently, perhaps the opportunity for increasing intercultural competence, but research examining the openness of learners' perspectives as revealed in their discourse suggests that this area remains a challenge (Belz, 2003).

The purpose of research investigating technology use is better to understand and improve practices in software development and technology use. At the same time, however, these studies display a range of possibilities that teachers and learners are using in the classroom and beyond. More than ever, learners in the language classroom need to be exposed to practices that will increase their strategic use of resources outside of class. Therefore, current principles for CALL pedagogy need to encompass not only what is known about language learning but also how learning can be improved in and out of the class through technology.

IV. Principles for CALL Pedagogy

Research on CALL will no doubt continue to inform the profession. In the meantime, the technological reality of many second language teachers and learners requires that knowledge about CALL be synthesized and communicated to and among teachers and learners. In other words, the principles that were laid out by Underwood need to be constantly updated. CALL pedagogy needs to take into account professional knowledge about SLA through technology, the range of technologies available to learners, and the teaching strategies that are need to teach successfully with technology.

Professional knowledge about instructed SLA suggests that qualities of learning materials should include such aspects as language learning potential, learner fit, meaning focus, and positive impact (Chapelle, 2001). CALL activities with language learning potential provide opportunities for learning by, for example, directing learners' attention to linguistic form, providing help with comprehension and production, and providing opportunities for error correction.

Activities with good learner fit match learners' linguistic ability level and individual characteristics such as age and interests. Activities with meaning focus require learners to work on constructing and interpreting meaning. Activities with positive impact have good effects extending beyond language learning to include learning of intercultural competence, strategies for using technology, and developing confidence.

These qualities are instantiated in a variety of ways through computer-learner interaction and computer-mediated communication for the study of vocabulary, grammar, reading, writing, listening, speaking, communication, and content-based language (Chapelle and Jamieson, 2008). For example, in teaching communication skills, teachers can give students a chance to engage in both oral face-to-face conversation and written interactive conversation through the use of synchronous written communication activities to provide opportunities for language focus. The interactive written communication offers learners the chance to slow down their conversation to reflect on the language (Warschauer, 1997). In teaching reading, teachers can look for electronic texts that fit their learners' level and interest to create good learner fit. In teaching listening, teachers can provide materials that offer learners opportunities to repeat the aural input as needed and to request subtitles to allow them to focus on the language.

As educators have pointed out, these new opportunities offered by technology create a novel environment for both teachers and learners (Sharples, Taylor, and Vavoula, 2007). For teachers this means that, with respect to the teaching skills they learned years ago, a different set of skills is needed for selecting and using technology in the classroom and for teaching students to succeed in a technology-rich world (Hauck and Stickler, 2006). Precisely what those skills are and how they should be taught in preservice and in-service teacher-education programs are topics of pressing importance in CALL today (Hubbard and Levy, 2006). They are likely to remain important as existing technology changes and more language technologies are developed. As learners are accustomed to working with language through technology, their language classes must increase not only their language knowledge but also their strategies for using the ubiquitous technology resources that can support their language use and language development.

V. Technology Today

The topic of CALL makes an ideal penultimate chapter for the *Handbook of Applied Linguistics* because it is the vehicle by which many of the concepts and findings in other aspects of an integral role in global communication. If research and practice in CALL is to contribute substantively to theory and practice in language teaching and learning, applied linguists' view of what constitutes appropriate CALL activities must constantly be updated on the basis of developments in theory and research in language teaching in addition to developments in technology. Current research is taking up this challenge, resulting in an intellectually stimulating and practically significant domain of applied linguistics, one that is currently being explored and expanded because technology constitutes such a significant focus in virtually all aspects of life.

CHAPTER 38

RESEARCH IN CORPUS LINGUISTICS

DOUGLAS BIBER, RANDI REPPEN, AND ERIC FRIGINAL

1. INTRODUCTION

Corpus linguistics is a research approach that has developed over the past several decades to support empirical investigations of language variation and use, resulting in research findings that are have much greater generalizability and validity than would otherwise be feasible. Corpus linguistics is not in itself a model of language. Rather, it can be regarded as primarily a methodological approach:

- It is empirical, analyzing the actual patterns of use in natural texts.
- It utilizes a large and principled collection of natural texts, known as a *corpus*, as the basis for analysis.
- It makes extensive use of computers for analysis, employing both automatic and interactive techniques.
- It depends on both quantitative and qualitative analytical techniques. (Biber, Conrad & Reppen, 1998: 4)

At the same time, corpus linguistics is more than a methodological approach, because these methodological innovations have enabled researchers to ask fundamentally different kinds of research questions, sometimes resulting in radically different perspectives on language variation and use from those taken in previous research. Corpus linguistic research offers strong support for the view that language variation is systematic and can be described using empirical, quantitative methods. Variation often involves complex patterns consisting of the interaction among several different linguistic parameters, but, in the end, it is systematic. Beyond this, the major contribution of corpus linguistics is to document the existence of linguistic constructs that are not recognized by current linguistic theories. Research of this type—referred to as a *corpus-driven* approach—identifies strong tendencies for words and grammatical constructions to pattern together in particular ways, whereas other theoretically possible combinations rarely occur.

A novice student of linguistics could be excused for believing that corpus linguistics evolved only recently, as a reaction against the standard practice of intuition-based linguistics. Introductory linguistics textbooks tend to present linguistic analysis (especially syntactic analysis) as it has been practiced over the past 50 years, employing the analyst's intuitions rather than being based on empirical analysis of natural texts. Against that background, it would be easy for a student to imagine that corpus linguistics developed only in the 1980s and 1990s, responding to the need to base linguistic descriptions on actual language use.

This view is far from accurate. In fact, intuition-based linguistics developed as a reaction to corpus-based linguistics. That is, the standard practice in linguistics up until the 1950s was to base language descriptions on analyses of collections of natural texts: precomputer corpora. Dictionaries have long been based on empirical analysis of word use in natural sentences. For example, Samuel Johnson's *Dictionary of the English Language*, published in 1755, was based on approximately 150,000 natural sentences recorded on slips of paper, to illustrate the natural usage of words. The *Oxford English Dictionary*, published in 1928, was based on approximately 5,000,000 citations from natural texts (totaling around 50 million words), compiled by over 2,000 volunteers over a 70-year period. (See the discussion in G. D. Kennedy, 1998: 14–15.) West's (1953) creation of the *General Service List* from a preelectronic corpus of newspapers was one of the first empirical vocabulary studies not motivated by the goal of creating a dictionary.

Grammars were also sometimes based on empirical analyses of natural text corpora before 1960. For example, Jespersen's grammars of English (1909–1949) used natural sentences from newspapers and novels to illustrate the various structures. An even more noteworthy example of this type is the work of C. C. Fries, who wrote two corpus-based grammars of American English. The first, published in 1940, had a focus on usage and social variation, based on a corpus of letters written to the government. The second is essentially a grammar of conversation: It was published in 1952, based on a 250,000-word corpus of telephone conversations. It includes authentic examples taken from the corpus and discussion of grammatical features that are especially characteristic of conversation (e.g., the words *well, oh, now*, and *why* when they initiate a "response utterance unit"; Fries, 1952: 101–102).

In the 1960s and 1970s, most research in linguistics shifted to intuition-based methods, arguing that language was a mental construct and that empirical analyses of corpora were not relevant for describing language competence. However, even during this period, some linguists continued the tradition of empirical linguistic analysis. For example, in the early 1960s, Randolph Quirk began the Survey of English Usage, a precomputer collection of 200 spoken and written texts (each around 5,000 words) that was subsequently used for descriptive grammars of English (e.g., Quirk et al., 1972). Functional linguists like Prince and Thompson also continued this descriptive tradition, arguing that (noncomputerized) collections of natural texts could be studied to identify systematic differences in the functional use of linguistic variants. For example, Prince (1978) compares the discourse functions of *WH*-clefts and *IT*-clefts in spoken and written texts. Thompson has been especially interested in the study of grammatical variation in conversation; for example, Thompson and Mulac (1991) analyzed factors influencing the retention versus omission of the complementizer that occur in conversation, whereas Fox and Thompson (1990) studied variation in the realization of relative clauses in conversation.

What changed in the 1980s were the widespread availability of large electronic corpora, and the increasing availability of computational tools that facilitated the linguistic analysis of those corpora. Work on large electronic corpora began in the 1960s, when Kucera and Francis (1967) compiled the Brown Corpus (a one-million word corpus of published AmE written texts). This was followed by a parallel corpus of BrE written texts: the LOB Corpus, published in the 1970s.

It was not until the 1980s, though, that major studies of language use based on large electronic corpora began to appear. Thus, in 1982, Francis and Kucera provide a frequency analysis of the words and grammatical part-of-speech categories found in the Brown Corpus, followed in 1989 by a similar analysis of the LOB Corpus (Johansson and Hofland, 1989). Book-length descriptive studies of linguistic features began to appear in this period (e.g., Granger, 1983, on passives; de Haan, 1989, on nominal postmodifiers) as did the first multidimensional studies of register variation (e.g., Biber, 1988). During this same period, English language learner dictionaries based on the analysis of large electronic corpora began to appear, such as the *Collins CoBuild English Language Dictionary* (1987) and the *Longman Dictionary of Contemporary English* (1987). Since that time, most descriptive studies of linguistic variation and use in English have been based on analysis of an electronic corpus, either a large standard corpus (such as the British National Corpus) or a small corpus designed for a specific study (e.g., a corpus of 20 biology research articles constructed for a genre analysis). Within applied linguistics, the subfields of English for specific purposes and English for academic purposes have been especially influenced by corpus research, so that nearly all articles published in these areas employ some kind of corpus analysis.

Studies in this research tradition have adopted the tools and techniques available from computer-based corpus linguistics, with its emphasis on the representativeness of the text collection, and its computational tools for investigating distributional patterns across registers and across discourse contexts in large text collections. The textbook treatments by Kennedy (1998), Biber, Conrad, and Reppen (1998), and McEnery, Xiao, and Tono (2006) provide good introductions to the methods used for these studies as well as surveys of previous research.

In the ensuing sections, we survey many of the most important linguistic studies over the past 25 years that have employed corpus analysis. These studies have been motivated by two major research goals (see Biber, Conrad, and Reppen, 1998: 5–8):

1. To describe linguistic features, such as vocabulary, lexical combinations, or grammatical features. These studies focus on variation in the choice among related linguistic features (e.g., the simple past tense versus present perfect aspect) or on the discourse functions of a single linguistic feature.
2. To describe the overall characteristics of a variety: a register or dialect. These studies provide relatively comprehensive linguistic descriptions of a single variety or of a set of related varieties.

Section 2, which follows, introduces studies of the first type, whereas section 3 surveys studies of the second type. Studies of both types have been undertaken for many of the world's languages. However, to limit the scope of the chapter, we survey only studies of English. Then, in section 4, we survey pedagogical applications of these descriptive corpus-based studies, discussing how classroom teaching and materials development have been influenced by the corpus revolution.

2. Descriptive Linguistic Studies

2.1. Corpus Studies with a Lexical Focus

Many of the earliest uses of corpora were designed to provide word lists ranked by frequency, comparing the most frequent words in different varieties. For example, Francis and Kucera (1982) and Johansson and Hofland (1989) catalog the most frequent words in the Brown and LOB Corpora, comparing word frequencies in the fiction versus nonfiction components of the corpora.

One of the major contributions of corpus-based lexical studies has been the insight that collocational associations are a central consideration for describing the meaning of a word. For example, the copular verbs *turn, come,* and *go* all have the same dictionary meaning: "to become, or to change to another state." However, corpus research (Biber et al., 1999: 444–445) shows that these three verbs have very different collocational associations: The most common adjectives following *turn* are color terms, like *black, brown, red,* and *white.* The most common adjectives following *come* describe processes representing a change to a more dynamic condition, such as *alive, awake, clean, loose,* and *unstuck.* And in contrast to both other verbs, the most common adjectives following *go* are all negative: *crazy, mad,* and *wrong.* It is not clear whether differences like these should be regarded as part of the core connotational meaning of a word, but it seems uncontroversial that this kind of information is crucially important for language learners.

There have been numerous corpus-based studies of collocation. Probably the best known is Sinclair (1991), who provides detailed descriptions on the collocations of *decline, yield,* and *set in.* Another excellent book-length introduction to the corpus-based study of collocation is by Partington (1998). For example, in chapter 2 of his book, Partington discusses the word *sheer* and its supposed synonyms *pure*, *complete*, and *absolute*, showing how these words are not at all interchangeable when considered from the perspective of their frequent collocates. Mahlberg (2005) provides a book-length treatment of general nouns in English (e.g., *time, day, man, woman, people, thing, way*), describing their meanings and use with respect to their collocational associations.

Most studies of collocation have disregarded register differences. One exception to this practice appears in a work by Biber, Conrad, and Reppen (1998: 43–53), which shows how the near-synonyms *big, large*, and *great* co-occur with very different sets of collocates (e.g., *big enough* versus *large number* versus *great deal*), and further shows how the collocational associations are very different in fiction versus academic writing. Other collocational studies taking a register perspective include those by Gledhill (2000) and Marco (2000), which both describe the functions of collocations in academic research writing.

Studies of collocation have in turn led to development of the notion of *semantic prosody* (Louw, 1993; Partington, 1998): the positive or negative connotations shared by the set of collocates that co-occur with a word. For example, the copular verb *go* (previously discussed) has a strong negative semantic prosody, whereas the copular verb *come* has a positive semantic prosody. Partington (1998: 66–67) discusses another example of this type: the verb *commit*, which has a strong negative semantic prosody, co-occurring with nouns like *crime, suicide*, and *offenses*. Similarly, Sinclair (1991: 74–75) notes that the nouns that co-occur as the subject of *set in* are mostly unpleasant states of affairs, such as *rot, decay, malaise, despair, infection, disillusion*, and so on. Studies have tended to focus on words with negative prosodies rather than positive prosodies. Other examples include *cause* (Stubbs, 1995), *signs of* (Stubbs, 2001: 458), and *sit through* (Hunston, 2002b: 60–62).

A related productive area of research has been the corpus-based (and corpus-driven) investigation of formulaic language in spoken and written registers. The methods and research goals of this line of research are quite different from the typical study of collocation. That is, studies of collocation have typically been case studies focused on a few particular words. These studies have typically disregarded register differences, and they have not attempted to generalize to the textual use of collocational combinations generally. In contrast, corpus studies of longer formulaic expressions are normally carried out in the context of a particular register or for the purposes of describing patterns of variation among multiple registers; in addition, the goals of these studies are to generalize about the use of formulaic language in the target registers rather than case studies restricted to one or two particular formulaic sequences. For example, Simpson (2004) and Simpson and Mendis (2003) describe the functions of idioms in academic spoken registers.

Many other studies have taken a corpus-driven approach to this research domain, identifying the sequences of words that are most common in different spoken and written registers (rather than starting with a set of formulaic expressions identified *a priori* based on their perceptual salience). These common word sequences, often referred to as *lexical bundles*, are usually not idiomatic and are not complete structures, but they are important building blocks of discourse. Thus, for example, Altenberg (1998) focuses on the recurrent word sequences in spoken English, whereas Biber et al. (1999, chapter 13) compare the lexical bundles in conversation and academic writing. Applying that framework, several studies have considered the types and functions of lexical bundles in additional registers: university classroom teaching and textbooks (Biber, Conrad, and Cortes, 2004; Nesi and Basturkmen, 2006), university student writing (Cortes, 2004), university institutional and advising registers (Biber and Barbieri, 2007), and political debate (Partington and Morley, 2004). N. Ellis et al. (2008) begin with a corpus analysis to identify a set of word sequences that are either frequent or that have strong collocational associations; they then test the psycholinguistic status of those sequences with respect to their perceptual salience and for their role in language production and comprehension (cf. Schmitt, Grandage, and Adolphs, 2004).

Corpus studies have shown that the types and functions of lexical bundles are very different among spoken and written registers (see, e.g., Biber, Conrad, and Cortes, 2004). First of all, there are generally more lexical bundles used in spoken registers than written registers. In terms of their structural characteristics, the bundles in speech tend to be composed of verb phrase and clause fragments, whereas the bundles in writing tend to be composed of noun phrase and prepositional phrase fragments. Those differences correspond to different discourse functions: The bundles in speech tend to be used for stance and discourse organizing functions, whereas the bundles in writing tend to have referential functions.

Of all subareas of applied linguistics, corpus research has probably had the greatest impact on lexical research and vocabulary studies. As previously noted, West (1953) created the *General Service List* of important vocabulary items based on analysis of a preelectronic corpus, and that list has been used in countless studies of vocabulary acquisition. One of the central concerns has been efforts to estimate the number of different words that a learner needs to know for different communicative purposes. Waring and Nation (1997) use corpus analysis to estimate the number of words needed to comprehend general written texts, whereas Coxhead (2000) analyzed a corpus of academic texts from several disciplines to develop a word list specifically for written academic language. Adolphs and Schmitt (2003) utilize analyses of spoken corpora to estimate the number of words required to understand conversational interactions.

Corpus research is similarly accepted as the standard practice in lexicography, so that all major ELT dictionaries are currently based on analysis of actual word use in large corpora (e.g., the *Collins CoBuild English Language Dictionary* [1987], the *Longman Dictionary of Contemporary English* [1987], and the *Cambridge Advanced Learner's Dictionary* [2005]). In sum, it would not be an overstatement to say that corpus research has revolutionized the way that lexicography, vocabulary acquisition, and word use in general are approached in linguistics.

2.2. Corpus Studies with a Grammatical Focus

Within descriptive linguistics, there have been numerous book-length studies over the past 20 years reporting corpus-based investigations of grammar and discourse: for example, Tottie (1991) on negation, Collins (1991) on clefts, Mair (1990) on infinitival complement clauses, Meyer (1992) on apposition, several books on nominal structures (e.g., de Haan, 1989; Geisler, 1995; Johansson, 1995), Mindt (1995) on modal verbs, Hunston and Francis (2000) on pattern grammar, Lindquist and Mair (2004) on grammaticalization, and Mair (2006) on recent grammatical change within American English and British English—in other words, during the twentieth century).

Most corpus-based grammatical studies take a register perspective. Many of these focus on the linguistic variants associated with a feature, using register differences as one factor to account for the patterns of linguistic variation. However, there are an even larger number of studies that have focused on the use of a particular linguistic feature in a single register; in this case, the goals of the study are to describe both the discourse functions of the linguistic feature as well as the target register itself. Studies of both types can be further subdivided according to the linguistic level of the target feature (e.g., grammatical class, dependent clause type). In addition, both types of studies include descriptions of synchronic patterns of use as well as descriptions of historical patterns of variation.

Corpus-based studies of linguistic features using register as a predictor have investigated linguistic variation from all grammatical levels, from simple part of speech categories to variation in the realization of syntactic phrase and clause types. These studies have shown that descriptions of grammatical variation and use are not valid for the language as a whole. Rather, characteristics of the textual environment interact with register differences so that strong patterns of use in one register often represent only weak patterns in other registers. The *Longman Grammar of Spoken and Written English* (Biber et al., 1999) and *Cambridge Grammar of English* (Carter and McCarthy, 2006) are comprehensive reference works with this goal, applying corpus-based analyses to show how any grammatical feature can be described for structural characteristics as well as patterns of use across spoken and written registers.

As previously noted, many corpus-based studies use register differences as a predictor of linguistic variation, whereas others study linguistic features in the context of a single register. Thus, for example, Tottie (1991) contrasts the choices between synthetic and analytic negation, as in

He could find *no* words to express his pain.
versus
He could*n't* find any words to express his pain.

Among other factors, Tottie shows that synthetic negation is strongly preferred in written rather than in spoken registers, whereas analytic negation is more commonly used in spoken registers. In contrast, Hyland (1998a) focuses on the single register of scientific research articles, describing variation in the use of hedges within that register.

As noted earlier, these studies have documented the use of lexico-grammatical features at all linguistic levels. Several studies analyze a single part-of-speech category, documenting the patterns of variation and use in particular registers. Studies taking the perspective of register variation include Barbieri (2005) on quotative verbs and Römer (2005a) on progressive verbs.

Several other studies describe linguistic variation within the context of a single spoken register, such as conversation. Quaglio and Biber (2006) survey the distinctive grammatical characteristics of conversation identified through corpus research, whereas other studies provide detailed descriptions of a particular feature in conversation. For example, McCarthy (2002) describes nonminimal response tokens; Aijmer (2002) provides a book-length description of discourse particles; Carter and McCarthy (2006) describe the discourse functions of the *get* passive; Tao and McCarthy (2001) focus on nonrestrictive *which* clauses; and Norrick (2008) describes the discourse functions of interjections in conversational narratives. Other studies of a single spoken register have focused on academic speech in university settings, based on analysis of the Michigan Corpus of Academic Spoken English (MICASE). For example, Fortanet (2004) focuses on the pronoun *we* in university lectures; Lindemann and Mauranen (2001) describe the use of *just* in academic speech; and Swales (2001) provides a detailed description of the discourse functions served by *point* and *thing* in university academic speech.

A much larger number of studies have described linguistic variation within the context of a particular written register, most often a type of academic writing. Many of these have focused on the kinds of verbs used in research writing (e.g., Thomas and Hawes, 1994), or the referring expressions in research articles (e.g., Hyland, 2001, on the use of self-mentions and Kuo, 1999, on the role relationships expressed by personal pronouns). Other studies deal with simple grammatical structures, but again most often within the context of academic writing. For example, Hyland (2002a) and Swales et al. (1998) describe variation in the use of imperatives and the expression of directives, whereas Hyland (2002b) and Marley (2002) focus on the use of questions in written registers.

The study of linguistic variation related to the expression of stance and modality has been especially popular in corpus-based research. Several of these studies compare the ways in which stance is expressed in spoken versus written registers. Biber and Finegan (1988) and Conrad and Biber (2001) focus on adverbial markers of stance in speech and writing, whereas Biber and Finegan (1989a, 1989b) and Biber et al. (1999, chapter 12) survey variation in the use of numerous grammatical stance devices (including modal verbs, stance adverbials, and stance complement clause constructions), again contrasting the patterns of use in spoken versus written registers. Biber (2006a, 2006b) and Keck and Biber (2004) take a similar approach but applied to university spoken and written registers.

Many other studies focus exclusively on the expression of stance and modality in written registers (usually academic writing). These include Vohla's (1999) study of modality in medical research writing, the studies of stance by Charles (2003, 2006, 2007) on academic writing from different disciplines, and several studies that focus on hedging in academic writing (e.g., Grabe and Kaplan, 1997; Hyland, 1996, 1998a; Salager, 1994). Related studies have been carried out under the rubric of *evaluation*, again usually focusing on academic writing (e.g., Hunston and Thompson, 2000; Hyland and Tse, 2005; Römer, 2005b; Stotesbury, 2003; Tucker, 2003; cf. Bednarek's 2006 study of evaluation in newspaper language). Fewer studies have described the linguistic devices used to express stance and evaluation in spoken registers; some of these have focused on conversation (e.g., McCarthy and Carter, 1997, 2004; Tao, 2007), whereas others have focused on academic spoken registers (e.g., Mauranen, 2003, 2004; Mauranen and Bondi, 2003; Swales and Burke, 2003).

Dependent clauses and more complex syntactic structures have also been the focus of numerous corpus-based studies that consider register differences. Several studies contrast the patterns of use in spoken and written registers: Collins (1991) on cleft constructions, de Haan (1989) on nominal postmodifiers, Geisler (1995) on relative infinitives, Johansson (1995) on relative pronoun choice, and Biber et al. (1999) on complement clause constructions. Other studies have focused on the use of a syntactic construction in a particular register, like the study of conditionals in medical discourse (G. Ferguson, 2001) or the study of extraposed constructions in university student writing (Hewings and Hewings, 2002).

All of the kinds of studies surveyed in the preceding paragraphs can be approached from a historical (or diachronic) perspective rather than a synchronic perspective, and numerous studies have taken that approach. For example, many of the papers in the edited volumes by Nevalainen and Kahlas-Tarkka (1997) and Kytö, Rydén, and Smitterberg (2006) incorporate register comparisons to describe historical change for linguistic features like existential clauses, adverbial clauses, and relative clauses. Biber and Clark (2002) contrast the kinds of noun modifiers common in academic versus popular written registers. Several historical studies of stance and modality have included analysis of register differences, such as Kytö (1991) on modal verbs in written and speech-based registers, Culpeper and Kytö (1999) on hedges in Early Modern English dialogues, Salager-Meyer and Defives (1998) on hedges in academic writing over the last two centuries, Fitzmaurice (2002b, 2003) on stance and politeness in early eighteenth-century letters, and Biber (2004) on historical change in the use of stance and modal features across a range of speech-based and written registers. A few studies have focused on recent (i.e., twentieth-century) historical change; for example, Hundt and Mair (1999) contrast the rapid grammatical change observed in "agile" registers (like newspaper writing) with the much slower pace of change observed in "uptight" registers like academic prose. Leech, Hundt, Mair, and Smith (in press) track historical change in the twentieth century using the register categories distinguished in the Brown/LOB family of corpora.

3. Descriptions of Varieties

3.1. Register Descriptions

The studies surveyed in the preceding section focus on a particular linguistic feature, using register to describe the use of that feature. In the present section, the analytical perspective is reversed: These studies focus on the overall description of a register, considering a suite of linguistic features that are characteristic of the register.

Many studies of this type describe spoken registers, including conversation (e.g., Biber, 2008; Carter and McCarthy, 1997, 2004; Quaglio and Biber, 2006; Biber and Conrad, in press: chapter 4), service encounters (e.g., McCarthy, 2000), call center interactions (Friginal, 2009a, 2009b), spoken business English (McCarthy and Handford, 2004), television dialogue (Quaglio, 2009; Rey, 2001), spoken media discourse (O'Keeffe, 2006), and spoken university registers like classroom teaching, office hours, and teacher-mentoring sessions (e.g., Biber, 2006a; Biber, Conrad, and Leech, 2002; Csomay, 2005; Reppen and Vásquez, 2007). Ädel and Reppen (2008) include several papers that use corpus analysis to describe different registers from academic, workplace, and television settings.

However, written registers have received considerably more attention than spoken registers. Academic prose has been the best described written register (see, e.g., Biber, 2006a; Biber, Connor, and Upton, 2007; Connor and Mauranen, 1999; Connor and Upton, 2004b; Conrad, 1996, 2001; Freddi, 2005; McKenna, 1997; Tognini-Bonelli and Del Lungo Camiciotti, 2005). But many other written registers have also been described using corpus-based analysis, including personal letters (e.g., Connor and Upton, 2003; Fitzmaurice, 2002a; Precht, 1998), written advertise-ments (e.g., Bruthiaux, 1994, 1996, 2005), newspaper discourse (e.g., Bednarek, 2006; Herring, 2003; Jucker, 1992), and fiction (e.g., Thompson and Sealey, 2007; Mahlberg, in press; Semino and Short, 2004). Electronic registers that have emerged over the past few decades, from e-mail communication to weblogs and texting, have been an especially interesting and productive area of research (see, e.g., Biber and Conrad, in press: chapter 7; Danet and Herring; 2003, Gains, 1999; Herring and Paolillo, 2006; Hundt, Nesselhauf, and Biewer, 2007; Morrow, 2006).

3.2. Multidimensional Analyses of Register Variation

Most of the studies previously listed have the primary goal of describing a single register. However, corpus analysis can also be used to describe the overall patterns of variation among a set of spoken and/or written registers. Perhaps the best known approach used for descriptions of this type is multidimensional (MD) analysis: a corpus-driven methodological approach that identifies the frequent linguistic co-occurrence patterns in a language, relying on inductive empirical/quantitative analysis (see, e.g., Biber, 1988, 1995; Biber and Conrad, in press: chapter 8). Frequency plays a central role in the analysis, because each dimension represents a constellation of linguistic features that frequently co-occur in texts. These *dimensions* of variation can be regarded as linguistic constructs not previously recognized by linguistic theory. Thus, MD analysis is a corpus-driven (as opposed to corpus-based) methodology, in that the linguistic constructs—the dimensions—emerge from analysis of linguistic co-occurrence patterns in the corpus. The set of co-occurring linguistic features that comprise each dimension is identified quantitatively. That is, based on the actual distributions of linguistic features in a large corpus of texts, statistical techniques (specifically, factor analysis) are used to identify the sets of linguistic features that frequently co-occur in texts.

The original MD analyses (Biber, 1986, 1988) investigated the relations among general spoken and written registers in English, based on analysis of the Lancaster-Oslo/Bergen (LOB) Corpus (15 written registers) and the London-Lund Corpus (6 spoken registers). Sixty-seven different linguistic features were analyzed computationally in each text of the corpus. Then, the co-occurrence patterns among those linguistic features were analyzed using factor analysis, identifying the underlying parameters of variation—in other words, the factors or dimensions.

In the 1988 MD analysis, the 67 linguistic features were reduced to 7 underlying dimensions. (The technical details of the factor analysis are given in Biber, 1988: chapters 4–5; see also Biber, 1995: chapter 5). The dimensions are interpreted functionally, based on the assumption that linguistic co-occurrence reflects underlying communicative functions; that is, linguistic features occur together in texts because they serve related communicative functions. For example, table 38.1 lists the important co-occurring features for dimensions 1 and 2 from the 1988 MD analysis, together with the labels reflecting the functional interpretation.

Many subsequent studies have applied the 1988 dimensions of variation to study the linguistic characteristics of other more specialized registers and discourse domains (Conrad and Biber, 2001). The following are examples:

Table 38.1. Summary of Dimensions 1 and 2 from the 1988 MD analysis of general English registers

Dimension 1: "Involved versus Informational Production"
Positive features: mental verbs, present tense verbs, contractions, possibility modals, first- and second-person pronouns, demonstrative pronouns, emphatics, hedges, causative subordination, WH clauses, that-clauses with that omitted, WH questions

Negative features: nouns, long words, high type/token ratio, prepositional phrases, attributive adjectives, passive verbs

Dimension 2: "Narrative Discourse"
Positive features: past tense verbs, perfect aspect verbs, communication verbs, third-person pronouns
*Negative features:*present tense verbs, attributive adjectives

Source: Biber, 1988.

Present-Day Registers	*Studies*
Spoken and written university registers	Biber et al. (2002)
AmE versus BrE written registers	Biber (1987)
AmE versus BrE conversational registers	Helt (2001)
Student versus academic writing (biology, history)	Conrad (1996, 2001)
I-M-R-D sections in medical research articles	Biber and Finegan (1994)
Direct mail letters	Connor and Upton (2003)
Discourse moves in non-profit grant proposals	Connor and Upton (2004b)
Oral proficiency interviews	Connor-Linton and Shohamy (2001)
Academic lectures	Csomay (2005)
Conversation versus TV dialogue	Quaglio (2009)
Female/male conversational style	Rey (2001); Biber and Burges (2000)
Author styles	Connor-Linton (2001); Biber and Finegan (1994)

Historical Registers	*Studies*
• Written and speech-based registers, 1650–present	Biber and Finegan (1989a, 1997)
• Medical research articles and scientific research articles, 1650–present	Atkinson (1992, 1996, 1999)
• Nineteenth-century written registers	Geisler (2002)

However, other MD studies have undertaken new corpus-driven analyses to identify the distinctive sets of co-occurring linguistic features that appear in a particular discourse domain or in a language other than English. The following section surveys some of those studies.

3.2.1 *Comparison of the Multidimensional Patterns across Discourse Domains and Languages*

Numerous other studies have undertaken complete MD analyses, using factor analysis to identify the dimensions of variation operating in a particular discourse domain in English rather than applying the dimensions from the 1988 MD analysis (e.g., Biber, 1992, 2001, 2006a, 2008; Biber, Connor, and Upton, 2007; Biber and Jones, 2005; Biber and Kurjian, 2007; Friginal 2006, 2009b; Kanoksilapatham, 2005, 2007; Reppen, 2001).

Given that each of these studies is based on a different corpus of texts, representing a different discourse domain, it is reasonable to expect that they would each identify a unique set of dimensions. This expectation is reinforced by the fact that the more recent studies have included additional linguistic features not used in earlier MD studies (e.g., semantic classes of nouns and verbs). However, despite these differences in design and research focus, there are certain striking similarities in the set of dimensions identified by these studies.

Most important, in nearly all of these studies, the first dimension identified by the factor analysis is associated with a *literate*, informational focus (e.g., nouns, prepositional phrases, attributive adjectives, longer words) versus an *oral*, involved focus (personal involvement/stance, interactivity, and/or real time production features). For example, the MD studies of university spoken and written registers (Biber, 2006a), elementary school spoken and written registers (Reppen, 2001), and eighteenth-century written and speech-based registers Biber (2001) all identified a first dimension of this type. More surprisingly, a similar dimension has emerged even in MD studies that have focused exclusively on spoken registers, such as that of M. White (1994), which investigated register variation within the domain of job interviews, and of Biber (2008), which investigated register variation among the different types of conversation. A second parameter found in most MD analyses corresponds to narrative discourse, reflected by the co-occurrence of features like past tense, third-person pronouns, perfect aspect, and communication verbs (see, e.g., the Biber, 2006a study of university registers; Biber, 2001, on eighteenth-century registers; and the Biber, 2008, study of conversation text types).

However, most of these studies have also identified some dimensions that are unique to the particular discourse domain. For example, Reppen's (1994) factor analysis identified a dimension of "other-directed idea justification" in elementary student registers. The study of university spoken and written registers (Biber, 2006a) identified two dimensions that are specialized to the university discourse domain: "Procedural versus content-focused discourse" and "academic stance."

In sum, corpus-driven MD studies of English registers have uncovered both surprising similarities and notable differences in the underlying dimensions of variation. Two parameters seem to be fundamentally important, regardless of the discourse domain: a dimension associated with informational focus versus (inter) personal focus and a dimension associated with narrative discourse. At the same time, these MD studies have uncovered dimensions particular to the communicative functions and priorities of each different domain of use.

These same general patterns have emerged from MD studies of languages other than English, including Nukulaelae Tuvaluan (Besnier, 1988), Korean (Kim and Biber, 1994); Somali (Biber and Hared, 1992, 1994); Taiwanese (Jang, 1998), Spanish (Biber, Davies, Jones, and Tracy-Ventura, 2006; Biber and Tracy-Ventura, 2007; Parodi, 2007), and Dagbani (Purvis, 2008). Taken together, these studies provide the first comprehensive investigations of register variation in non-English languages.

Biber (1995) synthesizes several of these studies to investigate the extent to which the underlying dimensions of variation and the relations among registers are configured in similar ways across languages. These languages show striking similarities in their basic patterns of register variation, as reflected by the co-occurring linguistic features that define the dimensions of variation in each language, the functional considerations represented by those dimensions, and the linguistic/functional relations among analogous registers. For example, similar to the full MD analyses of English, these MD studies have all identified dimensions associated with informational versus (inter)personal purposes and with narrative discourse.

At the same time, each of these MD analyses has identified dimensions that are unique to a language, reflecting the particular communicative priorities of that language and culture. For example, the MD analysis of Somali identified a dimension interpreted as "distanced, directive interaction," represented by optative clauses, first- and second-person pronouns, directional preverbal particles, and other case particles. Only one register is especially marked for the frequent use of these co-occurring features in Somali—personal letters. This dimension reflects the particular communicative priorities of personal letters in Somali, which are typically interactive as well as explicitly directive.

The cross-linguistic comparisons further show that languages as diverse as English and Somali have undergone similar patterns of historical evolution following the introduction of written registers. For example, specialist written registers in both languages have evolved over time to styles with an increasingly dense use of noun phrase modification. Historical shifts in the use of dependent clauses are also surprising: in both languages, certain types of clausal embedding—especially complement clauses—turn out to be associated with spoken registers rather than with written registers.

These synchronic and diachronic similarities raise the possibility of universals of register variation. Synchronically, such universals reflect the operation of underlying form/function associations tied to basic aspects of human communication; diachronically, such universals relate to the historical development of written registers in response to the pressures of modernization and language adaptation.

3.3. Corpus-Based Studies of Historical Registers

Corpus analysis has been especially important for historical descriptions of registers (see Biber and Conrad, in press: chapter 6). Multidimensional analysis has been used to document historical patterns of register variation (e.g., Atkinson, 1992, 1996, 1999; Biber, 2001; Biber and Finegan, 1989a, 1997; Geisler, 2002). However, there has been an even larger number of studies that provide a detailed description of a single historical register. A few MD studies have focused on a specific register, such as the study of historical change in fictional dialogue by Biber and Burges (2000) or the study of recent changes in television dialogue (Rey, 2001). But most of these studies provide detailed descriptions of the linguistic characteristics of a historical register. Several of these studies analyze spoken registers from earlier historical periods (e.g., Culpeper and Kytö, 2000, forthcoming; Kahlas-Tarkka and Rissanen, 2007; Kryk-Kastovsky, 2000; 2006; Kytö and Walker, 2003). The largest majority, though, focus on written historical registers, such as letters (Fitzmaurice, 2002a; Nevala, 2004), medical recipes and herbals (Mäkinen, 2002; Taavitsainen, 2001), and medical and scientific writing (e.g., Taavitsainen and Pahta, 2000, 2004).

3.4. World Englishes and English as a Lingua Franca (ELF)

In general, sociolinguistics has been resistant to the application of corpus-based analyses, and so most studies of social and regional dialect variation continue to employ traditional methodologies. However, a few research projects have studied regional dialect variation from a corpus perspective. For the most part, these projects have been conducted in European universities (Freiburg, Helsinki, Newcastle) and have focused on British English dialects, resulting in the Newcastle Electronic Corpus of Tyneside English, the Helsinki Corpus of British English Dialects (see Ihalainen, 1990), and the Freiburg English Dialect Corpus (FRED; see Kortmann and Wagner, 2005; Anderwald and Wagner, 2005). We are aware of only one study to date that has applied a corpus approach to analyze American English regional dialects: Grieve's (2009) study of variation in a 50-million-word corpus of letters to the editor collected from 200 cities from across the United States.

In contrast, the linguistic study of global varieties of English—or "World Englishes"—is almost always carried out from a corpus perspective. The strengths of the corpus approach make it ideal for describing new varieties that have emerged as English adapts to changing circumstances of use and contact with local languages and cultures (see Breiteneder, 2008). Research efforts in this area have focused on two major subareas: the study of World Englishes (indigenous varieties of English) and the study of English as a Lingua Franca (ELF; English used by nonnative English speakers). (See J. Jenkins, 2006, for a full discussion of this topic.)

Corpus development efforts in the arena of World Englishes are best represented by the International Corpus of English (ICE) project. The ICE project is an attempt to construct comparable corpora for all varieties of English spoken around the world (see Greenbaum, 1988, 1990a, 1990b, 1990c, 1991, 1996; Greenbaum and Nelson, 1996). Each corpus in ICE ideally has the same design—in other words, a total size of one million words, with 500 texts of approximately 2,000 words each from the same registers (news, conversation, etc.). The texts in the corpus date from 1990 or later. The authors and speakers of the texts are aged 18 or over, are educated through the medium of English, and either were born in the target country or moved there at an early age (Nelson, 1996).

As part of the ICE project or other related efforts, individual corpora have been constructed for many of the varieties of English used around the world. These include corpora for the "inner-circle" varieties of English (e.g., for Australia, Canada, Great Britain, New Zealand, the United States; see http://www.ucl.ac.uk/english-usage/ice/) as well as corpora for numerous other varieties of English spoken around the world, such as Caribbean English, East African English, Fiji English, Filipino English, Hong Kong English, Indian English, Jamaican English, Nigerian English, Singaporean English, and Xhosa English (see, e.g., Banjo, 1996; Bolt and Kingsley, 1996; Bolton, 2000; Burridge and Kortmann, 2008; Friginal, 2009b; Holmes, 1996; Hundt 1998,

2006; Hundt and Biewer, 2007; Kortmann, 2006; Mair, 1992; Mair and Sand, 1998; Ooi, 1997; Rogers, 2002, 2003; Sand, 1998, 1999; Schmied, 1990, 1994, 2004a, 2004b, 2005, 2006, 2007; Schmied and Hudson-Ettle, 1996; Tent and Mugler, 1996, 2004).

A parallel research effort has focused on English as a lingua franca (ELF). Two especially important projects in this area have been the Vienna Oxford International Corpus of English (VOICE; see Seidlhofer, 2006, 2007; Seidlhofer, Breiteneder, and Pitzl, 2006; Breiteneder et al., 2006) and the corpus of English as Lingua Franca in Academic Settings (ELFA corpus; see Mauranen, 2003, 2006, 2007).

4. Corpus Linguistics, Language Learning, and Language Pedagogy

Explorations into the pedagogical applications of corpus linguistics continue to match ongoing advancements in corpus-based technology and classroom research. Vocabulary acquisition and the mastery of grammar for language learners have traditionally been the preferred areas of investigation by many corpus researchers involved in the design and creation of language teaching materials (Conrad, 1999, 2000; Hinkel, 2002). However, in recent years, corpus tools have been utilized in the teaching of specific skills particularly in genre-based writing (Hyland, 2004b; Swales, 2002) and speaking in various academic and professional contexts.

There are several points of intersection between corpus linguistics and directly applied issues that involve language teaching and learning. In the following sections, we address four of these:

- The compilation and analysis of *learner corpora*
- The use of corpora for language teaching and learning
- Applications of corpus research in ESP/EAP
- The extent to which corpus findings can be integrated into textbooks and other teaching materials

4.1. Learner Corpora

One major application of corpus methods has been in the construction of *learner corpora* and the analysis of those corpora to document differences across L1 backgrounds. The most important project of this type is the International Corpus of Learner English (ICLE), a collection of corpora produced by learners from several different language backgrounds (see, e.g., Granger, 1993, 1994, 1996, 1998a, 2003a, 2003b). Many studies have compared the patterns of use in learner corpora to those found in native-English corpora to document patterns of *overuse* or *underuse* by learners. Studies have focused on a wide range of grammatical features, such as passives, participle clauses, connectors, and so on (see Aarts and Granger, 1998; Granger,

1997a, 2004; Granger and Tyson, 1996; Granger, Hung, and Petch-Tyson, 2002). Many studies in this tradition have also focused on formulaic sequences and the lexico-grammatical patterns associated with different learner groups (see, e.g., Altenberg and Granger, 2001; De Cock, 1998; De Cock et al., 1998; Granger, 1998b; Meunier and Granger, 2008). Although most corpus studies of leaner language have been based on the ICLE, there have also been major studies with similar research goals undertaken from other perspectives (e.g., Hinkel, 2002, 2003; Reder, Harris, and Setzler, 2003).

4.2. Corpora for Language Teaching and Learning

An even larger number of studies address the use of corpora for language teaching, introducing the approaches and discussing potential pedagogical benefits. These include numerous book-length treatments (e.g., Aston, 2001a; Aston, Bernardini, and Stewart, 2004; Botley, McEnery, and Wilson, 2000; Burnard and McEnery, 2000; Ghadessy et al., 2001; Lewandowska-Tomaszczyk, 2003, 2004; McEnery and Wilson, 1997; Mukherjee and Rohrbach, 2006; O'Keeffe, McCarthy, and Carter, 2007; Sinclair, 2004; Thomas and Short, 1996; Tribble and Jones, 1997; Wichmann, Fligelstone, McEnery, and Knowles, 1997) as well as an even larger number of journal articles and book chapters (e.g., Alderson, 1996; Aston, 1995, 1997, 2001b; Barbieri and Eckhardt, 2007; Braun, 2005; Brodine, 2001; Donley and Reppen, 2001; Fligelstone, 1993; Huckin and Coady, 1999; "Kaltenböck and Mehlmauer-Larcher, 2005; Leech, 1997, 2000; McCarthy and Carter, 2001; McEnery and Wilson, 1993, 1997, 2001; Meunier, 2002; Milton, 1998; Mindt, 1996; Mudraya, 2006; Murphy, 1996; O'Keeffe and Farr, 2003; Partington, 2001; Salsbury and Crummer, 2008; Shirato and Stapleton, 2007; Thompson and Tribble, 2001; Tribble, 2001; Yoon and Hirvela, 2004; Zorzi, 2001).

One especially common topic of these studies is the use of concordancing activities in the classroom, especially for inductive, data-driven learning (in addition to many of the studies previously cited, see Cobb, 1997; Flowerdew, 2001; Gaskell and Cobb, 2004; Gavioli, 1997, 2001; Johns, 1994, 1997; Nesselhauf, 2003; Qiao and Sussex, 2001; Sinclair, 2003; Stevens, 1993; Todd, 2001; Wichmann, 1995). For instance, Cobb (1997) and Horst, Cobb, and Nicolae (2005) report specific learning gains in the transfer of vocabulary knowledge of language learners that are attributable to the use of concordance programs and corpus-based tools. Similar studies by Chan and Liou (2005), Charles (2005), and Friginal (2006) illustrate how web-based concordancing instruction and the use of concordancers in editing laboratory reports significantly help students' learning and use of verb-noun collocations, reporting verbs, passive and active sentence structures, and linking adverbials. Most participants in these studies see the use of concordancers as helpful. Innovative corpus tools that aid in the introduction of new words, collocations, and lexical bundles help learners to improve their awareness of word meanings and of the uses of words in various contexts. In addition, hands-on concordancing also aids in successful learning of new academic vocabulary, and enhances students' performance in activities and on tests (Altenberg and Granger, 2001; McCarthy and Carter, 2002; Nesselhauf, 2005).

Other studies focus more on the unexpected research findings that result from corpus investigations, discussing how such findings often indicate that we should be using radically different pedagogical approaches and different teaching materials than those traditionally used for language teaching (see, e.g. Carter and McCarthy, 1995; Conrad, 1999, 2000; Henry and Roseberry, 2001; Hughes and McCarthy, 1998; Hunston, 2002b; Hunston and Francis, 1998; Liu, 2003; Nesselhauf, 2003). For example, Biber and Reppen (2002) present corpus findings that identify the most common verbs in English conversation and then survey ESL grammar books to show that most of them fail to illustrate the use of those verbs.

4.3. Corpora and ESP/EAP

Research in the subfields of English for specific purposes (ESP) and English for academic purposes (EAP) has become almost entirely corpus based over the past 10 to 20 years. For example, a survey of articles in any recent issue of *English for Specific Purposes* or the *Journal of English for Academic Purposes* shows that recent linguistic descriptions of special/academic varieties in English are almost always based on corpus analysis.

Similarly, corpus approaches have become commonplace for ESP/EAP pedagogy. For example, Gilquin, Granger, and Paquot (2007), Hyland (2004b), Flowerdew (2005), and Gavioli (2005) all acknowledge the invaluable contribution of corpus approaches in the teaching of ESP/EAP, especially in increasing learners' awareness of the textual features of the target language. Yoon and Hirvela (2004) and Lee and Swales (2006) explore the use of corpora and corpus tools in EAP courses. For example, Lee and Swales piloted an innovative 13-week course in corpus-informed EAP, in which students were able to compare their writing with the linguistic patterns in a corpus of professional, published academic papers. These studies indicate that the corpus approach to academic writing facilitates the development of writing skills and contributes to learners' increased confidence; a majority of the participants in studies reported that they would recommend corpus-informed writing classes to other foreign students.

4.4. Corpus-Informed Language Textbooks

In contrast to the extremely large number of books and research papers that advocate the application of corpus approaches for language teaching, there are surprisingly few language textbooks that are based on corpus research. ELT dictionaries, which have been based on corpus research since the 1980s, are the major exception here (see sections 1 and 2). However, publishers have been more reluctant to break with tradition in ELT textbooks for vocabulary and grammar.

There are a few notable exceptions to this generalization. In some cases, textbooks have been shaped by corpus analysis, even though this influence is not acknowledged on the book cover or in the introduction. Such books include the series Vocabulary in Use (McCarthy and O'Dell, 2001, 2004, 2005) and Natural Grammar (Thornbury, 2004). In more recent years, though, publishers have become more willing to market ESL textbooks that are directly shaped by the results of corpus research. For example, the four-level EFL/ESL Touchstone series by McCarthy, McCarten, and Sandiford (2006) is advertised as drawing on "the Cambridge International Corpus...to build a syllabus based on how people actually use English" (back cover). Vocabulary books like those by Schmitt and Schmitt (2005) and Huntley (2006) are corpus based in two major respects:

1. They teach the words on the "Academic Word List": a list of the most common vocabulary items that occur in a large corpus of written academic texts (see Coxhead, 2000, previously discussed in section 2.1).
2. They provide practice in the typical "collocations" of those words, derived from further corpus analysis.

Corpus-based EAP curricula are widely used throughout Europe and Asia, but they are usually based on locally created materials rather than on a major textbook. One exception to this is the corpus-informed textbook on chemistry research writing by Robinson, Stoller, Costanza-Robinson, and Jones (2008). This book is actually targeted for all students of chemistry, because native speakers of English encounter many of the same challenges in learning advanced disciplinary writing skills as do language learners.

It is possible to make a distinction between corpus-informed textbooks and corpus-based textbooks: The former incorporate natural examples taken from a corpus, whereas in the latter, decisions about inclusion/exclusion of topics and the sequence of topics are made based on the results of prior corpus analysis. In many cases, a corpus-based book will present linguistic patterns of use that would not have even been acknowledged in a traditional textbook. The vocabulary books by Schmitt and Schmitt (2005) and Huntley (2006) are corpus based in this sense. The grammar book by Thornbury (2004) also seems to be corpus based in this sense, although there is nothing in the book introduction that acknowledges the role of corpus analysis.

Two recent books provide corpus-based introductions to English grammar for advanced students training to become language teachers: *The Longman Student Grammar of Spoken and Written English* (and the accompanying workbook; Biber, Conrad, and Leech, 2002; Conrad, Biber and Leech, 2002) and the *Teacher's Grammar of English* (Cowan, 2008). Finally, Conrad and Biber (in press) identifies 50 of the most important and surprising corpus research findings from the *Longman Grammar of Spoken and Written English*, presenting those as grammar units for ESL/EFL students.

5. FUTURE DIRECTIONS

The present chapter has surveyed the extensive body of research using corpus analysis to describe the patterns of language use in English (and other languages). In addition, there is no shortage of studies that advocate the application of corpus approaches for language teaching. However, as described in the last section, there has been much less effort given to the actual implementation of corpus research findings to develop teaching materials, especially textbooks that can provide the basis for a curriculum. At present, however, there are several such books in the works, and we anticipate that this state of affairs will change dramatically over the next few years.

One specific area that is currently receiving attention is the analysis of spoken corpora annotated for prosody in addition to lexico-grammatical information. Interestingly, the very first large spoken corpus of English—the London-Lund Corpus—included detailed coding to reflect pitch, length, and pausing phenomena (see Svartvik, 1990). However, this information was mostly disregarded in linguistic analyses of that corpus. More recently, though, spoken corpora are being analyzed to document systematic patterns of discourse intonation. Cheng, Greaves, and Warren's (2008; cf. Warren, 2004) study of the Hong Kong Corpus of Spoken English is one notable example of this type. Similarly, the C-ORAL-ROM project (Cresti and Moneglia, 2005) is a major research effort to develop acoustically analyzed spoken corpora for Italian, French, Spanish, and Portuguese.

Finally, multimodal annotation of spoken interactions should be another important area for future research (see, e.g., Gu, 2002, 2007). In addition to enhanced prosodic and acoustic transcriptions of spoken corpora, these projects link video recordings to nonlinguistic features that play a crucial role in communication, such as facial expressions, hand gestures, and body position (see, e.g., Carter and Adolphs, 2008; Dahlmann and Adolphs, in press; Knight and Adolphs, 2008). Studies like these indicate that the strengths of corpus analysis can be extended to include aspects of communication beyond the analysis of the lexico-grammatical fabric of spoken and written texts.

PART XIII

CONCLUSION

CHAPTER 39

WHERE TO FROM HERE?

ROBERT B. KAPLAN

> Practically speaking, there is no "creation from nothing"
> (*ex nihilo*). There is always something "before the
> beginning," just as there is always something "after the end."
> Put another way, everything is "all middle."...Beginning
> and ending "in the middle of things" (*in medias res*), [any
> work] moves in many directions and dimensions and
> constantly promises or threatens to turn into something
> else. Being one thing, it offers to become many others.
>
> —Pope (2005)

As noted in the preface, this second edition of the *Oxford Handbook of Applied Linguistics* has undertaken to examine where applied linguistics came from, what it has achieved, and where it might be going. The entire field is, after all, only a bit more than a century old—a relatively inconsequential time span in the context of other disciplines that can legitimately claim millennial histories. The activity of bringing this edition to fruition has proved to be a rather surprising undertaking; I had initially assumed that most of the chapters could easily be updated and a few new references provided. The amount of new work and the number of new areas of study that have emerged over the relatively short time since the completion of the first edition is substantial. Some of the new areas of inquiry promise to require rethinking not only the scope of applied linguistics but even the scope of linguistics itself as well as a number of other subsidiary disciplines. Corpus work, although not a new departure—rather, a new way of looking at data augmented by new technological achievements—has demonstrated that the patterns hidden in the syntactic and rhetorical structure of language suggest that some of the widespread beliefs locked in both theory and pedagogy may need to be reexamined. (See Biber et al., (chapter 41) in this volume.) At the same time, recent work in the analysis of the structure and function of the brain has the potential to overturn much of pedagogical practice and theory, including the understanding of language acquisition as well as such notions as Universal Grammar in language acquisition. (See Schumann (chapter 20) in this volume.) Thus, the Universal Grammar (UG) model, which assumes an equation between linguistic theory and grammatical theory, does not recognize that language is only one "tool set" for construing experience; as Halliday writes, "Language is the essential condition of knowing, the process by which experience *becomes* knowledge" (1993: 94, italics in the original). Language is significantly complemented by the resources of other semiotic systems, all of which have been developed over cultural history, shaping, and being shaped by, the various activities in which they are used. Language is not—cannot be—an isolated system, and grammar cannot be equated with language. As Enkvist puts it,

> The important point is to realize that the text is the father of the sentence, and that text strategies come before the syntactic formation of individual sentences. Giving a sentence its textual fit, its conformity with the text strategy, is not a cosmetic surface operation polishing the sentence after it is already there. Textual fit is a far more basic requirement, determining the choice of words as well as the syntactic structure of a sentence. To modern text and discourse linguists this is so obvious that it seems curious that grammarians and teachers of composition have, through the centuries, spent so much time and effort on syntactic phenomena within individual sentences, while overlooking the fundamental questions of text strategy and information flow. (1997: 199)

The radical changes emanating from these research areas are illustrated in the growth of such subdivisions of applied linguistics as translation and interpretation. (See part X elsewhere in this volume.)

Some of the questions that seemed to demand attention in the first edition have faded away and have been replaced by new questions, even if the earlier questions have not been completely answered. More important, the incredible growth in, and the increased sophistication of, technology and its rapid assimilation into practice has increased the possibility of accessing much larger pieces of data at vastly greater speeds in analysis. That growth has substantially altered some approaches to language teaching, moving away from the traditional emphasis on grammatical structures and moving toward a much greater emphasis on communication. (See Wesche, chapter 22 in this volume.) The growth has resulted in the recognition that language is not an isolate based on absolute rules but is rather foremost a communication vehicle, varying over time as the communicative needs of communities of speakers demands. That growth has also demonstrated that the "one-nation/one-language myth" is indeed a myth; rather, languages are interrelated in complex ways; they are not entities metaphorically existing as isolates in a genealogical tree.

> The characterization of languages as fixed grammatical codes is at best unnecessarily reductionist and at worst a contributing factor in the loss of linguistic diversity. Before the advent of European nation-states, there were a number of dialect continua such as the Germanic, stretching from the north of

Scandinavia to the north of Italy and consisting of an indefinite number of
varieties, of which the proximate ones were mutually intelligible and the more
distant ones were not. At present, this continuum has been overlaid by a number
of superimposed official (standard) languages such as Swedish, Norwegian,
German, Dutch, and Letzebuergisch, each associated with a nation-state. Such
national languages, as Haugen points out, are cultural artifacts. (Mühlhäusler,
chapter 32 in this volume)

Recognition does not eliminate the need for learning grammar; rather, it pushes
grammar back into earlier stages of language learning and revises language teaching/
learning to focus on communication by showing that such practices as the pattern
drills common in the time of the audiolingual instruction have little to recommend
them as learning practices and much to support the belief that they are great
soporifics.

This discussion suggests that there is in fact a beginning and an end and that
what is contained in this volume is the middle between origins in the nineteenth
century and a future in the twenty-first century. But nothing could be further from
the truth. As Pope notes in the brief quotation at the start of this chapter, "there is
always something 'before the beginning,' just as there is always something 'after the
end.'" Rather, "everything is 'all middle,'" and any given body of ideas "moves in
many directions and dimensions and constantly promises or threatens to turn into
something else." To a certain extent, that is demonstrated by applied linguistics
growing out of a number of disparate ideas that co-occurred during the late
nineteenth century, that emerged as a coherent set of ideas during the twentieth
century, but that began to fragment into a range of new ideas at the end of the
twentieth century. (See Hinkle, chapter 11 in this volume.) The impression of
fragmentation is the result of the disparate emergence of ideas, reaching different
audiences at different times with different outcomes.

Although I have spent a lifetime trying to understand applied linguistics and to
disseminate it to a wide variety of audiences, and recognizing that I have not been
enormously successful in my endeavors, I am still constantly amazed that in the face
of all the evidence to the contrary, education administrators around the world are
still happy to promulgate instructional programs in which the rate of forgetting is
quite likely to exceed the rate of learning, in which time on task is so tentative as
essentially to assure fractured learning, and in which teacher training, materials
development, and the assessment of achievement continue to be conducted in bliss-
ful ignorance of the accumulated wealth of information about language learning,
language teaching, and language testing. These problems arise in part because the
key decision makers in charge of the educational process appear to remain essentially ignorant of the extant research, isolated from expert researchers in the field,
and unlikely or unwilling to seek advice even from teachers at the chalk face—who
presumably must know something about the matter even though they may lack the
academic credentials allegedly to guarantee their wisdom—let alone from the ranks
of scholars across the broad range represented by applied linguistics. One holds the
probably vain hope that this volume will come to the attention of teachers, teacher

trainers, educational supervisors and inspectors, and politicians charged with the management of educational systems and other politically based language activities at all the various levels at which they function, will penetrate their isolation, will assist in the understanding of the information contained in the volume, and will encourage all those disparate folk to apply its lessons to the segments of the system for which they are responsible. But the responsibility is much more broadly dispersed than the list of players just enumerated, because the parents of the students studying in the educational systems have a role to play, as do their offspring—the contemporary victims of the educational systems—and as do all the other members of the societies that support the various educational systems.

There is no longer any serious debate about the larger interdisciplinary scope of applied linguistics, in juxtaposition to the earlier and more limited interpretation of the field as being concerned exclusively with language teaching and learning, language-teacher trainers, and language testers—a conception more in tune with what Spolsky (1999, 2008) has termed *educational linguistics*. To be sure, these essentially educational matters are still major components of applied linguistics, but the disciplinary discussions of the 1980s and 1990s have established applied linguistics as an interdisciplinary field addressing real-world language problems of various types, or, as Brumfit (1997a: 93) puts it, "A working definition of applied linguistics will then be the theoretical and empirical investigation of real-world problems in which language is a central issue." There seems to be general agreement that there is no overarching theory "in large part because of the complexity of the issues" (Ricento, 2006a: 10), and, as Hornberger asserts, "the field remains 'poised perpetually between theory and practice'" (2008a: 35).

Over the past decade, there have been a number of publications that have explored the nature and status of applied linguistics, with both North American and European emphases. (See, e.g., "List of Publications Exploring the Nature and Status of Applied Linguistics" at the end of chapter 1.) There is no longer serious debate about the larger interdisciplinary scope of applied linguistics, as opposed to the earlier and more limited interpretation. To be sure, the fields of language learning, language teaching, and language testing are still central components in applied linguistics, but the disciplinary discussions of the 1980s and 1990s have established applied linguistics as an interdisciplinary field that addresses real-world language problems of various types. Applied linguistics is a field that centrally involves linguistic knowledge and training. That knowledge is combined with one or two other specialized concerns and is "applied" to problems that arise in the normal (and sometimes abnormal) course of daily life. These problems include, at least

- Needing to learn and use a second or third language
- Being taught effectively in an L2
- Being assessed and evaluated in an L2
- Negotiating services or health care in an L2
- Being impacted by language policies (whether planned or unplanned) that apply in educational, institutional, civic, or employment settings

- Needing skilled interpreter services for various reasons
- Maintaining home languages in dominant L2 contexts

These problems, and others like them, are at the core of the field of applied linguistics. Seeing the field from the perspective of language problems makes clear the fact that no single academic discipline can be sufficient to meet the needs of people facing multilingual/multicultural settings, language contact and bi/multilingualism, and translation. Language learning in the conventional sense cannot be, in and of itself, sufficient because it is not merely a matter of learning phonology, lexicon, and grammar but rather implicates behavior in multicultural environments and all the communicative skills implicit in such activity. Applied linguistics is also a major contributor to research in literacy, corpus linguistics, lexicography, teacher training, and sociolinguistics. Somewhat more distantly, it has linkages to such allied disciplines as education, cognitive psychology, English studies (stylistics, rhetoric, discourse studies, and literary studies), foreign language studies (discourse, culture, and literary studies), dialectal studies (stylistics, rhetoric, etc.), speech pathology, and communication sciences. The goal of representing applied linguistics in these wider terms is to establish the taxonomy of applied linguistics research that has been reviewed in this volume. Taking a broad view not only reflects the current nature of applied linguistics, at least as understood in North America, but also ensures that the work of applied linguistics from various backgrounds is reasonably represented. In covering research over the past decade, the following taxonomy representing the core of applied linguistics has been invoked:

01. Corpus linguistics
02. Discourse analysis
03. Language assessment
04. Language learning and teaching
    a. Second language teaching
    b. Foreign language teaching
    c. Bilingual and language minority education
    d. Dialect variation
    e. Instructional approaches
    f. Uses of technology
05. Language policy and planning
06. Language use in professional contexts
07. Neurobiology of language
08. Second language acquisition
09. Second language reading and writing research
10. Second language speaking and listening
11. Societal bilingualism and language contact
12. Translation and interpretation

As suggested, this volume represents what is in the middle. The end is not in sight. In all probability there will be a need for a third edition, probably no later than a decade from now. It is unlikely that I will be able to undertake that third edition; although my present age makes my future ability questionable, it is altogether fitting and proper that a younger editor should be selected—one aware of what came before the beginning and what is part of a longer middle as well as the reality that there will not be an end.

Perhaps, by the time an extended middle becomes available, a larger potential audience may be eager to be made aware of the importance of language.

References

Aarts, J., and S. Granger (1998). Tag sequences in learner corpora: A key to interlanguage grammar and discourse. In S. Granger (Ed.), *Learner English on Computer* (pp. 132–141). London & New York: Addison Wesley Longman.

Abasi, A., N. Akbari, and B. Graves (2006). Discourse appropriation, construction of identities and the complex issue of plagiarisim: ESL students writing in graduate school. *Journal of Second Language Writing* 15, 102–117.

Abbs, B., and I. Freebairn (1977). *Starting Strategies*. London: Longman.

Abbs, B., and M. Sexton (1978). *Challenges*. London: Longman.

Abd-Kadir, J., and F. Hardman (2007). The discourse of whole class teaching: A comparative study of Kenyan and Nigerian primary English lessons. *Language and Education* 21, 1–15.

Abraham, R. G., and H.-C. Liou (1991). Interaction generated by three computer programs. In P. Dunkel (Ed.), *Computer-Assisted Language Learning and Testing* (pp. 85–109). New York: Newbury House.

Abutalebi, J., and D. Green (2007). Bilingual language production: The neurocognition of language representation and control, *Journal of Neurolinguistics* 20, 242–275.

ACT COMPASS Planform [Online]. Available: http://www.act.org/compass

Adams, R. (2007). Do second language learners benefit from interacting with each other? In A. Mackey (Ed.), *Conversational Interaction in Second Language Acquisition* (pp. 29–51). Oxford: Oxford University Press.

Ädel, A., and R. Reppen (Eds.). (2008). *Corpora and Discourse: The Challenges of Different Settings*. Amsterdam: John Benjamins.

Adolphs, S., and N. Schmitt (2003). Lexical coverage of spoken discourse. *Applied Linguistics* 24, 425–438.

Ahn, I.-K. (2005). Pedagogical considerations of perspective coherence problems in simultaneous interpreting as a result of linguistic structure, illustrated by German-English examples. *Meta: Translators' Journal* 50(2), 696–712.

Ahn, H. J. (2005). Child care teachers' strategies in children's socialization of emotion. *Early Childhood Development and Care* 175(1), 49–61.

Aijmer, K. (2002). *English Discourse Particles*. Amsterdam: John Benjamins.

Aikhenvald, A. Y. (1999). Areal diffusion and language contact in the Içana-Vaupés basin, North West Amazonia. In A. Y. Aikhenvald, and R. M. W. Dixon (Eds.), *The Amazonian Languages* (pp. 385–415). Cambridge: Cambridge University Press.

Ainsworth-Vaughn, N. (1998). *Claiming Power in Doctor-Patient Talk*. New York: Oxford University Press.

Alatis, J. E. (1989). *Quest for Quality: The First Twenty-One Years of TESOL*. Arlington, VA: TESOL.

Albl-Mikasa, M. (2008). (Non-) sense in note-taking for consecutive interpreting. *Interpreting* 10(2), 197–231.

Albright, J., and A. Luke (2008). *Pierre Bourdieu and Literacy Education*. Mahwah, NJ: Lawrence Erlbaum.

Alcina, A. (2008). Translation technologies: Scope, tools and resources. *Target* 20(1), 79–102.

Alderson, J. C. (2000). *Assessing reading*. Cambridge: Cambridge University Press.

Alderson, J. C. (1999). Reading constructs and reading assessment. In M. Chalhoub-Deville (Ed.), *Issues in Computer-Adaptive Testing of Reading Proficiency* (pp. 49–78). Cambridge: Cambridge University Press.

Alderson, J. C. (1996). Do corpora have a role in language assessment? In J. Thomas, and M. Short (Eds.), *Using Corpora for Language Research: Studies in the Honour of Geoffrey Leech* (pp. 248–259). London: Longman.

Alexander, L. G. (1967). *New Concept English: First Things First*. London: Longman.

Alexieva, B. (1997). A typology of interpreter-mediated events. *Translator* 3(2), 153–174.

Alisjahbana, S. T. (1971). Language policy, language engineering and literacy in Indonesia and Malaysia. In T. A. Sebeok (Ed.), *Current Trends in Linguistics* (vol. 8, pp. 1087–1109). The Hague: Mouton.

Allen, J. P. B. (1989). *COLT observation scheme: Definition categories*. Toronto, Ontario.

Allen, J. P. B., and A. Davies (1977). *Testing and Experimental Methods* (vol. 4). London: Oxford University Press.

Allen, J. P. B., and S. P. Corder (1973–1975). *The Edinburgh Course in Applied Linguistics* (vol. 1, 1973); *Papers in Applied Linguistics* (vol. 2, 1975); *Techniques in Applied Linguistics* (vol. 3, 1974). London: Oxford University Press.

Alleyne, M. (1994). Problems of standardization of creole languages. In M. Morgan (Ed.), *The Social Construction of Identity in Creole Situations* (pp. 7–18). Los Angeles: Center for Afro-American Studies, UCLA.

Alleyne, M. (1980). *Comparative Afro-American: An Historical-Comparative Study of English-Based Afro-American Dialects of the New World*. Ann Arbor, MI: Karoma.

Alleyne, M. C. (1971). Acculturation and the cultural matrix of creolization. In D. Hymes (Ed.), *Pidginization and Creolization of Languages* (pp. 169–186). Cambridge: Cambridge University Press.

Allwright, D. (2005). Developing principles for practitioner research: The case of exploratory practice. *Modern Language Journal* 89, 353–366.

Allwright, R. (1984). The importance of interaction in classroom language learning. *Applied Linguistics* 5, 156–171.

Al-Salman, S., and R. Al-Khanji (2002). The native language factor in simultaneous interpretation in an Arabic/English context. *Meta: Translators' Journal* 47(4), 607–626.

Altabev, M. (1998). The effect of dominant discourses on the vitality of Judeo-Spanish in the Turkish social context. *Journal of Multilingual and Multicultural Development* 19(4), 263–281.

Altarriba, J., and K. M. Mathis (1997). Conceptual and lexical development in second language acquisition. *Journal of Memory and Language* 36, 550–568.

Altenberg, B. (1998). On the phraseology of spoken English: The evidence of recurrent word-combinations. In A. Cowie (Ed.), *Phraseology: Theory, Analysis and Applications* (pp. 101–122). Oxford: Oxford University Press.

Altenberg, B., and S. Granger (2001). The grammatical and lexical patterning of MAKE in native and non-native student writing. *Applied Linguistics* 22(2), 173–194.

Altmann, G. T. M., and M. Steedman (1988). Interaction with context during human sentence processing. *Cognition* 30, 191–238.

Amato, I. (2003). *Supervision: A New View of Nature*. New York: Harry N. Abrams.

Ambridge, B., and A. E. Goldberg (2008). The island status of clausal complements: Evidence in favor of an information structure explanation. *Cognitive Linguistics* 19, 357–389.

Amery, R. (2000). *"Warrabarna Kaurna!": Reclaiming an Australian Language*. Lisse, The Netherlands: Swets & Zeitlinger.

Amin, N. (1997). Race and the identity of the nonnative ESL teacher. *TESOL Quarterly* 31, 580–583.

Ammon, U. (1998). *Ist Deutsch noch internationale Wissenschaftssprache? Englishe auch für die Lehre an den deutschsprachigen Hochschulen.* [Is German still an International Language of Science? A proposal to also use German in German-speaking Universities]. Berlin/New York: Walter de Gruyter.

Ammon, U. (1997). Language spread policy. *Language Problems & Language Planning* 21, 51–57.

Ammon, U. (1994). Language spread policy. Vol. 2: Languages of the former colonial powers and former colonies [Special issue]. *International Journal of the Sociology of Language* 107.

Ammon, U. (1992). The Federal Republic of Germany's policy of spreading German. *International Journal of the Sociology of Language* 95, 33–50.

Ammon, U., and H. Kleinedam (Eds.). (1992). Language spread policy. Vol. 1: Languages of former colonial powers [Special issue]. *International Journal of the Sociology of Language* 95.

Anderman, G., and M. Rogers (Eds.). (2008). *Incorporating Corpora: The Linguist and the Translator*. Clevedon, Avon, UK: Multilingual Matters.

Anderson, A., and T. Lynch (1988). *Listening*. Oxford: Oxford University Press.

Anderson, B. (1991). *Imagined communities: Reflections on the origin and spread of nationalism* (Rev. ed.). New York: Verso.

Anderson, B. R. (1990). Language, fantasy, revolution: Java, 1900–1945. *Prisma* 50, 25–39.

Anderson, F. (1995). Classroom discourse and language socialization in a Japanese elementary-school setting: An ethnographic-linguistic study. PhD dissertation, University of Hawai'i, Honolulu.

Anderson, J. (1982). Acquisition of cognitive skill. *Psychological Review* 89, 369–406.

Anderson, J. R. (2007). *How Can the Human Mind Occur in the Physical Universe?* New York: Oxford University Press.

Anderson, J. R. (1985). *Cognitive Psychology and Its Implications*. New York: Freeman.

Andresen, J. T. (1990). *Linguistics in America 1769–1924*. New York: Routledge.

Anderson, K. O., W. Allen, and L. Narváez (1993). The applied foreign language component in the humanities and the sciences. In M. Krueger, and F. Ryan (Eds.), *Language and Content: Discipline- and Content-Based Approaches to Language Study* (pp. 103–113). Lexington, MA: D.C. Heath.

Anderson, N. (2009). ACTIVE Reading: The research base for a pedagogical approach to the reading classroom. In Z.-H. Han, and N. Anderson (Eds.), *Second Language Reading: Research and Instruction* (pp. 192–205). Ann Arbor: University of Michigan Press.

Anderwald, L., and S. Wagner (2005). The Freiburg English Dialect Corpus (FRED)— applying corpus-linguistic research tools to the analysis of dialect data. In J. Beal, K. Corrigan, and H. Moisl (Eds.), *Using Unconventional Digital Language Corpora. Vol. I: Synchronic Corpora*. Basingstoke: Palgrave Macmillan.

Angelelli, C. (2006). Validating professional standards and codes: Challenges and opportunities. *Interpreting* 8(2), 175–193.

Angelelli, C. (2004a). *Medical Interpreting and Cross-Cultural Communication*. Cambridge: Cambridge University Press.

Angelelli, C. (2004b). *Revisiting the Interpreter's Role: A Study of Conference, Court and Medical Interpreters in Canada, Mexico and the United States*. Amsterdam/Philadelphia: John Benjamins.

Angelil-Carter, S. (1997). Second language acquisition of spoken and written English: Acquiring the skeptron. *TESOL Quarterly* 31, 263–287.

Angelis, P. (2001). The roots of applied linguistics in North America. *Australian Review of Applied Linguistics* 24(1), 1–12.

Angelis, P. (1987 December). Applied linguistics: Realities and projections. Paper presented at the 1987 Annual Conference of the American Association for Applied Linguistics, San Francisco.

Angermeyer, P. (2006). "Speak English or what?" Codeswitching and interpreter use in New York Small Claims Courts. PhD dissertation, New York University.

Angermeyer, P. (2005). Who is "you"? Polite forms of address and ambiguous participant roles in court interpreting. *Target: International Journal of Translation Studies* 17, 203–226.

Antonek, J., R. Donato, and G. R. Tucker (2000). Differential linguistic development of Japanese language learners in elementary school. *Canadian Modern Language Review* 57, 325–351.

Appel, R., and L. Verhoeven (1994). Decolonization, language planning and education. In J. Arends, P. Muysken, and N. Smith (Eds.), *Pidgins and Creoles: An Introduction* (pp. 65–74). Amsterdam: John Benjamins.

Apronti, E. O. (1974). Sociolinguistics and the question of a national language: The case of Ghana. *Studies in African Linguistics* (Suppl. 5), 1–20.

Arabski, J. (Ed.). (2006). *Cross-Linguistic Influence in the Second Language Lexicon.* Clevedon, Avon, UK: Multilingual Matters.

Aranguan, M. L., and S. Moore (1999). Reply to Choate. *Proteus* 8(3/4), 21.

Archibald, J. (Ed.). (2000). *Second Language Acquisition and Linguistic Theory.* Oxford: Basil Blackwell.

Archibald, J. (1998). *Second Language Phonology.* Philadelphia: John Benjamins.

Archibald, J. (1993). *Language Learnability and L2 Phonology: The Acquisition of Metrical Parameters.* Dordrecht & Boston: Kluwer Academic.

Arends, J., P. Muysken, and N. Smith (Eds.). (1994). *Pidgins and Creoles: An Introduction.* Amsterdam: John Benjamins.

Arkoudis, S., and C. Davison (Eds.). (2008). Chinese students: Perspectives on their social, cognitive, and linguistic investment in English medium interaction [Special issue]. *Journal of Asian Pacific Communication* 18(1).

Armstrong, S. (1997). Corpus-based methods for NLP and translation studies. *Interpreting* 2(1/2), 141–162.

Arndt, V. (1987). Six writers in search of texts: A protocol based study of L1 and L2 writing. *ELT Journal* 41, 257–267.

Arsenian, S. (1945). Bilingualism in the post-war world. *Psychological Bulletin* 42, 65–86.

Artigal, J. (1997). The Catalán immersion program. In R. K. Johnson, and M. Swain (Eds.), *Immersion Education: International Perspectives* (pp. 133–150). Cambridge: Cambridge University Press.

Asher, J. (1977). *Learning Another Language through Actions: The Complete Teachers' Guidebook.* Los Gatos, CA: Sky Oaks.

Aston, G. (Ed.). (2001a). *Learning with Corpora.* Houston, TX: Athelstan.

Aston, G. (2001b). Learning with Corpora: An overview. In G. Aston (Ed.), *Learning with Corpora* (pp. 4–45). Houston, TX: Athelstan.

Aston, G. (1997). Enriching the learning environment: Corpora in ELT. In A. Wichmann, S. Fligelstone, T. McEnery, and G. Knowles (Eds.), *Teaching and Language Corpora* (pp. 51–64). London: Longman.

Aston, G. (1995). Corpora in language pedagogy: Matching theory and practice. In G. Cook, and B. Seidlhofer (Eds.), *Principle and Practice in Applied Linguistics* (pp. 257–270). Oxford: Oxford University Press.

Aston, G., S. Bernardini, and D. Stewart (Eds.). (2004). *Corpora and Language Learners.* Amsterdam: John Benjamins.

Atkinson, D. (1999). *Scientific Discourse in Sociohistorical Context: The Philosophical Transactions of the Royal Society of London, 1675–1975.* Hillsdale, NJ: Lawrence Erlbaum.

Atkinson, D. (1996). The Philosophical Transactions of the Royal Society of London, 1675–1975: A sociohistorical discourse analysis. *Language in Society* 25, 333–371.

Atkinson, D. (1992). The evolution of medical research writing from 1735 to 1985: The case of the Edinburgh Medical Journal. *Applied Linguistics* 13, 337–374.

Atkinson, P., and S. Delamont (2006). Rescuing narrative from qualitative research. *Narrative Inquiry* 16(1), 164–172.

Attali, Y. (2004). Exploring the feedback and revision features of Criterion. Paper presented at the annual meeting of the National Council onMeasurement in Education, San Diego, CA.

Attali, Y., and J. Burstein (2006). Automated essay scoring with e-rater v.2. *Journal of Technology, Learning and Assessment* 4(3).

Austin, J. L. (1962). *How to Do Things with Words.* Oxford: Oxford University Press.

Australian Telephone Interpreting Service (2009). Available from http://www.appliedlanguage.com/interpreting_services.shtml

Avineri, N. (2010). The interactive organization of 'insight': Clinical interviews with frontotemporal dementia patients. In A. W. Mates, L. Mikesell, and M. S. Smith (Eds.), *Language, Interaction and Frontotemporal Dementia: Reverse Engineering the Social Mind* (chapter 5). London: Equinox.

Awoniyi, T. A. (1995). Problems related to curriculum development and teaching mother tongues in Nigeria: A historical survey 1800–1974. *Audio Visual Language Journal* 13(1), 31–41.

Bachman, L. (1990). *Fundamental considerations inlanguage testing.* Oxford: Oxford University Press.

Bachman, L., and A. Palmer (1996). *Language Testing in Practice.* Oxford: Oxford University Press.

Baddeley, A. D. (2006). Working memory: An overview. In S. Pickering (Ed.), *Working Memory and Education* (pp. 1–31). Burlington, MA: Academic Press.

Baddeley, A. D., and G. J. Hitch (1974). Working memory. In G. A. Bower (Ed.), *Recent Advances in Learning and Motivation* (vol. 8, pp. 47–89). New York: Academic Press.

Baetens-Beadsmore, H. (1993). The European school model. In H. Baetens Beardsmore (Ed.), *European Models of Bilingual Education* (pp. 121–154). Clevedon, Avon, UK: Multilingual Matters.

Bailey, G., and M. Dyer (1992). An approach to sampling in dialectology. *American Speech* 67, 3–20.

Bailey, G., and N. Maynor (1998). Decreolization? In P. Trudgill, and J. Cheshire (Eds.), *The Sociolinguistics Reader* (pp. 249–262). London: Arnold. (Originally published in 1987 *Language in Society* 16).

Baker, C. (2008). Survey methods in researching language and education. In K. King, and N. H. Hornberger (Eds.), *Research Methods in Language and Education: Encyclopedia of Language and Education* (vol. 10, pp. 55–68). New York: Springer.

Baker, C. (2007). *A Parents and Teachers Guide to Bilingualism* (3rd ed.). Clevedon, Avon, UK: Multilingual Matters.

Baker, C. (2006). *Foundations of Bilingual Education and Bilingualism* (4th ed.). Clevedon, Avon, UK: Multilingual Matters.

Baker, C., and S. P. Jones (1998). *Encyclopedia of Bilingualism and Bilingual Education*. Clevedon, Avon, UK: Multilingual Matters.

Baker, M. (1993). Corpus linguistics and translation studies: Applications and implications. In M. Baker, G. Francis, and E. Tognini-Bonelli (Eds.), *Text and Technology: In Honour of John Sinclair* (pp. 233–250). Amsterdam and Philadelphia: John Benjamins.

Baker, P. (1991). Column: Writing the wronged. *Journal of Pidgin and Creole Languages* 6, 107–122.

Baker, P., and P. Mühlhäusler (1990). From business to pidgin. *Journal of Asian Pacific Communication* 1, 87–115.

Bakhtin, M. (1984). *Problems of Dostoevsky's Poetics* (Trans. C. Emerson). Minneapolis: University of Minnesota Press.

Bakhtin, M. (1981). *The Dialogic Imagination: Four Essays by M. M. Bakhtin*. Austin: University of Texas Press.

Baldauf, R. B., Jr. (1994). "Unplanned" language planning. In W. Grabe et al. (Eds.), *Annual Review of Applied Linguistics: Vol. 14. Language Policy and Planning* (pp. 82–89). Cambridge: Cambridge University Press.

Baldauf, R. B., Jr., and B. H. Jernudd (1983). Language of publications as a variable in scientific communication. *Australian Review of Applied Linguistics* 6(2), 97–108.

Baldauf, R. B., Jr., and R. B. Kaplan (Eds.). (2000). *Language Planning in Nepal, Taiwan and Sweden*. Clevedon, Avon, UK: Multilingual Matters.

Baldauf, R. B., Jr., and A. Luke (Eds.). (1990). *Language Planning and Education in Australasia and the South Pacific*. Clevedon, Avon, UK: Multilingual Matters.

Balliu, C. (2007). Cognition et déverbalisation. *Meta: Translators' Journal* 52(1), 3–12.

Bamberg, M. G. W. (Ed.). (1998). Oral versions of personal experience: Three decades of narrative analysis [Special issue]. *Journal of Narrative and Life History* 7(1–4).

Bankston, C. L., and J. M. Henry (1998). The silence of the gators: Cajun ethnicity and intergenerational transmission of Louisiana French. *Journal of Multilingual and Multicultural Development* 19, 1–22.

Banjo, A. (1996). The sociolinguistics of English in Nigeria and the ICE project. In S. Greenbaum (Ed.), *Comparing English Worldwide: The International Corpus of English* (pp. 239–248). Oxford: Clarendon Press.

Banton, M. (1998). Research note: Judicial training in ethnic minority issues in England and Wales. *Journal of Ethnic and Migration Studies* 24(3), 561–573.

Bar-Acher, M., and F. Kaufmann (1998). The functions and activities of the Academy of the Hebrew Language in the orientation and development of Hebrew. *Meta* 43, 10–18.

Barbassa, J. (2003, June 6). Interpreters to become court employees. *Contra Costa Times*. (Page numbers unavailable.)

Barbieri, F. (2005). Quotative use in American English: A corpus-based, cross-register comparison. *Journal of English Linguistics* 33 (3), 222–256.

Barbieri, F., and S. Eckhardt (2007). Applying corpus-based findings to form focused instruction: The case of reported speech. *Language Teaching Research* 11(3), 319–346.

Bardovi-Harlig, K. (in press). Exploring the pragmatics of interlanguage pragmatics: Definition by design. In A. Trosborg (Ed.), *Handbook of Pragmatics: Pragmatics across Language and Cultures* (vol. 7). Berlin: Mouton de Gruyter.

Bardovi-Harlig, K. (1999a). The interlanguage of interlanguage pragmatics: A research agenda for acquisitional pragmatics. *Language Learning* 49, 677–713.

Bardovi-Harlig, K. (1999b). Researching method. In L. F. Boulfton (Ed.), *Pragmatics and Language Learning* (vol. 9, pp. 237–264). Champaign, IL: University of Illinois, Urbana-Champaign–Division of English as an International Language (DEIL).

Bardovi-Harlig, K. (1996). Pragmatics and language teaching: Bringing pragmatics and pedagogy together. In L. F. Boulton (Ed.) *Pragmatics and Language Learning.* Urbana-Champaign: University of Illinois, Division of English as an International Language [DEIL] 7, 21–39.

Bardovi-Harlig, K., M.-T. Bastos, B. Burghardt, E. Chappetto, E. L. Nickels, and M. Rose (in press). The use of conventional expressions and utterance length in L2 pragmatics. In G. Kasper, D. R. Yoshimi, T. N. Hanh, and J. Yoshioka (Eds.), *Pragmatics and Language Learning* (vol. 12). Honolulu: University of Hawai'i, National Foreign Language Resource Center.

Bardovi-Harlig, K., and Z. Dörnyei (1998). Do language learners recognize pragmatic violations? Pragmatic vs. grammatical awareness in instructed L2 learning. *TESOL Quarterly* 32, 233–259.

Bardovi-Harlig, K., and B. S. Hartford (1993). Learning the rules of academic talk: A longitudinal study of pragmatic development. *Studies in Second Language Acquisition* 15, 279–304.

Bardovi-Harlig, K., and B. S. Hartford (1990). Congruence in native and nonnative conversations: Status balance in the academic advising session. *Language Learning* 40, 467–501.

Bardovi-Harlig, K., and T. Salsbury (2004). The organization of turns in the disagreements of L2 learners: A longitudinal perspective. In D. Boxer, and A. D. Cohen (Eds.), *Studying Speaking to Inform Second Language Learning* (pp. 199–227). Clevedon, Avon, UK: Multilingual Matters.

Bargiela-Chiappini, F., and S. Harris (Eds.). (1997). *The Languages of Business: An International Perspective.* Edinburgh: Edinburgh University Press.

Barik, H. (1994). A description of various types of omissions, additions and error translation encountered in simultaneous interpretation. In S. Lambert, and B. Moser-Mercer (Eds.), *Bridging the Gap* (pp. 121–137). Amsterdam: John Benjamins.

Barik, H. (1969). A study of simultaneous interpretation. PhD dissertation, University of North Carolina, Chapel Hill.

Barley, S., and G. Kunda (2001). Bringing work back. *Organization Science* 12, 76–95.

Barlow, M. (2005). Computer-based analysis of learner language. In R. Ellis & G. Barkhuizen (Eds.), *Analyzing Learner Language* (pp. 335–357). New York: Oxford University Press.

Bartlett, C. (1932). *Remembering.* Cambridge: Cambridge University Press.

Barnard, R., and M. Torres-Guzman (Eds.). (2009). *Creating Communities of Learning in Schools.* Clevedon, Avon, UK: Multilingual Matters.

Bassnett, S. (2007). Culture and translation. In P. Kuhiwczak, and K. Littau (Eds.), *A Companion to Translation Studies* (pp. 13–23). Clevedon, Avon, UK: Multilingual Matters.

Bassnett, S. (1980). *Translation Studies.* London: Methuen.

Bassnett, S., and A. Lefevere (Eds.). (1990). *Translation, History and Culture.* London: Pinter.

Bates, D. L. (1991). Mäori language: Some observations upon its use in criminal proceedings. *New Zealand Law Journal* February: 55–60.

Bates, E., and B. MacWhinney (1989). Functionalism and the competition model. In B. MacWhinney, and E. Bates (Eds.), *The Crosslinguistic Study of Sentence Processing* (pp. 3–76). New York: Cambridge University Press.

Battenburg, J. (1999). The gradual death of the Berber language in Tunisia. *International Journal of the Sociology of Language* 137, 147–161.

Beattie, G. W. (1980). The role of language production processes in the organisation of behaviour in face-to-face interaction. In B. Butterworth (Ed.), *Language Production* (vol. 1, pp. 69–107). London: Academic Press.

Bebel-Gisler, D. (1981). *La Langue Créole force Jugulée*. Paris and Montréal: L'Harmattan and Nouvelle-Optique.

Beck, M.-L. (1998). L2 acquisition and obligatory head-movement: English-speaking learners of German and the local impairment hypothesis. *Studies in Second Language Acquisition* 20, 311–348.

Becker, H., B. Geer, E. Hughes, and A. Strauss (1961). *Boys in White: Student Culture in Medical School*. Chicago: University of Chicago Press.

Bednarek, M. (2006). *Evaluation in Media Discourse: Analysis of a Newspaper Corpus*. London: Continuum.

Bejar, I. I. (1993). A generative approach to psychological and educational measurement. In N. Frederiksen, R. J. Mislevy, and I. I. Bejar (Eds.), *Test Theory for a New Generation of Test* (pp. 323–357). Hillsdale, NJ: Lawrence Erlbaum.

Belcher, D. (2006). English for specific purposes: Teaching to perceived needs and imagined futures in worlds of work, study and everyday life. *TESOL Quarterly* 40, 133–156.

Belcher, D. (2004). Trends in teaching English for specific purposes. In M. McGroarty et al. (Eds.), *Annual Review of Applied Linguistics: Vol. 24. Advances in Language Pedagogy* (pp. 165–186). New York: Cambridge University Press.

Belcher, D. (1997). An argument for nonadversarial argumentation: On the relevance of the feminist critique of academic discourse to L2 writing pedagogy. *Journal of Second Language Writing* 6, 1–21.

Belcher, D., and U. Connor (Eds.). (2001). *Reflections on Multiliterate Lives*. Clevedon, Avon, UK: Multilingual Matters.

Bell, A. (1991). *The Language of News Media*. Oxford: Blackwell.

Bell, A., and J. Holmes (Eds.). (1990). *New Zealand Ways of Speaking English*. Clevedon, Avon, UK: Multilingual Matters.

Belz, J. A. (2003). Linguistic perspectives on the development of intercultural competence in telecollaboration. *Language Learning & Technology* 7(2), 68–117.

Belz, J. A. (2001). Institutional and individual dimensions of transatlantic group work in network-based language teaching. *ReCALL* 13(2), 213–231.

Belz, J. A., and S. L. Thorne (2006). Introduction: Internet-mediated intercultural foreign language education and the intercultural speaker. In J. A. Belz, and S. L. Thorne (Eds.), *Internet-Mediated Intercultural Foreign Language Education*. Boston, MA: Thomson Heinle.

Belz, J. A., and N. Vyatkina (2008). The pedagogical mediation of a developmental learner corpus for classroom-based language instruction. *Language Learning & Technology* 12(3), 33–52.

Bender, B. W. (1970). Micronesian languages. *Current Trends in Linguistics* 8, 426–65.

Benesch, S. (2001). *Critical English for Academic Purposes: Theory, Politics, and Practice*. Mahwah, NJ: Lawrence Erlbaum.

Benesch, S. (1993). ESL, ideology, and the politics of pragmatism. *TESOL Quarterly* 27, 705–717.

Benhabib, S. (1999). Citizens, residents and aliens in a changing world: Political membership in a global era. *Social Research* 66, 709–744.

Benhabib, S. (1997). Strange multiplicities: The politics of identity and difference in a global context. In A. Samatar (Ed.), *The Divided Self: Identity and Globalizatio* (pp. 27–56). St. Paul, MN: Macalester College International Studies and Programming.

Benmaman, V. (1997). Legal interpreting by any other name is still legal interpreting. In S. E. Carr, R. Roberts, A. Dufour, and D. Steyn (Eds.), *The Critical Link: Interpreters in the Community* (pp. 179–190). Amsterdam/Philadelphia: John Benjamins.

Bennett, R. E. (1999). Using new technology to improve assessment. *Educational Measurement: Issues and Practice* 18, 5–12.

Benrabah, M. (2007). Language in education planning in Algeria: Historical development and current issues. *Language Policy* 6, 225–252.

Benrabah, M. (2005). The language planning situation in Algeria. *Current Issues in Language Planning* 6(4), 379–502.

Bentolila, A. (1987). Haitian Creole: A challenge for education. *Diogenes* 137, 73–87.

Benton, N. (1998). Education, language decline and language revitalisation: The case of Mäori in New Zealand. *Language and Education* 3(2), 65–82.

Benton, R. A. (1991a). Notes on the case for Mäori language television. *New Language Planning Newsletter* 5(4), 1–4.

Benton, R. A. (1991b). Tomorrow's Schools and the revitalisation of Mäori: Stimulus or tranquiliser? In O. Garcia (Ed.), *Bilingual Education: Focusschrift in Honour of Joshua A. Fishman on the Occasion of his 65th Birthday* (vol. 1, pp. 136–147). Amsterdam: John Benjamins.

Benton, R. A. (1981). *The Flight of the Amokura: Oceanic Languages and Formal Education in the South Pacific.* Wellington: New Zealand Council for Educational Research.

Benton, R. A., and N. Benton (2001). RLS in Aotearoa: New Zealand 1989–1999. In J. A. Fishman (Ed.), *Can Threatened Languages Be Saved?* Clevedon: Multilingual Matters, 423–450.

Bergeron, G. (2002). L'interprétation en milieu judiciaire [Interpreting in the judicial context]. *Meta: Translators' Journal* 4(2), 225–232.

Bergman, M. M. (Ed.). (2008). *Advances in Mixed Methods Research.* London: Sage.

Berk-Seligson, S. (2008). Judicial systems in contact: Access to justice and the right to interpreting/translating services among the Quichua of Ecuador. *Interpreting* 10 (1), 9–33.

Bernabé, J. (2001). *La Graphie Créole.* Martinique: Ibis Rouge Editions.

Bernaus, M., E. Moore, and A. C. Azevedo (2007). Affective factors influencing plurilingual students' acquisition of Catalan in a Catalan-Spanish bilingual context. *Modern Language Journal 91*, 235–246.

Bernhardt, E. (1999). If reading is reader-based, can there be a computer-adaptive test of reading? In M. Chalhoub-Deville (Ed.), *Issues in Computer-Adaptive Testing of Reading Proficiency* (pp. 1–10). Cambridge: Cambridge University.

Bernhardt, E. (1991). A psycholinguistic perspective on second language literacy. *AILA Review* 8, 45–60.

Berninger, V., and T. Richards (2002). *Brain Literacy for Educators and Psychologists.* San Diego, CA: Academic Press.

Berns, M., K. de Bot, and U. Hasebrink (2007). *In the Presence of English: Media and European Youth.* New York: Springer.

Bernstein, R. J. (1971). *Praxis and Action.* Philadelphia: University of Pennsylvania Press.

Bernsten, J. (1998). Runyakitara: Uganda's "new" language. *Journal of Multilingual and Multicultural Development* 19(2), 93–107.

Berry, R., and J. Hudson (1997). *Making the Jump: A Resource Book for Teachers of Aboriginal Students.* Broome, Western Australia: Catholic Education Office, Kimberley Region.

Besnier, N. (1988). The linguistic relationships of spoken and written Nukulaelae registers. *Language* 64, 707–736.

Best, C. T. (1995). A direct realist view of cross-language speech perception. In W. Strange (Ed.), *Speech Perception and Linguistic Experience: Issues in Crosslanguage Research* (pp. 171–204). Timonium, MD: York Press.

Bhatia, V. K. (2008). Genre analysis, ESP and professional practice. *English for Specific Purposes* 27, 161–174.

Bhatia, V. K. (2000). Genres in conflict. In A. Trosborg (Ed.), *Analysing Professional Genres* (pp. 147–161). Amsterdam: John Benjamins.

Bhatia, V. K. (1993). *Analyzing Genre: Language in Professional Settings*. London: Longman.

Bhimji, F. (2002). "Dile Famile": Socializing language skills with directives in three families in South Central Los Angeles. PhD dissertation, University of California, Los Angeles.

Bialystok, E. (2005). Consequences of bilingualism for cognitive development. In J. F. Kroll, and A. M. B. De Groot (Eds.), *Handbook of Bilingualism: Psycholinguistic Approaches* (pp. 417–432). New York: Oxford University Press.

Bialystok, E. (2001). *Bilingualism in Development: Language, Literacy and Cognition*. Cambridge: Cambridge University Press.

Bialystok, E. (1993). Symbolic representation and attentional control in pragmatic competence. In G. Kasper, and S. Blum-Kulka (Eds.), *Interlanguage Pragmatics* (pp. 43–59). New York: Oxford University Press.

Bialystok, E. (1990). *Communication Strategies*. Oxford: Blackwell.

Bialystok, E., F. I. M. Craik, R. Klein, and M. Viswanathan (2004). Bilingualism, aging and cognitive control: Evidence from the Simon Task. *Psychology and Aging* 19, 290–303.

Biber, D. (2008). Corpus-based analyses of discourse: Dimensions of variation in conversation. In V. K. Bhatia, J. Flowerdew, and R. Jones (Eds.), *Advances in Discourse Studies* (pp. 100–114). London: Routledge.

Biber, D. (2006a). *University Language*. Amsterdam: John Benjamins.

Biber, D. (2006b). Stance in spoken and written university registers. *Journal of English for Academic Purposes* 5, 97–116.

Biber, D. (2004). Historical patterns for the grammatical marking of stance: A cross-register comparison. *Journal of Historical Pragmatics* 5, 107–135.

Biber, D. (2001). Dimensions of variation among 18th century registers. In H.-J. Diller, and M. Gorlach (Eds.), *Towards a History of English as a History of Genres* (pp. 89–110). Heidelberg: C. Winter. (Reprinted in Conrad and Biber 2001, pp. 200–214).

Biber, D. (1995). *Dimensions of Register Variation: A Cross-Linguistic Comparison*. Cambridge: Cambridge University Press.

Biber, D. (1992). On the complexity of discourse complexity: A multidimensional analysis. *Discourse Processes* 15, 133–163. (Reprinted in Conrad and Biber, 2001, pp. 215–240).

Biber, D. (1988). *Variation across Speech and Writing*. Cambridge: Cambridge University Press.

Biber, D. (1987). A textual comparison of British and American writing. *American Speech* 62, 99–119.

Biber, D. (1986). Spoken and written textual dimensions in English: Resolving the contradictory findings. *Language* 62, 384–414.

Biber, D., and F. Barbieri (2007). Lexical bundles in university spoken and written registers. *English for Specific Purposes* 26, 263–86.

Biber, D., and J. Burges (2000). Historical change in the language use of women and men: Gender differences in dramatic dialogue. *Journal of English Linguistics* 28, 21–37.

Biber, D., and V. Clark (2002). Historical shifts in modification patterns with complex noun phrase structures: How long can you go without a verb? In T. Fanego, M. J. Lopez-Couso, and J. Perez-Guerra (Eds.), *English Historical Syntax and Morphology* (pp. 43–66). Amsterdam: John Benjamins.

Biber, D., U. Connor, and T. Upton (2007). *Discourse on the Move: Using Corpus Analysis to Describe Discourse Structure*. Amsterdam: John Benjamins.

Biber, D., and S. Conrad (in press). *Register, Genre and Style*. Cambridge: Cambridge University Press.

Biber, D., S. Conrad, and V. Cortes (2004). If you look at...: Lexical bundles in university teaching and textbooks. *Applied Linguistics* 25, 371–405.

Biber, D., S. Conrad, and G. Leech (2002). *The Longman Student Grammar of Spoken and Written English*. London: Longman.

Biber, D., S. Conrad, and R. Reppen (1998). *Corpus Linguistics: Investigating Language Structure and Use*. Cambridge: Cambridge University Press.

Biber, D., S. Conrad, and R. Reppen (1994). Corpus-based approaches in applied linguistics. *Applied Linguistics* 15, 169–189.

Biber, D., M. Davies, J. K. Jones, and N. Tracy-Ventura (2006). Spoken and written register variation in Spanish: A multi-dimensional analysis. *Corpora* 1, 7–38.

Biber, D., and E. Finegan (1997). Diachronic relations among speech-based and written registers in English. In T. Nevalainen, and L. Kahlas-Tarkka (Eds.), *To Explain the Present: Studies in the Changing English Language in Honour of Matti Rissanen* (pp. 253–275). Helsinki: Societe Neophilologique. (Reprinted in Conrad and Biber, 2001, pp. 66–83).

Biber, D., and E. Finegan (Eds.). (1994). *Sociolinguistic Perspectives on Register*. New York: Oxford University Press.

Biber, D., and E. Finegan (1989a). Drift and the evolution of English style: A history of three genres. *Language* 65, 487–517.

Biber, D., and E. Finegan (1989b). Styles of stance in English: Lexical and grammatical marking of evidentiality and affect. *Text* 9, 93–124.

Biber, D., and E. Finegan (1988). Adverbial stance types in English. *Discourse Processes* 11, 1–34.

Biber, D., and M. Hared (1994). Linguistic correlates of the transition to literacy in Somali: Language adaptation in six press registers. In D. Biber, and E. Finegan (Eds.), *Sociolinguistic Perspectives on Register* (pp. 182–216). New York: Oxford University Press.

Biber, D., and M. Hared (1992). Dimensions of register variation in Somali. *Language Variation and Change* 4, 41–75.

Biber, D., S. Johansson, G. Leech, S. Conrad, and E. Finegan (1999). *The Longman Grammar of Spoken and Written English*. London: Longman.

Biber, D., and J. K. Jones (2005). Merging corpus linguistic and discourse analytic research goals: Discourse units in biology research articles. *Corpus Linguistics and Linguistic Theory* 1, 151–182.

Biber, D., and J. Kurjian (2007). Towards a taxonomy of web registers and text types: A multi-dimensional analysis. In M. Hundt, N. Nesselhauf, and C. Biewer (Eds.), *Corpus Linguistics and the Web* (pp. 109–132). Amsterdam: Rodopi.

Biber, D., and R. Reppen (2002). What does frequency have to do with grammar teaching? *Studies in Second Language Acquisition* 24, 199–208.

Biber, D., and N. Tracy-Ventura (2007). Dimensions of register variation in Spanish. In G. Parodi (Ed.), *Working with Spanish Corpora* (pp. 54–89). London: Continuum.

Bickerton, D. (1984). The language bioprogram hypothesis. *Behavioral and Brain Sciences* 7, 173–221.

Bickerton, D. (1981). *Roots of Language*. Ann Arbor, MI: Karoma.

Bickerton, D. (1975). *Dynamics of a Creole System*. Cambridge: Cambridge University Press.

Bickerton, D., and C. Odo (1976). *Change and Variation in Hawaiian English. Vol. 1: General Phonology and Pidgin Syntax*. Honolulu: Social Sciences and Linguistics Institute, University of Hawai'i.

Billmyer, K. (1990). "I really like your lifestyle": ESL learners learning how to compliment. *Penn Working Papers in Educational Linguistics* 62, 31–48.

Birdsong, D. (1989). *Metalinguistic Performance and Interlinguistic Competence*. New York: Springer Verlag.

Black, P., C. Harrison, C. Lee, B. Marshall, and D. Wiliam (2004). Working inside the black box: Assessment for learning in the classroom. *Phi Delta Kappan* 86(1), 8–21.

Blackledge, A. (2003). Imagining a monocultural community: Racialization of cultural practice in educational discourse. *Journal of Language, Identity and Education* 2(4), 331–347.

Bland, S. K., J. S. Noblitt, S. Armington, and G. Gay (1990). The naive lexical hypothesis: Evidence from computer-assisted language learning. *Modern Language Journal* 74, 440–450.

Blake, R. (2000). Computer-mediated communication: A window on L2 Spanish interlanguage. *Language Learning & Technology* 4(1), 120–136.

Bley-Vroman, R. (1989). What is the logical problem of foreign language learning? In S. M. Gass, and J. Schachter (Eds.), *Linguistic Perspectives on Second Language Acquisition* (pp. 41–68). Cambridge: Cambridge University Press.

Bley-Vroman, R., and L. Loschky (1993). Grammar and task-based methodology. In S. Gass, & G. Crookes (Eds.), *Tasks and Language Learning: Integrating Theory and Practice* (pp. 123–167). Clevedon, Avon, UK: Multilingual Matters.

Block, C., and S. Parris (Eds.). (2008). *Comprehension Instruction: Research-Based Best Practices*. New York: Guilford.

Block, D. (2007). *Second Language Identities*. London, UK: Continuum.

Block, D., and D. Cameron (2002). *Globalization and Language Teaching*. London: Routledge.

Blommaert, J. (1996). Language planning as a discourse on language and society: The linguistic ideology of a scholarly tradition. *Language Problems and Language Planning* 20, 199–222.

Bloomfield, L. (1942). *Outline guide for the practical studies of foreign languages*. Baltimore: Linguistics Society of America.

Blum-Kulka, S. (1982). Learning to say what you mean in a second language: A study of speech act performance of learners of Hebrew as a second language. *Applied Linguistics* 3, 29–59.

Blum-Kulka, S., J. House, and G. Kasper (Eds.). (1989). *Cross-Cultural Pragmatics: Requests and Apologies*. Norwood, NJ: Ablex.

Blum-Kulka, S., and E. Olshtain (1986). Too many words: Length of utterance and pragmatic failure. *Studies in Second Language Acquisition* 8, 165–180.

Blum-Kulka, S., and E. Olshtain (1984). Requests and apologies: A cross-cultural study of speech act realization patterns (CCSARP). *Applied Linguistics* 5, 196–213.

Bock, J. (1986). Meaning, sound and syntax: Lexical priming in sentence production. *Journal of Experimental Psychology: Learning, Memory and Cognition* 12, 575–586.

Bock, K., and W. J. M. Levelt (1994). Language production: Grammatical encoding. In M. A. Gernsbacher (Ed.), *Handbook of Psycholinguistics* (pp. 945–984). San Diego, CA: Academic Press.

Boekaerts, M. (1986). The measurement of state and trait motivational orientation: Refining our measures. In J. H. L. van den Bercken, E. E. J. De Bruyn, and C. M. Bergen (Eds.), *Achievement and Task Motivation* (pp. 229–245). Lisse: Swets & Zeitlinger.

Boggs, S. T. (1985). *Speaking, Relating and Learning: A Study of Hawaiian Children at Home and at School.* Norwood, NJ: Ablex.

Bohnacker, U. (2005). Nonnative acquisition of Verb Second: On the empirical underpinnings of universal L2. In M. den Dikken, and C. Tortora (Eds.), *The Function of Function Words and Functional Categories* (pp. 41–77). Amsterdam: John Benjamins.

Bolinger, D. (1975). Meaning and memory. *Forum Linguisticum* 1, 2–14.

Bollée, A. (1993). Language policy in the Seychelles and its consequences. *International Journal of the Sociology of Language* 102, 85–99.

Bolt, P., and B. Kingsley (1996). The international corpus of English in Hong Kong. In S. Greenbaum (Ed.). *Comparing English Worldwide: The International Corpus of English* (pp. 157–214). Oxford: Clarendon Press.

Bolton, K. (Ed.). (2000). Hong Kong English: Autonomy and creativity [Special issue]. *World Englishes* 19(3).

Booth, R., and K. Davison (2003). Relating to our worlds in a psychobiological context: The impact of disclosure on self-generation and immunity. In J. Wilce (Ed.), *Social and Cultural Lives of Immune Systems* (pp. 36–49). London: Routledge.

Borrás, I., and R. C. Lafayette (1994). Effects of multimedia courseware subtitling on the speaking performance of college students of French. *Modern Language Journal* 78, 61–75.

Borsley, R. (1998). *Syntactic Theory.* Oxford: Arnold.

Bot, H. (2005). *Dialogue Interpreting in Mental Health (Utrecht Studies in Language and Communication* 19). Amsterdam/New York: Rodopi.

Botley, S., T. McEnery, and A. Wilson (Eds.). (2000). *Multilingual Corpora in Teaching and Research.* Amsterdam: Rodopi.

Bourdieu, P. (1977). The economics of linguistic exchanges. *Social Science Information* 16(6), 645–668.

Bourdieu, P., and J. Passeron (1977). *Reproduction in Education, Society and Culture.* London/Beverly Hills, CA: Sage.

Bourhis, R. Y. (1997). Language policies and language attitudes: Le Monde de la Francophone. In N. Coupland, and A. Jaworski (Eds.), *Sociolinguistics: A Reader* (pp. 306–322). New York: St. Martin's Press.

Bouton, L. F. (1994a). Can NNS skill in interpreting implicatures in American English beimproved through explicit instruction? In L. F. Bouton, and Y. Kachru (Eds.), *Pragmatics and Language Learning* (vol. 5, pp. 88–109). Urbana-Champaign, IL: University of Illinois, Urbana-Champaign, Division of English as an International Language (DEIL).

Bouton, L. F. (1994b). Conversational implicature in a second language: Learned slowly when not deliberately taught. *Journal of Pragmatics* 22, 157–167.

Boyd, M., and V. M. Maloof (2000). How teachers can build upon student proposed intertextual links to facilitate student talk in the ESL classroom. In J. K. Hall, and L. S. Verplaetse (Eds.), *Second and Foreign Language Learning through Classroom Interaction* (pp. 162–182). Mahwah, NJ: Lawrence Erlbaum.

Braine, G. (2005). The challenge of academic publishing: A Hong Kong perspective. *TESOL Quarterly* 39, 707–716.

Brandt, E. A., and V. Ayoungman (1989). Language renewal and language maintenance: A practical guide. *Canadian Journal of Native Education* 16(2), 42–77.

Braun, S. (2007). Interpreting in small-group bilingual videoconferences: Challenges and adaptation processes. *Interpreting* 9(1), 21–46.

Braun, S. (2005). From pedagogically relevant corpora to authentic language learning contents. *ReCALL* 17(1), 47–64.

Braun, S., and A. Clarici (1997). Inaccuracy for numerals in simultaneous interpretation: Neurolinguistic and neuropsychological perspective. *Interpreters' Newsletter* 7, 85–102.

Breen, M. P. (Ed.) (2001). *Learner Contributions to Language Learning: New Directions in Research*. London: Pearson Education.

Breen, M. P. (1987). Contemporary paradigms in syllabus design. *Language Teaching* 20, 81–92, 157–174.

Breen, M. P., and C. N. Candlin (1980). The essentials of a communicative curriculum in language teaching. *Applied Linguistics* 1, 89–112.

Breen, M. P., and A. Littlejohn (Eds.). (2000). *Classroom Decision-Making: Negotiation and Process Syllabuses in Practice*. Cambridge: Cambridge University Press.

Breinberg, P. (1986). Language attitudes: The case of Caribbean language. In D. Sutcliffe, and A. Wong (Eds.), *The Language of Black Experience* (pp. 136–142). Oxford: Blackwell.

Breiteneder, A. (2008). Challenging issues in corpus linguistics and World Englishes. Book review of *Corpus Linguistics and World Englishes: An Analysis of Xhosa English*. *International Journal of Corpus Linguistics* 13(2), 251–260.

Breiteneder, A., M.-L. Pitzl, S. Majewski, and T. Klimpfinger (2006). VOICE recording—methodological challenges in the compilation of a corpus of spoken ELF. *Nordic Journal of English Studies* 5(2), 161–188. Available at http://hdl.handle.net/2077/3153

Bremer, K., C. Roberts, M. Vasseur, M. Simonot, and P. Broeder (1996). *Achieving Understanding: Discourse in International Encounters*. London: Longman.

Brenzinger, M. (1997). Language contact and language displacement. In F. Coulmas (Ed.), *Handbook of Sociolinguistics* (pp. 273–284). Oxford: Blackwell.

Bresnan, J. (2001). *Lexical-Functional Grammar*. Oxford: Blackwells.

Brewer, R. (1988). *The Science of Ecology*. Philadelphia: Saunders College.

Bright, W. (Ed.). (1991). *Oxford International Encyclopedia of Linguistics* (4 vols.). New York: Oxford University Press.

Brindley, G. (2001). Assessment. In R. Carter, and D. Nunan (Eds.), *Teaching English to Speakers of Other Languages* (pp. 137–143). Cambridge: Cambridge University Press.

Brinton, D. M. (2007). Two for one? Language-enhanced content instruction in English for academic purposes. In D. Brinton, A. Koester, and T. Orr (Eds.), *A TESOL Symposium: Teaching English for Specific Purposes: Meeting Our Learners' Needs* (pp. 1–16). Alexandria, VA: TESOL.

Brinton, D. M., and C. A. Holten (2001). Does the emperor have no clothes? A re-examination of grammar in content-based instruction. In J. Flowerdew, and M. Peacock (Eds.), *Research Perspectives on English for Academic Purposes* (pp. 239–251). Cambridge: Cambridge University Press.

Brinton, D. M., and L. Jensen (2002). Appropriating the adjunct model: English for academic purposes at the university level. In J. A. Crandall, and D. Kaufman (Eds.), *Content-Based Instruction in Higher Education Settings* (pp. 125–137). Alexandria, VA: Teachers of English to Speakers of Other Languages.

Brinton, D., M. Snow, and M. Wesche (2003). *Content-Based Second Language Instruction: Classics Edition* (with updates). Ann Arbor: University of Michigan Press.

Brinton, D., M. Snow, and M. Wesche (1989). *Content-Based Second Language Instruction*. Rowley, MA: Newbury House.

Brisk, M. (2005). Bilingual education. In E. Hinkel (Ed.), *Handbook of Research in Second Language Teaching and Learning* (pp. 7–24). Mahwah, NJ: Lawrence Erlbaum.

Brodine, R. (2001). Integrating corpus work into an academic reading course. In G. Aston (Ed.), *Learning with Corpora* (pp. 138–176). Houston, TX: Athelstan.

Broeder, P., and K. Plunkett (1994). Connectionism and second language acquisition. In N. Ellis (Ed.), *Implicit and Explicit Learning of Languages* (pp. 421–454). San Diego, CA: Academic Press.

Brosnahan, L. F. (1963). Some historical cases of language imposition. In J. Spencer (Ed.), *Language in Africa* (pp. 7–24). Cambridge: Cambridge University Press.

Broughton, G. (1968–1970). *Success with English* (3 vols.). Harmondsworth, UK: Penguin.

Brown, C. (2000). The interrelation between speech perception and phonological acquisition. In J. Archibald (Ed.), *Second Language Acquisition and Linguistic Theory* (pp. 4–63). Oxford: Blackwell.

Brown, C. (1998). The role of the L1 grammar in the acquisition of L2 segmental structure. *Second Language Research* 14, 136–193.

Brown, G. (1995). *Speakers, Listeners and Communication*. Cambridge: Cambridge University Press.

Brown, G. (1986). Investigating listening comprehension in context. *Applied Linguistics* 7(3), 284–302.

Brown, G., and G. Yule (1983). *Teaching the Spoken Language*. Cambridge: Cambridge University Press.

Brown, J. D. (2004). Research methods for applied linguistics: Scope, characteristics and standards. In A. Davies, and C. Elder (Eds.), *The Handbook of Applied Linguistics* (pp. 476–500). Oxford: Blackwell.

Brown, J. D. (1992). Statistics as a foreign language—part 2: More things to consider in reading statistical language studies. *TESOL Quarterly* 26, 629–664.

Brown, J. D. (1991). Statistics as a foreign language—part 1: What to look for in reading statistical language studies. *TESOL Quarterly* 25, 569–586.

Brown, J. D., and T. S. Rogers (2002). *Doing Second Language Research*. Oxford: Oxford University Press.

Brown, K. (Ed.). (2006). *Encyclopedia of Language and Linguistics* (2nd ed., 14 vols.). Amsterdam: Elsevier.

Brown, P., and S. Levinson (1988). *Politeness*. Cambridge: Cambridge University Press.

Brown-Blake, C. (2008). The right to linguistic non-discrimination and Creole language situations: The case of Jamaica. *Journal of Pidgin and Creole Languages* 23(1), 32–74.

Brown-Blake, C., and P. Chambers (2007). The Jamaican Creole speaker in the UK criminal justice system. *International Journal of Speech, Language and the Law* 14(2), 269–294.

Bruder, M. N. (1973). *MMC: Developing Communicative Competence in English as a Second Language*. Pittsburgh, PA: University of Pittsburgh Press.

Brumfit, C. J. (2004). Applied linguistics in 2004: Unity in diversity? *AILA Review* 17, 133–136.

Brumfit, C. J. (1997a). How applied linguistics is the same as any other science. *International Journal of Applied Linguistics* 7(1), 86–94.

Brumfit, C. J. (1997b). Theoretical practice: Applied linguistics as pure and practical science. *AILA Review* 12, 18–30.

Brumfit, C. J. (1984). *Communicative Methodology in Language Teaching*. Cambridge: Cambridge University Press.

Brumfit, C. J., and K. Johnson (Eds.). (1979). *The Communicative Approach to Language Teaching*. Oxford: Oxford University Press.

Brunette, L., G. Bastin, I. Hemlin, and H. Clarke (Eds.). (2003). *The Critical Link 3: Interpreters in the Community*. Amsterdam and Philadelphia: John Benjamins.

Bruthiaux, P. (2008). Language Education, Economic Development and Participation in the Greater Mekong Subregion. *The International Journal of Bilingual Education and Bilingualism* 11(2), 134–148.

Bruthiaux, P. (2005). In a nutshell: Persuasion in the spatially constrained language of advertising. In H. Halmari, and T. Virtanen (Eds.) *Persuasion across genres* (pp. 35–152). Amsterdam: John Benjamins.

Bruthiaux, P. (1996). *The Discourse of Classified Advertising: Exploring the Nature of Linguistic Simplicity*. Oxford: Oxford University Press.

Bruthiaux, P. (1994). Me Tarzan, you Jane: Linguistic simplification in "personal ads" register. In D. Biber, and E. Finegan (Eds.), *Sociolinguistic Perspectives on Register* (pp. 136–154). New York: Oxford University Press.

Brutt-Griffler, J. (2002). *World English: A Study of Its Development*. Clevedon, Avon, UK and Buffalo, NY: Multilingual Matters.

Brysbaert, M. (1998). Word recognition in bilinguals: Evidence against the existence of two separate lexicons. *Psychologica Belgica* 38, 163–175.

Bucholtz, M. (2003). Theories of discourse as theories of gender: Discourse analysis in language and gender studies. In J. Holmes, and M. Meyerhoff (Eds.), *The Handbook of Language and Gender* (pp. 43–68). Malden, MA: Blackwell.

Buck, G. (1994). The appropriacy of psychometric measurement models for testing second language listening comprehension. *Language Testing* 11, 145–70.

Buck, G., and K. Tatsuoka (1998). Application of the rule-space procedure to language testing: Examining attributes of a free-response listening test. *Language Testing* 15(2), 119–157.

Buck, G., K. Tatsuoka, and I. Kostin (1997). The subskills of reading: Rule-space analysis of a multiple-choice test of second language reading comprehension. *Language Learning* 47, 423–466.

Bunderson, C. V., D. K. Inouye, and J. B. Olson (1989). The four generations of computerized educational measurement. In R. L. Linn (Ed.), *Educational Measurement* (pp. 367–407). Washington, DC: American Council on Education.

Burger, S., and M. Chrétien (2001). The development of oral production in content-based second language courses at the University of Ottawa. *Canadian Modern Language Review* 58(1), 84–102.

Burger, S., and A. Weinberg (2009). From institution to students: Evaluation of the new "French Immersion Studies" program at the University of Ottawa. Unpublished manuscript.

Burger, S., M. Wesche, and M. Migneron (1997). Late, late immersion, or discipline-based second language teaching at the University of Ottawa. In R. K. Johnson, and M. Swain (Eds.), *Immersion Education: International Perspectives* (pp. 65–84). Cambridge: Cambridge University Press.

Burnard, L., and T. McEnery (Eds.). (2000). *Rethinking Language Pedagogy from a Corpus Perspective: Papers from the Third International Conference on Teaching and Language Corpora*. Frankfurt: Lang.

Burningham, L. (1998). Factors Influencing Language Policy and Planning in a Utah School District. Unpublished MA Thesis, Brigham Young University, Provo, Utah.

Burns, A. (1998). Teaching speaking. In W. Grabe et al. (Eds.), *Annual Review of Applied Linguistics: Vol. 18. Foundation of Second Language Teaching* (pp. 102–123). New York: Cambridge University Press.

Burns, A., and S. Moore (2008). Questioning in simulated accountant-client consultations: Exploring implications for ESP Teaching. *English for Specific Purposes* 27, 322–337.

Burridge, K., and B. Kortmann (Eds.). (2008). *Handbook of Varieties: Australia, Pacific and Australasia*. Berlin/New York: Mouton de Gruyter.

Burstein, J., M. Chodorow, and C. Leacock (2004). Automated essay evaluation: The Criterion Online Writing Evaluation service. *AI Magazine* 25(3), 27–36.

Burstein, J., K. Kukich, S. Wolff, C. Lu, M. Chodorow, L. Braden-Harder, and M. D. Harris (1998). Automated scoring using a hybrid feature identification technique. In *Proceedings of the Annual Meeting of the Association of Computational Linguistics* Montreal, Canada.

Burstein, J., D. Marcu, and K. Knight (2003). Finding the WRITE stuff: Automatic identification of discourse structure in student essays. In S. Harabagiu, and F. Ciravegna (Eds.) *IEEE Intelligent Systems: Special Issue on Advances in Natural Language Processing* 18(1), 32–39.

Bybee, J. (2006). *Frequency of Use and the Organization of Language*. Oxford, UK: Oxford University Press.

Bygate, M. (2005). Applied linguistics: A pragmatic discipline, a generic discipline? *Applied Linguistics* 26, 568–581.

Bygate, M. (1999). Task as context for the framing, reframing and unframing of language. *System* 27, 33–48.

Bygate, M. (1996). Effects of task repetition: Appraising the developing language of learners. In D. Willis, and J. Willis (Eds.), *Challenge and Change in Language Teaching* (pp. 136–146). London: Heinemann.

Byon, A. S. (2006). Language socialization in Korean-as-a-foreign-language classrooms. *Bilingual Research Journal* 30, 265–291.

Cadierno, T. (2008). Learning to talk about motion in a foreign language. In P. Robinson, and N. Ellis (Eds.), *Handbook of Cognitive Linguistics and Second Language Acquisition* (pp. 239–275). New York: Routledge.

Calvé, P. (1991). Vingt-cinq ans d'immersion au Canada: 1965–1990 [Twenty-five years of immersion in Canada]. *Êtudes de Linguistique Appliquée: L'immersion au Canada [Studies in Applied Linguistics: Immersion in Canada]* [P. Calvé, Coordinator] 82, 7–23.

Calvet, L. J. (2006). *Towards an Ecology of World Languages*. Cambridge: Polity Press.

Calvet, L. J. (1999). *La guerre des langues et les politiques linguistiques* [*Language War and Linguistic Politics*] (2nd ed.). Paris: Hachette.

Calvet, L. J. (1997). Cities and languages. *Diagonales* 42, 32–33.

Camayd-Freixas, E. (2008). Statement to the profession. *Proteus* 17(3), 5–8.

Cambridge Advanced Learner's Dictionary (2005). Cambridge: Cambridge University Press.

Cameron, D. (1992). *Feminism and Linguistic Theory* (2nd ed.). New York: St. Martin's Press.

Cameron, D., E. Frazer, P. Harvey, M. B. H. Rampton, and K. Richardson (Eds.). (1992). *Researching Language: Issues of Power and Method*. London: Routledge.

Cameron, D., and D. Kulick (2003). *Language and Sexuality*. Cambridge: Cambridge University Press.

Cameron, L., J. Moon, and M. Bygate (1996). Language development of bilingual pupils in the mainstream. *Language and Education* 10, 221–236.

Campbell, S., and C. Roberts (2007). Migration, ethnicity and competing discourses in the job interview: Synthesizing the institutional and personal. *Discourse & Society* 18(3), 243–271.

Canadian Parents for French [CPF] (2008). *The State of French-second Language Education in Canada 2008*. Ottawa: CPF.

Canagarajah, A. S. (2006). Ethnographic methods in language policy. In T. Ricento (Ed.), *An Introduction to Language Policy: Theory and Method* (pp. 153–169). Oxford: Blackwell.

Canagarajah, A. S. (2002). *Critical Academic Writing and Multilingual Students*. Ann Arbor: University of Michigan Press.

Canagarajah, A. S. (1999). *Resisting Linguistic Imperialism in English Language Teaching*. Oxford: Oxford University Press.

Canagarajah, A. S. (1993). Comment on Ann Raimes's "Out of the Woods: Emerging traditions in the teaching of writing": Up the garden path: Second language writing approaches, local knowledge and pluralism. *TESOL Quarterly* 27, 301–306.

Canale, M., and M. Swain (1980). Theoretical bases of communicative approaches to second language teaching and testing. *Applied Linguistics* 1, 1–47.

Candlin, C. N., and S. Candlin (2003). Health care communication: A problematic site for applied linguistics research. In M. McGroarty et al. (Eds.), *Annual Review of Applied Linguistics: Vol. 23. Language Contact and Change* (pp. 134–154). New York: Cambridge University Press.

Candlin, C., and S. Sarangi (2004). Making applied linguistics matter. *Journal of Applied Linguistics* 1, 1–8.

Cantoni, G. (Ed.). (1996). *Stabilizing Indigenous Languages*. Flagstone, Az: Northern Arizona University Center for Excellence in Education.

CAPE website. Brigham Young University Humanities Research Center [Online]. Available: http://creativeworks.byu.edu/hrc

Caplan, D., G. Waters, and G. Dede (2007). Specialized verbal working memory for language comprehension. In A. R. A. Conway, C. Jarrold, M. J. Kane, A. Miyake, and J. N. Towse (Eds.), *Variation in Working Memory*. New York: Oxford University Press.

CARLA website. University of Minnesota Computer Adaptive Tests [Online]. Available: http://www.carla.umn.edu/index.html.

Carlet, L. (1998). G. V. Chernov's psycholinguistic model in simultaneous interpretation: An experimental contribution. *Interpreters' Newsletter* 8, 75–92.

Carpenter, H., K. Jeon, D. MacGregor, and A. Mackey (2006). Learners' interpretations of recasts. *Studies in Second Language Acquisition* 28, 209–236.

Carr, S. E., R. Roberts, A. Dufour, and D. Steyn (Eds.). (1997). *The Critical Link: Interpreters in the Community*. Amsterdam/Philadelphia: John Benjamins.

Carrell, P. (1979). Indirect speech acts in ESL: Indirect answers. In C. A. Yorio, K. Perkins, and J. Schachter (Eds.), *On TESOL '79: The Learner in Focus* (pp. 275–287). Washington, DC: TESOL.

Carroll, J. B., and S. M. Sapon (1959). *Modern Language Aptitude Test*. New York: Psychological Corporation.

Carroll, M., J. Murcia-Serra, M. Watorek, and A. Bendiscioli (2000). The relevance of information organization to second language acquisitions studies: The descriptive discourse of advanced adult learners of German. *Studies in Second Language Acquisition* 22, 441–466.

Carter, R., and S. Adolphs (2008). Linking the verbal and visual: New directions for corpus linguistics. In Language and computers [Special issue]. *Language, People, Numbers* 64, 275–291.

Carter, R., and M. McCarthy (2006). *Cambridge Grammar of English: A Comprehensive Guide to Spoken and Written English Grammar and Usage*. Cambridge: Cambridge University Press.

Carter, R., and M. McCarthy (2004). Talking creating: Interactional language, creativity and context. *Applied Linguistics* 25(1), 62–88.

Carter, R., and M. McCarthy (1997). *Exploring Spoken English*. Cambridge: Cambridge University Press.

Carter, R., and M. McCarthy (1995). Grammar and the spoken language. *Applied Linguistics* 16(2), 141–158.

Casanave, C. (2004). *Controversies in Second Language Writing: Dilemmas and Decisions in Research*. Ann Arbor: University of Michigan Press.

Casanave, C. (1998). Transitions: The balancing act of bilingual academics. *Journal of Second Language Writing* 7, 175–203.

Casanave, C. (1992). Cultural diversity and socialization: A case study of a Hispanic woman in a doctoral program in sociology/ In D. Murray (Ed.), *Diversity as Resource* (pp. 148–182). Alexandria, VA: TESOL.

Casse, P. (1981). *Training for the Cross-Cultural Mind: A Handbook for Cross-Cultural Trainers and Consultants*. Washington, DC: Sietar.

Cassidy, F. G. (1993). Short note: On Creole orthography. *Journal of Pidgin and Creole Languages* 8, 135–137.

Cassidy, F. G. (1961). *Jamaica Talk: Three Hundred Years of the English Language in Jamaica*. London: Macmillan.

Catford, J. C. (1965). *A Linguistic Theory of Translation: An Essay in Applied Linguistics*. London: Oxford University Press.

Catholic Education Office, Kimberley Region (1994). *FELIKS: Fostering English Language in Kimberley Schools*. Broome: Catholic Education Commission of Western Australia.

Cavalli, M. (1997). Social representations and linguistic planning: The case of Val d'Aoste. *Travaux neuchatelois de linguistique* 27, 83–97.

Cazden, C. (2001). *Classroom Discourse: The Language of Teaching and Learning* (2nd ed.). Portsmouth, NH: Heinemann.

Cazden, C. (1992). *Whole Language Plus: Essays on Literacy in the United States and New Zealand*. New York: Teachers College Press.

Cazden, C. (1987). *Classroom Discourse*. Portsmouth, NH: Heinemann.

Celce-Murcia, M. (Ed.). (2001). *Teaching English as a Second or Foreign Language* (3rd ed.). Boston: Heinle & Heinle.

Cenoz, J., B. Hufeisen, and U. Jessner (Eds.) (2001). *Cross-linguistic Influence in Third Language Acquisition: Psycholinguistic Perspectives*. Clevedon, UK: Multilingual Matters.

Chafe, W. L. (1985). Linguistic differences produced by differences between speaking and writing. In D. R. Olson, N. Torrence, and A. Hildyard (Eds.), *Literacy, Language and Learning: The Nature and Consequences of Reading and Writing* (pp. 105–123). Cambridge: Cambridge University Press.

Chalhoub-Deville, M. (2003). Second language interaction: Current perspectives and future trends. *Language Testing* 20, 369–383.

Chalhoub-Deville, M. (2002). Technology in standardized language assessments. In R. B. Kaplan (Ed.), *Oxford Handbook of Applied Linguistics* (pp. 471–484). New York: Oxford University Press.

Chalhoub-Deville, M. (Ed.). (1999). *Issues in Computer Adaptive Testing of Reading Proficiency: Studies in Language Testing*. Cambridge: Cambridge University Press.

Chalhoub-Deville, M. (1997). Theoretical models, operational frameworks, and test construction. *Language Testing* 14, 3–22.

Chalhoub-Deville, M., C. Alcaya, and V. Lozier (1997). Language and measurement issues in developing computer-adaptive tests of reading ability: The University of Minnesota model. In A. Huhta, V. Kohonen, L. Kurki-Suonio, and S. Luoma (Eds.), *Current Developments and Alternatives in Language Assessment* (pp. 546–585). Jyväskylä, Finland: Center for Applied Language Studies, University of Jyväskylä.

Chalhoub-Deville, M., C. Chapelle, and P. Duff (Eds.). (2006). *Inference and Generalizability in Applied Linguistics: Multiple Perspectives.* Amsterdam: John Benjamins.

Chalhoub-Deville, M., and C. Deville (2008). Utilizing psychometric developments in assessment. In E. Shohamy, and N. H. Hornberger (Eds.), *Language Testing and Assessment: Encyclopedia of Language and Education* (2nd ed., vol. 7, pp. 211–223). New York: Springer.

Chalhoub-Deville, M., and C. Deville (2006). Old, borrowed and new thoughts in second language testing. In R. L. Brennan (Ed.), *Educational Measurement* (4th ed., pp. 517–530). Westport, CT: American Council on Education/Praeger.

Chalhoub-Deville, M., and C. Deville (2005). A look back at and forward to what language testers measure. In E. Hinkel (Ed.), *Handbook of Research in Second Language Teaching and Learning* (pp. 815–832). Mahwah, NJ: Lawrence Erlbaum.

Chalhoub-Deville, M., and C. Deville (1999). Computer adaptive testing in second language contexts. In W. Grabe et al. (Eds.), *Annual Review of Applied Linguistics: Vol. 19. A Survey of Applied Linguistics* (pp. 273–299). New York: Cambridge University Press.

Chall, J. S., and E. Dale (1995). *Readability Revised: The New Dale–Chall Readability Formula.* Cambridge, MA: Brookline.

Chan, T., and H.-C. Liou (2005). Effects of web-based concordancing instruction on EFL students' learning of verb-noun collocations. *Computer Assisted Language Learning* 18(3), 232–250.

Chang, C.-C., and D. Schallert (2007). The impact of directionality on Chinese-English simultaneous interpreting. *Interpreting* 9(2), 137–176.

Chapelle, C. A. (2007). Challenges in evaluation of innovation: Observations from technology research. *Innovation in Language Learning and Teaching* 1(1), 30–45.

Chapelle, C. A. (2005). Interactionist SLA theory in CALL Research. In J. Egbert, and G. Petrie (Eds.), *Research Perspectives on CALL* (pp. 53–64). Mahwah, NJ: Lawrence Erlbaum.

Chapelle, C. A. (2003). *English Language Learning and Technology: Lectures Applied Linguistics in the Age of Information and Communication.* Amsterdam: John Benjamins.

Chapelle, C. A. (2001). *Computer Applications in Second Language Acquisition: Foundations for Teaching, Testing and Research.* Cambridge: Cambridge University Press.

Chapelle, C. A. (1999). Validity in language assessment. In W. Grabe et al. (Eds.), *Annual Review of Applied Linguistics: Vol. 19. Survey of Applied Linguistics* (pp. 154–272). New York: Cambridge University Press.

Chapelle, C. A. (1998). Multimedia CALL: Lessons to be learned from research on instructed SLA. *Language Learning & Technology* 2(1), 22–34.

Chapelle, C. A. (1990). The discourse of computer assisted language learning: Toward a context for descriptive research. *TESOL Quarterly* 24(2), 199–225.

Chapelle, C. A., and P. Duff (Eds.). (2003). Some guidelines for conducting quantitative and qualitative research in TESOL. *TESOL Quarterly* 37, 157–178.

Chapelle, C. A., M. Enright, and J. Jamieson (Eds.). (2008). *Building a Validity Argument For the Test of English as a Foreign Language.* New York: Routledge.

Chapelle, C. A., and J. Jamieson (2008). *Tips for Teaching with CALL: Practical Approaches to Computer Assisted Language Learning.* White Plains, NY: Pearson Education.

Charge, N., and L. Taylor (1997). Recent developments in IELTS. *ELT Journal* 51, 374–80.

Charles, M. (2007). Argument or evidence? Disciplinary variation in the use of the noun that pattern. *English for Specific Purposes* 26, 203–218.

Charles, M. (2006). The construction of stance in reporting clauses: A cross-disciplinary study of theses. *Applied Linguistics* 27(3), 492–518.

Charles, M. (2005). Phraseological patterns in reporting clauses used in citation: A corpus-based study of theses in two disciplines. *English for Specific Purposes* 17, 113–134.

Charles, M. (2003). "This mystery…": A corpus-based study of the use of nouns to construct stance in theses from two contrasting disciplines. *Journal of English for Academic Purposes* 2, 313–326.

Charpentier, J.-M. (1997). Literacy in a pidgin vernacular. In A. Tabouret-Keller, R. B. LePage, P. Gardner-Chloros, and G. Varro (Eds.) *Vernacular Literacy: A Re-evaluation* (pp. 222–245). Oxford: Clarendon Press.

Chater, N., and M. H. Christiansen (2008). Computational models of psycholinguistics. In R. Sun (Ed.), *The Cambridge Handbook of Computational Psychology* (pp. 477–504). New York: Cambridge University Press.

Chaudenson, R. (2001). *Creolization of Language and Culture* (revised in collaboration with S. S. Mufwene). London: Routledge.

Chaudenson, R. (1992). *Des Iles, des Hommes, des Langues.* Paris: L'Harmattan.

Chaudron, C. (1988). *Second Language Classrooms.* Cambridge: Cambridge University Press.

Chen, H.-C. (1992). Lexical processing in bilingual or multilingual speakers. In R. J. Harris (Ed.), *Cognitive Processing in Bilinguals* (pp. 253–264). Amsterdam: Elsevier.

Chen, H.-C., and Y. S. Leung (1989). Patterns of lexical processing in a nonnative language. *Journal of Experimental Psychology: Learning, Memory and Cognition* 15, 316–325.

Chen, J. (2007). Strategies for abating intercultural noise in interpreting. *Meta: Translators' Journal* 52(3), 529–541.

Chen, J., S. Belkada, and T. Okamoto (2004). How a Web-based course facilitates acquisition of English for academic purposes. *Language Learning & Technology* 8(2), 33–49.

Chen, L.-C. (1999). The organization of teacher-student interaction in Chinese EFL classroom lessons. MA thesis, San Diego State University, San Diego, CA.

Chen, Y. (2005). Barriers to acquiring listening strategies for EFL learners and their pedagogical applications. *TESL-EJ* 8(4). Retrieved May 27, 2006, from http://www-writing.berkeley.edu:16080/tesl-ej/ej32/a2.html

Cheng, A. (2008a). Analyzing genre exemplars in preparation for writing: The case of an L2 graduate student in the ESP genre-based instructional framework for academic literacy. *Applied Linguistics* 29, 50–71.

Cheng, A. (2008b). Individualized engagement with genre in academic literacy tasks. *English for Specific Purposes* 27, 387–411.

Cheng, A. (2007). Transferring generic features and recontextualizing genre awareness: Understanding writing performance in the ESP genre-based literacy framework. *English for Specific Purposes* 26, 287–307.

Cheng, W., C. Greaves, and M. Warren (2008). *A Corpus-Driven Study of Discourse Intonation.* Amsterdam: John Benjamins.

Chenoweth, N. A., and K. Murday (2003). Measuring student learning in an online French course. *CALICO Journal* 20(2), 285–314.

Chernov, G. V. (1994). Message redundancy and message anticipation in simultaneous interpretation. In S. Lambert, and B. Moser-Mercer (Eds.), *Bridging the Gap: Empirical*

Research in Simultaneous Interpretation (pp. 139–154). Amsterdam/Philadelphia: John Benjamins.

Chesterman, A. (2008). On Explanation. In A. Pym, M. Shlesinger, and D. Simeoni (Eds.), *Beyond Descriptive Translation Studies: Investigations in Homage to Gideon Toury* (pp. 363–379). Amsterdam and Philadelphia: John Benjamins.

Chesterman, A. (2005). Causality in translator training. In M. Tennent (Ed.), *Training for the New Millennium* (pp. 191–208). Amsterdam and Philadelphia: John Benjamins.

Chesterman, A. (2000). A causal model for translation studies. In M. Olohan (Ed.), *Intercultural Faultlines: Research Models in Translation Studies I. Textual and Cognitive Aspects* (pp. 17–27). Manchester, UK: St. Jerome.

Chew, P. G.-L. (2007). Remaking Singapore: Language, culture and identity in a globalized world. In A. B. M. Tsui, and J. W. Tollefson (Eds.), *Language Policy, Culture and Identity in Asian Contexts* (pp. 73–94). Mahwah, NJ: Lawrence Erlbaum.

Chiang, J., and P. Dunkel (1992). The effect of speech modification, prior knowledge and listening proficiency in English. *TESOL Quarterly* 26, 345–374.

Chick, J. K. (1992). Addressing contextual issues relevant to language teaching in South Africa: Implications for policy and practice. *Working Papers in Educational Linguistics* 8(2), 1–16.

Chick, K. (1996). Safe-talk: Collusion in apartheid education. In H. Coleman (Ed.), *Society and the Language Classroom* (pp. 21–39). Cambridge: Cambridge University Press.

Chick, K. (1988, March 8–13). Contribution of ethnography to applied linguistics and to the in-service education of English language teachers. Paper presented at the 22nd Annual Convention of Teachers of English to Speakers of Other Languages, Chicago.

Chilton, P. (2004). *Analysing Political Discourse: Theory and Practice.* London: Routledge.

Chincotta, D., and G. Underwood (1998). Simultaneous interpreters and the effect of concurrent articulation on immediate memory. *Interpreting* 3(1), 1–20.

Choate, D. L. (1999). Labor issues and interpreters in the California courts: An exchange (Letter to the Editors). *Proteus* 8(3/4), 20–21.

Chodorow, M., and C. Leacock (2000). An unsupervised method for detecting grammatical errors. In *Proceedings of the first conference of the North American Chapter of the Association of Computational Linguistics* (pp. 140–147). Seattle.

Chomsky, N. (1995). *The Minimalist Program.* Cambridge, MA: MIT Press.

Chomsky, N. (1991). Some notes on economy of derivation and representation. In R. Freidin (Ed.), *Principles and Parameters in Generative Grammar* (pp. 417–454). Cambridge, MA: MIT Press.

Chomsky, N. (1988). *Language and Problems of Knowledge: The Managua Lectures.* Cambridge, MA: MIT Press.

Chomsky, N. (1986). *Knowledge of Language.* New York: Praeger.

Chomsky, N. (1981). *Lectures on Government and Binding.* Dordrecht: Foris.

Chomsky, N. (1977). On *WH-* movement. In P. Culicover, T. Wasow, and A. Akmajian (Eds.). *Formal Syntax* (pp. 71–132). New York: Academic Press.

Chomsky, N. (1966). Linguistic theory. In R. G. Mead, Jr. (Ed.), *Language Teaching: Broader Contexts* (pp. 43–49). New York: MLA Materials Center.

Chomsky, N. (1959). Review of B. F. Skinner's *Verbal Behavior. Language* 35(1), 26–58.

Chomsky, N., and M. Halle (1968). *The Sound Pattern of English.* New York: Harper and Row.

Chrisp, S. (1997a). He Taonga Te Reo: The use of a theme year to promote a minority language. *Journal of Multilingual and Multicultural Development* 18(2), 100–106.

Chrisp, S. (1997b). Home and community language revitalization. *New Zealand Studies in Applied Linguistics* 4, 1–15.

Christian, D. (1999). Applied linguistics in 2000 and beyond. *AAALetter* 21: 6–9.

Christensen, C. (1997). *The Innovator's Dilemma: When New Technologies Cause Great Firms to Fail.* Boston, MA: Harvard Business School Press.

Christiansen, M. H., and N. Chater (1999). Connectionist natural language processing: The state of the art. *Cognitive Science* 23, 417–430.

Christie, F. (1999). Genre theory and ESL teaching: A systemic functional perspective. *TESOL Quarterly* 33, 759–763.

Christie, F. (1987). Genres as choice. In I. Reid (Ed.), *The Place of Genre in Learning: Current Debates* (pp. 22–34). Geelong, Australia: Deakin University.

Chun, D. M. (1994). Using computer networking to facilitate the acquisition of interactive competence. *System* 22(1), 17–31.

Chun, D. M., and J. L. Plass (1996). Effects of multimedia annotations on vocabulary acquisition. *Modern Language Journal* 80, 183–198.

Chung, Y.-G. (2005). Korean-English Internet Chat in Tandem for Learning Language and Culture: A Curricular Innovation in an International Languages Program. PhD dissertation, University of Ottawa.

Chung, Y.-G., B. Graves, M. Wesche, and M. Barfurth (2005). Computer-mediated communication in Korean-English chat rooms: Tandem learning in an International Languages Program. *The Canadian Modern Language Review* 62, 49–86.

Churchill, E. F. (1999). Pragmatic development in L2 request strategies by lower level learners. Paper presented at the Second Language Research Forum, Minneapolis, MN.

Cicourel, A. (1992). The interpenetration of communicative contexts: Examples from medical encounters. In A. Duranti, and C. Goodwin (Eds.), *Rethinking Context* (pp. 291–322). Cambridge: Cambridge University Press.

Cisar, D. P., and M. Z. Sudermann (1992). Foreign language across the curriculum: A critical appraisal. *Modern Language Journal* 76(3), 295–308.

Clahsen, H. M., and C. Felser (2006a). Grammatical processing in language learners. *Applied Psycholinguistics* 27, 3–42.

Clahsen, H. M., and C. Felser (2006b). How native-like is non-native processing? *Trends in Cognitive Science* 10, 564–570.

Clahsen, H., and P. Muysken (1986). The availability of UG to adult and child learners: A study of acquisition of German word order. *Second Language Research* 2, 93–119.

Clandinin, D. (Ed.). (2007). *Handbook of Narrative Inquiry.* Thousand Oaks: Sage.

Clandinin, D., and F. M. Connelly (2000). *Narrative Inquiry: Experience and Story in Qualitative Research.* San Francisco: Jossey-Bass.

Clark, R., and R. Ivanic (1997). *The Politics of Writing.* New York: Routledge.

Clarke, D. F. (1991). The negotiated syllabus: What is it and how is it likely to work? *Applied Linguistics* 12, 13–28.

Clarke, M. (2008). *Language Teacher Identities: Co-constructing Discourse and Community.* Clevedon, Avon, UK: Multilingual Matters.

Clayton, T. (1999). Decentering language in world-system inquiry. *Language Problems & Language Planning* 23, 133–156.

Clément, R. (1980). Ethnicity, contact and communicative competence in a second language. In H. Giles, P. Robinson, and P. M. Smith (Eds.), *Language: Social Psychological Perspectives* (pp. 147–154) Oxford: Pergamon.

Clément, R., Z. Dörnyei, and K. A. Noels (1994). Motivation, self-confidence and group cohesion in the foreign language classroom. *Language Learning* 44, 415–448.

Clément, R., and R. C. Gardner (2001). Second Language Mastery. In W. P. Robinson, and H. Giles (Eds.). *The New Handbook of Language and Social Psychology* (pp. 489–504). New York: Wiley.

Clément, R., and B. Kruidenier (1983). Orientations on second language acquisition: 1. The effects of ethnicity, milieu, and their target language on their emergence. *Language Learning* 33, 273–291.

Clementi, L. (2008). NAJIT supports Iraqi interpreters. *Proteus* 17(3), 3–4.

Clements, G. (1985). The geometry of phonological features. *Phonology Yearbook* 2, 225–252.

Cluver, A. D. de V. (1992). Language planning models for a post-apartheid South Africa. *Language Problems & Language Planning* 16, 105–136.

Cluver, A. D. de V. (1991). A systems approach to language planning: The case of Namibia. *Language Problems & Language Planning* 15, 43–64.

Clyne, M. (2001). Can the shift from immigrant languages be reversed in Australia? In J. A. Fishman (Ed.), *Can Threatened Languages Be Saved?* (pp. 364–390). Clevedon, Avon, UK: Multilingual Matters.

Clyne, M. (1997a). Language policy in Australia achievements, disappointments, prospects. *Journal of Intercultural Studies* 18, 63–71.

Clyne, M. (1997b). Managing language diversity and second language programmes in Australia. *Current Issues in Language and Society* 4, 94–119.

Clyne, M. (1994). *Intercultural Communication at Work: Cultural Values in Discourse*. Cambridge: Cambridge University Press.

Clyne, M. (1991). Australia's language policies: Are we going backwards? *Australian Review of Applied Linguistics* S8, 3–22.

Clyne, M. (1987a). Constraints on code-switching: How universal are they? *Linguistics* 25, 739–764.

Clyne, M. (1987b). Cultural differences in the organization of academic texts: English and German. *Journal of Pragmatics* 11(2), 211–247.

Clyne, M. (1982). *Multilingual Australia*. Melbourne: River Seine.

Clyne, M., and S. Kipp (1997). Trends and changes in home language use and shift in Australia, 1986–1996. *Journal of Multilingual and Multicultural Development* 18(6), 451–473.

Cobarrubias, J. (1990). The spread of the Spanish language in the Americas. In L. Laforgue, and G. D. McCommell (Eds.), *Language Spread and Social Change: Dynamics and Measurement* (pp. 49–92). Ste-Foy, Québec: Les Presses de l'Universite Laval.

Cobarrubias, J. (1983). Ethical issues in status planning. In J. Cobarrubias, and J. A. Fishman (Eds.), *Progress in Language Planning* (pp. 41–85). Berlin: Mouton.

Cobb, T. (2005). The case for computer-assisted extensive reading. *Contact* 31, 55–83.

Cobb, T. (1997). Is there any measurable learning from hands-on concordancing? *System* 25(3), 301–315.

Coelho, E. (1991). *Caribbean Students in Canadian Schools, Book 2*. Toronto: Pippin.

Coelho, E. (1988). *Caribbean Students in Canadian Schools, Book 1*. Toronto: Carib-Can.

Coffey, S., and B. Street (2008). Narrative and identity in the "language learning project." *Modern Language Journal* 92(3), 452–464.

Cohen, A. D. (1998). *Strategies in Learning and Using a Second Language*. London: Longman.

Cohen, A. D. (1997). Developing pragmatic ability: Insights from accelerated study of Japanese. In H. M. Cook, K. Hijirida, and M. Tahara (Eds.), *New Trends and Issues in Teaching Japanese Language and Culture*. Technical Report #15 (pp. 133–159). Honolulu: University of Hawai'i, Second Language Teaching and Curriculum Center.

Cohen, A. D. (1996). Developing the ability to perform speech acts. *Studies in Second Language Acquisition* 18, 253–267.

Cohen, A. D. (1994). *Assessing Language Ability in the Classroom* (2nd ed.). Boston, MA: Heinle & Heinle.

Cohen, A. D., and E. Macaro (Eds.). (2007). *Language Learning Strategies: Thirty Years of Research and Practice*. New York: Oxford University Press.

Cohen, A. D., and E. Olshtain (1993). The production of speech acts by EFL learners. *TESOL Quarterly* 27, 33–56.

Cohen, A. D., and E. Olshtain (1981). Developing a measure of sociocultural competence: The case of apology. *Language Learning* 31, 113–134.

Cohen, A. D., and R. Shively (2007). Acquisition of requests and apologies in Spanish and French: Impact of study and strategy-building intervention. *Modern Language Journal* 91, 89–212.

Cole, M. (1996). *Cultural Psychology: A Once and Future Discipline*. Cambridge, MA: Bradford Books.

Coleman, M., and T. L. Liau (1975). A computer readability formula designed for machine scoring. *Journal of Applied Psychology* 60, 283–284.

Collier, V. P. (1992). A synthesis of studies examining long-term language minority student data on academic achievement. *Bilingual Research Journal* 16(1&2), 187–212.

Collins CoBuild English Language Dictionary (1987). London: CoBuild.

Collins, L. (2002). The roles of L1 influence and lexical aspect in the acquisition of temporal morphology. *Language Learning* 52, 43–94.

Collins, P. (1991). *Cleft and Pseudo-cleft Constructions in English*. London: Routledge.

Colomer, J. M. (1996). To translate or learn languages? An evaluation of social efficiency. *International Journal of the Sociology of Language* 121, 181–197.

CommuniCAT. University of Cambridge Language Examination Syndicate [Online]. Available: http://www.ucles.org.uk

Computerized Adaptive Placement Test (CAPT) informational website [Online]. Available: http://eric.ed.gov:80/ERICWebPortal/custom/portlets/recordDetails/detailmini.jsp.

Conklin, N., and M. Lourie (1983). *A Host of Tongues: Language Communities in the U.S.* New York: Free Press.

Conley, J. M., and W. M. O'Barr (1998). *Just Words: Law, Language, and Power*. Chicago: University of Chicago Press.

Conley, J. M., and W. M. O'Barr (1990). *Rules versus Relationships: The Ethnography of Legal Discourse*. Chicago: University of Chicago Press.

Connor, U. (2004). Intercultural rhetoric research: Beyond texts. *Journal of English for Academic Purposes* 3, 291–304.

Connor, U. (2002). New directions in contrastive rhetoric. *TESOL Quarterly* 36, 493–510.

Connor, U. (1996). *Contrastive Rhetoric: Cross-Cultural Aspects of Second-Language Writing*. New York: Cambridge University Press University Press.

Connor, U., and A. Mauranen (1999). Linguistic analysis of grant proposals: European Union research grants. *English for Specific Purposes* 18(1), 47–62.

Connor, U., and T. Upton (Eds.). (2004a). *Discourse in the Professions: Perspectives from Corpus Linguistics*. Philadelphia: John Benjamins.

Connor, U., and T. Upton (2004b). The genre of grant proposals: A corpus linguistic analysis. In U. Connor, and T. Upton (Eds.), *Applied Corpus Linguistics: A Multidimensional Perspective* (pp. 235–256). Amsterdam: Rodopi.

Connor, U., and T. Upton (2003). Linguistic dimensions of direct-mail letters. In C. Meyer, and P. Leistyna (Eds.), *Corpus Analysis: Language Structure and Language Use* (pp. 71–86). Amsterdam: Rodopi.

Connor-Linton, J. (2001). Authors style and world-view: A comparison of texts about nuclear arms policy. In S. Conrad, and D. Biber (Eds.), *Variation in English: Multi-Dimensional Studies* (pp. 84–93). London: Longman.

Connor-Linton, J., and E. Shohamy (2001). Register variation, oral proficiency sampling and the promise of multi-dimensional analysis. In S. Conrad, and D. Biber (Eds.). *Variation in English: Multi-Dimensional Studies* (pp. 124–137). London: Longman.

Conrad, S. (2001). Variation among disciplinary texts: A comparison of textbooks and journal articles. In S. Conrad, and D. Biber (Eds.), *Variation in English: Multi-Dimensional Studies* (pp. 94–107). London: Longman.

Conrad, S. (2000). Will corpus linguistics revolutionize grammar teaching in the 21st century? *TESOL Quarterly* 34(3), 548–560.

Conrad, S. (1999). The importance of corpus-based research for language teachers. *System* 27(1), 1–18.

Conrad, S. (1996). Investigating academic texts with corpus based techniques: An example from biology. *Linguistics and Education* 8, 299–326.

Conrad, S., and D. Biber (in press). *Real Grammar: A Corpus-Based Approach to English.* Pearson/Longman.

Conrad, S., and D. Biber (Eds.). (2001). *Variation in English: Multi-dimensional Studies.* Harlow, Essex: Longman.

Conrad, S., D. Biber, and G. Leech (2002). *Workbook for the Student Grammar of Spoken and Written English.* London: Longman.

Conrad, S., and L. Goldstein (1999). ESL student revision after teacher-written comments: Text, contexts, and individuals. *Journal of Second Language Writing* 8, 147–179.

Cook, G. (2003). *Applied Linguistics.* Oxford: Oxford University Press.

Cook, G., and G. Kasper (Eds.). (2005). Applied linguistics and real world issues [Special issue]. *Applied Linguistics* 26(4).

Cook, H. M. (1999). Language socialization in Japanese elementary schools: Attentive listening and reaction turns. *Journal of Pragmatics* 31, 1443–1465.

Cook, V. J., and M. Newson (1996). *Chomsky's Universal Grammar.* Oxford: Basil Blackwell.

Cook-Gumperz, J., and K. Hanna (1997). Nurses' work, women's work: Some recent issues of professional literacy and practice. In G. Hull (Ed.) *Changing Work, Changing Workers: Critical Perspectives on Language, Literacy and Skills* (pp. 316–334). Albany: State University of New York Press.

Cooper, R. L. (1989). *Language Planning and Social Change.* Cambridge: Cambridge University Press.

Cooper, R. L. (1982a). A framework for the study of language spread. In R. L. Cooper (Ed.), *Language Spread: Studies in Diffusion and Social Change* (pp. 5–36). Bloomington: Indiana University Press.

Cooper, R. L. (Ed.). (1982b). *Language Spread: Studies in Diffusion and Social Change.* Bloomington: Indiana University Press.

Cooper, R. L., and B. Danet (1980). Language in the melting pot: The sociolinguistic context for language planning in Israel. *Language Problems & Language Planning* 4, 1–28.

Cope, B., and M. Kalantzis (Eds.). (1993). *The Powers of Literacy: A Genre Approach to Teaching Writing.* London: Falmer.

Corder, S. P. (1978a). Applied linguistics in Edinburgh. Unpublished paper written for inclusion in a proposed series—*Trends in Linguistics*—edited by Thomas Sebeok, but never realized.

Corder, S. P. (1978b). Language-learner language. In J. Richards (Ed.), *Understanding second and foreign language learning* (pp. 71–92). Rowley, MA: Newbury House.

Corder, S. P. (1974). Teaching linguistics: Edinburgh. Unpublished report written to Norman Petterson, English Teaching Information Centre, British Counsel.

Corder, S. P. (1973). *Introducing Applied Linguistics.* Harmondsworth, UK: Penguin.

Corder, S. P. (1971). Idiosyncratic dialects and error analysis. *IRAL* 9(2), 147–160.

Corder, S. P. (1967). The significance of learners' errors. *IRAL* 5(4), 16–170.

Corona, D., and O. García (1996). English in Cuba: From imperialist design to imperative need. In J. A. Fishman, A. Conrad, and A. Rubal-Lopez (Eds.), *Post-Imperialist English* (pp. 85–112). Berlin: Mouton de Gruyter.

Cortes, V. (2004). Lexical bundles in published and student disciplinary writing: Examples from history and biology. *English for Specific Purposes* 23, 397–423.

Costa, A. (2005). Lexical access in bilingual production. In J. F. Kroll, and A. M. B. De Groot (Eds.), *Handbook of Bilingualism: Psycholinguistic Approaches* (pp. 308–325). New York: Oxford University Press.

Costa, A., and A. Caramazza (1999). Is lexical selection in bilingual speech production language-specific? Further evidence from Spanish-English and English-Spanish bilinguals. *Bilingualism: Language and Cognition* 2, 231–244.

Costa, A., M. Miozzo, and A. Caramazza (1999). Lexical selection in bilinguals: Do words in the bilingual's two lexicons compete for selection? *Journal of Memory and Language* 41, 365–397.

Coulthard, M. (1977). *An Introduction to Discourse Analysis*. London: Longman.

Coulthard, M. (Ed.). (1991). *Advances in Spoken Discourse*. London: Routledge.

Coulthard, M., and A. Johnson (2007). *An Introduction to Forensic Linguistics: Language in Evidence*. London: Routledge.

Council of Europe (2001). *A Common European Framework of Reference for Modern Languages: Learning, Teaching, Assessment*. Cambridge: Cambridge University Press.

Council of Europe (2000). *Common European Framework of Reference for Languages: Learning, Teaching, Assessment*. Language Policy Division, Strasbourg. Available: http://www.coe.int/t/dg4/linguistic/CADRE_EN.asp

Coupland, N., and A. Jaworski (2006). *The New Sociolinguistics Reader*. Houndmills, UK: Palgrave.

Cowan, R. (2008). *Teacher's Grammar of English*. Cambridge: Cambridge University Press.

Coxhead, A. (2000). A new academic word list. *TESOL Quarterly* 34(2), 213–238.

Craig, C. G. (1997). Language contact and language degeneration In F. Coulmas (Ed.), *Handbook of Sociolinguistics* (pp. 257–270). Oxford: Blackwell.

Craig, D. R. (1999). *Teaching Language and Literacy: Policies and Procedures for Vernacular Situations*. Georgetown, Guyana: Education and Development Services.

Craig, D. R. (1983). Teaching standard English to nonstandard speakers: Some methodological issues. *Journal of Negro Education* 52, 65–74.

Craig, D. R. (1976). Bidialectal education: Creole and standard in the West Indies. *International Journal of the Sociology of Language* 8, 93–134.

Craig, D. R. (1966). Teaching English to Jamaican Creole speakers: A model of a multi-dialect situation. *Language Learning* 16(1&2), 49–61.

Crandall, J. A. (1994). Strategic integration: Preparing language and content teachers for linguistically and culturally diverse classrooms. In J. Alatis (Ed.), *Strategic Interaction and Language Acquisition: Theory, Practice and Research* (pp. 225–274). Washington, DC: Georgetown University Press.

Crandall, J., and D. Kaufman (Ed.). (2002). *Content-Based Instruction in Higher Educational Settings*. Alexandria, VA: Teachers of English to Speakers of Other Languages.

Crawford, J. (2003). James Crawford's language policy website. Retrieved December 10, 2008, from http://www.languagepolicy.net/.

Creese, A., P. W. Martin, and N. H. Hornberger (Eds.). (2008). *Language Ecology: Encyclopedia of Language and Education* (vol. 9). New York: Springer.

Cresswell, J. W. (2005). *Research Design: Qualitative, Quantitative, and Mixed Methods Approaches* (2nd ed.). Thousand Oaks, CA: Sage.

Cresti, E., and M. Moneglia (Eds.). (2005). *C-ORAL-ROM: Integrated Reference Corpora for Spoken Romance Languages*. Amsterdam: John Benjamins.

Crooker, C. (1996). *The Art of Legal Interpretation: A Guide for Court Interpreters*. Portland, OR: Continuing Education Press, Portland State University.

Crookes, G., and S. M. Gass (Eds.). (1993). *Tasks in a Pedagogical Context: Integrating Theory and Practice*. Clevedon, Avon, UK: Multilingual Matters.

Crookes, G., and R. W. Schmidt (1991). Motivation: Reopening the research agenda. *Language Learning* 41, 469–512.

Crowley, S. (1998). *Composition in the University*. Pittsburgh, PA: University of Pittsburg.

Crowley, T. (2000). The language situation in Vanuatu. *Current Issues in Language Planning* 1(1), 47–132.

Crowley, T. (1994). Linguistic demography: Interpreting the 1989 census results in Vanuatu. *Journal of Multilingual and Multicultural Development* 15, 1–16.

Crowley, T. (1987). *Introdaksen long stadi blong Bislama (Kos buk wan, Kos buk tu, Buk blong ridim)* [*Introduction to the Study of Bislama (Course Book One, Course Book Two, Book of Readings)*]. Suva: Extension Services, University of the South Pacific.

Crystal, D. (2003). *English as a Global Language* (2nd ed.). Cambridge: Cambridge University Press.

Crystal, D. (Ed.). (1997). *The Cambridge Encyclopedia of Language* (2nd ed.). Cambridge: Cambridge University Press.

Crystal, D. (Ed.). (1987). *The Cambridge Encyclopedia of Language*. Cambridge: Cambridge University Press.

Csapó, B. (Ed.). (2002). *Az iskolai műveltség* [*School Literacy*]. Budapest: Osiris.

Csapó, B. (Ed.). (1998). *Az iskolai tudás* [*School Knowledge*]. Budapest: Osiris.

Csomay, E. (2005). Linguistic variation within university classroom talk: A corpus-based perspective. *Linguistics and Education* 15, 243–74.

Culpeper, J., and M. Kytö (In press). *Early Modern English Dialogues: Spoken Interaction as Writing*. Cambridge: Cambridge University Press.

Culpeper, J., and M. Kytö (2000). Data in historical pragmatics: Spoken interaction (re)cast as writing. *Journal of Historical Pragmatics* 1(2), 175–199.

Culpeper, J., and M. Kytö (1999). Modifying pragmatic force: Hedges in early modern English dialogues. In A. H. Jucker, G. Fritz, and F. Lebsanft (Eds.), *Historical Dialogue Analysis* (Pragmatics and Beyond New Series 66) (pp. 293–312). Amsterdam and Philadelphia: John Benjamins.

Cumming, A. (Ed.). (2006). *Goals for Academic Writing: ESL Students and Their Instructors*. Philadelphia: John Benjamins.

Cumming, A. (2000). Profile of H. H. Stern. In M. Byram (Ed.), *Routledge Encyclopedia of Language Teaching and Learning* (pp. 576–577). London: Routledge.

Cumming, A. (1998). Theoretical perspectives on writing. In W. Grabe et al. (Eds.). *Annual Review of Applied Linguistics: Vol. 18. Foundations of Second Language Teaching* (pp. 61–78). New York: Cambridge University Press.

Cumming, A. (ed.). (1994). Alternatives in TESOL research: Descriptive, interpretive, and ideological orientations. *TESOL Quarterly* 28, 673–703.

Cumming, A. (1989). Writing expertise and second language proficiency. *Language Learning* 39, 81–141.

Cumming, A., and J. Gill (1991). Learning ESL literacy among Indo-Canadian women. *Language, Culture and Curriculum* 4, 181–200.

Cummins, J. (2006). Identity texts: The imaginative construction of self through multiliteracies pedagogy. In O. Garcia, T. Skutnabb-Kangas, and M. Torres-Guzman (Eds.). *Imagining Multilingual Schools: Language in Education and Globalization*. Clevedon, Avon, UK: Multilingual Matters.

Cummins, J. (2000a). Biliteracy, empowerment, and transformative pedagogy. In J. Tinajero, and R. A. DeVillar (Eds.). *The Power of Two Languages 2000* (pp. 9–19). New York: McGraw-Hill.

Cummins, J. (2000b). *Language, Power and Pedagogy: Bilingual Children in the Crossfire*. Clevedon, Avon, UK: Multilingual Matters.

Cummins, J. (1999). Alternative paradigms in bilingual education research: Does theory have a place? *Educational Researcher* 28, 26–32, 41.

Cummins, J. (1998). Immersion education for the millennium: What have we learned from 30 years of research on second language immersion? In M. R. Childs, and R. M. Bostwick (Eds.). *Learning Through Two Languages: Research and Practice* (pp. 34–47). Second Katoh Gakuen International Symposium on immersion and bilingual education, Katoh Gakuen. Also available at http://www.carla.umn.edu.

Cummins, J. (1996). *Negotiating Identities: Education for Empowerment in a Diverse Society*. Ontario, CA: California Association for Bilingual Education.

Cummins, J. (1986). The role of primary language development in promoting success for language minority students. In D. Holt (Ed.), *Schooling and Language Minority Students: A Theoretical Framework* (pp. 3–49). Los Angeles: Evaluation, Dissemination and Assessment Center, California State University.

Cummins, J. (1984). *Bilingualism and Special Education: Issues in Assessment and Pedagogy*. Clevedon, Avon, UK: Multilingual Matters.

Cummins, J., and N. H. Hornberger (2008). (Eds.). *Encyclopedia of Language and Education* (vol. 5: *Bilingual Education*, 2nd ed.). New York: Springer.

Currie, A.-M., J. Cohan, and L. Zlatic (2000). Linguistic approaches in information retrieval in medical texts. In J. Alatis, H. Hamilton, and A.-H. Tan (Eds.). *Linguistics, Language and the Professions* (*Georgetown University Round Table on Languages and Linguistics, 2000*) (pp. 220–233). Washington, DC: Georgetown University Press.

Currie, P. (1998). Staying out of trouble: Apparent plagiarism and academic survival. *Journal of Second Language Writing* 7, 1–18.

Curry, M., and T. Lillis (2004). Multilingual scholars and the imperative to publish in English: Negotiating interests, demands, and rewards. *TESOL Quarterly* 38, 663–688.

Curtis, A., and M. Romney (2006). *Color, Race and English Language Teaching: Shades of Meaning*. Mahwah, NJ: Lawrence Erlbaum.

Cushing, S. (1994). *Communication Clashes and Aircraft Crashes*. Chicago: University of Chicago Press.

Cutler, A. (2000). Listening to a second language through the ears of a first. *Interpreting* 5, 1–23.

Cutler, A., D. Dahan, and W. van Donselaar (1997). Prosody in the comprehension of spoken language: Literature review. *Language and Speech* 40(2), 141–202.

Cutting, J. C., and V. S. Ferreira (1999). Semantic and phonological information flow in the production lexicon. *Journal of Experimental Psychology: Learning, Memory and Cognition* 25, 318–344.

Dąbrowska, E. (2008). Questions with long-distance dependencies: A usage-based perspective. *Cognitive Linguistics* 19, 391–425.

Dąbrowska, E. (2004). *Language, Mind, and Brain*. Washington, DC: Georgetown University Press.

Dąbrowska, E. (1997). The LAD goes to school: A cautionary tale for nativists. *Linguistics* 35, 735–66.

Dagenais, D., D. Moore, S. Lamarre, C. Sabatier, and F. Armand (2008). Linguistic landscape and language awareness. In E. Shohamy, and D. Gorter (Eds.), *Linguistic Landscape: Expanding the Scenery* (pp. 253–269). London: Routledge/Taylor & Francis Group.

Dahlmann, I., and S. Adolphs (in press). Multi-modal spoken corpus analysis and language description: The case of multi-word expressions. In P. Baker (Ed.), *Contemporary Approaches to Corpus Linguistics.* London: Continuum Press.

Dallas, A., and E. Kaan (2008). Second language processing of filler-gap dependencies by late learners. *Language and Linguistics Compass* 2, 372–388.

Dalphinis, M. (1991). The Afro-English Creole speech community. In S. Alladina, and V. Edwards (Eds.), *Multilingualism in the British Isles, Vol. 2: Africa, the Middle East and Asia* (pp. 42–56). London: Longman.

Dalphinis, M. (1985). *Caribbean and African Languages: Social History, Language, Literature and Education.* London: Karia Press.

Dam, H. V. (2004). Interpreters' notes: On the choice of language. *Interpreting* 6(1), 3–17.

Dam, H. V. (1998). Lexical similarity vs. lexical dissimilarity in consecutive interpreting. *The Translator* 4 (1), 49–68.

Damasio, A. R. (1994). *Descartes' Error: Emotion, Reason and the Human Brain.* New York: G. P. Putnam's Sons.

Damian, M. F., and R. C. Martin (1999). Semantic and phonological codes interact in single word production. *Journal of Experimental Psychology: Learning, Memory and Cognition* 25, 345–361.

Danet, B., and S. C. Herring (Eds.). (2003). The multilingual Internet: Language, culture and communication in instant messaging, email and chat [Special issue]. *Journal of Computer Mediated Communication* 9(1).

Daniels, H. (2007). Pedagogy. In H. Daniels, M. Cole, and J. V. Wertsch (Eds.), *The Cambridge Companion to Vygotsky* (pp. 307–331). Cambridge: Cambridge University Press.

Danks, J., G. M. Shreve, S. B. Fountain, and M. K. McBeath (Eds.). (1997). *Cognitive Processes in Translation and Interpreting.* Thousand Oaks, CA: Sage.

Daoust, D. (1992). The role of occupation as a factor of change in the terminological habits of a Montreal private business. *Revue de l'ACLA* 14(2) 71–93.

Da Pidgin Coup (1999). Pidgin and education. Unpublished position paper, University of Hawai'i. Available at http://www.hawaii.edu./sls/pidgin.html

Darò, V. (1997). Experimental studies on memory in conference interpretation. *Meta: Translators' Journal* 42(4), 622–628.

Darrah, C. (1997). Complicating the concept of skill requirements: Scenes from a workplace. In G. Hull (Ed.), *Changing Work, Changing Workers: Critical Perspectives on Language, Literacy and Skills* (pp. 249–272). Albany: State University of New York Press.

Darrah, C. (1990). Skills in context: An exploration in industrial ethnography. PhD dissertation, Stanford University, Stanford, CA.

Das Gupta, J. (1970). *Language Conflict and National Development.* Berkeley, CA: University of California Press.

Dasgupta, P. (1990). Editorial perspectives: A new decade and a new direction. *Language Problems & Language Planning* 14, 85–88.

Daud, B. (1996). Bahasa Indonesia: The struggle for a national language. *Working Papers in Linguistics—University of Melbourne* 16, 17–28.

Davies, A. (1999). *An Introduction to Applied Linguistics: From Practice to Theory.* Edinburgh: Edinburgh University Press.

Davies, A. (Ed.). (1997). Ethics in language testing [Special issue]. *Language Testing* 14(3).

Davies, A., and C. Elder (2004a). General introduction: Applied linguistics: Subject to discipline? In A. Davies, and C. Elder (Eds.), *The Handbook of Applied Linguistics* (pp. 1–15). Malden, MA: Blackwell.

Davies, A., and C. Elder (Eds.). (2004b). *The Handbook of Applied Linguistics.* Malden, MA: Blackwell.

Davies, B., and R. Harré (1990). Positioning: The discursive production of selves. *Journal for the Theory of Social Behaviour* 20(1), 43–63.

Davis, K. (1995). Qualitative theory and methods in applied linguistics research. *TESOL Quarterly* 29, 427–453.

Davison, C. (2007). Views from the chalkface: English language school-based assessment in Hong Kong. *Language Assessment Quarterly* 4, 37–68.

Davydov, V. V. (2004). *Problems of Developmental Instruction: A Theoretical and Experimental Psychological Study* (Trans. Peter Moxhay). Moscow: Akademiya Press.

Davydov, V. V. (1988). Problems of developmental teaching: The experience of theoretical and experimental psychological research. *Soviet Education* 30, 3–83.

Davydov, V. V., and A. K. Markova (1983). A concept of educational activity for school children. *Soviet Psychology* 21, 50–76.

Day, E. (2002). *Identity and the Young English Language Learner.* Clevedon, Avon, UK: Multilingual Matters.

Day, R., and J. Bamford (1998). *Extensive Reading in the Second Language Classroom.* New York: Cambridge University Press.

DeAngelis, G. (2007). *Third or Additional Language Acquisition.* Clevedon, Avon, UK: Multilingual Matters.

de Bot, C. L. J. (2008). The imaging of what in the multilingual mind. *Second Language Research* 24, 111–133.

de Bot, K. (2008). Editor's introduction. In M. McGroarty et al. (Eds.) and Guest Ed. K. de Bot, *Annual Review of Applied Linguistics: Vol. 28. Neurolinguistics and Cognitive Aspects of Language Processing* (pp. vii–xi). New York: Cambridge University Press.

de Bot, K. (2007a). Dynamic systems theory, life span development and language attrition. In B. Köpke et al. (Eds), *Language Attrition: Theoretical Perspectives* (pp. 53–68). Amsterdam and Philadelphia: John Benjamins.

de Bot, K. (2007b). Language teaching in a changing world. *Modern Language Journal* 91, 274–276.

de Bot, K. (2007c). The imaging of what in the multilingual mind? *Second Language Research* 24, 1.

de Bot, K. (2006). Applied linguistics in Europe. In M. Berns (Ed.), *Elsevier Encyclopedia on Language and Linguists: Applied Linguistics.* New York: Elsevier.

de Bot, K. (2004). The multilingual lexicon: Modeling selection and control. *International Journal of Multilingualism* 1, 17–32.

de Bot, K. (2002). Cognitive processes in bilinguals: Language choice and code-switching. In R. B. Kaplan (Ed.), *The Oxford Handbook of Applied Linguistics* (pp. 287–300). New York: Oxford University Press.

de Bot, K. (1997). Nelde's law revisited. In W. Wölck, and A. De Houwer (Eds.), *Recent Studies in Contact Linguistics* (pp. 51–59). Bonn: Duemmler.

de Bot, K. (1992). A bilingual production model: Levelt's speaking model adapted. *Applied Linguistics* 13, 1–24.

de Bot, K., and W. Lowie (2009). On the stability of representations in the multilingual lexicon. In M. Pütz, and L. Sicora (Eds.), *Proceedings: LAUD Conference 2008.* Amsterdam: John Benjamins.

de Bot, K., and R. Schreuder (1993). Word production and the bilingual lexicon. In R. Schreuder, and B. Weltens (Eds.), *The Bilingual Lexicon* (pp. 191–214). Amsterdam: John Benjamins.

de Bot, K., M. Verspoor, and W. Lowie (2007). A dynamic systems theory approach to second language acquisition. *Bilingualism, Language and Cognition* 10, 7–21.

Decker, K. (1995). Orthography development for Belize Creole. Paper presented at the Society for Caribbean Linguistics Conference, Georgetown, Guyana. Online at http://www.kriol.org.bz/LanguagePages/Language.

De Cock, S. (1998). A recurrent word combination approach to the study of formulae in the speech of native and non-native speakers of English. *International Journal of Corpus Linguistics* 3(1), 59–80.

De Cock, S., S. Granger, G. Leech, and T. McEnery (1998). An automated approach to the phrasicon of EFL learners. In S. Granger (Ed.), *Learner English on Computer* (pp. 67–79). London and New York: Addison Wesley Longman.

Deetz, S. (1995). *Transforming Communication, Transforming Business.* Cresskill, NJ: Hampton Press.

DeGraff, M. (2001a). Morphology in creole genesis: Linguistics and ideology. In M. Kenstowicz (Ed.), *Ken Hale: A Life in Language* (pp. 53–121). Cambridge, MA: MIT Press.

DeGraff, M. (2001b). On the origins of creoles: A Cartesian critique of neo-Darwinian linguistics. *Linguistic Typology* 5(2/3), 213–310.

DeGraff, M. (Ed.). (1999). *Language Creation and Language Change: Creolization, Diachrony and Development.* Cambridge, MA: MIT Press.

De Groot, A. M. B. (1995). Determinants of bilingual lexicosemantic organization. *Computer Assisted Language Learning* 8, 151–180.

De Groot, A. M. B. (1993). Word-type effects in bilingual processing tasks: Support for a mixed representational system. In R. Schreuder, and B. Weltens (Eds.). *The Bilingual Lexicon* (pp. 27–51). Amsterdam: John Benjamins.

De Groot, A. M. B., P. Delmaar, and S. J. Lupker (2000). The processing of interlexical homographs in a bilingual and a monolingual task: Support for nonselective access to bilingual memory. *Quarterly Journal of Experimental Psychology* 53A, 397–428.

De Groot, A. M. B., L. Dannenburg, and J. G. Van Hell (1994). Forward and backward word translation by bilinguals. *Journal of Memory and Language* 33, 600–629.

De Groot, A. M. B., and R. Poot (1997). Word translation at three levels of proficiency in a second language: The ubiquitous involvement of conceptual memory. *Language Learning* 47, 215–264.

de Haan, P. (1989). *Postmodifying Clauses in the English Noun Phrase: A Corpus-Based Study.* Amsterdam: Rodopi.

Dejean, Y. (1993). An overview of the language situation in Haiti. *International Journal of the Sociology of Language* 102, 73–84.

Déjean le Féal, K. (1998a). Acquisition d'une langue de travail supplémentaire: Expérience récente d'une interprète de conférence [Acquiring an extra working language: A conference interpreter's recent experience]. *Traduire* 178–179, 71–84.

Déjean le Féal, K. (1998b). Non nova, sed nove [New Perspectives on Old Issues]. *Interpreters' Newsletter* 8, 41–49.

Déjean le Féal, K. (1997). Simultaneous interpretation with "training wheels." *Meta: Translators' Journal* 42(4), 616–621.

Déjean le Féal, K. (1978). Lectures et improvisations: Incidences de la forme de l'énonciation sur la traduction simultanée [Reading and speaking spontaneously: Effects of the statement's form on simultaneous interpreting]. PhD dissertation, Université de la Sorbonne Nouvelle, Paris.

de Jongh, E. M. (1992). *An Introduction to Court Interpreting*. Lanham, MD: University Press of America.

de Klerk, G. (2000). Mother tongue instruction and military dictatorships: How fascist ideology can set the stage for human rights. Paper presented at the Colloquium on Revisiting the Mother Tongue Question in Language Policy, American Association for Applied Linguistics Annual Conference, Vancouver, BC., Canada.

de Klerk, V., and G. P. Barkhuizen (1998). Language policy in the SANDF: A case for biting the bullet? *Language Problems & Language Planning* 22, 215–236.

Dekydtspotter, L. (2001). The universal parser and interlanguage: Domain-specific organization in the comprehension of combien interrogatives in English-French interrogatives. *Second Language Research* 17, 91–143.

Dekydtspotter, L., and R. Sprouse (2001). Mental design and (second) language epistemology: Adjectival restrictions of wh-quantifiers and tense in English-French interlanguage. *Second Language Research* 17, 1–36.

Delabatie, B., and D. Bradley (1995). Resolving word boundaries in spoken French: Native and nonnative strategies. *Applied Psycholinguistics* 16(1), 59–81.

De la Fuente, M. J. (2003). Is SLA interactionist theory relevant to CALL? A study of the effects of computer-mediated interaction in L2 vocabulary acquisition. *Computer Assisted Language Learning* 16(1), 47–81.

Dell, G. S. (1988). The retrieval of phonological forms in production: Tests of predictions from a connectionist model. *Journal of Memory and Language* 27, 124–142.

Dell, G. S., and P. G. O'Seaghdha (1991). Mediated and convergent lexical priming in language production: A comment on Levelt, et al. *Psychological Review* 98, 604–614.

Denison, N. (1982). A linguistics ecology for Europe. *Folia Linguistica* 16(1), 1–16.

Denzin, N. K. (2008). The new paradigm dialogs and qualitative inquiry. *International Journal of Qualitative Studies in Education* 21(4), 15–25.

Denzin, N. K., and Y. S. Lincoln (2005a). Introduction: The discipline and practice of qualitative research. In N. K. Denzin, and Y. S. Lincoln (Eds.), *The Handbook of Qualitative Research* (3rd ed., pp. 1–32). Thousand Oaks, CA: Sage.

Denzin, N. K., and Y. S. Lincoln (Eds.). (2005b). *The Handbook of Qualitative Research* (3rd ed.). Thousand Oaks, CA: Sage.

Denzin, N. K., Y. S. Lincoln, and L. Smith (Eds.). (2008). *Handbook of Critical and Indigenous Methodologies*. Thousand Oaks: Sage.

Department of Education and Training (DEET). (1991). *Australia's Language: The Australian Language and Literacy Policy*. Canberra: Australian Government Printing Service.

Department of Employment, Education, Training and Youth Affairs (DEETYA). (1998). *Literacy for All: The Challenge for Australian Schools* (Australian School Monograph Series 1/98). Canberra: DEETYA.

Department of Employment, Education, Training and Youth Affairs (DEETYA). (1996). *Desert Schools*, 1. Canberra: DEETYA.

Depue, R. A., and J. V. Moronne-Strupinsky (2005). A neurobehavioral model of affiliative bonding: Implications for conceptualizing a human trait of affiliation. *Behavioral and Brain Sciences* 28, 313–395.

Der-Kévorkian, I. (2008, February). Delivering multilingual justice: A look at the International Criminal Tribunal for the Former Yugoslavia. *ATA Chronicle*, 24–26.

de Swaan, A. (1998). A political sociology of the world language system (1): The dynamics of language spread. *Language Problems & Language Planning* 22(11), 63–75.

de Villiers, J., and T. Roeper (1995). Relative clauses are barriers to *wh*-movement for young children. *Journal of Child Language* 22, 389–404.

Devlin, B., S. Harris, P. Black, and I. G. Enemburu (Eds.). (1995). *Australian Aborigines and Torres Strait Islanders: Sociolinguistic and Educational Perspectives: International Journal of the Sociology of Language* 1995(113), 5–6.

Devlin, K., and D. Rosenberg (1996). *Language at Work: Analyzing Communication Breakdown in the Workplace to Inform System Design*. Stanford, CA: Center for the Study of Language and Information.

Devonish, H. S. (2007). *Language and Liberation: Creole Language and Politics in the Caribbean* (2nd ed.). Kingston: Arawak.

Devonish, H. S., and K. Carpenter (2007). *Full Bilingual Education in a Creole Language Situation: The Jamaican Bilingual Primary Education Project* (Occasional Paper No. 35). St Augustine, Trinidad and Tobago: Society for Caribbean Linguistics.

DIALANG Computer Adaptive Test informational website [Online]. Available: http://www.jyu.fi/~dialang/general.html

Dicker, S. J. (2003). *Languages in America: A Pluralist View* (2nd Edition). Clevedon, Avon, UK: Multilingual Matters.

Dieu, M. (1991). National languages and rice cultivation in Northern Cameroon. *Terminologies Nouvelles* 6 (December), 7–12.

Dijkhoff, M. (1993). [Report on the Netherlands Antilles]. *Pidgins and Creoles in Education (PACE) Newsletter* 4, 1–2.

Dijkstra, A., E. De Bruijn, H. Schriefers, and S. Ten Brinke (2000). More on interlingual homograph recognition: Language intermixing versus explicitness of instruction. *Bilingualism: Language and Cognition* 3, 69–78.

Dijkstra, A., J. Grainger, and W. J. B. Van Heuven (1999). Recognizing cognates and interlingual homographs: The neglected role of phonology. *Journal of Memory and Language* 41, 496–518.

Dijkstra, A., M. Timmermans, and H. Schriefers (2000). On being blinded by your other language: Effects of task demands on interlingual homograph recognition. *Journal of Memory and Language* 42, 445–464.

Dijkstra, A., and W. J. B. Van Heuven (1998). The BIA model and bilingual word recognition. In J. Grainger, and A. Jacobs (Eds.), *Localist Connectionist Approaches to Human Cognition* (pp. 189–225). Hillsdale, NJ: Lawrence Erlbaum.

Dijkstra, A., W. J. B. Van Heuven, and J. Grainger (1998). Simulating cross-language competition with the bilingual interactive activation model. *Psychologica Belgica* 38, 177–197.

Dijkstra, A., H. Van Jaarsveld, and S. Ten Brinke (1998). Interlingual homograph recognition: Effects of task demands and language intermixing. *Bilingualism: Language and Cognition* 1, 51–66.

Dijkstra, T. (2005). Bilingual word recognition and lexical access. In J. F. Kroll, and A. M. B. De Groot (Eds.), *Handbook of Bilingualism: Psycholinguistic Approaches* (pp. 179–201). New York: Oxford University Press.

Dirven, R., and M. Pütz (1996–1997). *Sprachkonflikt* [Language conflict]. In P. H. Nelde et al. (Eds.), *Contact Linguistics: An International Handbook of Contemporary Research.* (pp. 684–691). Berlin: de Gruyter.

Dodson, C., and S. Thomas (1988). The effect of total L2 immersion education on concept development. *Journal of Multilingual and Multicultural Development* 9, 467–485.

Dodge, E., and G. Lakoff (2005). Image schemas: From linguistic analysis to neural grounding. In B. Hampe (Ed.), *From Perception to Meaning: Image Schemas in Cognitive Linguistics* (pp. 57–91). Berlin: Mouton de Gruyter.

Dogançay-Aktuna, S. (1995). An evaluation of the Turkish language reform after 60 years. *Language Problems & Language Planning* 19, 221–249.

Donahue, T. S. (2001). Language planning and the perils of ideological solipsism. In J. W. Tollefson (Ed.), *Language Policies in Education: Critical Issues*. Mahwah, NJ: Lawrence Erlbaum.

Dong, Y. R. (1998). Non-native speaker graduate students' thesis/dissertation writing in science: Self-reports by students and their advisors from two US institutions. *English for Specific Purposes* 17, 369–90.

Dong, Y. R., and Z. Cai (2007). Representing lexical semantics in the competition model: Argument specification satisfaction. *Foreign Language Teaching and Research* 39, 169–176.

Donley, K. M., and R. Reppen (2001). Using corpus tools to highlight academic vocabulary in SCLT. *TESOL Journal* 12, 7–12.

Dorian, N. (1994). Purism vs. compromise in language revitalization and language revival. *Language in Society* 23, 479–494.

Dorian, N. (1982). Language loss and maintenance in language contact situations. In R. D. Lambert, and B. F. Freed (Eds.), *The Loss of Language Skills* (pp. 44–59). Rowley, MA: Newbury House.

Dorian, N. (1981). *Language Death: The Life Cycle of a Scottish Gaelic Dialect*. Philadelphia: University of Pennsylvania Press.

Döring, M. (2002). "Vereint hinterm Deich"—Die metaphorische Konstruktion der Wiedervereinigung in der deutschen Presseberichterstattung zur Oderfut ["Unified behind the Dike"—The Metaphorical Construction of Unification in German Press Reports about the River Oder Flood] 1997. In A. Fill, H. Penz, and W. Trampe (Eds.), *Colourful Green Ideas* (pp. 255–273). Bern: Peter Lang.

Dörnyei, Z. (in press). *The Psychology of Second Language Acquisition*. Oxford: Oxford University Press.

Dörnyei, Z. (2007). *Research Methods in Applied Linguistics*. Oxford: Oxford University Press.

Dörnyei, Z. (2003). *Questionnaires in Second Language Research: Construction, Administration and Processing*. Mahwah, NJ: Lawrence Erlbaum.

Dörnyei, Z. (2001). *Motivational Strategies in the Language Classroom*. Cambridge: Cambridge University Press.

Dörnyei, Z. (1994). Motivation and motivating in the foreign language classroom. *Modern Language Journal* 78, 273–284.

Dörnyei, Z. (1990). Conceptualizing motivation in foreign language learning. *Language Learning* 40, 46–78.

Dörnyei, Z., and K. Csizèr (1998). Ten commandments for motivating language learners: Results of an empirical study. *Language Teaching Research* 2, 203–229.

Dörnyei, Z., K. Csizér, and N. Németh (2006). *Motivation, Language Attitudes and Globalisation: A Hungarian Perspective*. Clevedon, Avon, UK: Multilingual Matters.

Dörnyei, Z., and J. Kormos (1998). Problem-solving mechanisms in L2 communication. *Studies in Second Language Acquisition* 20, 349–385.

Dörnyei, Z., and I. Otto (1998). Motivation in action: A process model of L2 motivation. *Working Papers in Applied Linguistics* 4, 43–69.

Dörnyei, Z., and S. Thurrell (1992). *Conversation and Dialogues in Action*. New York: Prentice-Hall International.

Doughty, C. (1991). Second language instruction does make a difference: Evidence from an empirical study of SL relativization. *Studies in Second Language Acquisition* 13, 431–469.

Doughty, C., and M. H. Long (Eds.). (2003). *The Handbook of Second Language Acquisition.* Malden, MA: Blackwell.

Doughty, C., and T. Pica (1986). "Information gap" tasks: Do they facilitate second language acquisition? *TESOL Quarterly* 20, 305–325.

Doughty, C., and J. Williams (1998a.) Pedagogical choices in focus on form. In C. Doughty, and J. Williams (Eds.), *Focus on form in classroom second language acquisition* (pp. 197–261). Cambridge: Cambridge University Press.

Doughty, C., and J. Williams (Eds.). (1998b). *Focus on Form in Classroom Second Language Acquisition.* New York: Cambridge University Press.

Drechsel, E. J. (1997). *Mobilian Jargon: Linguistic and Sociohistorical Aspects of a Native American Pidgin.* Oxford: Clarendon Press.

Dressler, C., and M. Kamil (2006). First- and second-language literacy. In D. August, and T. Shanahan (Eds.), *Developing Literacy in Second-Language Learners* (pp. 197–241). Mahwah, NJ: L. Lawrence Erlbaum.

Dua, H. (1996). The politics of language conflict: Implications for language planning and political theory. *Language Problems & Language Planning* 20, 1–17.

Dubin, F., and E. Olshtain (2008). *Course Design: Developing Programs and Materials for Language Learning.* Cambridge: Cambridge University Press.

Dubrowska, E. (2008). Questions with long-distance dependencies: A usage-based Prespective. *Congnitive Linguistics* 19, 391–425.

Dudley-Evans, T., and M. St. John (1998). *Developments in ESP: A Multi-Disciplinary Approach.* Cambridge: Cambridge University Press.

Dueñas, M. (2004). A description of prototype models for content-based instruction in higher education. *BELLS: Barcelona English Language and Literature Studies* 12. Retrieved February 2, 2009, from http://www.publicacions.ub.es/revistes/bells12/articulos.asp?codart=33.

Duff, P. A. (2008). *Case Study Research in Second Language Acquisition.* New York: Lawrence Erlbaum/Taylor & Francis.

Duff, P. A. (2006). Beyond generalizability: Contextualization, complexity and credibility in applied linguistics research. In M. Chalhoub-Deville, C. Chapelle, and P. Duff (Eds.), *Inference and Generalizability in Applied Linguistics: Multiple Research Perspectives* (pp. 65–95). Amsterdam: John Benjamins.

Duff, P. A. (2002a). Research approaches in applied linguistics. In R. B. Kaplan (Ed.), *The Oxford Handbook of Applied Linguistics* (pp 13–23). New York: Oxford University Press.

Duff, P. A. (2002b). The discursive co-construction of knowledge, identity and difference: An ethnography of communication in the high school mainstream. *Applied Linguistics* 23, 289–322.

Duff, P. A. (2001). Language, literacy, content and (pop) culture: Challenges for ESL students in mainstream courses. *Canadian Modern Language Review* 58(1), 103–133.

Duff, P. A. (1995). An ethnography of communication in immersion classrooms in Hungary. *TESOL Quarterly* 29, 505–537.

Duff, P. A. (1993). Tasks and interlanguage performance: An SLA perspective. In G. Crookes, and S. M. Gass (Eds.), *Tasks and Language Learning: Integrating Theory and Practice* (pp. 57–95). Clevedon, Avon, UK: Multilingual Matters.

Duff, P. A., and N. H. Hornberger (Eds.). (2008). *Language Socialization: Encyclopedia of Language and Education* (vol. 8). New York: Springer.

Dunkel, P. (1999). Research and development of a computer-adaptive test of listening comprehension in the less-commonly taught language Hausa. In M. Chalhoub-Deville

(Ed.), *Issues in Computer-Adaptive Testing of Reading Proficiency* (pp. 119–121). Cambridge: Press Syndicate of the University of Cambridge.

Dunkel, P. (1998). Considerations in developing or using second/foreign language proficiency computer-adaptive test. *Language Learning and Technology* 2, 77–93.

Dunkel, P. (1997). Computer-adaptive testing of listening comprehension: A blueprint for CAT development. *Language Teacher Online* 21, 10.

Dunkel, P. (1991). The effectiveness research on computer-assisted instruction and computer-assisted language learning. In P. Dunkel (Ed.), *Computer-Assisted Language Learning and Testing: Research Issues and Practice* (pp. 5–36). New York: Newbury House.

Dupoux, E., C. Paillier, N. Sebastien, and J. Mehler (1997). A destressing deafness in French? *Journal of Memory and Language* 36, 406–421.

Durie, A. (1999). Emancipatory Mäori education: Speaking from the heart. In S. May (Ed.) *Indigenous Community-based Education* (pp. 67–78). Clevedon, Avon, UK: Multilingual Matters.

Dussias, P. E. (2003). Syntactic ambiguity resolution in L2 learners: Some effects of bilinguality on LI and L2 processing strategies. *Studies in Second Language Acquisition* 25, 529–557.

Dussias, P. E., and N. Sagarra (2007). The effect of exposure on syntactic parsing in Spanish-English bilinguals. *Bilingualism: Language and Cognition* 10, 101–116.

Dutcher, N. (2004). *Expanding Educational Opportunity in Linguistically Diverse Societies* (2nd ed.). Washington, DC: Center for Applied Linguistics.

Dutton, T. E. (1983). Hiri-Motu—Iena Sivarai. Port Moresby: University of Papua New Guinea Press.

Duyck, W., E. Van Assche, D. Drieghe, and R. J. Hartsuiker (2007). Visual word recognition by bilinguals in a sentence context: Evidence for nonselective access. *Journal of Experimental Psychology: Learning, Memory and Cognition* 33, 663–679.

Eades, D. (in press). Sociolinguistics and the law. In R. Mesthrie, and W. Wolfram (Eds.), *Cambridge Handbook of Sociolinguistics*. Cambridge: Cambridge University Press.

Eades, D. (2003). Participation of second language and second dialect speakers in the legal system. In M. McGroarty et al. (Eds.), *Annual Review of Applied Linguistics: Vol. 23. Language Contact and Change* (pp. 113–133). New York: Cambridge University Press.

Eades, D. (1997). Language in court: The acceptance of linguistic evidence about indigenous Australians in the criminal justice system. *Australian Aboriginal Studies* 1, 15–27.

Eades, D. (1994). A case of communicative clash: Aboriginal English and the legal system. In J. Gibbons (Ed.), *Language and the Law* (pp. 234–264). London: Longman.

Eades, D., S. Jacobs, E. Hargrove, and T. Menacker (2006). Pidgin, local identity and schooling in Hawai'i. In S. J. Nero (Ed.), *Dialects, Englishes, Creoles and Education* (pp. 149–163). Mahwah, NJ: Lawrence Erlbaum.

Eagleson, R. (1994). Forensic analysis of personal written texts. In J. Gibbons (Ed.), *Language and the Law* (pp. 362–373). London: Longman.

Early, M. (2001). Language and content in social practice: A case study. *Canadian Modern Language Review* 58(1), 156–179.

Early, M., B. Mohan, and H. Hooper (1989). The Vancouver School Board Language and Content Project. In J. Esling (Ed.), *Multicultural Education and Policy: ESL in the 1990s*. Toronto: Ontario Institute for Studies in Education Press.

Eastman, C. A. (1983a). *Language Planning: An Introduction*. San Francisco: Chandler and Sharp.

Eastman, C. A. (1983b). Language-planning method. In *Language Planning: An Introduction* (pp. 177–203). San Francisco: Chandler and Sharp.

Eckman, F. R. (2008). Typological markedness and second language phonology. In J. G. Hansen Edwards, and M. L. Zampini (Eds.), *Phonology and Second Language Acquisition* (pp. 95–115). Philadelphia: John Benjamins.

Eckman, F. R. (2004). From phonetic differences to constraint rankings: Research on second language phonology. *Studies in Second Language Acquisition* 26, 513–550.

Edelman, G. M. (1987). *Neural Darwinism: The Theory of Neuronal Group Selection*. New York: Basic Books.

Edge, J., and K. Richards (1998). May I see your warrant, please? Justifying outcomes in qualitative research. *Applied Linguistics* 19, 334–356.

Edmondson, W., J. House, G. Kasper, and B. Stemmer (1984). Learning the pragmatics of discourse: A project report. *Applied Linguistics* 5, 113–127.

Educational Testing Service (ETS). (1998). *Computer-Based TOEFL: Score User Guide*. Princeton, NJ: Educational Testing Service.

Edwards, A. B. (1995). *The Practice of Court Interpreting*. Amsterdam/Philadelphia: John Benjamins.

Edwards, H., M. Wesche, S. Krashen, R. Clément, and B. Kruidenier (1984). Second language acquisition through subject-matter learning: A study of sheltered psychology classes at the University of Ottawa. *Canadian Modern Language Review* 41(2), 268–282.

Edwards, J. (2001). The ecology of language revival. *Current Issues in Language Planning* 2(2–3), 231–241.

Edwards, J. (1993). Language revival: Specifics and generalities. *Studies in Second Language Acquisition* 15, 107–113.

Edwards, J. (1992). Sociopolitical aspects of language maintenance and loss: Towards a typology of minority language situations. In W. Fase, K. Jaspaert, and S. Kroon (Eds.), *Maintenance and Loss of Minority Languages* (pp. 37–54). Philadelphia: John Benjamins.

Edwards, J. (1985). *Language, Society and Identity*. Oxford: Basil Blackwell.

Edwards, V. (1979). *The West Indian Language Issue in British Schools: Challenges and Responses*. London: Routledge & Kegan Paul.

Edwards, W. (1983). Code selection and code shifting in Guyana. *Langauge in Society* 12, 295–311.

Eggington, W. G. (1997). The English language metaphors we live by. In W. Eggington, and H. Wren (Eds.), *Language Policy: Dominant English, Pluralist Challenges* (pp. 29–46). Amsterdam: John Benjamins.

Eggington, W. G. (1994). Language policy and planning in Australia. In W. Grabe et al. (Eds.), *Annual Review of Applied Linguistics: Vol. 14. Language Planning and Policy* (pp. 137–155). New York: Cambridge University Press.

Eggington, W. G. (1985). Toward a language plan for the Southern California area: The Hacienda-La Puente sociolinguistic survey. PhD dissertation., University of Southern California, Los Angeles.

Eggington, W., and R. B. Baldauf, Jr. (1990). Towards evaluating the Aboriginal bilingual education program in the Northern Territory. In R. B. Baldauf, Jr., and A. Luke (Eds.), *Language Planning in Australasia and the South Pacific* (pp. 89–105). Clevedon, Avon, UK: Multilingual Matters.

Eggins, S. (1994). *An Introduction to Systemic Functional Linguistics*. London: Pinter.

Eggins, S., and D. Slade (1997). *Analyzing Casual Conversation*. London: Cassell.

Egi, T. (2007). Recasts, learners' interpretations and L2 development. In A. Mackey (Ed.), *Conversational Interaction in Second Language Acquisition* (pp. 249–267). Oxford: Oxford University Press.

Ehrlich, S. (1997). Gender as social practice. *Studies in Second Language Acquisition* 19, 421–446.

Eisner, F., and J. McQueen (2006). Perceptual learning in speech: Stability over time. *JASA* 4, 1950–1953.

Ellis, N. C. (2008). Usage-based and form-focused language acquisition: The associative learning of constructions, learned attention and the limited L2 endstate. In P. Robinson, and N. Ellis (Eds.), *Handbook of Cognitive Linguistics and Second Language Acquisition* (pp. 372–405). New York: Routledge.

Ellis, N. C. (2007). The associative–cognitive CREED. In B. VanPatten, and J. Williams (Eds.), *Theories of Second Language Acquisition*. Mahwah, NJ: Lawrence Erlbaum.

Ellis, N. C. (2005). At the interface: Dynamic interactions of explicit and implicit language knowledge. *Studies in Second Language Acquisition* 27, 305–352.

Ellis, N. C. (2003). Constructions, chunking, and connectionism: The emergence of second language structure. In C. Doughty, and M. Long (Eds.), *Handbook of Second Language Acquisition* (pp. 63–103). Oxford: Blackwell.

Ellis, N. C. (1999). Cognitive approaches to SLA. In W. Grabe, et al (Eds.) *Annual Review of Applied Linguistics* 19. *A Survey of Applied Linguistics* (pp. 22–42). New York: Cambridge University Press.

Ellis, N. C. (1998). Emergentism, connectionism and language learning. *Language Learning* 48, 631–644.

Ellis, N. C. (1996). Sequencing in SLA: Phonological memory, chunking, and points of order. *Studies in Second Language Acquisition* 18, 91–126.

Ellis, N. C., and R. Schmidt (1998). Rules or associations in the acquisition of morphology? The frequency by regularity interaction in human and PDP learning of morphosyntax. *Language and Cognitive Processes* 13, 307–336.

Ellis, N. C., and R. Schmidt (1997). Morphology and long-distance dependencies: Laboratory research illuminating the A in SLA. *Studies in Second Language Acquisition* 19, 145–171.

Ellis, N. C., R. Simpson-Vlach, and C. Maynard (2008). Formulaic language in native and second-language speakers: Psycholinguistics, corpus linguistics and TESOL. *TESOL Quarterly* 42, 375–396.

Ellis, R. (2007). The differential effects of corrective feedback on two grammatical structures. In A. Mackey (Ed.), *Conversational Interaction in Second Language Acquisition: A Series of Empirical Studies* (pp. 339–360). Oxford: Oxford University Press.

Ellis, R. (2003). *Task-Based Language Learning and Teaching*. Oxford: Oxford University Press.

Ellis, R. (1994). *The Study of Second Language Acquisition*. Oxford: Oxford University Press.

Ellis, R. (1992). Learning to communicate in the classroom: A study of two language learners' requests. *Studies in Second Language Acquisition* 14, 1–23.

Ellis, R. (1990). *Instructed second language acquisition*. Cambridge: Basil Blackwell.

Ellis, R., and G. Barkhuizen (Eds.). (2005). *Analysing Learner Language*. Oxford: Oxford University Press.

Ellis, R., S. Loewen, and R. Erlam (2006). Implicit and explicit corrective feedback and the acquisition of L2 grammar. *Studies in Second Language Acquisition* 28, 339–368.

Ellis, R., Y. Tanaka, and A. Yamazaki (1994). Classroom interaction, comprehension and the acquisition of L2 word meanings. *Language Learning* 44(4), 449–491.

Elman, J. L. (1995). Language as a dynamical system. In R. Port, and T. van Gelder (Eds.), *Mind in Motion: Explorations of the Dynamics of Cognition* (pp. 195–225). Cambridge, MA: MIT Press.

Elman, J. L. (1993). Learning and development in neural networks: The importance of starting small. *Cognition* 48, 71–99.

Elsasser, N., and P. Irvine (1987). English and Creole: The dialectics of choice in a college writing program. In I. Shor (Ed.), *Freire for the Classroom: A Sourcebook for Literacy Teaching* (pp. 129–149). Portsmouth, MA: Boynton/Cook.

Elston-Güttler, K. E., and T. C. Gunter (2009). Fine-tuned: Phonology and semantics affect first- to second-language zooming. In *Journal of Cognitive Neuroscience* 21(1), 180–196.

Elugbe, B. O. (1994). Minority language development in Nigeria: A situation report on Rivers and Bendel states. In R. Fardon, and G. Furniss (Eds.), *African Languages: Development and the State* (pp. 62–75). London: Routledge.

Embretson, S. E. (1985). Multicomponent content trait models for test design. In S. E. Embertson (Ed.), *Test Design: Developments in Psychology and Psychometrics* (pp. 195–218). Orlando, FL: Academic Press.

Emig, J. (1971). *The Composing Process of Twelfth Graders*. Urbana, IL: National Council of Teachers of English.

Emmorey, K., H. B. Borinstein, R. Thompson, and T. H. Gollan (2008). Bimodal bilingualism. *Bilingualism: Language and Cognition* 11, 43–61.

Engeström, Y. (1993). Developmental studies of work as a testbench of activity theory: The case of primary care medical practice. In S. Chaikin, and J. Lave (Eds.), *Understanding Practice* (pp. 64–103). Cambridge: Cambridge University Press.

Engeström, Y. (1987). *Learning by Expanding: An Activity-Theoretical Approach to Developmental Research*. Helsinki: Orienta-Konsultiti.

English Language Services (1964). *English 900*. New York: Collier Macmillan.

Englund Dimitrova, B. (2005). Literal translation in the translation process of professional translators. In K. Aijmer, and C. Alvstad (Eds.), *New Tendencies in Translation Studies* (pp. 29–39). Göteborg: Göteborg University.

Enkvist, N. E. (1997). Why we need contrastive rhetoric. Alter*nation* 4(1), 188–206.

Enninger, W., and L. Haynes (1984). Language ecology—a revived paradigm? In W. Enninger, W. Haynes, and L. Haynes (Eds.), *Studies in Language Ecology* (pp. 235–236). Wiesbaden, Germany: Steiner.

Entwisle, D. R. (1971). Developmental sociolinguistics: Inner-city children. *American Journal of Sociology* 74, 37–49.

Enyedi, Á., and P. Medgyes (1998). ELT in Central and Eastern Europe. *Language Teaching* 31, 1–12.

Epstein, S. (2007). *Inclusion: The Politics of Difference in Medical Research*. Chicago: University of Chicago Press.

Epstein, S., S. Flynn, and G. Martohardjono (1996). Second language acquisition: Theoretical and experimental issues in contemporary research. *Behavioral and Brain Sciences* 19, 677–758.

Ericsson, K. A., R. T. Krampe, and C. Tesch-Römer (1993). The role of deliberate practice in the acquisition of expert performance. *Psychological Review* 100, 363–406.

Erlich, S., and J. Sidnell (2006). "I think that's not an assumption you ought to make": Challenging presuppositions in inquiry testimony. *Language in Society* 35, 655–676.

Etzioni, A. (1969). *The Semi-Professions and Their Organization: Teachers, Nurses and Social Workers*. New York: Free Press.

Eubank, L. (1993/1994). On the transfer of parametric values in L2 development. *Language Acquisition* 3, 183–208.

Eubank, L. (1993). Optionality and the initial state in L2 development. In B. D. Schwartz, and T. Hoekstra (Eds.), *Language Acquisition Studies in Generative Grammar* (pp. 369–388). Philadelphia: John Benjamins.

Eubank, L., J. Bischof, A. Huffstutler, P. Leek, and C. West (1997). "Tom eats slowly cooked eggs": Thematic verb raising in L2 knowledge. *Language Acquisition* 6, 171–199.

Europeans and Languages (2005). European Commission, Eurobarometer, Brussels. Retrieved March 20, 2005, from http://europa.eu.int/comm/public_opinion/archives/ebs/ebs_237.en.pdf

Europeans and Languages: A Eurobarometer Special Survey (2001). European Commission, Directorate-General for Education and Culture, Brussels. Retrieved March 20, 2005, from http://europa.eu.int/comm/dgs/education_culture/index_en.htm

Evans, C. (1996). Ethnolinguistic vitality, prejudice, and family language transmission. *Bilingual Research Journal* 20, 177–207.

Extra, G. (1995). Ethnic minorities, language diversity and home language instruction: Crosscultural perspectives on the Netherlands. In T. F. Shannon, and J. P. Snapper (Eds.), *Berkeley Conference on Dutch Linguistics 1993: Dutch Linguistics in a Changing Europe* (pp. 17–39). Lanham, MD: University Press of America.

Faerch, C., and G. Kasper (1986). The role of comprehension in second language learning. *Applied Linguistics* 7(3), 257–274.

Færch, C., and G. Kasper (Eds.). (1983). *Strategies of Interlanguage Communication*. London: Longman.

Fairclough, N. (2003). *Analysing Discourse: Textual Analysis for Social Research*. London: Routledge.

Fairclough, N. (1995a). *Critical Discourse Analysis*. New York: Longman.

Fairclough, N. (1995b). *Media Discourse*. London: Edward Arnold.

Fairclough, N. (1989). *Language and Power*. Longman: New York.

Falbo, C. (1998). Analyse des erreurs en interprétation simultanée [Error analysis in simultaneous interpreting]. *Interpreters' Newsletter* 8, 107–120.

Falbo, C. (1995). Interprétation consécutive et exercices préparatoires [Consecutive interpreting and preparatory exercises]. *Interpreters' Newsletter* 6, 87–91.

Faltis, C., and S. Hudelson (1998). *Bilingual Education in Elementary and Secondary School Communities: Toward Understanding and Caring*. Needham Heights, MA: Allyn and Bacon.

Farhady, H. (1982). Measures of language proficiency from the learner's perspective. *TESOL Quarterly*, 16, 43–59.

Farrell, T., and C. Mallard (2006). The use of reception strategies by learners of French as a foreign language. *Modern Language Journal* 90(3), 338–352.

Fasold, R. (1984). *The Sociolinguistics of Society*. Oxford: Basil Blackwell.

Faure, E. (2000). Report: Guadeloupe. *Pidgins and Creoles in Education (PACE) Newsletter* 11, 3–4.

Feldman, C. F., A. Stone, and B. Renderer (1990). Stage, transfer and academic achievement in dialect-speaking Hawaiian adolescents. *Child Development* 61, 472–484.

Félix-Brasdefer, J. C. (2007). Pragmatic development in the Spanish as a foreign language classroom: A cross-sectional study of learner requests. *Intercultural Pragmatics* 4, 253–286.

Félix-Brasdefer, J. C. (2004). Interlanguage refusals: Linguistic politeness and length of residence in the target community. *Language Learning* 54, 587–653.

Fellman, J. (1974). The role of Eliezer Ben Yehuda in the revival of the Hebrew language: An assessment. In J. Fishman (Ed.), *Advances in Language Planning* (pp. 427–455). The Hague: Mouton.

Felser, C., and L. Roberts (2007). Processing wh- dependencies in a second language: A cross-modal priming study. *Second Language Research* 23, 9–36.

Fenton, S. (1997). The role of the interpreter in the adversarial courtroom. In S. E. Carr, R. Roberts, A. Dufour, and D. Steyn (Eds.), *The Critical Link: Interpreters in the Community* (pp. 29–34). Amsterdam/Philadelphia: John Benjamins.

Ferguson, C. A. (1982). Religious factors in language spread. In R. L. Cooper (Ed.), *Language Spread: Studies in Diffusion and Social Change* (pp. 95–106). Bloomington: Indiana University Press.

Ferguson, C. A. (1975). Towards a characterization of English foreigner talk. *Anthropological Linguistics* 17, 1–14.

Ferguson, C. A. (1971). Absence of copula and the notion of simplicity: A study of normal speech, baby talk, foreigner talk and pidgins. In D. Hymes (Ed.), *Pidginization and Creolization of Languages* (pp. 141–150). Cambridge: Cambridge University Press.

Ferguson, G. (2006). *Language Planning and Education*. Edinburgh: Edinburgh University Press.

Ferguson, G. (2001). "If you pop over there": A corpus-based study of conditionals in medical discourse. *English for Specific Purposes* 20, 61–82.

Ferrara, K. W. (1994). *Therapeutic Ways with Words*. New York: Oxford University Press.

Ferreira, M. (2005). A concept-based approach to writing instruction: From the abstract concept to the concrete performance. PhD dissertation, Pennsylvania State University, University Park.

Ferrier, K. (n.d.). Educational system on the island of Aruba. Retrieved February, 25, 2005, from http://minority.homac.at/schoolsys/aruba.html

Ferris, D. (2002). *Treatment of Error in Second Language Student Writing*. Ann Arbor: University of Michigan Press.

Ferris, D. (1999). The case for grammar correction in L2 writing classes: A response to Truscott (1996). *Journal of Second Language Writing* 8, 1–11.

Ferris, D. (1997). Influence of teacher commentary on student revision. *TESOL Quarterly* 31, 315–339.

Ferris, D., and J. Hedgcock (2004). *Teaching ESL Composition* (2nd ed.). Mahwah, NJ: Lawrence Erlbaum.

Fesl, E. (1987). Language death among Australian languages. *Australian Review of Applied Linguistics* 10(2), 12–22.

Festinger, N. (1999). When is a team not a team? *Proteus* 8(3/4), 6–7.

Fettes, M. (1998). Life on the edge: Canada's aboriginal languages under official bilingualism. In T. Ricento, and B. Burnaby (Eds.), *Language and Politics in the United States and Canada: Myths and Realities* (pp. 117–149). Mahwah, NJ: Lawrence Erlbaum.

Fettes, M. (1997). Language planning and education. In R. Wodak, and D. Corson (Eds.), *Encyclopedia of Language and Education* (8 vols.): *Language Policy and Political Issues in Education* (vol. 1, pp. 13–22). Dordrecht, Netherlands: Kluwer Academic.

Field, J. (2000). "Not waving but drowning": Do we measure the depth of the water or throw a lifebelt? *ELT Journal* 54(2), 186–195.

Field, J. (1998). Skills and strategies: Towards a new methodology for listening. *ELT Journal* 52(2), 110–118.

Fill, A. (Ed.). (1996). *Sprachökologie und Ökolinguistik* [*Language Ecology and Ecolinguistics*]. Tübingen: Stauffenburg.

Fill, A. (1993). *Ökolinguistik: Eine Einführung* [*An Introduction to Ecolinguistics*]. Tübingen: Narr.

Fill, A., H. Penz, and W. Trampe (Eds.). (2002). *Colourful Green Ideas*. Bern: Peter Lang.

Finegan, E., and J. Rickford (Eds.). (2004). *Language in the U.S.A.* New York: Cambridge University Press.

Fiori, M. L. (2005). The development of grammatical competence through synchronous computer-mediated communication. *CALICO Journal* 22(3), 567–602.

Fischer, K. (1992). Educating speakers of Caribbean English in the United States. In J. Siegel (Ed.), *Pidgins, Creoles and Nonstandard Dialects in Education* (pp. 99–123). Melbourne: Applied Linguistics Association of Australia.

Fischer, S. A. (1992). Homogeneity in Old Rapanui. *Oceanic Linguistics* 31(2), 181–190.

Fisher, S. (1995). *Nursing Wounds: Nurse Practitioners, Doctors, Women Patients and the Negotiation of Meaning.* New Brunswick, NJ: Rutgers University Press.

Fisher, S., and A. D. Todd (Eds.). (1983). *The Social Organization of Doctor Patient Communication.* Washington, DC: Center for Applied Linguistics.

Fishman, J. A. (Ed.). (2001). *Can Threatened Languages Be Saved?* Clevedon, Avon, UK: Multilingual Matters.

Fishman, J. A. (Ed.). (2000). *Can Threatened Languages Be Saved? "Reversing Language Shift" Revisited.* Clevedon, Avon, UK: Multilingual Matters.

Fishman, J. A. (1994). Critiques of language planning: A minority language perspective. *Journal of Multilingual and Multicultural Development* 15, 91–99.

Fishman, J. A. (1993). The content of positive ethnolinguistic consciousness. *Geolinguistics* 19, 16–26.

Fishman, J. A. (1992). Forward: What can sociology contribute to the sociolinguistic enterprise? In G. Williams (Ed.), *Sociolinguistics: A Sociological Critique* (pp. vii–ix). London: Routledge.

Fishman, J. A. (1991a). Mäori: The native language of New Zealand. In J. A. Fishman (Ed.), *Reversing Language Shift* (pp. 230–251). Clevedon, Avon, UK: Multilingual Matters.

Fishman, J. A. (1991b). *Reversing Language Shift: Theoretical and Empirical Foundations of Assistance to Threatened Languages.* Clevedon, Avon, UK: Multilingual Matters.

Fishman, J. A. (1991c). Theoretical recapitulation: What is reversing language shift (RLS) and how can it succeed? In J. Fishman (Ed.), *Reversing Language Shift* (pp. 381–419). Clevedon, Avon, UK: Multilingual Matters.

Fishman, J. A. (1988). Language spread and language policy for endangered languages. In P. H. Lowenberg (Ed.), *Language Spread and Language Policy Issues: Implications and Case Studies (Georgetown University Round Table on Languages and Linguistics)* (pp. 1–15). Washington, DC: Georgetown University Press.

Fishman, J. A. (1980). Prefatory notes. In P. H. Nelde (Ed.) *Languages in Contact and in Conflict* (p. xi). Wiesbaden, Germany: Steiner.

Fishman, J. A. (1977). The spread of English as a new perspective for the study of language maintenance and language shift. In J. A. Fishman, R. L. Cooper, and A. W. Conrad (Eds.), *The Spread of English: The Sociology of English as an Additional Language* (pp. 108–136). Rowley, MA: Newbury House.

Fishman, J. A. (Ed.) (1974). *Advances in Language Planning.* The Hague: Mouton.

Fishman, J. A. (1972). *The Sociology of Language.* Rowley, MA: Newbury House.

Fishman, J. A. (Ed.). (1971). *Advances in the Sociology of Language* (2 vols.). The Hague: Mouton.

Fishman, J. A. (1968). The sociology of language. In J. A. Fishman (Ed.), *Readings in the Sociology of Language* (vol. 1, pp. 5–13). The Hague: Mouton.

Fishman, J. A. (1966). *Language Loyalty in the United States: The Maintenance and Perpetuation of Non-English Mother-Tongues by American Ethnic and Religious Groups.* The Hague: Mouton.

Fishman, J. A. (1965). Language maintenance and language shift: The American immigrant case within a general theoretical perspective. *Sociologus* 16, 19–38.

Fishman, J. A. (1964). Language maintenance and language shift as a field of inquiry: A definition of the field and suggestions for its further development. *Linguistics* 9, 32–70.

Fishman, J. A., A. Conrad, and A. Rubal-Lopez (Eds.). (1996). *Post Imperialist English*. Berlin: Mouton de Gruyter.

Fishman, J. A., R. L. Cooper, and A. Conrad (Eds.). (1977). *The Spread of English: The Sociology of English as an Additional Language*. Rowley, MA: Newbury House.

Fishman, J. A., R. L. Cooper, and Y. Rosenbaum (1977). English around the world. In J. A. Fishman, R. L. Cooper, and A. Conrad (Eds.). *The Spread of English: The Sociology of English as an Additional Language* (pp. 77–107). Rowley, MA: Newbury House.

Fishman, J. A., C. A. Ferguson, and J. Das Gupta (Eds.). (1968). *Language Problems of Developing Nations*. New York: John Wiley & Sons.

Fitzmaurice, S. (2003). The grammar of stance in early eighteenth-century English epistolary language. In P. Leistyna, and C. Meyer (Eds.), *Corpus Analysis: Language Structure and Language Use* (pp. 107–132). Amsterdam: Rodopi.

Fitzmaurice, S. (2002a). *The Familiar Letter in Early Modern English*. Amsterdam/Philadelphia: John Benjamins.

Fitzmaurice, S. (2002b). Politeness and modal meaning in the construction of humiliative discourse in an early eighteenth-century network of patron-client relationships. *English Language and Linguistics* 6, 239–66.

Flavell, J. (1976). Metacognitive aspects of problem solving. In L. B. Resnick (Ed.), *The Nature of Intelligence* (pp. 231–235). Hillsdale, NJ: Lawrence Erlbaum.

Flege, J. E. (1995). Second language and speech learning: Theory, findings and problems. In W. Strange (Ed.), *Speech Perception and Linguistic Experience: Issues in Crosslinguistic Research* (pp. 233–277). Timonium, MD: York Press.

Flege, J. E. (1990). English vowel production by Dutch talkers: More evidence for the "similar" vs. "new" distinction. In J. Leather, and A. James (Eds.), *New Sounds '90: Proceedings of the 1990 Amsterdam Symposium on the Acquisition of Second Language Speech* (pp. 255–293). Amsterdam: University of Amsterdam.

Flege, J. E., D. Birdsong, E. Bialystok, M. Mack, H. Sung, and K. Tsukaa (2005). Degree of foreign accent in English sentences produced by Korean children and adults. *Journal of Phonetics* 33, 262–290.

Fligelstone, S. (1993). Some reflections on the question of teaching, from a corpus linguistics perspective. *ICAME Journal* 17, 97–109.

Flowerdew, J. (2001). Concordancing as a tool in course design. In M. Ghadessy, H. Mohsen, A. Henry, and R. Roseberry (Eds.), *Small Corpus Studies and ELT: Theory and Practice* (pp. 71–92). Amsterdam: John Benjamins.

Flowerdew, J. (2000). Discourse community, legitimate peripheral participation and the nonnative-English-speaking scholar. *TESOL Quarterly* 34, 127–150.

Flowerdew, J. (1999). Problems in writing for scholarly publication in English: The case of Hong Kong. *Journal of Second Language Writing* 8, 253–264.

Flowerdew, J. (1993). An educational, or process approach to the teaching of professional genres. *ELT Journal* 47, 305–316.

Flowerdew, L. (2005). An integration of corpus-based and genre-based approaches to text analysis in EAP/ESP: Countering criticisms against corpus-based methodologies. *English for Specific Purposes* 24, 321–332.

Foltz, P. W., W. Kintsch, and T. K. Landauer (1998). Analysis of text coherence using latent semantic analysis. *Discourse Processes* 25 (2–3), 285–307.

Fontaine, N., and J. Leather (1992). *Kwéyòl Usage and Attitudes of Dominican Second-Formers*. Canefield, Dominica: Folk Research Institute.

Forman, R. (2008). Using notions of scaffolding and intertextuality to understand the bilingual teaching of English in Thailand. *Linguistics and Education* 19, 319–332.

Fortanet, I. (2004). The use of "*we*" in university lectures: Reference and function. *English for Specific Purposes* 23, 45–66.

Foster-Carter, A. (1985). The sociology of development. In M. Haralambos (Ed.), *Sociology: New Directions* (pp. 1–21). Ormskirk: Causeway Press.

Fowler, Y. (1997). The courtroom interpreter: Paragon *and* intruder? In S. E. Carr, R. Roberts, A. Dufour, and D. Steyn (Eds.), *The Critical Link: Interpreters in the Community* (pp. 191–201). Amsterdam/Philadelphia: John Benjamins.

Fox, B., and S. Thompson (1990). A discourse explanation of the grammar of relative clauses in English conversation. *Language* 66, 297–316.

Fox, E. (1996). Cross-language priming from ignored words: Evidence for a common representational system in bilinguals. *Journal of Memory and Language* 35, 353–370.

Fox, M. J. (1975). *Language and Development: A Retrospective Survey of Ford Foundation Language Projects, 1952–1974.* New York: Ford Foundation.

Francis, W. (1999). Cognitive integration of language and memory in bilinguals: Semantic representation. *Psychological Bulletin* 125, 193–222.

Francis, W. N., and H. Kucera (1982). *Frequency Analysis of English Usage: Lexicon and Grammar.* Boston: Houghton Mifflin.

Frank, D. B. (1993). Political, religious and economic factors affecting language choice in St. Lucia. *International Journal of the Sociology of Language* 102, 39–56.

Frankel, R. M. (2001a). Clinical care and conversational contingencies: The role of patients' self-diagnosis in medical encounters. *Text* 21, 83–111.

Frankel, R. M. (2001b). Cracking the code: Theory and method in clinical communication analysis. *Health Communication* 13, 101–110.

Frankel, R. M. (2000). The (socio)linguistic turn in physician-patient communication research. In J. Alatis, H. Hamilton, and A.-H. Tan (Eds.), *Linguistics, Language and the Professions* (*Georgetown University Round Table on Languages and Linguistics, 2000*) (pp. 81–103). Washington, DC: Georgetown University Press.

Frauenfelder, U., and H. Schriefers (1997). A psycho-linguistic perspective on simultaneous interpretation. *Interpreting* 2(1/2), 55–89.

Frawley, W. (Ed.). (2003). *Oxford International Encyclopedia of Linguistics* (2nd ed., 4 vols.). New York: Oxford University Press.

Frawley, W., and J. P. Lantolf (1985). Second language discourse: A Vygotskyan perspective. *Applied Linguistics* 6, 19–44.

Frazier, L. (1987). Sentence processing: A tutorial review. In M. Coltheart (Ed.), *Attention and Performance XII: The Psychology of Reading* (pp. 601–681). Hillsdale, NJ: Lawrence Erlbaum.

Frazier, L., and J. Fodor (1978). The sausage machine: A new two-stage parsing model. *Cognition* 6, 1–34.

Frazier, S. (2007). Conversational structures of "reports" in writing class group work. *Semiotica* 164, 53–80.

Freddi, M. (2005). Arguing linguistics: Corpus investigation of one functional variety of academic discourse. *Journal of English for Academic Purposes* 4, 5–26.

Frederiksen, N., R. J. Mislevy, and I. I. Bejar (Eds.). (1993). *Test Theory for a New Generation of Tests.* Hillsdale, NJ: Lawrence Erlbaum.

Freebody, P. (1997). Assessment as communal versus punitive practice: Six new literacy crises for Australia. *Literacy and Numeracy Studies* 117(2), 5–17.

Freed, B. (1995). Language learning and study abroad. In B. Freed (Ed.), *Second Language Acquisition in a Study-Abroad Context* (pp. 3–33). Philadelphia: John Benjamins.

Freeland, J. (Ed.). (1999). Indigenous language maintenance in Latin America. *International Journal of Bilingual Education and Bilingualism* 2(3).

Freeland, J., and D. Patrick (Eds.). (2004). *Language Rights and Language Survival: Sociolinguistic and Sociocultural Perspectives.* Manchester, UK: St. Jerome.

Freeman, D. (1998). *Doing Teacher Research: From Inquiry to Understanding.* Pacific Grove, CA: Heinle and Heinle.

Freeman, M., K. deMarrais, J. Preissle, K. Roulston, and E. St. Peirre (2007). Standards of evidence in qualitative research: An incitement to discourse. *Educational Researcher* 36(1), 25–32.

Freeman, R. D. (1997). Researching gender in language use. In N. Hornberger, and D. Corson (Eds.), *Research Methods in Language and Education: Encyclopedia of Language and Education* (vol. 8, pp. 47–56). Dordrecht: Kluwer.

Freidson, E. (Ed.). (1973). *The Professions and Their Prospects.* Beverly Hills, CA: Sage.

Frenck-Mestre, C. (2005). Eye-movement recording as a tool for studying syntactic processing in a second language: A review of methodologies and experimental findings. *Second Language Research* 21, 175–198.

Frenck-Mestre, C., and P. Prince (1997). Second language autonomy. *Journal of Memory and Language* 37, 481–501.

Fries, C. C. (1952). *The Structure of English.* London: Longman.

Fries, C. C. (1945). *Teaching and Learning English as a Foreign Language.* Ann Arbor: University of Michigan Press.

Friginal, E. (2009a). Threats to the sustainability of the outsourced call center industry in the Philippines: Implications for language policy. *Language Policy* 2(1), 51–68.

Friginal, E. (2009b). *The Language of Outsourced Call Centers: A Corpus-Based Study of Cross-Cultural Interaction.* Amsterdam: John Benjamins.

Friginal, E. (2007). Outsourced call centers and English in the Philippines. *World Englishes* 26, 331–345.

Friginal, E. (2006). Developing technical writing skills in forestry using corpus-informed instruction and tools. Paper presented at the American Association of Applied Corpus Linguistics Conference, Flagstaff, AZ.

Frost, R. (1998). Toward a strong phonological theory of visual word recognition: True issues and false trails. *Psychological Review* 123, 71–99.

Fullan, M. (1982). *The Meaning of Educational Change.* New York: Columbia University, Teachers College Press.

Furstenberg, G., S. Levet, K. English, and K. Maillet (2001). Giving a virtual voice to the silent language of culture: The CULTURA project. *Language Learning and Technology* 5(1), 55–102.

Fusco, M. A. (1995). On teaching conference interpretation between cognate languages: Towards a workable methodology. *Interpreters' Newsletter* 6, 93–109.

Fuster, J. M., and G. E. Alexander (1971). Neuron activity related to short term memory. *Science* 173, 319–333.

Fyle, C. M. (1994). Official and unofficial attitudes and policy towards Krio as the main language of Sierra Leone. In R. Fardon, and G. Furniss (Eds.), *African Languages, Development and the State* (pp. 44–54). London: Routledge.

Gaarder, A. B. (1977). Language maintenance or language shift. In W. F. Mackey, and T. Andersson (Eds.), *Bilingualism in Early Childhood* (pp. 409–434). Rowley, MA: Newbury House.

Gains, J. (1999). Electronic mail—a new style of communication or just a new medium? An investigation into the text features of emails. *English for Specific Purposes* 18(1), 81–101.

Gal, S. (1979). *Language Shift: Social Determinants of Linguistic Change in Bilingual Austria.* New York: Academic Press.

Gall, J. P., M. D. Gall, and W. T. Borg (2005). *Applying Educational Research* (5th ed.). Boston: Pearson Education.

Gall, M. D., J. P. Gall, and W. T. Borg (2003). *Educational Research* (7th ed.). White Plains, NY: Pearson Education.

Gambier, Y. (2007). Réseaux de traducteurs/interprètes bénévoles [Networks of volunteer translators and interpreters]. *Meta: Translators' Journal* 52(4), 658–672.

Gambier, Y., D. Gile, and C. Taylor (Eds.). (1997). *Conference Interpreting: Current Trends in Research.* Amsterdam/Philadelphia: John Benjamins.

García, O. (2009). *Bilingual Education in the 21st Century: A Global Perspective.* Malden, MA & Oxford: Wiley/Blackwell.

García, O. (1999). Latin America. In J. A. Fishman (Ed.), *Latin America: Handbook of Language and Ethnic Identity* (pp. 226–243). Oxford: Oxford University Press.

García, O., and R. Otheguy (1989). *English across Cultures: Cultures Across English. A Reader in Cross-Cultural Communication.* Berlin: Mouton de Gruyter.

García, O., R. Peltz, H. F. Schiffman, and G. S. Fishman (Eds.). (2006). *Language Loyalty, Continuity and Change: Joshua A. Fishman's Contributions to International Sociolinguistics.* Clevedon, Avon, UK: Multilingual Matters.

Garcia-Landa, M. (1998). A theoretical framework for oral and written translation research. *Interpreters' Newsletter* 8, 5–40.

Gardner, R. C. (2007). Motivation and second language acquisition. *Porta Linguarum* 8, 9–20.

Gardner, R. C. (2006). The socio-educational model of second language acquisition: A research paradigm. In S. H. Foster-Cohen, M. Medved Krajnovic, and J. Mihaljecic Djigunovic (Eds.), *Eurosla Yearbook* (vol. 6). Amsterdam: John Benjamins.

Gardner, R. C. (2005). Integrative motivation and second language acquisition. Invited address to the Canadian Association of Applied Linguistics/Canadian Linguistics Association, London, Canada (see also http://publish.uwo.ca/~Gardner).

Gardner, R. C. (2002). Social psychological perspectives on second language acquisition. In R. B. Kaplan (Ed.), *Oxford Handbook of Applied Linguistics* (pp. 160–169). New York: Oxford University Press.

Gardner, R. C. (2000). Correlation, causation, motivation, and second language acquisition. *Canadian Psychology* 41, 10–24.

Gardner, R. C. (1985). *Social Psychology and Second Language Learning: The Role of Attitudes and Motivation.* London: Edward Arnold.

Gardner, R. C., and W. E. Lambert (1972). *Attitudes and Motivation in Second Language Learning.* Rowley, MA: Newbury House.

Gardner, R. C., and W. E. Lambert (1959). Motivational variables in second language acquisition. *Canadian Journal of Psychology* 13, 266–272.

Gardner, R. C., A.-M. Masgoret, J. Tennant, and L. Mihic (2004). Integrative motivation: Changes during a year-long intermediate-level language course. *Language Learning* 54, 1–34.

Gardner, R. C., and P. C. Smythe (1975). *Second Language Acquisition: A Social Psychological Approach* (Research Bulletin No. 332). London, Canada: University of Western Ontario, Department of Psychology.

Garmendia, M. C. (1994). The linguistic normalisation process in Basque country: Data of a decade. *International Journal of the Sociology of Language* 109, 97–107.

Garrett, N. (1991). Technology in the service of language teaching: Trends and issues. *Modern Language Journal* 75, 74–101.

Gaskell, D., and T. Cobb (2004). Can learners use concordance feedback for writing errors? *System* 32(3), 301–319.

Gass, S. M. (2003). Input and interaction. In C. Doughty, and M. H. Long (Eds.), *The Handbook of Second Language Acquisition* (pp. 224–255). Oxford: Basil Blackwell.

Gass, S. M. (1997). *Input, Interaction and the Second Language Learner*. Mahwah, NJ: Lawrence Erlbaum.

Gass, S. M., and M. Alvarez Torres (2005). Attention when? An investigation of the ordering effect of input and interaction. *Studies in Second Language Acquisition* 27, 1–31.

Gass, S. M., J. Behney, and B. Uzum (in preparation). Working memory capacity, inhibitory control and interaction-based learning.

Gass, S. M., and N. Houck (1999). *Interlanguage Refusals: A Cross-Cultural Study of Japanese-English*. New York: Mouton de Gruyter.

Gass, S. M., and K. Lewis (2007). Perceptions of interactional feedback: Differences between heritage language learners and non-heritage language learners. In A. Mackey (Ed.), *Conversational Interaction in Second Language Acquisition: A Series of Empirical Studies* (pp. 173–196). Oxford: Oxford University Press.

Gass, S. M., and A. Mackey (2007a). *Data Elicitation for Second and Foreign Language Research*. Mahwah, NJ: Lawrence Erlbaum.

Gass, S. M., and A. Mackey (2007b). Input, interaction and output in second language acquisition. In J. Williams, and B. VanPatten (Eds.), *Theories in Second Language Acquisition* (pp. 175–199). Mahwah, NJ: Lawrence Erlbaum.

Gass, S. M., and A. Mackey (2000). *Stimulated Research Methodology in Second Language Research*. Mahwah, NJ: Lawrence Erlbaum.

Gass, S. M., and S. Makoni (Eds.). (2004). *World Applied Linguistics: AILA Review*, 17. Philadelphia and Amsterdam: John Benjamins.

Gass, S. M., I. Svetics, and S. Lemelin (2003). Differential effects of attention. *Language Learning* 53, 497–545.

Gass, S., and E. Varonis (1994). Input, interaction and second language production. *Studies in Second Language Acquisition Research* 16, 283–302.

Gass, S., and E. Varonis (1989). Incorporated repairs in NNS discourse. In M. Eisenstein (Ed.), *The Dynamic Interlanguage* (pp. 71–86). New York: Plenum Press.

Gass, S., and E. Varonis (1985). Variation in native speaker speech modification to non-native speakers. *Studies in Second Language Acquisition* 7, 37–57.

Gasser, M. (1990). Connectionism and universals of second language acquisition. *Studies in Second Language Acquisition* 12, 179–199.

Gavioli, L. (2005). *Exploring Corpora for ESP Learning*. Philadelphia: John Benjamins.

Gavioli, L. (2001). The learner as researcher: introducing corpus concordancing in the classroom. In G. Aston (Ed.), *Learning with Corpora* (pp. 108–137). Houston, TX: Athelstan.

Gavioli, L. (1997). Exploring texts through the concordancer: Guiding the learner. In Wichmann, A., S. Fligelstone, T. McEnery, and G. Knowles (Eds.), *Teaching and Language Corpora* (pp. 83–99). London: Longman.

Geddes, M. (1986). *Fast Forward 3*. Oxford: Oxford University Press.

Geddes, M., and G. Sturtridge (1981). *Reading Links*. London: Heineman.

Geddes, M., and G. Sturtridge (1979). *Listening Links*. London: Heinemann.

Gee, J. (1996). *Social Linguistics and Literacies: Ideology in Discourses* (2nd ed.). London: Falmer.

Gegeo, D. W., and K. A. Watson-Gegeo (2004). The critical villager: Transforming language and education in Solomon Islands. In J. W. Tollefson (Ed.), *Language Policies in Education: Critical Issues* (pp. 309–325). Mahwah, NJ: Lawrence Erlbaum.

Geisler, C. (2002). Investigating register variation in nineteenth-century English: A multi-dimensional comparison. In R. Reppen, S. M. Fitzmaurice, and D. Biber (Eds.), *Using Corpora to Explore Linguistic Variation* (pp. 249–271). Amsterdam: John Benjamins.

Geisler, C. (1995). *Relative Infinitives in English*. Uppsala, Sweden: Uppsala University.

Genesee, F. (Ed.). (1994). *Educating Second Language Children*. Cambridge: Cambridge University Press.

Genesee, F. (1987). *Learning through Two Languages: Studies of Immersion and Bilingual Education*. Rowley, MA: Newbury House.

Genesee, F., E. Geva, C. Dressler, and M. Kamil (2006). Synthesis: Cross-linguistic relationships. In D. August, and T. Shanahan (Eds.), *Developing Literacy in Second-Language Learners: Report of the National Panel on Language Minority Children and Youth* (pp. 153–183). Mahwah, NJ: Lawrence Erlbaum.

Gentzler, E. (2002). What's Different about Translation in the Americas? *CTIS Occasional Papers* 2, 7–19.

Gentzler, E. (2001). *Contemporary Translation Theories*. Clevedon, Avon, UK: Multilingual Matters.

Gernsbacher, M. A., and M. Shlesinger (1997). The proposed role of suppression in simultaneous interpretation. *Interpreting* 2(1/2), 119–140.

Ghadessy, M., H. Mohsen, A. Henry, and R. Roseberry (Eds.). (2001). *Small Corpus Studies and ELT: Theory and Practice*. Amsterdam: John Benjamins.

Giambagli, A. (1998). La prise de notes peut-elle détourner d'une bonne qualité de l'écoute en interprétation consécutive? [Can note-taking distract from attentive listening in consecutive interpreting?]. *Interpreters' Newsletter* 8, 121–134.

Gibbons, J. (2004). *Forensic Linguistics*. Malden, MA: Blackwell.

Gibbons, P. (2002). *Scaffolding Language, Scaffolding Learning: Teaching Second Language Learners in the Mainstream*. Portsmouth, NH: Heinemann.

Gibson, E. (1998). Linguistic complexity: Locality of syntactic dependencies. *Cognition* 68, 1–76.

Gibson, E., and T. Warren (2004). Reading-time evidence for intermediate linguistic structure in long-distance dependencies. *Syntax* 7, 55–78.

Gick, B., B. Bernhardt, P. Bacsfalvi, and I. Wilson (2008). Ultrasound imaging applications in second language acquisition. In J. G. Hansen Edwards, and M. L. Zampini (Eds.), *Phonology and Second Language Acquisition* (pp. 309–322). Philadelphia: John Benjamins.

Gierl, M. J. (2007). Assessment Engineering Using the Attribute Hierarchy Method. Paper presented at the Annual Meeting of the National Council on Measurement in Education, Chicago.

Gierl, M. J., J. Zhou, and C. Alves (2008). Developing a Taxonomy of Item Model Types to Promote Assessment Engineering. *Journal of Technology, Learning and Assessment* 7. Available: http://escholarship.bc.edu/jtla/.

Giles, H., R. Y. Bourhis, and D. M. Taylor (1977). Towards a theory of language in ethnic group relations. In H. Giles (Ed.), *Language, Ethnicity, and Intergroup Relations* (pp. 307–349). New York: Academic Press.

Gill, C., and W. E. Hewitt (1996). Improving court interpreting services: What the states are doing. *State Court Journal* 20(1), 34–41.

Gillies, A. (2005). *Note-Taking for Consecutive Interpreting: A Short Course*. Manchester, UK and Northampton, MA: St. Jerome.

Gilquin, G., S. Granger, and M. Paquot (2007). Learner corpora: The missing link in EAP pedagogy. *Journal of English for Academic Purposes* 6, 319–335.

Gledhill, C. (2000). The discourse function of collocation in research article introductions. *English for Specific Purposes* 19, 115–135.

Gleitman, L. (1990). The structural sources of verb meaning. *Language Acquisition* 1, 3–55.

Glenn, C. L. (1997). The languages of immigrants. *READ Perspectives* 4(1), 17–58.

Glinert, L. (1998). Lexicographic function and the relation between supply and demand. *International Journal of Lexicography* 11(2), 111–124.

Goffman, E. (1961). *Asylums*. Garden City, NY: Doubleday.

Goffman, E. (1959). *The Presentation of Self in Everyday Life*. Garden City, NY: Doubleday.

Goh, C. (2002). Exploring listening comprehension tactics and their interaction patterns. *System* 30(2), 185–206.

Goh, C. (2000). A cognitive perspective on language learners' listening comprehension problems. *System* 28(1), 55–75.

Goh, C. (1997). Metacognitive awareness and second language listeners. *ELT Journal* 51(4), 361–369.

Goh, C., and Y. Taib (2006). Metacognitive instruction in listening for young learners. *ELT Journal* 60(3), 222–232.

Goldberg, A. (2006). *Constructions at Work: The Nature of Generalization in Language*. Oxford: Oxford University Press.

Goldberg, A., and D. Casenhiser (2008). Construction learning and SLA. In N. Ellis, and P. Robinson (Eds.), *Handbook of Cognitive Linguistics and Second Language Acquisition* (197–215). Mahwah, NJ: Lawrence Erlbaum.

Goldenberg, C., and G. Patthey-Chavez (1995). Discourse processes in instructional conversations: Interactions between teacher and transition readers. *Discourse Processes* 19, 57–74.

Goldsmith, J. (1976). An overview of autosegmental phonology. *Linguistic Analysis* 2, 23–68.

Goldstein, L. (2005). *Teacher Written Commentary in Second Language Writing Classrooms*. Ann Arbor: University of Michigan Press.

Goldstein, L., and S. Conrad (1990). Student input and negotiation of meaning in ESL writing conferences. *TESOL Quarterly* 24, 443–460.

Goldstein, T. (2003). *Teaching and Learning in a Multilingual School: Choices, Risks, and Dilemmas*. Mahwah, NJ: Lawrence Erlbaum.

Goldstein, T. (2001). Hong Kong, Canada: Playwriting as critical ethnography. *Qualitative Inquiry* 7(3), 279–303.

Goldstein, T. (1997). *Two Languages at Work: Bilingual Life on the Production Floor*. Berlin: Mouton de Gruyter.

Gollan, T., K. I. Forster, and R. Frost (1997). Translation priming with different scripts: Masked priming with cognates and noncognates in Hebrew-English bilinguals. *Journal of Experimental Psychology: Learning, Memory and Cognition* 23, 1122–1139.

Gomm, R., M. Hammersley, and P. Foster (2000). *Case Study Method*. Thousand Oaks, CA: Sage.

Gonsalvez, G. E. (1999). [Report]. *Pidgins and Creoles in Education (PACE) Newsletter* 10, 1.

Gonsalvez, G. E. (1996). Language policy and education reform: The case of Cape Verdean. In C. E. Walsh (Ed.), *Education Reform and Social Change: Multicultural Voices, Struggles and Visions* (pp. 31–36). Mahwah, NJ: Lawrence Erlbaum.

Gonzalez, A. (1989). Sociolinguistics in the Philippines. *Philippine Journal of Linguistics* 20(1), 57–58.

González, R. D., V. F. Vásquez, and H. Mikkelson (1991). *Fundamentals of Court Interpretation*. Durham, NC: Carolina Academic Press.

Goodwin, C., and A. Duranti (1992). Rethinking context: An introduction. In C. Goodwin, and A. Duranti (Eds.), *Rethinking Context: Language as an Interactive Phenomenon* (pp. 1–42). New York: Cambridge University Press.

Goodwin, J. M. (2001). EAP support for matriculated university students. In J. Murphy, and P. Byrd (Eds.), *Understanding the Courses We Teach: Local Perspectives on English Language Teaching* (pp. 259–280). Ann Arbor: University of Michigan Press.

Gordon, R. G., Jr. (Ed.). (2005). *Ethnologue: Languages of the World* (15th ed.). Dallas, TX: SIL International.

Gorter, D. (1987). Surveys of the Frisian language situation: Some considerations of research methods on language maintenance and shift. *International Journal of the Sociology of Language* 68, 41–56.

Gosden, H. (1996). Verbal reports of Japanese novices' research writing practices in English. *Journal of Second Language Writing* 5, 109–128.

Gottlob, L. R., S. D. Goldinger, G. O. Stone, and G. C. Van Orden (1999). Reading homographs: Orthographic, phonologic and semantic dynamics. *Journal of Experimental Psychology: Human Perception and Performance* 25, 561–574.

Gouadec, D. (1994, December). The introduction of official computer terminology: Attestations, Gallicization, normalization, assimilation. *Terminologies Nouvelles* 12, 141–147.

Goyvaerts, D. L. (1997). Power, ethnicity and the remarkable rise of Lingala in Bukavu, eastern Zaire. *International Journal of the Sociology of Language* 128, 25–44.

Grabau, C. M. (1996). Court interpreting: View from the bench. *State Court Journal* 20(1), 6–11.

Grabe, W. (2009). *Reading in a Second Language: Moving from Theory to Practice.* New York: Cambridge University Press.

Grabe, W. (2004). Perspectives in applied linguistics: A North American view. In S. M. Gass, and S. Makoni (Eds.), *World Applied Linguistics: AILA Review* 17, 105–132.

Grabe, W. (2002). Applied linguistics: An emerging discipline for the twenty-first century. In R. B. Kaplan (Ed.), *The Oxford Handbook of Applied Linguistics* (pp. 3–12). New York: Oxford University Press.

Grabe, W. (2001). Reading-writing relations: Theoretical perspectives and instructional practices. In D. Belcher, and A. Hirvela (Eds.), *Proceedings of the Ohio State Conference on Second Language Reading/Writing Connections* (pp. 15–47). Ann Arbor: University of Michigan Press.

Grabe, W. (1999). Developments in reading research and their implications for computer-adaptive reading assessment. In M. Chalhoub-Deville (Ed.), *Issues in Computer-Adaptive Testing of Reading Proficiency* (pp. 11–47). Cambridge: Cambridge University Press.

Grabe, W., and R. B. Kaplan (2006). Applied linguistics in North America. In K. Brown (Ed.), *Encyclopedia of Language and Linguistics* (14 vols.; 2nd ed., vol. 1, pp. 363–369). Amsterdam: Elsevier.

Grabe, W., and R. B. Kaplan (1997). On the writing of science and the science of writing: Hedging in science text and elsewhere. In R. Markkanen, and H. Schroder (Eds.), *Hedging and Discourse: Approaches to the Analysis of a Pragmatic Phenomenon in Academic Texts* (pp. 151–167). Berlin: Walter de Gruyter.

Grabe, W., and R. B. Kaplan (Eds.). (1991). *Introduction to Applied Linguistics.* Reading, MA: Addison Wesley.

Grabe, W., and F. Stoller (1997). Content-based instruction: Research foundations. In M. A. Snow, and D. M. Brinton (Eds.), *The Content-Based Classroom: Perspectives on Integrating Language and Content* (pp. 158–174). New York: Longman.

Grace, G. (1993). What Are Languages? *Ethnolinguistic Notes* 3(45), 1–17.

Graddol, D. (2006). *English Next*. London: British Council.

Graddol, D. (1997). *The Future of English? A Guide to Forecasting the Popularity of the English Language in the 21st Century*. London: British Council.

Graham, S., D. Santos, and R. Vanderplank (2008). Listening comprehension and strategy use: A longitudinal exploration. *System* 36(1), 52–68.

Gran, L., and B. Bellini (1996). Short-term memory and simultaneous interpretation: An experimental study on verbatim recall. *Interpreters' Newsletter* 7, 103–112.

Grandin, J. M. (1993). The University of Rhode Island's international engineering program. In M. Krueger, and F. Ryan (Eds.), *Language and Content: Discipline- and Content-Based Approaches to Language Study* (pp. 130–137). Lexington, MA: D.C. Heath.

Granger, S. (2004). Computer learner corpus research: Current status and future prospects. In U. Connor, and T. Upton (Eds.), *Applied Corpus Linguistics: A Multidimensional Perspective* (pp. 123–145). Amsterdam: Rodopi.

Granger, S. (2003a). Error-tagged learner corpora and CALL: A promising synergy. In Error analysis and error correction in computer-assisted language learning [Special issue]. *CALICO* 20(3), 465–480.

Granger, S. (2003b). The International Corpus of Learner English: A new resource for foreign language learning and teaching and second language acquisition research. *TESOL Quarterly* 37(3), 538–546.

Granger, S. (Ed.). (1998a). *Learner English on Computer*. London & New York: Addison Wesley Longman.

Granger, S. (1998b). Prefabricated patterns in advanced EFL writing: Collocations and formulae. In A. Cowie (Ed.), *Phraseology: Theory, Analysis and Applications* (pp. 145–160). Oxford: Oxford University Press.

Granger, S. (1997a). Automated retrieval of passives from native and learner corpora: Precision and recall. *Journal of English Linguistics* 25(4), 365–374.

Granger, S. (1997b). On identifying the syntactic and discourse features of participle clauses in academic English: Native and non-native writers compared. In J. Aarts, I. de Mönnink, and H. Wekker (Eds.), *Studies in English Language and Teaching* (pp. 185–198). Amsterdam: Rodopi.

Granger, S. (1996). Learner English around the world. In S. Greenbaum (Ed.), *Comparing English Worldwide: The International Corpus of English* (pp. 13–24). Oxford: Clarendon Press.

Granger, S. (1994). The learner corpus: A revolution in applied linguistics. *English Today* 39, 25–29.

Granger, S. (1993). International Corpus of Learner English. In J. Aarts, P. de Haan, and N. Oostdijk (Eds.), *English Language Corpora: Design, Analysis and Exploitation* (pp. 57–71). Amsterdam: Rodopi.

Granger, S. (1983). *The BE + Past Participle Construction in Spoken English (with Special Emphasis on the Passive)*. Amsterdam: Elsevier.

Granger, S., J. Hung, and S. Petch-Tyson (Eds.). (2002). *Computer Learner Corpora, Second Language Acquisition and Foreign Language Teaching*. Amsterdam: John Benjamins.

Granger, S., and S. Tyson (1996). Connector usage in the English essay writing of native and non-native EFL speakers of English. *World Englishes* 15, 17–27.

Graves, K. (2008). The language curriculum: A social contextual perspective. *Language Teaching* 41, 147–181.

Grbi, N. (2008). Constructing interpreting quality. *Interpreting* 10(2), 232–257.

Green, A., N. Schweda-Nicholson, J. Vaid, N. White, and R. Steiner (1990). Hemispheric involvement in shadowing vs. interpretation: A time-sharing study of simultaneous interpreters with matched bilingual and monolingual controls. *Brain and Language* 39, 107–133.

Green, A., J. Vaid, N. Schweda-Nicholson, N. White, and R. Steiner (1994). Lateralization for shadowing vs. interpretation: A comparison of interpreters with bilingual and monolingual controls. In S. Lambert, and B. Moser-Mercer (Eds.), *Bridging the Gap: Empirical Research in Simultaneous Interpretation* (pp. 331–355). Amsterdam/ Philadelphia: John Benjamins.

Green, B., J. Hodgens, and A. Luke (1994). *Debating Literacy in Australia: A Documentary History, 1945–1994*. Melbourne: Australian Literacy Foundation.

Green, D. W. (1998). Mental control of the bilingual lexico-semantic system. *Bilingualism: Language and Cognition* 1, 67–81.

Green, D. W. (1993). Towards a model of L2 comprehension and production. In R. Schreuder, and B. Weltens (Eds.), *The Bilingual Lexicon* (pp. 249–277). Amsterdam: John Benjamins.

Green, D. W. (1986). Control, activation and resource: A framework and a model for the control of speech in bilinguals. *Brain and Language* 27, 210–223.

Greenbaum, S. (Ed.). (1996). *Comparing English Worldwide: The International Corpus of English*. Oxford: Clarendon Press.

Greenbaum, S. (1991). ICE: The International Corpus of English. *English Today* 28, 3–7.

Greenbaum, S. (1990a). The International Corpus of English. *ICAME Journal* 14, 106–108.

Greenbaum, S. (1990b). Standard English and the International Corpus of English. *World Englishes* 9, 79–83.

Greenbaum, S. (1990c). The International Corpus of English: A progress report. *World Englishes* 9, 121–122.

Greenbaum, S. (1988). A proposal for an international computerized corpus of English. *World Englishes* 7, 315.

Greenbaum, S., and G. Nelson (1996). The International Corpus of English (ICE) project. *World Englishes* 15, 3–15.

Gregg, K. R. (2003). The state of emergentism in SLA. *Second Language Research* 19, 95–128.

Gregg, K. R. (1989). Second language acquisition theory: The case for a generative perspective. In S. Gass, and J. Schachter (Eds.), *Linguistic Perspectives on Second Language Acquisition* (pp. 15–40). Cambridge: Cambridge University Press.

Grenoble, L. A., and L. J. Whaley (2006). *Saving Languages: An Introduction to Language Revitalisation*. New York: Cambridge University Press.

Grenoble, L. A., and L. J. Whaley (1998). *Endangered Languages: Current Issues and Future Prospects*. Cambridge: Cambridge University Press.

Grice, H. P. (1975). Logic and conversation. In P. Cole, and J. L. Morgan (Eds.), *Syntax and Semantics: Speech Acts* (pp. 41–58). New York: Academic Press.

Gries, S. T. (2008). Corpus-based methods in analyses of SLA data. In P. Robinson, and N. C. Ellis (Eds.), *Handbook of Cognitive Linguistics and Second Language Acquisition* (pp. 406–431). New York: Routledge.

Grieve, J. (2009). A corpus-based study of dialect variation in the United States. PhD dissertation, Northern Arizona University, Flagstaff.

Grieve, J. (2007). Quantitative authorship attribution: An evaluation of techniques. *Literary and Linguistic Computing* 22, 251–270.

Grillo, R. (1989). Anthropology, language, politics. *Social Anthropology and the Politics of Language, Sociological Review Monograph* 36, 1–24.

Grin, F. (1996). The economics of language: Survey assessment, prospects. *International Journal of the Sociology of Language* 121, 17–44.

Grin, F., and F. Vaillancourt (2000). On the financing of language policies and distributive justice. In R. Phillipson (Ed.), *Rights to Language. Equity, Power and Education* (pp. 102–110). New York: Lawrence Erlbaum.

Grin, F., and F. Vaillancourt (1998). *Language Revitalisation Policy: An Analytical Survey. Theoretical Framework, Policy Experience and Application to Te Reo Māori*. Report to the [Department of the] Treasury. Wellington, New Zealand/Aotearoa. Released under the Official Education Act.

Grommes, P., and R. Dietrich (2000). Coherence in operating room team and cockpit communication: A psycholinguistic contribution to applied linguistics. In J. Alatis, H. Hamilton, and A.-H. Tan (Eds.), *Linguistics, Language and the Professions* (*Georgetown University Round Table on Languages and Linguistics, 2000*) (pp. 81–103). Washington, DC: Georgetown University Press.

Grosjean, F. (2001). The bilingual's language modes. In J. Nicol (Ed.), *One Mind, Two Languages: Bilingual Language Processing* (pp. 1–22). Oxford: Blackwell.

Grosjean, F. (1998). Studying bilinguals: Methodological and conceptual issues. *Bilingualism: Language and Cognition* 1, 131–149.

Grosjean, F. (1997a). The bilingual individual. *Interpreting* 2(1/2), 163–187.

Grosjean, F. (1997b). Processing mixed language: Issues, findings and models. In A. M. B. De Groot, and J. F. Kroll (Eds.), *Tutorials in Bilingualism: Psycholinguistic Perspectives* (pp. 225–254). Mahwah, NJ: Lawrence Erlbaum.

Grosjean, F. (1988). Exploring the recognition of guest words in bilingual speech. *Language and Cognitive Processes* 3, 233–274.

Grove, C. D. (1999). The Official English debate in the United States Congress: A critical analysis. PhD dissertation, University of Washington, Seattle.

Gu, Y. (2007). Segmenting and annotating a multimodal corpus (with special reference to SCCSD). Retrieved January 22, 2007, from http://www.corpus.bham.ac.uk/guabstr.htm

Gu, Y. (2002). Towards an understanding of workplace discourse: A pilot study for compiling a spoken Chinese corpus of situated discourse. In C. Candlin (Ed.), *Research and Practice in Professional Discourse* (pp. 137–186). Hong Kong: City University of Hong Kong Press.

Guba, E. G., and Y. S. Lincoln (1994). Competing paradigms in qualitative research. In N. K. Denzin, and Y. S. Lincoln (Eds.), *Handbook of Qualitative Research* (pp. 105–117). Thousand Oaks, CA: Sage.

Gubertini, M. C. P. (1998). Des ajouts en interprétation. Pourquoi pas? [Additions in interpreting. Why not?] *Interpreters' Newsletter* 8, 135–149.

Gubrium, J. F., and J. A. Holstein (Eds.). (2002). *Handbook of Interview Research: Context and Method*. Thousand Oaks, CA: Sage.

Guénette, D. (2007). Is feedback pedagogically correct? Research design issues in studies of feedback on writing. *Journal of Second Language Writing* 16, 40–53.

Guichon, N., and S. McLornan (2008). The effects of multimodality on L2 learners: Implications for CALL resource design. *System* 36(1), 85–93.

Guilford, J. (1997). The attitudes of French youth toward English loan words. *Linguistique* 33, 117–135.

Guilloteaux, M. J., and Z. Dörnyei (2008). Motivating language learners: A classroom-oriented investigation of the effects of motivational strategies on student motivation. *TESOL Quarterly* 42, 55–77.

Gumperz, J. J. (1983). *Discourse Strategies*. Cambridge: Cambridge University Press.

Gumperz, J. J., and R. Wilson (1971). Convergence and Creolization: A case from the Indo-Aryan/Dravidian border. In D. Hymes (Ed.), *Pidginization and Creolization of Languages* (pp. 151–168). London: Cambridge University Press.

Gunnarsson, B.-L. (1997). Applied discourse analysis. In T. A. Van Dijk (Ed.), *Discourse as Social Interaction* (pp. 285–312). Thousand Oaks, CA: Sage.

Gunnarsson, B.-L., P. Linell, and B. Nordberg (Eds.). (1997). *The Construction of Professional Discourse* (pp. 190–219). London: Longman.

Haarmann, H. (1990). Language planning in the light of a general theory of language: A methodological framework. *International Journal of the Sociology of Language* 86, 103–126.

Haarmann, H. (1980). *Multilingualisms 2: Elemente einer Sprachökologie*. Tübingen: Narr.

Hadfield, J. (1987). *Advanced Communicative Games*. Walton-upon-Thames: Nelson.

Haenen, J. (1996). *Piotr Gal'perin: Psychologist in Vygotsky's Footsteps*. New York: Nova Science.

Haertel, E. H. (1984). An application of latent class models for assessment data. *Applied Psychological Measurement* 8, 333–346.

Haigh, C. A., and D. Jared (2007). The activation of phonological representations by bilinguals while reading silently: Evidence from interlingual homophones. *Journal of Experimental Psychology: Learning, Memory and Cognition* 33, 623–644.

Halász, G., and J. Lannert (2003). *Jelentés a magyar közoktatásról* [Report on Hungarian education]. Budapest: Országos Közoktatási Intézet.

Halász, G., and J. Lannert (1998). *Jelentés a magyar közoktatásról* [Report on Hungarian education]. Budapest: Országos Közoktatási Intézet.

Hald, L., M. Bastiaanse, and P. Hagoort (2006). EEG theta and gamma responses to semantic violations in online sentence processing. *Brain and Language* 96(1), 90–105.

Hale, K., and S. J. Keyser (1993). On argument structure and the lexical expression of syntactic relations. In K. Hale, and S. J. Keyser (Eds.), *The View from Building 20: Essays in Linguistics in Honor of Sylvain Bromberger* (pp. 53–110). Cambridge, MA: MIT.

Hale, S. (2007). *Community Interpreting*. New York: Palgrave Macmillan.

Hale, S. (2004). *The Discourse of Court Interpreting: Discourse Practices of the Law, the Witness and the Interpreter*. Amsterdam/Philadelphia: John Benjamins.

Hale, S. (1997). The treatment of register variation in court interpreting. *Translator* 3(1), 39–54.

Hall, C. (1995). Formal linguistics and mental representation: Psycholinguistic contributions to the identification and explanation of morphological and syntactic competence. *Language and Cognitive Processes* 10, 169–187.

Hall, J. K. (2007). Redressing the roles of correction and repair in research on second and foreign language learning. *Modern Language Journal* 91, 511–526.

Hall, J. K. (1998). Differential teacher attention to student utterances: The construction of different opportunities for learning in the IRF. *Linguistics and Education* 9, 287–311.

Hall, J. K., A. Chen, and M. Carlson (2006). Reconceptualizing multicompetence as a theory of language knowledge. *Applied Linguistics* 27(2), 220–240.

Hall, J. K., and M. Walsh (2002). Teacher-student interaction and language learning. In M. McGroarty et al. (Eds.), *Annual Review of Applied Linguistics: Vol. 22. Discourse and Dialogue* (pp. 186–203). New York: Cambridge University Press.

Halliday, M. A. K. (1993). Towards a language-based theory of learning. *Linguistics and Education* 5, 93–116.

Halliday, M. A. K. (1978). *Language as Social Semiotic: The Social Interpretation of Language and Meaning*. London: Edward Arnold.

Halliday, M. A. K., and R. Hasan (1989). *Language, Context and Text: Aspects of Language in a Social-Semiotic Perspective*. Oxford: Oxford University Press.

Halliday, M. A. K., and R. Hasan (1976). *Cohesion in English*. London: Longman.

Halliday, M. A. K., A. McIntosh, and P. Strevens (1964). *The Linguistics Sciences and Language Teaching*. London: Longman.

Hamel, R. E. (1997). Language conflict and language shift: A sociolinguistic framework for linguistic human rights. *International Journal of the Sociology of Language* 127, 105–134.

Hamel, R. E. (1986). Language policy and interethnic conflict: Sociolinguistic research issues. *Escritos* 1(2), 7–36.

Hamidi, M., and F. Pöchhacker (2007). Simultaneous consecutive interpreting: A new technique put to the test. *Meta: Translators' Journal* 52(2), 276–289.

Hammersley, M., and P. Atkinson (2007). *Ethnography: Principles in Practice* (3rd ed.). London: Routledge.

Hammond, J. (2001). Literacies in school education in Australia: Disjunctions between policy and research. In New directions in literacy research: Policy, pedagogy, practice [Special issue]. *Language and Education* 15, 162–177.

Hamp-Lyons, L. (2001). Fourth generation writing assessment. In T. Silva, and P. Matsuda (Eds.), *On Second Language Writing* (pp. 117–127). Mahwah, NJ: Lawrence Erlbaum.

Hamp-Lyons, L. (1991a). Pre-text: Task-related influences on the writer. In L. Hamp-Lyons (Ed.), *Assessing Second Language Writing in Academic Contexts* (pp. 97–107). Norwood, NJ: Ablex.

Hamp-Lyons, L. (1991b). Reconstructing "academic writing proficiency." In L. Hamp-Lyons (Ed.), *Assessing Second Language Writing in Academic Contexts* (pp. 127–153). Norwood, NJ: Ablex.

Han, N. H. (2004). Language socialization of Korean-American preschoolers: Becoming a member of a community beyond the family. PhD dissertation, University of California, Los Angeles.

Han, N-R., M. Chodorow, and C. Leacock (2006). Detecting errors in English article usage by nonnative speakers. *Natural Language Engineering* 12(2), 115–129.

Han, Z.-H., and N. Anderson (Eds.). (2009). *Second Language Reading: Research and Instruction*. Ann Arbor: University of Michigan Press.

Hancin-Bhatt, B. (2008). Second language phonology in optimality theory. In J. G. Hansen Edwards, and M. L. Zampini (Eds.), *Phonology and Second Language Acquisition* (pp. 117–146). Philadelphia: John Benjamins.

Hancin-Bhatt, B., and R. Bhatt (1997). Optimal L2 syllables: Interaction of transfer and developmental effects. *Studies in Second Language Acquisition* 19, 331–378.

Haneda, M. (2005). Investing in foreign-language writing: A study of two multicultural learners. *Journal of Language, Identity and Education* 4(4), 269–290.

Hannahs, S. J., and M. Young-Scholten (Eds.). (1997). *Focus on Phonological Acquisition*. Philadelphia: John Benjamins.

Hansen, E., J. G. Zampini, and M. L. Zampini (Eds.). (2008). *Phonology and Second Language Acquisition*. Philadelphia: John Benjamins.

Hansen, I. G., and M. Shlesinger (2007). The silver lining: Technology and self-study in the interpreting classroom. *Interpreting* 9(1), 95–118.

Hansen, K. C. (1984). Communicability of some Western Desert communilects. In J. Hudson, and N. Pym (Eds.), *Language Survey*, Work Papers of SIL/AAB, B-11. Darwin: Summer Institute of Linguistics.

Hansen, M. (1999). Historical Summary of the Unz Initiative. MA Thesis, Brigham Young University, Provo, Utah.

Harklau, L. (2005). Ethnography and ethnographic research on second language teaching and learning. In E. Hinkel (Ed.), *Handbook of Research in Second Language Teaching and Learning* (pp. 179–194). Mahwah, NJ: Lawrence Erlbaum.

Harklau, L. (2000). From the "good kids" to the "worst": Representations of English language learners across educational settings. *TESOL Quarterly* 34, 35–67.

Harklau, L. (1999). Representing culture in the ESL writing classroom. In E. Hinkel (Ed.), *Culture in Second Language Teaching and Learning* (pp. 109–130). New York: Cambridge.

Harley, B. (1993). Instructional strategies and second language acquisition in French immersion: Patterns of second language development in French immersion. *Journal of French Language Studies* 2, 159–183.

Harley, B. (1984). The interlanguage of immersion students and its implications for second language teaching. In A. Davies, C. Criper, and A. Howatt (Eds.), *Interlanguage* (pp. 291–311). Edinburgh: Edinburgh University Press.

Harlow, R. (1991). Contemporary Mäori language. In G. McGregor, and M. Williams (Eds.), *Dirty Silence: Aspects of Language and Literature in New Zealand* (pp. 29–38). Auckland: Oxford University Press.

Harré, R., J. Brockmeier, and P. Mühlhäusler (1999). *Greenspeak*. Thousand Oaks: Sage.

Harrington, M. (2001). Sentence processing. In P. J. Robinson (Ed.), *Cognition and Second Language Instruction* (91–124). New York: Cambridge University Press.

Harrington, M. (1987). Processing strategies as a source of interlanguage variation. *Applied Psycholinguistics* 8, 351–378.

Harrington, M., and M. Sawyer (1992). L2 Working memory capacity and L2 reading skill. *Studies in Second Language Acquisition* 14, 25–38.

Harris, D. P. (1969). *Testing English as a Second Language*. New York: McGraw-Hill.

Harris, S. (1994). Ideological exchanges in British magistrates' courts. In J. Gibbons (Ed.), *Language and the Law* (pp. 156–170). London: Longman.

Harris, S., and Bargiela-Chiappini, F. (2003). Business as a site of language contact. In M. McGroarty et al. (Eds) *Annual Review of Applied Linguistics: Vol. 23. Language Contact and Change* (pp. 155–169). New York: Cambridge University Press.

Harris, S., and F. Bargiela-Chiappini (1997). The languages of business: Introduction and overview. In F. Bargiela-Chiappini, and S. Harris (Eds.), *The Languages of Business: An Interational Perspective* (pp. 1–18). Edinburgh: Edinburgh University Press.

Harris, T. (2003). Listening with your eyes: The importance of speech-related gestures in the language classroom. *Foreign Language Annals* 36, 180–187.

Harrison, K. D. (2007). *When Languages Die: The Extinction of the World's Languages and the Erosion of Human Knowledge*. New York: Oxford.

Hartford, B. S., and K. Bardovi-Harlig (1992). Closing the conversation: Evidence from the academic advising session. *Discourse Processes* 15, 93–116.

Hart-Landsberg, S., and S. Reder (1997). Teamwork and literacy: Teaching and learning at Hardy Industries. In G. Hull (Ed.), *Changing Work, Changing Workers: Critical Perspectives on Language, Literacy, and Skills* (pp. 350–382). Albany: State University of New York Press.

Hartsuiker, R., and M. Pickering (2007). Language integration in bilingual sentence production. *Acta Psychologica* 128, 479–489.

Hartsuiker, R., M. Pickering, and E. Veltkamp (2004). Is syntax separate or shared between languages? *Psychological Science* 15, 409–414.

Hassall, T. (2003). Requests by Australian learners of Indonesian. *Journal of Pragmatics* 35, 1903–1928.

Hatch, E. M. (1992). *Discourse and Language Education*. Cambridge: Cambridge University Press.

Hatch, E. M. (1983). *Psycholinguistics: A Second Language Approach*. Rowley, MA: Newbury House.

Hatch, E. M. (Ed.). (1978). *Second Language Acquisition*. Rowley, MA: Newbury House.

Hatch, E. M., and A. Lazaraton (1991). *The Research Manual: Design and Statistics for Applied Linguistics*. New York: Newbury House.

Hatch, E., and M. Long (1980). Discourse analysis: What's that? In D. Larsen-Freeman (Ed.), *Discourse Analysis in Second Language Research* (pp. 1–40). Rowley, MA: Newbury House.

Hatim, B., and J. Munday (2004). *Translation: An Advanced Resource Book*. London and New York: Routledge.

Hauck, M., and U. Stickler (2006). What does it take to teach online? *CALICO Journal* 23(3), 463–475.

Haugen, E. (1983). The implementation of corpus planning: Theory and practice. In J. Cobarrubias, and J. A. Fishman (Eds.). *Progress in Language Planning* (pp. 269–289). Berlin: Mouton.

Haugen, E. (1972). The ecology of language. In A. S. Kil (Ed.), *The Ecology of Language: Essays by Einar Haugen* (pp. 325–339). Stanford, CA: Stanford University Press.

Haugen, E. (1966). *Language planning and language conflict: The case of modern Norwegian*. Cambridge, MA: Harvard University Press.

Hauptman, P., M. Wesche, and D. Ready (1988). Second language acquisition through subject-matter learning: A follow-up study at the University of Ottawa. *Language Learning* 38(3), 433–475.

Hawkins, B. (1985). Is an "appropriate response" always so appropriate? In S. Gass, and C. Madden (Eds.), *Input in second language acquisition* (pp. 162–180). Rowley, MA: Newbury House.

Hawkins, E. (1987). *Awareness of Language: An Introduction* (revised ed.). Cambridge: Cambridge University Press.

Hawkins, R. (in press). Second language acquisition of morphosyntax. In W. Ritchie, and T. Baktia (Eds.), *The New Handbook of Second Language Acquisition*. Leeds, UK: Emerald.

Hawkins, R. (2008). Can linguistic knowledge be eliminated from theories of SLA? *Lingua* 118, 613–619.

Hawkins, R. (2001). *Second language syntax: A generative introduction*. Oxford, UK: Blackwell.

Hawkins, R., and C. Y.-H. Chan (1997). The partial availability of universal grammar in second language acquisition: The "failed functional features hypothesis." *Second Language Research* 13, 187–227.

Hawkins, R., and S. Liszka (2003). Locating the source of defective past tense marking in advanced L2 English speakers. In R. van Hout, A. Hulk, F. Kuiken, and R. Towell (Eds.), *The Lexicon-Syntax Interface in Second Language Acquisition* (pp. 21–44). Philadelphia: John Benjamins.

Hawley, C. (1987). Towards a language policy. In W. Hirsh (Ed.), *Living Languages: Bilingualism and Community Languages in New Zealand* (pp. 45–53). Auckland: Heinemann.

Hazäel-Massieux, M.-C. (1993). *Ecrire en Créole* [Writing in Creole]. Paris: L'Harmattan.

Haznedar, B., and B. Schwartz (1997). Are there optional infinitives in child L2 acquisition? *Proceedings of the Boston University Conference on Language Development* 21, 257–268.

He, A. W. (2000). The grammatical and interactional organization of teacher's directives: Implications for socialization of Chinese American children. *Linguistics and Education* 11(2), 119–140.

Heath, S. B. (2000). Linguistics in the study of language in education. *Harvard Educational Review* 70, 49–59.

Heath, S. B. (1982). What no bedtime story means: Narrative skills at home and school. *Language in Society* 11, 49–77.

Heath, S. B. (1972). *Telling Tongues: Language Policy in Mexico: Colony to Nation*. New York: Teachers College Press.

Heath, S. B., and B. Street (2008). *On Ethnography: Approaches to Language and Literacy Research*. New York: Teachers College Press.

Hefer, S. (2007). Interpretation in the Israeli legal system. *Proteus* 16(4), 1, 5–9.

Heh, Y.-C., and Q. Hu (1997). Over-the-phone interpretation: A new way of communication between speech communities. In M. Jérôme-O'Keeffe (Ed.), *Proceedings of the 1997 American Translators Association Annual Conference* (pp. 51–62). Medford, NJ: Information Today.

Heift, T., and M. Schulze (2007). *Errors and Intelligence in Computer-Assisted Language Learning: Parsers and Pedagogues*. London: Routledge.

Heinz, P. (1993). Towards enhanced, authentic second language reading comprehension assessment, research and theory building: The development and analysis of an automated recall protocol scoring system. PhD dissertation, Ohio State University, Columbus.

Heller, M. (2008). Bourdieu and "literacy education." In J. Albright, and A. Luke (Eds.), *Pierre Bourdieu and Literacy Education*. New York: Routledge.

Heller, M. (2007). *Linguistic Minorities and Modernity: A Sociolinguistic Ethnography* (2nd ed.). London, UK: Continuum.

Helms-Park, R. (2003). Transfer in SLA and creoles: The implications of causative serial verbs in the interlanguage of Vietnamese ESL learners. *Studies in Second Language Acquisition* 25, 211–244.

Helt, M. E. (2001). A multi-dimensional comparison of British and American spoken English. In S. Conrad, and D. Biber (Eds.), *Variation in English: Multi-Dimensional Studies* (pp. 157–170). London: Longman.

Hendry, B. (1997). Constructing linguistic and ethnic boundries in a Basque boarderland: Negotiating identity in Rioja Alavesa, Spain. *Language Problems & Language Planning* 21, 216–233.

Henry, A., and R. Roseberry (2001). Using a small corpus to obtain data for teaching a genre. In M. Ghadessy, H. Mohsen, A. Henry, and R. Roseberry (Eds.), *Small Corpus Studies and ELT: Theory and Practice* (pp. 93–133). Amsterdam: John Benjamins.

Henry, A., and R. L. Roseberry (1998). An evaluation of a genre-based approach to the teaching of EAP/ESP writing. *TESOL Quarterly* 32, 147–156.

Henry, J. (1997). The Louisiana French movement: Actors and actions in social change. In A. Valdman (Ed.), *French and Creole in Louisiana* (pp. 183–213). New York: Plenum.

Henze, R., and K. A. Davis (1999). Authenticity and identity: Lessons from indigenous language education. *Anthropology and Education Quarterly* 30(1), 3–21.

Heritage, J., and D. Maynard (Eds.). (2006). *Communication in Medical Care: Interaction between Primary Care Physicians and Patients*. New York: Cambridge University Press.

Hermans, D., T. Bongaerts, K. de Bot, and R. Schreuder (1998). Producing words in a foreign language: Can speakers prevent interference from their first language? *Bilingualism: Language and Cognition* 1, 213–229.

Hermans, T. (Ed.). (2002). *Crosscultural Transgressions: Research Models in Translation Studies II: Historical and Ideological Issues*. Manchester, UK: St. Jerome.

Hermans, T. (1999). *Translation in Systems: Descriptive and System-Oriented Approaches Explained*. Manchester, UK: St. Jerome.

Hermans, T. (Ed.). (1985). *The Manipulation of Literature: Studies in Literary Translation*. London and Sydney: Croom Helm.

Herrara, H. (2001). Getting organized: Lessons to be learned. *Proteus* 10(3). (Page numbers unavailable.)

Herring, S. C. (Ed.). (2003). Media and language change [Special issue]. *Journal of Historical Pragmatics* 4(1).

Herring, S. C., and J. C. Paolillo (2006). Gender and genre variation in weblogs. *Journal of Sociolinguistics* 10(4), 439–459.

Hewings, M., and A. Hewings (2002). "It is interesting to note that…": A comparative study of anticipatory "it" in student and published writing. *English for Specific Purposes* 21, 367–383.

Hewitt, W. E. (2000). *Language Interpreting over the Telephone: A Primer for Court Policy Makers and Managers*. Williamsburg, VA: National Center for State Courts.

Hewitt, W. E. (1997). Letter announcing the National Center for State Courts' Court Telephone Interpretation Service, May 15. Williamsburg, VA: National Center for State Courts.

Hewitt, W. E., and R. J. Lee (1996). Beyond the language barrier, or "You say you were eating an orange?" *State Court Journal* 20(1), 23–31.

Hill, J. H. (1978). Language contact systems and adaptations. *Journal of Anthropological Research* 34(1), 1–26.

Hill, J., and K. Hill (1986). *Speaking Mexicano: Dynamics of Syncretic Language in Central Mexico*. Tucson: University of Arizona Press.

Hill, T. (1997). The development of pragmatic competence in an EFL context. PhD dissertation, Temple University, Tokyo.

Hinkel, E. (2006). Current perspectives on teaching the four skills. *TESOL Quarterly*, 40(1), 109–131.

Hinkel, E. (Ed.). (2005). *Handbook of Research in Second Language Teaching and Learning*. Mahwah, NJ: Lawrence Erlbaum.

Hinkel, E. (2004). *Teaching Academic ESL Writing: Practical Techniques in Vocabulary and Grammar*. Mahwah, NJ: Lawrence Erlbaum.

Hinkel, E. (2003). Simplicity without elegance: Features of sentences in L1 and L2 academic texts. *TESOL Quarterly* 37(2), 275–301.

Hinkel, E. (2002). *Second Language Writers Texts: Linguistic and Rhetorical Features*. Mahwah, NJ: Lawrence Erlbaum.

Hinkel, E. (Ed.). (1999). *Culture in Second Language Teaching and Learning*. New York: Cambridge University Press.

Hinton, L. (2002). *How to Keep Your Language Alive: A Commonsense Approach to One-on-One Language Learning*. Berkeley, CA: Heyday Books.

Hinton, L. (1998). Language loss and revitalization in California: Overview. *International Journal of the Sociology of Language* 132, 83–93.

Hinton, L., and K. Hale (Eds.). (2001). *The Green Book of Language Revitalization in Practice*. San Diego, CA/New York, Academic Press.

Hirsh, W. (Ed.). (1987). *Living Languages: Bilingualism and Community Languages in New Zealand*. Auckland: Heinemann.

Hoey, M. (1991). Some properties of spoken discourses. In R. Bowers, and C. J. Brumfit (Eds.), *Applied Linguistics and English Language Teaching* (pp. 65–84). London: Modern English Publications in association with the British Council.

Hoffmann, A. (1998). The contribution of applied linguists to recent language policy initiatives in New Zealand: An argument for greater involvement. *TESOLANZ Journal* 6, 1–11.

Hoffman, R. R. (1997). The cognitive psychology of expertise and the domain of interpreting. *Interpreting* 2(1/2), 189–230.

Hogan-Brun, G., U. Ozolins, M. Ramonien, and M. Rannut (2007). Language politics and practices in the Baltic States. *Current Issues in Language Planning*, 8(4), 469–631.

Hohepa, M. K. (2006). Biliterate practices in the home: Supporting indigenous language regeneration. *Journal of Language, Identity, and Education* 5(4), 293–301.

Hohepa, P. (2000). *Towards 2030 AD (1): Mäori Language Regeneration: Examining Mäori Language Health*. Wellington: Te Taura Whiri i te Reo Mäori [Mäori Language Commission].

Holliday, A. (1994). *Appropriate Methodology and Social Context*. Cambridge: Cambridge University Press.

Holm, J. (1989). *Pidgins and Creoles, Vol. II: Reference Survey*. Cambridge: Cambridge University Press.

Holm, J. (1988). *Pidgins and Creoles*. Cambridge: Cambridge University Press.

Holmes, J. (1997). Keeping tabs on language shift in New Zealand: Some methodological considerations. *Journal of Multilingual and Multicultural Development* 18, 17–39.

Holmes, J. (1996). The New Zealand spoken component of ICE: Some methodological challenges. In S. Greenbaum (Ed.), *Comparing English Worldwide: The International Corpus of English* (pp. 163–178). Oxford: Clarendon Press.

Holmes, J. S. (2004). The name and nature of translation studies. In L. Venuti (Ed.), *The Translation Studies Reader* (2nd ed., pp. 180–192). London and New York: Routledge.

Holmes, J. S. (2000). The name and nature of translation studies. In L. Venuti (Ed.), *The Translation Studies Reader* (pp. 172–185). London and New York: Routledge.

Holmes, J. S. (1988/1994). The name and nature of translation studies. In J. S. Holmes *Translated! Papers on Literary Translation and Translation Studies* (Ed. Raymond van den Broeck, pp. 67–80). Amsterdam: Rodopi.

Holmes, J. S. (1987). The name and nature of translation studies. In G. Toury (Ed.), *Translation across Cultures* (pp. 9–24). New Delhi: Bahri.

Holmes, J. S. (1972). *The Name and Nature of Translation Studies*. Amsterdam: Translation Studies Section, University of Amsterdam, Department of General Literary Studies.

Hookoomsingh, V. (2004). Proposal for a harmonized orthography for Mauritian Creole Language (MCL). Retrieved April 27, 2005, from http://www.edutech.mu/?q+node/view/336

Hopp, H. (2006). Syntactic features and reanalysis in near-native processing. *Second Language Research* 22, 369–397.

Hopper, P. J. (1998). Emergent grammar. In M. Tomasello (Ed.), *The New Psychology of Language* (pp.155–175). Mahwah, NJ: Lawrence Erlbaum.

Hornberger, N. H. (Ed.). (2008a). *Can Schools Save Indigenous Languages? Policy and Practice on Four Continents* (*Studies in Minority Languages and Communities*). Basingstoke: Palgrave Macmillan.

Hornberger, N. H. (Gen. Ed.). (2008b). *Encyclopedia of Language and Education* (2nd ed., 10 vols.). New York: Springer.

Hornberger, N. H. (2006a). Negotiating methodological rich points in applied linguistics research: An ethnographer's view. In M. Chalhoub-Deville, C. Chapelle, and P. Duff (Eds.), *Inference and Gernalizability in Applied Linguistics* (pp. 221–240). Amsterdam: John Benjamins.

Hornberger, N. H. (2006b). Voice and biliteracy in indigenous language revitalization: Contentious educational practices in Quechua, Guarani, and Mäori contexts. *Journal of Language, Identity and Education* 5(4), 277–292.

Hornberger, N. H. (Ed.). (2003). *Continua of Biliteracy: An Ecological Framework for Educational Policy, Research and Practice in Multilingual Settings*. Clevedon, Avon, UK: Multilingual Matters.

Hornberger, N. H. (1997a). *Indigenous Literacies in the Americas: Language Planning from the Bottom Up*. Berlin & New York: Mouton de Gruyter.

Hornberger, N. H. (1997b). Literacy, language maintenance and linguistic human rights: Three telling cases. *International Journal of the Sociology of Language* 127, 87–103.

Hornberger, N. H. (1996). *Indigenous Literacies in the Americas: Language Planning from the Bottom Up*. Berlin: Mouton de Gruyter.

Hornberger, N. H. (1989). Can Peru's rural schools be agents for Quechua language maintenance? *Journal of Multilingual and Multicultural Development* 10(2), 145–159.

Hornberger, N. H. (1988). *Bilingual Education and Language Maintenance: A Southern Peruvian Quechua Case*. Dordrecht, Holland: Foris.

Hornberger, N. H., and S. M. Coronel-Molina (2004). Quechua language shift, maintenance and revitalization in the Andes: The case for language planning. *International Journal of the Sociology of Language* 167, 9–67.

Hornberger, N. H., and D. Corson (Eds.). (1997). *Research Methods in Language and Education: Encyclopedia of Language and Education* (vol. 8). Dordrecht: Kluwer.

Hornberger, N. H., and K. A. King (2000). Reversing Quechua language shift in South America. In J. A. Fishman (Ed.), *Can Threatened Languages Be Saved? Reversing Language Shift Revisited: A 21st Century Perspective* (pp. 166–194). Clevedon, Avon, UK: Multilingual Matters.

Hornberger, N. H., and K. A. King (1996). Language revitalisation in the Andes: Can the schools reverse language shift? *Journal of Multilingual and Multicultural Development* 17(6), 427–441.

Hornberger, N. H., and M. Pütz (Eds.). (2006). *Language Loyalty, Language Planning and Language Revitalization: Recent Writings and Reflections from Joshua A. Fishman: Bilingual Education and Bilingualism*. Clevedon, Avov, UK: Multilingual Matters.

Hornstein, N., and D. Lightfoot (Eds.). (1981). *Explanation in Linguistics: The Logical Problem of Language Acquisition*. London: Longman.

Horst, M., T. Cobb, and I. Nicolae (2005). Expanding academic vocabulary with an interactive on-line database. *Language Learning and Technology* 9(2), 90–110.

Horvath, B. (1985). *Variation in Australian English: The Sociolects of Sydney*. Cambridge: Cambridge University Press.

Hoshino, N., and J. F. Kroll (2008). Cognate effects in picture naming: Does cross-language activation survive a change of script? *Cognition* 106, 501–511.

Hossain, T., and J. W. Tollefson (2007). Language policy in education in Bangladesh. In A. B. M. Tsui, and J. W. Tollefson (Eds.), *Language Policy, Culture and Identity in Asian Contexts* (pp. 241–257). Mahwah, NJ: Lawrence Erlbaum.

Houck, N., and S. M. Gass (1996). Non-native refusals: A methodological study. In S. M. Gass, and J. Neu (Eds.), *Speech Acts across Cultures: Challenge to Communication in a Second Language* (pp. 45–64). Berlin: Mouton de Gruyter.

House, J. (1996). Developing pragmatic fluency in English as a foreign language: Routines and metapragmatic awareness. *Studies in Second Language Acquisition* 17, 225–252.

Hoven, D. (1999). A model for listening and viewing comprehension in multimedia environments. *Language Learning and Technology* 3(1), 88–103.

Howard, K. (2004). Socializing respect at school in northern Thailand. *Working Papers in Educational Linguistics* 20(1), 1–30.

Howatt, A. P. R. (2004). *A History of English Language Teaching* (2nd ed.). Oxford: Oxford University Press.

Howatt, A. P. R. (1999). History of second language teaching. In B. Spolsky (Ed.), *Concise Encyclopedia of Educational Linguistics* (pp. 618–625). Amsterdam: Elsevier.

Howatt, A. P. R. (1984). *A History of English Language Teaching*. Oxford: Oxford University Press.

Howatt, A. P. R., and H. Widdowson (2004). *A History of English Language Teaching* (2nd ed.). Oxford: Oxford University Press.

Hubbard, P., and M. Levy (Eds.). (2006). *Teacher Education in CALL*. Amsterdam: John Benjamins.

Huckin, T., and J. Coady (1999). Incidental vocabulary acquisition in a second language: A review. *Studies in Second Language Acquisition* 21, 121–138.

Huddleston, R., and G. Pullum (2002). *The Cambridge Grammar of the English Language*. New York: Cambridge University Press.

Hudson, T. (2007). *Teaching Second Language Reading*. New York: Oxford University Press.

Hughes, A. (2003). *Testing for Language Teachers* (2nd ed.). New York: Cambridge University Press.

Hughes, R., and M. McCarthy (1998). From sentence to discourse: Discourse grammar and English language teaching. *TESOL Quarterly* 32(2), 263–287.

Hull, G. (2007). Mobile texts and migrant audiences: Rethinking literacy in a new media age. Plenary Presentation to the Annual National Reading Conference, Austin, TX.

Hull, G. (Ed.). (1997). *Changing Work, Changing Workers: Critical Perspectives on Language, Literacy and Skills*. Albany: State University of New York Press.

Hulstijn, J. (2003). Connectionist models of language processing and the training of listening skills with the aid of multimedia software. *Computer Assisted Language Learning* 16(5), 413–425.

Hulstijn, J., and R. DeKeyser (Eds.). (1997). Testing SLA theory in the research laboratory [Special issue]. *Studies in Second Language Acquisition* 19, 2.

Hundt, M. (2006). "The committee *has/have* decided…": On concord patterns with collective nouns in inner and outer circle varieties of English. *Journal of English Linguistics* 34(3), 206–232.

Hundt, M. (1998). *New Zealand English Grammar: Fact or Fiction? A Corpus-Based Study in Morphosyntactic Variation*. Amsterdam: John Benjamins.

Hundt, M., and C. Biewer (2007). The dynamics of inner and outer circle varieties in the Pacific. In M. Hundt et al. (Eds.), *Corpus Linguistics and the Web* (pp. 253–273). Amsterdam: Rodopi.

Hundt, M., and C. Mair (1999). "*Agile*" and "*uptight*" genres: The corpus-based approach to language change in progress. *International Journal of Corpus Linguistics* 4, 221–242.

Hundt, M., N. Nesselhauf, and C. Biewer (Eds.). (2007). *Corpus Linguistics and the Web*. Amsterdam: Rodopi.

Hungarian Ministry of Education (2007). *Nemzeti alaptanterv* [National core curriculum—NCC]. Retrieved August 5, 2008, from http://www.okm.gov.hu/letolt/kozokt/nat_070926.pdf

Hungarian Ministry of Education (2003). *Nemzeti alaptanterv* [National core curriculum—NCC]. Budapest: Oktatási Minisztérium.

Hungarian Ministry of Education (1995). *Nemzeti alaptanterv* [National core curriculum—NCC]. Budapest: Oktatási Minisztérium.

Hunston, S. (2002a). *Corpora in Applied Linguistics*. Cambridge: Cambridge University Press.

Hunston, S. (2002b). Pattern grammar, language teaching and linguistic variation: Applications of a corpus-driven grammar. In R. Reppen, S. Fitzmaurice, and D. Biber (Eds.), *Using Corpora to Explore Linguistic Variation* (pp. 167–183). Amsterdam: John Benjamins.

Hunston, S., and G. Francis (2000). *Pattern Grammar: A Corpus-Driven Approach to the Lexical Grammar of English*. Amsterdam: John Benjamins.

Hunston, S., and G. Francis (1998). Verbs observed: A corpus-driven pedagogic grammar. *Applied Linguistics* 19(1), 45–72.

Hunston, S., and G. Thompson (Eds.). (2000). *Evaluation in Text: Authorial Stance and the Construction of Discourse*. New York: Oxford University Press.

Huntley, H. (2006). *Essential Academic Vocabulary*. New York: Houghton Mifflin.

Huss, L. (1999). *Reversing Language Shift in the Far North: Linguistic Revitalization in Northern Scandinavia and Finland*. Uppsala, Sweden: Uppsala University Library.

Huss, L., A. Camilleri, and K. A. King (Eds.). (2003). *Transcending Monolingualism: Linguistic Revitalisation in Education: Multilingualism and Linguistic Diversity*. Lisse, The Netherlands: Swets & Zeitlinger.

Huth, T. (2006). Negotiating structure and culture: L2 learners' realization of L2 compliment-response sequences in talk-in-interaction. *Journal of Pragmatics* 38, 2025–2050.

Hyland, K. (2008). Genre and academic writing in the disciplines. *Language Teaching* 41, 543–562.

Hyland, K. (2005). Stance and engagement: A model of interaction in academic discourse. *Discourse Studies* 7, 173–192.

Hyland, K. (2004a). *Disciplinary Discourses*. Ann Arbor: University of Michigan Press.

Hyland, K. (2004b). *Genre and Second Language Writing*. Ann Arbor: University of Michigan Press.

Hyland, K. (2002a). Directives: Argument and engagement in academic writing. *Applied Linguistics* 23(2), 215–239.

Hyland, K. (2002b). What do they mean? Questions in academic writing. *Text* 22(4), 529–557.

Hyland, K. (2001). Humble servants of the discipline? Self-mention in research articles. *English for Specific Purposes* 20, 207–226.

Hyland, K. (2000). *Disciplinary Discourses: Social Interaction in Academic Writing*. Harlow, UK: Longman.

Hyland, K. (1998a). *Hedging in Scientific Research Articles*. Amsterdam: John Benjamins.

Hyland, K. (1998b). The impact of teacher-written feedback on individual writers. *Journal of Second Language Writing* 7, 255–286.

Hyland, K. (1996). Writing without Conviction? Hedging in science research articles. *Applied Linguistics* 17(4), 433–454.

Hyland, K., and P. Tse (2005). Hooking the reader: A corpus study of evaluative that in abstracts. *English for Specific Purposes* 24, 123–139.

Hyltenstam, K., and C. Stroud (1996). Language maintenance. In H. Goeble, P. Nelde, A. Stary, and W. Wölck (Eds.), *Contact Linguistics* (pp. 567–578). Berlin: Walter de Gruyter.

Hymes, D. H. (1972a). Models of the interaction of language and social life (Revised from a 1967 paper). In J. Gumperz, and D. Hymes (Eds.), *Directions in Sociolinguistics: The Ethnography of Communication* (pp. 35–71). Blackwell.

Hymes, D. H. (1972b). On communicative competence. In J. Pride, and J. Holmes (Eds.), *Sociolinguistics* (pp. 269–293). Harmondsworth, UK: Penguin.

Hymes, D. H. (1971). *On Communicative Competence*. Philadelphia: University of Pennsylvania Press.

Hyon, S. (2002). Genre and ESL reading: A classroom study. In A. M. Johns (Ed.), *Genre in the Classroom: Multiple Perspectives* (pp. 121–141). Mahwah, NJ: Lawrence Erlbaum.

Hyon, S. (2001). Long-term effects of genre-based instruction: A follow-up study of an EAP reading course. *English for Specific Purposes* 20, 417–438.

Hyon, S. (1996). Genre in three traditions: Implications for ESL. *TESOL Quarterly* 30, 693–722.

Ihalainen, O. (1990). A source data for the study of English dialect syntax: The Helsinki Corpus. In J. Aarts, and W. Meijs (Eds.), *Theory and Practice in Corpus Linguistics* (pp. 83–103). Amsterdam: Rodopi.

ILEA Afro-Caribbean Language and Literacy Project in Further Adult Education (1990). *Language and Power*. London: Harcourt Brace Jovanovich.

Ilyenkov, E. V. (1974). Activity and knowledge. Available: http://www.marxists.org/archive/ilyenkov/works/activity/index.htm

Indefrey, P. (2006). A meta-analysis of hemodynamic studies on first and second language processing: Which suggestions can we trust and what do they mean? In P. Indefrey, and M. Gullberg (Eds.), *The Cognitive Neuroscience of Second Language Acquisition* (pp. 279–304). Malden, MA: Blackwell.

Inglehart, R. F., and M. Woodward (1972). Language conflicts and political community. In P. P. Giglioli (Ed.), *Language and Social Context* (pp. 358–377). Baltimore: Penguin.

Ingram, D. E. (2003). Language planning: Education and policy issues. In W. Bright et al. (Eds.), *International Encyclopedia of Linguistics* (4 vols.; vol. 2, pp. 412–414). New York: Oxford University Press.

Ingram, D. E. (1994). Language policy in Australia in the 1990s. In R. D. Lambert (Ed.), *Language Planning around the World: Contexts and Systemic Change* (pp. 69–105). Washington, DC: National Foreign Language Center.

Ingram, D. E. (1989). Language-in-education planning. In R. B. Kaplan et al. (Eds.), *Annual Review of Applied Linguistics: Vol. 10. Survey of Applied Linguistics Broadly Defined* (pp. 53–78). New York: Cambridge University Press.

Inoue, A. (2007). Copula patterns in Hawai'i creole: Creole origin and decreolization. In M. Huber, and V. Velupillai (Eds.), *Synchronic and Diachronic Perspectives on Contact Languages* (pp. 199–212). Amsterdam/Philadelphia: Benjamins.

International Corpus of English (ICE). http://ice-corpora.net/ice/.

Interpretation and translation: The challenges ahead. (2005). *ICC Newsletter* 5, 6.

Iwashita, N. (2003). Negative feedback and positive evidence in task-based interaction: Differential effects on L2 development. *Studies in Second Language Acquisition* 25, 1–36.

Jääskeläinen, R. (1998). Think-aloud protocols. In M. Baker (Ed.), *Routledge Encyclopedia of Translation Studies* (pp. 265–269). London and New York: Routledge.

Jackendoff, R. S. (2002). *Foundations of Language*. New York: Oxford University Press.

Jackendoff, R. S. (1990). *Semantic structures*. Cambridge, MA: MIT Press.

Jackson, P. W. (Ed.). (1992). *Handbook of Research on Curriculum: A Project of the American Educational Research Association*. New York: Macmillan.

Jacobsen, B. (2008). Interactional pragmatics and court interpreting: An analysis of face. *Interpreting* 10(1), 128–158.

Jacobson, R. (1959). On linguistic aspects of translation. In R. A. Brower (Ed.), *On Translation* (pp. 232–239). Cambridge: Harvard University Press.

James, C. T. (1975). The role of information in lexical decisions. *Journal of Experimental Psychology: Human Perception and Performance* 1, 130–136.

James, M. (2006). Transfer of learning from a university content-based EAP course. *TESOL Quarterly* 40, 783–806.

Jamieson, J., and C. A. Chapelle (1987). Working styles on computers as evidence for second language learning strategies. *Language Learning* 37(4), 523–544.

Jang, S.-C. (1998). Dimensions of spoken and written Taiwanese: A corpus-based register study. PhD dissertation, University of Hawai'i, Honolulu.

Jared, D., and J. F. Kroll (2001). Do bilinguals activate phonological representations in one or both of their languages when naming words? *Journal of Memory and Language* 44, 2–31.

Jarvis, S. (2002). Topic continuity in L2 English article use. *Studies in Second Language Acquisition* 24, 387–418.

Jarvis, S., and A. Pavlenko (2008). *Cross-Linguistic Influence in Language and Cognition*. New York: Routledge.

Jenkins, H. M. (Ed.). (1982). *Educating Students from Other Nations*. San Francisco: Jossey Bass.

Jenkins, J. (2006). Current perspectives on teaching World Englishes and English as a Lingua Franca. *TESOL Quarterly* 40(1), 157–181.

Jensen, A. (2008). Discourse strategies in professional negotiation: A case study. *English for Specific Purposes* 28, 4–18.

Jensen, C., and C. Hansen (1995). The effect of prior knowledge on EAP listening test performance. *Language Testing* 12(1), 99–119.

Jeon, K. (2007). Interaction-driven L2 learning: Characterizing linguistic development. In A. Mackey (Ed.), *Conversational Interaction in Second Language Acquisition: A Series of Empirical Studies* (pp. 379–403). Oxford: Oxford University Press.

Jepson, K. (2005). Conversations—and negotiated interaction—in text and voice chat rooms. *Language Learning & Technology* 9(3), 79–98.

Jernudd, B. H. (1971). Social change and Aboriginal speech variation in Australia. *Anthropological Linguistics* 13, 16–32.

Jernudd, B. H., and J. Das Gupta (1971). Towards a theory of language planning. In J. Rubin, and B. H. Jernudd (Eds.) *Can Language be Planned? Sociolinguistic Theory and Practice for Developing Nations* (pp. 195–216). Honolulu: University Press of Hawai'i.

Jescheniak, J. D., and K. I. Schriefers (1998). Discrete serial versus cascading processing in lexical access in speech production: Further evidence from the coactivation of near-synonyms. *Journal of Experimental Psychology: Learning, Memory and Cognition* 24, 1256–1274.

Jiang, N. (1998). Testing processing explanations for the asymmetry in masked cross-language priming. *Bilingualism: Language and Cognition* 2, 59–75.

Joaquin, A. D. L. (2010). The prefrontal cortex: Through maturation, socialization and regression. In A. W. Mates, L. Mikesell, and M. S. Smith (Eds.), Language, Interaction and Frontotemporal Dementia: Reverse Engineering the Social Mind. (Chapter 7.) London: Equinox.

Johansson, C. (1995). *The Relativizers* Whose *and* Of Which *in Present-Day English: Description and Theory*. Uppsala, Sweden: Uppsala University.

Johansson, S., and K. Hofland (1989). *Frequency Analysis of English Vocabulary and Grammar* (vols. 1–2). Oxford: Clarendon Press.

Johns, A. M. (Ed.). (2002). *Genre in the Classroom*. Mahwah, NJ: Lawrence Erlbaum.

Johns, A. M. (1997). *Text, Role and Context*. New York: Cambridge University Press.

Johns, A. M. (1991). Interpreting an English competency examination: The frustrations of an ESL science student. *Written Communication* 8, 379–401.

Johns, A. M., and T. Dudley-Evans (1991). English for specific purposes: International in scope, specific in purpose. *TESOL Quarterly* 25, 297–315.

Johns, T. (1997). Contexts: The background, development and trialling of a concordance-based CALL Program. In A. Wichmann, S. Fligelstone, T. McEnery, and G. Knowles (Eds.), *Teaching and Language Corpora* (pp. 100–115). London: Longman.

Johns, T. (1994). From printout to handout: Grammar and vocabulary teaching in the context of data-driven learning. In T. Odlin (Ed.), *Perspectives on Pedagogical Grammar* (pp. 293–313). Cambridge: Cambridge University Press.

John-Steiner, V. (1985). The road to competence in an alien language: A Vygotskian perspective on bilingualism. In J. V. Wertsch (Ed.), *Culture, Communication and Cognition: Vygotskian Perspectives* (pp. 348–371). Cambridge: Cambridge University Press.

Johnson, K. (1996). *Language Teaching and Skill Learning.* Oxford: Blackwell.

Johnson, K., and H. Johnson (Eds.). (1998). *Encyclopedic Dictionary of Applied Linguistics.* Oxford: Blackwell.

Johnson, R. K. (1997). The Hong Kong education system: Late immersion under stress. In R. K. Johnson, and M. Swain (Eds.), *Immersion Education: International Perspectives* (pp. 171–189). Cambridge: Cambridge University Press.

Johnson, R. K. (Ed.). (1989). *The Second Language Curriculum.* Cambridge: Cambridge University Press.

Johnson, R. K., and M. Swain (Eds.). (1997). *Immersion Education: International Perspectives.* Cambridge: Cambridge University Press.

Johnston, B., G. Kasper, and S. Ross (1998). Effect of rejoinders in production questionnaires. *Applied Linguistics* 19, 157–182.

Johnstone, B. (2000). *Qualitative Methods in Sociolinguistics.* New York: Oxford University Press.

Jones, A. (1994). The limits of voice identification. In J. Gibbons (Ed.), *Language and the Law* (pp. 346–361). London: Longman.

Jones, D. V., and M. Martin-Jones (2004). Bilingual education and language revitalization in Wales: Past achievements and current issues. In J. W. Tollefson, and A. B. M. Tsui (Eds.), *Medium of Instruction Policies: Which Agenda? Whose Agenda?* (pp. 43–70). Mahwah, NJ: Lawrence Erlbaum.

Jones, L. C., and J. L. Plass (2002). Supporting listening comprehension and vocabulary acquisition in French with multimedia annotations. *Modern Language Journal* 86, 546–561.

Jones, M. C. (1998). Death of a language, birth of an identity: Brittany and the Bretons. *Language Problems and Language Planning* 22(2), 129–142.

Jones, R. L., and B. Spolsky (1975). *Testing Language Proficiency.* Arlington, VA: Center for Applied Linguistics.

Joseph, C. M. B. (1997). Haitian Creole in New York. In O. García, and J. A. Fishman (Eds.), *The Multilingual Apple: Language in New York City* (pp. 282–299). Berlin: Mouton de Gruyter.

Joseph, J., and L. R. Waugh (Eds.). (in press). *Cambridge History of Linguistics.* Cambridge: Cambridge University Press.

Jucker, A. H. (1992). *Social Stylistics: Syntactic Variation in British Newspapers.* Berlin: Mouton.

Judd, E. (1992). Language-in-education policy and planning. In W. Grabe, and R. B. Kaplan (Eds.), *Introduction to Applied Linguistics* (pp. 169–188). Reading, MA: Addison-Wesley.

Judicial Improvements and Access to Justice Act (1988). Public Law 100–702, Title VII: Court Interpreter Amendments, Sections 701–712.

Juffs, A. (in press). The second language acquisition of the lexicon. In W. Ritchie, and T. K. Bhatia (Eds.), *The New Handbook of Second Language Acquisition.* Leeds, UK: Emerald.

Juffs, A. (2006). Processing reduced relative vs. main verb ambiguity in English as a second language: A replication study with working memory. In R. Slabakova, S. Montrul, and

P. Prevost (Eds.), *Inquiries in Linguistic Development in Honor of Lydia White* (pp. 213–232). Amsterdam: John Benjamins.

Juffs, A. (2005). The influence of first language on the processing of *wh-* movement in English as a second language. *Second Language Research* 21, 121–51.

Juffs, A. (2004). Representation, processing and working memory in a second language. *Transactions of the Philological Society* 102, 199–226.

Juffs, A. (2001). Psycholinguistically oriented second language research. In M. McGroarty et al. (Eds.), *Annual Review of Applied Linguistics: Vol. 21. Language and Psychology* (pp. 207–223). New York: Cambridge University Press.

Juffs, A. (2000). An overview of the second language acquisition of the links between verb semantics and morpho-syntax. In J. Archibald (Ed.), *Second Language Acquisition and Linguistic Theory* (pp. 187–227). Oxford: Blackwells.

Juffs, A. (1998a). Some effects of first language argument structure and morphosyntax on second language sentence processing. *Second Language Research* 14, 406–424.

Juffs, A. (1998b). Main verb versus reduced relative clause ambiguity resolution in L2 sentence processing. *Language Learning* 48, 107–147.

Juffs, A. (1996). *Learnability and the Lexicon: Theories and Second Language Acquisition Research*. Amsterdam and Philadelphia, PA: John Benjamins.

Juffs, A., and M. Harrington (1996). Garden path sentences and error data in second language sentence processing. *Language Learning* 46, 283–326.

Juffs, A., and M. Harrington (1995). Parsing effects in L2 sentence processing: Subject and object asymmetries in WH- extraction. *Studies in Second Language Acquisition* 17, 483–512.

Jupp, T., C. Roberts, and J. Cook-Gumperz (1982). Language and disadvantage: The hidden process. In J. J. Gumperz (Ed.), *Language and Social Identity* (pp. 232–256). Cambridge: Cambridge University Press.

Jurasek, R. T. (1996). Languages across the curriculum across the country. In B. Turlington, and R. Schoenberg (Eds.), *Spreading the Word II: Promising Developments for Undergraduate Foreign Language Instruction* (pp. 27–34). Washington, DC: American Council on Education.

Jurasek, R. T. (1993). Languages across the curriculum: A case history from Earlham College and a generic rationale. In M. Krueger, and F. Ryan (Eds.), *Language and Content: Discipline-Based Approaches to Language Study* (pp. 85–102). Lexington, MA: D.C. Heath.

Kabanova, O. Y. (1985). The teaching of foreign languages. *Instructional Science* 14, 1–47.

Kachru, B. B. (Ed.). (1992). *The Other Tongue: English across Cultures* (2nd ed.). Urbana: University of Illinois Press.

Kachru, B. B. (1988). The spread of English and sacred linguistic cows. In P. H. Lowenberg (Ed.), *Language Spread and Language Policy: Issues, Implication and Case Studies* (*Georgetown University Round Table on Languages and Linguistics*) (pp. 207–228). Washington, DC: Georgetown University Press.

Kachru, B. B. (1986). *The Alchemy of English: The Spread, Functions and Models of Non-native Englishes*. Oxford: Pergamon.

Kachru, B. B. (1982). *The Indianization of English*. New Delhi: Oxford University Press.

Kahlas-Tarkka, L., and M. Rissanen (2007). The sullen and the talkative: Discourse strategies in the Salem examinations. *Journal of Historical Pragmatics* 8(1), 1–24.

Kalina, S. (2005). Quality assurance for interpreting processes. *Meta: Translators' Journal* 50(2), 768–784.

Kaltenböck, G., and B. Mehlmauer-Larcher (2005). Computer corpora and the language classroom: On the potential and limitations of computer corpora in language teaching. *ReCALL* 17(1), 65–84.

Kamwangamalu, N. M. (1997). Multilingualism and education policy in post-apartheid South Africa. *Language Problems & Language Planning* 21, 234–253.

Kanagy, R., and K. Igarashi (1997). Acquisition of pragmatic competence in a Japanese immersion kindergarten. In L. F. Bouton (Ed.), *Pragmatics and Language Learning* (vol. 8, pp. 243–265). Champaign: University of Illinois, Urbana-Champaign, Division of English as an International Language (DEIL).

Kane, M. (2006). Validation. In R. Brennan (Ed.), *Educational Measurement* (4th ed.). Westport, CT: Greenwood.

Kanno, Y. (2008). *Language and Education in Japan: Unequal Access to Bilingualism.* Basingstoke, UK: Palgrave, Macmillan.

Kanno, Y. (2003). *Negotiating Bilingual and Bicultural Identities: Japanese Returnees betwixt Two Worlds.* Mahwah, NJ: Lawrence Erlbaum.

Kanno, Y., and B. Norton (Eds.). (2003). Imagined communities and educational possibilities [Special issue]. *Journal of Language, Identity, and Education* 2(4).

Kanoksilapatham, B. (2007). Rhetorical moves in biochemistry research articles. In D. Biber, U. Connor, and T. Upton (Eds.), *Discourse on the Move: Using Corpus Analysis to Describe Discourse Structure* (pp. 73–120). Amsterdam: John Benjamins.

Kanoksilapatham, B. (2005). Rhetorical structure of biochemistry research articles. *English for Specific Purposes* 24, 269–292.

Kaplan, R. B. (2009a). Review essay: An introduction to applied linguistics: From practice to theory, by Alan Davies. *Journal of Multilingual and Multicultural Development* 30(2), 167–173.

Kaplan, R. B. (2009b). Review of Language polices and TESOL: Perspectives from practice, by V. Ramanathan, and B. Morgan. *Current Issues in Language Planning* 10 (2) 236–242.

Kaplan, R. B. (2005). Contrastive rhetoric. In E. Hinkel (Ed.), *Handbook of Research on Second Language Teaching and Learning* (pp. 375–391). Mahwah, NJ: Lawrence Erlbaum.

Kaplan, R. B. (2003). CATESOL, yesterday and today—tomorrow is left to younger hands. *CATESOL* 15(1), 7–18.

Kaplan, R. B. (2002a). Preface. In R. B. Kaplan (Ed.), *The Oxford Handbook of Applied Linguistics* (pp. v–x). New York: Oxford University Press.

Kaplan, R. B. (Ed.). (2002b). *The Oxford Handbook of Applied Linguistics.* Oxford: Oxford University Press.

Kaplan, R. B. (2001). English—the accidental language of science? In U. Ammon (Ed.), *The Dominance of English as a Language of Science: Effects on Other Language Communities* (pp. 3–26). Berlin: Mouton de Gruyter.

Kaplan, R. B. (1999). Applied Linguistics: (Yesterday,) Today and Tomorrow. Paper Delivered at the 12th World Congress of Applied Linguistics. Tokyo, 2 August.

Kaplan, R. B. (1997). An IEP is a many-splendored thing. In M. A. Christison, and F. L. Stoller (Eds.), *A Handbook for Language Program Administrators* (pp. 3–19). Burlingame, CA: Alta Book Center.

Kaplan, R. B. (1994). Language policy and planning in New Zealand. In W. Grabe et al. (Eds.), *Annual Review of Applied Linguistics: Vol. 14. Language Policy and Planning* (pp. 156–176). New York: Cambridge University Press.

Kaplan, R. B. (1993a). Conquest of paradise: Language planning in New Zealand. In M. Hoey, and G. Fox (Eds.), *Data, Description, Discourse: Papers on the English Language in Honour of John McH Sinclair on His 60th Birthday* (pp. 151–175). London: Harper-Collins.

Kaplan, R. B. (1993b). TESOL and applied linguistics in North America. In S. Silberstein (Ed.), *The State of the Art TESOL Essays* (pp. 373–381). Alexandria, VA: TESOL.

Kaplan, R. B. (1992). Applied linguistics and language policy and planning. In W. Grabe, and R. B. Kaplan (Eds.), *Introduction to Applied Linguistics* (pp. 143–165). Reading, MA: Addison-Wesley.

Kaplan, R. B. (1991). On applied linguistics and discourse analysis. *Annual Review of Applied Linguistics* 11, 199–204.

Kaplan, R. B. (1988). Contrastive rhetoric and second language learning: Notes towards a theory of contrastive rhetoric. In A. Purves (Ed.), *Writing across Languages and Cultures: Issues in Contrastive Rhetoric* (pp. 275–304). Newbury Park, CA: Sage.

Kaplan, R. B. (1986). Culture and the written language. In J. M. Valdes (Ed.), *Culture Bound: Bridging the Culture Gap in Language Teaching* (pp. 8–19). New York, Cambridge University Press.

Kaplan, R. B. (Ed.). (1980). *On the Scope of Applied Linguistics*. Rowley, MA: Newbury House.

Kaplan, R. B. (1979). *The Language Needs. of Migrant Workers*. Wellington, New Zealand: New Zealand Council for Educational Research.

Kaplan, R. B. (1970). Notes toward an applied rhetoric. In R. Lugton (Ed.), *Preparing the EFL Teacher: A Projection for the '70s* (pp. 45–74). Philadelphia: The Center for Curriculum Development.

Kaplan, R. B. (1966). Cultural thought patterns in inter-cultural education. *Language Learning* 16, 1–20.

Kaplan, R. B., and R. B. Baldauf, Jr. (2007). Language policy spread: Learning from health and social policy models. *Language Problems & Language Planning* 31(2), 107–129.

Kaplan, R. B., and R. B. Baldauf, Jr. (2001). Not only English: "English only" and the world. In R. D. Gonzalez, and I. Melis (Eds.), *Language Ideologies: Critical Perspectives on the Official English Movement. Vol. 2: History, Theory and Politics* (pp. 293–315). Urbana, IL: National Council of Teachers of English.

Kaplan, R. B., and R. B. Baldauf, Jr. (Eds.). (1999). *Language Planning in Malawi, Mozambique and the Philippines*. Clevedon, Avon, UK: Multilingual Matters.

Kaplan, R. B., and R. B. Baldauf, Jr. (1997a). Language planning processes. In R. B. Kaplan and R. B. Baldauf, Jr., *Language Planning from Practice to Theory* (pp. 87–121). Clevedon, Avon, UK: Multilingual Matters.

Kaplan, R. B., and R. B. Baldauf, Jr. (1997b). *Language Planning: From Practice to Theory*. Clevedon, Avon, UK: Multilingual Matters.

Kaplan, R. B., and W. Grabe (2002). A modern history of written discourse analysis. *Journal of Second Language Writing* 11, 191–223.

Kaplan, R. B., and W. Grabe (2000). Applied linguistics and the *Annual Review of Applied Linguistics*. In W. Grabe et al. (Eds.), *Annual Review of Applied Linguistics: Vol. 20. Applied Linguistics as an Emerging Discipline* (pp. 3–17). New York: Cambridge University Press.

Kaplan, R. B., and H. G. Widdowson (1992). Applied linguistics: An overview. In W. Bright et al. (Eds.), *Oxford International Encyclopedia of Linguistics* (4 vols.; vol. 1, pp. 76–80). New York: Oxford University Press.

Karavas-Doukas, E. (1996). Using attitude scales to investigate teachers' attitudes to the communicative approach. *ELT Journal* 50, 187–198.

Karetu, T. S. (1991). Te Ngahurutanga: A decade of protest, 1980–1990. In W. Hirsh (Ed.), *Living Languages: Bilingualism and Community Languages in New Zealand* (pp. 159–178). Auckland: Heinemann.

Karmani, S. (2005). Petro-linguistics: The emerging nexus between oil, English, and Islam. *Journal of Language, Identity and Education* 4(2), 87–102.

Karpov, Y. V. (2005). *The Neo-Vygotskian Approach to Child Development*. Cambridge: Cambridge University Press.

Karpov, Y. V. (2003). Vygotsky's doctrine of scientific concepts: Its role in contemporary education. In A. Kozulin, B. Gindis, V. S. Ageyev, and S. M. Miller (Eds.), *Vygotsky's Educational Theory in Cultural Context* (pp. 138–155). Cambridge: Cambridge University Press.

Kashoki, M. E. (1982). Achieving nationhood through language: The challenge of Namibia. *Third World Quarterly* 4, 182–190.

Kasper, G. (2006). Beyond repair: Conversation analysis as an approach to SLA. *AILA Review* 19, 83–99.

Kasper, G. (1992). Pragmatic transfer. *Second Language Research* 8, 203–231.

Kasper, G., and S. Blum-Kulka (Eds.). (1993). *Interlanguage Pragmatics*. New York: Oxford University Press.

Kasper, G., and M. Dahl (1991). Research methods in interlanguage pragmatics. *Studies in Second Language Acquisition* 13, 215–247.

Kasper, G., and E. Kellerman (Eds.). (1997). *Communication Strategies: Psycholinguistic and Sociolinguistic Perspectives*. London: Longman.

Kasper, G., and K. Rose (2002). *Pragmatic Development in a Second Language*. Malden, MA: Blackwell. (See also *Language Learning* 52, Supplement 1.)

Kasper, G., and K. R. Rose (1999). Pragmatics and SLA. In W. Grabe et al. (Eds.), *Annual Review of Applied Linguistics: Vol. 19. A Survey of Applied Linguistics* (pp. 81–104). New York: Cambridge University Press.

Kasper, G., and R. Schmidt (1996). Developmental issues in interlanguage pragmatics. *Studies in Second Language Acquisition* 18, 149–169.

Kaufmann, F. (1998). Eléments pour une histoire de l'interprétation simultanée en Israël [Basic principles for a history of simultaneous interpreting in Israel]. *Meta: Translators' Journal* 43(1), 98–109.

Kawamoto, A. H. (1993). Nonlinear dynamics in the resolution of lexical ambiguity: A parallel distributed processing account. *Journal of Memory and Language* 32, 474–516.

Kawamoto, A. H., and J. H. Zemblidge (1992). Pronunciation of homographs. *Journal of Memory and Language* 31, 349–374.

Kayambazinthu, E. (1999). The language planning situation in Malawi. In R. B. Kaplan, and R. B. Baldauf Jr. (Eds.), *Language Planning in Malawi, Mozambique and the Philippines* (pp. 15–85). Clevedon, Avon, UK: Multilingual Matters.

Keating, M. (2005). The International Criminal Court: An introduction. *Communicate!* (January–February). Available: http://www.aiic.net/ViewPage.cfm/page1660.htm.

Keatinge, M. W. (1910/2005). The Great Didactic of Jan Amos Comenius. Available on line in paper back from flipkart.com/reformation-schooles-jan-amos-comenius/1443772402–10x3f824ic

Keatley, C., J. Spinks, and B. De Gelder (1994). Asymmetrical semantic facilitation between languages. *Memory & Cognition* 22, 70–84.

Keck, C. M., and D. Biber (2004). Modal use in spoken and written university registers: A corpus-based study. In R. Facchinetti, and F. Palmer (Eds.), *English Modality in Perspective: Genre Analysis and Contrastive Studies* (pp. 3–25). Frankfurt am Main: Peter Lang Verlag.

Kellet, C. J. M. (1995). Video-aided testing of student delivery and presentation in consecutive interpretation. *Interpreters' Newsletter* 6, 43–66.

Kelly, D. (2005). *A Handbook for Translator Trainers*. Manchester, UK: St. Jerome.

Kelly, D., and C. Way (2007). Editorial: On the Launch of *ITT*. *Interpreter and Translator Trainer* 1(1), 1–13.

Kelly, N. (2007, January). Interpreter certification programs in the US: Where are we headed? *ATA Chronicle* 36(1), 31–39.

Kelly, P. (1991). Lexical ignorance: The main obstacle to listening comprehension with advanced foreign language learners. *International Review of Applied Linguistics* 39(2), 135–149.

Kelm, O. R. (1992). The use of synchronous computer networks in second language instruction: A preliminary report. *Foreign Language Annals* 25(5), 441–454.

Kempe, V., and B. MacWhinney (1998). Acquisition of case marking by adult learners of German and Russian. *Studies in Second Language Acquisition* 20, 543–587.

Kendall, S., and D. Tannen (1997). Gender and language in the workplace. In R. Wodak (Ed.), *Gender and Discourse* (pp. 81–105). London: Sage.

Kendrick, M., and S. Jones (2008). Girls' visual representations of literacy in a rural Ugandan community. *Canadian Journal of Education* 31(3), 372–404.

Kennedy, C. (1996). "La crème de la crème": Coercion and corpus change—an example from recruitment advertisements. In H. Coleman, and L. Cameron (Eds.), *Change and Language* (pp. 28–38). Clevedon, Avon, UK: British Association for Applied Linguistics.

Kennedy, C. (1988). Evaluation of the management of change in ELT projects. *Applied Linguistics* 9, 329–342.

Kennedy, G. D. (1998). *An Introduction to Corpus Linguistics*. London: Longman.

Kennedy, G. D. (1982). Language teaching in New Zealand. In R. B. Kaplan et al. (Eds.), *Annual Review of Applied Linguistics: Vol. 2. Language and Language-in-Education Policy*. Rowley, MA: Newbury House.

Kenrick, D. (1996). Romani literacy at the crossroads. *International Journal of the Sociology of Language* 119, 109–123.

Kenyon, D. (2007). Examining a large-scale language testing project through the lens of assessment engineering: What can language testers learn? Paper presented at the Annual Meeting of the East Coast Organization of Language Testers, Washington, DC.

Kephart, R. F. (1992). Reading creole English does not destroy your brain cells! In J. Siegel (Ed.), *Pidgins, Creoles and Nonstandard Dialects in Education* (pp. 67–86). Melbourne: Applied Linguistics Association of Australia.

Kerekes, J. (2006). Winning an interviewer's trust in a gatekeeping encounter. *Language in Society* 35, 27–57.

Kerekes, J. (1992). Development in nonnative speakers' use and perceptions of assertiveness and supportiveness in a mixed-sex conversation (Occasional Paper No. 21). Honolulu: University of Hawai'i at Manoa, Department of English as a Second Language.

Kern, R. G. (2006). Perspectives on technology in learning and teaching languages. *TESOL Quarterly* 40(1), 183–210.

Kern, R. G. (2000). *Literacy and Language Teaching*. Oxford: Oxford University Press.

Kern, R. G. (1995). Restructuring classroom interaction with networked computers: Effects on quantity and characteristics of language production. *Modern Language Journal* 79, 457–476.

Khalifa, H., and C. J. Weir (2009). *Examining Reading: Studies in Language Testing 29*. Cambridge: Cambridge University Press.

Khemlani-David, M. (1998). Language shift, cultural maintenance and ethnic identity; A study of a minority community: The Sindhis of Malaysia. *International Journal of the Sociology of Language* 129, 67–76.

Khubchandani, L. M. (1989). Language demography in the Indian context. *Sociolinguistics* 18(1–2), 75–84.

Kilborn, K. (1989). Sentence processing in a second language: The timing of transfer. *Language and Speech* 32, 1–23.

Kim, J-H., and Z. Han (2007). Recasts in communicative EFL classes: Do teacher intent and learner interpretation overlap? In A. Mackey (Ed.), *Conversational Interaction in Second Language Acquisition: A Series of Empirical Studies* (pp. 269–297). Oxford: Oxford University Press.

Kim, V. (2009). American justice in a foreign language. Retrieved February 21, 2009, from http://articles.latimes.com/2009/feb/21/local/me-interpret21.

Kim, Y.-J., and D. Biber (1994). A corpus-based analysis of register variation in Korean. In D. Biber, and E. Finegan (Eds.), *Sociolinguistic Perspectives on Register* (pp. 157–181). New York: Oxford University Press.

Kinard, J. T., Sr., and A. Kozulin (2008). *Rigorous Mathematical Thinking: Conceptual Formation in the Mathematics Classroom*. Cambridge: Cambridge University Press.

Kincaid, J. P., R. P. Fishburne, R. L. Rogers, and B. S. Chissom (1975), Derivation of new readability formulas (automated readability index, Fog count and Flesch reading ease formula) for navy enlisted personnel. (pp. 8–75) Memphis, TN: Naval Air Station.

Kindler, A. (2002). *Survey of the States' Limited English Proficient Students and Available Educational Programs and Services: 2000–2001 Summary Report*. Washington, DC: National Clearinghouse for English Language Acquisition. Available: http://www.ncela.gwu.edu/ncbepubs/reports/index.htm

King, K. A. (2000). *Language Revitalization Processes and Prospects: Quichua in the Ecuadorian Andes*. Clevedon, Avon, UK: Multilingual Matters.

King, K. A., and N. H. Hornberger (Eds.). (2008). *Research Methods in Language and Education: Encyclopedia of Language and Education* (vol. 10). New York: Springer.

King, K. A., N. Schilling-Estes, L. Fogle, J. J. Lou, and B. Soukup (Eds.). (2008). *Sustaining Linguistic Diversity: Endangered and Minority Languages and Language Varieties* (*Georgetown University Round Table on Languages and Linguistics*). Washington, DC: Georgetown University Press.

Kinginger, C. (2008). *Language Learning in Study Abroad: Case Histories of Americans in France. Modern Language Journal* (Monograph Series 92). Oxford: Blackwell.

Kinginger, C., and S. J. Savignon (1991). Four conversations: Task variation and learner discourse. In C. Faltis, and M. McGroarty (Eds.), *Language in School and Society: Policy and Pedagogy* (pp. 85–106). New York: Mouton de Gruyter.

Kintsch, W. (1998). *Comprehension: A Framework for Cognition*. Cambridge: Cambridge University Press.

Kintsch, W., and K. Rawson (2005). Comprehension. In M. Snowling, and C. Hulme (Eds.), *The Science of Reading: A Handbook* (pp. 209–226). Malden, MA: Blackwell.

Kiraly, D. C. (2003). From instruction to collaborative construction: A passing fad or the promise of a paradigm shift in translator education? In B. J. Baer, and G. S. Koby (Eds.), *Beyond the Ivory Tower: Rethinking Translation Pedagogy* (American Translators Association Scholarly Monograph Series, vol. 12, pp. 3–27). Amsterdam and Philadelphia: John Benjamins.

Kiraly, D. C. (2000). *A Social Constructivist Approach to Translator Education*. Manchester, UK: St. Jerome.

Kirkwood, M. (Ed.). (1990). *Language Planning in the Soviet Union*. New York: St. Martin's Press.

Klaudy, K. (1998). Explicitation. In M. Baker (Ed.), *Routledge Encyclopedia of Translation Studies* (pp. 80–84). London and New York: Routledge.

Klaus, D. (2003). The use of Indigenous languages in early basic education in Papua New Guinea: A model for elsewhere? *Language and Education* 17(2), 105–111.

Klee, C. (2000). Foreign language instruction. In J. Rosenthal (Ed.), *Handbook of Undergraduate Second Language Education* (pp. 49–72). Mahwah, NJ: Lawrence Erlbaum.

Klee, C., and D. Tedick (1997). The undergraduate foreign language immersion program in Spanish at the University of Minnesota. In S. Stryker, and B. Leaver (Eds.) *Content-based Instruction in Foreign Language Education: Models and Method.* (pp. 140–173). Washington, DC: Georgetown University Press.

Kleinginna, P. R., and A. M. Kleinginna (1981). A categorized list of motivational definitions with a suggestion for a consensual definition. *Motivation and Emotion*, 5, 263–291.

Kleinsasser, R. C. (2004). Australia and New Zealand applied linguistics (ANZAL): Taking stock. In S. M. Gass, and S. Makoni (Eds.), *World Applied Linguistics: AILA Review*, 17 31–56. Philadelphia and Amsterdam: John Benjamins.

Klippel, F. (1984). *Keep Talking: Communicative Fluency Activities for Language Learning.* Cambridge: Cambridge University Press.

Kloss, H. (1998/1977). *The American Bilingual Tradition.* Washington, DC, and McHenry, IL: Center for Applied Linguistics and Delta Systems.

Knapp, K., and G. Antos (in press). *Handbooks of Applied Linguistics* (9 vols.; vol. 5). Berlin: Mouton de Gruyter.

Knight, D., and S. Adolphs (2008). Multi-modal corpus pragmatics: The case of active listenership. In J. Romeo (Ed.), *Corpus and Pragmatics* (pp. 175–190). Berlin: Mouton de Gruyter.

Kobayashi, H., and C. Rinnert (2004). Composing competence: How L1 and L2 writing experience interact. In M. Baynham, A. Deignan, and G. White (Eds.), *Applied Linguistics at the Interface* (pp. 105–118). London: Equinox.

Koby, G. S., and B. J. Baer (2003). Task-based instruction and the new technology: Training translators for the modern language industry. In B. J. Baer, and G. S. Koby (Eds.), *Beyond the Ivory Tower: Rethinking Translation Pedagogy.* (American Translators Association Scholarly Monograph Series, vol. 12, pp. 211–227). Amsterdam and Philadelphia: John Benjamins.

Koch, H. (1991). Language and communication in Aboriginal land claim hearings. In S. Romaine (Ed.), *Language in Australia* (pp. 94–103). Cambridge: Cambridge University Press.

Koda, K. (2008a). Looking back and thinking forward. In K. Koda (Ed.), *Learning to Read across Languages* (pp. 222–234). New York: Lawrence Erlbaum.

Koda, K. (Ed.). (2008b). *Learning to Read across Languages.* New York: Lawrence Erlbaum.

Koda, K. (2005). *Insights into Second Language Reading.* Cambridge: Cambridge University Press.

Kohn, K., and S. Kalina (1996). The strategic dimension of interpreting. *Meta: Translators' Journal* 41(1), 118–138.

Koike, D. A. (1996). Transfer of pragmatic competence and suggestions in Spanish. In S. M. Gass, and J. Neu (Eds.), *Speech Acts across Cultures: Challenge to Communication in a Second Language* (pp. 257–281). Berlin: Mouton de Gruyter.

Kormos, J. (2006). *Speech Production and Second Language Acquisition.* Mahwah, NJ: Lawrence Erlbaum.

Kormos, J., and A. Safar (2008). Phonological short-term memory, working memory and foreign language performance in intensive language learning. *Bilingualism: Language and Cognition* 1, 261–271.

Kortmann, B. (2006). Syntactic Variation in English: A Global Perspective. In B. Aarts, and A. McMahon (Eds.), *Handbook of English Linguistics* (pp. 603–624). Oxford: Blackwell.

Kortmann, B., and S. Wagner (2005). The Freiburg English Dialect Project and Corpus. In B. Kortmann, T. Herrmann, L. Pietsch, and S. Wagner (Eds.), *A Comparative Grammar of British English Dialects: Agreement, Gender, Relative Clauses* (pp. 1–20). Berlin/New York: Mouton de Gruyter.

Koschmann, T. (1999). Meaning making [Special issue]. *Discourse Processes* 27(2).

Koshik, I. (2002). A conversation analytic study of yes/no questions which convey reversed polarity assertions. *Journal of Pragmatics* 34, 1851–1877.

Koshik, I. (1999). Practices of pedagogy in ESL writing conferences: A conversation analytic study of turns and sequences that assist student revision. PhD dissertation, University of California, Los Angeles.

Kouwenberg, S., and P. Muysken (1994). Papiamento. In J. Arends, P. Muysken, and N. Smith (Eds.), *Pidgins and Creoles: An Introduction* (pp. 205–218). Amsterdam: John Benjamins.

Kouritzen, S. (1999). *Face[t]s of First Language Loss*. Mahwah, NJ: Lawrence Erlbaum.

Kowal, M., and M. Swain (1997). From semantic to syntactic processing: How can we promote it in the immersion classroom? In R. K. Johnson, and M. Swain (Eds.), *Immersion Education: International Perspectives* (pp. 284–309). Cambridge: Cambridge University Press.

Kozulin, A. (1995). The learning process: Vygotsky's theory in the mirror of its interpretations. *School Psychology International* 16, 117–29.

Kraemer, R. (1993). Social psychological factors related to the study of Arabic among Israeli high school students. *Studies in Second Language Acquisition* 15, 83–105.

Kramsch, C. (2000). Expansion of the field. *AAAL Newsletter* 20, 1–2.

Kramsch, C. (1993). Redrawing the boundaries of foreign language study. In M. Krueger, and F. Ryan (Eds.), *Language and Content: Discipline- and Content-Based Approaches to Language Study* (pp. 203–217). Lexington, MA: Heath.

Kramsch, C., and S. Thorne (2002). Foreign language learning as global community practice. In D. Block, and D. Cameron (Eds.), *Globalization and Language Teaching* (pp. 83–100). New York: Routledge.

Krapels, A. (1990). An overview of second language writing process research. In B. Kroll (Ed.), *Second Language Writing: Research Insights for the Classroom* (pp. 37–56). New York: Cambridge University Press.

Krashen, S. D. (2004). *The Power of Reading* (2nd ed.). Portsmouth, NH: Heinemann.

Krashen, S. D. (1993). *The Power of Reading: Insights from the Research*. Englewood, CO: Libraries Unlimited.

Krashen, S. D. (1985). *The Input Hypothesis: Issues and Implications*. London: Longman.

Krashen, S. D. (1984). *Writing: Research, Theory and Applications*. Oxford: Pergamon.

Krashen, S. D. (1982). *Principles and Practice in Second Language Acquisition*. Oxford: Pergamon.

Krashen, S. D. (1981). *Second Language Acquisition and Second Language Learning*. Oxford: Pergamon Press.

Krashen, S. D., and T. D. Terrell (2000). *The Natural Approach: Language Acquisition in the Classroom*. Essex: Pearson Education.

Krashen, S. D., and T. D. Terrell (1983). *The Natural Approach: Language Acquisition in the Classroom*. Oxford: Pergamon.

Krauss, M. (1998). The scope of the language endangerment crisis and recent response to it. In K. Matsumara (Ed.), *Studies in Endangered Languages* (pp. 101–114). Tokyo: Hituzi Syobo.

Krauss, M. (1992). The world's languages in crisis. *Language* 68, 4–10.

Kremer, B. (2005). Réflexions d'un praticien sur une étape de la formation des interprètes de conférence: approche méthodologique et pédagogique [A practitioner's reflections on a stage in conference interpreter training: A methodological and pedagogical approach]. *Meta: Translators' Journal* 50(2), 785–794.

Kremer-Sadlik, T., and J. L. Kim (2007). Lessons from sports: Children's socialization to values through family interaction during sports activities. *Discourse and Society* 18(1), 35–52.

Kress, G. R., and T. Van Leeuwen (2002). *Multimodal Discourse: The Modes and Media of Contemporary Communication*. London: Edward Arnold.

Kroll, B. (Ed.). (2003). *Exploring the Dynamics of Second Language Writing*. Cambridge: Cambridge University Press.

Kroll, J. F. (1993). Accessing conceptual representation for words in a second language. In R. Schreuder, and B. Weltens (Eds.), *The Bilingual Lexicon* (pp. 53–81). Amsterdam: John Benjamins.

Kroll, J. F., S. C. Bobb, M. M. Misra, and T. Guo (2008). Language selection in bilingual speech: Evidence for inhibitory processes. *Acta Psychologica* 128, 416–430.

Kroll, J. F., and J. Curley (1988). Lexical memory in novice bilinguals: The role of concepts in retrieving second language words. In M. Gruneberg, P. Morris, and R. Sykes (Eds.), *Practical Aspects of Memory* (vol. 2, pp. 389–395). London: John Wiley & Sons.

Kroll, J. F., and A. M. B. De Groot (Eds.). (2005). *Handbook of Bilingualism*. New York: Oxford University Press.

Kroll, J. F., and A. M. B. De Groot (1997). Lexical and conceptual memory in the bilingual: Mapping form to meaning in two languages. In A. M. B. De Groot, and J. F. Kroll (Eds.), *Tutorials in Bilingualism: Psycholinguistic Perspectives* (pp. 169–199). Mahwah, NJ: Lawrence Erlbaum.

Kroll, J. F., F. Dietz, and D. W. Green (2000). Language switch costs in bilingual picture naming and translation. Invited paper presented as part of a symposium, *Bilingual Lexical and Conceptual Processing* (R. Sanchez-Casas, organizer), International Congress of Psychology, Stockholm, Sweden.

Kroll, J. F., A. Dijkstra, N. Janssen, and H. Schriefers (1999). Cross-language lexical activity during production: Evidence from cued picture naming. Invited paper presented as part of a symposium, *Bilingualism* (J. Grainger, organizer), European Society for Cognitive Psychology, Ghent, Belgium.

Kroll, J. F., C. Gerfen, and P. Dussias (2008). Laboratory designs and paradigms in psycholinguistics. In L. Wei, and M. Moyer (Eds.), *The Blackwell Guide to Research Methods in Bilingualism*. Cambridge, MA: Blackwell.

Kroll, J. F., E. Michael, and A. Sankaranarayanan (1998). A model of bilingual representation and its implications for second language acquisition. In A. F. Healy, and L. E. Bourne (Eds.), *Foreign Language Learning: Psycholinguistic Experiments on Training and Retention* (pp. 365–395). Mahwah, NJ: Lawrence Erlbaum.

Kroll, J. F., and A. Peck (1998). Competing activation across a bilingual's two languages: Evidence from picture naming. Paper presented at the 43rd Annual Meeting of the International Linguistic Association, New York University, New York.

Kroll, J. F., and E. Stewart (1994). Category interference in translation and picture naming: Evidence for asymmetric connections between bilingual memory representations. *Journal of Memory and Language* 33, 149–174.

Kroll, J. F., and N. Tokowicz (2001). The development of conceptual representation for words in a second language. In J. L. Nicol, and T. Langendoen (Eds.), *Language Processing in Bilinguals* (pp. 49–71). Cambridge, MA: Blackwell.

Krueger, M., and F. Ryan (Eds.). (1993). *Language and Content: Discipline- and Content-Based Approaches to Language Study*. Lexington, MA: Heath.

Kryk-Kastovsky, B. (2000). Representations of orality in Early Modern English trial records. *Journal of Historical Pragmatics* 1(2), 201–230.

Kubota, R. (1999). Japanese culture constructed by discourses: Implications for applied linguistics research and ELT. *TESOL Quarterly* 33, 9–35.

Kubota, R., and A. Lehner (2004). Toward critical contrastive rhetoric. *Journal of Second Language Writing* 13, 7–27.

Kubota, R., and A. Lin (Eds.). (2009). *Race, Culture and Identities in Second Language Education*. London: Routledge.

Kubota, R., and A. Lin (Eds.). (2006). Race and TESOL: Introduction to concepts and theories [Special Issue]. *TESOL Quarterly* 40(3), 471–493.

Kubota, R., and A. Lin (Eds.). (2009). *Race, Culture and Identities in Second Language Education*. London: Routledge.

Kubota, R., and A. Lin (Eds.). (2006). Race and TESOL: Introduction to concepts and theories [Special issue]. *TESOL Quarterly* 40(3), 471–493.

Kucera, H., and W. N. Francis (1967). *Computational Analysis of Present-Day American English*. Providence, RI: Brown University Press.

Kulick, D. (1992). *Language Shift and Cultural Reproduction: Socialization, Self and Syncretism in a Papua New Guinea Village*. Cambridge: Cambridge University Press.

Kumaravadivelu, B. (2006). Dangerous liaison: Globalization, empire and TESOL. In J. Edge (Ed.), *(Re)locating TESOL in an Age of Empire* (p. 1–26). New York: Palgrave Macmillan.

Kumaravadivelu, B. (2001). Toward a post-method pedagogy. *TESOL Quarterly* 35, 537–560.

Kunda, G. (1992). *Engineering Culture: Control and Commitment in a High Tech Corporation*. Philadelphia: Temple University Press.

Kunda, G., and J. Van Maanen (1999). Changing scripts at work: Managers and professionals. *Annals of the American Academy of Political and Social Sciences* 561, 64–80.

Kunnan, A. J. (1999). Recent developments in language testing. In W. Grabe et al. (Eds.), *Annual Review of Applied Linguistics: Vol. 19. A Survey of Applied Linguistics* (pp. 235–253). New York: Cambridge University Press.

Kuo, C. (1999). The use of personal pronouns: Role relationships in scientific journal articles. *English for Specific Purposes* 18(2), 121–138.

Kurz, I. (2001). Conference interpreting: Quality in the ears of the user. *Meta: Translators' Journal* 46(2), 394–409.

Kurz, I. (1995). Watching the brain at work—an exploratory study of EEG changes during simultaneous interpreting (SI). *Interpreters' Newsletter* 6, 3–16.

Kurz, I., E. Basel, D. Chiba, W. Patels, and J. Wolfframm (1996). Scribe or actor? A survey paper on personality profiles of translators and interpreters. *Interpreters' Newsletter* 7, 3–18.

Kvale, S. (2006). Dominance through interviews and dialogues. *Qualitative Inquiry* 12(3), 480–500.

Kymlicka, W. (1995). *Multicultural Citizenship: A Liberal Theory of Minority Rights*. Oxford: Clarendon Press.

Kyratzis, A., and J. Cook-Gumperz (2008). Language socialization and gendered practices in childhood. In P. Duff, and N. H. Hornberger (Eds.), *Language Socialization Encyclopedia of Language and Education* (vol. 8, pp. 145–156). New York: Springer.

Kytö, M. (1991). *Variation and Diachrony, with Early American English in Focus*. Frankfurt: Peter Lang.

Kytö, M., M. Rydén, and E. Smitterberg (Eds.) (2006). *Nineteenth-century English: Stability and Change*. Cambridge: Cambridge University Press.

Kytö, M., and T. Walker (2003). The linguistic study of Early Modern English speech-related texts: How 'Bad' can 'Bad' data be? *Journal of English Linguistics* 31(3), 221–248.

Labaree, L. W. (1959). *The Papers of Benjamin Franklin* (vol. 4). New Haven, CT: Yale University Press.

Labov, W., and D. Fanshel (1977). *Therapeutic Discourse: Psychotherapy as Conversation*. New York: Academic Press.

Labrie, N., P. Nelde, and P. J. Weber (1994). Project for the study of less widely used languages of the European community. *Europa Ethnica* 51(2), 67–70.

Lado, R. (1964). *Language teaching: A scientific approach*. New York: McGraw-Hill.

Lado, R. (1961). *Language Testing*. London: Longman.

Lado, R. (1957). *Linguistics across cultures: Applied linguistics for language teachers*. Ann Arbor: University of Michigan Press.

Lado, R., and C. C. Fries (1957). *English Sentence Patterns: Understanding and Producing English Grammatical Structures: An Oral Approach*. Ann Arbor: University of Michigan Press.

Laforgue, L., and G. D. McConnell (Eds.). (1990). *Language Spread and Social Change: Dynamics and Measurement*. Ste.-Foy, Québec: Les Presses de l'Université Laval.

La Heij, W. (1988). Components of Stroop-like interference in picture naming. *Memory & Cognition* 16, 400–410.

La Heij, W., E. De Bruyn, E. Elens, R. Hartsuiker, D. Helaha, and L. Van Schelven (1990). Orthographic facilitation and categorical interference in a word-translation variant of the Stroop task. *Canadian Journal of Psychology* 44, 76–83.

La Heij, W., R. Kerling, and E. Van der Velden (1996). Nonverbal context effects in forward and backward translation: Evidence for concept mediation. *Journal of Memory and Language* 35, 648–665.

Laitin, D., and C. M. Eastman (1989). Language conflict: Transactions and games in Kenya. *Cultural Anthropology* 4(1), 51–72.

Lam, W. S. E. (2008). Language socialization in online communities. In P. A. Duff, and N. H. Hornberger (Eds.), *Language Socialization: Encyclopedia of Language and Education* (vol. 8, pp. 301–311). New York: Springer.

Lam, W. S. E. (2006). Re-envisioning language, literacy and the immigrant subject in new mediascapes. *Pedagogies: An International Journal* 1(3), 171–195.

Lam, W. S. E. (2000). Second language literacy and the design of the self: A case study of a teenager writing on the Internet. *TESOL Quarterly* 34(3), 457–482.

Lambert, W. E. (1974). Culture and language as factors in learning and education. In F. E. Aboud, and R. D. Meade (Eds.), *Cultural Factors in Learning and Education*. Bellingham, WA: Western Washington State College.

Lambert, W. E. (1967). A social psychology of bilingualism. *Journal of Social Issues* 23, 91–109.

Lambert, W. E. (1956a). Developmental aspects of second-language acquisition: I. Associational fluency, stimulus provocativeness, and word order influence. *Journal of Social Psychology* 43, 83–89.

Lambert, W. E. (1956b). Developmental aspects of second-language acquisition: II. Associational stereotypy, associational form, vocabulary commonness, and pronunciation. *Journal of Social Psychology* 43, 91–98.

Lambert, W. E. (1956c). Developmental aspects of second-language acquisition: III. A description of developmental changes. *Journal of Social Psychology* 43, 99–104.

Lambert, W. E. (1955). Measurement of the linguistic dominance of bilinguals. *Journal of Abnormal and Social Psychology* 50, 197–200.

Lamy, M.-N., and R. Goodfellow (1999). "Reflective conversation" in the virtual language classroom. *Language Learning & Technology* 2(2), 43–61.

Landauer, T. K., P. W. Foltz, and D. Laham (1980). Introduction to latent semantic Analysis. *Discourse Processes* 25, 259–284.

Landauer, T. K., D. Laham, B. Rehder, and M. E. Schreiner (1997). How well can passage meaning be derived without using word order? A comparison of Latent Semantic Analysis and humans. In M. G. Shafto, and P. Langley (Eds.), *Proceedings of the 19th Annual Meeting of the Cognitive Science Society* (pp. 412–417). Mahwah, NJ: Lawrence Erlbaum.

Lane, C., et al. (1999). The right to interpreting and translation services in New Zealand courts. *Forensic Linguistics* 6(1), 115–136.

Language Teaching (2007). Forty years of language teaching. *Language Teaching*, 40, 1–15.

Lantolf, J. P. (2007). Conceptual knowledge and instructed second language learning: A sociocultural perspective. In S. Fotos, and H. Nassaji (Eds.), *Form Focused Instruction and Teacher Eeducation: Studies in Honour of Rod Ellis* (pp. 35–54). Oxford: Oxford University Press.

Lantolf, J. P. (2006). Sociocultural theory and second language learning: State of the art. *Studies in Second Language Acquisition* 28, 67–109.

Lantolf, J. P. (Ed.). (2000). *Sociocultural Theory and Second Language Learning*. New York: Oxford University Press.

Lantolf, J. P., and M. E. Poehner (Eds.). (2008). *Sociocultural Theory and the Teaching of Second Languages*. London: Equinox.

Lantolf, J. P., and S. L. Thorne (2007). Sociocultural theory and second language acquisition. In B. VanPatten, and J. Williams (Eds.), *Theories in Second Language Acquisition* (pp. 201–224). Mahwah, NJ: Lawrence Erlbaum.

Lantolf, J., and S. L. Thorne (2006). *Sociocultural Theory and the Genesis of Second Language Development*. Oxford: Oxford University Press.

Lardiere, D. (2006). *Ultimate Attainment in Second Language Acquisition: A Case Study*. New York: Routledge.

Lardiere, D. (2000). Mapping features to forms in second language acquisition. In J. Archibald (Ed.), *Second Language Acquisition and Linguistic Theory* (pp. 102–129). Oxford: Basil Blackwell.

Larkey, L. (1998). Automatic essay grading using text categorization techniques. In *Proceedings of the 21st ACM-SIGIR Conference on Research and Development in Information Retrieval* (pp, 90–95). Melbourne, Australia.

Larsen-Freeman, D. (2004). CA for SLA? It all depends…*Modern Language Journal* 88, 603–607.

Larsen-Freeman, D., and L. Cameron (2008a). *Complex Systems and Applied Linguistics*. Oxford: Oxford University Press.

Larsen-Freeman, D., and L. Cameron (2008b). Research methodology on language development from a complex systems perspective. *Modern Language Journal* 92, 200–213.

Larsen-Freeman, D., and M. H. Long (1991). *Introduction to Second Language Acquisition Research*. London: Longman.

Larson, J. W. (1999). Considerations for testing reading proficiency via computer-adaptive testing. In M. Chalhoub-Deville (Ed.), *Issues in Computer-Adaptive Testing of Reading Proficiency* (pp. 71–90). Cambridge: Cambridge University Press.

Larson, J. W. (1989). S-SCAPE: A Spanish computerized adaptive placement exam. In W. F. Smith (Ed.), *Modern Technology in Foreign Language Education: Applications and Projects*. New York: ACTFL Foreign Language Series.

Larson, J. W. (1987). Computerized adaptive language testing: A Spanish placement exam. In K. M. Bailey, T. L. Dale, and R. T. Clifford (Eds.), *Language Testing Research: Papers from the 1986 Colloquium* (pp. 1–10). Monterey, CA: Defense Language Institute.

Larson, J. W., and H. S. Madsen (1985). Computerized adaptive language testing: Moving beyond computer-assisted testing. *CALICO Journal* 2, 32–36.

Launer, M. K., T. L. Launer, and M. L. Pedro (1998). Do US-based interpreters have a future? *ATA Chronicle* (April), 18–20, 23.

Laurenzo, H. (2008). Note taking for consecutive interpreting. *ATA Chronicle* (October), 24–29.

Laurier, M. (1999). The development of an adaptive test for placement in French. In M. Chalhoub-Deville (Ed.), *Issues in Computer-Adaptive Testing of Reading Proficiency* (pp. 119–132). New York: Cambridge University Press.

Laurier, M. (1991). What we can do with computerized adaptive testing—and what we cannot do. In S. Anivan (Ed.), *Current Developments in Language Testing* (pp. 244–255). Singapore: SEAMEO Regional Language Centre.

Lave, J. (1988). *Cognition in Practice*. Boston, MA: Cambridge University Press.

Lave, J., and E. Wenger (1991). *Situated Learning: Legitimate Peripheral Participation*. New York: Cambridge University Press.

Laviosa, S. (2007). Studying Anglicisms with comparable and parallel corpora. In W. Vandeweghe, S. Vandepitte, and M. Van de Velde (Eds.), *The Study of Language and Translation: Belgian Journal of Linguistics* 21, 123–136.

Laviosa, S. (Ed.). (1998). L'approche basée sur le corpus [The corpus-based approach], *Meta* 43(4). Retrieved March 11, 2008, from www.erudit.org/revue/meta/.

Lawton, D. (1980). Language attitude, discreteness and code shifting in Jamaican Creole. *English World-Wide* 1, 221–226.

Laycock, D. C. (1981). Melanesian linguistic diversity: A Melanesian choice? In R. J. May, and H. Nelson (Eds.), *Melanesian beyond Diversity* (pp. 33–38). Canberra: Research School of Pacific Studies.

Laycock, D. C. (1979). Multilingualism: Linguistics boundaries and unsolved problems in Papua New Guinea. In S. A. Wurm (Ed.), *New Guinea and Neighbouring Areas: A Sociolinguistic Laboratory* (pp. 81–99). The Hague: Mouton.

Layne, P., and S. Lepeintre (1996). Distance instruction. In W. Grabe et al. (Eds.), *Annual Review of Applied Linguistics: Vol. 16. Technology and Language* (pp. 226–239). New York: Cambridge University Press.

Lazaraton, A. (2008). Utilizing qualitative methods for assessment. In E. Shohamy, and N. H. Hornberger (Eds.), *Language Testing and Assessment: Encyclopedia of Language and Education* (2nd ed., vol. 7, pp. 197–209). New York: Springer.

Lazaraton, A. (2003). Evaluating criteria for qualitative research in applied linguistics: Whose criteria and whose research? *Modern Language Journal* 87, 1–12.

Lazaraton, A. (2000). Current trends in research methodology and statistics in applied linguistics. *TESOL Quarterly* 34(3), 175–181.

Lazaraton, A. (1995). Qualitative research in applied linguistics: A progress report. *TESOL Quarterly* 29, 455–472.

Leather, J., and A. James (1996). Second language speech and the influence of the first language. In W. Ritchie, and T. K. Bhatt (Eds.), *Handbook of Second Language Acquisition* (pp. 269–316). New York: Academic.

Lederer, M. (1981). *La traduction simultanée: Expérience et théorie* (*Simultaneous Translation: Experience and Theory*). Paris: Minard.

Lederer, M. (1980). *La traduction simultanée. Fondements théoriques* (*Simultaneous Translation: Theoretical Foundations*). Lille: Université de Lille III.

Lee, D., and J. M. Swales (2006). A corpus-based EAP course for NNS doctoral students: Moving from available specialized corpora to self-compiled corpora. *English for Specific Purposes* 25, 56–75.

Lee, J. (2007). Telephone interpreting—seen from the interpreters' perspective. *Interpreting* 9(2), 231–252.

Lee, N., L. Mikesell, A. D. L. Joaquin, A. W. Mates, and J. H. Schumann (in press). *The Interactional Instinct: The Evolution and Acquisition of Language*. Oxford: Oxford University Press.

Lee, T.-H. (2002). Ear voice span in English into Korean simultaneous interpretation. *Meta: Translators' Journal* 47(4), 596–606.

Lee, T.-H. (1999). Speech proportion and accuracy in simultaneous interpretation from English to Korean. *Meta: Translators' Journal* 44(2), 260–267.

Lee, Y.-A. (2006). Respecifying display questions: Interactional resources for language teaching. *TESOL Quarterly* 40, 691–713.

Leech, G. (2000). Grammar of spoken English: New outcomes of corpus-oriented research. *Language Learning* 50(4), 675–724.

Leech, G. (1997). Teaching and language corpora: A convergence. In A. Wichmann, S. Fligelstone, T. McEnery, and G. Knowles (Eds.), *Teaching and Language Corpora* (pp. 1–23). London: Longman.

Leech, G., M. Hundt, C. Mair, and N. Smith (2009). *Contemporary Change in English: A Grammatical Study*. Cambridge: Cambridge University Press.

Leeser, M. J. (2007). Learner-based factors in L2 reading comprehension and processing grammatical form: Topic familiarity and working memory. *Language Learning* 57, 229–270.

Lefebvre, C. (1998). *Creole Genesis and the Acquisition of Grammar: The Case of Haitian Creole*. Cambridge: Cambridge University Press.

Lefebvre, C., L. White, and C. Jourdan (Eds.). (2006). *L2 acquisition and Creole Genesis*. Amsterdam/Philadelphia: Benjamins.

Lefevere, A. (1992). *Translation, Rewriting and the Manipulation of Literary Fame*. London and New York: Routledge.

Legutke, M., and H. Thomas (1991). *Process and Experience in the Language Classroom*. London: Longman.

Leidner, R. (1993). *Fast Food, Fast Talk: Service Work and the Routinization of Everyday Life*. Berkeley: University of California Press.

Leki, I. (2007). *Undergraduates in a Second Language: Challenges and Complexities of Academic Literacy Development*. Mahwah, NJ: Lawrence Erlbaum.

Leki, I. (2003). A challenge to L2 writing professionals: Is writing overrated? In B. Kroll (Ed.), *Exploring Second Language Writing* (pp. 315–331). New York: Cambridge University Press.

Leki, I. (1990). Coaching from the margins: Issues in written response. In B. Kroll (Ed.), *Second Language Writing: Research Insights for the Classroom* (pp. 57–68). New York: Cambridge University Press.

Leki, I., and J. Carson (1997). "Completely different worlds": EAP and the writing experiences of ESL students in university courses. *TESOL Quarterly* 31, 39–69.

Lemke, J. (1995). *Textual Politics: Discourse and Social Dynamics*. London: Taylor and Francis.

Lennon, P. (1998). Approaches to the teaching of idiomatic language. *IRAL* 36, 11–30.

Lennon, P. (1996). Getting "easy" verbs wrong at the advanced level. *IRAL* 34, 23–36.

Lennon, P. (1990). Investigating fluency in EFL: A quantitative approach. *Language Learning* 40, 387–417.

LePage, R. (1986, October–December). Acts of identity. *English Today* 8, 21–24.

LePage, R. B. (1977). Processes of pidginization and creolization. In A. Valdman (Ed.), *Pidgin and Creole Linguistics* (pp. 222–255). Bloomington: University of Indiana Press.

LePage, R. B. (1968). Problems to be faced in the use of English as a medium of education in four West Indian territories. In J. A. Fishman et al. (Eds.), *Language Problems of Developing Nations* (pp. 431–443). New York: Wiley.

LePage, R. B., and A. Tabouret-Keller (1985). *Acts of Identity: Creole-Based Approaches to Ethnicity and Language*. Cambridge: Cambridge University Press.

Levelt, W. J. M. (1989). *Speaking: From Intention to Articulation*. Cambridge, MA: MIT Press.

Levelt, W. J. M., A. Roelofs, and A. S. Meyer (1999). A theory of lexical access in speech production. *Behavioral and Brain Sciences* 22, 1–75.

Levelt, W. J. M., H. Schriefers, D. Vorberg, A. S. Meyer, T. Pechman, and J. Havinga (1991). The time course of lexical access in speech production: A study of picture naming. *Psychological Review* 98, 122–142.

Levinson, S. C. (2003). *Space in Language and Cognition*. Cambridge: Cambridge University Press.

Levinson, S. C. (1997). From outer to inner space: Linguistic categories and non-linguistic thinking. In J. Nuyts, and E. Pederson (Eds.), *Language and Linguistic Categorization* (pp. 13–45). Cambridge: Cambridge University Press.

Levinson, S. C. (1983). *Pragmatics*. Cambridge: Cambridge University Press.

Levy, M. (1997). *Computer-Assisted Language Learning: Context and Conceptualization*. Oxford: Oxford University Press.

Levy, M., and G. Stockwell (2006). CALL *Dimensions: Options and Issues in Computer-Assisted Language Learning*. Mahwah, NJ: Lawrence Erlbaum.

Lewandowska-Tomaszczyk, B. (Ed.) (2004). *PALC2003: Practical Applications in Language Corpora*. Frankfurt: Lang.

Lewandowska-Tomaszczyk, B. (Ed.) (2003). *PALC2001: Practical Applications in Language Corpora*. Frankfurt: Lang.

Lewis, C., and B. Fabos (2005). Instant messaging, literacies and social identities. *Reading Research Quarterly* 40(4), 470–501.

Lewis, E. G. (1982). Movements and agencies of language spread: Wales and the Soviet Union compared. In R. L. Cooper (Ed.), *Language Spread: Studies in Diffusion and Social Change* (pp. 214–259). Bloomington: Indiana University Press.

Lewis, E. G. (1972). *Multilingualism in the Soviet Union*. The Hague: Mouton.

Leyew, Z. (1998). An Ethiopian language on the verge of extinction: K'emant, a preliminary sociolinguistic survey. *International Journal of the Sociology of Language* 134, 69–84.

Li, P. (1996). Spoken word recognition of code-switched words by Chinese-English bilinguals. *Journal of Memory and Language* 35, 757–774.

Li, Y. (2007). Apprentice scholarly writing in a community of practice: An intraview of an NNES graduate student writing a research article. *TESOL Quarterly* 41, 55–79.

Liddicoat, A. J. (1996). The narrowing focus: Australia's changing language policy. *Babel* 31(1), 4–7, 33.

Liddicoat, A. (1991). (Ed.). *Language Planning and Policy in Australia*. Melbourne: Applied Linguistics Association of Australia.

Liddicoat, A. J., and R. B. Baldauf, Jr. (Eds.). (2008). *Language Planning in Local Contexts*. Clevedon, Avon, UK: Multilingual Matters.

Liddicoat, A. J., and P. Bryant (Eds.). (2001). Language planning and language revival: A current issue in language planning. *Current Issues in Language Planning* 2(2 & 3), 137–140.

Liddicoat, A. J., and C. Crozet (2001). Acquiring French interactional norms through instruction. In K. R. Rose, and G. Kasper (Eds.), *Pragmatics in Language Teaching* (pp. 125–144). Cambridge: Cambridge University Press.

Lightbown, P. M. (1998). The importance of timing in focus on form. In C. Doughty, and J. Williams (Eds.), *Focus on Form in Classroom Second Language Acquisition* (pp. 177–196). Cambridge: Cambridge University Press.

Lightbown, P. M., and N. M. Spada (2006). *How Languages Are Learned* (3rd ed.). Oxford: Oxford University Press.

Lightbown, P. M., and N. Spada (1990). Focus-on-form and corrective feedback in communicative language teaching: Effects on second language learning. *Studies in Second Language Acquisition* 12(3), 429–48.

Lightbown, P. M., and L. White (1987). The influence of linguistic theories on language acquisition research: Description and explanation. *Language Learning* 37, 483–510.

Lim, J. M. H. (2006). Method sections of management research articles: A pedagogically motivated qualitative study. *English for Specific Purposes* 25, 282–309.

Lin, A. M.-Y. (Ed) (2008). *Problematizing Identity: Everyday Struggles in Language, Culture and Identity*. Mahwah, NJ: Lawrence Erlbaum.

Lin, A. M. Y. (1999). Doing-English-lessons in the reproduction or transformation of social worlds? *TESOL Quarterly* 33, 393–412.

Lin, A. M. Y., R. Grant, R. Kubota, S. Motha, G. Tinker Sachs, and S. Vandrick (2004). Women faculty of color in TESOL: Theorizing our lived experiences. *TESOL Quarterly* 38(4), 487–504.

Lin, A. M. Y., and P. W. Martin (Eds.). (2005). *Decolonisation, Globalisation: Language-in-Education Policy and Practice*. Clevedon, Avon, UK: Multilingual Matters.

Lincoln, Y. S., and E. G. Guba (2000). Paradigmatic controversies, contradictions and emerging confluences. In N. K. Denzin, and Y. S. Lincoln (Eds.), *Handbook of Qualitative Research* (2nd ed., pp. 163–188). Thousand Oaks, CA: Sage.

Lindemann, S., and A. Mauranen (2001). "It's just really messy": The occurrence and function of *just* in a corpus of academic speech. *English for Specific Purposes* 20, 459–475.

Lindquist, H., and C. Mair (2004). *Corpus Approaches to Grammaticalization in English*. Amsterdam: John Benjamins.

Lippi-Green, R. (1997). *English with an Accent*. London: Routledge.

Lipkin, S. (2008). Norms, ethics and roles among military court interpreters: The unique case of the Yehuda Court. *Interpreting* 10(1), 84–98.

Littlewood, W. T. (1981). *Communicative Language Teaching: An Introduction*. Cambridge: Cambridge University Press.

Liu, D. (2003). The most frequently used spoken American English idioms: A corpus analysis and its implications. *TESOL Quarterly* 37(4), 671–699.

Loasby, H. A. (1998). A study of the effects of language switching and priming in a picture-naming task. Unpublished manuscript, University of Oxford, UK.

Lo Bianco, J. (1997). English and pluralistic policies: The case of Australia. In W. Eggington, and H. Wren (Eds.), *Language Policy: Dominant English, Pluralistic Challenges* (pp. 107–119). Amsterdam and Canberra: John Benjamins and Language Australia.

Lo Bianco, J. (1990). Making language policy: Australia's experience. In R. B. Baldauf, Jr., and A. Luke (Eds.), *Language Planning and Education in Australasia and the South Pacific* (pp. 47–79). Clevedon, Avon, UK: Multilingual Matters.

Lo Bianco, J. (1987). *National Policy on Languages*. Canberra: Australian Government Publishing Service.

Lo Bianco, J., and P. Freebody (2001). *Australian Literacies: Informing National Policy on Literacy Education* (2nd ed.). Canberra: Language Australia.

Lo Bianco, J., and M. Rhydwen (2001). Is the extinction of Australia's indigenous languages inevitable? In J. A. Fishman (Ed.), *Can Threatened Languages Be Saved?* Clevedon, Avon, UK: Multilingual Matters, 391–422.

Lo Bianco, J., and R. Wickert (Eds.). (2001). *Australian Policy Activism in Language and Literacy*. Melbourne: Language Australia.

Loewen, S. (2005). Incidental focus on form and second language learning. *Studies in Second Language Acquisition* 27, 361–386.

Loewen, S., and T. Nabei (2007). Measuring the effects of oral corrective feedback on L2 knowledge. In A. Mackey (Ed.), *Conversational Interaction in Second Language Acquisition: A Series of Empirical Studies* (pp. 361–377). Oxford: Oxford University Press.

Loewen, S., and J. Philp (2006). Recasts in the adult L2 classroom: Characteristics, explicitness and effectiveness. *Modern Language Journal* 90, 536–556.

Lohr, S. (2008, December 27). Health care that puts a computer on the team. *The New York Times*, pp. B1, B3.

Long, D. (1990). What you don't know can't help you: An exploratory study of background knowledge and second language listening comprehension. *Studies in Second Language Acquisition* 12(1), 65–80.

Long, M. H. (2007). *Problems in SLA*. Mahwah, NJ: Lawrence Erlbaum.

Long, M. H. (1998). SLA: Breaking the siege. *University of Hawai'i Working Papers in ESL* 17, 79–129.

Long, M. H. (1996). The role of linguistic environment in second language acquisition. In W. C. Ritchie, and T. K. Bhatia (Eds.), *Handbook of Second Language Acquisition* (pp. 413–468). San Diego, CA: Academic Press.

Long, M. H. (1990). The least a second language acquisition theory needs to explain. *TESOL Quarterly* 24, 649–666.

Long, M. H. (1983). Linguistic and conversational adjustments to non-native speakers. *Studies in Second Language Acquisition* 5, 177–193.

Long, M. H. (1981). Input, interaction and second language acquisition. In H. Winitz (Ed.), *Native Language and Foreign Language Acquisition: Annals of the New York Academy of Sciences* 379, 259–278.

Long, M. H. (1980). Input, interaction and second language acquisition. PhD dissertation, University of California at Los Angeles.

Long, M. H., and G. Crookes (1992). Three approaches to task-based language teaching. *TESOL Quarterly* 26(1), 27–56.

Long, M. H., and C. Doughty (Eds.). (2009). *Handbook of Second and Foreign Language Teaching*. Malden, MA: Blackwell.

Long, M. H., and C. J. Sato (1983). Classroom foreigner talk discourse: Forms and functions of teachers' questions. In H. W. Seliger, and M. H. Long (Eds.), *Classroom Oriented Research in Second Language Acquisition* (pp. 268–286). Rowley, MA: Newbury House.

Longman Dictionary of Contemporary English (1987). Harlow: Longman.

Lonsdale, D. (1997). Modeling cognition in SI: Methodological issues. *Interpreting* 2(1/2), 91–117.

Loschky, L. (1994). Comprehensible input and second language acquisition: What is the relationship? *Studies in Second Language Acquisition* 16, 303–324.

Louw, B. (1993). Irony in the text or insincerity in the writer? The diagnostic potential of semantic prosodies. In M. Baker et al. (Eds.), *Text and Technology: In Honour of John Sinclair* (pp. 157–176). Amsterdam: John Benjamins.

Lowell, A., and B. C. Devlin (1999). Miscommunication between Aboriginal students and their non-Aboriginal teachers in a bilingual school. In S. May (Ed.), *Indigenous Community-based Education.* (pp. 137–159). Clevedon, Avon, UK: Multilingual Matters.

Lowenberg, P. H. (Ed.). (1988). *Language Spread and Language Policy: Issues, Implication and Case Studies (Georgetown University Round Table on Languages and Linguistics).* Washington, DC: Georgetown University Press.

Lowi, R. (2007). Building understanding through language and interaction: Joint attention, social modals and directives in adult-directed speech to children in two preschool. Unpublished PhD dissertation, University of California, Los Angeles.

Lowney, R. (2005). Federal judiciary accomplishments of the last 10 years and the challenges of the future. *Proteus* 14(3), 9–11.

Luciana, M. (2001). Dopamine-opiate modulations of reward seeking behavior: Implications for the functional assessment of prefrontal development. In C. A. Nelson, and M. Luciana (Eds.), *Handbook of Developmental Cognitive Neuroscience* (pp. 647–662). Cambridge, MA: MIT Press.

Luecht, R. M. (2008). Assessment engineering in test design, development, assembly and scoring. Paper presented at the Annual meeting of the East Coast Organization of Language Testers, Washington, DC.

Luecht, R. M. (2007). Assessment engineering in language testing: From data models and templates to psychometrics. Paper presented at the Annual Meeting of the National Council on Measurement in Education. Chicago.

Luecht, R. M. (2006). Assessment engineering: An emerging discipline. Paper presented at the Centre for Research in Applied Measurement and Evaluation. University of Alberta, Edmonton, Canada.

Luk, J. C. M., and A. M.-Y. Lin (2006). *Classroom Interactions as Cross-Cultural Encounters: Native Speakers in EFL Lessons.* Mahwah, NJ: Lawrence Erlbaum.

Luke, A. (2009). Race and language as capital in school: A sociological template for language education reform. In R. Kubota, and A. Lin (Eds.), *Race, Culture and Identities in Second Language Education.* London: Routledge.

Luke, A. (2004). Teaching after the market: From commodity to cosmopolitan. *Teachers College Record* 106(7), 1422–1443.

Luke, A., and R. B. Baldauf, Jr. (1990). Language planning and education: A critical rereading. In R. B. Baldauf, Jr., and A. Luke (Eds.), *Language Planning and Education in Australasia and the South Pacific* (pp. 349–356). Clevedon, Avon, UK: Multilingual Matters.

Lynch, T. (2009). *Teaching Second Language Listening.* Oxford: Oxford University Press.

Lynch, T. (1991). Questioning roles in the classroom. *ELT Journal* 45(3), 201–210.

Lynch, T., and J. MacLean (2001). "A case of exercising": Effects of immediate task repetition on learners' performance. In M. Bygate, P. Skehan, and M. Swain (Eds.), *Researching Pedagogic Tasks: Second Language Learning, Teaching and Testing* (141–162). London: Longman.

Lyotard, J.-F. (1984/1979). *La condition postmoderne.* Paris: Minuit. Tr. G. Bennington and B. Massumi, as *The postmodern condition: A report on knowledge.* Manchester, UK: Manchester University Press.

Lyster, R. (2007). *Learning and Teaching Languages through Content: A Counterbalanced Approach.* Amsterdam: John Benjamins.

Lyster, R. (1998). Recasts, repetition and ambiguity in L2 classroom discourse. *Studies in Second Language Acquisition* 20, 51–81.

Lyster, R., and H. Mori (2006). Interactional feedback and instructional counterbalance. *Studies in Second Language Acquisition* 28, 269–300.

Lyster, R., and L. Ranta (1997). Corrective feedback and learner uptake: Negotiation of form in communicative classrooms. *Studies in Second Language Acquisition* 20, 37–66.

Macaro, E., R. Vanderplank, and S. Graham (2005). A systematic review of the role of prior knowledge in unidirectional listening comprehension. In *Research Evidence in Education Library.* London: EPPI-Centre, Social Science Research Unit, Institute of Education, University of London.

MacDonald, C., and G. MacDonald (Eds.). (1995). *Connectionism: Debates on Psychological Explanation.* Oxford: Basil Blackwell.

MacDonald, M. C., and M. S. Seidenberg (2006). Constraint satisfaction accounts of lexical and sentence comprehension. In M. Traxler, and M. Gernsbacher (Eds.), *Handbook of Psycholinguistics* (2nd ed., pp. 581–611). Amsterdam: Elsevier.

MacDonald, M. C., N. J. Perlmutter, and M. S. Seidenberg (1994). The lexical nature of syntactic ambiguity resolution. *Psychological Review* 89, 483–506.

MacDonald, N. H., L. T. Frase, P. S. Gingrich, and S. A. Keenan (1982). The Writer's Workbench: Computer Aids for Text Analysis. *IEEE Transactions on Communications* 30(1), 105–110.

MacFarlane, A., and M. Wesche (1995). Immersion outcomes: Beyond language proficiency. *Canadian Modern Language Review* 51, 250–273.

MacIntyre, P. D. (2007). Willingness to communicate in the second language: Understanding the decision to speak as a volitional process. *Modern Language Journal* 91, 564–576.

MacIntyre, P. D., R. Clément, Z. Dörnyei, and K. A. Noels (1998). Conceptualizing willingness to communicate in a L2: A situational model of L2 confidence and affiliation. *Modern Language Journal* 82, 545–562.

Macken, M., and D. Slade (1993). Assessment: A foundation for effective learning in the school context. In B. Cope, and M. Kalantizis (Eds.), *The Powers of Literacy: A Genre Approach to Teaching Writing* (pp. 203–230). Pittsburgh, PA: University of Pittsburgh Press.

Mackey, A. (2007). Introduction: The role of conversational interaction in second language acquisition. In A. Mackey (Ed.), *Conversational Interaction in Second Language Acquisition: A Series of Empirical Studies* (pp. 1–26). Oxford: Oxford University Press.

Mackey, A. (2006). Feedback, noticing and second language development: An empirical study of L2 classroom interaction. *Applied Linguistics* 27, 405–430.

Mackey, A. (2002). Beyond production: Learners' perceptions about interactional processes. *International Journal of Educational Research* 37, 379–394.

Mackey, A. (1999). Input, interaction and second language development. *Studies in Second Language Acquisition* 21, 557–587.

Mackey, A., and S. M. Gass (2005). *Second Language Research: Methodology and Design.* Mahwah, NJ: Lawrence Erlbaum.

Mackey, A., S. M. Gass, and K. McDonough (2000). How do learners perceive implicit negative feedback? *Studies in Second Language Acquisition* 22, 471–497.

Mackey, A., and J. Goo (2007). Interaction research in SLA: A meta-analysis and research synthesis. In A. Mackey (Ed.), *Conversational Interaction in Second Language Acquisition: A Series of Empirical Studies* (pp. 407–452). Oxford: Oxford University Press.

Mackey, A., and J. Philp (1998). Conversational interaction and second language development: Recasts, responses and red herrings. *Modern Language Journal* 82, 338–356.

Mackey, A., J. Philp, T. Egi, A. Fujii, and T. Tatsumi (2002). Individual differences in working memory, noticing of interactional feedback and L2 development. In P. Robinson (Ed.), *Individual Differences and Instructed Language Learning* (vol. 2, pp. 181–209). Amsterdam: John Benjamins.

Mackey, A., and R. Silver (2005). Interactional tasks and English L2 learning by immigrant children in Singapore. *System* 33, 239–260.

Mackey, W. F. (1990). Donnés et mesure de la dynamique de diffusion des languages: Quelques hypotheses (Principles and measurements of the dynamics of language diffusion: Some hypotheses). In L. Laforgue, and G. D. McConnell (Eds.), *Language Spread and Social Change: Dynamics and Measurement* (pp. 23–40). Ste.-Foy, Québec: Les Presses de l'Université Laval.

Mackey, W. F. (1980). The ecology of language shift. In P. Nelde (Ed.), *Sprachkontakt und Sprachkonflikt [Language Contact and Language Conflict]* (pp. 35–41). Wiesbaden, Germany: Steiner.

Mackey, W. F. (1972). A typology of bilingual education. In Joshua A. Fishman (Ed.), *Advances in the Sociology of Language: Vol. 2. Selected Studies and Applications.* (pp. 413–432). The Hague: Mouton.

Mackey, W. F. (1965). *Language Teaching Analysis.* Bloomington: Indiana University Press.

Macnamara, J. (1971). Successes and failures in the movement for the restoration of Irish. In J. Rubin, and B. Jernudd (Eds.), *Can Language Be Planned? Sociolinguistic Theory and Practice for Developing Nations* (pp. 65–94). Honolulu: University Press of Hawai'i.

MacWhinney, B. (2008). A unified model. In P. Robinson, and N. Ellis (Eds.), *Handbook of Cognitive Linguistics and Second Language Acquisition* (pp. 341–371). New York: Routledge.

MacWhinney, B. (2005). A unified model of language acquisition. In J. F. Kroll, and A. M. B. De Groot (Eds.), *Handbook of Bilingualism: Psycholinguistic Approaches* (pp. 49–67). Oxford: Oxford University Press.

MacWhinney, B. (2001). From CHILDES to TalkBank. In M. Almgren, A. Barreña, M. Ezeizaberrena, I. Idiazabal, and B. MacWhinney (Eds.), *Research on Child Language Acquisition* (pp. 17–34). Somerville, MA: Cascadia.

MacWhinney, B. (Ed.). (1999). *The Emergence of Language.* Mahwah, NJ: Lawrence Erlbaum.

MacWhinney, B. (1995a). Language-specific prediction in foreign language learning. *Language Testing* 12, 292–320.

MacWhinney, B. (1995b). *The CHILDES Project: Tools for Analyzing Talk* (2nd ed.). Mahwah, NJ: Lawrence Erlbaum.

MacWhinney, B., and E. Bates (Eds.). (1989). *The Crosslinguistic Study of Sentence Processing* (pp. 3–76). New York: Cambridge University Press.

Maddux, C. D. (1986). Issues and concerns in special education microcomputing. *Computers in the Schools* 3, 3–4.

Madison, S. (2005). *Critical Ethnography: Method, Ethics and Performance.* Thousand Oaks, CA: Sage.

Madrid, D. (2002). The power of the FL teacher's motivational strategies. *CAUCE, Revista de Filologia,y su Didactica* 25, 369–422.

Madsen, H. S. (1991). Computer-adaptive testing of listening and reading comprehension: The Brigham Young University approach. In P. Dunkel (Ed.), *Computer-Assisted*

Language Learning and Testing: Research Issues and Practice (pp. 237–257). New York: Newbury House.

Maeshiba, N., N. Yoshinaga, G. Kasper, and S. Ross (1996). Transfer and proficiency in interlanguage apologizing. In S. M. Gass, and J. Neu (Eds.), *Speech Acts across Cultures: Challenge to Communication in a Second Language* (pp. 155–187). Berlin: Mouton de Gruyter.

Mahlberg, M. (in press). *Corpus Stylistics and Dickens's Fiction*. London: Routledge.

Mahlberg, M. (2005). *English General Nouns: A Corpus Theoretical Approach*. Amsterdam: John Benjamins.

Mahoune, J.-C. P. (2000). Seychellois Creole: Development and evolution. *IIAS Newsletter Online* 22. Retrieved February 25, 2005, from http://iias.leidenuniv.nl/iiasn/22/regions/22ISA1.html

Mair, C. (2006). *Twentieth-century English: History, Variation and Standardization*. Cambridge: Cambridge University Press.

Mair, C. (1992). Problems in the compilation of a corpus of standard Caribbean English: A pilot study. In G. Leitner (Ed.), *New Directions in English Language Corpora* (pp. 75–96). Berlin: de Gruyter.

Mair, C. (1990). *Infinitival Complement Clauses in English*. New York: Cambridge University Press.

Mair, C., and A. Sand (1998). Caribbean English: Structure and status of an emerging variety. In R. Borgmeier, H. Grabes, and A. Jucker (Eds.), *Anglistentag 1997: Giessen- Proceedings* (pp. 187–198). Trier: Wissenschaftlicher Verlag.

Major, R. C. (2001). *Foreign Accent: The Ontogeny and Phylogeny of Second Language Phonology*. Mahwah, NJ: Lawrence Erlbaum.

Makey, A., and S. Gass (2005). *Second Language Research: Methodology*. Mahwah, NJ: Lawrence Erlbaum.

Mäkinen, M. (2002). On interaction in herbals from Middle English to Early Modern English. *Journal of Historical Pragmatics* 3(2), 229–251.

Makoni, S., and A. Pennycook (2007). *Disinventing and Reconstituting Languages*. Clevedon, Avon, UK: Multilingual Matters.

Maley, A., A. Duff, and F. Grellet (1980). *The Mind's Eye*. Cambridge: Cambridge University Press.

Manchón, R. (Ed.). (in press). *Learning, Teaching and Researching Writing in Foreign Language Contexts*. Clevedon, Avon, UK: Multilingual Matters.

Manchón, R., and P. de Haan (Guest Eds.). (2008). Writing in foreign language contexts: Research insights [Special issue]. *Journal of Second Language Writing* 17(1).

Marantz, A. (1995). The minimalist program. In G. Webelhuth (Ed.), *Government and Binding Theory and the Minimalist Program* (pp. 351–382). Oxford: Blackwell.

Marckwardt, A. H. (1948). Motives for the study of modern languages. *Language Learning* 1, 3–99. (Reprinted in *Language Learning* 38 [1988] 161–169.)

Marco, M. J. L. (2000). Collocational frameworks in medical research papers: A genre-based study. *English for Specific Purposes* 19, 63–86.

Marcus, G. F. (1998). Can connectionism save constructivism? *Cognition* 66, 153–182.

Marian, V., H. K. Blumenfeld, and O. V. Boukrina (2008). Sensitivity to phonological similarity within and across languages. *Journal of Psycholinguistic Research* 37, 141–170.

Marian, V., and M. Spivey (2003). Bilingual and monolingual processing of competing lexical items. *Applied Psycholinguistics* 24, 173–193.

Marinis, T. (2003). Psycholinguistic techniques in second language acquisition research. *Second Language Research* 19, 144–161.

Marinis, T., L. Roberts, C. Felser, and H. Clahsen (2005). Gaps in second language sentence processing. *Studies in Second Language Acquisition* 27, 53–78.

Markee, N. P. (2008). Toward a learning behavior tracking methodology for CA-for-SLA. *Applied Linguistics* 29, 404–427.

Markee, N. P. (Guest Ed.). (2007). *Annual Review of Applied Linguistics: Vol. 27. Language and Technology*. New York: Cambridge University Press.

Markee, N. P. (Ed.). (2004). Classroom talks [Special issue]. *Modern Language Journal* 84(4).

Markee, N. P. (2000). *Conversation Analysis*. Mahwah, NJ: Lawrence Erlbaum.

Markee, N. P. (1997). *Managing Curricular Innovation*. Cambridge: Cambridge University Press.

Markee, N. P. (1991). Toward an integrated approach to language planning. *Studies in the Linguistic Sciences* 21(1), 107–123.

Marley, C. (2002). Popping the question: Questions and modality in written dating advertisements. *Discourse Studies* 4(1), 75–98.

Martin, J. R. (2002). Meaning beyond the clause: SFL perspectives. In M. McGroarty et al. (Eds.), *Annual Review of Applied Linguistics: Vol. 22. Discourse and Dialogue* (pp. 52–74). New York: Cambridge University Press.

Martin, J. R. (1993). Genre and literacy: modeling context in educational linguistics. In W. Grabe et al (Eds.), *Annual Review of Applied Linguistics 13: Issues in Second Language Teaching and Learning* (pp. 141–172). New York: Cambridge University Press.

Martinez, G. (2008). Language-in-healthcare policy, interaction patterns, and unequal care on the U.S.-Mexico border. *Language Policy* 7, 345–363.

Marx, K. (1881/1972). Theses on Feuerbach. In R. C. Tucker (Ed.), *The Marx-Engels Reader* (pp. 143–145). New York: W. W. Norton.

Marzocchi, C. (1998). The case for an institution-specific component in interpreting research. *Interpreters' Newsletter* 8, 51–74.

Massaro, D. W., and M. Shlesinger (1997). Information processing and a computational approach to the study of simultaneous interpretation. *Interpreting* 2(1/2), 13–53.

Master, P. (2005). Research in English for specific purposes. In E. Hinkel (Ed.), *Handbook of Research in Second Language Teaching and Learning* (pp. 99–116). Mahwah, NJ: Lawrence Erlbaum.

Mates, A. W. (2010). Using social deficits in frontotemporal dementia to develop a neurobiology of person reference. In A. W. Mates, L. Mikesell, and M. S. Smith (Eds.), *Language, Interaction and Frontotemporal Dementia: Reverse Engineering the Social Mind* (Chapter 6). London: Equinox.

Matoesian, G. (1999). The grammaticalization of participant roles in the constitution of expert identity. *Language in Society* 28, 491–521.

Matsuda, M. J. (1991). Voices of America: Accent, antidiscrimination law and a jurisprudence for the last reconstruction. *Yale Law Journal* 100, 1329–1407.

Matsuda, P. K. (1999.) Composition studies and ESL writing: A disciplinary division of labor. *College Composition and Communication* 50, 699–721.

Matsuda, P. K. (1998). Situating ESL writing in a cross-disciplinary context. *Written Communication* 15, 99–121.

Matsuda, P. K., and D. Atkinson (2008). A conversation on contrastive rhetoric: Dwight Atkinson and Paul Kei Matsuda talk about issues, conceptualizations and the future of contrastive rhetoric. In U. Connor, E. Nagelhout, and W. Rozycki (Eds.), *Contrastive Rhetoric: Reaching to Intercultural Rhetoric* (pp. 277–298). Philadelphia, PA: John Benjamins.

Matsuda, P. K., C. Ortmeier-Hooper, and Y. You (Eds.). (2006). *The Politics of Second Language Writing: In Search of the Promised Land*. West Lafayette, IN: Parlor Press.

Mattheier, K. A. (1984). Sprachkonflikte in einsprachigen Ortsgemeinschaften [Language conflicts in monolingual settings]. In E. Oksaar (Ed.), *Spracherwerb–Sprachkontakt–Sprachkonflikt* [Language Acquisition–Language Contact–Language Conflict]. (pp. 197–204). Berlin: de Gruyter.

Matthews, A., and C. Read (1981). *Tandem*. London: Evans.

Mauranen, A. (2007). Investigating English as a Lingua Franca with a Spoken Corpus. In M. C. Campoy, and M. J. Luzón (Eds.), *Spoken Corpora in Applied Linguistics* (pp. 33–56). Berlin: Peter Lang.

Mauranen, A. (2006). A rich domain of ELF: the ELFA Corpus of academic discourse. *Nordic Journal of English Studies* 5(2), 145–159.

Mauranen, A. (2004). "They're a little bit different": Variation in hedging in academic speech. In K. Aijmer, and A.-B. Stenström (Eds.), *Discourse Patterns in Spoken and Written Corpora* (pp. 173–197). Amsterdam: John Benjamins.

Mauranen, A. (2003). The Corpus of English as Lingua Franca in Academic settings. *TESOL Quarterly* 37(3), 513–527.

Mauranen, A., and M. Bondi (2003). Evaluative language use in academic discourse. *Journal of English for Academic Purposes* 2, 269–271.

May, S. (2008). *Language and Minority Rights*. New York and London: Routledge.

May, S. (2006). Addressing the context and complexity of indigenous language revitalization. *Journal of Language, Identity and Education* 5(4), 301–308.

May, S. (2001). *Language and Minority Rights: Ethnicity, Nationalism and the Politics of Language*. London: Longman.

May, S. (Ed.). (1999). *Indigenous Community-Based Education*. Clevedon, Avon, UK: Multilingual Matters.

Maynard, D. W. (1992). On clinicians' co-implicating recipients' perspective in delivery of diagnostic news. In P. Drew, and J. Heritage (Eds.), *Talk at Work: Interaction in Institutional Settings* (pp. 331–359). Cambridge: Cambridge University Press.

Mazrui, A. A., and M. Tidy (1984). *Nationalism and New States in Africa*. Nairobi: Heinemann.

McCafferty, J. J. (1999). Mäori language realization. In B. Spolsky (Ed.), *Concise Encyclopedia of Educational Linguistics* (pp. 144–146). Amsterdam: Elsevier.

McCarthey, S., G. Garcia, A. Lopez-Velasquez, S. Lin, and Y. Guo (2004). Understanding writing contexts for English language learners. *Research in the Teaching of English* 38, 351–394.

McCarthy, M. (2008). Accessing and interpreting corpus information in the teacher education context. *Language Teaching* 41, 563–574.

McCarthy, M. (2002). Good listenership made plain: British and American non-minimal response tokens in everyday conversation. In R. Reppen et al. (Eds.), *Using Corpora to Explore Linguistic Variation* (pp. 49–71). Amsterdam: John Benjamins.

McCarthy, M. (2001). Discourse. In R. Carter, and D. Nunan (Eds.), *Teaching English to Speakers of Other Languages* (pp. 48–55). Cambridge: Cambridge University Press.

McCarthy, M. (2000). Captive audiences: The discourse of close contact service encounters. In Coupland, J. (Ed.), *Small Talk* (pp. 84–109). London: Longman.

McCarthy, M., and R. Carter (2004). There's millions of them: Hyperbole in everyday conversation. *Journal of Pragmatics* 36, 149–184.

McCarthy, M., and R. Carter (2001). Size isn't everything: Spoken English, Corpus and the Classroom. *TESOL Quarterly* 35(2), 337–340.

McCarthy, M., and R. Carter (1997). Grammar, tails, and affect: Constructing affective choices in discourse. *Text* 17, 405–429.

McCarthy, M., and M. Handford (2004). Invisible to us: A preliminary corpus-based study of spoken business English. In U. Connor, and T. Upton (Eds.) *Discourse in the Professions: Perspectives from Corpus Linguistics* (pp. 167–201). Amsterdam: John Benjamins.

McCarthy, M., J. McCarten, and H. Sandiford (2004/2006). *Touchstone 1–4.* Cambridge: Cambridge University Press.

McCarthy, M., and F. O'Dell (2005). *English Collocations in Use.* Cambridge: Cambridge University Press.

McCarthy, M., and F. O'Dell (2004). *English Phrasal Verbs in Use.* Cambridge: Cambridge University Press.

McCarthy, M., and F. O'Dell (2001). *Basic Vocabulary in Use.* Cambridge: Cambridge University Press.

McCarty, T. L. (2006). Voice and choice in indigenous language revitalization. *Journal of Language, Identity and Education* 5(4), 308–315.

McCarty, T. L. (2004). Dangerous difference: A critical-historical analysis of language education policies in the United States. In J. W. Tollefson, and A. B. M. Tsui (Eds.), *Medium of Instruction Policies: Which Agenda? Whose Agenda?* Mahwah, NJ: Lawrence Erlbaum.

McCarty, T. L. (2002). *A Place to Be Navajo—Rough Rock and the Struggle for Self-Determination in Indigenous Schooling.* Mahwah, NJ: Lawrence Erlbaum.

McCarty, T. L., and L. J. Watahomigie (1999). Indigenous education and grassroots language planning in the USA. *Practicing Anthropology* 20(2), 5–11.

McCarty, T. L., L. J. Watahomigie, and A. Y. Yamamoto (Eds.). (1999). Reversing language shift in indigenous America: Collaborations and views from the field. *Practicing Anthropology*, 21(2), 2–4.

McCarty, T. L., and O. Zepeda (Eds.). (2006). *One Voice, Many Voices: Recreating Indigenous Language Communities.* Tempe and Tucson, AZ: Arizona State University Center for Indian Education/University of Arizona American Indian Language Development Institute.

McCarty, T. L., and O. Zepeda (Eds.) (1998). *Indigenous Language use and Change in the Americas.* Special Issue of *International Journal of the Sociology of Language* 132.

McCarty, T. L., and O. Zepeda (Eds.). (1995). Indigenous language education and literacy. *Bilingual Research Journal* 19(1).

McClelland, J. L., and D. E. Rumelhart (1981). An interactive activation model of context effects in letter perception, Part 1: An account of basic findings. *Psychological Review* 88, 375–405.

McConnell, G. D. (1990). Language spread as a phenomenon and concept. In L. Laforgue, and G. D. McCinnell (Eds.), *Language Spread and Social Change: Dynamics and Measurement* (pp. 9–16). Ste.-Foy, Québec: Les Presses de l'Université Laval.

McCrea, L. (1998). Towards a framework for language policy and planning in the state of Utah. Unpublished MA thesis, Brigham Young University, Provo, UT.

McCuaig, M. G., and H. H. (David) Stern (1981). In A. S. Mollica (Ed.), In honour of H. H. Stern [Special issue]. *Canadian Modern Language Review* 37(3), 429–440.

McDonough, J., and C. Shaw (2003). *Materials and Methods in ELT: A Teacher's Guide* (2nd ed.). Oxford: Blackwell.

McDonough, K. (2007). Interactional feedback and the emergence of simple past activity verbs in L2 English. In A. Mackey (Ed.), *Conversational Interaction in Second Language Acquisition: A Series of Empirical Studies* (pp. 323–338). Oxford: Oxford University Press.

McDonough, K. (2006). Interaction and syntactic priming. *Studies in Second Language Acquisition* 28, 179–207.

McDonough, K. (2005). Identifying the impact of negative feedback and learners' responses on ESL question development. *Studies in Second Language Acquisition* 27, 79–103.

McDonough, K., and A. Mackey (2006). Responses to recasts: Repetitions, primed production and linguistic development. *Language Learning* 56, 693–720.

McEnery, T., and A. Wilson (2001). *Corpus Linguistics* (2nd ed.). Edinburgh: Edinburgh University Press.

McEnery, T., and A. Wilson (1997). Teaching and language corpora. *ReCall* 9(1), 5–14.

McEnery, T., and A. Wilson (1993). The role of corpora in computer-assisted language learning. *Computer Assisted Language Learning* 6(3), 233–48.

McEnery, T., R. Xiao, and Y. Tono (2006). *Corpus-Based Language Studies: An Advanced Resource Book*. London and New York: Routledge.

McGroarty, M., et al. (Eds.). (2006). *Annual Review of Applied Linguistics: Vol. 26. Lingua Franca Languages*. New York: Cambridge University Press.

McGroarty, M., et al. (Eds.). (2004). *Annual Review of Applied Linguistics: Vol. 24. Advances in Language Pedagogy*. New York: Cambridge University Press.

McGroarty, M., et al. (Eds.). (2003). *Annual Review of Applied Linguistics: Vol. 23. Language Contact and Change*. New York: Cambridge University Press.

McGroarty, M. (2002). Language uses in professional contexts. In R. B. Kaplan (Ed.), *The Oxford Handbook of Applied Linguistics* (pp. 262–274). Oxford: Oxford University Press.

McGroarty, M. (1996). Language contact in social service institutions. In H. Goebel, P. Nelde, Z. Star, and W. Wölck (Eds.), *Contact Linguistics: An International Handbook of Contemporary Research* (vol. 1, pp. 865–871). Berlin: Walter de Gruyter.

Mckay, S. L. (2006). *Researching Second Language Classrooms*. Mahwah, NJ: Lawrence Erlbaum.

McKay, S. L., and N. H. Hornberger (Eds.). (1996). *Sociolinguistics and Language Teaching*. New York: Cambridge University Press.

McKoon, G., and R. Ratcliff (2003). Meaning through syntax: Language comprehension and the reduced relative clause construction. *Psychological Review* 110, 490–525.

McLaughlin, D. (1992). *When Literacy Empowers: Navajo Language in Print*. Albuquerque: University of New Mexico Press.

McNamara, T. F. (2001a). The history of applied linguistics in Australia. *Australian Review of Applied Linguistics* 24(1), 13–29.

McNamara, T. F. (2001b). Ten years of the Language Testing Research Centre. In C. Elder, A. Brown, E. Grove, K. Hill, N. Iwashita, T. Lumley, T. McNamara, and K. O'Loughlin (Eds.), *Experimenting with Uncertainty: Essays in Honour of Alan Davies* (pp. 5–10). Cambridge: Cambridge University Press.

McNamara, T. F. (2000). *Language Testing*. Oxford: Oxford University Press.

McNamara, T. F. (1998). Policy and social consideration in language assessment. In W. Grabe, et al. (Eds.), *Annual Review of Applied Linguistics: Vol. 18. Foundations of Second Language Teaching* (pp. 304–319). New York: Cambridge University Press.

McNamara, T. F. (1997). "Interaction" in second language performance assessment: Whose performance? *Applied Linguistics* 18, 446–466.

McNamara, T. F. (1996). *Measuring Second Language Performance*. London & New York: Longman.

McNamara, T. F., and J. Lo Bianco (2001). The distinctiveness of applied linguistics in Australia: A historical perspective. In R. L. Cooper, E. Shohamy, and J. Walters (Eds.), *New Perspectives and Issues in Educational Language Policy: A Festschrift for Bernard Dov Spolsky* (pp. 261–269). Amsterdam: John Benjamins.

McNamara, T. F., and C. Roever (2006). *Language Testing: The Social Dimension*. Malden, MA: Blackwell.

McWhorter, J. H. (2001). The world's simplest grammars are Creole grammars. *Linguistic Typology* 5(2/3), 125–166.

McWhorter, J. H. (1998). Identifying the creole prototype: Vindicating a typological class. *Language* 74, 788–818.

Mecartty, F. (2000). Lexical and grammatical knowledge in reading and listening comprehension by foreign language learners of Spanish. *Applied Language Learning* 11, 323–348.

Medgyes, P. (1986). Queries from a communicative teacher. *ELT Journal* 40, 107–112.

Medgyes, P., and K. Miklósy (2005). The language situation in Hungary: An update. In R. B. Kaplan, and R. B. Baldauf, Jr. (Eds.), *Language Planning and Policy in Europe: Vol. 1. Hungary, Finland and Sweden* (pp. 117–124). Clevedon, Avon, UK: Multilingual Matters.

Medgyes, P., and K. Miklósy (2000). The language situation in Hungary. *Current Issues in Language Planning* 1(2), 148–242.

Mehan, H. (1986). The role of language and the language of role in institutional decision-making. In S. Fisher, and A. Todd (Eds.), *Discourse and Institutional Authority: Medicine, Education and Law* (pp. 140–163). Norwood, NJ: Ablex.

Mehan, H. (1979). *Learning Lessons: Social Organization in the Classroom*. Cambridge, MA: Harvard University Press.

Mehrotra, R. R. (1985). Sociolinguistic surveys in South Asia: An overview. *International Journal of the Sociology of Language* 55, 115–124.

Mejias, H., P. Anderson, and R. Carlson (2002). Attitudes toward Spanish language maintenance or shift (LMLS) in the Lower Rio Grande Valley of South Texas. *International Journal of the Sociology of Language* 158, 121–140.

Melinkoff, D. (1963). *The Language of the Law*. Boston: Little, Brown.

Mellow, D. J. (2004). Connectionism, HPSG signs and SLA representations: specifying principles of mapping between form and function. *Second Language Research* 20, 131–165.

Menard-Warwick, J. (2007). "Because she made beds every day": Social positioning, classroom discourse and language learning. *Applied Linguistics* 29(2), 267–289.

Menard-Warwick, J. (2006). Both a fiction and an existential fact: Theorizing identity in second language acquisition and literacy studies. *Linguistics and Education* 16, 253–274.

Mendelsohn, D. J. (1998). Teaching listening. In W. Grabe et al. (Eds.), *Annual Review of Applied Linguistics: Vol. 18. Foundations of Second Language Teaching* (pp. 81–101). New York: Cambridge University Press.

Merlini, R. (1996). Interprit—consecutive interpretation module. *Interpreters' Newsletter* 7, 31–41.

Merriam, S. (1998). *Qualitative Research and Case Study Applications in Education* (2nd ed.). San Francisco: Jossey-Bass.

Messick, S. (1999). Technology and the future of higher education assessment. In S. Messick (Ed.), *Assessment in Higher Education: Issues of Access, Student Development and Public Policy* (pp. 245–254). Hillsdale, NJ: Lawrence Erlbaum.

Messick, S. (1988). Validity. In R. L. Linn (Ed.), *Educational Measurement* (pp. 13–113). New York: MacMillan.

Messina, A. (1998). The reading aloud of English language texts in simultaneously interpreted conferences. *Interpreting* 3(2), 147–161.

Mesthrie, R. (1999). Language loyalty. In B. Spolsky (Ed.), *Concise Encyclopedia of Educational Linguistics* (pp. 42–47). Amsterdam: Elsevier.

Met, M., and E. Lorenz (1997). Lessons from U.S. immersion programs: Two decades of experience. In R. K. Johnson, and M. Swain (Eds.), *Immersion Education: International Perspectives* (pp. 243–264). Cambridge: Cambridge University Press.

Métellus, J. (1998). The process of creolization in Haiti and the pitfalls of the graphic form. In K. M. Balutansky, and M.-A. Sourieau (Eds.), *Caribbean Creolization: Reflections on the Cultural Dynamics of Language, Literature and Identity* (pp. 118–128). Gainsville: University Press of Florida and Barbados: The Press University of the West Indies.

Meunier, F. (2002). The pedagogical value of native and learner corpora in EFL grammar teaching. In S. Granger, J. Hung, and S. Petch-Tyson (Eds.), *Computer Learner Corpora, Second Language Acquisition and Foreign Language Teaching* (pp. 119–141). Amsterdam: John Benjamins.

Meunier, F., and S. Granger (Eds.). (2008). *Phraseology in Foreign Language Learning and Teaching.* Amsterdam & Philadelphia: John Benjamins.

Meuter, R. F. I., and A. Allport (1999). Bilingual language switching in naming: Asymmetrical costs of language selection. *Journal of Memory and Language* 40, 25–40.

Mey, J. L. (1993). *Pragmatics: An introduction.* Oxford: Blackwell.

Meyer, B. (1998). What transcriptions of authentic discourse can reveal about interpreting. *Interpreting* 3(1), 65–83.

Meyer, C. (1992). *Apposition in Contemporary English.* Cambridge: Cambridge University Press.

Michaelis, S. (Ed.). (2008). *Roots of Creole Structures: Weighing the Contribution of Substrates and Superstrates.* Amsterdam/Philadelphia: Benjamins.

Michelman, F. (1995). French and British colonial policies: A comparative view of their impact on African Literature. *Research in African Literatures* 26, 216–225.

Miguélez, C. (1999). Current issues in court interpreting: Spain, a case study. *Proteus* 7(2), 5–8.

Mikesell, L. (2010). Examining preservative behaviors of a frontotemporal dementia patient and caregiver responses: The benefits of observing ordinary interactions and reflections on caregiver stress. In A. W. Mates, L. Mikesell and M. S. Smith (Eds.), Language, Interaction and Frontotemporal Dementia: Reverse Engineering the Social Mind (Chapter 4). London: Equinox.

Mikesell, L. (2004). Examining argument structure in conversation: A matter of indexical grounding. Unpublished MA thesis, University of California at Los Angeles.

Mikkelson, H. (2000). *Introduction to Court Interpreting.* Manchester, UK and Northampton, MA: St. Jerome.

Mikkelson, H. (1998). Towards a redefinition of the role of the court interpreter. *Interpreting* 3(1), 21–45.

Mikkelson, H. (1996). Community interpreting: An emerging profession. *Interpreting* 1(1), 125–129.

Miller, J. (2003). *Audible Difference.* Clevedon, Avon, UK: Multilingual Matters.

Miller, N. (1997). The influence of word form and meaning in bilingual language production. Master's Thesis. The Pennsylvania State University, University Park, PA.

Mills, S. (Ed.). (1995). *Language and Gender.* London: Longman.

Milton, J. (1998). Exploiting L1 and interlanguage corpora in the design of an electronic language learning and production environment. In S. Granger (Ed.), *Learner English on Computer* (pp. 186–198). London: Longman.

Ministry of Education (1956). *Report of the Official Committee on the Teaching of English Overseas*. London: Ministry of Education.

Mintz, D. (1998). Hold the phone: Telephone interpreting scrutinized. *Proteus* 7(1), 1, 3–5.

Mindt, D. (1996). English corpus linguistics and the foreign language-teaching syllabus. In J. Thomas, and M. Short (Eds.), *Using Corpora for Language Research: Studies in the Honour of Geoffrey Leech* (pp. 232–247). London: Longman.

Mishler, E. (1984). *The Discourse of Medicine: The Dialectics of Medical Interviews*. Norwood, NJ: Ablex.

Mislevy, R. J. (2006). Prospectus for the PADI design framework in language testing. Paper presented at the Annual Meeting of the East Coast Organization of Language Testers, Washington, DC.

Mislevy, R. J. (1996). Test theory reconceived. *Journal of Educational Measurement* 33, 379–416.

Mislevy, R. J. (1995). Probability-based inference in cognitive diagnosis. In P. Nichols, S. Chipman, and R. Brennan (Eds.), *Cognitively Diagnostic Assessment* (pp. 43–71). Hillsdale, NJ: Lawrence Erlbaum.

Mislevy, R. J., R. G. Almond, and J. F. Lukas (2003). A Brief Introduction to Evidence-Centered Design (Research Report Number RR-03-16). Princeton, NJ: Educational Testing Service.

Mislevy, R. J., and G. Haertel (2007). Implications of Evidence-Centered Design for Educational Testing: Lessons from the PADI Project. Paper presented at the Annual Meeting of the National Council on Measurement in Education. Chicago.

Mislevy, R. J., L. Hamel, R. G. Fried, T. Gaffney, G. Haertel, and A. Hafter (2003). *Design Patterns for Assessing Science Inquiry (PADI Technical Report 1)*. Menlo Park, CA: SRI International.

Mislevy, R. J., and M. M. Riconscente (2005). Evidence-centered assessment design. In S. M. Downing, and T. M. Haladyna (Eds.), *Handbook of Test Development* (pp. 61–90). Mahwah, NJ: Lawrence Erlbaum.

Mislevy, R. J., L. S. Steinberg, F. J. Breyer, R. G. Almond, and L. Johnson (1999). A cognitive analysis, with implications for designing simulation-based performance assessment. *Computers in Human Behavior* 15, 335–374.

Mitchell, C., and K. Vidal (2001). Weighing the ways of the flow: Twentieth century language instruction. *Modern Language Journal* 85(1), 26–38.

Mitchell, D. C., F. Cuetos, M. M. B. Corley, and M. Brysbaert (1995). Exposure-based models of human parsing: Evidence for the use of coarse-grained (nonlexical) statistical records. *Journal of Psycholinguistic Research* 24, 469–488.

Mitchell, D. C., and M. Brysbaert (1998). Challenges to recent theories of crosslinguistic variation in parsing: Evidence from Dutch. In D. Hillert (Ed.), *Sentence Processing: A Crosslinguistic Perspective* (pp. 313–335). San Diego, CA: Academic Press.

Miyake, A., and P. Shah (Eds.). (1999). *Models of Working Memory: Mechanisms of Active Maintenance and Executive Control*. Cambridge: Cambridge University Press.

Mizuno, A. (2005). Process model for simultaneous interpreting and working memory. *Meta: Translators' Journal* 50(2), 739–752.

Mizuno, A. (1995). A brief review of interpretation research in Japan. *Hermes* 14, 131–144.

Moeketsi, R. (1999). Redefining the role of the South African court interpreter. *Proteus* VI 8 (3/4), 12–15.

Moeketsi, R., and N. Mollema (2006). Towards perfect practice in South African court interpreting: A quality assurance and quality management model. *International Journal of Speech, Language and the Law* 13(1), 76–88.

Moeketsi, R., and K. Wallmach (2005). From *sphaza* to *makoya!*: A BA for court interpreters in South Africa. *International Journal of Speech, Language and the Law* 12(1), 77–108.

Mohan, B. (1992). Models of the role of the computer in second language development. In M. Pennington, and V. Stevens (Eds.), *Computers in Applied Linguistics: An International Perspective* (pp. 110–126). Clevedon, Avon, UK: Multilingual Matters.

Mohan, B. (1986). *Language and Content*. Reading, MA: Addison-Wesley.

Mohan, B., and G. H. Beckett (2001). A functional approach to research on content-based language learning: Recasts in causal explanations. *Canadian Modern Language Review* 58(1), 133–155.

Mohan, B., C. Leung, and C. Davison (2001). *English as a Second Language in the Mainstream: Teaching, Learning and Identity*. Harlow, Essex: Longman.

Mollica, A. S. (Ed.). (1981). In honour of H. H. Stern [Special issue]. *Canadian Modern Language Review* 37, 3.

Montrul, S. A. (1999). Causative errors with unaccusative verbs in L2 Spanish. *Second Language Research* 15, 191–219.

Montrul, S. A. (1998). The L2 acquisition of dative experiencer subject. *Second Language Research* 14, 27–61.

Moore, H. (2001). Rendering ESL accountable: Educational and bureaucratic technologies in the Australian context. In C. Elder, A. Brown, K. Grove, K. Hill, N. Iwasdhita, T. Lumley, T. Mcnamara, and K. O'Loughlin (Eds.), *Experimenting with Uncertainty: Essays in Honour of Alan Davies* (pp. 177–190). Cambridge: Cambridge University Press.

Moore, H. (1996). Language policies as virtual realities: Two Australian examples. *TESOL Quarterly* 30, 473–97.

Moore, J. I. (Ed.). (1999). *Immigrants in Courts*. Seattle WA: University of Washington Press.

Moore, L. C. (2008). Language socialization and second/foreign language and multilingual education in non-Western settings. In P. A. Duff, and N. H. Hornberger (Eds.), *Language Socialization: Encyclopedia of Language and Education* (vol. 8, pp. 175–185). New York: Springer.

Mora, M., D. Villa, and A. Davila (2006). Language shift and maintenance among the children of immigrants in the U.S. *Spanish in Context* 3(2), 239–254.

Morgan, B., and V. Ramanathan (2005). Critical literacies and language education: Global and local perspectives. In M. Mcgroarty et al. (Eds.), *Annual Review of Applied Linguistics: Vol. 25. A Survey A Survey of Applied* (pp. 151–169). New York: Cambridge University Press.

Mori, J. (2007). Border crossings? Exploring the intersection of second language acquisition, conversation analysis, and foreign language pedagogy. *Modern Language Journal* 91, 849–862.

Mori, J. (2004). Negotiating sequential boundaries and learning opportunities: A case from a Japanese language classroom. *Modern Language Journal* 88, 536–550.

Morita, N. (2004). Negotiating participation and identity in second language academic communities. *TESOL Quarterly* 38, 573–603.

Morphet, T. (1996). Afterword. In M. Prinsloo, and M. Breier (Eds.), *The Social Uses of Literacy: Theory and Practice in Contemporary South Africa* (pp. 257–264). Bertsham, South Africa: Sached Books.

Morren, R. C. (2001). Creole-based trilingual education in the Caribbean archipelago of San Andres, Providence and Santa Catalina. *Journal of Multilingual and Multicultural Development* 22(3), 227–241.

Morris, G., and R. Chenail (Eds.). (1995). *The Talk of the Clinic: Explorations in the Analysis of Medical and Therapeutic Discourse*. Hillsdale, NJ: Lawrence Erlbaum.

Morris, R. (2008). Missing stitches: An overview of judicial attitudes to interlingual interpreting in the criminal justice systems of Canada and Israel. *Interpreting* 10(1), 34–64.

Morris, R. (1998). Justice in Jerusalem—Interpreting in Israeli legal proceedings. *Meta: Translators' Journal* 43(1), 110–118.

Morrow, K., and K. Johnson (1979). *Communicate 1*. Cambridge: Cambridge University Press.

Morrow, P. R. (2006). Telling about problems and giving advice in an Internet discussion forum: Some discourse features. *Discourse Studies* 8(4), 531–548.

Moser-Mercer, B. (1997). Editorial: Methodological issues in interpreting research: An introduction to the Ascona workshops. *Interpreting* 2(1/2), 1–11.

Moser-Mercer, B. (1996). Quality in interpreting: Some methodological issues. *Interpreters' Newsletter* 7, 43–55.

Moser-Mercer, B., A. Künzli, and M. Korac (1998). Prolonged turns in interpreting: Effects on quality, physiological and psychological stress (pilot study). *Interpreting* 3(1), 47–64.

Moskowitz, G. (1978). *Caring and Sharing in the Foreign Language Class*. Rowley, MA: Newbury House.

Motha, S. (2006). Racializing ESOL teacher identities in US K12 public schools. *TESOL Quarterly* 40(3), 495–518.

Mounin, G. (1963). *Les problèmes théoriques de la traduction (Theoretical Problems in Translation)*. Paris: Gallimard.

Mouzourakis, P. (1996). Videoconferencing:Techniques and challenges. *Interpreting* 1(1), 21–38.

Mudraya, O. (2006). Engineering English: A lexical frequency instructional model. *English for Specific Purposes* 25, 235–256.

Mueller, G. (1980). Visual contextual clues and listening comprehension: An experiment. *Modern Language Journal* 64(3), 335–340.

Mueller, J. L. (2005). Electrophysiological correlates of second language processing. *Second Language Research* 21, 152–174.

Mufwene, S. S. (2001). *The Ecology of Language Evolution*. Cambridge: Cambridge University Press.

Mühleisen, S. (2002). *Creole Discourse: Exploring Prestige Formation and Change across Caribbean English-Lexicon Creoles*. Amsterdam/Philadelphia: Benjamins.

Mühlhäusler, P. (2006). Naming languages, drawing language boundaries and maintaining languages with special reference to the linguistic situation in Papua New Guinea. In D. Cunningham, D. E. Ingram, and S. Sumbuk (Eds.), *Language Diversity in the Pacific* (pp. 24–39). Clevedon, Avon, UK: Multilingual Matters.

Mühlhäusler, P. (2003a). *Language of Environment, Environment of Language: A Course in Ecolinguistics*. London: Battlebridge.

Mühlhäusler, P. (2003b). English as an exotic language. In C. Mair (Ed.), *The Politics of English as a World Language* (pp. 67–86). Amsterdam: Rodopi.

Mülhäusler, P. (2000). Language planning and language ecology. *Current Issues in Language Planning* 1(3), 306–367.

Mühlhäusler, P. (1998). Some Pacific island utopias and their languages. *Plurilinguismes* 15, 27–47.

Mühlhäusler, P. (1996a). The value of low candidature languages at university level. *Australian Language Matters* 4(1), 8–9, 15.

Mühlhäusler, P. (1996b). *Linguistic Ecology: Language Change and Linguistic Imperialism in the Pacific Region*. London: Routledge.

Mühlhäusler, P. (1995). Attitudes to literacy in the pidgins and creoles of the Pacific area. *English World-Wide* 16, 251–71.

Mühlhäusler, P., and A. Peace (2006). Environmental discourses. *Annual Review of Anthropology* 35, 457–479.

Mukherjee, J., and J-M. Rohrbach (2006). Rethinking applied corpus linguistics from a language-pedagogical perspective: New departures in learner corpus research. In B. Kettemann, and G. Marko (Eds.), *Planning, Gluing and Painting Corpora: Inside the Applied Corpus Linguist's Workshop* (pp. 205–232). Frankfurt: Peter Lang.

MultiCAT informational website [Online]. Available: http://www.cohums.ohio-state.edu/multicat.htm.

Munby, J. (1978). *Communicative Syllabus Design*. Cambridge: Cambridge University Press.

Munday, J. (2001). *Introducing Translation Studies: Theories and Applications*. London and New York: Routledge.

Murphy, B. (1996). Computer corpora and vocabulary study. *Language Learning Journal* 14, 53–57.

Murphy, J. M., and F. L. Stoller (Eds.). (2001). Sustained-content language teaching: An emerging definition [Special issue]. *TESOL Journal* 10(2/3).

Murray, D. E. (1995). *Knowledge Machines: Language and Information in a Technological Society*. London: Longman.

Murtagh, E. J. (1982). Creole and English as languages of instruction in bilingual education with Aboriginal Australians: Some research findings. *International Journal of the Sociology of Language* 36, 15–33.

Musacchio, M. T. (2005). The influence of English on Italian: The case of translations of economics articles. In G. Anderman, and M. Rogers (Eds.), *In and Out of English: For Better, For Worse?* (pp. 71–96). Clevedon, Avon, UK: Multilingual Matters.

Musau, P. M. (1999). Constraints on the acquisition planning of indigenous African languages: The case of Kiswahili in Kenya. *Language, Culture and Curriculum* 12, 117–127.

Mutonyi, H., and B. Norton (2007). ICT on the margins: Lessons for Ugandan education. *Language and Education* 21(3), 264–270.

Myers, G. (2000). Powerpoints: Technology, lectures and changing genres. In A. Trosborg (Ed.), *Analysing Professional Genres* (pp. 177–189). Amsterdam: John Benjamins.

Myers, G. (1999). *Ad Worlds: Brands, Media, Audiences*. London: Arnold.

Myers-Scotton, C. (1995). A lexically based model of code-switching. In L. Milroy, and P. Muysken (Eds.), *One Speaker, Two Languages. Cross-Disciplinary Perspectives on Code-Switching* (pp. 233–256). Cambridge: Cambridge University Press.

Myhill, J. (1999). Identity, territoriality and minority language survival. *Journal of Multilingual and Multicultural Development* 20(1), 35–50.

Myles, F. (2005). Review article: Interlanguage corpora and second language acquisition research. *Second Language Research* 21, 373–391.

Nagai, Y., and R. Lister (2003). What is our culture? What is our language? Dialogue toward the maintenance of Indigenous culture and language in Papua New Guinea. *Language and Education* 17(2), 87–104.

Nagata, N. (1993). Intelligent computer feedback for second language instruction. *Modern Language Journal* 77(3), 330–339.

Nahir, M. (1984). Language planning goals: A classification. *Language Problems and Language Planning* 8(3), 294–327.

Nahir, M. (1977). The five aspects of language planning: A classification. *Language Problems and Language Planning* 1(2), 107–122.

Naiman, N., M. Fröhlich, H. H. Stern, and A. Todesco (1978). *The Good Language Learner*. Toronto: Ontario Institute for Studies in Education.

Nassaji, H., and G. Wells (2000). What's the use of "triadic dialogue"? An investigation of teacher-student interaction. *Applied Linguistics* 21, 376–406.

Nation, P. (1990). *Teaching and Learning Vocabulary*. New York: Newbury House.

National Core Curriculum (NCC): First draft (1990). *Nemzeti alaptanterv: Els? fogalmazvány*. Székesfehérvár [Manuscript].

National Core Curriculum (NCC): Second draft (1993). *Nemzeti alaptanterv: Második fogalmazvány*. Budapest [Manuscript].

Nattinger, J. R., and J. S. DeCarrico (1992). *Lexical Phrases and Language Teaching*. Oxford: Oxford University Press.

Negueruela, E. (2003). A sociocultural approach to the teaching and learning of second languages: Systemic-theoretical instruction and L2 development. PhD dissertation, Pennsylvania State University, University Park.

Negueruela, E., and J. P. Lantolf (2006). A concept-based approach to teaching Spanish grammar. In R. Salaberry, and B. Lafford (Eds.), *Spanish Second Language Acquisition: State of the Art* (pp. 79–102). Washington, DC: Georgetown University Press.

Nelde, P. H. (1995). *Euromosaic: The Production and Reproduction of the Minority Language Groups in the European Union*. Luxembourg: Office for Official publications of the European Community.

Nelde, P. H. (1987). Language contact means language conflict. In G. Mac Eoin, A. Ahlqvist, and C. ÓhAodha (Eds.), *Third International Conference on Minority Languages* (pp. 33–42). Clevedon, Avon, UK: Multilingual Matters.

Nelde, P. H., H. Göebl, Z. Starý, and W. Wölck (Eds.) (1996). *Contact Linguistics: An International Handbook of Contemporary Research*. Berlin: de Gruyter.

Nelson, C. (2008). *Sexual Identities in English Language Education: Classroom Conversations*. New York: Routledge.

Nelson, G. (1996). The design of the corpus. In S. Greenbaum (Ed.), *Comparing English Worldwide: The International Corpus of English* (pp. 27–35). Oxford: Clarendon Press.

Nelson, G., and J. Carson (1998). ESL students' perceptions of effectiveness in peer response groups. *Journal of Second Language Writing* 7, 113–131.

Nelson, G., and J. Murphy (1992). An L2 writing group: Task and social dimensions. *Journal of Second Language Writing* 1, 171–194.

Nesi, H., and H. Basturkmen (2006). Lexical bundles and discourse signaling in academic lectures. *International Journal of Corpus Linguistics* 11, 283–304.

Nesselhauf, N. (2005). *Collocations in a Learner Corpus*. Amsterdam: John Benjamins.

Nesselhauf, N. (2003). The use of collocations by advanced learners of English and some implications for teaching. *Applied Linguistics* 24, 223–242.

Nettle, D. (1999). *Linguistic Diversity*. Oxford: Oxford University Press.

Nettle, D., and S. Romaine (2000). *Vanishing Voices: The Extinction of the World's Languages*. Oxford: Oxford University Press.

Nevala, M. (2004). Accessing politeness axes: Forms of address and terms of reference in early English correspondence. *Journal of Pragmatics* 36(12), 2125–2160.

Nevalainen, T., and L. Kahlas-Tarkka (Eds.). (1997). *To Explain the Present*. Helsinki: Societe Neophilologique.

Nevile, M. (2008). Being out of order: Overlapping talk as evidence of trouble in airline pilots' work. In V. Bhatia, J. Flowerdew, and R. Jones (Eds.), *Advances in Discourse Studies* (pp. 36–50). London: Routledge.

Nevile, M. (2007). Action in time: Ensuring timeliness for collaborative work in the airline cockpit. *Language in Society* 36, 233–257.

New Jersey per diems seek a fair deal (no author). (2001). *Proteus* 10(2). (Page numbers unavailable.)

Ng, R. (1993). A woman out of control: Deconstructing racism and sexism in the university. *Canadian Journal of Education* 18, 189–205.

Nguyen, T. C. P., and F. V. Tochon (1998). Influence comparée de la carte de concepts et du résumé sur la compréhension et la production orales durant l'interprétation consecutive [The comparative influence of a concept map and a summary on oral comprehension and production during consecutive interpreting]. *Meta: Translators' Journal* 43(2), 220–235.

Nicholas, H., P. M. Lightbown, and N. Spada (2001). Recasts as feedback to language learners. *Language Learning* 51(4), 719–758.

Nichols, J. (1997). Modeling ancient population structures and movement in linguistics. *Annual Review of Anthropology* 26, 359–384.

Nichols, P. C. (1996). Pidgins and creoles. In S. L. McKay, and N. H. Hornberger (Eds.), *Sociolinguistics and Language Teaching* (pp. 195–217). Cambridge: Cambridge University Press.

Nickels, E. L. (2006). Interlanguage pragmatics and the effects of setting. In K. Bardovi-Harlig, C. Félix-Brasdefer, and A. Omar (Eds.), *Pragmatics and Language Learning* (vol. 11, pp. 253–280). Honolulu: University of Hawai'i, National Foreign Language Resource Center.

Nida, E. A. (1964). *Toward a Science of Translating*. Leiden: E.J. Brill.

Nida, E. A. (1956). Motivation in second-language learning. *Language Learning* 7, 11–16.

Nidue, J. (1988). A survey of teachers' attitudes towards the use of Tok Pisin as a medium of instruction in community schools in Papua New Guinea. *Papua New Guinea Journal of Education* 24, 214–231.

Nielson, F. A., L. K. Hansen, and D. Balslev (2004). Mining for associations between text and brain activation in a functional neuroimaging database. *Neuroinformatics* 2, 369–380.

Nieuwland, M., and J. van Berkum (2006). When peanuts fall in love: N400 evidence for the power of discourse. *Journal of Cognitive Neuroscience* 18, 1098–1111.

Nikolic, M. (2005). Interpretation after Nuremberg: International war crimes trials. *Proteus* 14(1), 1, 6–8.

Nikolov, M. (2003). Angolul és németül tanuló diákok nyelvtanulási attitűdje és motivációja [Attitudes and motivation of learners of English and German]. *Iskolakultúra* 13(8), 61–73.

Nikolov, M. (Ed.). (1999a). *English Language Education in Hungary: A Baseline Study*. Budapest: British Council.

Nikolov, M. (1999b). Classroom observation project. In M. Nikolov (Ed.), *English Language Education in Hungary: A Baseline Study* (pp. 221–246). Budapest: British Council.

Nikolov, M., and K. Józsa (2006). Relationships between language achievements in English and German and classroom-related variables. In M. Nikolov, and J. Horváth (Eds.), *UPRT 2006: Empirical Studies in English Applied Linguistics* (pp. 197–224). Pécs, Hungary: Lingua Franca Csoport, PTE.

Nolan, F. (1994). Auditory and acoustic analysis in speaker recognition. In J. Gibbons (Ed.), *Language and the Law* (pp. 325–345). London: Longman.

Nolan, J. (2005). *Interpretation: Techniques and Exercises*. Bristol, UK: Multilingual Matters.

Nord, C. (1997). *Translating as a Purposeful Activity*. Manchester, UK: St. Jerome.

Nord, C. (1991/2005). *Text Analysis in Translation: Theory, Methodology, and Didactic Application of a Model for Translation-Oriented Text Analysis* (2nd ed.). Amsterdam and New York: Rodopi.

Norgate, S. (1997). Research methods for studying the language of blind children. In N. Hornberger, and D. Corson (Eds.), *Research Methods in Language and Education: Encyclopedia of Language and Education* (vol. 8, pp. 165–173). Dordrecht: Kluwer.

Norrick, N. (2008). Using large corpora of conversation to investigate narrative: The case of interjections in conversational storytelling performance. *International Journal of Corpus Linguistics* 13, 438–64.

Norris, J. M., and L. Ortega (2007). The future of research synthesis in applied linguistics: Beyond art or science. *TESOL Quarterly* 41, 805–815.

Norris, J. M., and L. Ortega (2006a). The value and practice of research synthesis for language learning and teaching. In J. Norris, and L. Ortega (Eds.), *Synthesizing Research on Language Learning and Teaching* (pp. 3–50). Philadelphia: John Benjamins.

Norris, J. M., and L. Ortega (Eds.). (2006b). *Synthesizing Research on Language Learning and Teaching.* Philadelphia: John Benjamins.

Northeast Conference on the Teaching of Foreign Languages (NEC). (1962). *Current Issues in Language Testing* (Ed., W. F. Bottiglia). Middlebury, VT: Northeast Conference on the Teaching of Foreign Languages.

Northern Territory Department of Education (1995). *1994 Annual Reports from Specialist Staff in Bilingual Programs in Northern Territory Schools.* Darwin: Northern Territory Department of Education.

Norton, B. (2001). Non-participation, imagined communities and the language classroom. In M. Breen (Ed.), *Learner Contributions to Language Learning: New Directions in Research* (pp. 159–171). London: Pearson Education.

Norton, B. (2000). *Identity and Language Learning: Gender, Ethnicity and Educational Change.* London: Longman/Pearson Education.

Norton, B. (1997a). Language, identity and the ownership of English. *TESOL Quarterly* 31(3), 409–430.

Norton, B. (Ed.). (1997b). Language and identity [Special issue]. *TESOL Quarterly* 31(3).

Norton, B., and K. Toohey (Eds.). (2004). *Critical Pedagogies and Language Learning.* New York: Cambridge University Press.

Norton, B., and K. Toohey (2002). Identity and language learning. In R. B. Kaplan (Ed.), *The Oxford Handbook of Applied Linguistics* (PP. 115–123). New York: Oxford University Press.

Norton, B., and K. Toohey (2001). Changing perspectives on good language learners. *TESOL Quarterly* 35(2), 307–322.

Norton Peirce, B. (1995). Social identity, investment and language learning. *TESOL Quarterly* 29(1), 9–31.

Nunan, D. (2001). Syllabus design. In M. Celce-Murcia (Ed.), *Teaching English as a Second or Foreign Language* (3rd ed., pp. 55–65). Boston: Heinle & Heinle.

Nunan, D. (1995a). *Atlas 1.* New York: Heinle and Heinle.

Nunan, D. (1995b). *Atlas 2.* Boston, MA: Heinle and Heinle.

Nunan, D. (1992). *Research Methods in Language Learning.* Cambridge: Cambridge University Press.

Nunan, D. (1991). Communicative tasks and the language curriculum. *TESOL Quarterly* 25, 279–295.

Nunan, D. (1989). *Designing Tasks for the Communicative Classroom.* Cambridge: Cambridge University Press.

Nwenmely, H. (1996). *Language Reclamation: French Creole Language Teaching in the UK and the Caribbean.* Clevedon, Avon, UK: Multilingual Matters.

Nystrand, M. (1997). Dialogic instruction: When recitation becomes conversation. In M. Nystrand, A. Gamoran, R. Kachur, and C. Prendergast (Eds.), *Opening Dialogue:*

Understanding the Dynamics of Language Learning and Teaching in the English Classroom. (pp. 1–29). New York: Teachers College Press.

O'Barr, W. M., and J. Conley (1996). Ideological dissonance in the American legal system. In C. Briggs (Ed.), *Disorderly Discourse: Narrative, Conflict and Inequality* (pp. 114–134). New York: Oxford University Press.

Ochs, E. (1988). *Culture and Language Development: Language Acquisition and Language Socialization in a Samoan Village.* Cambridge: Cambridge University Press.

Ochs, E., and C. Taylor (1992). Family narrative as political activity. *Discourse and Society* 3, 301–340.

Ockenden, M. (1972). *Situational Dialogues.* London: Longman.

Odlin, T. (2008a). Conceptual transfer and meaning extensions. In P. Robinson, and N. Ellis (Eds.), *Handbook of Cognitive Linguistics and Second Language Acquisition* (pp. 306–340). New York: Routledge.

Odlin, T. (2008b). Focus constructions and language transfer. In D. Gabry-Barker (Ed.), *Morphosyntactic Issues in Second Language Acquisition Studies* (pp. 3–28). Clevedon, Avon, UK: Multilingual Matters.

Odlin, T. (2005). Cross-linguistic influence and conceptual transfer: What are the concepts? In M. McGroarty et al. (Eds.), *Annual Review of Applied Linguistics: Vol. 25. A Survey of Applied Linguistics* (pp. 3–25). New York: Cambridge University Press.

Odlin, T. (2003). Cross-linguistic influence. In C. Doughty, and M. Long (Eds.), *Handbook of Second Language Acquisition* (pp. 436–486). Oxford: Blackwell.

Odlin, T. (2002). Language transfer and cross-linguistic studies: Relativism, universalism and the native language. In R. B. Kaplan (Ed.), *The Oxford Handbook of Applied Linguistics* (pp. 253–261). New York: Oxford University Press.

Odlin, T. (2001). Language transfer and substrate influence. In R. Mesthrie (Ed.), *Concise Encyclopedia of Sociolinguistics* (pp. 499–503). Amsterdam: Elsevier.

Odlin, T. (1989). *Language Transfer: Cross-Linguistic Influence in Language Learning.* Cambridge: Cambridge University Press.

OECD (2006). PISA 2006. Összefoglaló jelentés [Summary report]. Retrieved August 5, 2008, from http://www.okm.gov.hu/letolt/kozokt/pisa_2006_vegl_071205.pdf.

Ohly, R. (1989). Linguistic ecology: The African language case. *Logos* 9, 79–90.

Ohta, A. (2001). *Second Language Acquisition Processes in the Classroom: Learning Japanese.* Mahwah, NJ: Lawrence Erlbaum.

Ohta, A. S. (1999). Interactional routines and the socialization of interactional style in adult learners of Japanese. *Journal of Pragmatics* 31, 1493–1512.

O'Keeffe, A. (2006). *Investigating Media Discourse.* London: Routledge.

O'Keeffe, A., and F. Farr (2003). Using language corpora in initial teacher education: Pedagogic issues and practical applications. *TESOL Quarterly* 37(3), 389–418.

O'Keeffe, A., M. McCarthy, and R. Carter (2007). *From Corpus to Classroom: Language Use and Language Teaching.* Cambridge: Cambridge University Press.

Oksaar, E. (1980). *Mehrsprachigkeit, Sprachkontakt, Sprachkonflikt* [Multilingualism, Language Contact, Language Conflict]. In P. H. Nelde (Ed.), *Sprachkontakt und Sprachkonflikt* [Language Contact and Language Conflict] (pp. 43–52). Wiesbaden, Germany: Steiner.

Oliver, R. (1995). Negative feedback in child NS-NNS conversation. *Studies in Second Language Acquisition* 17, 459–481.

Oller, J. W., Jr. (1979). *Language Tests at School: A Pragmatic Approach.* London: Longman.

Oller, J., and K. Perkins (1980). *Research in Language Testing.* Rowley, MA: Newbury House.

Oller, J., and K. Perkins (1978). *Language in Education: Testing the Tests*. Rowley, MA: Newbury House.

Olohan, M. (2004). *Introducing Corpora in Translation Studies*. London and New York: Routledge.

Olohan, M. (Ed.). (2000). *Intercultural Faultlines: Research Models in Translation Studies I: Textual and Cognitive Aspects*. Manchester, UK: St. Jerome.

Olsher, D. A. (2004). Collaborative Group Work in Second and Foreign Language Classrooms: Talk, Embodiment, and Sequential Organization. PhD dissertation. University of California at Los Angeles.

Olshtain, E., and S. Blum-Kulka (1985). Degree of approximation: Nonnative reactions to native speech act behavior. In S. M. Gass, and C. Madden (Eds.). *Input in Second Language Acquisition* (pp. 303–325). Rowley, MA: Newbury House.

Olsson, J. (2008). *Forensic Linguistics* (2nd ed.). London: Continuum.

Omar, A. S. (1993). Closing Kiswahili conversations: The performance of native and non- native speakers. In L. F. Bouton, and Y. Kachru (Eds.), *Pragmatics and Language Learning* (vol. 4, pp. 104–125). Urbana-Champaign: University of Illinois, Division of English as an International Language (DEIL).

Omar, A. S. (1992). Conversational openings in Kiswahili: The pragmatic performance of native and nonnative speakers. In L. F. Bouton, and Y. Kachru (Eds.), *Pragmatics and Language Learning* (vol. 3, pp. 20–32). Urbana-Champaign: University of Illinois, Division of English as an International Language (DEIL).

Ondelli, S. (1998). Medium shift in interpretation: Do interpreters produce oral texts? *Interpreters' Newsletter* 8, 181–193.

O'Neill, R. (1981). *American Kernel Lessons: Beginning*. New York: Longman.

O'Neill, R. (1970). *English in Situations*. Oxford: Oxford University Press.

Ooi, V. (1997). Analysing the Singapore ICE corpus for lexicographic evidence. In M. Ljung (Ed.), *Corpus-based studies in English* (pp. 245–260). Amsterdam: Rodopi.

O'Reilly, R. C., and Y. Munakata (2000). *Computational Explorations in Cognitive Neuroscience: Understanding the Mind by Simulating the Brain*. Cambridge, MA: MIT Press.

O'Riagain, P. (1988). Bilingualism in Ireland 1973–1983: An overview of national sociolinguistic surveys. *International Journal of the Sociology of Language* 70, 29–51.

Orr, G. (1987). Aspects of the second language acquisition of Chichewa noun class morphology. PhD dissertation, University of California at Los Angeles.

Orrantia, D. (2002). The SSTI/NAJIT translation and interpretation national certification examination. *ATA Chronicle* (June), 19–22.

Ortega, L. (2009). *Understanding Second Language Acquisition*. London: Hodder Education.

Ortega, L. (2007). Second language acquisition explained? SLA across nine contemporary theories. In B. VanPatten, and J. Williams (Eds.), *Theories in Second Language Acquisition* (pp. 225–250). Mahwah, NJ: Lawrence Erlbaum.

Ortega, L. (Ed.). (2005). Methodology, epistemology and ethics in instructed SLA research [Special issue]. *Modern Language Journal* 89(3).

Ortega, L., and H. Byrnes (Eds.). (2008). *The Longitudinal Study of Advanced L2 Capacities*. New York: Routledge.

Ortega, L., and J. Carson (in press). Multicompetence, social context and L2 writing research praxis. In T. Silva, and P. K. Matsuda (Ed.), *Practicing Theory in Second Language Writing*. Mahwah, NJ: Lawrence Erlbaum.

Ortega, L., and G. Iberri-Shea (2005). Longitudinal research in SLA: Recent trends and future direction. In M. McGroarty et al. (Eds.), *Annual Review of Applied Linguistics:*

Vol. 25. A Survey of Applied Linguistics (pp. 26–45). New York: Cambridge University Press.

Osterhout, L., J. McLaughlin, L. Pitkänen, C. Frenck-Mestre, and N. Molinaro (2006). Novice learners, longitudinal designs, and event-related potentials: A means for exploring the neurocognition of second language processing. *Language Learning* 56, 199–230.

Otheguy, R. (1995). When contact speakers talk, linguistic theory listens. In E. Contini-Morova, and B. Goldberg (Eds.), *Meaning as Explanations: Advances in Linguistic Sign Theory* (pp. 213–242). Berlin: Mouton de Gruyter.

Otheguy, R. (1993). A reconsideration of the notion of loan translation in the analysis of US Spanish. In A. Roca, and J. Lipski (Eds.), *Spanish in the United States: Linguistic Contact and Diversity* (pp. 21–41). Berlin: Mouton de Druyter.

Otto, S. (1991). German as a second language in France—a view from the outside. *Germanistische Mitteilungen* 34, 81–88.

Oxford, R. L. (2002). Sources of variation in language learning. In R. B. Kaplan (Ed.), *Oxford Handbook of Applied Linguistics* (pp. 245–252). Oxford: Oxford University Press.

Oxford, R. L. (1996). New pathways of language learning motivation. In R. L. Oxford (Ed.), *Language Learning Motivation: Pathways to a New Century* (Technical Report #11) (pp. 1–8). Honolulu: The University of Hawai'i at Manoa, Second Language Teaching and Curriculum Center.

Oxford, R. L. (1993). Research update on teaching L2 listening. *System* 21(2), 205–211.

Oxford, R. L., and N. Anderson (1995). A cross-cultural view of learning styles. *Language Teaching* 28, 201–215.

Ozolins, U. (1993). *The Politics of Language in Australia*. Melbourne: Cambridge University Press.

Page, E. B. (1966). The Imminence of grading essays by computer. *Phi Delta Kappan* 48, 238–243.

Page, E. B., and N. S. Petersen (1995). The computer moves into essay grading: Updating the ancient test. *Phi Delta Kappan* 76, 561–565.

Pakir, A. (1993). Making bilingualism work: Developments in bilingual education in ASEAN. *Language, Culture and Curriculum* 6, 209–223.

Palionis, J. (1997). On the Lithuanian language during the Soviet dictatorship. *Gimtoji Kalba* 6(362), 1–3.

Pally, M. (Ed.). (2000). *Sustained Content Teaching in Academic ESL/EFL*. Boston: Houghton Mifflin.

Pally, M. (1997). Critical thinking in ESL: An argument for sustained content. *Journal of Second Language Writing* 6, 293–311.

Papadopoulou, D. (2005). Reading-time studies of second language ambiguity resolution. *Second Language Research* 21, 98–120.

Papadopoulou, D., and H. Clahsen (2003). Parsing strategies in L1 and L2 sentence processing: A study of relative clause attachment in Greek. *Studies in Second Language Acquisition* 24, 501–528.

Paradis, M. (2004). *A Neurolinguistic Theory of Bilingualism*. Amsterdam/Philadelphia: John Benjamins.

Paradis, M. (1998). Aphasia in bilinguals: How atypical is it? In P. Coppens, Y. Lebrun, and A. Basso (Eds.), *Aphasia in Atypical Populations* (pp. 35–66). Mahwah NJ: Lawrence Erlbaum.

Parks, S. (2000). Professional writing and the role of incidental collaboration: Evidence from a medical setting. *Journal of Second Language Writing* 9, 101–122.

Parodi, G. (2007). *Working with Spanish Corpora*. London: Continuum.

Partington, A. (2001). Corpus-based description in teaching and learning. In Aston, G. (Ed.), *Learning with Corpora* (pp. 63–84). Houston, Texas: Athelstan.

Partington, A. (1998). *Patterns and Meanings*. Amsterdam: John Benjamins.

Patrick, G. (2008). Attorneys need trained professionals. *Proteus* 17(2), 1, 9.

Patrick, P. L. (1999). *Urban Jamaican Creole: Variation in the Mesolect* (*Varieties of English around the world* G 17). Amsterdam: John Benjamins.

Patrick, P. L., and S. W. Buell (2000). Competing creole transcipts on trial. *Essex Research Reports in Linguistics* 32, 103–132.

Patthey-Chavez, G. G., and L. Clare (1996). Task, talk and text: The influence of instructional conversation on transitional bilingual writers. *Written Communication* 13, 515–563.

Paulsen Christensen, T. (2008). Judges' deviations from norm-based direct speech in court. *Interpreting* 10(1), 99–127.

Paulston, C. B. (1974). Linguistic and communicative competence. *TESOL Quarterly*, 8(2), 347–362.

Paulston, C. B., and M. Bruder (1975). *From Substitution to Substance*. Rowley, MA: Newbury House.

Pavlenko, A. (2008a). "I'm very not about the law part": Nonnative speakers of English and the Miranda warnings. *TESOL Quarterly* 42, 1–30.

Pavlenko, A. (2008b). Research methods in the study of gender in second/foreign language education. In K. King (Ed.), *Research Methods in Language and Education Encyclopedia of Language and Education* (vol. 10, pp. 165–174). New York: Springer.

Pavlenko, A. (2007a). Autobiographic narratives as data in applied linguistics. *Applied Linguistics* 28, 163–188.

Pavlenko, A. (2007b). Narrative analysis. In L. Wei and M. G. Moyer (Eds.), *The Blackwell Guide to Research Methods in Bilingualism and Multilingualism* (pp. 311–325). Malden, MA: Blackwell.

Pavlenko, A. (1999). New approaches to concepts in bilingual memory. *Bilingualism: Language and Cognition* 2, 209–230.

Pavlenko, A., and A. Blackledge (Eds.). (2003). *Negotiation of Identities in Multilingual Contexts*. Clevedon, Avon, UK: Multilingual Matters.

Pavlenko, A., and J. P. Lantolf (2000). Second language learning as participation and the (re)construction of selves. In J. P. Lantolf (Ed.), *Sociocultural Theory and Second Language Learning* (pp. 155–177). New York: Oxford University Press.

Pavlenko, A., and B. Norton (2007). Imagined communities, identity and English language teaching. In J. Cummins, and C. Davison (Eds.), *International Handbook of English Language Teaching* (pp. 669–680). New York: Springer.

Pavlenko, A., and I. Piller (2007). Language education and gender. In S. May (Ed.), *Language policy and political issues in education: Encyclopedia of Language and Education* (vol. 1, pp. 57–69). New York: Springer.

Pawley, A., and F. H. Syder (1983). Two puzzles for linguistic theory: Nativelike selection and nativelike fluency. In J. C. Richards, and R. W. Schmidt (Eds.), *Language and Communication* (pp. 191–226). London: Longman.

Pawlikova-Vihanova, V. (1996). Swahili and the dilemma of Ugandan language policy. *Asian and African Studies* 5(2), 158–170.

Payne, S., and P. J. Whitney (2002). Developing L2 oral proficiency through synchronous CMC: Output, working memory and interlanguage development. *CALICO Journal* 20(1), 7–32.

Pearson, B. A., and R. Berch (1994). Video depositions: Linguistic endorsement and caveats. In J. Gibbons (Ed.), *Language and the Law* (pp. 171–187). London: Longman.

Pearson, L. (2006). Teaching pragmatics in Spanish L2 courses: What do learners think? In K. Bardovi-Harlig, C. Félix-Brasdefer, and A. Omar (Eds.), *Pragmatics and Language Learning* (vol. 11, pp. 109–134). Honolulu: University of Hawai'i, Foreign Language Resource Center.

Pecorari, D. (2008). *Academic Writing and Plagiarism: A Linguistic Analysis*. London: Continuum.

Peddie, R. A. (1991a). Coming—ready or not? Language policy development in New Zealand. *Language Problems & Language Planning* 15, 25–42.

Peddie, R. A. (1991b). *One, Two, or Many? The Development and Implementation of Language Policy in New Zealand*. Auckland, NZ: University of Auckland.

Pederson, K. M. (1987). Research on CALL. In W. F. Smith (Ed.), *Modern Media in Foreign Language Education: Theory and Implementation* (pp. 99–132). Lincolnwood, IL: National Textbook Company.

Pellegrino, M. (2007). Assessment design driven by cognitive theory and research: Practical reality or pipe dream? Paper presented at the Annual Meeting of the National Council on Measurement in Education, Chicago.

Pellettieri, J. (2000). Negotiation in cyberspace: The role of *chatting* in the development of grammatical competence in the virtual foreign language classroom. In M. Warschauer, and R. Kern (Eds.), *Network-Based Language Teaching: Concepts and Practice* (pp. 59–86). Cambridge: Cambridge University Press.

Penning, R. (1996). History of the community interpreting industry: Gaining respect for the profession. In M. Jérôme-O'Keeffe (Ed.), *Proceedings of the 37th Annual Conference of the American Translators Association* (pp. 91–97). Medford, NJ: Learned Information.

Pennebaker, J. (2003). Telling stories: The health benefits of disclosure. In J. Wilce (Ed.), *The Social and Cultural Lives of Immune Systems* (pp. 19–34). London: Routledge.

Pennycook, A. (2008). Critical applied linguistics and language education. In S. May, and N. H. Hornberger (Eds.), *Language Policy and Political Issues in Education Encyclopedia of Language and Education* (vol. 1, pp. 169–181). New York: Springer.

Pennycook, A. (2004). Language policy and the ecological turn. *Language Policy* 3(3), 213–239.

Pennycook, A. (2001). *Critical Applied Linguistics: A Critical Introduction*. Mahwah, NJ: Lawrence Erlbaum.

Pennycook, A. (2000). English, politics, ideology: From colonial celebration to postcolonial performativity. In T. Ricento, and T. Wiley (Eds.), *Ideology, Politics and Language Policies: Focus on English* (pp. 107–119). Amsterdam: John Benjamins.

Pennycook, A. (Ed.). (1999). Critical approaches to TESOL [Special issue]. *TESOL Quarterly* 33(3).

Pennycook, A. (1998). *English and the Discourses of Colonialism*. New York: Routledge.

Pennycook, A. (1997). Borrowing others' words: Text, ownership, memory and plagiarism. *TESOL Quarterly* 30, 201–230.

Pennycook, A. (1995). English in the world/the world in English. In J. W. Tollefson (Ed.), *Power and Inequality in Language Education* (pp. 34–58). Cambridge: Cambridge University Press.

Pennycook, A. (1994). *The Cultural Politics of English as an International Language*. New York: Longman.

Perez-Chambers, M. (2000, March 20). Personal communication.

Perfetti, C., N. Landi, and J. Oakhill (2005). The acquisition of reading comprehension skill. In M. Snowling, and C. Hulme (Eds.), *The Science of Reading* (pp. 227–247). Malden, MA: Blackwell.

Peters, A. (1983). *Units of language acquisition*. Cambridge: Cambridge University Press.

Peterson, P. W. (1997). Knowledge, skills and attitudes in preparing teachers for content-based and language-enhanced settings. In M. A. Snow, and D. M. Brinton (Eds.), *The Content Based Classroom: Perspectives on Integrating Language and Content* (pp. 158–174). White Plains, NY: Longman.

Peterson, R. R., and P. Savoy (1998). Lexical selection and phonological encoding during language production: Evidence for cascaded processing. *Journal of Experimental Psychology: Learning, Memory and Cognition* 24, 539–557.

Philips, S. U. (1998). *Ideology in the Language of Judges: How Judges Practice Law, Politics and Courtroom Control*. Oxford: Oxford University Press.

Phillipson, R. (2003). *English Only Europe? Challenging Language Policy*. New York: Routledge.

Phillipson, R. (1994a). English language spread policy. *International Journal of the Sociology of Language* 107, 7–24.

Phillipson, R. (1994b). The spread of dominant languages (English, French, German) in multilingual Europe (ROLIG Paper No. 51, pp. 18–22). Roskilde, Denmark: Roskilde Universitets.

Phillipson, R. (1992). *Linguistic Imperialism*. Oxford: Oxford University Press.

Phillipson, R., and T. Skutnabb-Kangas (2000). Englishisation: One dimension of globalization. *AILA Review* 13, 19–36.

Phillipson, R., and T. Skutnabb-Kangas (1997). Linguistic human rights and English in Europe. *World Englishes* 16(1), 27–43.

Philp, J. (2003). Constraints on noticing the gap: Nonnative speakers' noticing of recasts in NS-NNS interaction. *Studies in Second Language Acquisition* 25, 99–126.

Pica, T. (2002). Subject-matter content: How does it assist the interactional and linguistic needs of classroom language learners? *Modern Language Journal* 86, 1–29.

Pica, T. (1994). Research on negotiation: What does it reveal about second-language learning conditions, processes, and outcomes? *Language Learning* 44(3), 493–527.

Pica, T. (1988). Interlanguage adjustments as an outcome of NS-NNS negotiated interaction. *Language Learning* 38, 45–73.

Pica, T. (1987). Second language acquisition, social interaction and the classroom. *Applied Linguistics* 8, 3–21.

Pica, T., and C. Doughty (1985). Input and interaction in the communicative language classroom: A comparison of teacher-fronted and group activities. In S. Gass, and C. Madden (Eds.), *Input in Second Language Acquisition* (pp. 115–132). Rowley, MA: Newbury House.

Pica, T., C. Doughty, and R. Young (1986). Making input comprehensible: Do interactional modifications help? *ITL Review of Applied Linguistics* 72, 1–25.

Pica, T., R. Kanagy, and J. Falodun (1993). Choosing and using communication tasks for second language instruction. In G. Crookes, and S. M. Gass (Eds.), *Tasks and language learning* (pp. 9–34). Clevedon, Avon, UK: Multilingual Matters.

Pica, T., H. S. Kang, and S. Sauro (2006). Information gap tasks: Their multiple roles and contributions to interaction research methodology. *Studies in Second Language Acquisition* 28, 301–338.

Pica, T., R. Young, and C. Doughty (1987). The impact of interaction on comprehension. TESOL *Quarterly* 21, 737–758.

Pickering, M. J., and S. Garrod (2004). Toward a mechanistic psychology of dialogue. *Behavioral and Brain Sciences* 27, 169–190.

Pickering, M. J., M. J. Traxler, and M. W. Crocker (2000). Ambiguity resolution in sentence processing: Evidence against frequency-based accounts. *Journal of Memory and Language* 43, 447–475.

Pickering, M. J., and R. P. G. Van Gompel (2006). Syntactic parsing. In M. Traxler, and M. Gernsbacher (Eds.), *Handbook of Psycholinguistics* (2nd ed., pp. 455–503). Amsterdam: Elsevier.

Picone, M. (1997). Enclave dialect contraction: An external overview of Louisiana French. *American Speech* 72(2), 117–144.

Piehl, A. (1996). Language standardization and guidance on correct usage. *Virttaja*. *Virittaja* 100, 490–503.

Pienemann, M., B. Di Biase, S. Kawaguchi, and G. Hakansson (2005). Processing constraints on L1 transfer. In J. F. Kroll, and A. M. B. de Groot (Eds.), *Handbook of Bilingualism: Psycholinguistic Approaches* (pp. 128–153). Oxford: Oxford University Press.

Pierce, B. N. (1994). The test of English as a foreign language: Developing items for reading comprehension. In C. Hill, and K. Parry (Eds.), *From Testing to Assessment* (pp. 33–60). New York: Longman.

Piggott, G. (1992). Variability in feature dependency: The case of nasality. *Natural Language and Linguistic Theory* 10, 33–77.

Piller, I. (2003). Advertising as a site of language contact. In M. McGroarty et al. (Eds.), *Annual Review of Applied Linguistics: Vol. 23. Language Contact and Change* (pp. 170–183). New York: Cambridge University Press.

Pimsleur, P. (1966). *Language Aptitude Battery*. New York: Harcourt, Brace, Jovanovich.

Pinker, S. (1994). *The Language Instinct*. New York: Morrow.

Pinker, S. (1989). *Learnability and Cognition: The Acquisition of Argument Structure*. Cambridge, MA: MIT Press.

Pinker, S., and A. Prince (1994). Regular and irregular morphology and the psychological status of rules. In S. D. Lima, R. L. Corrigan, and G. K. Iverson (Eds.), *The Reality of Linguistic Rules* (pp. 321–351). Philadelphia, PA: John Benjamins.

Pinker, S., and A. Prince (1988). On language and connectionism: Analysis of a parallel distributing model of language acquisition. *Cognition* 28, 73–193.

Piper, A. (1986). Conversation and the computer: A study of the conversational spin-off generated among learners of English as a foreign language working in groups. *System* 14(2), 187–198.

Pittaway, D. (2004). Investment and second language acquisition. *Critical Inquiry in Language Studies* 4(1), 203–218.

Planelles-Ivanez, M. (1996). The influence of linguistic planning on the feminization of job titles in France and Quebec: Two different results concerning usage. *Revue quebecoise de linguistique* 24(2), 71–106.

Plough, I. (1995). Indirect negative evidence, inductive inferencing and second language acquisition. In L. Eubank, L. Selinker, and M. Sharwood Smith (Eds.), *The Current State of Interlanguage: Studies in Honor of William E. Rutherford* (pp. 89–105). Amsterdam: John Benjamins.

Plough, I. (1994). A role for indirect negative evidence in second language acquisition. PhD dissertation, Michigan State University, East Lansing.

Plunkett, K., and V. Marchman (1993). From rote learning to system building: Acquiring verb morphology in children and connectionist nets. *Cognition* 48, 21–69.

Pöchhacker, F. (2005). From operation to action: Process-orientation in interpreting studies. *Meta: Translators' Journal* 50(2), 682–695.

Pöchhacker, F. (2001). Quality assessment in conference and community interpreting. *Meta: Translators' Journal* 46(2), 410–425.

Pöchhacker, F. (1995). Writings and research on interpreting: A bibliographic analysis. *Interpreters' Newsletter* 6, 17–31.

Poehner, M. E. (2008). *Dynamic Assessment: A Vygotskian Approach to Understanding and Promoting L2 Development*. Berlin: Springer.

Poirier, C. (1998). Toward a new image of Québec French: Twenty years of Tresor. *French Review* 71, 912–929.

Poldrack, R. A. (2006). Can cognitive processing be inferred from neuroimaging data? *TRENDS in Cognitive Sciences* 10, 59–63.

Polio, C., C. Fleck, and N. Leder (1998). "If only I had more time": ESL learners' changes in linguistic accuracy on essay revisions. *Journal of Second Language Writing* 7, 43–68.

Polkinghorne, D. (2007). Validity issues in narrative research. *Qualitative Inquiry* 13(4) 471–486.

Pollard, C. J., and I. Sag (1994). *Head-Driven Phrase Structure Grammar*. Chicago: University of Chicago Press.

Pollard, V. (1993). *From Jamaican Creole to Standard English: A Handbook for Teachers*. Brooklyn, NY: Caribbean Research Center, Medgar Evers College.

Pollock, J.-Y. (1989). Verb movement, universal grammar, and the structure of IP. *Linguistic Inquiry* 20, 365–424.

Pomerantz, A. (1984). Agreeing and disagreeing with assessments: Some features of preferred/dispreferred turn shapes. In J. M. Atkinson, and J. Heritage (Eds.), *Structures of Social Action: Studies in Conversation Analysis* (pp. 57–101). Cambridge: Cambridge University Press.

Poole, D. (2008). The messiness of language socialization in reading groups: Participation in and resistance to the values of essayist literacy. *Linguistics and Education* 19, 378–403.

Poole, D. (2005). Cross-cultural variation in classroom turn-taking practices. In P. D. Bruthiaux, D. Atkinson, W. G. Eggington, W. Grabe, and V. Ramanathan (Eds.), *Directions in Applied Linguistics: Essays in Honor of Robert B. Kaplan* (pp. 201–219). Clevedon, Avon, UK: Multilingual Matters.

Poole, D. (2003). Linguistic connections between co-occurring speech and writing in a classroom literacy event. *Discourse Processes* 35, 103–134.

Poole, D. (1992). Language socialization in the second language classroom. *Language Learning* 42, 593–616.

Pope, R. (2005). Preface. *Creativity: Theory, History, Practice*. London: Routledge.

Popper, K. (1961). *The Poverty of Historicism*. London: Routledge.

Porcel, J. (2006). The paradox of Spanish among Miami Cubans. *Journal of Sociolinguistics* 10(1), 93–110.

Porges, S. W. (2003). Social engagement and attachment: A philogenetic perspective. *Annals of the New York Academy of Sciences* 1008, 31–47.

Port, R., and T. van Gelder (1995). *Mind as Motion: Explorations in the Dynamics of Cognition*. Cambridge, MA: MIT Press.

Porter-Ladousse, G. (1987). *Role Play*. Cambridge: Cambridge University Press.

Portes, A., and R. Schauffler (1994). Language and the second generation: Bilingualism yesterday and today. *International Migration Review* 28(4), 640–661.

Poth, J. (1996). A methodological outline of language planning in Africa. *Etudes de Linguistic Appliquee* 103, 351–356.

Potowski, K. (2007). *Language and Identity in a Dual Immersion School*. Clevedon, Avon, UK: Multilingual Matters.

Potowski, K. (2004). Spanish language shift in Chicago. *Southwest Journal of Linguistics*, 2004, 23(1), 87–116.

Potter, M. C., K.-F. So, B. Von Eckardt, and L. B. Feldman (1984). Lexical and conceptual representation in beginning and more proficient bilinguals. *Journal of Verbal Learning and Verbal Behavior* 23, 23–38.

Poulisse, N. (1999). *Slips of the Tongue: Speech Errors in First and Second Language Production*. Amsterdam: John Benjamins.

Poulisse, N. (1997). Language production in bilinguals. In A. M. B. De Groot, and J. F. Kroll (Eds.), *Tutorials in Bilingualism: Psycholinguistic Perspectives* (pp. 201–224). Mahwah, NJ: Lawrence Erlbaum.

Poulisse, N., and T. Bongaerts (1994). First language use in second language production. *Applied Linguistics* 15, 36–57.

Powers, D. E., J. Burstein, M. Chodorow, M. E. Fowles, and K. Kukich (2000). Comparing the Validity of Automated and Human Essay Scoring GRE Board Research. Report No. 98–08a, ETS RR-00–10. Princeton, NJ: Educational Testing Services.

Prabhu, N. S. (1987). *Second Language Pedagogy*. Oxford: Oxford University Press.

Prasada, S., and S. Pinker (1993). Similarity-based and rule-based generalizations in inflectional morphology. *Language and Cognitive Processes* 8, 1–56.

Pratt, D., and E. C. Short (1994). Curriculum management. In T. Husén, and T. N. Postlethwaite (Eds.), *The International Encyclopedia of Education* (2nd ed., pp. 1320–1325). Oxford: Pergamon.

Pratt-Johnson, Y. (1993). Curriculum for Jamaican Creole-speaking students in New York City. *World Englishes* 12(2), 257–264.

Precht, K. (1998). A cross-cultural comparison of letters of recommendation. *English for Specific Purposes* 17(3), 241–265.

Pressley, M. (2006). *Reading Instruction that Works* (3rd ed.). New York: Guilford Press.

Preston, D. R. (1989). *Sociolinguistics and Second Language Acquisition*. Oxford: Blackwell.

Prévost, P., and L. White (2000). Missing surface inflection or impairment in second language acquisition. *Second Language Research* 16, 103–134.

Price, C. J., and K. J. Friston (2005). Functional ontologies for cognition: The systemic definition of structure and function. *Cognitive Neuropsychology* 22(3/4), 262–275.

Prince, E. (1978). A comparison of *WH*-clefts and *IT*-clefts in discourse. *Language* 54, 883–906.

Prior, P. A. (1998). *Writing Disciplinarity: A Sociohistoric Account of Literate Activity in the Academy*. Mahwah, NJ: Lawrence Erlbaum.

Pritchett, B. (1992). *Grammatical Competence and Parsing Performance*. Chicago: University of Chicago Press.

Provenzo, E. F., Jr., A. Brett, and G. N. McCloskey (1999). *Computers, Curriculum and Cultural Change: An Introduction for Teachers*. Mahwah, NJ: Lawrence Erlbaum.

Puetz, M. (1997). Language choices—contact and conflict. In Puetz, M. (Ed.), *Language Choices* (pp. ix–xxi). Amsterdam: Benjamins.

Puetz, M. (1994). *Language Contact and Language Conflict*. Amsterdam: Benjamins.

Purves, A. C. (Ed.). (1989). *Writing across Languages and Cultures: Issues in Contrastive Rhetoric* (pp. 275–304). Beverly Hills, CA: Sage. (*Written Communication Annual* 2.)

Purvis, T. (2008). A Linguistic and Discursive Analysis of Register Variation in Dagbani. PhD dissertation, Indiana University.

Pusponegroro, S. D. (1972). Address at the opening of the 7th RELC Regional Seminar. In *Report of the Regional Seminar on Instructional Materials for English Language Teaching*. Singapore: RELC.

Pyöli, R. (1998). Karelian under pressure from Russian—internal and external Russification. *Journal of Multilingual and Multicultural Development* 19, 128–142.

Qiao, H. L., and R. Sussex (1996). Using the Longman Mini-Concordancer on tagged and parsed corpora, with special reference to their use as an aid to grammar learning. *System* 24(1), 41–64.

Quaglio, P. (2009). *Television Dialogue: The Sitcom "Friends" versus Natural Conversation*. Amsterdam: John Benjamins.

Quaglio, P., and D. Biber (2006). The grammar of conversation. In B. Aarts, and A. McMahon (Eds.), *The Handbook of English Linguistics* (pp. 692–723). Oxford: Blackwell.

Quah, C. K. (2006). *Translation and Technology*. Houndmills and New York: Palgrave Macmillan.

Quinn, T. J. (1985). Functional approaches in language pedagogy. In R. B. Kaplan et al. (Eds.), *Annual Review of Applied Linguistics: 5 Broad Survey of Applied Linguistics* (pp. 60–80). New York: Cambridge University Press.

Quirk, R. (1988). The question of standards in the international use of English. In P. H. Lowenberg (Ed.), *Language Spread and Language Policy: Issues, Implications and Case Studies (Georgetown University Round Table on Languages and Linguistics)* (pp. 229–241). Washington, DC: Georgetown University Press.

Quirk, R., S. Greenbaum, G. Leech, and J. Svartvik (1972). *A Grammar of Contemporary English*. London: Longman.

Rabin, C. (1971). Spelling reform—Israel 1968. In J. Rubin, and B. Jernudd (Eds.), *Can Language Be Planned? Sociolinguistic Theory and Practice for Developing Nations* (pp. 95–122). Honolulu: University Press of Hawai'i.

Radecki, P., and J. Swales (1988). ESL student reaction to written comments on their written work. *System* 16, 355–365.

Rahman, T. (1995). The Siraiki movement in Pakistan. *Language Problems & Language Planning* 19, 1–25.

Raimes, A. (1985). What unskilled writers do as they write: A classroom study of composing. *TESOL Quarterly* 19, 229–258.

Rampton, B. (1997a). A socio-linguistic perspective on L2 communication strategies. In G. Kasper, and E. Kellerman (Eds.), *Communication strategies: Psycholinguistic and sociolinguistic perspectives* (pp. 279–303). London: Longman.

Rampton, B. (1997b). Retuning in applied linguistics. *International Journal of Applied Linguistics* 7, 3–25.

Rampton, B. (1995). Politics and change in research in applied linguistics. *Applied Linguistics* 12, 229–248.

Ratnaparkhi, A. (1998). Maximum entropy models for natural language ambiguity resolution. PhD dissertation., University of Pennsylvania.

Ratnaparkhi, A. (1996). A maximum entropy part-of-speech tagger. In *Proceedings of the Empirical Methods in Natural Language Processing Conference*. Philadelphia: University of Pennsylvania.

Raudenbush, S. W., and A. S. Bryk (2002). *Hierarchical Minear models: Applications and Data Analysis Methods*. Thousand Oaks, CA: Sage.

Ravel, J.-L., and P. Thomas (1985). *État de la Réforme de l'Enseignement aux Seychelles (1981–1985)*. Paris: Ministère des Relations Extérieures, Coopération et Développement.

Ray, C. (1996). Report: Papua New Guinea. *Pidgins and Creoles in Education (PACE) Newsletter* 7, 3.

Rayner, K., M. Carlson, and L. Frazier (1983). The interaction of syntax and semantics during sentence processing: Eye movements in the analysis of semantically biased sentences. *Journal of Verbal Learning and Verbal Behavior* 22, 358–374.

Rea-Dickins, P. (2006). Currents and eddies in the discourse of assessment: A learning-focused interpretation. *International Journal of Applied Linguistics* 16, 163–188.

Ready, D., and M. Wesche (1992). An evaluation of the University of Ottawa's sheltered program: Language teaching strategies that work. In R. Courchêne, J. Glidden,

J. St. John, and C. Thérien (Eds.), *Comprehension-Based Second Language Instruction* (pp. 389–405). Ottawa: University of Ottawa.

Reagan, T. (1983). The economics of language: Implications for language planning. *Language Problems & Language Planning* 7, 148–161.

Reder, S., K. Harris, and K. Setzler (2003). A multimedia adult learner corpus. *TESOL Quarterly* 37, 546–557.

Reedy, T. (2000). Te Reo Mäori: The past 20 years and looking forward. *Oceanic Linguistics* 39(1), 157–169.

Reid, J. (1994). Responding to ESL students' texts: The myths of appropriation. *TESOL Quarterly* 28, 273–292.

Rennert, S. (2008). Visual input in simultaneous interpreting. *Meta: Translators' Journal* 53(1), 204–217.

Reppen, R. (2001). Register variation in student and adult speech and writing. In S. Conrad, and D. Biber (Eds.), *Variation in English: Multi-Dimensional Studies* (pp. 187–199). London: Longman.

Reppen, R. (1994). Variation in Elementary Student Language: A Multi-Dimensional Perspective. PhD dissertation., Northern Arizona University, Flagstaff.

Reppen, R., and C. Vásquez (2007). Using corpus linguistics to investigate the language of teacher training. In J. Walinski, K. Kredens, and S. Gozdz-Roszkowski (Eds.), *Corpora and ICT in Language Studies* (pp. 13–29). Frankfurt: Peter Lang.

Research New Zealand (*Te Puni Kokiri*) (Ministry of Mäori Development). (2007). *The Health of the Mäori Language in 2006*. Wellington, New Zealand: Te Puni Kokiri.

Resolution (1997). Presented to the Judicial Council Court Interpreter Advisory Panel on June 7 by the Bay Area Court Interpreters (BACI). Berkeley, CA.

Rey, J. (2001). Historical shifts in the language of women and men: Gender differences in dramatic dialogue. In S. Conrad, and D. Biber (Eds.), *Variation in English: Multi-Dimensional Studies* (pp. 138–156). London: Longman.

Reyhner, J. (Ed.). (1997). *Teaching Indigenous Languages*. Flagstaff: Northern Arizona University Center for Excellence in Education.

Reyhner, J., G. Cantoni, R. N. St. Clair, and E. P. Yazzie (Eds.). (1999). *Revitalizing Indigenous Languages*. Flagstaff: Northern Arizona University Center for Excellence in Education.

Rhodes, N., D. Christian, and S. Barfield (1997). Innovations in immersion: The Key School two-way model. In R. K. Johnson, and M. Swain (Eds.), *Immersion Education: International Perspectives* (pp. 265–283). Cambridge: Cambridge University Press.

Riazi, A. (1997). Acquiring disciplinary literacy: A social-cognitive analysis of text production and learning among Iranian graduate students of education. *Journal of Second Language Writing* 6, 105–137.

Riccardi, A. (2005). On the evolution of interpreting strategies in simultaneous interpreting. *Meta: Translators' Journal* 50(2), 753–767.

Riccardi, A., G. Marinuzzi, and S. Zecchin (1998). Interpretation and stress. *Interpreters' Newsletter* 8, 93–106.

Ricento, T. (Ed.). (2006a). *An Introduction to Language Policy: Theory and Method*. Oxford: Blackwell.

Ricento, T. (2006b). Methodological perspectives in language policy. In T. Ricento (Ed.), *An Introduction to Language Policy: Theory and Method* (pp. 129–134). Malden, MA: Blackwell.

Ricento, T. (2005). Considerations of identity in L2 learning. In E. Hinkel (Ed.), *Handbook of Research on Second Language Teaching and Learning* (pp. 895–911). Mahwah, NJ: Lawrence Erlbaum.

Richards, J. C. (2005). *Communicative Language Teaching Today*. Singapore: RELC.

Richards, J. C. (2001). *Curriculum Development in Language Teaching*. New York: Cambridge University Press.

Richards, J. C., J. Hull, and S. Proctor (1991). *Interchange 2*. Cambridge: Cambridge University Press.

Richards, J. C., J. Platt, and H. Weber (1985). *Longman Dictionary of Applied Linguistics*. London: Longman.

Richards, J. C., and T. Rodgers (2001). *Approaches and Methods in Language Teaching* (2nd ed.). Cambridge: Cambridge University Press.

Richards, K. (2009). Trends in qualitative research in language teaching since 2000. *Language Teaching* 42(2), 147–180.

Richards, K. (2003). *Qualitative Inquiry in TESOL*. New York: Palgrave Macmillan.

Richardson, J. G. (1996). Court interpreting for deaf persons: Culture, communication and the courts. *State Court Journal* 20(1), 16–22.

Rickford, J. R. (1999). *African American Vernacular English: Features, Evolution, Educational Implications*. Oxford: Blackwell.

Rickford, J. R. (1997). The evolution of the ebonics issue. *Pidgins and Creoles in Education (PACE) Newsletter* 8, 8–10.

Rickford, J. R., and J. McWhorter (1997). Language contact and language generation: Pidgins and creoles. In F. Coulmas (Ed.), *The Handbook of Sociolinguistics* (pp. 238–256). Oxford: Blackwell.

Rickford, J. R., and E. C. Traugott (1985). Symbol of powerlessness and degeneracy, or symbol of solidarity and truth? Paradoxical attitudes toward pidgins and creoles. In S. Greenbaum (Ed.), *The English Language Today* (pp. 252–261). Oxford: Pergamon Institute of English.

Ridge, S. (2004). Language planning in a rapidly changing multilingual society: The case of English in South Africa. *Language Problems & Language Planning* 28(2), 199–215.

Ridgway, T. (2000). Listening strategies—I beg your pardon? *ELT Journal* 54(2), 179–185.

Riessman, C. K. (2008). *Narrative Methods for the Human Sciences*. Los Angeles: Sage.

Riggenbach, H. (1999). *Discourse Analysis in the Language Classroom: Vol. 1. The Spoken Language*. Ann Arbor: University of Michigan Press.

Riggenbach, H., and V. Samuda (2000). *Grammar Dimensions: Form, Meaning and Use 2*. [Platinum Edition.] Boston, MA: Heinle and Heinle.

Riggins, S. H. (Ed.). (1997). *The Language and Politics of Exclusion: Others in Discourse*. Thousand Oaks, CA: Sage.

Riley, P. (1981). Viewing comprehension: *L'oeil écoute*. In British Council, *The Teaching of Listening Comprehension* (pp. 143–155). Oxford: Pergamon/British Council.

Ringbom, H. (2007). *Cross-Linguistic Similarity in Foreign Language Learning*. Clevedon, Avon, UK: Multilingual Matters.

Rivera, K. (1999). From developing one's voice to making oneself heard: Affecting language policy from the bottom up. In T. Huebner, and K. Davis (Eds.), *Sociopolitical Perspectives on Language Policy and Planning in the USA* (pp. 333–346). Amsterdam: John Benjamins.

Rivers, W. M. (1968a). *Teaching Foreign Language Skills*. Chicago: University of Chicago Press.

Rivers, W. M. (1968b). *The Psychologist and the Foreign Language Teacher*. Chicago: University of Chicago Press.

Rivers, W. M., and M. S. Temperley (1978). *A Practical Guide to the Teaching of English as a Second Language*. New York: Oxford University Press.

Roberts, C., E. Davies, and T. Jupp (1992). *Language and Discrimination*. New York: Longman.

Roberts, R., and N. Schweda Nicholson (2003). Translation and interpretation. In W. Frawley (Ed.), *Oxford International Encyclopedia of Linguistics* (2nd ed., 4 vols; vol. 4, pp. 281–285). New York: Oxford University Press.

Robinson, C. D. W. (1994). Is sauce for the goose sauce for the gander? Some comparative reflections on minority language planning in North and South. *Journal of Multilingual and Multicultural Development* 15, 129–145.

Robinson, D. (1997/2003). *Becoming a Translator: An Introduction to the Theory and Practice of Translation* (2nd ed.). London and New York: Routledge.

Robinson, I. (1998). *The Establishment of Modern English Prose in the Reformation and the Enlightenment*. Cambridge: Cambridge University Press.

Robinson, M. A. (1992). Introspective methodology in interlanguage pragmatics research. In G. Kasper (Ed.), *Pragmatics of Japanese as a Native and Target Language* (pp. 27–82). Honolulu: University of Hawaii Press.

Robinson, M. A., F. Stoller, M. Constanza-Robinson, and J. Jones (2008). *Write Like a Chemist*. New York: Oxford University Press.

Robinson, P. (Ed.) (2000). *Cognition and Second Language Instruction*. New York: Cambridge University Press.

Robinson, P., and N. C. Ellis (Eds.). (2008). *Handbook of Cognitive Linguistics and Second Language Acquisition*. New York: Routledge.

Roca de Larios, J., L. Murphy, and R. Manchón (1999). The use of restructuring strategies in EFL writing: A study of Spanish learners of English as a foreign language. *Journal of Second Language Writing* 8, 13–44.

Rocca, S. (2007). *Child Second Language Acquisition: A Bi-directional Study of English and Italian Tense-Aspect Morphology*. Amsterdam: Benjamins.

Roder, T. (2000). Court interpreters join Communications Workers of America. *ATA Chronicle* (January), 18.

Rodgers, D. (2006). Developing content and form: Encouraging evidence from Italian content-based instruction. *Modern Language Journal* 90(3), 373–386.

Rodríguez, G. (2008). Second language sentence processing: Is it fundamentally different? Unpublished PhD dissertation, University of Pittsburgh, PA.

Roelofs, A. (1992). A spreading-activation theory of lemma retrieval in speaking. *Cognition* 42(1–3), 107–142.

Roelofs, A., and K. Verhoef (2006). Modeling the control of phonological encoding in bilingual speakers. *Bilingualism: Language and Cognition* 9, 167–176.

Rogers, C. (2003). Register variation in Indian English. PhD dissertation, Northern Arizona University, Flagstaff.

Rogers, C. (2002). Syntactic features of Indian English: An examination of written Indian English. In R. Reppen, S. M. Fitzmaurice, and D. Biber (Eds.), *Using Corpora to Explore Linguistic Variation* (pp. 249–271). Amsterdam: John Benjamins.

Rogers, C. R. (1969). *Freedom to Learn for the 80s*. Columbus, OH: Charles Merrill.

Rogerson-Revell, P. (2008). Participation and performance in international business meetings. *English for Specific Purposes* 27, 338–360.

Rogoff, B. (2003). *The Cultural Nature of Human Development*. Oxford: Oxford University Press.

Rogoff, B. (1995). Observing sociocultural activity on three planes: Participatory appropriation, guided participation and apprenticeship. In J. V. Wertsch, P. del Rio, and A. Alvarez (Eds.), *Sociocultural Studies of Mind* (pp. 139–164). Cambridge: Cambridge University Press.

Romaine, S. (2006). Planning for the survival of linguistic diversity. *Language Policy* 5, 441–473.

Romaine, S. (1994a). Language standardization and linguistic fragmentation in Tok Pisin. In M. Morgan (Ed.), *The Social Construction of Identity in Creole Situations* (pp. 19–42). Los Angeles: Center for Afro-American Studies, University of California at Los Angeles.

Romaine, S. (1994b). Hawai'i Creole as a literary language. *Language in Society* 23, 527–554.

Romaine, S. (1992). *Language, Education and Development: Urban and Rural Tok Pisin in Papua New Guinea.* Oxford: Oxford University Press.

Römer, U. (2005a). *Progressives, Patterns, Pedagogy.* Amsterdam: John Benjamins.

Römer, U. (2005b). "This seems counterintuitive, though…": Negative evaluation in linguistic book reviews by male and female authors. In E. Tognini-Bonelli and G. Del Lungo Camiciotti (Eds.) *Strategies in Academic Discourse* (pp. 97–116). Amsterdam/Philadelphia: John Benjamins.

Romero-Little, M., T. McCarty, L. Warhol, and O. Zepeda (2007). Language policies in practice: Preliminary findings from a large-scale national study of native American shift. *TESOL Quarterly* 41(3), 607–618.

Rose, K. R. (2000). An exploratory cross-sectional study of interlanguage pragmatic development. *Studies in Second Language Acquisition* 22, 27–67.

Rose, K. R., and G. Kasper (Eds.). (2001). *Pragmatics in Language Teaching.* Oxford: Oxford University Press.

Rosenthal, J. W. (Ed.). (2000). *Handbook of Undergraduate Second Language Education.* Mahwah, NJ: Lawrence Erlbaum.

Ross, J. R. (1967/1974). Constraints on variables in syntax. In G. Harman (Ed.), *On Noam Chomsky* (pp. 165–200). New York: Anchor/Doubleday.

Ross, S. (1997). An introspective analysis of listener inferencing on a second language listening test. In G. Kasper, and E. Kellerman (Eds.), *Communication Strategies: Psycholinguistic and Sociolinguistic Perspectives* (pp. 216–237). London: Longman.

Rost, M. (1994). On-line summaries as representations of lecture understanding. In J. Flowerdew (Ed.), *Academic Listening: Research Perspectives* (pp. 93–127). Cambridge: Cambridge University Press.

Rost, M. (1990). *Listening in Language Learning.* Harlow, UK: Longman.

Rostow, W. W. (1960). *The Stages of Economic Growth.* Cambridge: Cambridge University Press.

Rounds, P. L., and R. Kanagy (1998). Acquiring linguistic cues to identifying AGENT: Evidence from children using Japanese as a second language. *Studies in Second Language Acquisition* 20, 509–541.

Rowlands, S. (2000). Turning Vygotsky on his head: Vygotsky's "scientifically based method" and the socioculturalist social order. *Science and Education* 9, 537–575.

Rubin, J. (1994). A review of second language listening comprehension research. *Modern Language Journal* 78, 199–221.

Rubin, J. (1971). Evaluation and language planning. In J. Rubin, and B. H. Jernudd (Eds.), *Can Language Be Planned?* (pp. 217–252). Honolulu: University of Hawai'i Press.

Rubin, J., and B. H. Jernudd (Eds.). (1971). *Can Language Be Planned? Sociolinguistic Theory and Practice for Developing Nations.* Honolulu: University of Hawai'i Press.

Rubin, J., and R. Shuy (Eds.). (1973). *Language Planning: Current Issues and Research.* Washington, DC: Georgetown University School of Languages and Linguistics.

Rudvin, M. (2007). Professionalism and ethics in community interpreting: The impact of individualist versus collective group identity. *Interpreting* 9(1), 47–69.

Rumelhart, D. E., and J. L. McClelland (1986). On learning the past tenses of English verbs. In J. L. McClelland, D. E. Rumelhart, and the PDP Research Group (Eds.), *Parallel Distributed Processing: Explorations in the Microstructure of Cognition* (vol. 2, pp. 216–271). Cambridge, MA: MIT Press.

Russell, D. (2001). Looking beyond the interface: Activity theory and distributed learning. In M. Lea (Ed.), *Understanding Distributed Learning* (pp. 64–82). London: Routledge.

Russell, D. (1991). *Writing in the Academic Disciplines: 1870–1990*. Carbondale, IL: Southern Illinois University.

Russell, J., and N. Spada (2006). The effectiveness of corrective feedback for the acquisition of L2 grammar. In. J. Norris, and L. Ortega (Eds.), *Synthesizing Research on Language Learning and Teaching* (pp. 133–164). Amsterdam: John Benjamins.

Russo, C. P., and Baldauf, R. B., Jr. (1986). Language development without planning: A case study of tribal Aborigines in the Northern Territory, Australia. *Journal of Multilingual and Multicultural Development* 7, 301–317.

Russo, M. (1995). Self-evaluation: The awareness of one's own difficulties as a training tool for simultaneous interpretation. *Interpreters' Newsletter* 6, 75–85.

Russo, M., and P. Salvador (2004). Aptitude to interpreting: Preliminary results of a testing methodology based on paraphrase. *Meta Translators' Journal* 49(2), 409–432.

Ryan, W., M. Gobeil, A. Hope, and M. Toews-Janzen (2008). Evaluation of the French immersion studies academic stream: Year 2. University of Ottawa. Internal document.

Rymes, B. (in press). *Classroom Discourse Analysis: A Tool for Critical Reflection*. Cresskill, NJ: Hampton Press.

Rymes, B. (2003a). Eliciting narratives: Drawing attention to the margins of classroom talk. *Research in the Teaching of English* 37, 380–407.

Rymes, B. (2003b). Contrasting zones of comfortable competence: Popular culture in a phonics lesson. *Linguistics and Education* 14, 321–335.

Rynkofs, J. T. (1993). Culturally responsive talk between a second grade teacher and Hawaiian children during writing workshop. PhD dissertation, University of New Hampshire, West Haven.

Sabourin, L. (2001). L1 effects on the processing of grammatical gender in L2. *EUROSLA Yearbook* 1: 159–169.

Sabourin, L., and L. A. Stowe (2008). When are first and second languages processed similarly? *Second Language Research* 24, 397–430.

Sachs, R., and B.-R. Suh (2007). Textually enhanced recasts, learner awareness and L2 outcomes in synchronous computer-mediated interaction. In A. Mackey (Ed.), *Conversational Interaction in Second Language Acquisition: A Series of Empirical Studies* (pp. 197–227). Oxford: Oxford University Press.

Sacks, H., E. A. Schegloff, and G. Jefferson (1974). A simplest systematics for the organization of turn-taking for conversation. *Language* 50, 696–735.

Sagarra, N. (2008). Working memory and L2 processing of redundant grammatical forms. In Z. Han (Ed.), *Understanding Second Language Process* (pp. 133–147). Clevedon, Avon, UK: Multilingual Matters.

Sagarra, N. (2007). From CALL to face-to-face interaction: The effect of computer-delivered recasts and working memory on L2 development. In A. Mackey (Ed.), *Conversational Interaction in Second Language Acquisition: A Series of Empirical Studies* (pp. 229–248). Oxford: Oxford University Press.

Salaberry, M. R. (2008). *Marking Past Tense in a Second Language: A Theoretical Model*. London: Continuum.

Salager, F. (1994). Hedges and textual communicative function in medical English written discourse. *English for Specific Purposes* 13, 149–170.

Salomon, G. (1993). Editor's introduction. In G. Salomon (Ed.), *Distributed Cognitions: Psychological and Educational Considerations* (pp. ix–xxi). Cambridge: Cambridge University Press.

Salager-Meyer, F., and G. Defives (1998). From the gentleman's courtesy to the scientist's caution: A diachronic study of hedges in academic writing (1810–1995). In. I. Fortanet, S. Posteguillo, J. C. Palmer, and J. F. Coll (Eds.), *Genre studies in English for Academic Purposes* (pp. 133–172) Valencia: Universitat Jaume I Collección Summa, Filología.

Salsbury, T., and K. Bardovi-Harlig (2000). Oppositional talk and the acquisition of modality in L2 English. In B. Swierzbin, F. Morris, M. E. Anderson, C. A. Kleem, and E. Tarone (Eds.), *Social and Cognitive Factors in Second Language Acquisition: Selected Proceedings of the 1999 Second Language Research Forum* (pp. 57–76). Somerville, MA: Cascadilla Press.

Salsbury, T., and C. Crummer (2008). Using teacher-developed corpora in the CBI Classroom. *English Teaching Forum* 2, 28–37.

Salton, G. (1989). *Automatic Text Processing: The Transformation, Analysis and Retrieval of Information by Computer.* Reading, MA: Addison-Wesley.

Samborn, H. V. (1996). Tongue-tied. *ABA Journal* (February), 22–23.

Samejima, F. (1995). A cognitive diagnosis method using latent trait models: Competency space approach and its relationship with Dibello and Stout's unified cognitive psychometric diagnosis model. In P. Nichols, S. Chipman, and R. Brennan (Eds.), *Cognitively Diagnostic Assessment* (pp. 391–410). Hillsdale, NJ: Lawrence Erlbaum.

Samraj, B. (2005). An exploration of a genre set: Research article abstracts and introductions in two disciplines. *English for Specific Purposes* 24, 141–156.

Samraj, B. (2004). Discourse features of the student-produced academic research paper: Variations across disciplinary courses. *Journal of English for Academic Purposes* 3, 5–22.

Samuda, V. (2001). Guiding relationships between form and meaning during task performance: The role of the teacher. In M. Bygate, P. Skehan, and M. Swain (Eds.), *Researching Pedagogic Tasks: Second Language Learning, Teaching and Testing.* London: Pearson Educational.

Samuda, V., and M. Bygate (2008). *Tasks in Second Language Learning.* London: Palgrave.

Samuels, S. (2006). Toward a model of reading fluency. In S. Samuels, and A. Farstrup (Eds.), *What Research Has to Say about Fluency Instruction* (pp. 24–46). Newark, DE: International Reading Association.

Sanchez Vazquez, A. (1977). *The Philosophy of Praxis.* London: Merlin Press.

Sand, A. (1999). *Linguistic Variation in Jamaica: A Corpus-Based Study of Radio and Newspaper Usage.* Tübingen: Narr.

Sand, A. (1998). First findings from ICE-Jamaica: the verb phrase. In A. Renouf (Ed.), *Explorations in Corpus Linguistics* (pp. 201–216). Amsterdam: Rodopi.

Santos, T., D. Atkinson, M. Erickson, P. Matsuda, and T. Silva (2000). On the future of L2 writing. *Journal of Second Language Writing* 9, 1–20.

Sarangi, S. (2001). On demarcating the space between "lay expertise" and "expert laity." *Text* 21, 3–11.

Sasaki, Y. (1994). Paths of processing strategy transfers in learning Japanese and English as foreign languages: A competition model approach. *Studies in Second Language Acquisition* 16, 43–72.

Sato, C. J. (1991). Sociolinguistic variation and attitudes in Hawaii. In J. Cheshire (Ed.), *English around the World* (pp. 647–663). Cambridge: Cambridge University Press.

Sato, C. J. (1989). A nonstandard approach to standard English. *TESOL Quarterly* 23, 259–282.

Sato, C. J. (1985). Linguistic inequality in Hawaii: The post-Creole dilemma. In N. Wolfson, and J. Manes (Eds.), *Language of Inequality* (pp. 255–272). Berlin: Mouton.

Sato, M., and R. Lyster (2007). Modified output of Japanese EFL learners: Variable effects of interlocutor versus feedback types. In A. Mackey (Ed.), *Conversational Interaction in Second Language Acquisition: A Series of Empirical Studies* (pp. 123–142). Oxford: Oxford University Press.

Saussure, F. de (1966). *Course in General Linguistics* (Trans. W. Baskin [1916]). New York: McGraw Hill.

Savignon, S. (1991). Communicative language teaching: State of the art. *TESOL Quarterly* 25, 261–278.

Savignon, S. (1990). Communicative language teaching: Definitions and directions. In J. Alatis (Ed.), *Georgetown University Round Table on Language and Linguistics* (pp. 205–217). Washington, DC: Georgetown University Press.

Savignon, S. (1983). *Communicative Ccompetence: Theory and Classroom Practice*. Reading, MA: Addison-Wesley.

Savignon, S. (1972). *Communicative Competence: An Experiment in Foreign Language Teaching*. Philadelphia: Center for Curriculum Development.

Sawyer, M. (1992). The development of pragmatics in Japanese as a second language: The sentence-final particle *ne*. In G. Kasper (Ed.), *Pragmatics of Japanese as a Native and Foreign Language* (Tech. Rep. No. 3, pp. 83–125). Honolulu: University of Hawai'i at Manoa, Second Language Teaching and Curriculum Center.

Saxton, M. (1997). The contrast theory of negative input. *Journal of Child Language* 24, 139–161.

Sayers, J. (1996). Accidental language policy: Creating an ESL/bilingual teacher endorsement program in Utah. *TESOL Quarterly* 30, 611–615.

Scarcella, R. (1979). On speaking politely in a second language. In C. A. Yorio, K. Perkins, and J. Schachter (Eds.), *On TESOL '79* (pp. 275–287). Washington, DC: TESOL.

Schachter, J. (1989). Testing a proposed universal. In S. Gass, and J. Schachter (Eds.), *Linguistic Perspectives on Second Language Acquisition* (pp. 73–88). Cambridge: Cambridge University Press.

Schachter, J., and V. Yip (1990). Why does anyone object to subject extraction? *Studies in Second Language Acquisition* 12, 379–392.

Schane, S. (2006). *Language and Law*. London: Continuum.

Schauer, G. A. (2007). Finding the right words in the study abroad context: The development of German learners' use of external modifiers in English. *Intercultural Pragmatics* 4, 193–220.

Schegloff, E. A. (1991). Reflections on talk and social structure. In D. Boden, and D. H. Zimmerman (Eds.), *Talk and Social Structure: Studies in Ethnomethodology and Conversation Analysis* (pp. 44–70). Berkeley: University of California Press.

Schegloff, E. A., I. Koshik, S. Jacoby, and D. Olsher (2002). Conversation analysis and applied linguistics. In M. McGroarty et al. (Eds.), *Annual Review of Applied Linguistics: Vol. 22. Discourse and Dialogue* (pp. 3–31). New York: Cambridge University Press.

Schegloff, E. A., and H. Sacks (1973). Opening up closings. *Semiotica* 8, 289–327.

Scherer, K. R. (1984). Emotion as a multicomponent process: A model and some cross-culture data. In P. Shaver (Ed.), *Review of Personality and Social Psychology: Emotions, Relationships and Health* (vol. 5, pp. 37–63). Beverly Hills, CA: Sage.

Schieffelin, B. B., and R. C. Doucet (1994). The "real" Haitian Creole: Ideology, metalinguistics and orthographic choice. *American Ethnologist* 21, 176–200.

Schieffelin, B. B., and E. Ochs (1986). Language socialization. *Annual Review of Anthropology* 15, 163–191.

Schiffman, H. F. (1994). Diglossia, linguistic culture and language policy in Southeast Asia. In K. L. Adams, and T. J. Huduk (Eds.), *Papers from the Second Annual Meeting of the Southeast Asian Linguistics Society 1992* (pp. 279–307). Tempe: Arizona State University.

Schmidt, A. (1990). *The Loss of Australia's Aboriginal Language Heritage*. Canberra: Aboriginal Studies Press.

Schmidt, R. (2002). Racialization and language policy: The case of the U.S.A. *Multilingua* 21, 141–161.

Schmidt, R. (1993). Consciousness, learning and interlanguage pragmatics. In G. Kasper, and S. Blum-Kulka (Eds.), *Interlanguage Pragmatics* (pp. 21–42). Oxford: Oxford University Press.

Schmidt, R. (1990b). The role of consciousness in second language learning. *Applied Linguistics* 11, 129–158.

Schmidt, R. (1983). Interaction, acculturation, and the acquisition of communicative competence: A case study of an adult. In E. Judd, and N. Wolfson (Eds.), *Sociolinguistics and Language Acquisition* (pp. 137–174). Rowley, MA: Newbury House.

Schmidt, R., D. Boraie, and O. Kassabgy (1996). Foreign language motivation: Internal structure and external connections. In R. L. Oxford (Ed.), *Language Learning Motivation: Pathways to the New Century* (pp. 13–87). Honolulu: University of Hawai'i at Manoa, Second Language Teaching and Curriculum Center.

Schmidt, R., and S. N. Frota (1986). Developing basic conversational ability in a second language: A case study of a learner of Portuguese. In R. Day (Ed.), *Talking to Learn* (pp. 237–326). Rowley, MA: Newbury House.

Schmidt, R., and W. Savage (1992). Challenge, skill and motivation. *PASAA* 22, 14–28.

Schmied, J. (2007). Exploiting the Corpus of East-African English. In R. Facchinetti (Ed.), *Corpus Linguistics 25 Years On* (pp. 317–332). Amsterdam/New York: Rodopi.

Schmied, J. (2006). East African Englishes. In B. Kachru, Y. Kachru, and C. Nelson (Eds.), *The Handbook of World Englishes* (pp. 188–202). Basingstoke: Blackwell.

Schmied, J. (2005). English in Africa. In A. D. Cruse, et al (Eds.), *Handbook of Lexicology* (pp. 1270–1274). Berlin: Mouton.

Schmeid, J. (2004a). Cultural discourse in the East African Corpus of English and beyond: Possibilities and problems of lexical and collocational research in a one million word corpus. *World Englishes* 23(2), 251–260.

Schmied, J. (2004b). East African English (Kenya, Uganda, Tanzania) morphology and syntax. In B. Kortmann, et al. (Eds.), *A Handbook of Varieties of English: Volume 2, Morphology and Syntax* (pp. 929–947). Berlin: Mouton de Gruyter. [Reprinted in R. Mestrie (2008)] *Varieties of English 4: Africa, South and Southeast Asia.* (pp. 150–163). Berlin: Mouton de Gruyter.

Schmied, J. (1994). Analysing style variation in the East African Corpus of English. In U. Fries, G. Tottie, and P. Schneider (Eds.), *Creating and Using English Language Corpora* (pp. 169–174). Amsterdam: Rodopi.

Schmied, J. (1990). Corpus linguistics and non-native varieties of English. *World Englishes* 9, 255–268.

Schmied, J., and D. Hudson-Ettle (1996). Analyzing the style of East African newspapers in English. *World Englishes* 15, 103–113.

Schmitt, D., and N. Schmitt (2005). *Focus on Vocabulary*. Harlow: England: Longman.

Schmitt, N. (Ed.). (2002). *An Introduction to Applied Linguistics*. London: Arnold.

Schmitt, N., S. Grandage, and S. Adolphs (2004). Are corpus-derived recurrent clusters psycholinguistically valid? In N. Schmitt (Ed.), *Formulaic Sequences* (pp. 127–152). Amsterdam: John Benjamins.

Schneider, W., and R. Shiffrin (1977). Controlled and automatic human processing.
    I: Detection, search, and attention. *Psychological Review* 84, 1–66.
Schön, D. (1983). *The Reflective Practitioner: How Professionals Think in Action*. Aldershot,
    UK: Ashgate Arena.
Schoonbaert, S., R. Hartsuiker, and M. Pickering (2007). The representation of lexical and
    syntactic information in bilinguals: Evidence from syntactic priming. *Journal of
    Memory and Language* 56, 153–171.
Schoonen, R., K. de Glopper, J. Hulstijn, A. Simis, M. Stevenson, A. van Gelderen, and
    P. Snellings (2000, March). Secondary school writing in EFL and L1 (Dutch): The role
    of higher-order and lower-order skills. Paper presented at the annual meeting of the
    American Association of Applied Linguistics, Vancouver, British Columbia.
Schreffler, S. (2007). Hispanic heritage language speakers in the United States: Linguistic
    exclusion in education. *Critical Inquiry in Language Studies* 4(1), 25–34.
Schriefers, H., A. S. Meyer, and W. J. M. Levelt (1990). Exploring the time-course of lexical
    access in production: Picture-word interference studies. *Journal of Memory and
    Language* 29, 86–102.
Schubert, K. (1990). Editorial perspectives: A new decade and a new direction. *Language
    Problems & Language Planning* 14, 88–90.
Schumann, J. H. (2007). A linguistics for the evolution and neurobiology of language.
    Journal of English Linguistics 35, 278–287.
Schumann, J. H. (1997). *The Neurobiology of Affect in Language*. Boston: Blackwell. (Also
    published by *Language Learning* as a supplement to vol. 48, 1998.)
Schumann, J. H., S. Crowell, N. Jones, N. Lee, S. Schuchert, and L. Wood (2004). *The
    Neurobiology of Learning*. Mahwah, NJ: Lawrence Erlbaum.
Schumann, J. H., D. Favareau, N. Lee, L. Mikesell, H. Tao, D. Veronique, and A. Wray
    (2006). Language evolution: What evolved? *Marges Linguistique* 11, 167–199.
Schwartz, A. I., and J. F. Kroll (2006). Bilingual lexical activation in sentence context.
    Journal of Memory and Language 55, 197–212.
Schwartz, B. D. (1999). Let's make up your mind: "Special nativist" perspectives on
    language, modularity of mind, and nonnative language acquisition. *Studies in Second
    Language Acquisition* 21, 635–654.
Schwartz, B. D., and R. Sprouse (2000). When syntactic theories evolve: Consequences for
    L2 acquisition research. In J. Archibald (Ed.), *Second Language Acquisition and
    Lingusitic Theory* (pp. 156–186). Oxford: Blackwell.
Schwartz, B. D., and R. Sprouse (1996). L2 cognitive states and the full transfer/full access
    model. *Second Language Research* 12, 40–72.
Schwartz, B. D., and R. Sprouse (1994). Word order and nominative case in non-native
    language acquisition: A longitudinal study of (L1 Turkish) German interlanguage.
    In T. Hoekstra, and B. D. Schwartz (Eds.), *Language Acquisiton Studies in Generative
    Grammar* (pp. 317–368). Amsterdam: Benjamins.
Schweda Nicholson, N. (forthcoming). Interpreting at the International Criminal Tribunal
    for the Former Yugoslavia (ICTY): Linguistic and cultural challenges. *Proceedings of "The
    Translator as Mediator of Culture" Conference*. Amsterdam/Philadelphia: John Benjamins.
Schweda Nicholson, N. (2007a). European Union law: The journey of a proposal re:
    language services in criminal proceedings. *Proteus* 16(4), 3–5.
Schweda Nicholson, N. (2007b, July). Language and the law in the European Union (EU):
    Efforts to establish uniform standards for interpreter services in criminal matters.
    Paper presented at the International Association of Forensic Linguists (IAFL) Biennial
    Conference, Seattle, WA.

Schweda Nicholson, N. (2005a). Proactive efforts to educate attorneys and judges on the role of the court interpreter in the United States (U.S.) at the International Criminal Tribunal for the Former Yugoslavia (ICTY) and at the International Criminal Court. *FORUM, the International Journal of Interpretation and Translation* 3(2), 167–192.

Schweda Nicholson, N. (2005b). The Court Interpreters Act of 1978: A 25-year retrospective: Part II. *ATA Chronicle* (September), 32–37, 39.

Schweda Nicholson, N. (2005c). The Court Interpreters Act of 1978: A 25-year retrospective: Part I. *ATA Chronicle* (August) 36–41.

Schweda Nicholson, N. (2005d). The European Commission's Proposal for a Council Framework Decision: The United States' perspective. In H. Keijzer-Lambooy, and W. J. Gasille (Eds.), *Aequilibrium: Instruments for Lifting Language Barriers in Intercultural Legal Proceedings* (pp. 35–53). Utrecht, The Netherlands: ITV Hogeschool voor Tolken en Vertalen.

Schweda Nicholson, N. (2005e). What makes a good interpreter? A study of interpreter trainees' personality traits. *Conference Interpretation and Translation* (Korean Society of Conference Interpretation Journal) 7(2), 61–100.

Schweda Nicholson, N. (1999). Language policy development for interpreter services at the Executive Office for Immigration Review. *Language Problems & Language Planning* 23(1), 37–63.

Schweda Nicholson, N. (1997). Court interpretation in Denmark. In S. E. Carr, R. Roberts, A. Dufour, and D. Steyn (Eds.), *The Critical Link: Interpreters in the Community* (pp. 259–270). Amsterdam/Philadelphia: John Benjamins.

Schweda Nicholson, N. (1995). Translation and interpretation. In W. Grabe et al. (Eds.), *Annual Review of Applied Linguistics: Vol. 15. Survey of the Field of Applied Linguistics* (pp. 42–62). New York: Cambridge University Press.

Schweda Nicholson, N. (1994a). Community interpreter training in the United States and the United Kingdom: An overview of selected initiatives. *Hermes* 12, 127–139.

Schweda Nicholson, N. (1994b). Professional ethics for court and community interpreters. In D. Hammond (Ed.), *Professional Issues for Translators and Interpreters* (pp. 79–97). Amsterdam: John Benjamins.

Schweda Nicholson, N. (1994c). Training for refugee mental health interpreters. In C. Dollerup, and A. Lindegaard (Eds.), *Teaching Translation and Interpreting 2: Insights, Aims, Visions* (pp. 211–215). Amsterdam/Philadelphia: John Benjamins.

Schweda Nicholson, N. (1989). Documentation and text preparation for simultaneous interpretation. In D. L. Hammond (Ed.), *Proceedings of the 1989 American Translators Association Conference* (pp. 163–182). Medford, NJ: Learned Information.

Scida, E. E., and R. E. Saury (2006). Hybrid courses and their impact on student and classroom performance: A case study at the University of Virginia. *CALICO Journal* 23(3), 517–532.

Scollon, R., and S. B. K. Scollon (1983). Face in interethnic communication. In J. C. Richards, and R. W. Schmidt (Eds.), *Language and Communication* (pp. 156–188). London: Longman.

Scotton, C. M. (1988). Patterns of bilingualism in East Africa. In C. B. Paulston (Ed.), *International Handbook of Bilingualism and Bilingual Education*, (pp. 203–24). Westport CT: Grenwood Press.

Scotton, C. M. (1982). Learning lingua franca and socioeconomic integration: Evidence from Africa. In R. L. Cooper (Ed.), *Language Spread: Studies in Diffusion and Social Change* (pp. 63–97). Bloomington: Indiana University Press.

Scovel, T. (1998). *Psycholinguistics*. Oxford: Oxford University Press.

Scribner, S., and M. Cole (1981). *The Psychology of Literacy*. Cambridge, MA: Harvard University Press.

Searle, J. R. (1976). A classification of illocutionary acts. *Language and Society* 5, 1–23.

Searle, J. R. (1969). *Speech Acts*. Cambridge: Cambridge University Press.

Sebba, M. (2000). Orthography and ideology: Issues in Sranan spelling. *Linguistics* 38(5), 925–948.

Sebba, M. (1997). *Contact Languages: Pidgins and Creoles*. New York: St. Martin's Press.

Seeber, K., and C. Zelger (2007). Betrayal—vice or virtue? An ethical perspective on accuracy in simultaneous interpreting. *Meta: Translators' Journal* 52(2), 290–298.

Seedhouse, P. (2004). *The Interactional Architecture of the Language Classroom: A Conversation Analysis Perspective*. Malden, MA: Blackwell.

Segalowitz, N., and J. Hulstijn (2003). Automaticity in bilingualism and second language learning. In J. Kroll, and A. De Groot (Eds.), *Handbook of Bilingualism: Psycholinguistic Perspectives* (pp. 371–388). Oxford: Oxford University Press.

Seidenberg, M. S., and M. C. MacDonald (1999). A probabilistic constraints approach to language acquisition and processing. *Cognitive Science* 23, 569–588.

Seidlhofer, B. (2007). Common Property: English as a Lingua Franca in Europe. In J. Cummins, and C. Davison (Eds.), *International Handbook of English Language Teaching* (pp. 137–153). New York: Springer.

Seidlhofer, B. (2006). English as a lingua franca in the expanding circle: What it isn't. In R. Rubdy, and M. Saraceni (Eds.), *English in the World: Global Rules, Global Roles* (pp. 40–50). London: Continuum.

Seidlhofer, B. (2004). Research perspectives on teaching English as a lingua franca. In M. McGroarty et al. (Eds.), *Annual Review of Applied Linguistics: Vol. 24. Advances in Language Pedagogy* (pp. 209–239). New York: Cambridge University Press.

Seidlhofer, B. (Ed.). (2003). *Controversies in Applied Linguistics*. New York: Oxford University Press.

Seidlhofer, B., A. Breiteneder, and M.-L. Pitzl (2006). English as a lingua franca in Europe. In M. McGroarty, et al. (Eds.) *Annual Review of Applied Linguistics 26: Lingua Franca Languages* (pp. 1–34). New York: Cambridge University Press.

Selinker, L., and D. Douglas (1985). Wrestling with "context" in interlanguage theory. *Applied Linguistics* 6, 190–204.

Semino, E., and M. Short (2004). *Corpus Stylistics: Speech, Writing and Thought Presentation in a Corpus of English Writing*. London: Routledge.

Sergio, F. S. (1998). Notes on cultural mediation. *Interpreters' Newsletter* 8, 151–168.

Séror, J. (2005). Computers and qualitative data analysis: Paper, pens and highlighters vs. screen, mouse and keyboard. *TESOL Quarterly* 39(2) 321–328.

Setton, R. (1998). Meaning assembly in simultaneous interpretation. *Interpreting* 3(2), 163–199.

Setton, R., and M. Motta (2007). Syntacrobatics: Quality and reformulation in simultaneous-with-text. *Interpreting* 9(2), 199–230.

Shakir, A., and M. Farghal (1997). When the focus of the text is blurred: A textlinguistic approach for analyzing student interpreters' errors. *Meta: Translators' Journal* 42(4), 629–640.

Shamsudin, S., and H. Nesi (2006). Computer-mediated communication in English for specific purposes: A case study with computer science students at Universiti Teknologi Malaysia. *Computer Assisted Language Learning* 19(4–5), 317–339.

Shardakova, M. (2005). Intercultural pragmatics in the speech of American L2 learners of Russian: Apologies offered by Americans in Russian. *Intercultural Pragmatics* 2, 423–451.

Sharkey, N. (1996). Fundamental issues for connectionist language processing. In G. Brown, K. Malmkjaer, and J. Williams (Eds.), *Performance and Competence in Second Language Acquisition* (pp. 155–184). Cambridge: Cambridge University Press.

Sharples, M., J. Taylor, and G. Vavoula (2007). A theory of learning for the mobile age. In R. Andrews, and C. Haythornthwaite (Eds.), *The Sage Handbook of e-Learning Research* (pp. 221–247). Los Angeles: Sage.

Sharwood Smith, M. (1993). Input enhancement in instructed SLA: Theoretical bases. *Studies in Second Language Acquisition* 15, 165–179.

Sharwood Smith, M. (1991). Speaking to many minds: On the relevance of different types of language information for the L2 learner. *Second Language Research* 7, 118–132.

Shaw, P. (1996). Voices for improved learning: The ethnographer as co-agent of pedagogic change. In K. M. Bailey, and D. Nunan (Eds.), *Voices from the Language Classroom* (pp. 318–337). New York: Cambridge University Press.

Shaywitz, S., and B. Shaywitz (2004). Neurobiologic basis for reading and reading disability. In P. McCardle, and V. Chhabra (Eds.), *The Voice of Evidence in Reading Research* (pp. 417–442). Baltimore, MD: Brookes.

Sheen, Y. (2007). The effects of corrective feedback, language aptitude and learner attitudes on the acquisition of English articles. In A. Mackey (Ed.), *Conversational Interaction in Second Language Acquisition: A Series of Empirical Studies* (pp. 301–322). Oxford: Oxford University Press.

Shermis, M. D. (1996). Computerized adaptive testing for reading placement and diagnostic assessment. *Journal of Developmental Education* 38, 45–52.

Sherr, D. (2008). An Iraqi interpreter stateside. *Proteus* 17(3), 1, 4.

Sherr, D. (1999a). Interpreting in Spain and Colombia: Two perspectives. *Proteus* 8(3/4), 1, 3–4.

Shevyakov, M. B. (1987). On language policy in Ghana. *Vestnik Leningradskogo Universiteta, Istoriya yazyk literatura* [Bulletin of the University of Leningrad; History, Language, Literature] 42 (4), 88–91.

Shirato, J., and P. Stapleton (2007). Comparing English vocabulary in a spoken learner corpus with a native speaker corpus: Pedagogical implications arising from an empirical study in Japan. *Language Teaching Research* 11(4), 393–412.

Shirts, R. G. (1977). *BaFa' BaFa': A cross-culture simulation.* Del Mar, CA: Simulation Training Systems.

Shlesinger, M. (1998). Corpus-based interpreting studies as an offshoot of corpus-based translation studies. *Meta: Translators' Journal* 43(4), 486–493.

Shnukal, A. (1992). The case against a transfer bilingual program of Torres Strait Creole to English in Torres Strait schools. In J. Siegel (Ed.), *Pidgins, Creoles and Nonstandard Dialects in Education* (pp. 1–12). Melbourne: Applied Linguistics Association of Australia.

Shohamy, E. (2006). *Language Policy: Hidden Agendas and New Approaches.* London: Routledge.

Sholl, A., A. Sankaranarayanan, and J. F. Kroll (1995). Transfer between picture naming and translation: A test of asymmetries in bilingual memory. *Psychological Science* 6, 45–49.

Shonerd, H. G. (1990). Domesticating the barbarous tongue: Language policy for the Navajo in historical perspective. *Language Problems & Language Planning* 14, 193–208.

Shuck, G. (2006). Racializing the nonnative English speaker. *Journal of Language, Identity and Education* 5(4), 259–276.

Shuttleworth, M., and M. Cowie (1997). *Dictionary of Translation Studies.* Manchester, UK: St. Jerome.

Shuy, R. (2008). *Fighting over Words: Language and Civil Law Cases*. New York: Oxford University Press.

Shuy, R. (2002). *Linguistic Battles in Trademark Disputes*. London: Palgrave.

Shuy, R. (1998). *The Language of Confession, Interrogation and Deception*. Thousand Oaks, CA: Sage.

Shuy, R. (1996). *Language Crimes: The Use and Abuse of Language Evidence in the Courtroom*. (2nd ed.) Malden, MA: Blackwell.

Shuy, R. (1993). *Language Crimes: The Use and Abuse of Language Evidence in the Courtroom*. Oxford: Blackwell.

Siegel, J. (2008). *The Emergence of Pidgin and Creole Languages*. New York: Oxford University Press.

Siegel, J. (2007). Creoles and minority dialects in education: An update. *Language and Education* 21(1), 66–86.

Siegel, J. (2006). Keeping Creoles and dialects out of the classroom: Is it justified? In S. J. Nero (Ed.), *Dialects, Englishes, Creoles and Education* (pp. 39–67). Mahwah, NJ: Lawrence Erlbaum.

Siegel, J. (1999a). Stigmatized and standardized varieties in the classroom: Interference or separation? *TESOL Quarterly* 33, 701–278.

Siegel, J. (1999b). Creole and minority dialects in education: An overview. *Journal of Mulitlingual and Multicultural Development* 20(6), 508–531.

Siegel, J. (1998). Literacy in Melanesian and Australian pidgins and creoles. *English World-Wide* 16, 104–133.

Siegel, J. (1997a). Pidgins and English in Melanesia: Is there a continuum? *World Englishes* 16, 185–204.

Siegel, J. (1997b). Using a pidgin language in formal education: Help or hindrance? *Applied Linguistics* 18, 86–100.

Siegel, J. (1993). Pidgins and Creoles in education in Australia and the Southwest Pacific. In F. Byrne, and J. Holm (Eds.), *Atlantic Meets Pacific: A Global View of Pidginization and Creolization* (pp. 299–308). Amsterdam: John Benjamins.

Siegel, M. (1996). The role of learner subjectivity in second language sociolinguistic competency: Western women learning Japanese. *Applied Linguistics* 17, 356–382.

Silva, R., and H. Clahsen (2008). Morphologically complex words in L1 and L2 processing: Evidence from masked priming experiments in English. *Bilingualism: Language and Cognition* 11, 245–260.

Silva, T. (1993). Toward an understanding of the distinct nature of L2 writing: The ESL research and its implications. *TESOL Quarterly* 24, 657–671.

Silverman, D. (2001). *Interpreting Qualitative Data: Methods for Analysing Talk, Text and Interaction* (2nd ed.). Thousand Oaks, CA: Sage.

Simon, S. (1996). *Gender in Translation: Cultural Identity and the Politics of Translation*. London and New York: Routledge.

Simmons-McDonald, H. (2004). Trends in teaching standard varieties to Creole and vernacular speakers. In M. McGroarty, et al. (Eds.), *Annual Review of Applied Linguistics 24: Advances in Language Pedagofy* (pp. 187–208). New York: Cambridge University Press.

Simpson, G. B. (1984). Lexical ambiguity and its role in models of word recognition. *Psychological Bulletin* 96, 316–340.

Simpson, R. (2004). Stylistic features of spoken academic discourse: The role of formulaic expressions. In U. Connor, and T. Upton (Eds.), *Applied Corpus Linguistics: A Multidimensional Perspective* (pp. 37–64). Amsterdam: Rodopi.

Simpson, R., and D. Mendis (2003). A corpus-based study of idioms in academic speech. *TESOL Quarterly* 37, 419–441.

Sinclair, J. McH. (Ed.). (2004). *How to Use Corpora in Language Teaching*. Amsterdam: John Benjamins.

Sinclair, J. McH. (2003). *Reading Concordances*. Harlow, Essex: Pearson.

Sinclair, J. McH. (1991). *Corpus, Concordance, Collocation*. Oxford: Oxford University Press.

Sinclair, J. McH. (1987). Classroom discourse: Progress and prospects. *RELC Journal* 18, 1–14.

Sinclair, J. McH., and M. Coulthard (1975). *Towards an Analysis of Discourse: The English Used by Teachers and Pupils*. Oxford: Oxford University Press.

Singleton, D. (2000). Helping a jury understand witness deception. In J. Alatis, H. Hamilton, and A.-H. Tan (Eds.), *Linguistics, Language, and the Professions* (*Georgetown University Round Table on Languages and Linguistics*) (pp. 176–189). Washington, DC: Georgetown University Press.

Singler, J. V., and S. Kouwenberg (Eds.). (2008). *The Handbook of Pidgin and Creole Studies*. Oxford/New York: Wiley-Blackwell.

Skehan, P. (2003). Task-based instruction (Review article). *Language Teaching* 36(1), 1–14.

Skehan, P. (1998). *A Cognitive Approach to Language Learning*. Oxford: Oxford University Press.

Skehan, P. (1996). A framework for the implementation of task-based instruction. *Applied Linguistics* 17, 38–62.

Skilbeck, M. (1994). Curriculum renewal. In T. Husén, and T. N. Postlethwaite (Eds.), *The International Encyclopedia of Education* (2nd ed., pp. 1338–1343). Oxford: Pergamon.

Skilton-Sylvester, E. (2002). Should I stay or should I go? Investigating Cambodian women's participation and investment in adults ESL programs. *Adult Education Quarterly* 53(1), 9–26.

Skutnabb-Kangas, T. (2003). Revitalisation of indigenous languages in education: Contextualising the Papua New Guinea experience. *Language and Education* 17(2), 81–86.

Skutnabb-Kangas, T. (2000a). *Linguistic Genocide in Education—or Worldwide Diversity and Human Rights?* Mahwah, NJ: Lawrence Erlbaum.

Skutnabb-Kangas, T. (2000b). Linguistic human rights and teachers of English. In J. K. Hall, and W. Eggington (Eds.), *The Sociopolitics of English Language Teaching* (pp. 22–44). Clevedon, Avon, UK: Multilingual Matters.

Skutnabb-Kangas, T., and R. Phillipson (Eds.). (1994). *Linguistic Human Rights: Overcoming Linguistic Discrimination*. Berlin: Mouton.

Slaughter, H. (1997). Indigenous language immersion in Hawai'i: A case study of Kula Kaiapuni Hawai'i, an effort to save the indigenous language of Hawai'i. In R. K. Johnson, and M. Swain (Eds.), *Immersion Education: International Perspectives* (pp. 105–129). Cambridge: Cambridge University Press.

Slobin, D. (1997). Mind, code and text. In J. Bybee, J. Haiman, and S. Thompson (Eds.), *Essays on Language Function and Language Type* (pp. 437–467). Amsterdam: John Benjamins.

Slobin, D. (1996). From "thought and language" to "thinking for speaking." In J. Gumperz, and S. Levinson (Eds.), *Rethinking Linguistic Relativity* (pp. 97–114). Cambridge: Cambridge University Press.

Slobin, D. (1993). Adult language acquisition: A view from child language study. In C. Perdue (Ed.), *Adult Language Acquisition: Cross-Linguistic Perspectives. Volume II: The Results* (pp. 239–252). Cambridge: Cambridge University Press.

Smalley, W. A. (1988). Thailand's hierarchy of multilingualism. *Language Sciences* 10, 245–261.

Smith, D. J. (2006). Thresholds leading to *shift:* Spanish/English codeswitching and convergence in Georgia, U.S.A. *International Journal of Bilingualism* 10(2), 207–240.

Smith, L. T. (1999). *Decolonizing Methodologies: Research and Indigenous Peoples.* Dunedin, NZ: University of Otago Press.

Smith, M. C. (1997). How do bilinguals access lexical information? In A. M. B. De Groot, and J. F. Kroll (Eds.), *Tutorials in Bilingualism: Psycholinguistic Perspectives* (pp. 145–168). Mahwah, NJ: Lawrence Erlbaum.

Smith, M. S. (2010). Exploring the moral basis of social action in frontotemporal Dementia. In A. W. Mates, L. Mikesell, and M. S. Smith (Eds.), *Language, Interaction and Frontotemporal Dementia: Reverse Engineering the Social Mind.* London: Equinox.

Smith, N. V., and D. Wilson (1979). *The Results of Chomsky's Revolution.* Harmondsworth, UK: Penguin.

Smith, W. (1994). Computers, statistics, and disputed authorship. In J. Gibbons (Ed.), *Language and the Law* (pp. 374–413). London: Longman.

Smits, E., D. Sandra, H. Martensen, and T. Dijkstra (2009). Phonological inconsistency in word naming: Determinants of the interference effect between languages. *Bilingualism: Language and Cognition* 12, 23–39.

Smits, E., H. Martensen, T. Dijkstra, and D. Sandra (2006). Naming interlingual homographs: Variable competition and the role of the decision system. *Bilingualism: Language and Cognition* 9, 281–297.

Snow, C. E. (1990). Rationales for native language instruction: Evidence from research. In A. M. Padilla, H. H. Fairchild, and C. M. Valdez (Eds.), *Bilingual Education: Issues and Strategies* (pp. 60–74). Newbury Park: Sage.

Snow, C. E., P. Griffin, and S. Burns (2005). *Knowledge to Support the Teaching of Reading.* San Francisco: Jossey-Bass.

Snow, C. E., M. Porche, P. Tabors, and S. Harris (2007). *Is Literacy Enough? Pathways to Academic Success for Adolescents.* Baltimore: Brookes.

Snow, M. A. (2005). A model of academic literacy for integrated language and content instruction. In E. Hinkel (Ed.), *Handbook of Research in Second Language Teaching and Learning* (pp. 693–712). Mahwah, NJ: Lawrence Erlbaum.

Snow, M. A. (1998). Trends and issues in content-based instruction. In W. Grabe et al. (Eds.), *Annual Review of Applied Linguistics: Vol. 18. Foundations of Second Language Teaching* (pp. 243–267). New York: Cambridge University Press.

Snow, M. A. (1997). Teaching academic literacy skills: Discipline faculty take responsibility. In M. A. Snow, and D. M. Brinton (Eds.), *The Content-Based Classroom: Perspectives on Integrating Language and Content* (pp. 290–304). New York: Longman.

Snow, M. A., M. S. Andrade, and J. Harper Makaafi (2001). Guidelines for establishing adjunct courses at the university level. *TESOL Journal* (Autumn), 34–39.

Snow, M. A., and D. M. Brinton (Eds.). (1997). *The Content-Based Classroom: Perspectives on Integrating Language and Content.* New York: Longman.

Snow, M. A., and L. D. Kamhi-Stein (1997). Teaching academic literacy skills: A new twist on the adjunct model. *Journal of Intensive English Studies* 11, 93–108.

Snow, M. A., L. D. Kamhi-Stein, and D. Brinton (2006). Teacher training for English as a lingua franca. In M. McGroarty et al. (Eds.), *Annual Review of Applied Linguistics: Vol. 26. Lingua Franca Languages* (pp. 261–281). New York: Cambridge University Press.

Snow, M. A., M. Met, and F. Genessee (1989). A conceptual framework for the integration of language and content in second/foreign language instruction. *TESOL Quarterly* 23, 201–217.

Snyder, I. (2008). Research approaches to the study of literacy, technology and learning. In K. King, and N. H. Hornberger (Eds.), *Research Methods in Language and Education: Encyclopedia of Language and Education* (2nd ed., vol. 10, pp. 299–308). New York: Springer.

Snyder, I., and M. Prinsloo (Eds.). (2007). The digital literacy practices of young people in marginal contexts [Special issue]. *Language and Education: An International Journal* 21(3).

Sohrabi, B. (1997). Ethnolinguistic vitality and patterns of communication among the second generation of Iranian immigrants in Sweden. *International Journal of the Sociology of Language* 128, 45–72.

Sokolik, M. E. (1990). Learning without rules: PDP and a resolution of the adult language learning paradox. *TESOL Quarterly* 24, 685–696.

Sokolik, M. E., and M. E. Smith (1992). Assignment of gender to French nouns in primary and secondary language: A connectionist model. *Second Language Research* 8, 39–58.

Solan, L. (1993). *The Language of Judges*. Chicago: University of Chicago Press.

Sommer, G. (1991). Gradual language shift in Egypt and Botswana: Two case examples [Special issue]. *Afrikanistische-Arbeitspapiere*, 351–368.

Song, B. (2005). Content-based ESL instruction: Long-term effects and outcomes. *English for Specific Purposes* 25, 420–437.

Sonnenfeldt, R. (2006). *Witness to Nuremberg*. New York: Arcade Press.

Sonntag, S. K. (2003). *The Local Politics of Global English: Case Studies in Linguistic Globalization*. Lanham, MD: Lexington Books.

Sonntag, S. K. (1996). The political saliency of language in Bihar and Uttar Pradesh. *Journal of Commonwealth and Comparative Politics* 34(2), 1–18.

Sorace, A. (2000). Introduction: Optionality in second language acquisition. *Second Language Research* 16, 93–102.

Spack, R. (1997). The acquisition of academic literacy in a second language. *Written Communication* 14, 3–62.

Spada, N. M. (1997). Form-focused instruction and second-language acquisition: A review of classroom and laboratory research. *Language Teaching* 30, 73–87.

Spada, N. M. (1997). Form-focused instruction and second-language acquisition: A review of classroom and laboratory research. *Language Teaching* 30, 73–87.

Spada, N. M., and M. Fröhlich (1995). *Communicative Orientation of Language Teaching Observation Scheme: Coding Conventions and Applications*. Sydney: Macquarie University, NCELTR.

Spilka, R. (Ed.). (1993). *Writing in the Workplace: New Research Perspectives*. Carbondale: Southern Illinois University Press.

Spinner, P., and A. Juffs (2008). L2 grammatical gender in a complex morphological system: The case of German. *International Review of Applied Linguistics* 46, 315–348.

Spivey, M. J. (2007). *The Continuity of Mind*. Oxford: Oxford University Press.

Spivey, M. J., and V. Marian (1999). Cross-talk between native and second languages: Partial activation of an irrelevant lexicon. *Psychological Science* 10, 281–284.

Spolsky, B. (2008). Introduction: What is educational linguistics? In B. Spolsky, and F. M. Hult (Eds.) *The Handbook of Educational Linguistics* (pp. 1–9). Malden, MA: Blackwell.

Spolsky, B. (2004). *Language Policy*. Cambridge: Cambridge University Press.

Spolsky, B. (2003). Reassessing Māori regeneration. *Language in Society* 32(4), 553–578.

Spolsky, B. (Ed.). (1999). *Concise Encyclopedia of Educational Linguistics*. Amsterdam: Elsevier.

Spolsky, B. (1998). *Sociolinguistics*. Oxford: Oxford University Press.

Spolsky, B. (1997). The ethics of gatekeeping tests: What have we learned in one hundred years? *Language Testing* 14, 242–47.

Spolsky, B. (1996). Conditions for language revitalization: A comparison of the cases of Hebrew and Mäori. In S. Wright (Ed.), *Language and the State: Revitalization and Revival in Israel and Eire* (pp. 5–29). Clevedon, Avon, UK: Multilingual Matters.

Spolsky, B. (1995a). *Measured Words*. Oxford: Oxford University Press.

Spolsky, B. (1995b). Prognostication and language aptitude testing, 1925–62. *Language Testing* 12, 321–340.

Spolsky, B. (1987). *Report of* Mäori-*English Bilingual Education*. Wellington: New Zealand Department of Education.

Spolsky, B., and F. M. Hult (Eds.). (2008). *The Handbook of Educational Linguistics*. Malden, MA: Blackwell.

Spolsky, B., and E. Shohamy (1999a). Language in Israeli society and education. *International Journal of the Sociology of Language* 137, 93–114.

Spolsky, B., and E. Shohamy (1999b). *The Languages of Israel: Policy, Ideology and Practice*. Clevedon, Avon, UK: Multilingual Matters.

Spring, M. (1999). A view from down under. *Proteus* 8(2), 3–4.

Sprouse, R. (1998). Some notes on the relationship between inflectional morphology and parameter setting in first and second language acquisition. In M.-L. Beck (Ed.), *Morphology and Its Interfaces in Second Language Knowledge* (pp. 41–68). Philadelphia: John Benjamins.

Sridhar, S. N. (1990). What are applied linguistics? *Studies in the Linguistic Sciences* 20(2), 165–176.

Stalnaker, R. C. (1972). Pragmatics. In D. Davidson, and G. Harman (Eds.), *Semantics of Natural Language* (pp. 380–397). Dordrecht, The Netherlands: Reidel.

Stanovich, K. (2000). *Progress in Understanding Reading: Scientific Foundations and New Frontiers*. New York: Guilford Press.

Starreveld, P. A. (2000). On the interpretation of onsets of auditory context effects in word production. *Journal of Memory and Language* 42, 497–525.

Starreveld, P. A., and W. La Heij (1995). Semantic interference, orthographic facilitation and their interaction in naming tasks. *Journal of Experimental Psychology: Learning, Memory and Cognition* 21, 686–698.

Stein, P. (2008). *Multimodal Pedagogies in Diverse Classrooms: Representation, Rights and Resources*. London and New York: Routledge.

Stenhouse, L. (1975). *An Introduction to Curriculum Research and Development*. London: Heinemann.

Stephan, L. (1999). Political correctness versus freedom of speech: Social uses of language ideology. PhD dissertation, University of Washington, Seattle.

Stern, H. H. (1992). *Issues and Opinions in Language Teaching* (Ed. J. P. B. Allen and B. Harley). Oxford: Oxford University Press.

Stern, H. H. (1989). Analysis and experience as variables in second language pedagogy. In B. Harley, P. Allen, J. Cummins, and M. Swain (Eds.), *The Development of Bilingual Proficiency* (pp. 93–109). Cambridge: Cambridge University Press.

Stern, H. H. (1983). *Fundamental Concepts of Language Teaching*. Oxford: Oxford University Press.

Stern, H. H. (1970). *Perspectives on Second Language Teaching*. Toronto: Modern Language Center.

Stern, H. H. (1969). *Languages and the Young School Child*. Oxford: Oxford University Press.

Stern, H. H. (1967). *Foreign Languages in Primary Education*. Oxford: Oxford University Press.

Sterponi, L. (2007). Clandestine interactional reading: Intertextuality and double-voicing under the desk. *Linguistics and Education* 18, 1–23.

Stetsenko, A., and I. Arievitch (2002). Teaching, learning and development: A post-Vygotskian perspective. In G. Wells, and G. Claxton (Eds.), *Learning for Life in the 21st Century: Sociocultural Perspectives on the Future of Education* (pp. 84–96). Oxford: Blackwell.

Stevens, V. (1993). Concordances as enhancements to language competence. *TESOL Matters* 2(6), 11–21.

Stevick, E. W. (1990). *Humanism in Language Teaching*. Oxford: Oxford University Press.

Stevick, E. W. (1980). *Teaching Languages: A Way and Ways*. Rowley, MA: Newbury House.

Stewart, W. A. (1989). Structural mimicry in decreolization and its effect on pseudo-comprehension. In O. García, and R. Otheguy (Eds.), *English aross Cultures: Cultures across English. A Reader in Cross-Cultural Communication* (pp. 263–280). Berlin: Mouton de Gruyter.

Stewart, W. A. (1968). A sociolinguistic typology for describing national multilingualism. In J. Fishman (Ed.), *Readings in the Sociology of Language* (pp. 531–545). The Hague: Mouton.

St Fort, H. (2000). What is Haitian Creole?/Ki sa kreyòl ayisyen ye? Available at http://www.ahadonline.org/eLibrary/creoleconnection/Number20/haitiancreole.htm.

Stilling, N. A., S. E. Weisler, C. H. Chase, M. H. Feinstein, J. L. Garfield, and E. L. Rissland (1995). *Cognitive Science: An Introduction*. Cambridge, MA: MIT Press.

Stivers, T. (2007). *Prescribing under Pressure: Parent-Physician Conversations and Antibiotics*. New York: Oxford University Press.

Stotesbury, H. (2003). Evaluation in research article abstracts in the narrative and hard sciences. *Journal of English for Academic Purposes* 2, 327–241.

Stowe, L. A. (1986). Parsing *WH*-constructions: Evidence for on-line gap location. *Language and Cognitive Processes* 1, 227–245.

Straight, H. S. (Ed.). (1994). *Languages Across the Curriculum: Translation Perspectives VII*. Binghamton: State University of New York at Binghamton, Center for Research in Translation.

Street, B. (1984). *Literacy in Theory and Practice*. Cambridge: Cambridge University Press.

Street, R., and H. Giles (1982). Speech accommodation theory: A social cognitive approach to language and speech behavior. In M. Roloff, and C. R. Berger (Eds.), *Social Cognition and Communication* (pp. 193–226). Beverly Hills, CA: Sage.

Strevens, P. (2003). Applied linguistics. In W. J. Frawley (Ed.), *Oxford International Encyclopedia of Linguistics* (2nd ed., 4 vols.; vol. I, pp. 112–114). New York: Oxford University Press.

Strevens, P. (1992). Applied linguistics: An overview. In W. Grabe, and R. B. Kaplan (Eds.), *Introduction to Applied Linguistics* (pp. 13–31). Reading, MA: Addison-Wesley.

Strevens, P. (1978). Historical ruminations upon the 19th AGM. *BAAL Newsletter* 4, 3.

Strevens, P. (1977). *New Orientations in the Teaching of English*. Oxford: Oxford University Press.

Stroop, J. R. (1935). Studies of interference in serial verbal reactions. *Journal of Experimental Psychology* 18, 643–662.

Stryker, S. B., and B. L. Leaver (Eds.). (1997). *Content-Based Instruction in Foreign Language Education: Models and Methods*. Washington DC: Georgetown University Press.

Stuart, S. (1993). Dominican Patwa—mother tongue or cultural relic? *International Journal of the Sociology of Language* 102, 57–72.

Stubbs, M. (2001). Texts, corpora, and problems of interpretation: A response to Widdowson. *Applied Linguistics* 22, 149–172.

Stubbs, M. (1996). *Text and Corpus Analysis: Computer-Assisted Studies of Language and Culture*. Oxford: Blackwell.

Stubbs, M. (1995). Collocations and semantic profiles: On the cause of the trouble with quantitative methods. *Functions of Language* 2, 1–33.

Strubell, M. (1996). Language planning and bilingual education in Catalonia. *Journal of Multilingual and Multicultural Development* 17, 262–275.

Strunk, W., and E. B. White (1955). *The Elements of Style*. New York: Macmillan.

Sunderman, G., and J. F. Kroll (2006). First language activation during second language lexical processing: An investigation of lexical form, meaning, and grammatical class. *Studies in Second Language Acquisition* 28, 387–422.

Sutton, P. (1991). Language in Aboriginal Australia: Social dialects in a geographicidiom. In S. Romaine (Ed.), *Language in Australia*. Cambridge: Cambridge University Press.

Svanes, B. (1992). En undersoekelse av realisasjonsmoenstret for spraakhandlingen "aa be noen om aa gjoere noen" [A study of the realization pattern of the linguistic action "to ask someone to do something"]. Maal og Minne (English translation) 1–2, 89–107.

Svartvik, J. (Ed.) (1990). The London Corpus of Spoken English: Description and Research. *Lund Studies in English 82*. Lund, Sweden: Lund University Press.

Swain, M. (2006). Languaging, agency and collaboration in advanced language proficiency. In H. Byrnes (Ed.), *Advanced Language Learning: The Contribution of Halliday and Vigotsky* (pp. 95–108). London: Continuum.

Swain, M. (2005). The output hypothesis: Theory and research. In E. Hinkel (Ed.), *The Handbook of Research in Second Language Teaching and Learning* (pp. 471–483). Mahwah, NJ: Lawrence Erlbaum.

Swain, M. (2001a). Examining dialogue: Another approach to content specification and to validating inferences drawn from test scores. *Language Testing* 18, 275–302.

Swain, M. (2001b). Integrating language and content teaching through collaborative tasks. *Canadian Modern Language Review* 58(1), 44–63.

Swain, M. (2000a). French immersion research in Canada: Recent contributions to SLA and applied linguistics. In W. Grabe et al. (Eds.), *Annual Review of Applied Linguistics: Vol. 20. Applied Linguistics as an Emerging Discipline* (pp. 199–212). New York: Cambridge University Press.

Swain, M. (2000b). The output hypothesis and beyond: Mediating acquisition through collaborative dialogue. In J. P. Lantolf (Ed.), *Sociocultural Theory and Second Language Learning* (pp. 99–116). Oxford: Oxford University Press.

Swain, M. (1998). Focus on form through conscious reflection. In C. Doughty, and J. Williams (Eds.), *Focus on Form in Classroom Second Language Acquisition* (pp. 64–81). Cambridge: Cambridge University Press.

Swain, M. (1995). Three functions of output in second language learning. In G. Cook, and B. Seidlhofer (Eds.), *Principle and Practice in Applied Linguistics: Studies in Honour of H. G. Widdowson* (pp. 125–144). Oxford: Oxford University Press.

Swain, M. (1993). The output hypothesis: Just speaking and writing aren't enough. *Canadian Modern Language Review* 50, 158–164.

Swain, M. (1991). Manipulating and complementing content teaching to maximize second language learning. In E. Kellerman, R. Phillipson, L. Selinker, M. Sharwood Smith, and M. Swain (Eds.), *Foreign/Second Language Pedagogical Research* (pp. 234–50). Clevedon, Avon, UK: Multilingual Matters.

Swain, M. (1985). Communicative competence: Some roles of comprehensible input and comprehensible output in its development. In S. M. Gass, and C. Madden (Eds.), *Input in Second Language Acquisition* (pp. 235–253). Rowley, MA: Newbury House.

Swain, M., and P. Deters (2007). "New" mainstream SLA theory: Expanded and enriched. *Modern Language Journal* 91, 820–836.

Swain, M., and R. K. Johnson (1987). Immersion education: A category within bilingual education. In R. K. Johnson, and M. Swain (Eds.), *Immersion Education: International Perspectives* (pp. 1–18). Cambridge: Cambridge University Press.

Swain, M., and S. Lapkin (2002). Talking it through: Two French immersion learners' response to reformulation. *International Journal of Educational Research* 37(3–4), 285–304.

Swain, M., and S. Lapkin (2001). Focus on form through collaborative dialogue: Exploring tasks effects. In M. Bygate, P. Skehan, and M. Swain (Eds.), *Task-Based Learning: Language Teaching, Learning and Assessment*. London: Longman.

Swain, M., and S. Lapkin (2000). Task-based language learning: The uses of first language use. *Language Teaching Research* 4, 251–274.

Swain, M., and S. Lapkin (1998). Interaction and second language learning: Two adolescent French immersion students working together. *Modern Language Journal* 82, 320–337.

Swain, M., and S. Lapkin (1995). Problems in output and the cognitive processes they generate: A step toward second language learning. *Applied Linguistics* 16, 371–391.

Swain, M., and S. Lapkin (1982). *Evaluating Bilingual Education: A Canadian Case Study*. Clevedon, Avon, UK: Multilingual Matters.

Swales, J. M. (2004). *Research Genres: Explorations and Applications*. New York: Cambridge University Press.

Swales, J. M. (2002). Integrated and fragmented worlds: EAP materials and corpus linguistics. In J. Flowerdew (Ed.), *Academic Discourse* (pp. 150–164). London: Longman, Pearson Education.

Swales, J. M. (2001). Metatalk in American academic talk: The cases of POINT and THING. *Journal of English Linguistics* 29, 34–54.

Swales, J. M. (2000). Languages for specific purposes. In W. Grabe et al. (Eds.), *Annual Review of Applied Linguistics: Vol. 20. Applied Linguistics as an Emerging Discipline* (59–76). New York: Cambridge University Press.

Swales, J. M. (1996). Occluded genres in the academy: The case of the submission letter. In E. Ventola, and A. Mauranen (Eds.), *Academic Writing: Intercultural and Textual Issues* (pp. 45–58). Amsterdam: John Benjamins.

Swales, J. M. (1990). *Genre Analysis: English in Academic and Research Settings*. New York: Cambridge University Press.

Swales, J. M., U. Ahmad, Y-Y. Chang, D. Chavez, D. Dressen, and R. Seymour (1998). Consider this: The role of imperatives in scholarly writing. *Applied Linguistics* 19(1), 97–121.

Swales, J. M., and A. Burke (2003). "It's really fascinating work": Differences in evaluative adjectives across academic registers. In P. Leistyna, and C. F. Meyer (Eds.), *Corpus Analysis: Language Structure and Language Use* (pp. 1–18). New York: Rodopi.

Swales, J. M., and C. M. Feak (2004). *Academic Writing for Graduate Students: Essential Tasks and Tasks* (2nd ed.). Ann Arbor: University of Michigan Press.

Swales, J. M., and C. M. Feak (2000). *English in Today's Research World: A Writing Guide*. Ann Arbor: University of Michigan Press.

Swales, J. M., and S. Lindemann (2002). Teaching the literature review to international graduate students. In A. M. Johns (Ed.), *Genre in the Classroom: Multiple Perspectives* (pp. 105–119). Mahwah, NJ: Lawrence Erlbaum.

Swan, M. (2005). Legislation by hypothesis: The case of task-based instruction. *Applied Linguistics* 26(3), 376–401.

Swan, M. (1985). A critical look at the communicative approach. *ELT Journal* 39, 1–12, 76–87.

Swan, M., and C. Walter (1992). *The New Cambridge English Course, 3.* Cambridge: Cambridge University Press.

Sweedler-Brown, C. (1993). ESL essay evaluation: The influence of sentence-level and rhetorical features. *Journal of Second Language* 2, 3–17.

Szabo, C. (2006). Language choice for note-taking in consecutive interpreting. *Interpreting* 8(2), 129–147.

Taavitsainen, I. (2001). Middle English recipes: Genre characteristics, text type features and underlying traditions of writing. *Journal of Historical Pragmatics* 2(1), 85–113.

Taavitsainen, I., and P. Pahta (Eds.). (2004). *Medical and Scientific Writing in Late Medieval English.* Cambridge: Cambridge University Press.

Taavitsainen, I., and P. Pahta (2000). Conventions of professional writing: The medical case report in a historical perspective. *Journal of English Linguistics* 28(1), 60–76.

Tabor, W., C. Juliano, and M. K. Tanenhaus (1997). Parsing in a dynamical system: An attractor-based account of the interaction of lexical and structural constraints in sentence processing. *Language and Cognitive Processes* 12, 211–271.

Taguchi, N. (2005). Comprehending implied meaning in English as a foreign language. *Modern Language Journal* 89, 543–562.

Takahashi, S. (1996). Pragmatic transferability. *Studies in Second Language Acquisition* 18, 189–223.

Takahashi, S., and M. A. DuFon (1989). Cross-linguistic influence in indirectness: The case of English directives performed by native Japanese speakers. Unpublished manuscript, University of Hawai'i at Manoa (ERIC ED 370 439).

Takahashi, T., and L. Beebe (1987). The development of pragmatic competence by Japanese learners of English. *Japan Association of Language Teachers (JALT) Journal* 8, 131–155.

Takeda, K. (2008). Interpreting at the Tokyo War Crimes Tribunal. *Interpreting* 10(1), 65–83.

Takenoya, M. (2003). *Terms of Address in Japanese: An Interlanguage Pragmatics Approach.* Sapporo, Japan: Hokkaido University Press.

Takenoya, M. (1995). Address terms in Japanese: Patterns of use by native and nonnative speakers. PhD dissertation, Indiana University, Bloomington.

Talmy, S. (2008). The cultural productions of ESL student at Tradewinds High: Contingency, multidirectionality and identity in L2 socialization. *Applied Linguistics* 29, 619–644.

Talmy, S., and K. Richards (Eds.). (forthcoming). Qualitative interviews in applied linguistics: Discursive perspectives [Special issue]. *Applied Linguistics* 31.

Talyzina, N. (1981). *The Psychology of Learning.* Moscow: Progress Press.

Tamosiunaite, A. (2008). The Lithuanian language in the United States: Shift or maintenance? *Lituanus* 54(3), 60–78.

Tanenhaus, M. K., and J. C. Trueswell (1995). Sentence comprehension. In J. L. Miller, and P. D. Eimas (Eds.), *Speech, Language and Communication* (pp. 217–262). San Diego, CA: Academic Press.

Tang, G. (1992). The effects of graphic representation of knowledge structures on ESL reading comprehension. *Studies in Second Language Acquisition* 14, 177–195.

Tannen, D., and C. Wallat (1993). Doctor/mother/child communication: Linguistic analysis of a pediatric interaction. In A. D. Todd, and S. Fisher (Eds.), *The Social Organization of Doctor-Patient Communication* (2nd ed., pp. 31–47). Norwood, NJ: Ablex.

Tao, H. (2007). A corpus-based investigation of absolutely and related phenomena in spoken American English. *Journal of English Linguistics* 35(1), 5–29.

Tao, H., and M. McCarthy (2001). Understanding non-restrictive WHICH-clauses in spoken English, which is not an easy thing. *Language Sciences* 23, 651–677.

Tao, H., and C. F. Meyer (2008). Gapped coordinations in English: Form, usage and implications for linguistic theory. *Corpus Linguistics and Linguistic Theory* 2(2), 129–163.

Tarone, E. (2007). Sociolinguistic approaches to second language acquisition research 1997–2007. *Modern Language Journal* 91, 837–348.

Tarone, E., and M. Bigelow (2007). Alphabetic print literacy and oral language processing in SLA. In A. Mackey (Ed.), *Conversational Interaction in Second Language Acquisition: A Series of Empirical Studies* (pp. 101–121). Oxford: Oxford University Press.

Tarone, E., M. Bigelow, and K. Hansen (2009). *Literacy and Second Language Oracy.* Oxford: Oxford University Press.

Tashakkori, A., and C. Teddlie (Eds.). (2003). *Handbook of Mixed Methods in Social and Behavioral Research.* Thousand Oaks, CA: Sage.

Tashakkori, A., and C. Teddlie (1998). *Mixed Methodology: Combining Qualitative and Quantitative Approaches.* Thousand Oaks, CA: Sage.

Tatsuoka, K. K. (1993). Item construction and psychometric models appropriate for constructed responses. In R. E. Bennet, and W. C. Ward (Eds.), *Construction versus Choice in Cognitive Measurement: Issues in Constructed Response, Performance Testing and Portfolio Assessment* (pp. 107–134). Hillsdale, NJ: Lawrence Erlbaum.

Tauli, V. (1968). *Introduction to a Theory of Language Planning.* Acta Universitatis Upsaliensis, Studia Philologiae Scandinavicae Upsaliensia, 6. Uppsala, Sweden: University of Uppsala.

Tauroza, S. (1997). Using students' listening comprehension problems. *Perspectives* 9(1), 161–178.

Taylor, L. (1993). Text-removed summary completion as a means of assessing reading comprehension ability. Paper presented at the Language Testing Forum, Lancaster University, UK.

Taylor, M. C. (2008). Arts-based approaches to inquiry in language education. In K. King, and N. H. Hornberger (Eds.), *Research Methods in Language and Education: Encyclopedia of Language and Education* (2nd ed., vol. 10, pp. 243–254). New York: Springer.

Taylor, P. (2009). *Text-to-Speech Synthesis.* Cambridge: Cambridge University Press.

Taylor Torsello, C. (1996). Theme as the interpreter's path indicator through the unfolding text. *Interpreters' Newsletter* 7, 113–149.

Teaching translation throughout the world (2005). *Meta: Translators Journal* 50(1), 1–335.

Teddlie, C., and A. Tashakkori (2009). *Foundations of Mixed Methods Research: Integrating Quantitative and Qualitative Approaches in the Social and Behavioral Sciences.* Thousand Oaks, CA: Sage.

Tent, J., and F. Mugler (2004). The morphology and syntax of Fiji English. In B. Kortmann, E. Schneider, K. Burridge, R. Mesthrie, and C. Upton (Eds.) *A Handbook of Varieties of English, Vol. 2: Morphology and Syntax* (pp. 229–247). Amsterdam: Mouton de Gruyter.

Tent, J., and F. Mugler (1996). Why a Fiji corpus? In S. Greenbaum (Ed.), *Comparing English Worldwide: The International Corpus of English* (pp. 249–261). Oxford: Clarendon Press.

Terestyéni, T. (1996). Vizsgálat az idegennyelv-tudásról [A survey on foreign language knowledge]. *Modern Nyelvoktatás* 2, 3–16.

Terms of the profession (2008). *Proteus* 17(2), 12–14.

Tetreault, J., and M. Chodorow (2008). *The ups and downs of preposition error detection in ESL writing.* Manchester: COLING.

Tharp, R., and R. Gallimore (1991). *Rousing Minds to Life: Teaching, Learning and Schooling in Social Context.* Cambridge: Cambridge University Press.

Thatcher, B. (2000). L2 professional writing in a US and South American context. *Journal of Second Language Writing* 9, 41–69.

Theories and practices of translation and interpretation in Korea (2006). *Meta: Translators' Journal* 51(2), 185–429.

Thierry, G., and Y. J. Wu (2007). Brain potentials reveal unconscious translation during foreign-language comprehension. *Proceedings of the National Academy of Sciences* 104, 12530–12535.

Thomas, J. (1983). Cross-cultural pragmatics. *Applied Linguistics* 4, 91–112.

Thomas, J., and M. Short (Eds.). (1996). *Using Corpora for Language Research.* London: Longman.

Thomas, M. (1998). Programmatic ahistoricity in second language acquisition theory. *Studies in Second Language Acquisition* 20, 387–405.

Thomas, S., and T. Hawes (1994). Reporting verbs in medical journal articles. *English for Specific Purposes* 13(2), 129–148.

Thomas, W. P., and V. P. Collier (2002). *A National Study of School Effectiveness for Language Minority Students' Long-Term Academic Achievement.* Santa Cruz, CA: Center for Research on Education, Diversity and Excellence.

Thompson, I., and I. Rubin (1996). Can strategy instruction improve listening comprehension? *Foreign Language Annals* 29, 331–342.

Thompson, P. (1999). Exploring the contexts of writing: Interviews with Ph.D. supervisors. In P. Thompson (Ed.), *Issues in EAP Writing Research and Instruction.* (pp. 37–54). Reading, UK: CALS.

Thompson, P., and A. Sealey (2007). Through children's eyes? Corpus evidence of the features of children's literature. *International Journal of Corpus Linguistics* 12, 1–23.

Thompson, P., and C. Tribble (2001). Looking at citations: Using corpora in English for academic purposes. *Language Learning and Technology* 5(3), 91–105.

Thompson, S., and P. J. Hopper (2001). Transitivity, clause structure and argument structure: Evidence from conversation. In J. L. Bybee, and P. J. Hopper (Eds.), *Frequency and the Emergence of Linguistic Structure* (pp. 27–60). Amsterdam: Benjamins.

Thompson, S. A., and A. Mulac (1991). The discourse conditions for the use of the complementizer *That* in conversational English. *Journal of Pragmatics* 15, 237–251.

Thornbury, S. (2004). *Natural Grammar.* Oxford: Oxford University Press.

Thorne, S. L. (2003). Artifacts and cultures-of-use in intercultural communication. *Language Learning & Technology* 7(2), 38–67.

Thorne, S. L., and S. Payne (2005). Evolutionary trajectories, internet-mediated expression and language education. *CALICO Journal* 22(3), 371–398.

Thornell, C. (1997). The Songo language and its lexicon. *Travaux de l'Institut de Linguistique de Lund* 32, 3–195.

Thuerk, S. (2006, December 1). Court interpreter pay examined. *Wilson Daily Times* (NC). (Page numbers unavailable.)

Thumboo, E. (1987). The literary dimension of the spread of English: Creativity in a second tongue. In P. H. Lowenberg (Ed.), *Language Spread and Language Policy Issues: Implications and Case Studies (Georgetown University Round Table on Languages and Linguistics)* (pp. 361–401). Washington DC: Georgetown University Press.

Thurston, W. R. (1987). *Process of Changes in the Language of North-Western New Britain.* Canberra: Pacific Linguistics.

Tiersma, P. M. (1999). *Legal Language.* Chicago: University of Chicago Press.

Tindale, N. B. (1974). *Aboriginal Tribes of Australia.* Berkeley: University of California Press.

Titscher, S., R. Wodak, M. Meyer, and E. Vetter (1998). *Methoden der Textanalyse [Text Analysis Method].* Wiesbaden, Germany: Westdeutscher Verlag.

Tocalli-Beller, A., and M. Swain (2007). Riddles and puns in the ESL classroom: Adults talk to learn. In A. Mackey (Ed.), *Conversational Interaction in Second Language Acquisition: A Series of Empirical Studies* (pp. 143–167). Oxford: Oxford University Press.

Todal, J. (1999). Minorities with a minority: Language and the school in the Sámi areas of Norway. In S. May (Ed.), *Indigenous Community-Based Education* (pp. 124–136). Clevedon, Avon, UK: Multilingual Matters.

Todd, A. D. (1993). A diagnosis of doctor-patient communication in the prescription of contraception. In A. D. Todd, and S. Fisher (Eds.), *The Social Organization of Doctor-Patient Communication* (2nd ed., pp. 183–209). Norwood, NJ: Ablex.

Todd, A. D., and S. Fisher (1993). *The Social Organization of Doctor-Patient Communication* (2nd ed.). Norwood, NJ: Ablex.

Todd, L. (1990). *Pidgins and Creoles* (2nd ed.). London: Routledge.

Todd, R. (2001). Induction from self-selected concordances and self-correction. *System* 29(1), 91–102.

Tognini-Bonelli, E., and G. Del Lungo Camiciotti (2005). *Strategies in Academic Discourse.* Amsterdam/Philadelphia: John Benjamins.

Tokowicz, N., and B. MacWhinney (2005). Implicit and explicit measures of sensitivity to violations in second language acquisition in second language grammar: An event-related potential investigation. *Studies in Second Language Acquisition* 27, 173–204.

Tollefson, J. W. (2004). Medium of instruction in Slovenia: European integration and ethnolinguistic nationalism. In J. W. Tollefson, and A. B. M. Tsui (Eds.), *Medium of Instruction Policies: Which Agenda? Whose Agenda?* (pp. 263–281). Mahwah, NJ: Lawrence Erlbaum.

Tollefson, J. W. (Ed.). (2001). *Language Policies in Education: Critical Issues.* Mahwah, NJ: Lawrence Erlbaum.

Tollefson, J. W. (1997). Language policy in independent Slovenia. *International Journal of the Sociology of Language* 124, 29–50.

Tollefson, J. W. (1995). *Power and Inequality in Language Education.* New York: Cambridge University Press.

Tollefson, J. W. (1989). *Alien Winds: The Reeducation of America's Indochinese Refugees.* New York: Praeger.

Tomasello, M. (2003). *Constructing a Language: A Usage-Based Theory of Language Acquisition.* Cambridge, MA: Harvard University Press.

Tonelli, L., and A. Riccardi (1995). Speech errors, shadowing and simultaneous interpretation. *Interpreters' Newsletter* 6, 67–74.

Toohey, K. (2008). Ethnography and language education. In N. H. Hornberger, and K. King (Eds.), *Encyclopedia of Language and Education: Research Methods in Language and Education* (2nd ed., vol. 10, pp. 177–187). New York: Springer.

Toohey, K. (2001). Disputes in child L2 learning. *TESOL Quarterly* 35(2), 257–278.

Toohey, K. (2000). *Learning English at School: Identity, Social Relations and Classroom Practice.* Clevedon, Avon, UK: Multilingual Matters.

Torrisi, S. J. (2010). Social regulation in frontotemporal lobar degeneration: A case study. In A. W. Mates, L. Mikesell, and M. S. Smith (Eds.), Language, Interaction and Frontotemporal Dementia: Reverse Engineering the Social Mind (chapter 2). London: Equinox.

Toth, P. D. (2008). Teacher and learner led discourse in task-based grammar instruction: Providing procedural assistance for L2 morphosyntactic development. *Language Learning* 58, 237–285.

Toth, P. D. (2000). The interaction of instruction and learner internal factors in the acquisition of L2 morphosyntax. *Studies in Second Language Acquisition* 22, 169–208.

Tottie, G. (1991). *Negation in English Speech and Writing: A Study in Variation*. San Diego, CA: Academic Press.

Toury, G. (1995). *Descriptive Translation Studies and Beyond*. Amsterdam and Philadelphia: John Benjamins.

Toury, G. (Ed.). (1987). *Translation across Cultures*. New Delhi: Bahri Publications.

Toury, G. (1980). *In Search of a Theory of Translation*. Tel Aviv: Porter Institute for Poetics and Semiotics.

Towell, R., R. Hawkins, and N. Bazergui (1996). The development of fluency in advanced learners of French. *Applied Linguistics* 17, 84–119.

Townsend, D., and T. Bever (2001). *Sentence Comprehension: The Integration of Habits and Rules*. Cambridge, MA: MIT Press.

Trahey, M., and L. White (1993). Positive evidence and pre-emption in the second language classroom. *Studies in Second Language Acquisition* 15, 181–204.

Traxler, M. J., and R. P. G. van Gompel (2006). Syntactic parsing. In M. J. Traxler, and M. Gernsbacher (Eds.), *Handbook of Psycholinguistics* (2nd ed., pp. 455–503). New York: Elsevier.

Tremblay, P. F., and R. C. Gardner (1995). Expanding the motivation construct in language learning. *Modern Language Journal* 79, 505–518.

Trezise, P. (1996). Use of language and the Anunga Rules: *R v Jean Denise Izumi*. *Aboriginal Law Bulletin* 79(3), 17–18.

Tribble, C. (2001). Small corpora and teaching writing: Towards a corpus-informed pedagogy of writing. In M. Ghadessy, H. Mohsen, A. Henry, and R. Roseberry (Eds.) *Small Corpus Studies and ELT: Theory and Practice* (pp. 381–408). Amsterdam: John Benjamins.

Tribble, C., and G. Jones (1997). *Concordances in the Classroom*. Houston/Texas: Athelstan.

Trim, J. (2004). AILA's recollections. *AILA News* 5(2), no. 11. Available: http://www.aila.info/download/publications/news/news_11_2004_03.pdf.

Trofimovich, P., A. Ammar, and E. Gatbonton (2007). How effective are recasts? The role of attention, memory and analytical ability. In A. Mackey (Ed.), *Conversational Interaction in Second Language Acquisition: A Series of Empirical Studies* (pp. 171–195). Oxford: Oxford University Press.

Trofimovich, P., E. Gatbonton, and N. Segalowitz (2007). A dynamic look at L2 phonological learning: Seeking processing explanations for implicational phenomena. *Studies in Second Language Acquisition* 29, 407–448.

Trosborg, A. (1995). *Interlanguage Pragmatics: Requests, Complaints and Apologies*. Berlin: Mouton de Gruyter.

Trosborg, A. (1987). Apology strategies in natives/non-natives. *Journal of Pragmatics* 11, 147–167.

Trueswell, J. C., M. K. Tanenhaus, and S. M. Garnsey (1994). Semantic influences on parsing: Use of thematic role information in syntactic ambiguity resolution. *Journal of Memory and Language* 33, 285–318.

Truscott, J. (1998). Noticing in second language acquisition: A critical review. *Second Language Research* 14, 103–135.

Truscott, J. (1996). The case against grammar correction in L2 writing classes. *Language Learning* 46, 327–369.

Tse, J. K. P. (1982). Some advantages of sociolinguistic surveys for language planning purposes. *Ying Yu Yen Chiu Chi K'an* [*Studies in English Literature and Linguistics*] 8 (April), 157–167.

Tsuda, M. (1997). Human rights problems of foreigners in Japan's criminal justice system. *Migrationworld* 25(1/2), 22–28.

Tsuda, Y. (1997). Hegemony of English vs. ecology of language: Building equality in international communication. In L. Smith, and M. Forman (Eds.), *World Englishes 2000* (vol. 14). Honolulu: University of Hawai'i Press.

Tsuda, Y. (1994). The diffusion of English: Its impact on culture and communication. *Keio Communication Review* 16, 49–61.

Tsui, A. B. M., and J. Fullilove (1998). Bottom-up or top-down processing as a discriminator of L2 listening performance. *Applied Linguistics* 19(4), 432–451.

Tsui, A. B. M., and J. Tollefson (2007). *Language Policy, Culture and Identity in Asian Contexts.* Mahwah, NJ: Lawrence Erlbaum.

Tucker, G. R. (2003). Language contact and language change: Summary observations. In W. Grabe et al. (Eds.), *Annual Review of Applied Linguistics: Vol. 23. Language Contact and Change* (pp. 243–249). New York: Cambridge University Press.

Tucker, G. R. (2000). Concluding thoughts: Applied linguistics at the juncture of millennia. In W. Grabe et al. (Eds.), *Annual Review of Applied Linguistics: Vol. 20. Applied Linguistics as an Emerging Discipline* (pp. 241–249). New York: Cambridge University Press.

Tucker, G. R. (1997). Developing a language competent American society: Implications of the English-only movement. In T. Bongaerts, and K. De Bot (Eds.), *Perspectives on Foreign-Language Policy: Studies in Honour of Theo Van Els* (pp. 87–98). Amsterdam: John Benjamins.

Tudor, I. (1997). *Learner-Centredness in Language Education.* Cambridge: Cambridge University Press.

Tulung, G. (2008). Communicative task-generated oral discourse in a second language: A case study of peer interaction and non-native teacher talk in an EFL classroom. PhD dissertation, University of Ottawa.

Turlington, B., and R. Schoenberg (Eds.). (1996). *Spreading the Word II: Promising Developments for Undergraduate Foreign Language Instruction.* Washington, D.C.: American council on Education.

Turner, C. (1997). The Injinoo Home Language Program: A positive community response to marginalisation and institutional racism. *Australian Journal of Indigenous Education* 25, 1–9.

Tyler, M. (2001). Resource consumption as a function of topic knowledge in non-native and native comprehension. *Language Learning* 51, 257–280.

Tymoczko, M. (2007). *Enlarging Translation: Empowering Translators.* Manchester, UK: St. Jerome.

Tymoczko, M., and E. Gentzler (Eds.). (2002). *Translation and Power.* Amherst: University of Massachusetts Press.

UCLES (University of Cambridge Local Examinations Syndicate) Computerized Adaptive Placement Examination (CAPE) informational website. Available: http://www.cambridgeesol.org/contact.html.

Ullman, M. T. (2006). Language and the brain. In R. Fasold, and J. Connor-Linton (Eds.), *An Introduction to Language and Linguistics* (pp. 235–274). Cambridge: Cambridge University Press.

Ullman, M. T. (2001). The neural basis of lexicon and grammar in first and second language: The declarative/procedural model. *Bilingualism: Language and Cognition* 4, 105–122.

Underwood, J. (1984). *Linguistics, computers and the language teacher*. Rowley, MA: Newbury House.

UNESCO (1968). The use of vernacular languages in education: The report of the UNESCO meeting of specialists, 1951. In J. A. Fishman (Ed.), *Readings in the Sociology of Language* (pp. 688–716). The Hague: Mouton.

Ur, P. (1996). *A Course in Language Teaching: Practice and Theory*. Cambridge: Cambridge University Press.

Ur, P. (1981). *Discussions that work*. Cambridge: Cambridge University Press.

Uysal, H. H., L. Plakans, and S. Demobovskaya (2007). English language spread in local contexts: Turkey, Latvia and France. *Current Issues in Language Planning* 8(2), 192–216.

Vainikka, A., and M. Young-Scholten (1998a). The initial state in the L2 acquisition of phrase structure. In S. Flynn, G. Martohardjono, and W. O'Neil (Eds.), *The Generative Study of Second Language Acquisition* (pp. 17–34). Mahwah, NJ: Lawrence Erlbaum.

Vainikka, A., and M. Young-Scholten (1998b). Morphosyntactic triggers in adult second language acquisition. In M.-L. Beck (Ed.), *Morphology and Interfaces in Second Language Acquisition Knowledge* (pp. 89–113). Philadelphia: John Benjamins.

Vainikka, A., and M. Young-Scholten (1996). The gradual development of L2 phrase structure. *Second Language Research* 12, 7–39.

Vainikka, A., and M. Young-Scholten (1994). Direct access to X'-theory: Evidence from Turkish and Korean adults learning German. In B. D. Schwartz, and T. Hoekstra (Eds.), *Language Acquisition Studies in Generative Grammar* (pp. 265–316). Philadelphia: Benjamins.

Vaish, V. (2008). Interactional patterns in Singapore's English classrooms. *Linguistics and Education* 19, 366–377.

Valdez, G. (2001). *Learning and Not Learning English: Latino Students in American Schools*. New York: Teacher's College Press.

Valdman, A. (2004). Réflections sur l'histoire de l'AILA [Reflections on the history of AILA]. In S. Gass, and C. Makoni (Eds.), *World Applied Linguistics: A Celebration of 40 Years of AILA: AILA Review* 17, 25.

Valdman, A. (1991). Decreolization or dialect contact in Haiti? In F. Byrne, and T. Huebner (Eds.), *Development and Structures of Creole Languages: Essays in Honor of Derek Bickerton* (pp. 75–88). Amsterdam: John Benjamins.

Valdman, A. (1989). The use of Creole as a school medium and decreolization in Haiti. In W. Z. Sonino (Ed.), *Literacy in School and Society: Multidisciplinary Perspectives* (pp. 55–79). New York: Plennum Press.

Valette, R. (1977). *Modern Language Testing* (2nd ed.). New York: Harcourt Brace Jovanovich.

Van Besien, F. (1999). Anticipation in simultaneous interpretation. *Meta: Translators' Journal* 44(2), 250–259.

Vandergrift, L. (2007). Recent developments in second and foreign language listening research. *Language Teaching* 40, 191–210.

Vandergrift, L. (2006). Second language listening: Listening ability or language proficiency? *Modern Language Journal* 90, 6–18.

Vandergrift, L. (2003). Orchestrating strategy use: Toward a model of the skilled second language listener. *Language Learning* 53, 463–496.

Vandergrift, L. (1999). Facilitating second language listening comprehension: Acquiring successful strategies. *ELT Journal* 53(3), 168–176.

Vandergrift, L., C. Goh, C. Mareschal, and M. Tafaghodtari (2006). The metacognitive awareness listening questionnaire: Development and validation. *Language Learning* 56(3), 431–462.

van Ek, J. A. (1977). *The Threshold Level for Modern Language Learning in Schools.* Strasbourg: Council of Europe.

van Els, T. (2005). Multilingualism in the European Union. *International Journal of Applied Linguistics* 15, 263–281.

van Geert, P. (1994). *Dynamic Systems of Development: Change between Complexity and Chaos.* New York: Harvester.

van Gelder, T. (1998). The dynamical hypothesis in cognitive science. *Behavioral and Brain Sciences* 21, 615–656.

van Gelder, T., and R. Port (1995). It's about time: An overview of the dynamical approach to cognition. In R. Port, and T. van Gelder (Eds.), *Mind as Motion: Exploration in the Dynamics of Cognition* (pp. 1–45). Cambridge, MA: MIT Press.

Van Hell, J. G., and A. M. B. De Groot (2008). Sentence context modulates visual word recognition and translation in bilinguals. *Acta Psychologica* 128, 431–451.

Van Hell, J. G., and T. Dijkstra (2002). Foreign language knowledge can influence native language performance in exclusively native contexts. *Psychonomic Bulletin & Review* 9, 780–789.

Van Heuven, W. J. B., A. Dijkstra, and J. Grainger (1998). Orthographic neighborhood effects in bilingual word recognition. *Journal of Memory and Language* 39, 458–483.

Van Heuven, W. J. B., H. Schriefers, T. Dijkstra, and P. Hagoort (2008). Language conflict in the bilingual brain. *Cerebral Cortex* 18, 2706–2716.

van Lier, L. (2004). *The Ecology and Semiotics of Language Learning: A Sociocultural Perspective.* New York: Kluwer Academic.

van Lier, L. (1997). Apply within, apply without? *International Journal of Applied Linguistics* 7, 95–105.

van Lier, L. (1988). *The Classroom and the Learner.* London: Longman.

VanPatten, B. (Ed.). (2003). *Processing Instruction.* Mahwah, NJ: Lawrence Erlbaum.

VanPatten, B., and J. Williams (Eds.). (2007). *Theories in Second Language Acquisition.* Mahwah, NJ: Lawrence Erlbaum.

Van Valin, R. (1995). Toward a functionalist account of so-called "extraction constraints." In B. Divriendt (Ed.), *Complex Structures: A Functionalist Perspective* (pp. 29–60). Berlin: Mouton de Gruyter.

Van Valin, R., and R. La Polla (1997). *Syntax: Structure, Meaning and Function.* Cambridge: Cambridge University Press.

Van Weeren, J. (1995). European language qualifications. Information on standards of proficiency. *System* 23, 481–490.

Varga, D. (1995). Creation of a language: Rumantsch Grischun. *Studia Romancia et Anglica Zabrabiensia* 40, 181–190.

Varonis, E., and S. Gass (1985a). Non-native/non-native conversations: A model for negotiation of meaning. *Applied Linguistics* 6, 71–90.

Varonis, E., and S. Gass (1985b). Miscommunication in native/non-native conversation. *Language in Society* 14, 327–343.

Varro, G. (1997). Bilinguals sacrificed, or what are native languages good for? *Cahiers de l'Institut de Linguistique de Louvain* 23(3–4), 61–70.

Venuti, L. (Ed.). (2004). *The Translation Studies Reader* (2nd ed.). London and New York: Routledge.

Venuti, L. (1998). American tradition. In M. Baker (Ed.), *Routledge Encyclopedia of Translation Studies* (pp. 305–315). London and New York: Routledge.

Venuti, L. (1995). *The Translator's Invisibility: A History of Translation.* London and New York: Routledge.

Verdoodt, A. (1971). The differential impact of immigrant French speakers on indigenous German speakers: A case study in the light of two theories. *International Migration Review* 5, 138–146.

Verhoef, M. (1998). Toward a theory of language attitude planning in South Africa. *South African Journal of Linguistics* 16, 27–33.

Verhoeven, L. (1997). Acquisition of literacy by immigrant children. In *Writing Development: An Interdisciplinary View* (pp. 219–240). Amsterdam: John Benjamins.

Vermeer, H. J. (1998). Didactics of translation. In M. Baker (Ed.), *Routledge Encyclopedia of Translation Studies*. (pp. 60–63). London and New York: Routledge.

Vermeer, H. J. (1989). *Skopos* and commission in translational action (Trans. A. Chesterman). In A. Chesterman (Ed.), *Readings in Translation* (pp. 173–187). Helsinki: Oy Finn Lectura Ab.

Viaggio, S. (2006). *A General Theory of Interlingual Mediation*. Berlin: Frank & Timme.

Viaggio, S. (1996a). Elementary, my dear colleague! Educating our students' guesses. *Interpreters' Newsletter* 7, 57–71.

Viaggio, S. (1996b). Research in simultaneous interpretation: An outsider's overview. *Interpreters' Newsletter* 7, 73–84.

Viaggio, S. (1995). The praise of sight translation (and squeezing the last drop thereout of). *Interpreters' Newsletter* 6, 33–42.

Vidal, M. (1998). Telephone interpreting: Technological advance or due process impediment? *Proteus* 7(3), 1, 3–6.

Vihla, M. (1999). *Medical Writing: Modality in Focus* Amsterdam: Rodopi.

Viikberg, J. (1999). Language shift among Siberian Estonians: Pro and contra. *International Journal of the Sociology of Language* 139, 105–124.

Vinay, J.-P., and J. Darbelnet (1958/1995). *Stylistique comparée du français et de l'anglais: Méthode de traduction*. Paris: Didier. Translated and edited by J. C. Sager and M. J. Hamel (1995) as *Comparative Stylistics of French and English: A Methodology for Translation*. Amsterdam and Philadelphia: John Benjamins.

Voegelin, C. F., F. M. Voegelin, and N. W. Schutz, Jr. (1967). The language situation in Arizona as part of the Southwest cultural area. In D. Hymes, and W. E. Bittle (Eds.), *Studies in South Western Ethnolinguistics* (pp. 403–451). The Hague: Mouton.

Von Flotow, L. (1997). *Translation and Gender: Translating in the "Era of Feminism."* Manchester, UK: St. Jerome.

Von Studnitz, R., and D. Green (2002). Interlingual homograph interference in German-English bilinguals: Its modulation and locus of control. *Bilingualism: Language and Cognition* 5, 1–23.

von Stutterheim, C. (2003). Linguistic structure and information organisation: The case of very advanced learners. *EUROSLA Yearbook* 3, 183–206.

Vygotsky, L. S. (1986). *Thought and Language*. Cambridge, MA: MIT Press.

Vygotsky, L. S. (1978). *Mind in Society: The Development of Higher Psychological Processes*. Cambridge, MA: Harvard University Press.

Vygotsky, L. S. (1934/1986). *Thought and Language* (Ed. and intro. by A. Kozulin). Cambridge, MA: MIT Press.

Vygotsky, L. S. (1927/2004). The historical meaning of the crisis in psychology: A methodological investigation. In R. W. Rieber, and D. K. Robinson (Eds.), *The Essential Vygotsky* (pp. 227–243). New York: Kluwer/Plenum.

Vygotsky, L. S. (1926/1997). *Educational Psychology*. Boca Raton, FL: Nova Science

Wadensj, C. (2008). In and off the show: Co-constructing "invisibility" in an interpreter-mediated talk show interview. *Meta: Translators' Journal* 53(1), 184–203.

Wagner-Gough, J., and E. Hatch (1975). The importance of input data in second language acquisition studies. *Language Learning* 25, 297–307.

Waite, J. (1992). *Aoteareo: Speaking for Ourselves: Issues for the Development of a New Zealand Languages Policy*. Wellington: New Zealand Ministry of Education.

Waldinger, R. (Ed.). (2001). *Strangers at the Gates: New Immigrants in Urban America*. Berkeley: University of California Press.

Waldinger, R., and M. Lichter (2003). *How the Other Half Works: Immigration and the Social Organization of Labor*. Berkeley: University of California Press.

Walker, C., S. Ranney, and T. W. Fortune (2005). Preparing preservice teachers for English language learners: A content-based approach. In D. J. Tedick (Ed.), *Second Language Teacher Education* (pp. 313–333). Mahwah, NJ: Lawrence Erlbaum.

Walker, L. (2008). Observations in a Mexican courtroom. *Proteus* 17(4), 5–6.

Walsh, M. (1994). Interactional styles in the courtroom: An example from northern Australia. In J. Gibbons (Ed.), *Language and the Law* (pp. 217–233). London: Longman.

Wang, W., and Q. Wen (2002). L1 use in the L2 composing process: An exploratory study of 16 Chinese EFL writers. *Journal of Second Language Writing* 11, 225–247.

Ward, J. (2006). *The Students' Guide to Cognitive Neurosciences*. New York: Psychology Press.

Waring, R., and I. S. P. Nation (1997). Vocabulary size, text coverage and word lists. In N. Schmitt, and M. McCarthy (Eds.), *Vocabulary: Description, Acquisition and Pedagogy* (pp. 6–19). Cambridge: Cambridge University Press.

Warner, S. L. N. (1999). Kuleana: The right, responsibility, and authority of indigenous peoples to speak and make decisions for themselves in language and cultural revitalization. *Anthropology and Education Quarterly* 30, 68–93.

Warren, M. (2004). // so what have YOU been WORking on Recently//: Compiling a specialized corpus of spoken business English. In U. Connor, and T. Upton (Eds.), *Discourse in the Professions: Perspectives from Corpus Linguistics* (pp. 115–140). Amsterdam: John Benjamins.

Warschauer, M. (2003). *Technology and Social Inclusion: Rethinking the Digital Divide*. Boston: MIT Press.

Warschauer, M. (2000). The changing global economy and the future of English teaching. *TESOL Quarterly* 34, 511–535.

Warschauer, M. (1999). *Electronic Literacies: Language, Culture and Power in Online Education*. Mahwah, NJ: Lawrence Erlbaum.

Warschauer, M. (1997). Computer-mediated collaborative learning: Theory and practice. *Modern Language Journal* 81, 470–481

Warschauer, M. (1995/1996). Comparing face-to-face and electronic discussion in the second language classroom. *CALICO Journal* 13(2&3), 7–25.

Warschauer, M., and C. Meskill (2000). Technology and second language teaching. In J. W. Rosenthal (Ed.), *Handbook of Undergraduate Second Language Education* (pp. 303–318). Mahwah, NJ: Lawrence Erlbaum.

Watson, J. L. (Ed.). (1997). *Golden Arches East: McDonald's in East Asia*. Stanford, CA: Stanford University Press.

Watson, T. J. (1997). Languages within languages: A social constructivist perspective on multiple managerial discourses. In F. Bargiela-Chiappini, and S. Harris (Eds.), *The Languages of Business: An International Perspective* (pp. 211–227). Edinburgh: Edinburgh University Press.

Watson-Gegeo, K. A. (2004). Mind, language, and epistemology: Toward a language socialization paradigm for SLA. *Modern Language Journal* 88, 331–350.

Watson-Gegeo, K. A. (1994). Language and education in Hawai'i: Sociopolitical and economic implications of Hawai'i Creole English. In M. Morgan (Ed.), *The Social Construction of Identity in Creole Situations* (pp. 101–120). Los Angeles: Center for Afro-American Studies, UCLA.

Watson-Gegeo, K. A. (1988). Ethnography in ESL: Defining the essentials. *TESOL Quarterly* 22, 575–592.

Wattendorf, E., and J. Festman (2008). Images of the multilingual brain: The effect of age of second language acquisition. In K. de Bot (Guest Ed.), *Annual Review of Applied Linguistics: Vol. 28. Aspects of Language Processing* (pp. 3–24). New York: Cambridge University Press.

Weber, A., and A. Cutler (2003). Lexical competition in non-native spoken word recognition. *Journal of Memory and Language* 50, 1–25.

Weedon, C. (1987/1997). *Feminist Practice and Poststructuralist Theory* (2nd ed.) London: Blackwell.

Wei, L., and M. G. Moyer (Eds.). (2007). *The Blackwell Guide to Research Methods in Bilingualism and Multilingualism*. Malden, MA: Blackwell.

Wei, L., V. Saravanan, and J. N. L. Hoon (1997). Language shift in the Teochew community in Singapore: A family domain analysis. *Journal of Multilingual and Multicultural Development* 18(5), 364–384.

Weigle, S. C. (2002). *Assessing Writing*. Cambridge: Cambridge University Press.

Weigle, S. C., and L. Jensen (1997). Assessment issues for content-based instruction. In M. A. Snow, and D. Brinton (Eds.), *The Content-Based Classroom: Perspectives on Integrating Language and Content* (pp. 201–212). White Plains, NY: Addison Wesley Longman.

Weinberg, A., S. Burger, and A. Hope (2008). Evaluating the effectiveness of content-based language teaching. *Contact: Research Symposium Issue* 34(2), 68–80.

Weinstein-Shr, G. (1993). Literacy and social process: A community in transition. In B. Street (Ed.), *Cross-Cultural Approaches to Literacy* (pp. 272–293). Cambridge: Cambridge University Press.

Weir, C. J. (2005). *Language Testing and Validation: An Evidenced Based Approach*. New York: Palgrave Mcmillian.

Weissberg, B. (2000). Developmental relationships in the acquisition of English syntax: Writing vs. speech. *Learning and Instruction* 10, 37–53.

Weller, G. (2008). Training interpreters in Mexican Indian languages: A multi-national problem. *Proteus* 17(4), 3–4, 6.

Wells, G. (1993). Reevaluating the IRF sequence: A proposal for the articulation of theories of activity and discourse for the analysis of teaching and learning in the classroom. *Linguistics and Education* 5, 1–17.

Wenger, E. (1998). *Communities of Practice: Learning, Meaning and Identity*. Cambridge: Cambridge University Press.

Wesche, M. (2002). Early French immersion: How has the original Canadian model stood the test of time? In P. Burmeister, T. Piske, and A. Rhode (Eds.), *An Integrated View of Language Development—Papers in Honor of Henning Wode* (pp. 357–379). Trier, Germany: Wissenschaftlicher Verlag.

Wesche, M. (Ed.). (2001). French immersion and content-based language teaching in Canada [Special issue]. *Canadian Modern Language Review* 58(1).

Wesche, M. (2000). A Canadian perspective: Second language teaching and learning in the university. In J. Rosenthal (Ed.), *Handbook of Undergraduate Second Language Education* (pp. 187–208). Mahwah, NJ: Lawrence Erlbaum.

Wesche, M. (1994). Input and interaction in second language acquisition. In C. Gallaway, and B. Richards (Eds.), *Input and Interaction in Language Acquisition* (pp. 219–249). Cambridge: Cambridge University Press.

Wesche, M. (1993a). French immersion graduates at university and beyond: What difference has it made? In J. Alatis (Ed.), *Language,Communication and Social Meaning* (*Georgetown University Round Table on Languages and Linguistics*) (pp. 208–240). Washington, DC: Georgetown University Press.

Wesche, M. (1993b). Discipline-based approaches to foreign and second language study: Research issues and outcomes. In M. Krueger, and F. Ryan (Eds.), *Language and Content: Discipline-Based Approaches to Language Study* (pp. 57–58). Lexington, MA: D.C. Heath.

Wesche, M. (1985). What can the universities offer to the bilingual student? *Canadian Modern Language Review* 41, 956–961.

Wesche, M., and D. Ready (1985). Foreigner talk in the university classroom. In S. M. Gass, and C. Madden (Eds.), *Input in Second Language Acquisition* (pp. 89–114). Cambridge, MA: Newbury House.

Wesche, M., and P. Skehan (2002). Communicative, task-based and content-based language instruction. In R. B. Kaplan (Ed.), *Oxford Handbook of Applied Linguistics* (pp. 207–228). Oxford: Oxford University Press.

West, M. (Ed.) (1953). *A General Service List of English Words: With Semantic Frequencies and a Supplementary Word-list for the Writing of Popular Science and Technology.* London: Longman.

White, C. (2007). Innovation and identity in distance language learning and teaching. *Innovation in Language Learning and Teaching* 1(1), 97–110.

White, L. (2007). Linguistic theory, Universal Grammar and second language acquisition. In B. VanPatten (Ed.), *Theories in Second Language Acquisition* (pp. 37–56). Mahwah, NJ: Lawrence Erlbaum.

White, L. (2003). *Second Language Acquisition and Universal Grammar.* Cambridge: Cambridge University Press.

White, L. (2000). Second language acquisition: From initial state to final state. In J. Archibald (Ed.), *Second Language Acquisition and Linguistic Theory* (pp. 130–155). Oxford: Blackwell.

White, L. (1996). Clitics in L2 French. In H. Clahsen (Ed.), *Generative Perspectives on Language Acquisition* (pp. 334–368). Philadelphia: John Benjamins.

White, L. (1992). Long and short verb movement in second language acquisition. *Canadian Journal of Linguistics* 37, 273–286.

White, L. (1991a). Adverb placement in second language acquisition: Some effects of positive and negative evidence in the classroom. *Second Language Research* 7, 133–161.

White, L. (1991b). The verb-movement parameter in second language acquisition. *Language Acquisition* 1(4), 337–360.

White, L., J. Bruhn-Garavito, T. Kawasaki, J. Pater, and P. Prévost (1997). The researcher gave the subject a test about himself: Problems of ambiguity and preference in the investigation of reflexive binding. *Language Learning* 47, 145–172.

White, L., and A. Juffs (1998). Constraints on WH-movement in two different contexts of non-native language acquisition: Competence and processing. In S. Flynn, G. Martohardjono, and W. O'Neill (Eds.), *The Generative Study of Second Language Acquisition* (pp. 111–130). Hillsdale, NJ: Lawrence Erlbaum.

White, M. (1994). Language in job interviews: Differences relating to success and socioeconomic variables. PhD dissertation, Northern Arizona University, Flagstaff.

White, R. V. (1993). Innovation in curriculum planning and program development. In W. Grabe et al. (Eds.), *Annual Review of Applied Linguistics: Vol. 13. Issues in Second Language Teaching and Learning* (pp. 244–259). New York: Cambridge University Press.

Whitley, M. S. (1986). *Spanish/English Contrasts*. Washington, DC: Georgetown University.

Wichmann, A. (1995). Using concordances for the teaching of modern languages in higher education. *Language Learning Journal* 11, 61–63.

Wichmann, A., S. Fligelstone, T. McEnery, and G. Knowles (Eds.). (1997). *Teaching and Language Corpora*. London: Longman.

Widdowson, H. G. (2006). Applied linguistics and interdisciplinarity. *International Journal of Applied Linguistics* 16, 93–96.

Widdowson, H. G. (2005). Applied linguistics, interdisciplinarity and disparate realities. In P. Bruthiaux, D. Atkinson, W. Eggington, W. Grabe, and V. Ramanathan (Eds.), *Directions in Applied Linguistics: Essays in Honor of Robert B. Kaplan* (pp. 3–25). Clevedon, Avon, UK: Multilingual Matters.

Widdowson, H. G. (2004). A perspective on recent trends. In A. P. R. Howatt, *A History of English Language Teaching* (2nd ed., pp. 353–372). Oxford: Oxford University Press.

Widdowson, H. G. (2003). *Defining Issues in English Language Teaching*. Oxford: Oxford University Press.

Widdowson, H. G. (2000). Object language and the language subject: On the mediating role of applied linguistics. In W. Grabe et al. (Eds.), *Annual Review of Applied Linguistics: Vol. 20. Applied Linguistics as an Emerging Discipline* (pp. 21–33). Cambridge: Cambridge University Press.

Widdowson, H. G. (1998a). Skills, abilities and contexts of reality. In W. Grabe et al. (Eds.), *Annual Review of Applied Linguistics: Vol. 18. Foundations of Second Language Teaching* (323–333). Cambridge: Cambridge University Press.

Widdowson, H. G. (1998b). The theory and practice of critical discourse analysis. *Applied Linguistics* 19, 136–151.

Widdowson, H. G. (1993). Perspectives on communicative language teaching: Syllabus design and methodology. In J. Alatis (Ed.), *Georgetown University Roundtable on Language and Linguistics: Language Communication and Social Meaning* (pp. 501–507). Washington DC: Georgetown University Press.

Widdowson, H. G. (1990). *Aspects of Language Teaching*. Oxford: Oxford University Press.

Widdowson, H. G. (1983). *Learning Purpose and Language Use*. Oxford: Oxford University Press.

Widdowson, H. G. (1980). Applied linguistics: The pursuit of relevance In R. B. Kaplan (Ed.), *The Scope of Applied Linguistics* (pp. 74–87). Rowley, MA: Newbury House.

Widdowson, H. G. (1979/1984). *Explorations in Applied Linguistics* (2 vols.). Oxford: Oxford University Press.

Widdowson, H. G. (1978). *Teaching Language as Communication*. London: Oxford University Press.

Widdowson, H. G., and R. B. Kaplan (2003). Applied linguistics (concerns and related disciplines). In W. J. Frawley (Ed.), *Oxford International Encyclopedia of Linguistics* (2nd ed. 4 vols.; vol. I, pp. 114–118). New York: Oxford University Press.

Wilce, J. (2003). Introduction: Social and cultural lives of immune systems in a semiotic universe. In J. Wilce (Ed.), *Social and Cultural Lives of Immune Systems* (pp. 1–16). London: Routledge.

Wiley, T. G. (2006). The lessons of historical investigation: Implications for the study of language policy and planning. In T. Ricento (Ed.), *An Introduction to Language Policy: Theory and Method* (pp. 135–152). Malden, MA: Blackwell.

Wiley, T. G., and M. Lukes (1996). English-only and standard English ideologies in the U.S. *TESOL Quarterly* 30, 511–525.

Wiliam, D., and M. Thompson (2007). Integrating assessment and instruction: What will it take to make it work? In C. Dwyer (Ed.), *The Future of Assessment: Shaping Teaching and Learning* (pp. 53–82). Mahwah, NJ: Lawrence Erlbaum.

Wilkins, D. A. (1976). *Notional Syllabuses*. Oxford: Oxford University Press.

Willemyns, R. (1997). Language shift through erosion: The case of French-Flemish "Westhoek." *Journal of Multilingual and Multicultural Development* 18(1), 54–66.

Williams, C. H. (1991). Language planning and social change: Ecological speculations. In J. R. Dow, O. Garcia, and D. F. Marshall (Eds.), *Language Planning: Focusschrift in Honour of Joshua A. Fishman on the Occasion of His 65th Birthday* (vol. 3, pp. 53–74). Amsterdam/Philadelphia: John Benjamins.

Williams, G. (1992). *Sociolinguistics: A Sociological Critique*. London: Routledge.

Williams, H., and D. Thorne (2000). The value of teletext subtitling as a medium for language learning. *System* 28, 217–228.

Williams, J. (1999). Learner-generated attention to form. *Language Learning* 49, 583–625.

Williams, J. N. (2006). Incremental interpretation in second language sentence processing. *Bilingualism: Language and Cognition* 9, 71–88.

Williams, J. N., and C. Kuribara (2008). Comparing a nativist and emergentist approach to the initial stage of SLA: An investigation of Japanese scrambling. *Lingua* 118, 522–553.

Williams, J. N., P. Möbius, and C. Kim (2001). Native and non-native processing of English *WH-* questions: Parsing strategies and plausibility constraints. *Applied Psycholinguistics* 22, 509–540.

Williams, M., and R. L. Burden (1997). *Psychology for Language Teachers: A Social Constructive Approach*. Cambridge: Cambridge University Press.

Williams, R. M. (1947). The reduction of intergroup tensions. *Social Sciences Research Council Bulletin* 57, 40–43.

Willing, K. (1992). *Talking It Through: Clarification and Problem-Solving in Professional Work*. Sydney: Macquarie University, National Centre for English Language Teaching and Research.

Willis, D. (1990). *The Lexical Syllabus*. London: Collins CoBuild.

Willis, J. (1996). *A Framework for Task-Based Learning*. London: Longman.

Willis, J., and D. Willis (1988). *Collins COBUILD English Course*. London: Collins.

Wilson, M. (2007). Constructing measures. Paper presented at the Annual Meeting of the National Council on Measurement in Education, Chicago.

Winer, L. (1993). Teaching speakers of Caribbean English Creoles in North American classrooms. In A. W. Glowka, and D. M. Lance (Eds.), *Language Variation in North American English: Research and Teaching* (pp. 191–198). New York: Modern Language Association of America.

Winer, L. (1990). Orthographic standardization for Trinidad and Tobago: Linguistic and sociopolitical considerations. *Language Problems & Language Planning* 14(3). 237–268.

Winer, L. (1989). Variation and transfer in English Creole—Standard English language learning. In M. R. Eisenstein (Ed.), *The Dynamic Interlanguage: Empirical Studies in Second Language Variation* (pp. 155–173). New York: Plenum Press.

Winer, L., and L. Jack (1997). Caribbean English Creole in New York. In O. García, and J. A. Fishman (Eds.), *The Multilingual Apple: Language in New York City* (pp. 301–337). Berlin: Mouton de Gruyter.

Winford, D. (1998). On the origins of African American Vernacular English—A creolist perspective. Part II: Linguistic features. *Diachronica* 15, 99–54.

Winford, D. (1997a). Re-examining Caribbean English Creole continua. *World Englishes* 16(2), 233–279.

Winford, D. (1997b). On the origins of African American Vernacular English—A creolist perspective. Part I: The sociohistorical background. *Diachronica* 14, 305–344.

Winford, D. (1994). Sociolinguistic approaches to language use in the Anglophone Caribbean. In M. Morgan (Ed.), *The Social Construction of Identity in Creole Situations* (pp. 43–62). Los Angeles: Center for Afro-American Studies, UCLA.

Winter, J. (1992). Discourse as a resource: Methods of collecting language attitudes. *Australian Review of Applied Linguistics* 15(1), 1–2.

Wiruk, E. (2000). Report: Papua New Guinea. *Pidgins and Creoles in Education (PACE) Newsletter* 11, 1.

Wiruk, E. (1996). Report. *Pidgins and Creoles in Education (PACE) Newsletter* 7, 3.

Wodak, R. (2006). Linguistic analyses in language policies. In T. Ricento (Ed.), *An Introduction to Language Policy: Theory and Method* (pp. 170–193). Oxford: Blackwell.

Wodak, R. (2003). Auf der Suche nach einer neuen Europäischen Identität. In R. de Cillia, H. J. Krumm, and R. Wodak (Eds.), *DieKosten der Mehrsprachigkeit: Globalisierung und sprachliche Vielfalt* [*The Cost of Multilingualism: Globalisation and Linguistic Diversity*]. (pp. 125–134). London: Sage.

Wodak, R. (1997). Introduction: Some important issues in the research of gender and discourse. In R. Wodak (Ed.), *Gender and Discourse*. London: Sage.

Wodak, R. (1993). The development and forms of racist discourse in Austria since 1989. In D. Graddol, and S. Thomas (Eds.), *Language in a Changing Europe* (pp. 1–15). Bristol, PA: Multilingual Matters.

Wolf, M. (2007). *Proust and the Squid: The Story and Science of the Reading Brain*. New York: HarperCollins.

Wolff, D. (1987). Some assumptions about second language text comprehension. *Studies in Second Language Acquisition* 9, 307–326.

Wong, L. (1999). Authenticity and the revitalization of Hawaiian. *Anthropology and Education Quarterly* 30, 94–115.

Wooffitt, R. (2005). *Conversation Analysis and Discourse Analysis: A Comparative and Critical Introduction*. London: Sage.

Woolard, K. A. (1999). Simultaneity and bivalency as strategies in bilingualism *Journal of Linguistic Anthropology* 8, 3–29.

Worsley, P. (1987). Development. In P. Worsley (Ed.), *Sociology* (pp. 48–83). Harmondsworth, UK: Penguin Books.

Wray, A. (2002). *Formulaic Language and the Lexicon*. Cambridge: Cambridge University Press.

Wright, S. (2007). The right to speak one's own language: Reflections on theory and practice. *Language Policy* 6, 203–224.

Wu, Y. (1998). What do tests of listening comprehension test? A retrospection study of EFL test-takers performing a multiple-choice task. *Language Testing* 15(1), 21–44.

Wurm, S. A. (1999). Language revivalism and revitalization in Pacific and Asian areas. *International Journal of the Sociology of Language* 137, 163–172.

Wurm, S. A. (1985). Writing systems and the orthography of Tok Pisin. In S. A. Wurm, and P. Mühlhäusler (Eds.), *Handbook of Tok Pisin (New Guinea Pidgin)* (pp. 167–176). Canberra: Australian National University (Pacific Linguistics C-70).

Wurm, S. A. (1980). Standardisation and intrumentalisation in Tok Pisin. In A. Valdman, and A. Highfield (Eds.), *Theoretical Orientations in Creole Studies* (pp. 237–244). New York: Academic Press.

Xiao, H. (1998). Minority languages in Dehong, China: Policy and reality. *Journal of Multilingual and Multicultural Development* 19(3), 221–235.

Yagi, S. M. (1999). Computational discourse analysis for interpretation. *Meta: Translators' Journal* 44(2), 268–279.

Yagmur, K., K. de Bot, and H. Korzilius (1999). Language attrition, language shift and ethno-linguistic vitality of Turkish in Australia. *Journal of Multilingual and Multicultural Development* 20, 51–69.

Yalden, J. (1987). *Principles of Course Design for Language Teaching.* New York: Cambridge University Press.

Yang, R., and D. Allison (2003). Research articles in applied linguistics: Moving from results to conclusions. *English for Specific Purposes* 22, 365–385.

Yáñez-Prieto, C. M. (2008). On literature and the secret art of invisible words: Teaching literature through language. PhD dissertation, Pennsylvania State University, University Park.

Yashima, T. (2002). Willingness to communicate in a second language: The Japanese EFL context. *Modern Language Journal* 86, 54–56.

Yin, R. K. (2009). *Case Study Research: Design and Methods* (4th ed.). Thousand Oaks, CA: Sage.

Ying, H. G. (1996). Multiple constraints on processing ambiguous sentences: Evidence from adult L2 learners. *Language Learning* 46, 681–711.

Yngve, V. (1996). *From Grammar to Science: New Foundations for General Linguistics.* Amsterdam: John Benjamins.

Yoon, H., and A. Hirvela (2004). ESL student attitudes toward corpus use in L2 writing. *Journal of Second-Language Writing* 13, 257–283.

Yoshii, M., and J. Flaitz (2002). Second language incidental vocabulary retention: The effect of text and picture annotation types. *CALICO Journal* 20(1), 33–58.

Young, R. F. (2000, March). Interactional competence: Challenges for validity. Paper presented at the Language Testing Research Colloquium, Vancouver, British Columbia.

Young, R. F., and A. W. He (1998). *Talking and Testing: Discourse Approaches to the Assessment of Oral Proficiency.* Amsterdam: John Benjamins.

Young, Y., M. D. Shermis, S. R. Brutten, and K. Perkins (1996). From conventional to computer-adaptive testing of ESL reading comprehension. *System* 24, 23–40.

Young-Scholten, M., and J. Archibald (2000). Second language syllable structure. In J. Archibald (Ed.), *Second Language Acquisition and Linguistic Theory* (pp. 64–102). Oxford: Blackwell.

Yu, L. (1996). The role of cross-linguistic lexical similarity in the use of motion verbs in English by Chinese and Japanese learners. EdD dissertation, University of Toronto.

Yule, G. (1997). *Referential comunication tasks.* Mahwah, NJ: Lawrence Erlbaum.

Yule, G. (1996). *Pragmatics.* Oxford: Oxford University Press.

Zamel, V. (1983). The composing processes of advanced ESL students: Six case studies. *TESOL Quarterly* 17, 165–187.

Zappa-Hollman, S. (2007). Academic presentations across post-secondary contexts: The discourse socialization of non-native English speakers. *Canadian Modern Language Review* 63, 455–485.

Zavodny, M. (1998). The effects of Official English laws on limited-English-proficient workers (Working Paper 98–4a). Atlanta: Federal Reserve Bank of Atlanta.

Zeier, H. (1997). Psychophysiological stress research. *Interpreting* 2(1/2), 231–249.

Zepeda, O. (1998). Voices in the desert: Contemporary approaches to language maintenance and survival of an ancient language, Tohono O'odham. *International Journal of the Sociology of Language* 132, 47–57.

Zéphir, F. (1997). Haitian Creole language and bilingual education in the United States: Problem, right, or resource? *Journal of Multilingual and Multicultural Development* 18(3), 223–37.

Zhang, S. (1995). Reexamining the affective advantage of peer feedback in the ESL writing class. *Journal of Second Language Writing* 4, 209–222.

Zhou, M. (2006). Theorizing language contact, spread and variation in status planning: A case study of Modern Standard Chinese. *Journal of Asian Pacific Communication* 16(2), 159–174.

Zielinski, B. (2008). The listener: No longer the silent partner in intelligibility. *System* 36, 69–84.

Zimmermann, R. (2000). L2 writing: Subprocesses, a model of formulating and empirical findings. *Learning and Instruction* 10, 73–99.

Zobl, H. (1998). Representational changes: From listed representations to independent representations of verbal affixes. In M.-L. Beck (Ed.), *Morphology and Its Interfaces in Second Language Acquisition* (pp. 339–371). Philadelphia: John Benjamins.

Zorzi, D. (2001). The pedagogic use of spoken corpora. In G. Aston (Ed.), *Learning with Corpora* (pp. 85–107). Houston, Texas: Athelstan.

Zuengler, J. (2003). Jackie Chan drinks Mountain Dew: Constructing cultural models of citizenship. *Linguistics and Education* 14, 277–303.

Zuengler, J., and E. Miller (2006). Cognitive and sociocultural perspectives: Two parallel SLA worlds? *TESOL Quarterly* 40(1), 35–58.

Zuengler, J., and J. Mori (2002). Micro-analyses of classroom discourse: A critical consideration of method [Special issue]. *Applied Linguistics* 23(3).

Name Index

SUBJECT INDEX

academic language proficiency, 240, 368–369
academic writing, 108, 552, 553, 555, 556, 559, 565
accuracy, 68, 73, 123, 152, 218, 286, 288–289, 292, 309, 478, 495, 499, 534
achievement, 18, 78, 122, 204, 207, 209, 214, 272, 302, 328, 394, 464, 521, 573
acquisition hypothesis, 166, 176, 276
acrolect, 384, 386
ACT COMPASS Platform, 525
action research, 37, 38, 48, 218
ACTIVE Reading, 340
adaptation of language input, 278
additive, 184, 207, 400, 405, 406, 515
adjacency pairs, 233, 242
adjunct CBI, 283, 289
Administrative Office of the United States Courts (AO), 501
Adult Migrant English Language Program, 21
African American Vernacular English (AAVE), 384–385
ALANZ newsletter, 24
American Association of Applied Linguistics (AAAL), 7, 8, 17, 18, 28, 42
American Translators Association (ATA), 504
analytic negation, 554
analyzing actual patterns of use in natural texts, 548
Annual Review of Applied Linguistics (ARAL), 8, 17, 35, 56
anticipation techniques, 492
apartheid, 467
Applied Linguistics (AL), 3–59, 127–140, 233, 235, 244–259, 311, 318, 319, 321, 373–374, 432–434, 572, 574
Applied Linguistics Association of Australia (ALAA), 21, 22, 23
Applied Linguistics Association of New Zealand (ALANZ), 24
applied translation studies, 477, 483–486
apprenticeship model, 165
aptitude, 49, 205, 207, 245, 483, 496
Arabic, 150, 281, 398, 402, 404, 407, 410, 456, 492, 495, 502
Articulation, 23, 63, 64, 67–68, 71, 369, 459, 492
Articulator, 336, 337
assessing validity, 537–538
Assessment Engineering (AE), 518–519
assessment of bilingual dominance, 205
assimilation

of ethnic minorities, 205
of immigrant minorities, 294
Association Phonetique Internstionale (International Phonetic Association [IPA]), 29
Attitude, 92, 93, 207, 208, 212, 213, 291, 295, 328, 375, 385, 386, 391, 394, 446, 461
Attitude/Motivation Test Battery (AMTB), 208, 212, 213, 214, 215, 216
audiolingual methodology, 102
Australian Advisory Council on Languages and Multicultural Education (AACLAME), 21
Australian Review of Applied Linguistics, 21, 23
Australian Telephone Interpreting Service, 500
authentic texts, 279, 489, 524
automated essay evaluation, 529–538
automaticity, 40, 89, 92, 97, 193, 195, 196, 337, 515
autonomic nervous system, 246
aviation English, 426
avoiding verbalism, 169–170

Baby Talk, 219
back channeling, 233
Bahasa, 428
Bahasa Indonesia, 238, 431
Basa, 428
Basilect, 384
basolateral and extended amygdala, 245
Basque, 295, 299, 414, 432, 448
Bay Area [CA] Court Interpreters' (BACI), 501
Bayesian inference networks, 517
Behaviorism, 50, 53, 57, 112, 149, 166, 192, 206, 212, 219
bilingual aphasia, 338
bilingual education, 18, 39, 276, 294–303, 447, 459, 460
Bilingual Interactive Activation Model (BIA), 352–354
bilingual lexicon, 349–370
bilingual signage, 295
bilingualism, 8, 16, 35, 39, 50, 134, 184, 205, 296, 298, 299, 333–370, 400, 406
biliteracy, 296, 297, 298, 299, 388, 419
Bloomfieldian linguistic, 110, 111
Bologna Process, 483, 489
Boundedness, 176, 177
Bourguiba Institute, 5
brain studies, 39